Lecture Notes in Computer Science 3882

Mong Li Lee Kian Lee Tan
Vilas Wuwongse (Eds.)

Database Systems for Advanced Applications

11th International Conference, DASFAA 2006
Singapore, April 12-15, 2006
Proceedings

Volume Editors

Mong Li Lee
Kian Lee Tan
National University of Singapore
School of Computing
3 Science Drive 2, Singapore 117543, Singapore
E-mail: {leeml,tankl}@comp.nus.edu.sg

Vilas Wuwongse
Asian Institute of Technology
School of Advanced Technologies
Computer Science and Information Management Program
P.O. Box 4, Klong Luang, Pathumthani 12120, Thailand
E-mail: vw@cs.ait.ac.th

Library of Congress Control Number: 2006922864

CR Subject Classification (1998): H.2, H.3, H.4, H.5, J.1

LNCS Sublibrary: SL 3 – Information Systems and Application, incl. Internet/Web and HCI

ISSN 0302-9743
ISBN-10 3-540-33337-1 Springer Berlin Heidelberg New York
ISBN-13 978-3-540-33337-1 Springer Berlin Heidelberg New York

Springer is a part of Springer Science+Business Media

springer.com

Printed in Germany

Typesetting: Camera-ready by author, data conversion by Scientific Publishing Services, Chennai, India
Printed on acid-free paper SPIN: 11733836 06/3142 5 4 3 2 1 0

Foreword

Welcome to the 11th International Conference on Database Systems for Advanced Applications (DASFAA 2006)! This year's conference was held in Singapore where DASFAA was last held in 1997. DASFAA 2006 continued the tradition of providing an international forum for technical discussion among researchers, developers and users of database systems from academia, business and industry. Organizing DASFAA 2006 was a very rewarding experience—it gave me an excellent opportunity to work with many fine colleagues both within and outside Singapore.

I would like to thank Kian-Lee Tan and Vilas Wuwongse for putting together a world-class Program Committee. The committee worked very hard to bring a high-quality technical program to the conference. DASFAA 2006 also included an industrial track. David Cheung and Hwee Hwa Pang co-chaired this track and set up a separate committee to assess the quality of the submitted papers.

The conference also featured three tutorials: (1) Database Watermarking by Radu Sion, (2) Multilingual Database Systems by Jayant R. Haritsa, and (3) Video Sequence Indexing and Query Processing by Xiaofang Zhou, and a panel session. I would like to thank Ee Peng Lim and Krithi Ramamritham for their effort in organizing the tutorials and panel, respectively.

This conference would not have been possible without the support of many other colleagues: Tok-Wang Ling (Honorary Conference Chair), Mong Li Lee (Publication Chair), Masatoshi Yoshikawa (Publicity Chair), Sourav Saha Bhowmick and Anthony Kum Hoe Tung (Local Arrangement Co-chairs), Chee Yong Chan (Treasurer), and Mrs. Siew Foong Ho (Secretary).

Finally, I greatly appreciated the support of the National University of Singapore (NUS) and the Nanyang Technological University. In particular, I was happy that DASFAA 2006 participated in the NUS Centennial Celebrations as an event organized by the NUS academic staff.

April 2006

Beng Chin Ooi
Conference Chair

Message from the Program Co-chairs

The 11th International Conference on Database Systems for Advanced Applications (DASFAA 2006) was held in Singapore from April 12 to 15, 2006. As an annual international conference in the Pacific Asia region, DASFAA 2006 kept the traditions of the conference in promoting research and development activities in the database field among participants and their institutions from Pacific Asia and the rest of the world.

This year, the conference received 188 (research-track) submissions from over 28 different countries. The submitted papers were rigorously reviewed by the Program Committee members, and 46 full papers and 16 short papers were accepted for presentation.

The papers chosen for presentation spanned a wide range of topics, ranging from well-established areas such as XML, spatial and temporal databases, and data mining to upcoming areas like sensor networks, uncertainty and data streams, and subsequence matching and bioinformatics. The combination of selected papers made the conference interesting and provided the basis for discussion and exchange of ideas and for future development.

The conference was privileged to have keynote addresses delivered by Alon Y. Halevy of Google Inc. and University of Washington, Krithi Ramamritham of IIT Bombay, and Christian Jensen of Aalborg University. They provided insightful thoughts into various research challenges on information management, dissemination of dynamic data and geo-enabled mobile services.

DASFAA 2006 also included an industrial track with the aim of drawing industry practitioners and the academic community to share practical experience and real-world challenges that require research attention, and to advance the state of the art by integrating new techniques and research results in novel systems and applications. This track included a paper on automating the maintenance of the statistics for query optimization in Sybase ASE 15.0, a paper on automatically finding a mapping that transforms an XML schema into a relational counterpart that is tuned to the application workload, and a third paper that treats the problem of missing data from sensors deployed to monitor elderly dementia patients.

The research and industrial tracks were both supported by their respective Technical Program Committees. Both teams comprised renowned and hardworking researchers from around the world. Their invaluable efforts in reviewing the papers ensured the high quality of the accepted papers. We would like to take this opportunity to thank them again!

The technical program also consisted of three tutorials and a panel session. The three tutorials featured were Database Watermarking by Radu Sion, Multilingual Database Systems by Jayant R. Haritsa, and Video Sequence Indexing and Query Processing by Xiaofang Zhou.

The conference would not have been a success without the help and contributions of many individuals, and we would like to acknowledge them here: Tok-Wang Ling, Beng Chin Ooi, Ee Peng Lim, Krithi Ramamritham, Masatoshi Yoshikawa, Mong Li Lee, Sourav Saha Bhowmick, Anthony Kum Hoe Tung, Chee Yong Chan and Mrs. Ho Siew Foong. Finally, we would like to thank the session chairs, tutorial speakers, authors and participants, who contributed to making this conference a success.

April 2006

Kian-Lee Tan and Vilas Wuwongse
Research Track Co-chairs

David Cheung and Hwee Hwa Pang
Industrial Track Co-chairs

Conference Organization

Honorary Chair
Tok Wang Ling — National University of Singapore, Singapore

Conference Chair
Beng Chin Ooi — National University of Singapore, Singapore

Program Co-chairs
Kian Lee Tan — National University of Singapore, Singapore
Vilas Wuwongse — Asian Institute of Technology, Thailand

Tutorial Chair
Ee Peng Lim — Nanyang Technological University, Singapore

Panel Chair
Krithi Ramamritham — Indian Institute of Technology, Bombay

Industrial Program Co-chairs
David Wai-Lok Cheung — The University of Hong Kong, China
Hwee Hwa Pang — Singapore Management University, Singapore

Publicity Chair
Masatoshi Yoshikawa — Nagoya University, Japan

Publication Chair
Mong Li Lee — National University of Singapore, Singapore

Local Arrangement Co-chairs
Sourav Saha Bhowmick — Nanyang Technological University, Singapore
Anthony Kum Hoe Tung — National University of Singapore, Singapore

Treasurer
Chee Yong Chan — National University of Singapore, Singapore

Secretary
Mrs. Ho Siew Foong — National University of Singapore, Singapore

Jointly Organized by

School of Computing, National University of Singapore
School of Computer Engineering, Nanyang Technological University

As part of the National University of Singapore Centennial Celebrations

Program Committee

Regular Track

Charu Aggarwal	IBM T.J. Watson Research Center, USA
Chutiporn Anutariya	Shinawatra University, Thailand
Vijay Atluri	Rutgers University, USA
Sonia Berman	University of Cape Town, South Africa
Sourav S Bhowmick	Nanyang Technological University, Singapore
Luc Bouganim	INRIA, France
Athman Bouguettaya	Virginia Tech, USA
Stephane Bressan	National University of Singapore, Singapore
K. Selcuk Candan	Arizona State University, USA
Barbara Catania	University of Genova, Italy
Arbee L.P.Chen	National Tshing Hua University, Taiwan
Ming-Syan Chen	National Taiwan University, Taiwan
Ying Chen	IBM China Research Lab, China
Brian F Cooper	Georgia Institute of Technology, USA
Isabel F. Cruz	University of Illinois at Chicago, USA
Manoranjan Dash	Nanyang Technological University, Singapore
Amol Deshpande	University of Maryland, USA
Klaus Dittrich	University of Zurich, Switzerland
Gillian Dobbie	University of Auckland, New Zealand
Curtis Dyreson	Washington State University, USA
David W. Embley	Brigham Young University, USA
Hakan Ferhatosmanoglu	Ohio State University, USA
Elena Ferrari	University of Insubria at Como, Italy
Ada Waichee Fu	Chinese University of Hong Kong, China
Cong Gao	University of Edinburgh, UK
Minos Garofalakis	Bell Labs-Lucent Technologies, USA
Shahram Ghandeharizadeh	University of Southern California, USA
Jonathan Goldstein	Microsoft Research, USA
Dimitrios Gunopulos	University of California, Riverside, USA
Theo Haerder	TU Kaiserslautern, Germany
Takahiro Hara	Osaka University, Japan
Arantza Illarramendi	Basque Country University, Spain
Bala Iyer	IBM Silicon Valley Lab, USA
H.V. Jagadish	University of Michigan, USA
Arnd Christian Konig	Microsoft Research, USA
Panagiotis Kalnis	National University of Singapore, Singapore
Ibrahim Kamel	Zayed University, United Arab Emirates
Hyunchul Kang	Chung-Ang University, Korea
George Karypis	University of Minnesota, USA
Masaru Kitsuregawa	Institute of Industrial Science, Japan
Donald Kossmann	University of Heidelberg, Germany
Manolis Koubarakis	Technical University of Crete, Greece
Chiang Lee	National Cheng-Kung University, Taiwan

Dik Lun Lee	Hong Kong University of Science and Technology, China
Wang-Chien Lee	Penn State University, USA
Yoon-Joon Lee	KAIST, Korea
Jianzhong Li	Harbin Institute of Technology, China
Jinyan Li	Institute for InfoComm Research, Singapore
Wen-Syan Li	IBM Almaden Research Center, USA
Sergio Lifschitz	PUC-Rio, Brazil
Sanjay Madria	University of Missouri-Rolla, USA
Stefan Manegold	CWI, The Netherlands
Ioana Manolescu	INRIA Futurs, France
Volker Markl	IBM Almaden Research Center, USA
Weiyi Meng	Binghamton University, USA
Xiaofeng Meng	Renmin University of China, China
Mukesh Mohania	IBM India Research Lab, India
Atsuyuki Morishima	University of Tsukuba, Japan
S. Muthukrishnan	Rutgers University, USA
Mario A Nascimento	University of Alberta, Canada
Wolfgang Nejdl	University of Hannover, Germany
Raymond T. Ng	University of British Columbia, Canada
Aris Ouksel	University of Illinois at Chicago, USA
Sanghyun Park	Yonsei University, Korea
Evaggelia Pitoura	University of Ioannina, Greece
Sunil Prabhakar	Purdue University, USA
Weining Qian	Fudan University, China
Tore Risch	Uppsala University of Sweden
Prasan Roy	IBM India Research Lab, India
Simonas Saltenis	Aalborg University, Denmark
Markus Schneider	University of Florida, USA
Thomas Seidl	RWTH Aachen University, Germany
Oded Shmueli	Technion-Israel Institute of Technology, Israel
Ambuj K. Singh	University of Californa at Santa Barbara, USA
Dan Suciu	University of Washington, USA
Keishi Tajima	JAIST, Japan
Wang-Chiew Tan	University of California, Santa Cruz, USA
Katsumi Tanaka	Kyoto University, Japan
David Taniar	Monash University, Australia
Yufei Tao	City University of Hong Kong, China
Ozgur Ulusoy	Bilkent University, Turkey
Vasilis A. Vassalos	Athens University of Economics and Business, Greece
Haixun Wang	IBM T.J. Watson Research Center, USA
Wei Wang	University of North Carolina at Chapel Hill, USA
Yan Wang	Macquarie University, Australia
Kyu-Young Whang	KAIST, Korea
Jonker Willem	Philips Research, The Netherlands
Masatoshi Yoshikawa	Nagoya University, Japan
Xu Yu, Jeffrey	Chinese University of Hong Kong, China
Arkady Zaslavsky	Monash University, Australia
Yanchun Zhang	Victoria University, Australia

Jingren Zhou	Microsoft Research, USA
Shuigeng Zhou	Fudan University, China
Xiaofang Zhou	University of Queensland, Australia

Industrial Track

Manish Bhide	IBM India Research Lab, India
Qiong Luo	Hong Kong University of Science and Technology, China
Jussi Myllymaki	Google Inc., USA
Il-Yeol Song	Drexel University, USA
Kam-Fai Wong	The Chinese University of Hong Kong, China
Bai-Hua Zheng	Singapore Management University, Singapore

External Referees

Christoph Brochhaus	RWTH Aachen
Jost Enderle	RWTH Aachen
Ralph Krieger	RWTH Aachen
Guanling Lee	Pennsylvania State University
Ken Lee	Pennsylvania State University
Mei Li	Pennsylvania State University
Jinze Liu	University of North Carolina at Chapel Hill
Feng Pan	University of North Carolina at Chapel Hill
Wen-Chi Peng	Pennsylvania State University
Qingzhao Tan	Pennsylvania State University
Marc Wichterich	RWTH Aachen
Julian Winter	Pennsylvania State University

Table of Contents

Keynote Addresses

Sensor Networks

Subsequence Matching and Repeating Patterns

Spatial-temporal Databases

Data Mining

XML Compression and Indexing

XPath Query Evaluation

Uncertainty and Streams

Peer-to-Peer and Distributed Networks

Performance and Authentication

XML Query Processing

OLAP and Data Warehouse

Web and Web Services

Query Processing

Design: Modeling and Dependencies

Labeling Scheme and Graph Queries in XML

Document Retrieval

Industrial Papers

Short Papers

Dataspaces: A New Abstraction for Information Management

Alon Y. Halevy[1], Michael J. Franklin[2], and David Maier[3]

[1] Google Inc.
halevy@google.com
[2] University of California at Berkeley
franklin@cs.berkeley.edu
[3] Portland State University
maier@cs.pdx.edu

Most data management scenarios today rarely have a situation in which all the data that needs to be managed can fit nicely into a conventional relational DBMS, or into any other single data model or system. Instead, we see a set of loosely connected data sources, typically with the following recurring challenges:

- Users want be able to search the entire collection without having knowledge of individual sources, their schemas or interfaces. In some cases, they merely want to know where the information exists as a starting point to further exploration.
- An organization may want to enforce certain rules, integrity constraints, or conventions (e.g., on naming entities) across the entire collection, or track flow and lineage between systems. Furthermore, the organization needs to create a coherent external view of the data.
- The administrators may want to impose a single "support system" in terms of recovery, availability, and redundancy, as well as uniform security and access controls.
- Users and administrators need to manage the evolution of the data, both in terms of content and schemas, in particular as new data sources get added (e.g., as a result of mergers or new partnerships).

The aforementioned data management challenges are ubiquitous – they arise in enterprises (large or small), coordination within and across government agencies, data analysis in large science-related research or development projects, management of libraries (digital or otherwise), information collection and dissemination in the battlefield, search on one's PC desktop or other personal devices, coordination between devices in a "smart" home, and in search for structured objects on the web. In these scenarios, there is some well-understood scope and control across the data and systems within these organizations, and hence one can identify a space of data, which, if managed in a principled way, will offer significant benefits to the organization.

We recently introduced *dataspaces* [1] as a new abstraction for data management for such scenarios, and proposed the development of DataSpace Support Platforms (DSSPs) as an important agenda item for the data management field. In a nutshell, a DSSP offers a suite of interrelated services and guarantees that enables an application developer to focus on the specific challenges of an application, rather than the recurring challenges involved in dealing consistently and efficiently with large amounts of interrelated but disparately managed data.

M.L. Lee, K.L. Tan, and V. Wuwongse (Eds.): DASFAA 2006, LNCS 3882, pp. 1–2, 2006.

Traditionally, data integration and data exchange systems have aimed to offer many of the purported services of dataspace systems. In fact, DSSPs can be viewed as the next step in the evolution of data integration architectures, but are distinct from current data integration systems in the following way. Data integration systems require *semantic integration* before any services can be provided. Hence, although there is not a single schema to which all the data conforms, the system knows the precise relationships between the terms used in each schema. As a result, significant upfront effort is required in order to set up a data integration system.

Dataspace management is not a data integration approach; rather, it is more of a *data co-existence* approach. The goal of DSSPs is to provide base functionality over all data sources, regardless of how integrated they are. For example, a DSSP can provide keyword search over all of the data sources it contains, similar to the way that existing desktop search systems. When more sophisticated operations are required, such as relational-style query processing, data mining, over certain sources, then additional effort can be applied to more closely integrate those sources, in an incremental, "pay-as-you-go" fashion. Furthermore, as we perform more integration tasks, we expect the cost of integration to decrease. Similarly, along the administrative dimension, initially a DSSP can only provide weaker guarantees of consistency and durability. As stronger guarantees are desired, more effort can be put into making agreements among the various owners of data sources, and opening up certain interfaces (e.g., for commit protocols).

To summarize, the distinguishing properties of dataspace systems are the following:

- A DSSP must deal with data and applications in a wide variety of formats accessible through many systems with different interfaces. A DSSP is required to manage *all* the data in the dataspace rather than leaving some out, as with DBMSs.
- Although a DSSP offers an integrated means of searching, querying, updating, and administering the dataspace, often the same data may also be accessible and modifiable through an interface native to the system hosting the data. Thus, unlike a DBMS, a DSSP is not in full control of its data.
- Queries to a DSSP may offer varying levels of service, and in some cases may return *best-effort* or approximate answers. For example, when individual data sources are unavailable, a DSSP may be capable of producing the best results it can, using the data accessible to it at the time of the query.
- A DSSP should offer the tools to create tighter integration of data in the space as necessary.

Reference

1. M. Franklin, A. Halevy and D. Maier. From Databases to Dataspaces: a new abstraction for information management. *SIGMOD Record*, Volume 34(4), pp. 27-33, December, 2005.

Dissemination of Dynamic Data: Semantics, Algorithms, and Performance
(Extended Abstract)

Krithi Ramamritham

Indian Institute of Technology, Bombay
krithi@iitb.ac.in

The Internet and the Web are increasingly used to disseminate fast changing data such as sensor data, traffic and weather information, stock prices, sports scores, and even health monitoring information. These data items are highly dynamic, i.e., the data changes continuously and rapidly, streamed in real-time, i.e., new data can be viewed as being appended to the old or historical data, and aperiodic, i.e., the time between the updates and the value of the updates are not known a priori. Increasingly, users are interested in monitoring such data for online decision making. To provide users with dynamic, interactive, and personalized experiences, websites are relying on dynamic content generation applications, which build Web pages on the fly based on the run-time state of the website and the user session on the site. These applications make use of database backends. But, these benefits come at a cost, each request for a dynamic page requires computation as well as communication across multiple components inside the data dissemination and information processing infrastructure.

Consider the following scenario.

A company involved in developing IT enabled services responds to Request For proposals (RFPs). Often RFPs are brought to its attention by customers, sometimes through word of mouth. Won't it be convenient if the posting of a relevant RFP at a (potential) customer's website is automatically brought to the attention of the appropriate business unit or group within company? Our work is motivated by such needs -- the need to constantly track and monitor the dynamics of information sources -- some of which are identified through historical access patterns, others by monitoring potentially useful sites judiciously. Also, often a company responding to RFPs is looking to bolster its case by citing completed projects where the relevant skillsets have been demonstrated. The needed information can be retrieved by maintaining a knowledge repository and setting the following query that continuously sends up-to-date information, as the knowledge base gets updated, to the proposal writer(s).

```
CQ RFP_tracker:
   SELECT project_name, contact_info
   FROM RFP_DB
   WHERE skill_set_required ⊆ available_skills
```

Such a knowledge repository can be seen as an aggregator of data from specific dynamic sources. As another example, consider a user who wants to track a portfolio of

M.L. Lee, K.L. Tan, and V. Wuwongse (Eds.): DASFAA 2006, LNCS 3882, pp. 3 – 5, 2006.

stocks, in different (brokerage) accounts. He or she might be using a third party data aggregator which provides a unified view of financial information of interest by periodically obtaining information from multiple independent sources.

These examples reflect applications which make use of information that experience rapid and unpredictable changes for on-line decision making in time critical or value critical environments. The growth of the Internet as well as Intranets has made the problem of managing and disseminating such dynamic data both interesting and challenging. Resource limitations at a source of dynamic data or within the dissemination infrastructure will limit the number of users that can be served directly by the source. As user load on a site increases, the computation and communication costs can result in significant delays, leading to poor scalability and availability of dynamic data. Solutions needed to mitigate these problems involve techniques from multiple domains:

- *WWW and the internet* -- caching, replication, dynamic page generation techniques, edge servers;
- *Distributed systems* -- replication, load balancing, distribution of data;
- *Networking* -- content distribution networks, application level multicasting, peer-to-peer networks; and
- *Databases* -- active, real-time databases, caching.

There is a lot of excitement about this topic if the papers in conferences related to all the above areas are any indication. As part of our work, we have contributed to this excitement, but many questions remain. In this keynote talk, we will discuss the following issues, focusing on the open problems (see reference for details):

Specification of user QoS needs

The focus in many applications such as traffic monitoring, network fault management, etc., has been on the dissemination of important events as opposed to data, and on the execution of continuous queries. There are several alternative ways in which these can be expressed; Event-condition-action rules have been used for situation monitoring, profiles have been proposed for retrieving data or changes from the web and other sources, and continuous SQL-like queries have been used for processing dynamic data. In spite of the communication and computation overheads being non-negligible, the system should provide temporally coherent responses to queries over distributed data. So, in addition to specifying the queries, users' QoS should also be formulated to quantify the required coherency in the responses.

Caching-based approaches

Caching and replicating are widely used approaches to mitigate the performance degradations due to content distribution and delivery. But, unless updates to the data are carefully disseminated from sources to caches (to keep them coherent with the sources), the communication and computation overheads involved can lead to further losses of coherence in the results of queries executed over dynamic data.

Content Distribution Networks (CDNs) for dynamic data

Resource limitations at a source of dynamic data will limit the number of users that can be served directly by the source. A natural solution to this is to have CDNs for Dynamic Data, formed by a set of repositories which replicate the source data and serve it to geographically closer users. Services like Akamai and IBM's edge server technology are exemplars of such networks of repositories, which aim to provide better services by shifting most of the work to the edge of the network (closer to the end users). Although such systems scale quite well, when the data is changing rapidly, the quality of service at a repository farther from the data source will deteriorate. In general, replication can reduce the load on the sources, but replication of time-varying data introduces new challenges. Unless updates to the data are carefully disseminated from sources to repositories (to keep them coherent with the sources), the communication and computation overheads involved can result in delays as well as scalability, further contributing to loss of data coherence.

Change detection and monitoring
This is a critical requirement for many dynamic data intensive applications. Timely dissemination of changes to interested information sources is especially critical as periodic pull by humans (current usage) is a waste of resources. Algorithms for detecting changes to the contents of HTML and XML pages have been developed and used in many systems. In general, it is important for the change tracking procedure to be adaptive. Rather than having a periodic fetching of pages, the time of next fetch needs to be determined depending on the observed trend of changes in fetched pages. This would further reduce the amount of resources consumed for tracking and monitoring.

While discussing solutions to the above topics, we will make connections to those from peer-to-peer systems, stream processing, as well as sensor networks.

Reference

http://www.cse.iitb.ac.in/~krithi/ddd.html

Geo-Enabled, Mobile Services—A Tale of Routes, Detours, and Dead Ends

Christian S. Jensen

Department of Computer Science, Aalborg University, Denmark
csj@cs.aau.dk

Abstract. We are witnessing the emergence of a global infrastructure that enables the widespread deployment of geo-enabled, mobile services in practice. At the same time, the research community has also paid increasing attention to data management aspects of mobile services. This paper offers me an opportunity to characterize this research area and to describe some of their challenges and pitfalls, and it affords me an opportunity to look back and reflect upon some of the general challenges we face as researchers. I hope that my views and experiences as expressed in this paper may enable others to challenge their own views about this exciting research area and about how to best carry out their research in their own unique contexts.

1 Introduction

Driven in large part by rapid and sustained advances in key computing and communication hardware technologies, an infrastructure is emerging that contains vast quantities of interconnected computing and sensory devices.

Notably, we are witnessing continued improvements in the capabilities of consumer electronics such as mobile phones, personal digital assistants, personal computers, cameras, mp3 players, watches, navigation systems, and driver assistance systems. The performance and performance/price ratios associated with key technologies utilized by such systems and devices continue to increase quite rapidly.

Geo-positioning is also becoming increasingly available. For example, network assisted GPS promises to eliminate the excessive power consumption of GPS receivers, thus rendering GPS practical for outdoor, battery powered devices. The first satellite of the Galileo positioning system has already been launched, and Galileo is expected to be operational in 2010 [20]. Galileo will offer better positioning than does GPS with respect to several aspects, including the accuracy, penetration, and time to fix [1]. For example, the best-case accuracy (without the use of ground stations) of Galileo is 45 cm as opposed to 2 m for GPS. Next generation GPS will also offer better positioning, and Galileo and GPS are expected to be interoperable.

Further, the trend is towards the ability of consumer electronics devices to communicate with one another and their becoming Internet-worked.

This emerging infrastructure has the potential for enabling entirely new, geo-enabled applications and services that were either not relevant or of little use in fixed desktop computing settings.

M.L. Lee, K.L. Tan, and V. Wuwongse (Eds.): DASFAA 2006, LNCS 3882, pp. 6–19, 2006.

The range of possible applications and services is virtually limitless. For example, it includes traffic and transportation related services such as "fleet" management, including emergency vehicle dispatching and hazardous cargo and traffic offender tracking; road-pricing where payment is dependent on where, when, and how much a vehicle drives; other "metered" services, such as insurance and parking. It includes services that warn drivers about accidents, slow-moving vehicles, and icy and slippery road conditions on the road ahead. It also includes a wider range of safety-related services, such as services that track senile senior citizens, tourists traveling in potentially dangerous environments, and prisoners serving time at home. Next, it includes the oft-mentioned point-of-interest services that identify gas stations, restaurants, hospitals, etc. Finally, it includes the emerging and challenging area of games and "-tainment" (edu-, info-, enter-) services. One theme is to move games from taking part in a virtual world behind a small computer screen to taking part in reality. Virtual objects, e.g., treasures (or caches, cf. geocaching [6]), monsters, and bullets, are given geographical coordinates along with real, physical objects. This arrangement then enables games that aim to find treasures, catch or escape monsters, and hit with (virtual!) bullets.

Adopting a data centric view, I believe that by capturing pertinent aspects of reality in digital form—in semantically rich and appropriately organized structures, and with powerful update and retrieval techniques available—an ideal foundation for delivering a wide range of mobile services is obtained.

Members of the database research community are increasingly engaging in research in this exciting area, for good reasons. Geo-enabled, mobile services have great potential for being applied throughout society. Data management is a central element of such services. Further, this area offers ample new challenges to data management.

The remainder of this paper consists of four sections. In the next section, I discuss several general issues that relate to conducting use-inspired research and that reach beyond this research area. Section 3 elaborates on the data centric view of geo-enabled, mobile services espoused above. Then, Sect. 4 presents selected challenges and pitfalls specific to research within geo-enabled, mobile services. Finally, Sect. 5 summarizes the paper and points to further readings.

2 Aspects of Conducting Use-Inspired Research

This section considers first the positioning of research activities according to the degrees to which they are use inspired. Then, the positioning of research activities with respect to when their results can be expected to find practical application is discussed. Finally, Sect. 2.3 covers possible sources of inspiration for research ideas.

2.1 Solutions to Real Problems and Fundamental Insights

In his book "Pasteur's Quadrant," Donald E. Stokes [18] discusses the traditional dichotomy between basic research and applied research. He argues for a new, two-dimensional taxonomy. One dimension distinguishes between research that is use inspired and research that is not. The other distinguishes between research that yields (or aims for) fundamental understanding and research that does not. Stokes names the other two interesting quadrants after Bohr (fundamental insight, not use inspired) and Edison (no fundamental insight, use inspired). He gracefully leaves the last quadrant unnamed.

Our different research activities may be categorized according to Stokes' concepts. In particular, we may position our activities with respect to how use inspired they are. At the one extreme, we find application development. Here, we may well have a requirements specification that details what it takes to meet users' needs. At the other extreme, we typically find mathematical works that simply aim to solve open problems, e.g., to establish new complexity bounds for theoretical problems.

Much research in the database area—certainly in relation to the specific area considered in this paper—belongs in-between these two extremes. On the one hand, we do not base our work on articulated requirements specifications from real applications. On the other hand, we do tend to state practical concerns as motivation for our research.

Both extremes have merit, as do positions in-between these two. However, there are also dangers associated with in-between positions. In particular, when aiming for in-between positions, we run the risk of neither meeting any real needs nor solving any fundamental problems, thus ending up in the unnamed quadrant. Some years ago, I discussed this issue with a senior researcher. He told me that when he reviews papers, he is happy with a paper if it is able to simply point to one real application where its contribution is useful. At first, I thought that these were low stakes. I have since realized that this is not the case. It can actually be quite hard to identify such an application. A single paper often represents only one step towards a contribution that may have practical applications.

If we simply list, as an afterthought, specific applications in the motivational part of the introduction to a paper when the research is being written up, the results are often not convincing, and we run the risk of fooling ourselves. I believe that some of our research activities may benefit from us spending more time thinking about their positioning with respect to (specific or classes of) applications.

2.2 Timing

In many of our research activities, we aim for results that may eventually find application in practice. For this research, it seems to make sense for us to consider early on *when* we expect the results to be applied and then to formulate expectations to the state of reality as of that future time. The point is that the research results should apply to that reality.

It is of course not possible to accurately predict the state of reality, or even the aspects of reality that may be most relevant for our research, in, say, five or ten years from now. However, I still advocate that we spend a bit of time in formulating some expectations. The alternative would be to work totally in the dark.

One starting point is to extrapolate technology trends. Moore's Law effectively states that processor speeds double every 2 years (the numbers of a transistors on a chip doubles every 2 years) [8]. This self-fulfilling prophecy was put forward by Intel co-founder Gordon Moore in the mid 1960s, and it has roughly held true for four decades. Similar statements, with shorter doubling times, may be made for disk capacities and computer network bandwidths.

Let us consider what I term the Bicycle Analogy: *How fast will a bicyclist be able to go if Moore's Law applied?* Making the reasonable assumptions that the bicyclist is able to travel at 30 km/h originally and that the speed doubles every 2 years for 40 years, the current speed is 31,457,280 km/h!

This analogy illustrates several points: First, it illustrates my view that quantitative advances in hardware technologies are very important drivers of the research in software technologies. They have a profound impact on the software research agenda. (Qualitative advances, e.g., in the form of new types of sensors, are also important.) Second, sustained, exponential improvements such as these are dramatic and difficult to imagine. Indeed, they are counter-intuitive—we are simply not used to such rates of improvements in our daily lives. So, even if we have heard about exponential improvements, they are not natural to us.

I still remember how thrilled I was when, in 1991, I was able to get an external disk for my Mac. This disk was heavier than my current laptop, it sounded like a jet plane when it was turned on, and its capacity was less than 20 MB! At that time, if someone had told me about today's disks, or that I could get, e.g., a Secure Digital memory card that weighs 2 grams, uses very little power, and has a capacity of 2 GB, I am not sure that I would have believed it or acted wholeheartedly upon it in my research.

Third, the humans are the constant parts of the equation. While we perhaps think we are getting a lot smarter as the years go by, the improvements are negligible in comparison to the technology improvements.

Jim Gray's DBLP listing [5] has a significant concentration of papers that concern technology trends and is a good starting point for continued studies.

However, just because something is technically possible, this does not mean that that something is being deployed in practice. If we simply adopt a very technological focus, we may end up with overly optimistic predictions. Many technological possibilities do not materialize in practice, or do so only much later than possible. For example, third-generation mobile telephony has been technically possible for quite a few years, but is only now being deployed in many parts of the world.

People and enterprises are often conservative. The availability of existing infrastructures, or legacy systems, that to a large extent are capable of meeting needs block the deployment of new technologies. For new technologies to actually be deployed, a plausible business case must exist.

Incidentally, one big difference between academia and business is the importance of timing. In academia, it is probably not a disaster if a particular research result finds application only a few years later than expected. Rather, it is likely to be considered a success that the result found application at all! In business, where the potential financial rewards are higher, timing is of the essence. Once an enterprise has invested in new technology, that investment needs to generate revenue, so that salaries, etc. can be paid.

2.3 Inspiration

One important aspect of doing well in research is to work on great research ideas. There are many approaches to seeking inspiration that may lead to great ideas. Here, I discuss three.

A traditional way of getting ideas is to study the body of related work within one's area. In any event, it is important to be familiar with past, related work. One reason is that research results have little value if they are not new. Another is that it is important to build on past results where possible. By reading the literature, it is possible to get great ideas. However, this approach may also have a tendency to foster research activities and results that are closely related to existing activities and results. What has already been done had a tendency to define the "universe," and it is difficult to step well outside this universe.

For example, the research literature contains several dozen proposals for temporal data models and query languages. It seems that as everybody in the temporal database community read the many interesting papers about data models and query languages, they had to also study these subjects and also had to propose their own. As more and more proposals accumulated, it became increasingly harder to invent new and interesting proposals. And at some point, it probably became more constructive to study other problems.

The second approach to seeking inspiration is to interact with entrepreneurs. While researchers are constantly on the lookout for interesting problems to work on and thus thrive on problems, entrepreneurs thrive on solutions—they have plenty of problems.

During my interactions with entrepreneurs—e.g., via participation in advisory boards or boards of directors for technology start-ups, via industrial collaborations in research projects, and via participation in industry associations—many of my "great" ideas have been shot down as either not a "real" problem (because there is an easy 80% solution that does the job) or not an "important" problem (because there are many, more pressing problems).

While entrepreneurs have their own agendas and can be quite strong minded, they offer a different perspective. They serve as a filter that helps eliminate bad ideas and prioritize the remaining ones. In my experience, this has a positive effect on relevance and impact.

The third approach is to obtain inspiration from domain experts. One of the problems with relying solely on the first approach is that the research literature is generally quite abstract when it comes to the requirements of real problems. In contrast, domain experts have much richer views of problems and requirements. By interacting with domain experts, it becomes possible to "see" problems that would otherwise have remained invisible. For example, I have benefited from interacting with traffic researchers. This way, I have learned about problems that I would otherwise not have imagined.

3 Geo-Enabled Mobile Services

This section first elaborates on the data centric view of mobile services as formulated in the introduction. It then discusses the various types of content of relevance for mobile services, including business content (e.g., point-of-interest data), generic geo-content, also termed infrastructure, and user-specific geo-context.

3.1 Overview

The introduction states that "by capturing pertinent aspects of reality in digital form—in semantically rich and appropriately organized structures, and with powerful update and retrieval techniques available—an ideal foundation for delivering a wide range of mobile services is obtained." This section elaborates some on this statement.

First, this statement represents a data centric view of mobile services. The idea is that a service request by a mobile user translates into queries against the database envisioned in the statement. A key challenge in the delivery of mobile services then becomes a data processing problem.

The phrase "digital mirror of reality" has been used for describing the envisioned database. While this concise phrase is certainly to the point, it only partially reflects the desirable capabilities of this database, which go well beyond simply being a mirror. In particular, the database may capture past states of reality and one or more perceived future states, in addition to the current state. In more technical terms, the database supports the valid-time aspect of data. Further, if accountability is a concern, the database may include an incorruptible record of its past states. In technical terms, this is called transaction-time support.

Next, the database and the database management system used may not be a single relational or object-relational database stored in a centralized system. Rather, the database and system may well be distributed and heterogeneous in a number of respects. For example, the data may be physically distributed and may not adhere to the same common schema or data model. The control and data processing may also be distributed.

3.2 Infrastructure and Business Content

The delivery of geo-enabled mobile services in practice is dependent on relevant content being available. Examples of content include weather data; traffic condition data, including information about accidents and congestion; information about sights and attractions, e.g., for tourists; information about hotel rooms, etc. available for booking; and information about the current locations of populations of service users.

The management of such content includes several aspects. An information technology infrastructure, as discussed briefly in the previous section, must exist that is capable of capturing the content and capable of absorbing the content as it is made available, while being able simultaneously to make the content available to services.

We may distinguish between two types of content: the geographical infrastructure itself and all the other, "real" content that may be given geographical references and that must reference the infrastructure. So-called points of interest exemplify real content.

The *geographical infrastructure*, or *geo-content*, concerns the geographical space "itself," with hills, lakes, rivers, fjords, etc. It also concerns the road networks for use by vehicles and the transportation infrastructures for, e.g., pedestrians, trains, aircraft, and ships. The infrastructure for vehicles is of high interest because users may frequently be either constrained to, or at least using, this infrastructure.

Geo-content is essential. Users think of the real content as being located in a transportation infrastructure, and they access the content via the infrastructure. For example, the location of a point of interest is typically given in terms of the road along which it is located, and directions for how to reach the location are given in terms of the transportation infrastructure.

For the delivery of a range of geo-enabled mobile services, it is particularly important that a representation of the road infrastructure is available that supports multiple functions, including content capture; content update and querying, including route planning and way finding; and user display. This representation may be composed of several constituent representations [11].

It is common practice to specify the location of some content relative to the nearest kilometer post along a specific road. For example, the entry to a new parking area may be indicated by a road, a kilometer post on that road, and an offset. One representation, using linear referencing, is used in connection with the capture of such content.

A weighted, directed-graph representation may also be used that represents a quite abstract view of an infrastructure. This representation ignores geographical detail, but preserves the topology, and it may be used for connectivity-type queries, such as route guidance and way finding.

Next, a geo-representation is also needed that captures the geographical coordinates of the road infrastructure. With this representation, it is possible to map a location given in terms of geographical coordinates, e.g., from GPS receivers or point-on-a-map-and-click interfaces, to a location in the infrastructure. Finally, these three representations must be integrated.

All the *real content* encompasses any content that may reference, directly or indirectly, the geographical infrastructure. A museum, a store, or a movie theatre may have both a set of coordinates and a location in the road network. This type of content is open-ended and extremely voluminous. For example, it may include listings of movies currently running in the movie theatre, it may include seat availability information for the different shows, and it may include reviews of the movies. Often, the real content is the primary interest of the users.

Content is generally dynamic. This applies to road networks, where road construction and accidents change the characteristics of the networks with varying degrees of permanence. Other content is also dynamic. Examples abound. New stores open and existing stores relocate or close. The opening hours of a facility may change. The program of a movie theater changes. The sales available in a store change. This dynamicity of content implies that a representation of content must be designed to accommodate updates.

Content is more or less dynamic. The content that derives from the sampling of the positions of moving objects belongs at the highly dynamic end of the spectrum. Capturing the present positions, and possibly the past as well as anticipated future positions, of a large population of mobile users requires special techniques, as discussed next.

3.3 User-Specific Geo-Context—Locations, Destinations, Routes, and Trajectories

User-specific geo-context is another kind of content. Among such content, the *current position* of a service user is the traditional geo-context used in location-based services.

To maintain an up-to-date record of the current position of a service user, we may envision a scenario where a central server maintains a representation of the user's movement and where the local client, e.g., a mobile phone, is aware of the server-side representation. The client frequently compares its GPS position to the server-side position, and when the two differ by a threshold slightly smaller than the accuracy required, an update is issued to the server, which then revises its representation of the client's movement and sends this new representation to the client [3, 4]. This arrangement, termed shared-prediction-based tracking, aims to reduce the number of updates needed in order to main a current position at a given accuracy.

Different representations of a user's movement result in different rates of update. We consider several possible representations in turn. First, we may represent the movement of a user as a constant function, i.e., as a point. With this representation, an update is needed every time the user has moved a (Euclidean) distance equal to the threshold away from the previous position. This is a simple representation, and it may be useful when the user is barely moving or is moving erratically within an area that is small in comparison to the area given by the threshold used.

Second, we may represent the movement by a linear function, i.e., by a vector. When the user exceeds the threshold, the user sends the current GPS location and the current speed and direction (which GPS receivers also provide) to the server. The server then uses this information to predict the user's to-be-current positions.

Third, we may utilize the infrastructure in the representation of a user's movement. This requires that we are able to locate the user with respect to the infrastructure. One possibility is to assume that the user is moving at constant speed along the road on which the user is currently located. We may use the GPS speed as the constant speed, and we may assume that the user stops when reaching the end of the current road segment. Depending on the lengths of the segments, this representation can be expected to be better or worse than the vector representation. However, for realistic segments, this representation has the potential for outperforming the vector representation.

Next, we may use the route of the user in place of the segments. Folklore has it that most humans who travel do so towards a known destination. Most often, we do not move around aimlessly. Further, being creatures of habit, and perhaps for maximum efficiency, we tend to follow routes we have previously followed. Therefore, it is a good assumption that we are frequently able to predict correctly the route on which a service user travels. Using the correct route in place of a road segment means that the number of updates needed to maintain a user's position with the desired accuracy decreases further. Indeed, updates occur only because of incorrectly predicted speeds—no updates are caused by incorrectly predicted "locations." It should also be observed that if a route is predicted incorrectly, e.g., because the user makes a turn, this does not lead to a breakdown. Rather, this simply forces an update and a new prediction.

The infrastructures currently available for mobile services support the accumulation of GPS data from vehicles. Based on this data, it is possible to gradually create usage patterns for vehicles that consist of the routes traveled by the vehicles along with usage meta-data, which are temporal patterns that describe for each vehicle and route when the route is being used by that vehicle [2]. For example, a pattern may specify that a route is being used in the morning on weekdays. The resulting route and destination data may subsequently be used in services. By also attaching travel speeds to routes, we obtain trajectories, which are routes "lifted" into the time dimension [7].

4 Pitfalls and Specific Recommendations

This section presents six recommendations for conducting research. These are intended to apply to the area of geo-enabled, mobile services, but are to varying degrees applicable also to other areas of research. These are all recommendations that I am trying to follow myself, with the hope that my research is going to benefit.

4.1 Perceived Reality

For application-oriented research, estimate the time of application and formulate expectations to the reality as of that time; then design for that reality.

This recommendation was discussed in an abstract setting in Sect. 2.2. My different research activities[1] have quite different use horizons. For example, my research on tracking (e.g., [3, 4]) is applicable here and now, and is expect to remain applicable for the foreseeable future. For this research activity, we take care to only make assumptions that are met by current infrastructures. Assumptions concern the available computing and storage capabilities of mobile terminals, the available communication technologies, the available positioning technologies, the available digital road networks, and existing legislation.

Towards the other extreme, I expect that much of my research on the indexing of the positions of moving objects (e.g., [12, 14, 15, 16, 17]) is only applicable in the longer term. For disk-based indexing to be of interest, the sets of data items to be indexed must be much larger than the data sets seen today. For indexes that consider the current states of objects, the data sets should probably contain positions of hundreds of thousands of objects, while for indexes that consider the entire lifetimes of objects, data sets that concern thousands or tens of thousands of objects suffice to render disk-based indexing relevant.

This line of research is more speculative than the research on tracking, and it is also somewhat more removed from specific applications. Some of the results may not offer the final answers, but may serve as inspiration for further work. Also, although this research is generally cast in the setting of indexing of moving object, it might be that the results will be applied in other settings, e.g., settings with low-dimensional, continuous variables.

4.2 Architectural Setting

Ensure that at least one appropriate architectural setting exists or may be envisioned for the research contribution.

For some research, it is important to be specific about the architectural assumptions underlying the research. For other research, it may be sufficient to ensure that an appropriate architectural setting exists or can be envisioned. And for yet other research, architectural settings may not be an important concern.

In particular, for research that is expected to have practical application in the short term, the architectural setting is likely to be a concern. In keeping with this, the research I have conducted with my colleagues on tracking and also route acquisitioning and provisioning [2] is fairly explicit about architecture, and attempts have been made to ensure

[1] I will generally concern myself with my own research, to avoid making bold statements about the research of others.

that the assumptions about the possible application contexts are reasonable. In particular, we believe that the contributions are applicable in current application contexts, e.g., existing server-side systems, existing mobile terminals that use GPS for positioning and for GPRS data communication, and existing digital road networks. To justify these claims, we have built and demonstrated proof-of-concept prototype implementations.

Considering next the research on the indexing of moving objects, which is less directly applicable in practice and only in the longer term, the issue seems to be to ensure that architectural settings will indeed exist at the time when the various proposed indexes become widely applicable.

One point here is that it appears unrealistic to assume that the many indexes for moving objects will find their way into conventional object-relational database management systems. Other areas of data management and computer science research are also quite prolific when it comes to the invention of new indexes, so these observations apply also to those other areas. We may instead assume that the indexes may be applied in more componentized and open data management architectures.

4.3 Composability

Invent solutions for composable functionality.

When research on query processing in relation to moving objects first took off, the efficient processing of many basic types of queries had yet to be explored in the new moving-object settings. Examples included one-time and continuous range queries, nearest-neighbor queries, and reverse nearest-neighbor queries, to name but a few.

As techniques for the processing of these basic types of queries accumulate, it is natural that attention shifts to as yet unexplored or lightly explored types of queries. A potential pitfall is that we start producing highly optimized solutions to very specialized types of queries. This path is not advisable, as the prospects of these solutions finding practical applications are likely to decrease with the degree of specialization of the functionality.

To appreciate the point, consider SQL and the relational algebra as examples: We should avoid following the path where we invent highly efficient algorithms for increasingly complex SQL queries. Rather, we should focus on developing efficient algorithms for the relational algebra operators in terms of which the SQL queries may be expressed. At some point, query optimization should take over from efficient, standalone algorithms.

4.4 Versatility and Robustness

Prioritize versatile and robust solutions over specialized and brittle, although possibly highly performant, solutions.

One lesson to be learned from current, commercial data management technology and existing applications is that versatile and robust solutions have better chances of finding practical use than do very specialized ones, even if these exhibit very high performance in some cases. The objective of a query optimizer is quite modest: it should avoid the clearly inefficient ways of computing a query and identify one good way of executing the query. (Even meeting this objective can be a challenge.)

In the area of data processing for moving objects, the parameter space—the number of parameters and parameter settings that characterize a data processing workload—is very large. One consequence of this is that there is "room" for many solutions that offer superior performance for certain settings, but may be clearly inefficient for other settings.

The recommendation is that we try to aim for solutions that are versatile in terms of the functionality they offer and that are robust in terms of the settings. A solution for which there exist other solutions so that for every possible parameter setting, at least one of these other solutions has twice the performance may still be preferable if it is much more robust than its competitors.

One concern here is that is seems to be much easier to produce an experimental study that demonstrates the merits of a highly performant, but possibly brittle, solution than a study that demonstrates the merits of a robust solution with performance that is dominated by existing solutions.

4.5 Context

Design query processing techniques that exploit the entire context.

Mobile services are delivered to devices that are typically without (qwerty) keyboards and that have only small screens. Further, a service may be expected to be delivered in situations where the main focus of attention of its user is not the service, but rather that of, e.g., navigating safely in traffic. For these reasons, it is much more important than in a desktop computing situation that the user receives only the relevant information and service, with as little interaction with the system as possible. One approach to obtaining these qualities is to make the mobile services aware of the user's context, as covered in Sects. 3.2 and 3.3. Another benefit of taking the entire context into account is that better functionality can be provided.

The user's current location is one possible geo-context, and the user's destination is another. Yet another is the route that takes the user from the current location to the destination. Also, the trajectory that takes the user to the destination is a possible context.

Routes are interesting for at least two reasons. First, as also discussed in Sect. 3.3, mobile users typically travel towards destinations. A user often, or typically, follows the same route when going from one location to another. For example, a user typically travels along the same route from home to work.

Second, routes are significant as context for a range of services. For example, a service that knows the route of a user may alert the user about travel conditions, e.g., congestion and accidents, on the route ahead, while not bothering the user with conditions that do not relate to the user's route. As another example, routes may be used when users request the locations of "nearby" points of interest.

Another type of geo-context is the infrastructure, e.g., the transportation infrastructure, into which the users are embedded.

When we design query processing techniques, I recommend that we try to use as arguments all the context that we can reasonably expect to have available. So if we can assume to know the likely route of a moving vehicle, we may suggest restaurants or gas stations to the driver that are near to the expected route, rather than merely to the driver's current location, which is the best a service can do if it ignores the route. And, utilizing knowledge of the road network, we can use network distances as opposed to Euclidean distances in our calculations, and we can augment the answers with distances, detour distances, and suggested routes to the points of interest returned.

4.6 Queries and Updates

Pay attention to both query performance and update performance.

Many indexing and query processing techniques for geographical data were originally developed for largely static data. For example, R-trees do not contend well with workloads with frequent updates.

In contrast, mobile-service application scenarios exist that are characterized by frequent position updates. This puts focus on techniques that are capable of supporting workloads consisting of frequent updates as well as queries, and it puts focus on studies of the trade-off between query performance and update performance.

Updates of moving-object positions correspond to the sampling of continuous, position-valued variables. One implication of this is that our record of the position of a moving object is inaccurate. Different services may tolerate different inaccuracies. For example, a localized-weather service may tolerate a relatively high degree of inaccuracy without this affecting the functionality of the service, while a navigation service is dependent on more accurate positions.

An obvious approach to taking advantage of the different accuracy tolerances of different services is to perform updates only when needed to maintain the accuracies needed (cf. Sect. 3.3). Indexing and query processing techniques should be able to exploit this approach to updates.

By forming predictions of the future movements of the objects, the numbers of updates can be further reduced. Indexing techniques for moving objects that represent the current and near-future positions of the objects as linear functions from time to points in space predict that the objects move in linear fashion. Techniques that represent object positions as points in space predict that the objects do not move. One study of the movements of vehicles [3, 4] shows that constant prediction leads to almost three times as many updates as does linear prediction for a range of reasonable accuracies.

5 Summary

Based on my own research experience and with a focus on my research in the area of geo-enabled mobile services, this paper first presents some of my general thoughts about conducting use-inspired research. Following a data centric characterization of geo-enabled mobile services and the content of relevance to such services, the paper presents six recommendations for future work in mobile services.

Although I try to maintain a portfolio of research activities that range from ones with practical applicability in the short term to ones that are more speculative and that may only have indirect applications in the long term, the paper mainly concerns research with intended applications in the near and medium terms. Thus, those who conduct research in an abstract setting that is unrelated to perceived applications may not find the paper relevant.

It is important to realize that there is no single best approach to obtaining good research results. I hope that the thoughts presented in this paper can inspire others to possibly adjust the approaches they favor, so that they avoid detours and dead ends in their research and instead are able to identify direct routes to even better results.

For those who are interested in introductions to the general area covered in this paper, the recent books by Voisard and Schiller [19] and Güting and Schneider [7] come highly recommended. Reaching beyond data management, the first offers a broad coverage of location-based services, while the second is devoted specifically to data management for moving objects. Also, two recent special issues [9, 10] of the IEEE Data Engineering Bulletin are good starting points for those interested in doing research in indexing and query processing for moving objects.

Acknowledgments

I would like to thank my current Ph.D. students and colleagues with whom I conduct research on geo-enabled mobile services: Agnė Brilingaitė, Alinas Čivilis, Xuegang Huang, Stardas Pakalnis, Torben Bach Pedersen, Simonas Šaltenis, Albrecht Schmidt, Laurynas Speičys, Dalia Tiešytė, Kristian Torp, and Nerius Tradišauskas. Thanks also to my other recent collaborators within this paper's area: Rimantas Benetis, Michael Böhlen, Martin Breunig, Bin Cui, Anders Friis-Christensen, Ralf Hartmut Güting, Christian Hage, Zhiyong Huang, Wynne Hsu, Gytis Karčiauskas, Augustas Kligys, Jan Kolář, Harry Lahrmann, Mong Li Lee, Dan Lin, Hua Lu, Jovita Nenotaitė, Beng Chin Ooi, Dieter Pfoser, Rosanne Price, Keng Lik Teo, Igor Timko, Nectaria Tryfona, Rui Zhang, and Nora Zokaitė.

It is in large measure my interactions with these dedicated and capable individuals that have led me to formulate the views expressed in this paper (but for which I am solely responsible!).

References

1. BBC News: Q&A Europe's Galileo project. news.bbc.co.uk/1/hi/sci/tech/4555276.stm(2006)
2. Brilingaitė, A., Jensen, C.S., Zokaitė, N.: Enabling routes as context in mobile services. In: Proc. ACM GIS (2004) 127–136
3. Čivilis, A., Jensen, C.S., J. Nenortaitė, J., Pakalnis, S.: Efficient tracking of moving objects with precision guarantees. In: Proc. MobiQuitous (2004) 164–173
4. Čivilis, A., Jensen, C.S., Pakalnis, S.: Techniques for Efficient Tracking of Road-Network-Based Moving Objects. IEEE TKDE **17** (2005) 698–712
5. DBLP: Jim Gray. www.informatik.uni-trier.de/~ley/db/indices/a-tree/g/Gray:Jim.html (2006)
6. Groundspeak: Geocaching. www.geocaching.com (2006)
7. Güting, R.H., Schneider, M.: Moving Objects Databases. Morgan Kaufmann (2005)
8. Intel Corporation: Moore's Law. www.intel.com/technology/silicon/mooreslaw/ (2006)

9. Jensen, C.S. (ed): Special Issue on Indexing of Moving Objects. IEEE Data Engineering Bulletin **25(2)** (2002).
10. Jensen, C.S. (ed): Special Issue on Infrastructure for Research in Spatio-Temporal Query Processing. IEEE Data Engineering Bulletin **26(2)** (2003).
11. Jensen, C.S.: Database Aspects of Location-Based Services. In: [19] (2004) 115–147
12. Jensen, C.S., Lin, D., Ooi, B.C.: Query and update efficient B+-tree based indexing of moving objects. In: Proc. VLDB (2004) 768–779
13. Jensen, C.S., Šaltenis, S.: Towards Increasingly Update Efficient Moving-Object Indexing. In: [9] (2002) 35–40
14. Lee, M.L., Hsu, W., Jensen, C.S., Cui, B., Teo, K.L.: Supporting frequent updates in R-trees: a bottom-up approach. In: Proc. VLDB (2003) 608–619
15. Lin, D., Jensen, C.S., Ooi, B.C.: Efficient indexing of the historical, present, and future positions of moving objects. In: Proc. MDM (2005) 59–66
16. Pelanis, M., Šaltenis, S., Jensen, C.S.: Indexing the past, present and anticipated future positions of moving objects. ACM TODS **31** (2006, to appear)
17. Šaltenis, S., Jensen, C.S., Leutenegger, S.T., Lopez, M.A.: Indexing the positions of continuously moving objects. In: Proc. ACM SIGMOD (2000) 331–342
18. Stokes, D. E.: Pasteur's Quadrant. Brookings (1997)
19. Voisard, A., Schiller, J.: Location-Based Services. Morgan Kaufmann (2004)
20. Wikipedia: Galileo positioning system. en.wikipedia.org/wiki/Galileo_positioning_system (2006)

Processing Multiple Aggregation Queries in Geo-Sensor Networks

Ken C.K. Lee[1], Wang-Chien Lee[1], Baihua Zheng[2], and Julian Winter[1]

[1] Pennsylvania State University, USA
{cklee, wlee, jwinter}@cse.psu.edu
[2] Singapore Management University, Singapore
bhzheng@smu.edu.sg

Abstract. To process aggregation queries issued through different sensors as access points in sensor networks, existing algorithms handle queries independently and perform in-network aggregation only at the query time. As a result of ad-hoc and independent execution of queries, no partial result is sharable and reusable among the queries. Consequently, scarce sensor network resources can be easily overconsumed, particularly, those sensors commonly accessed by queries. In this paper, we address this issue by examining strategies to maintain **M**aterialized **I**n-**N**etwork **V**iews (*MINVs*) that pre-compute and store commonly used aggregation results in the sensor network. With MINVs, aggregated sensed results for some spatial regions are available and sharable to queries. Thus, the number of sensor accesses is greatly reduced. Through simulations, we validate the effectiveness of proposed strategies.

1 Introduction

Sensor network applications are often interested in the sensed data in ceratin geographical regions (typically in form of spatial windows) rather than on some specific sensors. Examples of such applications include pollution monitoring and city road traffic control. Through sensor networks, those environmental data (i.e., pollution and traffic) are tracked and made available for querying. Due to the expensive energy cost of communication in wireless sensor networks, a summary of readings (i.e., aggregated readings) is preferred over a collection of all individual sensor readings. This kind of queries that collect aggregated readings from sensors within a geographical area is called *spatial aggregation query*. In such queries, aggregate functions such as sum, count, average, max and min are frequently used. Example queries include: "What is the average pollution index value in the 10-meter space surrounding me?" and "How many available parking slots in the car park?".

In-network aggregation has been studied in sensor database projects (for example, Cougar [1] and TinyDB [2]). These works focus on the construction and optimization of a routing tree, an ad-hoc network topology over which query results are aggregated and routed toward the root where the result is collected. However, the design of these works focuses only on a single query. For a large-scale sensor network, multiple queries may be issued from different locations with

M.L. Lee, K.L. Tan, and V. Wuwongse (Eds.): DASFAA 2006, LNCS 3882, pp. 20–34, 2006.

sensors close to the users serving as *access points*. With existing techniques, individual queries can be processed by forming independent routing trees with access points as the roots. Due to independent topologies, the aggregated results cannot be naturally shared with and reused by other queries. The scarce sensor resources (in particular, the battery power) are therefore easily overconsumed. Thus, the lifetime of a sensor network (or a certain portion of network) is quickly shortened when a large number of queries are issued.

Sharing results of multiple aggregation queries and optimizing the query performance presents some technical challenges that must be faced. An independent executing query does not take other queries into consideration. Therefore, it is difficult to (1) determine what partial aggregated result of a query will be reusable (if any) by other queries; (2) decide which sensors to store sharable results for later access; and (3) make other queries aware of the availability of the stored query results. Moreover, processing on-demand queries issued from arbitrary sensors is already a challenging issue.

In this paper, we address these challenges by maintaining **M**aterialized **I**n-**N**etwork **V**iews (*MINVs*) in the sensor networks. By identifying a set of frequently-used sensor readings at the planning stage, a MINV can be defined to store an aggregated result of readings from the set of sensors in support for processing queries at the run time. Obviously, the deployment of MINVs has several advantages. First, the study of query compatibility in multiple query optimizations is reduced to the matching between the view and the queries. A query can take full advantage of the view if the aggregation required by the query is the same as the view. Thus, multiple queries can be supported through the view. Second, the views are distributed in the sensor network, so it does not overload any single sensor and it does not require any *super sensor* (i.e., a more powerful sensor) for data storage or processing. Queries are executed by traversing sensors in the network to collect readings, either the raw data or aggregated results from the views, based on the real requirements.

The rest of the paper is organized as follows. Section 2 describes the system model our proposals are based on and reviews related work. Section 3 details the proposed schemes to support multiple spatial aggregation queries. Section 4 evaluates the impact of different factors on the performance through simulation. Finally, Section 5 concludes the paper.

2 Preliminaries

In this section, we first describe the characteristics of sensor networks and our assumptions. Then, we discuss spatial aggregation queries followed by the review of some approaches in data dissemination reported in literature.

2.1 System Model and Assumptions

We consider the sensor network formed by homogeneous and stationary sensors as shown in Fig. 1(a) where dots represent sensors. We assume that sensors are densely and uniformly distributed in a geographical area. Sensors have four

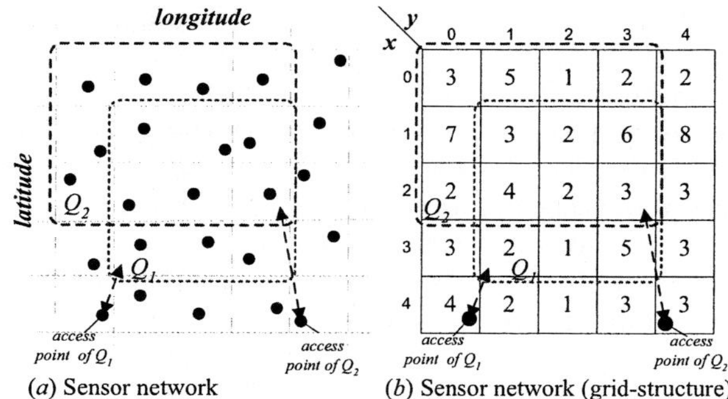

Fig. 1. Grid structure of sensor network

basic capabilities: (1) sensing, (2) storage, (3) computation, and (4) wireless communication. Sensors can sense and collect its readings, and serve as storage for its own collected readings and a partial content of a MINV. Computation enables some query processing tasks and wireless communication enables a sensor to relay messages from one sensor to its neighbors. All sensors are considered identical in terms of processing power, memory size, radio transmission coverage and energy. No task or data is sent to a specific *super* sensor for storage or processing. All sensors either operate independently or collaborate with others. We further assume the sensors are location-aware (i.e., each sensor obtains its geographical location) and time synchronized, (i.e., each sensor obtains the global clock) through GPS or other positioning techniques [3, 4].

As many well-known research in sensor data routing such as GAF [5] and data dissemination such as TTDD [6] and Comb-needle [7], we model the sensor network as a grid. We define the side length of a grid bound by $R/\sqrt{5}$ with R the transmission range of each sensor based on GAF [5]. Each cell is uniquely identified by a grid coordinate (x,y). For convenience, we refer to the cell at (x,y) as grid(x,y). We assume the cell side length is at most $R/\sqrt{5}$, therefore the signal of a sensor in a cell is conservatively reachable to other sensors in adjacent cells. To be specific, a message from a sensor located in grid(x, y) can be received by all other sensors within the same cell and neighboring cells (above, below, left and right) can also hear the message, but not sensors in diagonally adjacent cells. For simplicity, each cell is assumed to have only one sensor located at the center of grid(x, y) and denoted by $s_{x,y}$. Fig. 1(b) shows a logical presentation of the grid-structured sensor network. Further, we indicate a number in each cell as the reading of a corresponding sensor located inside the cell. Based on a grid-structured sensor network, we focus on the processing of spatial aggregation queries.

2.2 Spatial Aggregation Queries

Without loss of generality, we assume that each sensor maintains data in the following form: $\langle readings, loc \rangle$. Based on the grid structured sensor network, our spatial aggregation query is expressed in an SQL-like syntax as exemplified in the following:

SELECT $\mathbf{AGG}(readings)$ FROM SensorNetwork
WHERE loc IN $\langle[x_1, x_2], [y_1, y_2]\rangle$;

This expression means collecting ($\mathbf{AGG}(readings)$), aggregated readings from sensors in a logical relation, SensorNetwork, whose locations (loc) are within a region specified by $\langle[x_1, x_2], [y_1, y_2]\rangle$ where x_1, x_2, y_1 and y_2 are the grid coordinates. Referring to the Fig. 1(a), two aggregation queries, denoted by Q_1 and Q_2, are issued at two different sensors (called *access points*) to aggregate readings received at all the sensors within the specified spatial window. Later, the query results are routed back to the user via the corresponding access points.

2.3 Related Work

A number of ongoing research projects focus on guiding the sensors to disseminate their measurements to interested users. In general, those works can be grouped in three major categories, namely, *pure push*, *pure pull* and *hybrid* approaches. They are briefly reviewed as follows.

Pure Push Approaches. Pure push approaches proactively propagate readings from individual sensors assuming that queries located in different parts of the sensor network may be interested in their readings. This approach is suitable when multiple queries are scattered in the network and their locations are not known in advance. Example push approaches include flooding, SPIN [8] and TTDD [6].

Pure Pull Approach. In pure pull approach, sensors are silent unless a request arrives. Queries play an active role to traverse the network to collect readings. After having been triggered by a query, interested sensors deliver their readings toward an access point (also called sink point) where the query is issued. Example pull approaches include directed diffusion [9], TAG [10] and Cougar [1].

Hybrid Push and Pull Approach. Hybrid approaches combine the advantages of both push and pull approaches. These approaches are composed of two steps. First, sensors push their readings to collection points determined by dissemination algorithms. Second, from collection points, queries pull the readings depending on requirements. Several distributed approaches are proposed such as geographic hash-tables (GHTs) [11], DIM [12] and Comb-needle [7].

Our approaches proposed in this paper are also hybrid approaches, but are very different from existing work. First, we consider multiple queries with more complicated aggregation, which have not been considered in sensor networks. Second, we assume each sensor can serve as an access point and queries can be issued at any access point.

3 Materialized In-Network View

Motivated by the needs of sharing query results for multiple queries, we examine the use of MINVs to support multiple spatial aggregation queries. The materialized view has been widely used in data warehouse and OLAP applications [13] to improve the query response time. It computes aggregated values among a collection of disk resident operational data and stores the results as database views on disks. When a query is issued, the partial results of interested views are retrieved to ease query computation. We employ the similar idea in the context of sensor networks.

However, techniques designed for manipulating materialized views in a centralized database system cannot be directly applied to sensor networks due to the constraints of sensor networks. First, wireless communication is very energy expensive. Thus, both the message size and quantity need to be minimized. Second, each sensor has only a limited amount of memory and therefore a MINV needs to be distributed among sensors. Third, in-network view maintenance technique, rather than central approaches, are applied to keep the size of messages (intermediate view change) transferred among sensors compact.

Based upon the above factors, we propose three different approaches, namely, *full scanning*, *replication cluster*, and *prefix sum*, for managing a MINV and process spatial aggregation queries. Full scanning does not maintain any view. Replication cluster, as its name suggests, maintains a view of a pre-defined cluster and replicates the view to all the nodes inside the cluster. Prefix sum, good for supporting range sum queries, allows sensors to maintain cumulated readings over a range of sensors [13].

For the sake of simplicity, the following discussion focuses on the aggregation function, sum. Thus, a query accumulates sensor readings within a specified spatial window $\langle[x_1, x_2], [y_1, y_2]\rangle$. A given sum-aggregation query Q is to retrieve $\sum_{i=x_1}^{x_2} \sum_{j=y_1}^{y_2} r(s_{i,j})$, with $r(s_{i,j})$ the reading received from a sensor $s_{i,j}$. Let us revisit the query Q_1 depicted in Fig. 1(*b*). The specified spatial window is $\langle[1,3],[1,3]\rangle$ and the corresponding sum is 28 $(= 2+1+5+4+2+3+3+2+6)$.

3.1 Full Scanning

Full scanning is a pure pull approach. It maintains no view and serves as our baseline algorithm. Every query has to traverse all sensors within the query window to collect and aggregate readings. Initially, a query is routed from an access point to the closest sensor, named *originating node*, on the boundary of the spatial window. The query traversal follows two sorts of paths, namely, *border path* and *interior paths*. The border path runs along the window boundary and readings are recorded from encountered nodes until the originating node is met again. The interior paths are linear paths horizontally or vertically crossing the window. Employing both border and interior paths has the following advantages: (1) They ensure a complete coverage (and traversal) of all sensors in the window. (2) Parallel traversal of border path and interior paths improves response time. (3) The originating node where the scanning ends is the closest sensor to the access point; facilitating the efficient final result delivery.

The detailed description of scanning process of Q_1 is illustrated in Fig. 2. Initiated at the access point $(4, 0)$, Q_1 is first routed to the originating node $(3, 1)$ and traverses the border path in the clockwise direction. At $(2, 1)$, Q_1 finds a row of nodes ($(2, 1)$ through $(2, 3)$) not yet visited and forks a child query

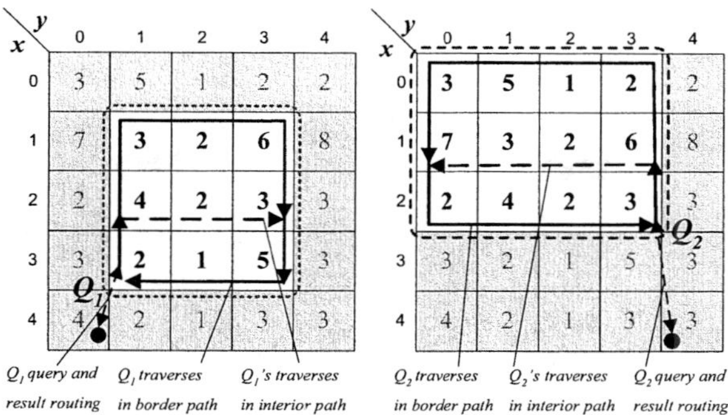

Fig. 2. Full scanning

Q'_1 to traverse along the interior path to collect the reading of the sensor at $(2,2)$. Meanwhile, Q_1 continues the traversal to $(1,1)$, $(1,2)$, and $(1,3)$. Then, at $(2,3)$, the intersection between the interior and border paths, Q_1 collects Q'_1's result (i.e., 2) and aggregates it with the tentative result (i.e., 20). Thereafter, Q_1 carries the aggregated reading of 22 and scans through $(3,3)$, $(3,2)$, and $(3,1)$, with the final reading of 28. The final answer is sent back to the access point. Q_2 traverses in the same fashion but with a counter-clockwise border path. The description is omitted for space saving.

For every single query, full scanning takes one pass and visits all required sensors once. However, sensors within a common query-interested region could be accessed multiple times. In Fig. 2, sensors within the common region of Q_1 and Q_2 (i.e. $\langle[1,2],[1,3]\rangle$), are accessed twice. Therefore, the saving/sharing among queries can be obtained if a sharable partial result is available somewhere.

3.2 Replication Cluster

The replication cluster approach is motivated by spatial access locality of queries, i.e., sensors closely located are very likely to be accessed by a same query. Here, we assume that certain clusters are determined at the system planning stage based on analysis of query patterns and other system, network, and application factors. Further, this cluster information is assumed known to both sensors and issued queries via pre-programming. Our idea is to let each sensor within a cluster maintain (and replicate) the view of an entire cluster. Thereafter, a query fully covering a cluster can obtain the view by visiting any single sensor within the cluster. Thus, the traversal of all the member nodes of a cluster is replaced by one sensor visit, significantly reducing the number of sensor accesses.

To maintain the freshness of a view inside a cluster, every sensor knows other member sensors in the same cluster and they adopt a flooding mechanism to update the view. When a sensor obtains a new reading, it updates its own replica of the view and then broadcasts the change (the difference between previous and new readings for sum semantic) to intermediate neighbor nodes. The broadcast is marked by a unique tuple $\langle ID_s, ID_b\rangle$, with ID_s the ID of the sender sensor

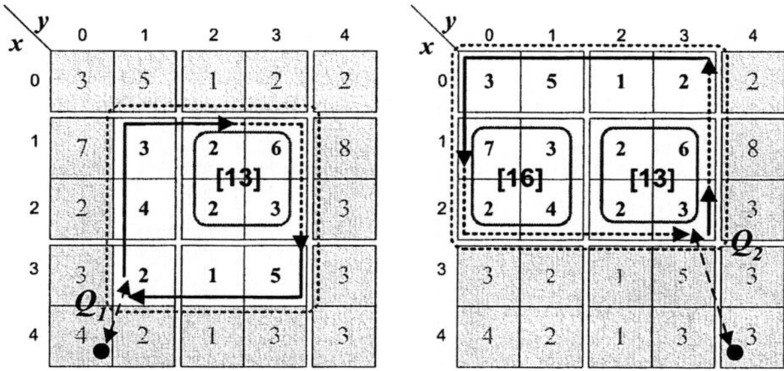

Fig. 3. Replication cluster

and ID_b the ID of the sender's broadcast. Once neighbor nodes receive the change, they update their own view replica and rebroadcast the same message. The flooding-based view update terminates at those nodes outside the cluster.

Fig. 3 shows query processing with replication cluster. Suppose two clusters are formed, located at $\langle[1,2],[0,1]\rangle$ and $\langle[1,2],[2,3]\rangle$. Like full scanning, Q_1 is first routed to node $(3,1)$ and starts traversal in the clockwise direction. However, a child query at $(2,1)$ can be avoided because the sensor at $(2,2)$ is part of a cluster fully covered by the query. Thus, it takes only the border path and aggregated result is 28 $(= 2+4+3+13+5+1)$. The result is sent back to the access point. Although Q_1 traverses both $(1,3)$ and $(2,3)$ (the path annotated by a dotted line), the query and the partial result are routed through the two sensors without invoking computation at the application level in sensors. Q_2 performs similarly. Note that the cluster $\langle[1,2],[2,3]\rangle$ is shared by both Q_1 and Q_2. Q_1 obtains the aggregated result (13) at node $(1,2)$ while Q_2 obtains it at node $(2,3)$. The workload of sensors within a cluster is also shared.

The cluster size has an impact on the performance. If the cluster size is relatively large to a query, a query will be less likely to be completely covered by a cluster; resulting in full scanning. If the cluster size is too small, the saving is limited since it still needs to fork child queries to scan interior sensors, and the sharing of aggregated readings is also limited.

3.3 Prefix Sum

The third approach is prefix sum view [13] which accumulates readings throughout the network. Each sensor maintains a partial cumulated sum of readings. We present two variants, namely, *1-dimensional (1-D) prefix sum* and *2-dimensional (2-D) prefix sum*. They employ the same aggregation concepts but are different in scopes of aggregation.

1-Dimensional Prefix Sum. With 1-D prefix sum, every sensor, $s_{i,j}$ in a sensor network maintains its own reading $r(s_{i,j})$, and a cumulated sum of readings denoted by $V_{i,j-1} = \sum_{k=0}^{j-1} r(s_{i,k})$ (or simply $V_{i,j-1} = r(s_{i,j-1}) + V_{i,j-2}$ where $V_{i,-1} = 0$). Sensor $s_{i,j}$ knows the sum of the readings of all the preceding nodes namely $s_{i,0}, s_{i,1} \cdots s_{i,j-1}$ in the row i. Fig. 4(a) depicts a sample sensor network

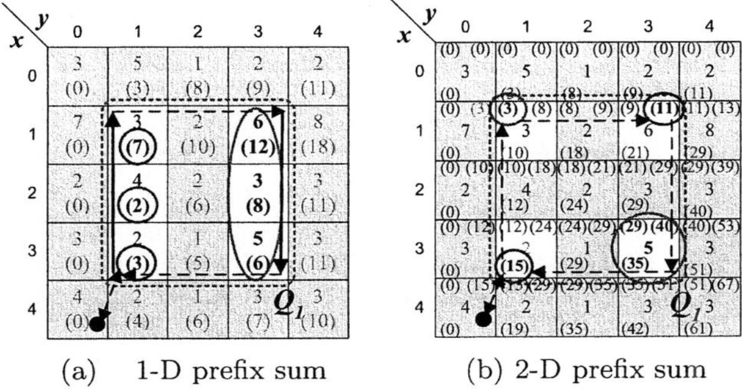

(a) 1-D prefix sum (b) 2-D prefix sum

Fig. 4. Linear Access on a Wireless Broadcast Channel

partitioned into 5 rows. In the top row, sensors $s_{0,j}$ keep readings: 3, 5, 1, 2 and 2 and the corresponding cumulated sums $V_{0,j-1}$ shown in braces: 0, 3, 8, 9 and 11 respectively, with $0 < j \leq 5$.

Instead of sending a sequence of readings along a row to initialize and update a view, in-network maintenance is used to propagate the sum of readings. At row i, the first node, $s_{i,0}$ starts propagating its own readings as $V_{i,0}$ $(= r(s_{i,0}))$ to the second node, $s_{i,1}$. Then $s_{i,1}$ keeps this received reading, and computes $V_{i,1}$, i.e., $V_{i,0} + r(s_{i,1})$ and sends it to $s_{i,2}$. The propagation repeats until the last sensor of the row is reached.

Upon request, a sensor $s_{i,j}$ can report any of the three readings: (1) its reading, $r(s_{i,j})$; (2) $V_{i,j-1}$, a stored cumulated sum of $r(s_{i,0})$ through $r(s_{i,j-1})$; and (3) $V_{i,j}$, a derived cumulated sum from readings of $s_{i,0}$ through $s_{i,j}$ (i.e., $V_{i,j-1} + r(s_{i,j})$). Thus, it is efficient to find out the cumulated sum from $s_{i,a}$ to $s_{i,b}$ $(a \leq b)$ in a row i by subtracting $V_{i,a-1}$ from $V_{i,b}$, since they are obtainable in $s_{i,a}$ and $s_{i,b}$. In Fig. 4(a), accessing sensors at $(0, 2)$ and $(0, 4)$ can get the cumulated sum from $(0, 2)$ to $(0, 4)$. The sensor at $(0, 2)$ provides $V_{0,1} = 8$ and the sensor at $(0, 4)$ reports $V_{0,4} = V_{0,3} + r(s_{0,4}) = 11 + 2 = 13$. The cumulated sum for the range is $V_{0,4} - V_{0,1} = 5$.

Spatial aggregation query processing is reduced to accessing the two ending nodes of rows covered by a query. For example, Q_1 in Fig. 4(a) covers three rows. Q_1 is first routed to the originating node at $(3, 1)$ to start clockwise border path traversal. It visits sensors at $(3, 1)$, $(2, 1)$ and $(1, 1)$ to collect $V_{3,0}(= 3)$, $V_{2,0}(= 2)$, and $V_{1,0}(= 7)$, respectively. Then the query is routed to $(1, 3)$, and it visits $(1, 3)$, $(2, 3)$, and $(3, 3)$ in sequence, collecting $V_{1,3}(= 18)$, $V_{2,3}(= 11)$, and $V_{3,3}(= 11)$. Finally the query result of 28 $(= -3 - 2 - 7 + 18 + 11 + 11)$ is sent back to the user.

2-Dimensional Prefix Sum. 2-D prefix sum view is in a 2-dimensional fashion. Before the discussion, we define the notation $W_{i,j}$ as the cumulated sum of reading of $s_{0,0}$ through $s_{i,j}$, i.e., $W_{i,j} = \sum_{a=0}^{i} \sum_{b=0}^{j} r(s_{a,b})$. Different from 1-D prefix sum view, each sensor $s_{i,j}$ has to maintain four readings, including (1) the local reading, $r(s_{i,j})$; (2) the cumulated sum $W_{i,j-1}$ provided by node $s_{i,j-1}$; (3) the cumulated sum $W_{i-1,j}$ provided by node $s_{i-1,j}$; and (4) the cumulated sum

$W_{i-1,j-1}$ from node $s_{i-1,j-1}$. With these four readings, $s_{i,j}$ can determine $W_{i,j}$ that is $r(s_{i,j})+W_{i,j-1}+W_{i-1,j}-W_{i-1,j-1}$. Illustrated in Fig. 4(b), a sensor, $s_{2,2}$, maintains four readings $r(s_{2,2})(=2)$, $W_{2,1}(=24)$, $W_{1,2}(=21)$ and $W_{1,1}(=18)$. The cumulated sum, $W_{2,2}$, is then $2+24+21-18=29$.

2-D prefix sum takes an entire 2D sensor network as a whole and maintain a network-wise view starting from $s_{0,0}$. When a sensor $s_{i,j}$ receives all the cumulated sums, i.e., $W_{i,j-1}$, $W_{i-1,j}$, and $W_{i-1,j-1}$ from its neighbors, it calculates $W_{i,j}$ and broadcasts two readings, $W_{i,j}$ and $W_{i,j-1}$ to sensors $s_{i,j+1}$ and $s_{i+1,j}$. The reason to broadcast $W_{i,j-1}$ is that $s_{i+1,j}$ may be located out of the transmission range of $s_{i,j-1}$ and may not receive $W_{i,j-1}$ during $s_{i,j-1}$'s broadcast.

The aggregated readings for a query can be efficiently derived with fewer sensor visits. For a region $\langle[x_1,x_2],[y_1,y_2]\rangle$, the aggregated reading is $W_{x_2,y_2}-W_{x_2,y_1-1}-W_{x_1-1,y_2}+W_{x_1-1,y_1-1}$. Since fewer nodes are visited, spatial aggregation queries can be performed at a much lower cost. As an example, Q_1 in Fig. 4(b) specifies $\langle[1,3],[1,3]\rangle$ as its traversal window. First, Q_1 visits the sensor at $(3,1)$ where $W_{3,0}(=15)$ is collected. Second, it visits the sensor at $(1,1)$ to collect $W_{0,0}(=3)$. Then Q_1 goes to sensors at $(1,3)$ and $(3,3)$ to collect $W_{0,3}(=11)$ and $W_{3,3}(=51)$. The final result is 28 $(=-15+3-11+51)$.

Discussion. Unlike replication cluster, prefix sum does not reinforce any cluster boundary. It provides better reuse of a MINV by simple addition and subtraction. With an 1-D prefix sum view, a range query can be answered by visiting nodes along two ending columns while with a 2-D prefix sum view, readings from four corner sensors are energy sufficient. 1-D prefix sum view has a slightly lower maintenance cost, and higher concurrency in view update than 2-D prefix sum view. Consider a sensor network of $m \times n$ nodes with insignificant signal interference. 1-D prefix sum view update performs a row-based update that involves at most $(n-1)$ propagations. 2-D prefix sum view maintenance starts at $s_{0,0}$, the top-left grid, and terminates at $s_{m-1,n-1}$. It requires $(n-1)$ propagations to reach the top-right side of the sensor network and another $(m-1)$ propagations to reach the bottom. Consequently, the time to update the entire network is about the same as the time to propagate $(m+n-2)$ messages. Besides, the storage overhead for 1-D prefix sum view is less than 2-D prefix sum view.

3.4 Extensions

In the above discussion, we have only considered the aggregate function sum. Here, we discuss the necessary extensions to the three approaches in support of other aggregate functions, such as max, min, count, average[1], and median, as shown in Table 1. To allow replication cluster to support max/min/median, the view definition can be modified such that all other possible sensor readings are maintained in the view. Keeping additional readings is useful to maintain the min/max and median. From the table we can observe that optimization is highly dependent on aggregate function types. Full-scanning can support all types of aggregate functions but it generally performs worse than the other two schemes

[1] average can be determined by the dividing sum by count.

Table 1. Support of aggregate functions

Approach	count/sum/average	max/min	median
Full scanning	Yes	Yes	Yes
Replication cluster	Yes	Additional readings required	
Prefix sum	Yes	No	No

due to the high traversal cost. Other approaches incur view update cost. Depending on the aggregate functions, appropriate approaches can be chosen or used in a combined way to evaluate a query. This observation inspires our future research work, i.e., how to combine different approaches to process aggregate queries.

4 Performance Evaluation

In this section, we provide performance evaluation of proposed approaches. We use simulation which is developed with CSIM18 [14] to examine the efficiency of our proposal in terms of total message costs, energy consumption and query response time. The system parameters are set as in Table 2. For simplicity, we assume sensor network, window queries, and clusters are squares, i.e. $m = n$, $q_x = q_y$ and $c_x = c_y$. We take sum as the aggregation function. Periodically or triggered by any sensor, update of a MINV is performed. We consider R_q as the ratio of the query issuing frequency (r_q) to the frequency of the update happening (r_u), i.e., the average number of queries issued between two consecutive updates. In addition to the proposed schemes, namely, full scanning (FS), replication cluster (RC), 1-D prefix sum (1DPS) and 2-D prefix sum (2DPS), we considered an alternative that all *raw* sensor readings are pulled out of the sensor network and maintained at a remote base station. We label this scheme **Base Station** (BS). All queries are routed to and processed at the base station. Assuming the base station is resident at grid(0,0) in the network, the message relay cost for a sensor at grid(i,j) is $i + j$.

To compare the performance of the three proposed approaches and the BS scheme, our simulation varies *query window size*, *ratio of query/update rates* and

Table 2. Parameters

Parameter	Notation	Settings	Default Value
Sensor network size	$m \times n$	$60^2, \cdots 140^2$	100^2
Query window size	$q_x \times q_y$	$10^2, \cdots 100^2$	20^2
Query rate (10^{-3} event per sec)	r_q	50, 5, 0.5, 0.05	0.5
Update rate (10^{-3} events per sec)	r_u	50	50
Ratio of query/update events	$R_q = r_u/r_q$	$1, 10, 100, 1000$	100
Cluster size	$c_x \times c_y$	2×2, 4×4	
Message Latency between two sensors		30ns	
Energy consumption per every message		21,600nj (send),3,600nj(receive)	

network size and study their impact on the *number of message relays*, *energy consumption* and *query response time*. The number of message relays counts the message passings between sensors. Energy consumption refers to the energy consumed per sensor in processing view updates and queries. For each sensor, the energy consumed to send a message takes 21,600 nano-joules (nj) and that to receive a message takes 3,600nj [15]. Query response time refers to the duration between query issue time and corresponding result collection time. On average, transmission of a message between sensors takes 30ms. In our evaluation, all results to present are averaged by the number of queries executed, so the average cost per query is reported. In the following subsections, the impacts of each factor is studied.

Evaluation 1. Impact of Query Window Size: Our first evaluation studies the impact of query window size which affects the query traversal costs. Generally speaking, a larger query window is expected to yield a larger number of messages transmitted for all proposed approaches. BS is however not affected by the query window size. We vary the query window size (side length in $10, \cdots 100$, with a step of 10) and fix the ratio of query rate and update rate (R_q) at 100 (by fixing query rate, r_q, at 0.5×10^{-3}/sec and update rate, r_u at 50×10^{-3}/sec).

The result is shown in Fig. 5. Firstly, Fig. 5(a) shows the number of message relays (in log scale). In the figure, we can see that 1DPS and 2DPS provide the least number of message relays, outperforming all other approaches. FS perform better than RC (both 2×2 and 4×4 clusters) only when small query sizes are experimented. As the query size larger than 30×30, FC and RC(2×2) are very

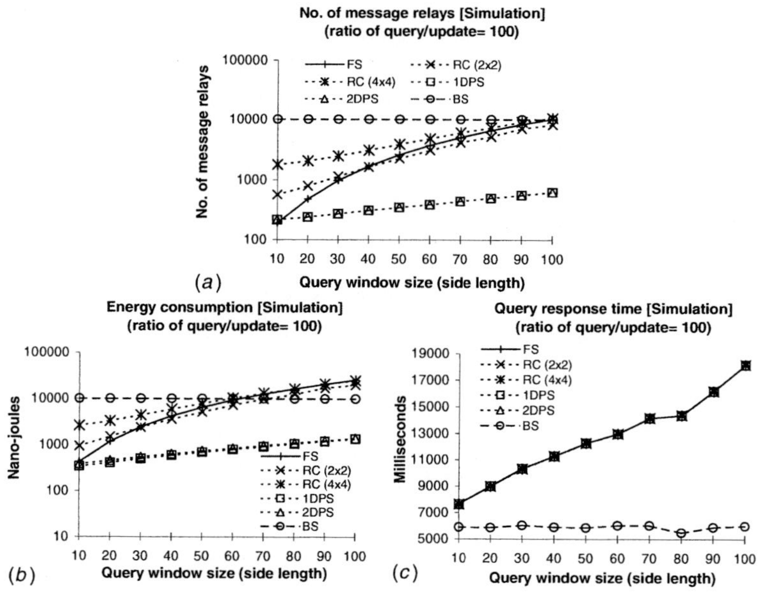

Fig. 5. Impact of query window size

close. Finally BS maintains the constant and largest number of message relays due to its high update costs.

Next, we study the impact of query size on energy consumption and query response time in Fig. 5(*b*) and Fig. 5(*c*), respectively. In Fig. 5(*b*), observation of energy consumption per sensor is very similar to that of message relays since message passing constitutes the major source of energy consumption. With this reason, we can see both 1DPS and 2DPS perform reasonably better than all others. BS maintains a constant level of energy consumption since it is independent of query size. In Fig. 5(*c*), query response time of all proposed schemes are the same since they involve the same longest query path, i.e., the border path for a same query window. Meanwhile, BS provides the shortest response time since queries do not need to traverse the query windows.

To sum up, this evaluation shows that the increase of query window size causes the message relays, energy consumption and response time increased for our proposed approaches. 1DPS and 2DPS perform the best and RC performs better than FC only when larger queries are experimented. BS provides constant performance and it performs the best in term of response time, otherwise, it is the weakest in the evaluation.

Evaluation 2. Impact of Ratio Between Query Rate and Update Rate: In the second evaluation, we study the effect of the ratio between query rate and update rate. The objective of this evaluation is to study the benefit of our proposed approaches when many queries are executed in a sensor network.

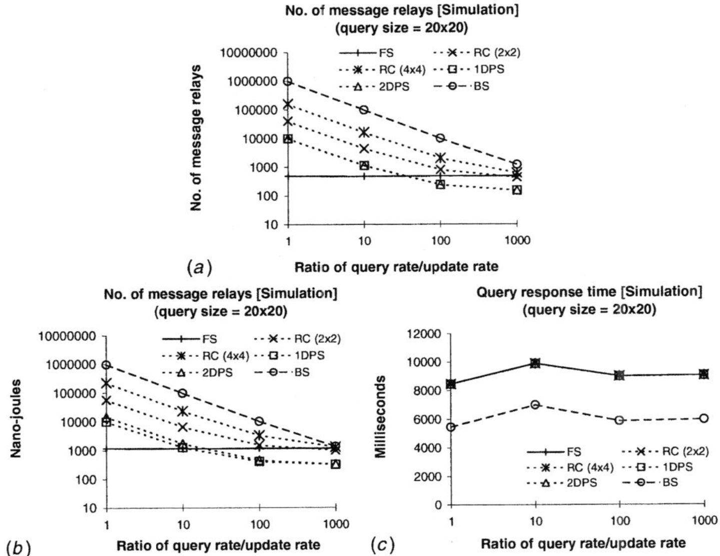

Fig. 6. Impact of query/update ratio

When the query rate is relatively high to update rate, the cost of MINV update is shared among queries for PS, RC and BS. FS is expected to have a fixed number of messages relays. We reuse the same settings as Evaluation 1 except that we vary the ratio of query rate and update rate between 1, 10, 100 and 1000 (by fixing query rate, r_q, at 50, 5, 0.5, 0.05 ($\times 10^{-3}$/sec) and fixing the update rate, r_u, at 50×10^{-3}/sec) and we retain the query window size at 20×20. Fig. 6 shows different performance metrics against the specified variation of ratio query/update rates. Fig. 6(a) shows the result in term of the number of message relays (in log scale). When a small query/update ratio (1 and 10) is experimented, all schemes except FS incurs higher costs due to heavy view update cost. Later, they decrease dramatically when higher query/update ratio (100 and 1000) is evaluated. Both 1DPS and 2DPS perform the same and better than RCs. BS is the weakest in this evaluation. Fig. 6(b) shows the energy consumption. The trends are similar to that of number of message relays because the message transmission is the major source of energy consumption. Fig. 6(c) depicts the query response time. BS performs the best and all other approaches have same query response time regardless of query/update ratio.

Evaluation 3. Impact of Network Size: The third evaluation investigates the scalability of our proposed approaches to the network size. We fix the query size and ratio of query/update rate at 20×20 and 100 respectively and we vary the network size from 60×60, to 80×80, to 100×100, to 120×120 and

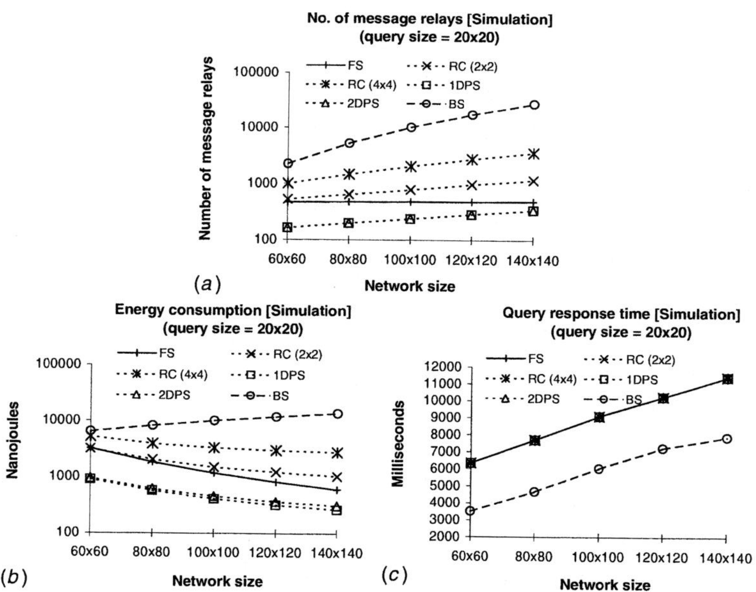

Fig. 7. Impact of network size

to 140 × 140. Fig. 7 plots the results. In Fig. 7(*a*), we can find the larger the network size is adopted, the larger the number of message relays produced by the schemes except for FS which does not maintain any view. Again, 1DPS and 2DPS perform the same and the best among all approaches while BS is the worst. Even worse, we can see that rate of increase of BS is higher than others because of increasing average distance between sensors and the base station; raising the average update costs. These results indicate that our 1DPS and 2DPS are good for various network size.

Fig. 7(*b*) depicts the impact of network sizes on energy consumption. It shows that the energy consumption all our proposed approaches generally decreases with the increase of the network size since queries (whose size equal to 20 × 20) become relatively small and they are scattered in the network. Therefore, the average energy consumed per node per query is much reduced. On the other hand, BS requires update propagation from every sensor, so that the update cost is increased with the network size. This observation points out the fact that the in-network query processing is more energy efficient. Fig. 7(*c*) shows the response time. This time all proposed approaches performs the same and BS remains the best.

5 Conclusion and Future Work

Aggregation queries are very important for sensor-network based systems. This paper identifies the limitations of existing ad-hoc based approaches for processing multiple aggregation queries and proposes materialized in-network views (MINVs) and associated access strategies, namely, *full scanning*, *replication cluster*, and *prefix sum*. Each approach has its own advantage and can support various types of the aggregation functions. Based on simulation, we compare their performance. Prefix sum provides the best performance in almost all the cases.

This is the first work addressing multiple spatial aggregation query processing in sensor networks. In the near future, we plan to work on a number of extensions. First, we are going to conduct in-depth analysis and extensive simulations and prototyping to validate our proposals and analysis. At the current stage, we consider queries issued in an one time fashion. To have continuous monitoring, sensors stream and aggregate their readings to the access points periodically or upon events of interest happen. As we have identified the minimum number of sensors to visit for a query using 1-D prefix sum and 2-D prefix sum in this paper, we will extend this model to register queries at those interested sensors in the spatial window. When changes of interested aggregated readings are detected at those query-registered sensors, the latest aggregated readings are propagated to the users. Further, as sensor memory is limited to accommodate a large number of views, we are studying the issue of memory management and selection criteria to maintain MINVs among sensors in sensor networks. Last but not least, as we explored in the paper, a query may include multiple aggregate functions and each approach has its own strength. It may be possible to execute the query using a combination of these proposed approaches.

Acknowledgements

In this research, Wang-Chien Lee and Ken C.K. Lee were supported in part by US National Science Foundation grant IIS-0328881.

References

1. Yao, Y., Gehrke, J.: Query Processing in Sensor Networks. In: CIDR, Asilomar, CA, USA, Jan 5-8. (2003)
2. Madden, S., Franklin, M.J., Hellerstein, J.M., Hong, W.: The Design of an Acquisitional Query Processor For Sensor Networks. In: SIGMOD Conf., San Diego, CA, USA, Jun 9-12. (2003) 491–502
3. Hightower, J., Borriello, G.: A Survey and Taxonomy of Location Systems for Ubiquitous Computing. (In: Technical Report UW-CSE 01-08-03, University of Washington)
4. MICA2 Environment/GPS Sensor Module MPR400/410/420, Crossbow Technology Inc. (http://www.xbow.com/Products/productsdetails.aspx?sid=72)
5. Xu, Y., Heidemann, J., Estrin, D.: Geography-informed Energy Conservation for Ad Hoc Routing. In: MOBICOM, Rome, Italy. (2001) 70–84
6. Ye, F., Luo, H., Cheng, J., Lu, S., Zhang, L.: A Two-Tier Data Dissemination Model for Large-Scale Wireless Sensor Networks. In: MOBICOM, Atlanta, GA. (Sep. 2002) 148–159
7. Li, X., Huang, Q., Zhang, Y.: Combs, Needles, Haystacks: Balancing Push and Pull for Discovery in Large-Scale Sensor Networks. In: ACM SenSys, Baltimore, MD. (Nov. 2004)
8. Heinzelman, W.R., Kulik, J., Balakrishnan, H.: Adaptive Protocols for Information Dissemination in Wireless Sensor Networks. In: MOBICOM, Seattle, WA. (Aug. 1999) 174–185
9. Intanagonwiwat, C., Govindan, R., Estrin, D.: Directed Diffusion: a Scalable and Robust Communication Paradigm for Sensor Networks. In: MOBICOM, Boston, MA. (Aug. 2000) 56–67
10. Maddan, S., Franklin, M.J., Hellerstein, J.M., Hong, W.: TAG: a Tiny AGgregation Service for Ad-Hoc Sensor Networks. In: OSDI. (Dec. 2002)
11. Ratnasamy, S., Karp, B., Yin, L., Yu, F., Estrin, D., Govindan, R., Shenker, S.: GHT: A Geographic Hash Table for Data-Centric Storage. In: WSNA, Altanta, GA. (Sep. 2002)
12. Li, X., Kim, Y.J., Govindan, R., Hong, W.: Multidimensional Range Queries in Sensor Networks. In: ACM SenSys, Los Angeles, CA. (Nov. 2004)
13. Ho, C.T., Agrawal, R., Megiddo, N., Srikant, R.: Range Queries in OLAP Data Cubes. In: SIGMOD Conf., Tucson, AZ. (May. 1997) 73–88
14. CSIM. (http://www.mesquite.com)
15. Lindsey, S., Raghavendra, C., Sivalingam, K.M.: Data Gathering Algorithms in Sensor Networks Using Energy Metrics. IEEE Transations on Parallel and Distributed Systems **13**(9) (2002)

In-Network Processing of Nearest Neighbor Queries for Wireless Sensor Networks

Yuxia Yao, Xueyan Tang, and Ee-Peng Lim

School of Computer Engineering,
Nanyang Technological University,
Singapore 639798
{yaoy0003, asxytang, aseplim}@ntu.edu.sg

Abstract. Wireless sensor networks have been widely used for civilian and military applications, such as environmental monitoring and vehicle tracking. The sensor nodes in the network have the abilities to sense, store, compute and communicate. To enable object tracking applications, spatial queries such as nearest neighbor queries are to be supported in these networks. The queries can be injected by the user at any sensor node. Due to the limited power supply for sensor nodes, energy efficiency is the major concern in query processing. Centralized data storage and query processing schemes do not favor energy efficiency. In this paper, we propose a distributed scheme called DNN for in-network processing of nearest neighbor queries. A cost model is built to analyze the performance of DNN. Experimental results show that DNN outperforms the centralized scheme significantly in terms of energy consumption and network lifetime.

1 Introduction

A sensor network is a distributed *ad-hoc* network comprised of a large number of sensor nodes equipped with capabilities of computing, storing and communicating [1]. The sensor nodes are usually battery operated and are deployed in an unattended manner to gather and process information without human intervention. Therefore, *energy efficiency* is the major concern in accessing the data captured by the sensor network.

A simple centralized method is to send all collected data to the base station for storage [2, 3]. The queries are also forwarded to and processed at a central base station. This approach involves unnecessary communication cost if only a portion of the data are accessed by the user. Moreover, due to message relay, the energy consumed by the sensor nodes closer to the base station is much higher than that by the nodes further from the base station. Unbalanced energy consumption reduces network lifetime [4, 5]. To improve energy efficiency, it is desirable to store the data at the sensor nodes in a distributed manner and apply *in-network processing* techniques to user queries [6, 7]. In this way, only the relevant data are extracted from the network and the communication cost is greatly reduced compared to the centralized scheme. Existing in-network query processing techniques have focused on aggregation and join queries [7, 8, 9, 10]. However, not much work has been done on spatial queries.

Nearest neighbor queries are an important class of spatial queries in object tracking applications [11]. In this paper, we consider in-network processing of nearest neighbor

M.L. Lee, K.L. Tan, and V. Wuwongse (Eds.): DASFAA 2006, LNCS 3882, pp. 35–49, 2006.

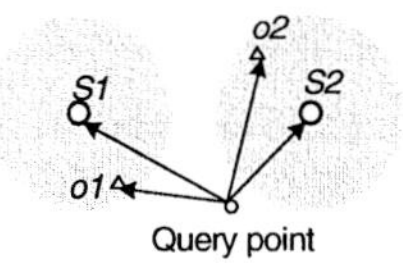

Fig. 1. Nearest Sensor Node vs. Nearest Object

queries. Our objective is to locate the nearest objects to a given query point. For example, consider a sensor network tracking the movement of taxies. The pedestrians carry devices, such as PDAs, to interact with the sensor network. Each PDA accepts from its user queries for nearest taxies and their locations, and injects the queries into the network by sending them to nearby sensor nodes. The data will be extracted from the relevant sensor nodes to respond to the user.

Existing work on nearest neighbor queries has focused on finding the *nearest sensor nodes* to a specified query point [12, 13]. This is different from our objective to locate the *nearest objects* to the query point because the nearest object may not be detected by the nearest sensor node. Figure 1 shows an example where S_1 and S_2 are two sensor nodes that detect objects o_1 and o_2 respectively. S_2 is closer to the query point than S_1. However, the nearest object to the query point is o_1.

In this paper, we propose a distributed scheme called *DNN* for in-network processing of nearest neighbor queries in wireless sensor networks. A grid structure is constructed for in-network storage of the collected data. Query processing in DNN proceeds in four steps: query routing, preliminary search, expanded search and result routing. We build a cost model to analyze the energy consumption of DNN and compare it with the centralized scheme. Experimental results show that DNN achieves significant energy saving over the centralized scheme.

The rest of the paper is organized as follows. Section 2 summarizes the related work. Section 3 presents the DNN scheme for in-network processing of nearest neighbor queries. Section 4 develops a cost model. Section 5 describes the experimental setup and discusses the experimental results. Finally, Section 6 concludes the paper.

2 Related Work

R-tree is a widely used indexing structure to support spatial queries in these databases [14]. M. Demirbas and Hakan [12] applied R-tree to locate the nearest sensor nodes in wireless sensor networks. In their approach, the sensor nodes are organized into a distributed R-tree in a bottom-up fashion. Each node keeps pointers to the lower level children and the higher level parent in the tree. Queries may be injected at any sensor node. However, to locate the nearest sensor nodes, the query has to trace back to the root of the tree making it a hotspot in the network. In addition, the tree structure is difficult to maintain in a dynamic environment.

Lee *et al.* [13] proposed an algorithm to locate k nearest sensor nodes in wireless sensor networks. They first locate the nearest sensor node to the query point and a set of perimeter nodes around the query point. A circle centered at the query point is then determined and is further divided into a set of subspaces each containing a perimeter node. The information of each subspace is collected by the perimeter node through a tree structure. After the query is resolved, the perimeter tree is destroyed to avoid the high cost of tree maintenance.

The above work has focused on locating the nearest sensor nodes. The locations of sensor nodes usually do not change over time. Different from [12, 13], we focus on the moving objects tracked by the sensor network. Our objective is to locate the nearest objects to a given query point. Although a number of indexing schemes have been proposed for moving object databases [15, 16], they targeted at centralized databases only and therefore do not apply to in-network processing in wireless sensor networks.

3 In-Network Processing of Nearest Neighbor Queries

In this section, we propose a distributed scheme called DNN for in-network processing of nearest neighbor queries in wireless sensor networks.

3.1 Distributed Data Storage

We consider a sensor network with the sensor nodes spreading over a 2-dimensional space. The sensor nodes are aware of their locations through GPS [17] or other localization algorithms [18]. The sensor nodes can sense the moving objects and collect their location information. Instead of sending all collected data to a central repository, we propose to store them at the sensor nodes in a distributed manner by partitioning the sensor network into a set of grid cells.

As shown in Figure 2, each grid cell has an area of $\alpha \times \alpha$, where α is a system parameter known to all sensor nodes in the network. The grid structure is constructed by designating a reference point (x_r, y_r) as the corner of a grid cell. Then, given any point (x, y) on the plane, the centroid of the grid cell containing (x, y) is given by $\big(x_r + (\lfloor \frac{x-x_r}{\alpha} \rfloor + \frac{1}{2}) \cdot \alpha, y_r + (\lfloor \frac{y-y_r}{\alpha} \rfloor + \frac{1}{2}) \cdot \alpha\big)$. The sensor node closest to the centroid of a grid cell is called a *grid index node* (shown by a solid dot in Figure 2). It is responsible for maintaining the location data of the objects detected in the grid cell. The object locations are periodically sampled by the sensor nodes and reported to the

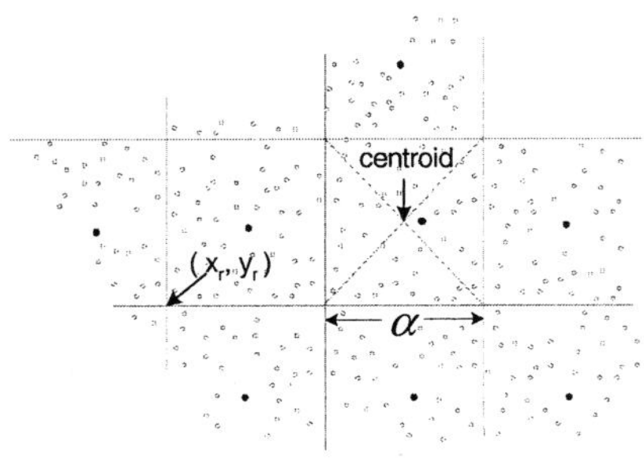

Fig. 2. Grid Structure in Sensor Network

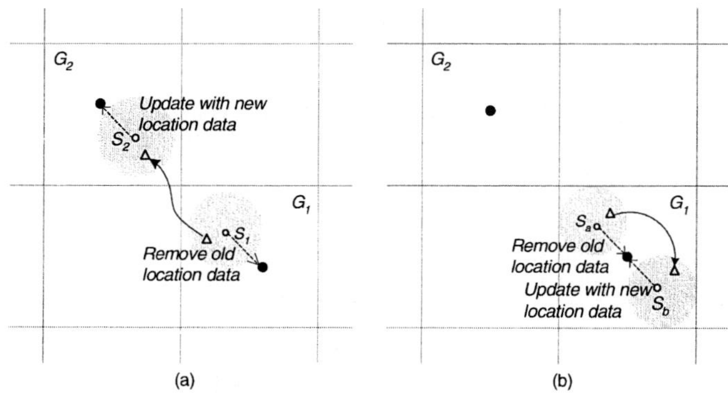

Fig. 3. Update of Object Location

grid index node[1]. The location data can be sent to the corresponding grid index node through GPSR routing[2] [22] by setting the centroid position of the grid cell as the destination.

To save communication cost, at each sampling, the location of an object is reported to the grid index node only if its location has changed since the last sample. We shall call it a *location update*. We assume that the objects being tracked are identifiable. They are electronically tagged or are identified based on the pre-embedded object code table in the sensor nodes [20, 21]. When the object location changes, at most two messages are needed to update the data at the grid index nodes. One message is used to signal the grid index node to remove the old location data and the other message is used to update the grid index node with the new location data. For example, Figure 3(a) shows the case where an object moves from one grid cell G_1 to another cell G_2. The location of the object is detected by sensor nodes S_1 and S_2 at two successive samplings. At the latter sampling, S_1 sends a message to the grid index node in G_1 to remove the old location data. Meanwhile, S_2 sends the new location data to the grid index node in G_2. Figure 3(b) shows another case where an object moves within a grid cell G_1. The location of the object is detected by sensor nodes S_a and S_b at two successive samplings. At the latter sampling, both S_a and S_b send a message to the grid index node in G_1. S_a's message signals the index node to remove the old location data while S_b's message feeds the index node with the new location data. If the object moves within a grid cell and its location is detected by the same sensor node in two successive samplings, only one message is sent from the sensor node to the grid index node for location update.

[1] Although the sensor nodes may work collaboratively to determine the location of an object in their vicinity [19], we assume that for each object, only one sensor node (the sensing leader or cluster head) is responsible for reporting its location at each sampling [20, 21]. For simplicity, the detecting sensor node in the rest of this paper refers to this node.

[2] GPSR is a greedy location-based routing scheme. Given the geographic locations of the source and the destination, GPSR routes the message to the node closest to the destination location. All message routing in this paper refers to GPSR routing.

3.2 Query Processing

In the preliminary search, we need a rule to determine the visiting order of grid cells. Since the location of boundary object determines the search circle for expanded search, to reduce the search cost, we would like the boundary object to be as close to the query point as possible. Thus, it is intuitive to visit the grid cells based on their distances to the cell G_0 containing the query point. We propose a *circle* approach to determine the visiting order of grid cells. Users issue queries for the locations of the nearest objects to given query points. In this paper, we focus on one-shot queries which complete once the results are returned. The queries can be injected into the sensor network at any sensor node (e.g., depending on the locations of the users). Each query Q is characterized by two locations (x_s, y_s) and (x_0, y_0), where (x_s, y_s) is the location where the query is issued (called the *query source*), and (x_0, y_0) is the location of the *query point*. If a user queries for the nearest object in his proximity, then $(x_s, y_s) = (x_0, y_0)$.

Query processing in DNN proceeds in four steps: *query routing*, *preliminary search*, *expanded search* and *result routing*. When a sensor node receives a query message, it calculates the centroid position of the grid cell G_0 containing the query point (x_0, y_0). In the query routing step, the query message is routed to the grid index node in G_0. The purpose of preliminary search is to find an object (called the *boundary object*) and define the search space. In this step, the grid cells surrounding G_0 (more specifically, the index nodes in these grid cells) are visited by message passing until a grid cell containing at least one object is found. Among the objects detected in that grid cell, the one closest to the query point is selected as the boundary object. A search circle centered at the query point and with a radius of the distance between the query point and the boundary object is defined as the search space. The nearest object to the query point is guaranteed to be located within the circle. The next step is expanded search. In this step, the grid cells within or intersecting with the circle, excluding those visited in the preliminary search, are visited by message passing to locate the nearest object. Finally, the query result is routed back to the user at (x_s, y_s).

Now, we discuss the preliminary search and the expanded search in detail.

Preliminary Search. The search is divided into rounds. In each round i, the unvisited grid cells intersecting with the circle centered at the centroid of G_0 and with a radius of $i \cdot \alpha$ are visited in clockwise order (see Figure 4(a)). This is done by sequentially passing a message from the grid index node of one cell to that of another. The message contains the locations of the query source and query point. Note that given the location of the query point, each grid index node can determine autonomously which grid cell to visit next. Figure 4(b) shows the route of the message in the preliminary search. The preliminary search completes when a grid cell containing at least one object is found.

Expanded Search. On completion of the preliminary search, a search circle centered at the query point and with a radius of the distance between the query point and the boundary object is defined. Let d be the radius of the circle. Intuitively, if the minimum distance between a grid cell and the query point is smaller than d, the grid cell is likely to contain objects less than distance d away from the query point. Therefore, a *search list* for the expanded search is given by all grid cells within or intersecting with the search circle, excluding those visited in the preliminary search. Figure 5 shows an example.

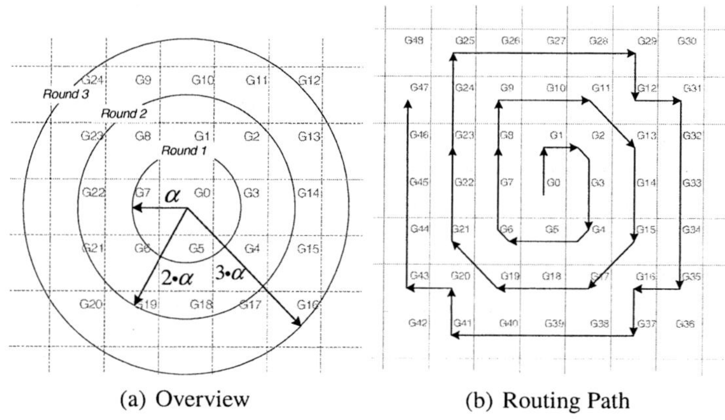

(a) Overview (b) Routing Path

Fig. 4. Preliminary Search

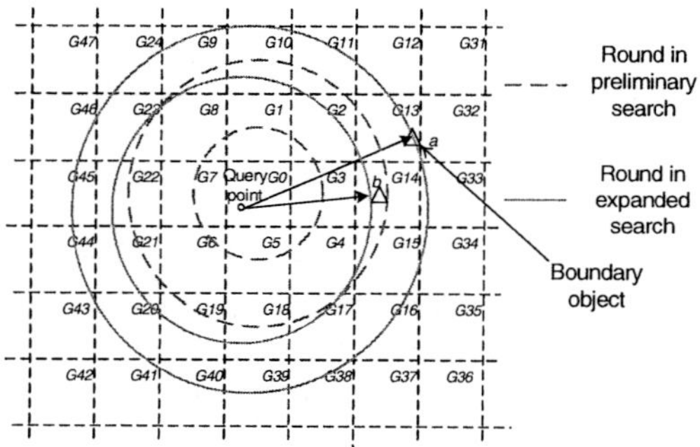

Fig. 5. Expanded Search

Suppose the query point (x_0, y_0) is in G_0 and the boundary object a is found in grid cell G_{13}. The grid index node in G_{13} determines the search circle (shown by the outer solid circle in Figure 5) and derives the set of grid cells within or intersecting with it: $Set_1 = \{G_0 - G_{24}, G_{33}, G_{34}, G_{38} - G_{41}, G_{43} - G_{46}\}$. The grid index node in G_{13} also computes the set of grid cells that have been visited in the preliminary search (based on the rounds shown by the dashed circles in Figure 5): $Set_2 = \{G_0 - G_{11}, G_{13}\}$[3]. Therefore, the search list in the expanded search is given by $Set_3 = Set_1 - Set_2 = \{G_{12}, G_{14} - G_{24}, G_{33}, G_{34}, G_{38} - G_{41}, G_{43} - G_{46}\}$.

The message passed between cells in the expanded search contains the search list and the locations of the boundary object, query source and query point. At each step, the message is routed to the grid cell on the search list that is closest to the cell currently holding the message. When a grid cell G_c receives the message, it first removes itself from the search list. One of the following three cases can occur: (i) no object is detected in G_c; (ii) all the objects detected in G_c are further away from the query point than

[3] The preliminary search completes in the middle of round 2, so the sensor nodes G_{14}– G_{15}, $G_{17} - G_{19}$ and G_{21}– G_{23} have not been visited in the preliminary search.

the boundary object; (iii) at least one object detected in G_c is closer to the query point than the boundary object. In cases (i) and (ii), the search list is not updated and the message is simply routed to the next grid cell on the search list that is closest to G_c. In case (iii), the object detected in G_c that is closest to the query point is selected as the new boundary object by updating the message content. A new search circle is derived accordingly. The search list is then updated by removing all grid cells outside the new search circle. The message is then routed to the next grid cell on the updated search list that is closest to G_c. The expanded search continues until the search list becomes empty. On completion of the expanded search, the message is routed to the query source and the location of boundary object is returned to the user as the query result.

In the example of Figure 5, the message is first routed to cell G_{14} in the expanded search (among the cells on the search list, G_{14} is closest to the grid cell G_{13} last visited in the preliminary search). Object b detected in G_{14} is closer to the query point than the current boundary object a. Thus, the search circle is shrunk and the search list is updated by removing cells G_{16}, G_{38}, G_{39}, G_{40}, G_{41}, G_{43}, G_{44}, G_{45}, G_{46} and G_{24} from the search list because they are outside the new search circle (shown by the inner solid circle in Figure 5). Among the cells on the updated search list, G_{15} is closest to cell G_{14}. So, the message is routed to G_{15} to continue the expanded search.

4 Cost Model and Analysis

In this section, we analyze the cost of the DNN scheme presented in Section 3. It is known that the energy consumption in wireless sensor networks is dominated by the communication cost [1]. We assume a dense network. In this case, the cost of message routing, i.e., the number of hops on the route from a source to a destination, is proportional to the Euclidean distance between the source and the destination. Therefore, we shall analyze the distance travelled by messages. We consider a square sensor field of size $s \times s$. It is divided into grid cells of size $\alpha \times \alpha$. A total number of N sensor nodes are randomly deployed in the network. A total of n objects are tracked by the sensor network.

4.1 Cost Model for DNN

In DNN, query processing and location update both involve communication.[4] For query processing, let C_{query}, C_{pre}, C_{exp} and C_{result} be the expected costs of query routing, preliminary search, expanded search and result routing per query respectively. The expected cost of a location update shall be denoted by C_{update}.

Query Routing and Result Routing. The expected costs of query and result routing are approximated by the distance between the query source and the query point. Assume the query source and query point are both randomly distributed in the network. Then, the expected routing distance is given by the average distance between any two points in the sensor network:

[4] Since this paper focuses on energy-efficient query processing, we do not include the communication overhead in sensing and data fusion. Such overhead is the same for the proposed DNN scheme and the centralized scheme we shall compare.

$$\frac{\int_0^s \int_0^s \int_0^s \int_0^s \sqrt{(x_i - x_j)^2 + (y_i - y_j)^2} dx_i dx_j dy_i dy_j}{(s \cdot s)^2}.$$

It follows from the mathematical results [23] that

$$C_{query} = C_{result} = \frac{s}{15}[\sqrt{2} + 2 + 5ln(1 + \sqrt{2})] = 0.5214 \cdot s.$$

Preliminary Search. To derive the cost of preliminary search, we need to know the number of grid cells visited. For simplicity, we assume that the probabilities of detecting objects in different cells are identical and independent. We use p to denote the probability that at least one object is detected in a grid cell. If the number of objects n is much smaller than the number of grid cells $(s \times s)/(\alpha \times \alpha)$, p is approximated by $\frac{n}{(s \times s)/(\alpha \times \alpha)}$. Then, the probability that we need to visit i grid cells in the preliminary search to locate a boundary object is $p(1-p)^{i-1}$. Therefore, the average number of grid cells visited in the preliminary search is given by

$$p + 2p(1-p) + 3p(1-p)^2 + \cdots = \frac{1}{p}.$$

Starting from the grid cell containing the query point, to visit i cells, the message needs to be sent between $i-1$ pairs of neighboring cells. Since the distance between a pair of neighboring cells is bounded by $\sqrt{2}\alpha$, the cost of preliminary search is bounded by

$$C_{pre} = (\frac{1}{p} - 1) \cdot \sqrt{2}\alpha.$$

Expanded Search. Similar to the preliminary search, we need to derive the number of grid cells visited in the expanded search. As described in Section 3.2, a search circle is derived at the end of preliminary search. If we know the total number of grid cells in the circle and the number of grid cells visited in the preliminary search, we can calculate the upper bound on the number of grid cells to visit in the expanded search.

We start by analyzing the relationship between the radius of a circle and the number of grid cells within or intersecting with the circle. It is intuitive that the number of cells is proportional to the area of the circle. Therefore, we used quadratic regression. The regression result shows that, given the circle radius r (r is a multiple of α), the number of grid cells within or intersecting with the circle is: $ar^2 + br + c$, where $a = \frac{3.1417}{\alpha^2}, b = \frac{4.1178}{\alpha}, c = 2.3241$. Figure 6 shows that the regression result (i.e., the number of grid cells computed by $ar^2 + br + c$) well matches the empirical result (i.e., the actual number of grid cells within or intersecting with the circle).

Let i be the number of grid cells visited in the preliminary search. We assume that the last grid cell visited in the preliminary search is in round x_i, i.e., the circle with radius $r_i = x_i \cdot \alpha$. Note that $a(r_i - \alpha)^2 + b(r_i - \alpha) + c$ indicates the number of grid cells visited in the first $x_i - 1$ rounds, and $ar_i^2 + br_i + c$ is the number of grid cells visited if round x_i completes. It follows that

$$a(r_i - \alpha)^2 + b(r_i - \alpha) + c \leq i \leq ar_i^2 + br_i + c.$$

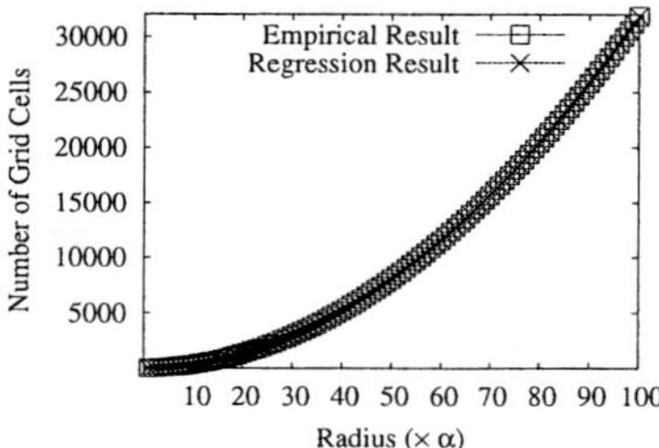

Fig. 6. Number of Grid Cells in a Circle

Therefore,

$$\frac{-b+\sqrt{b^2-4a(c-i)}}{2a} \leq r_i \leq \frac{-b+\sqrt{b^2-4a(c-i)}}{2a} + \alpha.$$

So, we approximate r_i by

$$r_i = \frac{-b+\sqrt{b^2-4a(c-i)}}{2a} + \frac{1}{2}\alpha.$$

We then derive the average number of grid cells visited in the expanded search as

$$\sum_{i=1}^{\infty} p(1-p)^{i-1} \cdot (ar_i^2 + br_i + c - i), \tag{1}$$

where $p(1-p)^{i-1}$ is the probability that i cells are visited in the preliminary search, and $ar_i^2+br_i+c-i$ is the corresponding number of grid cells to visit in the expanded search. Since the sum (1) converges when i approaches infinity, we can compute it numerically.

Similar to the preliminary search, we use $\sqrt{2}\alpha$ as a bound on the distance between neighboring grid cells. Thus, the cost of expanded search is bounded by

$$C_{exp} = \sum_{i=1}^{\infty} p(1-p)^{i-1} \cdot (ar_i^2 + br_i + c - i) \cdot \sqrt{2}\alpha.$$

Location Update. The communication cost of each location update is determined by the following factors: average distance from any point in a grid cell to the centroid of the grid cell; and the number of messages per location update. Following the mathematical results [23], the average distance is given by

$$\frac{\int_0^{\frac{\alpha}{2}} \int_0^{\frac{\alpha}{2}} \sqrt{x^2+y^2}\,dxdy}{\frac{\alpha}{2} \cdot \frac{\alpha}{2}} = 0.3825 \cdot \alpha.$$

As discussed in Section 3.1, at most two messages are required for each location update. Therefore, the cost per location update is bounded by

$$C_{update} = 2 \cdot 0.3825 \cdot \alpha = 0.7650 \cdot \alpha.$$

Let q be the rate at which queries are injected into the network. Let u be the total number of location updates per time unit for all objects in the network (it is obvious that u depends on the movement pattern of objects). Then, to summarize, the total communication cost of DNN is given by

$$\begin{aligned} C_{DNN} &= (C_{query} + C_{pre} + C_{exp} + C_{result}) \cdot q + C_{update} \cdot u \\ &= (2 \cdot 0.5214 \cdot s + \frac{1-p}{p} \cdot \sqrt{2}\alpha \\ &\quad + \sum_{i=1}^{\infty} p(1-p)^{i-1} \cdot (ar_i^2 + br_i + c - i) \cdot \sqrt{2}\alpha) \cdot q + 0.7650 \cdot \alpha \cdot u. \end{aligned}$$

4.2 Cost Model for Centralized Scheme

For comparison purpose, we also derive the communication cost of the centralized scheme in which all sensor nodes send the collected data to the base station and all queries are also forwarded to the base station for processing. We refer to this scheme as *CNN*. We assume the base station is located at the centroid of the network.[5] The cost of CNN consists of three parts: query routing, result routing and location update. The expected costs of query and result routing as well as the cost of per location update are all given by the average distance between any point in the network and the centroid of the network, i.e.,

$$C_{query} = C_{result} = C_{update} = \frac{\int_0^{\frac{s}{2}} \int_0^{\frac{s}{2}} \sqrt{x^2 + y^2}\, dx dy}{\frac{s}{2} \cdot \frac{s}{2}} = 0.3825 \cdot s.$$

In CNN, all collected data are maintained at the base station. Thus, only one message needs to be sent from the detecting sensor node to the base station at each location update. Therefore, the total communication cost of CNN is given by

$$C_{CNN} = (C_{query} + C_{result}) \cdot q + C_{update} \cdot u = 2 \cdot 0.3825 \cdot s \cdot q + 0.3825 \cdot s \cdot u.$$

5 Performance Evaluation

5.1 Experiment Setup

We conducted a wide range of experiments to evaluate the performance of the proposed DNN scheme and compared it with CNN. Table 1 summarizes the system parameters and their settings. We simulated a sensor network geographically covering a $50000m \times 50000m$ area. The number of sensor nodes deployed in the sensor network was set at 4×10^6, implying that on average, there is one sensor node in each $25m \times 25m$ square. The default size of a grid cell was set at $125m \times 125m$. The default number of objects being tracked was set at 800. The object were initially placed in the network at random. Their movement followed the random walk model. Specifically, time was divided into

[5] We set the base station at the centroid of the network to favor the centralized scheme.

Table 1. System Parameters and Settings

Parameters	Description	Default Value	Range
N	Number of sensor nodes	4×10^6	—
R	Communication range	$40m$	—
$s \times s$	Size of sensor network	$50000m \times 50000m$	—
$\alpha \times \alpha$	Size of grid cell	$125m \times 125m$	$[125m \times 125m, 3125m \times 3125m]$
n	Number of objects tracked	800	[160, 1600]
r	Sampling rate of sensor nodes	1 per time unit	—
v	Object moving velocity	$50m$ per time unit	—
P_{move}	Probability of object moving in each time interval	0.5	[0.1, 0.9]
q	Query rate	50 per time unit	[10, 100]

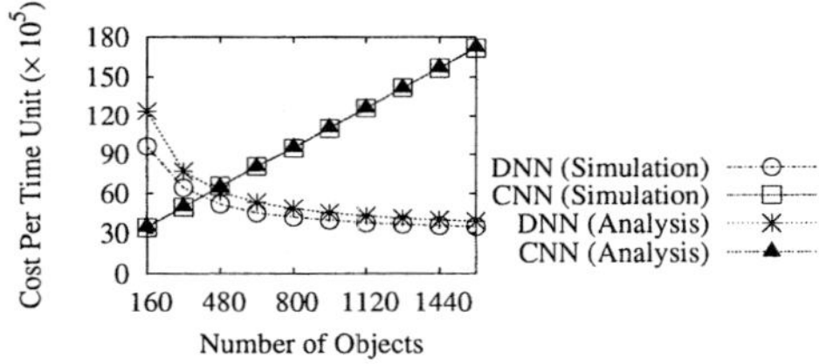

Fig. 7. Cost vs. Number of Objects

intervals. At the beginning of each interval, the object decided whether to *move* or *pause* according to the probabilities P_{move} and P_{pause} ($P_{move} + P_{pause} = 1$). If it decided to move, the move direction was randomly selected between 0 and 2π. The moving speed was set at $50m$ per time unit. The default length of the interval was set at 1 time unit. The default value for P_{move} was set at 0.5. The object locations were sampled by the sensor network once every time unit. At each sampling, the sensor node closest to an object was assumed to report the object location to the grid index node (in DNN) or the base station (in CNN). The default query rate was set at 50 per time unit. Both the query source and query point were randomly distributed in the network. The default communication range of each sensor node is set at $40m$.

5.2 Impact of Number of Objects

Figure 7 shows the simulation and analytical results of the Euclidean distance travelled by messages[6] as a function of number of objects. As seen from Figure 7(a), the analytical and simulation results match well. The analytical cost of DNN is slightly higher than the simulation result. This is because the DNN cost analyzed in Section 4 is an upper bound. As shall be explained soon, the cost of CNN increases with the number of objects, while that of DNN decreases with increasing number of objects. DNN outperforms CNN over a wide range of object numbers.

[6] We measured the total number of location updates per time unit in the simulation experiments and plugged it into the analytical model presented in Section 4.

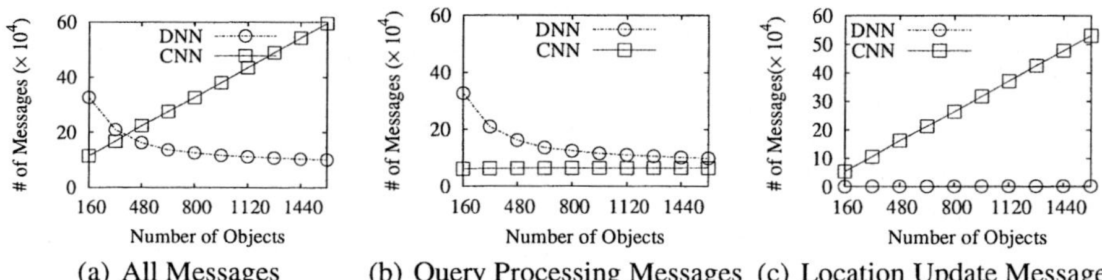

(a) All Messages (b) Query Processing Messages (c) Location Update Messages

Fig. 8. Number of Messages vs. Number of Objects

Figure 8(a) shows the total number of messages sent by the sensor nodes in the simulation experiments. It is seen that the curves have the same trend as those in Figure 7. This verifies that the cost defined using Euclidean distance (Section 4) is a good measure of message complexity. Figures 8(b) and 8(c) show the breakdown of query processing and location update messages. As shown in Figure 8(b), when the number of objects increases, the number of query processing messages in CNN remains unchanged. This is because in CNN, query processing consists of query routing and result routing only, the cost of which are independent of the number of objects. For DNN, the number of query processing messages reduces with increasing number of objects because the boundary object is located closer to the query point. This not only cuts down the number of grid cells visited in the preliminary search but also reduces the size of the search circle and hence the number of cells to visit in the expanded search. Figure 8(c) shows that the number of location update messages in DNN is considerably lower than that of CNN. It also grows much slower compared to that of CNN when the number of objects increases. With large number of objects, the overall message complexity of CNN is dominated by the location update messages and is much higher than that of DNN.

Figure 9 shows the distribution of the number of messages sent by the sensor nodes for DNN and CNN when the object number is 800. A point (x, y) on the curve means that a fraction x of all sensor nodes send more than y messages each. As shown in Figure 9, the workload distribution among the sensor nodes is highly unbalanced in CNN. The top 0.1% of the nodes send substantially high numbers of messages than the remaining nodes. On the other hand, the workload hence energy consumption is much more balanced among the sensor nodes in DNN. The numbers of messages sent by the top nodes are more than two orders of magnitude lower than those in CNN. If we define the network lifetime as the time duration before the first sensor node runs out

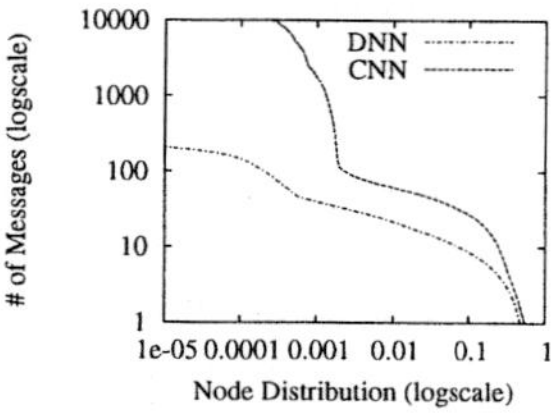

Fig. 9. Workload for Sensor Nodes

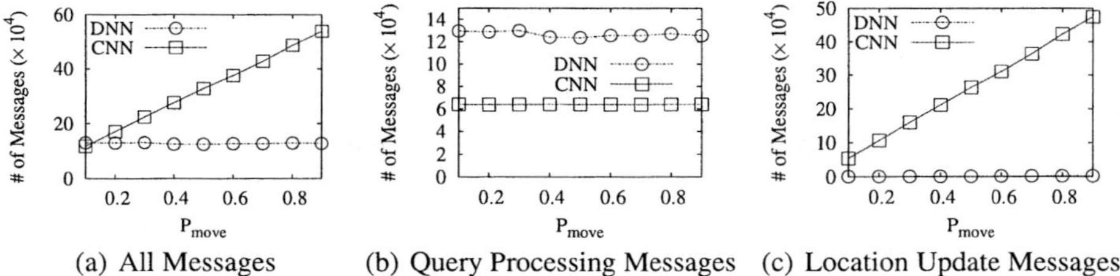

(a) All Messages (b) Query Processing Messages (c) Location Update Messages

Fig. 10. Number of Messages vs. P_{move}

of energy [24], DNN would prolong the network lifetime by a factor of more than 100 over CNN.

5.3 Impact of Object Movement

Figure 10 shows the performance results for different P_{move} values. It is intuitive that the objects move faster and hence incur more location updates at larger P_{move} values. Since the number of location update messages in DNN is much lower than the number of query processing messages (recall Figures 8(b) and (c)), the total number of messages in DNN is not significantly affected by the increase in P_{move}. The overall message complexity of CNN, on the other hand, substantially increases with P_{move}. This is because the total number of messages in CNN is dominated by that of location update messages. As shown in Figure 10(a), DNN considerably outperforms CNN over a wide range of P_{move} values.

5.4 Impact of Query Rate

Figure 11 shows the performance results for different query rates. The results indicate that the overall message complexity increases with query rate for both DNN and CNN. As shown in Figure 11(b), the number of location update messages is independent of the query rate for both schemes. Figure 11(c) shows that the number of query processing messages increases with query rate, leading to an increase in the overall message complexity. DNN outperforms CNN over a wide range of query rates. In general, the improvement of DNN over CNN is smaller for larger query rate.

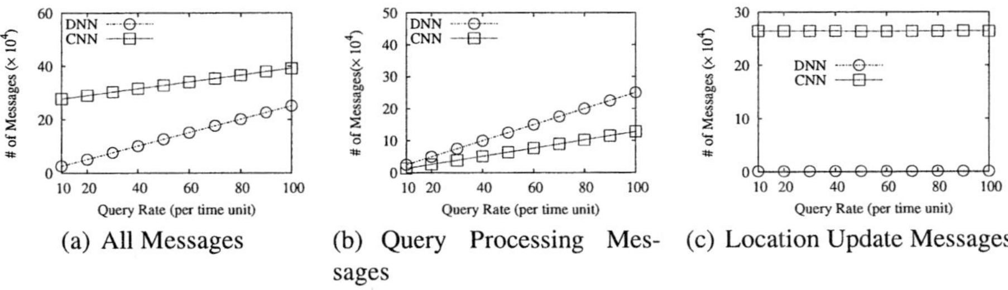

(a) All Messages (b) Query Processing Messages (c) Location Update Messages

Fig. 11. Number of Messages vs. Query Rate

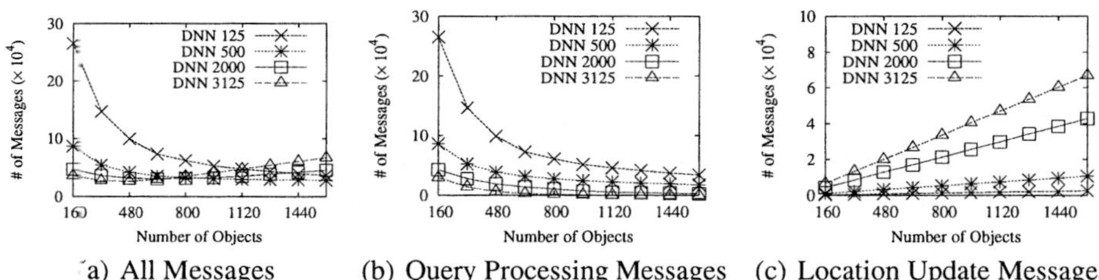

(a) All Messages (b) Query Processing Messages (c) Location Update Messages

Fig. 12. Number of Messages vs. Grid Cell Size

5.5 Impact of Grid Cell Size

We also investigate the impact of grid cell size. Figure 12 shows the message complexity for different α values $125m$, $500m$, $2000m$ and $3125m$ when the number of objects increases from 160 to 1600. In general, the number of query processing messages in DNN decreases with increasing grid cell size (see Figure 12(b)). On the other hand, the number of location update messages increases with grid cell size (see Figure 12(c)). When the number of objects is small, the location update messages take up a negligible portion of the total number of messages. Therefore, the overall message complexity of DNN decreases with increasing grid cell size. When the number of objects is large, the location update messages take up a larger portion of the total number of messages. As a result, the overall message complexity of DNN may increase with grid cell size beyond certain value. For example, when there are more than 800 objects being tracked, the cost for $\alpha = 3125$ is higher than that for $\alpha = 2000$.

6 Conclusion

In this paper, we have proposed a distributed scheme called DNN for in-network processing of nearest neighbor queries in wireless sensor networks. To avoid sending data to a central repository, a grid structure is constructed for in-network storage of the collected data. By localizing the location updates, DNN eliminates hotspots in the system. Query processing in DNN proceeds in four steps: query routing, preliminary search, expanded search and result routing. Experimental results show that DNN can significantly reduce and balance network-wide energy consumption compared to the centralized scheme.

References

1. G. Pottie. Wireless integrated network sensors. *Communications of the ACM* **43** (2000), pages 51–58.
2. P. Bonnet, J. Gehrke, P. Seshadri. Towards sensor database systems. In *Proceedings of IEEE MDM'01*, Hong Kong, China (2001), pages 3–14
3. R. Govindan, J. Hellerstein, W. Hong, S. Madden, M. Franklin. Shenker, S.: The sensor network as a database. Technical Report 02-771, Computer Science Department, University of Southern California (2002).

4. X. Tang, J. Xu. Extending network lifetime for precision-constrained data aggregation in wireless sensor networks. Accepted to appear in *Proceedings of IEEE INFOCOM'06*, Barcelona, Spain (2006).
5. I.F. Akyildiz, W. Su, Y. Sankarasubramaniam, E. Cayirci. A survey on sensor networks. In *IEEE Communication Magazine* **40** (2002), pages 102–114.
6. c. Intanagonwiwat, R. Govindan, D. Estrin. Directed diffusion: A scalable and robust communication paradigm for sensor networks. In *Proceedings of the 6th Annual ACM/IEEE Mobicom'00*, Boston, MA, USA (2000).
7. S. Madden, M. Franklin, J. Hellerstein, W. Hong. The design of an acquisitional query processor for sensor networks. In *Proceedings of ACM SIGMOD'03*, San Diego, CA, USA (2003).
8. N. Chowdhary, H. Gupta. Communication-efficient implementation of join in sensor networks. In *Proceedings of DASFAA'05*, Beijin, China (2005).
9. M. Sharaf, J. Beaver, A. Labrinidis, P. Chrysanthis. TiNA: A scheme for temporal coherency-aware in-network aggregation. In *Proceedings of the 3rd International ACM Workshop on Data Engineering for Wireless and Mobile Access*, San Diego, CA, USA (2003), pages 69–76.
10. Y. Yao, J. Gehrke. Query processing for sensor networks. In *Proceedings of the 1st Conference on Innovative Data System Research*, Asilomar, CA (2003).
11. N. Roussopoulos, S. Kelley, F. Vincent. Nearest neighbor queries. In *Proceedings of ACM SIGMOD'95*, San Jose, CA, USA (1995).
12. M. Demirbas, H. Ferhatosmanoglus. Peer-to-peer spatial queries in sensor networks. In *Proceedings of the 3rd IEEE International Conference on Peer-to-Peer Computing*, Linkoping, Sweden (2003).
13. J. Winter, W.-C. Lee. KPT: A dynamic KNN query processing algorithm for location-aware sensor networks. In *The 1st VLDB Workshop DMSN'04*, Toronto, Canada (2004).
14. A. Guttman. R-trees: a dynamic index structure for spatial searching. In *Proceedings of SIGMOD'84*, Boston, Massachusetts (1984).
15. S. Saltenis, C. Jensen, S. Leutenegger, M. Lopez. Indexing the positions of continuously moving objects. In *Proceedings of the ACM SIGMOD'01*, Santa Barbara, CA, USA (2001).
16. Y. Tao, D. Papadias, A. Shen. Continuous nearest neighbor search. In *Proceedings of VLDB'02*, Hong Kong, China (2002).
17. B.H. Wellenhof, H. Lichtenegger and J. Collins. Gps theory and practice. 2nd Ed, Springer-Verlag, New York.
18. D. Niculescu, B. Nathi. Ad hoc positioning system. In *Proceedings of INFOCOM'03*, San Francisco, CA (2003).
19. D. Li, K. Wong, Y. Hu, A. Sayeed. Detection, classification and tracking of targets in distributed sensor networks. *IEEE Signal Processing Magazine* **19** (2002).
20. J. Xu, X. Tang, W.-C. Lee. Ease: An energy-efficient in-network storage scheme for object tracking in sensor networks. In *Proceedings of IEEE SECON'05*, Santa Clara, CA, USA (2005).
21. Y. Xu, J. Winter, W.-C. Lee. Prediction-based strategies for energy saving in object tracking sensor networks. In *Proceedings of IEEE MDM'04*, Berkeley, CA, USA (2004).
22. B. Karp, H. Kung. GPSR: Greey perimeter stateless routing for wireless networks. In *Proceedings of the 6th Annual ACM/IEEE Mobicom'00*, Boston, MA, USA (2000).
23. E. Weisstein. Hypercube line picking. MathWorld–http://mathworld.wolfram.com/HypercubeLinePicking.html.
24. C. Buragohain, D. Agrawal, S. Suri. Power aware routing for sensor databases. In *Proceedings of IEEE INFOCOM'05*.

Associated Load Shedding Strategies for Computing Multi-joins in Sensor Networks

Xiaochun Yang[1,⋆], Lin Li[1], Yiu-Kai Ng[2], Bin Wang[1,⋆⋆], and Ge Yu[1,⋆⋆⋆]

[1] School of Information Science and Engineering,
Northeastern University, Liaoning 110004, China
yangxc@mail.neu.edu.cn
[2] Computer Science Department,
Brigham Young University, Provo, UT 84602, USA
ng@cs.byu.edu

Abstract. In sensor networks, multi-join queries are processed by joining sensor data generated at different sensor nodes. Due to the energy constraint, however, sometimes only partial sensor data can be transmitted to the join site. In handling the energy constraint on each sensor node, the load shedding strategy under the MAX-subset principle has been considered for shedding selected data at each node so that transmitted data may yield the maximal possible results in a multi-join. Existing load shedding approaches, however, isolate sensor data to be joined, which often do not yield the maximal results. To obtain as many results as possible, we propose two load shedding strategies, the *basic local associated shedding strategy* and the *global associated shedding strategy*, based on different shedding constraints in this paper. We also present the *max-loss-first associated shedding strategy* and the *multi-round associated shedding strategy* for improving the basic local associated shedding strategy. Experimental results show that the proposed strategies generate as many results as possible on multi-joins.

1 Introduction

In recent years, wireless sensor networks have been developing as an effect of advanced communications and electronics [2, 9]. Wireless sensor networks, however, have some notable constraints. First, sensor networks run for a long time when habitat monitoring is required. Second, sensor nodes are limited in power, computation capacity, and memory. Third, the number of sensor nodes in a sensor network can be very large [2, 5, 12]. These constraints cause the energy efficiency problem to become the most significant problem in sensor networks [9, 17], since communication between nodes is more energy consuming than processes that are performed locally [10]. In order to improve the energy efficiency in sensor

⋆ Supported by National Natural Science Foundation of China No. 60503036 and Natural Science Foundation for Doctoral Career Award of Liaoning Province No. 20041016.

⋆⋆ Supported by National Natural Science Foundation of China No. 60473074.

⋆⋆⋆ Supported by National Natural Science Foundation of China No. 60473073.

M.L. Lee, K.L. Tan, and V. Wuwongse (Eds.): DASFAA 2006, LNCS 3882, pp. 50–64, 2006.

networks, communication and data transmitting among different nodes should be minimized.

Assume that in a sensor network there are two kinds of nodes: the *ordinary* sensor nodes, which sense the environmental data and perform user specified simple queries (such as selection, projection, etc.), and the *proxy* nodes, which collect sensor data from ordinary sensor nodes and process join queries [11]. Ordinary sensor nodes are power constrained while the proxy nodes have no such restriction. In such a network, we note that processing multi-join operations requires large amount of communications and data transmission between nodes. In at least two different scenarios, only a portion (or none) of the sensing data should be transferred: (1) some sensing data collected from different nodes may not produce any join result and hence transferring them wastes energy, and (2) if the remaining energy in a sensor node is insufficient to transfer all the sensing data to the proxy node, then only a subset of data can be transmitted to satisfy the energy constraint. Whenever one or the other scenario occurs, some sensor data must be dropped (i.e., they are not transferred to the proxy node to be joined). Hence, the problem of choosing which portions of the data set to drop is of crucial importance for processing multi-joins in sensor networks, since different input data sets yield different join results. This is the *load shedding problem for multi-joins* in sensor networks. A well-known measurement is MAX-subset [8], which uses the size of the final join, i.e., the results after shedding of stream data, to determine the shedding decision.

In this paper we focus on the problem of load shedding over multi-joins in sensor networks using the measure of MAX-subset. We first define two shedding constraints, the *local shedding constraint* and the *global shedding constraint*, each of which represents a different multi-join shedding problem in sensor networks. Hereafter, we propose three different strategies, the *basic local associated shedding strategy*, *max-loss-first associated shedding strategy*, and the *multi-round associated shedding strategy* in solving the shedding problem under local shedding constraint, and apply the *global associated shedding strategy* in solving shedding problem under the global shedding constraint. We will provide experimental results to verify the effect of the proposed strategies.

The rest of the paper is organized as follows. In Section 2, we survey related work. In Section 3, we define the problem of load shedding for multi-joins in sensor networks. In Section 4, we describe our load shedding strategies. In Section 5, we present the experimental results on the proposed load shedding strategies. In Section 6, we give a concluding remark.

2 Related Work

The load shedding problem in data stream systems has been widely studied during the past few years. In a data stream management system, the incoming rate of stream data is unpredictable. Thus, when the incoming rate exceeds the processing rate, it is necessary to drop some data in order to make sure that the system load is below the accepted upper bound. Most of the existing data stream management systems, such as STREAM [3,4,13,15], AURORA [7,16], and TelegraphCQ [1,6,14], have their own load shedding mechanisms. There are two fundamental types of drop operators: *random drop* and *semantic drop*. The former randomly chooses tuples passed through the operator to drop with probability ρ, which expresses the fraction of tuples that should be dropped, whereas the latter looks like a filter, since it checks the value of each tuple and then decides whether the tuple should be dropped. When performing the semantic load shedding, there are also several measurements, such as QoS [16] that uses the importance of tuple's content to measure whether it should be dropped, and MAX-subset [8] that uses the number of join results generated by each input tuple to determine whether this input tuple should be dropped. [15] defines two different stream arrival models, the frequency-based model and the age-based model, when performing MAX-subset load shedding on data streams. In the *frequency-based* model, the number of join results produced by each input tuple is determined by the attribute value, whereas in the *age-based* model, the number of join results that a tuple produces is a function of the age of the tuple in the window. Based on various drop operators, measures, and models, different load shedding approaches are proposed in previous research works.

[8] views the join approximation problem in sensor networks as the static join approximation problem (as opposite to the dynamic join approximation problem in data streams). [8] also surveys possible error measures in approximated join queries (i.e., when some input tuples have to be evicted), and propose the measurement of MAX-subset, since most of the popular and common set approximation errors actually reduce to MAX-subset. [8] reduces the static join approximation problem into a bipartite graph problem and proposes the optimal dynamic programming solution and two fast 2-approximation algorithms, i.e., the node degree greedy (NDG) algorithm and the average degree greedy (ADG) algorithm, in solving the static join approximation problem. Among the two approximate algorithms, the former is applicable to the formulation when H_A and H_B tuples from the two relations R_A and R_B are to be deleted, respectively, while the latter is applicable when H number of tuples are to be deleted from R_A and R_B overall.

[8] also considers m-relations-joins, $m > 2$. It has been proved [8] that the static join approximation problem for maximizing the size of results of a multi-join is an NP-hard problem. An approximate algorithm is also proposed [8] for maximizing the size of results while H_i tuples are evicted from relation R_i ($1 \leq i \leq m$). We call this method the *independent shedding strategy* (IS for short), since IS independently chooses tuples from each relation that produce the lowest number of join results to be dropped. [8] proves that IS is an m-approximation algorithm. [8], however, does not consider another shedding constraint for multi-joins, i.e., when altogether a total of H tuples need to be deleted from relations involved in a multi-join. Furthermore, IS does not always generate the maximal results of a multi-join, which is a major design fault of IS.

We have investigated the features of multi-joins, as well as the sensor networks, and have developed several shedding strategies for performing multi-joins in sensor networks. We consider the shedding problem according to two different constraints: the *local shedding constraint* and the *global shedding constraint.* We show that our methods are better than IS, which is the only work directly related to ours, i.e., in solving the load shedding problem of multi-joins under the static assumption in sensor networks.

3 Problem Statement

In this section, we first discuss the multi-join shedding constraints in sensor networks. Hereafter, we introduce the measure of MAX-subset in load shedding and illustrate the approach proposed in [8] through a simple example.

Throughout this paper, it is assumed that relations $R_1, R_2, ..., R_m$ join with each other according to the order $R_1 \bowtie_1 R_2 \bowtie_2 ... \bowtie_{m-1} R_m$, where $\bowtie_i$ $(1 \leq i \leq m-1)$ is the equal join operation over attributes shared by R_i and R_{i+1}, and X_i is the combination of join attributes in R_i. Further assume that R_i $(2 \leq i \leq m-1)$ uses two different attributes to join with R_{i-1} and R_{i+1}, respectively.

3.1 Load Shedding Constraints

According to different applications discussed in Section 1, we design two kinds of load shedding constraint, which are local shedding constraint and global shedding constraint.

Definition 1 *(Local shedding constraint). Given relations $R_1, R_2, ..., R_m$ involved in a multi-join. For each relation R_i, it is required to remove $H_i (\leq |R_i|)$ tuples from R_i. We call $\langle H_1, \ldots, H_m \rangle$ the local shedding constraint with respect to $R_1, R_2, ...,$ R_m, and H_i the local shedding constraint value of relation R_i.*

Definition 2 *(Global shedding constraint). Given relations $R_1, R_2, ..., R_m$ involved in a multi-join. It is required to remove a total of H tuples from the m relations, where $1 \leq H \leq |R_1| + |R_2| + \cdots + |R_m|$. We call $\langle H \rangle$ the global shedding constraint over $R_1, R_2, ..., R_m$.*

Adopting different shedding decisions for multi-joins yield different results, and the size of each join resultant tuple is used as the measure of corresponding shedding decision, based on the assumption that each resultant set is equally important to the query user. We apply the measurement of MAX-subset [8] to load shedding over multi-joins, and propose several load shedding strategies based on the two constraints as given in Definitions 1 and 2 to obtain larger possible retained join results than the results computed by using existing approach.

3.2 Overview of the Independent Shedding (IS) Strategy

[8] proposes an approximate algorithm IS that handles load shedding based on the *local shedding constraint.* IS independently deletes H_i $(1 \leq i \leq m)$ tuples that produce the fewest join results from R_i in a multi-join. We illustrate how IS works through Example 1.

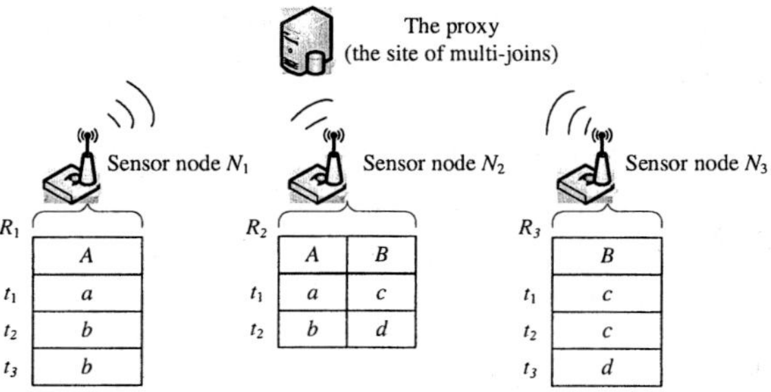

Fig. 1. $R_1 \bowtie_1 R_2 \bowtie_2 R_3$, where $\bowtie_1$ is $R_1[A] = R_2[A]$ and $\bowtie_2$ is $R_2[B] = R_3[B]$

Example 1. Assume that relations R_1, R_2, and R_3 are joined together in the order of $R_1 \bowtie_1 R_2 \bowtie_2 R_3$ such that the predicate of $\bowtie_1$ is $R_1[A] = R_2[A]$ and the predicate of $\bowtie_2$ is $R_2[B] = R_3[B]$ as shown in Fig. 1.

As shown in Fig. 1, if no shedding is performed on any relation, t_1 in R_1 can produce 2 results, while t_2 and t_3 each can produce 1 result, whereas t_1 and t_2 in R_3 each can produce 1 result, while t_3 in R_3 can produce 2 results. Given a *local shedding constraint* $\langle 2, 0, 2 \rangle$ applied to R_1, R_2, and R_3, IS drops t_2 and t_3 from R_1, and t_1 and t_2 from R_3, since they are the ones that produce fewest results when considering load shedding on the three relations independently. Unfortunately, IS obtains zero-join results after shedding, i.e., after shedding, $R_1 \bowtie_1 R_2 \bowtie_2 R_3 = \emptyset$. Instead, if we drop t_2 and t_3 from R_1, and t_2 and t_3 from R_3, then $R_1 \bowtie_1 R_2 \bowtie_2 R_3$ yields 1 result, which is a better solution than IS in terms of generating maximal join results. Since IS considers tuples from different relations independently, it isolates the complex relationships among all the tuples in different relations involved in a multi-join, and as a result, its multi-joins may not obtain the maximum resultant sets.

4 Our Load Shedding Strategies

In this section, we introduce our load shedding techniques, which include three shedding strategies conforming to local shedding constraint: (1) the *basic local associated shedding strategy*, (2) the *max-loss-first associated shedding strategy*, and (3) the *multi-round associated shedding strategy*, and *global associated shedding strategy* to global shedding constraint.

The basic local associated shedding strategy performs shedding in an ordered manner, through which larger join results can be retained than the ones computed by using strategy adopted by IS [8]. The max-loss-first and the multi-round strategy are designed for improving the basic local associated shedding strategy by quickly defining a shedding order and multiplying the number of rounds of shedding, respectively. The global associated shedding strategy, on the other hand, solves the shedding problem under the global shedding constraint using a global ranking of tuples on all relations. Prior to introducing the proposed strategies, we define different terms used in the strategies.

4.1 Output_rate

In a multi-join $R_1 \bowtie_1 R_2 \bowtie_2 \ldots \bowtie_{m-1} R_m$, suppose t is a join attribute value in relation R_i $(1 \leq i \leq m)$, then *output_rate*(t) is defined as the number of tuples generated by each input tuple that has the join attribute value t, i.e.,

$$output\_rate(t) = \frac{1}{|\delta_{X_{i-1}=t}(R_i)|} |R_1 \bowtie_1 \ldots \bowtie_{i-1} \delta_{X_{i-1}=t}(R_i) \bowtie_i \ldots \bowtie_{m-1} R_m|.$$

Note that if two tuples in one relation have the same join attribute value, then they must have the same *output_rate*. Hence, we only compute the *output_rate* of each join attribute value, instead of tuples.

It is not desired to obtain output_rate using the above equation, since we can only obtain the result of multi-join after the join-operation has been processed at the proxy node. In order to calculate output_rate before computing the join-operation at proxy node, we calculate the frequency of each join attribute value and send those frequencies to proxy node to compute the output_rate of each join attribute value. For relation R_1 (R_m, respectively), the frequency $f_1(v)$ ($f_m(v)$, respectively) of join attribute value v is defined as the number of tuples in $\delta_{X_1=v}(R_1)$ ($\delta_{X_m=v}(R_m)$, respectively). For relation R_i $(2 \leq i \leq m-1)$, the frequency $f_i(u,v)$ of join attribute values (u,v) in a tuple of R_i is defined as the number of tuples in $\delta_{X_i=(u,v)}(R_i)$.

The output_rate of each attribute value v in relation R_1 (R_m, similarly) is defined as follows:

$$output\_rate(v) = \sum_{(v,u)\in R_2[X_2]} (f_2(v,u) \sum_{(u,w)\in R_3[X_3]} (\ldots \sum_{(g,h)\in R_{m-1}[X_{m-1}]} (f_{m-1}(g,h) \cdot f_m(h))\ldots))$$

The *output_rate* of each attribute value in relation R_i $(2 \leq i \leq m-1)$ is defined as follows:

$$output\_rate(u,v) = \Big(\sum_{(w,u)\in R_{i-1}[X_{i-1}]} (f_{i-1}(w,u) \ldots \sum_{(k,p)\in R_2[X_2]} (f_2(k,p) \cdot f_1(k)) \ldots) \cdot \Big(\sum_{(v,o)\in R_{i+1}[X_{i+1}]} (f_{i+1}(v,o) \ldots \sum_{(g,h)\in R_{m-1}[X_{m-1}]} (f_{m-1}(g,h) \cdot f_m(h)) \ldots)\Big)$$

We demonstrate in Example 2 the process of computing the *output_rates* using frequency information on various join attributes.

Example 2. Assume that three relations R_1, R_2, and R_3 are joined in the order of $R_1 \bowtie_1 R_2 \bowtie_2 R_3$, and each relation involved in the join has eight tuples. The frequency information of join attribute value in R_1, R_2 and R_3 (denoted as

R_1

Join attribute value	frequency
a	2
b	3
c	3

R_2

Join attribute value	frequency
a, a	2
b, a	1
b, c	3
c, a	1
c, c	1

R_3

Join attribute value	frequency
a	5
b	2
c	1

(a)

R_1

Join attribute value	frequency	output_rate
a	2	10
b	3	8
c	3	6

R_2

Join attribute value	frequency	output_rate
a, a	2	10
b, a	1	15
b, c	3	3
c, a	1	15
c, c	1	3

R_3

Join attribute value	frequency	output_rate
a	5	10
b	2	0
c	1	12

(b)

Fig. 2. (a) Frequencies of join attribute values. (b) *Output_rates* of join attribute values.

f_1, f_2, and f_3, respectively) are shown in Fig. 2(a), which are used to compute the *output_rates* as shown in Fig. 2(b). For example, the *output_rate* of the join attribute value 'b' in R_1 is

$$output\_rate(b) = f_2(b,a) \cdot f_3(a) + f_2(b,c) \cdot f_3(c) = 1 \cdot 5 + 3 \cdot 1 = 8.$$

The *output_rate* of the attribute value '(a,a)' in

$$output\_rate(a,a) = f_1(a) \cdot f_3(a) = 2 \cdot 5 = 10.$$

The *output_rate* values of other tuples can be computed likewise and are shown in Fig. 2(b).

4.2 The Basic Local Associated Shedding (BLAS) Strategy

IS considers tuples from different relations independently, and often can not generate the maximum results of a multi-join. In order to improve IS, we propose the *basic local associated shedding strategy* (BLAS for short), which is designed to consider the load shedding on tuples in an associate way, in stead of independently. First, BLAS arranges relations in an order, which is called the *shedding order* in BLAS. For example, consider the three-relations-join $R_1 \bowtie R_2 \bowtie R_3$ under the shedding constraint $\langle H_1, H_2, H_3 \rangle$, there are six possible shedding orders, e.g., $R_1 \rightarrow R_2 \rightarrow R_3$ and $R_3 \rightarrow R_2 \rightarrow R_1$. In a shedding order, BLAS starts from the first relation $R_i (1 \leq i \leq 3)$ and drops H_i tuples with the lowest *output_rate*

Table 1. Different shedding orders on relations in Example 2 lead to different join results under the local shedding constraint $\langle 4, 4, 4\rangle$. Item " 3·c " under the "Drop Tuples from R_1" column denotes that three tuples with the attribute value 'c' are removed from relation R_1 when shedding is performed.

Shedding Order	# of Join Results	Drop Tuples from R_1	Drop Tuples from R_2	Drop Tuples from R_3
$R_1 \to R_2 \to R_3$	24	1·b, 3·c	2·(b,c), 1·(c,a), 1·(c,c)	1·a, 2·b, 1·c
$R_1 \to R_3 \to R_2$	24	1·b, 3·c	2·(b,c), 1·(c,a), 1·(c,c)	1·a, 2·b, 1·c
$R_2 \to R_1 \to R_3$	24	1·b, 3·c	3·(b,c), 1·(c,c)	1·a, 2·b, 1·c
$R_2 \to R_3 \to R_1$	24	1·b, 3·c	3·(b,c), 1·(c,c)	1·a, 2·b, 1·c
$R_3 \to R_1 \to R_2$	18	1·a, 3·c	2·(a,a), 1·(c,a), 1·(c,c)	2·a, 2·b
$R_3 \to R_2 \to R_1$	18	1·b, 3·c	3·(b,c), 1·(c,c)	2·a, 2·b

values among all tuples in R_i. Hereafter, the *output_rate* values of tuples in the second relation in the shedding order are updated, which is followed by choosing tuples that yield the smallest join results in the second relation to drop. This process is repeated until shedding over the last relation in the shedding order is accomplished.

Consider Example 1 again. Given the local shedding constraint $\langle 2, 0, 2\rangle$ (i.e., does not drop any tuples from R_2). If the shedding order is $R_1 \to R_3 \to R_2$, then BLAS first drops t_2 and t_3 from R_1. While noting that retaining t_3 in R_3 would yield empty result, BLAS will drop t_3 from R_3. Hereafter, another tuple in R_3 will be dropped, and BLAS will randomly select t_1 or t_2 to drop. As a result, BLAS can generate 1 result, instead of none using IS.

Note that different shedding orders result in different performances of BLAS. In Example 2, suppose the local shedding constraint is $\langle 4, 4, 4\rangle$, which yield 6 different shedding orders, and the number of join results are shown in Table 1. Note that different shedding orders yield the same number of join results if the number of shed tuple values of each corresponding relation is the same, since $\bowtie_i$ is associative and commutative. (See, for example, the first two shedding orders in Table 1.)

In order to obtain the largest join results, BLAS explores the shedding order space and chooses the one with the join result with the largest number of tuples to be the final shedding decision.

4.3 The Max-Loss-First Associated Shedding (MxLF) Strategy

BLAS searches the order space to find the best order, i.e., selects one of the shedding orders that yields the largest results among all the orders in the order space, as the final shedding decision. However, when m ($m > 1$) relations are joined, there are $m!$ different shedding orders. If m is very large, the searching cost could be very high. In solving this problem, we propose the *max-loss-first associated shedding strategy* (MxLF for short), which computes only one shedding order in a multi-join, instead of $m!$ shedding orders. For example, instead of considering the six shedding orders as shown in Table 1, MxLF computes only the shedding order $R_1 \to R_3 \to R_2$.

When performing shedding over relations, the *shedding loss* of a relation R is the number of lost join tuples caused by shedding over R. In MxLF, the larger the *shedding loss* is, the higher the priority it is in the shedding order to be adopted.

We define two different methods that follow the design philosophy of MxLF. In the first method, MxLF calculates the *shedding loss* of each relation while shedding is being performed. First of all, MxLF computes the shedding loss of each relation, given that the sets of lowest producing tuples are dropped (i.e., for each relation R_i, H_i tuples are dropped). The relation with the largest loss value is chosen as the first one in the shedding order. Hereafter, MxLF computes the revised shedding losses of the remaining relations, i.e., updating the shedding losses of the other relations involved in the multi-join due to the shedding on the first relation. This process is repeated for choosing the next relation in the shedding order.

In the second method, MxLF computes the *shedding loss* of each relation only once before all shedding is processed. Hereafter, the loss values are used to rank relations in a descending order, and this order is used as the shedding order by MxLF.

We call the two MxLF methods MAX_1 and MAX_2, respectively. Note that MAX_1 is the real max-loss-first method, whereas MAX_2 uses only the loss value before shedding of each relation involved in a multi-join without prorated adjustments on shedding losses on other involved relations to estimate the real loss value during the shedding process. Obviously, MAX_2 is more practical since its computational cost is lower than MAX_1. Furthermore, MxLF is just an approximate method that chooses a shedding order quickly in order to avoid the cost of searching the order space in BLAS. Whether MxLF can choose the optimal shedding order is largely dependent on the data sets to be joined. We have experimented many data sets in which MxLF yields the optimal shedding order in most cases; however, occasionally MxLF fails, which is anticipated.

4.4 The Multi-round Associated Shedding (MLAS) Strategy

Even though in most cases, MxLF can find the best shedding order among all $m!$ possible orders when m relations are joined, it may not yield the maximum resultant set. For instance, consider the shedding order $R_2 \rightarrow R_1 \rightarrow R_3 \rightarrow ... \rightarrow R_m$ is chosen by MxLF when joining $R_1, R_2, ..., R_m$ under the local shedding constraint $\langle H_1, H_2, ..., H_m \rangle$. MxLF first removes H_2 number of the least productive tuples from R_2, which is followed by computing the *output_rates* of tuples in R_1 and dropping H_1 number of the least productive tuples from R_1. Suppose in R_2, tuple t that matches with tuples $s_1, s_2, ..., s_i$ $(i \geq 1)$ in R_1 is retained, but $s_1, s_2, ..., s_i$ are all removed from R_1 in the subsequent shedding step. This causes $t \in R_2$ to become "useless," as shedding using a shedding order is irreversible, i.e., shedding using shedding orders can only work forward, but not backward.

To further enhance BLAS (or MxLF), we propose the *multi-round associated shedding strategy* (MLAS for short). MLAS satisfies the local shedding constraint through multi-rounds of BLAS, and in each shedding round the local shedding constraint values are fractions of the original ones. For example, if the original local shedding constraint is 10 tuples for each relation and the round number is set to be 5, then MLAS processes the shedding through 5 rounds of consecutive shedding. In each round BLAS is adopted to drop the two least productive tuples from each relation. The shedding rounds are performed one after the other, thus in the latter rounds the *output_rates* of tuples which are retained from the former rounds are calculated and the least productive tuples in each relation are dropped. Adopting this strategy, MLAS can minimize the probability of retaining least productive tuples or shedding tuples that yield the largest resultant sets. In the example above, if tuple $t \in R_2$ becomes "useless" after the first shedding round, t will be dropped by MLAS in the subsequent shedding round.

In MLAS, the number of rounds to be processed has the impact on the resultant size of multi-joins. In most cases, more rounds yield larger resultant sizes, even though occasionally more rounds lead to smaller resultant sizes. As shown in Fig. 6(a), the resultant size of the 5th round is smaller than the resultant size of the 4th round.

4.5 The Global Associated Shedding (GAS) Strategy

The *global associated shedding strategy* (GAS for short) considers tuples to be shed from all relations globally under global shedding constraint $\langle H \rangle$ rather than shedding individual relations. Before shedding, the *output_rate* of each tuple in each relation involved in a multi-join is calculated and a global ranking of all the tuples is established according to the *output_rate* value of each tuple in the descending order. Tuples at the end of the ranking, regardless which relation they come from, are dropped because they have the smallest *output_rate* values among all the tuples (and thus are treated as "least productive" tuples).

We can also adopt the multi-round shedding strategy on GAS, in which a set of tuples with the smallest *output_rates* among others are dropped from the global ranking in each shedding round, and the dropped set size in each round is a fraction of H. This process is similar to that of MLAS.

5 Experimental Results

In this section, we study the effect of our proposed load shedding strategies through 3-relations equi-join. First, we compare the number of results obtained by applying the local associated shedding approaches and IS considering different types of data distributions, data sizes under different local shedding constraint. Second, we study the performance of the global shedding approach GAS and the local shedding approach BLAS.

We generated five synthetic data sets as shown in Table 2 by considering two common types of data distributions, i.e., *uniform distribution* and *normal distribution*. Three data sets are uniformly distribution, whereas the other two data sets are normally distribution. In each data set, let $|R_1| = |R_2| = |R_3|$ (where $|R_i|$ is the number of tuples in R_i, $i = 1, 2, 3$). In the case of 3-relations equi-join, each of R_1 and R_3 provides an join attribute to join with R_2, while

Table 2. Synthetic data sets, in which "Size" means the number of tuples in each relation

Data set	Size	Distribution	Parameters
1	$100K$	Uniform	$D_1{=}D_2{=}D_3{=}D_4$, $\lvert D_1\rvert{=}50$
2	$100K$	Uniform	$D_1{=}D_2{\subset}D_3{=}D_4$, $\lvert D_1\rvert{=}30$, $\lvert D_3\rvert{=}60$
3	10	Uniform	$D_1{=}D_2{=}D_3{=}D_4$, $\lvert D_1\rvert{=}3$
4	$100K$	Normal	$\mu_1{=}0$, $\mu_2{=}20$, $\mu_3{=}40$, $\mu_4{=}60$, $\sigma_1{=}\sigma_2{=}\sigma_3{=}\sigma_4{=}10$
5	$100K$	Normal	$\mu_1{=}\mu_2{=}\mu_3{=}\mu_4{=}0$, $\sigma_1{=}\sigma_2{=}\sigma_3{=}\sigma_4{=}1$

R_2 provides two join attributes to join with R_1 and R_3, respectively. We assume that the involved four join attributes come from the value domain D_1, D_2, D_3, and D_4, respectively. For uniform distribution, we generated different data sets by adjusting the number of value domains, i.e. $|D_i|$. For normal distribution, we generated different data sets by setting different distribution expectations and standard deviations of D_i $(i = 1, ..., 4)$, i.e. μ_i and σ_i, respectively.

We ran each test for 10 times to obtain average results over the five data sets. Through the experiments on different data sets. We conclude that the proposed local shedding strategies come very close to generate the optimal solution. We also compared the experimental results of GAS and BLAS.

The configuration on the hardware and software used in the experiments were (1) hardware: CPU P3 1.0GHz, memory: 384MB RAM, disk size: 40G; (2) operating system: Microsoft Windows 2000 Professional; (3) programming environment: Microsoft Visual C++ 6.0.

5.1 Effect of Data Distribution

We compared the effect of two common types of data distributions, i.e., *uniform distribution* and *normal distribution* using data sets 1, 2, 4, and 5. We randomly chose tuples from data sets to form R_i $(i = 1, 2, 3)$ and varied the number of tuples in $|R_i|$ from 10K to 100K. In both uniform and normal data distributions, we compared the number of results using different load shedding strategies. Let $T_i = \frac{H_i}{|R_i|}$, where H_i is the local shedding constraint value, and R_i is the number of records in relation R_i. Fig. 3 shows the comparison results on data sets 1 and 2, and Fig. 4 shows the comparison results on data sets 4 and 5.

Earlier, we have mentioned that BLAS exhaustively searches the order space to find the best order which generates the maximal results. Fig. 3 shows that the number of join results using BLAS and MxLF are significantly higher than that of IS. When the number of tuples in each relation R_i increases, the gap between BLAS (MxLF, respectively) and IS becomes wider, which indicates that BLAS and MxLF are especially good for large data set.

Fig. 4 shows that when the attribute values follow normal distribution, both BLAS and MxLF outperform IS, even though the differences between BLAS (MxLF, respectively) and IS are not as significant as that in the data sets 1 and 2 with uniform distribution. It is interesting to know that in Fig. 4(c), when all the join attributes are in standard normal distribution, the BLAS, MxLF, and the IS superposed with one another. The reason is that join attributes in data

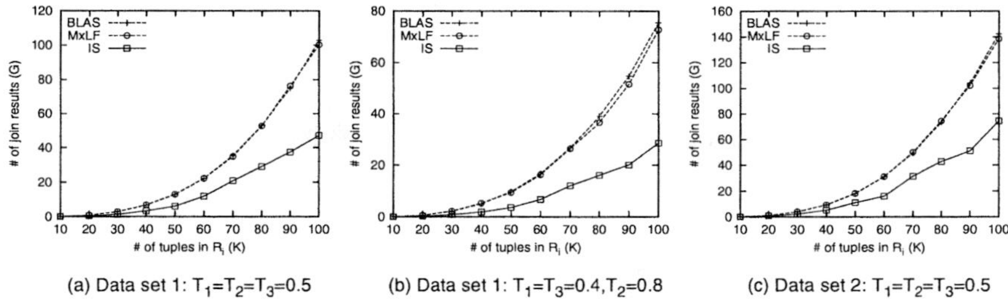

(a) Data set 1: T_1=T_2=T_3=0.5 (b) Data set 1: T_1=T_3=0.4,T_2=0.8 (c) Data set 2: T_1=T_2=T_3=0.5

Fig. 3. Comparisons between local associated shedding approaches and IS using various data sets with uniform distribution

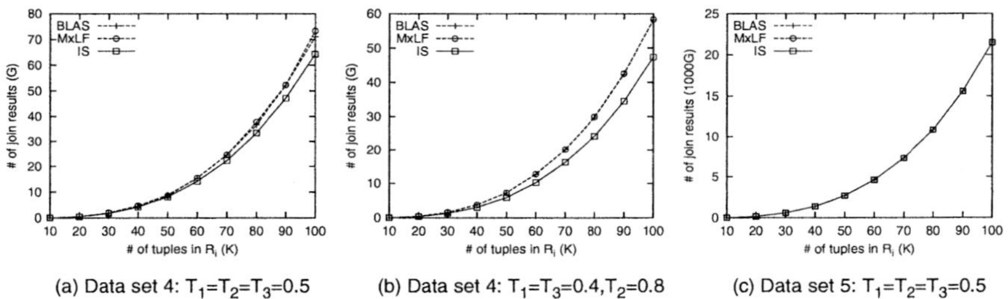

(a) Data set 4: T_1=T_2=T_3=0.5 (b) Data set 4: T_1=T_3=0.4,T_2=0.8 (c) Data set 5: T_1=T_2=T_3=0.5

Fig. 4. Comparisons between local associated shedding approaches and IS using various data sets with normal distribution

set 5 conform to standard normal data distribution. That is, for a join attribute value v, if v has high (low, respectively) frequency in one relation, v must also have high (low, respectively) frequency in other relations. When IS is adopted to perform load shedding, tuples that produce the smallest amount of tuples in the multi-join results may be ranked at the beginning (end, respectively) of the associated relation. In this scenario, all involved relations will be consistent in making the decision to drop the same join attributes. Since there is little conflict between relations in making deletion decisions, the number of join results is maximized and there is little room for BLAS to improve.

Both Fig. 3 and Fig. 4 indicate that the curves of MxLF rarely fall below the curves of BLAS, which implies that in most cases MxLF often chooses the best shedding orders.

5.2 Effect of Different Local Shedding Constraint

We used three different data sets (i.e., 1, 3, and 4) to test the effect of applying different local shedding constraint by varying T_i from 0.1 to 0.9.

Figs. 5 (a) and (b) show the comparison results using data sets 1 and 4 with uniform and normal data distribution, respectively. No matter which data distribution, i.e. normal or uniform distribution, is adopted and various numbers of tuples to be dropped from different relations, BLAS and MxLF always perform

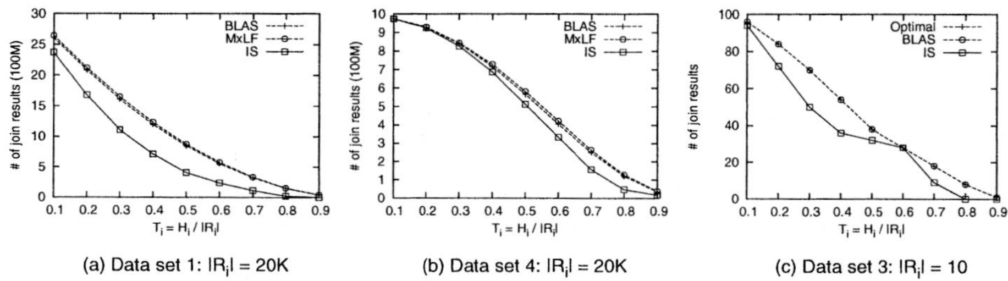

Fig. 5. Comparisons of various local shedding constraint

better than IS. Figs. 5 (a) and (b) also show that MxLF behaves well under various local shedding constraint.

Fig. 5 (c) shows the comparisons between different approaches and the optimal solution using data set 3 (a small data set). We plotted the number of join results in Fig. 5(c) generated by IS, BLAS, and the optimal solution. The figure shows that the curves of BLAS and the optimal solution are superposed with one another, and IS does not catch up with the optimal solution in most cases. We have observed that in most cases BLAS comes very close to the optimal solution.

5.3 Effect of Round Numbers in MLAS

Intuitively, one may think that more rounds lead to a larger resultant set. We have verified this hypothesis through a number of test cases. We used data sets 1 and 4, and randomly chose a number of tuples from these data sets to form R_i ($i \geq 1$) and $|R_i|$=20K. Figs. 6(a) and (b) show the number of join results using different round numbers in MLAS (BLAS is the special case when the round number equals to 1). The round numbers were changed from 1 to 50.

Figs. 6(a) and (b) show that when the shedding round number is small, the multi-round approach significantly increases the number of tuples in the multi-join result, and when the round number increases to a certain value, the number of tuples in the multi-join result remains stable. We conclude that a balance point can be found to obtain a large number of tuples in a multi-join result through small numbers of multi-rounds. For example, we can set the round number in

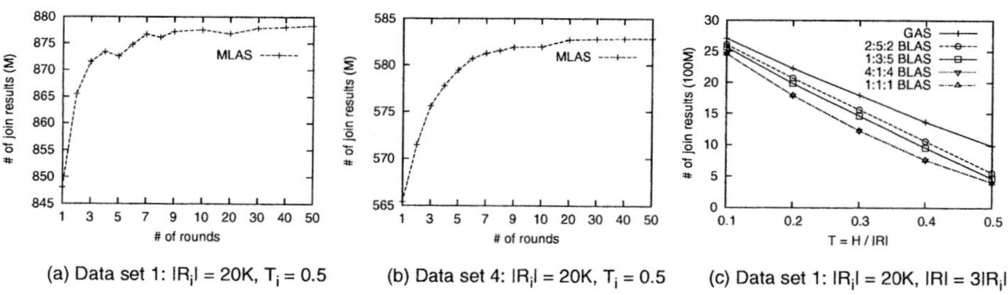

Fig. 6. Experimental results of MLAS, GAS, and BLAS with different local constraint values "$H_1 : H_2 : H_3$"

the uniform data set (as shown in Fig. 6(a)) to be 7 so that we can obtain 876M join results.

5.4 Comparison Between GAS and BLAS

In order to compare global shedding approach with local shedding approaches, we let the global constraint value H to be the sum of three local constraint values, i.e. H=H_1+H_2+H_3. We used data set 1 and assume that each relation R_i (i = 1, 2, 3) has 20K tuples.

Fig. 6 (c) compares GAS and BLAS under different local shedding constraint values for different relations. The figure shows that the number of results generated by GAS is always greater than that of BLAS. This is easy to understand, since GAS globally ranks output_rates of tuples from different relations, whereas local shedding approaches cannot. Fig. 6 (c) shows that under different local shedding constraint, the number of tuples in multi-join results are different. The curve marked with "2:5:2" denotes that $H_1 : H_2 : H_3$ = 2:5:2, which yields the maximal number of results among the four BLAS curves in Fig. 6 (c), while the curves marked with "1:1:1" and "4:1:4" have the worst performance among all the possible local shedding constraint value allocations. These indicate the existence of potential rules of the optimal load shedding decision in multi-joins, which will be further investigated in our future work.

6 Conclusion

In this paper we have proposed several associated shedding strategies for multi-joins in sensor networks, which include (1) the basic local associated shedding strategy (BLAS), (2) the max-loss-first associated shedding strategy (MxLF), (3) the multi-round associated shedding strategy (MLAS), and (4) the global associated shedding strategy (GAS). BLAS improves existing approaches and obtains large number of multi-join results, whereas MxLF and MLAS further enhance the performance of BLAS. MxLF can quickly find a shedding order, whereas MLAS can retain more join results by increasing the shedding rounds. We have also considered the global shedding constraint for which GAS is proposed. Finally, we have identified the effect of the proposed load shedding strategies through experimental results, which show that the proposed strategies generate much larger number of multi-join results than the ones using existing approaches.

References

1. Avnur, R., Hellerstein, J.M.: Eddies: Continuously Adaptive Query Processing. In Proceedings of ACM SIGMOD (2000) 261–272
2. Akyildiz, L.F., Su, W., Sankarasubramaniam, Y., Cayirci, E.: A Survey on Sensor Networks. IEEE Communications Magazine, Vol. 40(8)(2002) 102–114
3. Babcock, B., Babu, S. (eds.): Models and Issues in Data Stream Systems. In Proceedings of ACM PODS (2002) 1–16

4. Babcock, B., Datar, M., Motwani R.: Load Shedding for Aggregation over Data Streams. In Proceedings of ICDE (2004) 350–361
5. Cerpa, A., Elson, J., (eds.): Habitat Monitoring: Application Driver for Wireless Communications Technology. In Proceedings of the ACM SIGCOMM Workshop on Data Communications in Latin America and the Carribean (2001)
6. Chandrasekaran, S., Franklin, M.: Remembrance of Streams Past: Overload-Sensitive Management of Archived Streams. In VLDB (2004) 348–359
7. Carney, D., Çetintemel, U. (eds.): Monitoring Streams-A New Class of Data Management Applications. In Proceedings of VLDB (2002) 469–477
8. Das, A., Gehrke, J., Riedewald, M.: Approximate Join Processing Over Data Streams. In Proceedings of ACM SIGMOD(2003) 40–51; Extended version: Semantic Approximation of Data Stream Joins. In IEEE TKDE (2005), Vol. 17 44–59
9. Heinzelman, W.R., Chandrakasan, A., Balakrishnan, H.: Energy Efficient Communication Protocol for Wireless Micro-sensor Networks. In Proceedings of the 33rd Hawaii International Conference on System Sciences. (2000) 3005-3014
10. Li, J., Li, J., Shi, S.: Concepts, Issues and Advance of Sensor Networks and Data Management of Sensor Networks. Journal of Software, Vol. 14. (2002) 1717–1727
11. Madden, S., Franklin, M.J.: Fjording the Stream: An Architecture for Queries over Streaming Sensor Data. In Proceedings of ICDE (2002) 555–666
12. Mainwaring, A., Polastre, J., (eds.): Wireless Sensor Networks for Habitat Monitoring. In WSAN, 2002
13. Motwani, R., Widom, J. (eds.): Query Processing, Resource Management, and Approximation in a Data Stream Management System. In CIDR (2003) 245–256
14. Reiss, F., Hellerstein, J.M.: Data Triage: An Adaptive Architecture for Load Shedding in TelegraphCQ. In Proceedings of ICDE (2005) 155–156
15. Srivastava, U., Widom, J.: Memory-Limited Execution of Windowed Stream Joins. In Proceedings of VLDB (2004) 324–335
16. Tatbul, N., Çetintemel, U. (eds.): Load Shedding in a Data Manager. In Proceedings of VLDB (2003) 309–320
17. Xu, Y., Heidemann, J., Estrin, D.: Geography-informed Energy Conservation for Ad Hoc Routing. In Proceedings of the ACM/IEEE Mobicom (2001) 70–84

Using Multiple Indexes for Efficient Subsequence Matching in Time-Series Databases

Seung-Hwan Lim, Hee-Jin Park, and Sang-Wook Kim

College of Information and Communications, Hanyang University, Korea
{firemoon, hjpark, wook}@hanyang.ac.kr

Abstract. *Time-series subsequence matching* is an operation that searches for such data subsequences whose changing patterns are similar to a query sequence from a time-series database. This paper addresses a performance issue of time-series subsequence matching. First, we quantitatively examine the performance degradation caused by the *window size effect*, and then show that the performance of subsequence matching with a single index is not satisfactory in real applications. We claim that *index interpolation* is a fairly effective tool to resolve this problem. Index interpolation performs subsequence matching by selecting the most appropriate one from multiple indexes built on windows of their distinct sizes. For index interpolation, we need to decide the sizes of windows for multiple indexes to be built. In this paper, we solve the problem of selecting optimal window sizes in the perspective of *physical database design*. For this, given a set of pairs $\langle length, frequency \rangle$ of query sequences to be performed in a target application and a set of window sizes for building multiple indexes, we devise a formula that estimates the overall cost of all the subsequence matchings. By using this formula, we propose an algorithm that determines the optimal window sizes for maximizing the performance of entire subsequence matchings. We formally prove the optimality as well as the effectiveness of the algorithm. Finally, we perform a series of experiments with a real-life stock data set and a large volume of a synthetic data set to show the superiority of our approach.

1 Introduction

Around us, there are a variety of objects such as stock prices, temperature values, and money exchange rates whose values change as time goes by. The list of such changing values sampled at a time interval is called a *data sequence* for the object[1, 2, 7]. For example, a list of temperature values in New York, which were measured at every 1:00 AM during a year, could be a data sequence. Also, a set of data sequences stored in a database is called a *time-series database*[1, 2, 6, 7, 9, 10, 12].

In a time-series database, it is possible to predict future values of an object by analyzing its past values. Let us assume that we have a time-series database consisting of stock price sequences of several companies for past 10 years. We can predict how the stock price of our company will fluctuate next week by referencing to sequences whose changing patterns are similar to that of our

M.L. Lee, K.L. Tan, and V. Wuwongse (Eds.): DASFAA 2006, LNCS 3882, pp. 65–79, 2006.

company's in the last week. *Similar sequence matching* is an operation that finds such sequences whose changing patterns are similar to that of a given *query sequence* from a time-series database[1, 2, 7, 12]. Similar sequence matching is classified into two categories as follows[7, 12]:

(1) *Whole matching*: Given N data sequences $S_1, \ldots, S_N$, a query sequence Q, and a tolerance ϵ, we find such data sequences S_i that are similar to Q. Here, we note that the data and query sequences should be of the same length.
(2) *Subsequence matching*: Given N data sequences $S_1, \ldots, S_N$, a query sequence Q, and a tolerance ϵ, we find all the sequences S_i, one or more subsequences of which are similar to Q, and the offsets in S_i of those subsequences.

Since subsequence matching is a generalization of whole matching, it is applicable to practical applications more than whole matching. In this paper, we focus our attention on subsequence matching.

As a measure for determining the similarity for arbitrary two sequences $X(=[x_0, x_1, \ldots, x_{n-1}])$ and $Y(=[y_0, y_1, \ldots, y_{n-1}])$ of the same length n, the *Euclidean distance* $D(X, Y)$ defined below is widely used as a *basic* similarity measure[1, 4, 5, 7, 8, 13, 14][1]. Two sequences X and Y whose $D(X, Y)$ is below a user-specified tolerance value ϵ are regarded *similar* and are also said to be in ϵ-*match*[12].

$$D(X,Y) = \sqrt{\sum_{i=0}^{n-1} (x_i - y_i)^2} \quad (1)$$

There have been two basic methods proposed in references [7] and [12] for subsequence matching. Following reference[12], we call them *FRM*[7] and *Dual-Match*[12], respectively. Both of them use an index for efficient processing of subsequence matching. Also, they employ the concept of a *window* as an indexing unit. The window is a subsequence of a fixed-size w extracted from query and data sequences. Their common idea for performing subsequence matching is summarized as follows.

For indexing, windows of size w are extracted from every data sequence. Then, each window is transformed into a point in $f(\ll w)$-dimensional space by using the *Discrete Fourier transform*(DFT) or *wavelet transform*. All these points are stored into an R*-tree[3], a multidimensional index structure.

For subsequence matching with a tolerance ϵ, windows of size w are extracted from a query sequence of length $l(\geq w)$, and are transformed into points in f-dimensional space. For each point, a range query of a range $\epsilon/\sqrt{p}(p = \lfloor l/w \rfloor)$ is performed on the R*-tree built in the indexing stage. This process is called an *index searching step*. As a result, candidate subsequences, each of which

[1] In addition to the Euclidean distance, the Manhattan distance, the maximum distance in any pair elements[2], and the time warping distance can be also used as a similarity measure.

has a high possibility to be in ϵ-match with a query sequence, are found. For resolving *false alarms*[1, 7], which are recommended as the candidates but not true answers, each candidate subsequence is accessed from disk, and its actual *Euclidean distance* to the query sequence is computed. This process is called a *post-processing step*.

In both methods, the performance of subsequence matching is highly dependent on the window size. That is, the performance tends to deteriorate as the difference between the size of a window and the length of a query sequence gets larger. This phenomenon is called a *window size effect*[12]. In *FRM* and *Dual-Match*, the size of a window is determined by the minimum among lengths of query sequences to be issued, and subsequence matching performs by using *only one* R*-tree. This approach, however, has a problem that the performance of subsequence matching degrades seriously as the length of a query sequence increases. We can consider building of indexes for all the lengths of query sequences to be issued in a target application. This requires a large cost of maintaining a large number of indexes, thereby being infeasible in real applications.

In this paper, we propose a novel subsequence matching method based on the concept of *index interpolation*[11]. *Index interpolation* constructs multiple indexes on different sizes of windows and processes subsequence matching by selecting the most appropriate one for a given query sequence. Index interpolation is applicable to both *FRM* and *Dual-Match*, and is expected to enhance the performance of subsequence matching significantly.

In index interpolation, more indexes provide better performance, but require a higher cost for their maintenance. This paper mainly focuses on the selection of the sizes for multiple windows that maximize the performance of subsequence matching when the number of indexes is given.

We summarize the contributions of the paper in the following. First, we quantitatively show the performance degradation of subsequence matching due to the window size effect, and then reveal that the overall performance of subsequence matchings using a single index is not satisfactory in real applications. We claim that the concept of index interpolation is quite useful for solving this problem. For subsequence matching by using index interpolation, we need to determine the sizes of windows on which multiple indexes are built. We employ the *physical database design methodology* to select optimal sizes of windows. That is, we devise a formula that estimates the entire cost of performing all the subsequence matchings when there are a set of pairs ⟨length, frequency⟩ of query sequences to be issued and a set of sizes of windows on which indexes are built. By using this formula, we propose an algorithm that decides the optimal sizes of windows that maximize the overall performance of all the subsequence matchings. We also formally verify the optimality and effectiveness of the proposed algorithm. Finally, we show the effect of performance enhancement by the proposed algorithm over previous ones via extensive experiments.

The paper is organized as follows. Section 2 briefly introduces previous methods for subsequence matching, and discusses their advantages and disadvantages. Section 3 presents a result of preliminary experiments that show how the gap between the length of a query sequence and the size of a window affects the performance of subsequence matching. Section 4 proposes a new method based on index interpolation, and addresses the selection of multiple window sizes for optimizing the performance of subsequence matching. Section 5 verifies the superiority of the proposed method via a series of experiments. Finally, Section 6 summarizes and concludes the paper.

2 Related Work

2.1 FRM

Reference [7] proposed a subsequence matching method that allows data and query sequences of arbitrary lengths. Following reference [12], we call this method *FRM*. *FRM* uses the concept of a *window* of a fixed length for R*-tree indexing.

For indexing, *FRM* extracts *sliding windows* of size w from every possible position inside each data sequence S of length $len(S)(\geq w)$, and then it converts every sliding window into a point in $f(\ll w)$-dimensional space by using *DFT*. The number of points extracted from each data sequence S is $(len(S)-w+1)$. As a result, a large number of points appear in this way, and thus storage overhead for storing these points individually also gets large. For alleviating this problem, *FRM* forms the minimum bounding rectangles(*MBR*) enclosing multiple points and builds an R*-tree[3] on these *MBR*s instead of points.

For subsequence matching, *FRM* extracts p *disjoint windows* of size w from a query sequence of length $len(Q)(\geq w)$ where $p = \lfloor len(Q)/w \rfloor$, and then converts every disjoint window into a point in f-dimensional space by using *DFT*. For each point, *FRM* performs a range query on an R*-tree by using the point as a center and $\epsilon/\sqrt{p}$ as a range. This *index searching step* finds the points that correspond to the candidate subsequences that are highly likely to be true answers. To discard false alarms, it performs the *post-processing step*; i.e., it accesses all the sequences containing the candidate subsequences from the disk, and computes their *Euclidean* distance to the query sequence. Finally, it returns the final result set containing only the true answers after leaving out the false alarms.

2.2 Dual-Match

In order to reduce storage overhead, *FRM* stores the *MBR*s, each of which encloses multiple points, instead of storing individual points in an R*-tree. Inherently, these *MBR*s have *dead space*[3] inside. This dead space is the primary cause of false alarms, and thus degrades the overall performance of subsequence matching[12]. Moon et al.[12] proposed a method called *Dual-Match* to overcome this problem.

In contrast to *FRM* that locates sliding windows on data sequences and disjoint windows on a query sequence, *Dual-Match* extracts disjoint windows from data sequences and sliding windows from a query sequence. By this simple role exchange, *Dual-Match* reduces the number of points to be stored in the R*-tree by the ratio of $1/w$. This makes it possible to store individual points themselves rather than *MBRs* in an R*-tree. As a result, *Dual-Match* does not suffer from the problem caused by the dead space inside *MBRs* any longer, and thus achieves considerable performance improvement.

3 Motivation

3.1 Window Size Effect

Given a query sequence, subsequence matching with *FRM* or *Dual-Match* tends to incur more false alarms as the window size gets smaller. For example, the window size for an R*-tree R1 is larger than that for an R*-tree R2. In this case, the candidate set returned by searching R2 would contain extra false alarms, which do not exist in the set returned by searching R1. More false alarms require more time in the post processing step, thereby degrading the overall performance of subsequence matching. This phenomenon is called *window size effect*[12]. Therefore, the choice of a large window in R*-tree construction is so beneficial to efficient processing of subsequence matching.

On the other hand, the R*-tree thus built is useless in subsequence matching when its window size is larger than the length of (in *FRM*) and half the length of (in *Dual-Match*) a query sequence[7, 12]. In this case, subsequence matching takes much time since the *sequential scan* should be employed for finding matched subsequences. Therefore, it is crucial to choose a proper size of windows in the indexing stage for efficient processing of subsequence matchings.

Let us denote *minQLen* as the minimum among the lengths of query sequences to be used in a target application. The previous methods determine the window size for indexing as *minQLen* (in *FRM*) or $\lfloor(minQLen + 1)/2\rfloor$ (in *Dual-Match*). In real applications, however, query sequences of various lengths are issued regardless of the window size employed in indexing. Thus, the performance degradation of subsequence matching becomes fairly serious in case the difference between the length of a query sequence and the size of window is large.

3.2 Preliminary Experiments

We used 620 Korean stock price sequences of length 1,024 in experiments. Other experiment environments such as hardware and software settings, extraction of windows from data sequences, the lower-dimensional transform, and construction of indexes are the same as those explained in detail in Section 5.

We performed two preliminary experiments. The first experiment used only a single index of the fixed window size and observed the performance tendency of subsequence matching while changing the length of query sequences. The window size was set to $w = 64$ and the lengths of query sequences were set to $Len(Q) =$ 64, 128, 256, 512, and 1,024. The second experiment used query sequences of the fixed length and observed the performance tendency of subsequence matching while changing the window size. The length of query sequences used was $Len(Q)$ $=$ 1,024, and the window sizes were $w =$ 64, 128, 256, 512, and 1,024.

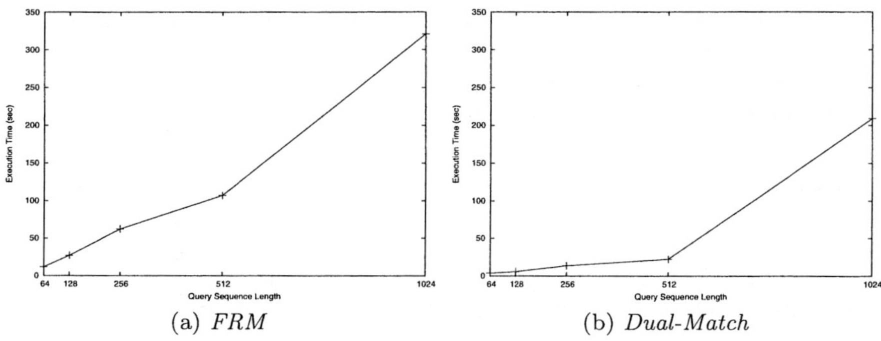

(a) *FRM* (b) *Dual-Match*

Fig. 1. Variation of Total Execution Time According to Query Sequence Lengths

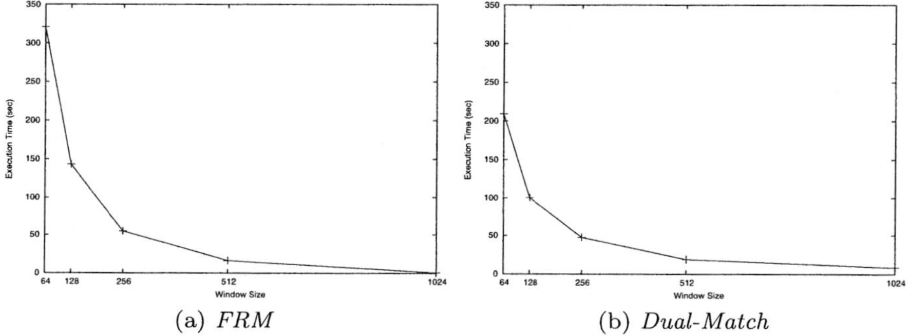

(a) *FRM* (b) *Dual-Match*

Fig. 2. Variation of Total Execution Time According to Window Sizes

We used the total execution time of subsequence matchings for all the query sequences as a performance factor. For every query, we adjusted a tolerance ϵ so that 20 subsequences should be returned as a final result set.

Figures 1(a) and 1(b) show the results of the first experiment for *FRM* and *Dual-Match*, respectively. In the figures, the horizontal axes represent the length of query sequences, and the vertical axes the total execution time in the unit of seconds. The results show that the total execution time increases as the query sequence gets longer for both *FRM* and *Dual-Match*. The rationale of the results is that, as the difference between the length of query sequences and the size of windows increases, the number of candidate subsequences obtained from the index searching step also increases due to the window size effect.

Figures 2(a) and 2(b) show the results of the second experiment. The horizontal axes represent the window size, and the vertical axes the total execution time. The results show that the total execution time rapidly decreases as the window size increases for both *FRM* and *Dual-Match*. The rationale of the results is the same as that of the first experiment.

In summary, the performance of subsequence matching dramatically deteriorates as the gap of the length of query sequences and the size of windows increases. This implies that the performance of subsequence matchings is not satisfactory to users when their processing is done with only a single R*-tree built on windows whose size is determined by considering the minimum length of query sequences as in the prior work.

4 The Proposed Method

In this section, we propose a novel method based on the concept of index interpolation to overcome the performance degradation caused by the window size effect. In index interpolation, we build multiple indexes on windows of different window sizes, and then use an index whose window size is the most appropriate for a given query sequence in subsequence matching.

As the number of indexes increases, the cost for maintaining indexes also increases while subsequence matching performs better. The cost includes not only the storage space for storing indexes but also the time for updating indexes when data is inserted, deleted, or modified. Thus, it is necessary to build as few indexes as possible.

In this section, we consider determining a list of *optimal window sizes* for a given set of pairs ⟨lengths and its frequencies⟩ of query sequences. The lengths and frequencies of query sequences can be easily obtained by analyzing a target application, which is a widely-accepted assumption in physical database design.

4.1 Optimal Window Size

For further presentation, we first introduce some notations and definitions. We denote the length of a query sequence by l_i, $i \geq 1$, and do the list of n query sequence lengths by $\langle l_1, l_2, \ldots, l_n \rangle$ where $l_1 < l_2 < \cdots < l_n$. Similarly, we denote the frequency of a query sequence length l_i by f_i and do accordingly the frequency list of $\langle l_1, l_2, \ldots, l_n \rangle$ by $\langle f_1, f_2, \ldots, f_n \rangle$. We denote a window size by w_i, $i \geq 1$, and do the list of m window sizes by $\langle w_1, w_2, \ldots, w_m \rangle$ where $w_1 < w_2 < \cdots < w_m$. In index interpolation, we perform subsequence matching by selecting the most appropriate one from $\langle w_1, w_2, \ldots, w_m \rangle$ and by using its corresponding index. We call this window size *an optimal one for the length of the query sequence,* l_k, and denote it by $w_{opt}(l_k)$.

We show that the optimal window size $w_{opt}(l_k)$ for a query sequence length l_k in a window list $\langle w_1, w_2, \ldots, w_m \rangle$ is computed by

$$w_p = max\{w_i | w_i \leq l_k \ (1 \leq i \leq m)\} \text{ for } FRM \text{ and} \quad (2)$$

$$w_q = max\{w_i | w_i \leq \lfloor (l_k + 1)/2 \rfloor \ (1 \leq i \leq m)\} \text{ for } Dual\text{-}Match \quad (3)$$

We show that w_p is the optimal window size for *FRM.* (One can show w_q is the optimal window size for *Dual-Match* in a similar way.) We first show any window size in $\langle w_{p+1}, \ldots, w_m \rangle$ cannot be the optimal one for query sequence length l_k. By definition of w_p, windows sizes $w_{p+1}, \ldots, w_m$ are all larger than l_k and the indexes for those window sizes cannot be used in subsequence matching for a query sequence of length l_k[7]. Thus, in this case, we have to perform sequential scan for a query sequence of length l_k, which shows as poor performance as no indexes are built.

Now, we show that w_p is the optimal window size for l_k among $\langle w_1, \ldots, w_p \rangle$. Every window in $\langle w_1, \ldots, w_p \rangle$ is not larger than l_k and thus an index built for any window size in $\langle w_1, \ldots, w_p \rangle$ can be used for processing a query sequence of length l_k without any concern of false dismissal[7]. According to the window size effect, as a window size is nearer to l_k, the performance becomes better. Therefor, it is hold that w_p is $w_{opt}(l_k)$ the optimal window size for l_k.

4.2 Cost Function

Given a query sequence length l_k and its frequency f_k, the cost of processing a query sequence of length l_k over the list of window sizes $W = \langle w_1, w_2, \ldots, w_m \rangle$, denoted by $C(l_k, f_k, W)$, is defined as follows.

$$C(l_k, f_k, W) = f_k l_k / w_{opt(k)}$$

This cost function is inferred from the observation from our preliminary experiments in Section 3: The cost of subsequence matching was found to be roughly proportional to the query sequence length and to be inversely proportional to the window size.

Now, we extend the cost function to a more general case. Given a list of query sequence lengths $L = \langle l_1, l_2, \ldots, l_n \rangle$ and a list of their frequencies $F = \langle f_1, f_2, \ldots, f_n \rangle$, the processing cost of subsequence matchings using W, denoted by $C(L, F, W)$, is the sum of $C(l_k, f_k, W)$'s for all $1 \leq k \leq n$, i.e.,

$$C(L, F, W) = \sum_{k=1}^{n} f_k l_k / w_{opt(k)}. \tag{4}$$

Also, the cost function for a sublist $L[i..j] = \langle l_i, \ldots, l_j \rangle$ and $F[i..j] = \langle f_i, \ldots, f_j \rangle$ over W is defined analogously.

$$C(L[i..j], F[i..j], W) = \sum_{k=i}^{j} f_k l_k / w_{opt(k)}. \tag{5}$$

4.3 Computing of Optimal Window Size List

In this section, we present an algorithm for determining a list of optimal window sizes W when L and F are given. First, we give a formal definition of W, the optimal window size list.

Definition 1. *For $L = \langle l_1, l_2, \ldots, l_n \rangle$, $F = \langle f_1, f_2, \ldots, f_n \rangle$, and m, a window size list $W = \langle w_1, w_2, \ldots, w_m \rangle$ is considered optimal if and only if $C(L, F, W) \leq C(L, F, W')$ for any window size list W' of length m. The cost $C(L, F, W)$ is called the optimal cost of L and F over the window size lists of length m and also denoted by $O_m(L, F)$.*

We show that every window size in W, the optimal window size list, corresponds to *some* query sequence length l_j in the next lemma. This implies that, for determining W, we just need to consider ${}_nC_m$, instead of l_nC_m, lists of windows sizes, where C represents *combination*.

Lemma 1. *If a window size list* $\langle w_1, w_2, \ldots, w_m \rangle$ *is an optimal window size list of length* $m(\leq n)$ *for* $L = \langle l_1, l_2, \ldots, l_n \rangle$ *and* $F = \langle f_1, f_2, \ldots, f_n \rangle$, $\langle w_1, w_2, \ldots, w_m \rangle = \langle l_{g(1)}, l_{g(2)}, \ldots, l_{g(m)} \rangle$ *for some* $1 \leq g(1) < g(2) < \cdots < g(m) \leq n$.

Proof. We only need to show that each window size w_i for $1 \leq i \leq m$ is the same as l_j for some $1 \leq j \leq n$. We prove it by contradiction. Assume that w_i' is a window size that is not same as any l_j for $1 \leq j \leq n$. Then, there exist two consecutive query sequence lengths l_{a-1} and l_a satisfying $l_{a-1} < w_i' < l_a$. One can show that the cost of subsequence matchings of L and F by using $\langle w_1, \ldots, w_i', \ldots, w_m \rangle$ is larger than that by using $\langle w_1, \ldots, l_a, \ldots, w_m \rangle$, which contradicts that $\langle w_1, w_2, \ldots, w_m \rangle$ is optimal. Hence, every window size w_i is the same as some l_j.

Next, we show how to compute the optimal cost $O_m(L, F)$ for $L = \langle l_1, l_2, \ldots, l_n \rangle$ and $F = \langle f_1, f_2, \ldots, f_n \rangle$. We note that we can obtain the optimal window size list of length m as a result of computing the optimal cost $O_m(L, F)$. One can consider a naive approach that computes the costs over all possible window size lists of length m and then gets the minimum of them. However, this approach should compute $O(n^m)$ values, which are too much. In this paper, we present an algorithm that computes the optimal cost $O_m(L, F)$ in $O(mn^2)$ time using *dynamic programming*. The main idea is that we first compute the optimal costs for query sequence sublists and then extend them to get the optimal cost for the whole query sequence list.

The computation of the optimal cost $O_m(L, F)$ consists of two steps. In step 1, we compute an $n \times n$ array NC where each entry $NC(i, j)$ for $1 \leq i \leq j \leq n$ stores $C(L[i..j], F[i..j], \langle l_i \rangle)$, i.e., the cost of the sublists $\langle l_i, \ldots, l_j \rangle$ and $\langle f_i, \ldots, f_j \rangle$ over the window size list $\langle l_i \rangle$. In step 2, we compute the optimal cost $O_m(L, F)$ using the array NC.

Step 1. Compute the array NC: We compute $C(L[i..j], F[i..j], \langle l_i \rangle)$ for each $1 \leq i \leq j \leq n$ and store it into $NC(i, j)$. We show how to compute all $NC(i, j)$'s in $O(n^2)$ time. By equation (5), $NC(i, j) = \sum_{k=i}^{j} f_k l_k / l_i$. Thus, $NC(i, i) = f_i$ and $NC(i, j) = NC(i, j-1) + f_j l_j / l_i$ for all $1 \leq i < j \leq n$, which means that we can compute $NC(i, i)$ in $O(1)$ time, and we also can compute $NC(i, j)$ in $O(1)$ time from $NC(i, j-1)$. Hence, we get the following lemma.

Lemma 2. *We can compute all* $NC(i, j)$*'s for* $1 \leq i \leq j \leq n$ *in* $O(n^2)$ *time.*

Step 2. We compute the optimal cost $O_m(L, F)$: Let $C'(i, j)$ for $1 \leq i \leq n$ and $1 \leq j \leq m$ denote the optimal cost of the sublists $\langle l_i, \ldots, l_n \rangle$ and $\langle f_i, \ldots, f_n \rangle$ over the list of j window sizes whose smallest window size w_1 is l_i. Then, $O_m(L, F) = C'(1, m)$. We show that we can compute $C'(1, m)$ by dynamic programming. We first show the following recurrence is satisfied for $C'(i, j)$ for $1 \leq i \leq n$ and $1 \leq j \leq m$.

Lemma 3. $C'(i,j) = \min_{k=i+1}^{n-j+2}\{NC(i,k-1) + C'(k,j-1)\}$.

Proof. By definition of $C'(i,j)$, the smallest window size w_1 is l_i. Consider the second smallest window size w_2. The window size w_2 can be one of the query sequence lengths $l_{i+1},\ldots,l_{n-i+1}$ by Lemma 1. If w_2 is l_k, $C'(i,j) = NC(i,k-1) + C'(k,j-1) \leq NC(i,k'-1) + C'(k',j-1)$ for any $i+1 \leq k' \leq n-i+1$. Hence, the recurrence is satisfied for $C'(i,j)$.

Finally, we show we can compute $C'(1,m)$ in $O(mn^2)$ time. Since we can compute $C'(i,j)$ in $O(n)$ time by Lemma 3, and we compute at most mn values of $C'(i,j)$'s, we can compute $C'(1,m)$ in $O(mn^2)$ time and we get the following lemma.

Lemma 4. *We can compute the optimal cost $O_m(L,F)$ in $O(mn^2)$ time.*

The pseudo-code for computing $C'(1,m)$ is depicted in Figure 3. In lines 1-4, we compute the array NC. In lines 5-10, we initialize some elements of the C' array. In lines 11-15, we compute all the elements of the C' array.

```
1: for i := 1 to n do
2:     NC[i][i] := f_i
3:     for j := i + 1 to n do
4:         NC[i][j] := NC[i][j − 1] + f_j l_j / l_i
5: for i := 1 to n do
6:     C[i][1] := NC[i][n]
7:     for j := 2 to n − i do
8:         C[i][j] := ∞
9:     for j := n − i + 1 to m do
10:        C[i][j] := 0
11: for i := n − 2 downto 1 do
12:     for j := 2 to min{m, n − i} do
13:         for k := i + 1 to n − j + 2 do
14:             temp := NC[i][k − 1] + C[k][j − 1]
15:             if (temp < C[i][j]) C[i][j] := temp
```

Fig. 3. Pseudo-code for computing $C'(1,m)$

5 Performance Evaluation

5.1 Experiment Environment

We used a real-life data set called *K_Stock_Data* and a synthetic data called *Syn_Data*. *K_Stock_Data*, the same one used for our preliminary experiments presented in Section 3, consists of 620 stock price sequences whose length is 1,024. *Syn_Data* is a synthetic data set comprising random walk data sequences s = $<s_1, s_2, \ldots, s_n>$ generated as follows[1].

$$s_{i+1} = s_i + z_i \tag{6}$$

Here, z_i is a random variable that takes an arbitrary value from an interval [-0.1, 0.1] and s_1, the first element of a sequence, is a special value obtained randomly from the interval [1, 10]. For performing our experiments extensively, we generated five sets of *Syn_Data* that comprise 2,000, 3,000, 4,000, and 5,000 data sequences of length 1,024, respectively and another five sets of *Syn_Data* that consist of 1,000 data sequences whose lengths are 2,000, 3,000, 4,000, and 5,000, respectively. On all these data sets, we built R*-trees in the same way as in our preliminary experiments.

Table 1. Number of Query Sequences in Each Group

Number of query sequence groups	Number of query sequences in each group	Sub-total number of query sequences
4	30	120
5	10	50
6	5	30
16	1	16
Total: 31		216

Also, query sequences have their lengths of multiples of 32 in the range [64, 1,024], and each query sequence belongs to a group by its length. The total number of groups is 31. We generated query sequences over groups as in Table 1, which follow the features in real applications. We see that query sequences in four groups frequently appear, and those in 16 groups do not. As a performance factor, we used the average execution time for subsequence matchings with the total of 216 query sequences. We also adjusted a tolerance ϵ so that 20 final answers are returned.

The hardware platform used in our experiments is a 2.8 GHz Pentium 4 PC equipped with 512MB RAM and 9GB hard disk. The software platform is MS Windows 2000 Server. The language used in development is Microsoft Visual C++. We set the size of a page for storing both data and R*-trees to 1KB. For dimensionality reduction, we used the *DFT*, and extracted six features for indexing. Since reference [12] already verified that *Dual-Match* performs much better than *FRM*, we only used *Dual-Match* in our experiments.

We compared the performance of the three methods: (A) *Dual-Match* with only one index (as in the original approach), (B) *Dual-Match* with multiple indexes whose window sizes are evenly chosen in the range of the minimum and maximum query sequence lengths, (C) *Dual-Match* with multiple indexes whose window sizes are chosen by our approach as shown in Section 4. Hereafter, we shortly call them methods (A), (B), and (C), respectively.

5.2 Results and Analyses

We ran three types of experiments for performance evaluation. In Experiment 1, we compared the performance of the three methods (A), (B), and (C) using

K_Stock_Data with different numbers of indexes. In Experiment 2 and Experiment 3, we compared the performance of the three methods using *Syn_Data* while changing the number and the length of data sequences, respectively.

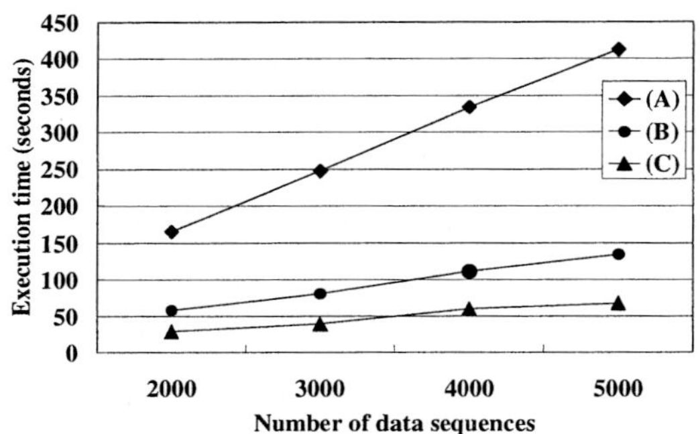

Fig. 4. Performance with Different Numbers of Data Sequences

Figure 4 shows the results of Experiment 1. The horizontal axis represents the number of R*-trees employed for subsequence matchings, and the vertical axis does the average execution time in the unit of seconds. As shown in the figure, method (A) showed the worst performance, and method (C) showed the best performance. When using five R*-trees, method (C) performs 7.8 times and 1.5 times better than methods (A) and (C), respectively. Also, it showed performance 5.6 times and 3.2 times better than methods (A) and (C), respectively. The performance gain tends to get larger with a smaller number of R*-trees employed in methods (B) and (C).

In Experiment 2, we examined the performance tendency of the three methods while changing the number of data sequences of length 1,024 to 2,000, 3,000, 4,000, and 5,000. We built four R*-trees for methods (B) and (C).

Figure 5 shows the results of Experiment 2. The horizontal axis represents the number of data sequences, and the vertical axis does the average execution time.

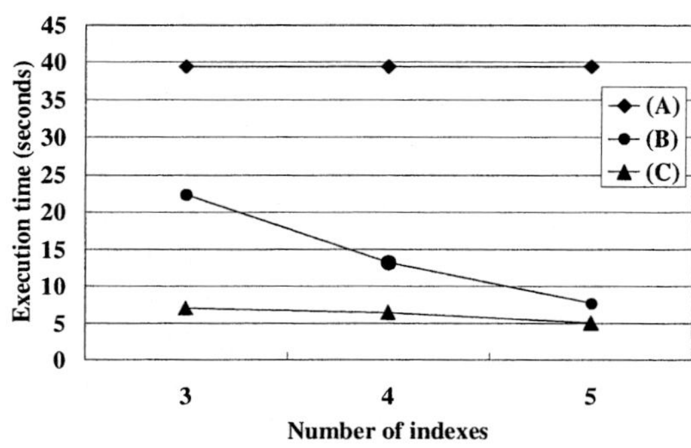

Fig. 5. Performance with Different Numbers of Indexes

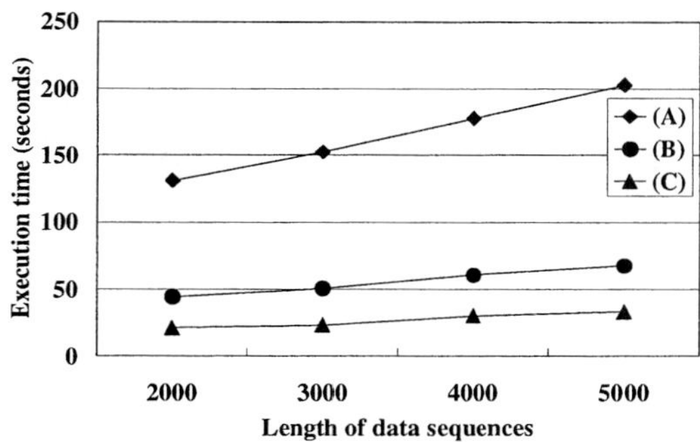

Fig. 6. Performance with Different Lengths of Data Sequences

In all cases, the performance of method (C) was shown to be better than that of method (B), which was shown to have better performance than method (A). Also, the performance gain of method (C) was shown to be about 5.7 times to 6.1 times when compared with method (A), and about 1.9 to 2.1 when compared with method (B).

In Experiment 3, we investigated the performance change of the three methods with 1,000 synthetic data sequences of length 2,000, 3,000, 4,000, and 5,000. As in Experiment 2, we employed four R*-trees for methods (B) and (C).

Figure 6 shows the results of Experiment 3. The horizontal axis represents the length of data sequences, and the vertical axis does the average execution time. The results appeared to be quite similar to that of Experiment 2. Regardless of the length of data sequences, method (C) showed the best performance, and achieved significant speedup about 6.2 times and 2.0 times over methods (A) and (B), respectively.

In summary, by employing the concept of index interpolation, we could improve the performance of subsequence matching significantly compared with the prior approach that uses only a single R*-tree. Also, our method for selecting the optimal window sizes for multiple R*-trees was shown to be fairly effective when compared with the simple one that chooses window sizes from even positions within a possible range.

6 Conclusions

In this paper, we have proposed a novel method for time-series subsequence matching based on index interpolation[11] that resolves the performance degradation caused by the window size effect.

The main contributions can be summarized as follows.

(1) Via preliminary experiments, we have first verified that the performance of subsequence matching by previous methods that employ only one R*-tree is not satisfactory to users. Then, we have claimed that index interpolation is a good choice to resolve this performance problem.

(2) We have derived a formula that estimates the cost for all the subsequence matchings when a set of pairs ⟨length, frequency⟩ of query sequences to be issued and a set of windows sizes for the R*-tree building are provided.
(3) Using the cost formula, we have proposed an efficient algorithm that determines an optimal set of window sizes that maximize the overall performance of all the subsequence matchings performed in a target application. We have formally shown the optimality and effectiveness of the proposed algorithm.
(4) We have quantitatively verified the effect of performance improvement obtained from the proposed method through a series of experiments.

The results reveal that the proposed approach outperforms the previous one up to 7.8 times. Currently, the proposed method provides the optimal list of window sizes, but not the optimal number of indexes. As a future study, we are considering tackling this issue by reflecting the update costs as well as subsequence matching costs.

Acknowledgement

This research was supported by the MIC (Ministry of Information and Communication), Korea, under the ITRC (Information Technology Research Center) support program supervised by the IITA (Institute of Information Technology Assessment) (IITA–2005–C1090–0502–0009).

References

1. R. Agrawal, C. Faloutsos, and A. Swami: Efficient Similarity Search in Sequence DataBases, In Proc. Int'l Conf. on Foundations of Data Organization and Algorithms (FODO), pp. 69-84, Chicago, Illinois, Oct. 1993.
2. R. Agrawal et al: Fast Similarity Search in the Presence of Noise, Scaling, and Translation in Time-Series Database, In Proc. Int'l Conf. on Very Large Data Bases (VLDB), pp. 490-501, Zurich, Switzerland, Sept. 1995.
3. N. Beckmann et al: The R*-tree: An efficient and Robust Access Method for Points and Rectangles, In Proc. Int'l Conf. on Management of Data, ACM SIGMOD, pp. 322-331, Atlantic City, New Jersey, May 1990.
4. K. P. Chan and A. W. C. Fu: Efficient Time Series Matching by Wavelets, In Proc. Int'l Conf. on Data Engineering (ICDE), IEEE, pp. 126-133, Sydney, Australia, Mar. 1999.
5. K. K. W. Chu and M. H. Wong: Fast Time-Series Searching with Scaling and Shifting, In Proc. ACM SIGACT-SIGMOD-SIGART Symposium on Principles of Database Systems (PODS), ACM, pp. 237-248, Philadelphia, Pennsylvania, May 1999.
6. T. Argyros, C. Ermopoulos: Efficient Subsequence Matching in Time Series Databases Under Time and Amplitude Transformations, ICDM, 2003
7. C. Faloutsos et al: Fast Subsequence Matching in Time-Series Databases, In Proc. Int'l Conf. on Management of Data, ACM SIGMOD, pp. 419-429, Minneapolis, Minnesota, May 1994.

8. D. Q. Goldin and P. C. Kanellakis: On Similarity Queries for Time-Series Data: Constraint Specification and Implementation, In Proc. Int'l Conf. on Principles and Practice of Constraint Programming, pp. 137-153, Cassis, France, Sept. 1995.
9. T. Kahveci, K. S. Ambuj: Variable Length Queries for Time Series Data, In Proc. Int'l Conf. on Data Engineering, 2001
10. T. Kahveci, K. S. Ambuj: Optimizing Similarity Search for Arbitrary Length Time Series Queries, IEEE Trans. Knowl. Data Eng. Vol. 16, No. 4, 418-433, 2004
11. W. K. Loh, S. W. Kim and K. Y. Whang: A Subsequence Matching Algorithm that Supports Normalization Transform in Time-Series Databases, Data Mining and Knowledge Discovery Journal, Vol. 9, No. 1, pp. 5-28, Jul. 2004.
12. Y. S. Moon et al: Duality-Based Subsequence Matching in Time-Series Databases, In Proc. Int'l Conf. on Data Engineering (ICDE), IEEE, pp. 263-272, Heidelberg, Germany, Apr. 2001.
13. D. Rafiei and A. Mendelzon: Similarity-based Queries for Time-Series Data, In Proc. Int'l Conf. on Management of Data, ACM SIGMOD, pp. 13-24, Tucson, Arizona, June 1997.
14. D. Rafiei: On Similarity-Based Queries for Time Series Data, In Proc. Int'l Conf. on Data Engineering (ICDE), IEEE, pp. 410-417, Sydney, Australia, Mar. 1999.
15. Weber, R. et al: A Quantitative Analysis and Performance Study for Similarity-Search Methods in High-Dimensional Spaces, In Proc. Int'l Conf. on Very Large Data Bases (VLDB), pp. 194-205, New York, Aug. 1998.

DAPSS: Exact Subsequence Matching for Data Streams

Yasuhiro Fujiwara, Yasushi Sakurai, and Masashi Yamamuro

NTT Cyber Space Laboratories, NTT Corporation,
1-1 Hikarinooka, Yokosuka-Shi, Kanagawa, 239-0847, Japan
{fujiwara.yasuhiro, sakurai.yasushi, yamamuro.masashi}@lab.ntt.co.jp

Abstract. There is much interest in the processing of data streams for applications in the fields such as financial analysis, network monitoring, mobile services, and sensor network management. The key characteristic of stream data, that it continues to arrive, demands a new approach. This paper focuses on the problem of detecting, exactly, similar pairs of subsequences of arbitrary length in streaming fashion. We propose DAPSS (DAta stream Processing for Store and Search), an efficient and effective method to detect the similar pairs, which keeps (1) the feature data of each sequence in the memory space and (2) the compressed data of the original sequences in the disk space. Experiments on synthetic and real data sets show that DAPSS is significantly (up to 35 times) faster than the naive method while it guarantees the correctness of query results.

1 Introduction

The focus on data engineering has recently shifted towards data stream applications. Examples include financial analysis, network monitoring, mobile services, sensor network management. In such applications, the data of interest comprises multiple sequences that each evolve over time. Generally the time-series data streams arrive online at high bit rates and are potentially unbounded in size. A fundamental challenge faced by these applications is that the data sources generate semi-infinite sequences. The resource limitations unavoidably imply a trade-off — it is practically impossible to keep all historical data in the memory space, but fast query processing must be ensured.

To analyze the co-evolving sequences in real time, the techniques for data stream processing should fulfill two important requirements:

1. Memory space requirements are limited to handle the co-evolving data streams.
2. High-speed computation is provided for update and query processing.

Previous studies assumed that data would be discarded after the processing to meet the above conditions; unfortunately, this sacrifices matching accuracy. We, therefore, try to remove this drawback, and add the following essential requirement:

3. The correctness of query results is guaranteed.

M.L. Lee, K.L. Tan, and V. Wuwongse (Eds.): DASFAA 2006, LNCS 3882, pp. 80–94, 2006.

To the best of our knowledge, this is the first study on the similarity search problem for streaming data sequences that considers output exactness in bounded memory.

We focus on the problem of detecting, exactly, similar pairs in multiple streaming data sequences with similarity queries of unknown, arbitrary length. Typical queries would be '*Find articles that have similar sales trend in on-line manner*', '*Find persons who have similar movements in real time*', or '*Find sites that shake in the same way during an earthquake*'. This problem is applicable to various services, but the naive approach has excessive CPU and memory requirements due to the unbounded nature of the voluminous data streams.

This paper proposes not only a new technique for sequence approximation, but also a framework in which multiple resolutions of (1) archiving compressed data streams, (2) updating the feature data of the streams, and (3) query processing, can be generated efficiently. We introduce DAPSS (DAta stream Processing for Store and Search) for monitoring multiple data streams. DAPSS has the following nice characteristics:

– **High-speed processing:** It detects similar pairs in a few seconds given hundreds of streaming data sequences in our experiments.
– **Correctness:** It returns all the qualifying pairs without omission (i.e., no false negatives and no false positives).
– **Low memory consumption:** Pairs are detected using bounded memory.
– **Data archiving:** Streaming data sequences are compressed and stored rapidly on a disk.
– **No restriction on query length:** It achieves fast subsequence matching for similarity queries of unknown, arbitrary length.

To achieve both high performance and output exactness, DAPSS first prunes a significant number of sequences at low computation cost by using a new approximation technique and if necessary to ensure the correctness of query results, examines the original data sequences held on a disk. We conducted several experiments on synthetic and real data sets to verify the effectiveness of DAPSS. The results show that DAPSS is up to 35 times faster than the naive method.

The remainder of the paper is organized as follows. Section 2 describes related work on sequence matching. In Section 3 we give the problem definition and introduces our proposed method for monitoring high-speed data stream. Section 4 presents our experiments and performance study of our method. In Section 5 we list the conclusions.

2 Related Work

While there has been much work on sequence matching, none of the previously published methods meets the requirements described in the introduction.

The majority of previous studies have targeted sequence indexing for stored data sets. Agrawal et al. studied whole sequence matching (similarity searches tackling equal length sequences) [1]. They utilize the Discrete Fourier Transform

(DFT) to approximate sequences and use R*-tree [2] to index the first few DFT coefficients. Faloutsos et al. introduced a technique for subsequence matching (similarity searches that target arbitrary length sequences) [3]. They divide the data sequences into sliding windows and the query sequence into disjoint windows; DFT is then applied to each window. They also use R*-tree to index the stored sequences. Moon et al.'s search method [4] is also based on sliding windows and represents an improvement over the one of [3]. Indyk et al. address the problem of identifying "representative trends" in time-series data. A representative trend is a subsequence that has the smallest sum of distances from all other subsequences. The representative trend can be derived from "sketches", which are the polynomial convolutions of the sequence and random vectors. They efficiently compute the sketches by using FFT (Fast Fourier Transformation). They efficiently compute the sum of distances by using random projections and FFT (Fast Fourier Transformation). However, their proposed method does not guarantees the exactness of results. Sakurai et al. studied similarity search problem for DTW (Dynamic Time Warping) [6]. They proposed a lower bounding measure for the DTW distance to guarantee no false negatives.

Recently, studies on data stream have been attracting much interest [7, 8]. Various algorithms and architectures of data stream management systems (DSMSs) have been presented so far [9, 10, 11, 12]; they are slightly related to our work. Many recent works focus on stream mining, including frequent items [13], clustering [14]. Sakurai et al. introduced an approximation technique for estimating the cross-correlation function. They detect lag correlations between data streams [15].

The similarity search problem has been studied also in the data stream domain. Zhu et al. studied the problem of detecting strongly correlated streaming data sequences [16]. They divide sequences among basic windows to compute DFT coefficients, and superimpose a grid on an approximated space to detect similar pairs. Unfortunately, their method is for fixed length queries and does not achieve output exactness. Bulut et al. studied the problem of detecting highly correlated sequences among many streaming data sequences given arbitrary length queries [17]. They use minimum bounding rectangles (MBRs) of R*-tree to calculate the coefficients of the Discrete Wavelet Transform (DWT) [18] at multiple resolutions. They use R*-tree to detect similar pairs with arbitrary length queries, but their method does not guarantee the correctness of query results.

3 Proposed Method

This paper focuses on the problem of detecting, exactly, similar pairs of subsequences of arbitrary length in data streams, that is, subsequence matching in streaming fashion. Table 1 lists the symbols and their definitions. Most proofs are omitted in this paper due to the space limitations. We employ the Euclidean distance as a dissimilarity measure. Note that the correlation coefficient would be fine; the correlation coefficient can be obtained from the Euclidean distance and basic statistics (i.e., sums and square sums) [16].

Table 1. Definition of main symbols

Symbols	Definitions
x_t	Value of a sequence X at time $t = 1, \cdots, n$
n	Sequence length
m	Number of sequences
l	Query length ($1 \leq l \leq n$)
X_l	Subsequence of X from $n - l + 1$ to n
ϵ	Threshold for similarity queries
$D(X,Y)$	Euclidean distance between sequences X and Y
$\hat{X}$	Approximation of X
$L(\hat{X},\hat{Y})$	Lower bound of $D(X,Y)$
$U(\hat{X},\hat{Y})$	Upper bound of $D(X,Y)$
K	Number of reference points
O_i	reference point ($1 \leq i \leq K$)

3.1 Preliminaries

Given two sequences $X = (x_1, x_2, \ldots, x_n)$ and $Y = (y_1, y_2, \ldots, y_n)$, their Euclidean distance $D(X, Y)$ is defined as $\sqrt{\sum_{t=1}^{n}(x_t - y_t)^2}$. The problem we address in this paper is the following:

Problem . Given a query, length l, and a distance threshold, ϵ, find sequence pairs in data streams as the set that satisfies the following condition:

$$D(X_l, Y_l) = \sqrt{\sum_{t=n-l+1}^{n}(x_t - y_t)^2} \leq \epsilon \tag{1}$$

This problem is associated with similarity search in multi-dimensional spaces [2, 19, 20, 21], but differs from traditional problems in that n continues to increase as new sequences continue to arrive.

Two technical barriers prevent the naive method from efficiently solving this problem. (1) Too much memory is required. This is due the unbounded length of the sequences; $O(mn)$ memory is required to store all data sequences and n continues to increase. (2) The CPU cost is excessive. This is mainly due to the number of sequences m; $O(m^2 l)$ CPU cost is incurred to calculate the combinations of all sequences.

3.2 Ideas Behind DAPSS

DAPSS is composed of the following three ideas.

Lossless compression. Since it is a practical impossibility to keep all historical data in the memory space, we exploit the disk space. DAPSS compresses the original sequences to reduce the I/O cost for accessing the archive on the disk. We employ lossless compression to guarantee the correctness of query results.

PSA: Piecewise Statistical Approximation. Previous works on sequence matching have introduced many approximation techniques such as the Fourier transform, Wavelet transform, APCA (Adaptive Piecewise Constant Approximation) [22], SVD (Singular Value Decomposition) [23]. We propose a new approximation technique, referred to as PSA (Piecewise Statistical Approximation), which yields low computation cost and high accuracy. PSA consists of the mean values and standard deviations of sequences. The major advantage of PSA is that, if we divide a sequence into multiple segments, the PSA representations of the segments are easily combined. Rather keeping the original sequences in the memory space, we keep only the PSA of each sequence. PSA enables the lower and upper bounding distances to be calculated by using our proposed distance function, and to detect similar pairs with low CPU cost and virtually no disk access.

Feature matrix. We introduce an index structure, called the feature matrix, to accelerate search performance. The feature matrix allows similar pairs to be detected by using distances from several reference points in the metric space. While PSA allows high-speed comparisons, the number of comparisons increases rapidly with the number of sequences (i.e., $O(m^2)$). The matrix reinforces PSA and reduces the number of comparisons that must be performed since it eliminates dissimilar pairs quickly; its construction cost is low. Therefore, similar sequences can be detected quickly any time users require.

3.3 Lossless Compression

The first idea is to save the I/O cost for accessing the archived streams by compressing the original data. In the lossless compression, each value of sequences is reorganized byte by byte to achieve high compression ratios. Our compression technique, used here, is slightly similar to Burrows-Wheeler Transform (BWT) [24] in that it sorts data before compressing, but differs in that it divides data before reorganizing.

Preprocessing. The inner structure of each sequence value is reorganized as the preprocessing. As shown in Fig. 1, each sequence value is expressed as a set of several bytes (e.g., 16.84 is expressed as 01000001 10000110 10111000 01010010

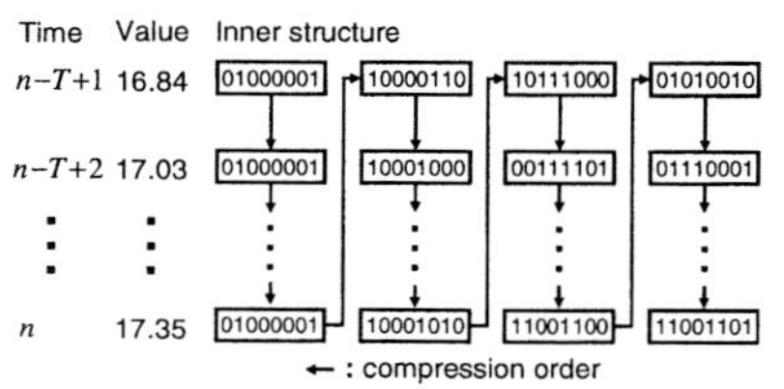

Fig. 1. Example of the inner structure of sequence values

Algorithm StoreData(X_T)
//B is the number of bytes of sequence values
for i to B **do**
  combine the i-th bytes of X_T;
end for
compress the combined data by RLE;
append the compressed data to the sequential file on the disk:

Fig. 2. Algorithm for the lossless compression

in IEEE-754). A single sequence value by itself can not be compressed effectively because neighboring bytes are not similar. Typically, most sequence data has the property of fluctuating gradually, so the sign part and fixed-point part tend to be similar (e.g., the sign part and fixed-point part of 16.84, 17.03 and 17.35 are all 01000001). We therefore reorganize sequence values every T time ticks for compression. For example, the set of each first byte of the T data values is compressed; the set of each second byte is then compressed. Fig. 2 shows the algorithm of the lossless compression.

Compressing and archiving. We employ RLE (Run-Length Encoding) for compressing data streams. There are many other encoding methods such as Huffman encoding [25] and Lempel-Ziv 77[26], but RLE is preferable since it offers one-pass encoding. The compressed data of each sequence are appended to the sequential file on the disk. Note that the sequential file is not a fixed-size structure; the compressed data are stored with information about the number of bytes to be read.

3.4 PSA

PSA consists of mean values and standard deviations, and its distance function gives lower and upper bounds of the distance of sequences, which guarantee no false positives and no false negatives, respectively.

Computing sequence features. We partition each sequence into S segments of predetermined length (i.e., the i-th segment of length s_i) and use their averages and standard deviations as features.

Definition 1 *(PSA). Let μ_i and σ_i be the average, standard deviation of the i-th segment of a sequence X, respectively. The PSA representation of X is defined as:*

$$\hat{X} = (\langle \mu_1, \sigma_1, s_1 \rangle, \langle \mu_2, \sigma_2, s_2 \rangle, \ldots, \langle \mu_S, \sigma_S, s_S \rangle) \quad (2)$$

$$\mu_i = \frac{1}{s_i} \sum_{j=t_i}^{t_{i+1}-1} x_j, \qquad \sigma_i = \sqrt{\frac{1}{s_i} \sum_{j=t_i}^{t_{i+1}-1} x_j^2 - \mu_i^2}$$

where $n = \sum_{i=1}^{S} s_i$, and t_i denotes the starting time tick of the i-th segment.

The major advantage of PSA is that the segments are easily combined since the segments consist of their average and standard deviation. We utilize this advantage, as described later.

Computing lower and upper bounding Distances. We introduce the lower bounding distance $L(\hat{X}, \hat{Y})$ of $D(X, Y)$ and its upper bounding distance $U(\hat{X}, \hat{Y})$. As shown in Fig.3, the lower/upper bounding distance is computed from consecutive segments shorter/longer than the query length.

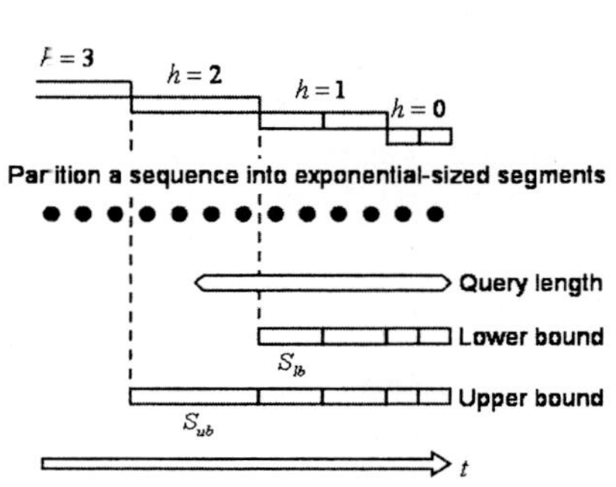

Fig. 3. Sequence segmentation

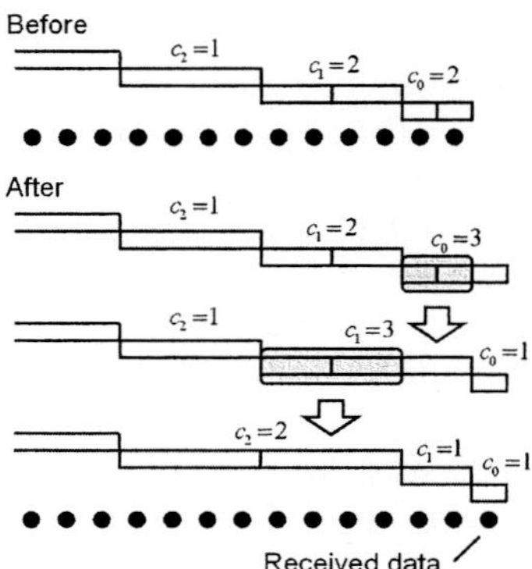

Fig. 4. Illustration of updating segments

Theorem 1. *Given two subsequences $X_l = (x_{n-l+1}, \dots, x_n)$ and $Y_l = (y_{n-l+1}, \dots, y_n)$ of length l, then we have*

$$L(\hat{X}_l, \hat{Y}_l) \leq D(X_l, Y_l) \tag{3}$$

where

$$L(\hat{X}_l, \hat{Y}_l) = \sqrt{\sum_{i=S_{lb}}^{S} s_i \left\{ \left(\mu_i^X - \mu_i^Y\right)^2 + \left(\sigma_i^X - \sigma_i^Y\right)^2 \right\}}$$

$$S_{lb} = \min(j \Big| \sum_{i=j}^{S} s_i \leq l)$$

Lemma 1. *The similarity search based on $L(\hat{X}_l, \hat{Y}_l)$ is sufficient to guarantee no false negatives.*

Lemma 1 is well-known as the lower bounding lemma [1].

Theorem 2. *Given two subsequences X_l and Y_l, the following holds.*

$$U(\hat{X}_l, \hat{Y}_l) \geq D(X_l, Y_l) \tag{4}$$

where

$$U(\hat{X}_l, \hat{Y}_l) = \sqrt{\sum_{i=S_{ub}}^{S} s_i \left\{ \left(\mu_i^X - \mu_i^Y\right)^2 + \left(\sigma_i^X + \sigma_i^Y\right)^2 \right\}}$$

$$S_{ub} = \max(j \Big| \sum_{i=j}^{S} s_i \geq l)$$

Similarly, we derive the upper bounding lemma as follows.

Lemma 2. *The similarity search based on $U(\hat{X}_l, \hat{Y}_l)$ is sufficient to guarantee no false positives.*

Management of segment lengths. We vary the segment length for each sequence; it yields an equal approximation error even when the query length is different. The segment length depends on the elapsed time starting when data arrive, as shown in Fig. 4. The length s_i of the i-th segment depends on level h, and the more the level h becomes, the longer s_i becomes. Length s_i is 2^h. Therefore DAPSS can handle arbitrary length queries. That is, relative errors are similarly small for both short and long queries.

The PSA representations are incrementally updated by combining segments when the number of segments of level h exceeds capacity C. We use Fig. 4 to illustrate our update procedure in case of $C = 2$. Let c_h be the number of segments of level h. Before updating, the number of segments for each level is $c_0 = 2$, $c_1 = 2$ and $c_2 = 1$. Suppose we receive one sequence value, then we have $c_0 = 3$, which is larger than $C = 2$. We combine the two segments at level 0 into one segment, and move it to level 1. Since we have $c_1 = 3$, another combination is done in the same way. As a result, the number of segments for each level is $c_0 = 1$, $c_1 = 1$ and $c_2 = 2$.

Such segments are easily combined; a new segment $\langle \mu'_i, \sigma'_i, s'_i \rangle$ can be computed from the i-th and $(i+1)$-th segments as: $\mu'_i = (\mu_i + \mu_{i+1})/2$, $\sigma'_i = \sqrt{(\sigma_i^2 + \sigma_{i+1}^2)/2 + (\mu_i - \mu_{i+1})^2/4}$ and $s'_i = 2s_i$, respectively. Fig. 5 shows the update algorithm of PSA.

As discussed in 3.3, since DAPSS stores the original sequences on the disk, it maintains the offset (i.e., file pointer) in the sequential file, which corresponds to each segment. After the i-th and $(i+1)$-th segments are combined, we use the offset of the i-th segment as the offset of the combined segment.

```
Algorithm UpdatePSA(x_{n+1})
 compute the (S + 1)-th segment from x_{n+1};
 S = S + 1;
 i = S - c_0;
 c_0 = c_0 + 1;
 //H is the maximum number of h for X
 for h = 0 to H do
   if c_h > C then
     combine the i-th and (i + 1)-th segments
     (compute a new segment for level h + 1);
     c_h = c_h - 2;
     S = S - 1;
     i = i - c_{h+1};
     c_{h+1} = c_{h+1} + 1;
   else
     break;
   end if
 end for
```

Fig. 5. PSA update Algorithm

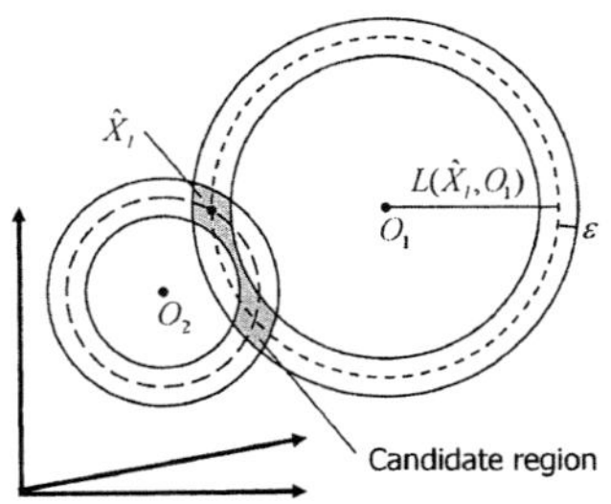

Fig. 6. Metric space formed by two reference points

	O_1	O_2	O_3	O_4
$\hat{X}_l$	3	3	4	3
$\hat{Y}_l$	4	5	3	7
$\hat{Z}_l$	1	3	2	3

$\epsilon = 3$

Fig. 7. Example of data structure

3.5 Feature Matrix

We use the feature matrix, which contains the distances between several reference points and the PSA of each sequence, to eliminate dissimilar sequence pairs efficiently. This implies that metric space is formed by the feature matrix. Many index structures have been proposed such as M-tree [27], mvp-tree [28], but the feature matrix is non-hierarchical since we need high-speed processing for constructing index structures. The feature matrix also guarantees no false negatives.

Data structure. We randomly select several reference points $O_i (1 \leq i \leq K)$ from the set of PSA representations for all sequences. Each sequence is assigned K values, $L(\hat{X}_l, O_i)$, which are the lower bounding distances between its PSA (referred to as $\hat{X}_l$) and O_i. In the metric space formed by the reference points, these values mean K concentric circles whose centers are O_i and radii are $L(\hat{X}_l, O_i)$ themselves (See Fig. 6). As shown in Fig. 7, the data structure of the feature matrix is simply an array of the distances between $\hat{X}_l$ and O_i. Fig. 8 shows an algorithm for computing the feature matrix.

```
Algorithm ComputeMatrix
  select K reference points O_i (1 ≤ i ≤ K)
  randomly from the PSA set;
  //compute the matrix elements
  for each PSA X̂_l do
    for i = 0 to K do
      compute L(X̂_l, O_i);
    end for
  end for
```

Fig. 8. Algorithm for computing the feature matrix

```
Algorithm MatrixFiltering (X̂_l)
  input: X̂_l
  output: the candidate set, Set{Ŷ_l}
  for each PSA Ŷ_l do
    if ∀O_i : |L(X̂_l,O_i) − L(Ŷ_l,O_i)| ≤ ε then
      report Ŷ_l as a candidate;
    end if
  end for
```

Fig. 9. Filtering algorithm

Filtering. The feature matrix filters out dissimilar sequence pairs with no false positives by using the following lemma.

Lemma 3. *Let $\hat{X}_l$ and $\hat{Y}_l$ be the PSA representations of X_l and Y_l, and let O be a reference point, then we have*

$$|L(\hat{X}_l, O) - L(\hat{Y}_l, O)| \leq D(X_l, Y_l) \tag{5}$$

Fig. 9 shows the filtering algorithm. For all reference points, it checks whether $|L(\hat{X}_l, O_i) - L(\hat{Y}_l, O_i)| \leq \epsilon$ holds. For example in Fig. 7, if $\epsilon = 3$, X_l and Y_l are not similar since $|3 - 7| > \epsilon$ at O_4. However, the pair of X_l and Z_l is a similar candidate since $|L(\hat{X}_l, O_i) - L(\hat{Y}_l, O_i)| \leq \epsilon$ for all reference points.

3.6 Update Algorithm

DAPSS performs update processing whenever it receives new data. Fig. 10 shows the update algorithm of DAPSS. It updates the PSA of each sequence for the received data. In addition, the subsequences of length T are compressed and stored on the disk every T time ticks.

```
Algorithm Update
 input: new values at t for m
         sequences X_1,···,X_m
 for each sequence X do
   X̂ =UpdatePSA(x_t);
   if t mod T = 0 then
     StoreData(X_T);
   end if
 end for
```

Fig. 10. Update algorithm

```
Algorithm Search
 input: ε, l
 output: all similar subsequence pairs
 ComputeMatrix;
 for each subsequence X_l do
   Set{Ŷ_l} =MatrixFiltering(X̂_l);
   for each subsequence Ŷ_l do
     if L(X̂_l, Ŷ_l) ≤ ε then
       if U(X̂_l, Ŷ_l) ≤ ε then
         report X_l and Y_l as a similar pair;
       else
         //load X_l and Y_l from the sequential files
         LoadData(X_l);
         LoadData(Y_l);
         if D(X_l, Y_l) ≤ ε then
           report X_l and Y_l as a similar pair;
         end if
       end if
     end if
   end for
 end for
```

Fig. 11. Search algorithm

3.7 Search Algorithm

When output is required by users or applications, DAPSS performs query processing to report similar pairs. Fig. 11 shows the search algorithm of DAPSS. We first compute the feature matrix, then extract similar pair candidates by using the matrix. The extracted candidates are examined on the lower and upper bounding distances computed from their PSA. If the lower bounding distance exceeds ϵ, we discard the candidate since it cannot be one of the similar pairs. Inversely, if the upper bounding distance does not exceed ϵ, we determine that the candidate is one of the similar pairs since its exact distance does not exceed the threshold either. Otherwise, the original sequences are fetched from the disk, and their exact distance is computed.

3.8 Complexity

We discuss how DAPSS can effectively detect similar pairs. Let m be the number of sequences of length n.

Lemma 4. *Let l be query length. The naive method requires $O(mn)$ space and $O(m^2l)$ time.*

Proof. The naive method keeps m sequences of length n in the memory space. It computes the distances of all possible pairs for a similarity query of length l. □

Lemma 5. *DAPSS requires $O(m \log(n) + l)$ memory space.*

Proof. Keeping the PSA of m sequences requires $O(mC \log(n))$ memory space since PSA has $\log(n)$ levels and each level has C segments. For query processing, computing the feature matrix of K reference points and the exact distance of the query length l need $O(mK)$ and $O(l)$, respectively. Since C and K are small constant values, and the space for compressing is negligible, the space complexity is $O(m \log(n) + l)$. □

Lemma 6. *DAPSS requires $O(m)$ amortized time per time-tick for update processing.*

Proof. The PSA coefficients on level h needs to be computed every 2^h time ticks ($h = 0, \cdots, \log n$). On average, DAPSS computes $O(m)$ coefficients per time-tick for m sequences since $\sum_{h=0}^{\log n} 1/2^h = 2$. Compressing with RLE for m subsequences needs $O(mT)$ every T time ticks. Overall, update processing requires amortized time $O(m)$ per time-tick. □

Note that the time complexity of DAPSS for update processing is constant, $O(m)$; it does not depend on n. The time complexity for query processing depends on the effectiveness of filtering due to the use of the feature matrix and PSA. In the next section, we will show the effectiveness by processing several data sets.

4 Experimental Evaluation

We performed experiments to demonstrate the effectiveness of DAPSS. We compared DAPSS with the naive method since none of the previously published methods meets the requirements described in the introduction. Note that the naive method requires $O(mn)$ memory space, which is much larger than the space DAPSS requires (i.e., $O(m \log(n) + l)$). All experiments were conducted on a 3.2GHz Pentium 4 PC with 1GB of main memory. We used the following real and synthetic data sets:

- *RandomWalk*: we generated 500 sequences as $x_t = \alpha + \sum_{i=1}^{t} \beta_i$, where α and β_i are uniform random numbers in the ranges [-100,100] and [-0.5,0.5], respectively.
- *Humidity*: humidity readings from 55 sensors within several buildings. Each sensor gives a reading every 30 seconds. We chose 50 sequences in the experiments.
- *Trajectory*: We kept track of the trajectory of 80 people's movements in an exhibition. This is the set of 2-dimensional time-series data of length 10,000. Each sensor gives a reading every 0.1 seconds.

The threshold for query processing increases as query length l grows; $\epsilon = 0.1 \cdot l$ for *RandomWalk*, $\epsilon = 0.02 \cdot l$ for *Humidity* and $\epsilon = 0.04 \cdot l$ for *Trajectory*. In our method, we used the time interval of $T = 64$ for the sequence compression, the capacity of segments $C = 40$, and there are 5 reference points (i.e., $K = 5$). In our experiments, we forbade the use of the disk cache; we cleared the disk cache before every trial.

4.1 Search Cost

We measured the search process time of DAPSS in a comparison with the naive method. Sequence length n was set at $10,000$. Fig. 12 depicts the wall clock time of DAPSS and the naive method for various query lengths, l. We used the sequence sets of $m = 500$ for *RandomWalk*, $m = 50$ for *Humidity* and $m = 80$ for *Trajectory*. The results show that DAPSS can efficiently detect similar data sequences; it is up to 35 times faster than the naive method.

Fig. 13 shows the wall clock time for various numbers of sequences when $l = 8000$. The results show that DAPSS can find similar sequences pairs much faster then the naive method. Instead of $O(m^2)$ time taken by the naive method, the search cost of DAPSS is close to $O(m)$ in Fig. 13. The result corresponds with our expectations. This is because the feature matrix causes a drastic reduction by pruning similar candidate pairs.

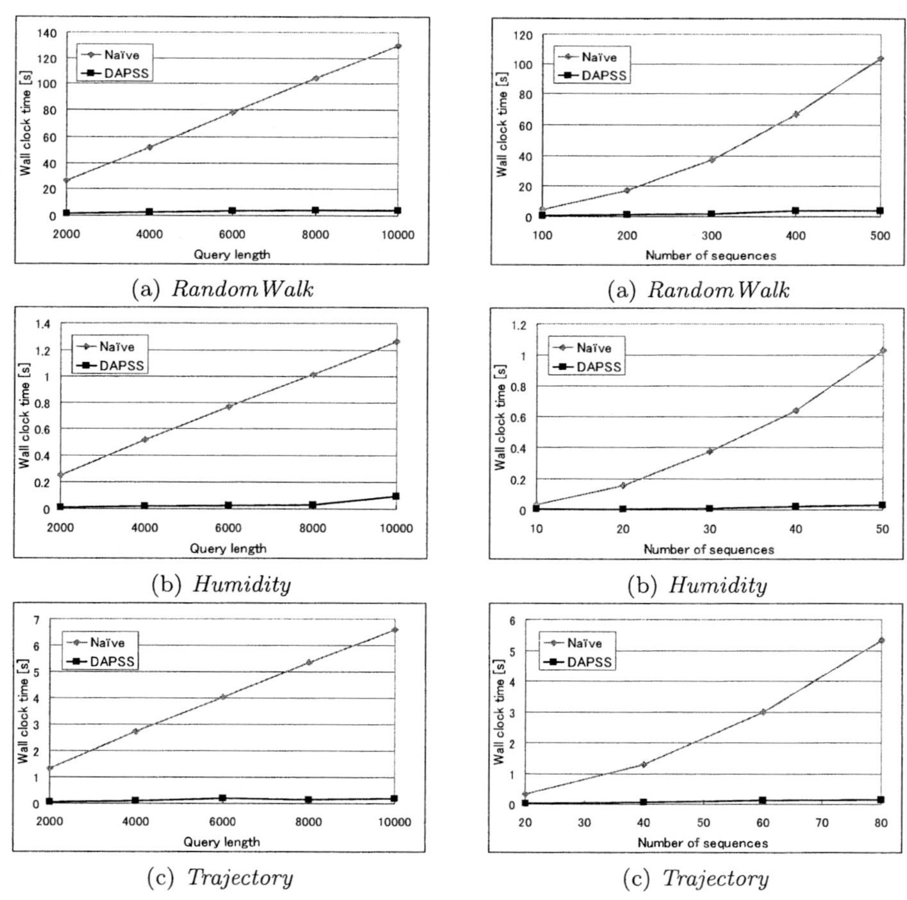

Fig. 12. Wall clock time for search processing versus query length

Fig. 13. Wall clock time for search processing versus the number of sequences

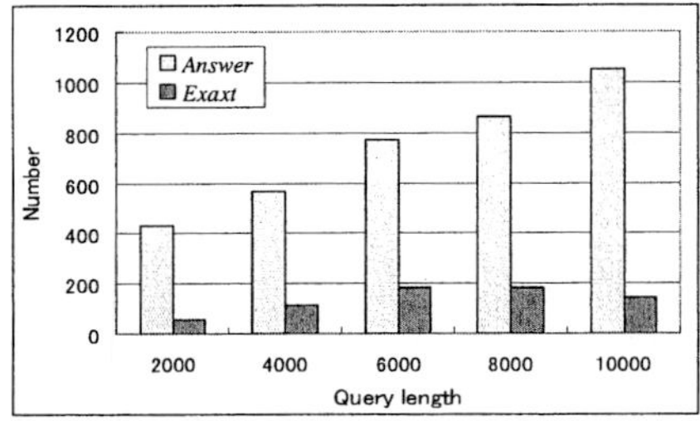

Fig. 14. Number of exact distance computations

4.2 Frequency of Exact Distance Computations

For our method, the search cost depends primarily on the number of exact distance computations since they trigger disk access. Fig. 14 shows the number of exact distance computations for query processing. In this figure, "*Answer*" represents the number of data sequence pairs included in answer set $\{X_l, Y_l | D(X_l, Y_l) \leq \epsilon\}$. "*Exact*" denotes the number of exact distance computations using the original sequences. We used *RandomWalk* for this experiment. The sequence length is $n = 10,000$ and the number of sequences is $m = 500$.

This figure shows that DAPSS can reduce the number of exact computations; *Exact* is even lower than *Answer*. If the upper bounding distance does not exceed ϵ, we can determine that the candidate is one of the similar pairs without computing its exact distance. The effectiveness of the upper bounding distance reduces the number of exact computations, which yields high performance as shown in Figs. 12 and 13.

4.3 Update Cost

Fig. 15 shows the update cost upon receiving new sequence data. In this figure "*RandomWalk (store)*" and "*Trajectory (store)*" represent the results, which include the cost of storing data streams. In here, we omit the results for *Humidity* since they are similar to those of *RandomWalk*.

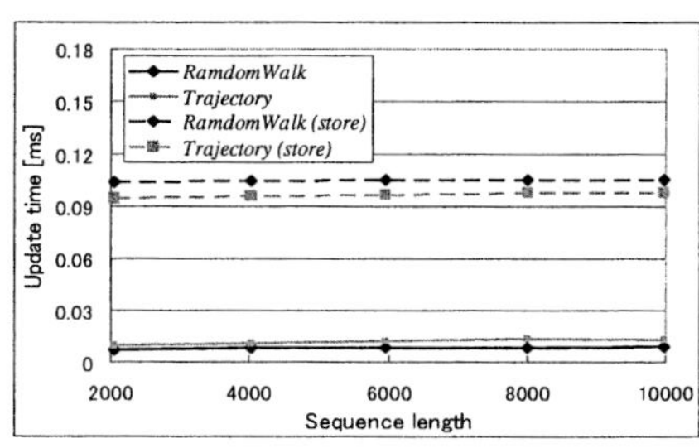

Fig. 15. Wall clock time for update processing

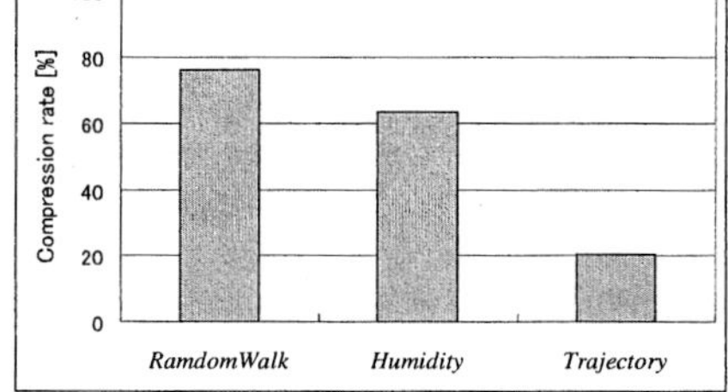

Fig. 16. Compression rate

The update cost is extremely low compared to the search cost. Moreover, the update cost is constant for all sequence lengths, n. We theoretically discussed the complexity of DAPSS in Section 3.8. DAPSS requires $O(m)$ time for update processing; it does not depend on n. Our theoretical analysis is confirmed by this experimental result.

We observe that the cost of "*Trajectory (store)*" is lower than that of "*RandomWalk (store)*" even though *Trajectory* is 2-dimensional time-series data. The reason for this is that RLE achieves better compression rate for *Trajectory* as shown in Fig. 16. Because many of the moving objects stopped often, *Trajectory* could be compressed more strongly and thus stored on the disk more efficiently.

5 Conclusion

In this paper, we address on the problem of detecting similar pairs of streaming data sequences given arbitrary length queries. We proposed DAPSS, which is based on three ideas: With lossless compression, streaming data sequences are compressed efficiently. With PSA, similar pair candidates are found rapidly even in long data sequences. With the feature matrix, similar pair candidates are found rapidly even if there are many data sequences. DAPSS achieves all of the following goals: (1) *High-speed processing*, (2) *Correctness*, and (3) *Low memory consumption*. Moreover, DAPSS has the following nice characteristics: (4) *Data archiving*, and (5) *No restriction on query length*. Our experimental results show that DAPSS can efficiently detect similar data sequences; it is significantly (up to 35 times) faster than the naive method.

References

1. Agrawal, R., Faloutsos, C., Swami, A.N.: Efficient similarity search in sequence databases. In: FODO. (1993) 69–84
2. Beckmann, N., Kriegel, H.P., Schneider, R., Seeger, B.: The r*-tree: An efficient and robust access method for points and rectangles. In: SIGMOD Conference. (1990) 322–331
3. Faloutsos, C., Ranganathan, M., Manolopoulos, Y.: Fast subsequence matching in time-series databases. In: SIGMOD Conference. (1994) 419–429
4. Moon, Y.S., Whang, K.Y., Han, W.S.: General match: a subsequence matching method in time-series databases based on generalized windows. In: SIGMOD Conference. (2002) 382–393
5. Indyk, P., Koudas, N., Muthukrishnan, S.: Identifying representative trends in massive time series data sets using sketches. In: VLDB. (2000) 363–372
6. Sakurai, Y., Yoshikawa, M., Faloutsos, C.: Ftw: Fast similarity search under the time warping distance. In: PODS. (2005) 326–337
7. Golab, L., Özsu, M.T.: Issues in data stream management. SIGMOD Record **32** (2003) 5–14
8. Babcock, B., Babu, S., Datar, M., Motwani, R., Widom, J.: Models and issues in data stream systems. In: PODS. (2002) 1–16
9. Law, Y.N., Wang, H., Zaniolo, C.: Query languages and data models for database sequences and data streams. In: VLDB. (2004) 492–503

10. Balakrishnan, H., Balazinska, M., Carney, D., Çetintemel, U., Cherniack, M., Convey, C., Galvez, E.F., Salz, J., Stonebraker, M., Tatbul, N., Tibbetts, R., Zdonik, S.B.: Retrospective on aurora. VLDB J. **13** (2004) 370–383
11. Johnson, T., Muthukrishnan, S., Rozenbaum, I.: Sampling algorithms in a stream operator. In: SIGMOD Conference. (2005) 1–12
12. Chandrasekaran, S., Franklin, M.J.: Remembrance of streams past: Overload-sensitive management of archived streams. In: VLDB. (2004) 348–359
13. Yu, J.X., Chong, Z., Lu, H., Zhou, A.: False positive or false negative: Mining frequent itemsets from high speed transactional data streams. In: VLDB. (2004) 204–215
14. Aggarwal, C.C., Han, J., Wang, J., Yu, P.S.: A framework for projected clustering of high dimensional data streams. In: VLDB. (2004) 852–863
15. Sakurai, Y., Papadimitriou, S., Faloutsos, C.: Braid: Stream mining through group lag correlations. In: SIGMOD Conference. (2005) 599–610
16. Zhu, Y., Shasha, D.: Statstream: Statistical monitoring of thousands of data streams in real time. In: VLDB. (2002) 358–369
17. Bulut, A., Singh, A.K.: A unified framework for monitoring data streams in real time. In: ICDE. (2005) 44–55
18. pong Chan, K., Fu, A.W.C.: Efficient time series matching by wavelets. In: ICDE. (1999) 126–133
19. Katayama, N., Satoh, S.: The sr-tree: An index structure for high-dimensional nearest neighbor queries. In: SIGMOD Conference. (1997) 369–380
20. Sakurai, Y., Yoshikawa, M., Uemura, S., Kojima, H.: The a-tree: An index structure for high-dimensional spaces using relative approximation. In: VLDB. (2000) 516–526
21. Kollios, G., Papadopoulos, D., Gunopulos, D., Tsotras, V.J.: Indexing mobile objects using dual transformations. VLDB J. **14** (2005) 238–256
22. Keogh, E.J., Chakrabarti, K., Mehrotra, S., Pazzani, M.J.: Locally adaptive dimensionality reduction for indexing large time series databases. In: SIGMOD Conference. (2001) 188–228
23. Korn, F., Jagadish, H.V., Faloutsos, C.: Efficiently supporting ad hoc queries in large datasets of time sequences. In: SIGMOD Conference. (1997) 289–300
24. Burrows, M., Wheeler, D.J.: A block-sorting lossless data compression algorithm. Technical Report 124, SRC Research Report (1994)
25. Huffman, D.: A method for the construction of minimum redundancy codes. Proc. IRE **40** (1952) 1098–1101
26. Ziv, J., Lempel, A.: A universal algorithm for sequential data compression. IEEE Transactions on Information Theory **23** (1977) 337–343
27. Ciaccia, P., Patella, M., Zezula, P.: M-tree: An efficient access method for similarity search in metric spaces. In: VLDB. (1997) 426–435
28. Bozkaya, T., Özsoyoglu, Z.M.: Distance-based indexing for high-dimensional metric spaces. In: SIGMOD Conference. (1997) 357–368

An Efficient Approach for Mining Top-K Fault-Tolerant Repeating Patterns*

Jia-Ling Koh and Yu-Ting Kung

Department of Information and Computer Education,
National Taiwan Normal University, Taipei, Taiwan 106, R.O.C
jlkoh@ice.ntnu.edu.tw

Abstract. In this paper, an efficient strategy for mining top-K non-trivial fault-tolerant repeating patterns (FT-RPs in short) with lengths no less than *min_len* from data sequences is provided. By extending the idea of appearing bit sequences, fault-tolerant appearing bit sequences are defined to represent the locations where candidate patterns appear in a data sequence with insertion/deletion errors being allowed. Two algorithms, named **TFTRP-Mine**(**T**op-K non-trivial **FT-RP**s **Mining**) and **RE-TFTRP-Mine** (**RE**finement of **TFTRP-Mine**), respectively, are proposed. Both of these two algorithms use the recursive formulas to obtain the fault-tolerant appearing bit sequence of a pattern systematically and then the fault-tolerant frequency of each candidate pattern could be counted quickly. Besides, RE-TFTRP-Mine adopts two additional strategies for pruning the searching space in order to improve the mining efficiency. The experimental results show that RE-TFTRP-Mine outperforms TFTRP-Mine algorithm when *K* and *min_len* are small. In addition, more important and implicit repeating patterns could be found from real music objects by adopting fault tolerant mining.

1 Introduction

Repeating patterns represent the important sub-patterns in a data sequence because they appear repeatedly. There have been many approaches proposed for mining repeating patterns[1][3][4]. However, in most approaches, only exact pattern matching was considered during the mining process. It may cause some implicit repeating patterns not being found because of insertion/deletion errors occurring. For example, suppose two data sequences: S1="ACDE...ACEDE...", and S2 ="ACD E... ADE..." are given. The pattern "ACEDE" approximately matches "ACDE" with one insertion error in S1. Besides, the pattern "ADE" approximately matches "ACDE" with one deletion error in S2. However, the exact matching approach will lost the implicit repeating pattern "ACDE" in these two sequences.

To solve the above problem, this paper focuses on the strategy for mining "*fault-tolerant*" repeating patterns, *FT-RP*s in short. In other words, the insertion/deletion errors are allowed when counting the appearing frequency of a pattern. Besides, to avoid duplicated information and many short patterns being found, only "non-trivial" FT-RPs, i.e., those FT-RPs containing no super-pattern with the same fault-tolerant

* This work was partially supported by the R.O.C. N.S.C. under Contract No. 94-2213-E-003-010.

M.L. Lee, K.L. Tan, and V. Wuwongse (Eds.): DASFAA 2006, LNCS 3882, pp. 95 – 110, 2006.

frequency, and their lengths no less than a given *min_len* are mined out. Moreover, by giving the desired number of non-trivial FT-RPs to be mined, we propose an approach of mining "top-K non-trivial fault-tolerant repeating patterns with length no less than min_len" to avoid finding a huge amount of non-representative patterns.

A data structure called *correlative matrix* was proposed in [3] to aid the process for extracting repeating patterns in a music object. The main disadvantage of this approach is that the processing cost is proportional to the square of the length of the music object. To solve this problem, the same authors developed the *String-Join* algorithm [1] to extract the *non-trivial* repeating patterns in a music object. In [4], the representation of *bit index sequence* was designed to characterize note sequences of music objects. In the mining process, the frequency of a candidate pattern was obtained by performing **shift** and **and** operations on bit sequences and then counting the number of 1s in the resultant bit sequence. Therefore, frequency checking could be performed quickly.

Fault-tolerant data mining would discover more general and useful information for real-world dirty data. The problem of fault-tolerant frequent patterns (itemsets) was defined and solved in [6] by proposing FT-Apriori algorithm. Similar to the Apriori-like algorithms, FT-Apriori algorithm suffered from generating a large number of candidates and scanning database repeatedly. This problem became worse when the fault tolerance was increasing or the support thresholds were decreasing. To speed up the mining of fault tolerant frequent patterns, we proposed an algorithm named FFT-Mine (Fast Fault Tolerant frequent patterns Mining) in [5]. By extending the form of appearing vectors, the fault-tolerant appearing vectors were defined to represent the distribution that the candidate patterns were contained in database with fault tolerance. FFT-Mine algorithm provided a systematically method to reduce the number of operations performed on bit vectors to get the fault-tolerant appearing vectors of candidates. Then whether a candidate is a fault-tolerant frequent itemset could be judged quickly.

When mining frequent patterns, it is difficult for users to set an appropriate minimum support threshold without knowing the distribution of data in the database. Moreover, if long patterns exist in a database, the mining result may return many short or tedious patterns with duplicated information. To prevent the above problems occurring, [2] proposed a TFP algorithm to discover top-K frequent closed patterns with length no less than *min_l*. For solving the similar problems when mining frequent sequential patterns, TSP algorithm was proposed in [7]. It adopted the similar idea proposed in TFP algorithm to raise the minimum support during the mining process for discovering top-K closed sequential patterns. Then the searching space would be pruned dramatically to speed up the mining process.

In summarizing the interesting strategies proposed in the related works, an efficient way of mining top-K non-trivial fault-tolerant repeating patterns (FT-RPs in short) with length no less than *min_len* for data sequences is proposed in this paper. By extending the idea of appearing bit sequences, fault-tolerant appearing bit sequences are defined to represent the locations where candidate patterns appear in a data sequence with insertion/deletion errors allowed. Then the fault-tolerant frequency of a candidate pattern could be counted from its fault-tolerant appearing bit sequence quickly. The recursive formulas are designed for obtaining the fault-tolerant appearing bit sequence of a pattern systematically in order to eliminate the duplicate computations. Two algorithms, named **TFTRP-Mine** and **RE-TFTRP-Mine**, respectively, are proposed. The TFTRP-Mine algorithm generates candidate patterns by performing a depth-first searching approach. The RE-TFTRP-Mine algorithm adopts two additional strategies to increase the mining efficiency. The first one is to assign priorities of found repeating patterns for generating candidates according to their fault-tolerant frequencies. Moreover, the minimum frequency is raised dynamically when K numbers of FT-RPs have been found. The experimental results show these two strategies will prune the searching space dramatically when K is small proportional to the number of whole FT-RPs.

This paper is organized as follows. Section 2 defines the relative terms used in this paper. The appearing bit sequences and the way of getting fault-tolerant appearing bit sequences are introduced in Section 3. Section 4 describes the whole processing steps of TFTRP-Mine and RE-TFTRP-Mine algorithms. The performance evaluation of proposed algorithms is shown in Section 5. Finally, in Section 6, we propose the conclusion and feature works of this paper.

2 Preliminaries

[*Def.* 2.1] Let E={l_1, l_2, …, l_k} denote the set of data items in a specific application domain. $DSeq=D_1D_2\ldots D_n$ is a **data sequence**, where $D_i\in$E(i=1…n) denoting the data item on the ith position of the sequence. The length of *DSeq* is denoted as $|DSeq|$.

[*Def.* 2.2] Let S_1 and S_2 denote two data sequences, where $S_1=X_1X_{2\ldots}X_m$ and $S_2=Y_1Y_{2\ldots}Y_n$. S_2 is a **sub-sequence** of S_1 iff there exists an integer sequence i_1, i_2, …, i_n such that $1\le i_1\le i_2 \ldots \le m$ and $X_{ik}=Y_k$ for k = 1to n.

[*Def.* 2.3] Given a data sequence $DSeq=D_1D_2\ldots D_n$ and another data sequence (also named a pattern) $P=P_1P_{2\ldots}P_m$, P **appears** in *DSeq* on position i iff there exists an integer $1\le i\le$ n, such that $D_iD_{i+1}\ldots D_{i+m-1}= P_1P_{2\ldots}P_m$. It is also said *DSeq* **contains** *P* on position i and *P* is a **sub-pattern** of *DSeq*. The **frequency** of a pattern *P* in *DSeq* is the number of various positions in *DSeq* where *DSeq* contains *P*.

[*Def.* 2.4] A data sequence $DSeq=D_1D_2\ldots D_n$ is said to **FT-contain** pattern $P=P_1P_{2\ldots}P_m$ (m≥2) on position i **with δ insertion errors** iff there exist an integer $1\le i \le$ n, such that $D_i=P_1$, $D_{(i+m-1)+\delta}=P_m$, and P is a sub-sequence of $D_iD_{i+1}\ldots D_{(i+m-1)+\delta}$. Given a fault tolerance δ_I (δ_I >0), *DSeq* is said to **insertion FT-contain** pattern *P* under fault tolerance δ_I, denoted as **IFT-contain** in short, iff *DSeq* FT-contains *P* with **δ** insertion errors and $\delta\le\delta_I$. In other words, there exists a sub-pattern of *DSeq* starting from position i which is gotten by inserting at most δ_I data items in the *middle* of *P*. The pattern is also said to **IFT-appear** in *DSeq*.

[Example 2.1] Suppose *DSeq*=ABCDABCA, and δ_I**=2**. Given patterns P_1=ABCA, P_2=BCAC, and P_3=ABBC. According to [Def. 2.4], *DSeq* FT-contains P_1 on position 1 with 1 insertion error. Besides, *DSeq* FT-contains P_1 on position 5 with 0 insertion error. Similarly, *DSeq* FT-contains P_2 on position 2 with two insertion errors. Therefore, *DSeq* IFT-contains P_1 and P_2. However, P_3 doesn't IFT-appear in *DSeq*.

[*Def.* 2.5] A data sequence $DSeq=D_1D_2\ldots D_n$ is said to **FT-contain** a pattern $P=P_1P_{2\ldots}P_m$ (m>δ) on position i **with δ deletion errors** iff there exist an integer

$1 \le i \le n$, such that $D_i D_{i+1} \ldots D_{(i+m-1)-\delta}$ is a sub-sequence of P. Given a fault tolerance $\boldsymbol{\delta_D}(\boldsymbol{\delta_D} > \mathbf{0})$, *DSeq* is said to **deletion FT-contain** pattern *P*, denoted as **DFT-contain** in short, iff *DSeq* FT-contains *P* on position *i* with $\boldsymbol{\delta}$ deletion errors, where D_i=P_1 and $\boldsymbol{\delta} \le \boldsymbol{\delta_D}$. That is, there exists a sub-pattern of *DSeq* starting from position *i* which is gotten by deleting *at most* $\boldsymbol{\delta_D}$ data items from *P* except the first data item. The pattern *P* is also said to **DFT-appear** in *DSeq*.

[Example 2.2] Suppose *DSeq*=ABCBCA, and $\boldsymbol{\delta_D}$**=3**. Given patterns P_1=BCDA and P_2=EFB. *DSeq* FT-contains P_1 on position 4 with 1 deletion error (by deleting "D" from P_1). Therefore, P_1 DFT-appears in *DSeq*. Although *DSeq* FT-contains P_2 on positions 2 and 4, respectively, with 2 deletion errors, P_2 doesn't DFT-appear in *DSeq* because the deletion error on the first data item of P_2 is not allowed.

[*Def.* 2.6] The **fault tolerant frequency** of a pattern *P* in *DSeq*, denoted as $FT\text{-}freq_{DSeq}(P)$, is the number of various positions in *DSeq* where *DSeq* IFT/DFT-contains *P*. The pattern *P* is named a **fault-tolerant repeating pattern, FT-RP** in short, if and only if $FT\text{-}freq_{DSeq}(P) \ge$ a required minimum frequency *min_freq*.

[*Def.* 2.7] A FT-RP *P* is a **non-trivial FT-RP** if there does not exist any FT-RP *P'* such that *P* is a sub-pattern of *P'*, and $FT\text{-}freq_{DSeq}(P') = FT\text{-}freq_{DSeq}(P)$.

3 Bit Sequence Representation

In this section, section 3.1 will introduce the design of appearing bit sequences. How to apply the *appearing bit sequences* of patterns to compute the frequency of candidate patterns with fault tolerance quickly is introduced in section 3.2 and 3.3.

3.1 Appearing Bit Sequences

For each kind of data item *N* in the data sequence, *N* has a corresponding *appearing bit sequence* (denoted as $Appear_N$). The length of each appearing bit sequence equals the length of the data sequence. The leftmost bit is numbered as bit 1 and the numbering increases to the rightmost bit. If some data item appears on the *i*th position of the data sequence, bit *i* in the appearance bit sequence of this data item is set to be 1; otherwise, it is set to be 0. A bit index table is used to store the appearing bit sequences for all the data items in the data sequence. Therefore, the frequency of a data item is obtained according to the number of bits with value 1 in its appearing bit sequence, without needing to scan the data sequence repeatedly. The idea is also applicable for a longer pattern as explained in the following example.

[Example 3.1] The bit index table of "ABCDABCACDEEABCCDEAC" is given as shown in Table 1.

1) Suppose we would like to get $Appear_{AB}$. A position *i* where "AB" appears implies "A" must appear on position *i* and "B" appears on the next position (*i*+1).
Step1. Get $Appear_B$=01000100000001000000 from Table 1.

Table 1. The bit index table of *DSeq*

Data Item	Appearing Bit Sequence
A	10001001000010000010
B	01000100000001000000
C	00100010100000110001
D	00010000010000001000
E	00000000001100000100

Step2. Perform **left shift** 1 (=|AB|-1) bit operation on $Appear_B$ (shift bit (i+1) to bit i, where $1 \leq i \leq 19$, and set bit 20 to be 0), $L\_shift(Appear_B, 1)$ = 10001000000010000000.

Step3. $Appear_{AB} = Appear_A \wedge L\_shift(Appear_B, 1)$ = 10001000000010000000.

2) Suppose we would like to get $Appear_{ABC}$ after getting $Appear_{AB}$. A position i where "ABC" appears implies "AB" must appears on position i and "C" appears on position i+2.

Step1. Obtain $Appear_C$=00100010100000110001 from Table 1.

Step2. Perform **left shift** 2 (=|ABC|-1) bits on $Appear_C$, $L\_shift(Appear_C, 2)$ = 10001010000011000100.

Step3. $Appear_{ABC} = Appear_{AB} \wedge L\_shift(Appear_C, 2)$ = 10001000000010000000.

Accordingly, the frequency of "ABC" in *DSeq* equals the number of bits with value 1 in $Appear_{ABC}$ (that is 3 in this case).

Suppose pattern $P=P_1P_{2...}P_m$ ($m \geq 2$), where P_i (i=1, …,m) is a data item. Let $P'=P_1P_{2...}P_{m-1}$ and $X=P_m$. Then $Appear_P$ could be deduced from $Appear_{P'}$ and $Appear_X$ according to the recursive formula 3.1 shown below.

If |P|=1, $Appear_P = Appear_P$;

Otherwise, $Appear_P = Appear_{P'} \wedge L\_shift(Appear_X, |P|-1)$. (3.1)

The function $L\_shift(b, n, c)$ performs **left shift** n bits on b, and the rightmost bits on b are filled with constant c(c=0 or 1). If the parameter c is omitted from the function, the default value of c is set to be 0.

3.2 Appearing Bit Sequences with Insertion Fault Tolerance

By extending appearing bit sequences, the fault-tolerant appearing bit sequences are designed to represent the appearing positions of a pattern with fault tolerance. Given a fault-tolerance δ(δ_I or δ_D), the fault-tolerant appearing bit sequence of a pattern P in a data sequence, denoted as $FT\text{-}Appear_P^+(\delta)/FT\text{-}Appear_P^-(\delta)$, represents the positions where the data sequence IFT/DFT-contains P.

By considering the insertion fault tolerance, the appearing bit sequence of a pattern P with E numbers of insertion errors, denoted as $Appear_P^+(E)$, is defined. The bits with value 1 in $Appear_P^+(\delta)$ represent those positions where the data sequence FT-contains P with E insertion errors. According to **[*Def.* 2.4]**, there are (δ_I+1) situations that a pattern P IFT-appears in *DSeq* under fault tolerance δ_I. That is, *DSeq* FT-contains P with 0, 1, 2, …, or δ_I insertion errors. In other words, performing δ_I **or** operations on (δ_I+1) appearing bit sequences: $Appear_P^+(0)$, $Appear_P^+(1)$, $Appear_P^+(2)$,

…, and $Appear_P^+(\delta_I)$, $FT\text{-}Appear_P^+(\delta_I)$ could be obtained. According to the definition, $Appear_P^+(E)$ with $|P|=1$ is obtained from the following rule:

[Rule 3.1] Suppose the insertion fault-tolerance is set to be δ_I. If $|P|=1$, $Appear_P^+(E)=0$ for all $1 \le E \le \delta_I$. (3.2)

The remaining problem is how to get $Appear_P^+(E)$ for $|P|>1$ and $0 \le E \le \delta_I$. Since $Appear_P^+(0)$ represents the locations where *DSeq* FT-contains *P* with *zero* insertion error, the way of getting $Appear_P^+(0)$ is the same as getting $Appear_P$. When $1 \le E \le \delta_I$, $Appear_P^+(E)$ could be obtained by performing bit operations on appearing bit sequences of the prefix of *P* with length |P-1| and the last data item in P according to the following lemma.

[Lemma 3.1] Given a pattern $P=P_1P_{2...}P_m$, where P_i (i=1,…,m) is a data item. Let P' denote $P_1P_{2...}P_{m-1}$ and *X* denote P_m. *DSeq* FT-contains pattern *P* with *E* insertion errors on position *i*, iff *DSeq* FT-contains pattern P' with *k* insertion errors on position *i* $(0 \le k \le E)$ and *X* appears on position i+(|P|+E)-1.

Proof. P' appears in *DSeq* from position *i* to (i+|P|-1)+k (with k insertion errors) and E-k insertion errors occurs between P' and *X*. Besides, |P'|+1=|P|. It induces that *X* appears on position (i+|P|-1)+k+(E-k)+1=i+(|P'|+1)+E-1= i+(|P|+E)-1.

In other words, *X* must appear on the (|P|+E-1)*th* position on the right hand side of position *i*. Therefore, the way of getting $Appear_P^+(E)$ is expressed as the following recursive formula for $0<E \le \delta_I$.

If |P|=1, $Appear_P^+(E)=0$;

Otherwise, $Appear_P^+(E)=(\bigvee_{k=0}^{E} Appear_{P'}^+(k)) \wedge L\_shift(Appear_X, |P|+E-1)$. (3.3)

To combine Formulas (3.1) and (3.3), a recursive function of getting $Appear_P^+(E)$, where $0<E \le \delta_I$ is defined as follows.

[*Def.* 3.1] Recursive function of getting $Appear_P^+(E)$: Suppose a pattern $P=P_1P_{2...}P_m$ is given, where P_i (i=1,…,m) is a data item. Let P' denote $P_1P_{2...}P_{m-1}$ and *X* denote P_m. When insertion fault tolerance δ_I is given, $Appear_P^+(E)$ is obtained from the following recursive function for $0 \le E \le \delta_I$.

If |P|=1, **then** $Appear_P^+(0)=Appear_P$; $\forall 1 \le E \le \delta_I$, $Appear_P^+(E)=0$;

Else $Appear_P^+(E)=(\bigvee_{k=0}^{E} Appear_{P'}^+(k)) \wedge L\_shift(Appear_X, |P|+E-1)$.

[Example 3.2] Suppose δ_I is set to be 1. According to the bit index table shown in Table 1, the process of getting $Appear_{AB}^+(1)$ and $Appear_{ABC}^+(1)$ is shown as follows.

(1) $Appear_{AB}^+(1)$

Step1. Get $Appear_B$ = 010001000000010000000 from the bit index table.

Step2. Perform an **or** operation on $Appear_A^+(0)$ and $Appear_A^+(1)$. According to formula (3.2), $Appear_A^+(1)=0$, and $Appear_A^+(0)=Appear_A$.

$s = Appear_A^+(0) \vee Appear_A^+(1)$=100010010000100000010.

Step3. Perform **left shift** 2 (= |AB|+1-1) bits on $Appear_B$,

$t = L\_shift(Appear_B, 2) =$ 00010000000100000000.

Step4. Perform an **and** operation on s and t to get $Appear_{AB}^+(1)$. Thus the resultant bit sequence: $s \wedge t =$ 00000000000000000000.

(2) $Appear_{ABC}^+(1)$

Step1. Get $Appear_C =$ 00100010100000110001.

Step2. Perform an **or** operation on $Appear_{AB}^+(0)$ and $Appear_{AB}^+(1)$. Since $Appear_{AB}^+(0)$ is gotten based on formula (3.1) and $Appear_{AB}^+(1)$ is known from the previous result of this example, the resultant appearing bit sequence: $s = Appear_{AB}^+(0) \vee Appear_{AB}^+(1) =$ 10001000000010000000.

Step3. Perform **left shift** 3 (=|ABC|+1-1) bits on $Appear_C$,

$t = L\_shift(Appear_C, 3) =$ 00010100000110001000.

Step4. Perform an **and** operation on s and t to get $Appear_{ABC}^+(1)$. Thus the resultant bit sequence: $s \wedge t =$ 00000000000010000000.

Finally, $FT\text{-}Appear_P^+(\delta_I)$ is obtained by performing $\bigvee_{i=0}^{\delta_I} Appear_P^+(i)$. $FT\text{-}freq_{DSeq}(P)$ equals to the number of bits with value 1 in $FT\text{-}Appear_P^+(\delta_I)$. Therefore, the insertion fault-tolerant frequency of a pattern P could be counted quickly.

[Example 3.3] Follows the results shown in Example 3.1 and Example 3.2, $FT\text{-}Appear_{ABC}^+(1) = Appear_{ABC}^+(0) \vee Appear_{ABC}^+(1) =$ 10001000000010000000 and $FT\text{-}freq_{DSeq}$("ABC") = 3.

To avoid duplicate computations of **or** and **left shift** operations to get $Appear_P^+(E)$ for various E, the function of getting $Appear_P^+(E)$ is re-defined to use recurrent relations between temporary results for getting $Appear_P^+(E)$ and $Appear_P^+(E\text{-}1)$.

[*Def.* 3.2] Modified recursive function of getting $Appear_P^+(E)$**:** Suppose a pattern $P=P_1P_2...P_m$ is given. Let $P' = P_1P_2...P_{m-1}$ and X denote P_m. $Appear_P^+(E)$ is obtained from the following recursive function for $0 \le E \le \delta_I$.

If |P|=1, **then** $Appear_P^+(0) = Appear_P$; $\forall 1 \le E \le \delta_I$, $Appear_P^+(E)=0$;
Else If E =0, **then** $temp_1(E) = Appear_{P'}^+(0)$; $temp_2(E) = L\_shift(Appear_X, |P|\text{-}1)$;
Else $temp_1(E) = temp_1(E\text{-}1) \vee Appear_{P'}^+(E)$; $temp_2(E) = L\_shift(temp_2(E\text{-}1), 1)$;
$Appear_P^+(E) = temp_1(E) \wedge temp_2(E)$.

3.3 Appearing Bit Sequences with Deletion Fault Tolerance

The appearing bit sequence of a pattern P with E numbers of deletion errors is denoted as $Appear_P^-(E)$. The bits with value 1 in $Appear_P^-(E)$ represent those positions where the data sequence FT-contains P with E deletion errors.

Suppose a pattern $P=P_1P_2...P_m$ is given. Let Y denote the first data item P_1 and P'' denote $P_2P_3...P_m$. $FT\text{-}Appear_P^-(\delta_I)$ represents the positions where Y appears and $DSeq$ FT-contains P'' on the next positions with at most δ_D deletion errors. Therefore, when finding a position j where $DSeq$ FT-contains P'' with 0, 1, 2, …, or δ_D deletion errors, if implies $DSeq$ DFT-contains P on position (j-1) if position (j-1) contains Y. In other words, after performing **or** operations on (δ_D+1) appearing bit sequences:

$Appear_{P''}^{+}(0)$, $Appear_{P''}^{+}(1)$,..., $Appear_{P''}^{+}(\delta_D-1)$, and $Appear_{P''}^{+}(\delta_D)$, then performing a **left shift** operation on the previous result, and finally performing an **and** operation with $Appear_Y$, $FT\text{-}Appear_P^{-}(\delta_D)$ could be obtained. Note that if $|P| \le \delta_D+1$, when performing the left shift operation, the rightmost bit is filled with 1 because the bit is considered as "don't care" bit on the next performed **and** operation. Otherwise, 0 is filled to the rightmost bit. According to the definition, $Appear_{P''}^{-}(E)$ is obtained from the following rule for all $|P''| \le E \le \delta_D$:

[Rule 3.2] Suppose the deletion fault-tolerance is set to be δ_D. If $|P''| \le \delta_D$, $Appear_{P''}^{-}(E)=0$ for all $|P''|<E\le\delta_D$; $Appear_{P''}^{-}(E)$=complement($Appear_{P''}$) for $E=|P''|$. (3.4)

Accordingly, the remaining problem is to get $Appear_{P''}^{-}(E)$ for $0 \le E < |P''|$. Since $Appear_P^{-}(0)$ represents the positions where *DSeq* FT-contains P" with *zero* deletion error, it implies the same information represented in $Appear_{P''}$. Therefore, the way of getting $Appear_P^{-}(0)$ is the same as getting $Appear_{P''}$. When $1 \le E \le |P''|$, $Appear_{P''}^{-}(E)$ is obtained by performing bit operations on appearing bit sequences of the prefix of P" with length $|P''-1|$ and the last data item in P" according to the following lemma.

[Lemma 3.2] Given a pattern $P''=P_2P_3...P_m$, where (i=2 , ...,m) is a data item. Let Q denote $P_2P_3...P_{m-1}$, and X denote the last data item P_m. *DSeq* FT-contains pattern P"with E deletion errors on position i, iff

1) *DSeq* FT-contains pattern Q with E deletion errors on position i and X appears on position $i+(|P''|-1-E)$, or
2) *DSeq* FT-contains pattern Q with (E-1) deletion errors on position i and FT-contains X on position $i+(|P''|-E)$ with 1 deletion error.

Proof

1) Q appears in *DSeq* from position i to $i+(|Q|-E)-1$ (with E deletion errors). If *DSeq* FT-contains P" on position i with E deletion errors, X must appear on position $i+(|P''|-1-E)$ (because $|Q|=|P''|-1$).
2) Q appears in *DSeq* from position i to $i+(|Q|-(E-1))-1= i+(|Q|-E)$ (with E-1 deletion errors). Then X is forced to be absent on position $i+(|Q|-E)+1$. That is, *DSeq* FT-contains X with 1 deletion error on position $i+(|P''|-1-E)+1=i+(|P''|-E)$.

Therefore, the way of getting $Appear_{P''}^{-}(E)$ is expressed as the following recursive function for $0 < E \le \delta_D$.

If $|P''| < E$, $Appear_{P''}^{-}(E) = 0$;
Else if $|P''| = E$, $Appear_{P''}^{-}(E)$ = complement($Appear_{P''}$);
Else $Appear_{P''}^{-}(E)=(Appear_Q^{-}(E) \wedge \text{L\_shift}(Appear_X, |P''|\text{-E-1},0))\vee$
$(Appear_Q^{-}(E\text{-}1) \wedge \text{L\_shift}(Appear_X^{-}(1), |P''|\text{-E},1))$. (3.5)

To combine Formulas (3.1) and (3.5), a recursive function of getting $Appear_{P''}^{-}(E)$, where $0 \le E \le \delta_D$ is defined as follows.

[*Def.* 3.3] (Recursive function of getting $Appear_{P''}^{-}(E)$**):** Suppose a pattern $P''= P_2P_3...P_m$ is given. Let Q denote $P_2P_3...P_{m-1}$ and X denote P_m. When deletion fault tolerance δ_D is given, $Appear_{P''}^{-}(E)$ is obtained from the following recursive function for $0 \le E \le \delta_D$.

IF |P"|=1, **then** $Appear_{P"}^{-}(0)= Appear_P(E)$; $Appear_{P"}^{-}(1)$=complement($Appear_P$);
Else if $E = 0$, **then** $Appear_{P"}^{-}(0)=Appear_Q^{-}(0) \wedge L\_shift(Appear_x, |P"|-1)$;
Else if $E >|P"|$, **then** $Appear_{P"}^{-}(E) = 0$;
Else if $E =|P"|$, **then** $Appear_{P"}^{-}(E)$ = complement($Appear_{P"}^{-}(0)$);
Else $Appear_{P"}^{-}(E) = (Appear_Q^{-}(E) \wedge L\_shift(Appear_x, |P"|-E-1,0)) \vee$
$(Appear_Q^{-}(E-1) \wedge L\_shift(Appear_x^{-}(1), |P"|-E,1))$.

[Example 3.4] Suppose δ_D is set to be 1. According to the bit index table shown in Table 1, the process of getting $Appear_B^{-}(1)$, $Appear_{BC}^{-}(1)$ and $Appear_{BCD}^{-}(1)$ is described as follows.

(1) $Appear_B^{-}(1)$ = complement($Appear_B$).
Step1. Get $Appear_B$ = 01000100000001000000.
Step2. $Appear_B^{-}(1) = \neg Appear_B$ = 10111011111110111111.
(2) $Appear_{BC}^{-}(1) = (Appear_B^{-}(1) \wedge L\_shift(Appear_C,0,0) \vee$
$(Appear_B^{-}(0) \wedge L\_shift(Appear_C^{-}(1),1,1)$
Step1. Get $Appear_C$ = 00100010100000110001.
Step2. Perform **left shift** 0 (=|BC|-1-1) bit on $Appear_C$,
s= $L\_shift(Appear_C,0,0)$=00100010100000110001.
Step3. Perform an **and** operation on s and $Appear_B^{-}(1)$, where the result of $Appear_B^{-}(1)$ has been obtained previously. $u=s\wedge Appear_B^{-}(1)$=00100010100000110001.
Step4. $Appear_C^{-}(1)= \neg Appear_C$ =11011101011111001110.
Step5. Perform **left shift** 1 (=|BC|-1) bit on $Appear_C^{-}(1)$ (the rightmost bit is filled with 1). $t= L\_shift(Appear_C^{-}(1),1,1)$ = 10111010111110011101.
Step6. Perform an **and** operation on t and $Appear_B^{-}(0)$.
$v = t\wedge Appear_B$=00000000000000000000.
Step7. Perform an **or** operation on u and v. Then the resultant bit sequence is $w= u\vee v$ = 00100010100000110001.
(3) $Appear_{BCD}^{-}(1) = (Appear_{BC}^{-}(1) \wedge L\_shift(Appear_D,1,0) \vee$
$(Appear_{BC}^{-}(0)\wedge L\_shift(Appear_D^{-}(1),2,1)$
Step1. Get $Appear_D$ = 00010000010000001000.
Step2. Perform **left shift** 1 (=|BCD|-1-1) bit on $Appear_D$.
$s= L\_shift(Appear_D(1),1,0)$ =00100000100000010000.
Step3. Perform an **and** operation on s and $Appear_{BC}^{-}(1)$, where the result of $Appear_{BC}^{-}(1)$ has been obtained previously.
$u=s\wedge Appear_{BC}^{-}(1)$=00100000100000010000
Step4. $Appear_D^{-}(1)= \neg Appear_D$=11101111101111110111.
Step5. Perform **left shift** 2 (=|BCD|-1) bits on $Appear_D^{-}(1)$.
$t=L\_shift(Appear_D^{-}(1),2,1)$=10111110111111011111.
Step6. Perform an **and** operation on t and $Appear_{BC}^{-}(0)$.
$v = t\wedge Appear_{BC}^{-}(0)$=00000100000001000000.
Step7. Perform an **or** operation on u and v. Then the resultant bit sequence is $w = u\wedge v$ = 00100100100001010000.

Let $temp(E)$ denote the results of $\bigvee_{k=0}^{E} Appear_{p"}^{-}(k)$. To combine formulas 3.4 and 3.5, a recursive function of getting $FT\_Appear_P^{-}(\delta_D)$ is defined as follows.

[*Def.* 3.4] (Recursive function of getting $FT\_Appear_P^{-}(\delta_D)$**):** Suppose a pattern $P=P_1P_2...P_m$ is given, where P_i (i=1,...,m) is a data item. Let Y denote P_1, P'' denote $P_2P_3...P_m$, Q denote $P_2P_3...P_{m-1}$, and X denote P_m. When deletion fault tolerance δ_D is given, $FT\_Appear_P^{-}(\delta_D)$ is obtained from the following recursive function.

If $|P| \leq \delta_D + 1$, **then** $FT\_Appear_P^{-}(\delta_D) = Appear_Y$;
Else $temp_{P'}(\delta_D\text{-}1) = Appear_Q \vee (Appear_Q^{-}(\delta_D\text{-}1) \wedge \text{L\_shift}(Appear_X, |P''|\text{-}\delta_D, 0))$;
$temp_{P'}(\delta_D) = temp_Q(\delta_D\text{-}1) \vee (Appear_Q^{-}(\delta_D) \wedge \text{L\_shift}(Appear_X, |P''|\text{-}\delta_D\text{-}1, 0))$;
$FT\_Appear_P^{-}(\delta_D) = Appear_Y \wedge \text{L\_shift}(temp_{P'}(\delta_D), 1, 0)$.

$FT\_Freq_{DSeq}^{-}(P)$ equals to the number of bits with value 1 in $FT\_Appear_P^{-}(\delta_D)$. Therefore the deletion fault-tolerant frequency of a pattern P could be counted efficiently to evaluate whether P is a FT-RP or not.

4 Mining Top-K Non-trivial FT-RPs with Min-length Constraint

In this section, two algorithms, called **TFTRP-Mine** and **RE-TFTRP-Mine,** are developed for finding Top-K non-trivial **FT-RP**s. These two algorithms are applicable for both situations considering insertion/deletion fault tolerance by exchanging the function of generating fault-tolerant appearing bit sequences.

4.1 TFTRP-Mine Algorithm

TFTRP-Mine Algorithm is designed based on the representation of fault-tolerant appearing bit sequences to mine top-K non-trivial FT-RPs. First, the data sequence is scanned once to create the bit index table. Initially, the candidate pattern is a single data item in the data sequence. If the candidate is a FT-RP, an additional data item is appended to the FT-RP to generate a longer candidate pattern. In other words, the candidate patterns are generated in *depth-firs* order. So the fault-tolerant appearing bit sequence of a candidate pattern is obtained according to the recursive function defined in the previous section. Then, the fault-tolerant frequency of a candidate pattern is counted efficiently to decide whether it is a FT-RP. According to the *anti-monotonic* property, it is not necessary to generate candidate patterns by appending additional data items to a non-FT-RP. Moreover, a FT-RP must satisfy the minimum length and non-trivial constraints before being outputted to the mining result. Finally, after sorting the mining result according to the fault-tolerant frequencies, the top-K non-trivial FT-RPs satisfying the *min_len* constraints are obtained from the first K patterns in the result. In summarizing the above descriptions, the mining process of TFTRP-Mine algorithm consists of the following steps.

Algorithm TFTRP-Mine:
Input: a data sequence *DSeq*, fault tolerance δ_I / δ_D, *min_len*, and *K*.
Output: Top-K non-trivial FT-RPs with length no less than *min_len*.
Step1. Scan *DSeq* once to construct the bit index table.
Let $D = \{D_1, D_2, ...D_n\}$denote the set of data items in *DSeq*.
Step2. Set *P* to be an empty data sequence. Set $l = 1$ and $j_l = 1$.

Step3. Generate longer candidate patterns:

Step3-1. Generate a new candidate P' by appending data item D_{jl} to *P*, and compute $FT\text{-}Appear_{P'}^{+}(\delta_I)$ or $FT\text{-}Appear_{P'}^{-}(\delta_D)$.

Step3-2. Count the number of bits with value 1 in $FT\text{-}Appear_{P'}^{+}(\delta_I)$ or $FT\text{-}Appear_{P'}^{-}(\delta_D)$ to get FT_freq_{DSeq}(P'). If $FT\_freq_{DSeq}(P') < min\_freq$, proceed to **Step3-6.**

Step3-3. Check whether *P'* satisfies the minimum length constraint. If $|P'| \geq min\_len$, insert *P'* into Minlen set.

Step3-4. Set $P=P'$, $l = l + 1$, $j_l = 1$, and recursively call **Step3.**

Step3-5. Check whether *P'*, is non-trivial by calling procedure **Non_Trivial**(*P'*, temporal results).

Step3-6. Set $j_l = j_l + 1$, If $j_l \leq$ n, proceed to **Step3-1.**

Step3-7. $l = l\text{-}1$. If $l > 0$, return the recursive call; otherwise, proceed to **Step4.**

Step4. Sort the temporal results in fault-tolerant frequency descending order. Extract the first *K* patterns from the temporal results.

If S is non-trivial among the patterns found until now according to the results in *Temp*, the procedure Non_Trieval(*S*, *Temp*) will insert S into *Temp.* Moreover, all the sub-patterns of S in Temp, which have the same frequencies with S, will be removed.

4.2 RE-TFTRP-Mine Algorithm

In TFTRP-Mine algorithm, all the FT-RPs in the data sequence are found first. Then, top-K non-trivial FT-RPs are extracted from the results. If huge amounts of FT-RPs exist, all FT-RPs still have to be mined out even only the top-K non-trivial FT-RPs need to be outputted. It causes the mining process costly even for a small K setting. Therefore, the refinement of TFTRP-Mine, RE-TFTRP-Mine algorithm is designed. In the refined algorithm, those FT-RPs which are not possible the top-K non-trivial FT-RPs are pruned as early as possible by raising *min_freq* during the mining process. The idea is to raise *min_freq* to be a higher value if the least frequency among the most updated top-K FT-RPs has became larger than *min_freq*. Then, the FT-RPs with fault-tolerant frequencies less than the new *min_freq* will not be used to generate longer candidate patterns in the following mining process. Moreover, in order to get the FT-RPs with high fault-tolerant frequencies as early as possible, among the FT-RPs which have been discovered, the FT-RPs with higher frequencies are assigned higher priorities used to generate new candidates.

The mining process of RE-TFTRP-Mine algorithm is shown below. Since the minimum length constraint is required, the two strategies described above are applied only after all the FT-RPs with length equal to *min_len* have been found and stored in Minlen_Heap. Then, the patterns in Minlen_Heap are sorted according to their fault-tolerant frequencies to decide their priorities for generating the following candidates.

Algorithm RE-TFTRP-Mine:

Input: a data sequence *DSeq*, fault tolerance δ_I / δ_D, *min_len*, and *K*.

Output: Top-K non-trivial FT-RPs with length no less than *min_len*.

Step1. Scan *DSeq* once to construct the bit index table.
Let $D = \{D_1, D_2, \ldots D_n\}$ denote the set of data items in *DSeq*.

Step2. Set P to be an empty data sequence. Set $l = 1$ and $j_l = 1$.

Step3. Generate longer candidate patterns:

Step3-1. Generate a new candidate P' by appending data item D_{jl} to P, and compute $FT\text{-}Appear_{P'}^{+}(\delta_I)$ or $FT\text{-}Appear_{P'}^{-}(\delta_D)$.

Step3-2. Count the number of bits with value 1 in $FT\text{-}Appear_{P'}^{+}(\delta_I)$ or $FT\text{-}Appear_{P'}^{-}(\delta_D)$ to get FT_freq_{DSeq}(P'). If $FT\_freq_{DSeq}(P') < min\_freq$, proceed to **Step3-5**.

Step3-3. Check whether P' satisfies the minimum length constraint. If $|P'| \geq min\_len$, insert P' into Minlen_Heap and proceed to **Step3-5**.

Step3-4. If $|P'| < min\_len$, set $P=P'$, $l = l + 1$, $j_l = 1$, and recursively call **Step3**.

Step3-5. Set $j_l = j_l + 1$. If $j_l \leq n$, go back to **Step3-1.**

Step3-6. $l = l - 1$, if $l > 0$, return the recursive call; else if $l = 0$, copy the K patterns in Minlen-Heap with top-K fault tolerant frequencies to temporal top-K set, and proceed to **Step4**.

Step4. Select a FT-RP to generate candidates:

Step4.1. Maintain the non-trivial FT-RPs patterns with Top-K fault tolerant frequencies in the temporal top-K set. Let S denote the pattern that has the least frequency among the Top-K patterns currently. If FT_freq_{DSeq}(S)> *min_freq*, set $min\text{-}freq = FT\_freq_{DSeq}$(S). Remove those patterns with fault-tolerant frequencies being less than the new *min_freq* from Minlen_Heap.

Step4.2. Set $P=\{Q|\ Q$ has maximum fault-tolerant frequency in Minlen_Heap$\}$ and remove P from Minlen_heap. Set $l=|P|$, $l = l+1$, $j_l=1$, and recursively call **Step3**.

Step4.3. Check whether P is non-trivial by calling procedure **Non_Trivial**(*P*, temporal top-K set).

Step5. Repeat **Step 4** until Minlen_Heap is empty.

Step6. Extract the first K patterns from the temporal top-K set to be the mining result.

5 Performance Study

We implemented TFTRP-Mine and RE-TFTRP-Mine algorithms using Borland C++ Builder 5.0. The experiments are performed on a 2.4GHz Intel Pentium IV PC machine with 512 megabytes main memory and running Microsoft XP Professional.

In the first five experiments, data sequences are produced from a synthesis data generator. Two input parameters are required when running the data generator, where L denotes the length and E denotes the number of various data items in the generated data sequence. The scalabilities of TFTRP-Mine and RE-TFTRP-Mine algorithms on execution time are compared under various parameters setting. Moreover, the results of mining repeating patterns in real music objects without fault tolerance and with fault tolerance are compared in the last experiment. According to theses experiment results, the effectiveness of mining with fault tolerance is observed.

In addition to the data parameters L and E defined previously, δ_I(the insertion fault tolerance), *min_len*(the minimum length constraint) and K(the desired number of non-trivial FT-RPs to be mined) also influence the mining results and execution time of the proposed algorithms. By varying one of these five factors (*L*, *E*, δ_I, *min_len*, and *K*) in each experiment, the scalabilities of TFTRP-Mine and RE-TFTRP-Mine on execution time are observed. Besides, in order to show the pruning effect of RE-TFTRP-Mine, the numbers of generated candidate patterns of two algorithms are also illustrated. In the following five experiments, *min_freq* is fixed to be 10.

[Experiment 1] Changing the size of a data sequence (L)
In this experiment, $\delta_I = 2$, *min_len* = 8, *K* = 5 and *E* = 5 are given. *L* is varied from 1000 to 5000. The experimental results in Fig. 1 show the execution efficiency of RE-TFTRP-Mine algorithm outperforms the one of TFTRP-Mine algorithm. The reason is that the former does not need to generate all candidate patterns when finding top-K non-trivial FT-RPs. Moreover, the number of generated candidate patterns increases as the value of *L* is raised. Therefore, when *L* increases, the execution efficiency of TFTRP-Mine is slower and slower than the one of RE-TFTRP-Mine algorithm.

[Experiment 2] Changing the number of various data items (E)
Fig. 2 shows the execution times of the proposed two algorithms on data sequences with *L*=2000, where δ_I=2, *min_len*=8 and *K*=5 are inputted. When *E* increases from 5 to 25, the generated candidate patterns also increases. Thus, the performance efficiencies of two algorithms decrease in this range. However, when *E*=30, the numbers of generated candidates in both algorithms become less than the ones generated when *E*=25 and the corresponding execution time of both algorithms is also lowered down. The reason is that more various data items may cause the data sequence becomes more "sparse". Therefore, fewer FT-RPs are found and fewer candidate patterns are generated even there are more various data items.

[Experiment 3] Changing insertion fault tolerance (δ_I)
This experiment is performed on data sequences with *L*=2000, where *E*=5, *min_len*=8 and *K*=5 are inputted. As the results shown in Fig. 3, when δ_I increases, the number of generated candidate patterns grows exponentially because much more FT-RPs are found due to the relaxed constraints. Therefore, the execution time of two algorithms also increases as δ_I increases. However, RE-TFTRP-Mine still prunes huge amount of unnecessary candidates dramatically.

[Experiment 4] Changing the minimum length (*min_le*)
This experiment is performed on data sequences with *L*=2000 and *E*=5, where δ_I=2 and *k*=5 are inputted. For the same data sequence, no matter what value the *min_len* is, the number of generated candidate patterns in TFTRP-Mine algorithm is the same (41,730) and the curve of execution time keeps almost steady. On the other hand, RE-TFTRP-Mine algorithm finds all the FT-RPs with lengths equal to *min_len* before tuning the *min_freq*. Therefore, the number of generated candidates of algorithm increases as *min_len* increases. In addition, because the longer patterns usually have lower frequencies, the larger *min_len* is, the less number of non-trivial FT-RPs are discovered. Thus, the number of non-trivial FT-RPs in the data sequence is less than 5 when *min_len* = 45 and 50. It implies that the setting of *min_freq* was not raised during the execution of RE-TFTRP-Mine algorithm. In this situation, RE-TFTRP-Mine

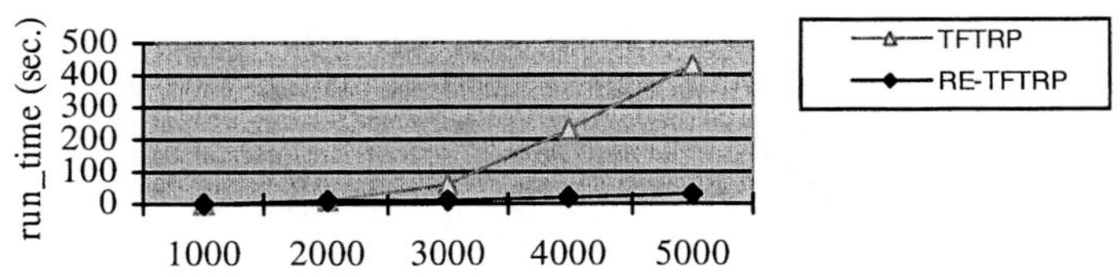

L	1000	2000	3000	4000	5000
TFTRP	10295	41730	120075	348610	533770
RE_TFTRP	8705	24300	24760	36090	41280

Number of generated candidates

Fig. 1. Result of Experiment 1

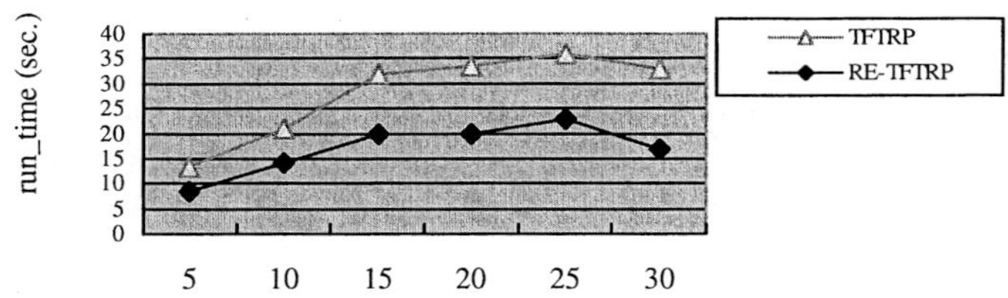

E	5	10	15	20	25	30
TFTRP	41730	70840	103110	112325	120780	111408
RE_TFTRP	24300	38540	154825	56760	66140	46656

Number of generated candidates

Fig. 2. Result of Experiment 2

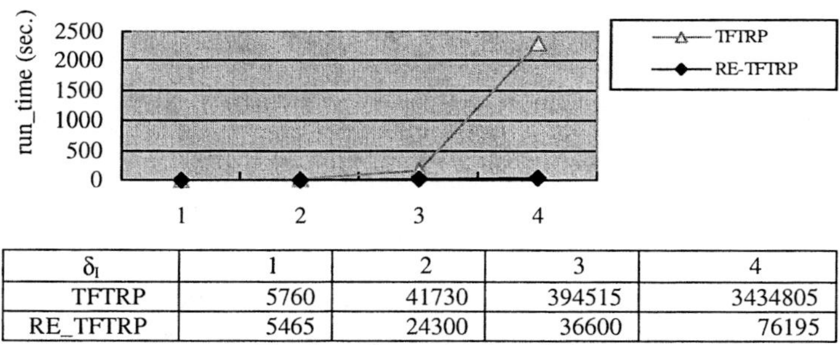

δ_I	1	2	3	4
TFTRP	5760	41730	394515	3434805
RE_TFTRP	5465	24300	36600	76195

Number of generated candidates

Fig. 3. Result of Experiment 3

algorithm generates the same candidate patterns as TFTRP-Mine does and needs additional cost to maintain the sorted FT-RPs and the top-Ks. So the execution time of RE-TFTRP-Mine is over the one of TFTRP-Mine when min_len is 45 and 50.

[Experiment 5] Changing the setting value of *K*

In this experiment, data sequences with L=2000 and E=5 are used as test data, where the run time parameters δ_I=2 and *min_len*=8 are given. Let *max_K* denote the number

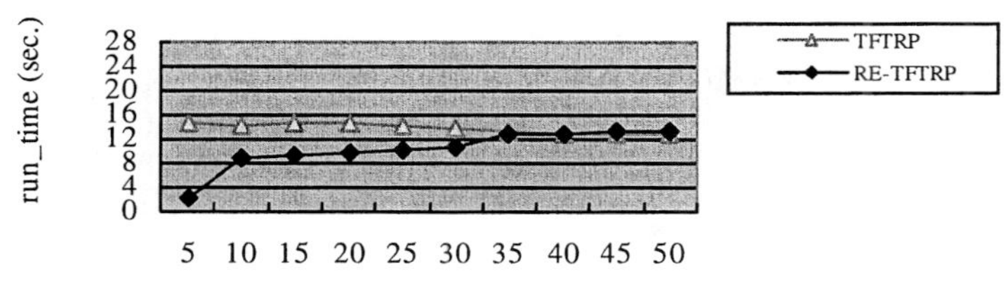

min_len	10	20	30	40	50
TFTRP	41730	41730	41730	41730	41730
RE_TFTRP	25240	27615	30500	39620	41730

Number of generated candidates

Fig. 4. Result of Experiment 4

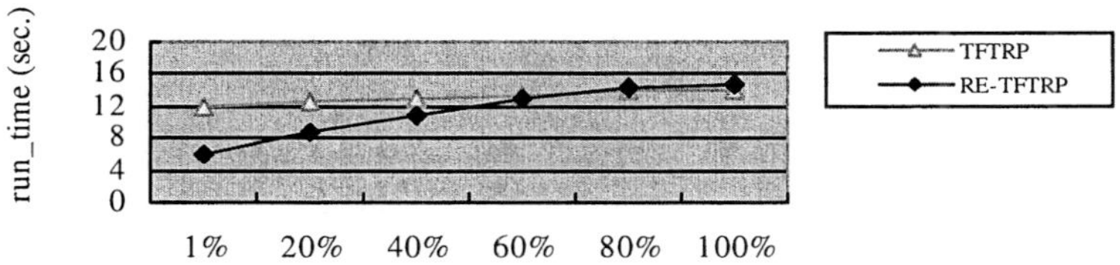

K/max_K	1%	20%	40%	60%	80%	100%
TFTRP	41730	41730	41730	41730	41730	41730
RE_TFTRP	14320	24300	31735	37325	41730	41730

Number of generated candidates

Fig. 5. Result of Experiment 5

of total non-trivial FT-RPs with *min_len* constraints discovered in this test data sequence. K is varied from $max\_K \times 1\%$ to $max\_K \times 100\%$. Fig. 5.5 shows that the number of generated candidates in RE-TFTRP-Mine is the same with the one generated in TFTRP-Mine when K/max_K is more than 80%. This case occurs because the least-frequency in the top 80% non-trivial FT-RPs is the same with *min_freq*. Therefore, the pruning strategy does not work and more processing cost of RE-TFTRP-Mine is required than TFTRP-Mine. However, the execution time of RE-TFTRP-Mine is about half of the time of TFTRP-Mine because RE-TFTRP-Mine prunes about two third of the candidate patterns when K/max_K is 1%.

[Experiment 6] Performance evaluation on effectiveness

In this experiment, five popular songs are selected as test data, whose total playing-times are between 4 and 5 minutes. The run-time parameters *min_freq* = 3, $K = 2$ and *min_len* =8 are given. We compare the found repeating patterns under various setting of δ_I or δ_D with the actual motifs in the music object. The results show that no non-trivial FT-RPs satisfying the *min_len* constraint could be found among the five music objects if fault-tolerant mapping is not allowed. When at most two insertion/deletion errors are allowed (δ_I or $\delta_D = 2$), the found patterns are most close to the motifs in the music objects. It shows that mining repeating patterns with fault tolerance is necessary.

6 Conclusion and Future Works

In this paper, two algorithms, named TFTRP-Mine and RE-TFTRP-Mine, are proposed to mine top-K non-trivial fault-tolerant repeating patterns with lengths no less than minimum length constraints from data sequences. By extending the idea of appearing bit sequences, fault-tolerant appearing bit sequences are defined to represent the positions where candidate patterns appear in a data sequence with Insertion/deletion errors. Both of two algorithms use the recursive formulas to obtain fault-tolerant appearing bit sequences of a pattern systematically and then the fault-tolerant frequency of each candidate pattern could be obtained quickly. Besides, RE-TFTRP-Mine adopts two additional strategies to improve the mining efficiency. The experimental results show that RE-TFTRP-Mine outperforms TFTRP-Mine algorithm when *K* and *min_len* are small. In addition, when adopting fault tolerant mining, more important and implicit repeating patterns could be found for music objects.

References

1. C. C. Liu, J. L. Hsu, and A. L. P. Chen, "Efficient Theme and Non-Trivial Repeating Pattern Discovering in Music Databases," in Proceedings of the 15th International Conference on Data Engineering (ICDE'99), 1999.
2. J. Han, J. Wang, Y. Lu, and P. Tzvetkov, "Mining Top-K Frequent Closed Patterns without Minimum Support", in Proceedings of 2002 International Conference on Data Mining (ICDM'02), 2002.
3. J. L. Hsu, C. C. Liu, and A. L.P. Chen, "Efficient Repeating Pattern Finding in Music Databases," in Proceedings of the Seventh International Conference on Information and Knowledge Management(ACM CIKM'98), 1998.
4. J. L. Koh and W. D. C. Yu, "Efficient Feature Mining in Music Objects," Lecture Notes in Computer Science: DEXA'01: Database and Expert Systems Applications, pp. 221-231, Springer-Verlag, 2001.
5. J. L. Koh and P. W. Yo, "An Efficient Approach for Mining Fault-Tolerant Frequent Itemsets based on Bit Sequences," Lecture Notes in Computer Science: DASFAA'05: Database Systems for Advanced Applications, Springer-Verlag, 2005.
6. J. Pei, A. K.H. Tung, and J. Han, "Fault-Tolerant Frequent Pattern Mining: Problem and Challenges," in Proceedings of ACM-SIGMOD International Workshop on Research Issues on Data Mining and Knowledge Discovery (DMKD'01), 2001.
7. P. Tzvetkov, X. Yan, and J. Han, "TSP: Mining Top-K Closed Sequential Patterns", in Proceedings of 2003 International Conference on Data Mining (ICDM'03), 2003.

Querying Multi-granular Compact Representations

Romāns Kasperovičs and Michael Böhlen

Free University of Bozen - Bolzano,
Dominikanerplatz - P.zza Domenicani 3,
39100 Bozen - Bolzano, Italy

Abstract. A common phenomenon of time-qualified data are temporal repetitions, i.e., the association of multiple time values with the same data. In order to deal with finite and infinite temporal repetitions in databases we must use compact representations. There have been many compact representations proposed, however, not all of them are equally efficient for query evaluation. In order to show it, we define a class of simple queries on compact representations. We compare a query evaluation time on our proposed multi-granular compact representation GSequences with a query evaluation time on single-granular compact representation PSets, based on periodical sets. We show experimentally how the performance of query evaluation can benefit from the compactness of a representation and from a special structure of GSequences.

1 Introduction

A temporal repetition takes place when the same data are associated with multiple time values. Table 1 shows a temporal repetition of a meeting of DB Group that takes place every Monday in January 2005.

When a temporal repetition is infinite (or infeasible large), some finite representer is used to store it in a database. Table 2 shows a representer for the temporal repetition from Table 1 with our proposed compact representation *GSequences.*

The name of GSequences stands for 'granularity sequences', because it consists of finite sequences of periodicities over granularities.

We assume a point-based representation of time, when the time domain is a discrete lineary-ordered set of time points forming the 'bottom granularity'. Additional granularities are partitionings of the bottom granularity defined with functions, allowing non-regular granules, when it is necessary.

A periodicity over a granularity is a five-element tuple, where the first element refers to the granularity and the remaining part defines a periodical repetition over the granularity. For example, periodicity $\langle \text{days}, 2, 1, 10, 20 \rangle$ defines a repetition of days described by the function $f(x) = 2x + 1$, where $10 \leq f(x) \leq 20$.

When two or more periodicities are combined into a sequence, each periodicity, except for the rightmost, is related to the following periodicity. We refer the

M.L. Lee, K.L. Tan, and V. Wuwongse (Eds.): DASFAA 2006, LNCS 3882, pp. 111–124, 2006.

Table 1. Temporal Repetition of DB Group Meeting

Group	Room	Time
DB Group	204	2005-01-03 14:00
DB Group	204	2005-01-10 14:00
DB Group	204	2005-01-17 14:00
DB Group	204	2005-01-24 14:00
DB Group	204	2005-01-31 14:00

Table 2. Representer of DB Group Meetings using GSequences

Group	Room	Time
DB Group	204	$(\langle \text{hours}, 1, 0, 14, 16\rangle, \langle \text{days}, 1, 0, 1, 1\rangle, \langle \text{weeks}, 1, 0, *, *\rangle,$ $\langle \text{years}, 1, 0, 2005, *\rangle)$

rightmost periodicity as *absolute* and the rest of periodicities as *relative*. Informally, each relative periodicity is happening *during* each granule of the following periodicy. For example, sequence $(\langle \text{months}, 1, 0, 1, 3\rangle, \langle \text{years}, 1, 0, 2005, 2006\rangle)$ defines first three months during year 2005 and during year 2006.

If the limits of an absolute periodicity are unset, the represented repetition is infinite. For relative periodicities, unset limits imply the limits of a granule of the following periodicity. For example, $\langle \text{months}, 2, 1, 1, *\rangle$ represents an infinite repetition of every second month starting from month 1. Sequence $(\langle \text{hours}, 3, 1, *, *\rangle,$ $\langle \text{days}, 2, 1, 10, 20\rangle)$ is equivalent to $(\langle \text{hours}, 3, 1, 1, 24\rangle, \langle \text{days}, 2, 1, 10, 20\rangle)$, because every day has 24 hours.

There have been many compact representations created during the last two decades [2, 4, 5, 6, 7, 8, 9, 10]. All of them can be used to store temporal repetitions in databases, however, depending on a representation, different performance results might be achieved evaluating the queries. All related works listed do not explore this particular issue.

Many temporal repetitions use common time granularities (e.g., hours, days, years) and periodicity (e.g., every 3rd, every 10th starting from 2nd). As a result, most popular compact representations use periodicity and/or granularities. Works [2, 5, 7, 8, 9, 10] combine multiple granularities in their proposed representation, whereas work [6] uses a single time granularity.

Most of the representations were shown to have the expressiveness equal to eventually periodical sets [5, 6, 7, 8, 10]. An eventually periodical set consists of a finite non-periodical subset and a periodical subset. A periodical set, consequently, is a possibly infinite set, each element of which can be obtained by adding or subtracting positive number p from some other element of this set. For example, eventually periodical set $\{1, 3, 4, 5, 10, 15, 20, \ldots\}$ consists of finite non-periodical subset $\{1, 3, 4\}$ and infinite periodical subset $\{5, 10, 15, 20, \ldots\}$.

Many of compact representations are based on algebraic expressions, where set operations are most common [2, 4, 7, 8, 9, 10]. Both, compact representation values and the relations between granularities, are defined with algebraic expressions. As a result, proposed algorithms assume inductive inference which might badly impact the performance of queries. However, the complexity of algorithms has been estimated only at the theoretical level and the real query evaluation time on different compact representations has never been compared.

Some of the works mentioned address implementation issues, suggest query evaluation algorithms or describe implemented prototypes. Work [3] describes an implementation of the representation proposed in [7] in a real database for use in temporal rules. Work [6] describes algorithms for the evaluation of relational operations on proposed representations. The work [8] describes an efficient algorithm for the evaluation of joins on proposed compact representation. Work [10] describes methods of simplification of representations at the symbolic level. Work [1] describes a simplification algorithm for minimising representations of periodical granularities.

We practically show that not all representations are equally efficient for query evaluation. We use single-granular representation, referred as PSets, with expressiveness equal to eventually periodical sets to compare the query evaluation time with GSequences. We define the compactness property of a representer and we prove that a representer with GSequences is as much or more compact than a representer with PSets of the same temporal repetition. The queries we consider have two boundaries and the target granularity. An example of such a query on a representer shown in Table 2 is 'days with meetings between 2005-03-01 and 2005-05-31'. The experiments we run confirm that the structure and the compactness of GSequences gives an advantage during query evaluation.

Section 2 defines compact representations GSequenses and PSets along with all necessary concepts we use in these definitions. In section 3 we analyse the compactness of both representations. Section 4 defines a class of simple queries on compact representation and gives complexity estimation for query evaluation algorithms on both compact representation. Section 5 contains the results of our experiments. Section 6 finishes this article with conclusions and future work.

2 Compact Representations

2.1 Time Domain and Granularities

All related works we refer assume discrete lineary-ordered time domain. For our representation we use the same assumption.

Definition 1 (time domain). *A time domain T is a discrete, lineary ordered set, infinite in the future and bounded in the past.*

Example 1. Sample time values are $1, 3, 10, 55009440$.

We define granularities as a partitioning of the time domain T.

Definition 2 (granularity). *Let $\mathcal{G} = \mathbb{N}$ be an index set and let $g \in \mathcal{G}$. A mapping $M_g : \mathbb{N} \mapsto 2^T$ is a granularity with an index g if*

1. $\forall i \in \mathbb{N} : (M_g(i) \neq \emptyset)$;
2. $\forall i \in \mathbb{N}$: *$M_g(i)$ is a finite set;*

3. $\forall i, j \in \mathbb{N} : (i \neq j \Rightarrow (M_g(i) \cap M_g(j) = \emptyset))$;
4. $\forall i, j \in \mathbb{N} : (i < j \Rightarrow (\forall m \in M_g(i), n \in M_g(j) : m < n))$;
5. $\bigcup_i M_g(i) = T$.

The first and the second conditions require all partitions to be non-empty and finite. The third condition disallows partitions to overlap. The fourth and the fifth conditions require that there are no gaps between the partitions.

Example 2. According to Def. 2, proper granularities are days, weeks, Gregorian months, Gregorian years, moon months, milliseconds, centuries, summer and winter time periods, etc. Weekends, leap years, etc., are not granularities, because they allow gaps.

Definition 3 (base granularity). *A granularity* $M_b : \mathbb{N} \mapsto 2^T$ *is a base granularity iff* $\forall i \in \mathbb{N}(M_b(i) = \{i\})$.

Example 3. If the base granularity is equal to 'days', granularities 'weeks' and 'month' group the time domain T into the partitions as it is shown in Fig. 1.

Our definition of granularity allows us to specify mapping M_g with function $\mu_{g \to T} : \mathbb{N} \to T$, or just μ_g, where $\mu_g(x)$ returns the first element of T of granule x and $\mu_g(x+1) - 1$ returns the last element of T of granule x.

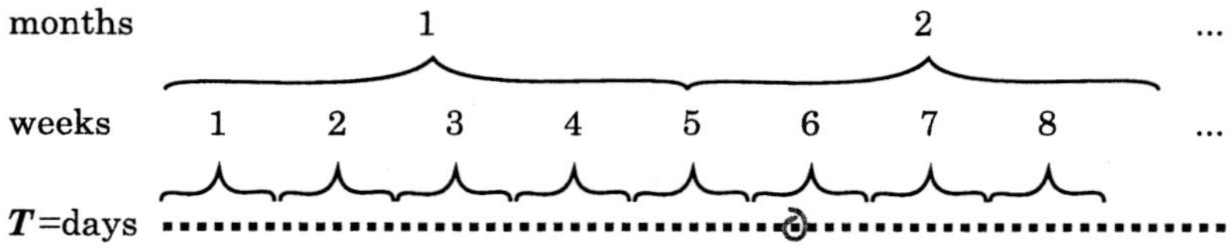

Fig. 1. Granularity as a Partitioning of the Time Domain T

In further sections we use also reverse mapping M_g^{-1} that can be defined with function $\mu_{g \to T}^{-1} : T \to \mathbb{N}$, or just μ_g^{-1}, that returns index $i \in \mathbb{N}$ of a granule of granularity g for given $t \in T$ if $\mu_g(i) \leq t < \mu_g(i+1)$.

Example 4. For the base granularity equal to 'days', function $\mu_{\text{years}}(x)$ returns the first day of year x. Function $\mu_{\text{years}}^{-1}(y)$ returns a year to which day y belongs.

$$\begin{aligned}
\mu_{\text{years}}(x) &= 365x + \lfloor x/4 \rfloor - \lfloor x/100 \rfloor + \lfloor x/400 \rfloor \\
\mu_{\text{years}}^{-1}(y) &= 400 \lfloor \frac{y}{146097} \rfloor + \\
&\quad +100 \min(3, \lfloor \frac{y \bmod 146097}{36524} \rfloor) + \\
&\quad +4 \lfloor \frac{(y \bmod 146097) \bmod 36524}{1461} \rfloor + \\
&\quad + \min(3, \lfloor \frac{((y \bmod 146097) \bmod 36524) \bmod 1461}{365} \rfloor)
\end{aligned}$$

A new granularity g can be defined using one already defined granularity h. In other words $\mu_g(x) = \mu_h(\mu_{g\to h}(x))$ and $\mu_g^{-1}(x) = \mu_h^{-1}(\mu_{g\to h}^{-1}(x))$. In this case to define g we define only $\mu_{g\to h}(x)$ and $\mu_{g\to h}^{-1}(x)$.

Example 5. If months are already defined with functions $\mu_{\text{months}}(x)$ and $\mu_{\text{months}}^{-1}(x)$, we can define years with $\mu_{\text{years}\to\text{months}}(x) = 12(x-1)+1$ and $\mu_{\text{years}\to\text{months}}^{-1}(x) = \lfloor x/12 \rfloor + 1$.

2.2 Temporal Repetition and Compact Representation

Let A be some combination of non-temporal domains and let a denote some element of A. Let T be the time domain.

Definition 4 (temporal repetition). *A temporal repetition of some data a is a relation $r_a \subseteq \{a\} \times T$.*

Example 6. Table 3 illustrates a temporal repetition of a bus no. 2 in Bozen-Bolzano. This temporal repetition is infinite, because buses are supposed to go forever.

Table 3. Bus no. 2 Schedule in Bozen-Bolzano

No.	Station	Time
2	Stazione 1	2005-01-03 7:48
2	Stazione 1	2005-01-03 8:00
2	Stazione 1	2005-01-03 8:12
...	...	...
2	Stazione 1	2005-01-04 7:48
2	Stazione 1	2005-01-04 8:00
2	Stazione 1	2005-01-04 8:12
...	...	...

Definition 5 (compact representation). *Let X be some domain. Let $\upsilon : X \to 2^T$ be a function that takes an element of X and returns a subset of time domain T. A compact representation is pair $\langle X, \upsilon\rangle$, where X is called the domain of the representation and υ is called the unfold operation of the representation.*

In sections 2.4 and 2.5 we define two particular compact representations PSets and GSequences, showing the use of this definition.

Definition 6 (relational unfold). *Let $\bar{r}_a \subset \{a\} \times X$ and $\bar{R} = \bigcup_{a,i} \bar{r}_{a,i}$ be a set of all possible $\bar{r}_{a,i}$. Let $r_a \subset \{a\} \times T$ and $R = \bigcup_{a,i} r_{a,i}$ be a set of all possible $r_{a,i}$. A relation operation $\Upsilon : \bar{R} \to R$ is relational unfold operation for the compact representation $\langle X, \upsilon\rangle$, if $\forall \bar{r} \in \bar{R}(\Upsilon(\bar{r}) = \{\langle a, t\rangle \mid \exists x \in X(\langle a, x\rangle \in \bar{r} \wedge t \in \upsilon(x))\})$.*

Definition 7 (representer). *A relation $\bar{r} \subset \{a\} \times X$ is a representer with the domain X of a temporal repetition r if there's such a relational unfold operation Υ, that $\Upsilon(\bar{r}) = r$ and $\bar{r}$ is finite and $|\bar{r}| \leq |r|$.*

Example 7. Let $\bar{r} = \{\langle a, x_1\rangle, \langle a, x_2\rangle\}$ be some representer, where $x_1, x_2 \in X$. Let $\upsilon(x_1) = \{2, 3, 4\}$ and $\upsilon(x_2) = \{7, 9\}$. The result of $\Upsilon(\bar{r})$ is a temporal repetition $\{\langle a, 2\rangle, \langle a, 3\rangle, \langle a, 4\rangle, \langle a, 7\rangle, \langle a, 9\rangle\}$.

Definition 8 (compactness). *The compactness of a representer $\bar{r} \subset \{a_1\} \times \ldots \times \{a_n\} \times X$ is its size in bytes occupied in a database.*

Example 8. Having attribute 'Group' as a fixed length character string of length 10, having an attribute 'Room' as a natural number and having granularity indexes encoded by natural numbers, the representer given in Table 2 has a length of $10 + 1 \cdot s + 4 \cdot 5 \cdot s$ bytes, where s is a size of one natural number in bytes.

2.3 Periodical Sets and Periodical Granularities

Definition 9 (periodical set). *Set $S \subseteq \mathbb{N}$ is a periodical set if there exists some $p \in \mathbb{N}$, called period, and finite subset $S' \subseteq S$, called repeating subset, such that:*

1. $\forall i \in S \setminus S'(\exists r \in S', x \in \mathbb{N}(i = r + xp))$;
2. $\forall i \in S(\exists r \in S', x \in \mathbb{N}(i = r + xp) \Rightarrow i \in S \setminus S')$.

The first condition of the definition ensures that all elements of set $S \setminus S'$ can be obtained by consequently adding period p to the elements of subset S' of S. The second condition ensures that S' is 'minimal'. In other words, no element of S' can be expressed subtracting or adding the same period to another element of subset S'.

Example 9. Set $S = \{2, 3, 6, 8, 13, 14, 17, 19, \ldots, 46, 47, 50, 52, \ldots\}$ is a periodical set with repeating subset $S' = \{2, 3, 6, 8\}$ and period $p = 11$.

With the appropriate base granularity many other granularities, including Gregorian calendar granularities, are periodical.

Definition 10 (periodical granularity). *Granularity M_g is a periodical granularity if $\bigcup_{i=1}^{\infty} \mu_g(i)$ is a periodical set.*

Example 10. If the base granularity is 'days', Gregorian years form a periodical set with a repeating subset of 400 elements (years) and the period equal to 146097 days. Gregorian months form a periodical set with a repeating subset of 400x12 elements (months) and the same period equal to 146097 days.

2.4 PSets

Definition 11 (periodicity). *Let $\mathbb{N}^* = \mathbb{N} \cup *$. A periodicity is a five tuple $\langle g, p, o, l, h\rangle$, where $g \in \mathcal{G}$ is a granularity index, $p, o \in \mathbb{N}$ are respectively a period and an offset of a linear function $f(x) = px + o$ and $l, h \in \mathbb{N}^*$ are respectively lower and upper bounds on the value of $f(x)$.*

Example 11. Sample periodicities are $\langle \text{minutes}, 11, 2, 0, 200\rangle$, $\langle \text{seconds}, 11, 3, 0, *\rangle$ and $\langle \text{days}, 11, 6, *, *\rangle$.

Definition 12 (X_{PS}). *The domain of the compact representation PSets* $X_{\text{PS}} = \mathcal{G} \times \mathbb{N} \times \mathbb{N} \times \mathbb{N}^* \times \mathbb{N}^*$ *is a set of all possible periodicities.*

Definition 13 (υ_{PS}). *Let* $x \in X_{\text{PS}}$ *and let* $x = \langle g, p, o, l, h\rangle$.

- *for* $l = * \wedge h = *$:
  $\upsilon_{\text{PS}}(x) = \{t \in T \mid \exists i \in \mathbb{N}(f = pi + o \wedge t \in M_g(f))\}$;
- *for* $l = * \wedge h \neq *$:
  $\upsilon_{\text{PS}}(x) = \{t \in T \mid \exists i \in \mathbb{N}(f = pi + o \wedge t \in M_g(f) \wedge f \leq h)\}$;
- *for* $l \neq * \wedge h = *$:
  $\upsilon_{\text{PS}}(x) = \{t \in T \mid \exists i \in \mathbb{N}(f = pi + o \wedge t \in M_g(f) \wedge l \leq f)\}$;
- *for* $l \neq * \wedge h \neq *$:
  $\upsilon_{\text{PS}}(x) = \{t \in T \mid \exists i \in \mathbb{N}(f = pi + o \wedge t \in M_g(f) \wedge l \leq f \leq h)\}$.

Example 12. Table 4 shows a fragment of a representer with PSets of the temporal repetition of the bus no 2 shown in Table 3. The values of the rightmost column encode a periodical set with a period 1 week = 10080 minutes, and repeating subset {7665, 7680, 7695}, where 7665 corresponds to 07:45 of the first Saturday, 7680 to 08:00, and 7695 to 08:15.

Table 4. Representer of Bus no. 2 Schedule in Bozen-Bolzano using PSets

No.	**Station**	X_{PS}
2	Stazione 1	minutes,10080,7665,*,*
2	Stazione 1	minutes,10080,7680,*,*
2	Stazione 1	minutes,10080,7695,*,*
...	...	...

2.5 GSequences

Definition 14 (X_{GS}). *Let P be a finite sequence of periodicities. The domain of the compact representation GSequences* $X_{\text{GS}} = \bigcup_i P_i$ *is a set of all possible* P_i.

To define υ_{GS} we introduce some helper functions. Function $\xi : \mathcal{G} \times \mathbb{N} \times \mathcal{G} \rightarrow \mathbb{N}$ takes tuple $\langle e, i, g\rangle$, where e and g are granularity indexes and i is an index of a partition of granularity e, and returns an index of a partition of granularity g:

$$\xi(e, i, g) = \begin{cases} \mu_g^{-1}(\mu_e(i)), & \text{if } \mu_g(\mu_g^{-1}(\mu_e(i))) \geq \mu_e(i); \\ \mu_g^{-1}(\mu_e(i)) + 1, & \text{if } \mu_g(\mu_g^{-1}(\mu_f(i))) < \mu_e(i). \end{cases}$$

Let x be some element of X_{GS}. Let x' denote x without the leftmost periodicity and let $r_1 \in x$ be the leftmost periodicity in x. For example, if $x = (\langle days, 1, 0, 1, 1\rangle, \langle weeks, 1, 0, *, *\rangle, \langle months, 1, 0, 1, 1\rangle, \langle years, 1, 0, 2005, 2005\rangle)$, then $x' = (\langle weeks, 1, 0, *, *\rangle, \langle months, 1, 0, 1, 1\rangle, \langle years, 1, 0, 2005, 2005\rangle)$ and $r_1 = \langle days, 1, 0, 1, 1\rangle$.

Let $\bar{\upsilon} : X_{\mathrm{GS}} \rightarrow 2^{\mathcal{G}\times\mathbb{N}}$ be a function and let $\bar{\upsilon}(P)$ be defined as follows.

1. if $(r_1 = \langle g,p,o,l,h\rangle) \wedge (x' = \emptyset)$:
   - for $l \neq * \wedge h \neq *$, $\bar{\upsilon}(x) = \{\langle g,i\rangle \mid l \leq i \leq h \wedge \exists j \in \mathbb{N}(i = pj + o)\}$;
   - for $l = * \wedge h \neq *$, $\bar{\upsilon}(x) = \{\langle g,i\rangle \mid 1 \leq i \leq h \wedge \exists j \in \mathbb{N}(i = pj + o)\}$;
   - for $l \neq * \wedge h = *$, $\bar{\upsilon}(x) = \{\langle g,i\rangle \mid i \geq l \wedge \exists j \in \mathbb{N}(i = pj + o)\}$;
   - for $l = * \wedge h = *$, $\bar{\upsilon}(x) = \{\langle g,i\rangle \mid i \geq 1 \wedge \exists j \in \mathbb{N}(i = pj + o)\}$;
2. if $r_1 = \langle g,p,o,l,h\rangle \wedge (x' \neq \emptyset)$:
   - for $l \neq * \wedge h \neq *$,
   $\bar{\upsilon}(x) = \{\langle g,i\rangle \mid \exists\langle e,k\rangle \in \bar{\upsilon}(x')(\langle g,i\rangle \in \bar{\upsilon}(g,p,o,l+\xi(e,k,g),h+\xi(e,k,g)))\}$
   - for $l = * \wedge h \neq *$,
   $\bar{\upsilon}(x) = \{\langle g,i\rangle \mid \exists\langle e,k\rangle \in \bar{\upsilon}(x')(\langle g,i\rangle \in \bar{\upsilon}(g,p,o,1,h+\xi(e,k,g)))\}$
   - for $l \neq * \wedge h = *$,
   $\bar{\upsilon}(x) = \{\langle g,i\rangle \mid \exists\langle e,k\rangle \in \bar{\upsilon}(x')(\langle g,i\rangle \in \bar{\upsilon}(g,p,o,l+\xi(e,k,g),\xi(e,k+1,g)))\}$
   - for $l = * \wedge h = *$,
   $\bar{\upsilon}(x) = \{\langle g,i\rangle \mid \exists\langle e,k\rangle \in \bar{\upsilon}(x')(\langle g,i\rangle \in \bar{\upsilon}(g,p,o,1,\xi(e,k+1,g)))\}$

Finally, $\upsilon_{\mathrm{GS}}(x) = \{t \in T \mid \exists\langle b,i\rangle \in \bar{\upsilon}(\langle b,1,0,*,*\rangle \cup x)(t = i)\}$, where b denotes the base granularity.

Example 13. Let us take $x = \{\langle weeks,1,0,*,*\rangle, \langle months,1,0,1,1\rangle\}$ as an example. An expression $\bar{\upsilon}(months,1,0,1,1)$ returns a set of one month $\{\langle \text{months},1\rangle\}$. An expression $\bar{\upsilon}(\{\langle weeks,1,0,*,*\rangle, \langle months,1,0,1,1\rangle\})$ returns a set of weeks whose index is between $\xi(\text{months},1,\text{weeks})$ and $\xi(\text{months},1,\text{weeks})$.

3 Compactness Analysis

As it is shown in [2], periodicity $\langle g,p,o,h,l\rangle$ over periodical granularity g with granularity period p_g and granularity repeating subset S'_g forms periodical set S_f with the period $p_f = p_g$ and repeating subset S'_f, $|S'_f| = |S'_g|/p$, if the $|S'_g|$ is divisible by p.

In other case resulting periodical set S_f has period $p_f = \frac{p_g \cdot \mathrm{LCM}(|S'_g|,p)}{|S'_g|}$ and repeating subset S'_f, $|S'_f| = \mathrm{LCM}(|S'_g|,p)/p$, where LCM stands for the least common multiple.

Example 14. A periodicity $\langle \text{months},3,0,*,*\rangle$ with the granularity period of 146097 days and the granularity repeating subset of 4800 months forms on $T =$ 'days' a periodical set S_f with a period of $p_f = 146097$ days and a repeating subset of $146097/3 = 48699$ elements.

For a periodicity $\langle \text{months},11,0,*,*\rangle$ in the same conditions $p_f = 146097 \cdot 11 = 1607067$ and $|S'_f| = (1607067 \cdot 11)/11 = 146097$ elements.

Lemma 1. *For any representer $\bar{r}_{\mathrm{PS}}$ there's a representer $\bar{r}_{\mathrm{GS}}$ of the same temporal repetition, that is as compact as $\bar{r}_{\mathrm{PS}}$.*

Proof. PSets is a trivial case of GSequences, when a sequence of periodicities contains only one periodicity. Hence, any representer $\langle g, p, o, l, h\rangle \in X_{\mathrm{PS}}$ can be constructed a representer $(\langle g, p, o, l, h\rangle) \in X_{\mathrm{GS}}$ of the same temporal repetition and with the same compactness.

Lemma 2. *For any periodical granularities $g_1, \ldots, g_m$ expression $\bar{\upsilon}_{\mathrm{GS}}$ $((\langle g_1, p_1, o_1, l_1, h_1\rangle, \ldots, \langle g_m, p_m, o_m, l_m, h_m\rangle))$ returns a periodical set of elements of time domain T.*

The idea of the proof of Lemma 2 is that the resulting periodical set has a period equal to the least common multiple of the periods of each $\langle g_i, p_i, o_i, l_i, h_i\rangle$.

Lemma 3. *For any periodical granularities $g_1, \ldots, g_m$ representer $\bar{r}_{\mathrm{GS}} = \{\langle a_1, \ldots, a_n, x\rangle\}$, where $x = (\langle g_1, p_1, o_1, l_1, h_1\rangle, \ldots, \langle g_m, p_m, o_m, l_m, h_m\rangle$, is more compact than a representer of the same temporal repetition with the domain X_{PS}, if the size of a periodical subset in $\bar{\upsilon}_{\mathrm{GS}}$ $((\langle g_1, p_1, o_1, l_1, h_1\rangle, \ldots, \langle g_m, p_m, o_m, l_m, h_m\rangle))$ is bigger than m.*

Theorem 1. *For any representer $\bar{r}_{\mathrm{PS}}$ there's a representer $\bar{r}_{\mathrm{GS}}$ of the same temporal repetition, which is as compact as $\bar{r}_{\mathrm{PS}}$ or even more compact.*

Proof. According to Lemma 1 for each representer with PSets there exists a representer with GSequences which is as compact as the representer with PSets. According to Lemma 3, if there is a periodical granularity g with periodical subset $|S'_g| > 1$, there exists a representer $\bar{r}_{\mathrm{GS}}$ which is more compact than any representer with PSets of the same temporal repetition.

4 Queries on Compact Representations

In this paper we investigate two types of queries on compact representations. The first type of query has a form

$$\pi[\xi(b, \mathrm{time}, g)](\sigma[C_1 \leq \mathrm{time} \leq C_2](\Upsilon(\bar{r}))) , \quad (1)$$

where where σ is a selection operation, $\bar{r}$ is a compact representation, time is an attribute of $\bar{r}$ of compact representation domain, C_1 and C_2 are some constants of the time domain, π is a projection operation, b is an index of the base granularity, g is an index of some given granularity and $\xi : \mathcal{G} \times \mathbb{N} \times \mathcal{G} \to \mathbb{N}$ is a granularity convertion function used in previous sections.

The second type of query has a form

$$\sigma[C_1 \leq \mathrm{time} \leq C_2](\Upsilon(\bar{r})) . \quad (2)$$

This type of queries is a specific case of the first type with $g = b$.

We distinguish two different approaches of the evaluation of queries 1 or 2. The naive approach is first to evaluate an operation $\Upsilon(\bar{r})$ and then to proceed with a regular query on temporal repetition. This naive approach fails in cases when a temporal repetition is infinite, because $\Upsilon(\bar{r})$ never stops.

4.1 Query Evaluation on PSets

The approach we use to evaluate queries on PSets produces a temporal repetition already inside given bounds. The algorithm contains two nested cycles (see Listing 1.1). The outer cycle goes through the tuples in a representer and the inner cycle produces tuples of the resulting temporal repetition. We can evaluate the complexity of this algorithm as $O(\Upsilon_{\mathrm{PS}}) = n^2$.

Listing 1.1. PSets Evaluation Algorithm

```
procedure ϒPS(r̄,C1,C2,g)
   for each tuple=(someA, periodicity) in r̄
      υPS(periodicity,C1,C2,g);
procedure υPS(periodicity,C1,C2,g)
   with periodicity = (e,p,o,l,h) do
     [a;b] = intersection ([l;h],[C1;C2]);
     xmin = minimum argument value of p*x+o in [a;b];
     xmax = maximum argument value of p*x+o in [a;b];
     for x = xmin to xmax
       result = convert(p*x+o→g);
       print result;
```

4.2 Query Evaluation on GSequences

The query evaluation algorithm for GSequences is shown in Listing 1.2. It consists of two procedures. The first procedure goes sequentially through the input tuples and calls the second procedure for each tuple. The second procedure generates the tuples of the resulting temporal repetition recursively going through the sequence of periodicities. The maximal depth of a recursion is equal to the length of the sequence. For each periodicity the procedure runs the cycle through its granularity values. Therefore, we can evaluate the complexity of the algorithm, as $O(\Upsilon_{\mathrm{GS}}) = n^n$.

It seems that the performance of Υ_{GS} should be worse than of Υ_{PS}, however, (1) the number of input tuples for υ_{PS} is normally bigger than for υ_{GS}, in order to produce the same output, (2) we use some specifics from the input to reduce the number of operations in υ_{GS}.

Sequential application of bounds. Because of a sequential structure of GSequences given bounds C_1 and C_2 are applied starting from the rightmost periodicity reducing the range for the following periodicities.

Example 15. Let us take a compact representation shown in Table 2 and a query σ[2005-01-01 00:00 $\leq$ time $\leq$ 2005-01-31 23:59]$(\Upsilon(\bar{r}))$. Evaluating this query the bounds are applied first to the years and then to the weeks of remaining years only, etc.

Listing 1.2. GSequences Evaluation Algorithm

```
procedure ΥGS(r̄,C1,C2,g)
   for each tuple=(someA,gsequence) in r̄
      υGS(gsequence,C1,C2,g,null);
procedure υGS(sequence,C1,C2,g,parent)
   with sequence=(X,(e,p,o,l,h)) do
      if parent is set then offset = convert(parent→e);
      else offset = 0;
      [a;b]=intersection([l+offset;h+offset],[C1;C2]);
      if parent is set then
         highparent = convert(parent+1→e);
         [a;b]=intersection([a;b],[a;highparent−1]);
      xmin = minimum argument value of p*x+o in [a;b];
      xmax = maximum argument value of p*x+o in [a;b];
      for x = xmin to xmax
         if X is empty then
            result = convert(p*x+o→g);
            print result;
         else if e = g then print result;
         else υGS(X,C1,C2,g,p*x+o);
```

Hierarchical definition of granularities. We define new granularities using already defined granularities. This allows us to perform granularity convertion operations without going to the base granularity (we avoid getting intermediate results with very big indexes).

Example 16. Let us take a compact representation shown in Table 2 in a database where the base granularity is equal to milliseconds. If both years and weeks are defined or transitively defined in terms of days, an index of the first week of the year can be calculated with the formula $\mu^{-1}_{\text{weeks}\rightarrow\text{days}}(\mu_{\text{years}\rightarrow\text{days}}(i))$.

Truncating sequences. When the target granularity is present in a sequence of periodicities, we process a sequence only till this periodicity.

Example 17. Let us take a compact representation shown in Table 2 and a query $\pi[\xi(\text{time},\text{days})](\sigma[\text{2005-01-01 00:00} \leq \text{time} \leq \text{2005-01-31 23:59}](\Upsilon(\bar{r})))$. Since there's a periodicity over days in the sequence of periodicities, the evaluation process stops on this periodicity without processing the remaining periodicities.

5 Experiments

In this section we show the results of three experiments in which we compare the performance of queries to GSequences and PSets representers.

In each experiment the same query (query 1 when the target granularity is given or query 2 otherwise) is applied to GSequences and PSets representers of

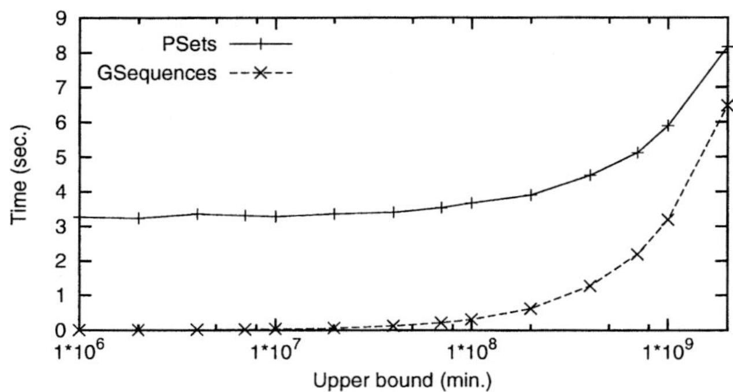

Fig. 2. Results of Experiment 1

the same temporal repetition. According to our assumptions, both representers might have different number of input tuples, but the query results are always identical.

Since it is not very convinient to control the number of output tuples through the query parameters, we compare the query processing time to the given bounds. In other words, horisontal axis in the following plots represents the difference $C_2 - C_1$, or just C_2 (upper bound) with $C_1 = 0$.

In all experiments the base granularity is equal to 'minutes'.

Experiment 1. A GSequences representer of a temporal repetition is illustrated in Table 5. A PSets representer of the same repetition consists of 327,000 tuples with a period equal to 210,378,241 minutes. The results of the experiment show, that the huge size of a representer with PSets gives a big advantage to GSequences.

Table 5. Representer with GSequences for Experiment 1

Some Domain	**Time**
Some Value	$(\langle \text{minutes}, 1, 0, 1, 10\rangle, \langle \text{hours}, 1, 0, 1, 10\rangle, \langle \text{days}, 1, 0, 1, 10\rangle,$ $\langle \text{months}, 11, 0, *, *\rangle)$

Experiment 2. In this experiment we used a real temporal repetition of a bus no. 2 of Bozen-Bolzano. A representer with GSequences consists of 51 tuples. A representer with PSets consists of 456 tuples. From the results of the experiment showed in Fig. 3 it is obvious that the difference in compactness is not sufficient for this kind of queries to beat the difference in complexity of the methods.

Experiment 3. For this experiment we took the same temporal repetition as for Exp.1 and we set the target granularity equal to days. The results illustrated in Fig. 4 show the advantage of truncating sequences.

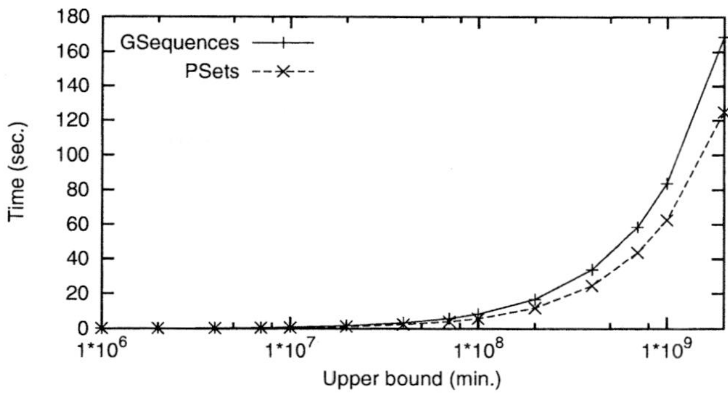

Fig. 3. Results of Experiment 2

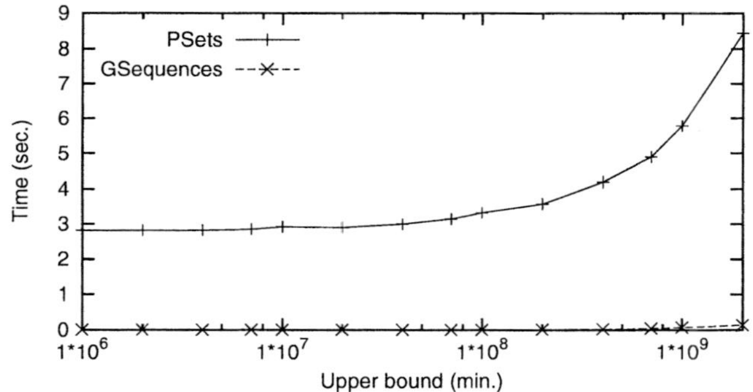

Fig. 4. Results of Experiment 3

6 Conclusions

Compact representations are used to store temporal repetitions in databases. It is essential that compact representations can be queried in the same way as they were temporal repetition, and query evaluation algorithm should take an advantage of querying compact representations.

In this paper we presented a compact representation of temporal repetitions GSequences that combines periodicity with a use of multiple temporal granularities. On this representation we showed that a query evaluation can benefit from a structure of a compact representation. To support this result we experimentally compared GSequences with other compact representation PSets with more simple structure. We introduced the compactness property of compact representations. We proved that besides more sophisticated structure of GSequences it has equal or better compactness than PSets. We also showed and proved experimentally that a compactness of a representer can significantly impact the query evaluation time.

In the future work we aim to implement more complicated queries containing joins and aggregation operations.

References

1. C. Bettini and S. Mascetti. An efficient algorithm for minimizing time granularity periodical representations. In *TIME*, pages 20–25, 2005.
2. C. Bettini and R. D. Sibi. Symbolic representation of user-defined time granularities. In *Proceedings of TIME'99*, pages 17–28. IEEE Computer Society, 1999.
3. R. Chandra, A. Segev, and M. Stonebraker. Implementing calendars and temporal rules in next generation databases. In *Proceedings of the Tenth International Conference on Data Engineering*, pages 264–273, Washington, DC, USA, 1994. IEEE Computer Society.
4. D. R. Cukierman and J. P. Delgrande. The sol theory: A formalization of structured temporal objects and repetition. In *Proceedings of TIME'04*. IEEE Computer Society, 2004.
5. L. Egidi and P. Terenziani. A mathematical framework for the semantics of symbolic languages representing periodic time. In *Proceedings of TIME'04*. IEEE Computer Society, 2004.
6. F. Kabanza, J.-M. Stevenne, and P. Wolper. Handling infinite temporal data. In *PODS*, pages 392–403, 1990.
7. B. Leban, D. D. McDonald, and D. R. Forster. A representation for collections of temporal intervals. In *Proceedings of AAAI'86*, pages 367–371, August 1986.
8. M. Niezette and J.-M. Stevenne. An efficient symbolic representation of periodic time. In *Proceedings of the First International Conference on Information and Knowledge Management*, November 1992.
9. P. Ning, X. S. Wang, and S. Jajodia. An algebraic representation of calendars. *Ann. Math. Artif. Intell.*, 36(1-2):5–38, 2002.
10. P. Terenziani. Symbolic user-defined periodicy in temporal relational databases. *IEEE TKDE*, 15(2), March/April 2003.

The COST Benchmark—Comparison and Evaluation of Spatio-temporal Indexes

Christian S. Jensen, Dalia Tiešytė, and Nerius Tradišauskas

Department of Computer Science, Aalborg University, Denmark
{csj, dalia, nerius}@cs.aau.dk

Abstract. An infrastructure is emerging that enables the positioning of populations of on-line, mobile service users. In step with this, research in the management of moving objects has attracted substantial attention. In particular, quite a few proposals now exist for the indexing of moving objects, and more are underway. As a result, there is an increasing need for an independent benchmark for spatio-temporal indexes.

This paper characterizes the spatio-temporal indexing problem and proposes a benchmark for the performance evaluation and comparison of spatio-temporal indexes. Notably, the benchmark takes into account that the available positions of the moving objects are inaccurate, an aspect largely ignored in previous indexing research. The concepts of data and query enlargement are introduced for addressing inaccuracy. As proof of concepts of the benchmark, the paper covers the application of the benchmark to three spatio-temporal indexes—the TPR-, TPR*-, and B^x-trees. Representative experimental results and consequent guidelines for the usage of these indexes are reported.

1 Introduction

With the availability of mobile computing technologies, geo-positioning, and wireless communication capabilities, it has become possible to accumulate the changing locations of populations of moving objects in real time. Consumer electronics are affordable, current Global Positioning System (GPS) [1] receivers are capable of geo-positioning with an accuracy of up to a few meters, the General Packet Radio Service (GPRS) [2] and similar technologies have become common and relatively cheap means of wireless data transfer. It is thus possible for an object to continually obtain and transmit its current position to a central server.

Applications are emerging that require or may benefit from the tracking of the locations of moving objects. These occur in areas such as logistics, traffic management, public transportation, and location-based services. Current applications usually track only relatively small numbers of objects, but as the underlying technologies continue to improve, applications that concern large numbers of objects are on the horizon.

The increasing interest in mobile location data has served as motivation for the development of spatio-temporal indexes for the current and near-future positions of moving objects. A number of spatio-temporal indexes have been proposed, such as R-tree-based indexes, e.g., the TPR-tree [3], the TPR*-tree [4], the STAR-tree [5], and the R^{EXP}-tree [6]; the quadtree-based index STRIPES [7], and the B^+-tree-based B^x-tree [8], to name but a few.

M.L. Lee, K.L. Tan, and V. Wuwongse (Eds.): DASFAA 2006, LNCS 3882, pp. 125–140, 2006.

This continuing proliferation of indexing techniques creates a need for a standard procedure for performance evaluation and comparison. Although mathematical complexity analysis is valuable, empirical evaluation [9] is indispensable for evaluation and comparison of spatio-temporal indexing techniques. The current state of affairs is that indexes being proposed are being evaluated empirically and are being compared to, typically, one other indexing technique. The empirical studies reported are rarely exhaustive and, not surprisingly, tend to focus on the favorable qualities of the index being proposed. The availability of an independent benchmark specification establishes an equal footing for obtaining experimental results and enables broader comparison.

This paper proposes a benchmark specification, termed COST, for the evaluation and comparison of spatio-temporal indexes. The benchmark is independent in the sense that it is proposed independently of a specific indexing technique. The benchmark aims to provide a unified procedure that covers an extensive variety of possible and realistic settings. In particular, the benchmark evaluates the index ability to accommodate uncertain object positions. Queries and updates are considered, as are both I/O and CPU performance.

The remainder of this paper is outlined as follows. Related work is covered in Sect. 2. The addressed indexing problem is detailed in Sect. 3. Sections 4 and 5 contain the benchmark specification. As proof of concepts, Sect. 6 reports on experimental results that were obtained using the benchmark. Section 7 concludes and offers directions of future work.

2 Related Work

We cover in turn existing benchmarks for spatio-temporal data, previous work on the indexing of uncertain data, and past empirical evaluations of spatio-temporal indexes.

A number of benchmarks exist that measure transaction performance in traditional database systems. For example, a set of benchmarks that evaluate system performance and price is provided by Gray [10]. However, these benchmarks are not applicable to spatio-temporal data.

Of relevance to moving objects, Theodoridis [11] provides a benchmark that includes a database description and 10 non-predictive queries for the static and moving spatial data. Myllymaki and Kaufman [12] also propose a benchmark, DynaMark, for moving objects. The query and update performance measure is CPU time, as a main-memory resident index is assumed. Future queries on anticipated future locations are not considered. Werstein [13] proposes a benchmark for 3-dimensional spatio-temporal data. The benchmark is oriented towards general operating system and database system performance comparison, including evaluation of the spatio-temporal and 3-dimensional capabilities. Tzouramanis et al. [14] perform an extensive, rigorous experimental comparison of four types of quadtree-based spatio-temporal indexes, using a benchmark specification when performing experiments with the four indexes. However, their proposal concerns raster data, generated with the G-TERD benchmark tool.

The concept of data uncertainty for moving object positions has previously been studied quite extensively (see, e.g., [15, 17, 18, 19]). While the bulk of this work has been conducted independently of indexing, some works (see, e.g., [16, 19]) offer insights into the indexing of uncertain positions. The present paper goes further by proposing a simple and yet effective method for storing and retrieving position data with accuracy guarantees. Existing indexes can straightforwardly be extended to accommodate such data.

Many authors of spatio-temporal indexes have compared their indexes to usually one other competitive index (e.g., [3, 4, 7, 8]). However, these comparisons tend to focus on exploring the properties of the new index being proposed; and with the new index being the main topic, the experimental specifications are relatively limited and lack independence.

The benchmarks covered above consider neither uncertain data nor accuracy guarantees. DynaMark shares similarities with COST benchmark with respect to the generated traffic data, but it lacks aspects to do with future positions. To the best of our knowledge, no independent benchmark exists that has been designed specifically for the evaluation of disk-based indexes for the current and near-future uncertain positions of moving objects.

3 Spatio-temporal Indexing

This paper is concerned with the indexing of large amounts of current and near-future, 2-dimensional moving object positions, and predictive queries are of interest. In this setting, position data are received from continuously moving objects capable of reporting their position and velocity. Mobile applications—e.g., those that provide location-enabled services to mobile users—issue queries on this data.

3.1 Spatio-temporal Data and Queries

The objects, represented as 2-dimensional points, update their positions periodically. As the server is recording the positions of a large amount of objects, updates should occur as rarely as possible. The current and anticipated future positions of the objects can be queried at any time. Therefore, continuous function that approximates the actual object movements and enables predictive queries is derived from the position data received.

An appropriate approximation function should satisfy the following requirements: (1) the parameters of the function can be obtained from the moving object; (2) the function reduces the amount of updates; (3) predicted positions are helpful in answering predictive queries; and (4) the function is easy to compute and its representation is compact.

It is common to predict an object's near-future position using a linear function of time [3, 4, 7, 8]. An object's position at time t is denoted by a 2-dimensional vector $\overrightarrow{P}$, and its velocity is given by a 2-dimensional vector $\overrightarrow{V}$. The function takes time as an argument, and returns the object's position:

$$\overrightarrow{P}(t) = \overrightarrow{P}(t_{\text{up}}) + \overrightarrow{V}(t_{\text{up}})(t - t_{\text{up}}) \tag{1}$$

Here t_{up} is the time of the last update, at which the object's position was $\overrightarrow{P}(t_{\text{up}})$; $\overrightarrow{V}(t_{\text{up}})$ is the velocity at time t_{up}, and $\overrightarrow{P}(t)$ is the predicted position at time t.

This function may be represented as a tuple $(\overrightarrow{P}(t_{\mathrm{ref}}), \overrightarrow{V}(t_{\mathrm{up}}))$, where time t_{ref} is an agreed upon, global reference time at which the object's position is stored. When an update of an object arrives at time t_{up}, its position $P(t_{\mathrm{ref}})$ at time t_{ref} is calculated using (1).

The linear function satisfies the four requirements for the approximation function. Velocity and position values are easy to obtain—they are output by GPS receivers [1], and the velocity can also be estimated based on previous positions (first requirement). The function's value is calculated in a constant time, and the representation is compact (fourth requirement). Studies show that using this function for vehicle positions, the average number of updates is reduced by more than a factor of two for accuracy thresholds below 200 meters, in comparison to the standard approach where the current position is assumed to be given by the most recently reported position [17] (second requirement). Finally, linear prediction offers better approximations of near-future positions than does constant prediction, yielding more reasonable answers to predictive queries (third requirement).

Three types of queries that a spatio-temporal index should support can be distinguished [3]. Let t, t_1, and t_2 be time points and let q_{r}, q_{r_1}, and q_{r_2} be 2-dimensional rectangles.

Q1. Timeslice query $Q1 = (q_{\mathrm{r}}, t)$ returns the objects that intersect with q_{r} at time t.

Q2. Window query $Q2 = (q_{\mathrm{r}}, t_1, t_2)$ returns objects that intersect with q_{r} at some time during time interval $[t_1, t_2]$. This query generalizes the timeslice query.

Q3. Moving window query $Q3 = (q_{\mathrm{r}_1}, q_{\mathrm{r}_2}, t_1, t_2)$ returns the objects that intersect, at some time during $[t_1, t_2]$, with the trapezoid obtained by connecting rectangles q_{r_1} and q_{r_2} at times t_1 and t_2, respectively. This query generalizes the window query.

Figure 1 offers an example encompassing four objects and three queries in 1-dimensional space. The *arrows* in the figure represent object movement.

The queries $q1$, $q2$, and $q3$ are timeslice, window, and moving window queries, respectively. Query $q3$ has spatial ranges $q3_{r_1} = [-20, -10]$, $q3_{r_2} = [-25, -10]$, and time range $[5, 6]$. The result of the query depends on when the query is issued. If issued before time $t = 3$, the result is $\{o1, o4\}$. Otherwise, the result is $\{o4\}$. Object $o1$ is updated at time 3 and its predicted trajectory changes. Its new trajectory does not intersect with the query.

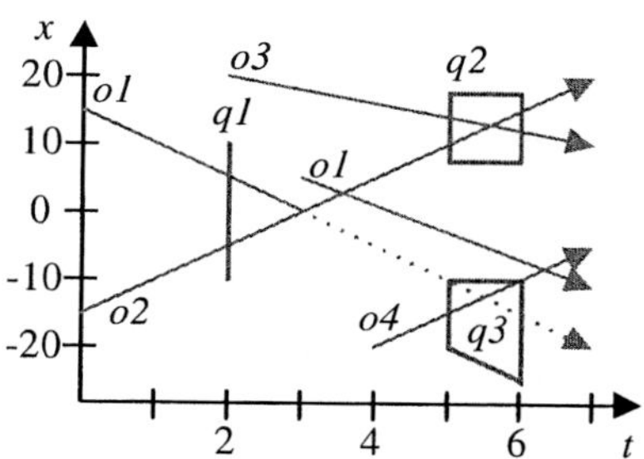

Fig. 1. Example of objects and queries in a 1-dimensional space

3.2 Update Policies

The inaccuracy of the moving object positions available at the server side stems from two sources. The positions measured by the moving objects (e.g., using GPS) are inaccurate, and the use of sampling introduces inaccuracy. Because the measurement inaccuracy is much smaller than the sampling inaccuracy in a typical setting, we assume that the measurements are accurate and focus on the inaccuracy due to sampling.

In particular, we assume an approach where, at any point in time, the actual position of an object deviates from the position assumed on the sever side, the predicted position, by no more than a chosen distance threshold thr. An update policy should be adopted that satisfies the accuracy guarantee with as few updates as possible.

The so-called *point-based* update policy requires an object to issue an update when the distance between the object's current and its most recently reported positions reaches the threshold value. With this policy, the server assumes that an object remains where it was when it most recently reported its position. Frequent updates result.

To reduce the cost of updates a *vector-based* policy may be adopted [17], where each moving object shares a linear prediction, as given by (1), of its position with the server. When the distance between an object's actual and predicted positions exceeds the distance threshold thr, the object issues an update to the server. The point-based policy is the special case of the vector-based policy, where the linear prediction function is constant ($\vec{V} = \vec{0}$, where $\vec{0}$ is the zero vector).

The point-based update policy is shown in Fig. 2 (a). Here, the position $\vec{P}(t_i)$ is updated at time t_i, and the actual position remains in the circle with center $\vec{P}(t_i)$ and radius thr for some time, yielding a predicted position of $\vec{P}(t_i)$. At time t_{i+1}, the difference between the actual and predicted positions reaches thr, and an update is issued.

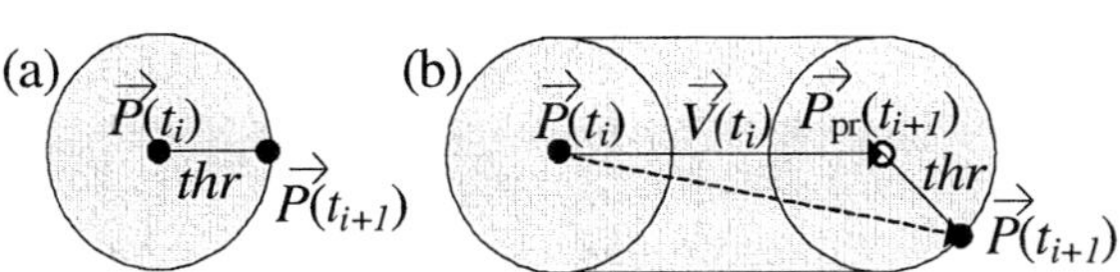

Fig. 2. Point-based (a) and vector-based (b) update policies with accuracy threshold *thr*

Next, the vector-based policy is illustrated in Fig. 2 (b). First, at time t_i, the object reports its actual position $\vec{P}(t_i)$ and velocity $\vec{V}(t_i)$ to the server. The server's prediction is illustrated by the *solid horizontal vector*. The object shares this prediction with the server. In addition, it repeatedly compares its actual position with the predicted position $\vec{P}_{\text{pr}}$. When at time t_{i+1}, the object's position is $\vec{P}(t_{i+1})$, the distance between the two positions is thr, and an update is generated. Updates are sent only when needed in order to maintain the accuracy guarantees.

As discussed in Sect. 3.1, the vector-based policy yields fewer updates than the point-based policy for the same accuracy guarantees and therefore is preferable.

3.3 Query and Data Enlargement

The notions of *precision* (p) and *recall* (r) [20] are commonly used for measuring the accuracy of a query result. The precision is the fraction of the objects in the result that actually satisfy the query predicate, and the recall is the fraction of the objects that satisfy the query predicate that are in the query result. Ideally, $p = r = 1$, meaning that the query result contains exactly the objects that satisfy the query.

However, the data are inaccurate—the positions of the objects are only known with accuracy thr. It is thus not possible to achieve $p = r = 1$; however, perfect recall can be achieved[1] and is a desirable requirement for an index. Thus, the query result is guaranteed to contain all objects that may satisfy the query predicate.

To achieve prefect recall, it is necessary to take the inaccuracy of the predicted positions into account. This may be done by means of either data or query enlargement.

Query enlargement addresses position inaccuracy by expanding the query area by thr in all directions. If different objects have different thresholds, the maximum threshold must be used. Perfect recall is achieved as all the objects that are actually in the query area have predicted positions that are no further than thr away from their actual positions.

The "fattened" query rectangle may be obtained as the Minkowski sum [21] of the two sets. Each point p_q that belongs to the query rectangle q_r is added to each point p_s that belongs to the segment s of length thr:

$$q_\mathrm{r} \oplus s = \{p_\mathrm{q} + p_\mathrm{s} | p_\mathrm{q} \in q_\mathrm{r} \wedge p_\mathrm{s} \in s\}$$

Figure 3 (a) shows query enlargement in a 2-dimensional space.

Next, with data enlargement object positions are expanded into spatial regions with extent. In particular, an object's position becomes a circle with radius thr, instead of being a point. The center of the circle is the predicted position. The object's actual position is always inside the circle. If the circle intersects with the query area, the object must be included in the query result. Figure 3 (b) illustrates data enlargement. The shaded area denotes the movement of the object.

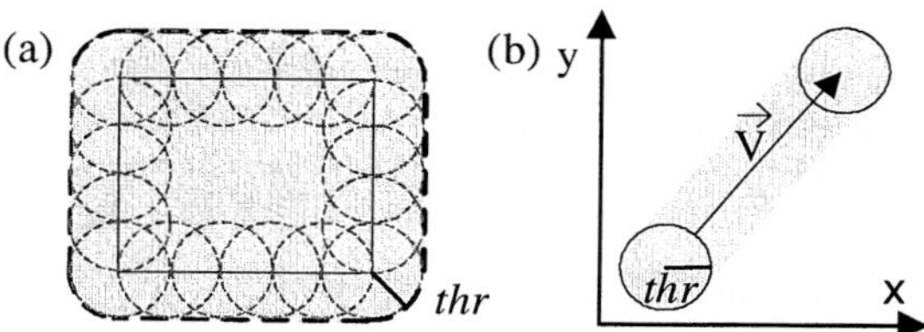

Fig. 3. Example of query (a) and data (b) enlargement

A spatio-temporal index should support either query or data enlargement. However, existing indexes tend to ignore position inaccuracy and simply assume that they know the exact position of each object, meaning that $thr = 0$. Such indexes must be adjusted to index positions with non-zero threshold values.

4 Benchmark Data and Settings

The workload for an index consists of a sequence of the updates and queries. The benchmark specification contains definitions of workloads and procedures of using them. The desired properties of the workloads and workload generation are discussed first. Definitions of benchmark procedures, termed *experiments*, then follow.

[1] We note that perfect recall for queries that concern future times is only possible when updates that occur between the time a query is issued and the future times specified in the query cannot affect the query result.

4.1 Workload Parameters

A set of update and query parameters defines the benchmark workloads. The workloads aim to simulate a wide range of situations in which an index may be used. The following parameters are of interest:

Number of Objects. The number of objects largely determines the size of the index and may be used to examine the scalability of the index.

Position and Velocity Skew. These parameters determine the distribution in space of the object positions and velocities. They are highly related, as velocity skew leads to position skew. An example of skew is the concentration of stationary vehicles in the suburbs at night and in business districts during working hours, and many moving vehicles during the morning and afternoon rush hours.

Update Arrival Pattern. The rate of updates depends on the chosen update policy as described in Sect. 3.2. With the vector-based policy, the durations in-between updates vary greatly. The update frequency depends on the movement trajectories and speeds of the objects. This parameter allows examination of how an index accommodates different frequencies of updates.

Position Accuracy Threshold. The distance threshold *thr* (defined in Sect. 3.2) affects the update arrival rate and the query or data extents. By varying this parameter, the index ability to support various update frequencies as well as data and query sizes can be studied.

Query Parameters. The required query types, their spatial and temporal extents and their time intervals are the query parameters of interest. The types of queries considered are described in Sect. 3.1.

Workload Duration. The workload duration is measured as a number of updates executed by the index. This parameter allows examination of how an amount of updates affects the performance of an index.

4.2 Workload Generator

The workloads in the COST benchmark are generated using a workload generator that extends the generator by Šaltenis et al. [22]. That generator was chosen as the starting point because it is capable of easily creating workloads according to many of the parameters discussed in Sect. 4.1 and because it is fast in comparison to such generators as CitySimulator [23, 24] and GSTD [25, 26], which use complex functions, e.g., functions that control the interactions among the objects. We proceed to explain the original generator, then describe the extensions implemented.

A workload intermixes queries and updates with a chosen proportion. An index is then subjected to these operations. In the generator, object movement is either random or network-based. To accommodate the latter, a number of "hubs" with random positions and links between these form a complete, bi-directional, spatial graph. Objects move between hubs until the end of a simulation. The maximum speed of an object is chosen randomly from a set of maximum speeds. An object accelerates and decelerates when moving from one hub to another. Updates are generated in average intervals of $UpdateInterval$ time durations. For any kind of data, these parameters can be set:

$Objects$. Total number of moving objects.
$Space$. The extent of the space where the objects are moving.
$Speed_i, i = 1, ..., 50$. Possible maximum speeds of the objects. For each object, its maximum speed is chosen at random.
$TotalUpdates$. The number of update operations performed in the simulation.
$UpdateInterval$. The average duration between two successive updates of an object.
$Hubs$. The number of destinations between which the objects are moving. Value 0 implies uniform (random) distribution.
$QuerySize$. The maximum spatial extent of a query in percentages of the indexed space.
$QueryTypes$. The fractions of timeslice, window, and moving window queries (see Sect. 3.1). The sum of the three fractions must add up to 1.
$QueryTime$. The maximum temporal extents of window and moving window queries.
$QueryWindow$. The maximum duration of time that queries may reach into the future.
$QueryingInterval$. Querying frequency relative to update operations.
$QueryQuantity$. The number of queries generated at each query generation event.

The generator was extended, enabling it to choose between its original update policy and the vector-based policy (as described in Sect. 3.2). The original policy was extended so that it is able to randomly select a different update interval for each object. Specifically, the generator was extended to accommodate three parameters:

$UpdatePolicy$. Either the shared prediction based vector policy (0) or the original time-based (1) policy is used.
$Threshold_i, i = 1, ..., 50$. The threshold distance between the predicted and the actual positions, used in the vector policy ($UpdatePolicy = 0$). Up to 50 thresholds may coexist. For each object, its threshold is chosen at random.
$UpdateInterval_i, i = 1, ..., 50$. The average duration between two successive updates of an object (as in the original generator). Up to 50 update intervals are possible. For each object, its average update interval is chosen at random. This parameter is used only when $UpdatePolicy = 1$.

With the vector-based update policy, updates are generated when the distance between the actual position of an object and the predicted position reaches $Threshold_i$. An additional update is generated when an object reaches a hub.

4.3 Evaluation Metrics

The COST benchmark uses two types of performance metrics: the average number of I/O operations per index operation, and the average CPU time per index operation (update, query). One I/O operation is one read of a page from disk to main memory or one write of a page to disk. Reads and writes from and to the available main memory buffer are not counted. The CPU time for one operation is the time of CPU usage from the moment when the operation is issued to the moment when the result of the operation is computed. I/O is typically considered to be the main cost factor in determining an index's performance, while the CPU time is a minor factor.

5 Definitions of Experiments

A benchmark experiment is defined by a set of workload parameters and disk page and main memory buffer size settings. In each experiment, one parameter, or a set of related parameters, as defined in Sect. 4.1, is varied. The set of experiments was chosen with the objective of varying the important workload parameters from Sect. 4.1. Parameter values are chosen so that the workloads cover a wide variety of situations. To ensure that the benchmark stress-tests the indexes under study, some experiments use extreme parameter values. The page and buffer size settings are kept constant for all experiments.

The default values for all workload parameters and settings are listed in Table 1. The chosen values are commonly used in existing evaluations of spatio-temporal indexes (e.g., [4, 8]). The default speeds are typical speeds of vehicles, and the number of hubs simulates a real-world road network with a substantial number of destinations. The page and buffer sizes are relatively small, the objective being to obtain the effects of large indexes with relatively small volumes of data. For each experiment, described shortly, only parameters with values that differ from the defaults are listed. Note that it is possible to use only a subset of parameters $Speed_i$, $Threshold_i$, and $UpdateInterval_i$, $i = 1, ..., 50$, e.g., it is possible to assign the same speed to all objects by setting $Speed_1$ and omitting parameters $Speed_i, i = 2, ..., 50$.

All experiments measure the average CPU time and number of I/O's per operation.

Table 1. Default workload parameters and settings used in experiments

Parameter	Value	Parameter	Value
$Page, Buffer$	1 KB, 50 KB (50 pages)	$QueryInterval$	400 updates
$Objects$	100 K	$QueryQuantity$	2 (in total 1000)
$Space$	$100,000 \times 100,000$ m^2	$QueryTime$	10 s
$Speed_i, i = 1, ..., 4$	12.5, 25, 37.5, 50 m/s	$QuerySize$	0.25% of $Space$
$TotalUpdates$	200 K	$QueryWindow$	50 s
$Hubs$	500	$QueryTypes$	0.6:0.2:0.2
$UpdatePolicy$	0	$Threshold_1$	100 m

Experiment 1. Number of Objects *Objective:* Examine index scalability.
Parameter values: $Points = 100, 200, ..., 1000$ K.
Number of workloads: 10.

Experiment 2. Position and Velocity Skew *Objective:* Examine the effects of position and velocity skew.
Parameter values: Part 1 (very high skew): $Hubs = 2, 4, ..., 20$. Part 2 (average skew): $Hubs = 20, 40, ..., 200$. Part 3 (low skew): $Hubs = 500, 1000, ..., 5000$, and 0 hubs (uniform distribution).
Number of workloads: 10 for parts 1 and 2, 11 for part 3.

Experiment 3. Maximum Speeds of Objects *Objective:* Examine the effects of varying maximum speeds as well as varying distributions of speeds among the objects. As fast objects are more likely to be updated than slow ones, the update frequency increases with increasing speeds.
Parameter values: Part 1 (distribution of speeds): All objects are assigned either speed 25 m/s or 200 m/s, and workloads are generated so that the fractions of objects with speed 200 m/s are: 0.02; 0.1; 0.2; 0.3; 0.4; 0.5; 0.6; 0.7; 0.8; 0.9; 0.98. Thus, all $Speed_i$ are assigned either 25 m/s or 200 m/s, and for each workload, the smallest i is chosen that allows us to obtain the needed fraction of fast objects. Part 2 (low maximum speeds): $Speed_1 = 0.05; 2; 4; 6; 8; 10; 12; 14; 16; 18$. Part 3 (high maximum speeds): $Speed_1 = 30, 60, ..., 300$ m/s.
Number of workloads: 11 for part 1, 10 for the parts 2 and 3.

Experiment 4. Position Accuracy Threshold *Objective:* Examine the influence of varying thresholds as well as the distribution of varying thresholds among the objects. Note that the update rate depends on the threshold and that the simulation time increases as updates become infrequent.
Parameter values: Part 1 (distribution of thresholds): All objects are assigned either a threshold of 100 m or a 1000 m, and workloads are generated so that the fractions of objects with speed 1000 m are : 0.02; 0.1; 0.2; 0.3; 0.4; 0.5; 0.6; 0.7; 0.8; 0.9; 0.98. Thus all $Threshold_i$ are assigned either 100 m or 1000 m, and for each workload the minimum i is chosen that allows us to obtain the needed fraction of objects with large (and small) threshold. Part 2 (equal thresholds for all objects): $Threshold_1 = 100, 200, ..., 1000$ m.
Number of workloads: 11 for part 1, 10 for part 2.

Experiment 5. Update Arrival Interval *Objective:* Examine the influence of varying update intervals as well as distribution of update intervals. The update frequency affects the time duration of a workload.
Parameter values: $UpdatePolicy = 1$. Part 1 (distribution of update intervals): Similarly to the two previous experiments, two values of a parameter, here $UpdateInterval_i$, are used—60 s (frequent) and 600 s (rare). The value of i is chosen so that workloads are obtained where the fractions of objects with an interval of 600 s are: 0.02; 0.1; 0.2; 0.3; 0.4; 0.5; 0.6; 0.7; 0.8; 0.9; 0.98. Part 2 (frequent updates): $UpdateInterval_1 = 20, 40, ..., 200$ s. Part 3 (rare updates): $UpdateInterval_1 = 120, 240, ..., 1200$ s.
Number of workloads: 11 for part 1, 10 for parts 2 and 3.

Experiment 6. Index Lifetime *Objective:* Examine the effect of varying index lifetime (in numbers of updates).
Parameter values: $TotalUpdates = 100, 200, ..., 1000$ K.
Number of workloads: 10.

Experiment 7. Query Types *Objective:* Examine the differences in performance for different types of queries: timeslice, window, and moving window queries.
Parameter values: $QueryTypes = 1:0:0, 0:1:0, 0:0:1$.
Number of workloads: 3.

Experiment 8. Query Parameters *Objective:* Examine the effects of varying spatial extents, temporal extents, and time windows of queries.

Parameter values: Part 1 (spatial extents): $QueryTypes = 0 : 1 : 0$, $QuerySize = 0.05, 0.15, ..., 0.95\%$. Part 2 (temporal extents): $QueryTypes = 0 : 1 : 0$, $QueryTime = 0, 20, ..., 120\,\text{s}$. Part 3 (time windows): $QueryTypes = 1 : 0 : 0$, $QueryWindow = 0, 20, ..., 120\,\text{s}$.
Number of workloads: 10 for part 1 and 7 for parts 2 and 3.

6 Application of the COST Benchmark

In order to ensure that the benchmark was well specified and yields useful results, it was applied for evaluating and comparing three existing indexes, namely the TPR-, TPR*-, and B^x-trees [3, 4, 8]. The TPR*- and B^x-trees were chosen because they are recent and represent the state of the art, and the TPR-tree is the predecessor of a dozen proposals for spatio-temporal indexes.

6.1 Introduction to the TPR-, TPR*-, and B^x-Trees

The TPR-tree (Time Parametrized R-tree) [3] and its descendant, the TPR*-tree [4], are based on the R*-tree [27]. These indexes are adapted for time-parametrized data and queries. Data objects are assigned to minimum bounding rectangles (MBRs) as in the R*-tree. Additionally, the TPR- and TPR*-trees use linear functions of time to represent the movements of the objects and MBRs.

Operations in the TPR-tree are handled similarly to the operations in the R*-tree, except that the penalty metrics of the R*-tree (e.g., MBR enlargement) are generalized to being integrals over a time period ranging from the current time and H time units into the future (calculated based on the update rate).

The authors of the TPR*-tree have modified the TPR-tree by introducing new insertion and deletion algorithms. An additional heap structure is used during insertions with the objective of achieving better insertions. Instead of the integral used in the TPR-tree, the TPR*-tree calculates penalty metrics based on sweeping regions (the area covered by a moving MBR from the current time and H time units into the future).

The B^x-tree uses the B^+-tree structure and algorithms to store and retrieve data. Spatial data are transformed into 1-dimensional data using space-filling curves.

The B^x-tree partitions the time axis into intervals with a duration equal to the maximum duration in-between two updates of any object. Each such interval is further partitioned into n phases. For each phase, an index partition is created, at most $n + 1$ partitions existing at a time. The partition in which to insert an object is chosen according to the object's insertion time. As time passes, partitions expire, and new partitions are created. Objects in an expiring partition are reinserted into the newest partition.

The index key of an object is calculated using the update time and position of the object that is stored at the reference time of object's partition. To achieve perfect recall (with the assumption that the accuracy threshold is 0), queries are expanded according to the maximum velocity of all objects and the query time. The objects that qualify for the query according to their velocities are selected; all other objects are filtered out.

For the experimental evaluation, the TPR- and TPR*-trees were extended to support data enlargement, and the B^x-tree was extended to support query enlargement. Enlarged data and query objects are approximated to squares and rectangles, respectively.

6.2 Experimental Evaluation Using the COST Benchmark

Implementations of the three indexes were obtained from their authors and modified where needed in order to perform the benchmark experiments. The indexes require a number of parameters to be set. For the B^{x}-tree, the maximum update interval is

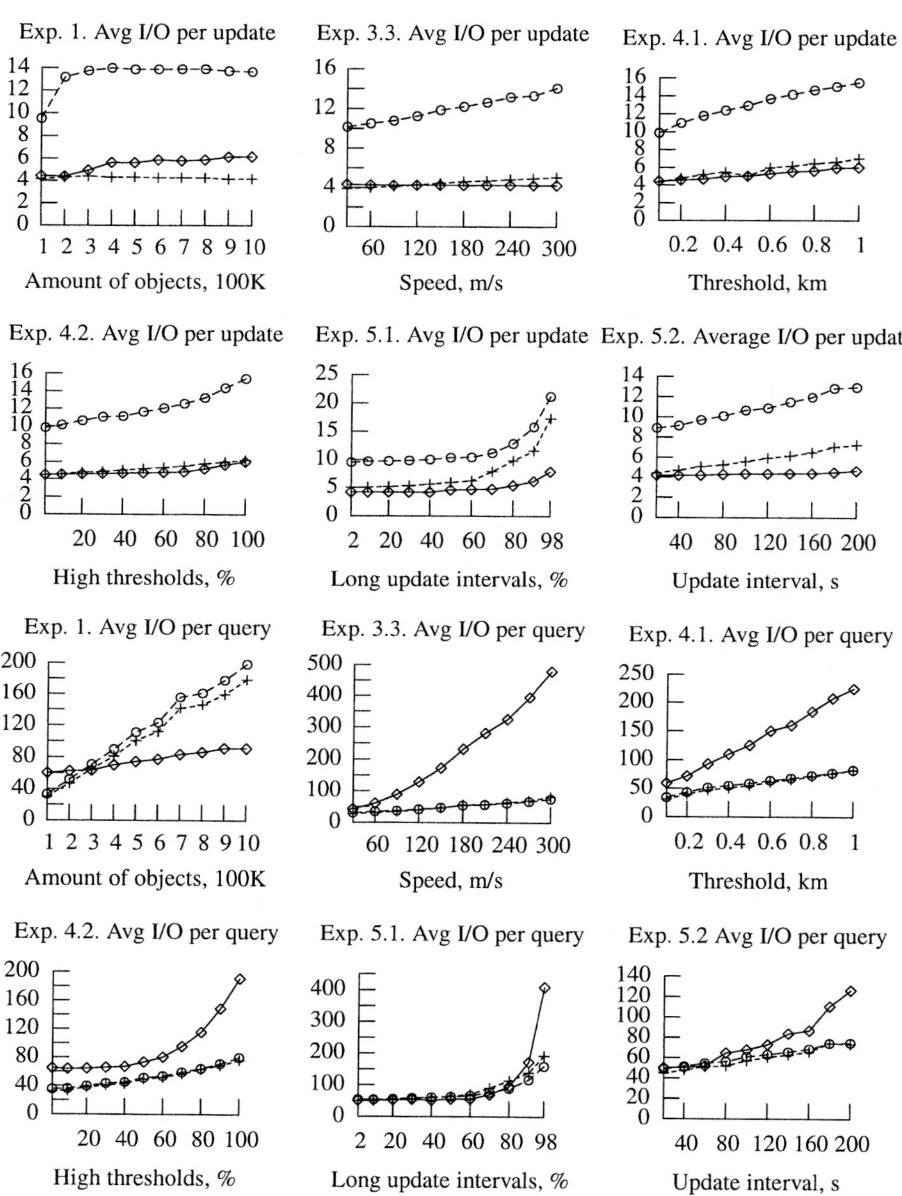

Fig. 4. Example experimental results obtained using the COST benchmark

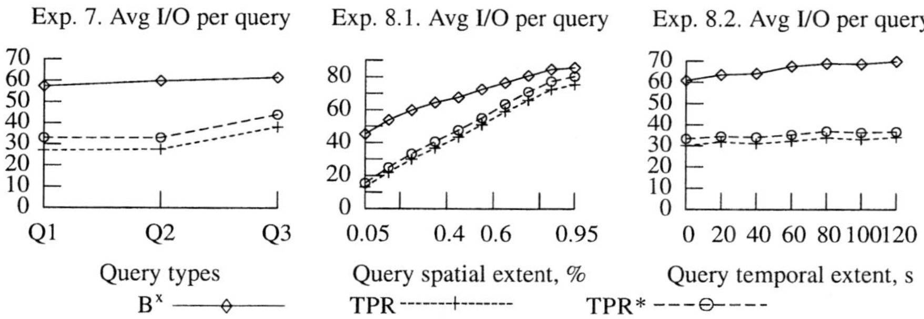

Fig. 5. An example of experimental results using the COST benchmark

120 s, there are 2 phases, the cell size is 100×100 m^2. For the TPR and TPR*-trees, $H = 120$ s.

Representative experimental results are provided in Fig. 4 and Fig. 5. The remaining results are omitted due to space limitations. The experimental results in Fig. 4 show that the indexes are sensitive to changing workloads. For example, high object speeds (more than 75 m/s, Exp. 3.3) or rare updates (less than once in 160 s on average, Exp. 5.1 and 5.2) significantly degrade the query I/O performance of the B^x-tree. However, the update performance of the B^x-tree tends to be more stable than for the TPR- and TPR*-trees (Exp. 3.3, 5.1, and 5.2). When the threshold increases, the query and update performances of the indexes degrade gradually (Exp. 4.1). However, when there is a high percentage of objects with large thresholds, the query performance of B^x-tree degrades significantly (Exp. 4.2). This is due to the resulting long update intervals and large query expansions (Exp. 5.1 and 5.2).

The TPR- and TPR*-trees exhibit inadequate query performance when the index size is large (in the benchmark experiments, above 600 K objects, Exp. 1). The B^x-tree scales well for both query and update performance (Exp. 1).

Experiments that concern query types are shown in Fig. 5. The indexes are largely insensitive to changing query types (Exp. 7). The B^x-tree has a higher overhead compared to the other indexes when query spatial extent is small, but query performance becomes similar for all indexes with larger queries (Exp. 8.1). Varying the temporal extent from 0 to 120 s has only a small effect on query performance (Exp. 8.2).

The experiments demonstrate that the benchmark fulfills its purpose: it has uncovered strengths and weaknesses of the indexes (only some of which were covered by the papers that introduced the indexes). For example, the experimental results identify situations in which the B^x-tree has lower query performance than the TPR-tree and that were not covered by the paper presenting the B^x-tree [8]. As another example, the benchmark shows that situations (not covered by the paper presenting the TPR*-tree [3]) exist where the TPR-tree outperforms the TPR*-tree for updates.

Summarizing the experimental results, the TPR-, TPR*-, and B^x-trees appear each to be the best choice in different situations, characterized by different workloads. The B^x-tree seems to be a good choice in situations with large numbers of objects, which degrade the performance of the TPR- and TPR*-trees. The B^x-tree also performs well when the maximum interval in-between the updates is known; the maximum position accuracy threshold is low; and the speeds of objects do not exceed the usual speeds of vehicles. In other cases, the TPR- or TPR*-trees, which most often exhibit very similar query performance, should be chosen. With extremely long update intervals, the TPR*-tree might be preferable over the TPR-tree.

The TPR- and TPR*-trees appear to be the most versatile indexes; however, the B^x-tree is based on the B^+-tree; which is already available in many DBMSs. Therefore, a creation of a more robust version of the B^x-tree may be promising direction for research.

7 Conclusions and Future Work

A number of indexes for the current and near-future positions of moving objects exist, and more are underway. This state of affairs creates an increasing need for a neutral and well-articulated experimental setting for evaluating and comparing these indexes.

This paper proposes a benchmark, termed COST, that is targeted specifically toward the evaluation of such indexes. The benchmark aims to make realistic assumptions about the experimental settings—data is inherently inaccurate, predictive queries that reach into the future are covered, the indexes are assumed to be stored persistently on disk. More specifically, an update technique is assumed where positions are guaranteed to be accurate within agreed-upon thresholds and where updates occur only when necessary in order to satisfy the guarantees. The indexes may use either query or data enlargement to account for the inaccurate data. The benchmark includes a workload generator, definitions of experiments, and evaluation metrics. It considers a wide range of workload parameters that cover many real-world situations.

As proof of concept and to evaluate the benchmark, it was applied to the TPR-, TPR*-, and B^x-trees. The experiment demonstrates that the benchmark is well-specified and is capable of covering a wide range of situations. Weaknesses and strengths of the indexes were detected by examining the sensitivity of the indexes to workloads with varying parameter values, including workloads with extreme settings. The experimental results cover situations that were not covered in the papers that introduced the indexes, due to more extensive experiments. The obtained results provide guidance as to when each of the indexes should and should not be used.

The benchmark may be extended by inclusion of such aspects as index size in disk pages, CPU time and numbers of I/O for bulkloading and bulk operations, and evaluation of concurrent accesses. Further studies of existing spatio-temporal indexes are also warranted, possibly including detailed studies of special cases and aspects specific to individual indexes. Examples include detailed studies of overlaps among MBRs, growth rates of MBRs, and the grouping of objects into MBRs in R-tree-based indexes. For the B^x-tree, such studies may cover query enlargement aspects and migration loads. For all indexes, it is of interest to investigate aspects such as tree depths and node fanouts. Studies such as these have the potential to offer insights that may guide the development of improved indexes.

Acknowledgments. This research was conducted within the project Telematics Applications Based on Ubiquitous Sensor Networks, funded by the Electronics and Telecommunications Research Institute, South Korea. C. S. Jensen is also an adjunct professor in Department of Technology, Agder University College, Norway.

References

1. Blewitt, G.: Basics of the GPS technique: observation equations. Geodetic Applications of GPS (1997) 10–54
2. Wikipedia: GPRS (2001–2005) http://en.wikipedia.org/wiki/GPRS.
3. Šaltenis, S., Jensen, C.S., Leutenegger, S.T., Lopez, M.A.: Indexing the positions of continuously moving objects. In: Proc. ACM SIGMOD. (2000) 331–342
4. Tao, Y., Papadias, D., Sun, J.: The TPR*-tree: an optimized spatio-temporal access method for predictive queries. In: Proc. VLDB. (2003) 790–801
5. Procopiuc, C.M., Agarwal, P.K., Har-Peled, S.: STAR-tree: an efficient self-adjusting index for moving objects. In: Revised Papers from the 4th International Workshop on Algorithm Engineering and Experiments. (2002) 178–193
6. Šaltenis, S., Jensen, C.S.: Indexing of Moving Objects for Location-Based Services. In: Proc. ICDE. (2002) 463–472
7. Patel, J.M., Arbor, A., Chen, Y., Chakka, V.P.: STRIPES: an efficient index for predicted trajectories. In: Proc. ACM SIGMOD. (2004) 635–646
8. Jensen, C.S., Lin, D., Ooi, B.C.: Query and update efficient B+-tree based indexing of moving objects. In: Proc. VLDB. (2004) 768–779
9. Zobel, J., Moffat, A., Ramamohanarao, K.: Guidelines for presentation and comparison of indexing techniques. SIGMOD Rec. **25** (1996) 10–15
10. Gray, J., ed.: The Benchmark Handbook for Database and Transaction Processing Systems. Morgan Kaufmann Publishers, Inc. (1993)
11. Theodoridis, Y.: Ten benchmark database queries for location-based services. The Computer Journal **46** (2003) 713–725
12. Myllymaki, J., Kaufman, J.: DynaMark: A Benchmark for Dynamic Spatial Indexing. In: Proc. MDM. (2003) 92–105
13. Werstein, P.F.: A performance benchmark for spatiotemporal databases. In: Proc. of the 10th Annual Colloquium of the Spatial Information Research Centre. (1998) 365–373
14. Tzouramanis, T., Vassilakopoulos, M., Manolopoulos, Y.: Benchmarking access methods for time-evolving regional data. Data Knowl. Eng. **49** (2004) 243–286
15. Cheng, R., Kalashnikov, D.V., Prabhakar, S.: Querying imprecise data in moving object environments. IEEE Trans. on Knowl. and Data Eng. **16** (2004) 1112–1127
16. Tao, Y., Cheng, R., Xiao, X., Ngai, W.K., Kao, B., Prabhakar, S.: Indexing multi-dimensional uncertain data with arbitrary probability density functions. In: Proc. VLDB. (2005) 922–933
17. Čivilis, A., Jensen, C.S., J. Nenortaitė, J., Pakalnis, S.: Efficient tracking of moving objects with precision guarantees. In: Proc. MobiQuitous. (2004) 164–173
18. Wolfson, O., Sistla, A.P., Chamberlain, S., Yesha, Y.: Updating and querying databases that track mobile units. Distrib. Parallel Databases **7** (1999) 257–387
19. Pfoser, D., Jensen, C.S.: Capturing the uncertainty of moving-object representations. In: Proc. SSD. (1999) 111–132
20. Lazaridis, I., Mehrotra, S.: Approximate selection queries over imprecise data. In: Proc. ICDE. (2004) 140–152
21. Weisstein, E.W.: Minkowski sum. From MathWorld—A Wolfram web resource (1999–2005) http://mathworld.wolfram.com/MinkowskiSum.html.
22. Šaltenis, S., Jensen, C.S., Leutenegger, S., Lopez, M.: Indexing the positions of continuously moving objects. Technical report, Aalborg University (November 1999)
23. Kaufman, J., Myllymaki, J., Jackson, J.: CitySimulator (2001) https://secure.alphaworks.ibm.com/aw.nsf/techs/citysimulator.
24. Myllymaki, J., Kaufman, J.: LOCUS: A testbed for dynamic spatial indexing. IEEE Data Eng. Bull. (Special Issue on Indexing of Moving Objects). **25** (2002) 48–55

25. Theodoridis, Y., Nascimento, M.A.: Generating spatiotemporal datasets on the WWW. SIGMOD Rec. **29** (2000) 39–43
26. Theodoridis, Y., Silva, J.R.O., Nascimento, M.A.: On the generation of spatiotemporal datasets. In: Proc. of the 6th International Symposium on Advances in Spatial Databases. (1999) 147–164
27. Beckmann, N., Kriegel, H.P., Schneider, R., Seeger, B.: The R*-tree: an efficient and robust access method for points and rectangles. In: Proc. SIGMOD. (1990) 322–331

Efficient Maintenance of Ephemeral Data

Albrecht Schmidt and Christian S. Jensen

Department of Computer Science, Aalborg University, Denmark
{al, csj}@cs.aau.dk

Abstract. Motivated by the increasing prominence of loosely-coupled systems, such as mobile and sensor networks, the characteristics of which include intermittent connectivity and volatile data, we study the tagging of data with so-called *expiration times*. More specifically, when data are inserted into a database, they may be stamped with time values indicating when they expire, i.e. when they are regarded as stale or invalid and thus are no longer considered part of the database. In a number of applications, expiration times are known and can be assigned at insertion time. We present data structures and algorithms for online management of data stamped with expiration times. The algorithms are based on fully functional treaps, which are a combination of binary search trees with respect to a primary attribute and heaps with respect to a secondary attribute. The primary attribute implements primary keys, and the secondary attribute stores expiration times in a minimum heap, thus keeping a priority queue of tuples to expire. A detailed and comprehensive experimental study demonstrates the well-behavedness and scalability of the approach as well as its efficiency with respect to a number of competitors.

1 Introduction

We explore aspects of implementing an extension to Codd's relational data model [5] where each tuple in a relation is timestamped with an *expiration time*. By looking at a tuple's timestamp, it is possible to see when the tuple ceases to be part of the current state of the database. Specifically, assume that, when a tuple r is inserted into the database, it is stamped with an *expiration time*, $t^{\text{exp}}(r)$. Tuple r is thus considered part of the current state of the database from the time of insertion until $t^{\text{exp}}(r)$. Expiration-time semantics now ensures that operations, most prominently queries, do not see tuples that have expired by the time associated with a query. Our study is motivated by the emergence and increasing prominence of data management applications which involve data for which the expiration time is known at the time of insertion, updates are frequent, and the connectivity of the data sources that issue the updates is intermittent. Applications which involve mobile networks, sensor networks, and the Internet generally qualify as examples.

Data produced by sensors that measure continuous processes are often short-lived. Consider a sensor network of temperature sensors that monitor a road network. It may be assumed that a temperature measurement is valid for at most a fixed number of minutes after it is measured, or the duration of validity may be determined by more advanced computations in the sensor network. A central database receives temperature measurements stamped with expiration times. A measurement from a sensor then automatically disappears if the sensor does not issue a new temperature measurement before

M.L. Lee, K.L. Tan, and V. Wuwongse (Eds.): DASFAA 2006, LNCS 3882, pp. 141–155, 2006.

the old measurement expires. While a temperature sensor network may be relatively static in nature, mobile devices that frequently log on to and log off from access points form a more dynamic network. In such a context, it is natural to tag records that capture log-ons with expiration times so that a session can be invalidated by the server after a period of inactivity. Closely related examples are cookies and session keys used where only stateless protocols like HTTP [20] are used for communication. Similarly, availability tactics like *heartbeats* [3], where devices periodically emit (heartbeat) messages to indicate that they are still online, go together with expiration times in a natural way. For a more detailed discussion about the role of expiration times in query processing see [17].

By adding the notion of expiration time to a database management system (DBMS), designers can help simplify software architectures and reduce code complexity while retaining transparent semantics. A user of an expiration time-enabled SQL engine needs not be aware of the new concept, as expiration time ∞ can be assumed for tuples for which no expiration time is provided explicitly. A further benefit of the integration of expiration times into a DBMS is that the number, and thus cost, of transactions especially in distributed systems can often be reduced significantly because no explicit delete statements to 'clean-up' previous transactions need be issued; since transaction costs in these settings are often an important bottleneck, overall system performance can increase significantly.

The *contributions of this paper* are as follows. (1) Motivated by the ubiquity of loosely-coupled distributed systems with unstable connections such as mobile and sensor networks, we argue that DBMS support for expiration time benefits applications, as pointed out above. (2) The main technical contribution of this paper are online main-memory algorithms and data structures that are capable of handling data expiration efficiently on a variety of devices; this implies that expired data are automatically removed as early as possible from the database without the need for user interaction. (3) A comprehensive experimental study offers insight into resource consumption and other performance characteristics such as scaling behaviour, response times, and throughput.

The remainder of the paper is structured as follows. The next section briefly outlines the assumed (simple) extension to the relational model and discusses functional treaps from an algorithmic point of view. Section 3 presents the results of a comprehensive evaluation of the performance characteristics of treaps and a comparative study of the performance of treaps with respect to various competing data structures; it also covers a variety of functional issues in relation to expiration times and the use of treaps. After a review of related work, the final section concludes the paper and identifies promising directions for future research.

2 Treaps in Detail

2.1 Setting

We assume the following basic setting for our research: data sources emit tuples stamped with expiration times. A relational view of these sources is provided, where only current, i.e. unexpired, tuples are exposed to queries. Thus, expiration times can be seen as a database-internal function t^{exp} : *tuples* $\rightarrow$ *timestamps* from tuples to timestamps. Assuming that a database $db^{\exp}$ of tuples with expiration times is given and that the time associated with a query q is given by τ_q, then the tuples seen by q are: $\{r \mid r \in db^{\exp} \wedge t^{\exp}(r) > \tau_q\}$. It is a fundamental decision to associate expiration times with tuples. Arguably, they could be associated with other constituents of the relational model, including individual attribute values, attributes or other schema elements. This design decision is motivated by a desire for clear semantics, simplicity, and practicality [17, 18].

2.2 Overview

A treap is a combination of a tree and a heap: with respect to a (primary) key attribute, it is a binary search tree; with respect to a second, non-key attribute, it is a heap. The idea we elaborate on in the remainder of this paper is to use the key attribute for indexing while managing expiration times using the second non-key attribute.

We use the term *(fully) functional* [16] for a data structure if an update of the data structure produces a new version, both physically and logically, without altering the original. Functional data structures enable concurrent access through versioning [4]. In particular, by using a functional treap then, as long as only one thread updates the treap (like any other fully functional data structure), concurrent (read) access can be implemented with a minimum of locking, which is desirable in a main-memory environment.

```
class Node;
class Inner extends < k, t, v > Node {
  left child: Node;
  key: k;
  expiration: t;
  data: v
  right child: Node;
} /* Instantiate with: Inner(l_c, k, t, c, r_c) */
class Leaf extends Node {};
  /* Instantiate with: Leaf */
```

Fig. 1. Treap node data type

The structure of a treap node is shown in Fig. 1. The layout of the tree is binary: each node has a left and a right child, a key, and an expiration time; it also has a value field, which may contain arbitrary data such as non-key attributes.

2.3 Example

We proceed to exemplify how functional treaps can be used to support expiration times efficiently. Focus lies on eager removal of expired data.

Figure 2 shows the construction of a treap given the following sequence of (key, expiration time) pairs to be inserted: $(1, 7), (2, 6), (3, 6), (4, 0), (5, 7), (6, 6), (7, 8)$. A pair (key, time) denotes a tuple with key 'key' and associated expiration time 'time'. Note that, for the time being, we assume that the key and the expiration time are statistically independent; in [18], we discuss in more detail what happens when we do not make this assumption; we now just remark that we can use a hash function on the key to achieve independence. The last step in Fig. 2 consists of removing the root node from the treap, i.e. carrying out an expiration, for example at time 1. The algorithms that do the actual work are discussed in the sequel.

Before presenting algorithms, however, we have a quick look at the notation used in this paper. First, the functional nature is reflected in the code by the absence of

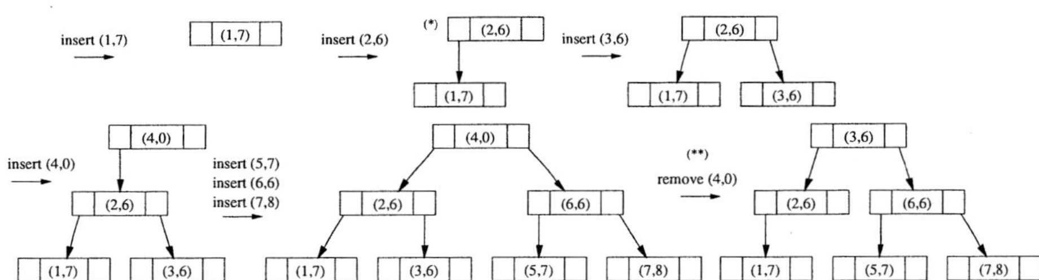

Fig. 2. Example treap

the assignment operator and, instead, the allocation of new objects with the **new** keyword whenever an update is performed. The function **new** t $(a_1, a_2, \ldots, a_n)$ allocates a new object of type t and initialises it by calling the respective constructor with the arguments $a_1, a_2, \ldots, a_n$. Second, extensive use of ML or Scala-style *pattern matching* [15] is made to bind parts of complex, nested data structures to variables in a concise manner avoiding combinations of nested if-statements. For example, assuming the class definitions of Fig. 1, using the second treap in the first row of Fig. 2 (marked (*)) and the find function of Fig. 3 then the first clause of Fig. 3 is executed as follows. Assume we want to find the node with the key 1, i.e. we call 'find $(treap, 1)$' where *treap* is bound (using the constructor notation) to 'Inner (Inner (Leaf, 1, 7, ⊥, Leaf), 2, 6, ⊥, Leaf)'. If we match against it the pattern 'Inner (_, k, _, item, _) **when** (key $= k$)' (line 3, Fig. 3), the following variable bindings are created: $k = 2$, item $= \perp$ ($\perp$ denotes a non-applicable variable in our case, i.e. we do not use the data field in this example). The underscore '_' in a constructor denotes a 'don't care' variable that is present in the class, but for which no binding is created. Since k is bound to 2 and the function argument key to 1, the **when** clause evaluates to false and the pattern does not match. However, the pattern in line 4 matches, and the following bindings are created: left $=$ Inner (Leaf, 1, 7, ⊥, Leaf), right $=$ Leaf, and $k = 2$. Since the **if** statement evaluates to true, function find is called recursively and terminates successfully.

```
1 function find (node, key) =
2   match node with
3   | Inner (_, k, _, item, _) when (key = k) → item
4   | Inner (left, k, _, _, right) →
5     if (key < k)
6     then find (left, key)
7     else find (right, key)
8   | Leaf → raise exception (Key is not in treap)
```

Fig. 3. Lookup of a primary key

If a treap is well-balanced, i.e. structurally similar to a height-balanced binary tree, it is guaranteed that we can execute look-up queries in logarithmic time. Treaps being also heaps implies that nodes with minimal expiration times cluster at the treap root. If the root node has expired, i.e. its expiration timestamp e is smaller than the current time, we can simply remove it.This is advantageous because we can keep the amount of stale data to a minimum using an eager deletion policy: as long as the root node is stale we remove it. Since stale data cluster at the root, no search is required. Furthermore, this strategy has the advantage that we essentially only need one procedure for both expiration and deletion: indeed, expiration is implemented as a small wrapper.

2.4 Operations on Treaps

This section introduces the most important operations on treaps. Since we are not aware of any other work that presents algorithms for the functional variant of treaps, we describe the operations in some detail.

Maintaining Balance. Like many other balanced tree structures, the insert and delete functions of treaps maintain balance through order-preserving node rotations. The insert function only rotates nodes on the path from a leaf, namely the newly inserted node, to the root. The delete function uses rotations to move an interior node to the leaf level without violating the order of the tree. Due to the functional nature of our kind of treap, rotations during inserts and deletes are implemented by slightly different code: for insertion (Fig. 4), the local function that implements the rotations is called *rebalance* (see second line in figure). We remark that it is the way the treap is rebalanced that destroys locality and makes it hard to adapt treaps to paginated secondary memory data structures.

Insertion. Insertion is a two-stage process. First, we insert a pair (key, time) as if the treap was a functional binary tree on key. We then execute rotations to re-establish the heap property (while retaining the binary tree property), which may have been violated. Insertion works as displayed in Fig. 4; it illustrated in several places in Fig. 2.

```
function insert (tree, key, time, item) =
  local function rebalance (node) =
    match node with
    | Inner(Inner(s1, u, t', i', s2), v, t, i, s3) when (t > t') →
      new Inner(s1, u, t', i', new Inner(s2, v, t, i, s3))
    | Inner(s1, u, t, i, Inner(s2, v, t', i', s3)) when (t > t') →
      new Inner(new Inner(s1, u, t, i, s2), v, t', i', s3)
    | _ → node;
  match tree with
  | Inner(_, k, _, _, _) when (key = k) → tree
  | Inner(left, k, t, i, right) →
    if (key < k)
    then rebalance (new Inner(insert(left, key, time, item), k, t, i, right))
    else rebalance (new Inner(left, k, t, i, insert(right, key, time, item)))
  | Leaf → new Inner(Leaf, key, time, item, Leaf)
```

Fig. 4. Insertion into treaps

The second phase allocates new memory as it re-establishes the heap property. This fact and because the function runs through the tree twice (top to bottom for insertion and bottom to top for rebalancing) may seem to make insertion a comparatively expensive operation; however, since the first phase already populates the CPU caches with the nodes needed in the second phase, the overhead is not too large. The performance figure later in this paper quantify the cost of insertion relative to expiration. The amortised cost of insertion is $O(\log n)$ time where n is the number of elements stored in the treap [19]. Additionally, each insertion also allocates $O(\log n)$ memory by producing a new version of the data structure; however, since we use node-copying [4] to implement concurrency rather than provide access to historical versions of the data, memory management automatically reclaims $O(\log n)$ memory per insertion once it is not used by other threads anymore. Thus, for single-threaded applications the overall memory requirements per insertion are not higher than for conventional treaps. In the case of multi-threaded applications, old treap versions are reclaimed as soon the owning thread terminates. For practical workloads, this usually implies that algorithms does not incur a memory overhead.

Removal and Expiration. Like insertion, removal is a two-stage process [18]. The first step consists of locating the node that contains a given key. The second step includes executing rotations so that the node sifts down and eventually becomes a leaf. After this has happened, it is simply discarded. Removal of a key is also exemplified in Fig. 2 (marked (**) in Fig. 2). Like insertion, it is purely functional. By repeatedly calling the deletion function as long as the root node is expired, we can eagerly remove all stale data from the treap. Since the removal algorithm returns a new version of the treap just like insert, the discussion of resource requirements is similar to the discussion of insertion.

Other Operations. Depending on the area of application, other operations on treaps make sense as well. For example, we can use full traversals of a treap to create snapshots of the current state of the database for statistics, billing, etc. Furthermore, if the less-than relationship between keys returns sensible values, range queries on keys can be used to quickly extract ordered intervals from the indexed keys. These operations are implemented exactly as for binary trees, so no code is provided here. However, a performance evaluation of full traversals is presented in the next section.

Concurrency Issues. The tactics used to achieve concurrency is *versioning* [4], implemented by the node-copying method [7]. This implies that each modification to the data structure produces a new version; the previous version can be then garbage-collected once all pointers to it become stale. Therefore, treaps are not ever-growing data structures since only, besides the most recent version, only versions currently in use are kept in memory. Thus, only one thread is allowed to update the data structure, but any number of threads can read from it. As pointed out earlier, this type of design pattern can be implemented in a nearly locking-free manner and provides for concurrent operations at the cost of increased memory allocation and deallocation but not increased overall memory usage. Modern generational garbage collectors [6] are optimised for this kind of allocation pattern and provide favourable performance. Despite the increased memory allocation and deallocation activity the overall storage requirements are asymptotically not higher than traditional single-version implementation (assuming a 'standard' database setting with a finite number of threads all of which feature finite running times).

3 Experiments and Evaluation

This section reports on empirical studies of the performance of treaps. We take the following approach: First, we present the formal framework of our evaluation which

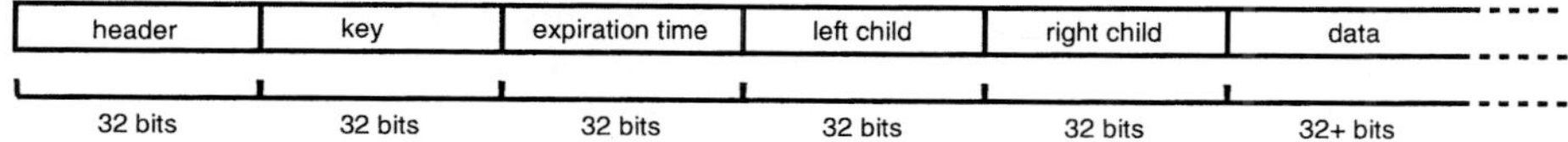

Fig. 5. Physical layout of an internal treap node

allows to reproduce results. Then we examine the performance of treaps for a diverse range of workloads. Lastly, we compare treaps to a number of competitors, including Red-Black trees and AVL trees.

3.1 Experimental Setup

The experiments were carried out on a PC running Gentoo Linux on an Intel Pentium IV processor at 1.5 GHz featuring 512 MB of main memory available; no hard disk was used during the experiments. The CPU caches comprise 8 KB at level 1 and 512 KB at level 2. The compiler used was gcc/g++ 3.2. The performance data from which the graphs displayed in this section were gathered from experiments lasting over 42 hours of runtime on a single machine. Figure 5 displays the physical layout of an internal treap node in our implementation. We fixed the size of the data field to 32 bits for our experiments. All relevant data are inlined, so to access a key or expiration time, we do not have follow a pointer, but we can read it locally in the record. This has been done mainly to improve cache utilisation [1]; in general, however, the data field may contain a pointer to non-local data. In order to explore the full potential and the limitations of treaps, we generated synthetic data to get the data volume needed to test the behaviour of treaps in the limit. The sensor and network hardware available to us are unable to deliver the data volumes necessary to determine the performance limitations of the data structure. Figure 6 plots counts of tuples across time and exemplifies a workload we used.

The dashed line indicates the numbers of tuples that arrive at each particular point in time. For example, the peak at approx. 20,000 milliseconds denotes that 4,000 tuples arrive during the respective interval and have to be inserted into the treap. Without support for expiration time, the network traffic would approximately double, and each spike indicating the arrival of new data would be followed by a spike indicating the deletion of the very data comprising the first spike (assuming that all data expire a fixed duration after their insertion).

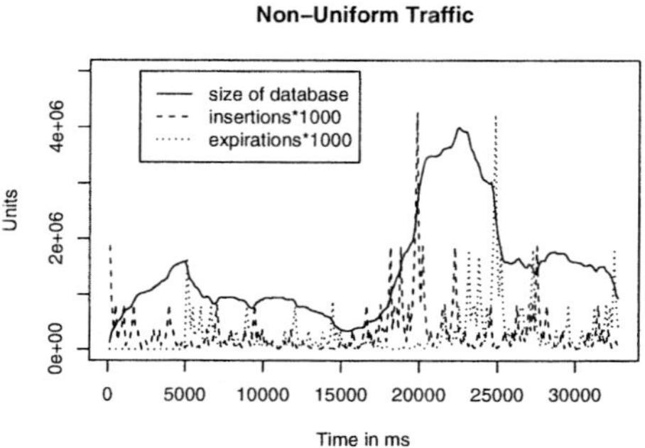

Fig. 6. Database size and operation for non-uniform traffic

We use the B-Model data generator proposed by Wang et al. [22], which is well suited for our purposes. This generator is capable of generating workloads while consuming only a fraction of available system resources. Thus, it provides enough performance not to flaw results. To make it fit our purposes, we extend the generator to work with four input parameters rather than the original three parameters. The three original parameters, b, l, and N, are the bias, the aggregation level, and the total volume, respectively; we refer to this model as $\mathrm{BModel}(b, l, N)$. The bias b describes the roughness of the traffic, i.e. how irregular it is and how pronounced the peaks are. The aggregation level l measures the resolution at which we observe the traffic. The parameter N equals the sum of all measurements and specifies the total amount of traffic. The new, fourth parameter is a random variable describing the distribution of the expiration times of arriving network traffic, i.e. the time interval we consider the $\mathrm{BModel}(b, l, N)$ arriving items valid.

To get an impression of both maximum throughput and response to extremely bursty traffic, we divided our experiments into two parts. We first consider uniform traffic, i.e. $\mathrm{BModel}(0.5, l, N)$. This is done to capture how treaps respond to continuous high workloads. Since the versioning semantics call for frequent allocations of memory, we can expect efficient memory management to be a key factor. Next, we consider $\mathrm{BModel}(b, l, N)$, $b \in]0.5, 1.0[$, i.e. bursty traffic. This is done to estimate how well treaps act under workloads with more or less pronounced peaks. In these settings, minimum and maximum throughput are of interest. Examining treaps in this context is a first step towards the consideration of stochastic quality-of-service guarantees. For experiments which try to illustrate scaling behaviour, N is the parameter used to generate databases of different size. However, when we talk about the size of a database, e.g. about 4 M tuples in Fig. 7(a), we mean the average number of unexpired tuples residing in the database, potentially after some bootstrap.

3.2 Discussion of Treap Performance

We now turn our attention to Figs. 7(a) through 8(b), which describe the performance of the data structure under different stress patterns and for different workloads. We first investigate the performance of updates; then we turn our attention to querying.

Insertions and Expirations. We first examine the behaviour of treaps under a uniform workload with insertions into a four million tuple database, i.e. after an initial bulk load, the database consists of four million tuples on average, with insertions and expirations basically cancelling out each other.

Figure 7(a) shows the throughput for such a setting. The conspicuous peaks are mainly due to comparatively cheap memory allocation cost after major garbage collections. Notice that the dotted line representing expiration remains, once expirations set in, above the dashed line representing insertions; thus, expirations are cheaper than insertions for large databases. This reflects the structure of the insertion algorithm, requiring to traversal from the root to a leaf and back. On the other hand, expiring the root only requires sifting the node to the leaf level before discarding it. Thus, expirations also require fewer memory allocations than insertions.

Since treaps only guarantee amortised performance, it is also interesting to learn to what degree the costs of the individual operations differ. Due to the high throughput, which may exceed 100,000 operations per second on our platform, is very hard to monitor the cost of an atomic operation without influencing the result to a degree that

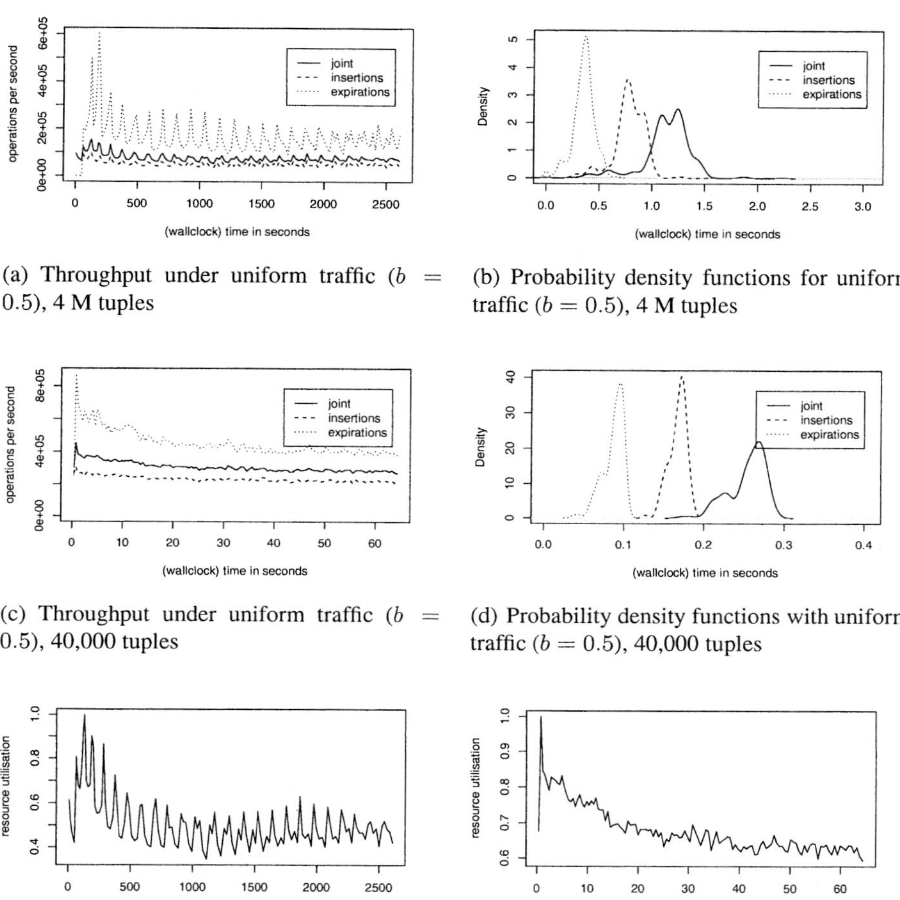

(a) Throughput under uniform traffic ($b = 0.5$), 4 M tuples

(b) Probability density functions for uniform traffic ($b = 0.5$), 4 M tuples

(c) Throughput under uniform traffic ($b = 0.5$), 40,000 tuples

(d) Probability density functions with uniform traffic ($b = 0.5$), 40,000 tuples

(e) Resource utilisation for run displayed in Fig. 7(a)

(f) Resource utilisation for run displayed in Fig. 7(c)

Fig. 7. Performance impressions, resource consumption, and peak performance

renders it unusable. Therefore, we move to a higher level of aggregation and consider the lengths of intervals containing a fixed number of insertions and expirations. This number was fixed to 80,000 for the experiments. While this rather large number theoretically may obscure the variance in the costs of individual operations, we did not experience this problem and found it a good trade-off between unobtrusiveness and intuition.

In Fig. 7(b), the Probability Density Function (PDF) of such an analysis displayed. We note that the local maximum of the solid line representing expirations at 0.0 indicates that the system wants to expire data, but there is no stale data present. This results in an operation with nearly zero cost. Figure 7(b) also shows that expirations are cheaper than insertions by a factor of approx. two and that the overall cost of a joint operation, insertions and expirations combined, is reasonable. Disregarding the phantom expirations of nearly-zero cost, one can assume that the execution time of 80,000 insertions lies between about 1.0 and 1.4 seconds. This suggests that treaps behave reliably and predictably in practical settings.

To provide some evidence that the performance peaks in Fig. 7(a) are indeed memory management-related, we concentrate on the results reported in Fig. 7(c). This time, the database contains 40,000 tuples on average. Now, the local maxima in the graph are noticeably less pronounced than in the large database. It turns out that because of the small size, major re-organisations of the storage space can be avoided, keeping the cost of individual memory allocations on about the same level. This is also reflected in the PDF displayed in Fig. 7(d). The bandwidths of insertions, expirations, and of the joint PDF are smaller in both absolute and relative terms. Figure 7(e) and 7(f) concern resource utilisation. It can be seen that most of the time, the treap is able to insert data at about half the maximum possible rate and that memory management causes some pronounced spikes. Again, for smaller databases the spikes remain less pronounced.

Uniform traffic can be considered the worst case for treaps in the sense that it always has to deliver as much performance as possible. In the case of non-uniform traffic, we can expect the system to consume few resources when there are few operations, while running resource-intensively when the numbers of operations peak. This is also demonstrated in Fig. 6. The straight line indicates the database size. Since we use an eager expiration and removal policy, the line also reflects the number of valid, i.e. non-expired, tuples in the database. A note on the choice of the parameter $b = 0.695234$ for non-uniform traffic: we chose b in this range because it is typical for Web traffic [22], a scenario which is probably closest to our area of application.

Retrieval. Concerning retrieval performance, Fig. 8(a) presents the cost profile of uncorrelated lookups while varying the database size. The graph shows that the number of lookups per second decreases as the database size grows and is thus consistent with $O(\log n)$ key lookup complexity. Figure 8(b) illustrates how expensive it is to traverse a treap in an in-order fashion. Traversal is an interesting operation, as it can be used for creating snapshots, computing joins, etc. The operation is linear in the size of the database, but benefits from caching: the path from the treap root the current node is very likely to be resident in the cache hierarchy. Thus, the operation is surprisingly fast; traversing a one million tuple database takes about one-third of a second on our test

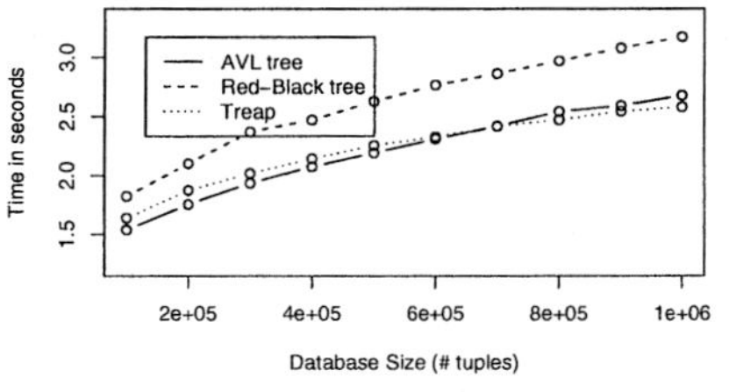

(a) Scaling of 100,000 uncorrelated lookups for AVL trees, Red-Black trees, and treaps

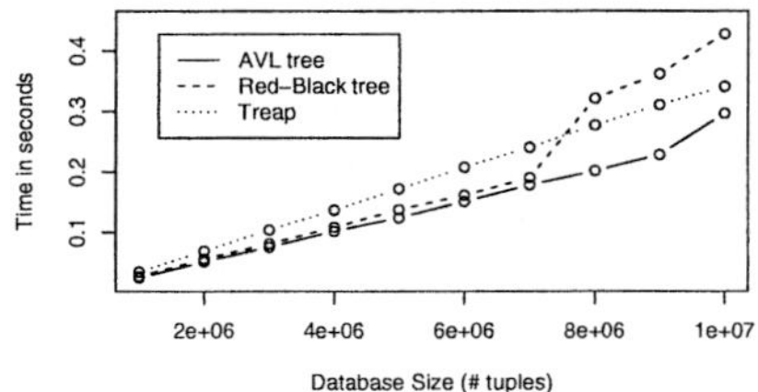

(b) Scaling of complete in-order traversal of AVL trees, Red-Black trees, and treaps

Fig. 8. Generated traffic; lookup and traversal in database containing up to 16 M tuples

platform. This indicates that the versioning semantics of our treaps does not impede full traversals since the number of arriving tuples is certainly limited. Figure 8 also displays the performance of the same operations on AVL trees and Red-Black trees, which are what we compare treaps against in the following subsection.

3.3 Comparing Treaps to Competitors

To estimate the performance and resource consumption of the treap index relative to other data structures, we compared the behaviour of treaps to a number of competing approaches. We use the following methodology: Besides requiring appropriate competitors to provide an index on the key attribute, we distinguish between structures which support *eager* expiration and structures which do not. Eager expiration implies that we can remove expired data in a timely fashion from the data structure so that, for example, ON EXPIRATION triggers can fire as soon as the item becomes stale and not at some arbitrary, later point in time. Thus, eager expiration calls for priority queue-like access to the data in addition to the index on the key values. We achieved this by combining the index structures with priority queues. Since our context requires us to work with main-memory data structures, we chose AVL trees and Red-Black trees [11] as competitors to treaps. To support expiration on these structures, we applied (1) periodic cleansing strategies, and (2) priority queue-supported, eager expiration strategies to both data structures. Since treaps may require us to apply a hash function to key values and, thus, may not support range queries under certain circumstances, we also compared the performance of treaps to main-memory hash tables [11]. Again, we use plain hash tables as well as heap-supported hash tables for eager expiration.

Maintenance Costs. To measure how dynamic a database instance is at a given point in time we look at how many tuples of a snapshot would expire during a given interval. Formally, we introduce the notion of *Rate of Expiration* (RoE), which is defined as the ration between expired data and the sum of expired and current data, in a given time interval. Thus, the Rate of Expiration is number between 0 and 1 (or 0% and 100%) which captures how dynamic or how static a particular database state is by relating the number of tuples expirations in a given time interval to the size of the database. Note that the RoE does not take into account insertions and expiration from insertions; it only measures the decay of a database state. An RoE of 100% would imply that, during the interval d, all data expire, whereas an RoE of 0% implies that there are no expirations. We note that expiration time-enabled data structures in general appear particularly useful when RoE is relatively low, i.e. a significant part of the database does not expire in the interval of interest; high RoEs imply that the we have to dispose of large parts of a database, which in turn implies that we have to scan a large part of the data—those to be expired—which we can do anyway without supporting data structures.

Figure 9 compares the cost of maintaining treaps to the cost of maintaining the other well-known data structures which were adapted to support expiration time. The RoE varies from very dynamic 100% to much more static 1%. It turns out that treaps never perform significantly worse than the other data structures but scale much better, both in terms of memory requirements and processor time, for databases with relatively small

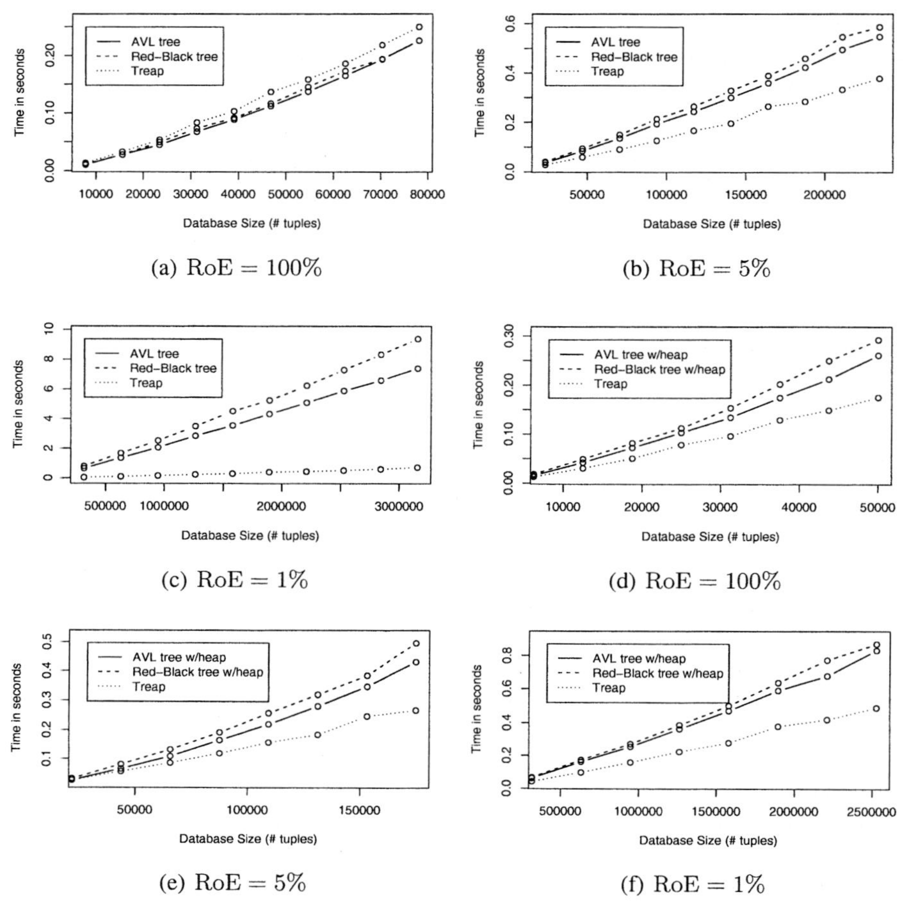

(a) RoE = 100% (b) RoE = 5%

(c) RoE = 1% (d) RoE = 100%

(e) RoE = 5% (f) RoE = 1%

Fig. 9. Performance comparison to AVL and Red-Black Trees with/without supporting heaps

Rate of Expiration, which we consider a typical case. In more detail, Figs. 9(a)–9(c) illustrate that treaps outperform AVL trees and Red-Black trees for RoEs of 5% and 1%, whereas they incur only a small overhead for an RoE of 100%. Note that in this case expiration is done on AVL and Red-Black using traversals at the end of each interval, but no additional memory is needed for supporting data structures; thus, expiration is not eager. However, eager expiration can be implemented with supporting heaps as shown in Figs. 9(d)–9(f). Note that in these figures AVL and Red-Black trees are combined with heaps to support eager expiration. However, this incurs a memory overhead for these data structures so that, given a fixed-size main memory, a treap could index more than twice the data size than the competitors. Nevertheless, treaps outperform the other data structures in all cases although not as clearly as in the heap-less experiment.

Query Performance. This subsection considers the question what *query* performance (rather than the cost of maintenance) treaps feature in comparison to AVL and

Red-Black trees. As mentioned earlier, Fig. 8 shows the performance for two important query primitives used frequently in data management: traversals and lookup queries. It turns out that, as Fig. 8(a) shows, treaps consistently outperform Red-Black trees and are *en par* with AVL trees with respect to point queries or lookups. For small databases AVL trees exhibit a slightly better performance where treaps are slightly ahead for larger databases. Similarly, for scanning the data set in sort order, treaps perform slightly worse than both, Red-Black and AVL trees, for small databases; for large databases, they are again ahead of Red-Black trees as Fig. 8(b) shows. However, the important point here is that the probabilistic performance guarantees of treaps do not incur a significant (if at all) penalty on query performance.

Further Issues. The full version of this paper [18] covers several practically relevant issues. Most notably, it relaxes the assumption of statistical independence between key values and expiration times, by introducing a hash function to enforce the independence. Additionally, the full version also compares treaps to expiration time-enabled hash tables and discusses main-memory performance issues. Many other issues are also discussed in somewhat more detail than presented here.

4 Related Work

At the level of query languages and data models, which are not the focus of this paper, the concept of expiration time relates to the concept of vacuuming [9]. With vacuuming, it is possible to specify rules that delete data: when the preconditions, e.g. related to time, in the head of a rule, are met, the data identified by the body of the rule are logically deleted from the database. Like expiration time, vacuuming separates logical deletion from physical deletion. But whereas expiration times are explicitly associated with the tuples in the database, vacuuming specifies which data to delete in separate rules. We believe that the techniques presented in this paper may be relevant for the efficient implementation of time-based vacuuming. Stream databases [2], on the other hand, allow users to specify query windows; in this sense, they take an approach which is opposite to expiration times, which let the data sources declare how long a tuple is to be considered current. Some works that refer to the term "expiration" are slightly related to expiration time and thus this paper's contribution. Expiration has been used in the context of view self-maintenance: Here the problem is which data that can be removed ("expired") without this affecting the results of a predetermined set of queries (views) [8].

The use of expiration time has been studied in the context of supporting moving objects [21]. The idea is that locations reported by moving objects that have not been updated explicitly for some time are considered inaccurate and should thus be expired. The R^{EXP}-tree extends the R-tree to index the current and anticipated future positions of two- and three-dimensional points, where the points are given by linear functions of time and are associated with expiration times. We are not aware of any related research on main memory based indexing that incorporates expiration time.

Okasaki [16] offers a very readable introduction to purely functional data structures. Our primary data structure, the *(functional) treap*, is described and analysed in substantial detail by Seidel and Aragon [19]; it was first introduced by McCreight [14]. Later, treaps were primarily seen and interpreted as randomised search trees [19]. Treaps have been used in a number of contexts; however, we are not aware of any time-related applications. Heaps are a classical data structure in computer science [11]. In this paper, we technically achieve concurrency on functional treaps through versioning [4] by implementing the node-copying method [7]. In a database context, Lomet and Salzberg [13] present versioning supporting variants of B-trees and discuss related issues. Finally, we remark that distributed garbage collection also shares similarities with expiring data in databases; especially eager collection is sensible when scarce resources have to be freed up.

5 Conclusion and Future Work

This paper argues that expiration time is an important concept for data management in a variety of application areas, including heartbeat patterns in mobile networks and short-lived data. It presents a functional, or versioned, variant of the previously proposed treap along with algorithms for supporting data with expiration time, and it argues that this is an efficient main-memory index for data with expiration times. Through comprehensive and comparative performance experiments, the paper demonstrates that its proposal scales well beyond data volumes produced by current mobile applications and thus is suited for advanced applications.

Data expiration is an important and natural concept in many volatile application settings where traditional ACID semantics are not appropriate. Often, devices such as mobile phones, PDAs, sensors, and RFID tags experience intermittent connectivity, but also do not need a full-blown transaction system for many tasks. In these settings, data management applications can benefit from the underlying platform being expiration time-enabled. Benefits include lower transaction workloads, reduced network traffic, and the ability to free memory occupied by stale data immediately.

Support in the underlying platform for expiration time also have the potential of simplifying application logic by removing the need for "clean-up" transactions. The paper demonstrates through experiments that a functional treap, which is a binary tree with respect to a key and a heap with respect to the expiration time, is an effective tool for handling expiration times in main-memory settings.

Several interesting directions for future research exist in relation to the support for expiration time in data management. When data are not as short-lived as assumed in this paper, it might be beneficial to develop strategies for extending standard secondary-memory data structures, e.g. heap files, B-trees, and hash files, with expiration time support. We anticipate that expiration for secondary-memory structures requires strategies different from those presented in this paper. Furthermore, to take full advantage of database management system technology, expiration times have to be sensibly integrated into SQL's isolation levels and transaction system.

Acknowledgments. The authors would like to thank Peter Schartner for helpful comments and pointers as well as Laurynas Speicys, Simonas Šaltenis, and Kristian Torp for helpful discussions and their collaboration. C. S. Jensen is also an adjunct professor in Department of Technology, Agder University College, Norway.

References

1. Ailamaki, A., DeWitt, D., Hill, M.: Data page layouts for relational databases on deep memory hierarchies. The VLDB Journal **11** (2002) 198–215
2. Arasu, A., Babu, S., Widom, J.: CQL: A Language for Continuous Queries over Streams and Relations. Proc. DBPL (2003) 1–19
3. Bass, L., Clements, P., Kazman, R.: Software Architecture in Practice. Addison Wesley, (2003)
4. Bernstein, P., Hadzilacos, V., Goodman, N.: Concurrency Control and Recovery in Database Systems. Addison Wesley (1987)
5. Codd, E. F.: A Relational Model of Data for Large Shared Data Banks. Comm. ACM **13** (1970) 377–387
6. Diwan, A., Tarditi, D., Moss, J.: Memory System Performance of Programs with Intensive Heap Allocation. ACM TOCS **13** (1995) 244–273
7. Driscoll, J., Sarnak, N., Sleator, D., Tarjan, R.: Making Data Structures Persistent. Journal of Computer and System Sciences **38** (1989) 86–124
8. Garcia-Molina, H., Labio, W., Yang, J.: Expiring Data in a Warehouse. Proc. VLDB (1998) 500–511
9. Jensen, C.§.: Vacuuming. The TSQL2 Temporal Query Language (1995) 447–460
10. Jensen, C. S., Lomet, D.: Transaction Timestamping in (Temporal) Databases. Proc. VLDB (2001) 441–450
11. Knuth, D.: The Art of Computer Programming, vol. 3, Sorting and Searching. Addison Wesley (1998)
12. Lehman, T., Carey, M.: Query Processing in Main Memory Database Management Systems. Proc. ACM SIGMOD (1986) 239–250
13. Lomet, D., Salzberg, B.: Access Methods for Multiversion Data. Proc. ACM SIGMOD (1989) 315–324
14. McCreight, E.: Priority Search Trees. SIAM Journal on Computing **14** (1985) 257–276
15. Odersky, M., *et al.*: The Scala Programming Language. http://scala.epfl.ch (2005)
16. Okasaki, C.: Purely Functional Data Structures. Cambridge University Press (1998)
17. Schmidt, A., Jensen, C. S., Šaltenis, S.: Expiration Times for Data Management. IEEE ICDE (2006, to appear)
18. Schmidt, A., Jensen, C. S.: Efficient Management of Short-Lived Data. Technical Report (2005) http://arxiv.org/abs/cs.DB/0505038
19. R. Seidel and C. Aragon. Randomized Search Trees. *Algorithmica*, 16(4/5): 464–497, 1996.
20. The World Wide Web Consortium. HTTP - Hypertext Transfer Protocol. http://www.w3.org/Protocols/ (2005)
21. Šaltenis, S., Jensen, C. S.: Indexing of Moving Objects for Location-Based Services. Proc. IEEE ICDE (2002) 463–472
22. Wang, M., Chan, N., Papadimitriou, S., Faloutsos, C., Madhyastha, T.: Data Mining Meets Performance Evaluation: Fast Algorithms for Modeling Bursty Traffic. Proc. IEEE ICDE (2002) 507–516

References containing URLs are valid as of 6 December 2005.

Mining Outliers in Spatial Networks

Wen Jin[1], Yuelong Jiang[1], Weining Qian[2], and Anthony K.H. Tung[3]

[1] School of Computing Science, Simon Fraser University
{wjin, yjiang}@cs.sfu.ca
[2] Department of Computer Science, Fudan University
wnqian@fudan.edu.cn
[3] Department of Computer Science, National University of Singapore
atung@comp.nus.edu.sg

Abstract. Outlier analysis is an important task in data mining and has attracted much attention in both research and applications. Previous work on outlier detection involves different types of databases such as spatial databases, time series databases, biomedical databases, etc. However, few of the existing studies have considered spatial networks where points reside on every edge. In this paper, we study the interesting problem of distance-based outliers in spatial networks. We propose an efficient mining method which partitions each edge of a spatial network into a set of length d segments, then quickly identifies the outliers in the remaining edges after pruning those unnecessary edges which cannot contain outliers. We also present algorithms that can be applied when the spatial network is updating points or the input parameters of outlier measures are changed. The experimental results verify the scalability and efficiency of our proposed methods.

1 Introduction

Outlier analysis, which aims to find a small number of exceptional objects in a database, is an important data mining task. Methods have been developed for different types of databases such as spatial databases [1, 2, 13, 17, 16, 19], time series databases [10, 14], biomedical databases [21, 22], etc. In these methods, the databases are typically considered static and relational, and the distance used in identifying outliers is always measured by Euclidean distance.

However, in many real applications where spatial data are managed, *spatial objects are often added or removed, and the position and accessibility of spatial objects are constrained by spatial networks* [21]. Examples include road networks, river networks, plane networks, rail networks, etc.

In general, a spatial network can be modeled as a graph where points are located on the edges. These points can be static objects such as buildings, or snapshots of mobile objects such as vehicles. Clearly, the actual distance between any two points, called *network distance*, is measured by the length of the shortest path connecting them in the network instead of Euclidean distance. Figure 1 depicts an example of a spatial network, where each node is denoted by a square, each edge is associated with a distance label, and each point (object) is denoted by a cross and lies exactly on an edge.

M.L. Lee, K.L. Tan, and V. Wuwongse (Eds.): DASFAA 2006, LNCS 3882, pp. 156–170, 2006.

Mining outlying objects in a spatial network can provide very useful knowledge to decision makers. For example, a road supervisor is interested to know which(or how many) vehicles are most deviant to other vehicles in distance during rush hour, or which roads or portions of a road have the least traffic. Such outlier information can be used to analyze traffic patterns in a network and help adjust the coverage of traffic volume.

Due to the features of network distance and the dynamics of spatial networks, state-of-the-art algorithms on mining outliers in traditional databases cannot be straightforwardly applied in spatial networks. As shown in Figure 1, point P_{12}, P_{19} and P_{26} are close to each other in Euclidean distance(if not considering network constraint). For instance, if we apply the well-known cell-based outlier detection method [12] to this graph, P_{12}, P_{19} and P_{26} will be grouped into a small cell, and will be treated as non-outliers. However, since the only route to P_{26} in the network is through the edge (n_7, n_4), and the remaining points have much larger network distances to P_{26} than to any other point, so P_{26} is an outlier in the network. This problem motivates us to design a novel method to find outliers in a spatial network efficiently. Some recent work has been done on identifying graph outliers [4, 8, 20], but the processed graph contains only nodes and edges, and is different from a spatial network where additional points reside on the edges. Furthermore, these existing methods basically aim to find exceptional nodes or exceptional edges.

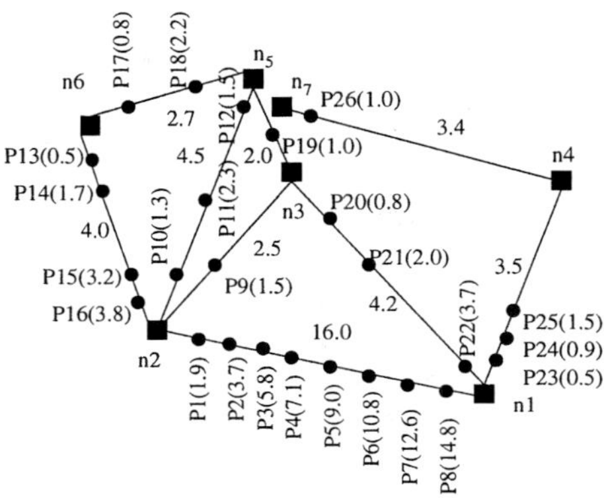

Fig. 1. An example of a spatial network

In this paper, we study the interesting problem of distance-based outliers in spatial networks. We propose an efficient mining method which partitions each edge of a spatial network into a set of length d segments, then quickly identifies the outliers in the remaining edges after pruning those unnecessary edges which cannot contain outliers. We also present algorithms for dynamical settings where points in a spatial network are inserted/removed, and for settings where the input parameters of outlier measures are changed. Our contributions are as follows:

- We introduce the problem of distance-based outliers in spatial networks.
- We develop very efficient algorithms for mining outliers in spatial networks in both static settings and dynamic settings, including when points in a spatial network or input parameters of outlier measures are updated.
- We perform extensive experiments on both synthetic datasets and real datasets.

The rest of the paper is organized as follows. Section 2 surveys related work. Section 3 introduces the preliminaries of outliers in spatial networks. Section 4 introduces the mining algorithm for static spatial networks. Section 5 introduces the mining algorithm for spatial networks in dynamic settings. Section 6 presents the performance analysis of these methods. We conclude the paper with a summary in Section 7.

2 Related Work

In the database point of view, recent research on outlier detection can be categorized into statistics-based, distance-based, density-based and clustering-based approaches [9].

Outlier research has its roots in statistics [7, 3], and this early work can be classified as distribution-based and depth-based. A distribution-based method uses some kind of data distribution model such as Normal, which is mostly univariate, to describe the properties of a dataset. It then tests for outliers based on the postulated distribution. The problem of this method is that it assumes that the dataset possesses some probability distribution beforehand. In real applications, it is difficult to know the underlying data distribution. A depth-based method uses computational statistics to represent data in different depths and outliers are probably those data in lower depths. However, as such a method relies on k-dimensional convex hulls computation with a lower bound cost of $\Omega(n^{k/2})$, it is not efficient for high dimensions.

The concept of distance-based outliers, proposed by Knorr and Ng [12], defines an object p being an outlier, if at most n objects are within distance d of p. Outliers pertain to the global view of a dataset. A cell-based outlier detection approach that partitions a dataset into cells is also presented in the work. The time complexity of this cell-based algorithm is $O(N + c^k)$ where k is dimension number, N is dataset size, and c is a number inversely proportional to d. For very large databases, this method achieves better performance than depth-based methods. However, it is still exponential to the number of dimensions. Ramaswamy et al. extended the notion of distance-based outliers by using distance to the k-nearest neighbor to rank outliers [19], where an efficient algorithm is given based on the technique of partitioning dataset and distance bounding [18].

Some clustering algorithms such as CLARANS [15], DBSCAN [5], BIRCH [25], and CURE [6] consider outliers, but only to the point of ensuring that they do not interfere with the clustering process. Further, outliers are only by-products in clustering algorithms, and generally, clustering algorithms cannot be applied directly to a spatial network to find outliers.

Breunig et al. introduced the concept of local outliers, which assigns each piece of data a local outlier factor (LOF) of being an outlier, depending on its neighborhood[2]. This outlier factor can be used to rank objects according to their outlierness. Computing the LOF of all objects in a database requires O(n*runtime of a knn query). The outlier factors can be computed very efficiently if OPTICS is used to analyze the clustering structure. A top-n based local outliers mining algorithm which uses the distance bound of a micro-cluster to estimate density was presented in [11].

3 Preliminaries

Before we introduce mining algorithms for the spatial network outliers. Let us revisit related concepts and notions of spatial networks and outliers, interesting readers can see the details in [23, 12]. Let a spatial network be a weighted graph $G = (V, E, W)$, and V is a set of nodes, and E is a set of edges. The function $W : E \rightarrow R^+$ associates each edge with a positive weight. Without loss of generality, W can be regarded as the distance in an edge. The position of a *point* (i.e. object) p in the network can be expressed by $< n_i, n_j, pos >$ where the $pos \in [0, W(e)]$ and $e = (n_i, n_j)$. It shows p has pos unit away from the node n_i along the edge (n_i, n_j). As shown in Figure 1, P_{15} lies on the edge (n_6,n_2) and it is 3.2 units away from n_6 along the edge, so it is represented by $< n_6, n_2, 3.2 >$. We assume the number of points in the spatial network G is N, and the edges in the spatial network satisfies the triangle inequality.

Definition 1. *Let p and q be two points whose positions are* (n_a, n_b, pos_p) *and* (n'_a, n'_b, pos_q)*, respectively. The* **direct distance** $ddist(p, q)$ *between points p and q is defined by* $|pos_p - pos_q|$ *if* $n_a = n'_a$ *and* $n_b = n'_b$ *(i.e., p and q lie on the same edge); otherwise, it is defined as* ∞. *Given a point p with position* (n_a, n_b, pos_p)*, the direct distance* $ddist(p, n_a)$ *between p and* n_a *is* pos_p. *The direct distance* $ddist(p, n_b)$ *is defined by* $W(n_a, n_b) - pos_p$*[23].*

Note that *ddist* only works for two points lying on the same edge, while the *ddist* of a point from a node works only when the point is lying on an edge adjacent to the node.

Definition 2. *Given nodes* n_i *and* n_j*, the* **network distance** $ndist(n_i, n_j)$ *is defined as the distance of the shortest path from* n_i *to* n_j *and vice versa[23].*

Definition 3. *Given points p and q, where p lies on the edge* (n_a, n_b) *and q lies on the edge* (n'_a, n'_b)*, the* **network distance** $ndist(p, q)$ *is the distance of the shortest path from p to q.* $ndist(p, q)$ *is defined by* $\min_{x \in \{a,b\}, y \in \{a',b'\}}(ddist(p, n_x) + ndist(n_x, n_y) + ddist(n_y, q))$ *if p and q lie on different edges; otherwise,* $ndist(p, q)$ *is the minimum of the previous quantity and* $ddist(p, q)$*[23].*

Since the number of nodes in the spatial networks is much smaller than that of points, so the network distance between each pair of nodes n_i and n_j can be materialized with little cost and will be used frequently to speed up distance comparisons in the stage of outliers detection. To facilitate efficient access, the adjacency list and points are stored in two separate flat files indexed by B+-trees[24], as shown in Figure 2 representing the spatial network of Figure 1.

Given a collection of N points that lie on a network, we aim to find a small group of points according to the following criteria.

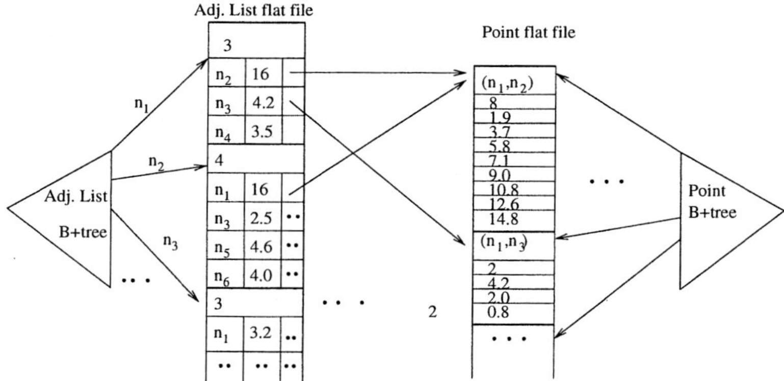

Fig. 2. Data structure of the network and segment trees

Definition 4. *Given user-defined parameters P and d, and a network distance function F, a point o in a spatial network G is a distance-based outlier if at least fraction P of points in G lie greater than* **network distance** *d from o.*

4 Mining Outliers in Static Spatial Networks

In this section, we first present a naive index-based method to identify the outliers among the points in network. Then we propose a novel edge-segmentation method which can significantly improve the performance of mining outliers.

4.1 A Naive Index-Based Method

For a point o in the spatial network G, the d-neighborhood of o contains the set of points that are within distance d of o. The fraction P is the minimum fraction of points in G that must be outside the d-neighborhood of an outlier. Obviously, given P and d, the problem of identifying distance-based outliers in the spatial network can be solved by answering a nearest neighbor search at each point o.

We can build an index by employing a range search with a network distance of d for each point o to find such outliers. If more than $(1-P)N$ points are found in the d-neighborhood, o is a non-outlier; otherwise, o is an outlier. When the d becomes larger, each range search costs larger which degrades the performance greatly, so the worst case of this method has the complexity of $O(N^2)$. Such an index can be maintained for answering outlier queries multiple times.

4.2 An Edge-Segmentation Method

Before introducing our outliers mining algorithms, we first consider preprocessing a spatial network. We partition each edge $e = (n_i, n_j)$ into $\lceil \frac{w(e)}{d} \rceil$ segments $S_1 = [n_i, n'_1)$, $S_2 = [n'_1, n'_2)$, $\ldots$, $S_{\lceil \frac{w(e)}{d} \rceil - 1} = [n'_{\lceil \frac{w(e)}{d} \rceil - 2}, n'_{\lceil \frac{w(e)}{d} \rceil - 1})$,

$S_{\lceil \frac{w(e)}{d} \rceil}$ $=[n'_{\lceil \frac{w(e)}{d} \rceil - 1}, n_j]$ where each segment has a length of d, and n'_1, n'_2, ..., $n'_{\lceil \frac{w(e)}{d} \rceil - 1}$ are the positions of the segment ends. In practice, one end segment in each edge such as $S_{\lceil \frac{w(e)}{d} \rceil}$ may not be of a length of exactly d, but an actual length $d^* < d$. As shown in Figure 3, edge (n_1, n_2) is equally partitioned into segments $[n_1, n'_1)$, $[n'_1, n'_2)$, $[n'_2, n'_3)$, $[n'_3, n'_4)$ and $[n'_4, n_2]$. The statistics information such as the number of points in each segment is also maintained.

Now each edge segment of a spatial network can be categorized into one of the following types: (1) *Outlier Segment(OS)* which consists of outliers; (2) *Non-outlier Segment(NS)* which cannot contain any outlier; and (3) *Undetermined Segment(US)* which may or may not have outliers. Without any pair-wise distance computation during the outlier detection, an *Outlier-Segments* returns objects that are outliers, or a *Non-outlier Segments* can be immediately pruned. The remaining outliers can be identified among the *Undetermined Segments.*

Now the problem is how to quickly identify the type of an edge as *Outlier-Segment*, *Non-outlier Segment* or *Undetermined Segment.*

Fig. 3. Edge segmentation

Fig. 4. OS and NS

Definition 5. *The smallest distance between segment* $S_i = [n_a, n_b]$ *and segment* $S_j = [n_c, n_d]$, $\mathbf{sdist}(S_i, S_j)$, *is* $\min\{ndist(n_a, n_c), ndist(n_a, n_d), ndist(n_b, n_c), ndist(n_b, n_d)\}$. *Segment* S_j *is* **adjacent** *to segment* S_i *if the smallest distance between* S_i *and* S_j, $sdist(S_i, S_j) < d$.

Here, S_j refers to the segment adjacent to S_i in either right side or left side. The adjacent segments of S_i are also called the d-neighborhood of S_i.

Definition 6. *The largest distance between segment* $S_i = [n_a, n_b]$ *and segment* $S_j = [n_c, n_d]$, $\mathbf{ldist}(S_i, S_j)$, *is* $\max\{ndist(n_a, n_c), ndist(n_a, n_d), ndist(n_b, n_c), ndist(n_b, n_d)\}$. *Segment* S_j *is* **complementary** *to segment* S_i *if the largest distance between* S_i *and* S_j, $ldist(S_i, S_j) \leq d$.

Here, S_i may also have multiple complementary segments. Specifically, if S_i is a segment with length d, there is no such complementary segment. If S_j is S_i's complementary segment, it must be S_i's adjacent segment; but if S_j is S_i's adjacent segment, it may not be S_i's complementary segment.

Lemma 1. *Given segment* S_i, S_j, *if* S_j *is not an adjacent segment to* S_i, *then any point* $p \in S_i$, $q \in S_j$ *must be more than d apart, i.e.* $ndist(p, q) > d$.

Lemma 2. *Given c_i points in segment S_i and c_j points in S_i's adjacent segments, S_i is an* **outlier segment (OS)** *if c_i+c_j < $(1 - P)N$.*

Lemma 3. *Given c_i points in segment S_i and c_j points in S_i's complementary segments, S_i is a* **non-outlier segment(NS)** *if c_i+c_j $\geq (1 - P)N$.*

As shown in Figure 4, the number of points in segments $[n_1',n_2']$, $[n_2',n_3']$, $[n_3',n_4']$ are c_1, c_2 and c_3 respectively. If $c_2 \geq (1 - P)N$, none of points in $[n_2',n_3']$ is an outlier. If $c_1 + c_2 + c_3 < (1 - P)N$, all the points in $[n_2',n_3']$ are outliers.

Those segments which are neither outlier segments nor non-outlier segments are **undetermined segments(US)**.

Thus, we can scan the spatial network once, and partitioning edges of the spatial network into segments of length d. Suppose there are **m** segments, and the whole points are categorized into three types of segments:**OS, NS** and **US**. Since the points in **OS** segments and **NS** segments can easily be identified as either outliers or non-outliers, the remaining mining task is obviously to further check those segments labeled as **"US"**. That is, each point p in such a **"US"** segment will be evaluated the distance *only* between the points in the d-neighborhood of the segment where p resides. If none of the points is identified as an outlier, the segment is labeled as **"NS"**, otherwise the segment is labeled as **"US(O)"**. The pseudo-code of the mining algorithm is as follows.

Algorithm 1. An Edge-Segmentation Outlier Detection Method.
Input: A spatial network $G = (V, E, W)$ partitioned into m segments, N, d, P
Output: Outliers in G
Method:

```
FOR i = 1 to m DO Count_i = 0
FOR each point p DO
    Map p to its segment S_i, increment Count_i by 1;
FOR i = 1 to m DO
    IF Count_i + Σ_{S_j is complementary to S_i} Count_j ≥ (1 − P)N THEN
        Label S_i as "NS";//S_i is a Non-Outlier Segment
    ELSE IF Count_i + Σ_{S_j is adjacent to S_i} Count_j < (1 − P)N THEN
        Label S_i as "OS";//S_i is an Outlier Segment
    ELSE//S_i is an Undetermined Segment, needs to check its points one by one
            FOR each object p ∈ S_i DO
                Count_P = Count_i;
                FOR each object q ∈ S_j where S_j adjacent to S_i DO
                    IF ndist(p, q) ≤ d THEN
                        Increment Count_p by 1;
                IF Count_p ≤ (1 − P)N THEN
                    P is an outlier, label S_i as "US(O)";//S_i an outlier
                IF S_i is not labeled as "US(O)" THEN
                    Label S_i as "NS";
Output outliers in G;
```

Step 1 takes m time(since there are m segments), where $m \ll N$ is the total number of segments. Step 2 to step 3 takes N time. For Step 4 to step 19, the worst case happens when each segment contains at most $N(1-P)$ objects, and each object in a segment is required to check up to $N(1-P)$ objects in each of the adjacent or complementary segments. As the number of adjacent or complementary segments is bounded by m, hence, step 4 to step 19 takes $O(m(N(1-P))^2)$ time. Thus the worst case time complexity is $O(m(N(1-P))^2+N) = O(m(N(1-P))^2)$. Furthermore, based on the similar analysis in [12], we know that since P is expected to be extremely close to 1 in practice, especially for large datasets, so $O(mN^2(1-P)^2)$ can be approximated by $O(m)$, thus under such circumstance the time complexity is $O(m+N)$.

5 Mining Outliers in Dynamic Settings

In the previous section, we introduce an edge-segmentation method to efficiently mine distance-based outliers in a static setting in which the whole points are available in a spatial network. In this section, we will discuss the dynamic settings for outliers detection in the following two cases:(1) the points are added to or removed from edges, or (2) users may query the outliers with respect to different input parameters d or p. In both cases, it requires to effectively maintain the existing segmentation structure and mine the changes of outliers in an incremental way.

5.1 Mining Outliers When Points Are Updated

From the perspective of data management, points in the spatial network are always updated in the case of m_1 insertions or m_2 deletions. Since the distance-based outlier is dependent on N, so after updating, if the number of points is changed to N' where $N' = N + m_1 - m_2$, each point in the spatial network needs to check whether there are $(1-p)N'$ points within its d neighborhood region. Thus we can apply the edge-segmentation algorithm to the updated spatial network to find the changes of outliers. The problem is how to make full use of the existing segmentation structure and avoid unnecessary distance computation as much as it can?

It is clear that each segment is labeled either **OS, NS** or **US** after the outlier detection in static setting. Such information can incrementally maintained in the case of points deletion or insertion. Since the number of points is changed after updating points, the type of each segment S_i needs to be quickly updated based on Lemma 2 and Lemma 3 given in the previous section.

The problem is that if S_i is labeled as **OS** or **NS**, we obviously know that the whole points in S_i are either outliers or non-outliers, but for those **undetermined segments(US)** S_i, we still need further check every point P in S_i to see if it is an outlier or not. *To reduce the cost of such pairwise computation and to improve the efficiency of incremental mining as much as possible, we store the points in each edge into a binary tree, and the points of each segment can be*

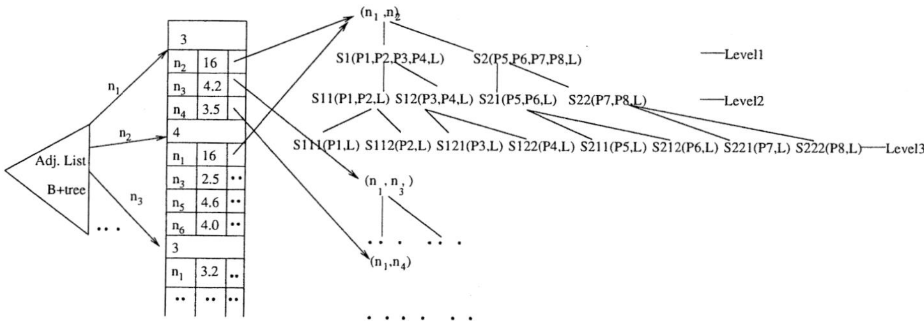

Fig. 5. Data structure of the network and segment trees

further partitioned till a length of u. For segment S_i, the points within it are organized as a binary tree. That is, if the parent node covers points in subsegment with length l, it will be expanded to two child nodes: the left child node covers points in left half of subsegment with length $l/2$ and the right child node covers points in right half. The tree expansion procedure starts with segment S_i (root node), and continues until one of following conditions is satisfied: (1)the node does not cover any points in current subsegment; (2) the length of subsegment is less than $2u$. Figure 5 shows the example of organizing edge segments ($d = 8$) and their subsegments corresponding to the network in Figure 1, into tree structures. The points of each segment are maintained into a binary segment tree. Each node in the tree is labeled (shown as "L" in Figure 5) in one of three types. We observe that the smaller the u, the larger size of the tree, and less number of points in each subsegment in the lowest level of the tree. As shown in the Figure 5, the tree only expands to the level 2 when $u = 4$, while it expands to the level 3(in dashed box) if $u = 2$.

Now we can **progressively check outlier points level-by-level instead of one by one**. If the current segment (subsegment) S_i is labeled as **US**, *the left and right child subsegments of* S_i *will be checked to see whether they are* **OS**, **NS** *or* **US**. Before checking Lemma 2 and Lemma 3, the number of points in current subsegment, its adjusted adjacent subsegments, and its adjusted complementary subsegments in same level of the trees should be obtained. Fortunately, all these information is stored in the trees and we do not need to access the points again. An example of progressive checking **US** segment is illustrated in Figure 6, where $d = 10$ and $u = 2$. Note that the length of segment S_{i3} is $d^* = 6$ since S_{i3} is the last segment in the edge.

If segment S_{i2} is undetermined, its subsegment S_{i21} and S_{i22} are checked. If subsegment S_{i21} is still undetermined, its subsegment S_{i211} and S_{i212} are further checked. For different segment S_{ik}, the range of its adjacent segments (shown in dashed lines) and the range of its complementary segments (shown in blacken lines) are adjusted correspondingly. We can see in Figure 6 that with the decreasing of the subsegment length, the gap between these two ranges becomes smaller and smaller, so does the chance that the subsegment is still labeled as **NS**. The pseudo-code of the mining algorithm is as follows.

Algorithm 2. A Dynamic Outlier Detection Method for Updated Points.
Input: Segment Trees of $G = (V, E, W)$, N, d, P, m_1 insertions, m_2 deletions
Output: Outliers in G
Method:

```
FOR i = 1 to m_1 + m_2 DO
    Update points in G and counts in corresponding segments and subsegments;
FOR i = 1 to m DO
    IF Count_i + Σ_{S_j is complementary to S_i} Count_j ≥ (1 − P)(N + m_1 − m_2) THEN
        Label S_i as "NS"; //S_i is a Non-Outlier Segment
    ELSE IF Count_i + Σ_{S_j is adjacent to S_i} Count_j < (1 − P)(N + m_1 − m_2) THEN
        Label S_i as "OS"; //S_i is an Outlier Segment
    ELSE //S_i is an Undetermined Segment, check its subsegments or points
        SubsegmentCheck(S_i);
Output outliers in G;
```

Procedure: *SubsegmentCheck*(S_i)

```
IF S_i is the subsegment in non-leaf node THEN
    FOR k = 1 to 2 DO //check the left and right child subsegments of S_i
        IF S_ik satisfies the condition of Lemma 3 or Lemma 2 THEN
            Label S_ik as "OS" or "NS"; //S_ik is an Outlier/Non-Outlier Subsegment
        ELSE //S_ik is an Undetermined Subsegment, check its subsegments or points
            SubsegmentCheck(S_ik);
ELSE //S_i is an Undetermined Subsegment in leaf node, check its points one by one
    FOR each point p in S_i DO
        Count_p = Count_i;
        FOR each point q ∈ S_j where S_j is adjacent to S_i DO
            IF ndist(p, q) ≤ d THEN
                Increment Count_p by 1;
        IF Count_p ≤ (1 − P)(N + m_1 − m_2) THEN
            p is an outlier, label S_i as "US(O)"; //S_i has outlier(s)
    IF S_i is not labeled as "US(O)" THEN
        Label S_i as "NS";
```

Note that the only difference between algorithm 2 and algorithm 1 is that in algorithm 2 if S_i is undetermined we make use of the subsegment points count information in binary trees to recursively check subsegments of S_i (by the procedure *SubsegmentCheck*(S_i)) . The points scan does not happen unless the subsegment in leaf node is still undetermined.

5.2 Mining Outliers When Parameter d or P Changes

As we know, the output of the distance-based outliers in a spatial network relies on two parameters d and P. So how to choose the meaningful value of d or P is crucial to the effectiveness of mining results. In practice, users have more experience and better understanding in using percentage P, i.e. the higher value of P means higher degree of the outlierness. On the other hand, since many users are not domain experts, they are not sure which value of d is suitable to the mining algorithm. Instead, they are more likely choosing different values of d

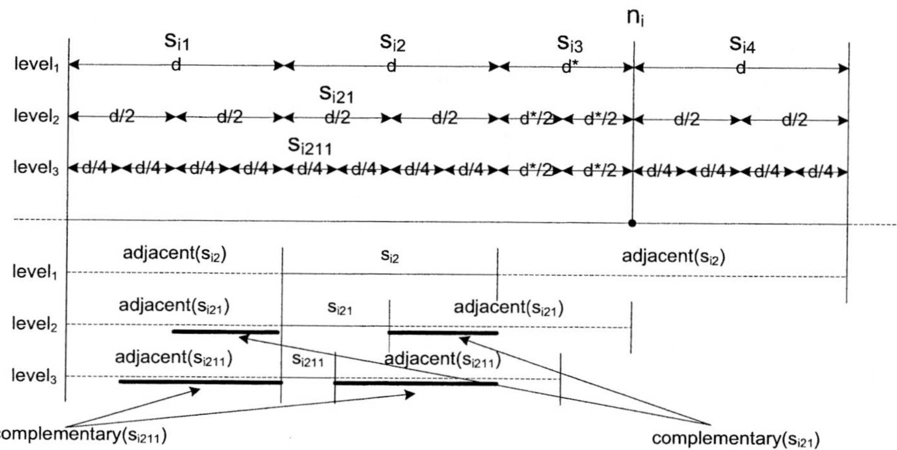

Fig. 6. Progressive check for "US" subsegments

for the outlier mining algorithm and evaluate the effectiveness by comparing the outliers with respect to different input parameters. As a result, it is necessary to develop efficient incremental methods for answering outliers in case of updates on d. Since d is always changed, the data structure used in the previous section: a binary tree with multiple level for each edge is not suitable, under such circumstance, we have to just keep one level in each binary tree.

Without loss of generality, we assume each time users input a new $d' = c \cdot u$, where c is a positive integer. Specifically, this corresponds to changing the segments based on the lowest level of subsegments with unit u described in Section 5.1.

Since each segment of length d consists of multiple subsegments where each has length u, thus for any new distance threshold d', it is not necessary to build the new edge-segments from scratch by re-partitioning the edges into segments of the new d' for storage. Instead, we can only maintain the existing edge-segments and each time "virtually" infer the corresponding segments of the new length d' when accessing the existing edge segments for outlier detection. Figure 7 shows

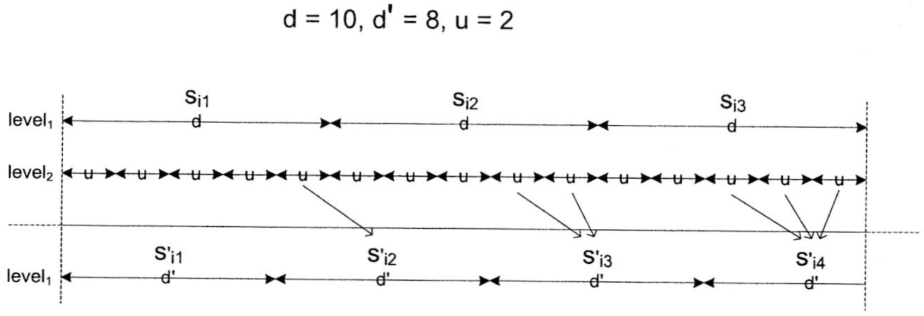

d = 10, d' = 8, u = 2

level_1 S_i1 d S_i2 d S_i3 d

level_2 u u u u u u u u u u u u u u u

level_1 S'_i1 d' S'_i2 d' S'_i3 d' S'_i4 d'

Fig. 7. Segments shifting when d changes to d'

the example that given the edge segments $S_{i1}, S_{i2}, \ldots$ of length d where S_{ij} consists of subsegments with unit length u in leaf nodes, the new edge segments $S'_{i1}, S'_{i2}, \ldots$ of length d' can be inferred by shifting the position of existing subsegment to that of a new subsegment. By updating the counts in the new segment, we can evaluate its new segment type accordingly. Those segments with label **"US"** will be further checked to identify the outlierness of each belonging point. Since the procedure outlier detection is similar to the previous subsection, we omit the detailed description due to the limitation of space. We also have the following interesting property for the inferred new edge segments.

Lemma 4. *Suppose the edge segments of length d' are inferred from edge segments of length d, if $d' > d$ and if segment S'_i of length d' contains any segment S_j of length d labeled as* **"NS"**, *S'_i is labeled as* **"NS"**; *if $d' < d$ and if any segment S'_i of length d' is contained in any segment S_j of length d labeled as* **"OS"**, *S'_i is labeled as* **"OS"**.

For the case of different values of P, there is no need to rebuild or infer the new edge segments, but only updating the type of each segment by applying the similar method in subsection 5.1 to reduce the unnecessary pairwise distance computations. We have the following interesting property for the type of edge segment in the case of new P'.

Lemma 5. *For the segment S_i, if new percentage threshold $P' > P$, then S_i will still be* **"NS"** *if S_i is* **"NS"** *w.r.t. P; if $P' < P$, then S_i will still be* **"OS"** *if S_i is* **"OS"** *w.r.t. P.*

6 Experimental Evaluation

In this section, we evaluate the performance of our proposed techniques. We implemented the naive index based method and the edge-segmentation method for mining outliers. We also implemented the algorithms for mining outliers in dynamic settings with the points being updated and when parameters changing. All algorithms are written in C++ and the experiments were run on a PC with a Pentium 4 CPU of 1.6GHz, a memory of 512Mb. We used the real road networks of Canada which can be obtained from www.maproom.psu.edu/dcw/ and did some cleaning to form a connected network. In the network, there are 42582 nodes and 46731 edges. The Euclidean distance of the connected nodes is set as the weights of the graph edges, and this is a natural way for the weight setting when we simulate the traffic of the road networks.

On the road networks, we generated points that simulate real world traffic. We start from a random node and use Dijkstra's algorithm to traverse the network and add points to the edges. The way to control the points generated is similar to [24] which focuses on generating the points to form clusters but we expand it to create the outliers. At the border of each cluster, we make the points especially sparse so as to control outlier. By adjusting the magnification factor F and the initial separation distance s_{init}[24], points are generated with different sparsity

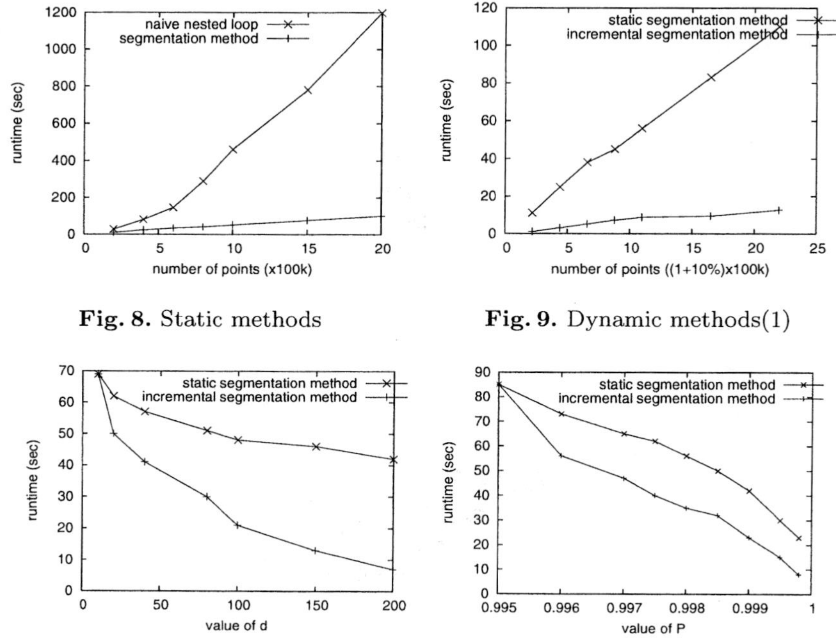

Fig. 8. Static methods

Fig. 9. Dynamic methods(1)

Fig. 10. Dynamic methods(2)

Fig. 11. Dynamic methods(3)

so that we can test different parameters for the outlier mining. For some fixed d and P, we run the naive nested loop and segmentation based algorithms and they all return the same results. It is also the same when we run our dynamic mining algorithms or compute it from scratch without using the existing results computed earlier. This proves the effectiveness of the algorithms, so we just focus on investigating the efficiency and the scalability of the methods.

To test efficiency and scalability, we generated sets of points with different cardinality. The cardinality of the points set is from 200k to 2000k where P is a fixed value (0.9985). Figure 8 shows the runtime for these different data sets. We can see that the naive nested loop method is much slower than the segmentation based method which is almost linearly increased with the number of points. If **10%** points is updated on each set of points listed in Figure 9, it shows that our incremental method runs much faster than iterating the static segmentation method on the updated points.

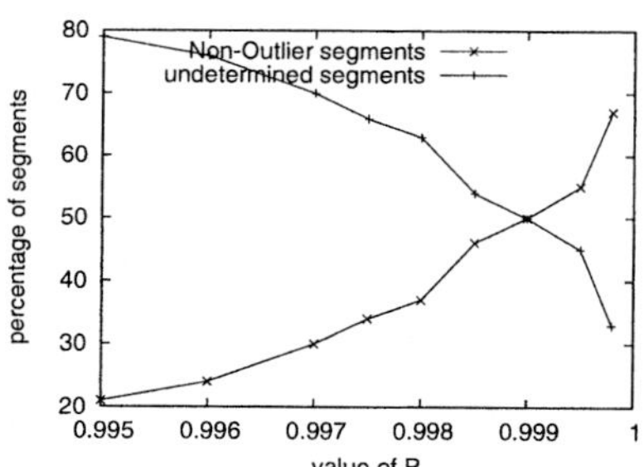

Fig. 12. Dynamic methods(4)

We use a set of 800k points to investigate the performance of proposed methods in the case of changing values of P and d. If d changes, we keep P as 99.5%;

while if P changes, d is kept as 20 units(outliers have been computed when $P = 99.5\%$). Both Figure 10 and Figure 11 show that the dynamic segmentation methods perform better than static methods.

Interestingly, we observe in Figure 12 that when P increases, the sum of percentage of **NS** and **US** is almost 100% with respect to the very small percentage of **OS**, which reflects the fact that the larger value of P, the less number of outliers in the spatial network. The similar result can be obtained if we increase the value of d since the larger value of d also leads to less number of outliers.

7 Conclusion

The achieved fruitful results in both research and applications have substantially demonstrated the important role of outlier analysis in data mining area. Existing work on outlier detection involves in different types of databases such as spatial databases, time series databases, bio-medical database etc., while few of them is applied on spatial networks where points reside in every edge. In this paper, we explore the interesting problem of distance-based outlier in spatial networks and propose an efficient mining method which partitions each edge of spatial network into a set of length d segments, then quickly identify the outliers in the remaining edges after pruning those unnecessary edges which cannot contain outliers. We also study the dynamic settings in the spatial network, including updating points or the input parameters of outlier measures are changed. The experimental results verify the scalability and efficiency of our proposed methods.

References

1. C. Aggarwal and P. Yu. Outlier detection for high dimensional data. In *SIGMOD* 2001
2. Markus M. Breunig, Hans-Peter Kriegel, Raymond T. Ng, Jorg Sander LOF: Identifying Density-Based Local Outliers. In *SIGMOD* 2000
3. V. Barnett and T. Lewis. In *Outliers in Statistical Data.* John Wiley & Sons, 1994.
4. Deepayan Chakrabarti: AutoPart: Parameter-Free Graph Partitioning and Outlier Detection. In *PKDD* 2004
5. M. Ester, H.-P. Kriegel, J. Sander, and X. Xu. A density-based algorithm for discovering clusters in large spatial databases. In *KDD* 1996
6. S. Guha, R. Rastogi, and K. Shim. Cure: An efficient clustering algorithm for large databases. In *SIGMOD* 1998
7. D. Hawkins. *Identification of Outliers.* Chapman and Hall, London, 1980.
8. V. Hautamki, I. Krkkinen and P. Frnti:Outlier detection using k-nearest neighbour graph, In *ICPR* 2004
9. Jiawei Han, Micheline Kamber: Data Mining: Concepts and Techniques. In *Morgan Kaufmann* Publishers.
10. H. Jagadish, N. Koudas, and S. Muthukrishnan:Mining deviants in a time series database. In *VLDB* 1999
11. W. Jin, Anthony.K.H. Tung and J.W. Han. Mining Top-n Local Outliers in Large Databases. In *KDD* 2001

12. Edwin M. Knorr, Raymond T. Ng: Algorithms for Mining Distance-Based Outliers in Large Datasets. In *VLDB* 1998
13. E. Knorr and R. Ng. Finding Intensional Knowledge of Distance-Based Outliers. In *VLDB* 1999
14. S. Muthukrishnan, Rahul Shah, Jeffrey Scott Vitter: Mining Deviants in Time Series Data Streams. In *SSDBM* 2004
15. R. Ng and J. Han. Efficient and effective clustering method for spatial data mining. In *VLDB* 1994
16. Spiros Papadimitriou, Hiroyuki Kitagawa, Phillip B. Gibbons, Christos Faloutsos. LOCI: Fast Outlier Detection Using the Local Correlation Integral. In *ICDE* 2003
17. Spiros Papadimitriou, Christos Faloutsos: Cross-Outlier Detection. In *SSTD* 2003
18. N. Roussopoulos, S. Kelley and F. Vincent. Nearest Neighbor Queries. In *SIGMOD* 1995
19. Sridhar Ramaswamy, Rajeev Rastogi, Kyuseok Shim: Efficient Algorithms for Mining Outliers from Large Data Sets. In *SIGMOD* 2000
20. Shashi Shekhar, Chang-Tien Lu, Pusheng Zhang: Detecting graph-based spatial outliers: algorithms and applications (a summary of results). In *KDD* 2001
21. Jorg Sander, Raymond T. Ng, Monica C. Sleumer, Man Saint Yuen, Steven J. Jones: A methodology for analyzing SAGE libraries for cancer profiling. In *ACM Trans. Inf. Syst.* 23(1): 35-60 (2005)
22. Weng-Keen Wong, Andrew W. Moore, Gregory F. Cooper, Michael Wagner: Rule-Based Anomaly Pattern Detection for Detecting Disease Outbreaks. In *AAAI* 2002
23. Man Lung Yiu, Nikos Mamoulis: Clustering Objects on a Spatial Network. In *SIGMOD* 2004
24. Man Lung Yiu, Nikos Mamoulis, Dimitris Papadias: Aggregate Nearest Neighbor Queries in Road Networks. In *IEEE Trans. Knowl. Data Eng.* 17(6): 820-833 (2005)
25. T. Zhang, R. Ramakrishnan, and M. Livny. BIRCH: an efficient data clustering method for very large databases. In *SIGMOD* 1996

Summarizing Frequent Patterns Using Profiles

Gao Cong[1], Bin Cui[2], Yingxin Li[3], and Zonghong Zhang[4]

[1] The University of Edinburgh, UK
gao.cong@ed.ac.uk
[2] Department of Computer Science and Technology, Peking University, Beijing, China
cuibin@pku.edu.cn
[3] Department of Anesthesiology, School of Medicine, University of Virginia, USA
[4] Service and Applications, Institute for Infocomm Research, A-Star, Singapore
zhzhang@i2r.a-star.edu.sg

Abstract. Frequent pattern mining is an important data mining problem with wide applications. The huge number of discovered frequent patterns pose great challenge for users to explore and understand them. It is desirable to accurately summarizing the set of frequent patterns into a small number of patterns or profiles so that users can easily explore them. In this paper, we employ a probability model to represent a set of frequent patterns and give two methods of estimating the support of a pattern from the model. Based on the model, we develop an approach to grouping a set of frequent patterns into k profiles and the support of frequent pattern can be estimated fairly accurately from a relative small number of profiles. Empirical studies show that our method can achieve compact and accurate summarization in real-life data and the support of frequent patterns can be restored much more accurately than the previous method.

1 Introduction

Mining frequent patterns or itemsets is a fundamental and essential problem in many data mining applications, such as association rule mining, classification, and clustering (e.g. [3, 7, 17]). There are a host of frequent pattern mining algorithms (e.g. [3, 9]) that discover the complete set of patterns that occur in at least ξ (*minimum support*) fraction of a dataset. The complete set of frequent patterns is often huge in number, which makes the interpretability of frequent patterns very difficult. The concepts of closed frequent patterns and maximal frequent patterns usually can help in reducing the output size. However, they can only partly alleviate the problem. The size of closed frequent patterns (or maximal frequent patterns) often remains to be very large and thus it is still difficult for users to examine and understand them.

Recently, several proposals were made to discover k patterns or profiles. This allows users to specify the value of k and thus only discover a small number of patterns or approximation. The concept of top-k patterns is proposed by Han et al [10]. Although this provides users the option to discover only the k most frequent patterns, this is not a generalization of all frequent patterns satisfying a support threshold. k *covering sets* was proposed by Afrati et al. [1] to approximate a collection of frequent patterns, i.e. each frequent pattern is covered by at least one of the k sets. The proposal is interesting in generalizing the collection of patterns into k sets. However, the support information is

M.L. Lee, K.L. Tan, and V. Wuwongse (Eds.): DASFAA 2006, LNCS 3882, pp. 171–186, 2006.

ignored in the approximation and it is unknown how to recover the support of a pattern from the k sets. Support is a very important property of a pattern and plays a key role in distinguishing patterns.

Yan et al [19] proposed an approach to summarizing patterns into k profiles by considering both pattern information and support information; each cluster (profile) is represented with three elements: the *master pattern*, i.e. the union of the patterns in the cluster, the number of transactions supporting the clusters, the probability of items of the master pattern in the set of transactions supporting the pattern. The supports of frequent patterns can be estimated from the k clusters. It is assumed in [19] that the items in the master pattern are independent in each profile. The independence model is simple and easy to learn, but it is fairly inaccurate since items are usually not independent. However, it is too expensive to consider n-dimensional probability distribution, where n is the number of items.

In this paper, we adopt an alternative probability model to represent a profile composed of a set of frequent patterns. Instead of assuming the independence among items in [19], we consider the pairwise probabilities that are still easy to compute. From the pairwise probabilities, we build simple Bayesian Network to estimate the n- dimensional probability distribution, and thus can estimate the supports of the patterns. Alternatively, we can also compute a rough support estimation for the patterns directly from the pairwise probability. With the model, we can measure the similarity between two profiles (and patterns) using Killback-Leibler divergence and a complementary distance score, and thus arrange all patterns into a set of (hierarchial) groups. In the hierarchical tree, users can explore the frequent patterns in a top-down manner as suggested in [19]. Our methods can successfully summarize patterns into tens of profiles while the support of patterns can be recovered accurately. We conduct extensive experiments on several real datasets. Our method can summarize thousands of patterns accurately using only tens of profiles on all real datasets we tested. Compared with method in [19], our methods make great improvement in summarization quality measured by restoration error.

The rest of this paper is organized as follows: Section 2 will give the problem statement. In Section 3, we present the probability model ro represent profiles and methods of estimating the supports of frequent patterns from the profiles. We introduce algorithms for grouping frequent patterns into profiles in Section 4. The experimental results are reported in Section 5. Section 6 discusses the related work. Finally we conclude this paper in Section 7.

2 Problem Statement

Let $I = \{i_1, i_2, ..., i_n\}$ be a set of **items** which represent attribute values in a transaction database DB. A pattern (or itemset) X is a non-empty subset of I. Given a DB, the **support** of a pattern X, denoted as $sup(X)$, is the fraction of tuples in the DB which contains X.

Definition 1. ***Frequent Pattern:*** *Given a minimum support threshold ξ ($0 \leq \xi \leq 1$) and a database DB, a pattern X is* **frequent** *if $sup(X) \geq \xi$.*

Definition 2. ***Closed Frequent Pattern:*** *A frequent pattern X is closed if there does not exits a pattern X' such that $X \subset X'$ and X is contained by the same set of tuples as X'.*

Closed frequent patterns are a lossless compression of frequent patterns and the complete set of frequent patterns and their supports can be derived from the set of closed frequent patterns. The size of closed frequent patterns is usually (much) smaller than the size of frequent patterns. Hence, in this paper we summarize closed frequent patterns as [19] while the proposed method equally applies to summarize frequent patterns.

Table 1. An example of database transactions

Transaction	Number of transactions
acd	100
bcd	100
abcd	800

Table 1 shows a sample dataset, where the first column represents the transactions and the second the number of transactions. For example, 100 transactions have only items a, c, and d; and 100 transactions have only items b, c, and d. There are totally 1000 transactions in this example. If we set the minimum support at 50%, clearly pattern $< abcd >$ is frequent. Additionally, we know that all its subsets are frequent as well, i.e. $< a, b, c, d, ab, ac, ad, bc, bd, cd, abc, abd, acd, bcd, abcd >$. Among these 15 frequent patterns, we can find 4 closed patterns according to the $definition$ 2, which are $< cd, acd, bcd, abcd >$. As one can see, the number of closed frequent patterns is much less than that of frequent patterns.

We observe that in this example the supports of all the 4 closed patterns are very close to each other and they are similar in terms of their items. We could summarize the 4 patterns into one fermentative pattern $< abcd >$.

Problem statement. Given a set of frequent closed patterns $CP = X_1, X_2, ..., X_m$ that are mined from database $DB = t_1, t_2, ...t_n$, pattern summarization is to group the m closed frequent patterns into k pattern profiles, each of which is represented with a probability model.

3 Model of Profiles

Suppose that patterns X_1, ... X_s are grouped together to form a profile. The profile can be characterized with two important properties: one is *master pattern* $\chi = X_1 \cup X_2 \cup ... \cup X_s$ generated by the union of the m patterns in the group; the other is the set of transactions $DB_u = DB_{X_1} \cup DB_{X_2} \cup ... \cup DB_{X_s}$. Consider these information, we propose a probability model to represent the profile.

Definition 3. ***Profile Model:*** *Let $X_1, X_2, ..., X_s$ be a set of patterns and $DB' = \cup_i DB_{X_i}$, $i = 1, ..., s$. A summarization profile over $X_1, X_2, ..., X_s$ is a triple $\Phi =< \chi, \rho, \theta >$. $\chi = X_1 \cup X_2 \cup ... \cup X_s$ is the master pattern of $X_1, X_2, ..., X_m$; $\rho = |DB'|/|DB|$ is defined as the support of the profile; suppose that $\chi = \{x_1, x_2, ..., x_t\}$, θ is composed of two parts:*

1. *$p(x_i = 1) = |DB_{x_i}|/|DB'|$, where $x_i \in \chi$ and DB_{x_i} is the set of tuples in DB' that contain item x_i.*
2. *$p(x_i = 1, x_j = 1) = |DB_{x_i \cup x_j}|/|DB'|$, where $x_i, x_j \in \chi \wedge i \neq j$ and $DB_{x_i \cup x_j}$ is the set of tuples in DB' that contain items x_i and x_j.*

Given $p(x_i = 1)$, $p(x_j = 1)$ and $p(x_i = 1, x_j = 1)$, one can obtain the probability distribution of $p(x_i, x_j)$ in the set of tuples DB' using the inclusion-exclusion principle: $p(x_i = 1, x_j = 0) = p(x_i = 1) - p(x_i = 1, x_j = 1)$; $p(x_i = 0, x_j = 1) = p(x_j = 1) - p(x_i = 1, x_j = 1)$; and $p(x_i = 0, x_j = 0) = 1 - p(x_i = 1) - p(x_j = 1) + p(x_i = 1, x_j = 1)$.

Table 2. An example of profile

	a	b	c	d	ab	ac	ad	bc	bd	cd
probability	0.9	0.9	1	1	0.8	0.9	0.9	0.9	0.9	1

Using the dataset in Table 1, we can build a pattern profile for $< abcd >$. Table 2 shows the profiles by deriving the distribution vectors for the sample datasets. For example, $p(a) = \frac{100+800}{1000} = 0.9$. In addition, without accessing the original dataset, we can infer that $< abd >$ is less frequent than the $< acd >$. Pattern profile actually provides more information than the master pattern itself; it encodes the distribution of sub-patterns.

The k-set model in [1] represents the collection of patterns only with a master pattern $\chi = X_1 \cup X_2 \cup ... \cup X_s$, and thus the support information is lost. In [1], the profile is represented not only by the master pattern but also by the probability distribution of items in χ in the set of transactions $DB' = DB_{X_1} \cup DB_{X_2} \cup ... \cup DB_{X_s}$. The key difference of our model from that in [19] is that we include the pair-wise probability distribution of items in DB', while it is assumed that items are independent boolean random variables in [19]. As to be shown, the pair-wise probability not only allows us to build more accurate probability model to characterize the patterns in a profile, but also provides better measures to group patterns into profiles.

3.1 Estimate Support Using Profiles

In this subsection, we will present two methods of estimating the support of a pattern given a profile. The first is based on a simple Bayesian model derived from the pairwise probability and then applies on chain rule to compute the joint probability of items in a pattern; the second is simplified version of the first method.

Before presenting our methods, we first give some background on estimating the probability. The support of a pattern in dataset DB can be regarded as the summary of the probability that the pattern occurs in each transaction.

$$p(X|DB) = \sum_{t \in DB} p(X|t) * p(t)$$

where $p(t) = 1/|DB|$ and $p(X|t) = 1$ if $X \in t$, 0 otherwise.

We regard the probability of observing a pattern as the probability that the pattern is generated by its profile times the probability of observing the profile from a transaction.

$$p(X|t) \approx p(X|\Phi, t) * p(\Phi|t) \approx p(X|\Phi) * p(\Phi|t),$$

where we assume the conditional independence $p(X|\Phi, t) = p(X|\Phi)$. According to the model, one can estimate the support for a given pattern X from the profile that it belongs to. Given a profile Φ over a set of patterns $X_1, X_2, ..., X_s$, the estimated support for X based on the profile Φ is

$$\widehat{s}(X) = \Phi.\rho * p(X|\Phi) \tag{1}$$

where $\Phi.\rho = |DB_{X_1} \cup ... \cup DB_{X_s}|/|DB|$.

The problem here is how to estimate the $p(X|\Phi)$. Our first approach to estimating probability $p(X|\Phi)$ is to build a simple Bayesian network, a Chow-Liu tree model, for each profile using the pairwise probability. We first compute the mutual information between each pair of items in a profile, and then compute the minimum spanning tree from the full graph whose nodes are the items and edges are the mutual information. After obtaining the minimum spanning tree, i.e. a polytree Bayesian network, we can use the Pearls' belief propagation algorithm [15] to compute $p(X|\Phi)$.

The Chow-Liu tree approximates an nth-order distribution by a product of n -1 second order component distributions. The Chow-Liu Tree structure is proved to be the optimal one in the sense of Maximum Likelihood criterion [6]. Before introducing the algorithm for building Chow-Liu tree model [6], we first give the formula to compute mutual information between two variables:

$$I(X,Y) = \sum_x \sum_y p(x,y) log \frac{p(x,y)}{p(x)p(y)} \tag{2}$$

Intuitively, $I(X,Y)$ measures the amount of information that random variable X contains about Y (and vice versa). The higher of the value, the more correlated are the two variables; $I(X,Y) = 0$ if X and Y are independent.

We need to perturb the probabilities $p(x,y)$, $p(x)$ and $p(y)$ to avoid zero probabilities. For example, we compute $p'(x)$ as follows:

$$p'(x) = \lambda u + (1 - \lambda)p(x) \tag{3}$$

where λ is a constant, $0 < \lambda < 1$, and u is the prior of x and can be the background distribution of item x.

Algorithm 1 outlines how to learn a Chow-Liu tree structure for a profile Φ. In the beginning, it computes the mutual information using Equation 2 between any pairs of items in the profile Φ. In lines 4-10, it repeats until a Chow-Liu tree is discovered. The algorithm in lines 4-10 aims to find a spanning tree with the maximal mutual information, which can be implemented with Kruskal's algorithm of Prim's algorithm [8] for finding minimum spanning tree.

Complexity analysis. In order to compute the mutual information of each pair, we need to scan the database once to compute the probability. It takes $O(f^2 n)$, where n is the number of tuples supporting the profile i.e. $\Phi.\rho \times |DB|$ and f is the size the largest

Input: Transaction database DB
Profile $\Phi = < \chi, \rho, \theta >$
Output: a Chow-Liu tree model.

1. let MI be the set of mutual information $I(x_i, x_j)$ between any two items x_i, x_j in $\Phi.\chi$;
2. initiate a tree $T(V, E)$, where each item in $\Phi.\chi$ becomes one node in V and $E = \emptyset$;
3. initiate $k = 0$;
4. **while** $k < |\Phi.\chi| - 1$
5.   select pair (x_i, x_j) such that $x_i, x_j = argmax_{x_i, x_j} I(x_i, x_j)$;
6.   **if** there is no cycle formed in T **then**
7.   add edge (x_i, x_j) into T;
8. $E = E \cup (x_i, x_j)$
9. $k = k + 1$;
10. $MI = MI \backslash \{(x_i, x_j)\}$;
11. **return** T;

Fig. 1. Algorithm CLtree

tuple. It takes $O(d^2)$ to compute the mutual information, where d is the size of $\Phi.\chi$. If one adopts Kruskal's algorithm to compute the minimum spanning tree (lines 4-10), it takes $O(d^2 logd)$; it takes $O(d^2 + dlogd)$ if one uses Prim's algorithm [8]. Hence, Algorithm 1 can finish in $O(f^2 n + d^2 + d^2 logd)$ using Kruskal's algorithm.

After the Chow-Liu tree model is learned, we can compute $p(X|\Phi)$ based on the chain rule and some specified order of the items in χ:

$$P(X|\Phi) = p(x_1, \Phi) \prod p(x_i | x_{i-1}, ..., x_1, \Phi) \tag{4}$$

$p(x_1, \Phi)$ is already in the profile Φ and the $p(x_i | x_{i-1}, ..., x_1, \Phi)$, $i = 2, ..., d$ (d is the size of X) can be computed using the belief propagation algorithm [15]. The belief propagation algorithm is a message-passing scheme that updates the probability distributions for each node in a Bayesian network in response to observations of one or more variables, i.e. to compute the probability of x_i after the values of $x_{i-1}, ..., x_1$ are set as evidence. Hence, $\prod p(x_i | x_{i-1}, ..., x_1, \Phi)$ can be computed by taking the product of belief measures. On a polytree (Chow-Liu tree is a polytree), the belief propagation algorithm converges in time proportional to the number of edges in the tree, i.e. $|\Phi.\chi| - 1$. Note that there is no need to propagate the impact of each instantiation to the entire polytree; the propagation are transmitted only to those variables in $P(X|\Phi)$. Interested readers can refer to [15] for the algorithm details.

Our second method further approximates the nth-order distribution by replacing the higher order conditional probabilities with second order ones:

$$P(X|\Phi) = p(x_1, \Phi) \prod p(x_i | x_{i-1}, \Phi) \tag{5}$$

The above formula approximates $p(x_i | x_{i-1}, ..., x_1, \Phi)$ with $p(x_i | x_{i-1}, \Phi)$, and thus learning Bayesian network is not required. The second method will be more efficient than the first one. As to be shown in experiment, this simplified model can also improve greatly the independent model in [19].

The probability model of profiles provides a method of representing a set of patterns in a compact way and methods of recovering their supports. The remaining problem is how to group the set of patterns into k profiles.

4 Grouping Patterns

In this section, we first introduce the similarity measures between the profiles and then describe a clustering algorithm using the similarity measures.

The key of clustering patterns into profiles with high quality is a good distance measure for the patterns and profiles as well. At the beginning of the clustering, each pattern can be regarded as a profile with triple elements as described in the previous section. Hence, one ideal distance measure between two profiles Φ_p and Φ_q should consider (1) the overlapping of master patterns $\Phi_p.\chi$ and $\Phi_q.\chi$; (2) the similarity of the probability distribution of items in the two profiles, which can reflect the correlation between the transactions that support the two profiles; (3) the support of the two profiles.

These three factors are correlated one another. Kullback-Leibler divergence (KL-divergence) is widely used to compute the divergence between two probability distributions and is also adopted in [19]. We choose KL-divergence to measure the distance between two profiles since it considers the three factors, especially the first two, of the profiles: if two patterns differ greatly in the items (of their master patterns), or the two probability distributions differ greatly, the KL distance will be large; if the profiles are similar in master patterns as well as probability, it is highly possible that their supports are similar (Note that it is not sufficient).

The KL-divergence of two variable can be computed as follows:

$$\mathrm{KL}(x||y) = \sum_{x,y} p(x)log\frac{p(x)}{p(y)} \tag{6}$$

When the $p(x)$ and $q(x)$ have zero probability, KL($x||y$)= ∞. This can be avoided by smoothing the $p(x)$ and $q(x)$ as Equation 3.

The smaller $KL(x||y)$ value is, the more similar of the distributions of variables x and y. In our profile model, there are distributions for pairwise variables and single variables and they contain overlapping information. We consider three combinations to compute the KL-divergence of the two profiles.

1. $\mathrm{KL}(\Phi_p||\Phi_q) = \sum_{x_i,x_j \in C} \mathrm{KL}(p(x_i,x_j)||q(x_i,x_j))$, where $C = \Phi_p.\chi \cup \Phi_q.\chi$;

   The formula is simple and computes the KL-divergence using joint distribution for every pair of items in the union of the master patterns of the two profiles.

2. $\mathrm{KL}(\Phi_p||\Phi_q) = \sum_{x_i,x_j \in C} \mathrm{KL}(p(x_i,x_j)||q(x_i,x_j)) + \sum_{x_i \in D} \mathrm{KL}(p(x_i)||q(x_i))$, where $C = \Phi_p.\chi \cap \Phi_q.\chi$ if $|\Phi_p.\chi \cap \Phi_q.\chi| > 1$; $C = \emptyset$ otherwise, and $D = \Phi_p.\chi \cup \Phi_q.\chi - C$;

   The formula computes the KL-divergence using the joint distribution for common pairs of items in the master patterns of the two profiles, and computes the KL-divergence using the distribution of single item for items that appear only in one master pattern of the two profiles.

3. $\mathrm{KL}(\Phi_p||\Phi_q) = \sum_{x_i,x_j \in \Phi_p.\chi \vee x_i,x_j \in \Phi_p.\chi} \mathrm{KL}(p(x_i,x_j)||q(x_i,x_j)) +$ $\alpha \times \mathrm{KL}(p(\Phi_p.\chi)||q(\Phi_p.\chi)) + \beta \times \mathrm{KL}(p(\Phi_q.\chi)||q(\Phi_q.\chi))$, where $\alpha = 1$ if $|\Phi_p.\chi| = 1$; 0 otherwise, and $\beta = 1$ if $|\Phi_q.\chi| = 1$; 0 otherwise.

   The formula can be regarded as a combination of the above two methods: it employs the pair wise distribution if a pair appears in at least one of the master patterns; it employs the distribution for single item if the master pattern is a single item.

We introduce one complementary measure when two patterns have the same KL-divergence score. This often happens especially when the profile is composed of one pattern in the beginning of clustering. For example, consider three patterns $X_1 = \{abcd, 100\}$, $X_2 = \{abef, 500\}$ and $X_3 = \{ab, 600\}$, where the pattern and its support are separated by comma. It is easy to verify that $\mathrm{KL}(X_1||X_2)$ and $\mathrm{KL}(X_1||X_3)$ are the same whichever the three combination we use. In this example, suppose that we want to cluster the three patterns into two groups. Intuitively we should group X_2 and X_3 together but not X_1 and X_2 although their KL-divergences are the same. This is because X_2 and X_3 have similar number of support and thus their transactions that support them likely have large overlapping. This example implies that KL-divergence score alone may not be sufficient sometimes.

We can accurately compute the overlapping of two patterns (or profiles) Φ_p and Φ_q by

$$D(\Phi_p, \Phi_q) = (DB_{\Phi_p} \cap DB_{\Phi_q})/(DB_{\Phi_p} \cup DB_{\Phi_q})$$

This measure is proposed in [18] to compute the similarity of patterns. But it takes $O(|DB|)$ to compute one pair of patterns and thus is relatively expensive. Instead, we use a simplified score and find it achieves reasonably good results in all our experiments.

$$D'(\Phi_p, \Phi_q) = |\Phi_p.\rho - \Phi_q.\rho|/max(\Phi_p.\rho, \Phi_q.\rho) \tag{7}$$

where $\Phi_p.\rho$, $\Phi_q.\rho$ are the support of Φ_p and Φ_q respectively.

In what follows, we will introduce how to cluster the patterns based on the two measures introduced above. We adopt hierarchical agglomerative clustering to group profiles. Hierarchical clustering is shown to obtain stable results in [19] in clustering frequent patterns. But other clustering methods, such as K-means, can be adopted to cluster profiles.

Hierarchical clustering can not only produce k profiles, but also generate a dendrogram which allows users to explore the k profiles in a top-down manner. Algorithm 2 outlines the hierarchical clustering method for profiles. In line 4, the algorithm computes the pair-wise KL-divergence (Equation 6) and computes the complementary distance measure (Equation 7) in line 5. Note that we only compute the KL-divergence score between Φ_i and Φ_j using $\mathrm{KL}(\Phi_i||\Phi_j)$ $(i < j)$ although the KL score is not symmetric. We found that the final clustering results are similar even if we compute $\mathrm{KL}(\Phi_j||\Phi_i)$. In lines 6-12, the algorithm repeats until the number of clusters becomes k. At each iteration, the algorithm picks two clusters that have the smallest KL-divergence score; if several pairs of clusters have the same smallest KL-divergence score, it picks

Input: Transaction database DB
Pattern set X= $\{X_1, X_2, ...X_m\}$
Number of profiles K
Output: a set of pattern profiles $\Phi_1, ..\Phi_k$.

1. initialize $k = m$ clusters, each of which contains one pattern;
2. **for** each Φ_i
3.   **for** each $\Phi_j, j < i$
        /* compute the pairwise KL divergence between Φ_i and Φ_j;*/
4. $DIST1_{ij} = KL(\Phi_i || \Phi_j)$
        /* compute the complementary distance between Φ_i and Φ_j;*/
5. $DIST2_{ij} = D'(\Phi_i, \Phi_j)$
6. **while** $k < K$
7.   select Φ_p and Φ_q such that $DIST1_{pq}$ is the smallest among all $DIST1_{ij}$ and $DIST2_{pq}$ is the smallest among all $DIST2_{ij}$ whose $DIST1_{ij} = DIST1_{pq}$;
8.   merge clusters Φ_p and Φ_q to a new cluster Φ_r;
9. $\Phi_r.\chi = \Phi_p.\chi \cup \Phi_q.\chi$
10. $DB_{\Phi_r} = DB_{\Phi_p} \cup DB_{\Phi_q}$
11.   update profile of Φ_r
12.   compute similarity scores between Φ_r and other profiles
13. scan dataset to update the K profiles
14. **return** Φ_i $(i = 1, ...K)$

Fig. 2. Algorithm HCluster

the pair of clusters with the minimum complementary distance. In line 9, the algorithm updates the master pattern of the new cluster by combining the master patterns from the two clusters generating the new cluster. In line 10, the algorithm computes the combined transactions supported by the new profile.

In line 11, the algorithm needs to update the probability of the new profile. One method is to rebuild the accurate profile after two profiles are combined. However, this is expensive since computing profile needs to scan the original dataset. Instead, we approximate the probability p(x,y) of the profiles (we approximate p(x) similarly):

$$p(x, y|\Phi_r) = \frac{\Phi_p.\rho}{\Phi_p.\rho + \Phi_q.\rho} p(x, y|\Phi_p) + \frac{\Phi_q.\rho}{\Phi_p.\rho + \Phi_q.\rho} p(x, y|\Phi_q) \tag{8}$$

Complexity analysis. The initial KL-divergence computation takes $O(m^2d^2)$, where m is the number of patterns and d is the size of the maximum master pattern of all profiles. The computation of initial complementary distance takes $O(m^2)$. For each cluster Φ_p, we maintain a distance list between Φ_p and other clusters and sort them in non-descending order. When a new cluster is generated, we create and sort a distance list for it in time $O(mlogm)$. Thus the hierarchical clustering itself can be done in $O(m^2logm)$. Since we adopt the approximation as Equation 8 to compute the profile of the merged cluster, and thus we do not need to scan the dataset. It can be updated in $O(d^2)$ time. Finally, we scan the dataset to update the K profiles, which takes d^2nK.

Quality evaluation. From a high quality profile, one should be able to estimate the support of a frequent pattern as close as possible. In this paper, we adopt the same quality measure as that used in [19], namely restoration error:

$$J = \frac{1}{|T|} \sum_{X \in T} \frac{|\widehat{s}(X) - s(X)|}{s(X)} \tag{9}$$

where T is the set of frequent patterns to be evaluated. Restoration error is the average relative error between the estimate support of a pattern and its real support. It is desirable that the restoration error is small, and thus profiles can provide an accurate estimation.

Given a pattern, it may be covered by the master patterns of several profiles. Hence, we need to estimate these supports for it. However, we only select the maximum one by following the method in [19].

$$\widehat{s}(X) = max_{\Phi_i} \widehat{s}(X|\Phi_i)(i \in [1, k]) \tag{10}$$

We realize that there are other options to make the selection. For example, given a pattern and several profiles whose master patterns cover the pattern, we can pick the profile whose master pattern is the most similar to the given pattern to estimate support for the given pattern.

5 Empirical Study

In this section, we report the performance evaluation of our summarization method. The algorithms were implemented with C++. All the experiments were conducted on 2.4GhZ, 512M memory Intel PC running Linux.

We used three real-life datasets:

- **Mushroom.** The Mushroom dataset consists of 8124 hypothetical mushroom samples with 119 distinct features; each sample has 23 features. This is a dense dataset and is available from the UCI machine leaning repository [1].
- **BMS-Webview1.** The BMS-Webview [22] is a web click-stream dataset. The dataset consists of 59602 web sessions (transactions) with 497 distinct product pages (items).
- **BMS-POS.** The BMS-POS [22] contains seven years worth of point-of-sale data from a large electronic retailer. Each item represents a product category and each transaction is a customer's purchase transaction consisting of all the product categories purchased at one time. The dataset consists of 515597 transactions with 1657 distinct items.

We first evaluate the three combinations of computing KL-divergence given in Section 4, then compare our methods with the existing method, and finally evaluate the effect of probability model on clustering results and restoration error. We employed restoration error as the evaluation metric as [19] does.

[1] http://www.ics.uci.edu/ mlearn/MLRepository.html

5.1 Comparison with Existing Method

Before we compare with the exiting summarizing method, we first evaluate the three combinations in Section 4 of computing the KL-divergence score. We apply the three combinations to compute the KL divergence in the clustering algorithm while using the Equation 5 to estimate the supports of frequent patterns. Figure 3 shows the results on the dataset BMS-Webview1. The combination 2 and combination 3 consistently outperform combination 1 while the difference between combination 2 and 3 is trivial. We have obtained qualitatively similar results on the other two datasets. One possible reason for the worse performance of combination 1 is that it considers some pairs of items that do not appear in the same profile, i.e. such pairs do not represent any profile, and thus it is not meaningful to compute the divergence of such pairs.

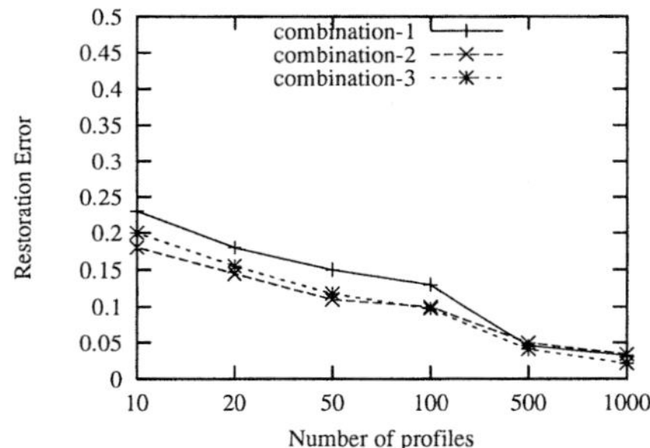

Fig. 3. The effect of different combinations to compute KL score on BMS-Webview1

We compare our algorithms against the latest work in [19] in terms of restoration error. The algorithm *summary* denotes the summarization method in [19]. According to the results of comparing three combinations given in Section 4, we use third combination to compute the KL divergence score for our methods. Furthermore, the algorithm *summary+* denotes the summarization method that uses the Equation 5 to estimate the support of a pattern; and the algorithm *summary++* employs the Equation 4 to estimate the support of a pattern.

We generated a set of 688 frequent closed patterns from Mushroom dataset by setting minimum support at 25% (The same set of frequent closed patterns was used in [19]). The maximum length of frequent patterns is 8. Figure 4 shows the average restoration error over the closed frequent patterns. Compared with the *summary* [19], both *summary+* and *summary++* can reduce the restoration error by at least 50%. The 688 patterns can be successfully summarized into 10 profiles with reasonable good quality: the average restoration error is less than 0.1.

We generated a set of 4195 frequent closed patterns from BMS-Webview by setting minimum support at 0.1% (the setting is the same as in [19]) and the maximum length of pattern is 6. Figure 5 shows the average restoration error over the set of closed frequent patterns. Both *summary+* and *summary++* outperform the *summary* by several times in terms of restoration errors. The *summary++* can reduce the restoration error of *summary+* by 50%. The 4195 patterns can be successfully summarized into 50 profiles

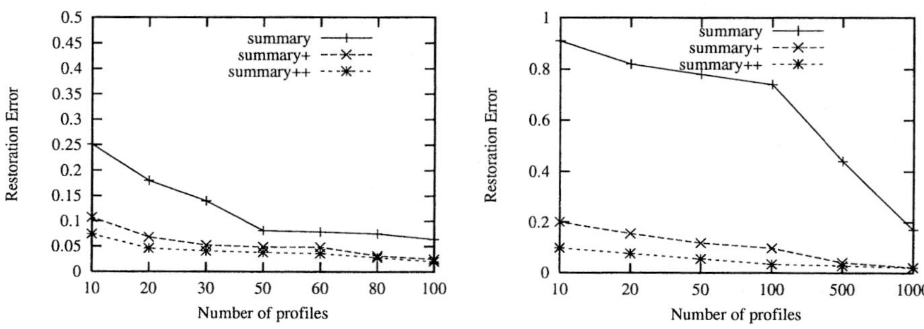

Fig. 4. Restoration Error for Mushroom

Fig. 5. Restoration Error for BMS-Webview1

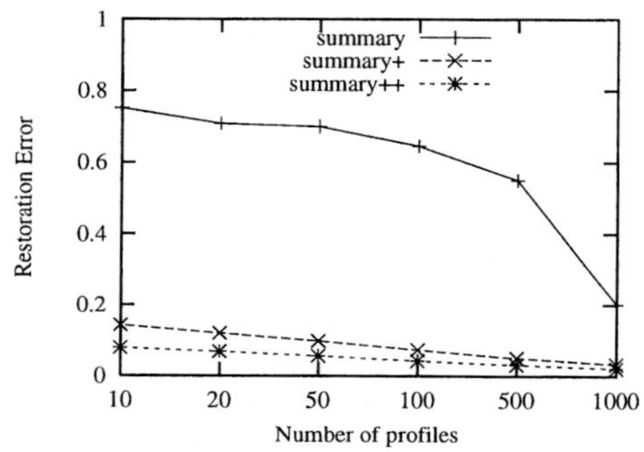

Fig. 6. Restoration Error for BMS-POS

with reasonable good quality: the average restoration error is 0.11 for *summary*+ and 0.05 for *summary*++ while it is 0.82 for *summary*. The restoration error is only 0.20 for *summary*+ and 0.09 for *summary*++ compared with 0.92 for algorithm *summary* when we cluster patterns into 10 profiles.

We generated a set of 6646 frequent closed patterns from BMS-POS by setting minimum support at 0.4% and the maximum length of frequent patterns is 6. Figure 6 shows the average restoration error over the set of closed frequent patterns. Both *summary*+ and *summary*++ outperform the *summary* by several times in terms of restoration errors. The *summary*++ can reduce the restoration error of *summary*+ by 50%. The 6646 patterns can be successfully summarized into 50 profiles with reasonable good quality: the average restoration error is less than 0.1 (0.096 for *summary*+ and 0.053 for *summary*++). The restoration error is only 0.142 for *summary*+ and 0.077 for *summary*++ compared with 0.752 for the *summary* when we summarize patterns into 10 profiles.

5.2 The Effect of Probability Model

In this subsection, we try to distinguish the effect of profile model on the quality of support restoration (Section 3) and the quality of the clustering results (Section 4) although the support restoration is closely related to clustering quality. We group the set of frequent patterns based on the model of algorithm *summary*, then build our probability model in each profile by accessing the dataset and use the Equation 5 to restore the support information. This is a hybrid of *summary* and *summary+*. We have found that it will yield qualitatively similar results if we make a hybrid from *summary* and *summary++*.

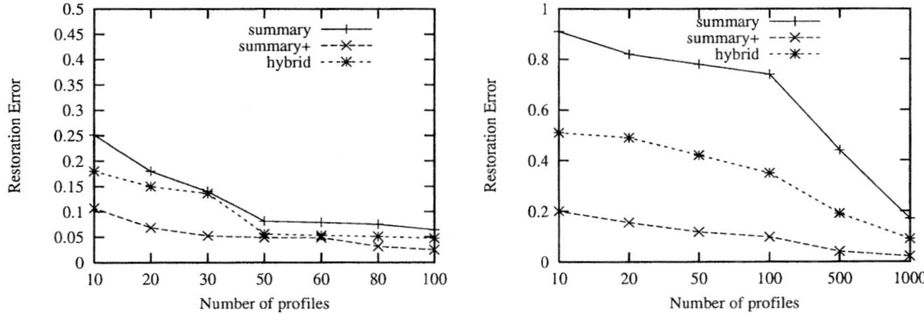

Fig. 7. Mushroom

Fig. 8. BMS-Webview1

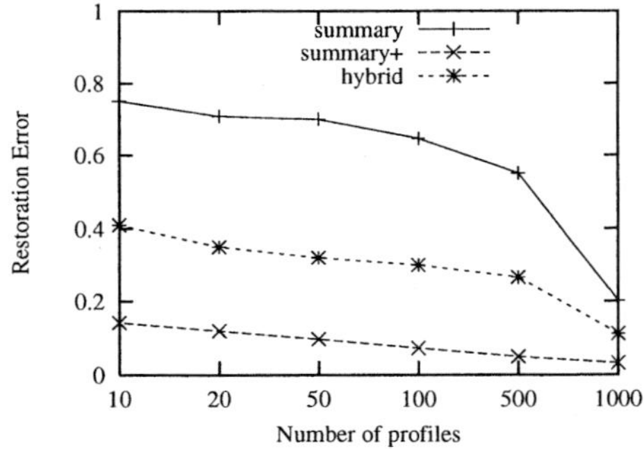

Fig. 9. BMS-POS

Figures 7-9 show the comparisons of the hybrid method with the *summary* and *summary+* on three datasets. We use the same setting for three datasets as that in the last subsection. The line of hybrid method lies between the those of *summary* and *summary+*. This means that the support estimation methods based on the probability model in Section 3 alone cannot achieve the improvement of *summary+* over *summary*. This implies that the clustering based on the probability model in Section 3 results in better clusters of frequent patterns than [19]. In other words, the probability model of this paper characterizes the frequent patterns better than the model in [19] does, and thus the calculated distances between clusters based on such model are more effective.

As a summary, both *summary+* and *summary++* greatly outperform *summary*. *Summary++* usually can improve *summary+* by 50% in terms of restoration accuracy while *summary+* is simple and is fast in terms of computation.

6 Related Work

Frequent pattern mining has received much attention in the past decade. Many frequent pattern mining algorithms have been proposed (e.g. [3, 9]). The number of frequent patterns can be very large and many of these frequent patterns may be redundant. To reduce the frequent patterns to a compact size, mining frequent closed patterns (e.g. [13]) has been proposed, which is a lossless compression of frequent patterns. Lossless here means that all frequent patterns together with their supports can be recovered from the closed patterns. Another lossless compression patterns of frequent patterns has been proposed to mine non-derivable frequent patterns [5].

There have been some other proposals to mine a subset of all frequent patterns. These methods are lossy in the sense that not all information about frequent patterns can be recovered. Maximal frequent pattern (e.g. [2]) is one of the most typical concepts in this category. In maximal frequent pattern, all frequent sub-patterns are removed, and thus the number of patterns is greatly reduced. However, the support information of all the sub-patterns are lost and maximal patterns can be large in number. Other lossy compression proposals include error-tolerant patterns [20], top-k patterns [10], condensed frequent pattern base [16], compressed frequent pattern sets [18].

The closest work to our study is the k approximation frequent sets [1] and k summarizing profiles [19]. The k approximation frequent sets use k frequent itemsets to cover a collection of frequent itemsets while trying to minimize the negative positive patterns; the set of frequent patterns can be deducted from the k approximate frequent sets. However, the support information of patterns is lost. The k summarizing profiles use a simple independence probability model to represent a set of patterns and cluster the profiles. One salient feature of k summarizing profiles is that support information can be restored relatively accurately. In this paper, we improve the probability model to represent model and propose new methods to derive support using our proposed probability model. Our profile model is also related to the probabilistic models developed in [14] for query approximation, where frequent patterns and their supports are used to estimate query selectivity, and independence model and Chow-Liu tree model are used for query approximation.

There are also many proposals about mining interesting rules with various interestingness measures [12]: post-processing to remove uninteresting rules [11], mining interesting rules [4], mining non-redundant association rules[21], and mining top-k covering rule groups [7]. There studies are very different from the pattern summarization.

7 Conclusion and Discussions

In this paper, we have revisited the pattern summarization problem. We proposed a probability model to represent a set of frequent patterns and two methods of estimating the support of a pattern from the model. With the model, we can arrange all patterns into a set of (hierarchial) clusters and thus users can explore the patterns in a top-down manner. Our methods can successfully summarize patterns into tens of profiles while the supports of patterns can be recovered reasonably accurately. Empirical studies show that our method can achieve accurate summarization in real-life data and the supports of frequent patterns can be restored more accurately than the previous method.

In future, we plan to investigate the application of other distance measure, such as Jensen-Shannon divergence, to compute the similarity of profiles and other clustering methods, such as the co-clustering based on information theory. We also plan to apply for clustering algorithms and co-clustering algorithm to the transaction database directly to obtain some clusters of items (one item could be in multiple clusters) and build a probability model for each cluster. It would be interesting to investigate the quality of such clusters to estimate the supports of frequent patterns.

References

1. F. Afrati, A. Gionis, and H. Mannila. Approximating a collection of frequent sets. In *Proceedings of the tenth ACM SIGKDD international conference on Knowledge discovery and data mining*, pages 12–19, 2004.
2. R. Agarwal, C. Aggarwal, and V. V. V. Prasad. Depth first generation of long patterns. In *Proc. of KDD*, 2000.
3. R. Agrawal and R. Srikant. Fast algorithms for mining association rules. In *Proc. 1994 Int. Conf. Very Large Data Bases (VLDB'94)*, pages 487–499, Sept. 1994.
4. R. J. Bayardo and R. Agrawal. Mining the most intersting rules. In *Proc. of ACM SIGKDD*, 1999.
5. T. Calders and B. Goethals. Mining all non-derivable frequent itemsets. In *Proceedings of the 6th European Conference on Principles of Data Mining and Knowledge Discovery*, 2002.
6. C. Chow and C. Liu. Approximating discrete probability distributions with dependence trees. *IEEE Transactions on Information Theory*, 14:462–467, 1968.
7. G. Cong, K.-L. Tan, A. K. H. Tung, and X. Xu. Mining top-k covering rule groups for gene expression data. In *Proceedings of the ACM SIGMOD international conference on Management of data*, 2005.
8. T. Cormen, C. Leiserson, and R. Rivest. *Introduction to Algorithms*. The MIT Press, 1990.
9. J. Han, J. Pei, and Y. Yin. Mining frequent patterns without candidate generation. In *Proc. 2000 ACM-SIGMOD Int. Conf. Management of Data (SIGMOD'00)*, 2000.
10. J. Han, J. Wang, Y. Lu, and P. Tzvetkov. Mining top.k frequent closed patterns without minimum support. In *Proceedings of the 2002 IEEE International Conference on Data Mining (ICDM)*, 2002.
11. B. Liu, W. Hsu, and Y. Ma. Pruning and summarizing the discovered associations. In *ACM KDD*, 1999.
12. E. R. Omiecinski. Alternative interest measures for mining associations in databases. *IEEE Transactions on Knowledge and Data Engineering*, 15(1):57–69, 2003.
13. N. Pasquier, Y. Bastide, R. Taouil, and L. Lakhal. Discovering frequent closed itemsets for association rules. In *Proc. 7th Int. Conf. Database Theory (ICDT'99)*, Jan. 1999.
14. D. Pavlov, H. Mannila, and P. Smyth. Beyond independence: Probabilistic models for query approximation on binary transaction data. *IEEE Transactions on Knowledge and Data Engineering*, 15(6):1409–1421, 2003.
15. J. Pearl. *Probabilistic reasoning in intelligent systems: networks of plausible inference*. Morgan Kaufmann Publishers Inc., San Francisco, CA, USA, 1988.
16. J. Pei, G. Dong, W. Zou, and J. Han. Mining condensed frequent-pattern bases. *Knowl. Inf. Syst.*, 6(5):570–594, 2004.
17. J. Wang and G. Karypis. SUMMARY: Efficiently summarizing transactions for clustering. In *Proceedings of the 2004 IEEE International Conference on Data Mining (ICDM)*, 2004.
18. D. Xin, J. Han, X. Yan, and H. Cheng. Mining compressed frequent-pattern sets. In *VLDB*, 2005.

19. X. Yan, H. Cheng, J. Han, and D. Xin. Summarizing itemset patterns: a profile-based approach. In *Proceeding of the eleventh ACM SIGKDD international conference on Knowledge discovery in data mining*, 2005.
20. C. Yang, U. Fayyad, and P. S. Bradley. Efficient discovery of error-tolerant frequent itemsets in high dimensions. In *Proceedings of the seventh ACM SIGKDD international conference on Knowledge discovery and data mining*, 2001.
21. M. Zaki. Generating non-redundant association rules. In *Proc. 2000 Int. Conf. Knowledge Discovery and Data Mining (KDD'00)*, 2000.
22. Z. Zheng, R. Kohavi, and L. Mason. Real world performance of association rule algorithms. In *Proceedings of the Seventh ACM SIGKDD International Conference on Knowledge Discovery and Data Mining*, 2001.

Mining Spatio-temporal Association Rules, Sources, Sinks, Stationary Regions and Thoroughfares in Object Mobility Databases

Florian Verhein and Sanjay Chawla

School of Information Technologies, University of Sydney, NSW, Australia
{fverhein, chawla}@it.usyd.edu

Abstract. As mobile devices proliferate and networks become more location-aware, the corresponding growth in spatio-temporal data will demand analysis techniques to mine patterns that take into account the semantics of such data. Association Rule Mining has been one of the more extensively studied data mining techniques, but it considers discrete transactional data (supermarket or sequential). Most attempts to apply this technique to spatial-temporal domains maps the data to transactions, thus losing the spatio-temporal characteristics. We provide a comprehensive definition of *spatio-temporal association rules (STARs)* that describe how objects move between regions over time. We define *support* in the spatio-temporal domain to effectively deal with the semantics of such data. We also introduce other patterns that are useful for mobility data; *stationary regions* and *high traffic regions*. The latter consists of *sources*, *sinks* and *thoroughfares*. These patterns describe important temporal characteristics of regions and we show that they can be considered as special STARs. We provide efficient algorithms to find these patterns by exploiting several pruning properties[1].

1 Introduction

The need for spatio-temporal data mining and analysis techniques is growing. Some specific examples include managing cell phone networks and dealing with the data generated by Radio Frequency Identification Tags. Mining such data could detect patterns for applications as diverse as intelligent traffic management, sensor networks, stock control and wildlife monitoring. For example, consider the movement of users between cells of a mobile phone (or similar) network. Being able to predict where users will go would make cell hand-over decisions easier and improve bandwidth management. Also, since most people own a mobile phone these days, the data could be used for fast and inexpensive population movement studies. Local governments would find the ability to answer questions such as "how much is this park being used?", "which areas are congested?" and "what are the main routes that people take through the city" useful. The latter query would help design better pedestrian and vehicle routes to take into account the main flows of people.

We therefore consider a set of regions, which may be any shape or size, and a set of objects moving throughout these regions. We assume that it is possible to determine which objects are in a region, but we do not know precisely where an object is in that

[1] This research was partially funded by the ARC Discovery Grant, Project ID: DP0559005.

M.L. Lee, K.L. Tan, and V. Wuwongse (Eds.): DASFAA 2006, LNCS 3882, pp. 187–201, 2006.

region. We do not assume that objects are always somewhere in the region set, so in the example of a mobile phone network, turning the phone off poses no problems for our methods. We are interested in finding regions with useful temporal characteristics (thoroughfares, sinks, sources, and stationary regions) and rules that predict how objects will move through the regions (spatio-temporal association rules). A source occurs when the number of objects leaving a region is high enough. A sink has a high number of objects entering it. A thoroughfare is a region through which many objects move - that is, many objects enter and leave. A stationary region is where many objects tend to stay over time, while a STAR describes how an object moves between regions. Together, these patterns describe many mobility characteristics and can be used to predict future movements.

We take the approach of mining our patterns on a time window by time window basis. We think this is important because it allows us to see the changing nature of the patterns over time, and allows for interactive mining - including changing the mining parameters. Even though the patterns we consider occur in a spatial settings, they are all temporal patterns because they describe objects movements *over time*, as well as capturing *changes* in the way the objects move over time. To understand this, consider each pattern set ξ_i as capturing object movements over a 'short' period of time. In our algorithms this is the interval pair $[TI_i, TI_{i+1}]$. That is, ξ_i captures how the objects move between the time intervals TI_i and TI_{i+1}. Then, as the algorithm processes subsequent time intervals, the patterns mined at these points will in general change, forming a *sequence* of pattern sets $< \xi_i, \xi_{i+1}, ... >$. This change in the *patterns* that are output can be considered longer term changes. Such changes in the patterns describe the changes in the objects behavior over time. Another way to think about this is to consider the objects motion as a random process. If the process is stationary, we would expect the patterns to remain the same over time. If the process is not stationary, the patterns will change with time to reflect the change in the way the objects move.

There are a number of challenges when mining spatio-temporal data. First, dealing with the interaction of space and time is complicated by the fact that they have different semantics. Secondly, we also need to deal with these semantics effectively. This includes considering the effects of area and the time-interval width not only on the the patterns we mine, but also in the algorithms that find those patterns. Finally, handling updates efficiently in a dynamic environment is challenging - especially when the algorithm must be applied in real time. We adopt a *data stream* model where spatial data arrives continuously as a sequence of snapshots $S_1, S_2, ...$, and the model that we mine must keep up with this. Unless sampling techniques are used, such algorithms cannot do better than scale linearly with time. Since processing the spatial snapshots is expensive in general, we focus our attention there. We deal with exact techniques in this paper, but it is possible to use probabilistic counting techniques together with our algorithms, as demonstrated in one of our experiments.

2 Contributions

We make the following contributions:

– We give a rigorous definition of Spatio-Temporal Association Rules (STARs) that preserve spatial and temporal semantics. We define the concepts of *spatial coverage,*

spatial support, temporal coverage and *temporal support*. Because these definitions retain the semantics of the spatial and temporal dimensions, it allows us to mine data with regions of any size without skewing the results. That is, we successfully extend association rules to the spatio-temporal domain.
- We define useful spatio-temporal regions that apply to objects moving through such regions. These are *stationary regions* and *high traffic regions*. The latter may be further broken into *sources, sinks* and *thoroughfares*. We stress that these are temporal properties of a spatial region set, and show that they are special types of STARs. We also describe a technique for mining these regions efficiently by employing a pruning property.
- We propose a novel and efficient algorithm for mining the STARs by devising a pruning property based on the high traffic regions. This allows the algorithm to prune as much of the search space as possible (for a given dataset) before doing the computationally expensive part.

Our algorithms do not assume or rely on any form of index (such as an R-tree, or aggregated R-tree) to function or to obtain time savings. If such an index is available, the algorithms will perform even better. Our time savings come about due to a set of pruning properties, which are spatial in nature, based on the observation that only those patterns that have a support and confidence above a threshold are interesting to a user (in the sense that they model the data).

The rest of the paper is organized as follows. In Section 3 we survey related work and place our contributions in context. In Section 4 we give several related definitions of STARs that highlight some of the differences in interpreting STARs. We close the section with a detailed example to illustrate the subtleties. In Section 5 we define hot spots, stationary regions and high traffic regions. In Section 6 we describe our algorithm for mining STARs. The results of our experiments on STAR mining are described in Section 7. We conclude in Section 8 with a summary and directions for future work.

3 Related Work

There has been work on spatial association rules (examples include [1, 2]) and temporal association rules (examples include [3, 4]) but very little work has addressed both spatial and temporal dimensions. Most of the work that does can be categorised as traditional association rule mining [5] or sequential association rule mining *applied* to a spatio-temporal problem, such as in [6].

The work by Tao et al. [7] is the only research found that addressed the problem of STARs (albeit briefly) in the Spatial-Temporal domain. As an application of their work they show a brute force algorithm for mining specific spatio-temporal association rules. They consider association rules of the form $(r_i, \tau, p) \Rightarrow r_j$, with the following interpretation: "If an object is in region r_i at some time t, then with probability p it will appear in region r_j by time $t + \tau$". Their algorithm is a brute force technique that takes time quadratic in the number of regions. They use FM-PCSA sketches [8] for speed, have a simple STAR definition and ignore the spatial and temporal semantics of the data (such as the area of the regions or the time interval width).

Other interesting work that deals with spatio-temporal patterns in the spatio-temporal domain includes [9, 10, 11, 12, 7]. Mamoulis et al. [12] mine periodic patterns in objects moving between regions. Wang et al. [10] introduce what they call *flow patterns,* which describe the changes of events over space and time. They consider events occurring in regions, and how these events are connected with changes in neighbouring regions as time progresses. Ishikawa et al. [11] describe a technique for mining object mobility patterns in the form of markov transition probabilities from an indexed spatio temporal dataset of moving points. In this case, the transition probability p_{ij} of an (order 1) markov chain is $P(r_j|r_i)$ where r_i and r_j are regions, which is the confidence of a spatio-temporal association rule, although this is not mentioned by the authors. Tsoukatos et al. [9] mine frequent sequences of non spatio-temporal values for regions.

The work we have listed above is quite different from ours. Tao et al. [7] consider a simple spatio-temporal association rule definition, and the algorithm for finding the rules is brute force. Patterns that can be interpreted as STARs are considered by [11, 10], but they focus on very different research problems. The algorithm of [11] will find all transition probabilities, even if they are small. Amongst other things, our algorithm makes use of the fact that users will not be interested in rules below a support threshold, and uses this to prune the search space. And most importantly, none of the related work consider the spatial semantics of the regions, such as area, nor do they consider spatial support or similar concepts.

Dealing with the area of regions correctly is important for interpretation of the results. Many authors implicitly assume that the spatial regions can be specified to suit the algorithm. However, this is usually not the case. Cells in a mobile phone network are fixed, and have a wide range of sizes and geometries depending on geographic and population factors. Data mining applications have to be developed to work with the given region set, and we cannot ignore the influence of different sized regions. In the case of mining mobility patterns of moving objects (including sources, sinks, stationary regions, thoroughfares and STARs), ignoring area will skew the results in favour of larger regions because they will have more objects in them on average. By taking the region sizes into account, we avoid skewing the results and make our STARs comparable across different sized regions. Finally, although it is possible to scale most patterns by the area after they have been mined, this is undesirable because it prevents pruning of the search space. Our algorithms deal with the spatio-temporal semantics such as area effectively throughout the mining process and prune the search space as much as possible.

No previous work could be found, despite our efforts, that considers sources, sinks, stationary regions and thoroughfares. We think these patterns are very important because they capture temporal aspects of the way that objects move in space.

4 Spatio-temporal Association Rules

Given a dataset T of spatio-temporal data, define a language L that is able to express properties or groupings of the data (in both time, space, and object attributes). Given two sentences $\varphi_1 \in L$ and $\varphi_2 \in L$ that have no common terms, define a spatio-temporal association rule as $\varphi_1 \Rightarrow \varphi_2$. For example, the rule "late shift workers head into the city in the evening" can be expressed as $LateShiftWorker(x) \wedge InRegion(OutsideCity) \wedge Time(Evening) \Rightarrow InRegion(City) \wedge Time(Night)$. To evaluate whether such a spatio-temporal rule is interesting in T, a selection predicate $q(T, \varphi_1 \Rightarrow \varphi_2)$ maps the rule to $\{true, false\}$. The selection predicate will in general be a combination of support and confidence measures. For example, if the support and confidence of a rule R_1 are above their respective thresholds, then $q(T, R_1)$ evaluates to true.

The language L can be arbitrarily complex. We consider the special case where objects satisfying a query move between regions. A query q allows the expression of predicates on the set of non spatio-temporal attributes of the objects. We explore a number of definitions of such STARs in this section to highlight subtleties. We deal only with the STAR of Definition 2 outside this section, so the reader can safely focus on this on the first reading, without missing the main ideas of the paper.

Definition 1. STAR (alternatives): *Objects in region r_i satisfying q at time t will:*

(a) **appear** *in region r_j* **for the first time at** *time $t + \tau$.* Notation: $(r_i, t, @\tau, q) \Rightarrow r_j$.
(b) **be in region** r_j **at** *time $t + \tau$.* Notation: $(r_i, t, \tau, q) \Rightarrow r_j$.
(c) **appear** *in region r_j* **by (at or before)** *time $t + \tau$.* Notation: $(r_i, [t, \tau], q) \Rightarrow r_j$.

Note that (a) distinctly defines the time in r_j at which the objects must arrive. (b) is less rigid and allows objects that arrived earlier than time $t + \tau$ to be counted as long as they are still present *at* time $t + \tau$. (c) counts the objects as long as they have made an appearance in r_j at any time within $[t, t + \tau]$. We generalise (c) in our final definition:

Definition 2. STAR: *Objects appearing in region r_i satisfying q during time interval TI_s will appear in region r_j during time interval TI_e, where $TI_s \cap TI_e = \emptyset$ and TI_s is before[2] TI_e.* Notation: $(r_i, TI_s, q) \Rightarrow (r_j, TI_e)$.

Note that all the definitions are equivalent when $TI_s = t$, $TI_e = t + 1$ and $\tau = 1$. We are interested in the rules that have a high confidence and high support . We will use the notation $r_i \Rightarrow r_j$ or ζ for a STAR when we are not concerned with its exact definition. We will consider the problem of more rigorous support definitions that are more appropriate in a spatio-temporal setting later.

Definition 3. *Define* **support** *of a rule ζ, denoted by $\sigma(\zeta)$, to be the number of objects that follow the rule, and the support (with respect to q) of a region r during TI, denoted by $\sigma(r, TI, q)$, to be the number of distinct objects within r during TI satisfying q.*

Definition 4. *Define the* **confidence** *of a rule ζ whose antecedent contains region r_i during TI, denoted by $c(\zeta)$, as the conditional probability that the consequent is true given that the antecedent is true. This is the probability that the rule holds and is analogous to the traditional definition of confidence and is given by $c(\zeta) = \sigma(\zeta)/\sigma(r_i, TI, q)$.*

We illustrate the above definitions with an example.

Example 1. Consider Figure 1(a) which shows the movement of the set of objects $S = \{a, b, c, d, e, f, g\}$ in the time-frame $[t, t + 3]$ captured at the four snapshots $t, t + 1, t + 2, t + 3$. Assume that $q = `true'$ so that all objects satisfy the query.

[2] We actually mine rules where TI_s and TI_e are adjacent, but it is easy to generalise our methods so that this restriction does not hold.

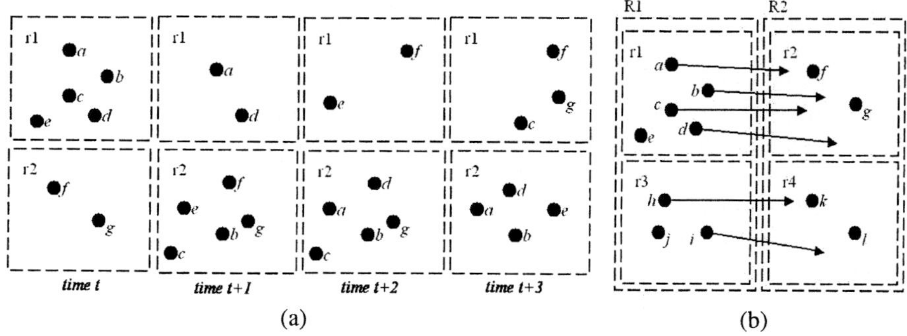

(a) (b)

Fig. 1. Example data for STAR mining

Consider the STAR $\zeta = (r_1, t, @1, q) \Rightarrow r_2$. From the diagram, $\{b, c, e\}$ follow this rule, so the support of the rule is $\sigma(\zeta) = 3$. Since the total number of objects that started in r_1 is $5 = \sigma(r_1, t, q) = |\{a, b, c, d, e\}|$, the confidence of the rule is $c(\zeta) = \frac{3}{5}$. For $\zeta = (r_1, t, @2, q) \Rightarrow r_2$ we have $\sigma(\zeta) = 2$ because $\{a, d\}$ follow the rule, and $c(\zeta) = \frac{2}{5}$. For $\zeta = (r_1, t, @3, q) \Rightarrow r_2$ we have $\sigma(\zeta) = 0$ because no object appears in r_2 for the first time at time $t + 3$.

The STAR $\zeta = (r_1, t, 1, q) \Rightarrow r_2$ is equivalent to $\zeta = (r_1, t, @1, q) \Rightarrow r_2$. But for $\zeta = (r_1, t, 2, q) \Rightarrow r_2$ we have $\sigma(\zeta) = 4$ because $\{a, b, c, d\}$ follow the rule (for this STAR definition we count them as long as they are still there at time $t + 2$), and $c(\zeta) = \frac{4}{5}$. For $\zeta = (r_1, t, 3, q) \Rightarrow r_2$ we have $\sigma(\zeta) = 4$ since $\{a, b, d, e\}$ follow the rule (we don't count c because it is no longer in r_2 at time $t + 3$), and $c(\zeta) = \frac{4}{5}$.

$(r_1, [t, 1], q) \Rightarrow r_2 = (r_1, t, 1, q) \Rightarrow r_2 = (r_1, t, @1, q) \Rightarrow r_2$. For $\zeta = (r_1, [t, 2], q) \Rightarrow r_2$ we have $\sigma(\zeta) = 5$ because $\{a, b, c, d, e\}$ satisfy the rule. e satisfies even though it has left by $t + 2$. Since all objects from r_1 have made an appearance in r_2 by $t + 2$ we must have $\sigma((r_1, [t, k], q) \Rightarrow r_2) = 5$ for all $k \geq 2$. For $\zeta = (r_1, [t + 1, 1], q) \Rightarrow r_2$ we have $\sigma(\zeta) = 2$ and $c(\zeta) = \frac{2}{2} = 1$.

The STAR $\zeta = (r_1, [t, t], q) \Rightarrow (r_2, [t+1, t+k])$ is equivalent to $(r_1, [t, k], q) \Rightarrow r_2$ for $k \geq 1$. For the STAR $\zeta = (r_1, [t, t + 1], q) \Rightarrow (r_2, [t + 2, t + 3])$ we have 5 distinct objects ($\{a, b, c, d, e\}$) appearing in r_1 during $[t, t + 1]$ and 6 distinct objects ($\{a, b, c, d, e, g\}$) appearing in r_2 during $[t + 2, t + 3]$. The objects following the rule are $\{a, b, c, d, e\}$ so the support of the rule is 5 and its confidence is $\frac{5}{5} = 1$. For $\zeta = (r_1, [t + 1, t + 2], q) \Rightarrow (r_2, [t + 3])$ we have $\sigma(\zeta) = 3$ and $c(\zeta) = \frac{3}{4}$.

Counting the objects that move between regions is a simple task. The main idea is that if S_1 is the set of objects in r_1 at time t and S_2 is the set of objects in r_2 at time $t + 1$ then the number of objects moving from r_1 to r_2 during that time is $|S_1 \cap S_2|$ (assuming objects don't appear in more than one region at a time).

4.1 Extending Support into the Spatio-temporal Setting

Defining support in a spatio-temporal setting is more complicated than we have considered so far. Specifically, the size of any spatial atom or term in the rule should affect the support. That is, given the support in Definition 3, two rules whose only difference is the area of the region in which they apply will have identical support. Consider Figure 1(b) where $r_1 \subset R_1$, and objects $\{a, b, c, d\}$ move from r_1 to r_2 between time t and $t+1$. Then the rules $r_1 \Rightarrow r_2$ and $R_1 \Rightarrow r_2$ have the same support[3]. However, among these sets of equivalent rules we would prefer the rule covering the smallest area because it is more precise. A similar issue arises when we wish to compare the support of rules that cover different sized regions. Consider again Figure 1(b). The support of $r_1 \Rightarrow r_2$ is 4 and $\sigma(r_3 \Rightarrow r_4) = 2$ while $\sigma(R_1 \Rightarrow R_2) = 6$ which is higher than the other rules but only because it has a greater coverage. This leads to the conclusion that support should be defined in terms of the coverage of a rule.

Definition 5. *The* **spatial coverage** *of a spatio-temporal association rule ζ, denoted by $\phi_s(\zeta)$, is the sum of the area referenced in the antecedent and consequent of that rule. Trivially, the spatial coverage of a region r_i is defined as $\phi_s(r_i) = area(r_i)$.*

For example, the coverage of the rule $r_1 \Rightarrow r_2$ is $area(r_1) + area(r_2)$. This remains true even if $r_1 = r_2$ so that STARs with this property are not artificially advantaged over the others. We solve the problem of different sized regions by scaling the support $\sigma(\zeta)$ of a rule by the area that it covers, to give *spatial support.*

Definition 6. *The* **spatial support**, *denoted by $\sigma_s(\zeta)$, is the spatial coverage scaled support of the rule. That is, $\sigma_s(\zeta) = \sigma(\zeta)/\phi_s(\zeta)$. The spatial support of a region r_i during TI and with respect to q is $\sigma_s(r_i, TI, q) = \sigma(r_i, TI, q)/\phi_s(r_i)$.*

Consider again Figure 1(b) and assume the r_i have unit area and the R_i are completely composed of the r_i they cover. Then we have $\sigma_s(r_1 \Rightarrow r_2) = \sigma(r_1 \Rightarrow r_2)/\phi_s(r_1 \Rightarrow r_2) = 4/2 = 2$, $\sigma_s(r_3 \Rightarrow r_4) = 2/2 = 1$ and $\sigma_s(R_1 \Rightarrow R_2) = \sigma(R_1 \Rightarrow R_2)/\phi_s(R_1 \Rightarrow R_2) = 6/4 = \frac{3}{2}$. The rule $R_1 \Rightarrow R_2$ no longer has an advantage, and in-fact its spatial support is the weighted average of its two composing rules.

We do not need to scale confidence because it does not suffer from these problems. Indeed, increasing the size of the regions in a rule will on average increase both $\sigma(\zeta)$ and $\sigma(r_i, TI_s)$, so larger regions are not advantaged. Confidence is also a (conditional) probability, so scaling it by spatial coverage would remove this property.

In a spatio-temporal database we must also consider the *temporal support* and *temporal coverage*.

Definition 7. *The* temporal coverage *of a rule ζ, denoted by $\phi_t(\zeta)$, is the total length of the time intervals in the rule definition.*

For example, the temporal coverage of the rule $(r_i, TI_s, q) \Rightarrow (r_j, TI_e)$ is $|TI_s| + |TI_e|$ where $|TI|$ is an appropriate measure of the time interval width.

Definition 8. *The* temporal support *of a rule ζ, denoted by $\sigma_t(\zeta)$, is the number of time interval pairs $TI' = [TI_s, TI_e]$ over which it holds*[4].

Note that we did not perform scaling by temporal coverage. In short, this is because we view the temporal coverage as being defined by the user and so each rule mined

[3] Since $\{a, b, c, d\}$ follow the rules, the support is 4 in both cases.

[4] Of course, we then omit TI_s and TI_e from the notation of ζ.

will necessarily have the same temporal coverage. A more complicated reason presents itself when we consider mining the actual rules. For example, assume the temporal coverage of a rule ζ is τ. We have at least two options, either we count the temporal support of the rule during $[t, t+\tau], [t+1, t+1+\tau], [t+2, t+2+\tau], ...$ or during $[t, t+\tau], [t+\tau, t+2\tau], [t+2\tau, t+3\tau], ...$ Scaling by temporal coverage would only make sense in the second case. If we assume an open timescale (one that has no end, or is sufficiently large that we can assume this) then the number of opportunities to gain a support count (that is, for the rule to hold) in the first case does not depend on the size of τ. That is, the temporal coverage is not a factor. Note that *temporal support* only applies to the case where a user is interested in which STARs re-occur over time (and hence STARs which rarely occur are not interesting).

The reader should note that the definitions of STARs that we give apply to a specific time interval and describe how objects move during that time. This is quite general in the sense that the mined STARs can be analysed for changes over time, for periodicities, or simply aggregated in time (using temporal support) to find recurrent patterns.

Both temporal and spatial coverage are defined by the user or the application. Spatial coverage is inherent in the size of the regions. Temporal coverage is more flexible and determines the window for which rules must be valid, but this choice is the same for all rules. When mining STARs we attempt to find rules that have a *spatial support* above a threshold, $minSpatSup$ and *confidence* above $minConf$. If the user is interested in summarising STARs over time, we additionally output only those rules with *temporal support* above $minTempSup$.

5 Hot-Spots, High Traffic Areas and Stationary Regions

Definition 9. *A region r is a dense region or* **hot spot** *with respect to q during TI if $density(r, TI, q) \equiv \sigma_s(r, TI, q) \geq minDensity$, where $minDensity$ is a given density threshold. We also define r as dense during $TI' = [TI_i, TI_{i+1}]$ if it is dense during both both TI_i and TI_{i+1}.*

We define a region r to have high traffic (with respect to some query q) if the number of objects that satisfy q and are entering and/or leaving the region is above some threshold. A stationary region is one where enough objects remain in the region. These patterns are a special type of STAR. They are also easy to find. Consider two *successive* time intervals TI_1 and TI_2. Then the number of objects (satisfying q) that are in r in TI_2 that were not there in TI_1 is the number of objects that entered r between TI_1 and TI_2. Let S_1 be the set of objects (satisfying q) that are in r during TI_1, and let S_2 be the corresponding set for TI_2. We are clearly looking for $|S_2 - S_1|$, where $-$ is the set difference operation. Similarly, the number of objects leaving r is $|S_1 - S_2|$ and the number of objects that remain in r for both TI_1 and TI_2 is $|S_1 \cap S_2|$.

Example 2. Consider again Figure 1(a) during $TI' = [[t, t], [t+1, t+1]] \equiv [t, t+1]$ and assume the threshold is 3. $\{e, b, c\}$ enter r_2 during TI', so r_2 is a sink and because they came from r_1, r_1 is a source. During $TI' = [t+1, t+2]$, $\{g, b, c\}$ remain in r_2 so it is a stationary region during TI'. If the threshold is 2, it would also be a thoroughfare because $\{a, d\}$ enter while $\{e, f\}$ leave during TI'. r_2 is also a stationary region during $[t+2, t+3]$ because $\{a, b, d\}$ stay there.

To express high traffic regions as STARs, note that if we let $*$ be the set of regions excluding r but including a special region r_{else}, then the number of objects entering r during $TI' = [TI_i, TI_{i+1}]$ is just the support of $(*, TI_i, q) \Rightarrow (r, TI_{i+1})$. We need r_{else} to cater for the case that an object 'just' appears (disappears) from the region set. We model this as the object coming from (going to) r_{else}. This situation would happen in the mobile phone example when a user turns his/her phone on (off). We now formally define high traffic areas and stationary regions.

Definition 10. *A region r is a* **high traffic region** *with respect to query q if the number of objects (satisfying q) entering r (n_e) or leaving r (n_l) during $TI' = [TI_i, TI_{i+1}]$ satisfy*

$$\frac{\alpha}{\phi_s(r)} \geq minTraffic : \alpha = n_e \text{ or } n_l$$

where $minTraffic$ is a given density threshold and ϕ_s is given by definition 5. Note that $n_e \equiv \sigma((*, TI_i, q) \Rightarrow (r, TI_{i+1}))$ and $n_l \equiv \sigma((r, TI_i, q) \Rightarrow (*, TI_{i+1}))$.

Such regions can be further subdivided. If $n_e/\phi_s(r)$ is above $minTraffic$ we call that region a **sink.** *If $n_l/\phi_s(r)$ is above $minTraffic$ we call it a* **source,** *and if a region is classified as both a sink and a source we call it a* **thoroughfare.**

Definition 11. *If the number of objects remaining in r, denoted by n_s, satisfies $\frac{n_s}{\phi_s(r)} \equiv \sigma((r, TI_i, q) \Rightarrow (r, TI_{i+1}))/\phi_s(r) \geq minTraffic$ then we call r a* **stationary region**. *A stationary region may or may not be a high traffic region.*

Note that if we define $area(*) = 0$ then the definition of high traffic areas is a statement about the *spatial support* of special types of STARs. For stationary regions however, we get as a consequence of Definition 5 that $\frac{n_s}{\phi_s(r)} = 2 \cdot \sigma_s((r, TI_i, q) \Rightarrow (r, TI_{i+1}))$. We define $n_\alpha/\phi_s(r) : \alpha \in \{e, l, s\}$ as the *spatial support* of these patterns.

The following theorem allows us to prune the search space for finding high traffic regions and stationary regions.

Theorem 1. *If $minTraffic \geq minDensity$ then:*

1. The set of sources during $[TI_i, TI_{i+1}]$ are a subset of dense regions during TI_i
2. The set of sinks during $[TI_i, TI_{i+1}]$ are a subset of dense regions during TI_{i+1}
3. The set of stationary regions during $[TI_i, TI_{i+1}]$ are a subset of the regions that are both dense during TI_i and during TI_{i+1}.

Proof. Due to lack of space, it has been omitted. Please see [13].

As a consequence, if $minTraffic \geq minDensity$ then the set of thoroughfares during $[TI_i, TI_{i+1}]$ is a subset of the regions that are dense at time TI_i and at time TI_{i+1}. These properties prune the search for high traffic regions, so we can find high traffic regions by setting $minDensity = minTraffic$, mining all hot-spots and then mining the hot-spots for high traffic areas.

6 Mining Spatio-temporal Association Rules

In this section we exploit the high traffic area mining techniques to develop an efficient STAR mining algorithm for the STARs of definition 2 (omitting q for simplicity).

As a motivation to why this is useful, assume a set of regions R. Then there are $|R|^2$ possible rules for each TI', since there are $|R|$ starting regions and $|R|$ finishing regions. Using a brute force method, this would require $|R|^2$ counts of the number of objects in a region. Our algorithms address this quadratic time component.

The reader may find it useful to refer to Figure 2 while reading the following. We exploit the following theorem:

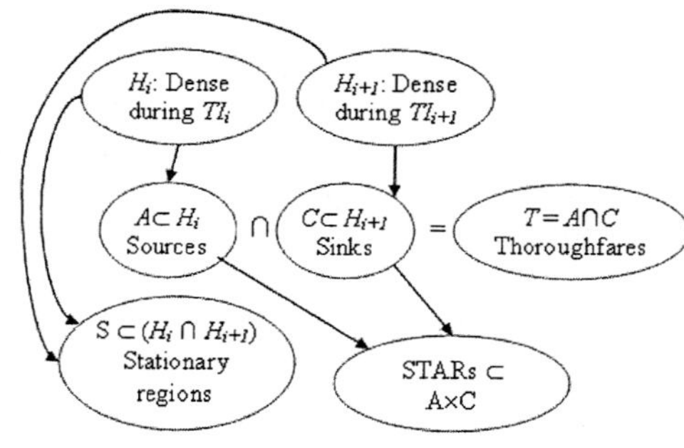

Fig. 2. Illustration of the complete mining procedure

Theorem 2. *Let* $sizeFactor = \frac{\max_k(area(r_k)) + \min_k(area(r_k))}{\max_k(area(r_k))}$. *If* $sizeFactor \cdot minSpatSup \geq minTraffic$ *then during* $TI' = [TI_i, TI_{i+1}]$*:*

1. The set of consequent regions of STARs with spatial support above $minSpatSup$ *is a subset of the set of sinks,* C*.*
2. The set of antecedent regions of STARs with spatial support above $minSpatSup$ *is a subset of the set of sources,* A*, and*
3. The set of STARs whose consequent and antecedent are the same and have a spatial support above $minSpatSup$ *correspond to a subset of stationary regions, with equality when* $2 \cdot minSpatSup = minTraffic$*.*

Proof. Due to lack of space, it has been omitted. Please see [13].

The steps to mine STARs of definition 2 with spatial support above $minSpatSup$ and confidence above $minConf$ during the time interval $TI'_i = [TI_i, TI_{i+i}]$ are as follows:

1. Set $minDensity = minSpatSup \cdot sizeFactor$ and mine all *hot-spots* during TI_i and during TI_{i+1} to produce the set H_i and H_{i+1}.
2. Set $minTraffic = minSpatSup \cdot sizeFactor$ and find the set of *high traffic areas* and *stationary regions* from H_i and H_{i+1}. Denote the set of *sources* by A, the set of *sinks* by C, the set of *thoroughfares* by T and the set of *stationary regions* by S. Recall from Theorem 1 that $A \subset H_i$, $C \subset H_{i+1}$, $S \subset H_i \cap H_{i+1}$ and $T = A \cap C \subset H_i \cap H_{i+1}$.
3. By Theorem 2, A contains all candidates for the antecedent of STARs, C contains all the candidates for consequents of STARs and S contains all the STARs where the antecedent is the same as the consequent. Using this we evaluate the rules corresponding to the elements of $A \times C - S \times S$ and S for spatial support and confidence[5]. We keep all rules that pass these tests.

[5] Note that S may or may not be contained in $A \cup C$ and may in fact be disjoint. This is why we need to evaluate all of S for STARs. Since some overlap may occur, we save repeated work by evaluating $A \times C - S \times S$ rather than $A \times C$.

We then apply the above procedure for the next successive set of timestamps $TI'_{i+1} = [TI_{i+1}, TI_{i+2}]$ and so on. We therefore generate a sequence of pattern sets (hot-spots, high traffic areas, stationary regions and STARs) $< \xi_i, \xi_{i+1}, \xi_{i+2}, ... >$ over time. If desired, we aggregate the patterns by counting the number of intervals TI' for which each of the the patterns hold. If the total number of these (its temporal support as defined earlier) is above the threshold $minTempSup$ after the procedure is complete, we output the pattern. The TI are given by a *schedule algorithm* that splits up the timestamps into a stream of time intervals. There are many possible choices for this algorithm, two examples of which we have considered in section 4.1.

If regions are of different sizes, then in the worst case situation where a very large region and a very small region exist the pruning will be least efficient. In the limiting case we obtain the choice which gives the lower bound $\min_{choice\ of\ region\ geometry} sizeFactor = 1$. On the other hand, the best pruning occurs when all the regions are the same size, in which case $sizeFactor = 2$ and set of stationary regions corresponds exactly to the set of STARs with the same antecedents and consequents. In this case we set $2 \cdot minSpatSupport = minTraffic = minDensity$ in the procedure above and we don't need to check the rules corresponding to S for support.

An optional pruning method may be applied that takes into account an objects maximum speed or other restrictions on its movement. That is, a STAR will not exist between two regions r_i and r_j if they are so far apart that it is impossible to reach r_j from r_i during the time interval TI'. Define a neighbourhood relation $N(R_i, R_j)$ that outputs the subset S of $R_i \times R_j$ such that $S = \{r_i, r_j : N(r_i, r_j) = 1, r_i \in R_i, r_j \in R_j\}$. Here, R_i, R_j are sets of regions, and $N(r_i, r_j)$ is 1 if and only if r_i and r_j are neighbours. By 'neighbours' we mean that r_j can be reached from r_j during TI'. This relation allows restrictions such as 'one way' areas, inaccessible areas, and maximum speed of objects to be exploited for further pruning the search space. If such a relation is available, we now need only to evaluate $N(A, C) - S \times S$.

The reader should note that $|A \times C - S \times S| \leq |R \times R|$, and that the amount by which it is smaller depends on the data and $minSpatSup$. We effectively prune the search space *as much as possible given the dataset and mining parameters* before doing the computationally expensive part. Our experiments show that this time saving is large in practice, even for very small spatial support thresholds.

Finally, to tie up the theory, we define the temporal support of a *hot-spot* as the number of TI's for which the region is dense. Consequently, the reader should note that the *hot-spots, stationary regions, high traffic areas* and *STARs* all have spatial and temporal support defined for them, and apply over two successive time intervals $TI' = [TI_i, TI_{i+1}]$.

7 Experiments

7.1 Efficiency and Scalability

We generated four datasets for our experiments consisting of $10,000$ points, each moving through $[0,1)^2$ at timestamps $0, 0.01, 0.02, ..., 1$ according to the rules $x \leftarrow x + X$, $y \leftarrow y + Y$ where $X \sim uniform(-0.01, 0.05)$ and $Y \sim uniform(-0.01, 0.1)$. We use $TI' = [t, t+1], [t+1, t+2], ...$ *Toroidal* adjustment was used so objects wrap around the unit square when they reach its boundary. The initial distributions were *Gaussian* with mean 0.5. Our four datasets differed only in the variance of the initial distributions, with $\sigma^2 \in \{0.05, 0.1, 0.2, 0.3\}$ corresponding to what we shall call our *Compact, Medium, Sparse and Very Sparse* datasets. The speed and the randomness of the motion has the effect of spreading the objects out rather quickly over the workspace, so all the datasets become sparse toward the end of the timestamps. Indeed, the datasets were chosen to thoroughly exercise our algorithm. We used six region configurations in $n \times n$ grids where the number of regions was varied $(36, 81, 144, 225, 324, 441)$, while keeping the total area covered constant at $15^4 = 50625$. [13] provides more detail.

We evaluate the performance gains of the algorithm over a brute force algorithm performing the same task on the various datasets, using different parameter settings. We did *not* use a neighbourhood relation to further prune the search space in these experiments. We varied the spatial support threshold: $minSpatSup \in \{0.05, 0.075, 0.1\}$. Due to our region configuration (which gives $sizeFactor = 2$), and using the results from the theory, we always have $minSpatSup \cdot 2 = minDensity = minTraffic$. We used $minConf = 0.0$ and $minTempSup = 1$.

The choice of a *very low* spatial support threshold ($minSpatSup = 0.05$) was made so that many rules were mined for all the datasets, and that a high proportion of regions would be dense and high traffic regions according to the corresponding thresholds. For example, for the 15 by 15 region set, $minSpatSup = 0.05$ corresponds to a region being dense (high traffic) if at least 22.5 objects occupy it (move into it or out of it). Since there are $10,000$ objects and only $15^2 = 225$ regions, on average each region would have more than 44 objects in it, more than sufficient for the support thresholds. Furthermore, since objects will move on average more than $2/3$ of the way across a region during each timestamp, there will be plenty of objects moving between regions to provide support for high traffic regions and STARs.

For the compact and medium dataset case (Figure 3(a) and (b)), the time taken by the pruning algorithm for all support thresholds grows significantly slower than the brute force approach. For the very sparse dataset (Figure 3(d)), the time for both algorithms grow at a similar rate for $minSpatSup = 0.05$, but the pruning algorithm is still significantly faster. Recall that for this *low* setting of the support threshold, almost every region becomes dense and a high traffic region. For the higher support thresholds, the pruning algorithm is able to prune more regions and subsequently performs much better. The other datasets fall between these two cases. Recall that the more regions are pruned, the smaller the quadratic component of the algorithm is. In all cases it can be seen that pruning is very beneficial and that the amount the search space can be pruned is determined by the properties of the dataset and the support thresholds. Since users will be looking for patterns with high support, this is ideal.

7.2 Performance When Using Sketches to Handle Real-Time Streaming Data

Handling millions of objects moving in real time, streaming data is generally not possible due to time and space considerations. We used FM-PCSA sketches [8] to reduce processing time and space at the cost of accuracy. Using the compact dataset we were able to achieve precision and recall values of 67% using only 8% of the space and less than 38% of the time of exact methods. Since the size of FM-PCSA sketches scale

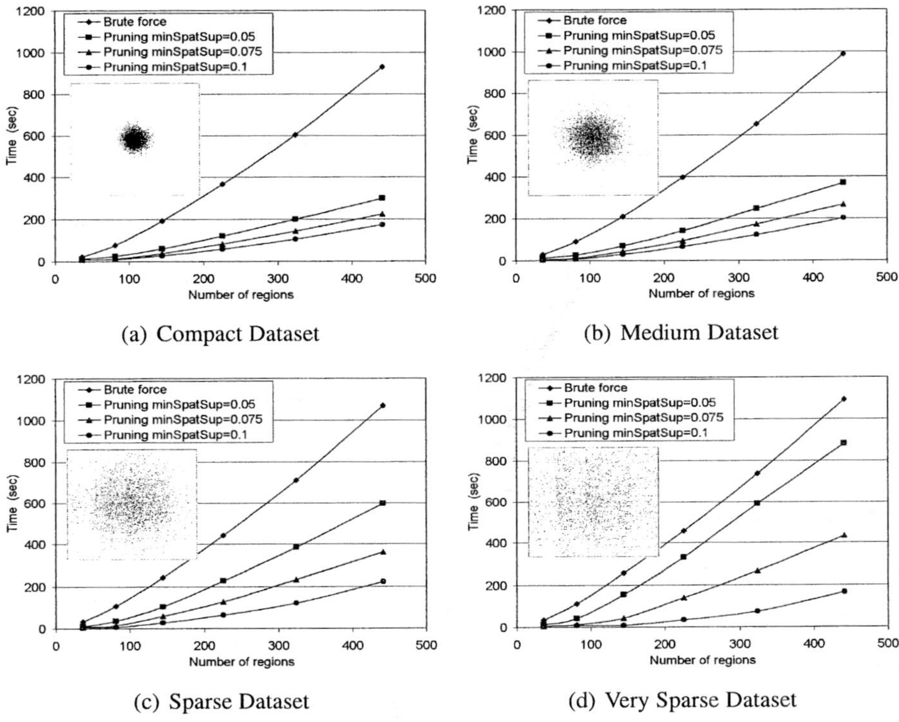

(a) Compact Dataset

(b) Medium Dataset

(c) Sparse Dataset

(d) Very Sparse Dataset

Fig. 3. Results on the different datasets with different support settings

logarithmically in the number of objects, they can be used to handle millions of objects. By increasing their size, errors can be reduced. More detail can be found in [13].

7.3 Finding Patterns in Noisy Data

In this experiment we generate a dataset with a known pattern and add noise to it. We used a 10×10 region layout. 100 objects were spread evenly (10 per region) over one row of the grid and made to move with a constant velocity of one region (0.1 of the unit square) per time stamp to the right. The grid was toroidal, so objects leaving on one side emerge on the other. We then added various numbers N of uniformly distributed objects to the region layout, moving with various speeds. We used $N \in \{1000, 2000, 3000, 4000, 5000\}$, and the distribution defining the objects' change in location was $X \sim Y \sim uniform(-\alpha, \alpha)$ with $\alpha \in \{0.05, 0.1, 0.15, 0.2\}$. The datasets were generated in the unit square, which was scaled up so that each (square) region had an area of 100. With a $minSpatSup \leq 0.05$ therefore, this creates the same 10 STARs at each time interval. We set $minSpatConf = 0$.

We first set $minSpatSup = 0.05$ (and hence $minTraffic = minDensity = 0.1$), thus ensuring a recall of 1, and examined the effect of the 'noisy objects' on precision. As illustrated in Figure 4(a), precision fell for all datasets as the number of objects was increased. We also note that the way the noisy objects moved impacted on the

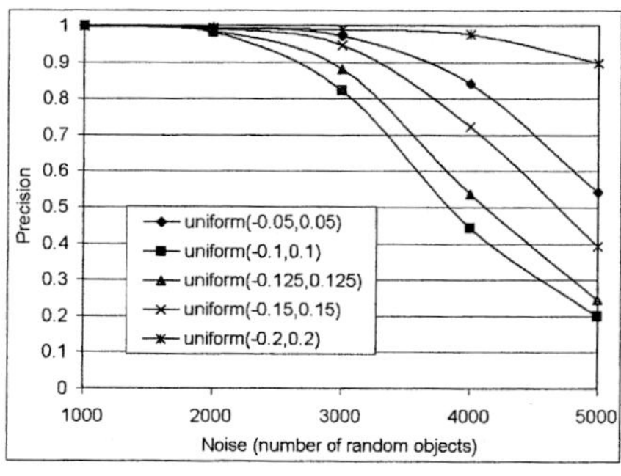

(a) Precision vs the amount of randomly moving objects (noise) for various mobility distributions. Recall is 1 in all cases.

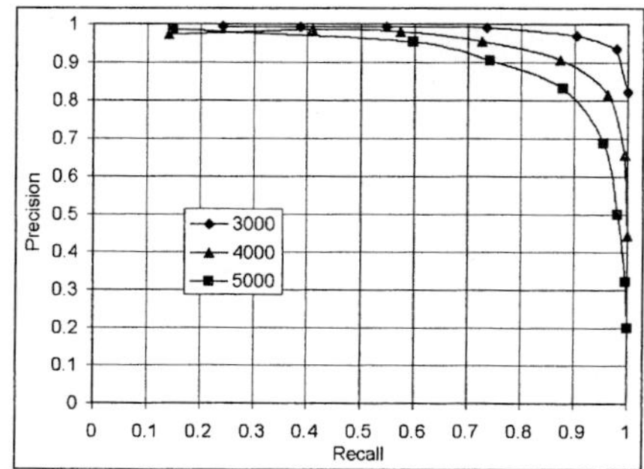

(b) Precision vs Recall for $uniform$ $(-0.1, 0.1)$, obtained by varying the $minSpatSup$

Fig. 4. Results for mining a pattern in noisy data

false positives. Objects that moved fast or slow created fewer false positive STARs. The worst drop in precision (supported by further experiments with finer grained variation of α) was for objects moving with $uniform(-0.1, 0.1)$. This meant that they moved enough on average to move between regions, but not enough to move too far away and thus 'dilute' their support.

Overall, the results were quite good: for a recall of 1 we achieved precision above 0.98 for all datasets with 2000 or fewer noisy objects. That is, when the number of noisy objects was twenty times the number of objects creating the target pattern (this meant there were two times as many noisy objects in regions of the STARs than objects supporting the desired pattern). For most of the datasets the performance for 3000 or more noisy objects was not very good. We therefore sacrifice our perfect recall score for some increases in precision by increasing $minSpatSup$. Generally, increasing $minSpatSup$ will reduce recall but increase precision. We use the *hardest* dataset for this. That is, with the noisy objects moving with $uniform(-0.1, 0.1)$. Figure 4(b) shows the resulting precision-recall curve. Clearly, even for the 5000 noisy object case we are able to achieve precision and recall above 0.85, which is an excellent result. That is, with noisy objects 50 times the number of objects supporting the desired pattern, moving over an area 10 times the area of the desired pattern, with α set to maximise the false positive rate, we are still able to get precision and recall above 0.85.

8 Conclusion

We have introduced rigorous definitions of important spatio-temporal patterns while retaining the semantics of space and time. Most notably, we have effectively extended association rule mining to the spatio-temporal domain. Furthermore, we presented efficient algorithms for finding these patterns in object mobility datasets. These algorithms prune the search space as much as possible before doing the computationally expensive part. By mining the patterns on a time interval by time interval basis, we can not only find current patterns in streaming data, but also see how these patterns evolve over longer periods of time. This will be the focus of future work.

References

1. Shekhar, S., Huang, Y.: Discovering spatial co-location patterns:a summary of results. In: Proceedings of the 7th International Symposium on Spatial and Temporal Databases SSTD01. (2001)
2. Huang, Y., Xiong, H., Shekhar, S., Pei, J.: Mining confident co-location rules without a support threshold. In: Proceedings of the 18th ACM Symposium on Applied Computing ACM SAC. (2003)
3. Ale, J.M., Rossi, G.H.: An approach to discovering temporal association rules. In: SAC '00: Proceedings of the 2000 ACM symposium on Applied computing, ACM Press (2000) 294–300
4. Li, Y., Ning, P., Wang, X.S., Jajodia, S.: Discovering calendar-based temporal association rules. Data Knowl. Eng. **44** (2003) 193–218
5. Agrawal, R., Srikant, R.: Fast algorithms for mining association rules. In: Proceedings of 20th International Conference on Very Large Data Bases VLDB, Morgan Kaufmann (1994) 487–499
6. Mennis, J., Liu, J.: Mining association rules in spatio-temporal data. In: Proceedings of the 7th International Conference on GeoComputation. (2003)
7. Tao, Y., Kollios, G., Considine, J., Li, F., Papadias, D.: Spatio-temporal aggregation using sketches. In: 20th International Conference on Data Engineering, IEEE (2004) 214–225
8. Flajolet, P., Martin, G.: Probabilistic counting algorithms for data base applications. Journal of Computer Systems Science **31** (1985) 182–209
9. Tsoukatos, I., Gunopulos, D.: Efficient mining of spatiotemporal patterns. In: SSTD '01: Proceedings of the 7th International Symposium on Advances in Spatial and Temporal Databases, London, UK, Springer-Verlag (2001) 425–442
10. Wang, J., Hsu, W., Lee, M.L., Wang, J.T.L.: Flowminer: Finding flow patterns in spatio-temporal databases. In: ICTAI. (2004) 14–21
11. Ishikawa, Y., Tsukamoto, Y., Kitagawa, H.: Extracting mobility statistics from indexed spatio-temporal datasets. In: STDBM. (2004) 9–16
12. Mamoulis, N., Cao, H., Kollios, G., Hadjieleftheriou, M., Tao, Y., Cheung, D.W.: Mining, indexing, and querying historical spatiotemporal data. In: KDD '04: Proceedings of the tenth ACM SIGKDD international conference on Knowledge discovery and data mining, New York, NY, USA, ACM Press (2004) 236–245
13. Verhein, F., Chawla, S.: Mining spatio-temporal association rules, sources, sinks, stationary regions and thoroughfares in object mobility databases (technical report 574). Technical report, School of IT, University of Sydney, NSW, Australia (2005)

Document Decomposition for XML Compression: A Heuristic Approach

Byron Choi

Nanyang Technological University
kkchoi@ntu.edu.sg

Abstract. Sharing of common subtrees has been reported useful not only for XML compression but also for main-memory XML query processing. This method compresses subtrees only when they exhibit identical structure. Even slight irregularities among subtrees dramatically reduce the performance of compression algorithms of this kind. Furthermore, when XML documents are large, the chance of having large number of identical subtrees is inherently low. In this paper, we proposed a method of decomposing XML documents for better compression. We proposed a heuristic method of locating minor irregularities in XML documents. The irregularities are then projected out from the original XML document. We refered this process to as *document decomposition*. We demonstrated that better compression can be achieved by compressing the decomposed documents separately. Experimental results demonstrated that the *compressed skeletons*, for *all* real-world datasets, to our knowledge, fit comfortably into main memory of commodity computers nowadays. Preliminary results on querying compressed skeletons validate the effectiveness our approach.

1 Introduction

XML has been the *defacto* standard for data exchange on the web. While XML has been useful for passing small messages between heterogeneous applications [15], XML has also been used to represent large amount of data [19, 12, 8, 13]. However, a major drawback of this use of XML is the increase in the size of data, due to the verboseness of XML syntax. What is desirable is an efficient compression technique for XML.

The main reason for storing data as XML is that (part of) the documents may need to be queried efficiently later. The two kinds of compression techniques, "syntactic" and "semantic", perform differently regarding query processing. "Syntactic" compression (*e.g.,* [22]) treats data as a sequence of bytes. While syntactic compression often produces good compression performance on a wide range of datasets, the semantics of data is often lost during compression. This often reduces query performance on the compressed data. An alternative is to derive a "semantic" compression technique, *e.g.,* [14, 4]. Typically, such technique compresses data based on its semantics. The semantics embedded in the compressed data has been reported useful for query evaluation [4, 3]. In this paper, we shall focus on semantic compression. It should also be remarked [10] that applying semantic compression followed by syntactic compression often results in better overall compression and query performance.

At the core of the "semantic" XML compression technique [4], it is a procedure of compressing/sharing identical subtrees. Its performance depends on the number and the

M.L. Lee, K.L. Tan, and V. Wuwongse (Eds.): DASFAA 2006, LNCS 3882, pp. 202–217, 2006.

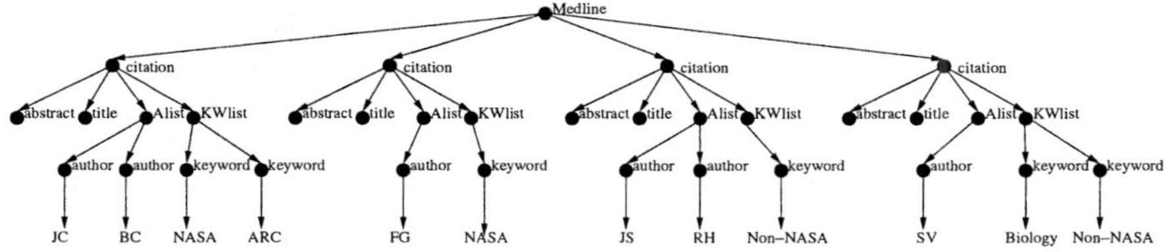

Fig. 1. An XML tree T

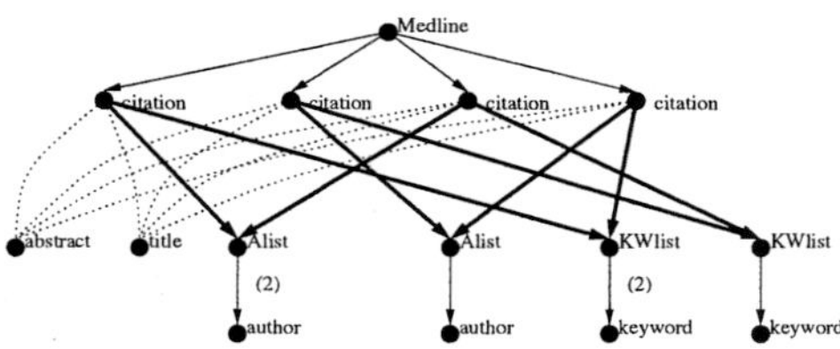

Fig. 2. Skeleton of T, G

size of identical subtrees being shared. However, when XML documents are large, the chance of having large identical subtrees is *inherently* low. Unfortunately, in practice, we encounter a case where the compressed instance produced by [4] is larger than the size of the memory of a commodity computer nowadays. Worse still, query evaluation on compressed XML [4, 3] assumed the compressed instance was stored in main memory. This necessitates further investigations on XML compression techniques.

To illustrate the problem studied in this paper, we present a real-world example and show the result of our proposed solution. Consider the simplified MEDLINE bibliography dataset [19] shown in Figure 1. A MEDLINE document contains a large number of citations, although four citations are shown in the example. Each citation has an abstract, a title, a list of authors and a list of keywords, among other things. We shall illustrate the compression presented in [4, 3] with this document.

Consider a depth-first traversal on the document. Suppose that during this traversal we also generate a tree in which each of the text nodes is replaced by a marker (#) indicating the presence of text nodes in the original document. We refer this tree to as the *skeleton* of the document. Consider the first two author (`author`) nodes. Once we have replaced the text nodes by the markers, these nodes exhibit identical structure. Therefore we can replace them by a single structure and put multiple edges from the `citation/Alist` node on top of the `author` node. Moreover, since these `Alist`-`author` edges occur *consecutively*, we can indicate this with a single edge together with a note of the number of occurrences. Thus, working bottom-up, we compress the skeleton into a DAG as shown in Figure 2. Multiple consecutive edges are indicated by an annotation (n), and an edge without annotation occurs once (in the DAG). This technique has been known as *subtree-sharing* [4, 3].

The edges in the middle of Figure 2 illustrate the reason of inefficient subtree-sharing. The `citation` nodes are not compressed because each `citation` node has a slightly different author list and keyword list. In fact, the identical sub-structures in

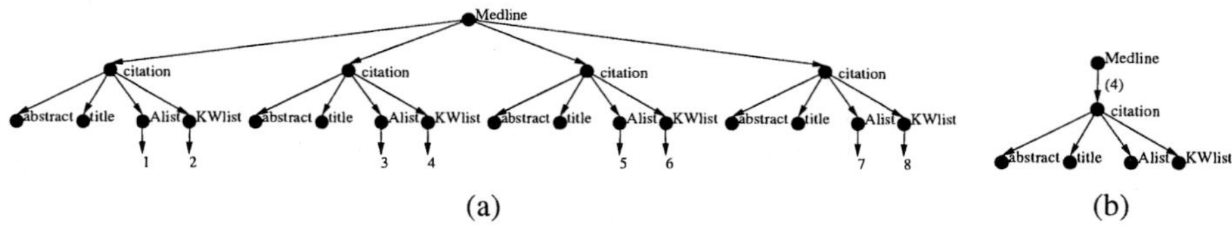

Fig. 3. (a) The reduced document of Figure 1 and (b) its compressed skeleton

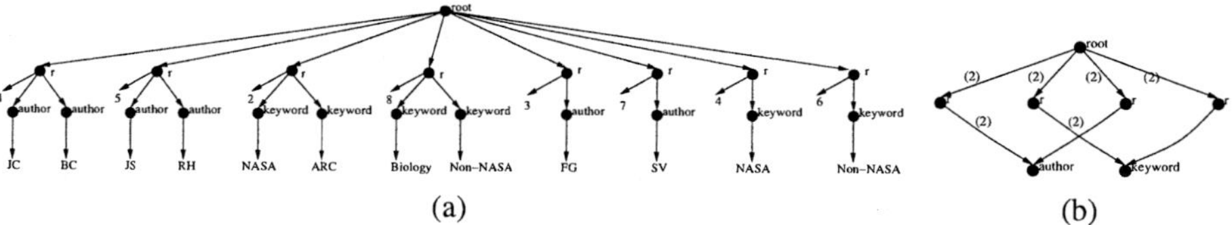

Fig. 4. (a) The outlier document of Figure 1 and (b) its compressed skeleton

`citation` dominate the others. Since the `citation` nodes are not compressed, the dashed edges are also necessary.

In this paper, we proposed an improved compression algorithm for XML. Our technique is inspired by *projected clustering techniques* for data mining applications (see Section 4). Our technique projects out the subtrees which stop [3] from compressing an input XML. The projected subtrees are grouped in an *outlier* document. The remaining document formed the *reduced* document. We call this process *document decomposition*.

Let us return to the simplified MEDLINE document. Suppose that we decompose the document at P, where P = {`/Medline/citation/Alist`,`/Medline/citation/KWlist`}. It means that we shall project out the subtrees underneath P and group them in an outlier document. The reduced document and the outlier document are shown in Figure 3 (a) and Figure 4 (a), respectively. We shall compress the reduced and the outlier documents by using [3] individually. The compressed skeletons of the reduced and the outlier documents are presented in Figure 3 (b) and Figure 4 (b), respectively. Note that the compressed skeletons contain neither the bold nor the dashed edges. The complicated edges in the middle of Figure 1 are encoded by data values. That is, they are no longer *embedded in* the compressed skeleton. Consequently, the decomposed documents can be compressed efficiently. However, we need to store these (uncompressed) edges on disk. Furthermore, there is a tradeoff between skeleton compression and query processing. Queries involving both the reduced and the outlier documents require extra joins to recover the relationship between the two documents. In this paper, we proposed a heuristic method to determine these edges.

The main contributions of this paper are listed as follows.

- We propose an algorithm for XML compression by decomposing an XML document into a reduced and an outlier document. The decomposition causes irregular subtrees to be grouped in the outlier document and leaves the subtrees remaining in the reduced document fairly similar. We noted that the decomposed-compressed skeletons of real-world XML documents fit in main memory comfortably.

– We proposed a query-rewriting algorithm for evaluating queries on the decomposed documents by leveraging existing query evaluation algorithms [3].
– We present experimental results on the effectiveness of the compression and preliminary experimental results on query evaluation on decomposed skeletons.

The remainder of this paper is structured as follows. Section 2 contains notations used and background information of this paper. Section 3 presents the representation, the construction and query evaluation of decomposed XML. Section 4 presents our heuristic algorithm for determining good decomposition. Section 5 shows an experimental study of our proposed algorithm. We discuss some related work in Section 6. Conclusions and future work are presented in Section 7.

2 Notations and Background

In this section, we list some notations used in the paper. We consider the compression algorithm VEC presented in [3] in this paper. Consider an XML document T. VEC(T) $\equiv$ (G, V), where G is the compressed skeleton of T and V is the representation for data nodes. A *cut* is the set of edges at where the decomposition occurs. We consider the cut to be specified by a set of simple downward paths P, which can also be considered as "projections" of subtrees. Thus, we may refer P to the cut. Suppose the DTD of T is available. The possible variations in subtree structure will be essentially [1] indicated by stars "*". Denote the set of stars in the DTD to be $\mathcal{S}$. For identifying irregularities, projections make sense at stars only. In addition, we assume that the cuts in T are not nested. Justifications shall be provided followed by the discussion of our solution in Section 4. Given a projection P, we decomposed an XML document into the reduced document T_r^P and the outlier document T_o^P. We may omit P from the notation if it is clear from the context. Similarly, we denote the decomposed, compressed document as DVEC: DVEC(T,P) $\equiv$ (VEC(T_r), VEC(T_o)) $\equiv$ ((G_r, V_r), (G_o, V_o)).

The main challenge of our problem is to determine P at which the document is decomposed. The search space of the problem is $O(2^{|\mathcal{S}|})$. This daunting complexity indicates that there is a need to develop heuristics for the problem. In addition, the number of subtrees in the document is $O(2^{|T|})$, where $|T|$ is the number of nodes in T.

3 Document Decomposition

Consider a projection P of an input document T determined by the heuristic proposed in Section 4. We discussed the construction of the compressed reduced and outlier documents in one scan of T in Section 3.1 and Section 3.2. Section 3.2 contained no new ideas but completed the discussions on compression VEC on our simplified MEDLINE document. In Section 3.3, we re-write queries on T into queries on T_r^P and T_o^P and discuss how [4, 3] is used for efficient query evaluation. Technique presented in this section can be applied recursively to support multiple decompositions.

[1] For simplicity, we skip the discussions on "?".

3.1 Construction of the Reduced and the Outlier Documents

In this subsection, we present an algorithm for producing the reduced document T_r and the outlier document T_o of a given P, shown in Figure 5. The algorithm consists of a single depth first traversal of the original document T. The construction of T_o and T_r and the compression algorithm VEC can be easily incorporated into a single traversal of T. We decoupled the discussions of the two for simplicity.

The details of the algorithm is as follows. During the traversal of the document, we maintained the parent n' of the current node n and the path p from the root to n. We use a boolean variable *top* to indicate whether the current node belongs to T_r and r_{last} to record the last consecutive subtrees crossing the "boundary" of a path in P. A counter $\#ordinal$ is used to record the number of cut edges encountered.

Initially, T_r and T_o are empty. Line 12-13 show the simplest case where the traversal does not cross the cut: if *top* is true (resp. false), we continue to construct T_r (resp. T_o). If the traversal crosses the boundary of the projection (Line 01-10), we modified T_r (Line 02-06) and T_o (Line 07-10) as follows. First, we remove the cut edge from T_r (Line 03). Denote $n.l$ as the tag of a node. If n does not form consecutive l nodes

```
Procedure decompose(T, P)
Input: A doc. tree T and a projection P
Output: T_r and T_o
T_r = empty; T_o = empty; top = true; ordinal# = 0; r_last = null
Depth first traversal on T:
On entry of a node n:
Denote p to be the path from the root to n and (n',n) to be an edge in T
01 if path to n' ∈ P      //across the boundary
02   top = false
03   remove (n',n) from T_r      //due to Line 14
04   if the last child of n' is not an ordinal number
       //for the reduced doc.
05     append a new ordinal node w. ordinal# o and the edge (n', o) to T_r
06     ordinal#++; top = false
       //for the outlier doc.
07     merge_last_subtree(r_last,T_o)
08     create o' as a clone of o
09     create artificial nodes r; append o' to olist of r; create an edge (r, n)
10     r_last = r
     else
11     append n and (r_last, n) to T_o
   else
12   if top == true    append n and (n', n) to T_r
13   else    append n and (n', n) to the r_last-subtree
On exit of a node n:
if p ∈ P then top = true
```

Fig. 5. Construction of T_P^r and T_P^o, the decompose procedure

with previously visited children of n' (Line 04), we create a new ordinal (text) node o with a unique ordinal number $\#ordinal$ (Line 05) and append o to T_r. The construction of the outlier T_o involves grouping subtrees based on their structure. If the guard condition in Line 03 ensures that n does not form consecutive l-subtrees with r_{last}, this implies r_{last} has been completely traversed. We use the `merge_last_tree` procedure to append r_{last} to a group, in T_o, according to its structure. The grouping can be efficiently implemented by hashtables [4]. Then we create a new r node and append its corresponding ordinal number to r. r is set to be the new r_{last}-subtree. If the guard condition is satisfied, we continue to build the r_{last}-subtree (Line 11). The algorithm requires exactly one scan on T and maintains one r_{last}-subtree in main memory during the scan.

3.2 Compression of the Reduced and the Outlier Documents

The reduced and the outlier documents are yet another XML documents. Existing XML compression techniques can be directly applied to compress these documents. We resume our discussion on compressing the skeleton of XML [4]. Skeleton compression is also implemented in a depth first traversal of T. The implementation requires a main-memory hashtable of subtrees encountered during the traversal. On the exit of a node n, *i.e.,* the entire subtree rooted at n is traversed, we probe the hashtable and check if such a subtree (structure) is encountered before. If this is the case, we compress/share the subtree by adding a reference to the existing subtree in G, the compressed skeleton. Otherwise, we insert n into both G and the hashtable. For example, the outlier document shown in Figure 4 (a) is compressed to the structure shown in Figure 4 (b).

The data nodes are handled as follows. When a data node is encountered during the traversal, we *append* the data node to a container (vector) which is uniquely identified by the root-to-leaf path. For instance, at the end of the traversal, the data nodes in the outlier document shown in Figure 4 (a) are listed below.

```
/root/r/author: [JC, BC, WF, FG, JS, RH, SV]
/root/r/keyword: [NASA,ARC,NASA,ARC,Non-NASA,Biology,Non-NASA]
/root/r/@olist: [1, 5, 2, 8, 3, 7, 4, 6]
```

We shall discuss the implementation of the containers for ordinal numbers together with query processing in the next subsection. It should also be remarked that the compression algorithm can be readily incorporated into the `decompose` procedure. Neither the reduced document nor the outlier document is fully materialized.

3.3 Query Evaluation on Decomposed Documents

In this subsection, we illustrate how a query on a document is rewritten into a query on its decomposed documents. Subsequently, query evaluation on compressed XML [3] is reused for evaluating queries on decomposed documents.

Denote the query evaluation of [3] as $eval$. Consider a path query p, $/e_1/e_2/.../e_n$. The evaluation of p on VEC(T) are rewritten into a query on DVEC(T,P) as follows.

$eval(p, \text{VEC}(T))$
$\equiv eval(p, \text{DVEC}(T, P))$
$\equiv eval(p, \text{DVEC}.1)$
$\cup\, eval(F(/e_1, \text{DVEC}(T, P))/e_2/.../e_n, \text{DVEC}.2),$
$\cup\, eval(F(/e_1/e_2, \text{DVEC}(T, P))/e_3/.../e_n, \text{DVEC}.2), ...$
$\cup\, eval(F(/e_1/e_2/.../e_{n-1}, \text{DVEC}(T, P))/e_n, \text{DVEC}.2),$
where $F(p, \text{DVEC}(T, P))$ = `for` $\$x$ `in` DVEC.2/*root*
`where` $\$x$/`@o` = $eval(\text{DVEC}.1, p/\texttt{text()})$
`return` $\$x/r$
$\equiv eval(p, \text{DVEC}.1)$
$\bigcup_{1..n-1} eval(F(/e_1/../e_i, \text{DVEC}(T, P))/e_{i+1}/.../e_n, \text{DVEC}.2)$

The rewritten query on the right hand side of the formula comprises two parts. The first part states that the result of $eval(p, \text{VEC}(T))$ includes the results found in the reduced document, *i.e.,* DVEC.1 while the second part states that the result of $eval(p, \text{VEC}(T))$ also includes the ones found in (1) evaluating $/e_1/e_2/.../e_i$ in DVEC.1 followed by (2) evaluating $/e_{i+1}/e_{i+2}/.../e_n$ on the outlier document, *i.e.,* DVEC.2. This requires joins, denoted as F, of the intermediate results from (1) and (2) on ordinal numbers, which recover cross edges between DVEC.1 and DVEC.2.

Implementation. The overhead introduced by the rewriting involves exactly joins on ordinal numbers and projections on $\$x/r$. The joins are often needed, *e.g.,* queries with descendant steps "//". Hence, it is desirable to pre-compute the joins as well as the projection in F. A clustered index is built on the result of the joins [20]. That is, we do not store the containers for ordinal numbers but the join result in F. Consequently, F are implemented as a scan on the index, as opposed to a few joins on-the-fly. Cost estimation techniques can be incorporated to further optimize the joins. We plan to incorporate these techniques into our method in future.

4 Heuristic Algorithm for Determining a Cut

In previous sections, we illustrated the idea of document decomposition and showed how decomposition may improve compression. The key of the problem is to determine a good cut P of an input document T. The pseudo-code of our algorithm for this issue is shown in Figure 6. The overall algorithm can be roughly divided into four phases. (1) We infer a "schema" $\mathcal{S}$ from the input document T. (2) As we construct $\mathcal{S}$, we construct histograms N to summarize the structural property of T (Line 01). We reduce the number of stars in $\mathcal{S}$ in this phase. (3) Based on the histograms on reduced $\mathcal{S}$ and our cost function, we use a simulated-annealing procedure (Line 02) to progressively search for a good cut. (4) Finally, we refine the solution obtained (Line 03).

Next, we present a detailed discussion on the four phases of our proposed solution. The meaning of the parameters in Figure 6 are discussed as we proceed.

Phase 1. Schema inference phase. As remarked earlier, the major variations of the structure are indicated by the stars in DTDs. We shall consider stars as "*structural dimensions*" of a subtree and subsequently represent a subtree as a data point in a multi-dimensional space. In this phase, we shall determine all possible stars in a document.

Input: T, an XML tree; θ_{sup} θ_H, θ_C, θ_S, K
θ_{sup}: the minimum support of major stars; θ_H: the minimum entropy of major stars;
θ_C: the weight of the query part of Formula 1; θ_S: the weight of the storage part of Formula 1;
K: the number of scans used in the refinement phase
Output: $\mathcal{S}$: a set of stars where decomposition occurs,
01 $(\mathcal{S}, N) =$ `infer_major_stars`$(T, \theta_{sup}, \theta_H)$ //Phase 1 and 2
02 $\mathcal{S} =$ `simulated_annealing`$(\mathcal{S}, N, \theta_C, \theta_S)$ //Phase 3
03 **for** i **from** 0 **to** K //Phase 4
    $N_{2^i} =$ `recover_order`$(\mathcal{S}, 2^i)$
    $\mathcal{S} =$ `simulated_annealing`$(\mathcal{S}, N_{2^i}, \theta_C, \theta_S)$
04 **return** $\mathcal{S}$

Fig. 6. Algorithm `determine_cut` (T)

When the DTD of a document is present, we obtain the stars for free. Otherwise, we infer the probable stars from the document. First, we construct a prefix tree of the document. (The prefix tree will also be used in later phases.) A node in a prefix tree represents a prefix occurred in a document and is associated with the support, *sup*, of the prefix in the document. Second, we define a *support ratio* between each pair of parent-child nodes (A, B) to estimate the possible location of stars. There are three possible cases for the support ratio:

1. The support ratio is between 0 to 1. This implies B is probably A's optional child;
2. The support ratio is 1. This often implies a one-to-one relationship;
3. The support ratio is greater than one. This often indicates a one-to-many relationship. We regard the edges in this class as *star edges.*

There are exceptions of the above implications. Consider a pathological document in which half of the A nodes do not have B-child and half of the A nodes have exactly two B-children. The support ratio indicates a false one-to-one relationship. However, such exceptions are rare, in practice.

Example 1. We illustrate the support ratio with an example shown in Figure 7. The prefix tree is derived from the XML document shown in Figure 1. The support of the node is indicated inside the square bracket and the support ratio is indicated on the edge. We use a "*" to indicate the location of stars.

Phase 2. Initialization phase. A subtree can be readily summarized by a vector: each star is associated with an entry in the vector and the value of the entry is the number of repetitions of the star edge in the subtree. For example, consider again the `citation`

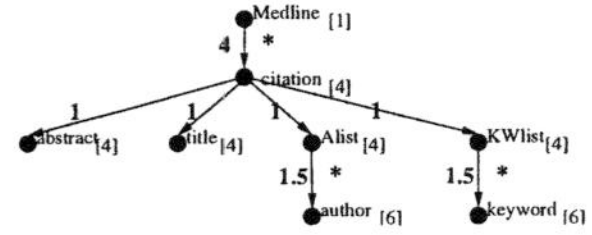

Fig. 7. The prefix tree of T in Figure 1

subtrees in the document shown in Figure 1. The vector of the subtrees are (2, 2), (1, 1), (2, 1) and (1, 2), respectively. Alternatively, subtrees can be viewed as data points in a structural-dimensional space.

Consider a depth first traversal on a given document T again. The vector of partially-traversed subtrees are kept in main memory which requires $O(d|S|)$ space. Typically, the number of stars $|S|$ in a prefix tree is small. However, large $|S|$ causes problems: (1) Summary structures are built for each stars later; when $|S|$ is large, large amount of memory is required; (2) A search in a high dimensional space is often inaccurate [2]. Unfortunately, we find a real-world case where S is large: The prefix tree of TREEBANK (linguistic dataset) contains thousands of stars. This motivates us to distinguish major and minor stars (dimensions) in the initialization phase. Subsequent search focuses on the major stars only. This phase consists of two methods.

The first method is to skip processing the stars with small support. A star with small support may lead to small impact on overall compression. Though simple, this method has been found effective. For example when we considered the minor stars to be the ones with a support smaller than 0.5% of the total number of edges in T, the method prunes more than 95% stars in the prefix tree of TREEBANK.

Another method involves computing the information content of a star (structural dimension). Specifically, we compute the entropy H of a (local) histogram N of a star $s \in S$ as: $-\sum_{x \in B} p_x log(\frac{1}{p_x})$, where B is the set of bins in the histogram, each bin represents a class of subtrees, p_x is the probability of encountering x in N, where $x \in B$ and two s-subtrees belong to the same bin (class) if and only if they have the same number of outgoing s-edges. We build such histogram of each star in S in one scan of T and compute the entropy of such histograms at the end of the scan. Large entropy implies the corresponding (star) edges in T are inherently incompressible and are considered candidates of irregularities in T. The intuition is to project out these irregularities from T which may leave the reduced subtree more compression-friendly. On the contrary, in later phases, we skip the stars with an entropy smaller than a threshold.

Specifically, we use two parameters θ_{sup} and θ_H to specify the minimum support and entropy of a major star. Any star with a support (resp. entropy) smaller than θ_{sup} (resp. θ_H) is considered a *minor star*. We shall remove minor stars from S and pass a reduced S to the next phase for determining good cuts. We refer this process to as *reduction of structural dimensions of subtrees*.

We remark that the histograms constructed in this phase summarize local structural information only. This method is sound: The entropy of histograms with global information is at least as large as the one with local information. The reduction based on local information, though space-efficient, may exclude some globally optimal cuts.

Phase 3. Simulated-annealing phase. Similar to most data-mining algorithms, our algorithm consists of a simulated-annealing phase which progressively improves the quality of the solution. We represent a subtree as a vector/data point in the reduced dimensions. For each star, a histogram of reduced vectors is constructed. Our search finds a set of stars P_{cur} whose decomposition cost is minimized, in the reduced dimensions.

Initially, we randomly choose a P_{cur}. We assume that the stars in P_{cur} are not nested. This property is preserved as the search proceeds. (Nested stars in P_{cur} are nested cuts, which interact and cause a model inaccurate.) The simulated-annealing process is guided by the cost (*a.k.a.* energy) function defined in Formula 1 and 2.

$$energy(T,P) = \theta_C \times \sum_{s \in P \cup \{r\}} s.sup + \theta_S \times \sum_{s \in P \cup \{r\}} |s.N| \times s.sup \times f(s,P), \tag{1}$$

$$f(n,P) = \begin{cases} 1 & \text{if } n \neq r \\ \prod_{s \in P}(1 - f(s)) \;\; where \\ \quad f(s) = \prod_{a \in A(s)} a.sup/S(a).sup \\ \quad\quad where\ A(s) = s.ancestors\ and\ S(a) = a.siblings \cup \{a\} & \text{if } n = r \end{cases} \tag{2}$$

The cost function models the query cost and the storage cost of a cut P. The parameter θ_C and θ_S are used to model the relative importance of the query cost and the storage cost, respectively. Below describes the meaning of the formulae for these costs.

Query cost. The query cost is linearly proportional to the total number of edges across the cut. The reason is that when a query involves multiple decomposed skeletons, joins are required to reconstruct (part of) the skeletons. With modern join algorithms, the joins can be implemented with runtime linear to the number of edges across the cut. Hence, we have $\sum_{s \in P \cup \{r\}} s.\mathtt{sup}$ in Formula 1.

Storage cost. The storage cost models the size of the compressed skeletons after decomposition. Assume that the size of compressed skeleton is proportional to the number of structurally distinct subtrees in T. Furthermore, as we shall see in experiments, nested projections often lead to small advantages in compressions. Since such projections are typically hard to estimate accurately and indeed complicated our model, we assume nested projections are not allowed. Based on these assumptions, we define the storage cost as follows. (1) The space required to store s-subtrees is proportional to the size of the histogram of s $|s.N|$ and the number of s-subtrees $\mathtt{sup}$. Hence we have $\sum_{s \in P} |s.N| \times s.\mathtt{sup}$. (2) To model the size of the reduced document (*i.e.*, the r-subtree), we need to model the effect of projecting out P on the r-subtree. We define an additional function f for this purpose. Consider an edge (n_1, n_2) in a prefix tree. We assume the storage required to store n_2-subtrees is proportional to $f(n_2)$, the percentage of $n_2.\mathtt{sup}$ among all children of n_1, *i.e.*, $n_2.\mathtt{sup}/S(n_2).\mathtt{sup}$, where $S(n_2)$ is the siblings of n_2 together with n_2. We model the cost of storing n_1 after projecting out n_2-subtree to be 1 - $f(n_2)$. Since we want to compute the effect of projecting out s-subtrees on the root r, we "propagate" the effect to the root by multiplying the value of $f(a)$ for all a in the ancestors of s. Therefore, we yield Formula 2.

The two costs described above interact in a non-trivial manner: (1) A star s with a small depth often implies a small *sup* and a small query cost. (2) However, the number of structurally distinct s-subtrees, $|s.N|$, could be large. (3) Projecting s has proximate impact on the compression of r, modeled by $f(r, P)$. The reverse of the three conditions applies to stars with a large depth.

Phase 4. Refinement phase. In this phase, we handle the node order (Line 04 of Figure 6). The order of nodes may cause (1) *false negatives* when the entropy of N

is small but identical subtrees occur mainly alternately or (2) *false positive* when the entropy of N is large but consecutive identical subtrees are frequently found. Possible false positives/negatives can be detected by additional scans on T: Similar to string compression, we construct histograms of k-consecutive s-subtrees. The order of XML is recovered as the value of k increases. The stars with sharp increase (resp. decrease) in entropy as k increases are the candidates of false positives (resp. negatives).

Complexities. The construction of prefix tree and the initialization phase are implemented in one scan of T. The simulated-annealing phase requires a scan of T for building histograms in the reduced dimension. Depending on the importance of the ordered-ness in determining the cut for T, another K scans on T are needed in the refinement phase. Hence, the I/O cost of the algorithm is $(2 + K) \times |T|$.

5 Experimental Evaluation

We conducted an experimental evaluation on the proposed document decomposition and the heuristic algorithm. We focused mainly on the quality of the cuts returned by the heuristics presented in Section 4 and briefly studied query performance on decomposed documents. To evaluate the query performance on decomposed documents, we used the query modules in [3]. We have implemented a prototype of the heuristics and decomposition algorithm in C/C++. The prototype is run on a LINUX box running REDHAT 9.0. The CPU was 1.8GHz PENTIUM 4, while the system had 2GB of physical memory. We allowed the heuristics five tries and a maximum 100K search steps. We defined a variable I, ranges from 0 to 1, whose value is directly proportional to the maximum number of stars (paths) allowed in a cut. We considered the stars with the support less than 0.5% of the total number of edges in the document as minor stars. θ_C and θ_S are the weights of the query component and the storage component of Formula 1, respectively.

Experiments on different datasets. We have applied the heuristics/decomposition algorithm on a few XML datasets: the Penn TREEBANK linguistic dataset, the XML benchmark XMARK with scaling factor 1, the computer science bibliography dataset DBLP, Shakespeare plays in XML, protein dataset SWISSPROT, MEDLINE biological dataset, and the SKYSERVER astronomical dataset. I and θ_S/θ_C are 1. We summarized our results in Table 1. $T^{|V|}$, $G^{|V|}$ and, $G^{|V|}_{r,o}$ are the number of nodes in skeleton

Table 1. Compression result

Doc	$T^{\|V\|}$	$G^{\|V\|}$	$G^{\|E\|}$	$G^{\|V\|}_{r,o}$	$G^{\|E\|}_{r,o}$
TREEBANK	7.1M	475K	1.3M	475K+0K	1.3M+0M
XMARK	1.7M	73K	381K	15K+45K	44K+272K
DBLP	2.6M	4.4K	225K	1.0K+0.4	83K+1K
Shakespr.	180K	1.5K	32K	0.5K+0.5K	2.6K+2.2K
SWISSPROT	3M	59K	778K	2K+7K	33K+241K
ML (3 yr)	36M	586K	5.8M	9.5K+219K	324K+2.1M
ML (all)	NA	NA	NA	54K + 2.8M	6.9M + 66M
SKYSERVER	5.2G	372	371	372+0	371+0

without compression, compressed skeleton and decomposed-compressed skeletons, respectively. Similarly, we use $|E|$ to denote the number of edges in these three structures.

We begin our discussions with the simple cases. The results from TREEBANK and SKYSERVER show that document decomposition produces negligible or no improvement on compression. TREEBANK contains numerous linguistic trees, where each tree often exhibits a unique structure. Almost all stars in the prefix tree of TREEBANK are minor. Hence document decomposition does not yield more common subtrees, when it is compared to the one without. In contrast, SKYSERVER dataset encodes a large relation; its prefix tree contains one star. The heuristics correctly returns an empty cut.

For the remaining datasets except XMARK, the heuristics returned cuts which improved compression over *already compressed skeletons* by using five tries only. The number of nodes in decomposed skeletons ranges from 15% (SWISSPROT) to 66% (Shakespeare) of that of original compressed skeleton; And the number of the edges in decomposed skeletons is reduced to 15% (Shakespeare) to 41% (MEDLINE) of the original compressed skeleton. Furthermore, by decomposing (all) MEDLINE dataset (39G bytes), we can store its compressed skeletons in main memory of a commodity computer, which was impossible before.

When the heuristics is applied to XMARK, we observed that the heuristics hits false local maxima frequently. The reason can be illustrated with the example shown in Figure 8. Figure 8 (a) shows a simplified XMARK data, in which open and closed auctions contain lists of paragraphs, specifically $listpar$-subtrees. Common subtree-sharing does not perform efficiently on $listpar$-subtrees because there are many distinct paragraph structures in XMARK. Hence, we encountered the complicated edges shown in Figure 8 (b). The heuristics sometimes places $/XMark/closed\_auction$ (alone) into the cut because this would separate *some* problematic subtrees from the original document. However, after this decomposition, *both* documents contain the problematic subtrees (see Figure 8 (c)). To project out all $listpar$-subtrees from XMARK, a path like $//listpar$ is needed. Unfortunately, $listpar$ is recursive. This means $//listpar$ specifies nested cuts, which is not modeled by our formulas. Worst still, $listpar$-subtrees appear at a few places in XMARK's prefix tree which lead to many false local maxima in the search space. Since the current heuristics does not model correlation between stars, the search skips such local maxima by chance only.

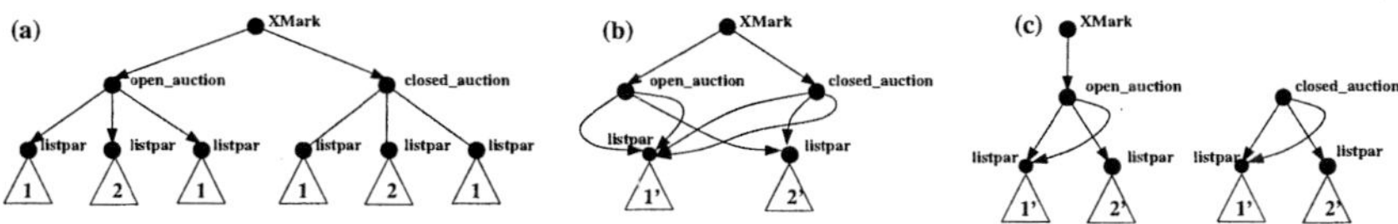

Fig. 8. Problematic case in XMARK: (a) sketch of XMARK; (b) compressed skeleton without decomposition; (c) compressed skeletons with decomposition

Experiments on parameters. We conducted another set of experiments to study the effects of some parameters of our method on XMARK and DBLP datasets. We reported the *average* of the local maxima returned by five tries of the heuristics. We fixed θ_C/θ_S to be 1 and varied the cut size by varying I. When I is 0, there is no decomposition.

I	0	0.2	0.4	0.6	0.8	1
$G_{r,o}^{\lvert V \rvert}$	73K	58K	66K	64K	58K	68K
$G_{r,o}^{\lvert E \rvert}$	381K	303K	339K	315K	300K	329K

Fig. 9. Dec. skeleton size vs cut size (XMark)

I	0	0.2	0.4	0.6	0.8	1
$G_{r,o}^{\lvert V \rvert}$	4.4K	2.1K	1.5K	2.0K	1.2K	1.6K
$G_{r,o}^{\lvert E \rvert}$	225K	153K	65K	130K	59K	134K

Fig. 10. Dec. skeleton size vs cut size (DBLP)

θ_C/θ_S	0.01	0.1	1	10	100
$G_{r,o}^{\lvert V \rvert}$	71K	74K	70K	74K	71K
$G_{r,o}^{\lvert E \rvert}$	360K	370K	351K	372K	356K
$\lvert C \rvert$	35K	38K	35K	32K	32K

Fig. 11. Dec. skeleton size vs θ_C/θ_S (XMark)

θ_C/θ_S	0.01	0.1	1	10	100
$G_{r,o}^{\lvert V \rvert}$	3K	2.8K	2.9K	2.9K	3.6K
$G_{r,o}^{\lvert E \rvert}$	163K	156K	166K	164K	195K
$\lvert C \rvert$	1.2M	932K	944K	810K	808K

Fig. 12. Dec. skeleton size vs θ_C/θ_S (DBLP)

For both XMARK and DBLP datasets, we noted that the effectiveness of our approach increases as the value of I increases until I is close to 1. The size of the search space of the heuristics increases as I increases. Thus, the heuristics has a higher chance of returning good cuts. However, when I is close to 1, the search space, hence the number of local maxima, becomes too large. In such cases, the quality of cuts returned by the heuristics reduces. The results from XMARK and DBLP datasets exhibited similar trends. However, the average case of DBLP (Figure 10) is relatively closer to the results in Figure 1, which were obtained from the best of the five tries. This can be explained by the problematic case in XMARK discussed earlier.

Consider each pair of adjacent columns in Figure 9 and Figure 10. We obtained the best compression improvement when I was switched from 0 to 0.2. The improvement between other consecutive columns was relatively minor. This indicated that in practice, if decomposition helped compression at all, a small number of stars was sufficient.

In the next experiment, we altered the value of θ_S and θ_C and observed the quality of cuts returned by the heuristics. I has been set to 0.8. The numbers reported are the average of local maxima returned by five tries. In addition, we reported the number of edges across the cut $|C|$. The results were summarized in Figure 11 and Figure 12. The heuristics reports better compression but worse $|C|$ as θ_C/θ_S decreases. The trend is not observable from the results of XMARK dataset as it contains poorly-compressed subtrees ($e.g., listpar$) not modeled by the cost function.

Figure 13 presented the effect of applying decomposition recursively on DBLP dataset. Consider the first decomposition. The number of nodes and edges in the decomposed skeletons are reduced to 23% and 37% of their original values. However, extra storage is needed to store 359K edges crossing the cut in data vectors. When decomposition is applied on the reduced document, further improvement on compression (40% for the nodes and 70% for the edges) can be achieved with an overhead of storing 116K cross edges. Not surprisingly, when the outlier document is further decomposed, the improvement on compression is negligible: The heuristics aimed at separating compression-unfriendly subtrees from the original skeleton and grouped them in the outlier document. Furthermore, the decomposition of the outlier document requires storing additional 153K edges. This experiment showed that the compression improvement of our method reduces as more decompositions are applied.

# dp.	$G_{r,o}^{\|V\|}$	$G_{r,o}^{\|E\|}$	$\|C\|$
0	4.4K	225K	0
1	1.0K + 0.6K	83K + 2K	359K
3	(0.6K + 48) + (0.5K + 36)	(25K + 0.1K) + (2K + 67)	359K + (116K + 153K)

Fig. 13. Efficiency of recursive cuts on DBLP

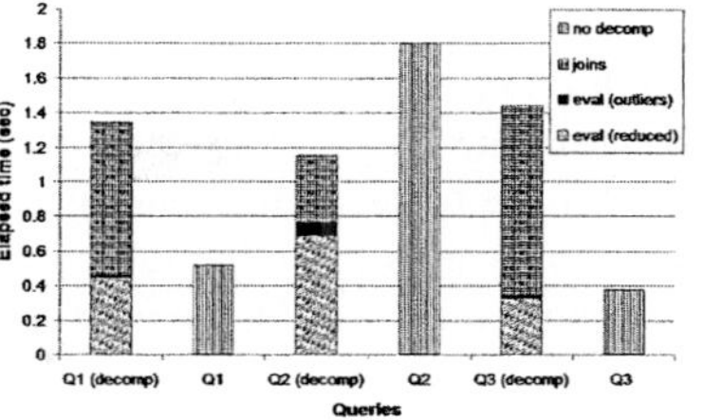

Fig. 14. Performance of XMark queries involving cross edges

Experiments on XMARK queries. We conducted an experiment on querying XMARK dataset with or without decomposition. The paths in the cut returned by our heuristics are listed below.

/site/regions/europe/item/incategory
/site/regions/namerica/item/incategory
/site/people/person/watches/watch
/site/open_auctions/open_auction/annotation/description/parlist/listitem
/site/closed_auctions/closed_auction/annotation/description/parlist/listitem

Except $Q6$, $Q7$, $Q15$, $Q19$, all queries in XMARK benchmark [17] can be evaluated by using the reduced document alone and hence query performance is improved by evaluating the queries on smaller skeletons. We summarized the performance of the queries involving cross edges in Figure 14. $Q1$, $Q2$ and $Q3$ are renaming of the relevant path queries in $Q6$/$Q19$, $Q15$ and $Q7$ in [17], respectively.

Sort-merge join algorithm is used for the joins on data vectors encoding the cross edges. The result of $Q1$ and $Q3$ are similar. The outlier skeleton participates the query because of the descendant step in the path queries. The join on the cross edges introduces a significant overhead on query processing. We noted retrospectively that the outlier skeleton is small and the queries on the outlier skeletons are evaluated to empty sets. In this case, the join could be eliminated by evaluating the corresponding path queries on the two skeletons prior to the join. By doing so, query performance on skeletons with and without decomposition were comparable. The selectivity of $Q2$ is low. The join in $Q2$ required less time than the joins in $Q1$ and $Q3$. In addition, path evaluation on the decomposed skeletons is faster simply because smaller skeletons are being processed.

6 Related Work

XML compression techniques can be roughly categorized into syntactic technique and semantic technique. The compression technique considered in this paper is a semantic compression technique derived from sharing of common subtrees [4, 3]. Semantic compressions have also been proposed to support data mining applications [1, 10, 11]. The objective of their schemes is to compute representative tuples of a relation. However, [1, 10, 11] assumed relational data and their support on XML remains unexplored.

Closest to our work is the STORED system [7]. The system transforms XML into a set of relations and subsequently, store, query and manage XML in a relational database system. The major distinction between our scheme and STORED is that we shred XML to XML, as opposed to relations. Note also that an extreme of our method, full decomposition, yields the edge table of an input document, where skeleton compression is no longer relevant. At the core of STORED is a data-mining algorithm for typical tree structures [21] in a set of trees. However, without projections, as discussed in [7], [21] would generate a relational schema that covers only a small portion of the data. Due to the impedance mismatch of the tree model and the relational model, storing the outliers (irregular or dissimilar structures) in relations can be space-inefficient. In comparison, we treat the outliers as an XML document and compress them with XML compression.

There is a host of work on mining transactional data [9]. Typically, a database consists of a set of transactions, each of which represents a set of items. There is a natural connection between our algorithm and this class of algorithms. Subtrees can be readily regarded as transactions. Unfortunately, the number of subtree structures in a document is $O(2^{|T|})$. We tackled this problem by pruning the minor subtrees (stars) through a coarse estimation followed by a scalable way of summarizing the subtree structures.

Finally, efforts are spent on syntactic XML compressors [6, 16, 5, 18]. [6, 16, 18, 5] treat XML data as tokens of elements, attributes and text. Customized syntactic compression is derived for handling these data separately. These techniques (*e.g.,* arithmetic coding, dictionary-based static coding) are fundamentally different from ours.

7 Conclusions and Future Work

We have proposed a heuristic approach of decomposing XML document for yielding better compression. By using our method, we have not encountered a real-world dataset whose decomposed-compressed skeletons could not be fit into the main memory of a commodity computer, which was not the case before. Despite the improvement on compression, the new compressed representation may introduce overhead on query processing. This paper presented an experimental study on the decomposition and the heuristic algorithm and preliminary results on querying decomposed-compressed skeletons.

We have planed to extend our algorithm for optimizing compression in the presence of query workload and statistics to optimize queries. We are investigating on applying the decomposition as a data partition algorithm of distributed XML query processing.

References

1. S. Babu, M. N. Garofalakis, and R. Rastogi. Spartan: A model-based semantic compression system for massive data tables. In *SIGMOD*, pages 283–294, 2001.
2. S. Berchtold, C. Bohm, D. A. Keim, and H.-P. Kriegel. A cost model for nearest neighbor search in high-dimensional data space. In *PODS*, pages 78–86, 1997.
3. P. Buneman, B. Choi, W. Fan, R. Hutchison, R. Mann, and S. Viglas. Vectorizing and querying large xml repositories. In *ICDE*, pages 261–272, 2005.
4. P. Buneman, M. Grohe, and C. Koch. Path Queries on Compressed XML. In *VLDB*, pages 141–152, 2003.

5. J. Cheney. Compressing XML with multiplexed hierarchical PPM models. In *Data Compression Conference*, pages 163–172, 2001.
6. J. Cheng and W. Ng. Xqzip: Querying compressed xml using structural indexing. In *EDBT*, pages 219–236, 2004.
7. A. Deutsch, M. F. Fernandez, and D. Suciu. Storing semistructured data with STORED. In *SIGMOD*, pages 431–442. ACM Press, Jun. 1999.
8. J. Gray, D. Slutz, A. Szalay, A. Thakar, J. vandenBerg, P. Kunszt, and C. Stoughton. Data mining the SDSS Skyserver database. Technical Report MSR-TR-2002-01, Microsoft, 2002.
9. J. Han and M. Kamber. *Data Mining: Concepts and Techniques*. Morgan Kaufmann, 2000.
10. H. V. Jagadish, J. Madar, and R. T. Ng. Semantic compression and pattern extraction with fascicles. In *VLDB*, pages 186–198, 1999.
11. H. V. Jagadish, R. T. Ng, B. C. Ooi, and A. K. H. Tung. Itcompress: An iterative semantic compression algorithm. In *ICDE*, pages 646–657, 2004.
12. Language and Information in Computation at Penn. Penn treebank project. Available at `http://www.cis.upenn.edu/~treebank/`.
13. M. Ley. Dblp bibliography. Available at `http://www.informatik.uni-trier.de/~ley/db/`, Mar 2005.
14. H. Liefke and D. Suciu. XMill: an efficient compressor for XML data. In *SIGMOD*, pages 153–164, 2000.
15. E. Miller, R. Swick, D. Brickley, B. McBride, J. Hendler, G. Schreiber, and D. Connolly. Semantic Web. W3C Working Group, August 2005. `http://www.w3.org/2001/sw/`.
16. J.-K. Min, M.-J. Park, and C.-W. Chung. Xpress: a queriable compression for xml data. In *SIGMOD*, pages 122–133, 2003.
17. A. Schmidt, F. Waas, M. Kersten, M. J. Carey, I. Manolescu, and R. Busse. XMark: A benchmark for XML data management. In *VLDB*, pages 974–985, 2002.
18. P. M. Tolani and J. R. Haritsa. Xgrind: A query-friendly xml compressor. In *ICDE*, pages 225–234, 2002.
19. U.S. National Library of Medicine. MEDLINE distributed in XML format. Available at `http://www.nlm.nih.gov/bsd/licensee/data_elements_doc.html`.
20. P. Valduriez. Join indices. *TODS*, 12(2):218–246, 1987.
21. K. Wang and H. Liu. Discovering typical structures of documents: a road map approach. In *SIGIR*, pages 146–154, 1998.
22. J. Ziv and A. Lempel. A Universal Algorithm for Sequential Data Compression. *IEEE Transactions on Information Theory*, 23(3):337–343, May 1977.

An Efficient Co-operative Framework for Multi-query Processing over Compressed XML Data

Juzhen He[1], Wilfred Ng[2], Xiaoling Wang[1], and Aoying Zhou[1]

[1] Department of Computer Science and Engineering, Fudan University, Shanghai 200433, China
{juzhenhe, wxling, ayzhou}@fudan.edu.cn
[2] Department of Computer Science, Hong Kong University of Science and Technology, Hong Kong
wilfred@cs.ust.hk

Abstract. XML is a de-facto standard for exchanging and presenting information on the Web. However, XML data is also recognized as verbose since it heavily inflates the size of the data due to the repeated tags and structures. The data verbosity problem gives rise to many challenges of conventional distributed database technologies. In this paper, we study the XML dissemination problem over the Internet, where the speed of information delivery can be rather slow in a server-client architecture which consists of a large number of geographically spanned users who access a large amount of correlated XML information. The problem becomes more severe when the users access closely related XML fragments, and in this case the usage of bandwidth is inefficient. In order to save bandwidth and process the queries efficiently, we propose an architecture that incorporates XML compression techniques and exploits the results of XPath containment. Within our framework, we demonstrate that the loading of the server is reduced, the network bandwidth can be more efficiently used and, consequently, all clients as a whole can benefit due to savings of various costs.

1 Introduction

XML has become the standard for data exchange on the Web, and database servers are employed to store large amounts of XML documents, such as XML digital libraries and XML dissemination systems. In these applications, XML repositories are employed to support queries from many clients. However XML data are verbose due to their repeated tags and structures. Most XML documents in the servers are compressed in order to reduce the storage size. Many previous works have studied techniques for efficient evaluation of XML path expression [11, 14], and other works have focused on different kinds of XML compression technologies [1, 6, 9, 10, 12, 13, 19]. However, these works do not consider how to process compressed XML documents in XML subscribe/dissemination applications, such as the RSS (Really Simple Syndication) news distribution system, which supports processing multiple queries imposed by a group of clients.

M.L. Lee, K.L. Tan, and V. Wuwongse (Eds.): DASFAA 2006, LNCS 3882, pp. 218–232, 2006.

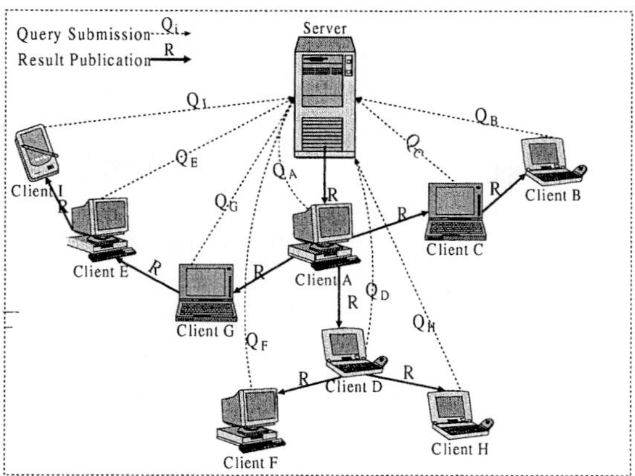

Fig. 1. Architecture of a Co-operative Framework

Assume that there are co-operative relationships among clients, as Fig. 1 shows. The server keeps the compressed large-scale XML document, and clients co-operate to obtain information or news from the server. In this scenario, it is important to adopt distributed techniques and XML compression approaches to save bandwidth in result delivery. For example, the server is in London and users from Beijing pose queries to the server. After query processing and result publication, some results on the users' local machines may be reusable in response to the subsequent queries posed from Shanghai.

One might also find that distributed SQL query techniques in traditional RDB have been extensively studied [2] and applied in server-client architectures. However, these conventional database techniques are not directly applicable to distributed XML query processing, especially over compressed XML documents. To our knowledge, this is the first paper to address the problem of efficiently processing XML queries over a co-operative framework with XML compression techniques. The main contributions of this paper can be summarized as follows:

- We propose a co-operative framework for multi-query processing over compressed XML data. We study how to process these XML queries in Internet-scale XML data dissemination applications, such as the RSS news dissemination system.
- We exploit XML compression technology to reduce the system's bandwidth consumption. Though some previous works have studied various XML compression techniques, none of them has studied how to handle co-operative clients to gain efficient dissemination on the Web.
- We develop a special index structure QIT, which helps the server to process queries efficiently and helps clients to obtain results from compressed XML fragments reserved by other clients. This technique is shown to benefit all clients as a whole, since the average network cost is greatly reduced.

- We carry out an empirical study. Our experimental results show that the proposed methods are efficient and practical.The loading of the server is reduced, the network bandwidth can be more efficiently used and consequently, all clients as a whole can benefit due to savings in various costs.

The rest of the paper is organized as follows. Related work is introduced in Section 2. Section 3 describes the preliminaries. Sections 4 and 5 present our approaches of building the index structure on the server side and processing queries over compressed XML. Section 6 gives the experimental results related to the efficiency of our framework. Finally, Section 7 concludes and discusses future work.

2 Related Works

Recently, several methods have been proposed for query optimization of an XML document [14], in which the structural index is an efficient approach for path/structure queries. There are also some research results [15, 16] that combine a structure index with keyword search for XML document retrieval. For example, the index introduced in [16] integrates both the advantages of a structural index and inverted lists. However, there is no previous work on efficient multi-query processing over compressed XML documents. We need to establish a better framework that is able to handle both structure and text queries in a smaller storage space. There are a few XML compression techniques [1, 6, 9, 10, 12, 13, 19] that can be classified into two categories according to whether the encoded document can be queried directly or not. XMill [6], which is an example of the first category, aims to minimize the size of the XML document as much as possible and achieves the highest compression ratio of all compressors. XGRIND [1] and XPRESS [9], two examples of homomorphism compressors in the second category, both support directly querying of compressed data by retaining the document structure after compression. XGRIND uses dictionary encoding and Huffman encoding for tags and data separately, whereas XPRESS adopts reverse arithmetic encoding and diverse encoding methods depending on the data type, which allows XPRESS to achieve a better compression ratio and higher query efficiency than XGRIND. In this paper, we design our framework based on XPRESS techniques to disseminate compressed XML documents over the co-operative server-client architecture.

3 Preliminaries

XPath, widely accepted as the core component of XML query languages, is adopted as our query language. We constrain our XPath in $XP^{\{/,//,*\}}$ in this paper. The grammar of $XP^{\{/,//,*\}}$ is given as:

$$q \rightarrow l \mid * \mid . \mid q/q \mid q//q \quad (1)$$

where "l" is the label of XML document, "$*$" is a wildcard and "." denotes current tag. "/" and "//" means child and descendant, respectively.

There exists containment relationships among different queries in $XP^{\{/,//,*\}}$, and it is necessary to exploit this containment relationship to speed up the publication of the query result. If query Q_A contains query Q_B after computing, we can send Q_A's result to corresponding client C_A and ask C_A to send Q_B's result to client C_B to avoid the server sending Q_B's result to both C_A and C_B. This approach reduces the server's load and saves the server's bandwidth.

Definition 1 (Containment of XPath). *For XPath Q_1 and Q_2, if the result of Q_1 is always contained in the result of Q_2 for every XML instance, we say Q_1 is contained by Q_2, and denote this fact as $Q_1 \subset Q_2$.*

The containment of the $XP^{\{/,//,*\}}$ expression is a CO-NP problem, and [7] gives an efficient but not complete PTIME algorithm to compute the containment. Each XPath expression can be expressed as a *one-arity* pattern tree, and vice versa (as Fig. 2 shows, p and p' are pattern trees of XP_p and $XP_{p'}$ respectively). Thus XPath expressions can be translated into tree patterns, and the containment is evaluated based on the homomorphism between the corresponding pattern trees. When there is a homomorphism between pattern trees, there also exists a containment relationship between these XPath queries.[7]

Definition 2 (Pattern Homomorphism). *For two tree patterns p and p', if there exists a homomorphism $h : p' \rightarrow p$, then $p \subset p'$.*

And one can determine in $O(|p||p'|)$ whether a homomorphism exists [7]. Fig. 2 is an example of one homomorphism from pattern tree p' to p. Thus, the query $XP_{p'}$ contains the query XP_p.

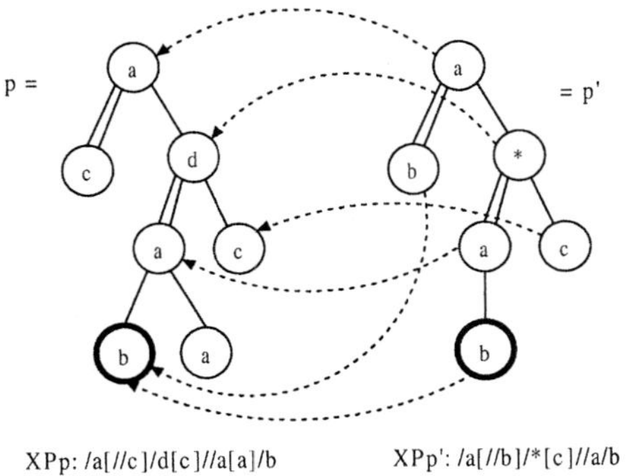

Fig. 2. A homomorphism from p' to p

Based on the containment relationship in Definition 2, we design a query-index in order to store these relationships. Fig. 3 shows that a query index tree is built on the server side to store this containment among queries.

On the other hand, in order to minimize the document's size and save bandwidth, we adopt an XML compression approach. We choose XPRESS [9] to be the compression tool in our framework. We also extend "intervals" technique to

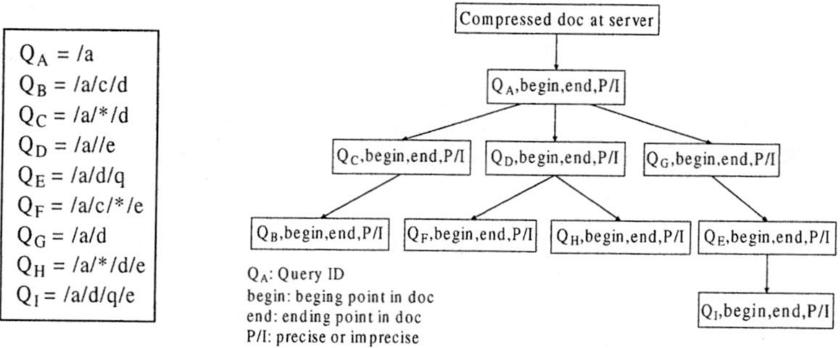

Fig. 3. An Example of QIT (Query Index Tree)

speed up the query processing. The "intervals", which are used to encode tags in XPRESS, are helpful to process the query on the compressed document. The containment among "intervals" indicates the containment of the suffix for simple paths, thus "intervals" technique can be used in complex query processing. The interval of a tag is computed based on the probability of this tag in the XML document, and each tag in the document has a simple path that contains its parent and ancestors. For a simple path $/p_1/p_2/\ldots/p_n$, assuming that the probability of p_i is $prob_i$, the original interval before compression of p_i is $[MIN_{io}, MAX_{io})$ and the compressed interval is $[MIN_i, MAX_i)$, where

$$MIN_{io} = \sum_{k=1}^{i-1} prob_k, MAX_{io} = \sum_{k=1}^{i} prob_k \tag{2}$$

$$MIN_i = MIN_{io} + prob_i * MIN_{i-1}, MAX_i = MIN_{io} + prob_i * MAX_{i-1} \tag{3}$$

For example, there are "a", "b", and "c" three different elements in an XML document. Assuming their probabilities are 0.3, 0.3 and 0.4, and their original intervals before compression are $[0.0, 0.3)$, $[0.3, 0.6)$ and $[0.6, 1.0)$ respectively. For query Q_A: $//c$, whose interval is $[0.6, 1.0)$, and query Q_B: $/a/c$, with interval $[0.6 + 0.4 * 0.0, 0.6 + 0.4 * 0.3)$, that is $[0.6, 0.72)$, because $[0.6, 0.72)$ is contained in $[0.6, 1.0)$, Q_B's results is contained in Q_A's result. Thus, by interval encoding approach, the containment relationship of XPath expressions can be obtained by the computation of interval values. We will further discuss in Section 5 how to use intervals for compressed XML fragments dissemination.

4 Building QIT and Sub-index

In this section we discuss the concept of QIT, which exploits the containment relationship for XPath expressions in order to avoid server sending repeated result fragments and to support more efficient multi-query evaluation.

4.1 Query Index Tree

Definition 3 (Query Index Tree). *A Query Index Tree (QIT) is an index in a server. Suppose that there are n XPath queries Q_1, Q_2, $\ldots Q_n$. According to the containment relationship among these queries, the query tree is defined as:*

1. *The root is marked as the queried document D; all the queries are its descendants.*
2. *Each node has a set of descendants (except the leaf node) whose queries are contained by the query of current node.*
3. *Each node is represented by "(Q_{id}, begin, end, P/I)", where Q_{id} denotes the query submitted by a client; "begin" and "end" record the locations of the result fragments in the original document; "P/I" means if the result is precise or imprecise, where an imprecise result means that the result is not exact for user's query and is a larger one.*

QIT reveals the containment among queries and compressed result. The result locations, which are the values of "begin" and "end", in QIT is for queries processing at intermediate clients. As Fig. 3 shows, clients from C_A to C_I submit queries from Q_A to Q_I. According to the containment among these queries, the corresponding QIT is obtained according to Definition 3. In next section, we will describe the algorithm for building QIT.

4.2 QIT Construction in the Server

The main goal of QIT is to build a hierarchical structure among queries based on their containment relationship. This problem is analogous to building hierarchy classification tree, such as Yahoo taxonomy. If query Q_A contains query Q_B, Q_A is the parent of Q_B. In Fig. 4a, Q_A contains all the other queries. Thus, node Q_A is the root as shown in Fig. 4b. In Fig. 4c, queries from Q_B to Q_I are classified into three classes. Then, the larger queries which contain smaller ones in each class is determined, shown in Fig. 4d. Finally, queries are organized as a tree in Fig. 4e.

We use stacks to implement this procedure where each stack represents one class, and the algorithm is described in Algorithm 1.

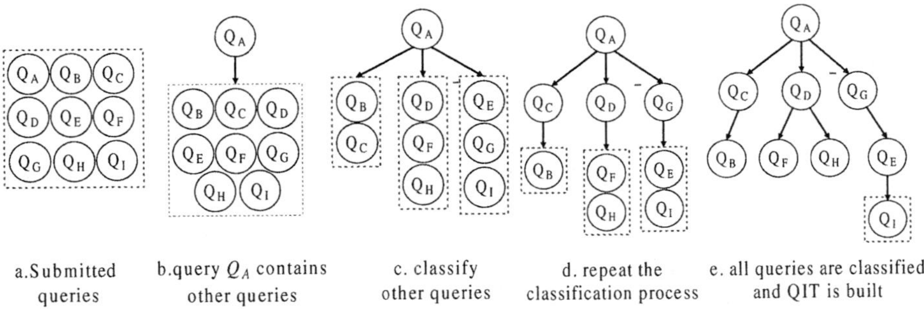

Fig. 4. Procedure of Building QIT

Algorithm 1. `BuildingQIT (Query Set` QS`, node` R`)`

Input: QS is a set containing simplified queries; node R is current root
Output: QIT tree

1: set up a new stack and add the first query into it;
2: **for** each query Q in QS **do**
3:    **for** each existing stack S **do**
4:       **if** Q contains S's top **then**
5:          S.push(Q);
6:          continue to check whether other stack tops are contained by Q and combine them;
7:       **else if** Q is contained by S's top **then**
8:          push Q into S and keep current top unchanged;
9:          **break**;
10:       **end if**
11:    **end for**
12:    **if** Q has not classified into existing stacks **then**
13:       set up a new stack and push Q into it as top;
14:       tops of current stacks become the children of R;
15:    **end if**
16: **end for**
17: **for** each stack S' **do**
18:    **if** S' has elements other than top **then**
19:       BuildingQIT (queries in this stack expect top, top of this stack);
20:    **end if**
21: **end for**

Initially, an empty stack is built and the first query is pushed into the stack. When a new query comes, we compare it to the tops of all current stacks. If this query is contained by the top query of a stack, it will be classified into that stack and the current stack top will remain unchanged (Steps 7–9). If this query contains the top query of a stack, we not only put it as the current stack top, but also continue to compare it with other stack, because there might exist other stack tops contained by this query. If that happens, we combine these two stacks and put this query as the new top (Steps 4–6). If there is no stack top that has containment with the current query, we have to set up a new stack for it (Steps 12–14). After all queries have been processed, each stack is a separate class. For the class that has more than one query, we recursively classify the queries and build the hierarchy according to the containment relationship (Steps 17–21). Then, the whole QIT is constructed.

The time complexity for BuildingQIT is $O(n^2)$ in the worst case, which happens when there is no containment relation among all the queries.

4.3 Sub-index Construction for Clients

In the procedure of result delivery, the naive traditional approach in the distributed environment is to evaluate queries in the server and extract the results for each client. However, this approach is time consuming and creates heavy loading on the server. Our framework is able to reduce the server workload and bandwidth with the help of intermediate clients to transmit some compressed results according to the containment described in QIT.

In order to obtain child queries' results at intermediate(inner) clients in QIT as quickly as possible, a **sub-index** is present for each client. This sub-index is to record the result location of subsequent queries. Each result fragment sent to an intermediate client is always affiliated with the corresponding sub-index. When intermediate clients need to publish their offspring's results contained in their own result fragments, the corresponding sub-index will help the clients to locate and extract required results quickly.

Definition 4 (Sub-index). *A sub-index of query Q is the sub-tree rooted at Q in the QIT. This index includes all the result-location information of node Q's children in the QIT.*

For example, in Fig. 4e, when we send Q_D's result to client C_D, the sub-tree rooted at node Q_D will be attached. This sub-tree includes all result-location information for Q_D's children. When client C_D receives the result fragment, it scans the sub-index first, and extracts the corresponding part for clients C_F and C_H (rather than decompressing the XML fragments and evaluating queries Q_F and Q_H), and then extracts sub-indices for C_F and C_H, respectively. This explains how and why a sub-index helps efficient query processing over compressed XML fragments.

5 Multi-query Evaluation

In this section, we discuss two issues related to query evaluation in our framework. One is how to evaluate queries using QIT over compressed XML documents. The other is how to support intermediate clients to locate results and corresponding sub-indices for its child clients. These two problems are related to how to use QIT for query processing. Here, our algorithm for query evaluation based on QIT is presented.

After compressing the XML document using XPRESS [9], the information on compression related to process queries is reserved. We use an "**Interval Table**" to keep the mapping of simple paths to the intervals. Each simple path in the document has a unique interval, which can be obtained from this Interval Table.

XPath expressions in our algorithm are considered as P, $P_1//P_2$, $P_1/*/P_2$, $P_1//P_2/*/P_3$, $P_1/*/P_2//P_3$, ..., where P_i is a simple path like $/p_{i1}/p_{i2}\cdots/p_{in}$, and p_{ij} is a label in the XML document. Thus, the P_i can be translated into "intervals" by using the Interval Table.

For XPath query containing double slash, such as $P_1//P_2$, it is translated into a group of intervals. Thus, XPath query $P_1//P_2$ is separated into P_1 and P_2 by "//", and interval values of these two parts are obtained from the Interval Table. For example, "*/a/b//c/d*" will be separated into "*/a/b*" and "*/c/d*", and intervals of "*/a/b*" and "*/c/d*" will be looked up in the Interval Table.

Algorithm 2. `TestNodes(Interval` I`, QuerySet` $QNodes$`, Boolean` B`, Structure` PS`)`

Input: I is the given interval; $QNodes$ is a set containing the query nodes which have not been tested; B indicates test all children in $QNodes$ ("true") or only complex ones ("false"); PS is the structure of I's tag.
Output: add matched children into PS.SatNodes and partly matched children into PS.WaitNodes.

for each query Q_c in $QNodes$ **do**
  if (Q_c is a simple path) && (I is contained Q_c's interval) **then**
    add Q_c into PS.SatNodes;
    TestChildren(I, Q_c.children, "true", PS);
  else if (Q_c contains "*" or "//") && (I is contained by Q_c's first interval) **then**
    add (Q_c,2) into PS.WaitNodes;
    TestChildren(I, Q_c.children, "false", PS);
  end if
end for

For XPath query containing wildcard, such as $P_1/*/P_2$, it is separated into P_1, "*", P_2, where $P_i = /p_{i1}/p_{i2} \ldots /p_{in}$ $(i = 1, 2)$. Then, we translate these three parts into their corresponding intervals. For example, "$/a/b/*/c/d$" is transformed into "$/a/b$", "*" and "$/c/d$".

XPath queries encoded into intervals by using Interval Table can be evaluated directly on the compressed document.

Before introducing the **QueryEvaluation** algorithm in Algorithm 3, we introduce four data structures.

UnsatNodes keeps the root of the sub-trees that cannot be matched with the current tag. Once the root cannot be matched, all its descendants cannot be matched according to the containment relationship.

WaitNodes For nodes whose queries contain "*" or "//", if parts of their intervals have been matched at or before this tag, WaitNodes keeps the next parts of unsatisfied intervals, and these parts will be tested with coming tags.

SatNodes keeps the query nodes that are matched with the current tag.

PathStack is a stack that keeps structures that contains the current tag, and its UnsatNodes, SatNodes and WaitNodes.

In Algorithm 3, a null PathStack is initially set up, and all child nodes of QIT's root are inserted into UnsatNodes of the root element(Steps 1–4). In processing of a start tag (encoded into an interval), WaitNodes and UnsatNodes of its parent element will be checked (Step 7). The nodes in these two structures will be classified into simple paths and complex ones. For each query in WaitNodes, the interval of the specific part is tested (Step 11), and when matched, its next interval of this query will be inserted into WaitNodes of the current tag (Step 16). However, it is possible that this part is the final part of the corresponding query.

Algorithm 3. `QueryEvaluation(Compressed doc` *Doc*`, Query tree` *QIT*`)`

Input: *Doc* is the compressed XML doc; *QIT* contains all submitted queries
Output: *QIT* containing all result locations

```
1: initiate PathStack into empty;
2: create a path structure rootPS for root element of Doc;
3: insert all children of QIT's root into rootPS.UnsatNodes;
4: push rootPS into PathStack;
5: begin to parse Doc:
6: for each coming interval I of start tag T do
7:    set parentPS as the top of PathStack;
8:    create a path structure PS for T;
9:    TestNodes(I, parentPS.UnsatNodes, "true", PS); {call Alogorithm 2}
10:   for each element (Q_t, loc) in parentPS.WaitNodes do
11:      if I is contained by the loc^th interval of Q_t then
12:         if loc^th interval is the final interval of Q_t then
13:            add Q_t into PS.SatNodes.
14:            TestNodes(I, Q_t.children, "true", PS);
15:         else
16:            add (Q_t,loc + 1) into PS.WaitNodes;
17:            TestNodes(I, Q_t.children, "false", PS);
18:         end if
19:      end if
20:   end for
21:   push PS into PathStack;
22: end for
```

Then this query has been totally matched at this tag and should be inserted into SatNodes of current tag(Step 13). Besides, the child nodes of this node in QIT need to be checked recursively (Steps 14 and 17).

For UnsatNodes, Algorithm 2 is called at step 9. In Algorithm **TestNodes**, for each query, its interval can be evaluated with current tag directly, and once satisfied, the child nodes of this query in QIT are checked recursively (Steps 2–4). For complex queries that contain "*" or "//", the first interval will be tested. Once satisfied, the following interval is inserted into WaitNodes and its children which have complex queries are checked recursively (Steps 5–7).

6 Experiments

In this section, we describe the implementation of this prototype and test our approach on the well-known XML benchmark XMark [21], whose compression ratio by XPRESS approach is approximately 60%. We conducted all the experiments on a platform with a machine of Pentium IV, 3.2 G CPU and 2 GB of RAM. This platform is used to simulate a distributed environment, where clients are simulated as threads and each client submits one query to the server. The number of clients ranges from 10 to 70.

The size of the original documents is varied from 1KB to 100MB, and the number of queries ranges from 20 to 1000. The queries used in our experiment are extracted randomly from the paths contained in the original XML document. We study these parts of our framework as follows. The first is to test the efficiency of query processing on the server side in Sections 6.1 and 6.2. The second is to verify the efficiency of reducing the server's load in Section 6.3. Finally, we compare our approach with a direct XML processing strategy in Sections 6.4 and 6.5, which demonstrate the overall benefits of our approach in terms of cost savings.

6.1 Time Performance of Building QIT

The objective in this experiment is to study the time cost of using BuildingQIT versus the synthetic data-set when running on the server side. We vary the query number and observe the CPU time changes when running BuildingQIT algorithms, in which the building time includes the cost of determining the containment relationship and constructing QIT trees for all queries.

As shown in Fig. 5, the time spent on building the query tree is roughly linearly scalable to the number of queries submitted to the server. It also indicates that the time used to build the QIT tree is negligible compared to processing XPath over a large-scale XML document when the clients increase. We also compare QIT to BloomFilter [17] on building time in order to study the efficiency of the QIT algorithm. BloomFilter is known to be highly efficient as a new tool used in XML filtering. The results confirm that the QIT building time is comparable to the building time in BloomFilter approach.

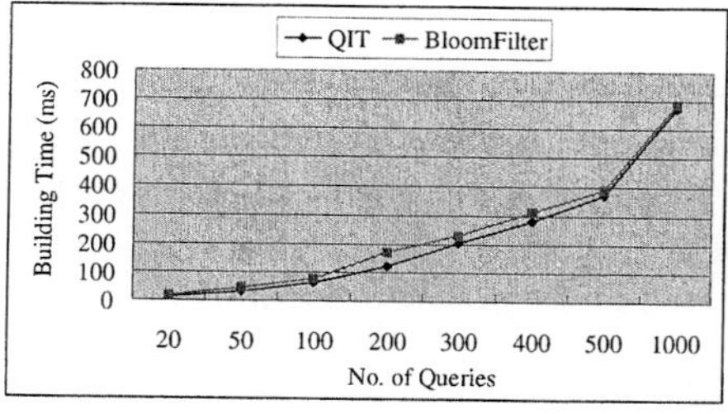

Fig. 5. QIT Vs. BloomFilter

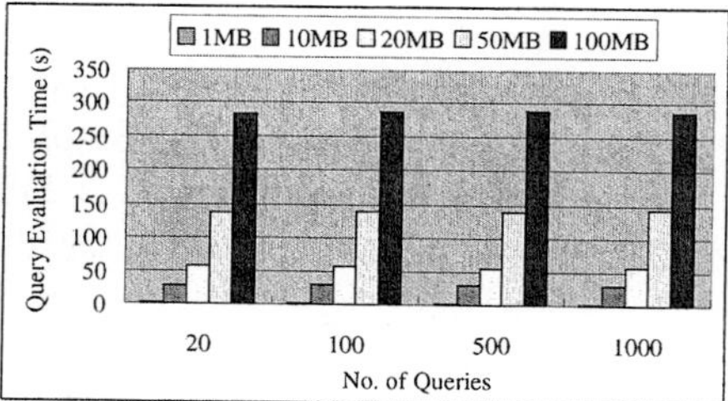

Fig. 6. Query Evaluation Performance

6.2 Performance of Query Evaluation

We now study the efficiency of query evaluation on the server side. As shown in Fig. 6, for each specified document size, the time spent on query evaluation is stable, even though the query number varies greatly from 20 to 1000 and the XML document size varies from 1MB to 100MB. This desirable feature is due to the use of QIT which is built for all queries. After translating the XPath expression into its corresponding encoded interval, the queries over the compressed document are transformed into computation of interval value according to QIT.

In order to obtain the "begin" and "end" information for QIT, the compressed document is parsed only once, thus the query processing time by our approach depends mainly on the document size.

6.3 Workload of Server

The experiments in this section are executed in the simulated distributed architecture. We fix the XML document to 1MB size and limit the client number to 70. We show the efficiency of our approach in reducing the server's load during the result publication. In Fig. 7, three kinds of size ratios are used to examine the load effect of the server. The parameters are explained as follows:

Sout is the size of server's output; *Tout* is the total data size published in the network; *Uout* is the size of the uncompressed results that will be sent by traditional approach without compression; *Dout* is presented for comparison to XML filtering in Sub/Pub mode [3, 4, 17] where the server will send the whole document once it is proved to match the query. *Dout* is thus the document size multiplied by query number.

As shown in Fig. 7, when the client number is small and when there is a low containment ratio existing among queries, most of the results should be processed and sent out by the server. In this case the $Sout/Tout$ approaches 1. When the client number is 10, $Sout/Uout$ is close to the compression ratio of XPRESS. When the client number becomes larger, the containment ratio will also increase. As a result, the publication load of the server will be shared by the intermediate clients. Then, the server's load in the whole network is reduced. Compared with the uncompressed cases, the server's load in our system has the advantages gained by XML compression and clients' co-operative transmission.

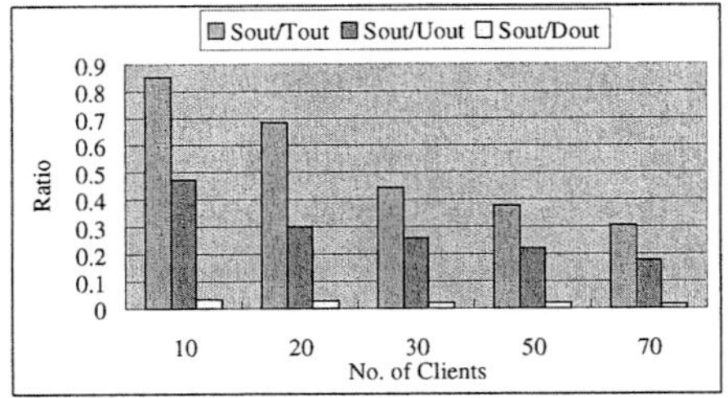

Fig. 7. Server Output Ratios

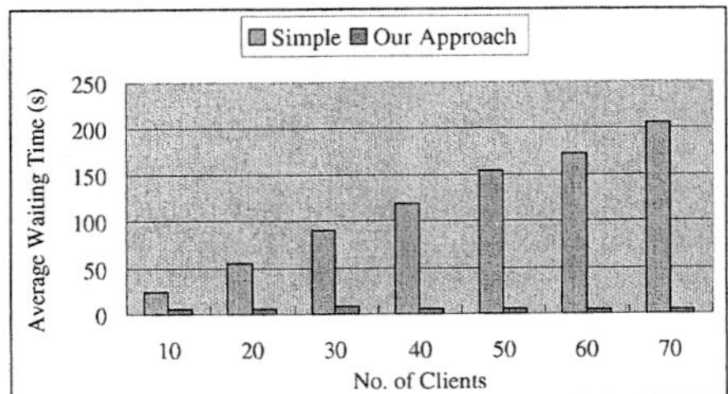

Fig. 8. Average Waiting Time

6.4 Comparison with Simple XML Processing Strategy

In order to gain better insight into the benefits of our approach, we compare our approach with the **simple strategy**, which has neither QIT nor co-operation among clients. For each submitted query, the server directly evaluates on the original XML document. Here, we adopt SAXParser to parse the document, and then to obtain the matched results for queries. The XML document used in this experiment is fixed at 1MB.

In a distributed server-client network, performance of a system will be determined not only by the query processing time, but also by the publishing time of results or the response time to the client. We use the parameter **average waiting time** given below in order to figure out the average response time for a client to receive the query result.

$$AverageWaitingTime = \frac{\sum(Tf_i - Ts)}{n} \tag{4}$$

where Tf_i is the time when the ith client finishes receiving its result, Ts is the time the server begins to publish the first result, and n is the number of clients.

As shown in Fig. 8, the server evaluates queries in a linear fashion when using the simple strategy, thus the waiting time of clients increases linearly with the total number of clients which submit queries. In our approach, query results are published by both the server and intermediate clients in a multi-thread fashion. In addition, the reduced size of the results by compression in our approach enhances the overall performance.

6.5 Overall Cost Savings

We have already demonstrated how the performance of our system can be enhanced by exploiting the containment relationships existing in submitted queries. The worst case is that no containment can be used and the server has to evaluate and publish all results as the simple strategy. Whereas we still have the advantage of bandwidth savings due to the XML compression even in worst case. We now formulate the cost in the worst case W and the cost A in our approach as follows.

$$W = \sum_{i=1}^{n}(Tp_i + Tr_i) \tag{5}$$

where Tp_i and Tr_i indicate the query processing time and result publication time for the ith client, respectively.

And we use A to indicate the actual condition of our approach.

$$A = Tqit + Tp + \sum_{i=1}^{n} Tr_i \tag{6}$$

where $Tqit$ is the QIT-building time of Algorithm 1, Tp is the query processing time of Algorithm 3, and Tr_i denotes the time of result publication to the ith client.

We establish a parameter called the **saving ratio** as follows:

$$S = \frac{W - A}{W} \tag{7}$$

The saving ratio for querying on a 1MB-size XML document is shown in Fig. 9. When the number of clients increases, the containment ratio increases and so does the saving ratio. As intermediate clients help the server to publish the contained results in our approach, the response time of the whole network decreases. We also note in Fig. 9 an interesting phenomenon that the efficiency

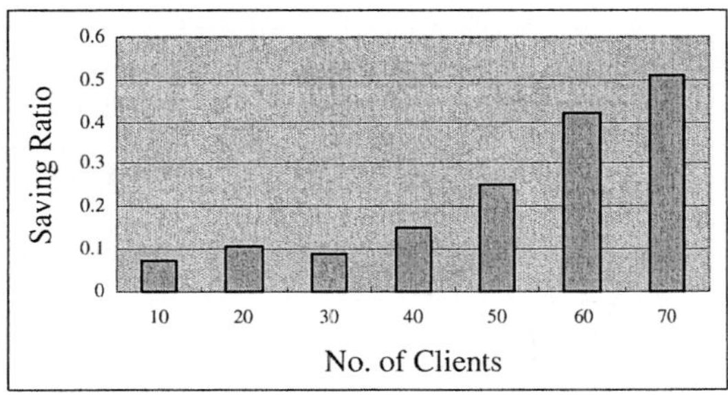

Fig. 9. Saving Ratios

of query processing improves when more clients participate in asking and distributing query results.

7 Conclusions and Future Work

In this paper, we tackle the problem of how to process queries efficiently over a server-client architecture that consists of a large number of geographically distributed users who access a large amount of correlated XML information. We present a framework that is able to save bandwidth and process the queries efficiently. The underlying idea is to take advantage of XML compression technology and the containment relationships among queries in a co-operative client-server environment to publish XML results on the network. We also discuss some techniques to support query processing in the server side and client sides. Experimental results show that our approach is efficient in Internet-scale XML dissemination. In the future work, we will discuss dynamical maintenance of QIT and extend our scope of queries further to include more expressive XML queries such as XQuery. An orthogonal problem related to fast information dissemination is that we need to exploit the use of cache to aid the sharing of XML data that have been obtained by clients.

Acknowledgement

This work is partially supported by NSFC under grant No. 60496325 and 60403019, and by RGC CERG under grant No. HKUST6185/02E and HKUST6185/03E.

References

1. Tolani, P. M., Haritsa, J. R.: XGRIND: A Query-Friendly XML Compressor. In Proc. of the 18th ICDE (2002) 225–234.
2. Chen, Z., Gehrke, J., Korn, F.: Query Optimization in Compressed Database Systems. In Proc. of SIGMOD (2001) 271–282.
3. Diao, Y., Rizvi, S., Franklin., M. J.: Towards an Internet-Scale XML Dissemination Service. In Proc. of the 30th VLDB (2004) 612–623.

4. Diao, Y., Altinel, M., Franklin, M. J., et al.: Path Sharing and Predicate Evaluation for High-Performance XML Filtering. ACM Trans. Database Sys. (2003) 467–516.
5. Buneman, P., Grohe, M., Koch, C.: Path Queries on Compressed XML. In Proc. of the 29th VLDB (2003) 141–152.
6. Liefke, H., Suciu, D.: XMill: An Efficient Compressor for XML Data. In Proc. of SIGMOD (2000) 153–164.
7. Miklau, G., Suciu, D.: Containment and Equivalence for an XPath Fragment. Journal of the ACM. Vol. 51 No. 1 (2004) 2–45.
8. Neven, F., Schwentick, T.: XPath Containment in the Presence of Disjunction, DTDs and Variables. In Proc. of ICDT (2003) 315–329.
9. Min, J., Park, M., Chung, C.: XPRESS: A Queryable Compression for XML Data. In Proc. of SIGMOD (2003) 22–33.
10. Cheng, J., Ng, W.: XQzip: Querying Compressed XML Using Structural Indexing. In Proc. of EDBT (2004) 219–236.
11. Bruno, N., Gravano, L., Koudas, N., et al.: Navigation- vs. Index-Based XML Multi-Query Processing. In Proc. of the 19th ICDE (2003) 139–150.
12. Ng, W., Lam, Y. W., Wood, P., et al.: XCQ: A Queriable XML Compression System. In Proc. of WWW (2003).
13. Ng, W., Lam, Y. W., Cheng, J.: Comparative Analysis of XML Compression Technologies. To appear: World Wide Web Journal (2005).
14. Jiang, H., Lu, H., Wang, W., et al.: XR-Tree: Indexing XML Data for Efficient Structural Joins. In Proc. of ICDE (2003) 253-263.
15. Amer-Yahia, S., Koudas, N., Marian, A., et al.: Structure and Content Scoring for XML. In Proc. of VLDB (2005) 361–372.
16. Kaushik, R., Krishnamurthy, R., Naughton, J., et al.: On the integration of structure indexes and inverted list. In Proc. of SIGMOD (2004) 779–790.
17. Gong, X., Qian, W., Yan, Y., et al.: Bloom Filter-based XML Packets Filtering for Millions of Path Queries. In Proc. of ICDE (2005) 890–901.
18. XPath. http://www.w3.org/TR/xpath20/.
19. gzip. http://www.gzip.org.
20. XML. http://www.xml.com/.
21. Xmark. http://www.xml-benchmark.org/.

Adaptively Indexing Dynamic XML

Damien K. Fisher and Raymond K. Wong

National ICT Australia Ltd,
and School of Computer Science and Engineering,
University of New South Wales, NSW 2052, Australia
{damienf, wong}@cse.unsw.edu.au
Tel.: +61 2 93855932; Fax: +61 2 93855995

Abstract. It is difficult to index XML in practice, as there is a great deal of structure that can be included in an index. Using feedback from the database user's queries can assist the indexer by highlighting the exact structure in which the user is interested. In this paper, adaptive index structure for XML documents is presented which captures the structure given by branching path expressions, a very important class of queries. By leveraging existing infrastructure, the structure can handle updates both to the underlying data, and to itself, with little additional cost.

1 Introduction

While the Extensible Markup Language (XML) has found practical application in numerous domains, its tree-based data model poses many challenges to efficient query evaluation. Early approaches to query evaluation over XML focused on constructed summaries of the XML document using bisimulations. There are now many indexes, such as the DataGuide [4], 1-, 2- and T-index [9], $M(k)$-index [5], $A(k)$-index [8], $D(k)$-index [11], and F/B index [6]. Most of these indexes can only handle a small subset of queries (typically variants of simple path expressions). While some update algorithms have been proposed [13, 7], updating is still a major limitation of this approach. Also, many of these indexes also have poor worst case size. The other major approach to XML query evaluation is through the use of joins, such as the structural join [1] and the twig join [2]. These operators take as input sorted sets containing all nodes in the database satisfying a predicate (such as an element label), and output all results satisfying a structural test.

It is natural to ask whether or not these two approaches can be combined over their common domain, tree structured XML data. Queries for which a graph index does not contain an exact answer can be evaluated using a straightforward combined approach: with each node in the graph index, we store the set of corresponding document nodes, sorted in document order. Using these sets as input, we can apply the various join based algorithms to evaluate a given query. This will be faster than a join on the complete document if the input sets are smaller, and if there are not too many matches in the index for the query.

There is clearly a tradeoff between index size and query efficiency. Our goal is to improve the performance of existing join operations, such as the twig join,

M.L. Lee, K.L. Tan, and V. Wuwongse (Eds.): DASFAA 2006, LNCS 3882, pp. 233–248, 2006.

by leveraging the additional structural information captured by graph synopses. The key insight which allows us to construct a workable solution to this problem is that while XML allows huge variation in the kinds of queries that can be asked, in reality the user is only interested in a very small subset of those queries.

We develop a graph index which captures the structure present in a query workload through the use of adaptive update operations. Updates to our index can be implemented as a side-effect of query evaluation, reducing their cost significantly. In contrast to other graph indexes, our index has the advantage of giving the user explicit control over the size of the index. Our index can also handle updates to the underlying database.

The rest of our paper is organized as follows. After the preliminaries in Section 2 and 3, two new join operators are presented in Section 4. The basic index structure is given in Section 5. In Section 6 we evaluate our scheme empirically, and Section 7 concludes the paper.

2 Related Work

Graph indexes for XML data have a relatively long and rich tradition, and hence there are many varieties. The DataGuide [4] was one of the first: it can answer simple path queries exactly and is easily updatable, but in the worst case suffers from a size exponential in the number of nodes in the database. Other indexes, such as the 1-index, 2-index, and T-index [9], can answer slightly more complicated queries, but these indexes can also be very large in practice, and only address relatively simple queries.

Due to the fact that long and complicated, but infrequently queried, path expressions often contribute to the complexity of these graph structures, recent work has focused on indexes which answer restricted classes of simple path expressions. For instance, the $A(k)$-index [8] uses a restricted form of bisimilarity, k-bisimilarity, which reduces the index size, at the cost of storing exact answers to only simple paths of length up to k. In a later work, Kaushik et al [7] demonstrated how to update many types of graph synopses efficiently, including the 1-index, $A(k)$-index, and F/B-index; Yi et al [13] have given update algorithms with quality guarantees for the 1-index and $A(k)$-index.

The above indexes only handle a very limited set of queries; if we wish to handle branching path queries, then we must use an F/B index. As shown by Kaushik et al [6], this is the smallest possible graph index that answers all branching path queries exactly. Unfortunately, it can be very large, and in practice this is the case more often than not. While Kaushik et al provided some ways of reducing the size of the index at some cost in efficiency, even with these improvements the index can remain large. Also, while Kaushik et al [7] demonstrated how to update the F/B-index, there are no guarantees on the quality of the resulting index and thus degradation over time can be expected.

Closest to our work are the adaptive indexes previously developed in the literature, such as the $D(k)$-index [11] and the $M(k)$-index [5], both osu which extend the $A(k)$-index. Chung et al [3] presented a workload-aware path index,

APEX, which can adapt to changes in the query workload. However, these can only handle simple path expressions.

In contrast to the above, our work supports more complicated queries and gives the user direct control over the size of the index. Moreover, it can reflect changes to the underlying database.

An alternative method of querying XML data is through the use of join algorithms. One of the most important of these was the structural join, proposed by by Al-Khalifa et al [1], which they demonstrated was asymptotically optimal. This operator can answer single-step ancestor-descendant queries, and can be chained together to answer general branching path queries. More recently, a holistic twig join algorithm has been proposed by Bruno et al [2] which substantially outperforms chained structural joins. Our work provides a new framework within which these join algorithms can be used with significant performance improvements.

3 Background

Given an alphabet of element labels Σ, we shall model XML documents as a tuple $D = \langle V_D, E_D, \lambda_D \rangle$, where $\langle V_D, E_D \rangle$ is a finite, unranked, ordered, labelled tree with vertex set V_D and edge set E_D, and $\lambda_D : V \to \Sigma$ maps nodes in the tree to their element label. We disregard IDREF edges and attributes. , and will drop subscripts on variables when there is no ambiguity.

An important encoding method for XML data is the region algebra approach, in which each node x is assigned an integer range $[s_x, e_x]$, where s_x is the start tag, e_x is the end tag, and $s_x < e_x$. Region algebras allow the efficient determination of ancestor-descendant queries, by requiring that a node x is an ancestor of a node y if and only if $s_x < s_y < e_x$. In this paper, we will disregard updating such encodings, as this is well-researched (e.g., [12]). We shall assume that each node has a persistent identifier through which we can access its start and end tags (along with other structural information such as its label); recent research has shown how this can be accomplished [12].

Finally, this paper makes use of an important fragment of XPath, the *branching path expressions*, which satisfy the grammar $q := a//q \mid a[q] \mid //a$, where $a \in \Sigma$ is any element label. For instance, the query $//a[//b]//c$ returns all nodes labelled c that have an ancestor node labelled a, which have at least one descendant labelled b. An intuitive way of thinking about such queries is as *twigs*,

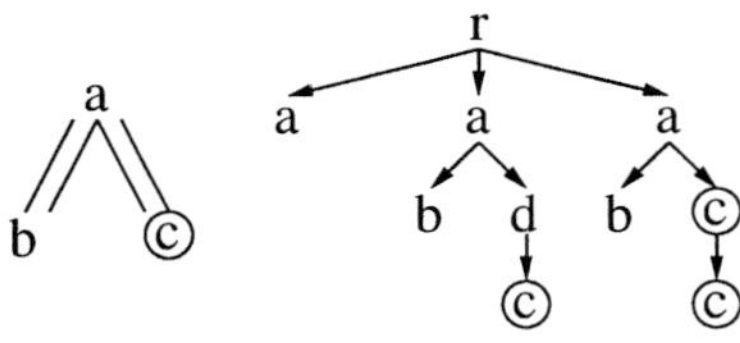

Fig. 1. A branching path query and its result set on a document

which are query trees with a single special node, the *match node*, indicating what the result should be. To find the result of the query, we find all matches of the query in the document tree, and return the nodes in these matches which correspond to the match node. Figure 1 gives the twig query for $//a[//b]//c$ and the corresponding result set for a small XML document — the match node in the query and matched nodes in the document are circled. We will also represent a query q as a tuple $\langle V_q, E_q, \lambda_q \rangle$, where $\langle V_q, E_q \rangle$ is the graph representing the query, and $\lambda_q : V_q \rightarrow \Sigma$ is a map giving the label of each node.

4 Split Operations

We now present two join operators which are key to updating the index. These joins are modifications of the standard structural join [1], which takes two input sets of nodes A and D, both sorted into document order, and returns the sorted set $A \bowtie D = \{(a, d) \mid \forall a \in A, \forall d \in D, a \text{ is an ancestor of } d\}$. Instead of returning pairs of nodes, our join operators return either only the matching ancestors or the matching descendants, plus the sets of non-matching ancestors or descendants, again in document order.

Our first join operator, the F-Join, is given in Algorithm 1. This join operator can be used to determine the matching ancestors of a structural join. We have:

Algorithm 1. F-JOIN

```
F-JOIN(A, D)
// Given two sorted input sets of nodes, return the smallest set
// A_m ⊆ A such that A ⋈ D = A_m ⋈ D, as well as its
// complement Ā_m, both sorted in document order.
A_m ← ∅, Ā_m ← ∅, S ← ∅
while (¬AT-END(A) ∧ ¬AT-END(D)) ∨ ¬EMPTY(S) do
    if SHOULD-POP(CURRENT(A), CURRENT(D), S) then
        x ← POP(S)
        if EMPTY(S) then
            Ā_m ← Ā_m ∪ {x.node} ∪ x.cache
        else
            TOP(S).cache ← TOP(S).cache ∪ x.cache
    else if START(CURRENT(A)) < START(CURRENT(D)) then
        PUSH({node = CURRENT(A), cache = ∅})
        ADVANCE(A)
    else
        for each x ∈ S from bottom to top do
            A_m ← A_m ∪ {x.node}
            Ā_m ← Ā_m ∪ x.cache
        S ← ∅
        ADVANCE(D)
while ¬AT-END(A) do
    Ā_m = Ā_m ∪ {CURRENT(A)}
    ADVANCE(A)

SHOULD-POP (A, D, S)
return ¬EMPTY(S)∧
    (AT-END(A) ∨ START(A) > END(TOP(S)))∧
    (AT-END(D) ∨ START(D) > END(TOP(S)))
```

Theorem 1. *Algorithm 1 returns the smallest set* $A_m \subseteq A$ *such that* $A \ltimes D = A_m \ltimes D$*, and* $\bar{A}_m = A - A_m$*, both sorted in document order, in worst case time* $O(|A| + |D|)$*, which is asymptotically optimal.*

Proof. (Sketch): Our algorithm maintains a stack of ancestor nodes, which represents all possible ancestors of the current descendant. If the top-most of these ancestor nodes matches a descendant node (that is, it is an ancestor of a node in the descendant set), then we can output all of them as matched ancestor nodes — this happens in lines 14–15.

For unmatched nodes, the algorithm is complicated by the difficulty in determining whether nested ancestor nodes are unmatched. For instance, if we have two ancestor nodes a and a', such that a is an ancestor of a', then if we determine that a' is a unmatched ancestor node, this does not necessarily mean that a is unmatched. Thus, to output unmatched nodes in document order, we cannot output a' immediately upon finding that a' is unmatched. For this reason, for each node in the stack we maintain a cache of nodes that we know are unmatched; lines 6 and 15 give the two cases where we output them.

Our second join operator, the B-Join, is given in Algorithm 2, and returns the matching and non-matching descendants in the structural join. We have:

Theorem 2. *Algorithm 2 returns the smallest set* $D_m \subseteq D$ *such that* $A \ltimes D = A \ltimes D_m$*, and* $\bar{D}_m = D - D_m$*, both sorted in document order, in worst case time* $O(|A| + |D|)$*, which is asymptotically optimal.*

Proof. Correctness relies on the verification of the four conditional statements. If the condition at line 3 is true, then the current ancestor node comes after the current descendant node, and hence the descendant node is unmatched. If

Algorithm 2. B-JOIN

B-JOIN(A, D)
// Given two sorted input sets of nodes, return the smallest set
// $D_m \subseteq D$ such that $A \ltimes D = A \ltimes D_m$, as well as its complement
// $\bar{D}_m$, both sorted in document order.
1: $D_m \leftarrow \emptyset$, $\bar{D}_m \leftarrow \emptyset$
2: **while** $\neg$AT-END(A) $\wedge$ $\neg$AT-END(D) **do**
3:     **if** START(CURRENT(A)) $>$ END(CURRENT(D)) **then**
4:         $\bar{D}_m = \bar{D}_m \cup$ CURRENT(D)
5:         ADVANCE(D)
6:     **else if** END(CURRENT(A)) $<$ START(CURRENT(D)) **then**
7:         ADVANCE(A)
8:     **else if** START(CURRENT(A)) $<$ START(CURRENT(D)) **then**
9:         $D_m = D_m \cup$ CURRENT(D)
10:         ADVANCE(D)
11:     **else**
12:         $\bar{D}_m = \bar{D}_m \cup$ CURRENT(D)
13:         ADVANCE(D)
14: **while** $\neg$AT-END(D) **do**
15:     $\bar{D}_m = \bar{D}_m \cup$ CURRENT(D)
16:     ADVANCE(D)

the condition at line 6 is true, then the current ancestor node comes before the current descendant node, and hence we must advance to the next ancestor node. If the condition at line 8 is true, then the current ancestor node is an ancestor of the current descendant node, and hence we have a match. Otherwise, the current ancestor node is a descendant of the current descendant node, and hence the descendant node cannot be matched.

Since each descendant node is placed into one of the sets D_m and $\bar{D}_m$, and the output sets are sorted (since we only ever advance the cursors), correctness is now clear. Moreover, the number of iterations through the loop is bounded by $O(|A| + |D|)$, and the second loop has complexity $O(|D|)$; hence, the total time is $O(|A| + |D|)$.

5 The Index Structure

5.1 Basic Definition

In this section, we give an overview of our index structure. First, we give our definition of a graph synopsis:

Definition 1 (Graph Synopsis). *A graph synopsis of an XML document D is a tuple $S(D) = \langle V_S, E_S, t, e \rangle$, where:*

1. *$\langle V_S, E_S \rangle$ is a graph;*
2. *$t : V_S \rightarrow 2^{V_D}$ gives the target sets for each $v \in V_S$;*
3. *$\forall v_s \in V_S$, $\forall u_d, v_d \in t(v_s)$, $\lambda_D(u_d) = \lambda_D(v_d)$;*
4. *$\dot{\bigcup}_{v \in V_S} t(v) = V_D$ (the union is disjoint);*
5. *$e : E_S \rightarrow \{possible, normal, F, B, FB\}$ is a map giving the type of each edge;*
6. *$\forall u_s, v_s \in V_S$, if $\langle u_s, v_s \rangle \in E_S$ and $e(\langle u_s, v_s \rangle) \neq possible$, then there exists $u_d \in t(u_s)$, $v_d \in t(v_s)$ such that u_d is an ancestor of v_d in D;*
7. *$\forall u_d, v_d \in V_D$, if u_d is an ancestor of v_d in D, then there exists $u_s, v_s \in V_S$ such that $u_d \in t(u_s)$, $v_d \in t(v_s)$, and $\langle u_s, v_s \rangle \in E_S$.*

Our definition varies from the standard definition of a graph synopsis. Our graph synopsis is closer to the *transitive closure* of such a synopsis, because the inclusion of an edge between two nodes in the synopsis implies an ancestor-descendant relation in the database, not a parent-child relation. Our reason for doing this is that it allows us to preserve more structural information during index updates, since we are interested in branching path queries with ancestor-descendant edges.

The other major difference in our definition of a graph synopsis is that each edge is labelled, which has important implications for query processing. The presence of a "possible" edge indicates that there is a possible linkage between nodes in the target sets of the two nodes, as opposed to the definite linkage given by a normal edge. The remaining edge types are related to two important concepts that we borrow from previous work, namely *forward and backward stability* [10]:

Definition 2 (Stability). *Consider two nodes u and v from a graph synopsis $S(D)$, with $\langle u_S, v_S \rangle \in E_S$. Then:*

1. *The edge $\langle u_S, v_S \rangle$ is "backwards" stable (B-stable) if and only if for all $v_D \in t(v_S)$, there exists a node $u_D \in t(u_S)$ that is an ancestor of v_D.*
2. *The edge $\langle u_S, v_S \rangle$ is "forwards" stable (F-stable) if and only if for all $u_D \in t(u_S)$, there exists a node $v_D \in t(v_S)$ that is a descendant of u_D.*

Thus, the remaining edge types denote whether we know whether that edge is forward stable, backward stable, or both. Note that a normal or possible edge might actually be forward or backward stable (or both): the edge type only reflects that fact if the index has been able to deduce it.

5.2 Overview of Approach

A sketch of our approach is found in Algorithm 3. The idea is to start with the coarsest possible graph synopsis; during query evaluation, we collect statistics which help us determine the structure that the user is interested in. Every k queries (for some user-defined constant k), we choose to split nodes in the index using this information, so as to focus on the structure that the user is querying; when the index grows beyond some upper bound U, we then combine nodes in the index to reduce its size. The issue then becomes how to detect what structure the user is interested in, and how to split and merge the nodes efficiently.

Algorithm 3. Overview of the Adaptive Index

```
I ← INITIALIZE-INDEX(D), i ← 0
while database is still running do
    q ← next query to be evaluated
    EVALUATE-AND-COLLECT-STATISTICS(I, q)
    if i ≡ 0 (mod k) then
        SPLIT(I)
    if index size ≥ U then
        while index size > L do
            MERGE(I)
    i ← i + 1
```

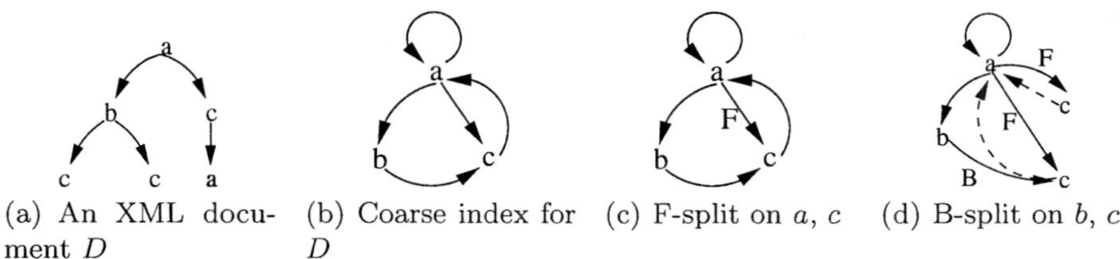

(a) An XML document D (b) Coarse index for D (c) F-split on a, c (d) B-split on b, c

Fig. 2. A sample adaptive index

Figure 2 gives an example of our approach. Given the sample XML document in Figure 2(a), the initial index is the coarse graph synopsis of Figure 2(b). Figures 2(c) and 2(d) demonstrate the effect of various split operations on the graph (we will discuss how these split operations occur later).

5.3 Index Construction

The initial bulk construction of the index is straightforward, and can be done in a single pass. The pseudocode is given in Algorithm 4; this algorithm can be implemented in a single preorder traversal of the document, maintaining only a stack that grows with the depth of the document. Since at each node we perform an amount of work proportional to the depth of the stack (due to line 3), the total amount of work for a document of n nodes and depth d is $O(nd)$; as the depth is generally very small this algorithm runs in linear time in practice.

Algorithm 4. INITIALIZE-INDEX

```
INITIALIZE-INDEX(D = ⟨V_D, E_D, λ⟩)
// Given an XML document, construct the initial index.
1: V_S ← Σ, E_S ← ∅, (∀v ∈ V_S) t_S(v) ← ∅
2: for each v ∈ V_D in document order do
3:     E_S ← E_S ∪ {⟨λ(u), λ(v)⟩ | ∀u ∈ ANCESTORS(v)}
4:     t(λ(v)) ← t(λ(v)) ∪ {v}
5: return S = ⟨V_S, E_S, t_S⟩
```

5.4 Query Evaluation

We now consider the evaluation of a query q on a graph synopsis $S(D)$. This is not as easy as evaluating a query using join operators on the traditional inverted list index, since there can be multiple matches of a given query in our index. Evaluating a query involves finding all embeddings into the synopsis:

Definition 3 (Embedding). *An embedding of a query q into a synopsis $S(D)$ is a map $m : V_q \rightarrow V_S$ satisfying:*

- $\forall u, v \in V_q$, *if* $\langle u, v\rangle \in E_q$ *then* $\langle m(u), m(v)\rangle \in E_S$.
- $\forall v \in V_q$, $\lambda_q(v) = \lambda_S(m(v))$.

We use exhaustive search to find the set of all embeddings of a query into the graph synopsis. The query could then be evaluated by taking the input sets for the join to be the target sets of the nodes given by the embedding, and returning the union of the results from all embeddings. We can increase the evaluation performance by taking advantage of stability, due to the following:

Lemma 1. *Given two nodes u and v from a graph synopsis $S(D)$, we have:*

1. *If $\langle u, v\rangle$ is B-stable, then evaluating the query $\lambda(u)//\lambda(v)$ on the sets $t(u)$ and $t(v)$ returns the set $t(v)$.*
2. *If $\langle u, v\rangle$ is F-stable, then evaluating the query $\lambda(u)[\lambda(v)]$ on the sets $t(u)$ and $t(v)$ returns the set $t(u)$.*

The idea is best seen when evaluating the query $//a[//c]$ on Figures 2(b) and 2(c). In Figure 2(c), because the edge between a and c is F-stable, we can immediately return the target set of node a as the result of the query; on the other hand, in

Figure 2(b), we must perform a join to filter out any nodes that do not occur in the result set.

For a general twig query, we can trim the query using the graph synopsis. An edge $\langle q_1, q_2 \rangle$ in the query is labelled F or B stable according to the following:

- If q_1 is the match node of the query, then we label $\langle q_1, q_2 \rangle$ F-stable.
- If q_2 or one of q_2's descendants is the match node, then we label $\langle q_1, q_2 \rangle$ B-stable.
- If neither q_1 nor any of its descendants is the match node of the query, then we label $\langle q_1, q_2 \rangle$ F-stable.

The labelling of edges in the query as B or F stable is consistent with the kind of joins that would be required to answer that query. Once we have annotated the twig query, we can trim nodes from the query using Algorithm 5: if the embedding of a query q maps an edge in the query to an edge in the index which preserves F- or B-stability, then we can delete that edge if it leads to a leaf node.

Algorithm 5. TRIM-QUERY

```
TRIM-QUERY(q, m, S(D))
// Trim a query q given an embedding m into a synopsis S(D).
repeat
    for each q2 ∈ V_q such that q2 is a leaf node do
        q1 ← PARENT(q2)
        if IS-F-STABLE(⟨q1, q2⟩) then
            if IS-F-STABLE(⟨m(q1), m(q2)⟩) then
                Delete q2 from q
                break
        else if CHILDREN(q1) = {q2} then
            if IS-B-STABLE(⟨q1, q2⟩) then
                if IS-B-STABLE(⟨m(q1), m(q2)⟩) then
                    Delete q1 from q, replacing it with q2
                    break
until no changes to the query occur
```

5.5 Splitting Nodes

We now describe how to update the index to capture structure the user is querying. The process involves choosing two nodes u and v in the synopsis, such that $\langle u, v \rangle \in E_S$, and splitting the node u (respectively v) into two nodes so that one of the resulting nodes is F-stable with respect to v (respectively B-stable with respect to u). We will first discuss the actual splitting process, before turning to the question of how to determine which nodes to split.

Suppose we have two nodes u and v in the graph synopsis, and we wish to split u into two nodes u_1 and u_2 such that u_1 is F-stable with respect to v (the case of performing a B-split is similar and is omitted). To split the nodes, we use the F-JOIN algorithm (see Algorithm 1) to split the target set of u into the two targets sets of u_1 and u_2. If the target set of u_1 is empty, then none of the nodes in the target set of u were ancestors of nodes in v, and hence the edge can be removed. If the target set of u_2 is empty, then the edge $\langle u, v \rangle$ is F-stable. We note that the F-JOIN algorithm can be used to answer join queries, and hence we can actually simultaneously evaluate a query and update our index, thus reducing the update cost to virtually nil.

Otherwise, we copy the edges incident on u over to u_1 and u_2 as follows: for any edge $e = \langle x, u \rangle$, we add edges $e_1 = \langle x, u_1 \rangle$ and $e_2 = \langle x, u_2 \rangle$. If e is B-stable, then we make both e_1 and e_2 B-stable. Otherwise, e_1 and e_2 are marked possible. Similarly, for any edge $e = \langle u, x \rangle$, we add edges $e_1 = \langle u_1, x \rangle$ and $e_2 = \langle u_2, x \rangle$. If e is F-stable, then we make both e_1 and e_2 F-stable. Otherwise, e_1 and e_2 are marked possible. Finally, we make the edge $\langle u_1, v \rangle$ F-stable, and ensure that there is no edge from u_2 to v.

As an example of node splitting, consider Figure 2. Figure 2(c) is equivalent to Figure 2(b) after it has undergone an F-split on node a with respect to node c. In this case, all nodes in $t(a)$ are ancestors of nodes in $t(c)$, and hence the edge is already F-stable. After this split, we then perform a B-split on the nodes b and c, with the result in Figure 2(d). In this case, we do need to split the nodes. The edges out of the c nodes are possible since we cannot be sure whether each c node has a relationship with the a node.

The final issue is how to determine which nodes should actually be split. We collect two sets of statistics about the workload, one for F- and one for B-stable splits; each is stored as a two dimensional integer array, indexed by nodes in the synopsis. The data stored in an entry $\langle u, v \rangle$ represent the amount of "work" the query processor performs which involves the nodes u and v in an F- or B-stable fashion. In our case, we used a very simple definition of work: the amount of work is the number of nodes in the target set that participated in computing the result (e.g., for twig joins, these would be the nodes from each target set that occur somewhere in a result tuple). Our experiments demonstrate the effectiveness of this definition.

We found that this statistic was quite easy to approximate for both structural joins and twig joins. As a simple example, suppose that we are answering the query $//a[//b]//c$ using composed structural joins. Suppose that we have three nodes a, b, and c, corresponding to each node in the query in the obvious way. One way of evaluating the query would be to join a and c in a F-stable way, and then join a and b in a B-stable way. For each pair of nodes, the information we collect is simply the number of nodes that end up in the result set at each step.

We use this information to split nodes as follows: when we decide to split a node, we find the largest entry in both the F-stable and B-stable arrays. We then perform an F-split or B-split on those two nodes, depending upon which array the entry occurs in. After each split, we reset the array entries to zero; this allows us to handle changes in the query workload dynamically.

5.6 Merges

At some point, the index structure will grow to a size that is unacceptable to the database user. In this case, we can merge nodes in the index until we reach a satisfactory size. We assume the user gives us two constants, L and U, such that $|\Sigma| \leq L < U$, which represent lower and upper bounds on the index size (the index must have size at least $|\Sigma|$ because that is the size of the coarsest graph synopsis). When the index size reaches U, we repeatedly merge nodes until we obtain an index of size L.

Given two nodes u and v in the graph synopsis such that $\lambda(u) = \lambda(v)$, merging them to create a new node w is straightforward. The target sets can be merged together in linear time using a standard merge algorithm — this can be delayed until a query is performed, in which case the new target set can be constructed on the fly. Incoming edges into u and v are added to w in the following way:

1. If there is an edge $\langle x, u \rangle$ but no edge $\langle x, v \rangle$, then $\langle x, w \rangle$ has the same type as $\langle x, u \rangle$.
2. If $\langle x, u \rangle$ is a possible edge, and $\langle x, v \rangle$ is a possible edge, then $\langle x, w \rangle$ is a possible edge.
3. If $\langle x, u \rangle$ or $\langle x, v \rangle$ is F-stable, then $\langle x, w \rangle$ is F-stable.
4. In all other cases, $\langle x, w \rangle$ is a normal edge.

For outgoing edges, case 3 is replaced with the analogous condition for B-stability.

The question then becomes how to determine which nodes u and v should be merged. Intuitively, we wish to merge nodes together which are frequently involved in similar queries, since this will save some effort. Recall that during the evaluation of a query q over a synopsis $S(D)$, we obtain the set M of all embeddings between q and $S(D)$. The sets $M_v = \{m(v) \mid m \in M\}$ represent the set of all nodes in $S(D)$ that each $v \in V_q$ is mapped to. In terms of evaluating this particular query, merging nodes appearing together in these sets makes sense.

Hence, we maintain a two-dimensional integer array, with the array indexes being the nodes in V_S, which counts the number of times two nodes $u, v \in V_S$ occur together in some set M_w. When we need to merge nodes, we merge the most frequently occurring pair in this array. In the rare event that every query has a unique embedding into $S(D)$ (and hence the array will be identically zero), we simply merge randomly chosen pairs of nodes having the same label.

5.7 Updates

We handle updates by storing for each element label a pointer to a special update node in the index. This pointer, initially null, points to the last synopsis node with an identical label created during an update. When a node is inserted and the pointer is null, we create a new synopsis node in the index, add a possible edge from every other node in the synopsis to this node, and set the pointer to this node. The further insertion of nodes then results in their addition to the target set of this update node. When the update node is split or merged, we reset the pointer to null.

This simple update scheme can be improved through several optimizations. If we have schema information, then we can restrict the addition of edges to only those synopsis nodes which can be an ancestor of this node. Also, the most common kinds of updates in practice are bulk insertions of documents or document fragments. In this case, it is much better to create a coarse graph synopsis of the newly inserted data (using Algorithm 4) and combine this with the index. Edges now only need to be added to the root of the document fragment, and hence we can capture structure more efficiently than with the node-by-node approach.

Deletions are handled more straightforwardly: when a node is deleted, we simply iterate through all target sets in the index and remove the node from each of them. If deletions are frequent, then this scheme can be improved by caching a list of deleted nodes. When evaluating queries over the index, we filter out any nodes that occur in the deleted list; once the deleted list reaches a suitable size, we then iterate through the target sets and delete all the nodes in the list simultaneously.

6 Experimental Evaluation

We now turn to the experimental evaluation of our adaptive index. All experiments were implemented in C++, and were conducted on a Pentium M 1.7 GHz PC with 1 GB of memory and 60 GB of hard drive space, using the Microsoft Windows XP Professional operating system. Our implementation is simple; for instance, we performed node splits instantly, instead of waiting for the next appropriate query. Thus, our experiments actually *overestimate* the cost of maintaining our index; a more complete implementation would be more efficient.

We chose a variety of data sets, of varying complexity and structure (their most relevant characteristics are summarized in Table 1): DBLP, SwissProt and XMark. These data sets exhibit a wide range of structural properties and thus are a good test for our adaptive index. Due to lack of space we have omitted the results for DBLP, on which our index performed even better than for the others.

6.1 Generating a Query Workload

One of the most important aspects of our experiments is to generate a realistic, but random, query workload. We restricted our queries to branching path queries having between l and u nodes (in our case, we chose the values $l = 3$ and $u = 5$ as queries are generally fairly small in practice).

There are two kinds of query workloads we are interested in testing: *positive* and *negative* query workloads, which have high and low selectivity respectively. Negative queries are easy to generate: we can simply generate random twigs over the label set of the data set (the vast majority of random twigs have zero selectivity in practice). We do not include results for negative queries since we found that our scheme handled them very easily. To generate positive queries, we

Table 1. Characteristics of experimental data sets

	DBLP	SwissProt	XMark
Size (MB)	150.68	109.50	113.06
Element Count	3760416	2977031	1666315
Maximum Depth	6	5	12
Average Depth	3.00	3.57	5.56
F/B Index Size	2896	699619	432851

make use of the F/B-index of the data set, which contains the exact answers for all branching path queries. We omit details due to lack of space, but essentially we picked random subtrees of the F/B-index as queries.

In practice, it is often the case that a small percentage of queries account for a large number of the actual queries to the database. Thus, in the following experiments, we chose a random subset $\mathcal{Q}_h \subseteq \mathcal{Q}$ of "hot" queries (in our case, $|\mathcal{Q}_h| = 0.2|\mathcal{Q}|$). We draw queries from $\mathcal{Q}$ by choosing each query using the following procedure: 70% of the time, we choose a query uniformly and randomly from $\mathcal{Q}_h$, the remaining 30% of the time we choose a query randomly from $\mathcal{Q} - \mathcal{Q}_h$.

6.2 Experiment 1: Testing Adaptibility

In this experiment, we verified that the basic principle of our index is indeed correct and results in a performance improvement. We created a query workload $\mathcal{Q}$ as described in the previous section, and initialized our adaptive index. We then repeatedly queried the adaptive index with queries drawn from $\mathcal{Q}$, and allowed the index to split as required. We did not restrict the index size in this experiment, so merge operations were not used; similarly, we kept the data set static, and hence updates were also not an issue. We performed split operations every $k = |\mathcal{Q}|$ queries. While we tested our index with queries workloads of size 50, 100, and 200, we do not include the similar results for $|Q| = 50$ and $|Q| = 100$ due to space limitations.

Every $|\mathcal{Q}|$ queries, we tested the index's performance by measuring the time taken to query a bag of $|\mathcal{Q}|$ queries drawn from $\mathcal{Q}$ — to ensure consistency, we used the same bag of queries for every test, and disabled statistics collection during the test so that it did not impact upon the index splitting behavior. We also measured the cost of updating the index during each block of $|\mathcal{Q}|$ queries.

Figure 3 gives the results for our data sets, for query workloads of size 200. The time taken during query evaluation is represented as a relative value, where 1.0 is the time taken to evaluate the queries using a structural join-based approach. We also give in the same graph the number of nodes in the index, which increases

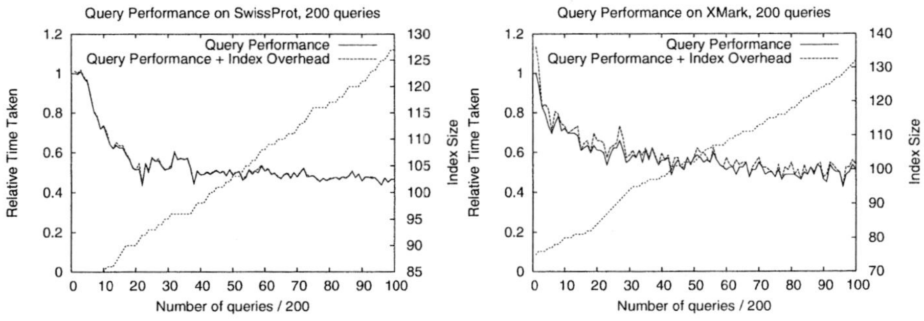

Fig. 3. Testing adaptability, $|\mathcal{Q}| = 200$

as split operations are performed. As can be seen, in each case the adaptive index relatively quickly provides a significant performance improvement of up to 60%, which is particularly impressive given how efficient the unoptimized join operators already are in evaluating branching query expressions. Even at the end of the experiment, all of the indexes are still very small compared to a typical graph index, with less than 150 nodes in all cases.

6.3 Experiment 2: Controlling Index Size

In this experiment, we test the impact of limiting the index's size on its performance. The previous experiment demonstrated that the indexes remain very small for even a fairly long-running database; nevertheless, restrictions on size are of course very useful. We chose to limit the index size for each data set to the following bounds: DBLP $[60, 75)$, SwissProt $[100, 120)$, and XMark $[90, 110)$.

Apart from the size restriction, the experimental setup was identical to that of Experiment 1. The results are shown in Figure 4 (we again omit the similar results for smaller query workloads due to lack of space). As can be seen, while the merge operation might adversely impact the performance in the short-term, the impact is not overly significant and is quickly corrected. It is hardly surprising that merging nodes reduces the performance of the index, given that we are forced to lose structural information.

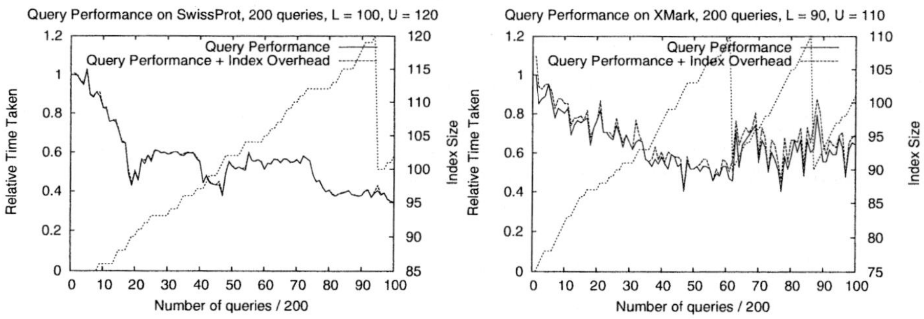

Fig. 4. Controlling index size, $|\mathcal{Q}| = 200$

6.4 Experiment 3: Testing Updatability

In this experiment, we test the impact of updates on the index. Our experimental setup was the same as Experiment 2, except that 30% of the way through the experiment, we appended a randomly generated document to the database, increasing its size by approximately 10% (we appended the document for simplicity only; where the document is inserted has no impact on the index's performance). Due to the ease with which random documents can be generated using XMark, we restricted this experiment to that data set only. Also, due to the larger number of nodes involved in the index, we also increased the lower and upper bounds to 140 and 180 respectively, which are more realistic bounds given that XMark has 74 unique elements.

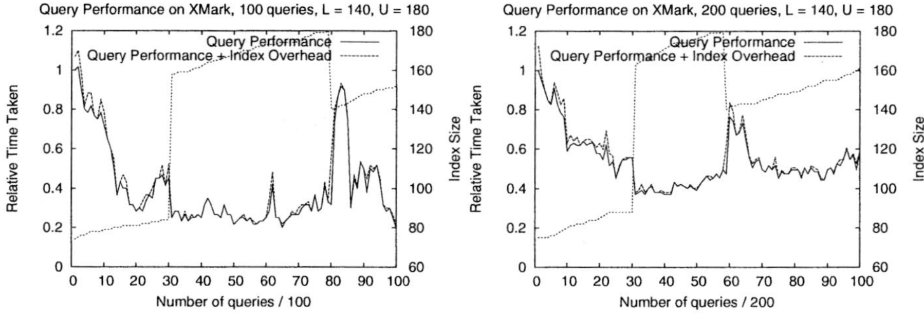

Fig. 5. Updating the index for the XMark data set

Our results are given in Figure 5 (we omit the results for $|Q| = 50$ for space reasons). The update point can be seen in the large jump in the number of nodes in the index. As can be seen, the updates have little adverse impact on the performance of the index; in fact, it is clear that the primary performance impact comes from the merge operation that occurs later. Intuitively this makes sense, since adding additional nodes does not reduce our knowledge of the structure of the underlying database, whereas taking them away does.

7 Conclusion

In this paper, we have described a new adaptive index scheme for XML documents which can efficiently process branching path expressions. The scheme optimizes the use of join operators, such as structural and twig joins, by capturing additional structural information from the query workload. By only what is needed, the index is able to efficiently evaluate branching path expressions using a fraction of the number of nodes that the F/B index would use. The index can also handle updates to the underlying database in an effective manner.

References

1. S. Al-Khalifa et al. Structural joins: A primitive for efficient XML query pattern matching. In *ICDE 2002*, pages 141–154, 2002.
2. N. Bruno, N. Koudas, and D. Srivastava. Holistic twig joins: optimal XML pattern matching. In *SIGMOD 2002*, pages 310–321. ACM, 2002.
3. C.-W. Chung, J.-K. Min, and K. Shim. APEX: an adaptive path index for XML data. In *VLDB 2002*, pages 121–132. Morgan Kaufmann, 2002.
4. R. Goldman and J. Widom. DataGuides: Enabling query formulation and optimization in semistructured databases. In *VLDB 1997*, pages 436–445. Morgan Kaufmann.
5. H. He and J. Yang. Multiresolution indexing of XML for frequent queries. In *ICDE 2004*, pages 683–694. IEEE Computer Society, 2004.
6. R. Kaushik, P. Bohannon, J. F. Naughton, and H. F. Korth. Covering indexes for branching path queries. In *SIGMOD 2002*, pages 133–144. ACM, 2002.

7. R. Kaushik, P. Bohannon, J. F. Naughton, and P. Shenoy. Updates for structure indexes. In *VLDB 2002*, pages 239–250. Morgan Kaufmann, 2002.
8. R. Kaushik, P. Shenoy, P. Bohannon, and E. Gudes. Exploiting local similarity for indexing paths in graph-structured data. In *ICDE*, pages 129–140. IEEE Computer Society, 2002.
9. T. Milo and D. Suciu. Index structures for path expressions. In *ICDT 1999*, pages 277–295. Springer, 1999.
10. N. Polyzotis and M. N. Garofalakis. Statistical synopses for graph-structured XML databases. In *SIGMOD 2002*, pages 358–369. ACM, 2002.
11. C. Qun, A. Lim, and K. W. Ong. $D(k)$-Index: An adaptive structural summary for graph-structured data. In *SIGMOD*, pages 134–144. ACM, 2003.
12. A. Silberstein, H. He, K. Yi, and J. Yang. BOXes: Efficient maintenance of order-based labeling for dynamic XML data. In *ICDE*, pages 285–296, 2005.
13. K. Yi, H. He, I. Stanoi, and J. Yang. Incremental maintenance of XML structural indexes. In *SIGMOD 2004*, pages 491–502. ACM, 2004.

TwigStackList¬: A Holistic Twig Join Algorithm for Twig Query with Not-Predicates on XML Data

Tian Yu, Tok Wang Ling, and Jiaheng Lu

School of Computing,
National University of Singapore
{yutian, lingtw, lujiahen}@comp.nus.edu.sg

Abstract. As business and enterprises generate and exchange XML data more often, there is an increasing need for searching and querying XML data. A lot of researches have been done to match XML twig queries. However, as far as we know, very little work has examined the efficient processing of XML twig queries with not-predicates. In this paper, we propose a novel holistic twig join algorithm, called *TwigStackList¬*, which is designed for efficient matching an XML twig pattern with negation. We show that *TwigStackList¬* can identify a large query class to guarantee the I/O optimality. Finally, we run extensive experiments that validate our algorithm and show the efficiency and effectiveness of *TwigStackList¬*.

1 Introduction

In the recent years, business and enterprises generate and exchange XML data more often. The XML data can be very complex and deeply nested. Therefore, there is a lot of interest in query processing over data that conforms to a tree-structured data model ([2, 7]). Efficiently matching all twig patterns in an XML database is a major concern of XML query processing. Among them, holistic twig join approach has been taken as an efficient way to match twig pattern since it has shown effectiveness by reducing the intermediate result ([2, 3, 4, 5]). We observe that, the existing work on holistic twig query matching only consider twig queries without not-predicate, such as:

$$\texttt{Q1}: \ suppliersDatabase/supplier[.//store]//part$$

This twig pattern is written in XPath [15] format. It selects *part* elements which are descendants of *supplier* elements having at least one descendent element *store*.

However, in real applications, XML queries is more complex and may contain logical-NOT predicates (or not-predicates), such as:

$$\texttt{Q2}: \ suppliersDatabase/supplier[NOT(.//store)]//part$$

The query selects *part* elements which are descendent of *supplier* elements having no descendant element *store*. Therefore, it is important for us to specify an algorithm to efficiently solve the twig patterns with not-predicates.

In general, the not-predicates can be used in a nested manner, such as:

$$\texttt{Q3}: suppliersDatabase/supplier[NOT(.//store[NOT(location = ''Singapore'')])]/part$$

M.L. Lee, K.L. Tan, and V. Wuwongse (Eds.): DASFAA 2006, LNCS 3882, pp. 249–263, 2006.

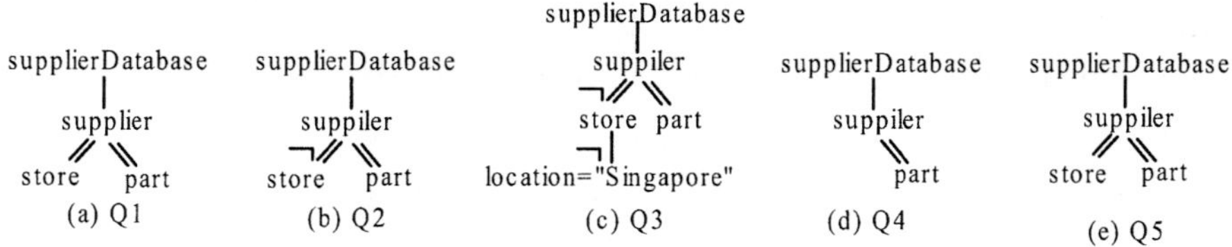

Fig. 1. Examples of XML Queries

It selects *part* elements which are descendent of *supplier* elements having no descendent element *store* that is not in *Singapore*. In another word, if the supplier only contains *store* that is in *"Singapore"*, its descendent *part* is in the answer to query Q3.

We call the general twig queries with not-predicates as NOT-twig queries. The queries without not-predicates are called normal-twig queries. The graphical representations of NOT-twig Q1, Q2, and Q3 are shown in Fig. 1(a), (b) and (c).

To match a twig query with not-predicates, a naïve method is to decompose it into several normal-twig queries (without not-predicates). Each decomposed normal-twig queries are individually evaluated using the existing method, and the final result can be calculated based on the results of the individual decomposed quires. Each not-predicate in the NOT-twig produce an additional decomposed query.

For example, we can evaluate query Q2 by solving the following two queries:

Q4: *suppliersDatabase/supplier//part*
Q5: *suppliersDatabase/supplier[.//store]//part*

Existing holistic algorithms, *TwigStack* [2] or *TwigStackList* [7] can be used to find the answers of Q4 and Q5, shown in Fig. 1(d) and (e). The query Q2 can be evaluated by calculating the difference of two answering set for Q4 and Q5. Clearly, this naïve approach is not optimal in most cases. For example, the elements in *supplier* and *part* has to be accessed twice in order to evaluate the two decomposed queries from query Q2.

Jiao et al. [6] proposed a holistic path join algorithm for path query with not-predicates. However, it cannot answer the problem of twig pattern with not-predicates. To the best of our knowledge, this paper is the first that address the problem of XML NOT-twig matching.

In this paper, we developed a new algorithm to match NOT-twig queries holistically without decomposing them into normal-twigs. The contributions of our work are:

– We discuss the problem of sub-query matching and propose a novel holistic twig join algorithm, namely *TwigStackList*$\neg$, based on the new concept of *Negation Children Extension* (for short *NCE*). Unlike naïve method, this approach ensures that all elements in the XML documents are scanned no more than once.
– We demonstrate that in a NOT-twig, when all the positive edges below branching nodes are ancestor-descendant relationships, the I/O cost is only proportional to the sum of sizes of the input and the final output. Therefore, our algorithm can guarantee the I/O optimality for a very large query set. Furthermore, even when there exist positive parent-child relationships below branching nodes, the intermediate solutions output by *TwigStackList*$\neg$ are guaranteed to be smaller than the naïve method.

– We present experimental results on a range of real and synthetic data, and query twig patterns. The results validate our analysis and show the superiority of *TwigStackList¬* in answering twig patterns with not-predicates.

The rest of the paper is organized as follows. Section 2 studies the related work. Section 3 defines the representation of twig queries with not-predicates and discusses the problem of sub-query matching. Section 4 explains our algorithm *TwigStackList¬*, and proves its correctness. Section 5 presents the performance study and the experimental results. Finally, section 6 concludes the paper.

2 Related Work

With the increasing popularity of XML data representation, XML query processing and optimization has attracted a lot of research interest. In this section, we summarize the literature on matching twig queries efficiently.

Zhang et al. [16] proposed a multi-predicate merge join (MPMGJN) algorithm based on (DocId, Start, End, Level) labeling of XML elements. The Twig join algorithms by Al-Khalifa et al. [1] gave a stack-based binary structural join algorithm. The later work by Bruno et al. [2] proposed a holistic twig join algorithm, *TwigStack*, to avoid producing a large intermediate result. However, this algorithm is only optimal for ancestor-descendent edges. Therefore, Lu et al. [7] developed a new algorithm called *TwigStackList*, in which a list data structure is used to cache limited elements to identify a larger optimal query class. Chen et al. [3] studied the relationship between different data partition strategies and the optimal query classes for holistic twig join. Recently, Lu et al. [8] proposed a new labeling scheme called extended Dewey to efficiently process XML twig pattern.

In order to solve complex twig queries, Jiang et al. [4] researched the problem of efficient evaluation of twig queries with OR predicates. Lu et al. [9] studied how to answer an ordered twig pattern using region encoding. Jiao et al. [6] proposed a holistic path join algorithm for path query with not-predicates.

In the recent years, two new algorithms, *ViST* [13] and *PRIX* [10], are proposed to transform both XML data and queries into sequences, and answer XML queries through subsequence matching. Their methods avoid join operations in query processing. However, to eliminate false alarm and false dismissal, they resort to time consuming operations (post-processing for false alarm and multiple isomorphism queries processing for false dismissal [12]).

3 Preliminaries

3.1 XML Data Model

We model XML documents as ordered trees. The edges between the tree nodes can be parent-child (for short PC) or ancestor-descendant (for short AD).

Many state of the art join algorithms on XML documents are based on certain numbering schemes. For example, the binary XML structural join in [1, 16], and the twig join in [2] use *(startPos: endPos, LevelNum)*. It is an example of using *region encoding* to label elements in an XML file. Fig. 2 shows an example XML data tree. *startPos* and *endPos* are calculated by performing a pre-order (document order) traversal of the document tree; *startPos* is the number in sequence assigned to an element when it is first encountered and *endPos* is equal to one plus the *endPos* of the last element visited. Leaf elements have same *startPos* and *endPos*. *LevelNum* is the level of a certain element in its data tree.

Formally, element *u* is an ancestor of element *v* iff *startPos(u)* $<$ *startPos(v)* and *endPos(u)* $>$ *endPos(v)*. Similarly, element u is the parent of element v iff *startPos(u)* $<$ *startPos(v)*, *endPos(u)* $>$ *endPos(v)*, and *levelNum(u)* + *1* = *levelNum(v)*.

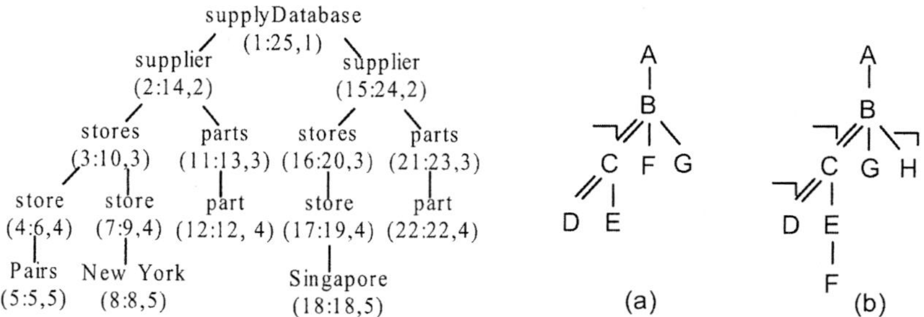

Fig. 2. XML data tree with region encoding

Fig. 3. Two NOT-twigs

3.2 NOT-Predicate and Node Operations

Each NOT-twig query has a corresponding tree representation, which contains all the nodes in the query, $\{n_1,n_2,...n_m\}$. Each node n_i and its ancestor (or parent respectively) n_j, are connected by an edge, denoted by *edge(*n_i*,* n_j*)*. The tree edges can be classified into one of the following four types: (1) positive ancestor/descendant edge, represented as "||"; (2) positive parent/child edge, represented "|"; (3) negative ancestor/descendant edge, represented as "||¬ "; (4) negative parent/child edge, represented as "|¬".

A negative edge corresponds to an *edge(*n_i*,*n_j*)* with a not-predicate in XQuery expression. It includes negative parent/child edge and negative ancestor/descendant edge. In this case, node n_j is called a *negative child* of node n_i. Similarly, a positive edge corresponds to an *edge(*n_i*,*n_j*)* without not-predicates in XQuery expression. Node n_j is considered to be a *positive child* of node n_i.

As an example, consider the NOT-twig in Fig. 3(b), *edge(B, C)* and *edge(C, D)* are negative ancestor/descendant edge, *edge(B, H)* is negative parent/child edge. Node B has three children, in which node G is a positive child, node C node H are negative children.

Given a query tree Q, a not-predicate is a subtree in Q such that the edge between the root of the subtree and its ancestor (or parent respectively) is a negative edge. We call the root of the subtree a negative child of its ancestor (or parent respectively).

As an example, the NOT-twig in Fig. 3(a) has one not-predicates (rooted at node C), and the NOT-twig in Fig. 3(b) has three not-predicates (rooted at node C, D and

H). The not-predicates are nested, therefore, we can see that not-predicate C contains not-predicate D.

In the following, we define some operations on query tree nodes. *isRoot(n)*, *isLeaf(n)*, and *isOutputNode(n)* respectively checks if a query node n is a root, a leaf node, or an output node. $is\_Neg\_Child(n)$ checks if the edge between node n and its ancestor (or parent respectively) has a not-predicate.

neg_children(n) and *pos_children(n)* respectively returns all the nodes that are the negative and positive children of n. *parent(n)* returns the parent node of n, and the function *children(n)* gets all child nodes of n. Therefore, we have *neg_children(n)*∪ *pos_children(n)* = *children(n)*. Function *AD_neg_children(n)* and *PC_neg_children(n)* returns all the negative AD child or negative PC child nodes of n. Similarly, function *AD_pos_children(n)* and *PC_pos_children(n)* returns all the positive AD child or PC child nodes of n.

3.3 Sub-query Matching and the Output Elements

In this paper, a *node* refers to a query node in twig query pattern and *element* refers to a data node in XML data tree. A NOT-twig matching problem can be decomposed into recursive sub-query matching problems.

Given a NOT-twig query Q, a query node n and a XML data tree D, we say that an element e_n(with the tag n) in the XML data tree D **satisfies** the sub-query rooted at n of Q iff:

(1) n is a leaf node of NOT-query Q; OR
(2) For each child node n_i of n in Q:

- (case i) If n_i is a positive PC child node of n, there is an element e_{n_i} in D such that e_{n_i} is a child element of e_n and satisfies the sub-query rooted at n_i in D.
- (case ii) If n_i is a positive AD child node of n, there is an element e_{n_i} in D such that e_{n_i} is a descendant element of e_n and satisfies the sub-query rooted at n_i in D.
- (case iii) If n_i is a negative PC child node of n, there does not exist any element e_{n_i} in D such that e_{n_i} is a child element of e_n and satisfies the sub-query rooted at n_i in D.
- (case iv) If n_i is a negative AD child node of n, there does not exist any element e_{n_i} in D such that e_{n_i} is a descendant element of e_n and satisfies the sub-query rooted at n_i in D.

We classify the nodes in a NOT-twig query into the following categories:

Definition 1 (output node, non-output node, output leaf node, leaf node). *A node n_i in a NOT-twig query is classified as an output node if n_i does not appear below any negative edge; otherwise, it is a non-output node. An output node with no positive children is called a output leaf node. A query node without any children is called a leaf node.*

For the NOT-twig in Fig. 3(b), $\{A, B, G\}$ and $\{C, D, E, F, H\}$ are the sets of output nodes and non-output nodes. Note that G is the output leaf node and $\{D, F, G, H\}$ are the leaf nodes.

The output elements for a NOT-twig query is defined in the following:

Definition 2 (Output elements for a NOT-twig Query). *Given an XML document* D *and a twig query with K output nodes,* $\{n_1, n_2... n_k\}$. *A tuple* $< e_1,..., e_k >$ *is defined to be a* ***matching answer*** *for the query iff (1)* e_i *has the same type (tag name) as* n_i*; (2) for each pair of elements* e_i *and* e_j *in the tuple,* e_j *is a descendant (or child respectively) element of* e_i *in* D *if* edge(n_i, n_j) *is a AD (or PC respectively) edge; and (3) Any output node* e_k *(with tag* K*) satisfies sub-query rooted at node* k *.*

For example, consider the document in Fig. 4(a), we want to match the NOT-twig in Fig. 4(b). $< A_1, B_1 >$ is not a matching answer since A_1 doesn't satisfy the sub-query rooted at A since it has a chid C_1 that satisfy the sub-query rooted at C. However, $< A_2, B_2 >$ is a matching answer.

For the NOT-twig in Fig. 4(c), both $< A_1, B_1 >$, and $< A_2, B_2 >$ are matching answers, because A_1 is an ancestor of B_1, A_2 is an ancestor of B_2, and all of A_1, B_1, A_2, B_2 satisfies the sub-query matching.

4 Negation Twig Join Algorithm

In this section, we present *TwigStackList*$\neg$, an algorithm for finding all the matching answers of a NOT-twig query against an XML document. We should know that although *TwigStackList*$\neg$ shares similarity with the *TwigStackList* algorithm in the previous work [7], it makes an important extension to handle the NOT-twigs.

4.1 Notation and Data Structures

For each node n in the query twig, a data stream T_n is associated with it. *Stream* is a posting list (or inverted list) accessed by a simple iterator. An XML document is partitioned into streams and an additional region coding label is assigned to each element in the streams. All elements in a stream are of the same tag and ordered by their *startPos*. We can only read the elements in a stream once from head to tail. Cursor c_n to access to the current element in T_n.

Our algorithm uses two types of data structure: list and stack. A chain of linked stacks is used to compactly represent partial results of individual query root-leaf paths. Lists L_n are used to cache limited number of items in the main memory, when the algorithm look-ahead read some elements. For each output node, we associate a list L_n and a stack S_n with it. Since non-output nodes do not contribute to the final solution, they don't have stacks associated with them. Therefore, we only maintain a list for each non-output node. At every point during computation: the nodes in stack S_n and L_n are guaranteed to lie on a root-leaf path in the database, which means each element is an ancestor or parent of that following it. Thus, the size of S_n and L_n are bounded by the maximum depth of the XML document. For each list L_n, we declare an integer variable p_n, as a cursor to point to an element in the list L_n.

Based on the data structure definition, we can now define the concept of *head element*:

Definition 3 (head element). *In* TwigStackList¬, *for each node in the query, if list L_n is not empty, we say that the element indicated by the cursor p_n of L_n is the head element of n. Otherwise, we say that element pointed by c_n in the stream T_n is the head element of n.*

In our algorithm, we use the function *getElement(n)* to get the *head element* of a query node n.

4.2 Negation Children Extension

We introduce a new concept: *Negation Children Extension* (for short *NCE*), which is important to determine whether an element likely be involves in the results of a NOT-twig query.

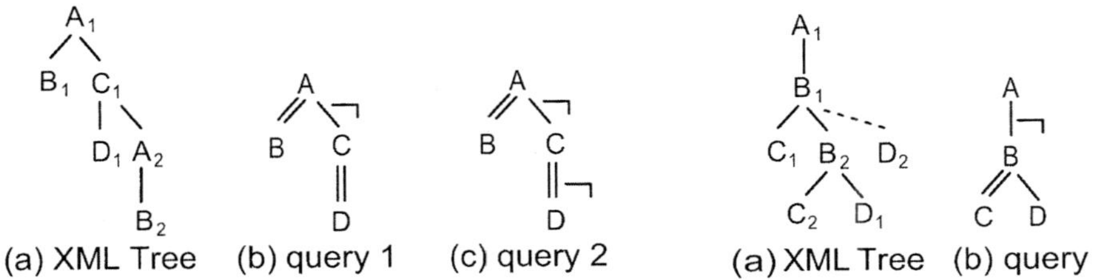

Fig. 4. Illustration of Sub-query Matching

Fig. 5. Sub-optimality example

Given an NOT-twig query *Q* and a dataset *D*, we say that an element e_n (tag *n*) in XML database *D* has a **Negation Children Extension** (for short *NCE*) based on the following conditions:

1. If in Q, query node n has no positive PC child or it is not an output node, the element e_n has a NCE iff it satisfies the sub-query rooted at n; OR
2. If in Q, query node n has positive PC child n_i and n is an output node, there is an element e'_n (with tag n) in the path from e_n to e_{n_i} such that e'_n is the parent of e_{n_i} and e_{n_i} also has *NCE*. The checking for the positive AD child, negative PC child and AD child nodes remains the same as sub-query matching.

The concept is different from sub-query matching method discussed in Section 3.3, since holistic algorithm cannot guarantee optimality when processing positive PC relationships. When the nodes are output nodes, we can eliminate the useless intermediate results using join operation, similar to the method used in $TwigStackList$. Condition (2) of NCE is based on this property. However, if the node is non-output nodes, the positive PC relationship has to be checked before the intermediate results are generated.

For example, consider the XML document and the two queries in Fig. 4(a), (b) and (c). Observe that *(1)* For both query 1 and query 2, B_1, B_2 and D_1 has *NCE* since they are leaf nodes. *(2)* For query 1, C_1 has *NCE* , since D_1 is a descendant of C_1. However, for query 2, C_1 doesn't have *NCE*. It is because since D_1 is a descendant of C_1 in the XML document, C_1 doesn't satisfy the sub-query rooted at C. *(3)* For query 1, since C_1

has *NCE*, we can safely say A_1 has no *NCE*. It is because C_1 is a child of A_1 and in the NOT-twig, node C is a negative PC child of node A. A_1 doesn't satisfy the sub-query rooted at A. *(4)* For query 2, in the XML document, there are no element with tag C that has *NCE*. Also, A_1 has a descendent B_1 with *NCE*. Therefore, A_1 has *NCE*. *(5)* For both query 1 and query 2, A_2 has *NCE* since A_2 has a descendent B_2 with *NCE*, and does not have any child with the tag C.

In the previous algorithm, both *TwigStack* and *TwigStackList* might output useless intermediate results when a branching node has at least one PC children. Now, we discuss the effect of this sub-optimality problem based on the concept PC-Branching node:

Definition 4 (PC-Branching node). *In a NOT-twig, a node n is called PC-Branching node if n has more than one positive children, among which at least one is a PC child.*

If a PC-Branching node is also an output node, we call it output PC-Branching node. Otherwise, it is called non-output PC-Branching node.

When we match a NOT-twig, the sub-optimality is caused by *PC-Branching* nodes in the query. If the PC-Branching node is an output node, the algorithm can use the method in *TwigStackList* and eliminate the useless intermediate results using join operation.

However, when the PC-Branching node is a non-output node, the useless intermediate result may result in false output. For example, the XML document and query are shown in Fig. 5(a) and (b), the query node B is a non-output PC-Branching node. Initially, the algorithm scans A_1, B_1, C_1 and D_1. Since only the first element of a stream is read, there is no way for the algorithm to decide if B_1 has an child element D_2. If the XML dataset does not has element D_2, the previous methods (*TwigStack* [2] or *TwigStackList* [7]) will still assume that B_1 has a child with tag D. In this case, the element A_1 cannot contribute to the final results and is deleted from the potential solution list. This operation is wrong since we will lose a matching answer A_1. Therefore, our algorithm solve negative PC child nodes differently. For a non-output PC-Branching node (of the type n), we need to use join operation to find the elements e_n with *NCE* before generating intermediate results. For example, to match the NOT-twig in 5(b), we search for elements of type B that has an descendent element C_i and a child element D_i. Since there is no matching element, we then conclude A_1 is in the matching answers.

In our algorithm, we use the function *isNonBranching(n)* to test if an node n is a non-output PC-Branching node.

4.3 Algorithm: TwigStackList¬

The main algorithm of *TwigStackList¬* (represented in algorithm 2), which computes answers to a NOT-tiwg, operates in two phases. In the first phase (line 1-12), the individual query root-leaf paths are output. In the second phase (line 13), these solutions are merged-joined to compute the matching answers to the whole query.

getNext(n) is an important procedure call in the main algorithm of *TwigStackList¬*. It returns a node n' (possibly n' = n). Assume that element $e_{n'}$ is the *head element* of node n'. In our algorithm, the element $e_{n'}$ has *NCE*.

In line 2, if the node is a non-output PC-Branching node, we call *TwigStackList Copy¬*. This function is a copy of *TwigStackList¬* but matches the sub-query Q_n (rooted at node n). It uses the same data streams C as the calling function, but terminates when the *getStart(n)* >*getEnd(Parent(n))*. Therefore, we only want to find the elements that are a potential descendants of the element *getElement(Parent(n))*. The final results are inserted to the list of n, L_n.

Algorithm 1. *getNext(n)*

1: **if**(isLeaf(n)) return n
2: **if**(isNonBranching(n)) TwigStackListCopy¬(Q_n,getEnd(Parent(n)))
3: **foreach** node n_i in pos_children(n) **do**
4: g_i=getNext(n_i)
5: **if**($g_i \neq n_i$) return g_i
6: $Posn_{max}$=$maxarg_{n_i \in children(n)} getStartPosn_{max}$
7: $Posn_{min}$=$maxarg_{n_i \in children(n)} getStartPosn_{min}$
8: **while** (getEnd(n) < getStart(n_{max})) proceed(n)
9: **foreach** node n_i in neg_children(n) **do**
10: **while**(getStart(n_i) <getStart(n)) proceed n_i
11: g_i=getNext(n_i)
12: **if**($g_i \neq n_i$)
13: **if**(getEnd(n_i) <getStart(g_i)) return n_i
14: **else** return g_i
15: **if**(is_Neg_AD_Child(n_i))
16: **while**(getElement(n) is the ancestor of getElement(n_i)) $proceed(n)$
17: **if** ($getStart(n)$>$getStart(n_{max})$) return n_{min}
18: **if**($n_{max}! = null$) MoveStreamToList(n,n_{max})
19: **foreach** node n_i in $PC\_neg\_children(n)$) **do**
20: **while**($c_n.start < getStart(n_i)$) **do**
21: **if**(c_n.*end*>*getEnd*(g)) $L_n.append(c_n)$
22: $advance(T_n)$
23: **if**(there is an element e_i in L_n such that e_i is the parent of getElement(n_i))
24: delete elements e_i and getElement(n_i)
25: **foreach** node n_i in $PC\_pos\_children(n)$ **do**
26: **if**(there is an element e_i in list L_n such that e_i is the parent of getElement(n_i))
27: **if**(n_i is the only child of n) move the cursor p_n of list L_n to point to e_i
28: **else** return n_i
29: return n

Line 3-8 check for positive PC child nodes for output nodes (details discussed in $TwigStackList$). Line 9-15 check for negative child nodes of n. We recursively call for every $n_i \in neg\_children(n)$. If any returned node g_i is not n_i , we return g_i, if *getStart*(g_i)<*getEnd*(n_i) (line 9). Otherwise, if the return value is n_i, we *proceed*(n_i) in the main algorithm and call *getNext(n)* again. If g_i=n_i and the *head element* of node n is the ancestor of the *head element* of node n_i (n_i is a negative AD child of n in the NOT-twig), the algorithm concludes the *head element* of n doesn't appear in the final answers(line 16).

If node n has at least one positive child, line 18 calls *MoveStreamToList* to push elements e_n into the list of node n. Then, line 19-24 check the negative PC relationship in condition (iv) of *NCE*. We push the potential parent of element e_{n_i} into the list of n

(line 21). In line 20-21, we make sure the elements are nested from top to end in the list. If we can find an element that is a negative child of an element in the list L_n, the parent element is deleted from the list (line 24). Finally, line 25-28 check the condition (ii) of *NCE*.

Now we discuss the main algorithm of *TwigStackList*¬ (in Algorithm 2). First of all, line 2 calls *getNext* to identify the next element to be processed. If returned node is non-output nodes, the algorithm just proceed the node in line 12. Otherwise, the algorithm check the output nodes the same way as *TwigStackList*.

Example 1. Consider the XML data and query shown in Fig. 4(a) and (b) again. Initially, the stream cursors are pointed to A_1, B_1, C_1 and D_1. In the first call of *getNext(A)*, the element A_1 is first pushed into the list L_A (in line 18 of *getNext*), then deleted from the list (in line 24 of *getNext*), since C_1 has NCE and is a child of A_1. After the second call of *getNext*, the cursors of A and B are forwarded to A_2, B_2, and the cursors of C and D are pointing to the end of the stream. The following steps push A_2 to stack and output the intermediate result $< A_2,B_2 >$. For this query, no merging operation is needed.

Algorithm 2. *TwigStackList*¬

1: **while**(¬ end( )) **do**
2: n_{act}=getNext(root)
3: **if**(!n_{act}.isNonOutputNode( ))
4: **if**(¬ isRoot(n_{act})) cleanParentStack(nact,getStart(n_{act}))
5: **if**(isRoot(n_{act}) ∨¬ empty(Sparent(n_{act})))
6: clearSelfStack(n_{act},getEnd(n_{act}))
7: moveToStack(n_{act},$S_{n_{act}}$,pointertotop($S_{parent(nact)}$))
8: **if**(isOutputleaf(n_{act}))
9: showSolutionsWithBlocking($S_{n_{act}}$,1)
10: pop($S_{n_{act}}$)
11: **else** proceed(n_{act})
12: **else** proceed(n_{act})
13: mergeAllPathSolutions( )

Example 2. We now consider the same XML data, but change the query to Fig. 4(c). Initially, the stream cursors points to A_1, B_1, C_1 and D_1. In the first call of *getNext(A)*, the node C is returned. It is because C_1 is first pushed into the list (in line 18 of *getNext*), then deleted from the list (in line 24 of *getNext*) since leaf node D_1 is a child of C_1 in the XML data. We advance the stream of C and reach the end of the stream. Therefore, in the next call of *getNext*, the element A_1 is pushed to stack and output the path solution $< A_1,B_1 >$. We call *getNext* again to advance stream A, and push element A_2 into stack S_A. The path $< A_2,B_2 >$ is then output by the algorithm.

4.4 Analysis of TwigStackList¬

In the section, we show the correctness of our algorithm and analyze its efficiency. Some proofs are omitted here due to space limitation.

Lemma 1. *For an arbitrary node n in the NOT-twig query we have* getNext(n)=n'. *Then the following properties hold:*

1. *n' has the* NCE
2. *Either (a) n=n' or (b) parent(n) does not have* NCE *due to the node n'.*

Lemma 2. *Suppose* getNext(n)=n' *returns a non-output query node. The head element does not contribute to any matching solutions, since it is not an output node. The Algorithm just proceed the node.*

Lemma 3. *Any element e that is inserted to stack S_n satisfy the not-predicates of the query. That is, if n has a negative descendant n' in query, then there is no element $e_{n'}$ in stream $T_{n'}$ such that $e_{n'}$ is a descendant of e_n. If element e has a negative PC child e_m (node type m. m is the negative PC child of node n in the query), e is deleted in line 24 of algorithm 1.*

Lemma 4. *In* TwigStackList¬, *when any element e is popped from stack , e is guaranteed not to participate a new solution any longer.*

Theorem 1. *Given a NOT-twig* Q *and an XML database* D. *Algorithm* TwigStackList¬ *correctly returns all matching answers for* Q *on* D.

Proof. Using Lemma 2, we know that when *getNext* returns a query node n in *getNext*, if the stack is empty, the head element e_n does not contribute to any matching solutions. Thus, any element in the ancestors of n that has positive child e_n with *NCE* is returned by the *getNext* before e_n. If n is negative child, we guarantee that each element e_n with *NCE* in the list L_n is checked to remove their corresponding parent elements by using lemma 3. Furthermore, with lemma 4, we can maintain that, for each node n in the query, the elements that involve in the root-leaf path solution are all in the stack S_n. Finally, each time that n = *getNext(root)* is an output leaf node, we output all solution for e_n (line 9 of *TwigStackList¬*).

We now analyze the optimality of *TwigStackList¬*. For the normal-twig join algorithms, *TwigStack* [2] is optimal for AD only twig patterns; *TwigStackList* [7] although identifies a larger optimal class than $TwigStack$, can not guarantee optimality for PC edges in non-branching node. In [3], the author proved that it is difficult to find an optimal normal-twig pattern matching method, since we cannot determine only from the first elements of various streams if any first element is in the match to a given twig pattern.

However, our algorithm can identify a larger optimal class than *TwigStackList* for NOT-twigs. In particular, the optimality of *TwigStackList¬* allows the existence of parent-child relationship in more than one negative branching edges, as illustrated below.

For example, we want to match the NOT-twig in Fig. 6(c) to the dataset in Fig. 6(a). If the naïve method uses *TwigStackList* to solve the problem, we removes the not-predicates and change the query to Fig. 6(b). In order to solve it, *TwigStackList* first scans A_1, C_1 and B_1, and pushes element A_1, A_2 and A_3 into the list L_A. However, since we can only read the head of a stream at a time, when we advance B, we

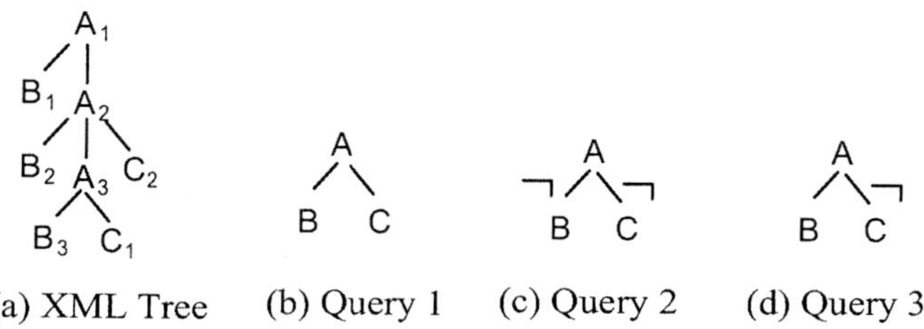

(a) XML Tree (b) Query 1 (c) Query 2 (d) Query 3

Fig. 6. Optimality study

could not decide whether A_1 has a child tagged with C. Therefore, this algorithm will output one useless solution $< A_1,B_1 >$.

If we use *TwigStackList¬* to directly match query 2 (in Fig. 6(c)). We first push element A_1, A_2 and A_3 into the list L_A. Then, we can immediately identify that A_3 has a child C_1. Since there is an not-predicate on *edge(A,C)*, A_3 is removed from the list. We advance C and since C_2 is a child of A_2, A_2 is deleted from L_A. We advance C again, since A_1 doesn't have any child element with the tag name C. We output the path $< A_1,B_1 >$ as output.

We use the similar method to match the NOT-twig in Fig. 6(d). After we push A_1, A_2 and A_3 into the stack L_A, we can identify that A_1 has a child B_1. Since there is an not-predicate on *edge(A, C)*, A_1 is removed from the list. B is advanced to B_2. Since it is a child of A_2, A_2 is deleted from the list. B is advanced to B_3, which is a child of A_3, A_3 is also deleted from the list. Therefore, there is no matching answers to query 3.

Thus, this example shows that our algorithm may guarantee the optimality for queries with parent-child relationship negative branching edge.

Theorem 2. *Consider an XML database* D *and an NOT-twig query* Q *without non-output PC-Branching nodes. The worst case I/O complexity of* TwigStackList¬ *is linear in the sum of the sizes of input and output lists. The worst-case space complexity of this algorithm is that the number of nodes in* Q *times the length of the longest path in* D.

5 Experimental Evaluation

We implements two naive twig join algorithms, *naïve-TwigStack* (for short *NTS*) and *naïve-TwigStackList* (for short *NTSL*), to be compared with our algorithm, *twigstack list¬*. The naive methods use the straightforward query decomposition approach. This approach first decomposes the NOT-twig into queries without not-predicates. The decomposed queries are then matched individually (using *TwigStack* [2] or *TwigStackList* [7], respectively) and the NOT-twig solution is calculated by the set-difference of the decomposed query results.

In our experiment, we use the following two metrics to compare the performance of the three algorithms.

- **Intermediate path solutions:** This metric measures the total number of intermediate path solutions. For the naïve methods, the total number is the sum of the intermediate results of all the decomposed queries.
- **Execution time:** We calculate this metric using the average time elapsed to answer a query with ten individual runs.

5.1 Experimental Setup

We use JDK 1.4 with the file system as a simple storage engine. All experiments run on a 1.7G Pentium IV processor with 768MB of main memory and 2GB quota of disk space, running windows XP system. We used three real-world and synthetic data sets for our experiments. The first one is a real dataset: TreeBank [11]. The file size is 82M bytes with 2.4 million nodes. The second one is the well-known benchmark data: XMark [14]. The size of file is 115M bytes with factor 1.0. The third one is a Random data set. We generated random uniformly distributed data trees using two parameters: fan-out, depth. We use seven different labels (tag: a, b, c, d, e, f and g) to generate the data sets.

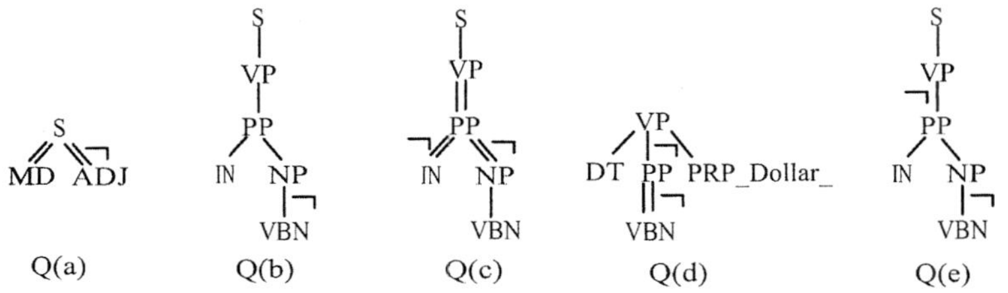

Fig. 7. Five NOT-twigs tested in TreeBank

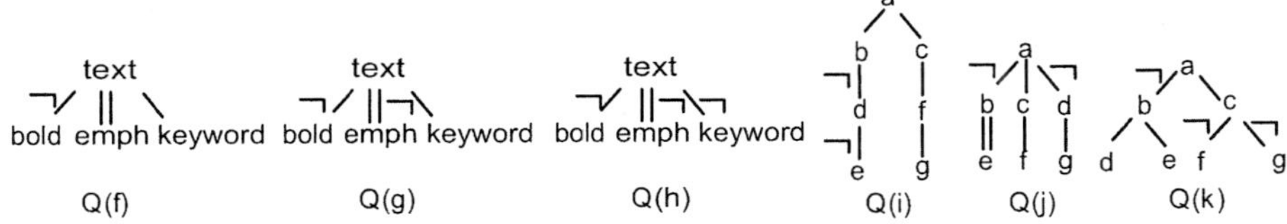

Fig. 8. Six NOT-twigs: Test Q(f), Q(g), Q(h) in XMark; Q(i), Q(j), Q(k) in Random data set

We tested five twig queries (in Fig. 7) in TreeBank, and three twig queries (in Fig. 8) in XMark and Random data set separately. The queries give a comprehensive comparison of the three algorithms, since the queries have different structures and combinations of positive and negative edges.

5.2 Performance Study

Fig. 9 shows the results on execution time in the three datasets. We can observe from the three figures that *TwigStackList¬* is more efficient than the two naïve methods for all the queries. It is because the naïve methods have to match more than one decomposed queries and generate more intermediate results.

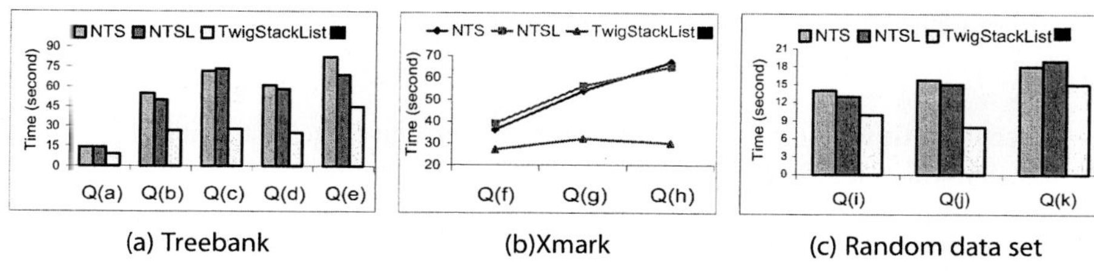

(a) Treebank (b)Xmark (c) Random data set

Fig. 9. Execution time of NOT-twig on three datasets

An interesting observation is made when we test the queries in XMark database. Query Q(f), Q(g), Q(h) have the same query nodes and structure, but the number of not-predicates is different. We can see from Fig. 9(b) that for *TwigStackList¬*, the time to match the three queries is almost constant. However, the results for *NTS* and *NTSL* show that when we increase the number of not-predicate, the total execution time increases linearly. It is because as we increase the number of not-predicates, we are increasing the number of decomposed queries that the naïve method need to match.

For each NOT-twig, the number of decomposed queries and the the intermediate results are listed in Table 1. The last column shows the number of path solutions in the matching answers. The results show that *TwigStackList¬* is sub-optimal if there are PC-Branching nodes in the queriy, e.g PP in Q(b), VP in Q(d), a in Q(i).

In Table 1, we can see that the number of intermediate results output by our *TwigStackList¬* is always less than the results output by *NTS* and *NTSL*. It is because when we output the intermediate results in *TwigStackList¬*, we already considered the not-predicates. Thus, the number of useless intermediate paths is largely reduced.

Therefore, according to the experimental results, we can conclude that our new algorithm *TwigStackList¬* could be used to evaluate twig pattern with not-predicates because it has obvious performance advantage over the straightforward approaches: NTS and $NTSL$. *TwigStackList¬* guarantees the I/O optimality for a large query class.

Table 1. The number of intermediate path solutions

Query	Dataset	Decomposed Queries	NTS	NTSL	TwigStackList¬	Useful Solutions
Q(a)	Treebank	2	31197	31197	31143	31143
Q(b)	Treebank	2	64053	61646	60356	58405
Q(c)	Treebank	3	355981	355981	14484	14484
Q(d)	Treebank	3	78857	78675	1789	1508
Q(e)	Treebank	3	215595	209652	78326	67312
Q(f)	XMark	2	181066	171392	22870	21050
Q(g)	XMark	3	228009	224027	12057	12057
Q(h)	XMark	4	308708	306602	7476	7476
Q(i)	Random	3	152	114	58	36
Q(j)	Random	3	1701	1461	138	138
Q(k)	Random	4	1731	1120	837	436

6 Conclusion and Future Work

In this paper, we proposed a new holistic twig join algorithm, called *TwigStackList¬*, to process NOT-twig query. Although holistic twig join has been proposed to solve normal-twig patterns, applying it to NOT-twig matching is nontrivial. We developed a new concept *Negation Children Extension* to determine whether an element is in the results of a NOT-twig query. We also make the contribution by identifying a large query class to guarantee I/O optimality for *TwigStackList¬*. The experimental results show that our algorithm is more effective and efficient than the naïve method.

In the future, we will improve the algorithm based on the following two issues: one is to design an efficient index scheme that might change the format of the input data. Another possible issue to improve our algorithm is to identify a larger optimal query class for NOT-twig matching.

References

1. Shurug Al-Khalifa, H. V. Jagadish, Nick Koudas, Jignesh M. Patel, Divesh Srivastava, and Yuqing Wu. Structural joins: A primitive for efficient XML query pattern matching. In *Proceedings of ICDE*, pages 141–152, 2002.
2. Nicolas Bruno, Nick Koudas, and Divesh Srivastava. Holistic twig joins: optimal XML pattern matching. In *Proceedings of SIGMOD*, pages 310–321, 2002.
3. Ting Chen, Jiaheng Lu, and Tok Wang Ling. On boosting holism in XML twig pattern matching using structural indexing techniques. In *Proceedings of SIGMOD*, 2005.
4. Haifeng Jiang, Hongjun Lu, and Wei Wang. Efficient processing of twig queries with or-predicates. In *In Proceeding of SIGMOD*, pages 59–70, 2004.
5. Haifeng Jiang, Wei Wang, Hongjun Lu, and Jeffrey Xu Yu. Holistic twig joins on indexed XML documents. In *In Proceeding of VLDB*, pages 273–284, 2003.
6. Enhua Jiao, Tok Wang Ling, Chee Yong Chan, and Philip S. Yu. Pathstack¬: A holistic path join algorithm for path query with not-predicates on XML data. In *Proceedings of DASFAA*, 2005.
7. Jiaheng Lu, Ting Chen, and Tok Wang Ling. Efficient processing of XML twig patterns with parent child edges: A look-ahead approach. In *Proceedings of CIKM*, pages 533–542, 2004.
8. Jiaheng Lu, Tok Wang Ling, Chee-Yong Chan, and Ting Chen. From region encoding to extended dewey: On efficient processing of XML twig pattern matching. In *In Proceeding of VLDB*, 2005.
9. Jiaheng Lu, Tok Wang Ling, Tian Yu, Changqing Li, and Wei Ni. Efficient processing of ordered XML twig pattern. In *In Proceeding of DEXA*, 2005.
10. Praveen Rao and Bongki Moon. PRIX: Indexing adnd quering XML using prüfer sequences. In *Proceedings of ICDE*, 2004.
11. Treebank. http://www.cs.washington.edu/research/xmldatasets/www/repository.html.
12. Haixun Wang and Xiaofeng Meng. On the sequencing of tree structures for XML indexing. In *In Proceeding of ICDE*, pages 372–383, 2005.
13. Haixun Wang, Sanghyun Park, Wei Fan, and Philip S. Yu. ViST: A dynamic index mathod for querying XML data by tree structure. In *Proceedings of SIGMOD*, 2003.
14. XMARK. http://monetdb.cwi.nl/xml.
15. XPath. http://www.w3.org/TR/xpath.
16. Chun Zhang, Jeffery Naughton, David DeWitt, Qiong Luo, and Guy Lohman. On supporting containment queries in relational database management systems. In *Proceedings of SIGMOD*, pages 425–436, 2001.

Efficient Schemes of Executing Star Operators in XPath Query Expressions*

Young Chul Park[1], Je Hyun Cho[1], Geum Ji Cha[1], and Peter Scheuermann[2]

[1] Kyungpook National University, Department of Computer Science,
1370, Sangyeok-dong, Buk-gu, Daegu 702-701, Korea
ycparkknu@hanmail.net, c2061@bcline.com, geumji@hotmail.com
[2] Northwestern University, Department of Electrical and Computer Engineering,
2145 Sheridan Road, Evanston IL 60208-3118, USA
peters@northwestern.edu

Abstract. Upon performing XPath queries on XML documents that are stored in relational databases, the execution of path expressions with steps of the star operator '*', which can be mapped to arbitrary names of either elements or attributes, has not been treated seriously in the literature. This paper presents schemes of acquiring *path identifiers* of query expressions that have steps of star operators in addition to steps of element names and attribute names. The contribution of this paper can be summarized as follows. First, we show that path identifiers of "/@*" and "//@*" can be obtained from the relation *Path* that holds path identifiers of path expressions in XML documents; by extending the relation Path, path identifiers of "//*" can be obtained from the extended relation; and some of "/*"s can be handled with the same way as "//*". Second, to obtain path identifiers of "/*" from the extended relation Path, we propose a new reserved character '$' that extends the string-pattern of the LIKE operator of SQL. The reserved character '$' followed by the restricting character string '[^patterns]' matches arbitrary number of arbitrary characters except for the characters listed in the restricting character string.

1 Introduction

XML [1] has been evolved as a standard format for expressing data, data exchanges, and data searching over Internet. A number of query languages for XML documents, such as XML-QL [2], XQL [3], XPath [4], and XQuery [5] have been proposed by the World Wide Web Consortium. As far as database management systems are concerned, the research on XML can be classified into two groups: one is publishing relational data as XML [8], [9] and the other is storing XML documents on database management systems and retrieving XML documents by querying the stored documents [6], [7], [10], [11], [12]. The latter can be classified further depending on whether the stored documents follow some specific DTD [13] or XML Schema [14]. This paper is concerned with publishing XML documents by issuing XPath queries on the stored XML documents that do not follow any DTD or XML Schema. In this

* This work was supported by KOSEF Grant (R01-2000-000-00403-0).

M.L. Lee, K.L. Tan, and V. Wuwongse (Eds.): DASFAA 2006, LNCS 3882, pp. 264 – 278, 2006.

context, the input XML documents are shredded into relations, and users can view the XML documents as XML trees and issue XPath queries against the XML trees. The system then translates XPath queries into SQL queries over those relations.

XRel [10], [11] introduced the concept of the *path identifier* as auxiliary retrieval information in addition to the stored XML documents. A path identifier is assigned to each path expression that represents a path in the XML tree starting at the root element node and ending at a specific node corresponding to an element or attribute. The path-based approach involves storing pairs of path expressions and path identifiers in a separate relation named *Path*. The processing of XPath queries using path identifiers reduces the number of joins performed on the relations that stores the actual data of the XML tree since it eliminates the cost of finding the intermediate element nodes on the path. In addition, XRel retrieval has the advantage that its performance is independent of the path length specified in the query expression. The work reported with XTABLES [12], [15] has also adopted the concept of a path identifier.

XPath queries can involve the star operator '*' that can be mapped to arbitrary names of either elements or attributes in conjunction with the delimiters '/' or '//'. The possible combinations include "/*" that maps arbitrary child element names, "//*" that maps arbitrary descendant element names, "/@*" that maps arbitrary child attribute names, and "//@*" that maps arbitrary descendant attribute names. XRel recommended the following two-phase procedure for the efficient processing of XPath expressions containing star operators. In the first phase, once a star operator is found in an expression, relation Path is used to find the path identifiers of the path up to and excluding the first step of the star operator in the expression. In the second phase, this step and all the remaining steps in the expression are supposed to be translated into join operations on the related relations. However, this approach does not take full advantage of using the path identifiers.

Chan et al. [21] introduced the *layer* axis as a scheme of minimizing star operators and also proposed its implementation by utilizing *levels* and *heights* of the nodes in the XML trees corresponding to the input XML documents. Although this scheme was proposed for the processing of star operators on any context node of the XML tree, it fails to find path identifiers for the whole XPath query. For example, for the XPath query "//a/b//*/*/e/f", the layer axis has the benefit of processing a partial path for "//*/*/e". The nodes that satisfy the path identifiers can work as context nodes for further processing of XQuery queries as in the XPath accelerator [7] and Chan et al. [21].

In this paper, steps in XPath expressions are classified into two types: *name-steps* and *star-steps*. *Name-steps* are the steps that specify either specific element names or attribute names (possibly prefixed with @); *star-steps* are the steps that specify the star operator '*' that matches any element name or attribute name (possibly prefixed with @). We consider '/' and '//' as the only delimiters of steps for XPath expressions. Given that we have eight combinations of delimiters and steps: "/name", "//name", "/@name", "//@name", "/*", "//*", "/@*", and "//@*". The goal of this paper is to find path identifiers of path expressions that are linear paths and are composed of the above eight combinations of delimiters and steps. Query expressions of twig patterns and other axes such as *sibling*, *ancestor*, etc are not in the scope of this paper.

The contribution of this paper can be summarized as follows. First, using relation Path, we suggest a method of retrieving path identifiers of "/@*" and "//@*" in query expressions, and by extending relation Path, we introduce a scheme that finds path identifiers of "//*" from the extended relation and show that some "/*"s can be handled the same way as "//*"s. Second, for the string match operation LIKE of SQL, we propose a new reserved character "$" that enables retrieving path identifiers of "/*" in query expressions from the extended relation Path. The reserved character "$" must be followed by some restricting characters and can be matched by any number of characters that are not listed in the restricting character set.

In this paper, we consider two different modes of XPath query evaluation [15]: the *select* mode and the *reconstruct* mode. The *select mode* (i.e., "node-selecting XPath queries" in [21]) takes the information of elements or attributes that satisfy the queries from the related relations, while the *reconstruct mode* (i.e., "standard XPath queries" in [21]) generates an XML document with the sub-trees that have as their roots the elements or attributes that satisfy the queries.

The rest of this paper is organized as follows. In Section 2, we describe the database schemas that are used in this paper for storing XML documents. In Section 3, we introduce four new schemes, denoted as PE, POE, PRE, and PME, for finding path identifiers of query expressions with star operators. We ascertain the effect of finding path identifiers for different lengths of steps in Section 4. In Section 5, our new reserved character '$' for the string-pattern of the LIKE operator of SQL is introduced and we conclude this paper in Section 6.

2 Database Schema

For storing contents of input XML documents and the search information on them, our database schema consist of the following four relations: Doc_Name, Path, Edge, and Element. Fig. 1 illustrates three hypothetical input XML documents.

The *XML tree* [11] of an XML document is an ordered tree of nodes and edges, where nodes of the tree represent root node, element nodes, attribute nodes, text nodes of the document, edges connecting the root node to the element node for the document element, element nodes to their child element nodes, their child text nodes

```
<A>
  <B C="CCC">
    <E> EEE </E>
    BBB
  </B>
  <G>GGG</G>
  AAA
</A>
```

(a) sample1.xml

```
<X>
  <Y> YYY </Y>
  XXX
</X>
```

(b) sample2.xml

```
<A>
  <G>
    <H M="MMM">
      <N>
        <K> KKK </K>
        NNN
      </N>
      HHH
    </H>
    ggg
  </G>
  <B C="CCC" D="DDD"/>
  aaa
</A>
```

(c) sample3.xml

Fig. 1. Examples of input XML documents

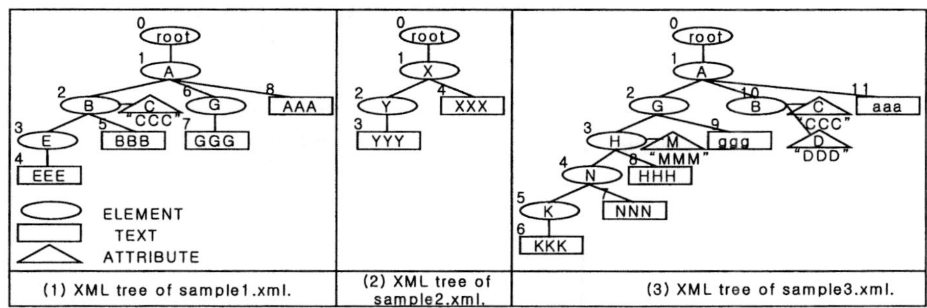

Fig. 2. XML trees

DOCID	DOCNAME
1	sample1
2	sample2
3	sample3

Fig. 3. Relation Doc_Name

PATHID	PATHEXP	PATHID	PATHEXP
1	#/A	7	#/X#/Y
2	#/A#/B	8	#/A#/G#/H
3	#/A#/B#/@C	9	#/A#/G#/H#/@M
4	#/A#/B#/E	10	#/A#/G#/H#/N
5	#/A#/G	11	#/A#/G#/H#/N#/K
6	#/X	12	#/A#/B#/@D

Fig. 4. Relation Path

and the attribute nodes for their attributes. Edges of each node that connect child nodes of the node have orders from left to right according to the order of appearance of elements or texts for the child nodes within the document. Every node in an XML tree except for the attribute nodes has its own *node identifier* for its identification information. Serial numbers starting from 0 are allocated to nodes of the root, elements and texts for their node identifiers while traversing the XML tree in the depth first order. Fig. 2 illustrates XML trees for the XML documents of Fig. 1. The number on top of each node in Fig. 2 signifies the node identifier allocated to that node. Note that attribute nodes having attribute names and attribute values, as properties of their enclosing element nodes, have the same node identifiers as their enclosing element nodes.

For each input XML document, one record of <docid, docname> pair is stored in relation Doc_Name. *Docid* is the document identifier that is allocated to the document and *docname* represents the name of the document, which is the file name of the input XML document in our current implementation. The document identifier starts from 1 and is incremented by one whenever a new XML document is inserted. Fig. 3 illustrates the contents of relation Doc_Name for the three XML documents in Fig. 1.

From the XML tree of every input XML document, for all the paths starting from the root element node to arbitrary element node or attribute node, relation Path stores <pathid, pathexp> pair for every different path expression, where pathid means the path identifier and pathexp signifies the path expression. Serial numbers starting from 1 are allocated to new paths upon storing path expressions in relation Path. Path expressions in relation Path have "#/" right before every element name and "#/@" right before every attribute name [11]. Fig. 4 illustrates the contents of relation Path for the XML documents in Fig. 1. It has 12 records. By using path identifiers, multiple join operations and/or recursive queries are replaced by a *SQL string match operation* using the XPath expression string, after applying the replacement function f% of XRel, against the pathexp attribute in relation Path. The function f% replaces occurrences of '/' in the input string by "#/" and occurrences of '//' by "#%/".

For each node in the XML tree, relation Edge stores a record that consists of <docid, id, parent_id, end_desc_id, pathid, type, value, ...> [12][16]. In the information, *docid* represents the document identifier of the document to which the node belongs, *id* means the node identifier of the node, *parent_id* signifies the node identifier of the parent node of the node, *end_desc_id* means the node identifier of the last descendant node such that it is the maximum number among the node identifier of the node and the node identifiers of the descendant nodes of the node, *pathid* identifies the path identifier of the node, *type* represents the type of the node, *value* holds element name, attribute name, attribute value, or string-value of the text depending on the type of the node. Other database attributes in relation Edge represent orders among sibling elements and sibling attributes. Since queries using these fields are not related to the topic of this paper, discussions about them are not treated in this paper. Fig. 5 illustrates some records of relation Edge. It has 31 records for the XML documents in Fig. 1.

DOCID	ID	PARENT_ID	END_DESC_ID	PATHID	TYPE	VALUE	...
1	1	-1	8	1	ELEM	A	...
1	2	1	5	2	ELEM	B	...
1	2	1	5	3	AT_N	C	...
1	2	1	5	3	AT_V	CCC	...
1	3	2	4	4	ELEM	E	...
1	4	3	4	4	TEXT	EEE	...
1	5	2	5	2	TEXT	BBB	...
...	...	...	...	...	...	...	...

Fig. 5. Relation Edge

To expedite the retrieval of root element nodes that satisfy XPath queries, we put relation *Element* that keeps the information of element nodes of XML trees. Therefore, relation Element is a subset of relation Edge and does not have the database attribute *type*. Relation Element for the XML documents of Fig. 1 has 12 records.

3 Processing Star-Steps

The replacement function f% of XRel can be applied only to the name-steps. Note that the function f% replaces occurrences of '/' in the input string by "#/" and occurrences of '//' by "#%/". This section classifies the star-steps into two groups: those that can be performed on relation Path and those that need an additional relation.

3.1 Path Identifiers of Star-Steps

We first identify the characteristics of partial paths that can be converted into the string match operation of SQL queries.

Observation 1. For the leading consecutive n + 1 (n ≥ 0) steps of XPath query expressions, assume that path identifiers of the leading partial paths of n steps can be found from relation Path.

(1) If the n + 1st step is "//*", the step can be replaced by "#/%" in the LIKE clause of SQL query and then the replaced one is applied either to all path expressions in relation Path whose last steps are elements if the step "//*" is the last step in the query expressions or to all path expressions in relation Path otherwise.

(2) If the n + 1st step is "/@*" (and "//@*"), the step can be replaced by "#/@%" (and "#%/@%", respectively) in the LIKE clause of SQL query and then be applied against all path expressions in relation Path.

According to Observation 1, to find path identifiers of the query expressions with the star-step "//*", we have modified relation Path to have an additional database attribute, *path_type*, such that path expressions having elements as their last steps hold 0 and those having attributes as their last steps hold 1 for the database attribute. Fig. 6 illustrates the contents of relation Path augmented by the database attribute *path_type* to relation Path of Fig. 4. In the rest of this paper, relation Path means relation Path augmented by the database attribute *path_type*.

PATHID	Path_Type	PATHEXP	PATHID	Path_Type	PATHEXP
1	0	#/A	7	0	#/X#/Y
2	0	#/A#/B	8	0	#/A#/G#/H
3	1	#/A#/B#/@C	9	1	#/A#/G#/H#/@M
4	0	#/A#/B#/E	10	0	#/A#/G#/H#/N
5	0	#/A#/G	11	0	#/A#/G#/H#/N#/K
6	0	#/X	12	1	#/A#/B#/@D

Fig. 6. Relation Path augmented by path_type

For example, in the case of the XPath query expression "/A//*/F/@V", path identifiers of it can be obtained from relation Path by the SQL query "pathexp like '#/A#/%#/F#/@V'". However, in the case of "/A//*", since the last step is "//*", the SQL query should be "pathexp like '#/A#/%' and path_type = 0".

Observation 2. In the XPath query expressions, for the *star partial path* W_n consisting of n (n > 0) consecutive star-steps of elements, let us denote W_n as (i) ES_n if all steps in W_n are "/*", (ii) DS_n if at least one step in W_n is "//*" and at least one step in W_n is "/*", and (iii) FDS_n if all steps in W_n are "//*".[1] In the XPath query expressions, the following formulas hold.

[1] ES, DS, and FDS stand for Exact_Star, Descendant_Star, and Full_Descendant_Star, respectively.

(1) $DS_n = FDS_n$.
(2) ES_n //name = DS_n /name = DS_n //name = FDS_n //name = FDS_n /name.
(3) ES_n //@name = DS_n /@name = DS_n //@name = FDS_n //@name = FDS_n /@name.
(4) ES_n //@* = DS_n /@* = DS_n //@* = FDS_n //@* = FDS_n /@*.
(5) ES_{n-1} $FDS_1 = DS_n$, where n > 1.

Even though Observation 1 does not present any mapping method for the star-step "/*", Observations 2-1 ~ 2-4 illustrate that some "/*"s have the same meaning as "//*". For example, the query expression "/A/*//*/B/C/*/*//G/*//@*" can be modified into "/A//*//*/B/C//*//*/G//*/@*" such that, by applying f% to the name-steps and Observation 1 to the star-steps, it can be translated into the SQL query "pathexp like '#/A#/%#/%#/B#/C#/%#/%#/G#/%#/@%'". Observation 2-5 illustrates that DS_n on query expressions has the same meaning as the concatenation of ES_{n-1} and FDS_1.

Observation 3. Let's denote a partial path of a query expression that consists of n (n > 0) consecutive "/*"s as ES_n. Suppose that the immediately preceding step (if any) of ES_n is not a star-step and the immediately following step (if any) of ES_n is not a star-step of element. The schemes of Observation 2 do not specify how to convert "/*" in ES_n into "//*" if ES_n is either the last partial path in the query expression or immediately followed by either "/name", "/@name", or "/@*".

Observation 3 introduces some patterns of "/*"s that cannot be converted into "//*"s. Consider the query expression "/*//*/B/*/*/E//G/*//*/K/*". Both the leading partial path "/*//*" and the partial path "/*//*" between "/G" and "/K" of the expression can be converted into "//*//*" according to Observation 2-1. However, both the partial path "/*/*" between "/B" and "/E", and the partial path "/*" after "/K" belong to the partial paths that are mentioned in Observation 3, that is, the "/*"s in the partial paths cannot be converted into "//*".

We denote partial paths that consist of some consecutive "/*"s that cannot be converted into the same number of consecutive "//*"s as *StringMatch_improper(SMI,* in short*) partial paths* and all other partial paths as *StringMatch_proper(SMP,* in short*) partial paths*. The name *SMP partial paths* come from the fact that they can be converted into the string match SQL queries according to the replacement function f% and Observations 1 and 2. In the above query expression, partial paths "/*//*/B" and "/E//G/*//*/K" are SMP partial paths and partial paths "/*/*" between "/B" and "/E", and "/*" after "/K" are SMI partial paths.

We denote the scheme that finds path identifiers of the leading SMP partial paths (if any) in query expressions from relation Path based on both f% and Observations 1 and 2, and then processes the remaining steps by the join operations on relation Element or Edge (depending on the last step of the expressions) as scheme *PE* (acronym of *P*ath and *E*lement).

3.2 SMI Partial Paths

XPath query expressions can be decomposed into one leading SMP partial path (if any) and the rest (if any) that has some SMI partial paths. The path identifiers of the leading SMP partial path can be obtained from relation Path. The rest of the query expressions can be viewed as either a sequence of steps with the parent/child and ancestor/descendant relationships or a sequence of <SMI partial path, SMP partial path> pairs. Based on the former view, we introduce two schemes *POE* and *PRE*; and based on the latter view a scheme *PME* is introduced in this section. For the explanation of these three schemes, we propose the notion of the *XML path tree* that is explained next.

For the set of path expressions of one XML document, if elements and attributes of each path expression are represented as nodes and parent/child relationships between steps of each path expression are represented as edges, they constitute a tree. However, their representation for the set of path expressions of all the stored XML documents might constitute a forest. In the forest, once a virtual node is put and edges are connected from the virtual node to every root node of the forest, the forest becomes a tree. We denote the tree as an *XML path tree*. Except for the root node of the XML path tree, each node in the tree has its own name of either element or attribute and the path identifier that corresponds to its path expression. The root node of the XML path tree has null as its name and 0 as its path identifier. Fig. 7 illustrates the XML path tree for the XML documents in Fig. 1. In Fig. 7, the number marked above each node shows the path identifier of the node and the string within each node represents either element name or attribute name of the node.

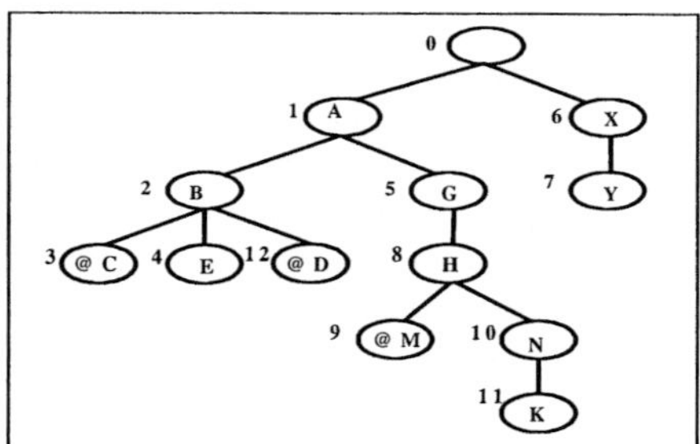

Fig. 7. XML path tree

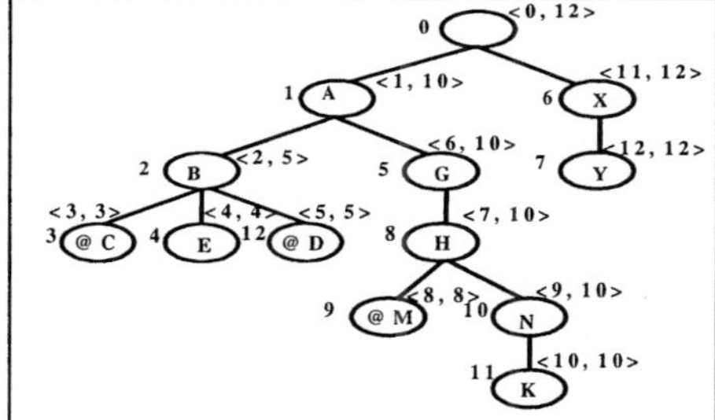

Fig. 8. MXL path_range tree

3.2.1 Scheme POE

Scheme *POE* (acronym of *P*ath, *O*neStep, and *E*lement) is the same as scheme *PE* except for using additional relation OneStep for finding path identifiers of leading steps with the parent/child relationship only in the remaining steps of scheme *PE*. Relation *OneStep* stores information of every edge in the XML path tree. The information of each edge is kept from the viewpoint of the child node of the edge and consists of <pathID, parent_pathID, path_type, name>. The database attributes pathID, parent_pathID, path_type, and name represent the pathID of the child node, the pathID of the parent node, the type of the child node (0 for the element node and 1 for the attribute node), and the name of the child node, respectively. The number of entries in relation OneStep is the same as that of relation Path.

Once path identifiers of some steps (possibly null) are given and the path expression is extended by a single step with the parent/child relationship (i.e., the delimiter '/') such as "/name", "/*", "/@name", and "/@*", the path identifiers of the extended path expression can be found at relation OneStep. In that, the *path_type* of the step has to be specified in the SQL query. Relation OneStep cannot be used for the steps with the ancestor/descendant relationships (i.e., the delimiter '//'). Nevertheless, since some delimiters of '//' can be transformed into '/' according to Observation 2, some steps with delimiters '//', after converting their delimiters into '/', can be processed at relation OneStep.

3.2.2 Scheme PRE

The XML path tree keeps the information of the parent/child relationships among nodes in the tree. In addition to that, to provide the ancestor/descendant relationships among nodes in the XML path tree, each node in the XML path tree can be extended to have a *range*. The *range* of each node consists of <*nodeID*, *end_desc_nodeID*> pair. The *nodeID* is the node identifier that is unique to each node and is assigned to each node of the tree while searching nodes of the tree by the depth-first search order. The root node of the tree is assigned 0 as its node identifier. The *end_desc_nodeID* of each node is the maximum value between the node identifier of the node and the node identifiers of the descendant nodes (if any) of the node. With the provisions of the *range* of each node, the descendant nodes of the node are those whose node identifiers are greater than the *nodeID* of the range and also less than or equal to the *end_desc_nodeID* of the range. The extended tree is denoted as the *XML path_range tree*. Fig. 8 illustrates the XML path_range tree for the XML path tree of Fig. 7.

Scheme *PRE* (acronym of *P*ath, OneStep_*R*ange, and *E*lement) is the same as scheme *PE* except for using additional relation OneStep_Range for finding path identifiers of the whole remaining steps. Relation *OneStep_Range* stores information of every edge in the XML path_range tree. Like relation *OneStep*, the information of each edge of the XML path_range tree is recorded in relation OneStep_Range from the viewpoint of the child node of the edge and consists of <pathID, parent_pathID, path_type, name, nodeID, end_desc_nodeID>. The number of entries in relation OneStep_Range is the same as that of relation Path.

3.2.3 Scheme PME

For each node in the XML path tree, there could be a set of element nodes that are reachable from the node by walking down one or more star-steps with the delimiter '/'. We call the context node and the set of element nodes reachable with k star-steps from the node the *ground node* and the root nodes of *k-StepSubtrees* of the ground node, respectively. The root nodes of k-StepSubtrees of a ground node might formulate some sub-trees of the XML path tree. For example, in the XML path tree of Fig. 7, if the element node 'A' is taken as a ground node, the number k can be 1, 2, 3, or 4. Fig. 9 illustrates k-StepSubtrees of the ground node 'A' with 2 as the value of k. In the Fig., the thick-circled nodes within the inner box represent the root nodes of the k-StepSubtrees and the thick-circled and shaded nodes below the box represent descendant nodes of them.

For each non-leaf node in the XML path tree, having it as a ground node, for every k that is between 1 and the height of the ground node in the tree, and for every node in the set of nodes in the sub-trees of k-StepSubtrees, relation *MultiStep_Subtree* keeps the information of <ground_pathID, star_count, target_pathID, path_type,

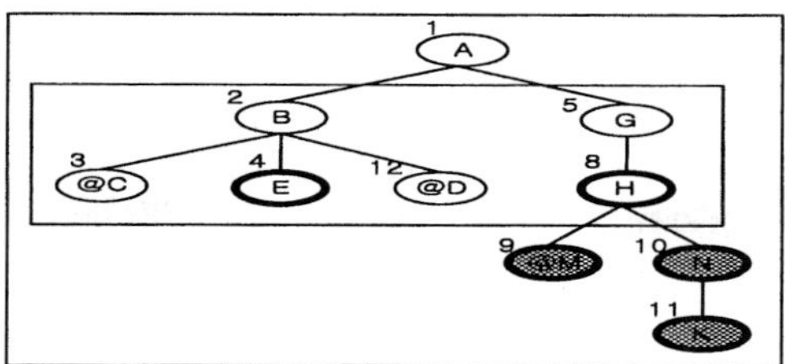

Fig. 9. The k-StepSubtrees of node 'A' with k = 2

from_root_path>. In that, ground_pathID, star_count, target_pathID, path_type, and from_root_path mean the path identifier of the ground node, the number k, the path identifier of the node that is reached, the type of the node that is reached, and the partial path to get to the node from some root of the k-StepSubtrees of the ground node, respectively. For example, the k-StepSubtrees of Fig. 9 can be mapped into relation MultiStep_Subtree as five entries. All the entries have 1 as ground_pathID and 2 as star_count. Relation MultiStep_Subtree for the XML path tree of Fig. 7 has 60 entries. Among them, 50% of them are entries with ground_pathID of 0.

Scheme *PME* (acronym of *P*ath, *M*ultiStep_Subtree, and *E*lement) is the same as scheme *PE* except for using additional relation MultiStep_Subtree for finding path identifiers of the whole remaining steps. In scheme PME, XPath query expressions are decomposed into one SMP partial path and a sequence of <SMI partial path, SMP partial path> pairs. By using relation MultiStep_Subtree, the acquisition of path identifiers for every <SMI partial path, SMP partial path> pair based on the given ground path identifier can be done as follows. First, for the SMI partial path, when the number of the star steps is k, set "star_count = k" in the SQL query. Second, based on the Observations 1 and 2, the string match SQL query for the SMP partial path can be processed exactly the same way as relation Path. Accordingly, if the last step in the SMP partial path is "//*", "path_type = 0" has to be given into the SQL query.

4 Performance Evaluation

We have implemented the schemes in this paper and carried out performance experiments over various XPath query expressions. We used Intel Pentium 4 CPU of 1.70 GHz with 768 MB of main memory as the hardware specification, Windows 2000 Server as the operating system, and Oracle 9i[18] as the database management system. We utilized Java as the system development language and JDBC as the connection interface between XPath query processing system and the database management system.

For each XPath query, two modes of execution, both the *select mode* and the *reconstruct mode*, were considered such that for each mode the query was converted into an SQL query and then its performance was evaluated. Each query has been executed five times and the average value of the execution times has been taken. To minimize effects of the previous queries to the next query, several queries have been executed in some mixed way. In this experiment, to clarify differences in the execution time among the schemes for the same XPath query, the time for parsing

XPath queries and converting them into SQL queries, the time for binding result columns of result tuples into host variables, and the time for displaying host variables on the screen have been excluded from the measurement of the query execution time. Instead, we measured only the times for executing the following two statements: "rs = stmt.executeQuery(SQL_stmt);" that executes the SQL statement that is already created; and "while (rs.next()) {count++;}" that fetches all the result tuples.

We stored 37 plays of Shakespeare [17] in XML documents into the relations of this paper after parsing them using Oracle XML Development Kit [19]. The documents take 7.6 MB, have 179,689 elements, no attribute, and 147,442 texts in total. In the documents, the numbers of some elements are extremely larger than those of other elements. For example, the number of element LINE is 107,833; the number of element SPEAKER is 31,081; and the number of element SPEECH is 31,028. It took about 16 minutes to parse the whole XML documents and store them into the relations. Relations Doc_Name, Element, Edge, Path, Onestep, Onestep_Range, and Multistep_Subtree take 37, 179689, 327131, 57, 57, 57, and 525 records, respectively.

In this performance evaluation, six schemes (*E, PE_Org, PE, POE, PRE,* and *PME*) are compared. Scheme *E* does not utilize path identifiers and finds root elements that satisfy query expressions by using relation Element. Scheme *PE_Org* finds path identifiers of the leading name-steps in query expressions from relation Path and then processes the remaining steps by join operations on relation Element. Other schemes are explained in Sections 3. To clarify the relative effectiveness of each scheme, we performed the experiment with the following three classes of XPath queries: (1) with SMP partial paths only, (2) with the leading SMP partial path and some SMI partial paths, and (3) without any leading SMP partial path.

Table 1 illustrates some XPath queries with SMP partial paths only. Because of the characteristics of the queries, path identifiers of the whole paths can be retrieved from relation Path in scheme PE. Schemes POE, PRE, and PME are not shown in the table because their additional relations are not used for the queries such that they have exactly the same results as scheme PE.

Table 1. XPath queries with SMP partial paths only

XPath Queries	**Execution time (sec): Select/Reconstruct mode**			**Number of result tuples**
	E	**PE_Org**	**PE**	
Q1: /PLAY/*//STAGEDIR	0.750/2.399	0.750/2.378	0.607/1.912	6,258/12,516
Q2: /PLAY/*/*//STAGEDIR	0.818/2.412	0.841/2.370	0.602/1.815	6,255/12,510
Q3: /PLAY/*/*/*//STAGEDIR	0.964/1.703	0.860/1.565	0.235/0.826	1,967/3,934
Q4: /PLAY/*/*/*/*//STAGEDIR	2.094/2.232	2.070/2.292	0.110/0.289	618/1,236

For the XPath queries in Table 1, schemes E and PE_Org made very similar results. In the select mode, the more '/*'s are put in the query expressions, the more execution time has been required. However, in scheme PE, the more star-steps are involved, the more query execution time has been diminished. Scheme PE has shown the following remarkable effects compared with scheme PE_Org: for query Q4, the performance has been improved by 94.7% (and 87.4%) in the select mode (and

Table 2. Queries with a leading SMP partial path and some SMI partial paths

XPath Queries	Execution time (sec): Select/Reconstruct mode					Number of result tuples
	E	PE	POE	PRE	PME	
Q5:/PLAY/ACT/SCENE/*/* /STAGEDIR	1.992/ 2.263	1.944/ 2.321	0.125/ 0.310	0.123/ 0.315	0.115/ 0.294	618/ 1,236
Q6:/PLAY/ACT/*/SPEECH /*/STAGEDIR	1.912/ 2.147	1.916/ 2.144	0.116/ 0.319	0.113/ 0.322	0.112/ 0.298	618/ 1,236
Q7:/PLAY/ACT/*/SPEECH //STAGEDIR	0.742/ 1.356	0.745/ 1.366	0.729/ 1.164	0.247/ 0.685	0.237/ 0.651	1,960/ 3,920
Q8: /PLAY/*/*/SPEECH// STAGEDIR	0.763/ 1.294	0.768/ 1.367	0.740/ 1.268	0.245/ 0.693	0.242/ 0.659	1,967/ 3,934

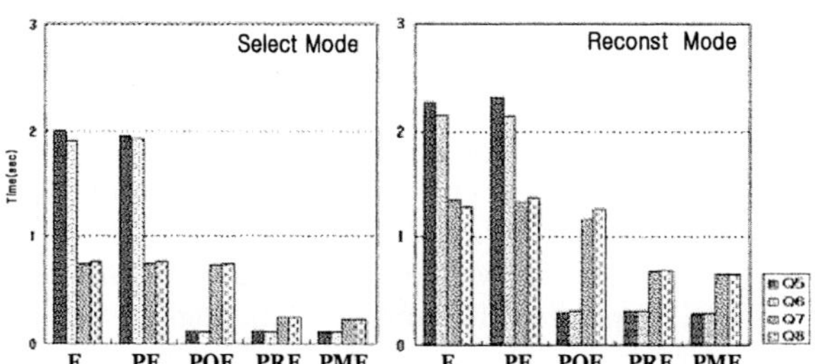

Fig. 10. The performance graph for Table 2

reconstruct mode, respectively).[2] In the rest of this experiment, method PE_Org will not be discussed anymore.

Table 2 illustrates some XPath queries with both a leading SMP partial path and some SMI partial paths, and Fig. 10 shows the performance graph for Table 2. In those queries, after the leading SMP partial path, queries Q5 and Q6 have steps of the parent/child relationship only and queries Q7 and Q8 have steps of parent/child and ancestor/descendant relationships.

For the XPath queries that do not have any leading SMP partial path, except for the fact that leading star-steps of the queries cannot be executed in relation Path, their execution characteristics are very similar to those of Table 2.

Through this performance evaluation, we have got the following observations: (1) once the path identifiers are used only for some leading steps and the rest steps are processed directly at relation Edge, the effect of using path identifiers are limited, and (2) the effect of using path identifiers is dependent on the selectivity of the result tuples. In other words, we agree upon the opinion of indexing method PRIX [22] that has the bottom-up processing strategy compared to the top-down processing of indexing scheme of ViST [23].

As we have seen in the performance evaluations, scheme PME has shown the best performance. Note that scheme SME provides path identifiers of path expressions that

---

[2] Let the execution time of scheme A be x and that of scheme B be y. We say that the execution time of scheme B is improved by ((x – y)/x) * 100% compared with that of scheme A.

are composed of the given eight combinations of delimiters and steps. Once we can get path identifiers for the whole XPath query expressions from relation Path, the performance could be better than any of the schemes in this paper. In the next section, to make mapping the star-step of element with the delimiter '/' in XPath query expression to its corresponding string match operation of SQL, we propose a new reserved character '$' that extends existing LIKE operation of SQL.

5 Proposal of a New Reserved Character '$'

The string-pattern of the LIKE operator of SQL supports the reserved character '%' that matches arbitrary number of arbitrary characters. For example, finding character strings that end with "BCD" and have *at least* one 'A' before that sub-string can be performed by "like '%A%BCD'". However, finding character strings that end with "BCD" and have *exactly* one 'A' before that sub-string, such as "ABCD", "MAKBCD", and "AKBCD", cannot be performed by using '%'. To make this possible, we need some reserved character that matches arbitrary number of characters *except for* the character 'A'.

For that purpose, we propose a new reserved character '$' that extends the existing string-pattern of the LIKE operator. The reserved character '$' must be followed by the restricting character string '[^patterns]'.[3] The pattern '$[^patterns]' matches arbitrary number of arbitrary characters except for the characters listed in the restricting character string. Once the reserved character '$' is supported, by utilizing '$[^A]' that matches arbitrary number of characters except for the character 'A', finding character strings that end with "BCD" and have *exactly* one 'A' before that sub-string can be performed by "like '$[^A]A$[^A]BCD'".

Observation 4. For the leading consecutive n + 1 ($n \geq 0$) steps of XPath query expressions, assume that path identifiers of the leading partial paths of n steps can be found from relation Path. Suppose that the reserved character '$' is provided. Once the leading n + 1st step is a star-step of element with the delimiter '/', the step can be mapped into "#/$[^#]" in the LIKE clause of SQL query and then the mapped one is applied either to all path expressions in relation Path whose last steps are elements if the step "/*" is the last step in the query expressions or to all path expressions in relation Path otherwise.

Provided that the reserved character '$' is supported, based on both the result on name-steps from [11] and the result on star-steps from Observations 1 and 4 of this paper, the mapping of steps in the XPath query expressions into some string match operations on relation Path can be summarized as Table 3. Table 3 means that, if the reserved character '$' is supported, path identifiers of the paths with all name-steps and star-steps can be obtained from relation Path. For example, path identifiers of the XPath query expression "/A/*/*/D" can be obtained by "pathexp like '#/A#/$[^#]#/$[^#]#/D'" and path identifiers of "/A/*/*/D/*" can be obtained by "pathexp like '#/A#/$[^#]#/$[^#]#/D#/$[^#]' and path_type = 0".

---

[3] The SQL Server [20] supports '[patterns]' for listing characters to be permitted and '[^patterns]' for listing characters to be restricted.

Table 3. Mapping of steps into string-patterns

Name-Step	String Match SQL query	Star-Step	String Match SQL query	
/name	#/name	/*	the last step	#/$[^#] and path_type = 0
			not the last step	#/$[^#]
//name	#%/name	//*	the last step	#/% and path_type = 0
			not the last step	#/%
/@name	#/@name	/@*	#/@%	
//@name	#%/@name	//@*	#%/@%	

6 Conclusion and Future Works

With the star-steps in XPath query expressions, depending on the length of steps whose path identifiers can be found, the query execution times vary tremendously. For finding path identifiers of path expressions with the given eight combinations of delimiters and steps, saying "/name", "//name", "/@name", "//@name", "/*", "//*", "/@*", and "//@*", this paper proposed a new reserved character '$' for the string-pattern of the LIKE operation of SQL and presented the mapping of steps of XPath query expressions into string match operations of SQL. Once the reserved character '$' is supported, since path identifiers of XPath query expressions can be obtained from relation Path, besides the fact that no additional relation is necessary to find path identifiers, since path identifiers for the whole path can be found from relation Path, the performance of the query execution can be always better than the scheme PME that has the best performance among schemes presented in this paper. Part of our ongoing research is developing efficient execution algorithms for XPath expressions with the star operator while supporting all XPath axes.

References

1. World Wide Web Consortium. Extensible Markup Language (XML) 1.0, W3C Recommendation, February 1998, "http://trio.co.kr/webrefer/xml/xml10.html."
2. World Wide Web Consortium. A. Deutsch, M. Fernandez, D. Florescu, A. Levy, and D. Suciu, XML-QL: A Query Language for XML. August 1998, "http:// www.w3.org/ TR/ NOTE-xml-ql/."
3. World Wide Web Consortium. J. Robie, J. Lapp, and D. Schach, XML Query Language (XQL). September 1998, "http://www.w3.org/TandS/QL/QL98/pp/xql.html."
4. World Wide Web Consortium. XML Path Language (XPath), Version 2.0, W3C Working Draft, 02 May 2003, "http://www.w3.org/TR/2003/WD-xpath20-20030502/." [4-1] World Wide Web Consortium. XML Path Language (XPath), Version 1.0, "http://www.w3.org/ TR/xpath."
5. World Wide Web Consortium. XQuery 1.0: An XML Query Language, W3C Working Draft, 12 November 2003.
6. T. Grust and M.V. Keulen, "Tree Awareness for Relational DBMS Kernels: Staircase Join," H. Blanken, H.-J. Schek, and G. Weikum, Eds. Lecture Notes in Computer Science, Vol. 2818. Springer-Verlag, Heidelberg, Germany, 2003.
7. T. Grust, M.V. Keulen, and J. Teubner, "Accelerating XPath Evaluation in Any RDBMS," *ACM Transactions on Database Systems*, Vol.29, No. 1, March 2004, Pages 91-131.

8. M. F. Fernandez, A. Morishima, D. Suciu, and W. C. Tan, "Publishing Relational Data in XML: The SilkRoute Approach," *IEEE Data Engineering Bulletin,* Vol. 24, No. 2, pp. 12-19, June 2001.
9. M. Carey, D. Florescu, Z. Ives, Y. Lu, J. Shanmugasundaram, E. Shekita, and S. Subramanian, "XPERANTO: Publishing Object-Relational Data as XML," in *Workshop on Web and Databases (WebDB)*, 2000. (Informal Proceedings)
10. T. Shimura, M. Yoshikawa, and S. Uemura, "Storing and Retrieval of XML Documents using Object-Relational Databases," in *DEXA '99, Proc. of 10th International Conference and Workshop on Database and Expert Systems Applications,* Vol. 1677, pp. 206-217, Florence, Italy, August 30 - September 3, 1999.
11. M. Yoshikawa, T. Amagasa, T. Shimura, and S. Uemura, "XREL: A Path-Based Approach to Storage and Retrieval of XML Documents using Relational Databases," *ACM Transactions on Internet Technology,* Vol. 1 , No. 1, pp. 110-141, August 2001.
12. J. Shanmugasundaram, I. Tatarinov, S. D. Viglas, K. Beyer, E. Shekita, and C. Zhang, "Storing and Querying Ordered XML using a Relational Database System," in *Proc. of ACM SIGMOD International Conference on Management of Data,* pp. 204-215, Madison, Wisconsin, U.S.A, June 2002.
13. World Wide Web Consortium. Document Type Definition (DTD), W3C Recommendation, 4 February 2004, "http://www.w3.org/TR/REC-xml#dt-doctype/."
14. World Wide Web Consortium. XML Schema Part 0: Primer, W3C Recommendation, 2 May 2001, "http://www.w3.org/TR/2001/REC-xmlschema-0-20010502/."
15. Sgrep, "http://www.cs.helsinki.fi/u/jjaakkol/sgrep.html."
16. J. E. Fnderburk, G. Kiernan, J. Shanmugasundaram, E. Shekita, and C. Wei, "XTABLES: Bridging Relational Technology and XML," *IBM Systems Journal*, Vol. 41, No. 4, pp. 616-641, 2002.
17. John Bosak, The Play of Shakespeare in XML, January 1998, "http://www.oasis-open.org/cover/bosakShakespeare200.html."
18. Oracle Enterprise Manager Administrator's Guide Release 9.0.2, Oracle Corporation, 2002.
19. Oracle9i Application Developer's Guide - XML, Release 1 (9.0.1), Part No. A88894-01, June 2001.
20. SQL2000 Server, Microsoft Corp, "http://www.microsoft.com/sql/default.asp."
21. C.Y. Chan, W. Fan, and Y. Zeng, "Taming XPath Queries by Minimizing Wildcard Steps," in *Proc. of VLDB Conference*, Toronto, Canada, 2004, Pages 156-167.
22. P. Rao and B. Moon, "PRIX: Indexing And Querying XML Using Prufer Sequences," in *Proc. of ICDE*, March 2004, Boston, MA, U.S.A.
23. H. Wang, S. Park, W. Fan, and P.S. Yu, "ViST: A Dynamic Index Method for Querying XML Data by Tree Structures," in *Proc. of ACM SIGMOD International Conference on Management of Data*, San Diego, CA, June 2003.

Exploit Sequencing to Accelerate XML Twig Query Answering*

Qian Qian, Jianhua Feng, Jianyong Wang, and Lizhu Zhou

Department of Computer Science and Technology,
Tsinghua University, Beijing 100084, P.R. China
qqpeter99@mails.tsinghua.edu.cn,
{fengjh, jianyong, dcszlz}@tsinghua.edu.cn

Abstract. Speeding up query evaluation in large XML repositories becomes a challenging and all-important problem with vast XML-related applications arising. In this paper, we present SCALER[1], an efficient algorithm for XML query answering based on UDFTS[2] and effective twig structure matching scheme. UDFTS not only constructs a one-to-one correspondence between trees and sequences but also maintains critical parent-child relationships for twig structure matching. With SCALER, XML queries can be performed by subsequence matching without breaking twigs into sub paths and evaluating these paths individually. Thus, costly join operations can be avoided elegantly. We also show the correctness of query answering by eliminating false dismissals and false alarms naturally in SCALER. By a thorough experimental study on various real-life data, we prove the efficiency and scalability of SCALER over the previous known alternative.

1 Introduction

With the rapid growth for the last decade, XML has become one of the most important collections of knowledge that the human being ever had. It is used as a standard for information representation and exchanging in commercial and scientific applications [5]. To exploit the power of XML, a database system should handle the major issues of storing, indexing and querying XML documents. How to efficiently query XML documents is one of the key problems in XML database system. Much research has been undertaken on providing flexible indexing and query mechanisms to extract data from XML documents [14, 22, 21, 11, 10, 19]. Due to the semi-structured nature of XML, XML documents are often modeled by tree hierarchies. As well, XML query languages (e.g., XPath [3] and XQuery [4]) are typically expressed by linear paths or twig patterns which comply with tree hierarchical structure. As an example, a twig query given in XPath is as follow:

Professor[Paper/Conference="DASFAA"]/Name

* The work was supported by the National Natural Science Foundation of China under Grant No.60573094, Tsinghua Basic Research Foundation under Grant No.JCqn2005022 and Zhejiang Natural Science Foundation under Grant No.Y105230.

[1] SCALER stands for SequenCe bAsed XML QuEry AlgoRithm.

[2] UDFTS stands for Unique Depth-First Traversal Sequence.

M.L. Lee, K.L. Tan, and V. Wuwongse (Eds.): DASFAA 2006, LNCS 3882, pp. 279 – 294, 2006.

The query qualifies XML documents by specifying a twig pattern composed of four elements Professor, Paper, Conference and Name, as well as a value predicate Conference="DASFAA". It is to find the names of all professors who published papers on "DASFAA".

The research for indexing and querying XML documents recent years mainly contributes two classes of approaches on answering XML queries.

Structural Index: It facilitates traversing through the hierarchy of XML documents by referencing the structural information of the documents. The representative works on structural index are DataGuide[14], 1-index[22], A(k)[18], D(k)[8], M(k)[16], APEX[10], F&B index[19].These indexing mechanisms can prune search space for processing of path and twig queries.

Coding Schemes: This class of approaches follows the strategy of encoding each element by its positional information within the hierarchy of XML document. With the help of effective tree traversal order or textural positions of start and end tags, the encoding scheme provides facilitation to identify parent-child and ancestor-descendant relationships between XML elements without traversing the entire tree hierarchies. The coding schemes mainly are addressed in Region Code: Dietz[11], Li2Moon(XISS)[21], Zhang coding[7], Bit-vector coding[Li 13], Dewey coding[17], PBiTree coding[28], as well as our former work BBTC[13], an update-aware coding scheme. Upon these coding schemes, many structural join algorithms have been developed to efficiently process path and twig queries [1, 6, 9, 21, 7].

However, most of previous approaches based on above two classes of methodologies process a twig query by breaking it into sub paths, evaluating these paths separately and finally joining the results. With the purpose to avoid costly join operations in query evaluation, we propose a novel XML query processing algorithm, SCALER. In our algorithm, the first pass is "sequencing", in which XML documents are transformed into UDFTSs which not only constructs one-to-one correspondences between trees and sequences but also maintains critical parent-child relationships for twig structure matching. The second pass is twig structure matching for finding all the documents satisfying the twig pattern.

Our Contributions: The contributions of this paper can be summarized as follows:

- First, we propose a sequencing method, UDFTS, which keeps one-to-one correspondences between trees and sequences. It captures the parent-child and sibling ordering constraints within the sequence representations which provide great facilitations in twig structure matching. It unifies structure and content nodes into the same sequencing method, which avoids additional cost of accessing structure and content respectively. UDFTS is also linearly scalable in terms of original XML document's size.
- Second, we develop a novel and efficient XML query answering algorithm SCALER, which treats twig query as a holistic query unit without breaking it into several sub paths for further evaluation. Benefited from UDFTS, SCALER effectively accommodates tree connectedness checking and twig structure matching in one pass without false dismissals and false alarms in query answers. It provides a significant enhancement in query performance through this "one pass".

- Third, once-scan indexing technique is proposed upon UDFTS, which is a simple and effective way to establish index hierarchy with the convenience supplied by parent-child relationships in UDFTS.
- Last, a thorough performance study is conducted to evaluate SCALER's efficiency and scalability in comparison with two state-of-the-art algorithms, PRIX[25] and ViST[26].

The reminder of this paper is organized as follows. Section 2 gives related work about sequence based query answering research. We formalize the twig query problem in our paper in Section 3. Section 4 presents our algorithm SCALER. Performance study is described in Section 5. Finally we conclude in Section 6.

2 Related Work

Much research effort has been focused on efficient XML indexing and query processing. As a core operation in XML data management, finding all occurrences of a query pattern in XML documents attracted more and more attentions. Exploiting sequencing techniques to speed up complex query evaluation is a new idea in XML query processing which is proposed recently. It provides significant performance enhancement over traditional methods. We will give brief introductions and discussions on the recent proposed works PRIX[25] and ViST[26]. Within the discussions of their drawbacks, we will elaborate the motivations of our approach. In our previous work [12], we also propose an approach for XML data mining based on sequencing technique.

PRIX: Rao et al. proposed prüfer sequences based indexing and querying method to evaluate XML query. It transforms XML documents and queries into prüfer sequences without false alarms and false dismissals. Four-pass refinement phases are performed to obtain correct answers including subsequence matching, connectedness refinement, twig structure refinement and leaf nodes matching refinement.

However, there are some limitations in prüfer sequencing. First, the prüfer sequencing is not a naturally connectedness-aware sequencing method, which doesn't maintain the parent-child relationship information between elements. As a result, during query processing, an additional connectedness refinement pass is introduced in PRIX. Second, PRIX can't unify the representations of non-leaf nodes and leaf nodes, as the prüfer sequences can only represent non-leaf nodes. For a complete twig match, another leaf nodes matching refinement needs to be applied. From the discussions on functionality and performance issues above, we concern that prüfer sequencing maybe not the best sequencing method for XML query answering.

ViST: It is a dynamic index method for querying XML data by tree structure, which uses tree structure as the basic unit of query to avoid expensive join operations. It provides a unified index on both content and the structure of XML documents.

But query answering in ViST may result in false alarms. As Figure 1, the structure-encoded sequence of query Q is a subsequence of the sequences of Doc1 and Doc2. However, the pattern Q only occurs in Doc2, and the query processing component should be aware to detect the false alarms for further elimination in query answers. In the work [27], constraint sequencing is proposed to solve this problem.

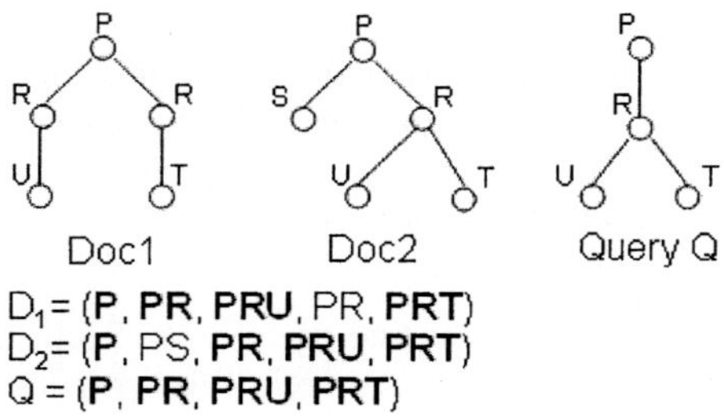

P R R U T S R U T P R U T P
Doc1 Doc2 Query Q

D_1= (**P**, **PR**, **PRU**, PR, **PRT**)
D_2= (**P**, PS, **PR**, **PRU**, **PRT**)
Q = (**P**, **PR**, **PRU**, **PRT**)

Fig. 1. False Alarms in ViST

Actually, it hints that a more natural and effective sequencing method should be investigated to facilitate the twig matching process. That's why we propose our algorithm to enhance the performance of XML query answering.

3 Preliminaries

Tree Sequencialization. Our approach starts with a valid and effective sequencing method for tree hierarchy. Ad hoc sequencing methods such as depth-first and Prüfer code have been used for XML indexing [18, 8]. The prüfer code [24, 25] is a succinct tree encoding method. In which, an n-node tree is labeled arbitrarily from 1 to n. We encode the tree by deleting the leaf node which has the smallest label and appending the label of its parent to the sequence. So the Prüfer sequence for the tree in Figure 2 is (2, 6, 3, 6, 6). While if we use depth-first traversal (called DFT in this paper) method, we can get the sequence as (P, R, T, D, T, N).

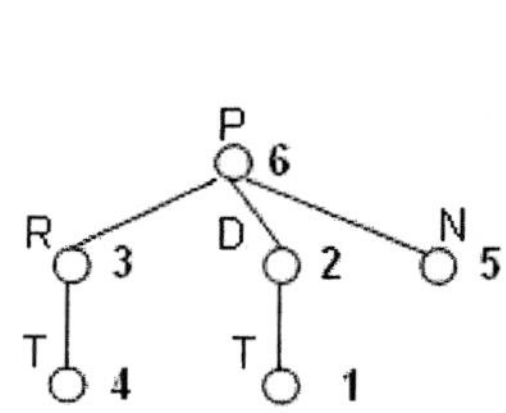

Fig. 2. A Sample Tree Structure

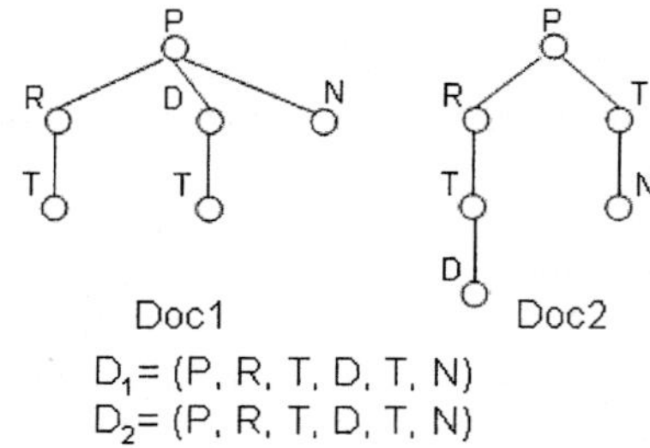

Fig. 3. The False Sequencing in DFT

However, DFT can't guarantee the one-to-one correspondences between trees and sequences. Figure 3 gives the example that two different trees are represented in the same depth-first traversal sequence.

Though there are some drawbacks in representing tree hierarchies by DFT, the DFT sequences still provide satisfied property which maintains the parent-child and sibling orders in left-to-right manner within their corresponding sequences. For example, the parent-child pair (R, T) in Doc1 is located in left-to-right order of sequence D_1, as well as the sibling pair (R, D). This nice feature is quite useful in our algorithm SCALER which will be demonstrated in following sections.

XML Twig Query Problem. Formally, the XML twig query answering can be stated as follows: *Given a collection of XML documents and a twig query Q, find all the documents that Q occurs.* Here Q can be expressed by involving wildcards '//' and '*'.

4 SCALER: An Efficient Sequence Based Algorithm for XML Query Answering

The whole XML twig query answering involves two passes. One is sequencing both XML documents and twig queries into UDFTSs, and the other is twig structure matching on UDFTSs.

4.1 UDFTS: Unique Depth-First Traversal Sequence

Given a set of input XML documents Docs = {Doc_1, Doc_2, …, Doc_n}, the first step of SCALER is to transform the tree hierarchy of an XML document into a sequence representation. In our algorithm, we adopt the depth-first traversal as our framework. Figure 4 depicts the input XML documents set in our running example, while Table 1 shows the corresponding sequences set generated by depth-first traversing the tree nodes of each document. Following we use DFTS to denote a sequence generated by DFT method.

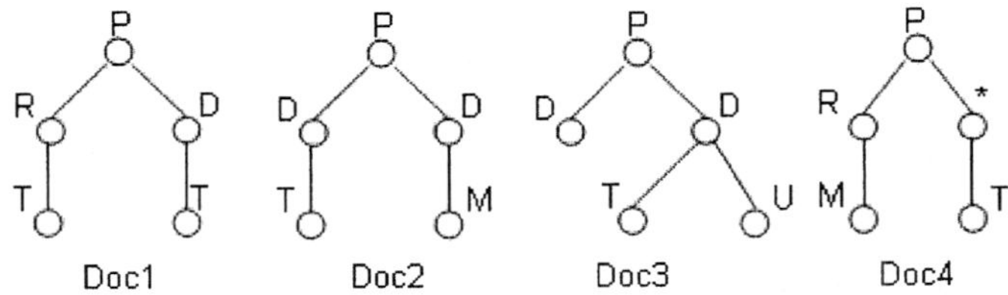

Fig. 4. An Example of XML Documents

Table 1. An Example of DFTSs

Sequence identifier	Sequence
1	P R T D T
2	P D T D M
3	P D D T U
4	P R M * T

False Sequencing Problem. It is evident that a DFTS preserves much structural information of the original XML document, such as the sibling ordering and ancestor-descendant ordering. That is, a node always appears before its descendants and its right siblings in the DFTS. However, DFTS representation does not preserve the complete structure information of an XML document. For example, if a node B appears before a node A in a certain DFTS, we cannot tell whether B is an ancestor or a left sibling of A. Thus, a DFTS cannot uniquely represent an XML document, and two different XML documents may have the same DFTS. Figure 5(1) and Figure 5(2) are apparently two different tree structures, whereas they have the same DFTS. A ramification from this problem is that the tree structure cannot be reconstructed from its DFTS. For example, the DFTS w.r.t. the XML document shown in Figure 5(3) is "PRRTD", we cannot determine which node among "P", "R" and "R" is the parent of "T".

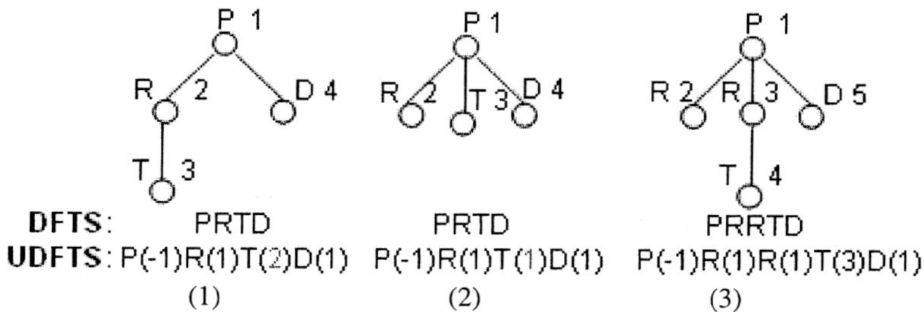

Fig. 5. XML Documents Sequencing in DFTS and UDFTS

To solve the above false sequencing problem, we propose a unique sequence representation method under the depth-first traversal framework. The unique sequence representation of an XML document in our method is denoted by UDFTS. Given an XML document, let its DFTS be (L_1, L_2, ..., L_n), its UDFTS is defined as ($L_1(P_1)$, $L_2(P_2)$, ..., $L_n(P_n)$), where P_i is a code used to uniquely identify the parent of L_i (i.e., P_i is a unique code of L_i's parent). In UDFTS, the code of L_1 is defined as 1 and the code of L_i is determined by the pre-order coding scheme under the depth-first traversal framework. Thus, the code of L_i equals i. In addition, the code of L_1's parent (i.e., P_1) is defined as -1. Figure 5 shows the UDFTSs of the corresponding XML documents.

Because a UDFTS preserves both the parent-child relationships and sibling ordering information, it uniquely represents an XML document and can be used to reconstruct the tree structure of the XML document. This sequencing method also facilitates once-scan index establishment for efficient parent-child and ancestor-descendent identification. Figure 6 shows the facilitation of parent-child checking in SCALER.

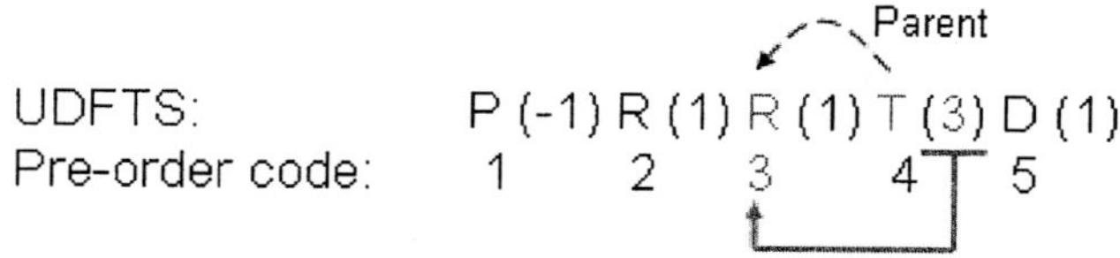

Fig. 6. Parent-Child Checking in UDFTS

Algorithm UDFTSBuilder is presented as follow, which is efficient in transforming both XML documents and XML queries into UDFTSs and once-scan index building.

It should be noted that the UDFTS construction and once-scan index are finished in the same phase with only once Depth-First Traversal of XML document. Extra cost about data scan on index building is saved by the nice feature of UDFTS. The detail structure about once-scan index is addressed in Section 4.4.

```
Algorithm:     UDFTSBuilder(doc,udfts,osi)
Input:         doc, an XML document
Output:        udfts, the UDFTS of doc
               osi, once-scan index
udfts :=ϕ;
osi := ϕ;
root := Root(doc);
addNode(udfts, root, -1);
nextNode := DFT(doc, root);
parentNode := root;
while(nextNode!= null)
  parentPreordercode := PreorderCode(doc,parentNode);
  addNode(udfts, nextNode, parentPreordercode);
  addToOSI(osi, parentNode, nextNode);
  nextNode := DFT(doc, nextNode);
  parentNode := Parent(doc, nextNode);
end while
```

4.2 Twig Structure Matching in SCALER

First, we elaborate the definition of subsequence in SCALER, which is the foundation of SCALER and can be stated below.

Definition 1: (Subsequence). *Given two UDFTSs* $S_1= (L_1(P_1), L_2(P_2), \ldots, L_n(P_n))$ *and* $S_2= (l_1(p_1), l_2(p_2), \ldots, l_m(p_m))$ $(m \le n)$, S_2 *is a subsequence of* S_1, *if*

1. *for each* $l_i(p_i)$ $(0<i\le m)$ *in* S_2, *there exists* $L_j(P_j)$ $(0<j\le n)$ *in* S_1, *s.t.* $l_i=L_j$ *and* $l(p_i)=L(P_j)$;
2. *for any two pairs label-equal nodes* $L_i=l_m$, $L_j=l_n$, $(i<j)$ *in* S_1, *then* $m<n$ *in* S_2.

For example, in Figure 7, UDFTS(Q) is a subsequence of UDFTS(Doc2) but not a subsequence of UDFTS (Doc1). Because for condition 1 in Definition 1, "T(2)" in UDFTS(Q) has parent label "R" but the node "T(4)" has parent label "S" in UDFTS(Doc1) which is conflicted with condition 1. In fact, Definition 1 proposes two consistent constraints on L and P in subsequence finding, which guarantee the equivalence between labels and its parent labels.

Upon the common sense stated in Definition 1, we move on to illustrate the algorithm SCALER by following definitions and theorems.

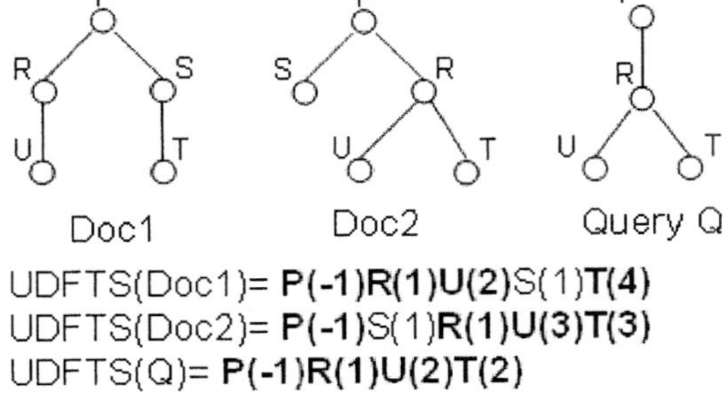

Fig. 7. An Example of Subsequence

Definition 2: (Leaf Item). *For a given UDFTS S= ($L_1(P_1)$, $L_2(P_2)$, …, $L_n(P_n)$), L_i a leaf item iff* $\neg \exists P_j=i$ $(i<j\leq n)$.

Definition 3: (Valid Sequence). *Let UDFTS S = ($L_1(P_1)$, $L_2(P_2)$, …, $L_n(P_n)$). If for each L_i ($1<i\leq n$), $P_i<i$, then S is a valid sequence.*

Definition 4: (Valid Local Item). *Given a local item L(P) w.r.t. a UDFTS ($L_1(P_1)$, $L_2(P_2)$, …, $L_n(P_n)$), L(P) is called a valid local item if* $\exists L_m$ $(1\leq m\leq n)$, *s.t.* $m=P$.

For example, the two XML documents in Figure 8 can be converted into two UDFTS. Suppose "P(-1)D(1)" is the current subsequence, where item P's pre-order code is 1, item D's is 2. As Figure 8(2) shows, for local item T, its parent is node R with pre-order code 3, which is greater than D's pre-order code, thus, T is not a valid local item and cannot be used to expand the subsequence "P(-1)D(1)".

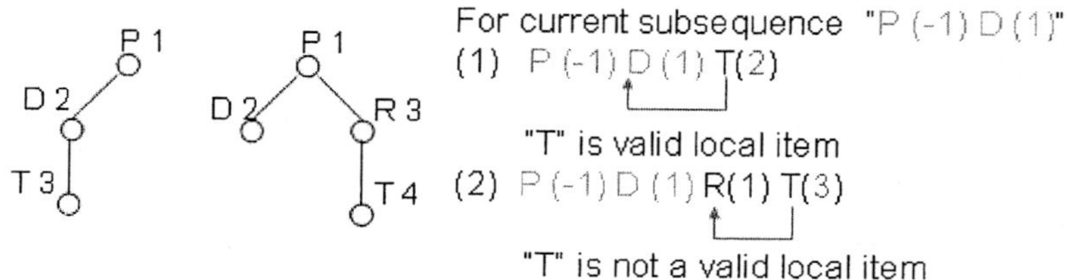

Fig. 8. An Example of Valid Local Item

Definition 5: (Valid Subsequence). *Let UDFTS S = ($L_1(P_1)$, $L_2(P_2)$, …, $L_n(P_n)$) be a subsequence of a tree T's UDFTS(T), S is a valid subsequence, if for any item $L_i(P_i)$ ($1<i\leq n$), it is a valid local item for the subsequence ($L_1(P_1)$, $L_2(P_2)$, …, $L_{i-1}(P_{i-1})$).*

In fact, the definition 5 shows how to identify the connectedness of each node in UDFTS through valid local item checking. However, from another angle, a valid subsequence of S also can be obtained by deleting zero or more leaf items from S. Basing on the observation in definition 5, we can guarantee to introduce no dismissals in finding subsequences of UDFTS.

Theorem 1: (Valid Subsequence Checking). *If twig query Q is a subgraph of tree T, then UDFTS(Q) is a valid subsequence of UDFTS(T).*

For example, in figure 7, because query Q is a subgraph of Doc2, thus Q is a valid sequence of UDFTS(T) according to the statement in Theorem 1. Being the case, the correct valid subsequence also can be deduced by deleting the leaf item "S" in UDFTS(Doc2). But UDFTS(Q) can't be produced from UDFTS (Doc1) because Q is not a subgraph of Doc1.

Theorem 1 gives us theoretic evidences to prove UDFTS' advantages in twig structure matching. In practice, we need following operational Theorem 2 to conduct our algorithm. As an advantage of UDFTS, connectedness between nodes is naturally indicated within the parent-child information. Beneficially, we can easily perform the matching of twig structure including structure and value nodes in one pass, which is handled in two passes in PRIX.

Definition 6: (Structural Consistency). *Given two UDFTSs S_a and S_b, $S_a = (LA_1(PA_1), LA_2(PA_2), \ldots, LA_n(PA_n))$ and $S_b = (LB_1(PB_1), LB_2(PB_2), \ldots, LB_n(PB_n))$, structural consistency happened between S_a and S_b iff $LA_i=LB_i$ and $PA_i=PB_i$ ($1 \le i \le n$).*

In Figure 9, for Doc3, S3' which is obtained after subsequence recoding is a valid subsequence of UDFTS(Doc3). As well, we know S3' is structural consistency with Sq, which is determined by Definition 6. Oppositely, S1' doesn't have structural consistency with Sq, because of the different parent codes of node E and F. Intuitively, Figure 9 indicates the twig query structure Q is contained in Doc3. We can see structural consistency is an important and useful principle in evaluating XML query on UDFTS. Finally, we step forward to give Theorem 2, an effective theorem to solve the XML twig query problem completely.

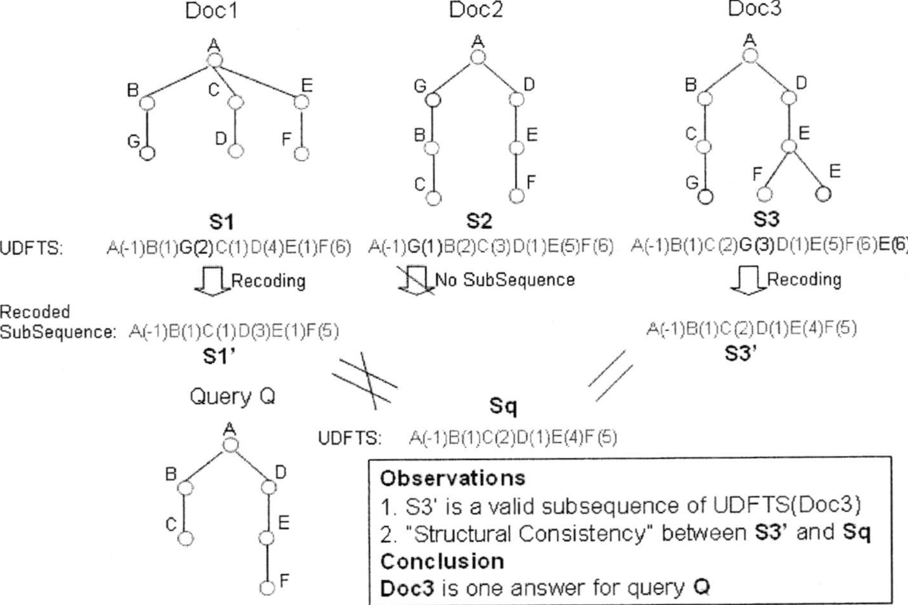

Fig. 9. An Example of Structural Consistency

Theorem 2: (Answer for Twig Query). *Given a twig query Q and an XML document Doc. Doc is said to be the answer of twig query Q, if there is at least one subsequence S of UDFTS(Doc) which is*

1. a valid subsequence of UDFTS(Doc);
2. structural consistency with UDFTS(Q).

Actually, the key observations of Theorem 2 are the following. First, the subsequence S must be a connected tree structure. Second, the twig structure of S must be the same as Q, which is guaranteed by Definition 6. The complete algorithm SCALER for XML query answering is described as follows.

```
Algorithm:     SCALER(docUDFTS, qUDFTS, OSI)
Input:         docUDFTS, the UDFTS of an XML document
               qUDFTS, the UDFTS of an XML twig query Q
               OSI, Once-Scan Index
Output:        Query Answers Set for Q
               No answer if return φ
resultSequenceQueue := φ;
qNextNode := FirstNode(qUDFTS);
firstSequence := new Sequence(qNextNode);
AddSequence(resultSequenceQueue, firstSequence);
while(qNextNode!=null)
   length := CurrentLength(ResultSequenceQueue);
   while( length > 0 )
      nextSequence := GetFirstSequence(
                              resultSequenceQueue);
      lastItem := GetLastItem(nextSequence);
      rightQNode := NextNode(qUDFTS,qNextNode);
      childItemSet := GetChildren(lastItem,
                                  rightQNode, OSI);
      for each child in childItemSet
          if(ValidLocalItem(nextSequence, child))
             newChild := Recode(nextSequence,child);
             if(newChild!=null and newChild
                                   == rightQNode)
                AppendNode(nextSequence, child);
                AddSequence(resultSequenceQueue,
                                   nextSequence)
      end for
      RemoveFirstSequence(resultSequenceQueue);
      length--;
   end while
   qNextNode:=NextNode(qUDFTS, qNextNode);
end while
return resultSequenceQueue;
```

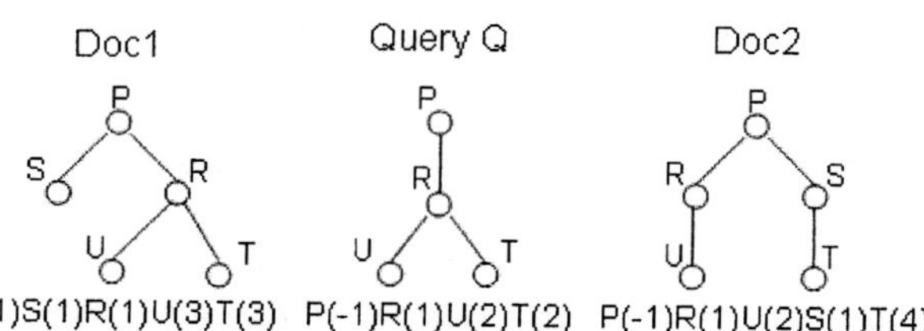

	ResultSequenceQueue for Doc1	ResultSequenceQueue for Doc2
Step 1	{ P(-1) }	{ P(-1) }
Step 2	{ P(-1)R(1) }	{ P(-1)R(1) }
Step 3	{ P(-1)R(1)U(3) } → { P(-1)R(1)U(2) }	{ P(-1)R(1)U(2) }
Step 4	{ P(-1)R(1)U(2)T(3) } → { P(-1)R(1)U(2)T(2) }	{ }
Result	Success	Failure

Fig. 10. An Example of Twig Query Answering Using SCALER

The key idea of SCALER algorithm is about valid local item checking, valid subsequence expanding, and structural consistency testing. In the algorithm description, line 12 describes the function "GetChildren" for getting all children of "lastItem" with OSI efficiently. Line 15 is the valid local item checking process based on Definition 4. The "recode" is performed by replacing the parent code of one node with the position of its parent node in the new generated subsequence. Figure 10 gives an example to explain the algorithm. For query Q, Doc1 is the correct answer while Doc2 is not. Four steps in the Figure 10 show the step-by-step changes in ResultSequenceQueue. At last, we find the final matched subsequence for Doc1 is same as UDFTS(Q).

4.3 Wildcard Query Support

In order to process twig queries with wildcards "//" and "*", we classify the issue into the following three different situations.

1) **"//" at the beginning of twig query**

This kind of query is easy to be handled as our method allows occurrence finding at anywhere in the UDFTS of a tree. For example, for query "//P/D/T", we can firstly match node "P" at anywhere in the document's UDFTS without root-start matching constraint.

2) **"//" at the middle of twig query**

For "//" in the middle of twig query's UDFTS, we extend our Valid Local Item and checking scheme in Definition 4. Here we propose a more flexible definition of Valid "//" Item.

Definition 7: (Valid "//" Item). *Given a local item L(P) w.r.t. a UDFTS ($L_1(P_1)$, $L_2(P_2)$, ..., $L_n(P_n)$), L(P) is called a Valid "//" Item if* $\exists L_m$ *($1 \leq m \leq n$), s.t.* L_m *is L's ancestor.*

During the matching process of node "//" in twig query, we use Valid "//" Item checking to replace Valid Local Item checking in Definition 4. This new checking process can be efficiently implemented by our once-scan index discussed in Section 4.4.

3) **"*" at the middle of twig query**

It could be noted that the node "*" in twig query actually represents all the Valid Local Items for the one-node UDFTS before it. For example, given twig query "P/D/*/T", the "*" indicates the Valid Local Items for the node "D". As a result, subsequence matching is performed by enumerating all the Valid Local Items for further processing. This enumeration process is also benefited from our once-scan index proposed in Section 4.4.

4.4 Once-Scan Indexing Technique

In order to achieve high performance in twig matching for XML query processing, all the UDFTSs are indexed on parent-child relationships which are always the first class of citizen to be accessed during the valid subsequence expanding. Especially, one nice feature of UDFTS is that parent-child and sibling orders in tree are maintained in left-to-right orders in UDFTS. Based on this observation, we figure out our once-scan index, which only once scan is needed on UDFTS to establish. During the scan from left to right in UDFTS, we can record the information of nodes' pre-order codes, child nodes and sibling nodes. Figure 11 shows an example about once-scan index. Each node entry in index can have both in and out links which can be used in two directions when identifying parent-child relationships between tree nodes.

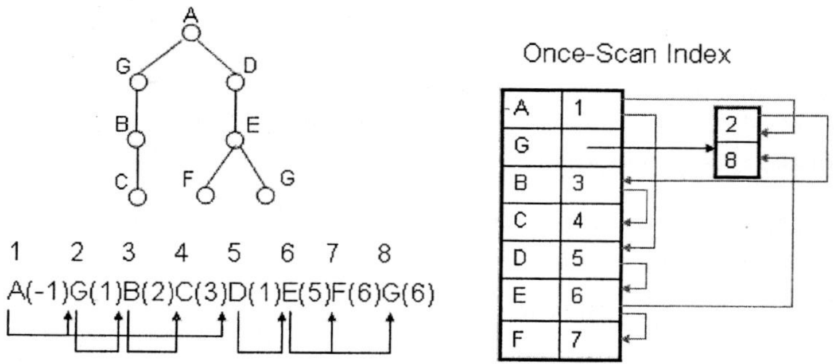

Fig. 11. An Example of Once-Scan Index

In once-scan index, we keep the pointers to denote the parent-child relationships, which are sufficient to discover all the ancestor-descendant relationships by performing transitive index accessing efficiently.

5 Performance Evaluations

In this section, we compare the performance of SCALER, PRIX and ViST. We use C++ in implementing these algorithms. For ViST, the symbol-prefix pairs in the structure-encoded sequences were directly stored in the D-Ancestorship B^+ tree. We carry out our experiments on a Windows2000 machine with an AMD 2.0MHz CPU and 1G MB RAM.

5.1 Datasets

In our experiments, we use public XML data DBLP [20] and XML benchmark data XMARK [29]. Table 2 presents the major characteristics of these two datasets with the terms of element number, document size, attribute number, max-depth and sequence number.

Table 2. Characteristics of Two Datasets

Item \ Dataset	XMark	DBLP
Number of Elements	101,271	133,755
Document Size (MB)	35.6	52.4
Number of Attributes	18,140	101,980
Max-depth	12	7
Number of Sequences	12,846	52,437

5.2 Queries

Table 3 shows the queries for performance testing on XMark and DBLP. These queries have different characteristics in terms of selectivity, presence of values and twig structure.

Table 3. XML Queries

Query	Expression	DataSet
Q1	/site//item/[location='USA']/mail/data[text='06/09/2001']	XMark
Q2	/site//person/*/age[text='40']	XMark
Q3	/site//person/*/city[text='Toronto']	XMark
Q4	//closed auction[seller/person='person11052']/date[text='09/19/2000']	XMark
Q5	/inproceedings/title	DBLP
Q6	/book/[key='Maier']/author	DBLP
Q7	/*/author[text='David']	DBLP
Q8	//author[text='James']	DBLP
Q9	//inproceedings[./author='Jim Gray'][./year='1995']	DBLP
Q10	//www[./editor]/url	DBLP
Q11	//title[text='Semantic Analysis Patterns']	DBLP

5.3 Experimental Results

We first demonstrate the scalability of SCALER with regard to varying the query complexity and data size. Figure 12 exhibits the performance under different queries and data conditions. For Figure 12(a), we can see that it takes more time to process longer queries, because longer queries require larger amount of index traversal. It also shows that our algorithm SCALER scales up sub-linearly with the increase of query complexity. As well, for varying data size, SCALER is scalable with ascending data size in Figure 12(b).

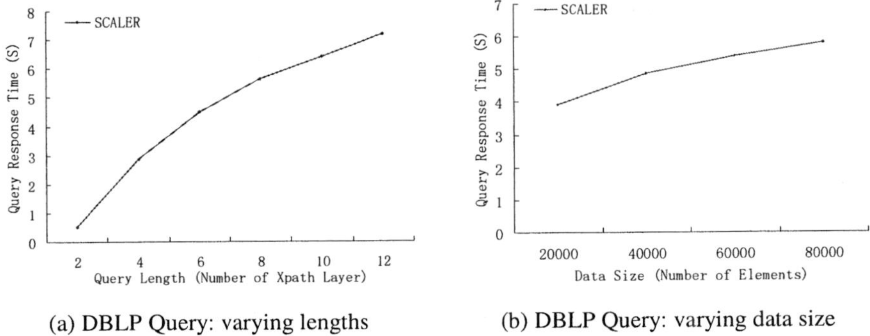

(a) DBLP Query: varying lengths

(b) DBLP Query: varying data size

Fig. 12. Query Response Times for XML Datasets

Figure 13 summaries the performance in comparison among SCALER, PRIX and ViST. We test twig queries Q1, Q2, Q3, Q4 on XMark, as well as Q5 to Q11 on DBLP. Obviously, we can see SCALER performs significantly better than ViST and

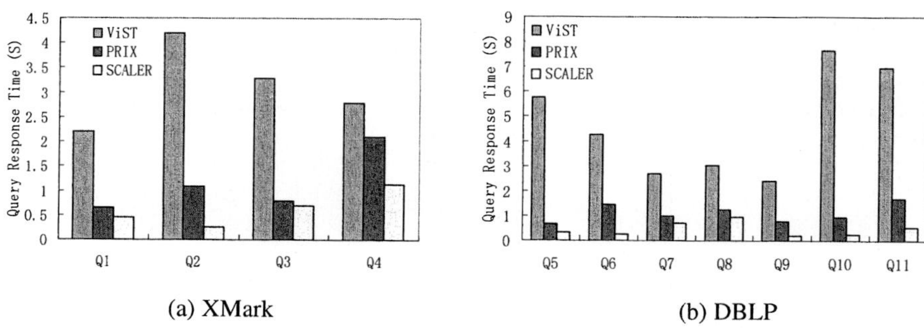

(a) XMark (b) DBLP

Fig. 13. Query Response Times for Three Methods

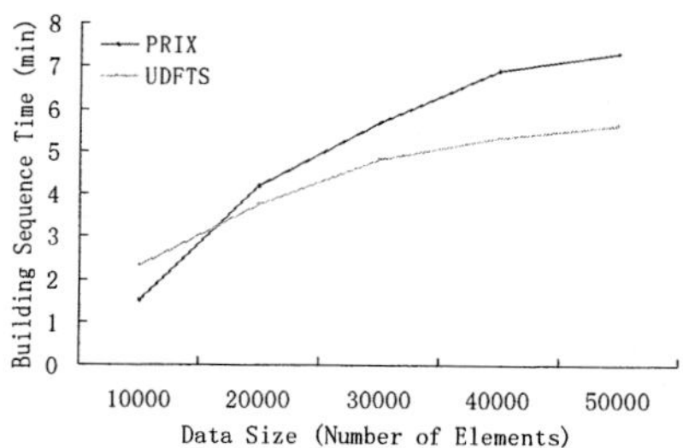

Fig. 14. Time for Sequences Building on XMark Datasets

PRIX. Through simplifying the twig structure matching process, the advantages of UDFTS become significant in comparing with prüfer sequencing in PRIX method.

Figure 14 shows the performance difference in sequencing XML documents between UDFTS and PRIX. The result shows UDFTS performs better in sequencing XML documents. Actually, because of the natural and efficient Depth-First Traversal of a tree, UDFTS achieved better performance and scalability than PRIX.

For our experimental datasets XMark and DBLP, Figure 15(a) shows the index sizes of SCALER and ViST. Figure 15(b) shows the linear building index time of SCALER, which is more efficient than the index construction in ViST.

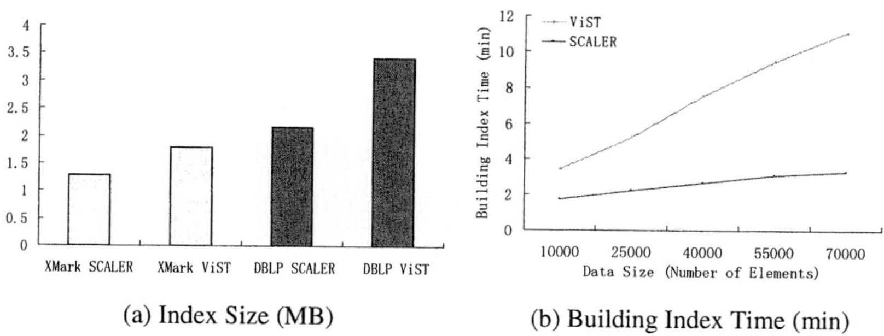

(a) Index Size (MB) (b) Building Index Time (min)

Fig. 15. Index Size and Building Index Time for DBLP Datasets

6 Conclusions

In this paper, we introduce an efficient and scalable approach for XML query answering. By transforming both XML documents and XML queries into UDFTSs, finding the occurrences of a twig query becomes equivalent with subsequence matching on UDFTS which is elegantly proved in our statement. We also provide the algorithm SCALER to match twig queries by valid local item and structural consistency checking. Benefited from once-scan indexing mechanism in SCALER, we achieve convincible performance enhancement in XML twig query answering. The performance study provides rich evidences to show SCALER's advantages in efficiency and scalability over previous known alternatives.

References

1. S. Al-Khalifa, H. V. Jagadish, N. Koudas, J.M. Patel, D. Srivastava, and Y.Wu. Structural joins: A primitive for efficient XML query pattern matching. ICDE 2002
2. S. Alstrup and T. Rauhe. Improved labeling scheme for ancestor queries. In Proc. ACM SIAM Symposium on Discrete Algorithms (SODA), 2002.
3. A.Berglund, S.Boag, D.Chamberlin,M.F.Fernandez, M.Kay, J.Robie, and J.Simon. XML path language(XPath)2.0 W3c working draft 16. World Wide Web Consortium, Aug.2002
4. S.Boag,D.Chamberlin,M.F.Fernandez,D.Florescu, J.Robie, and J.Simon. XQuery 1.0: An XML Query Language W3c working draft 16. World Wide Web Consortium, Aug.2002
5. T.Bray, J.Paoli, C.M.Sperberg-McQueen, and E.Maler. Extensible markup language (XML)1.0 second editon W3C recommendation.WorldWide Web Consortium, Oct.2000
6. N. Bruno, et.al. Holistic twig joins: Optimal XML pattern match-ing. SIGMOD02.
7. Zhang C, Naaghton J, DeWitt D , et al . On Supporting Containment Queries in Relational Database Management Systems. SIGMOD 2001
8. Q. Chen, A. Lim, and K. W. Ong. D(k)-index: An adaptive structural summary for graph-structured data. SIGMOD 2003
9. S. Y. Chien, Z. Vagena, D. Zhang, V. J. Tsotras, and C. Zaniolo. Efficient structural joins on indexed XML documents.VLDB 2002
10. C. Chung, J. Min, and K. Shim. APEX: An adaptive path index for XML data. SIGMOD02
11. B. F. Cooper, N. Sample, M. Franklin, G. Hjaltason, and M. Shadmon. A fast index for semistructured data. In VLDB, pages 341–350, September 2001.
12. Jianhua Feng, Qian Qian, Jianyong Wang, Lizhu Zhou. Exploit Sequencing to Accelerate Hot XML Query Pattern Mining. ACM SAC 2006.
13. Jianhua Feng, Guoliang Li, Lizhu Zhou, Na Ta, Qian Qian, Yuguo Liao. BBTC: A New Update-supporting Coding Scheme for XML Documents, WAIM05
14. R. Goldman and J. Widom. DataGuides: Enabling query formulation and optimization in semistructured databases. VLDB 1997
15. T. Grust. Accelerating XPath location steps. SIGMOD 2002
16. H. He and J. Yang. Multiresolution indexing of XML for frequent queries. ICDE, 2004
17. Igor Tatarinod, Stratis D. diglas, Kedin Beyer, Jayadel Shanmagasandaram, Eagene Shekita, and Chan Zhang. Storing and querying ordered XML using a relational database system. SIGMOD 2002
18. R. Kaushik, P. Shenoy, P. Bohannon, and E. Gudes. Exploiting Local Similarity for Efficient Indexing of Paths in Graph Structured Data. ICDE2002

19. R. Kaushik, P. Bohannon, J. F. Naughton and H. F. Korth. Covering indexes for branching path queries. SIGMOD. 2002
20. Michael Ley. DBLP database web site. http://www.informatik.uni-trier.de/ ley/db, 2000.
21. Q. Li , B. Moon. Indexing and querying XML data for regular path expressions. VLDB01
22. T. Milo and D. Suciu. Index structures for path expression. ICDT 1999.
23. Paul F Dietz, Maintaining order in a linked list, The 14th Annual ACM Symp on Theory of Computing , San Francisco , 1982
24. S. Picciotto. How to Encode a Tree. PhD thesis, University of California, San Diego, 1999.
25. Praveen Rao, Bongki Moon, PRIX: Indexing and querying XML using prüfer sequences. ICDE2004
26. H.Wang, S. Park,W. Fan, P. S. Yu. ViST: A Dynamic Index Method for Querying XML Data by Tree Structures. SIGMOD 2003
27. H. Wang, X Meng. On the sequencing of Tree structures for XML indexing, ICDE2005
28. Wei Wang, Haifeng Jiang, Hongjun Lu, and Jeffrey Xu Yu. PBiTree coding and efficient processing of containment joins. ICDE 2003
29. XMARK: The XML-benchmark project. http://monetdb.cwi.nl/ xml, 2002.

Probabilistic Similarity Join on Uncertain Data

Hans-Peter Kriegel, Peter Kunath, Martin Pfeifle, and Matthias Renz

University of Munich, Germany
{kriegel, kunath, pfeifle, renz}@dbs.ifi.lmu.de

Abstract. An important database primitive for commonly used feature databases is the similarity join. It combines two datasets based on some similarity predicate into one set such that the new set contains pairs of objects of the two original sets. In many different application areas, e.g. sensor databases, location based services or face recognition systems, distances between objects have to be computed based on vague and uncertain data. In this paper, we propose to express the similarity between two uncertain objects by probability density functions which assign a probability value to each possible distance value. By integrating these probabilistic distance functions directly into the join algorithms the full information provided by these functions is exploited. The resulting probabilistic similarity join assigns to each object pair a probability value indicating the likelihood that the object pair belongs to the result set. As the computation of these probability values is very expensive, we introduce an efficient join processing strategy exemplarily for the distance-range join. In a detailed experimental evaluation, we demonstrate the benefits of our probabilistic similarity join. The experiments show that we can achieve high quality join results with rather low computational cost.

1 Introduction

In many modern application ranges, e.g. spatio-temporal query processing of moving objects [9], sensor databases [8] or personal identification systems [28], usually only uncertain data is available. For instance, in the area of mobile services, the objects continuously change their positions so that exact positional information is almost impossible to obtain. In the area of multimedia databases, e.g. image or music databases, or in the area of personal identification systems based on face recognition and fingerprint analysis, there often exists the problem that a feature value cannot exactly be determined. This uncertain data can be handled by assigning confidence intervals to the feature values, or by specifying probability density functions indicating the likelihoods of certain feature values. In other application areas such as the clustering of distributed feature vectors [13], only approximated (uncertain) information is transmitted to a central server site due to security aspects or limited bandwidth. Let us note that the distance-range join can act as a preprocessing step to speed up clustering.

In order to join these uncertain object representations by traditional join methods, the similarity between the objects has to be measured by one numerical value, i.e. the complete probabilistic distance information is aggregated by only one distance value. Obviously, aggregation goes hand in hand with information loss. For instance, we have no information about the degree of uncertainty of such a single distance value. Even if we

M.L. Lee, K.L. Tan, and V. Wuwongse (Eds.): DASFAA 2006, LNCS 3882, pp. 295–309, 2006.

had one, it would be of no use because traditional join algorithms cannot handle this additional information.

In this paper, we propose to use probabilistic distance functions to measure the similarity between uncertain objects. Contrary to traditional approaches, we do not extract aggregated values from the probabilistic distance functions but enhance the join algorithms so that they can exploit the full information provided by these functions. The re-sulting probabilistic similarity join assigns a probability value to each object pair indicating the likelihood that the pair belongs to the result set, i.e. these probably values reflect the trustability of the result. In applications where wrong results have fatal consequences, e.g. medical treatment, users might only look at very certain results, whereas in commercial advertising, for instance, all results might be interesting. In this paper, we propose a solution for a probabilistic similarity join which is practically very important, the problematic distance-range join.

Probabilistic distance-range joins can be used in the area of location based services but also in many different other areas. For instance, like their non-probabilistic counterparts, they can serve as basic operations for data mining algorithms. Based on the result set of the probabilistic distance-range join, we can efficiently generate a density based clustering of uncertain data. We could group those objects together into one cluster which have a probability value higher than 0.5 that their distance is lower than a certain threshold value.

In this paper, we first present the theoretical foundations of probabilistic similarity joins, and then show how to compute them based on the generally applicable concept of monte-carlo sampling. Thereby, each uncertain object is described by a set of sample points. In order to guarantee efficient join processing, we group the sample points of one uncertain object into k clusters. Minimal bounding boxes of these clusters are then used to identify and skip unnecessary distance computations in a filter step. For the distance-range join, the filter step has an additional advantage. Often an incremental processing of the join query is desired which returns the results in descending order of their probabilities, i.e. the most promising results are returned first. Our approach allows us to determine an upper-bound probability value for each object pair in the filter step which can then be used to return the first results very early.

The remainder of this paper is organized as follows: In Section 2, we present the related work in the area of similarity join processing and query processing of uncertain data. In Section 3, we show how we can carry out a non-probabilistic similarity join on uncertain data. In Section 4, we propose our probabilistic similarity join, which is evaluated in detail in Section 5. We conclude this paper in Section 6 with a short summary and a few remarks on future work.

2 Related Work

In the past decade, a lot of work has been done in the field of similarity join processing. Recently some researchers have focused on the area of query processing of uncertain data. However, to the best of our knowledge no work has been done in the area of join processing of uncertain data. In the following, we present related work on both topics, similarity join processing and query processing of uncertain data.

2.1 Similarity Join

A join groups tuples of two relations R and S into pairs if a *join predicate* is fulfilled. In a *similarity join*, the join predicate is based on the similarity between the objects stored in the relations. This similarity is measured by a distance function d: $O \times O \rightarrow IR_0^+$, e.g. the Euclidean distance between two feature vectors. The most popular similarity join operation is the distance range join. The distance range join $R \bowtie_\varepsilon S$ of two multidimensional or metric sets R and S is the set of pairs where the distance of the objects does not exceed a given parameter ε:

Definition 1. Distance-range join (ε-join)
The distance range join $R \bowtie_\varepsilon S$ of two finite sets R and S is the set $R \bowtie_\varepsilon S := \{(r, s) \in R \times S: d(r, s) \leq \varepsilon\}$.

The distance range join can be applied in density-based clustering algorithms which often define the local data density as the number of objects in the ε-neighborhood of some data object. These clustering algorithms can beneficially be expressed by a self-join using the distance-range paradigm [3].

Most related work on efficient join processing is related to the spatial intersection join. These algorithms which are often based on multidimensional index structures can easily be adapted to distance based predicates for multidimensional point databases instead of the intersection of polygons. The most common technique is the *R-tree Spatial Join* (*RSJ*) [4] which processes R-tree like index structures built on both relations R and S. The RSJ algorithm traverses the indexes of R and S synchronously. When a pair of directory pages (P_R, P_S) is under consideration, the algorithm forms all pairs of the child pages of P_R and P_S having distances of at most ε. For these pairs of child pages, the algorithm is called recursively, i.e. the corresponding indexes are traversed in a depth-first order. Various optimizations of RSJ have been proposed such as the *BFRJ-algorithm* [12] which traverses the indexes according to a breadth-first strategy.

If no multidimensional index is available, it is possible to construct the index on the fly before starting the join algorithm. Several techniques for bulk-loading multidimensional index structures exist [5, 14]. The *seeded tree method* [19] joins two point sets provided that only one is supported by an R-tree. The partitioning of this R-tree is used for a fast construction of the second index on the fly. The *spatial hash-join* [20, 23] decomposes the set R into a number of partitions which is determined according to given system parameters.

A join algorithm particularly suited for similarity self joins is based on the *ε-kdB-tree* [25]. Koudas and Sevcik proposed the *Size Separation Spatial Join* [16] and the *Multidimensional Spatial Join* [15] which make use of space filling curves to order the points in a multidimensional space.

2.2 Query Processing of Uncertain Data

Many studies have focused on the management of uncertain data and on providing probabilistic queries on databases with uncertain data. A survey of the research area concerning uncertainty and incomplete information in databases is given in [1] and [22].

Recently, a lot of work has been published in the area of management and query processing of uncertain data in sensor databases [8] and especially in moving object environments [9, 26]. Similar to the approach presented in this paper, the approaches in [8, 9, 26] model uncertain data by means of probabilistic density functions (*pdfs*). In [26], for instance, moving objects send their new positions to the server, iff their new positions considerably vary from their last sent positions. Thus, the server always knows that an object can only be a certain threshold value away from the last sent position. The server, then assigns a pdf to each object reflecting the likelihood of the objects possible positions. Based on this information the server performs probabilistic range queries. Likewise, in [9] an approach is presented for probabilistic nearest neighbor queries. Note that both approaches assume non-uncertain query objects. Thus, they cannot be used as foundation for a join on uncertain objects where both query and database objects are uncertain.

Furthermore, most recently [10] an approach was proposed dealing with spatial query processing not on positionally uncertain data but on existentially uncertain data. This kind of data naturally occurs, if, for instance, objects are extracted from uncertain satellite images. The approach presented in this paper does not deal with existentially uncertain data but with positionally uncertain data which can be modelled by probability density functions.

Definition 2. Uncertain object representation
Let $o \in D \subseteq IR^d$ be an object from a database. An *uncertain object representation* is a function $o_{uncertain}$: $IR^d \rightarrow IR_0^+ \cup \infty$,for which the following condition holds:

$$\iint_{IR^d} o_{uncertain}(v)dv = 1$$

In the following, we will show that the above definition is a generalization of existing object description techniques used to describe uncertain data.

Modelling Distributed Feature Vectors. In [13], feature vectors were grouped together to small clusters at client site. Then each cluster is represented by a feature vector and a covering-radius and this information was transmitted to the server. If we assume that V is the volume of the hyper-sphere belonging to the micro-cluster of object o, the uncertain object representation $o_{uncertain}$ assigns to each feature vector contained in the hyper-sphere a value of $1/V$ and to each feature vector outside of the hyper-sphere a value of 0. Note that all objects within such a micro-cluster have the same uncertain object representation.

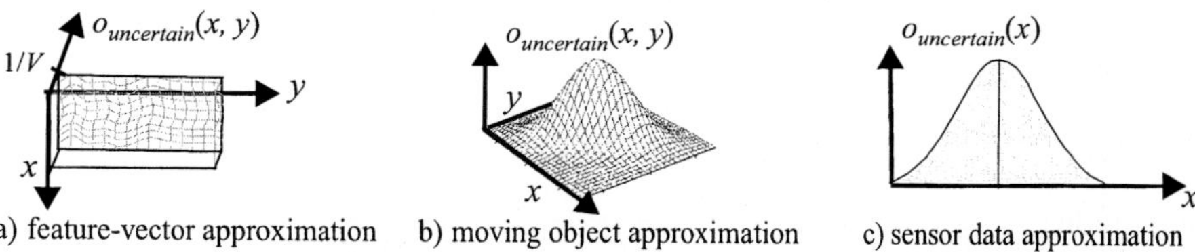

Fig. 1. Uncertain object descriptions

In [18], an approach for distributed clustering of high-dimensional feature vectors was introduced. In order to save transmission cost, only certain dimensions of a feature vector were transmitted to the server. For the dimensions which were not transmitted, the server can limit the possible values by an interval. Thus, the server can individually generate for each feature vector a conservative approximating box. If we assume that V is the volume of the box belonging to object o, the uncertain object representation $o_{uncertain}$ assigns to each feature vector co ntained in the box a value of $1/V$ and to each feature vector outside of the box a value of 0 (cf. Figure 1a). In this case, the uncertain object descriptions are different for the different objects.

Modelling Moving Objects. Technical problems with the GPS system, or outdated positional information force the server to approximate moving objects by one- or two-dimensional Gaussian probability density functions $o_{uncertain}$ (cf. Figure 1b). If we assume that the exact positions of the moving objects are available [27], the probability density functions $o_{uncertain}$ correspond to dirac-delta functions which assign to the exact position a value of infinity and to all other positions a value of 0.

Modelling Sensor Data. Many applications use sensors for monitoring values like wind speed, pressure or temperature. Due to continuous changes, a central database has at each time only approximated information of each of these attributes. In [8], it was suggested to model each of these values by appropriate density functions, which corresponds to a 1-dimensional uncertain object representation according to Definition 2 (cf. Figure 1c).

If clear from the context, we simply write o for the uncertain object representation $o_{uncertain}$ from now on. As already mentioned there exists a lot of work in the area of query processing on these uncertain object representations, but, to the best of our knowledge, there does not exist any work in the literature which tackles the complex problem of joining these uncertain objects.

3 Non-probabilistic Similarity Join on Uncertain Data

Traditional join algorithms require distance functions which express the similarity between two objects by exactly one numerical value. Based on these traditional distance functions, the join algorithms decide for each object pair unambiguously whether it belongs to the result set or not. Usually, this decision is based on 'sharp' object representations, i.e. the objects are assumed to be certain.

In this section, we introduce distance functions which do not express the similarity between two objects by a single numerical value. Instead, we propose distance functions expressing the similarity between two objects by means of a probability density function which we call *probabilistic distance function.* This function describes the probability distribution of all possible distances between two objects. A one-dimensional example is depicted in Figure 2. Figure 2a shows two uncertain objects o and o' according to Definition 2. The distance between these two objects is described by a probabilistic distance function.

a)

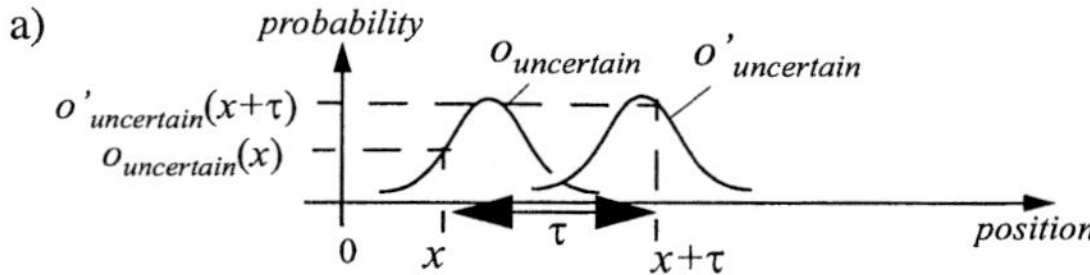

b)

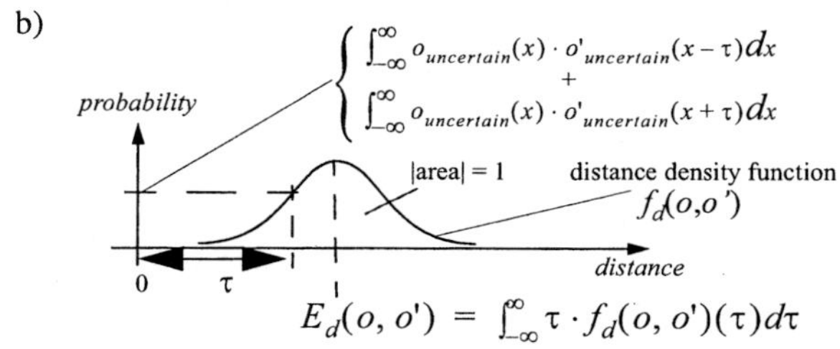

Fig. 2. Probabilistic distance function in an uncertain feature space. b) probabilistic distance function, a) reflecting the distance between two one-dimensional uncertain objects.

Definition 3. Probabilistic distance function

Let $d: D \times D \rightarrow IR_0^+$ be a distance function, and let $P(a \leq d(o, o') \leq b)$ denote the probability that $d(o, o')$ is between a and b. Then a probabilistic density function $f_d: D \times D \rightarrow (IR_0^+ \rightarrow IR_0^+ \cup \infty)$ is called a *probabilistic distance function* if the following condition holds:

$$P(a \leq d(o, o') \leq b) = \int_a^b f_d(o, o')(x)dx$$

If the distance $\tau = d(o,o')$ between two objects can exactly be determined, the probabilistic distance function f_d is equal to the dirac-delta-function δ, i.e. $f_d(o, o')(x) = \delta(x-\tau)$ [7]. Thus, the traditional approach can be regarded as a special case of Definition 3. Let us point out that the probability distribution of each uncertain data item is considered independent.

As traditional join algorithms can only handle distance functions which yield a unique distance value, we propose to extract the expected distance value from these probabilistic distance functions. The expected distance value $E_d: O \times O \rightarrow IR_0^+$ represents the probabilistic distance function by one single value $E_d(o, o') = \int_{-\infty}^{\infty} x \cdot f_d(o, o')(x)dx$ (cf. Figure 2b).

Although, this expected distance value expresses the distance between two uncertain objects in an appropriate way, similarity joins based on this distance measure might be misleading. Look at the example shown in Figure 3 depicting 4 uncertain objects o_A, o_B, o_C and o_D having different uncertainties. On the right hand side of Figure 3 the corresponding probabilistic distance functions of the object pairs are shown. This example demonstrates that both objects o_B and o_D are within the ε-range of object o_A, when simply using the expected distances. Although, the probabilities that the objects o_B and o_C are within the ε-range of o_A are very similar, o_B belongs to the result set and o_C not. Furthermore, although the expected distance between the uncertain objects o_A and o_B is lower

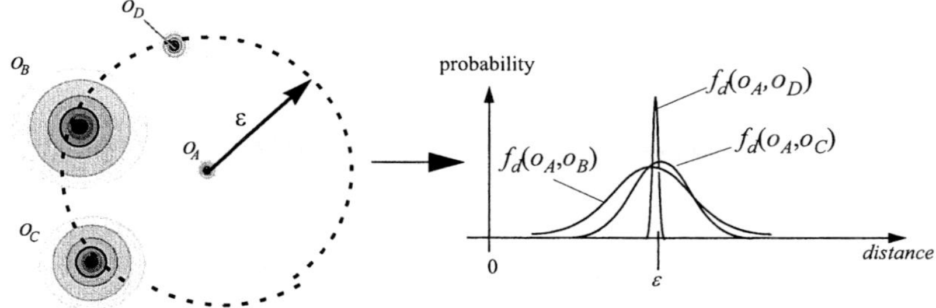

Fig. 3. Distance-range join based on the expected distance

than the expected distance between the objects o_A and o_D, the probability that o_B is within the ε-range of o_A is much smaller than the probability for o_D. To sum up, similarity joins based on the expected distances are not able to take the uncertainty of the object representations into account and thus fail to produce meaningful results.

4 Probabilistic Similarity Join on Uncertain Data

As outlined in Section 3, a non-probabilistic similarity join on uncertain data has some limitations which are overcome by the probabilistic similarity join introduced in this section. The probabilistic similarity join is based on a direct integration of the probabilistic distance functions rather than using only aggregated values. Our new *probabilistic similarity join* assigns to each object pair a probability value reflecting the likelihood that the object pair belongs to the join result set.

Definition 4. Probabilistic similarity join
Let R and S denote two relations, and let θ_d denote any similarity join predicate based on a given distance function d. Furthermore, let $P(r\ \theta_d\ s)$ denote the probability that $r\ \theta_d\ s$ is true for an object pair $(r, s) \in R \times S$. Then, the *probabilistic similarity join* $R \overset{\text{prob}}{\underset{\theta}{\bowtie}} S$ consists of object pairs $(r, s) \in R \times S$ for which $P(r\ \theta_d\ s) > 0$ holds, i.e.

$$R \overset{\text{prob}}{\underset{\theta}{\bowtie}} S = \{(r, s, P(r\ \theta_d\ s)) \mid P(r\ \theta_d\ s) > 0\} \subseteq R \times S \times [0,1]$$

4.1 Theoretical Foundations

In this section, we shortly show how we can theoretically compute the probability value $P(o\ \theta_d^{dr}\ o')$[1] underlying the probabilistic distance-range join.

Lemma 1. Let $\varepsilon \in IR_0^+$ and let d be an arbitrary distance function between feature vectors. For each pair of uncertain object representations (o, o'), we can compute the probability $P(o\ \theta_d^{dr}\ o')$ based on their probabilistic distance function $f_d(o, o')$ as follows:

$$P(o\ \theta_d^{dr} o') = \int_{-\infty}^{\varepsilon} f_d(o, o')(x)dx$$

Proof. Lemma 1 directly follows from the definition of the distance-range join (cf. Definition 1) and the definition of the probabilistic distance function (cf. Definition3). □

[1] In the remainder of the paper θ_d^{dr} denotes the join predicate of the distance-range join.

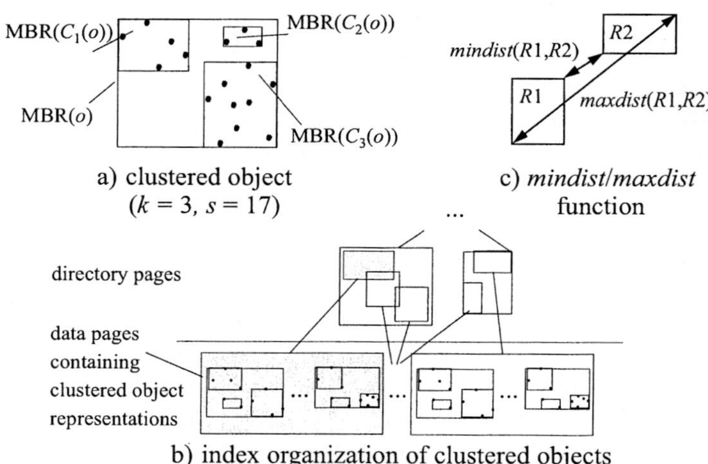

Fig. 4. Database Integration of Uncertain Data

4.2 Computational Aspects

Although for some uncertain object representations it would be possible to compute the probabilistic similarity join directly on Lemma 1, we propose to compute it based on the generally applicable concept of monte-carlo sampling. In many applications the uncertain objects might already be described by a discrete probability density function, i.e. we have the sample set already. If the uncertain object is described by a continuos probability density function, we can easily sample according to this function and derive a set of samples. In the following, we assume that each object o is represented by a set of s sample points, i.e. o is represented by s different representations $\{o_1, ..., o_s\}$. After having described how to organize these discrete object representations within a database (cf. Section 4.2.1), we show how to compute the probabilistic distance-range join (cf. Section 4.2.2) based on these discrete object representations.

4.2.1. Database Integration of Uncertain Data

In order to reduce the complexity of the join computations, we introduce efficient join variants which are based on groups of samples. Thereby two samples o_i and o_j of the same object o are grouped together to one cluster, if they are close to each other. We can generate such a clustering on the object samples by applying the partitioning clustering algorithm k-means [21] individually to each sample set $\{o_1, ..., o_s\}$. Thus, an object is no longer approximated by s samples, but by k clusters containing all the s sample points of the object (cf. Figure 4a).

Definition 5. Clustered object representation

Let $\{o_1, ..., o_s\}$ be a discrete object representation. Then, we call the set $\{\{o_{1,1}, ..., o_{1,n_1}\}, ..., \{o_{k,1}, ..., o_{k,n_k}\}\}$ a *clustered object representation* where $\bigcup_{i=1...k, j=1...n_i} o_{i,j} = \{o_1, ..., o_s\}$ and $n_1 + ... + n_k = s$.

We store these clustered object representations in R-tree [11] like index structures. Thereto, we determine the minimum bounding rectangle MBR($C_i(o)$) of each cluster

$C_i(o) = \{o_{i,1}, ..., o_{i,n_i}\}$, and the minimum bounding rectangle MBR(o) of $o = \{o_1, ..., o_s\}$. Then, we store the clustered object representations as depicted in Figure 4b in a standard index structure suitable for managing spatially extended objects. In the following section, we assume that there exist two functions *mindist* and *maxdist* which return the minimal and the maximal distance between two rectangles, between two points, or between a point and a rectangle (cf. Figure 4c).

4.2.2. Distance Range Join

Managing the uncertain objects in R-tree like index structures (cf. Figure 4) enables us to carry out a distance-range join based on a parallel R-tree run as described in [4]. In general, we can use this approach without any changes regarding the way we use the hierarchical directory structure for pruning branches in the R-tree. The only difference is on the leaf level where we assign a probability value to each object pair. Figure 5a shows the algorithm for computing such a probability value.

Definition 4 requires that the result set of the probabilistic similarity join contains all objects having a probability value higher than 0. Sometimes, it is desirable that this result set is sorted in descending order of the probability values. A straightforward approach would be to determine the complete result set, and then sort it. The disadvantage of this approach is that we have to wait rather long for getting the first element of the result set. In the following, we present an approach which allows us to determine the first element of the sorted result set very efficiently. The basic idea is to adapt the optimal multi-step k-nearest-neighbor approach presented in [24] to our needs.

First, we carry out an approximated probabilistic distance-range join based on a parallel R-tree run and on the probability function presented in Figure 5b. Note that, especially for high sample rates s, this function can be computed much more efficiently than the one presented in Figure 5a. Obviously, for the result set of this approximated join the following lemma holds.

Lemma 2. Let R $\bowtie^{prob}_{dr,exact}$ S denote the result set of a probabilistic similarity join based on the probability function presented in Figure 5a, and let R $\bowtie^{prob}_{dr,filter}$ S denote the result set of a probabilistic similarity join based on the probability function presented in Figure 5b. Then the following statement holds:

$$(r, s, p_{dr,exact}(r,s)) \in R \bowtie^{prob}_{dr,exact} S \Rightarrow \exists (r, s, p_{dr,filter}(r,s)) \in R \bowtie^{prob}_{dr,filter} S: p_{dr,exact}(r,s) \leq p_{dr,filter}(r,s)$$

Proof. As both join variants run through the R-tree directory in the same way, they only differ in the computation of the probability values of object pairs. If we assume an object pair (r,s), the value $p_{dr,filter}(r,s)$ (cf. Figure 5b) is always equal to or larger than $p_{dr,exact}(r,s)$ (cf. Figure 5a), as *mindist* (MBR($C_i(s)$), MBR($C_{i'}(r)$)) $\leq$ *maxdist* (MBR($C_i(s)$), MBR($C_{i'}(r)$)) holds. Furthermore, if *mindist* (MBR($C_i(s)$), MBR($C_{i'}(r)$)) $> \varepsilon$ holds, then for all sample points $s_{i,j}$ and $r_{i',j'}$ the distance $dist(s_{i,j}, r_{i',j'})$ is also larger than ε. □

Next, we sort the set $R \bowtie^{prob}_{dr,filter} S$ in descending order according to the filter probability values. In the refinement step, we incrementally walk through this sorted list and compute the exact probability values $p_{dr,exact}(r,s)$ as shown in Figure 5a. If the filter probability value $p_{dr,filter}$ of the currently considered join candidate pair is smaller or equal to the maximal exact probability value computed so far, we can immediately report the object pair having the maximal exact probability value. If we have already refined further object

a)

```
FUNCTION p_dr,exact /* computes the exact probability */
INPUT:
o = {{o_1,1, ..., o_1,n_1},...,{o_k,1, ..., o_k,n_k}}clustered_uncertain_object,
o' = {{o'_1,1, ..., o'_1,n'_1},..., {o'_k,1, ..., o'_k,n'_k}}clustered_uncertain_object
OUTPUT: numerical value p∈[0..1];

BEGIN
  IF mindist (MBR(o), MBR(o')) > ε THEN
     RETURN 0
  ELSE IF maxdist (MBR(o), MBR(o')) ≤ ε THEN
     RETURN 1
  ELSE BEGIN
     probability := 0;
     FOR i = 1 TO k DO
       FOR i' = 1 TO k DO
         IF maxdist (MBR(C_i(o)), MBR(C_i'(o'))) ≤ ε THEN
           probability := probability + n_i · n'_i'
         ELSE
           FOR j = 1 TO n_i DO
             FOR j' = 1 TO n'_i' DO
               IF dist (o_i,j , o'_i',j') ≤ ε THEN
                 probability := probability + 1;
     RETURN probability / s²;
  END;
END.
```

b)

```
FUNCTION p_dr,filter /* computes the filter probability */
INPUT:
o = {{o_1,1, ..., o_1,n_1},...,{o_k,1, ..., o_k,n_k}}clustered_unertain_object,
o' = {{o'_1,1, ..., o'_1,n'_1},..., {o'_k,1, ..., o'_k,n'_k}}clustered_uncertain_object
OUTPUT: numerical value p∈[0..1];

BEGIN
  IF mindist (MBR(o), MBR(o')) > ε THEN
     RETURN 0
  ELSE IF maxdist (MBR(o), MBR(o')) ≤ ε THEN
     RETURN 1
  ELSE BEGIN
     filter_probability := 0;
     FOR i = 1 TO k DO
          FOR i' = 1 TO k DO
            IF mindist (MBR(C_i(o)), MBR(C_i'(o'))) ≤ ε THEN
              filter_probability := filter_probability + n_i · n'_i'
     RETURN filter_probability / s²;
  END;
END.
```

Fig. 5. Probability functions underlying the distance-range join. a) Computation of the exact probability, b) Computation of the filter probability.

pairs for which the exact probability value is equal or higher than $p_{dr,filter}$, then all these pairs can be reported before starting the next refinement. Obviously, this process can iteratively be continued until the user decides that he has received enough object pairs.

5 Experimental Evaluation

In this section, we examine the effectiveness, i.e. the quality, and the efficiency of our proposed probabilistic similarity join approach. The efficiency of our approach was measured by the number of required distance computations which dominate the overall runtime cost. The depicted cost concerning the *probabilistic distance-range join* experiments reflect the overall number of required distance computations.

5.1 Experimental Setup

The following experiments are based on artificial datasets, each consisting of a set of 3- and 10-dimensional uncertain feature vectors. Additionally, we also applied our approaches to two distributed real-world datasets PLANE and PDB where the feature vectors were described by multi-dimensional boxes according to [18].

ART*d*(*u*) datasets. Each of these artificial datasets contains 1000 uncertain objects distributed equally in a *d*-dimensional normalized data space. Thereby the parameter *u* denotes the grade of uncertainty of the objects in the dataset. The uncertainty of the objects, i.e. the maximal variance of the feature values, is measured relatively to the data space. In our experiments, we used two different settings for the uncertainty. For the ART3 data set, *u* = *'low'* denotes an uncertainty of 3% of the data space and *u* = *'high'* denotes an uncertainty of 5% of the data space. For the ART10 data set, *u* = *'low'* denotes an uncertainty of 3% of the data space and *u* = *'high'* denotes an uncertainty of 4% of the data space.

PLANE dataset. The real world dataset PLANE consists of 1000 high-resolution 3D CAD objects provided by our industrial partner, an American airplane manufacturer. Each object is represented by a 42-dimensional feature vector which is derived from the cover sequence model as described in [17]. The average uncertainty of the PLANE data set is 1% of the data space.

PDB dataset. This 3D protein structure dataset is a real world dataset derived from the Brookhaven Protein Data Bank (PDB) [6]. The 1000 objects are represented by 3D shape histograms [2] resulting in a 120-dimensional feature vector per object. The average uncertainty of the PDB data set is 4% of the data space.

For the sampling of the possible object positions we assumed an equal distribution within the corresponding uncertainty areas. All *d*-dimensional datasets are normalized w.r.t. the unit space $[0,1]^d$. As distance measure we used the L_1-distance (Manhattan distance). We performed a self-join on the datasets where the ε-distance was set to 3% of the dataspace for all datasets, except of the PDB dataset for which we set $\varepsilon = 1\%$. If not stated otherwise, the size of the sample set of each uncertain object is initially set to 25 samples which are approximated by 7 clusters.

5.2 Experiments on the Sample Rate

In the first experiments, we examined the quality of our similarity join approaches by varying the number of used samples per object. We noticed that for sample rates higher

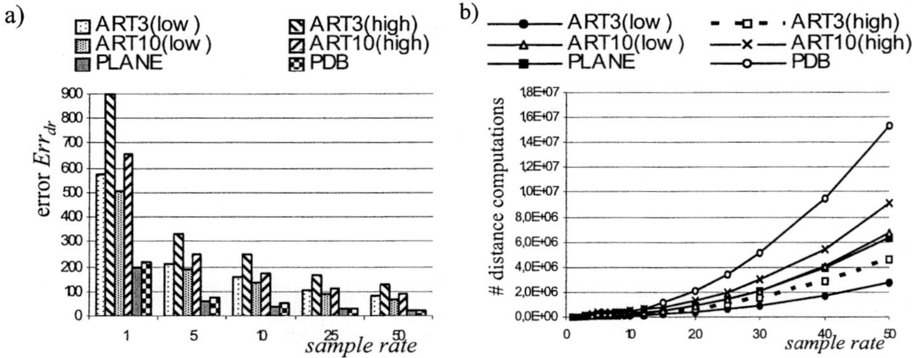

Fig. 6. Influence of the sample rate *sr*. a) Error, b) Number of distance computations.

than 100 the resulting probability values do not change any more considerably. Therefore, we used the probabilistic similarity join result $R_{exact} = \{(r, s, P_{exact}(r\ \theta_d\ s)) | P_{exact}(r\ \theta_d\ s) > 0\}$ (cf. Definition 4) based on 100 samples as reference join result for measuring the error of the probabilistic similarity join results $R_{approx} = \{(r, s, P_{approx}(r\ \theta_d\ s)) \mid P_{approx}(r\ \theta_d\ s) > 0\}$ based on sample rates $sr < 100$. The used error measure Err_{dr} for the distance-range joins is defined as follows:

$$Err_{dr}(R_{approx}, R_{exact}) = \sum_{(r,s) \in R \times S} \left| P_{approx}(r\ \theta_d^{dr}\ s) - P_{exact}(r\ \theta_d^{dr}\ s) \right|$$

Figure 6a shows the error of the *probabilistic distance-range join* for a varying sample rate *sr*. The figure shows clearly that the error decreases rapidly with increasing sample rates. At a sample rate $sr = 10$ the error is less than half the size compared to the error at $s = 1$ for all datasets. Furthermore, comparing the artificial datasets with high uncertainties (ART*d*(*high*)) to those with low uncertainties (ART*d*(*low*)), we can observe that a higher uncertainty leads to a higher error.

In the next experiment, we investigated how the sample rate influences the cost of the join processing. Figure 6b shows the number of distance computations required to perform the join for varying sample rates. We set the number *k* of clusters to 5 for a sample rate *sr* higher than 5, otherwise we set $k = sr$. The cost increase superlinear with increasing sample rates *s*. For high sample rates, the good quality (cf. Figure 6a) goes along with high join cost (cf. Figure 6b). In particular, the join processing on datasets with high uncertainty (ART*d*(*high*)) does not only lead to a lower quality of the results but is also more expensive than the processing on more accurate datasets (ART*d*(*low*)). Altogether, we achieve a good trade-off between the quality of the results and the required cost when using a sample rate of $sr = 25$.

5.3 Experiments on the Efficiency

In this subsection, we examine the runtime performance of our probabilistic join approach. At first, we consider the runtime behavior for different sample rates *s* and varying number of clusters *k*. The experimental results are depicted in Figure 7. On the

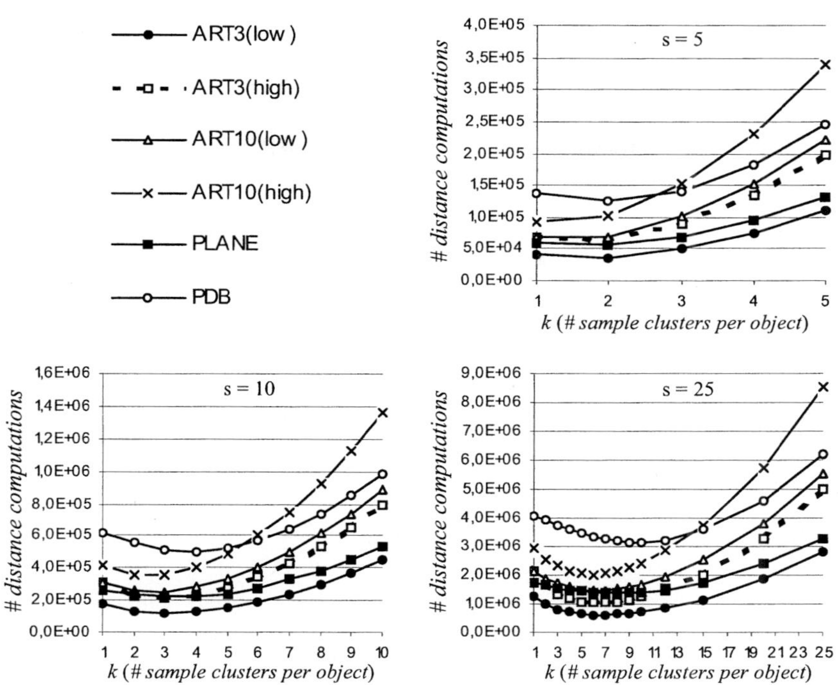

Fig. 7. Runtime performance for varying number of sample clusters

one hand, when using only one cluster per object ($k = 1$), we have only a few clusters for which we must compute the distances between them. On the other hand, the refinement of these clusters is very expensive. When using one cluster per object, the cluster covers the entire uncertain object, i.e. it has a large extension. The probability that the ε-range value is between the *mindist* value and the *maxdist* value of a pair of such clusters is very high, i.e. a lot of cluster pairs have to be refined. Very small clusters ($k = s$) also lead to an expensive join processing, because we have to compute a lot of distances between pairs of clusters when refining the object pairs. The best trade-off for k can be achieved somewhere in between these two extremes. As depicted in Figure 7, the optimal setting for k depends on the used sample rate. Generally, the higher the used sample rate s, the higher is the optimal value for k.

In the next experiments, we demonstrate the advantages of the filter step when enabling a ranked output of the results in descending order of their probabilities. As mentioned in Section 4.2.2, the proposed filter step enables an early output of the first join results. Figure 8a depicts the performance of the ranked distance-range join w.r.t. the probabilities of the results. Only 25% of the distance computations are required to output all certain results, i.e. results having a probability higher than 95%. Only 70% of the distance computations are required to output all results having a probability higher than 50%. The join cost w.r.t. the number of returned results are depicted in Figure 8b. Only 45% of the distance computations are required to return the first 10% of the result

a) 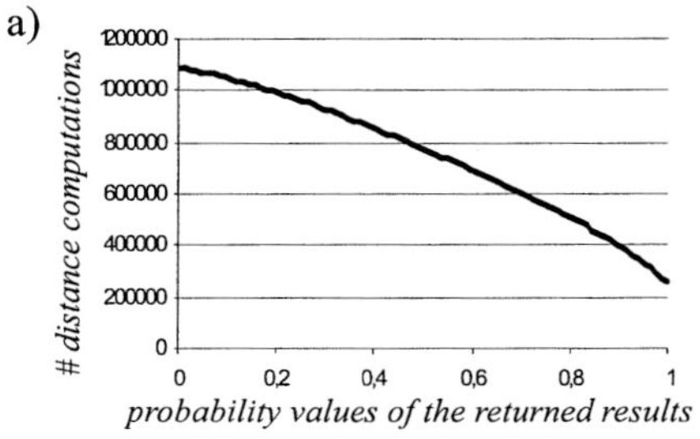

b) 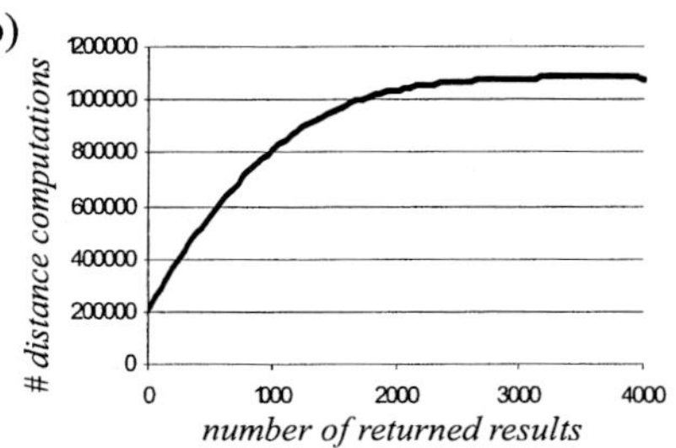

Fig. 8. Runtime ranked distance-range join (ART3(high)). a) performance with respect to the result probability, b) performance with respect to the number of returned results.

set. The proposed incremental join processing is particularly useful when the user wants to stop the query after getting either the most significant results or a small portion of the result set.

6 Conclusions

Similarity query processing on uncertain data is an important emerging topic in many modern database application areas. In this paper, we introduced the general concept of *probabilistic similarity joins* on uncertain objects which assign to each object pair a probability value indicating the likelihood that it belongs to the result set. In particular, we introduced in detail how to compute these probability values for the distance-range join. We showed how this similarity join can effectively be carried out based on the generally applicable concept of monte-carlo sampling. In order to improve the efficiency of the proposed probabilistic similarity join, we determined appropriate approximations of the object samples by means of clustering. Based on these approximations, the proposed probabilistic distance-range join algorithm also supports an incremental report of the join results ranked in descending order of their probability values. In a detailed experimental evaluation based on artificial and real-world data sets, we demonstrated that the incremental probabilistic distance-range join allows to report the most significant join results very early.

In our future work, we plan to extend our probabilistic algorithm to further similarity join predicates, e.g. the nearest-neighbor and reverse-nearest neighbor predicates. Furthermore, we will show that probabilistic similarity joins can beneficially be used as a basic operation for various data mining algorithms, e.g. clustering and classification algorithms, which have to process uncertain data.

References

1. Abiteboul S., Hull R., Vianu V.: *Foundations of Databases.* Addison Wesley, 1995.
2. Ankerst M., Kastenmüller G., Kriegel H.-P., Seidl T.: *3D Shape Histograms for Similarity Search and Classification in Spatial Databases.* SSD'99.
3. Böhm C., Braunmüller B., Breunig M., Kriegel H.-P.: *High Performance Clustering Based on the Similarity Join.* CIKM'00.

4. Brinkhoff T., Kriegel H.P., Seeger B.: *Efficient Processing of Spatial Joins Using R-trees.* SIGMOD '93.
5. van den Bercken J., Seeger B., Widmayer P.: *A General Approach to Bulk Loading Multidimensional Index Structures.* VLDB'97.
6. Bernstein F. C., Koetzle T. F., Williams G. J., Meyer E. F., Brice M. D., Rodgers J. R., Kennard O., Shimanovichi T., Tasumi M.: *The Protein Data Bank: a Computer-based Archival File for Macromolecular Structures.* Journal of Molecular Biology, Vol. 112 (1977).
7. Bracewell R.: *The Impulse Symbol.* Ch. 5 in The Fourier Transform and Its Applications, 3rd ed.: McGraw-Hill, 1999.
8. Cheng R., Kalashnikov D.V., Prabhakar S.: *Evaluating probabilistic queries over imprecise data.* SIGMOD'03.
9. Cheng R., Kalashnikov D. V., Prabhakar S.: *Querying imprecise data in moving object environments.* IEEE Transactions on Knowledge and Data Engineering, 2004.
10. Dai X., Yiu M., Mamoulis N., Tao Y., Vaitis M.: *Probabilistic Spatial Queries on Existentially Uncertain Data.* SSTD'05.
11. Guttman A.: *R-trees: A Dynamic Index Structure for Spatial Searching.* SIGMOD'84.
12. Huang Y.-W., Jing N., Rundensteiner E. A.: *Spatial Joins Using R-trees: Breadth-First Traversal with Global Optimizations.* VLDB'97.
13. Januzaj E., Kriegel H.-P., Pfeifle M.: *Scalable Density-Based Distributed Clustering.* PKDD'04.
14. Kamel I., Faloutsos C.: *Hilbert R-tree: An Improved R-tree using Fractals.* VLDB'94.
15. Koudas N., Sevcik K.: *High Dimensional Similarity Joins: Algorithms and Performance Evaluation.* ICDE'98.
16. Koudas N., Sevcik K.: *Size Separation Spatial Join.* SIGMOD'97.
17. Kriegel H.-P., Brecheisen S., Kröger P., Pfeifle M., Schubert M.: *Using Sets of Feature Vectors for Similarity Search on Voxelized CAD Objects.* SIGMOD'03.
18. Kriegel H.-P., Kunath P., Pfeifle M., Renz M.: *Approximated Clustering of Distributed High Dimensional Data.* PAKDD'05.
19. Lo M.-L., Ravishankar C. V.: *Spatial Joins Using Seeded Trees.* SIGMOD'94.
20. Lo M.-L., Ravishankar C. V.: *Spatial Hash Joins.* SIGMOD'96.
21. McQueen J.: *Some Methods for Classification and Analysis of Multivariate Observations.* In 5th Berkeley Symp. Math. Statist. Prob., volume 1, 1967.
22. Motro A.: *Management of Uncertainty in Database Systems.* In Modern Database Systems, Won Kim (Ed.), Addison Wesley, 1995.
23. Patel J.M., DeWitt D.J.: *Partition Based Spatial-Merge Join.* SIGMOD'96.
24. Seidl T., Kriegel H.-P: *Optimal Multi-Step k-Nearest Neighbor Search.* SIGMOD'98.
25. Shim K., Srikant R., Agrawal R.: *High-Dimensional Similarity Joins.* ICDE'97.
26. Wolfson O., Sistla A. P. , Chamberlain S., Yesha Y.: *Updating and Querying Databases that Track Mobile Units.* Distributed and Parallel Databases, 7(3), 1999.
27. Yiu M. L., N. Mamoulis N.: Clustering Objects on a Spatial Network. SIGMOD'04, pp. 443-454.
28. Zhao W., Chellappa R., Phillips P.J., Rosenfeld A.: *Face Recognition: A literature survey.* ACM Computational Survey, 35(4), 2000.

Handling Uncertainty and Ignorance in Databases: A Rule to Combine Dependent Data

Sunil Choenni[1,2], Henk Ernst Blok[2], and Erik Leertouwer[1]

[1] Dutch Ministry of Justice, Research & Documentation Centre (WODC), P.O.Box 20301, 2500 EH, The Hague, The Netherlands
{r.choenni, e.c.leertouwer}@minjus.nl
[2] University of Twente, Fac. of EEMCS, P.O. Box 217, 7500 AE, Enschede, The Netherlands
{r.s.choenni, h.e.blok}@utwente.nl

Abstract. In many applications, uncertainty and ignorance go hand in hand. Therefore, to deliver database support for effective decision making, an *integrated* view of uncertainty and ignorance should be taken. So far, most of the efforts attempted to capture uncertainty and ignorance with probability theory. In this paper, we discuss the weakness to capture ignorance with probability theory, and propose an approach inspired by the Dempster-Shafer theory to capture uncertainty and ignorance. Then, we present a rule to combine dependent data that are represented in different relations. Such a rule is required to perform joins in a consistent way. We illustrate that our rule is able to solve the so-called problem of information loss, which was considered as an open problem so far.

1 Introduction

Today, we distinguish several data models to represent and query data, such as the relational data model, object-oriented data models, XML data models, etc. Through the years a number of efforts has been devoted to capturing uncertainty in the context of relational databases [2,3,6,8,9,12,13,14,16]. Despite these efforts not all issues have been satisfactorily solved in the context of relational databases, while modelling uncertainty in other types of databases, such as XML databases is still in its childhood [1,7,10]. These approaches, except [13], are based on probability theory, and as a consequence they inherit the limitations of this theory. Probability theory is very suitable to capture uncertainty **but not** suitable to model ignorance. This has been noted and discussed in [2]. To overcome these limitations, Barbara et al. [2] introduced the so-called notion of missing probability, which is actually a way to model ignorance. However their approach suffers to a number of problems as will be illustrated in the next section.

Since uncertainty and ignorance go hand in hand in many applications, we feel that databases should support them in an integrated way. Suppose we have a document of which 80% is clearly visible and 20% of the document is damaged. This document

M.L. Lee, K.L. Tan, and V. Wuwongse (Eds.): DASFAA 2006, LNCS 3882, pp. 310 – 324, 2006.

contains an enormous amount of addresses, including addresses that give rise to suspicion. From the visible part, we can derive that 70% of the addresses is "normal" and 30% of them are considered as suspicious. So, if we have an arbitrary address A that comes from the visible part of the document, we know the distribution among normal and suspicious addresses, and therefore we are able to estimate whether A is a normal or a suspicious address. However, we will remain in *uncertainty* of the actual status of A, until we have checked in the document the details about A. For the damaged part of the document, we do not have any clue about the distribution of normal and suspicious addresses, therefore we are *ignorant* with regard to the addresses in this part of the document. If we want to estimate whether an arbitrary address B, of which it is unknown to what part of the document it belongs, is normal or suspicious, then we need to combine uncertainty and ignorance. Note, that estimating whether B is normal or suspicious on the basis of the distribution function that pertains only to the visible part will be unreliable. Therefore, to deliver database support for effective decision making, an *integrated* view of uncertainty and ignorance should be taken.

In this paper, we present how uncertainty and ignorance can be modelled in a relation, which consists of a set of tuples, and each tuple is a list of attribute values. Our approach is inspired by the Dempster-Shafer theory [5,11,15], but differs on main points of this theory (see Section 3). Then, we focus on how two relations, in which uncertainty and ignorance are captured can be combined in a consistent way to support joins in databases. We note that a join is an important operation to answer user queries posed on a relational database. The goal of this paper is to present the intuitive ideas behind our rule to combine dependent data and to show that we are able to solve the so-called problem of information loss (see Section 2), which was posed as an open problem in [2]. Therefore we will restrict ourselves in this paper to the combination of **two** relations. For the generalization of the rule to more than two relations we refer to a forthcoming paper and for the theoretical foundation of our model to capture uncertainty and ignorance in relational databases, we refer to [4].

The remainder of this paper is organised as follows. In Section 2, we discuss our problem definition in more detail and discuss why probability theory fails to solve the problem. Then, in Section 3, we briefly introduce our approach to model uncertainty and ignorance in databases. Then, in Section 4, we define our combination rule to combine dependent data represented in two different tables. In Section 5, we illustrate the application of our combination rule. Finally, Section 6 concludes the paper.

2 Problem Definition

In relational databases, a relation is defined over some attributes. An attribute takes a single value from a predefined domain. In our approach, we allow an attribute to take a *set* of values from a predefined domain **D**, and a function will be associated with this set, expressing the degree of uncertainty and ignorance among the elements in a set.

By means of the following example, which is similar to an example in [2], we introduce our problem definition in more detail. Suppose we want to predict the planting behaviour of farmers. Therefore, we need to model some data about the weather and some data about the planting behaviour of farmers in the past. Let us assume that for the weather the possible outcome is either wet or dry. Now the KNMI (Royal Dutch Meteorological Institute) has collected evidences that it will be a dry season with probability 0.6 and another set of evidences is pointing to a wet season with a probability of 0.2. Since the probability of a dry and a wet season sum up to (0.6 + 0.2 =) 0.8, the remaining 0.2 actually implies ignorance with regard to the weather. In [2] , the authors model ignorance by assigning the probability of 0.2 to the set {wet, dry}. The semantic of this solution is that we do not make any statement how the probability of 0.2 is distributed among the elements of the set {wet, dry}. In the left table of Figure 1, the weather data is modelled. Furthermore, we have the following statistics for a dry season: 30% of the farmers planted turnips and 70% of them planted wheat if they expected a dry season. If farmers expected a wet season, they planted turnips. In the right table of Figure 1, we have modelled this data.

source	weather
KNMI	0.6 [dry] 0.2 [wet] 0.2 [dry, wet]

weather	plant
dry	0.3 [turnips] 0.7 [wheat]
wet	1.0 [turnips]

Fig. 1. Two base relations to model weather data

To gain insight in the planting behaviour of a farmer in the next season, the tables of Figure 1 need to be joined. To combine the probabilities, we may use the conditional rule of Bayes, namely, **Pr**(weather="w", plant="p") = **Pr**(plant="p" | weather="w")***Pr**(weather ="w"), which results in Figure 2.

The first tuple in Figure 1 is telling us that the probability that it will be a dry season and a farmer will plant turnips is 0.18 and the probability that it will be a dry season and a farmer will plant wheat is 0.42. Note, the joined table contains answers to questions like: what is the probability that turnips/wheat will be planted next season?

source	weather plant
KNMI	(0.6*0.3 =) 0.18 [dry turnips] (0.6*0.7 =) 0.42 [dry wheat]
KNMI	(0.2 *1.0 =) 0.2 [wet turnips]

Fig. 2. Result of a join between the base relations depicted in Figure 1

As can be verified from Figure 2, ignorance (the probability of 0.2 assigned to {dry, wet}) has no influence on the join result. So, we have this information in one of our tables, but it is not used during the join, hence we have *information loss*.

From the above-mentioned example we observe the following. First of all, probability theory is not equipped to handle ignorance. For example, probability theory does not provide us the possibility to model the situation that 60% of the collected evidences points to a dry season and 20% to a wet season. Intuitively, we like to model this as **Pr**(dry) =0.6 and **Pr**(wet) = 0.2. However, this is in contradiction which one of the fundamental rules in probability theory. A corollary of the basic axioms of probability theory is the rule $\mathbf{Pr}(A)+\mathbf{Pr}(\neg A)=1$. Let A represent the event "dry" season, thus $\mathbf{Pr}(A)=0.6$. Actually, the probability of the event "wet" season is now determined and should be $\mathbf{Pr}(wet)=1-0.6=0.4$ which is in contradiction with the collected evidences that are pointing to 0.2. Perhaps one might think that this problem can be solved by modelling an outcome space as Ω = {(wet), (dry), (wet, dry)} and defining a probability function p: $\Omega \rightarrow [0,1]$. In Appendix 1, we show that this does *not* lead to a solution.

Second, the approach proposed by Barbara et al. [2] leads to information loss and the embedding of their approach in probability theory is dubious, since it is in contradiction with the axioms of this theory (see also [4]).

Third, modelling ignorance by assigning a mass to a whole set of events, instead of (equally) distributing the mass among the elements of the set, is an attractive option and is pursued in this paper.

From the observations, we learn that ignorance and uncertainty are strongly intertwined. Therefore, for data management purpose, we need a theory in which these notions are embedded in an *integrated* way. In the next section, we propose our approach to capture uncertainty and ignorance.

3 Modelling Uncertainty and Ignorance in Databases

In this section, we start by introducing some basic notions from Dempster-Shafer theory [11] to capture uncertainty and ignorance in a single relation. However, to combine data from two different relations we need to extend the theory. We will discuss the extension in Section 3.2.

3.1 Basics of Dempster-Shafer Theory

We propose to attach a mass function, called **b**asic **p**robability **a**ssignment (bpa) to a set of attribute values in a relation. Based on this function, we will define the notion of ignorance.

[Def. 2.1] Let X be a set and $D_x = \{S \mid S \subseteq X\}$, then a function $m: D_x \rightarrow [0,1]$ is a bpa whenever $m(\emptyset)=0$ and $\sum_{S \in D_X} m(S)=1$.

The quantity $m(S)$ expresses a relative confidence in exactly S and not in any (proper) subset of *S*. The total confidence in *S*, which we call *belief*, is the sum of the probability assignments committed to all subsets of *S*. The following definition describes the relation between a belief function and basic probability assignment.

[Def. 2.2] For a given bpa *m*, a belief function, called *Bel*, is defined over any $S \in D_x$ as $Bel(S) = \sum_{S' \subseteq S} m(S')$. Note, a bpa induces a belief function and conversely.

To define the notion of ignorance, we first define plausibility.

[Def. 2.3] The plausibility of any set $S \in D_x$ is defined as $Pl(S) = 1 - Bel(\neg S)$.

[Def. 2.4] The degree of ignorance for a set *S* is defined as $Ig(S) = Pl(S) - Bel(S)$.

Now, we are able to model smoothly the data collected by KNMI in our example introduced in Section 2, without being in conflict with the axioms that belief functions should satisfy [15]. Note, for two sets S_1 and S_2, the following should hold for a belief function *Bel*: $Bel(S_1 \cup S_2) \geq Bel(S_1) + Bel(S_2) - Bel(S_1 \cap S_2)$.

Recall, in example 1, the KNMI collected evidences to predict whether it will be a dry or a wet season, and 60% of the evidences was pointing to a dry season, 20% to a wet season, and the remaining 20% of the evidences was neither pointing to a wet nor a dry season. This can be modelled as follows: *m*({dry}) = 0.6, *m*({wet}) =0.2, and *m*({dry, wet}) = 0.2. The corresponding belief function to *m* is: *Bel*({dry}) = 0.6, *Bel*({wet}) =0.2, and *Bel*({dry, wet}) = *m*({dry}) + *m*({wet}) + *m*({dry, wet}) = 1.0.

The plausibility for a dry season is: $Pl(\{\text{dry}\}) = 1 - Bel(\neg\{\text{dry}\}) = 1 - Bel'(\{\text{wet}\}) = 0.8$, and the ignorance with regard to a dry season is $Ig(\{\text{dry}\}) = Pl(\{\text{dry}\}) - Bel(\{\text{dry}\}) = 0.8 - 0.6 = 0.2$. We note that this is in line with our intuition, since 60% of the evidences are pointing to a dry season and 20% of the evidences leave us in ignorance because they are neither supporting a dry nor a wet season. So, an optimistic estimation for a dry season is 0.8. A similar reasoning can be hold for the prediction of a wet season.

3.2 Extending the Dempster-Shafer Theory

As can be seen from Figure 2, the combination of the base relations of Figure 1 leads to a relation , in which we like to obtain a bpa defined on a set that in turn consists to two distinct sets namely $D_{weather}$={dry, wet} and D_{plant}={turnips, wheat}. Therefore, we need to extend the notion of bpa's to two distinct sets. Furthermore, the data in the weather table should be interpreted as that turnips will be planted with a bpa of 0.3, given the fact that it will be a dry season. So this means that the bpa defined on plant is dependent on the attribute weather. Therefore, we introduce the notion of dependent bpa. We start extending the Dempster-Shafer theory by defining a bpa on different sets.

[Def. 2.5] Let X and Y be two distinct sets and $D_x = \{S \mid S \subseteq X\}$ and $D_y = \{Q \mid Q \subseteq Y\}$. A function $m: D_x \times D_y \rightarrow [0,1]$ is a combined bpa on D_x and D_y whenever (1) $m(S,Q) = 0$, if $S = \varnothing$ or $Q = \varnothing$ and (2) $\sum_{S \in D_x} \sum_{Q \in D_y} m(S,Q) = 1$. A combined bpa will be denoted as c-bpa in the following.

Analogous to definitions 2.2 and 2.3, the belief and plausibility on D_x and D_y are defined as follows.

[Def. 2.6] Let *m* be a c-bpa defined over 2 distinct sets D_x and D_y, the belief in *(S,Q)*, in which $S \in D_x$ and $Q \in D_y$, is defined as $Bel(S,Q) = \sum_{S' \subseteq S} \sum_{Q' \subseteq Q} m(S', Q')$. The plausibility in the pair *(S,Q)* is defined as $Pl(S,Q) = 1 - Bel(\neg S, \neg Q)$.

[Def. 2.7] Let *m* be a c-bpa defined over two distinct sets D_x and D_y, and m_x a bpa defined on D_x, then *m* is called dependent on m_x whenever $\exists S \in D_x : \sum_{S_i \subseteq S} \sum_{Q \in D_y} m(S_i, Q) = 1$ and $m_x(S_i) > 0$. In the following we will denote a dependent bpa *m* on m_x as $m_{y|x}(.| S)$.

The intuition behind Def 2.7 is the following. The fact that a set $S \in D_x$ exists for which holds $\sum_{S_i \subseteq S} \sum_{Q \in D_y} m(S_i, Q) = 1$ means that we are talking about a "world" *S*, in which we distinguish all kinds of events *Q*, i.e., we reason about events *Q* given the world *S* or a subset of *S*. The fact $m_x(S_i) > 0$ implies that we have evidences that a world *S* exists, and therefore it is worthwhile to reason in world *S*.

Let us illustrate the notion of dependent bpa by means of our KNMI example, in which $D_{\text{weather}} = \{\text{dry}, \text{wet}\}$; and the bpa $m_{\text{weather}} = (\{\text{dry}\}) = 0.6$, $m_{\text{weather}} = (\{\text{wet}\}) = 0.2$ and $m_{\text{weather}} = (\{\text{dry}, \text{wet}\}) = 0.2$.

Then, the c-bpa *m*(dry, turnips) = 0.7 and *m*(dry, wheat) = 0.3 is dependent on m_{weather} since *m*(dry, turnips) + *m*(dry, wheat) =1.0 and $m_{\text{weather}} = (\{\text{dry}\}) > 0$. Note, in this case *S* = {dry}. If we formulate *m* as $m_{\text{plant|weather}}(\text{turnips} | \text{dry}) = 0.7$ and $m_{\text{plant|weather}}(\text{wheat} | \text{dry}) = 0.3$, then it is clear that it represents the first tuple in the right table of Figure 1.

The class of relational schemes that we consider in the remainder of this paper consists of a set of base relations, in which bpa's are defined on *single* attributes. Furthermore, we assume that there is a non stochastic attribute that serves as key and uniquely identifies a tuple in a *base* relation. All other attributes in the relation, including their bpa's, are dependent on the key. The relations introduced in Figure 1 are typically the base relations that we consider.

4 A Combination Rule

This section is devoted to the combination of a bpa m_x defined on a domain D_x and a dependent bpa, $m_{y|x}(.| S)$ defined on two domains D_x and D_y. In the following, a subset $S_i \subseteq S \in D_x$ or $Q_j \in D_y$ is called a focal element of a belief function if $m_x(S_i) > 0$ or $m_{y|x}(Q_j | S) > 0$. Consider two belief functions Bel_x and $Bel_{y|x}$, with

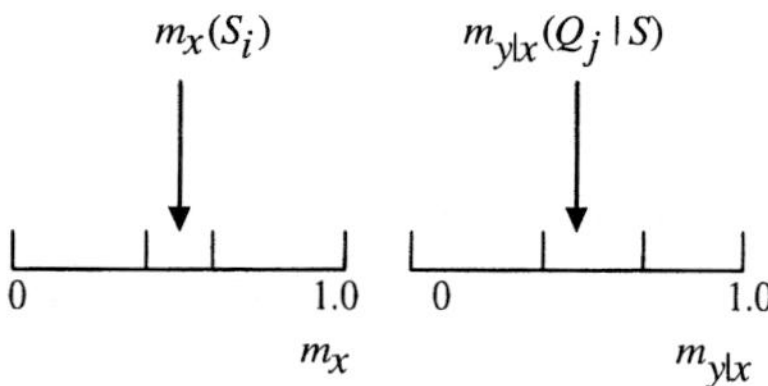

Fig. 3. Graphical representation of a bpa and a dependent bpa

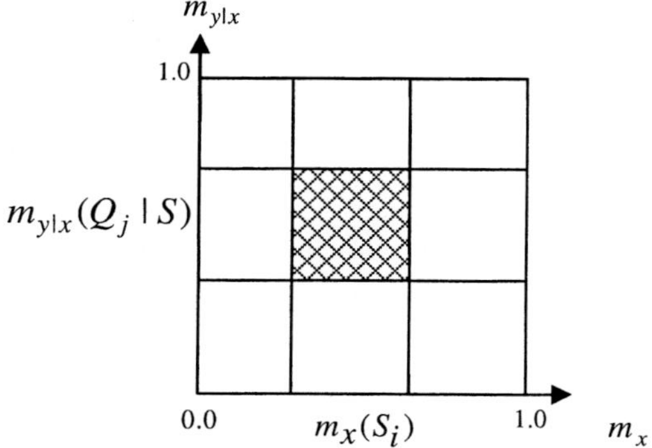

Fig. 4. Graphical representation of the combination of a bpa with a conditional bpa

corresponding bpa's m_x and $m_{y|x}(.\mid S)$. Let $S_i, i = 1,2,..., p$ and $Q_j, j = 1,2,..., q$ be the focal elements of Bel_x and $Bel_{y|x}$, respectively. A graphical representation of both belief functions is given in Figure 3, in which the bpa's of the focal elements are depicted as segments of a line segment of length 1.

In Figure 4, it is shown how the two bpa's can be orthogonally combined to obtain a square. The area of the total square is exactly 1. The area of a rectangle is the c-bpa value assigned to the combination of the focal elements S_i and $Q_j \mid S$.

Let us focus on answering the following question: what is the meaning and result of the combination of the focal elements S_i and $Q_j \mid S$ in Figure 4? The result of the combination of these two elements is either the pair (S_i, Q_j) or $(S_i, *)$, in which * represents the whole domain D_y. We use the wildcard symbol, since the interpretation of the pair $(S_i, *)$ is that the first element is S_i, while the second element could be any subset of D_y. We distinguish three situations for providing an explanation for obtaining either the pair (S_i, Q_j) or $(S_i, *)$. In the following, the sets S_i and $Q_j \mid S$ are focal elements, and, as said before, $S_i \subseteq S \in D_x$ and $Q_j \in D_y$.

In the first situation, we assume $S \cap S_i = \varnothing$, then the result of the combination of S_i and $Q_j \mid S$ is the pair $(S_i, *)$. Since the intersection between S and S_i results in an empty set, m_x does not have any focal elements that supports set S, and therefore no statement can be made about the support for Q_j. So, we have support for S_i due to m_x and no support for a specific subset of D_y on the basis of S_i. Therefore, we conclude the pair $(S_i,*)$ and the contribution to the exact support for this pair on the basis of $m_x(S_i)$ and $m_{y|x}(Q_j \mid S)$ is computed by multiplying those values. In the following $\oplus$ symbolizes the combination operator. We note that the value of $m_x \oplus m_{y|x}(S_i,*)$ is equal to the size of the area of the shaded rectangle in Figure 4.

Let us illustrate this situation by means of our running KNMI example. Suppose we want to combine $m_{\text{weather}} = (\{\text{wet}\}) = 0.2$ and $m_{\text{plant|weather}}(\text{turnips} \mid \text{dry}) = 0.7$. Note, $m_{\text{weather}} = (\{\text{wet}\}) = 0.2$ means that we have evidences for a wet season. However, $m_{\text{plant|weather}}(\text{turnips} \mid \text{dry}) = 0.7$ implies that there is support for planting turnips assuming that it will be dry. Since wet is in contradiction with dry, the conclusion should be that we have evidences for a wet season and no statement can be made about what to plant. Therefore, we conclude that the combination leads to $m_{weather} \oplus m_{plant|weather}(\{\text{wet}\},*) = 0.2 * 0.7 = 0.14$.

In the second situation, $S_i \subseteq S$, and therefore $S \cap S_i \neq \emptyset$. Then, the result of the combination of S_i and $Q_j \mid S$ is the pair (S_i, Q_j). In this case, we have support for set S_i which is expressed by means of m_x since $m_x(S_i) > 0$. Therefore, we have also support for set *S*, since *S* contains S_i. Consequently, we conclude support for Q_j. The contribution to the exact support for pair (S_i, Q_j), i.e., $m_x \oplus m_{y|x}(S_i, Q_j)$, on the basis of $m_x(S_i)$ and $m_{y|x}(Q_j \mid S)$, is again computed by multiplying the values $m_x(S_i)$ and $m_{y|x}(Q_j \mid S)$.

In the last situation, $S \cap S_i \neq \emptyset$ and $S_i \not\subseteq S$. Then, the result of the combination of S_i and $Q_j \mid S$ is the pair (S_i, Q_j) as well. Assume that *T* is the non empty set of the intersection between *S* and S_i. Since $m_x(S_i) > 0$ and we do not know anything about how this value is distributed among the elements or subsets of S_i, an option is to assign support to and to reason about *T*. Note, that this can be done for each subset of S_i that might be of interest. Since $T \subseteq S$ and we have support for *T*, this implies support for *S*. Consequently, we may conclude support for set Q_j, since $m_{y|x}(Q_j \mid S) > 0$ and we have support for *S* via *T*. Again, the bpa value for (S_i, Q_j) is computed as follows: $m_x \oplus m_{y|x}(S_i, Q_j) = m_x(S_i) m_{y|x}(Q_j, S)$.

We illustrate the last situation by means of our running example, where $m_{\text{weather}} = (\{\text{dry}\}) = 0.6$, $m_{\text{weather}} = (\{\text{wet}\}) = 0.2$, and $m_{\text{weather}} = (\{\text{dry, wet}\}) = 0.2$. Consider the following two dependent bpa's: $m^1_{\text{plant|weather}}(\text{turnips} \mid \text{dry}) = 0.7$ and $m^1_{\text{plant|weather}}(\text{wheat} \mid \text{dry}) = 0.3$ and $m^2_{\text{plant|weather}}(\text{turnips} \mid \text{wet}) = 1.0$, representing the first and the second tuple in the right table of Figure 1 respectively.

Combining $m_{\text{weather}} = (\{\text{dry, wet}\}) = 0.2$ with $m^1_{\text{plant|weather}}$ results into: $m_{\text{weather}} \oplus m^1_{\text{plant|weather}}(\text{dry, turnips}) = 0.2*0.7 = 0.14$ and $m_{\text{weather}} \oplus m^1_{\text{plant|weather}}(\text{dry, wheat}) = 0.2*0.3 = 0.06$. We note that $m_{\text{weather}} = (\{\text{dry, wet}\}) = 0.2$ implies support for the set $\{\text{dry, wet}\}$. However we do not know how the mass of 0.2 is distributed among the elements of $\{\text{dry, wet}\}$. Since for $m^1_{\text{plant|weather}}$, a dry weather is of interest, a possible distribution is the computed $m_{\text{weather}} \oplus m^1_{\text{plant|weather}}$. In $m^2_{\text{plant|weather}}$, a wet weather is of interest. Then, the combination of $m_{\text{weather}} = (\{\text{dry, wet}\}) = 0.2$ with $m^2_{\text{plant|weather}}$ results in $m_{\text{weather}} \oplus m^2_{\text{plant|weather}}(\text{wet, turnips}) = 0.2$. So, the combination of $m_{\text{weather}} = (\{\text{dry, wet}\}) = 0.2$ may result in different possible distributions depending on the set of weather that is of interest for a dependent bpa. This is in line with our intuition.

Let us formulate now our combination rule, in which sum up the rectangles that contribute to the bpa of a pair (S_i, Q_j).

$$m_x \oplus m_{y|x}(S_i, Q_j) = \begin{cases} \sum\limits_{S_i \cap S \neq \varnothing} m_x(S_i) m_{y|x}(Q_j \mid S) & \text{if } Q_j \neq * \\ \sum\limits_{\substack{S_i \cap S = \varnothing \\ Q \in D_y}} m_x(S_i) m_{y|x}(Q \mid S) + \sum\limits_{S_i \cap S \neq \varnothing} m_x(S_i) m_{y|x}(* \mid S) & \text{else} \end{cases} \tag{1}$$

As discussed in the foregoing, the combination of S_i and $Q_j \mid S$ results in $(S_i, *)$ whenever $S_i \cap S = \varnothing$. In the case, $S_i \cap S \neq \varnothing$ the pair $(S_i, *)$ can be obtained due to a combination of S_i and $* \mid S$ as well. Therefore, the *else* part of combination rule consists of two expressions.

The following proposition considers a special case of our combination rule. As will be illustrated in the next section, it appears that this special case is sufficient to solve the open problem posed in [2].

[Prop. 1] Let m_x be a bpa defined over D_x, and S_{fix} be a fixed set in a dependent c-bpa $m_{y|x}(. \mid S_{fix})$, which is defined over D_x and D_y. Then equation (1) reduces to

$$m_x \oplus m_{y|x}(S_i, Q_j) = \begin{cases} m_x(S_i) m_{y|x}(Q_j \mid S_{fix}) & \text{if } S_i \cap S_{fix} \neq \varnothing \\ m_x(S_i) & \text{else} \end{cases} \tag{2}$$

[*Proof.*] The intersection of S_i and S_{fix} is either empty or not empty. If the intersection between S_i and S_{fix} results in a non empty set then our combination rule, i.e., equation (1) reduces to

$$m_x \oplus m_{y|x}(S_i, Q_j) = \begin{cases} m_x(S_i) m_{y|x}(Q_j \mid S_{fix}) & \text{if } Q_j \neq * \\ m_x(S_i) m_{y|x}(* \mid S_{fix}) & \text{else} \end{cases}$$

which is equal to $m_x \oplus m_{y|x}(S_i, Q_j) = m_x(S_i) m_{y|x}(Q_j \mid S_{fix})$.

If the intersection between S_i and S_{fix} results in an empty set, then our combination rule, i.e., equation (1) reduces to $m_x \oplus m_{y|x}(S_i, Q_j) = \sum_{Q \in D_y} m_x(S_i) m_{y|x}(Q \mid S_{fix})$. According to Def 2.7, $\sum_{Q \in D_y} m_{y|x}(Q \mid S_{fix}) = 1$ since $m_{y|x}(. \mid S_{fix})$ is a dependent c-bpa.

Therefore,

$$m_x \oplus m_{y|x}(S_i, Q_j) = \sum_{Q \in D_y} m_x(S_i) m_{y|x}(Q \mid S_{fix}) = m_x(S_i) \sum_{Q \in D_y} m_{y|x}(Q \mid S_{fix}) = m_x(S_i). \quad \square$$

5 Illustrative Examples

In this section, we illustrate how our combination rule can be applied to support a join in relational databases. As noted before, a join is an important operator and combines data that is stored in different relations. We restrict ourselves to equi-joins due to the page limitations. Example 5.1 in this section is literally adopted from [2]. This example was posed as an open problem by its authors. We will illustrate how this problem can be solved by applying our combination rule. We start by elaborating on the value that a join attribute should assume after performing a join.

A traditional equi-join, is expressed by $R_1.A = R_2.A$, in which A is an attribute that appears in both relations R_1 and R_2. In this case, two tuples from the different relations are composed to a joined tuple if they have the same value for attribute *A*. Since in our extended relational model an attribute in R_1 as well as in R_2 may consist of a set of values, the question arises: what value attribute *A* should assume after a join?

Let A_1 and A_2 be the sets that contain the values for attribute *A* in relation R_1 and R_2 respectively. Then, the set $A_1 \cap A_2$ contains data that can be found in both relations. So, a joined tuple on the basis of *A* pertains to the set $A_1 \cap A_2$. Therefore, we define the value for attribute *A* after a join as the set $A_1 \cap A_2$. By means of examples, we illustrate how our combination rule can be applied in performing joins. The following example, adopted from [2], shows the results that we intuitively expect from a join in a relational model that is capable to deal with uncertainty and ignorance.

[Example 5.1] Consider the following instances of two relations R_1 and R_2.

R_1

Z	A
z	0.4 [a_1]
	0.6 [*]

R_2

A	B
a_1	0.7 [b_1]
	0.3 [b_2]

Each relation consists of two attributes. Attributes Z and A are the keys of R_1 and R_2 respectively. As argued in [2], intuitively, the join between these relations on attribute A should result for pair (a_1, b_1) in probability[1] range between 0.28 and 0.7 and for pair (a_1, b_2) in probability range between 0.12 and 0.3. How to obtain these values was left as an open problem in [2].

In the next example, we illustrate how we can obtain these desired values by applying proposition 1, which is a special case of our combination rule. Then, in Example 5.3 we discuss a more complicated case.

[Example 5.2] From the relations of example 5.1, it is clear that we have the following bpa defined on attribute A in relation R_1: $m_1(\{a_1\}) = 0.4$ and $m_1(*) = 0.6$. Recall that * represents the whole domain of an attribute. In relation R_2, we have a c-bpa defined over the attributes A and B and which is dependent on m_1. This bpa looks as follows: $m_{2|1}(\{b_1\} \mid \{a_1\}) = 0.7$ and $m_{2|1}(\{b_2\} \mid \{a_1\}) = 0.3$. From now on we omit the brackets for a set, if it is clear that we are dealing with a set. Although it seems that the bpa on attribute A in R_1 is treated differently than the bpa on attribute B in R_2, this is not the case. Due to space limitations, we informally touch on this issue in this paper. Actually m_1 is dependent on the bpa of key Z via $\{z\}$. Since there is no uncertainty about z and no other relations contains attribute Z, we can define the bpa on A in R_1 as an independent bpa m_1. Note that this reasoning does not hold for attribute B in R_2, since there is uncertainty about attribute A in R_1.

The combination of m_1 and $m_{2|1}(. \mid S)$, in which S is a subset of or equal to the domain of attribute A, is sketched in Figure 5. On the horizontal and vertical axis the bpa m_1 and the dependent bpa $m_{2|1}(. \mid S)$ are depicted respectively. We note that here the set S is a fixed set that consists of $\{a_1\}$, and therefore Proposition 1 is applied.

In Figure 5, for the sake of clarity, each rectangle contains the (new) combined pair of sets together with its corresponding bpa value. For example, the combination of the bpa values of the elements (a_1) (with value 0.4) and $(b_1 \mid a_1)$ (with value 0.7) results in a bpa of 0.4*0.7 = 0.28 for pair (a_1, b_1) (lower left rectangle in Figure 5). We note that the support for pair (a_1, b_1) is in line with our intuition. According to $m_{2|1}(b_1 \mid a_1) = 0.7$ there is support for b_1 whenever there is support for a_1. Since $m_1(a_1) > 0$ there is indeed support for a_1, and, therefore there is support for b_1. A similar reasoning holds for the support of pair (a_1, b_2).

The combination of the bpa values of (*) and $(b_1 \mid a_1)$ results in a bpa of 0.7*0.6 =0.42 for pair $(*, b_1)$ for the following reason. The intersection between $\{*\}$ and $\{a_1\}$ is the set $\{a_1\}$. So, the combination of the elements (*) and $(b_1 \mid a_1)$ is $(*, b_1)$. Note that $m_1(*) = 0.6$ means that there is support for the whole domain of attribute A.

[1] We note that probability is the term that is used by the authors in [2].

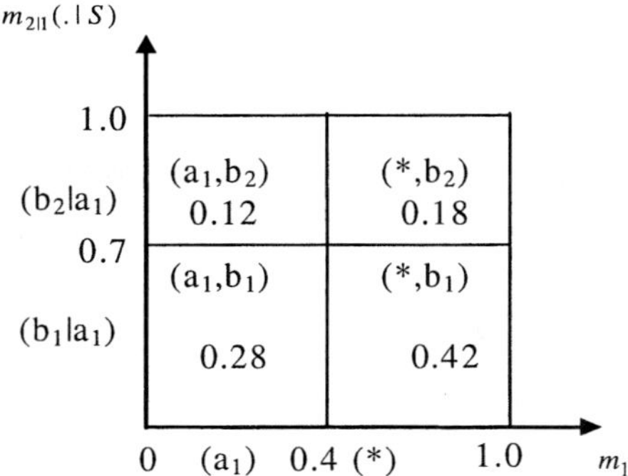

Fig. 5. Graphical representation of the combination of m_1 and $m_{2|1}(.|S)$

Z	*A B*
z	0.28 $[a_1, b_1]$ 0.12 $[a_1, b_2]$ 0.42 $[*, b_1]$ 0.18$[*, b_2]$

(a)

	Bel	*Pl*
$[a_1, b_1]$	0.28	0.7
$[a_1, b_2]$	0.12	0.3
$[*, b_1]$	0.7	0.7
$[*, b_2]$	0.3	0.3

(b)

Fig. 6. (a) Join result between R_1 and R_2 and (b) Corresponding belief and plausibility values

However, no statement can be made about the distribution of 0.6 among the subsets of the domain of A. Since now the subset $\{a_1\}$ is of interest, we consider this set as option. A similar reasoning holds for the support of pair $(*, b_2)$.

Consequently, the join between relations R_1 and R_2 is given in Fig. 6(a) and the corresponding belief and plausibility values for the different pairs are given in Fig 6(b).

The belief and plausibility values for attributes *A* and *B* are in line with the intuition as proposed in [2]. Note, that in this example we have support for the set $\{a_1\}$ with a bpa value of 0.4 and support for the set $\{b_1\}$ with value 0.7, given that there is support for $\{a_1\}$. Therefore, we have a belief of 0.4*0.7 = 0.28 for the pair (a_1, b_1). However, it might be that the support for $\{a_1\}$ is 1.0, since a bpa value 0.6 is assigned to the set $\{*\}$, which contains the set $\{a_1\}$. Therefore, intuitively, the plausibility that pair (a_1, b_1) may occur is 1.0*0.7 = 0.7.

[**Example 5.3]** Consider the snapshots of two relations called ship and description.

ship

name	type
Maria	0.6 [Frigate] 0.3 [Tugboat] 0.1[*]

description

type	max-speed
Frigate	0.7 [20-knots] 0.3 [30-knots]
Tugboat	1.0 [15-knots]

The relation ship describes the type of a ship that an observed ship might be. For example, intelligence has been gathered to conclude that Maria may be either a Frigate with confidence 0.6 or a Tugboat with confidence 0.3, while some evidences leave us in doubt about the type of Maria. Therefore, 0.1 is assigned to all possible types of ships. The relation description describes the maximal speed and the confidence in this speed under the condition that the type of a ship is known before-hand. So, the bpa assigned to the attribute max-speed is dependent on type. Perhaps unnecessarily, we note that if we want to answer a question like "What is the maximum speed of Maria?", we have to perform a join between above mentioned relations.

To compute a join between the relations ship and description on the attribute max-speed, we have to perform two combinations, namely a combination of the tuple of ship with the first tuple of description, and a combination of the tuple of ship with the second tuple of description.

The combination of the tuple (Maria {0.6 [Frigate], 0.3 [Tugboat], 0.1 [*]}) of ship with the tuple (Frigate, {0.7 [20-knots], 0.3 [30-knots]}) of description results in the left part of Figure 7. Note, Frigate is a fixed set in the left part of Figure 7, while in the right part of Figure 7 Tugboat is a fixed set. On the horizontal axis the bpa of attribute type of relation ship is depicted, called m_{ship}, and on the vertical axis the dependent bpa $m_{\text{desc} | \text{ship-Fr}}$ corresponding to the first tuple of relation description is depicted. For a similar reasoning as in Example 3.2, the bpa pertaining to relation ship is modeled as an independent bpa. The combination of the bpa values of the pairs (Tugboat) and (30-knots | Frigate) results in a bpa value 0.3 *0.7 =0.21 for the pair (Tugboat,*) (lower middle rectangle in the right part of Figure 7). In this case, we have support for Tugboat, but this definitely does not mean support for Frigate, and therefore there is no support for a specific set of values of max-speed. For the combination of the bpa's of the remaining sets, a similar reasoning can be followed as in Example 3.2.

The combination of (Maria {0.6 [Frigate], 0.3 [Tugboat], 0.1 [*]}) of relation ship with the second tuple (Tugboat, {1.0 [15-knots]}) of relation description results in the right part of Figure 7.

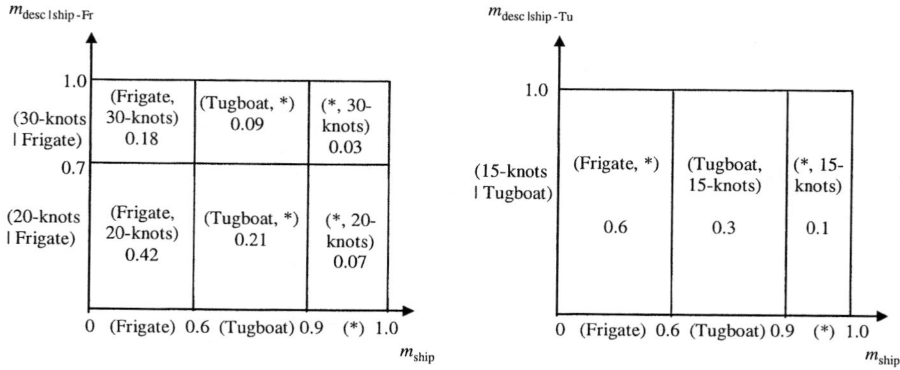

Fig. 7. Graphical representation of the combination of the bpa's corresponding to ship and description

Name		type max-speed
Maria	0.42	[Frigate, 20-knots]
	0.18	[Frigate, 30-knots]
	0.3	[Tugboat, *]
	0.07	[*, 20-knots]
	00.3	[*, 30-knots]
Maria	0.6	[Frigate,*]
	0.3	[Tugboat, 15-knots]
	0.1	[*, 15-knots]

(a)

	Bel	*Pl*
$m_{ship} \oplus m_{desc \mid ship\text{-}Fr}$		
[Frigate, 20-knots]	0.42	0.49
[Frigate, 30-knots]	0.18	0.21
[Tugboat,*]	0.3	0.4
[*, 20-knots]	0.49	0.49
[*, 30-knots]	0.21	0.21
$m_{ship} \oplus m_{desc \mid ship\text{-}Tu}$		
[Frigate,*]	0.6	0.7
[Tugboat, 15-knots]	0.3	0.4
[*, 15-knots]	0.4	0.4

(b)

Fig. 8. (a) Join result between ship and description and (b) Corresponding Bel and Pl values

The result of the join between the relations ship and description together with the corresponding belief and plausibility values is given in Figure 8.

We note that the belief and plausibility values are in line with our intuition. For example, the belief of 0.42 that Maria is a Frigate and has a maximum speed of 20-knots can be understood by the fact that the bpa for a Frigate recorded in the relation ship is 0.6 and the bpa that the maximum speed is 20-knots for a Frigate is 0.7 (recorded in the relation description). The plausibility value of 0.49 for the same pair can be understood by the fact that a bpa of 0.1 is assigned to each possible subset of ships in relation ship, implying ignorance. It might be the case that the bpa of 0.1 belongs to Frigate. Therefore, the plausibility that a ship is a Frigate with a maximum speed of 20 knots is (0.6 + 0.1)*0.7 = 0.49.

6 Conclusion and Further Research

Many researchers have pointed out that there is a need to handle uncertainty and ignorance in database applications. Most of the efforts applied probability theory to capture uncertainty and ignorance. As has been argued in Section 2, probability theory is suitable to capture uncertainty but *not* to capture ignorance. In this paper, we have proposed a framework to capture uncertainty and ignorance in an integrated way. Although our framework can be tailored to different type of data models, we elaborate it for the relational model. We assume that an attribute can assume a set of values instead of a single value. And we assign, inspired by the Dempster-Shafer theory [5,11,15], a so-called basic probability assignment (bpa) to an attribute. However, the properties of the Dempster-Shafer theory appeared insufficient to support joins. Therefore, we extended the theory with the notion of a "dependent" bpa. Such a bpa provides us the possibility to take dependencies between data into account. Based on the notion of dependent bpa, we came up with a combination rule to combine a bpa, m_1, with a bpa that is dependent on m_1. As has been shown, the application of this combination rule solves the problem of information loss that occurs as a consequence of joins. Until now, the problem of information loss was posed as an open problem in the literature [2]. Furthermore, in our model we have a clear semantics of ignorance.

A topic for further research is the formalization of the basic operators in the context of our model. The study of aggregation operators and nested operators is also a topic for further research. Furthermore, in the context of optimization our extended model gives cause for the study of a number of issues, such as the control of the complexity behavior of our combination rule, query optimization and so on.

References

1. Al-Khalifa, S., Yu, C., Jagadish, H.V., Querying Structured Text in XML Database, Int. Conf. ACM SIGMOD 2003.
2. Barbara, D., Garcia-Molina, H., Porter, D., A Probabilistic Relational Data Model, in Proc. Int. Conference on Extending Database Technology, 1990, pp. 60-74.
3. Cavallo, R., Pittarelli, M., The Theory of Probabilistic Databases, iProc. VLDB Int. Conf. on Very Large Databases 1987
4. Choenni, R., Blok, H.E., Fokkinga, M., Extending the Relational Model with Uncertainty and Ignorance, Technical Report, University of Twente.
5. Dempster, A.P., Upper and Lower Probabilities Induced by a Multi-Valued Mapping, in Annals Math. Stat. 38, pp.325-339.
6. Dey, D., Sarkar, S., A Probabilistic Relational Model and Algebra . ACM TODS 21(3), 1996, pp. 339-369.
7. Fuhr, N., A Probabilistic Relational Model for the Integration of IR and Databases, ACM SIGIR 93, pp. 309-317.
8. Güntzer, U., Kießling, W., Thöne, H. New Directions for Uncertainty Reasoning in Deductive Databases. In Proc. ACM SIGMOD, Int Conf. on Management of Data, 1991, pp. 178-187
9. Gelenbe, E., Hebrail, G., A Probability Model of Uncertainty in Databases, in Proc. ICDE Int. Conf. on Data Engineering, 1986, pp. 328-333.
10. Hung, E., Getoor, L., Subrahmaniam, PXML: A Probabilistic Semi-structured Data Model and Algebra, Int. Conf. on Data Engineering 2003.
11. Halpern, J.Y., Fagin, R., Two views of belief: belief as generalized probability and belief as evidence, in Artificial Intelligence 54, pp. 275-317.
12. Lakshmanan, L., Sadri, F., Modelling Uncertainty in Deductive Databases, in Proc. Databases, Expert Systems and Applications, 1994.
13. Lee, S-K, An Extended Relational Database Model for Uncertain and Imprecise Information, in Proc. VLDB, Int. Conf. on Very Large Databases, 1992, 211-220.
14. Raju, K, Majumdar, A. Fuzzy Functional Dependencies and Lossles Join Decomposition of Fuzzy Relational Database Systems, ACM TODS 13(2), 1988, 129-166.
15. Shafer, G., A Mathematical Theory of Evidence, Princeton University Press, Princeton 1976, 297p.
16. Wong, E., A Statistical Approach to Incomplete Information in Database Systems. ACM TODS 7(3), 1982.

Appendix

Perhaps one might think that the KNMI problem of Section 2 can be solved by probability theory by choosing a suitable model for the outcome space. One could argue to choose the outcome space as follows $\Omega = \{[\text{wet}], [\text{dry}], [\text{wet, dry}]\}$. Then we can use probability theory to reason about this space. We define now a probability function p: $\Omega \rightarrow [0,1]$. Let say p([dry]) = 0.6, p([wet]) = 0.2, and p([dry, wet]) =0.2. If we compute the probability of the union of wet and dry, then p([dry] $\cup$ [wet]) = p([dry]) + p([wet]) = 0.8, which is in contradiction with p([dry, wet]) =0.2.

PMJoin: Optimizing Distributed Multi-way Stream Joins by Stream Partitioning

Yongluan Zhou[1], Ying Yan[2], Feng Yu[1], and Aoying Zhou[2]

[1] National University of Singapore
[2] Fudan University

Abstract. In emerging data stream applications, data sources are typically distributed. Evaluating multi-join queries over streams from different sources may incur large communication cost. As queries run continuously, the precious bandwidths would be aggressively consumed without careful optimization of operator ordering and placement. In this paper, we focus on the optimization of continuous multi-join queries over distributed streams. We observe that by partitioning streams into substreams we can significantly reduce the communication cost and hence propose a novel partition-based join scheme - PMJoin. A few partitioning techniques are studied. To generate the query plan for each substream, a heuristic algorithm is proposed based on a rate-based model. Results from an extensive experimental study show that our techniques can sufficiently reduce the communication cost.

1 Introduction

Many recently emerging applications, such as network management, financial monitoring, sensor networks, stock tickers etc, fueled the development of continuous query processing techniques over data streams. In these applications, the data sources are typically distributed, e.g. the network hosts or routers in network management. Collecting all the data to a centralized server may not be cost-effective due to the high communication cost. Clearly, a distributed stream processing system is inevitable. Unlike traditional DBMS, where the processing in each node involves expensive I/O operations, stream processing systems often perform main memory operations. These operations are relatively inexpensive in comparison to the communication cost. As both the queries and data streams are continuous, a lot of existing work, such as [2], focus on minimizing the communication cost, especially when the source nodes are connected by a wide-area network. Furthermore, as the streams are continuous and unbounded, a rate-based cost model has to be used.

In this paper, we focus on multi-way window join query which is an important and expensive type of continuous queries. These queries may involve multiple streams from different source nodes. Let us look at an example drawn from the network management application.

Example 1. We want to monitor the traffic that passes through three routers and has the same destination host within the last 0.5 seconds. Data collected from

M.L. Lee, K.L. Tan, and V. Wuwongse (Eds.): DASFAA 2006, LNCS 3882, pp. 325–341, 2006.

Table 1. Distribution (tuples/ second)

S_i	S_1	S_2	S_3	$S_{1,2}$	$S_{1,3}$	$S_{2,3}$
λ_i	100.2	50.07	50.03	9.003	7.001	2.0008
λ_i^a	0.1	0.03	50	0.003	5	1.5
λ_i^b	0.1	50	0.01	5	0.001	0.5
λ_i^c	100	0.04	0.02	4	2	0.0008

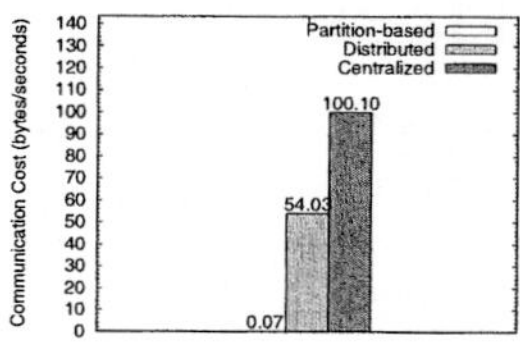

Fig. 1. Communication cost of plans

the three routers feed three streams s_1, s_2 and s_3 to three processing nodes n_1, n_2 and n_3. The content of each stream tuple includes the destination host ip *dest* of a data packet and possibly other information. This task can be represented in a three-way window join query $S_1 \bowtie_{S_1.dest=S_2.dest} S_2 \bowtie_{S_2.dest=S_3.dest} S_3$ where the window size of each stream is 0.5 seconds. □

In Table 1, λ_i denotes the rate of stream S_i and λ_i^a denotes the rate of tuples from S_i whose value in the *dest* attribute is a. Furthermore, $S_{i,j}$ is the result stream of $S_i \bowtie S_j$ and its rate is denoted as $\lambda_{i,j}$. The minimum communication cost that can be achieved under different schemes are as follows:

1. Centralized scheme: The best plan in this category is to send both S_2 and S_3 to n_1. If we assume the tuple size of every stream is 1 byte, then this scheme results in communication cost of $\lambda_2 + \lambda_3 = 100.1$(bytes/sec).
2. Distributed scheme: In this category, the best plan is to send S_3 to n_2 first and then ship the result $S_{2,3}$ to n_1. If we assume the tuple size of a join result tuple is the sum of the two input tuples, we can derive the communication cost of this plan as $\lambda_3 + \lambda_{2,3} \times 2 \approx 54.03$(bytes/sec).
3. Partitioned-based scheme: taking a closer look at the problem, we can find that the arrival rates of tuples vary with different values in the joining attributes. Furthermore, the popularity of the values in different streams also vary. Hence the optimal plans for these tuples are also different. For example in Table 1, $dest = a$ is popular in S_3 while it is unpopular in the other two streams. Hence the best plan for these tuples is to ship them from S_2 to n_1 to join with S_1 and then the resulting tuples are sent to n_3 to join with S_3. This results in the cost of 0.036 (bytes/sec). However, for those tuples with $dest = b$, the best plan is totally different: those tuples from S_3 should be sent to n_1 and then to n_2. By exploiting this characteristic, the minimum communication cost that we can get for Example 1 is approximately 0.07 (bytes/sec).

In this paper, we focus on the static optimization of multi-join queries. Static optimization can be applied to applications where the stream's characteristics are relatively stable and their changes are predictable. Moreover, given that our problem has not been previously studied, it is important to examine how static optimization can be performed before extending the work to a dynamic context. To summarize, our main contributions are as follows:

- We formulate the problem and propose a heuristic-based optimization algorithm to decide the join operation locations and the tuple routing orders based on a rate-based cost model.
- To further reduce the communication cost, we propose a novel join scheme: PMJoin. We also study different partitioning strategies (e.g., rate-based, hash, etc).
- We fully implemented the system and run a simulation study. The study shows the efficiency of our techniques.

The rest of the paper is organized as follows. Section 2 reviews the related work. Section 3 presents the proposed techniques. In Section 4, we perform extensive performance studies on our implementation. Section 6 concludes the paper.

2 Related Work

Distributed processing of multi-way join have already been extensively studied in the context of traditional relational database systems. [13] provides a thorough survey on this area. The optimizers in Distributed INGRES [9] and System R* [14] consider both CPU and I/O cost as well as the communication cost of processing a whole dataset. In these systems the I/O cost are so high that they cannot be omitted. SDD-1 [7] uses heuristics to optimize the utilization of semi-join. Semi-join is useful when a tuple is much larger than a single attribute and the selectivity is low. However, semi-join is not readily applicable to window join processing. This is because streams are normally continuous and queries should be evaluated in a nearly real time manner. For example, a tuple t_i may be pruned away because there is no matching tuples in the opposite window. However, new tuples may arrive at the opposite window which may match t_i. Extra complicated mechanisms have to be introduced to ensure the correctness. As shown in our study, we believe our PMJoin, together with the optimization heuristics, is a promising alternative to reduce the communication cost. Our techniques can also be adapted for traditional passive data processing whose performance needs further study. The above-mentioned systems and a considerable amount of work (e.g. [8, 16, 21]) have also exploited horizontal fragmentation of relations to increase the parallelism and consequently to reduce the response time. Static and dynamic data allocation [3, 17, 20] try to allocate replications to reduce communication cost or to balance the load on servers. However, none of the above techniques exploit generating different plans for different partitions. Furthermore, a rate-based cost model has to be used in our problem.

[12] studies techniques for the evaluation of window join queries over data streams. [19, 10] examine the processing of multiple joins over data streams. [4, 15, 5, 6] investigate the static and adaptive ordering of operators for continuous queries over data streams. However, all these studies focus on centralized processing. There are also several recent efforts devoted to extending centralized schemes to distributed context. [1] proposes the design of a distributed stream system. [2] studies the operator placement problem for stream processing. However, these approaches assume there is an already optimized query plan and then

allocate the operators, while our approach does not impose such an assumption. Furthermore, they do not explore partitioning of the streams to further optimize the plans. In [18], the operators are assumed to have been allocated, and the proposed scheme adaptively decides the routing order of the tuples.

3 Distributed Multi-join

In this section, we first formulate the problem and then present the scheme to generate a query plan for each substream. It also applies to the case without stream partitioning. Then we study how stream partitioning can be applied to minimize communication cost.

3.1 Problem Formulation

In our system, there is a set of geographically distributed data stream sources $\Sigma = \{S_1, S_2, \cdots, S_{|\Sigma|}\}$ and a set of distributed processing nodes $\mathcal{N} = \{n_1, n_2, \cdots, n_{|\mathcal{N}|}\}$ interconnected by a widely distributed overlay network. Since the data stream sources in practice may not have the ability to communicate with multiple nodes, we separate the data sources from the processing system by assigning nodes as delegations of data sources. Streams are routed to the various processing nodes through their delegated nodes. A multi-way window join query may involve streams from multiple nodes. For simplicity, we assume the queries do not involve stored tables.

As mentioned before, our main concern is to minimize the communication cost. We adopt the unit-time cost paradigm and hence communication cost of a processing scheme Ω can be computed as $C(\Omega) = \frac{Amount\ of\ communications\ (in\ bytes)}{Observation\ period}$.

The formal problem statement is: *Given a m-way window join* ($\forall m < |\Sigma|$) *query Q, which involves a set of streams* Σ *and they are located at a set of nodes* $\mathcal{N}$*, find a join scheme* Ω *so that the total communication cost* $C(\Omega)$ *is minimized.*

3.2 Join Operation Locations and Tuple Routing Orders

Before processing the queries, we have to first decide the placement of the join operators. Then we have to route the streams and the intermediate result streams (if necessary) around the nodes. In this subsection, we focus on how to decide the location of the join operations as well as the routing order of the tuples for each substream. Since it also applies to streams without partitioning and we treat each substream independently, we use the term "stream" instead of "substream" in the following discussions. The evaluation of the join operations allocated to each node can use any of the existing centralized join optimization and processing techniques, e.g. [19, 10]. In this paper, we assume the join operations in each node are evaluated using MJoin [19]. In this technique, one in-memory index structure, e.g. hash tables, is built for each joining stream. The joining stream could be a source stream or an intermediate result stream generated by another node. When a tuple from a joining stream arrives, it would be inserted into its corresponding index structure, and be used to probe other index structures one by one to evaluate the query. The optimization of the probing order has already been studied in centralized processing literatures [4, 6, 19] and would not be considered in this paper.

Notations and Cost Model. Let the set of streams and the set of nodes involved in the query Q be Σ and $\mathcal{N}$, respectively. The set of streams that are located in $n_i \in \mathcal{N}$ is denoted as Σ_i. The result stream of $S_i \bowtie S_j$ is denoted as $S_{i,j}$ and the result stream of $S_{i,j} \bowtie S_k$ is denoted as $S_{i,j,k}$ and so on. If two streams are located at one node, we say that they are co-located. A function $col_{i,j}$ is defined as follows:

$$col_{i,j} = \begin{cases} 0 & : \quad S_i \text{ and } S_j \text{ are co-located} \\ 1 & : \quad \text{otherwise} \end{cases} \tag{1}$$

We adopt a rate-based cost model similar to the one developed in [5]. The arrival rates of streams S_i and $S_{i,j}$ are denoted as λ_i and $\lambda_{i,j}$, respectively. Let W_i and W_j be the expected number of tuples in the window of S_i and S_j, respectively. For a tuple-based window, W_i is equal to the window size K_i, while for a time-based window, W_i is equal to $\lambda_i \cdot T_i$, where T_i is the window size. To estimate $\lambda_{i,j}$, we note that for every unit time, λ_i tuples from S_i and λ_j tuples from S_j would be used to probe the windows of S_j and S_i, respectively. Out of the $\lambda_i \cdot W_j + \lambda_j \cdot W_i$ pairs of tuples, $f \times (\lambda_i \cdot W_j + \lambda_j \cdot W_i)$ matches are expected to be found, where f is the join selectivity. Therefore the expected number of tuples generated by $S_i \bowtie S_j$ per unit time can be estimated as

$$\lambda_{i,j} = f \times (\lambda_i \cdot W_j + \lambda_j \cdot W_i) \tag{2}$$

The tuples in the active window of the result stream $S_{i,j}$ are composed of those result tuples that are the join results of the tuples in the active window of S_i and S_j. Hence the expected number of tuples in the active window of $S_{i,j}$ can be computed as

$$W_{i,j} = f \cdot W_i \cdot W_j \tag{3}$$

Eqs. (2) and (3) can be recursively applied to obtain the values for multiple joins. Furthermore, it should be noted that the output rate and the window of the join result of a set of streams are independent of how the join is performed. Hence for a given distributed query plan, we can compute its unit-time communication cost by computing the rates of the streams that are sent over the network.

A Heuristic Algorithm. Given the above cost model, we can use a specific searching algorithm to search a specific solution space. For example, we can use dynamic programming to select an optimal plan from all the left deep tree plans. The computation complexity of the algorithm is $O(n!)$. However, as we will see soon, the search algorithm has to be applied several times in our partition-based join approach. Hence we will propose a much cheaper algorithm which runs in $O(n^2)$ time. Algorithm 1 shows the proposed stream join optimization algorithm.

Algorithm 1. STREAMJOINOPT(Σ, G)

```
Input: Σ: A set of streams;
G: A join graph over Σ;
begin
    for each n_i ∈ N do
        Sort Σ_i in increasing arrival rates;
        for j = 0; j < |Σ_i|; j++ do
            for k = j + 1; k < |Σ_i|; k++ do
                if λ_{Σ_i[j]⋈Σ_i[k]} < λ_{Σ_i[j]} then
                    Label the join between Σ_i[j] and Σ_i[k] as local;
                    Σ_i[j] ← Σ_i[j] ⋈ Σ_i[k];
                    Σ_i ← Σ_i − Σ_i[k];
    Sort Σ in increasing arrival rates;
    while |Σ| > 1 do
        Σ_p ← the slowest stream S_i;
        Σ− = S_i;
        repeat
            cost ← MaxNumber;
            for each stream S_j joinable with any stream in Σ_p do
                if C(Σ_p + S_j) < cost then
                    k ← j;
                    cost ← C(Σ_p + S_j);
            label the edges that connect any stream in Σ_p and S_j as pending;
            if case (1) is chosen then
                assign all the pending join operations to the node of S_j;
                S_p ← Collapse Σ_p and S_k to one node ;
                Σ_p ← S_p;
            else
                Σ_p+ = S_k; Σ− = S_k;
        until |Σ_p| = 1;
        Insert Σ_p into Σ;
end
```

The input of the algorithm is the set of streams Σ involved by the query as well as the join graph representation G of the query. A join graph consists of a set of vertices each representing a stream and a set of edges each representing a join operation between the two connected streams. Furthermore, each vertex in the graph is annotated with the source node of the corresponding stream. We use the following example to illustrate.

Example 2. A query joins 5 streams: S_0, S_1, S_2, S_3 and S_4 which are spread over 3 nodes. Figure 2(a) shows the join graph of this query. The location of each stream is drawn around each vertex. The selectivities of the join operations are also drawn around the corresponding edges. Columns $2 - 6$ in Table 2 list the

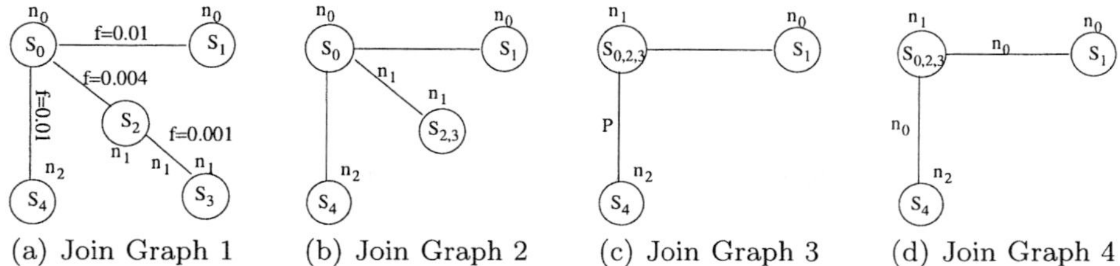

Fig. 2. Processing steps for an example query

Table 2. Parameters of streams

S_i	S_0	S_1	S_2	S_3	S_4	$S_{2,3}$	$S_{0,2,3}$
λ_i	10	35	25	30	15	15	9
W_i	100	350	250	300	150	75	30

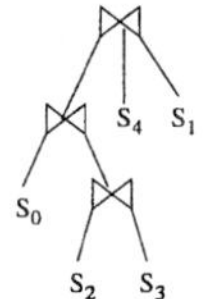

Fig. 3. The plan tree

arrival rates λ_i and the expected number of tuples in the window W_i of these source streams.

For brevity, we assume that tuples from every stream (either a source stream or an intermediate result stream) have the same sizes in the following discussions. The adoption of this assumption does not lose any generality as we can always incorporate the tuple sizes in the calculation of cost without changing the algorithm.

At the first step (lines 2 - 9) of the algorithm, we find whether there is any locally evaluable join operation which can result in a stream whose rate is smaller than both joining streams. Evaluating these joins locally tends to reduce the potential communication cost if some of the streams need to be shipped out to other sites. For Example 2, there are two locally evaluable joins: $S_0 \bowtie S_1$ and $S_2 \bowtie S_3$. By using Equations (2) and (3), $\lambda_{S_0 \bowtie S_1}$ and $\lambda_{S_2 \bowtie S_3}$ can be estimated as 70 and 15, respectively. Hence we choose to allocate $S_2 \bowtie S_3$ to n_1 and we label the corresponding edge with n_1. For ease of processing, once a join operation is allocated, we would collapse the two connected vertices in the join graph and the resulting vertex represents their join result stream. By applying this to Figure 2(a), we can derive Figure 2(b). The rate and window size of $S_{2,3}$ are also listed in column 6 of Table 2.

In the second part (lines 10 - 28) of the algorithm, we employ a heuristic approach to allocate the remaining join operations. There are two nested loops in this part. For each iteration of the outer loop, we will determine the location of a subset of join operations. First, we pick a stream with the smallest rate, say S_i. This is because it may result in less communication cost if S_i has to be transmitted over the network. Next, to evaluate the join between S_i and each of the other streams S_j that are joinable with S_i, we have two cases:

1. Send S_i to the node of S_j. The potential communication cost of this case is equal to the sum of the cost of sending S_i to the node of S_j and the potential cost of sending out the result stream of $S_i \bowtie S_j$, i.e. $\lambda_i \cdot col_{i,j} + \lambda_{i,j}$. The second term is to count the potential cost of sending out the result stream to perform other join operations.
2. Send both S_i and S_j to a third site. The potential cost of this case is $\lambda_i + \lambda_j$.

For each stream, the case with smaller cost is used. We greedily choose a stream S_k with the smallest estimated cost and move it from Σ to Σ_p. If case (1) is chosen for S_k, that means the join operation is already allocated. We will remove streams S_i and S_k from Σ and add the result stream $S_{i,k}$ to Σ and start a new iteration. Correspondingly, in the join graph, we will collapse nodes S_i and S_k into one node $S_{i,k}$. However, if case (2) is chosen for S_k, that means the join operation is still pending for allocation. We will search for another stream S_l that is joinable to any stream in Σ_p with the smallest cost. The cost estimation is similar to the above analysis. To ease the presentation of the algorithm, we define the following function:

$$C(\Sigma_p + S_j) = \min\{ \sum_{S_i \in \Sigma_p} \lambda_i + \lambda_j, \sum_{S_i \in \Sigma_p} \lambda_i \cdot col_{i,j} + \lambda_{\Sigma_p,i} \} \quad (4)$$

For example, in Figure 2(b), we first add the slowest stream S_0 to Σ_p. Then for the three joinable streams $S_1, S_{2,3}$ and S_4, using Eqs. (2), (3) and (4), we can find that $C(\Sigma_p + S_{2,3})$ is the smallest. Furthermore, case (1) should happen, i.e. S_0 will be sent to node n_1 to perform the join with $S_{2,3}$. Hence we label the edge between S_0 and $S_{2,3}$ with n_1. Then we collapse nodes S_0 and $S_{2,3}$ to one node $S_{0,2,3}$. This results in Figure 2(c). The rate and window of $S_{0,2,3}$ is computed using Eqs. (2) and (3) and listed in column 7 of Table 2. Now a new iteration of the outer loop in the second part of the algorithm has to be started. The currently slowest stream is $S_{0,2,3}$, hence it is added to Σ_p. Among the two joinable streams S_1 and S_4, the potential cost of adding S_4 is smaller. This time, case (2) is chosen, i.e. $S_{0,2,3}$ and S_4 have to be sent to a third site. We label the edge between node $S_{0,2,3}$ and S_4 with a P to indicate that the join operation is pending for allocation. Then the last stream S_1 has to be chosen and S_1 and $S_{0,2,3}$ have to be sent to n_0 to perform the joins. Now the two join operations can be labeled with n_0. Then all the join operations have already been allocated.

The output plan of Algorithm 1 can be represented using a tree. In the tree, each leaf node is a source stream and each intermediate node is an MJoin operator. Each MJoin operator is located in one node and has two or more input streams. We order these streams in the order such that the right most stream (or abbreviated as the right stream) have the same location with the MJoin operator. That means all the other input streams of this MJoin operator would be sent over to the location of the right stream to perform the join operations. Figure 3 shows the tree representation of the output plan of Example 2.

3.3 Stream Partitioning

In a partition-based scheme, each stream S_i may be partitioned into D substreams $S_i^1, S_i^2, \ldots, S_i^D$ based on the values on the joining attribute. This is based on the observation that the arrival rates of tuples with different values may vary much inside each single stream. Hence the optimal scheme for these tuples are different. We denote the rate of a substream S_i^k as λ_i^k.

PMJoin. In this subsection, we will look at how the partition-based join can be applied to a multi-way equijoin query whose join predicates are specified on a single attribute, say *attr*. This kind of queries is common in a lot of applications, such as Example 1 in Section 1. Furthermore, these could also be a subset of predicates in a multi-way join query that are specified on the same attribute. We propose a scheme that is called Partition-based Multi-way Join (PMJoin) to evaluate this set of join predicates. Every stream involved in these join predicates is partitioned into multiple substreams on *attr*. The substreams of all the streams can be grouped into D groups. The kth group of substreams is $\{S_1^k, S_2^k, \ldots, S_{|\mathcal{N}|}^k\}$. For each group of substreams, we can use Algorithm 1 to decide the allocation of the join operations.

We illustrate the plan of PMJoin by using Example 1. First, based on the value of the *dest* attribute, we partition each stream into three substreams S_i^a, S_i^b and S_i^c. These streams are grouped into three groups. Then for each group of substreams, we use Algorithm 1 to optimize the plan. The resulting plans for the three groups of substreams are shown in Figure 4.

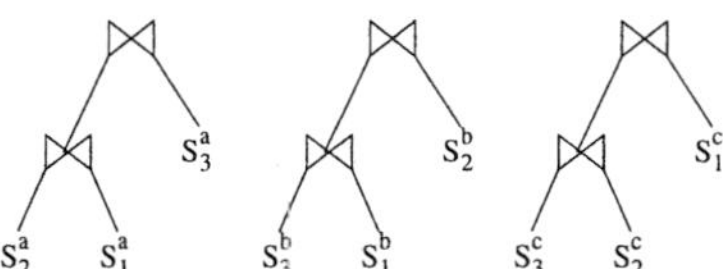

Fig. 4. Plans for the substreams in Example 1

To get the lowest cost, we can partition each stream into as many substreams as possible. For example, we can put tuples with each distinct value in the joining attribute into one substream. Let the number of these values be R then we could partition the stream into R substreams. However, it is clear that with more partitions, more plans have to be generated and it complicates the processing. So we adopt a more flexible approach where the number of partitions can be specified as any D. This can be viewed as clustering the above finest substreams (i.e., one substream per value) into D partitions. In the following discussions, we refer to these finest substreams as FStreams. FS_i^k stands for the kth FStream from stream S_i. And the unique *attr* value of the tuples of a FStream is called the value of the FStream. We consider three approaches:

1. Hash partition. A hash function can be applied to hash the values of the FStreams into one of the D buckets. The FStreams in each bucket compose a substream. This is actually a random partitioning method.

2. Range partition. Divide the data range into D sub-ranges. FStreams whose values fall into the ith sub-range compose the ith substream.

3. Rate-based partition. The above two approaches ignore the arrival rates of the various FStreams. A good partitioning method should put those groups of FStreams whose optimal plans are similar to each other in one partition. In this way, the generated plan for that partition would be good for all its FStreams. Here we use an approximate approach to estimate the similarity of the optimal plans of two groups of FStreams. For each group of FStreams, $\{FS_1^k, FS_2^k, \ldots, FS_{|\mathcal{N}|}^k\}$, we sort them in increasing order of their arrival rates. Then we create a vector V_k where the ith element indicates the position of FS_i^k in the above sorted list. For example, if we have a sorted list as $\langle FS_3^k, FS_1^k, FS_2^k \rangle$, then $V_k = \langle 2, 3, 1 \rangle$. So the distance between the kth and the lth groups of FStreams is measured by the distance between V_k and V_l, which is measured as $|V_k - V_l|$. The intuition is that the more similar the sorted lists of the two groups of FStreams are, the more similar their optimal plans would be. Now we can employ any clustering techniques to cluster the groups of FStreams into D clusters. In this paper, we adopt the k-Means approach [11].

To apply all the above mechanisms, we need to know the rate of each FStream. To reduce the cost of maintaining such statistics, we can use traditional histogram approaches. Only statistics of histogram buckets are maintained, and the rates of an FStream is estimated based on the statistics of the bucket it belongs to.

Multi-join on different attributes. For a generic multi-join query whose joins involve multiple attributes, our approach works as follows. We first run Algorithm 1 to determine the plan for the scheme without partitioning. Given the output plan of Algorithm 1, we will try to find out several sets of join predicates where we can apply PMJoin.

We call a MJoin operator to be *partitionable* on *attr* if the join predicates in the Mjoin operator are all (equalities) on the same attribute *attr*. The procedure to find the subset of join predicates to apply partitioning works in two steps. In the first step, from the output plan of Algorithm 1, we try to aggressively determine the subsets of join predicates that can be partitioned by using Algorithm 2. The algorithm starts from the root. If the current operator is found to be partitionable on an attribute, say *attr*, it would be marked as a PMJoin operator. Then if any child of the current operator is also partitionable on *attr*, it would merge that child with the current operator. Note that after the merge, the prior grandchildren would become children of the current operator. These new children would also be searched to see if they can be merged. After the merging attempt, we recursively call the algorithm on each child of the current operator.

In the second step, we try to select some of the PMJoins from those found by the above algorithm. Note that the output stream of a PMJoin consists of a number of substreams that would be located at several sites. For example, the result stream $S_{1,2,3}$ of Example 1 consists of three substreams that are located at n_1, n_2 and n_3. Now suppose the result stream has to join with another steam,

Algorithm 2. FINDPARTITION(O_i)

```
Input: O_i: an MJoin operator ;
R: an boolean array, R[i] is true if O_i is the right child of its parent;
begin
    if !R[i] AND O_i is partitionable on an attribute attr then
        Mark O_i as PMJoin ;
        for each child operator O_j of O_i do
            if O_j is partitionable on attr then
                Merge O_j to O_i;

    for each child operator O_j of O_i do
        FindPartition(O_j);
end
```

say S_i, on another attribute. If PMJoin is used to join $S_{1,2,3}$ and S_i, we have to repartition the substreams of $S_{1,2,3}$ that are located at the three nodes. Furthermore, the substreams of S_i may have to be sent to all these three nodes. This results in high communication cost. Therefore, we opt to impose two constraints on the application of PMJoin. (1) The input streams of a PMJoin should be located at a single node. That means a PMJoin cannot be the child of another PMJoin. (2) The right child of a MJoin operator cannot be a PMJoin operator. Otherwise, the other input streams of the MJoin operator have to be sent over to the output nodes of that PMJoin.

Our heuristic, which is given below, favors those PMJoins that have high input stream rates. This is because they may provide more opportunities to reduce the communication cost by using PMJoin.

1. Sort all the PMJoins on the total input stream rates.
2. Remove the one with the largest input stream rate.
3. Remove the parent PMJoin (if any) from the sorted list, and restore it back to one or more MJoin operators.
4. If the list is not empty go to step 2.

4 Performance Study

In this section, we present a performance study of our techniques. We fully implemented the system using Java. To ease the control of experiments, we use a discrete event simulation package JavaSim to simulate the distributed processing effect. For each experiment, we would collect the total communication cost for every second. Without loss of generality, we assume that tuples from all the streams and the join result tuples have the same sizes. Hence we only count the number of tuples that are transmitted over the network. Without loss of generality, we assume the joining attributes are of integer values and the windows are all time-based windows specified in seconds. All the arrival rates are specified in the unit of tuples/second. To model different data frequencies, we use various

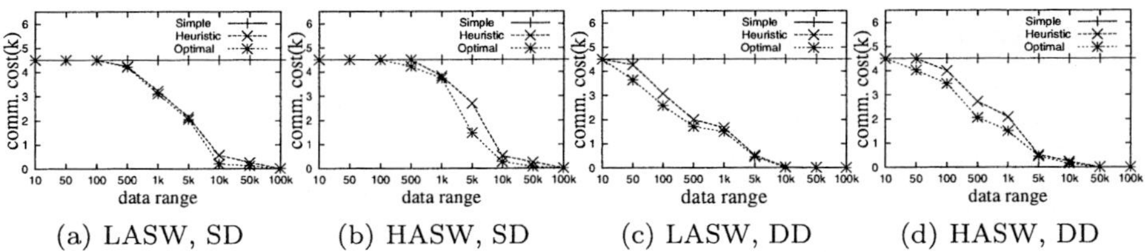

(a) LASW, SD (b) HASW, SD (c) LASW, DD (d) HASW, DD

Fig. 5. Performance of the Heuristic Algorithm

types of distributions. The value distributions are chosen from the following distributions: (1) Uniform distribution, (2) Normal distribution with the mean being the mid value and varied standard deviation, (3) Zipf distribution with the skew parameter θ varied from 0.1 to 1.5, (4) Self-Similar with the skew parameter h varied from 0.1 to 0.9. (For integers $1 \ldots N$, the first $h \cdot N$ integers gets $1 - h$ of the weight.) To examine the performance of our heuristic algorithm, we compare it with two algorithms: (1) Simple: send the other streams to the location of the stream with the highest rate; (2) Optimal: exhaustively enumerate the possible plans and choose the best one.

4.1 The Heuristic Optimization Algorithm

In the first experiment, we consider the following different situations: (1) streams with lower arrival rates have smaller window sizes (LASW); (2) streams with higher arrival rates have smaller window sizes (HASW). Both situations would be studied under two senarios: similar data distribution (SD) and different data distributions (DD). For the similar distribution scenarios, we randomly choose 10 zipfian distributions with the skew parameters varied from 0.1 to 0.3. For the case with different distributions, we randomly choose 10 distributions from all those listed above. We vary the data ranges from 1-10 to 1-100000. Note that query selectivities would be smaller with larger data ranges. Each stream is from a different node. Figure 5 presents the results of this experiment. From the figures, we can see that the communication cost of the Simple approach is constant to various data ranges. That is because this approach simply chooses to send all the other 9 streams to the location of the fastest stream. Thus, the communication cost is equal to the sum of these 9 streams. For the heuristic and the optimal approach, when data range is small, the communication cost are the same as that of Simple. The reason is the selectivities of the join operations are high and any intermediate result streams would have relatively large rates. Hence the best plan here is the same as Simple. However the communication cost of the heuristic and optimal approach drops with the increase in data ranges. That is because the join operations become more selective, hence it brings more benefits to perform distributed processing to minimize the communication cost. Furthermore, we can see that our heuristic algorithm performs very close to the optimal approaches under the 4 different situations.

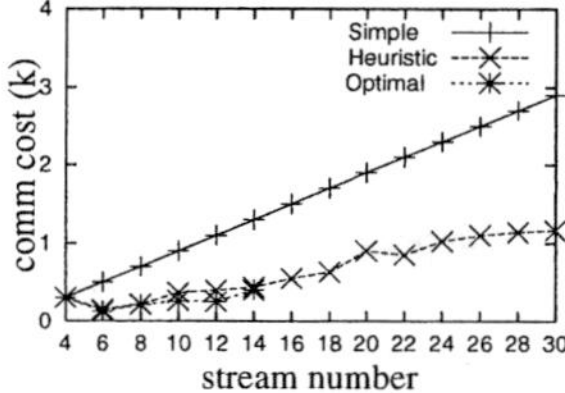

Fig. 6. #streams

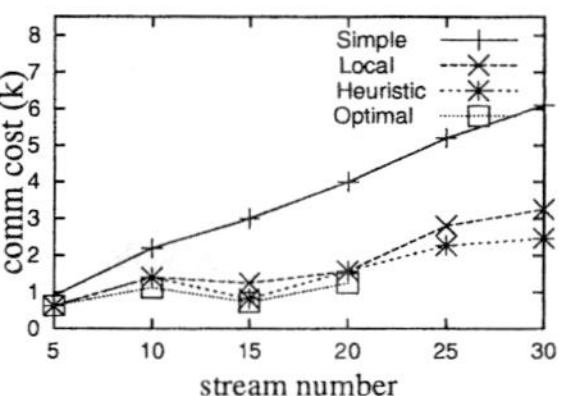

Fig. 7. #streams/node

In the second experiment, we study the effect of the number of streams. We fix the data range at 1-1000 and all the arrival rates at 100 tuples/second. We vary the number of streams and randomly choose the window sizes from 10 to 100 seconds. Data distributions are also randomly chosen. We compare our heuristic algorithm with the Simple method and the Optimal algorithm. Due to the long running time of the Optimal algorithm, we can only get the results up to 14 streams. The results are presented in Figure 6. We can see that the cost of the Simple method increases proportionally as the number of streams increases. The improvements of the heuristic approach and Optimal approach over the Simple method is larger with larger number of streams. That is because more steams provide more opportunities to optimize allocation of join operations to reduce the communication cost. Furthermore, we can see that the heuristic approach is very close to the Optimal algorithm.

In the third experiment, we examine the effect of the number of streams on each node, which is handled by the first step of our heuristic algorithm. We fix the number of nodes in this experiment to 5. The streams are randomly allocated to the nodes and their arrival rates are varied from 100 to 500. The other configurations are similar to the earlier experiment. We compare our heuristic to (a) Optimal: the optimal scheme and (b) Local: the one with the first step replaced by simply joining all the local streams. When the total number of streams increases, the average number of streams in each node also increases. The results are shown in Figure 7. We can see that our heuristic works better than Local. That is because it would only perform those joins that would reduce the rates, while Local would perform also those that may increase the rates.

4.2 PMJoin

In the first experiment, all the join predicates are equalities on a single attribute. Hence PMJoin can be used here. We use 10 streams with arrival rates varying from 10 to 1000 and window sizes randomly chosen from 10 to 100. We fix the data range of all the streams to 1-1000. Each stream is located at one node. We vary the partition number of our partition functions to examine the sensitivity of the PMJoin. Note that when the partition number is equal to 1, it is the same as the scheme without partitioning. When the partition number is the same as the data range, there is only one value in each partition. To examine the effect of the different partition methods, we study two cases: (1) the values in a "hot

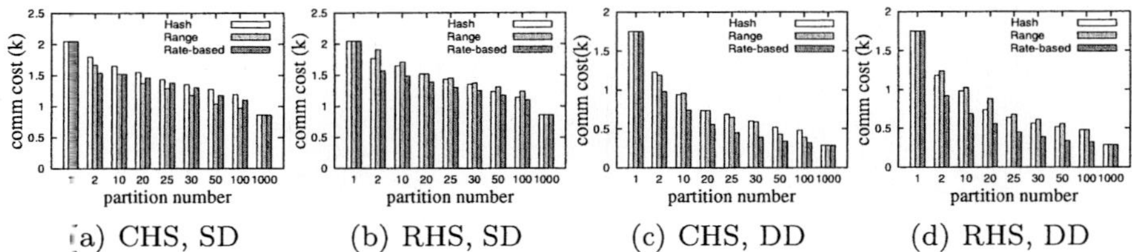

(a) CHS, SD (b) RHS, SD (c) CHS, DD (d) RHS, DD

Fig. 8. Performance of PMJoin

spot" is randomly spread over the data range (Random Hot Spot: RHS); (2) the values are contiguously located in the data range (Contiguous Hot Spot: CHS). Under each case, we also study two senarios: similar distribution (SD) and different distribution (DD) mentioned in Section 4.1. The results are shown in Figure 8. When streams have similar distributions, PMJoin has only moderate improvement over the non-partitioning approach. That is because the frequent values among the streams are similar. That means most of the substreams would have similar plans as that of the non-partitioning scheme. However, in the case of different distributions, we found that large communication cost can be saved even when the streams are partitioned into only two substreams. The reason is the optimal plans of the substreams are much different from each other. PMJoin optimizes their plans independently, hence results in less communication cost. Furthermore, as we can see, finer granularities of the partition function can result in larger improvements.

Furthermore, in Figure 8(a), range partition works the best most of the time. That is because in this situation, the groups of FStreams in a contiguous range would have similar optimal plans. Rate-based partition works better only when there are two partitions. The bad performance of Rate-based partition is due to the fact that the data distributions are all zipfian distributions. When there are more than two partitions, most of the groups of FStreams would have the same sorted list and hence the same vector V_k. So the distances between them are all 0. As a result, the k-Means clustering algorithm randomly places them into different partitions. However, for the other three conditions, rate-based partition works persistently the best. This is attributed to its ability to identify those groups of FStreams that have similar optimal plans. Range partition loses its advantage because those groups of FStreams having similar optimal plans are not contiguous. It works worse than hash partition when the hot spot is randomly spread over the data range.

One may worry that PMJoin would bring too much routing overheads due to its more complicated routing mechanisms (each substream has a different routing order). Here we conduct another experiment to measure its overhead. The configurations are the same as the experiment above. We use our implementation to compare the routing cost of PMJoin with different number of partitions. Figure 9 shows the cpu time used for routing in each second. Surprisingly, most of the time, PMJoin has even lower routing cost than the scheme without partitioning (i.e. partition number = 1). This can be attributed to the ability of PMJoin to

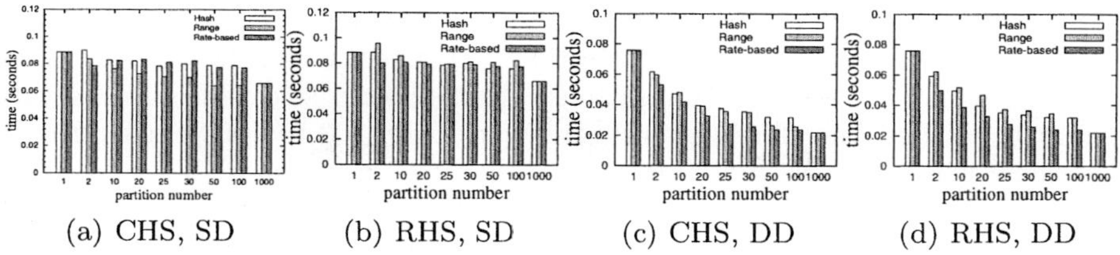

(a) CHS, SD (b) RHS, SD (c) CHS, DD (d) RHS, DD

Fig. 9. Routing overhead comparison

minimize the communication cost. Because fewer tuples are routed in PMJoin, its routing cost is smaller. PMJoin is more powerful in the case of different data distribution, hence its routing cost is much lower than the scheme without partitioning in this case. In addition, a better partitioning scheme further reduces more routing cost.

In the third experiment, we study the sensitivity of PMJoin to the number of streams. The distributions of the streams are randomly selected which is similar to the "Different Distributions" above. The results are presented in Figure 10. We only present the results when the partition number is 1, 500 and 1000, respectively. The others would lie between them. We can see that with increasing number of streams, PMJoin has larger improvement over the scheme without partitioning. Rate-based partition works the best under various number of streams. Range partition works better than hash partition for contiguous hot spot, while the reverse is true for randomly spread hot spot. Interestingly, with the increase in the number of streams, the cost of the scheme without partitioning increases while those of most of the PMJoin schemes decrease. Note that the distributions of the streams in this experiment are different, hence with more number of streams, the selectivity of the query is decreased. That means more tuples can be dropped before reaching the output, which can save the communication cost. PMJoin provides more opportunities to exploit this effect by using different plans for different group of substreams.

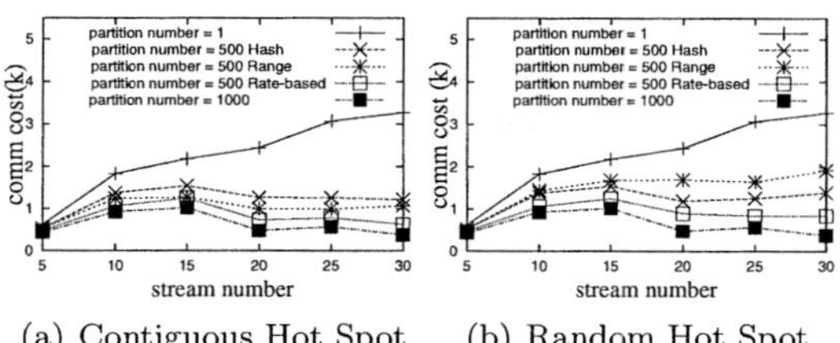

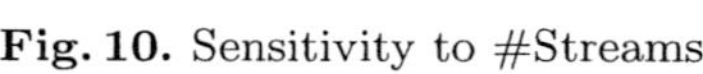
(a) Contiguous Hot Spot (b) Random Hot Spot

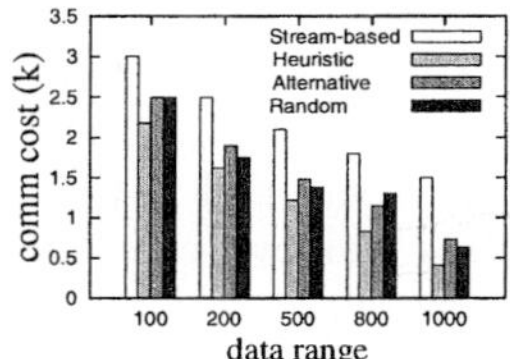

Fig. 10. Sensitivity to #Streams

Fig. 11. Different Attributes

4.3 Multi-joins on Different Attributes

In this section, we examine our techniques for multi-join queries whose equality predicates involve different attributes. We compare our heuristics to select the

PMJoin operator with two other approaches: (1) Random: replace the step 1 and 2 in the heuristic with a random selection; (2) Alternative: choose from those not selected by the heuristic algorithms. We randomly select 20 streams with different distributions. Their arrival rates vary from 100 to 1000 tuples/second and their window sizes vary from 10 seconds to 100 seconds. These streams are randomly allocated to 10 nodes. 200 random queries are generated with the number of joining attributes varied from 3 to 7. We get the average resulting cost of these queries under the three approaches. Figure 11 shows the results under different data ranges. In all the cases, the scheme without partitioning performs the worst. With larger data ranges (i.e. lower selectivity), the partition-based scheme is more beneficial. Furthermore, our heuristic outperforms the other two approaches.

5 Conclusion

In this paper, we studied the optimization of multi-join queries over distributed data streams. We proposed a heuristic optimization algorithm to minimize the communication cost. Furthermore, a partition-based join scheme: PMJoin was presented. Different partition techniques were discussed and heuristics to utilize PMJoins were also proposed. Our performance study showed that our techniques can sufficiently reduce the communication cost of the system. Although we propose the techniques under the context of distributed stream processing, the techniques can also be adapted to traditional distributed database systems. Further performance study in this context is required.

References

1. D. J. Abadi et al. The Design of the Borealis Stream Processing Engine. In *CIDR*, 2005.
2. Y. Ahmad and U. Çetintemel. Networked query processing for distributed stream-based applications. In *VLDB*, 2004.
3. P. M. G. Apers. Data allocation in distributed database systems. *ACM Trans. Database Syst.*, 1988.
4. R. Avnur and J. M. Hellerstein. Eddies: continuously adaptive query processing. In *SIGMOD*, 2000.
5. A. M. Ayad and J. F. Naughton. Static optimization of conjunctive queries with sliding windows over infinite streams. In *SIGMOD*, 2004.
6. S. Babu et al. Adaptive ordering of pipelined stream filters. In *SIGMOD*, 2004.
7. P. A. Bernstein et al. Query processing in a system for distributed databases (sdd-1). *ACM Trans. Database Syst.*, 1981.
8. D. J. DeWitt and R. H. Gerber. Multiprocessor hash-based join algorithms. In *VLDB*, 1985.
9. R. Epstein, M. Stonebraker, and E. Wong. Distributed query processing in a relational data base system. In *SIGMOD*, 1978.
10. L. Golab and M. T. Özsu. Processing sliding window multi-joins in continuous queries over data streams. In *VLDB*, 2003.

11. A. Jain and R. Dubes. *Algorithms for Clustering Data.* Prentice Hall, 1998.
12. J. Kang et al. Evaluating window joins over unbounded streams. In *ICDE*, 2003.
13. D. Kossmann. The state of the art in distributed query processing. *ACM Comput. Surv.*, 2000.
14. G. M. Lohman et al. Query processing in r*. In *Query Processing in Database Systems.* Springer, 1985.
15. S. Madden et al. Continuously adaptive continuous queries over streams. In *SIGMOD*, 2002.
16. D. Shasha and J. T.-L. Wang. Optimizing equijoin queries in distributed databases where relations are hash partitioned. *ACM Trans. Database Syst.*, 1991.
17. J. Sidell et al. Data replication in mariposa. In *ICDE*, 1996.
18. F. Tian and D. J. DeWitt. Tuple routing strategies for distributed eddies. In *VLDB*, 2003.
19. S. Viglas, J. F. Naughton, and J. Burger. Maximizing the output rate of multi-way join queries over streaming information sources. In *VLDB*, 2003.
20. O. Wolfson, S. Jajodia, and Y. Huang. An adaptive data replication algorithm. *ACM Trans. Database Syst.*, 1997.
21. C. T. Yu et al. Partition strategy for distributed query processing in fast local networks. *IEEE Trans. Software Eng.*, 1989.

Clustering Peers Based on Contents for Efficient Similarity Search

Yanfeng Shu and Bei Yu

School of Computing,
National University of Singapore, Singapore
{shuyanfe, yubei}@comp.nus.edu.sg

Abstract. Similarity search is becoming a norm in most real-life applications such as digital asset management systems. In such systems, users typically want to retrieve documents or objects similar to terms specified in the query or query examples. In this paper, we present a system for supporting similarity search in P2P networks that retains many desirable properties of existing P2P systems. To support efficient search, peers are formed into clusters based on their contents and clusters are organized as a structured overlay. Optimizations are employed to improve search performance. The experimental results confirm the effectiveness of our proposed system architecture.

1 Introduction

Peer-to-peer (P2P) has become a promising paradigm for developing large-scale distributed systems. In recent years, many P2P systems have been successfully deployed, and they can be broadly classified into two kinds: unstructured and structured. Unstructured P2P systems use simple protocols on network organization and administration: peers are organized randomly, and each peer maintains its own data. Naturally, their maintenance cost is low. Unfortunately, most systems perform their search based on flooding techniques. Consequently, they have to search a large portion of the network, making the system unscalable or compromising the quality of the results as a trade-off for a more efficient search. In other words, these unstructured systems offer no performance guarantee.

Different from unstructured systems, structured P2P systems enforce network structure and data placement within the network. For example, in Chord [23], peers are organized into a logical ring, and a data object is always assigned to the first peer whose identifier is the next or the same key in the identifier space. Thus, they are efficient in locating peers and data. However, their maintenance cost is high when there are frequent node membership and data changes. Also, they mainly support *exact*-key lookups while more complex search abilities are necessary for supporting most real-life applications. For example, in Information Retrieval, a user wants to retrieve documents containing terms or features that are most relevant to his queries.

In this paper, we examine the problem of supporting similarity search in P2P networks, and propose a P2P system architecture that retains many desirable properties of both unstructured and structured P2P systems while supporting efficient similarity search. For instance, in our system, by maintaining data by itself, each peer has more

M.L. Lee, K.L. Tan, and V. Wuwongse (Eds.): DASFAA 2006, LNCS 3882, pp. 342–356, 2006.

autonomy; by forming peers into clusters, maintenance becomes easier, and by organizing clusters in a structured way, queries can be routed more efficiently. The main design goal is to keep the maintenance cost caused by node membership or data changes low, while enabling efficient similarity search. Our approach is novel in three ways. First, we introduce the concept of Representative Points (RPs), which is used to characterize peers' contents. Based on RPs, peers with similar contents can be clustered together. Second, we propose several methods to organize clusters in a structured way. This "structured" property of our system brings about two benefits: one is efficient cluster formation. When a new peer joins the network, it can locate its cluster quickly. The other is efficient query routing. Given a query, a peer can route it to a relevant cluster within a few hops. Third, we employ effective optimization strategies for similarity search. When a query reaches a relevant cluster, nearby clusters may also need to be searched to improve search results. The main task of our optimization is to reduce the number of clusters to be searched as much as possible without compromising result quality. We have conducted extensive simulation studies to examine the effect of various parameters on the search performance, and our results confirm the effectiveness of our system.

The rest of the paper is organized as follows: we discuss related work in Section 2; we present the design details of our system in Section 3; we provide the results of our performance study in Section 4.2; and finally, we conclude the whole paper in Section 5.

2 Related Work

There has been much work done on P2P search. In the following, we discuss some of the work according to the overlay type.

2.1 Search in Unstructured Networks

Early unstructured systems (e.g., Gnutella) mainly depend on flooding for search. Thus, they have no performance guarantee. Also, they have limited search capability. For example, in Gnutella, queries are restricted to strings that can be contained in filenames. Thus, work based on the unstructured overlay mainly focuses on improving search performance or search capability [18, 12, 22, 7, 6, 14, 13]. [14] and [13] are most similar to our work, in that peers with similar contents are clustered together to support similarity search. However, both [14] and [13] depend on flooding for cluster formation. For example, in [13], when a new peer joins the network, it broadcasts a query to ask for signatures of peers within its neighborhood, and then establishes an attractive link with the one whose signature is most similar to its signature.

2.2 Search in Structured Networks

Structured P2P systems can be classified into two main kinds: DHT-based and skip-list based. DHT-based systems, such as Chord [23] and CAN [19], use a distributed hash table to distribute data over the network. One main difference among DHT systems is in their identifier space and neighbor definition. For example, in Chord, two peers are neighbors if the difference of their identifiers is 2^i $(i = 1..m)$ in *one*-dimensional identifier space $(0..2^m - 1)$, while in CAN, two peers are neighbors if their coordinate spans overlap along $d-1$ dimensions and abut along one dimension in a d-dimensional coordinate space. Skip graphs [1] and SkipNet [11] are two skip-list based systems. In skip graphs[1], each node is a member of multiple doubly linked lists at several levels. The bottom-level list consists of all nodes ordered by their keys. At upper levels, the list to which a node belongs is controlled by the node's membership vector, which is generated randomly. Specifically, a node is in the list L_w at level i, if and only if w is a prefix of its member vector of length i. Each node stores the addresses and keys of its left and right neighbors at each level. When searching, a node first checks its neighbors at the highest level. If there is a neighbor whose key is not past the search key, the search request is passed to the neighbor; otherwise, neighbors at a lower level are checked.

There is a great amount of work done on extending structured systems and thus supporting complex queries. For example, range queries are supported in [5, 2, 9, 21], and keyword queries are supported in [20, 16, 25, 24]. As one main application area of our work is Information Retrieval, we describe work on this aspect in more detail. Within the work in the context of keyword query search, pSearch [25] is most similar to ours in that contents are organized around their semantics. The main difference is that in pSearch, each semantic vector (corresponding to each document) needs to be published into CAN's space while in our work, there is no data publishing; instead, we introduce RPs to characterize peers' contents and form peers with similar RPs into clusters. The rest of the work [20, 16, 24] publishes keywords into Chord's space, with the difference in the decision about which keywords need to be published.

2.3 Search in Unstructured/Structured Networks

Some work has been reported on search on both unstructured and structured overlays, such as [17, 27, 15, 3]. By observing Gnutella's query processing and PIERSearch's (based on DHT systems) in latency and result quality, [17] proposes a hybrid system for keyword search, where Gnutella is used to locate popular items, and PIERSearch is used to handle rare items. [27] shares the spirit of [17]: Instead of indexing all data items owned by each peer, only a portion of them are registered with the index. Also, by the index, peers with shared interests can be clustered together. In SSW [15], peers are formed into semantic clusters, which are organized into a small world network. There are two main differences between SSW and our work: first, in SSW, the system has full control of data placement, while in our work, each node has full control of its data. With this increasing node autonomy, the system has more complexity in dealing with cluster formation. Second, in SSW, a search is finished when a query reaches its destination cluster (the cluster which covers the query) and nodes in the destination cluster are searched, while in our work, nearby clusters of the destination cluster are also searched to improve search results. Compared to SSW, our work focuses more on similarity searches. SETS [3] is most similar to our work. In SETS, each peer's content is represented by a peer vector, and peers with similar contents are arranged into a topic-segmented overlay (a small-world network). The main difference is, in SETS, peers are clustered by a central site, which has full knowledge about topic segments. Thus, during search, the similarity between the query vector and each topic centroid is

[1] As our system uses skip graphs to organize clusters, we describe it in more detail.

computed, and top R segments are selected. In contrast, there is no such central site in our system. That is, a peer has little knowledge about which clusters are most similar to the query. The problem with a central site is that it presents a single point of failure and a performance bottleneck. On the other hand, the flexibility and scalability provided by decoupling global information from the central site demand more sophisticated and efficient search strategies.

3 System Design

The basic idea of our system design is to cluster peers that have similar contents so that relevant information can be retrieved with a few hops around the neighborhood. Though the idea is straightforward, we need to address several issues in order to make it work effectively. The first main issue we need to address is the formation and organization of clusters. This issue is important, as it directly decides system scalability. In most previous work, either a centralized method [3] or a fully decentralized method [14, 13] is used for cluster formation. Both approaches are not scalable: The former may suffer from performance bottleneck. The latter may overload the network when there are a large number of peers in the network. In our system, we employ a *hybrid* method: Each cluster makes its own decision on how and when to form new clusters, and within a cluster, peers may need to exchange messages with each other. By organizing clusters in a structured way, a new peer can find its cluster efficiently. The other main issue is efficient support for similarity search. In query processing, a query is first routed to a relevant cluster, and subsequently forwarded to nearby clusters. It is therefore important for a system to be able to decide which clusters to search first and return the results of a certain degree of quality as soon as possible. Before describing these issues in more detail, in the following, we first introduce an important concept for peer clustering: *Representative Points*(RPs).

3.1 Representative Points (RPs)

Individuals tend to have certain interests and share data of certain topics. For example, a researcher may only be interested in papers on computer science while a doctor may only be interested in medical science papers. The data can therefore be associated with some representative points in the data space. We call such points that characterize peers' contents Representative Points – RPs. We do not place any restriction on the techniques used by peers to summarize data. For Information Retrieval, a peer can derive its RP as follows: First, each document is represented as a term vector by a Vector Space Model(VSM) [4], where each element is the term weight computed by TF*IDF (term frequency * inverse document frequency). Then each term vector is converted into a semantic vector with much lower dimentionalities by Latent Semantic Indexing (LSI) [8]. By normalizing the sum of all semantic vectors of its documents, a peer gets its RP. Instead of a single RP, multiple RPs may be derived for each peer and they can be obtained by using a data clustering algorithm such as K-Means. With multiple RPs, a peer may need to join multiple clusters. Without loss of generality, in what follows, we assume that each peer has only one RP.

3.2 Cluster Overlay

In this part, we describe how clusters are formed and organized. We also describe how an overlay with clusters is maintained.

Construction. Suppose each peer data item corresponds to a point in a data space, each cluster covers a subspace, and a peer only joins the cluster whose space covers its RP. The first peer in the network forms the only cluster with itself as a member. As more peers join the network, the cluster is split. We assume cluster size, the maximum number of peers within a cluster, is known system-wide.

We split clusters on the basis of similarity: When a cluster is split, two sub-clusters are generated, and we always assign a peer to the sub-cluster which is more similar to the peer. The similarity between a cluster and a peer is computed by some similarity function (e.g., cosine score or euclidean distance) between the cluster centroid (computed by averaging its current members' RPs) and the peer's RP. Specifically, we split a cluster as follows: First, two peers which are most dissimilar in the cluster to be split are chosen as the first peers of two sub-clusters. The selection of seeds is philosophically similar to most splitting process in which overall coverage and overlap are to be minimized; for example, the splitting in the R-tree [10]. Subsequently, for each peer not yet in either sub-cluster, the similarity between the peer and the centroid of each sub-cluster is computed, and the one with the greatest difference between its similarities to sub-clusters is selected next and assigned to the more similar sub-cluster whose centroid will be recomputed. After all peers are assigned, the cluster is split along the dimension which has the maximum span between the centroids of its two sub-clusters.

Currently, in our system, peers within a cluster are simply organized randomly. Each peer maintains a few links to peers within the same cluster, called *intra-cluster links*. The number of intra-cluster links is fixed at the outset, and flooding is used as the main strategy for searching within a cluster. Besides maintaining links to peers within its own cluster (i.e., intra-cluster links), each peer in a cluster also maintains a few links to peers in other clusters, called *inter-cluster links*. We may maintain inter-cluster links as defined in CAN. Two clusters have links (i.e., a peer in one cluster has a link to a peer in the other cluster), if they are spatial neighbors, i.e., their spaces overlap in d-1 dimensions and abut in one dimension in a d-dimensional space. We call such links *spatial links*. Alternatively, we may maintain inter-cluster links as defined in skip graphs. Each cluster has a randomly generated membership vector, and cluster ids are used as keys in skip graphs. Two clusters have links, if they are neighboring at any level of skip graphs. We call such links *skip links*. The cluster id is derived as follows: When a cluster is split, if one of its sub-clusters covers the space at the left of split dimension, the cluster id of the sub-cluster will be attached with "0"; otherwise, the cluster id of the sub-cluster will be attached with "1". For the initial cluster in the network, the cluster id is "". By comparing cluster ids sequentially, clusters in a network can be ordered. Figure 1 gives an example of these two kinds of inter-cluster links that could be maintained in a network (the data space is $two-$dimensional). From the figure, we can see that, if spatial links are maintained, cluster C_3 would have $five$ spatial links, connecting itself to C_1, C_2, C_4, C_5, and C_7 respectively; and if skip links are maintained, it would have $three$ skip links, which connect itself to C_2, C_4, and C_6 respectively.

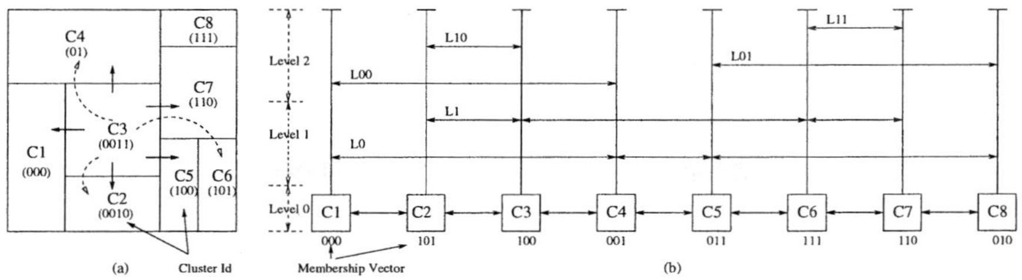

Fig. 1. An example of inter-cluster links in a 2-d space. (a) the cluster overlay (solid lines represent spatial links, while dashed lines represent skip links); (b) the corresponding skip graphs for organizing clusters.

While intra-cluster links facilitate query forwarding within a cluster, inter-cluster links facilitate query forwarding across clusters. Compared to intra-cluster links, inter-cluster links are more important for efficient similarity search, as they decide how a query can be routed to relevant clusters efficiently. For inter-cluster links, spatial links can facilitate similarity search greatly as they link clusters which are within close proximity in the data space. Skip links, on the other hand, may not do as well as spatial links for similarity search. As most skip links are randomly decided, they do not necessarily connect to nearby clusters. For example, in Figure 1, by skip links, C_3 only directly connects to two of its spatially close clusters. However, skip links incur much lower maintenance cost as compared to spatial links. Also, routing between any two clusters by skip links can be performed efficiently. Detailed comparison between spatial links and skip links will be given in our performance study. In the following, we mainly consider skip links as inter-cluster links, and present how we use them for similarity search. The case for spatial links as inter-cluster links can be dealt with as well.

Maintenance. Since each peer maintains its own data, there is no data publishing; thus, the corresponding maintenance cost that would otherwise be incurred is avoided. When there are data changes, a peer's RP may be affected, though compared to data changes, RP changes may not be so frequent. Periodically, a peer monitors its data changes and recomputes its RP when there are many changes (all is done locally). When a peer finds its RP not covered by the current cluster, it leaves and then rejoins the network. Before leaving, the peer notifies its neighbors, which will rebuild the corresponding links. The link reconstruction is very simple: The departing peer need only provide information about some other peers within its cluster. A peer that leaves the network follows the same process. In case of peer failure (detected by 'heartbeats'), a peer rebuilds its links by asking other peers within its cluster which have information about the clusters with which the peer wants to rebuild links. In summary, the clustering and use of representative points not only simplify network maintenance but also improve network robustness.

If a cluster disappears (i.e., the peer which leaves or fails is the only one in its cluster), maintenance proceeds as described in skip graphs [1]. That is, each cluster maintains a redundant cluster list of length $2r$, which includes the closest r left and r right clusters along the bottom level list in the skip graphs. If a cluster disappears, it is replaced by a cluster with the first live left or right cluster in its redundant cluster list. A background stabilization process runs periodically at each peer to fix neighbors at the upper levels in the skip graphs.

3.3 Similarity Search

Similarity search in our system involves three main steps: routing across clusters, flooding within a cluster, and searching clusters in the neighborhood. Given a query, a peer first checks whether its cluster covers the query. If not, it routes the query to the cluster which covers the query; otherwise, it floods the query within its own cluster. Meanwhile, it forwards the query to nearby clusters which may contain data relevant to the query. The pseudo-code of the search algorithm is given in Figure 2.

```
P.SimilaritySearch(q, SP, CQ)
    //SP is the search space, whose initial value is the whole space
    //CQ is the cluster queue, including clusters to be searched
    if q.key is not covered by the space of P's cluster
        Routing(q, SP, CQ)
    else
        flooding q within the cluster
        //search nearby clusters
        for i = P.clusterId.length() − 1 downto 0
            //get a nearby cluster C's id by P's clusterId b0...bl
            C.clusterId=b0...¬bi
            get C.space by the split history
            if SP ⊇ C.space
                insert C into CQ;
        while CQ is not empty or q is not satisfied
            get C from CQ;
            forward SimilaritySearch(q, C.space, CQ − C) to C
```

Fig. 2. The basic similarity search algorithm

Routing across clusters. Each peer maintains a split history of its cluster, which records the split dimension and position of each split. As we have described, all clusters can be ordered by their cluster ids. By comparing the query with its split history, a peer can decide how to route a query via its skip links (see Figure 3 for the pseudo-code). If the cluster id of the query's destination is smaller than its cluster id, the peer will check its left skip links. If the cluster id of the query's destination is larger than its cluster id, the peer will check its right skip links. When checking the links, the link which is at the highest level is always tried first, followed by links at the lower levels. This process continues until the destination cluster is reached.

Flooding within a cluster. When q arrives at its destination cluster, it will be flooded to all peers within the cluster. Each query has a unique id, and each peer maintains a query queue. If a peer has seen a query before, it simply discards the query; otherwise, it adds the query into its query queue, and then forwards the query to other peers within the same cluster via its intra-cluster links. Meanwhile, it searches its data, computes

```
P.Routing(q, QR, CQ)
1. if q.key is covered by P.clusterSpace
2.       q arrives at its destination
3. else for i = 0 to P.splitHistory.length − 1
4.             if A.clusterId[i] = 0
               and q.key[splitHistory[i].splitDim > splitHistory[i].splitPos
5.                   forward q via right inter-cluster links
6.             else if A.clusterId[i] = 1
               and q.key[splitHistory[i].splitDim <= splitHistory[i].splitPos
7.                   forward q via left inter-cluster links
```

Fig. 3. Routing procedure

similarities between the data and the query, and returns top k results, or results whose similarities exceed certain threshold.

Searching nearby clusters. As clusters are constructed only by peers' RPs, it may be possible that nearby clusters which are *spatially nearby* or *semantically close* to the destination cluster also contain relevant data. Thus, after q reaches its destination cluster, "nearby" clusters also need to be searched. For example, in Figure 1, suppose C_3 is q's destination cluster. After searching C_3, we need to search all its nearby clusters, i.e., C_1, C_2, C_4, C_5, and C_7, to improve search results.

Two problems need to be solved for searching nearby clusters. The first problem is *how to find a cluster's nearby clusters.* As we mentioned earlier, most skip links are randomly decided, and they do not necessarily connect to nearby clusters. The second problem is *which clusters to be searched first, given a set of nearby clusters.* For a set of nearby clusters, some may be more relevant to q than others. By searching the most relevant clusters first, we can return results with a certain degree of quality without having to search irrelevant clusters.

We address the first problem by analyzing the relationship between two clusters in the network. If two clusters, C_1 and C_2, are directly generated from the splitting of the same cluster C, then they are nearby, i.e., spatially nearby (based on Eulicidian distance) or semantically close (based on cosine similarity); otherwise, they may not be nearby. Suppose C_1 is further split, its sub-clusters and C_2 are only possibly nearby. With this property, for a cluster "$b_1 ... b_{i-1} b_i$" (its cluster id is "$b_1 ... b_{i-1} b_i$"), we check the following nonoverlapping i clusters which may be nearby to it, "$b_1 ... b_{i-1} \overline{b_i}$", "$b_1 ... \overline{b_{i-1}}$", ..., and "$\overline{b_1}$". And then forward q to each of these clusters, where the process is continued until q is satisfied (e.g., no more results are required), or all clusters in the network have been searched. Note that each nearby cluster may in fact contain some sub-clusters. To limit the search space, when q is forwarded, we attach the space of each nearby cluster (SP in Figure 2) with the query message. Though a cluster has little knowledge about whether a nearby cluster is further split or not, it can compute the nearby cluster's space by the cluster's id according to its split history.

For the second problem, i.e., the sequence of nearby clusters to be searched, we address it by ordering clusters according to their "closeness" to q, and searching the cluster which is the closest first. The closeness of a cluster is decided by the closeness of its peers to q. For a peer p, its closeness to q is noted as $Close(p, q)$. We measure closeness either in terms of the spatial distance or in terms of the cosine similarity. Note that Euclidean distance and cosine similarity produce the same ranking for normalized vectors. For all peers in a cluster C whose space is $[ll, hr]$ (ll and hr are the low-left point and high-right point of the space respectively), their closenesses to q are bounded by $Close(ll, q)$ and $Close(hr, q)$. We use $Close(ll, q)$ to represent the closeness of C to q. If a cluster has the smallest closeness value when closeness is measured in terms of the spatial distance, or has the largest closeness value when closeness is measured in terms of the cosine similarity, it is regarded as the closest. It is easy to compute a nearby cluster's closeness to q, since we can know its space as described before. When q is forwarded to a nearby cluster which is further split, it is always forwarded to the sub-cluster which is closest to q. With each query message, a cluster queue (CQ in Figure 2) is attached, which includes all clusters to be searched in the sequence of their closeness to q. When a cluster is searched, its nearby clusters will be inserted in the queue.

Following the above example, for C_3 whose id is "0011", we check the following clusters whose ids are "0010" (C_2), "000" (C_1), "01" (C_4), and "1" respectively, and forward q to each of these clusters by skip links. Among these clusters, cluster "1" is further split. If q is forwarded to cluster "1" randomly, it may be possible that q reaches a sub-cluster which is not the closest to C_3, e.g., C_6 or C_8 (suppose closeness is measured in terms of the spatial distance in this example). To avoid this, when q is forwarded to a cluster, it is always forwarded to the cluster which covers a point that has minimal spatial distance to q. Thus, when C_3 wants to forward q to cluster "1", it first finds such a point. Suppose the whole space is $[(0, 0), (1, 1)]$, the first split position is 0.6 at dimension 0, and q is $(0.5, 0.5)$, the space of cluster "1" will be [(0.6,0), (1,1)], and the point which has minimum distance to q in cluster "1" will be $(0.6, 0.5)$. C_3 then forwards q to the cluster which covers $(0.6, 0.5)$, e.g., C_7 (suppose the low-left point of C_7's space is (0.6,0.4)).

4 Performance Study

In this section, we evaluate the system via extensive simulations, and present the experimental results.

4.1 Experimental Setup

We generate different synthetic datasets with different data dimensionalities and data distributions, for a given number of peers in the network and a given number of data objects per peer. The data distribution is decided by the distribution of RPs and the distribution of data in each peer, both of which are based on multivariate normal distribution. When generating data, we first generate RPs for peers, which follow a normal distribution with variance σ_1^2 (the distribution mean is a random point in the data space); then we generate data for each peer, which also follow a normal distribution whose mean and variance are the peer's RP and σ_2^2 respectively. By varying σ_1^2, we can control the peer distribution in the space, and by varying σ_1^2, we can control the data similarity at each peer. Table 1 summarizes parameters and their default values for the

Table 1. Parameters used in the experiments

	Description	Default value
N	Network size (number of peers in the network)	6000
M	Cluster size (number of peers in a cluster)	30
m	Avg. outdegree within a cluster	4
n	Number of data items per peer	50
d	Dimensionality of data	10
σ_1^2	Variance of peer (RP) distribution in the space	0.04
σ_2^2	Variance of data distribution in each peer	0.04

evaluation on synthetic datasets. For each peer, we randomly generate 10 queries, and results are averaged over all peers. Euclidean distance is used as the similarity function.

The following metrics are used to evaluate the performance: (1) *Average lookup hops*. The average number of hops for a query to reach its destination cluster. (2) *Routing cost*. We differentiate two kinds of routing costs: inter-cluster routing cost, which is the average number of messages for routing a query across clusters, and intra-cluster routing cost, which is the average number of messages sent within clusters. We are interested in the aggregate inter-cluster and the aggregate intra-cluster routing costs during a search. (3) *Maintenance cost*. The average number of links (neighbors) each peer needs to maintain, which includes the average number of inter-cluster links and the average number of intra-cluster links. (4) *Processing cost*. The percentage of peers which are probed to evaluate a query and return results. (5) *Result quality*. The quality of returned results. We measure result quality in terms of the percentage of retrieved results among top k results in the whole network (in the experiments, we use 10 for k).

4.2 Experiment Results

We first compare these two kinds of inter-cluster links by measuring their effects on overlay performance and search performance respectively. For overlay performance measurement, we test average lookup hops and maintenance costs with both links by varying network size, data dimensionality, and cluster size. For search performance measurement, we test average aggregate inter-cluster and average aggregate intra-cluster routing costs, and processing costs incurred for a search to reach a certain result quality.

Average lookup hops. Figure 4 shows the results on average lookup hops. In (a) and (b), the cluster size is set to be the default value (30), and the cluster size is varied in (c). As shown in the figure, the number of average lookup hops with skip links increases logarithmically with network size, and changes little with dimensionality. The number of average lookup hops with spatial links is much affected by the dimensionality: when dimensionality is high, the number of hops needed for a query to reach its destination cluster is small; however, when dimensionality is low (< 4), the number of hops needed becomes big. This is mainly because the number of hops with spatial links needed for a query to reach its destination cluster largely depends on the number of neighbors maintained by each peer. As will be shown next, in a network with spatial links, each peer needs to maintain a large number of neighbors when dimensionality is high. When

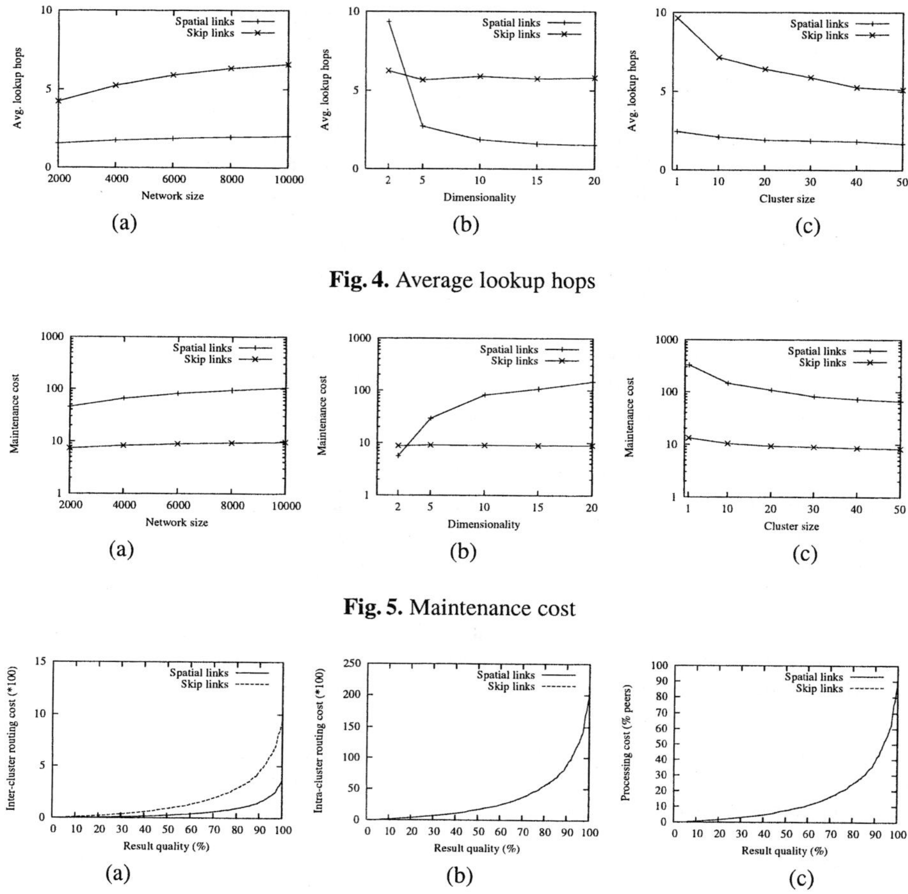

Fig. 4. Average lookup hops

Fig. 5. Maintenance cost

Fig. 6. Search performance

the cluster size increases, the number of average lookup hops decreases accordingly due to fewer number of clusters, as reflected in (c).

Maintenance cost. The maintenance cost is measured in terms of the average number of inter-cluster links maintained by each peer (the average number of intra-cluster links maintained by each peer is fixed). As shown in Figure 5, much higher maintenance cost is incurred when spatial links are maintained, especially when dimensionality is high. For skip links, maintenance cost increases logarithmically with network size, which is little affected by dimensionality. The effect of cluster size on the maintenance cost is shown in (c). For both links, maintenance costs decrease with larger cluster size.

Search performance. Figure 6 shows the search performance of both spatial and skip links, where (a) reflects average aggregate inter-cluster routing costs, (b) reflects average aggregate intra-cluster routing costs, and (c) reflects processing costs, which are incurred to achieve a certain result quality. To decrease routing costs (esp. inter-cluster routing costs), we employ the following strategy: whenever a peer receives a query, it checks whether a cluster in the cluster queue (attached with the query message) can be reached directly by its inter-cluster links, and attached the related routing information of the cluster to the query message if such a cluster exists, which can facilitate the future routing to the cluster.

As shown in the figure, for a certain result quality, intra-cluster routing costs and processing costs incurred for both links are nearly the same. However, there is a relatively big gap between inter-cluster routing costs for both links. This is mainly because of the following reasons: firstly, each peer with spatial links maintains much more neighbors, and thus a search request can be routed from one cluster to another at less cost. Secondly, spatial links connect to nearby clusters while skip links do not necessarily connect to nearby clusters, and thus more routing costs are needed for skip links to reach the same result quality.

From the above experiments, we can see that, there involves a tradeoff as for which kind of inter-cluster links is chosen. Though spatial links have good performance in average lookup hops and aggregate routing costs, they incur much maintenance cost, as each peer in the network with spatial links needs to maintain a large number of neighbors (though this is alleviated a little with larger cluster size), especially when the data dimensionality is high. Skip links, on the other hand, are little affected by the data dimensionality, and each peer in the network with skip links only needs to maintain a few number of neighbors. This makes skip links more suitable for large-scale distributed information retrieval where the data dimensionality is typically high and the network is typically dynamic. However, skip links incur more routing costs than skip links.

Next, we vary the cluster size and data distribution, and measure their effects on the search performance. As similar trends for spatial links are observed in all measurements, we only give results for skip links.

The effect of cluster size. Figure 7 shows the effect of cluster size on the search performance. The cluster size M is varied from 10 to 50. As shown in (a), as cluster size increases, the result quality decreases, though not significantly. When the cluster size is increased from 10 to 50, by probing 20% peers, the result quality is decreased by about 8% i.e., 8% less results are correctly retrieved. This is mainly because larger cluster size leads to less focussed clusters. Thus more clusters (peers) are probed to achieve a certain result quality.

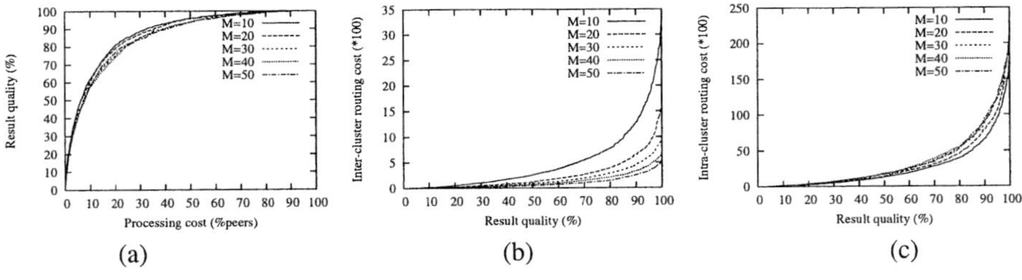

Fig. 7. The effect of cluster size

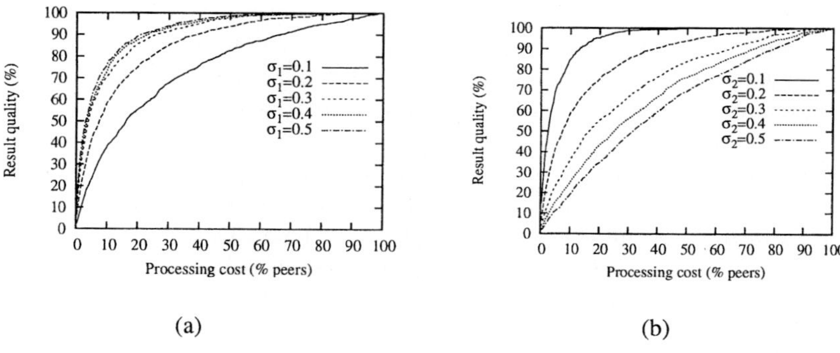

Fig. 8. The effect of data distribution

Figure 7(b) and (c) show the effect of cluster size on routing cost. As shown in the figure, as cluster size increases, inter-cluster routing cost decreases, while intra-cluster routing cost increases, for a certain result quality. This is because, with larger cluster size, each cluster becomes less focussed, thus more clusters need to be probed to achieve a certain result quality, which results in more intra-cluster messages; on the other hand, with larger cluster size, there are less clusters in the network, thus less messages are required for inter-cluster routing to reach a relevant cluster, and even more clusters need to be probed to reach a certain result quality, the total messages for inter-cluster routing are still decreased.

Thus, the choice of cluster size also involves a tradeoff. Given a certain result quality, we need to find an appropriate cluster size which is small enough to achieve the result quality we want with less peers probed, but is large enough not to incur much inter-cluster routing cost, which may dominate the total routing cost with small cluster size.

The effect of data distribution. Figure 8 shows the effect of data distribution on result quality, where (a) reflects the effect of RP distribution, and (b) reflects the effect of data distribution in each peer. In (a), we fix the data distribution at each peer and vary the distribution of RPs by increasing σ_1 from 0.1 to 0.5, while in (b), we fix the RP distribution and vary the data distribution at each peer by increasing σ_2 from 0.1 to 0.5. From the figure, we find that, both RP distribution and data distribution in each peer have great effect on the result quality. A certain result quality can be achieved with less peers probed by either increasing σ_1, or decreasing σ_2. The reason is, with larger σ_1, RPs are distributed more uniformly in the data space; since each peer uses its RP to join the network, peers become more distributed in the network, and thus clusters become more focussed in some sense for a certain cluster size. The same reasoning applies to data distribution at each peer. With smaller σ_2, the content of each peer becomes more focussed, and thus clusters become more focussed.

This experiment, from another perspective, also illustrates that, the effectiveness of our system may be affected by the data distribution. We have already evaluated our system on real datasets (AP Newswire documents in TREC [26] CDs 1 and 2), and our results show that our system is still effective. Due to space constrains, we omit them here.

5 Conclusion

In this paper, we have presented a system for similarity search in P2P networks. Our system retains many desirable properties of current P2P systems, and supports similarity search efficiently. By introducing Representative Points, peers are clustered according to their contents. By organizing clusters into a structured overlay, queries can be routed efficiently. Given a query, a peer need only route it to relevant clusters. Optimizations are employed to further improve search performance. Extensive simulation study has been done, and the results show the effectiveness of our system.

Acknowledgements. The work was in part funded by an A*STAR research grant on SpADE (R-252-000-193-30).

References

1. J. Aspnes and G. Shah. Skip graphs. In *Proceedings of the 14th Annual ACM-SIAM Symposium on Discrete Algorithms*, 2003.
2. F. Banaei-Kashani and C. Shahabir. Swam: A family of access methods for similarity-search in peer-to-peer data networks. In *Proceedings of the Thirteenth ACM conference on Information and knowledge management*, 2004.
3. M. Bawa, G. S. Manku, and P. Raghavan. Sets: Search enhanced by topic segmentation. In *Proceedings of the 26th annual international ACM SIGIR conference on Research and development in informaion retrieval*, 2003.
4. M. Berry, Z. Drmac, and E. Jessup. Matrices, vector spaces, and information retrieval. In *SIAM Review, 41(2)*, 1999.
5. A. Bharambe, M. Agrawal, and S. Seshan. Mercury: Supporting scalable multi-attribute range queries. In *Proceedings of the ACM Special Interest Group on Data Communication(SIGCOMM)*, 2004.
6. E. Cohen, A. Fiat, and H. Kaplan. Associative search in peer to peer networks: Harnessing latent semantics. In *Proceedings of IEEE INFOCOM*, 2003.
7. F. M. Cuenca-Acuna and T. D. Nguyen. Text-based content search and retrieval in ad hoc p2p communities. In *International Workshop om Peer-to-Peer Computing (co-located with Networking 2002)*, 2002.
8. S. C. Deerwester, S. Dumais, T. K. Landauer, G. Furnas, and R. Harshman. Indexing by latent semantic analysis. In *Journal of the American Society of Information Science, 41(6)*, 1990.
9. P. Ganesan, B. Yang, and H. G. Molina. One torus to rule them all: Multi-dimensional queries in p2p systems. In *Proceedings of the Seventh International Workshop on the Web and Databases*, 2004.
10. A. Guttman. R-trees: A dynamic index structure for spatial searching. In *Proceedings ACM SIGMOD Conference on Management of Data*, 1984.
11. N. J. A. Harvey, M. B. Jones, S. Saroiu, M. Theimer, and A. Wolman. Skipnet: A scalable overlay network with practical locality properties. In *Fourth USENIX Symposium on Internet Technologies and Systems (USITS'03)*, 2003.
12. V. Kalogeraki, D. Gunopulos, and D. Zeinalipour-Yazti. A local search mechanism for peer-to-peer networks. In *Proceedings of the Eleventh International Conference on Information and Knowledge Management*, 2002.

13. I. King, C. H. Ng, and K. C. Sia. Distributed content-based visual information retrieval system on peer-to-peer networks. In *ACM Transactions on Information Systems (TOIS), Volume 22, Issue 3*, 2004.
14. K. A. Klampanos and J. M. Jose. An architecture for information retrieval over semi-collaborating peer-to-peer networks. In *Proceedings of the 2004 ACM symposium on Applied computing*, 2004.
15. M. Li, W.-C. Lee, and A. Sivasubramaniam. Semantic small world: An overlay network for peer-to-peer search. In *Proceedings of the Network Protocols, 12th IEEE International Conference on (ICNP'04)*, 2004.
16. L. Liu, K. D. Ryu, and K.-W. Lee. Keyword fusion for efficient keyword-based search in p2p file sharing. In *Proceedings of the Fourth International Workshop on Global and Peer-to-Peer Computing*, 2004.
17. B. T. Loo, J. M. Hellerstein, R. Huebsch, S. Shenker, and I. Stoica. Enhancing p2p file-sharing with an internet-scale query processor. In *Proceedings of the 30th International Conference on. Very Large Data Bases*, 2004.
18. C. Lv, P. Cao, E. Cohen, K. LI, and S. Shenker. Search and replication in unstructured peer-to-peer networks. In *Proceedings of the 16th annual ACM International Conference on supercomputing*, 2002.
19. S. Ratnasamy, P. Francis, M. Handley, R. Karp, and S. Shenker. A scalable content-addressable network. In *Proceedings of the ACM Special Interest Group on Data Communication(SIGCOMM)*, 2001.
20. P. Reynolds and A. Vahdat. Efficient peer-to-peer keyword searching. In *Middleware 2003*, 2003.
21. Y. Shu, B. C. Ooi, and K. L. Tan. Supporting multi-dimensional range queries in peer-to-peer systems. In *Proceedings of IEEE P2P*, 2005.
22. K. Sripanidkulchai, B. Maggs, and H. Zhang. Efficient content location using interest-based locality in peer-topeer systems. In *Proceedings of IEEE INFOCOM*, 2003.
23. I. Stoica, R. Morris, D. Karger, F. Kaashoek, and H. Balakrishnan. Chord: A scalable peer-to-peer lookup service for internet applications. In *Proceedings of the ACM Special Interest Group on Data Communication(SIGCOMM)*, 2001.
24. C. Tang and S. Dwarkadas. Hybrid global-local indexing for efficient peer-to-peer information retrieval. In *Proceedings of the Symposium on Networked Systems Design and Implementation (NSDI)*, 2004.
25. C. Tang, Z. Xu, and S. Dwarkadas. Peer-to-peer information retrieval using self-organizing semantic overlay networks. In *Proceedings of the ACM Special Interest Group on Data Communication(SIGCOMM)*, 2003.
26. Text retrieval conference(trec). *http://trec.nist.org*.
27. R. Zhang and Y. C. Hu. Assisted peer-to-peer search with partial indexing. In *Proceedings of IEEE INFOCOM*, 2005.

Optimizing Peer Virtualization and Load Balancing

Wanxia Xie[1], Shamkant B. Navathe[1], Sushil K. Prasad[2], David Fisher[1], and Yong Yang[1]

[1] College of Computing, Georgia Institute of Technology, 801 Atlantic Drive, Atlanta, GA, USA
{wanxia.xie, sham, dfisher, yy}@cc.gatech.edu
[2] Dept. of Computer Science, Georgia State University, 34 Peachtree Street, Atlanta, GA, USA
sprasad@gsu.edu

Abstract. Structured peer-to-peer systems are popular solutions for large scale distributed computing and query processing. Heterogeneity among peers calls for peer virtualization to maintain a simple, yet powerful peer-to-peer overlay network. Nevertheless, peer virtualization generates a huge number of virtual peers and causes the unnecessary communication overhead in the routing process. In this paper, we propose a new peer-to-peer routing algorithm that reduces the number of hops of message forwarding and improves the performance of routing. We study the new and previous algorithms from the analytical perspective and through simulations. It shows that the average number of hops per query is improved by 15% to 25% in our algorithm. In addition, we propose a Top-k peer selection algorithm for load balancing to find out the top k best available nodes in the P2P network with 2(N-1) messages within 2O(logN) hops. (N is the number of physical nodes.) The load balancing scheme is based on multiple factors which could be optimized on cost, proximity, reputation and other factors.

1 Introduction

Peer-to-peer (P2P) research is a popular topic for the past several years. Distributed hash table (DHT) based P2P systems [8,9,10,12] have constituted the main-stream since Year 2000. As these P2P systems try to utilize all available resources in P2P network, load balancing and peer heterogeneity are two important issues to be addressed.

Peer heterogeneity focuses on the physical capabilities of a peer including computing, storage and bandwidth. It is an unavoidable situation that we had to handle in today's P2P computing environment as most peers are connected through the Internet. Intuitively peer virtualization is one way to address the heterogeneity among peers. In peer virtualization, a peer is a virtual concept and not exactly a physical node. The idea is to allocate more virtual peers to a more powerful physical peer instead of viewing all physical peers as being the same. This makes sense as the physical nodes with more capacities are assigned more load.

Recently a few peer virtualization schemes [2, 3, 7 and 13] are proposed. In [2, 3], the number of virtual peers assigned to a node is proportional to its capacity. [7]

M.L. Lee, K.L. Tan, and V. Wuwongse (Eds.): DASFAA 2006, LNCS 3882, pp. 357 – 373, 2006.

proposes a scheme to adapt the number of virtual peers in a node according to its load situation. [13] proposes a peer virtualization scheme to utilize the proximity among peer nodes in order to reduce the overhead of transferring the load from one peer node to another peer node.

During load balancing, the system moves one or more virtual peers from the overloaded physical node to another physical node. When peer virtualization is more fine-grained, the average size of load allocated to each virtual peer is smaller. Therefore we have a more accurate estimate of load being moved and the consumption of network bandwidth used to move load will be more efficient in this process.

One problem of these peer virtualization schemes is that they generate a much larger number of virtual peers than the number of physical peers. But the routing algorithm among peers still route the messages according to the virtual peers. The routing message may bounce back and forth among physical peers. This causes the unnecessary communication overhead in the routing process. The routing overhead is measured by $R_{overhead}$. As we know, $R_{overhead} = \frac{Hop_{Virtual}}{Hop_{baseline}}$, in which $Hop_{Virtual}$ is the average number of hops for a query in the virtualized P2P network and $Hop_{baseline}$ is the average number of hops for a query in the physical P2P network. Figure 1 shows the routing overhead that peer virtualization causes. The number of physical nodes is set to 1,000. The baseline calculation is based on Chord [10]. We can see that the routing overhead dramatically increases as peer virtualization generates a large number of virtual peers.

On the other hand, all these schemes ignore the shared information among virtual peers in the same physical peer node, to the best of our knowledge. We argue that such shared information could be used to improve the routing among peers. For example, the routing tables (i.e. finger tables in Chord [10]) and neighbor lists of all virtual peers residing at the same node could be searched to find the closer next node to the destination peer. Even if some existing schemes might utilize some of the shared information, which we do not see from their publications, they did not explore how the routing process is affected by the sharing, the degree of peer virtualization

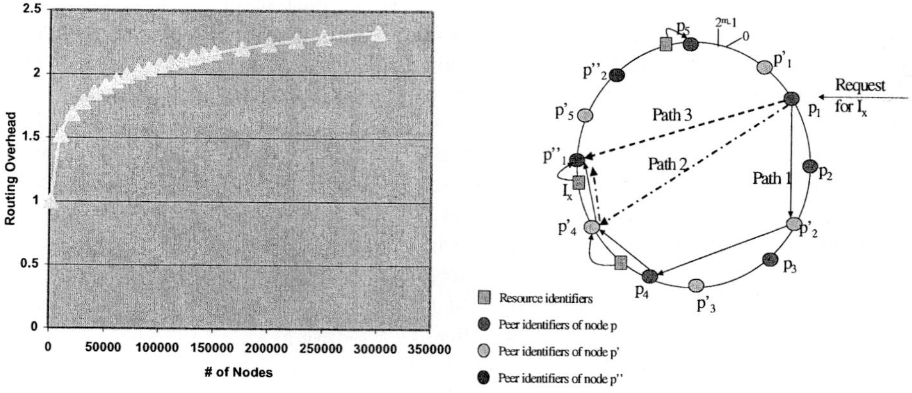

Fig. 1. Routing overhead

Fig. 2. Identifier Ring

and the degree of peer heterogeneity. For example, if virtual peers residing at the same node share all information, could we get a better routing performance if the number of virtual peers residing at the same node increases more as they will share more information and have a larger combined routing table?

Based on this information, we propose a new routing algorithm for the virtualized P2P network, which improves the average number of hops per query by 13% to 25% depends on the degree of peer heterogeneity and peer virtualization.

One of main problems in load balancing is to identify where the extra load should be assigned. Previous load balancing schemes need to periodically exchange load and capacity information when there are no overload nodes. In addition, they ignore many factors including the cost for capacity in different nodes. In reality, the cost is different depending on the reputation and reliability of the nodes. We propose a new scheme in which we could find the top k best available nodes with only 2(N-1) messages within 2O(logN) hops while we do not need to periodically exchange the load and capacity. (N is the number of physical nodes.) Moreover, our top k nodes could base on multiple factors such as load, cost, distance, reliability, reputation and security level. In addition, these factors are based on the latest information available in the P2P network.

The primary contributions of our work presented in this paper are as follows.

1) We propose a new routing algorithm for the virtual P2P network that improves the average number of hops per lookup by 13% to 25%.
2) We analytically show the optimality of the Chord protocol in physical P2P network, and compare the expected number of hops per query with our routing algorithm in a virtualized P2P network from analytical perspective and through simulations.
3) We propose a Top-k peer selection algorithm to find out the top k best available under-loaded nodes in the current P2P network with 2(N-1) messages within 2O(logN) hops. With this algorithm, peers only need to exchange load and other information when overloaded nodes send the request instead of periodically updating this information. The load balancing scheme is based on multiple factors which could be optimized on cost, proximity, reputation and other factors.

This paper is organized as follows. In Section 2, we introduce peer heterogeneity, peer virtualization, and load balancing. Section 3 provides the system model. Section 4 describes the new routing/query algorithm and top-k nodes algorithms. Section 5 provides the theoretical analysis. Section 6 presents the simulation results. Section 7 compares the related work. Section 8 contains a summary and future work.

2 Peer Heterogeneity and Load Balancing

2.1 Peer Heterogeneity and Virtualization

Typically peer nodes have different computing capabilities including CPU, memory, storage and network bandwidth. When we allocate the load, e.g., publish the resource's information, it would be natural to assign more load, e.g., publish larger number of resource objects, to the sites with more capabilities. As [6] mentioned, peer virtualization is one way to address peer heterogeneity. Existing approaches [3, 2] assign a static number of virtual peer identifiers to a node according to the capabilities of the node when the node joins the overlay network. One of the problems in these approaches is, after we assign these virtual peers to a node, the node always keeps these virtual peers no matter how the capabilities and the load of the node changes. Intuitively, the number of virtual peer identifiers assigned to the node at the first time may not be appropriate. Furthermore, in a dynamic environment, the capabilities and the load of a node may change dramatically. [7] proposes a scheme to adapt the number of virtual peers in a node according to its load situation.

Our peer virtualization scheme combines the adaptive approach proposed in [7] with node categories discussed in the following. In our adaptive design, the number of virtual peers assigned to a node dynamically changes depending on the load and capabilities of the node. We mainly focus on three capabilities: computing capability such as CPU and memory, storage capability such as disk spaces, and network capability including network bandwidth. We classify physical nodes based on computing, storage and network capabilities of nodes. When overload/hotspots occur, the overloaded node sends the load balancing request so the number of virtual peers assigned to a physical node may dynamically change. When the load of a node reaches a certain threshold in one or all three capabilities, e.g. when the CPU load exceeds 90%, we should reduce the number of virtual peer identifiers associated with the node.

2.2 Load Balancing

We can represent the capacity of a node p as $\mathrm{Capacity}_{\mathbf{p}}(c,s,b)$ and the load as $\mathrm{Load}_{\mathbf{p}}(c,s,b)$. There is load threshold $T_p(c, s, b)$. In the above terms, c denotes respectively computing capacity/load/threshold, s denotes storage capacity/ load/ threshold and b denotes network bandwidth capacity/load/threshold respectively. If $\mathrm{Load}_{\mathbf{p}}(c,s,b) > T_p(c, s, b)$, node p is overloaded. For the virtual peer i in the node p, the load is denoted as $\mathrm{Load}_{\mathbf{p,i}}(c,s,b)$.

Adapting an overloaded node to normal condition or achieving a state where every physical node is lowered below the threshold is called load balancing. The specific implementation of adaptation is to utilize the algorithm for a virtual peer to join or leave the virtual P2P network. That is, removing a virtual peer is equal to a virtual peer leaving the network, and adding a virtual peer is equal to a virtual peer identifier joining the network. The problems that we need to answer are therefore "*Which virtual peers should be moved*?" and "*Where should these virtual peers be moved to?*"

For the first problem, we want to find out the set of virtual peers in node p that minimize the load moved while satisfying the goal of reducing the load of overloaded node to normal. So we want to find out $(I_{p,1}, \ldots I_{p,n},)$ that minimize $\sum_{i=1}^{n} Load_{p,i}(c,s,b)$ so that $\mathrm{Load}_{\mathbf{p}}(c,s,b) < T_p(c, s, b)$ in which $I_{p,i}$ is the *i*th virtual peer in the node p.

For the second problem, we propose the top k peer selection algorithm to find the top k best nodes, which satisfy certain criteria, in the P2P network. "How to decide k?" is not the focus in this paper. But a rule of thumb is to choose k that equals to the number of virtual peers needed to be moved from p. We can get this information from the answer to the first problem.

A top-k peer selection query includes two kinds of criteria: Selection Criteria (SC) and Optimization Criteria (OC). SC is the criteria that peers must meet. OC is the criteria that the query should optimize. A sample query is described informally as follows.

```
            SELECT top k peers
Selection Criteria:
            T(c,s,b) - Load(c,s,b) > mLoad(c,s,b)
    AND     Security_level > 0
    AND     Reliability >99%
    AND     Location = 'USA'
    AND                      Reputation >='****'
    AND     Cost < $1,000
    AND     Distance < 500 miles
Optimization Criteria:     MIN(Cost)
```

In the above top k query, mLoad(c,s,b) is the additional capacity available to accommodate a virtual peer. So the peer should have enough spare capacity, the security level should be above 0, the reliability should be above 99%, the peer is located at USA, the reputation should be equal or above 4 stars, the cost for mLoad(c,s,b) is less than the budget $1,000 and the distance to the overloaded node is less than 500 miles. We want to select top k peers that satisfy the above condition and have the cheapest cost per capacity unit. This is a cost-based load balancing scheme.

By using the optimization criteria in the above top k query, we essentially transfer our load balancing scheme into a multi-dimension multi-criteria decision problem. For example, if we want a proximity aware scheme, we could use MIN(Distance) as the optimization criterion. If we need a reputation-based scheme, we could use MAX(Reputation) as the optimization criterion.

3 System Model

Structured P2P systems such as DHT based P2P systems provide an upper bound on the number of messages so that they guarantee the answer if the result is in the P2P network. As we can see from [3, 8, 9, 10, 11, 12], this feature is based on the design of identifiers in the distributed hash tables. There are two identifiers in a virtualized P2P system: peer identifier and resource identifier. In order to map a resource identifier to a peer identifier, both identifiers are carefully designed in an m-bit identifier ring modulo 2^m, where m is a system parameter (m=24 in our study) and 2^m is the identifier space, so that a peer node can be identified when a resource identifier is known. (A resource identifier could be seen as a keyword in Chord.) The identifier ring is depicted in Figure 2. A physical node could be associated with multiple virtual peer identifiers. P, P'', P''' are three physical nodes. Virtual peers P_1, P_2, P_3, P_4 and P_5

are located in node P. Virtual peers P_1', P_2', P_3', P_4' and P_5' are located in node P'. Virtual peers P_1'' and P_2'' are located in node P''.

There are two layers of P2P networks in our system. One is the virtualized P2P network that we use to publish/lookup resource objects. The other is the physical network that we use to do load balancing. Our top k peer algorithm is executed in the physical P2P network that has a much smaller number of peers than the virtualized P2P network. We use the new routing algorithm in the virtualized P2P network and Chord protocol in the physical one.

3.1 Peer Virtualization Data Model

Now we discuss the system model. Let Ip denote a peer identifier, Ir denote resource identifier, Np denote the number of peer identifiers, Nr denote the number of resource identifiers. Usually Nr >> Np.

Properties: Properties(Ip) of a peer identifier Ip describe the address, port, capabilities, node class and load information.

Predecessor: Predecessor(Ip) of a peer identifier Ip is the maximum peer identifier that is less than Ip in the peer identifier ring.

Successor Node Set: SuccessorSet (Ip) of a virtual peer identifier Ip is defined as:

$$\text{SuccessorSet (Ip)} = \{ \text{Ip}_i \mid \text{Ip}_i = \text{SUCC\_NODE (Ip, i)} \ (0<=i<r)\}$$

in which SUCC_NODE (x, i) returns the ith minimum peer identifier which satisfies two conditions: i) it is greater than x in the peer identifier ring and ii) the node associated with this peer identifier x is different from the nodes that are already in the successor node set, and r is the number of successive nodes maintained.

Routing Table: RoutingTable (Ip) of a peer identifier Ip for node p is defined as:

RoutingTable (Ip) = { (Ipi, Address(Ipi)) | Ipi = MIN_NODE ((Ip+2^{i-1}) mod 2^m) (0<=i<=Np)} in which MIN_NODE (x) returns the minimum peer identifier which is greater than or equal to x in the peer identifier ring, and Address (x) returns the physical IP address of the peer identifier x.

Peer Identifier Descriptor: PeerDescriptor(Ip) of a peer identifier can be defined as {Ip, Properties (Ip), Predecessor (Ip), SuccessorSet (Ip), RoutingTable (Ip)}.

Node Descriptor: NodeDescriptor(p) of a node p is defined as

$$\{(\text{Ip}_i, \text{PeerDescriptor}(\text{Ip}_i)) \mid \text{Ip}_i \text{ is one of virtual peers residing in node p.}\}$$

In our discussion, all comparisons assume modulo 2^m operations unless otherwise specified. If peer p' is said to be closer to peer p than p'' to p, that means p' is in the clockwise path from p'' to p in the identifier ring. (This is a very important point to understand the algorithms.) The routing table is used to route the information among virtual peer nodes. The successor node set is used for fault tolerance. As we will discuss in the routing algorithm, the successor node set could also be utilized to speed up routing.

4 Algorithm

4.1 Routing

In previous DHT protocols such as Chord, only the routing table of the peer identifier is used for the routing protocol. In our system, we utilize both the routing table and successor node set of *all* peer identifiers in the node for the routing of a message. As we previously discussed, we assign different numbers of virtual peers to a node according to the capabilities and the load of the node. A node p is associated with the node descriptor NodeDescriptor(p). The idea to speed up the routing process is to utilize the shared information in the node descriptor as the computation in the local node is much cheaper than the message communication among nodes. A typical situation of routing is to locate the proper peer identifier Ip given a resource identifier Ir. The algorithm to find the next peer identifier Ip' to which the request is forwarded from the current node p is described in Algorithm 1. FIND_CLOSEST_NODE () returns the peer identifier, which is the clockwise closest peer in the identifier ring to the destination peer.

Algorithm 1. Finding the next peer identifier (Routing algorithm)

```
0   Routing (Ir, Ip, p) {
1   If (Ir == Ip) return (Ip, p); // find the peer identifier and the node
2   Else {
3           (Ip', p') = (Ip, p) // initialize
4           For (i=0; i < GetNumberOfPeerIDs(p); i ++) {
5           // Find the closest peer identifier (Ip'', p'') in the routing table of this peer identifier
6                   (Ip'', p'') = FIND_CLOSEST_NODE (Ir, p.PeerIDs(i).RoutingTable);
7         // Find the closest peer identifier (Ip'', p'') in the successor node set
8         // of this peer identifier
9                   (Ip''', p''') =FIND_ CLOSEST_NODE(Ir, p.PeerIDs(i).SuccessorSet);
10          // Compare (Ip', p') with (Ip'', p'') and (Ip''', p''') to find the closet
11          // peer identifier in these three identifier pairs.
12        // Assign the closest peer identifier and its node to (Ip', p');
13          (Ip', p') = FIND_ CLOSEST_NODE (Ir, {(Ip', p'), (Ip'', p''), (Ip''',p''')});
14          }
15          return (Ip', p');        } }
```

In this paper, the old routing algorithm refers to Chord routing algorithm in the virtualized P2P network. The new routing algorithm refers to our routing algorithm. The key difference between this routing algorithm and the old one is the loop from Line 4 to Line 14. The old routing algorithm will not search the routing tables and successor node sets of *all* virtual peer servers residing in the same node. This routing algorithm is not limited to our peer virtualization scheme. If a peer virtualization scheme does not maintain a successor node set for each virtual peer, the routing algorithm could ignore Line 9.

Now we use an example to compare the new routing algorithm and the old routing algorithm. In Figure 2, a query request for resource Ix is made to the virtual peer P_1. PATH 1 (P_1->P'_2->P_4->P'_4->P''_1) shows the routing path in the old routing algorithm, which only searches the routing table of the virtual peer. PATH 2 (P_1-> P'_4->P''_1) shows the routing path if we search all the routing tables of all virtual peers residing at the same node. PATH 3 (P1-> P''_1) shows the routing path of the new routing algorithm, which searches all the routing tables and successive Node Set of all virtual peer servers residing in the same node. As we can see from Figure 2, PATH 1 needs 4 hops to reach the destination, PATH 2 needs 2 hops to reach the destination and PATH 3 only needs one hop to reach the destination.

Hypothesis 1: Let PATH (p', p, Ir) be the routing path from p' to p and PATH (p'', p, Ir) be the routing path from p'' to p. Let Distance (p', p, Ir) be the number of hops of PATH(p', p, Ir) and Distance(p'', p, Ir) be the number of hops of PATH(p'', p, Ir).

If p' is closer to p than p'' is close to p in the clockwise direction, we have

Distance (p', p, Ir) <= Distance (p'', p, Ir)

The hypothesis is correct if p' and p'' are virtual peers that reside in the same physical node p* since our routing algorithm will search routing tables and successor sets in p* to find the same or closer next peer so that Distance (p', p, Ir) <= Distance (p'', p, Ir). Is it correct in all cases? We will discuss the details in Section 5.

Hypothesis 2: If virtual peers residing at the same node share all information, could we get a better routing performance if the number of virtual peers residing at the same node increases more as they will share more information and have a larger combined routing table? Is it possibly better than Chord routing algorithm in the physical P2P network?

Intuitively it could be true. But we will use the simulation to verify part I of Hypothesis 2 and verify Part II in an analytical approach.

4.2 Top-K Peer Selection Algorithm

As we discussed in Section 2.2, one of main problems in load balancing is to find the appropriate nodes to transfer the extra load. Previous approaches need to maintain metadata information about load periodically in P2P system even if there are no overloaded nodes. Moreover, they could not find out the best available peers satisfying the requirement of an overloaded node.

In order to find top k physical under-loaded peers that optimize the optimization criteria, we need to have global information. Broadcast is one way to get this information. But regular broadcast approaches such as Gnutella [5] usually flood messages into the whole P2P network and it is uncertain when the query will end.

As we use Chord protocol in the physical P2P network, we already maintain a finger (/routing) table in each physical node. So why cannot we reuse these information to assist broadcasting?

Here we present a clever broadcast approach. The idea is to broadcast the messages to the nodes in the finger table. In the routing process, the message will be forwarded to only one node in its finger table. In the broadcast process, the message will be forwarded to multiple nodes in its finger table. The specific algorithm is presented as follows.

Algorithm 2. Top-k Peer Selection

Input: the overloaded node p, a Top-k query including Peer Selection Criteria (SC) and Optimization Criteria (OC),
Output: Top-k peers that satisfy SC
Phase I: Broadcast

1. p broadcasts the top k peer query into each node in its finger table.
2. Each node p'_i receiving a top-k peer query will check itself to see whether it satisfy the requirement of peer selection criteria. If yes, it will add itself into its qualifying peer list.
3. p'_i will forward the top k peer query to the nodes in its finger table if these node identifiers fall into the identifier space between p'_i and $p'_{(i+1)}$ (clockwise). If the number of queries p'_i forwards fno>0, and the number of responses p'_i receives rno<fno, p'_i will wait for the response from the nodes that it sends the query. Otherwise, p'_i enters the next phase.

Phase II: Aggregation

4. After p'_i collected all responses, it picks the top k peers from its qualifying peer list based on the selection criteria that we want to optimize. It could be cost, load, proximity, reputation or other criteria.
5. p'_i sends top k peers back to the source that it receives the request from.
6. p receives all responses from all nodes in its finger table, and picks the top k peers from all responses.

In this algorithm, the nodes select the top k peers based on the local information, peer selection criteria and optimization criteria in the query request. So the system does not need periodically exchange the dynamic metadata information such as load.

Theorem 1. Top-k peer selection algorithm takes exactly 2(N-1) messages with 2O(logN) hops. (N is the number of physical nodes.)

Proof. Let's first look at the broadcast phase. In this phase, every node other than p receives exactly one top-k query request. In aggregation phase, every node other than p sends a top-k query response back to the node that it receives the request from. So the algorithm will cost exactly 2(N-1) messages.

Based on Chord protocol, we know that the maximum number of hops that p is needed to reach any other nodes is O(logN). As the maximum number of hops for p to receive a top-k result is also O(logN). The maximum number of hops for the algorithm is 2O(logN).

Theorem 2 (Correctness). Top-k peer selection algorithm selects the top k peers, which satisfy the Selection Criteria (SC) and Optimization Criteria (OC), in the whole P2P network.

Proof. The assumption here is that the attributes in selection criteria and optimization criteria do not change during the top-k peer selection. This is reasonable as the process needs only 2(logN) hops. As we select these top k peers from all peers, the aggregation phase guarantees that there are no better peers available to satisfy SC and OC. Under the above assumption, we know that the algorithm selects the best k peers.

5 Theoretical Analysis

In this section, we will focus on the theoretical analysis of our algorithms.

Claim 1. Chord routing algorithm in the physical P2P network can be decomposed into a knapsack problem.

Proof. In Chord, each node maintains, in the steady state, a table of nodes at a fixed distance from that node. The distance from the start to the end node then becomes the knapsack; we want to fill the space provided with the lowest number of hops as we can.

Claim 2. Chord routing algorithm is optimal with its finger table in the physical P2P network.

Proof. Chord uses, at its base, a greedy algorithm, always taking as big steps as it can as soon as it can. Since Chord's finger table consists of nodes that are distant by powers of 2, this algorithm always finds the optimal route for that finger table.

Now let us look at part II of **Hypothesis 2**.

Our routing algorithm is also a greedy algorithm always taking as big steps as it can at each step since Algorithm 1 picks the closest next node from the routing tables of all virtual peers. However, the hops we can make are dependent on the hops we've already made, and the hop-sizes are no longer powers of two, so a greedy algorithm may not be optimal. Combining with the conclusion in Claim 2, the answer is "No".

Next we try to verify **Hypothesis 1**. Hypothesis I could be rephrased into the following question. **Question 2**: Will the new routing algorithm that combines routing tables amongst virtual peers residing in the same physical peer, always perform at least as well as the Chord algorithm without sharing routing table combination?

The answer is "no". Here is a counter-example. In a 2^4 identifier space, 0 needs only 1 hop to reach 8. 1 needs 3 hops to reach 8. So we can see that the new routing algorithm is not better than the previous algorithm in all cases, but we believe the average number of hops per query by using our new routing algorithm should be better than the old one. (We also verified this in the simulation section.)

In order to determine the number of hops taken by various key-based routing algorithms, it is necessary to build a mathematical model of the algorithm.

We start by making a number of simplifying assumptions. First, we assume that the number of active physical nodes $N=2^n$ for some positive integer n, and the address space is much larger than the number of physical or virtual nodes (which is a reasonable assumption, since Chord uses an address space of size 2^{160}). We further assume that the nodes are equally spaced around the address space. While this does not really reflect the actual state of affairs, it does allow us to examine the behavior of the system in the average case. This allows us to view the address space as continuous, but broken up into 2^n discrete, equal sections. While the sections will not be, in reality, equal, the random behavior of the algorithms allows us to make this approximation, since the more the number of nodes present in the system, the more it will approach this ideal.

When we introduce virtual nodes, we will make the assumption that the number of virtual nodes M = $2^{m'}$ for some positive integer m'. The degree of peer virtualization (PVR) we represent as $\gamma = \frac{M}{N}$.

In order to measure the expected behavior of the system, we introduce a random variable X. X represents a random target in the address space that we will attempt to locate using the algorithm (assuming a source location of 0, without loss of generality). We are interested then in H_X, the number of hops required to reach X from 0.

Theorem 3. In Chord, the expected number of hops required to reach a random target, $E(H_X)$, is $\frac{1}{2}n$.

Proof. In order to find this, we must count the number of possible targets for each potential $H_X = p$, which we call C(p). For p = 1, clearly, C(1) = n. More generally, C(p) = $\binom{n}{p}$. This number is difficult to analyze, but the fact that it is symmetrical around $\frac{1}{2}n$ gives an expected value for $p = H_X$, $E(H_X) = \frac{1}{2}n$. This result is also verified in the simulation results in Chord [10].

Lemma 1. In Chord with node virtualization, the expected number of hops,

$$E(H_X) = \frac{1}{2}m' = \frac{1}{2}(n + \log \gamma) \cdot$$

The proof of this theoretic is similar to the proof above, since peer virtualization results in an identical number of hops as if each of the virtual nodes were a physical node.

For comparison, we define an algorithm like Chord, called Random. The difference is that, instead of maintaining a finger table of nodes at fixed distances, Random nodes maintain finger tables of size k of nodes at random points around the address space. At each step, if the target is not within its finger table, the algorithm picks a random target.

Theorem 4. In Random, the expected number of hops, $E(H_X)$, is $\frac{N}{k}$.

Proof. At each step of Random's trip around its address space, its probability of reaching its target is $\frac{k}{N}$, since the current node has a size k finger table, and there is a $\frac{1}{N}$ chance that each particular target is the correct one. This therefore is a straightforward Poisson distribution, and $E(H_X)$ is $\frac{N}{k}$.

6 Performance Evaluation

In this section, simulations are done to demonstrate and validate our design. The experiment data is a collection of keywords, which originally come from 80,000 HTML documents collected from 1,000 websites. The total number of different keywords is around 21,000,000. In addition, 160,000 search terms collected from a real world search engine are used to measure the performance of queries.

The hop length of the routing is the number of hops of the routing path of a query. It is the average hop length from many sample queries. In our simulation, we measure 160,000 queries to find the average hop length of the queries. For each query, we randomly choose a virtual peer as the initiator node. We measure the number of hops for each query and find the average number of hops per query from 160,000 sample queries.

Let R_{hop} denote the hop length ratio, HIR_{hop} be the hop improvement ratio, PVR be the peer virtualization ratio, PHR be the peer heterogeneity ratio. We have

$$R_{hop} = \frac{Hop_{old}}{Hop_{new}}, \quad HIR_{hop} = R_{hop} - 1 = \frac{Hop_{old}}{Hop_{new}} - 1,$$

and $$PVR = \frac{Total\ Number\ of\ Virtual\ Peers}{Total\ Number\ of\ Physical\ Peers}$$

As we can see from the above formula, PVR will always be equal to or greater than 1.

In order to evaluate the impact of peer heterogeneity, we use two distributions for nodes: Gaussian distribution and Real distribution. In Gaussian distribution, we use PVR as the mean and PVR/3 as the standard deviation. Of course, the number of virtual peers in a physical node will always be greater than 0. Real distribution is the real world distribution that we deduced from the statistics analysis of 1000 websites. It gives the probability of 0.1%, 1%, 0.6%, 1%, 4.2%, 7.6%, 17.4%, 33.5%, 22.6% and 12% for capacities of 900, 700, 450, 350, 250, 175, 125, 75, 30 and 1. Peer Heterogeneity Ratio (PHR) is the ratio to measure the degree that the system assign load according to their peer heterogeneity. This ratio is between 0 and 1. If PHR = 0, the system views each node as being the same. This transfers into a uniform distribution with PVR=1. If PHR = 1, the system utilize the peer heterogeneity at the utmost degree.

In the simulation, we want to study the routing overhead, the average number of hops per query and routing improvement ratio with respect to peer virtualization ratio, peer heterogeneity ratio and the number of physical nodes. In addition, we want to verify Hypothesis 2.

6.1 Routing Overhead Comparison

Following up Figure 1, Figure 3(a) shows the routing overhead of two algorithms for 1000 physical nodes with Gaussian distribution. Routing overhead in both algorithms increases as PVR becomes larger since the total number of virtual peers (M=PVR*1000) also increases. We can see that the new routing algorithm reduces the

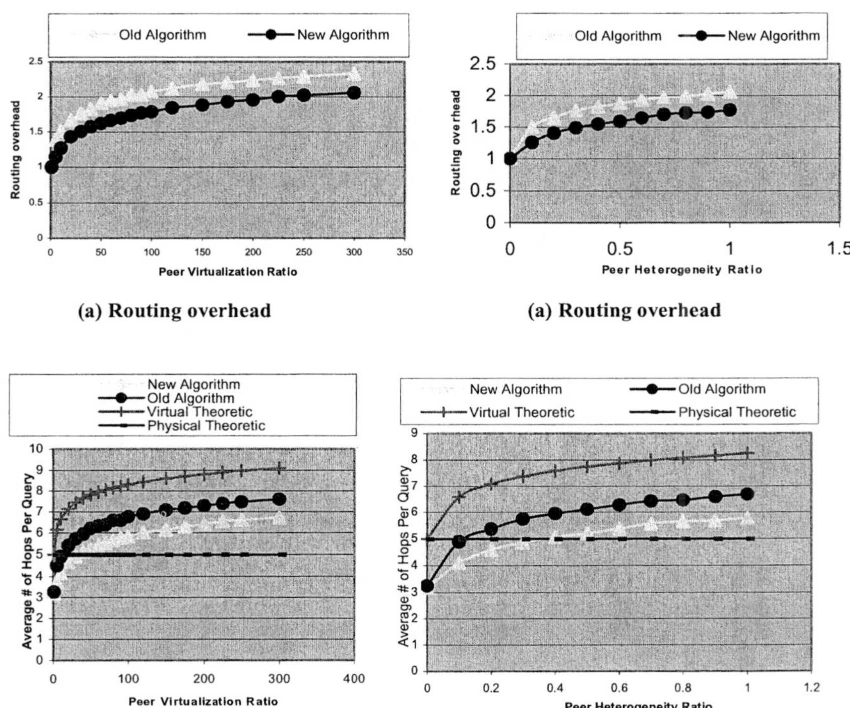

(b) Comparison of expected # of hops per query

(b) Comparison of expected # of hops per query

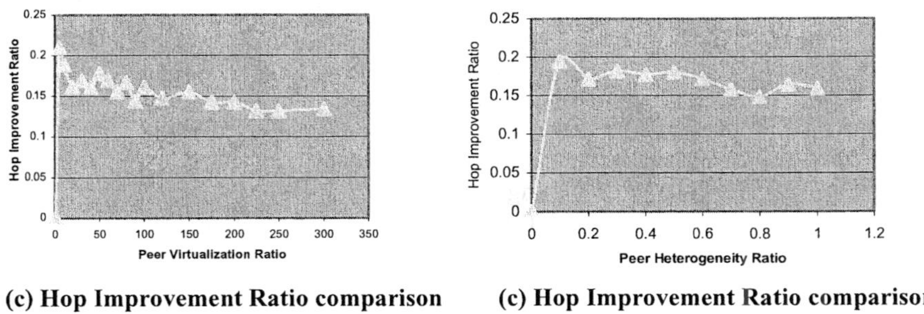

(c) Hop Improvement Ratio comparison

(c) Hop Improvement Ratio comparison

Fig 3. Impact of peer virtualization ratio (Gaussian distribution, # of nodes =1000)

Fig 4. Impact of peer heterogeneity ratio (Real Distribution, # of nodes =1000)

routing overhead by 30% compared to the old one. As we previously explained, therouting message may bounce between two nodes in the old routing algorithm when we use virtual peers. The new routing algorithm removes the bouncing among peers and utilizes routing tables and successor sets of all virtual peers in the node to improve the routing. Nevertheless, the routing overhead is still big in the new algorithm. As $R_{overhead}$ is always greater than or equal to 1, there is always routing overhead as long as there is peer virtualization. The baseline case could be seen as the optimal case.

Figure 4(a) shows the similar pattern for routing overhead of the two algorithms. The routing overhead increases as PHR increases since the total number of virtual peers increases becomes larger. The routing overhead in the new algorithm is improved by 0% to 27% compared to one in the old algorithm. This improvement increases as the PHR increases.

6.2 Comparison of Average Number of Hops Per Query

We can deduct the average number of hops per query from our theoretical analysis. From Theorem 3, we can know physical theoretical value of the average number of hops per query in a P2P network

$$PTV = \frac{1}{2} LogN$$

in which N is the number of physical nodes. From Lemma 1, we can know virtual theoretic value of the average number of hops per query in a P2P network

$$VTV = \frac{1}{2} M = \frac{1}{2} (LogN + LogPVR)$$

in which M is the number of virtual peers.

We now look at the average number of hops per query in the two algorithms. Figure 3(b) shows that the average number of hops increases when PVR increases. The average number of hops in the new algorithm is always equal or better than one in the old algorithm. The two algorithms always outperform the virtual theoretical case. As the number of physical nodes is set to 1000, the physical theoretic value is a constant. After PVR>=10, the old algorithm underperforms the physical theoretical case. While the new algorithm trails the physical theoretical case after PVR>=40. So after PVR>=40, the average number of hops per query falls between the physical theoretic value and the virtual theoretical value. Figure 4(b) shows the similar pattern as Figure 3(b). As PHR changes from 0 to 1, the average number of hops increases in both algorithms and the new algorithm always outperforms the old algorithm.

6.3 Impact of Peer Virtualization Ratio

Now we look at the impact of peer virtualization ratio. At first, we want to explain why PVR could be 100 or more in the simulation. The purpose is to see whether the load balance performance could be better when you have more virtual peers as each virtual peer is allocated a smaller number of load, assuming the load would be distributed uniformly. Figure 3(a) and (b) shows that the routing overhead and the average number of hops per query increase as PVR increases. This occurs as the number of virtual numbers dramatically increases. Figure 3(c) demonstrates that the new routing algorithm improves the average routing hop length of a query by 13% to 23% compared to the old algorithm. When PVR is smaller, the hop improvement ratio is better. As PVR increases, the total number of virtual peers increases but the size of each routing table does not change so the hop improvement ratio drops.

6.4 Impact of Peer Heterogeneity Ratio

Now we look at the impact of peer heterogeneity ratio. Figure 4(a) and (b) shows that the routing overhead and the average number of hops per query increase as PVR increases. This occurs as the increase of PHR incurs a larger number of virtual numbers. Figure 4(c) demonstrates that the new routing algorithm improves the average routing hop length of a query by 14% to 19% compared to the old algorithm. When PHR is smaller, the hop improvement ratio is better. As PHR increases, the total number of virtual peers increases but the size of each routing table does not change so the hop improvement ratio drops.

6.5 Impact of the Number of Physical Nodes

Figure 5(a) shows that the performance of two algorithms are between the physical theoretical case and the virtual theoretical case as PVR=50. As the number of physical nodes increases, the average number of hops in four situations also increases. The performance of the new algorithm is very close to the physical theoretical case. Figure 5(b) shows that the performance of two algorithms are between the physical theoretical case and the virtual theoretical case as PHR=1. As the number of physical nodes increases, the average number of hops in four situations also increases. In both figures, the new algorithm outperforms the old algorithm.

Overall the simulations verify that our routing algorithm always have a smaller expected number of hops per query than the previous routing algorithms. Routing overhead increases as PVRs increases. In order to control routing overhead, we need to control PVR. As we can see from the results, the answer to Hypothesis 2 is "no".

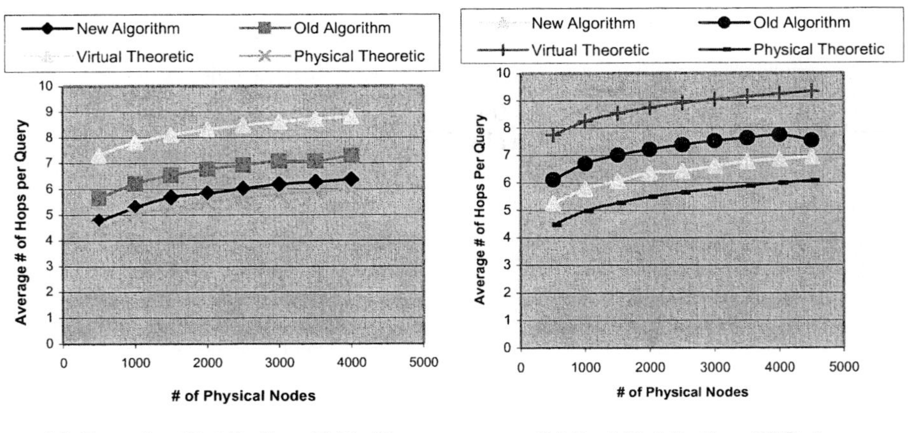

(a) Gaussian Distribution, PVR=50 (b) Real Distribution, PHR=1

Fig. 5. Impact of the number of Physical Nodes

7 Related Work

A few peer virtualization schemes [2, 3, 7, 13] are proposed to address load balancing and peer heterogeneity among peers. In [2, 3], the number of virtual peer servers assigned to a node is proportional to its capacity. [7] proposes a scheme to adapt the number of virtual peer servers in a node according to its load situation. [13] proposes a peer virtualization scheme to utilize the proximity among peer nodes in order to reduce the overhead of transferring the load from one peer node to another peer node. But they did not explore sharing information among virtual peers and study how the various factors affect the performance of the routing process. Super peer approach [11] separates super peers from simple peers so that super peer will have more responsibilities such as routing and computing. Nonetheless, this does not solve load balancing among super peers, as there is capacity heterogeneity among super peers. [14] proposes online load balancing algorithms that guarantee a constant imbalance ratio for horizontal range partitioning. Top-K algorithm [1] proposes a top-k query retrieval in a super-peer HyperCuP topology. But it does not have any connections with load balancing and it is designed for the specific topology. Our load balancing scheme such as top-k peer selection algorithm is not a replacement of other load balancing schemes. Rather it could be combined with other schemes to find a good match. For example, our scheme could be used when the overload/hotspots are not frequent. It provides a very useful mechanism to find the optimal k peers based on the design objective function.

8 Conclusion

In this paper, we propose a new routing algorithm for the virtual P2P network that improves the average number of hops per lookup by 13% to 25%. We analytically show the optimality of Chord protocol in physical P2P network, and compare the expected number of hops per query with our routing algorithm. We propose a top k load balancing algorithm to find out the top k best available under-loaded nodes in the current P2P network with 2(N-1) messages within 2O(logN) hops. With this algorithm, peers need to exchange load and other information only when overloaded nodes send the request instead of periodically updating this information.

References

1. W. Balke, W. Nejdl, W. Siberski, U. Thaden. " Progressive Distributed Top-k Retrieval in Peer-to-Peer Networks", Proceedings of ICDE 2005, Tokyo, Japan.
2. F. Dabek, M.F. Kaashoek, D. Karger, R. Morris, and I. Stoica. "Wide-area cooperative storage with CFS." Proceedings of the 18th ACM Symp. On Operating Systems Principles (SOSP 01), Oct. 2001.
3. B. Gedik and L. Liu. "PeerCQ: A Decentralized and Self-Configuring Peer-to-Peer Information Monitoring System". ICDCS 2003.
4. L. Galanis, Y. Wang, S. R. Jeffery, D. J. DeWitt. "Locating Data Sources in Large Distributed Systems." VLDB 2003.
5. Gnutella. http://gnutella.wego.com

6. D. Karger, E. Lehman and T. Leighton etc. "Consistent hashing and random trees: Distributed caching protocols for relieving hot spots on the World Wide Web". In ACM Symposium on Theory of Computing Author Index, pages 654–663, May 1997.
7. A. Rao, K. Lakshminarayanan, R. K. Sonesh Surana, and I. Stoica. "Load balancing in structured p2p systems." In Proceedings of the 2nd International Workshop on Peer-to-Peer Systems (IPTPS), Feb. 2003.
8. S. Ratnasamy, P. Francis, M. Handley, R. Karp, S. Shenker. "A Scalable Content-Addressable Network." SIGCOMM 2001.
9. A. Rowstron and P. Druschel, "Pastry: Scalable, distributed object location and routing for large-scale peer-to-peer systems". IFIP/ACM International Conference on Distributed Systems Platforms (Middleware), Heidelberg, Germany, pages 329-350, November 2001.
10. I. Stoica, R. Morris, D. Karger, F. Kaashoek, H. Balakrishnan. "Chord: A Scalable Peer-To-Peer Lookup Service for Internet Applications." SIGCOMM 2001.
11. B. Yang and H. Garcia-Molina. "Designing a super-peer network." In Proc. ICDE, March 2003.
12. B. Y. Zhao, L. Huang, J. Stribling, S. C. Rhea, A. D. Joseph, and J. Kubiatowicz , "Tapestry: A Resilient Global-scale Overlay for Service Deployment" IEEE Journal on Selected Areas in Communications.
13. Y. Zhu and Y. Hu, "Towards Efficient Load Balancing in Structured P2P Systems", IPDPS 2004.
14. P. Ganesan, M. Bawa, and H. Garcia-Molina. "Online balancing of range-partitioned data with applications to peer-to-peer systems", In VLDB 2004.

Distributed Network Querying with Bounded Approximate Caching

Badrish Chandramouli[1], Jun Yang[1], and Amin Vahdat[2]

[1] Dept. of Computer Science, Duke University
{badrish, junyang}@cs.duke.edu
[2] Dept. of Computer Science and Engg., University of California, San Diego
vahdat@cs.ucsd.edu

Abstract. As networks continue to grow in size and complexity, distributed network monitoring and resource querying are becoming increasingly difficult. Our aim is to design, build, and evaluate a scalable infrastructure for answering queries over distributed measurements, at reduced costs (in terms of both network traffic and query latency) while maintaining required precision. In this infrastructure, each network node owns a set of numerical measurements and actively maintains bounds on these values cached at other nodes. We can answer queries approximately, using bounds from nearby caches to avoid contacting the owners directly. We focus on developing efficient and scalable techniques to place, locate, and manage bounded approximate caches across a large network. We have developed two approaches: One uses a recursive partitioning of the network space to place caches in a static, controlled manner, while the other uses a locality-aware *distributed hash table* to place caches in a dynamic and decentralized manner. In this paper, we focus on the latter approach. Experiments over a large-scale emulated network show that our techniques are very effective in reducing query costs while generating an acceptable amount of background traffic; they are also able to exploit various forms of locality that are naturally present in queries, and adapt to volatility of measurements.

1 Introduction

Consider a network of nodes, each monitoring a number of numeric measurements. These measurements may be related to performance, e.g., per-node statistics such as CPU load and the amount of free memory, or pairwise statistics such as latency and bandwidth between nodes. Measurements may also be application-specific, e.g., progress of certain tasks, rate of requests for particular services, popularity of objects in terms of number of recent hits, etc. Such measurements are of interest to distributed monitoring systems (e.g., Ganglia [8]) as well as systems requiring support for querying distributed resources (e.g., PlanetLab [12] and the Grid [6]).

We consider the problem of efficiently supporting relational-style queries over these distributed measurements. For example, a network administrator may want to issue periodic monitoring queries from a workstation over a remote cluster

M.L. Lee, K.L. Tan, and V. Wuwongse (Eds.): DASFAA 2006, LNCS 3882, pp. 374–388, 2006.

of nodes; a team of scientists may be interested in monitoring the status of an ongoing distributed simulation running over the Grid. The results of these monitoring queries may be displayed in real time in a graphical interface on the querying node, or used in further analysis. As another example, consider relational-style querying of distributed resources. Suppose there are two sets of nodes. A query may request pairs of nodes (one from each set) satisfying the following condition: Both nodes have low load (which can be expressed as relational selection conditions), and the latency between them is low (which can be expressed as a relational join condition). Such queries are typical in resource discovery, e.g., when a Grid user wants to select a data replica and a compute server among candidate replicas/machines to perform a job, or when a distributed systems researcher wants to select some nodes on PlanetLab with desired load and connectivity requirements for running experiments.

With increasing network size and complexity, the task of querying distributed measurements has become exceedingly difficult and costly in terms of time and network traffic. Processing a query naively (by simply contacting the nodes responsible for the requested measurements) is very expensive, as we will demonstrate in our experiments. If kept unchecked, network activities caused by the queries could interfere with normal operations and lead to unintended artifacts in performance-related measurement values. These problems are exacerbated by periodic monitoring queries, by queries that request measurements from a large number of nodes, and by queries that return a large result set.

We seek to develop a better infrastructure for distributed network querying, by exploiting optimization opportunities that naturally arise in our target applications: (1) *Approximation*: For most network monitoring and resource querying applications, exact answers are not needed. Approximate values will suffice as long as the degree of inaccuracy is quantified and reported, and the user can control the degree of inaccuracy. Small errors usually have little bearing on how measurements are interpreted and used by these applications; at any rate, these applications already cope with errors that are inevitable due to the stochastic nature of measurements. (2) *Locality*: Many types of localities may be naturally present in queries. There is temporal locality in periodic monitoring queries and queries for popular resources. There may also be spatial locality among nodes that query the same measurements; for example, a cluster of nodes run similar client tasks that each check the load on a set of remote servers to decide which server to send their requests. Finally, there may be spatial locality among measurements requested by a query; for example, a network administrator monitors a cluster of nodes, which are close to each other in the network.

We have built a distributed querying infrastructure that exploits the optimization opportunities discussed above. The first opportunity can be exploited by *bounded approximate caching* [10] of measurement values. To ensure the quality of approximation, the system actively updates a cache whenever the actual value falls outside a prescribed bound around the cached value. The effectiveness of bounded approximate caching has been well established [10]. In this paper, we focus on developing efficient and scalable techniques to place, locate, and manage bounded approximate caches across a large network, so that locality, the second opportunity mentioned above, is also exploited in an effective manner.

The naive approach is to cache queried measurements just at the querying node. Unfortunately, this approach is not very effective in our setting. First, queries from other nodes have no efficient way of locating these caches. Second, bounded approximate caches are more expensive to maintain than regular caches, because nodes with the original measurements must actively update bounded approximate caches when their bounds are violated. For regular caches, because of low cache maintenance overhead, one can take an aggressive approach of caching every miss and discard it later if it turns out to be not beneficial. The naive approach may well work if such an aggressive approach is feasible. However, we do not have such luxury for bounded approximate caching; we must carefully weigh its cost and benefit before deciding to cache a measurement, because of the costs incurred in establishing, maintaining, and tearing down a bounded approximate cache. With the naive approach of caching only at the querying node, since caching only benefits the querying node itself, it is unlikely that this benefit will outweigh the cost of caching.

Therefore, we need to find an effective way to aggregate the benefits of caching by making caches easier to locate and more accessible to querying nodes. We would also like to exploit locality in query workload by encouraging the same node to cache measurements that are frequently queried together, and by encouraging a measurement to be cached close to nodes that are querying it. Moreover, we need to base our caching decision on a cost/benefit analysis that seeks to minimize the overall foreground traffic (for queries) and background traffic (for cache updates and maintaining statistics for caching decisions) in the system. Accomplishing these goals in a scalable manner, without relying on central servers and access to global knowledge of the system, is a challenging task.

We have developed two approaches. The first approach uses a recursive partitioning of the network space to place caches in a static, controlled manner, and is described briefly in Section 2. The second approach (described in Section 3) uses a *distributed hash table* (DHT) such as [14] to place caches in a scalable, dynamic and decentralized manner. Both approaches are designed to capture various forms of locality in queries to improve performance. We show how to make intelligent caching decisions using a cost/benefit analysis, and we show how to collect statistics necessary for making such decisions with minimum overhead. Using experiments running on ModelNet [16], a scalable Internet emulation environment, we show in Section 4 that our solution significantly reduces query costs while incurring low amounts of background traffic; it is also able to exploit localities in the query workload and adapt to volatility of measurements.

Although we focus on network monitoring and distributed resource querying as motivation for our work, our techniques can be adapted for use by many other interesting applications. In [3], we briefly describe how to generalize the notion of a "query region" from one in the network space to one in a semantic space. For example, a user might create a live bookmark of top ten Internet discussion forums about country music, approximately ranked according to some popularity measure (e.g., total number of posts and/or reads during the past three hours), and have this bookmark refreshed every five minutes using a periodic query. In this case, the query region is "discussion forums about country music," and the popularity measurements of these sites are requested. Generalization would allow our system to select a few nodes to cache all data needed to compute this bookmark, and periodic queries from users with similar bookmarks will be automatically directed to these caches.

2 System Overview

Data and queries. Our system consists of a collection of nodes over a network. Each node monitors various numerical quantities, such as the CPU load and the amount of free memory on the node, or the latency and available bandwidth between this and another node. These quantities can be either actively measured or passively observed from normal system and network activities. We call these quantities *measurements*, and the node responsible for monitoring them the *owner* of these measurements.

A query can be issued at any node for any set of measurements over the network. The term *query region* refers to the set of nodes that own the set of measurements requested. Our system allows a query to define its region either by listing its member nodes explicitly, or by describing it semantically, e.g., all nodes in some local-area network, or all nodes running public HTTP servers. By the manner in which it is defined and used, a query region often exhibits locality in some space, e.g., one in which nodes are clustered according to their proximity in the network, or one in which nodes are clustered according to the applications they run. For now, we will concentrate on the case where regions exhibit locality in terms of network proximity, which is common in practice. In [3], we briefly discuss how to handle locality in other spaces.

For a query that simply requests a set of measurements from a region, the result consists of the values of these measurements. Our system allows a query to specify an *error bound* $[-\delta_q^-, \delta_q^+]$; a stale measurement value can be returned in the result as long as the system can guarantee that the "current" measurement value (taking network delay into account) lies within the specified error bound around the value returned. To be more precise, suppose that the current time is t_{curr} and the result contains a measurement value v_{t_0} taken at time t_0. The system guarantees that v_t, the value of the measurement as monitored by its owner at time t, falls within $[v_{t_0} - \delta_q^-, v_{t_0} + \delta_q^+]$ for any time $t \in [t_0, t_{curr} - lag]$, where lag is the maximum network delay from the querying node to the owner of the measurement (under the routing scheme used by the system). More discussion on the consistency of query results in our system can be found in [3].

Beyond simple queries, our system also supports queries involving relational selections or joins over bounded approximate measurement values. Results of such queries may contain "may-be" as well as "must-be" answers. The details of the query language and its semantics are beyond the scope of this paper.

Bounded approximate caching. As discussed in Section 1, the brute-force approach of contacting each owner to obtain measurement values is unnecessary, expensive, and can cause interference with measurements. Caching is a natural and effective solution but classic caching is unable to bound the error in stale cached values. Instead, we use *bounded approximate caching*, where bounds on cached measurement values are actively maintained by the measurement owners (directly or indirectly).

The owner (or a cache) of a measurement is referred to as a *cache provider* (with respect to that measurement) if it is responsible for maintaining one or more other caches, called *child caches*, of that measurement. Each *cache entry* contains, among other information, the cached measurement value and a bound $[-\delta^-, \delta^+]$. A cache provider maintains a list of *guarantee entries*, one for each of its child caches. A guarantee entry mirrors the information contained in the corresponding child cache entry, and is used to ensure that the guaranteed bounds of child caches are maintained. We require the bound of a child cache to contain the bound of its provider cache.

Whenever the measurement value at a cache provider changes, it checks to see if any of its child caches need to be updated with a new value and bound. If yes, the provider notifies the affected child caches. The cache entries at these child caches and the guarantee entry at the provider are updated accordingly. This process continues from each provider to its child caches until we have contacted all the caches that need to be updated. This update of bounded approximate caches is similar to the update dissemination techniques described in [15]. We use a timeout mechanism to handle network failures (see [3] for details).

The choice of bounds is up to the application issuing queries. Tighter bounds provide better accuracy, but may cause more update traffic. There are sophisticated techniques for setting bounds dynamically and adaptively (e.g., [11]); such techniques are largely orthogonal to the contributions of this paper. Here, we focus on techniques for *selecting* bounded approximate caches to exploit locality and the tradeoff between query and update traffic, and for *locating* these caches quickly and efficiently to answer queries. These techniques are outlined next.

Selecting and locating caches. We have developed two approaches to selecting and locating caches in the network. The first is a controlled caching approach and is described in [3]. The idea is to use a coordinate space such as the one proposed by *Global Network Positioning* (*GNP*) [9] for all nodes in the network, and perform controlled caching based on a hierarchical partitioning of the GNP space. Each owner preselects a number of nodes as its potential caches, such that nearby owners have a good probability of selecting the same node for caching, allowing queries to obtain cached values of measurements in large regions from fewer nodes. The selection scheme also ensures that no single node is responsible for caching too many measurements, and that the caches are denser near the owner and sparser farther away; therefore, queries from nearby nodes get better performance. We show in [3] that this approach does quite well compared to the naive approach of contacting the node responsible for the requested measurements. This approach, however, exploits some but not all types of locality that we would like to exploit and also restricts the amount of caching at any node by design. There is also a concern of scalability because some nodes carry potentially much higher load than other nodes. Nevertheless, because of its simplicity, the GNP-based approach is still viable for small- to medium-sized systems.

This led us to develop a new approach which has a number of advantages over the first one and is the focus of this paper. This second approach uses a locality-aware DHT to achieve locality- and workload-aware caching in an adaptive manner. Not only do nearby owners tend to select the same nodes for caching (as in the controlled approach), queries issued from nearby nodes for the same measurements also encourage caching near the querying nodes. With the use of a DHT, the system is also more decentralized than in the controlled approach. We use DHTs because the technology scales to a large number of nodes, the amount of state at each node is limited, it uses no centralized directory, and it copes well with changing network conditions. The downside is a lesser degree of control in exploiting locality, and more complex protocols to avoid centralization. This approach is presented next.

3 DHT-Based Adaptive Caching

Background on DHTs. An *overlay network* is a distributed system whose nodes establish logical *neighbor* relationships with some subset of global participants, forming a logical network overlayed atop the IP substrate. One type of overlay network is a *Distributed Hash Table* (*DHT*). As the name implies, a DHT provides a hash table abstraction over the participating nodes. Nodes in a DHT store data items; each data item is identified by a unique key. An overlay routing scheme delivers requests for a key to the node responsible for storing the data item with that key. Routing proceeds in multiple hops and is done without any global knowledge: Each node maintains only a small set of neighbors, and routes messages to the neighbor that is in some sense "closest" to the destination.

Pastry [14] is a popular DHT that takes network proximity into account while routing messages. A number of properties of Pastry are relevant to our system. The *short-hops-first* property, a result of locality-aware routing, says that the expected distance traveled by a message during each successive routing step increases exponentially. The *short-routes* property says that the average distance traveled by a Pastry message is within a small factor of the network distance between the message's source and destination. The *route-convergence* property concerns the distance traveled by two messages sent to the same key before their routes converge. Studies [14] show that this distance is roughly the same as the distance between the two source nodes. These properties provide us a natural way to aggregate messages originated from close-by nodes.

Overview of caching with pastry. Our basic idea is to leverage a locality-aware DHT such as Pastry in building a caching infrastructure where two types of aggregation naturally take place. One type of aggregation happens on the owner side: Close-by owners select same caching nodes nearby, allowing us to exploit the spatial locality of measurements involved in region-based queries. The other type of aggregation happens on the querying node side: Close-by querying nodes can also find common caches nearby, allowing us to exploit the spatial locality among querying nodes.

Suppose that all nodes route towards a randomly selected root using Pastry. The Pastry routes naturally form a tree $\mathcal{T}$ (with bidirectional edges) exhibiting both types of aggregation, as illustrated in Figure 1. Queries first flow up the tree following normal (forward) Pastry routes, and then down to owners following reverse Pastry routes. Nodes along these routes are natural candidates for caches. Our system grows and shrinks the set of caches based on demand, according to a cost/benefit analysis using only locally maintained information. The operational details of our system are presented next. We do not discuss cache updates because the process is similar to that described in Section 2 (see [3] for details).

Initialization. A primary objective of the initialization phase is to build the structure $\mathcal{T}$. While Pastry itself already maintains the upward edges (forward Pastry hops), our system still needs to maintain the downward edges (reverse Pastry hops). To this end, every node in $\mathcal{T}$ maintains, for each of its child subtree in $\mathcal{T}$, a representation of the set of nodes found in that subtree, which we call a *subtree filter*. Subtree filters are used to forward messages on reverse Pastry paths, as we will discuss later in connection with querying. Nodes at lower levels can afford to maintain accurate subtree filters because the subtrees are small. Nodes at higher levels, on the other hand, maintain lossy subtree filters implemented with *Bloom filters* [1].

During the initialization phase, after the overlay network has been formed, each node in the system sends an `INIT` message containing its IP address towards the root. Each node along the path of this message adds the node IP to the subtree filter associated with the previous hop on the path. As an optimization, a node can combine multiple `INIT` messages received from its children into a single `INIT` message (containing the union of all IP addresses in the messages being combined), and then forward it.

Querying. When a query is issued for a set of measurements, the querying node routes a `READ` message towards the root via Pastry. This message contains the IP address of the querying node and the set of measurements requested (along with acceptable bounds). When a node N receives a `READ` message, it checks to

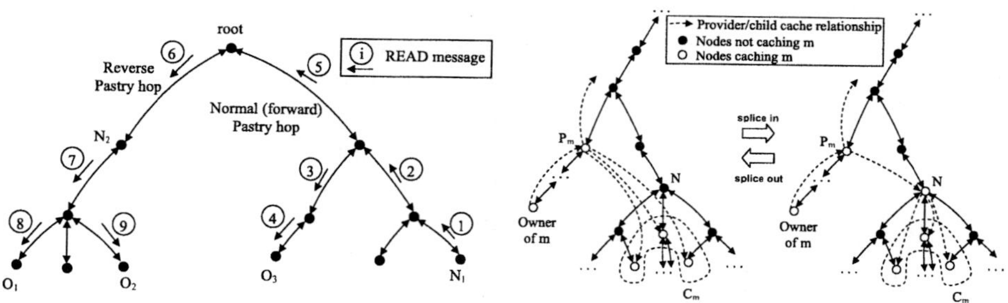

Fig. 1. Two-way aggregation with Pastry

Fig. 2. Splicing: add/remove a cache

see if it can provide any subset of the measurements requested. If yes, N sends back to the querying node a READ_REPLY message containing these measurement values (with cached bounds and timestamp, if applicable). If all requested measurements have been obtained, we are done. Otherwise, let $\mathcal{O}$ denote the set of nodes that own the remaining measurements. N checks each of its subtree filters $\mathcal{F}_i$: If $\mathcal{O} \cap \mathcal{F}_i \neq \varnothing$, N forwards the READ message to its i-th child with the remaining measurements owned by $\mathcal{O} \cap \mathcal{F}_i$ (unless the READ message received by N was sent from this child in the first place). Note that messages from N to its children follow reverse Pastry routes. Finally, if the READ message received by N was sent from a child (i.e., on a forward Pastry route), N also forwards the READ message to its parent unless N is able to determine that all requested measurements can be found at or below it.

As a concrete example, Figure 1 shows the flow of READ messages when node N_1 queries measurements owned by O_1, O_2, and O_3, assuming that no caching takes place. If node N_2 happens to cache measurements owned by O_1 and O_2, then messages 7 through 9 will be saved. It is possible to show that our system attempts to route queries towards measurement owners over $\mathcal{T}$ in an optimal manner. We do not discuss the effect of false positives in Bloom filters in this paper; the reader is referred to [3] for details.

Adding and removing caches. Each node in our system has a *cache controller* thread that periodically wakes up and makes caching decisions. We first describe the procedures for adding and removing a cache of a measurement.

Suppose that a node N decides to start caching a particular measurement m. Let P_m denote the first node that can be N's cache provider on the shortest path from N to the owner of m in $\mathcal{T}$. Let $\mathcal{C}_m$ denote the subset of P_m's child caches whose shortest paths to P_m go through N. An example of these nodes is shown in Figure 2. After N caches m, we would like P_m to be responsible for updating N, and N to take over the responsibility of updating $\mathcal{C}_m$, as illustrated in Figure 2 on the right. Note that at the beginning of this process, N does not know what P_m or $\mathcal{C}_m$ is. To initiate the process, N sends a SPLICE_IN message over $\mathcal{T}$, along the same path that a READ request for m would take. Forwarding of this message stops when it reaches P_m, the first node who can be a cache provider for m. We let each cache provider record the shortest incoming path from each of its child caches; thus, P_m can easily determine the subset $\mathcal{C}_m$ of its child caches by checking whether the recorded shortest paths from them to P_m go through N. Then, P_m removes the guarantee entries and shortest paths for $\mathcal{C}_m$; also, P_m adds N to its guarantee list and records the shortest path from N to P_m. Next, P_m sends back to N a SPLICE_IN_OK message containing the current measurement value and timestamp stored at P_m, as well as the removed guarantee entries and shortest paths for $\mathcal{C}_m$. Upon receiving this message, N caches the measurement value, adds the guarantee entries to its guarantee list, and records the shortest paths after truncating their suffixes beginning with N. Finally, N sends out a SPLICE_IN_OK message to each node in $\mathcal{C}_m$ to inform it of the change in cache provider. The cache removal procedure uses SPLICE_OUT and SPLICE_OUT_OK messages. It is similar to cache addition and slightly simpler (see [3] for a detailed description).

It can be shown that, in the absence of false positives in subtree filters, a cache update originated from the owner would be sent over a minimal multicast tree spanning all caches if update messages were routed over $\mathcal{T}$.

Caching decisions. Periodically, the cache controller thread at N wakes up and makes caching decisions. For each measurement m that N has information about, the thread computes the benefit and cost of caching m. We break down the benefit and cost of caching m into four components: (1) $B_{read}(m)$ is the benefit in terms of reduction in read traffic. For each READ message received by N requesting m, if m is cached at N, we avoid the cost of forwarding the request for m, which will be picked up eventually by the node that either owns m or caches m, and is the closest such node on the shortest path from N to m's owner in $\mathcal{T}$. Let d_m denote the distance (as measured by the number of hops in $\mathcal{T}$) between N and this node. The larger the distance, the greater the benefit. Thus, $B_{read}(m) \propto d_m \times H_m$, where H_m is the request rate of m at node N. (2) $B_{upd}(m)$ is the net benefit in terms of reduction in update traffic. It's computation requires the maintenance of a large number of parameters; hence we approximate it to be proportional to the reduction in update cost from the cache provider P_m's perspective (see [3] for details). (3) $C_{upd}(m)$ is the cost in terms of resources (processing, storage, and bandwidth) incurred by N for maintaining its child caches for m. (4) $C_{cache}(m)$ is the cost incurred by N for caching m (other than $C_{upd}(m)$). We omit the details of these last three components and refer the interested reader to [3].

Given a set $\mathcal{M}$ of candidate measurements to cache, the problem is to determine a subset $\mathcal{M}' \subseteq \mathcal{M}$ that maximizes $\sum_{m \in \mathcal{M}'} \left(B_{read}(m) + B_{upd}(m)\right)$ subject to the cost constraints that $\sum_{m \in \mathcal{M}'} C_{upd}(m) \leq T_{upd}$, and $\sum_{m \in \mathcal{M}'} C_{cache}(m) \leq T_{cache}$. Here, T_{upd} specifies the maximum amount of resources that the node is willing to spend on maintaining its child caches, and T_{cache} specifies the maximum cache size. This problem is an instance of the *multi-constraint* 0-1 *knapsack problem.* It is expensive to obtain the optimal solution because our constraints are not small integers; even the classic single-constraint 0-1 knapsack problem is NP-complete. So, we use a greedy algorithm by defining the *pseudo-utility* of caching m as

$$\frac{B_{read}(m) + B_{upd}(m)}{C_{upd}(m)/T_{upd} + C_{cache}(m)/T_{cache}}.$$

It is basically a benefit/weighted-cost ratio of caching m. The greedy algorithm simply decides to cache measurements with highest, non-negative pseudo-utility values above some threshold. Caches are added and removed as described earlier.

Maintaining statistics. We now turn to the problem of maintaining statistics needed for making caching decisions. For measurements currently being cached by N, we can easily maintain all necessary statistics with negligible overhead by piggybacking the statistics on various messages. A more challenging problem is how to maintain statistics for a measurement m that is not currently cached at N. Maintaining statistics for all measurements in the system is simply not scalable. Ignoring uncached measurements is not an option either, because we would be unable to identify good candidates among them. In classic caching, any miss will cause an item to be cached; if it later turns out that caching is not worthwhile, the item will be dropped. However, this simple approach does not work well for our system because the penalty of making a wrong decision is higher: Our caches must be actively maintained, and the cost of adding and removing caches is not negligible.

Fortunately, from the cost/benefit analysis, we observe that a measurement m is worth caching at N only if N sees a lot of read requests for m or there are a number of frequently updated caches that could use N as an intermediary. Hence, we focus on monitoring statistics for these measurements, over each *observation period* of a tunable duration. For example, the request rate H_m is maintained by N for each m requested during the observation period; request rates for unrequested, uncached measurements are assumed to be 0. Our techniques to estimate update rates and d_m over the observation period are more complex. More details on scalable maintenance of statistics are described in [3].

Overall, the space needed to maintain statistics for uncached measurements is linear in the total number of measurements requested plus the total number of downstream caches updated during an observation period. Thus, the amount of required space can be controlled by adjusting the observation period length.

4 Experiments and Results

Experimental setup. We have implemented the GNP- and the DHT-based approaches. We conduct our experiments over ModelNet [16], a scalable and highly accurate Internet emulation environment. We emulate 20,000-node INET [4] topologies with a subset of nodes participating in measurement and querying activities. We report results for subsets with 250 nodes acting as both owners and querying nodes. These nodes are emulated by twenty 2.0GHz Intel Pentium 4 edge emulation nodes running Linux 2.4.27. All traffic passes through a 1.4GHz Pentium III core emulation node running FreeBSD-4.9.

While all results in this paper use an emulated network, we have also deployed our system (with around 50 nodes) over PlanetLab [12]. Note that the number of owners and querying nodes in our experiments is not constrained by the system's scalability, but rather by the hardware resources available for deploying it over an emulated network. The advantage of deploying a full system over an emulated network is that it ensures that all costs are captured and we do not inadvertently miss out any important effects or interactions. As future work, we plan to develop a simpler simulation-based evaluation, which would allow us to demonstrate larger experiments at the expense of some realism.

Workloads. We wish to subject our system to workloads with different characteristics that may represent different application scenarios. To this end, we have designed a workload generator to produce a mix of four basic types of "query groups." The four types of query groups are: (1) *Near-query-near- owner* (*NQNO*): A set of n_q nearby nodes query the same set of n_o owners that are near one another (not necessarily close to the querying nodes). This group should benefit most from caching, since there is locality among both querying nodes and queried owners. (2) *Near-query-far-owner* (*NQFO*): A set of n_q nearby nodes query the same set of n_o owners that are randomly scattered in the network. There is good locality among the querying nodes, but no locality among the queried owners. (3) *Far-query-near-owner* (*FQNO*): A set of n_q distant nodes query the same set of n_o owners that are near one another. This group exhibits good locality among the queried owners, but no locality among the querying nodes. (4) *Far-query-far-owner* (*FQFO*): A set of n_q nodes query the same set of n_o owners; both the querying nodes and the queried owners are randomly scattered. This group should benefit least from caching.

A workload $[a, b, c, d]$ denotes a mix of a NQNO query groups, b NQFO query groups, c FQNO query groups, and d FQFO query groups. All query groups are generated independently. Each workload is further parameterized by n_q and n_o, the number and the size of queries in each group, and p, the period at which the queries will be reissued.

In this paper, we experiment with synthetic measurements, each generated by a random walk where each step is drawn from a normal distribution with mean 0 and standard deviation σ. If σ is large, bounds on this measurement will be violated more frequently, resulting in higher update cost. Synthetic measurements allow us to experiment with different update characteristics easily. Experiments with real node-to-node latency measurements demonstrate the effectiveness of bounded approximate caching, and are presented in [3].

4.1 Results for the DHT-Based Approach

Advantage of caching. To demonstrate the advantage of caching, we run a workload $W_1 = [1, 1, 1, 1]$ for 1000 seconds, with $n_q = 4$, $n_o = 10$, and $p = 16$ seconds. Effectively, during each 16-second interval, there are a total of 16 nodes querying a total of 40 owners, with each query requesting 10 measurements. This workload represents an equal mix of all four types of query groups, with some benefiting more than others from caching. The measurements in this experiment are synthetic, with $\sigma = 7$. Bounds requested by all queries are $[-10, 10]$. During the experiment, we record both *foreground traffic*, consisting of `READ` and `READ_REPLY` messages, and *background traffic*, consisting of all other messages including splice messages and `CACHE_UPDATE` messages.

Figure 3 shows the behavior of our system over time, with the size of each cache capped at 100 measurements (large enough to capture the working set of W_1). We also show the behavior of the system with caching turned off. The message rate shown on the vertical axes is the average number of messages per second generated by the entire system over the last 16 seconds (same as the period of monitoring queries). From Figure 3, for cache size 100 we see that after a burst of foreground traffic when queries start running, there is an increase in the background traffic as nodes decide to cache measurements. Once caches have been established, the foreground traffic falls dramatically due to the caches. As the set of caches in system stabilizes, the background traffic also reduces to mostly `CACHE_UPDATE` messages. On the other hand, with caching

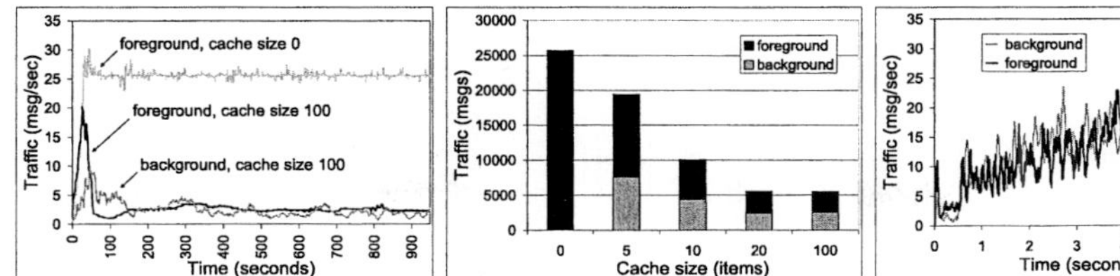

Fig. 3. Traffic vs. time **Fig. 4.** Traffic vs. cache size **Fig. 5.** Adapt to volatility

turned off (cache size 0) we see that the foreground traffic remains very high at all times (there is no background traffic). The high foreground traffic outweighs the benefit of having no background traffic. In sum, caching is extremely effective in reducing the overall traffic in the system.

Figure 4 compares the performance of the system under different cache sizes (in terms of the maximum number of measurements allowed in the cache of each node). We show the total number of foreground and background messages generated by the system over the length of the entire experiment (1000 seconds). As the cache size increases, the overall traffic decreases, although the benefit diminishes once the caches have grown large enough to hold the working set. Another interesting phenomenon is that for very small cache sizes, the background traffic is relatively high because of more splice operations caused by thrashing. Nevertheless, our system is able to handle this situation well.

Adapting to volatility in measurements. In this experiment, we use the same workload W_1 with cache size 100. We gradually increase the volatility of measurements by increasing the standard deviation σ of the random walk steps every 500 seconds. For the requested query bound of $[-10, 10]$, we effectively increase the update rate from 0.0 to 3.0 updates per second. The result of this experiment is shown in Figure 5. Initially, with a zero update rate, there is no cost to maintaining a cache, so all frequently requested measurements are cached, resulting in low foreground and background traffic. As we increase the update rate, however, the background traffic increases. This increase in cache update cost causes nodes to start dropping cached measurements; as a result, the foreground traffic also increases. Eventually, the update rate becomes so high that it is no longer beneficial to cache any measurements. Thus, the background traffic drops to zero, while the foreground traffic increases to the level when there is no caching (cf. Figure 3). To summarize, our system only performs caching if it leads to an overall reduction in total traffic; consequently, the total traffic in the system never rises above the level without caching. This shows that our system is able to adapt its caching strategy based on the volatility of measurements.

Aggregation effects. The next two sets of experiments demonstrate that our system can exploit locality in both querying nodes and queried owners. To illustrate aggregation on the querying node side, we perform a series of experiments using five workloads, $[0, 0, 2, 2]$, $[1, 0, 2, 1]$, $[2, 0, 2, 0]$, $[2, 1, 0, 1]$, and $[2, 2, 0, 0]$, where the percentage of queries issued from nearby nodes increases from 0% to

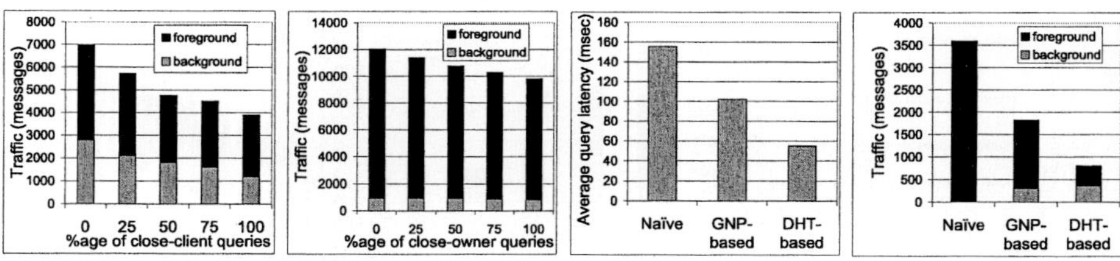

Fig. 6. Traffic vs. percentage of queries from nearby nodes.

Fig. 7. Traffic vs. percentage of queries to nearby owners.

Fig. 8. Comparison of average query latency.

Fig. 9. Comparison of total traffic.

100%. We set $n_q = 5$ and $n_o = 4$ for these five workloads. From the results in Figure 6, we see that the total traffic reduces as the percentage of queries from nearby nodes increases. Figure 7 shows the second set of experiments that illustrate owner-side aggregation by using five workloads where the percentage of queries requesting nearby owners increases from 0% to 100%. We again see that the total traffic reduces as the percentage of queries requesting nearby owners increases. These experiments show that our system derives performance benefits by exploiting locality both among querying nodes and in query regions.

Comparison with the naive and GNP approaches. Figure 8 compares the average query latency (as measured by the average time it takes to obtain the requested measurement, after all caches have been created) for a simple workload that exhibits locality among querying nodes. For baseline comparison, we also measure the average query latency of a naive approach, where each querying node simply contacts the owner directly for the measurement. From the figure, we see that the DHT-based approach has the lowest query latency, while the GNP-based approach performs a little worse, but both outperform the naive approach. Figure 9 compares the total network traffic generated by the system while processing a workload in which five querying nodes repeatedly query a faraway set of 12 nearby owners over 480 seconds, using the naive, GNP-based, and DHT-based approaches. Again, the DHT-based approach outperforms the other two approaches as it exploits querying node side locality effectively.

5 Related Work

Network monitoring. A large number of network monitoring systems have been developed by both the research community and commercial vendors. Astrolabe [17] is a system that continuously monitors the state of a collection of distributed resources and reports summarized information to the its users. Ganglia [8] is a system for monitoring a federation of clusters. While our work also considers the network monitoring problem, we focus on supporting set-valued queries approximately rather than aggregation queries. Our approach of bounded approximate caching and methods for locality-aware, cost-based cache management offer better flexibility and adaptability than these systems, which are preset to either push or pull each piece of information. Our techniques can be used to enhance these and other existing network monitoring systems.

Data processing on overlay networks. PIER [7] is a DHT-based massively distributed query engine that brings database query processing facilities to new, widely distributed environments. For network monitoring, also one of PIER's target applications, we believe that bounded approximate caching meshes well with PIER's relaxed consistency requirement, and our DHT-based caching techniques can also be applied to PIER. Locality-aware DHTs have been used to build SCRIBE [2], a scalable multicast system, and SDIMS [18], a hierarchical aggregation infrastructure. Our DHT-based approach also uses a locality-aware DHT, but for the different purpose of selecting and locating caches; in addition, we use reverse DHT routes to achieve aggregation effects on the owner side.

Approximate query processing for networked data. The idea of bounded approximate caching has been explored in detail by Olston [10], along with techniques such as adaptive bound setting, source cooperation in cache synchronization, etc. We apply bounded approximate caching in this paper, but we focus on how to select caches across the network to exploit locality, and how to locate these caches quickly and efficiently to answer queries. We also extend the approximate replication scheme by allowing guarantees to be provided not only by the owner, but also by any other cache with a tighter bound.

Web caching and web replication. Web caching [13] is often done by ISPs using web proxy servers. Web replication [13] refers to data sources spreading their content across the network, primarily for load balancing. In both cases, the cache content is stored exactly and most often relatively stable content (e.g. images) is replicated at static locations. They do not deal with the problem of rapidly updating data; this means that they can afford to establish a large number of caches/replicas. Our system deals with replication of dynamic measurements and therefore update costs are high. We reduce update costs by caching bounded measurements, and balance update and query costs by caching at dynamically chosen nodes in the network.

6 Conclusions

In this paper, we tackle the problem of querying distributed network measurements, with an emphasis on supporting set-valued queries using bounded approximate caching of individual measurements. We focus on efficient and scalable techniques for selecting, locating, and managing caches across the network to exploit locality in queries and tradeoff between query and update traffic. We have proposed, implemented, and evaluated a DHT-based adaptive caching approach and compared it with a GNP-based controlled caching approach. Experiments over a large-scale emulated network show that our caching techniques are very effective in reducing communication costs and query latencies while maintaining the accuracy of query results at an acceptable level. The DHT-based approach is shown to adapt well to different types of workloads. In addition to temporal locality in the query workload, the approach is able to exploit spatial localities in both querying nodes and measurements accessed by region-based queries.

Although the results are promising, techniques described in this paper represent only the first steps towards building a powerful distributed network querying system. As future work, we plan to investigate the hybrid approach of combining query shipping and data shipping, and consider more sophisticated caching schemes such as *semantic caching* [5].

Acknowledgement. We would like to thank Joe Hellerstein and David Oppenheimer for their ideas and suggestions. We would also like to thank Adolfo Rodriguez and Chip Killian for several discussions and help.

References

1. B.H. Bloom. Space/time trade-offs in hash coding with allowable errors. *CACM*,1970.
2. M. Castro, P. Druschel, A. Kermarrec, and A. Rowstron. SCRIBE: A large-scale and decentralized application-level multicast infrastructure. *IEEE JSAC*, 2002.
3. B. Chandramouli, J. Yang, and A. Vahdat. Distributed network querying with bounded approximate caching. Technical report, Department of Computer Science, Duke University, June 2004.
4. H. Chang, R. Govindan, S. Jamin, S. Shenker, and W. Willinger. Towards Capturing Representative AS-Level Internet Topologies. In *SIGMETRICS*, 2002.
5. S. Dar, M. J. Franklin, B. Jónsson, D. Srivastava, and M. Tan. Semantic data caching and replacement. In *VLDB*, 1996.
6. I. Foster and C. Kesselman. *The Grid: Blueprint for a New Computing Infrastructure.* Morgan Kaufmann, 1999.
7. R. Huebsch, J. M. Hellerstein, N. Lanham, B. T. Loo, S. Shenker, and I. Stoica. Querying the internet with PIER. In *VLDB*, 2003.
8. M. L. Massie, B. N. Chun, and D. E. Culler. The Ganglia distributed monitoring system: Design, implementation, and experience. *Parallel Computing*, 2004.
9. T. S. E. Ng and H. Zhang. Predicting internet network distance with coordinates-based approaches. In *IEEE INFOCOM*, 2002.
10. C. Olston. *Approximate Replication.* PhD thesis, Stanford University, 2003.
11. C. Olston, B. T. Loo, and J. Widom. Adaptive precision setting for cached approximate values. In *SIGMOD*, 2001.
12. PlanetLab. http://www.planet-lab.org.
13. M. Rabinovich and O. Spatschek. *Webcachingandreplication.* Addison-Wesley, 2002.
14. A. Rowstron and P. Druschel. Pastry: Scalable, decentralized object location, and routing for large-scale peer-to-peer systems. *Lecture Notes in Computer Science*, 2218, 2001.
15. S. Shah, K. Ramamritham, and P. J. Shenoy. Maintaining coherency of dynamic data in cooperating repositories. In *VLDB*, 2002.
16. A. Vahdat, K. Yocum, K. Walsh, P. Mahadevan, D. Kostić, J. Chase, and D. Becker. Scalability and accuracy in a large-scale network emulator. *ACM SIGOPS Operating Systems Review*, 2002.
17. R. Van Renesse, K. P. Birman, and W. Vogels. Astrolabe: A robust and scalable technology for distributed system monitoring, management, and data mining. *ACM TOCS*, 2003.
18. P. Yalagandula and M. Dahlin. A scalable distributed information management system. In *SIGCOMM*, 2004.

Type-Level Access Pattern View: A Technique for Enhancing Prefetching Performance

Wook-Shin Han*, Woong-Kee Loh**, and Kyu-Young Whang

Department of Computer Science &
Advanced Information Technology Research Center (AITrc),
Korea Advanced Institute of Science and Technology (KAIST),
Daejeon, Korea
{wshan, woong, kywhang}@mozart.kaist.ac.kr

Abstract. Navigational applications on Object-Relational DBMSs (ORDBMSs) access objects in the database related to one another via reference and collection attributes. When accessing an object, the applications first look up the object cache in the client and, if the object does not exist, fetch the object from the server. Prefetching is to identify the objects that are highly probable to be accessed in the future by the applications and to save these objects in the object cache in advance. Since prefetching reduces the number of high cost fetches, it is crucial for the performance of the applications. The prefetch method proposed by Han et al. [7] reduces the number of fetches by orders of magnitude compared with the previous methods. However, overall performance enhancement is not as significant as reduction of fetches. Since the performance of prefetching is determined by the number of disk accesses in the server as well as the number of fetches. In this paper, we propose a technique for minimizing the number of disk accesses to enhance the performance of the prefetch method proposed by Han et al. We propose a method for creating materialized views based on the type-level path access logs proposed by Han et al. [6]. We call the materialized view as the *type-level access pattern view*. We then present an algorithm for minimizing the number of disk accesses when prefetching the objects from the database in the server by using the type-level access pattern view. We perform a series of experiments using a variety of databases to show that the technique proposed in this paper significantly enhances the overall performance of the navigational applications. We show that the proposed technique reduces the number of disk accesses by up to 33.0 times and enhances the performance by up to 21.4 times compared with the original prefetch method by Han et al.

Keywords: navigational application, prefetch method, type-level path access log, type-level access pattern view.

1 Introduction

Object-Relational DBMS (ORDBMS) is an extension of Relational DBMS (RDBMS) incorporating the object-oriented features such as type, object, method, reference, and

* He is currently with the Department of Computer Engineering, Kyungpook National University, Korea.

** Corresponding author.

M.L. Lee, K.L. Tan, and V. Wuwongse (Eds.): DASFAA 2006, LNCS 3882, pp. 389–403, 2006.

inheritance [10]. ORDBMS represents the inter-related objects as complex objects via the reference and collection attributes. The applications on ORDBMS access the complex objects in the client and fetch the related objects from the database in the server when necessary. The applications are generally called *navigational applications*, and the examples are XML applications, Geographical Information Systems (GIS), and CAD/CAM systems.

When an object is requested by the navigational applications or external users, the applications first check if the object is in the object cache in the client. If exists, the applications just access the object. If not, the applications send the request to fetch the object to the server, and the server accesses the object from the database and then sends it to the client.

Due to the above characteristics of the navigational applications, they require a lot of object fetches between the client and server. Since the cost of object fetch is very high in the navigational applications, the frequent object fetches severely degrade the overall performance of the applications [2, 7]. To overcome the problem, many researches on prefetching for reducing the number of object fetches have been performed. Prefetching is to identify the objects that are highly probable to be accessed by the applications in the future and to save them in the object cache in advance [2, 8, 11]. The previous prefetch methods can be categorized into four groups: (1) page based, (2) object-level/page-level access pattern based, (3) user hint based, and (4) context based prefetch methods [7]. Recently, there are researches on applying the prefetch idea to web applications [5] and query optimization [3].

Han et al. [7] proposed a prefetch method based on the notions of *type-level access locality* and *type-level access pattern* in the navigational applications on ORDBMS. The type-level access locality is the phenomenon that the types of objects accessed by the applications appear repeatedly, and the type-level access pattern is the pattern of object types appearing repeatedly. Han et al. [7] showed the superiority of their prefetch method based on the type-level access pattern over the context based prefetch method [2], which had been the most efficient one before, through a series of experiments. That is, their prefetch method reduced the number of object fetches by up to 97.8 times, and enhanced the overall performance of the navigational applications by up to 6.39 times.

As can be seen in the result of experiments by Han et al. [7], the enhancement ratio of the overall performance of navigational applications is not as significant as the reduction ratio of the number of object fetches. In general, the two most important factors deciding the performance of prefetching are the number of object fetches and the number of disk accesses in the server. Even though the number of object fetches is reduced significantly, if the number of disk accesses remains unchanged, the overall performance would not be enhanced as much. For example, assuming that the costs of object fetches and disk accesses are equal, even when the number of object fetches is improved ten times (the number is reduced to 10%), the overall performance is improved only about two times $\left(\frac{1+1}{0.1+1} \approx 2\right)$. In this paper, we propose a technique for enhancing the performance of the prefetch method proposed by Han et al. [7] by minimizing the number of disk accesses. The major contributions of this paper are as follows:

(1) For the *iterative pattern*, which is the most frequent type-level access pattern, we propose a method for creating materialized views based on the type-level path access logs proposed by Han et al. [6]. We call the materialized view as the *type-level access pattern view*.
(2) We present an algorithm for minimizing the number of disk accesses when prefetching the objects from the database in the server by using the type-level access pattern views.
(3) We perform a series of experiments using a variety of databases to show that the technique proposed in this paper significantly enhances the overall performance of navigational applications. We show that the proposed technique reduces the number of disk accesses by up to 33.0 times and enhances the performance by up to 21.4 times compared with the original prefetch method by Han et al. [7].

The rest of this paper consists of the following. In Section 2, we briefly explain the type-level access pattern based prefetch method proposed by Han et al. [7]. In Section 3, we present the algorithms for creating the type-level access pattern views and for efficient prefetching using the views. In Section 4, we perform extensive experiments to show the superiority of the proposed technique over the prefetch method by Han et al. [7]. Finally, we conclude this paper in Section 5.

2 Type-Level Access Pattern Based Prefetching

We define several terms in Section 2.1, and explain the prefetch algorithm and the type-level path access log in Section 2.2 and Section 2.3, respectively. Figure 1 shows the example database schema used throughout this paper.

2.1 Terminologies

The general pattern of accessing objects by the navigational applications is that the applications first obtain the root objects to determine the navigational scope by executing SQL query statements and then access related objects via the reference and collection attributes from the root objects. The set of root objects for starting the navigation is called *navigational root set*, and is denoted by Ω. For example, the navigational root set can be constructed by executing a statement "SELECT * FROM Professor WHERE Salary $\geq$ \$100,000" on the database shown in Figure 1.

The *type-level path* (*TLP*) of an object o is the sequence of attributes referenced to access the object o starting from root objects. Han et al. [7] assumed the navigational root set as a virtual collection attribute of a virtual object to express the type-level path of the root objects, and denoted the virtual collection attribute as a_Ω. For example, assuming Course objects in Figure 1 as the root objects, the type-level path of Professor objects o is $a_\Omega.has\_sections.is\_taught\_by$.

The *type-level path graph* (*TLPG*) for a navigational root set Ω is a directed graph in which each node represents the type of the objects accessed in navigation and each edge the attributes referenced. The type-level path graph is created and extended while the navigational application accesses the related objects from the navigational root set Ω; whenever an object of a new type is accessed in navigation, the corresponding edge

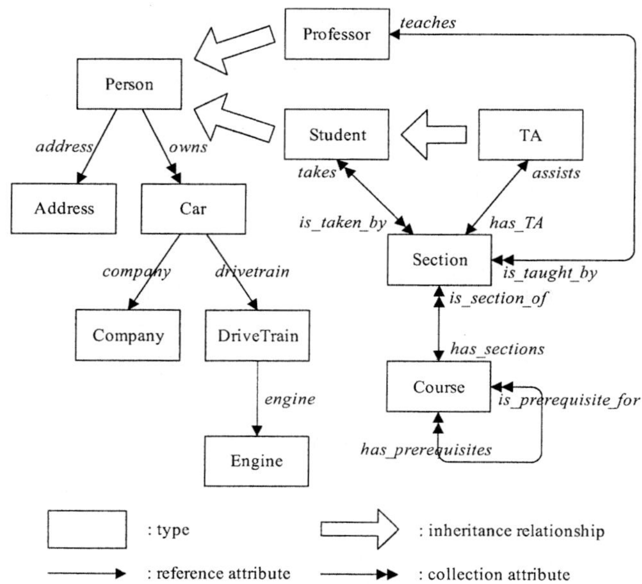

Fig. 1. University Database Schema

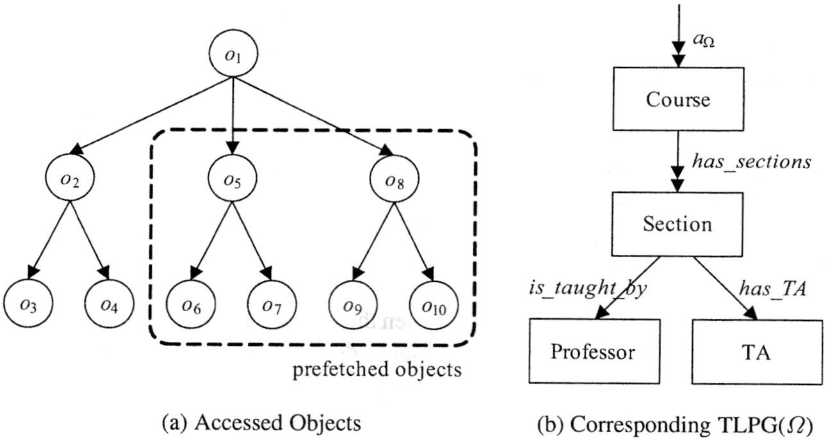

(a) Accessed Objects (b) Corresponding TLPG(Ω)

Fig. 2. Accessed Objects and the Type-Level Path Graph

and node are appended to the graph. The type-level path graph is used to detect the repetitive type-level access patterns. All the nodes corresponding to the types of the objects accessed in navigation are connected directly or indirectly from the root node which corresponds to Ω. Figure 2 shows a simple example. Figure 2(a) shows the objects accessed in the database shown in Figure 1, and the object number indicates the access order of the objects. Figure 2(b) is the TLPG(Ω) generated while accessing the objects in navigation. Table 1 summarizes the notations used throughout this paper.

Table 1. Summary of Notations

Notation	Description
o	an object
TLP(o)	type-level path of an object o
Ω	a navigational root set
TLPG(Ω)	type-level path graph for a navigational root set Ω
TLAG(Ω)	type-level path access log graph for a navigational root set Ω

2.2 Prefetch Algorithm

When the navigational applications access the related objects, they tend to repetitively access the same attributes of the objects. Han et al. [7] defined the phenomenon as the *type-level access locality* and the repetitive pattern of accessing the attributes in the related objects as the *type-level access pattern*. Prefetch algorithm selects the objects to prefetch using the type-level access patterns.

There can be diverse forms of type-level access patterns depending on the navigational applications. In this paper, we deal with the *iterative pattern*, which is the most frequent type-level access pattern for prefetching. The iterative pattern is the type-level access pattern that generates type-level paths that appear repetitively when accessing the objects via the collection attributes in complex objects.

We explain how the prefetch algorithm works for the iterative pattern with the example shown in Figure 2. At first, the navigational application retrieves objects for specific courses by executing an SQL query statement, and the returned objects constitute the root objects in the navigational root set Ω. In Figure 2(a), the object o_1 is the root object. Next, the application accesses the objects corresponding to the sections for each course and then the objects for the professor and TA for each section. In the database in Figure 1, since the attribute $has\_sections$ of type Course is a collection attribute, one Course object can contain one or more Section objects.

When the navigation is started from the navigational root set Ω, the TLPG(Ω) consists of only the edge a_Ω and the root node Course corresponding to the type of root objects. The TLPG in Figure 2(b) is generated while the application accesses the root object o_1 and the related objects $o_2 \sim o_4$; when the object o_2 is accessed, the TLPG(Ω) is appended with the edge $has\_sections$ and node Section, and when the objects o_3 and o_4 are accessed, it is appended with the edges is_taught_by and has_TA and the nodes Professor and TA. Next, when the navigational application tries to access the Section objects o_5 next to o_2, since the type-level path $a_\Omega.has\_sections$ of o_5 is already contained in the TLPG(Ω), the application detects the iterative pattern by the collection attribute $has\_sections$. The application marks the edge in the TPLG as the iterative pattern edge, and prefetches objects $o_5 \sim o_{10}$ based on the iterative pattern. The prefetched objects are transferred to the client at the same time.

2.3 Type-Level Path Access Log

In most cases, the navigational applications reference the small subset of attributes of the objects accessed in navigation. The unit of prefetching in the existing prefetch

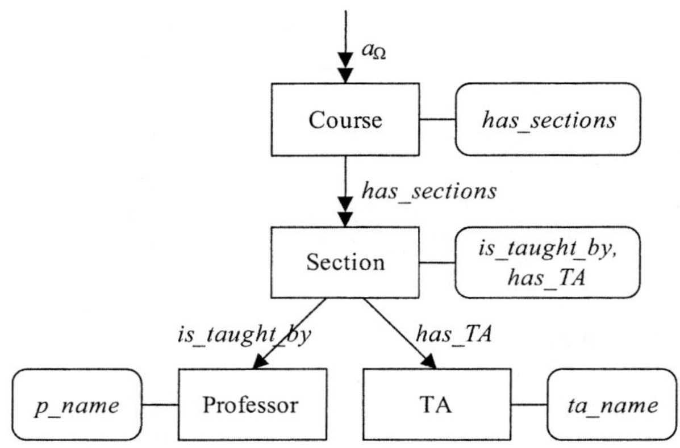

Fig. 3. Type-Level Path Access Log Graph

methods including the one by Han et al. [7] is an object. However, if the size of the objects is greater than the size of the attributes actually referenced by the navigational applications, it can cause the overhead on transferring data between the client and server. Han et al. [6] proposed the notion of type-level path access log for prefetching only the attributes that are highly probable to be actually referenced by the applications. For the object o having the type-level path P from the navigational root set Ω, the set of attributes actually referenced by the navigational application is defined as the *access log for type-level path* P and denoted as $\{a_1, \ldots, a_n\}$, where $a_i (1 \leq i \leq n)$ are the attributes of object o that are actually referenced in the navigation.

The navigational applications use *type-level path access log graph* (*TLAG*) to detect the repetitive type-level path access logs. The TLAG is an extension of the TLPG explained in Section 2.2, and each node corresponding to the type-level path P in the TLAG is associated with an access log for the path P. Figure 3 shows a TLAG extended from the TLPG in Figure 2(b). The rounded rectangle in the figure represents the access log for the type-level path corresponding to each node.

3 Type-Level Access Pattern View

In this section, we propose a prefetch technique using the materialized views for enhancing the performance of the type-level access pattern based prefetch method proposed by Han et al. [7]. In this paper, the type-level access pattern view for the iterative pattern is called the *iterative pattern view*. A type-level access pattern view is created for each of the type-level access patterns newly detected by the navigational application, and is used for prefetching objects according to the similar type-level access patterns detected by the application. In Sections 3.1 and 3.2, we explain on creating and matching the iterative pattern view, respectively.

3.1 Creating the Iterative Pattern View

The iterative pattern view is a materialized view that stores the objects accessed based on the iterative pattern. Since a type-level access pattern corresponds to an edge in the TLAG marked as the iterative pattern edge, an iterative pattern view is created for the TLAG subgraph rooted by the node pointed by the iterative pattern edge. First, a type corresponding to each of the nodes in the TLAG subgraph is defined so that the type should contain the attributes in the access log of the corresponding node. The type is called the *navigational view type* in this paper. Next, an iterative pattern view of the navigational view type corresponding to the root node of the TLAG subgraph is defined. Optionally, an index on the object identifier (OID) of the root objects can be constructed for efficient retrieval of the iterative pattern view objects.

In this paper, we use the nested type to combine an object o and the objects related via the collection attributes of object o in a single object. The nested type is the type defined in the other type, and the collection attribute is defined as the nested set type in the iterative pattern view. The following Rules 1 and 2 are for defining the navigational view types corresponding to the nodes of the TLAG subgraph and the iterative pattern view for the TLAG subgraph, respectively [1].

Rule 1 . Let A be the type of the node pointed by an edge a in the TLAG subgraph, $B_1, \ldots, B_n$ be the types of the nodes pointed by the edges $b_1, \ldots, b_n$ from the node A, and $B'_1, \ldots, B'_n$ be the navigational view types corresponding to the nodes $B_1, \ldots, B_n$, respectively. And let $c_1, \ldots, c_k$ be the remaining attributes except the attributes $b_1, \ldots,$ b_n in the access log of the node A, and $T_1, \ldots, T_k$ be the types of the remaining attributes, respectively. The navigational view type A' corresponding to the node A is defined as follows:

CREATE TYPE {
    oid REF TYPE(A)
    c_1 T_1;
    ...
    c_k T_k;
    b_1 ITER(b_1, B'_1);
    ...
    b_n ITER(b_n, B'_n);
} A';

where REF TYPE(A) represents the OID type for the objects of type A. ITER(b_i, B'_i) $(1 \leq i \leq n)$ is replaced either with SETOF(B'_i) if b_i is a collection attribute, or with B'_i if it is a reference attribute. □

Rule 2 . In addition to the settings in Rule 1, let R be the type of the root node of the TLAG subgraph, r be the edge pointing to the node R, and R' be the navigational view type corresponding to the node R defined by the Rule 1. The iterative pattern view for the TLAG subgraph and the index on the iterative pattern view is defined as follows:

[1] The syntax used to define the navigational view type and the iterative pattern view in Rules 1 and 2 follows the one proposed by Stonebraker and Moore [10], and most of the recent commercial database systems provide the statements for the similar features [9].

CREATE VIEW $view\_name$ **OF** R' **AS**
ITER_ATTR_COL(r);

CREATE INDEX idx_name **ON** $view\_name(oid)$;

ITER_ATTR_COL(a) ::=
 SELECT
  REF(O),
  $c_1, \ldots, c_k$,
  ITER_ATTR(b_1), ... , ITER_ATTR(b_n)
 FROM A O

ITER_ATTR_REF(a) ::=
 A'(REF(A), $c_1, \ldots, c_k$, ITER_ATTR(b_1), ... , ITER_ATTR(b_n)) ,

where O is the alias for the objects of type A, and REF(A) or REF(O) represents the OID of the object O of type A. If a is a collection attribute, ITER_ATTR(a) is replaced with SETOF(ITER_ATTR_COL(a)); otherwise, it is replaced with ITER_ATTR _REF(a). □

Figure 4 shows the iterative pattern view for the TLAG shown in Figure 3 on the assumption that the edge a_Ω pointing to the root node of the TLAG is marked as the iterative pattern edge. In Figure 4(a), the navigational view types are defined for each of four nodes in the TLAG, and the nested set type is defined for the collection attribute $has\_sections$ of navigational view type course_t. Figure 4(b) shows the iterative pattern view v1 of the root type course_t defined in Figure 4(a) and the index v1_idx defined on the attribute oid of the view v1. The SELECT statement for defining the iterative pattern view v1 contains the nested SELECT statement to retrieve all the section_t objects connected from the collection attribute $has\_sections$. We focus on creating the type-level access pattern views in this paper, and the general management of the views is not mentioned since it is studied in the existing literatures [1, 4].

3.2 Matching the Iterative Pattern View

In this section, we explain on finding the iterative pattern view among those in the database that best matches the type-level access pattern detected by the navigational application. In this paper, the problem to find the matching iterative pattern view to be used for prefetching is defined as the graph matching problem between the TLAG corresponding to the type-level access pattern detected by the application and the TLAG for the iterative pattern view in the database. We need the following definition to solve the problem:

Definition 1 . For a path $P = a_1..a_k$ and the TLAG T, the path P is defined as the *reachable path in* T if both of two conditions below are satisfied:

```
CREATE TYPE {
    oid             REF Course;
    has_sections    SETOF(section_t);
} course_t;

CREATE TYPE {
    oid             REF Section;
    is_taught_by    professor_t;
    has_TA          ta_t;
} section_t;

CREATE TYPE {
    oid             REF Professor;
    p_name          VARCHAR(50);
} professor_t;

CREATE TYPE {
    oid             REF TA;
    ta_name         VARCHAR(50);
} ta_t;
```

(a) Navigational View Types

```
CREATE VIEW v1 OF course_t AS  /* Iterative Pattern View */
SELECT
    REF(C),
    SETOF(
        SELECT
            REF(S),
            professor_t(REF(S.is_taught_by), S.is_taught_by.p_name),
            ta_t(REF(S.has_TA), S.has_TA.ta_name)
        FROM C.has_sections S)
FROM Cource C;

CREATE INDEX v1_idx ON v1(oid);
```

(b) Iterative Pattern View and the Index

Fig. 4. Iterative Pattern View for the TLAG in Figure 3

Condition (1). The type of the attribute a_1 is one of the attribute types of the root node of the TLAG T.

Condition (2). There exists a node reachable through the path $a_1..a_{k-1}$ from the root node of TLAG T and the access log of the node contains the attribute a_k. □

We need the following idea to define the matching of iterative pattern views. Let $P_S = a_\Omega..a_s$ be the type-level path of the root node of the subgraph S of a TLAG T. Among all the possible subgraphs of TLAG T, the graphs $S_\Omega(= T)$, S_1, ... , S_{s-1} rooted by the nodes of the type-level paths a_Ω, $a_\Omega.a_1$, ... , $a_\Omega..a_{s-1}$, respectively, are called the *supergraphs* of S. By extending the idea of supergraph, S itself can be regarded as a supergraph of S. The following Definition 2 defines the matching of iterative pattern views using the ideas of reachable path and supergraph.

Definition 2 . For a subgraph S of a TLAG T and a TLAG T_V for an iterative pattern view V, let $b_1, \ldots, b_k$ be all the attributes in the access logs in S. It is defined

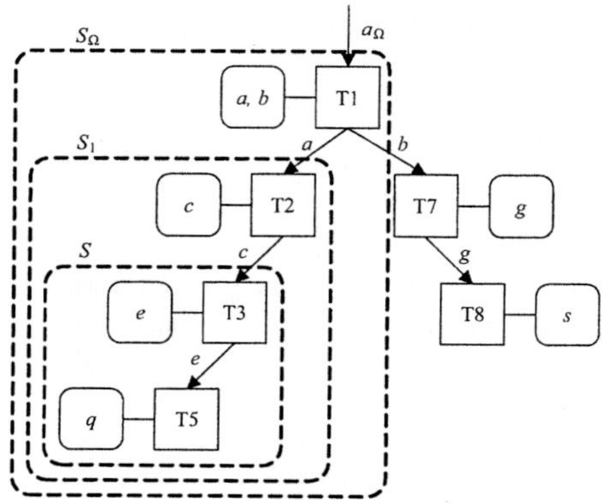

(a) TLAG T and a Subgraph S

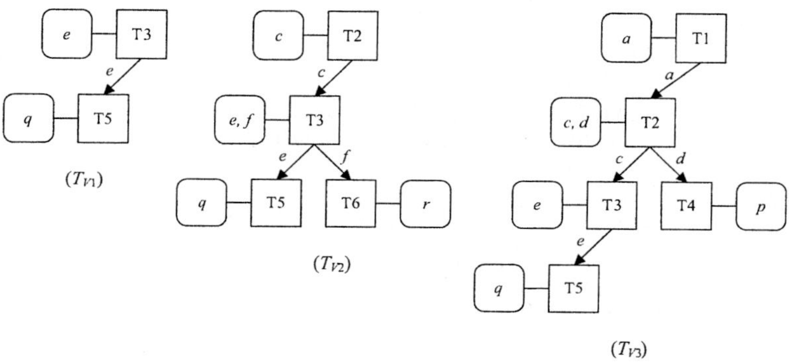

(b) TLAGs T_V for the Iterative Pattern Views Matching the Subgraph S

Fig. 5. Subgraph S of TLAG T and TLAGs T_V for Iterative Pattern Views Matching S

that the TLAG T_V matches the subgraph S, if either one of two cases below is satisfied:

CASE (1). All the paths $P_1, \ldots, P_k$ to the attributes $b_1, \ldots, b_k$ from the root node of S are reachable paths in T_V.

CASE (2). Among the graphs $S_\Omega, \ldots, S_s$, which are the subgraphs of the TLAG T and the supergraphs of S at the same time, there exists a graph $S_i (\Omega \leq i \leq s)$ satisfying the CASE (1) above. That is, all the paths $P_1^i, \ldots, P_k^i$ to the attributes $b_1^i, \ldots, b_k^i$ from the root node of S_i are reachable paths in T_V. □

By extending the idea of supergraph to regard S itself as a supergraph of S, two cases in Definition 2 can be merged into one. Figure 5 shows the subgraph S of the TLAG T and the TLAGs T_V for the iterative pattern views matching S. In Figure 5(a), S_Ω and S_1 are the supergraphs of S. Each TLAG in Figure 5(b) matches S, S_1, and S_Ω and satisfies CASE (1), (2), and (2) in Definition 2, respectively.

```
Procedure ViewMatchingAlgorithm
Input:
        T: TLAG
        S: Subgraph of T
Output:
        V: Matched View
begin
(1)     CandidateViews = φ;
        /* Find the candidate views that match S based on Definition 2. */
(2)     for each TLAG T_V for an iterative pattern view V in the database begin
            /* CASE (1) */
(3)         isMatching = CheckMatch(S, T_V);
(4)         if isMatching == TRUE begin
(5)             CandidateViews = CandidateViews ∪ {V};
(6)             continue;
(7)         end if
            /* CASE (2) */
(8)         for each path P' from the root of T to the root of S begin
(9)             S' = SuperGraph(P', S);
(10)            isMatching = CheckMatch(S', T_V);
(11)            if isMatching == TRUE begin
(12)                CandidateViews = CandidateViews ∪ {V};
(13)                break;
(14)            end if
(15)        end for
(16)    end for
        /* Get the minimum cost view from the candidate views. */
(17)    V = MinCost(S, CandidateViews);
(18)    return V;
end.
```

Fig. 6. Iterative Pattern View Matching Algorithm

Figure 6 shows the algorithm that returns an iterative pattern view V that best matches the given subgraph S of a TLAG T based on Definitions 1 and 2. The algorithm first finds all the iterative pattern views matching the given subgraph S in the lines (1) $\sim$ (16), and then selects an iterative pattern view with the minimal cost in the lines (17) $\sim$ (18). To find all the matching iterative pattern views, for each of the TLAGs T_V for the iterative pattern views in the database, the algorithm checks if CASE (1) in Definition 2 is satisfied in the lines (3) $\sim$ (7), and CASE (2) in the lines (8) $\sim$ (15). The function CheckMatch(S, T_V) in the lines (3) and (10) returns TRUE if CASE (1) in Definition 2 is satisfied for the given subgraph S and TLAG T_V, or FALSE otherwise. The function SuperGraph(P', S) in the line (9) returns a supergraph of S rooted by the node having the type-level path P'. The function MinCost(S, CandidateViews) in the line (17) returns an iterative pattern view with the minimal cost among those contained in CandidateViews. Using a complicated method for computing the cost of a view in the function could cause the overhead on the performance of the navigational application. In this paper, we define the cost of a view as the number of disk pages occupied by the view, and select the view with the smallest size as the minimal cost view.

4 Performance Evaluation

In this section, we perform a series of experiments to compare the performance of the prefetch method based on the type-level access pattern view proposed in this paper (denoted as *ViewPrefetch*) and the original prefetch method proposed by Han et al. (denoted as *TypePrefetch*) [7]. In Sections 4.1 and 4.2, we explain the environment and the result of our experiments, respectively.

4.1 Experiment Environment

We performed two groups of experiments evaluating the performance of (1) the navigational application on the database in Figure 1 and (2) the XML database application. Since the performance of the navigational applications is affected by the degree of clustering of the objects, we performed the experiments (1) and (2) on the clustered database (denoted as *ClusteredDB*) and the non-clustered database (denoted as *NonClusteredDB*) separately. The objects in the ClusteredDB are stored in the order that they are accessed by the navigational application, and those in the NonClusteredDB are stored in a random order.

In the experiment (1), the number of all the professors is 20,000, and the number of those whose salaries are above $100,000 is 1,000 (5% of selectivity). All the professors own a car, and the number of car manufacturers is 100. The XML data used in the experiment (2) are the bibliography data for a publishing company. We defined a navigational view type for each element in DTD, and mapped the asterisk (*) representing multiple sub-elements as the collection attribute [2]. In the experiment (2), the number of all the XML objects in the XML database is 40,000, and the arbitrary 2,000 XML objects (5% of selectivity) among them are chosen and transformed into XML documents. The XML application starts navigation from the root objects in the database corresponding to the root elements in DTD, and accesses the objects connected from the root objects directly or indirectly according to the hierarchical architecture of the DTD. Then the application generates XML documents by integrating the XML tags corresponding to the accessed objects.

We implemented both of the prefetch methods ViewPrefetch and TypePrefetch on the ODYSSEUS [13], an ORDBMS under development at KAIST. The hardware platforms are Sun Ultra-2 Workstation for the client and Sun Ultra-60 Workstation for the server. The size of object cache in the client is 8MB, and the size of page buffer in the server is 16MB. To remove the buffering effects by the Operating System, we used our own disk manager that accesses directly the raw disks. We computed the ratios $\frac{TypePrefetch}{ViewPrefetch}$ of the number of disk I/O's and the execution times for each of the experiments. We performed each of the experiments five times and presented the average value as the final result.

4.2 Experiment Results

Figure 7 shows the result of experiment (1). In the figure, the Y axis represents the value $\frac{TypePrefetch}{ViewPrefetch}$, i.e., the improvement ratio of ViewPrefetch compared with

[2] The XML data and DTD are obtained from http://www.cs.wisc.edu/niagara/data.html. In our experiment, we generated additional XML data based on the DTD.

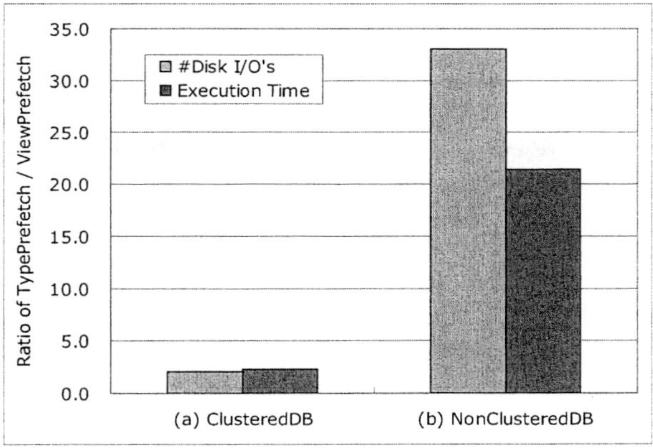

Fig. 7. Experiment Result of the Navigational Application

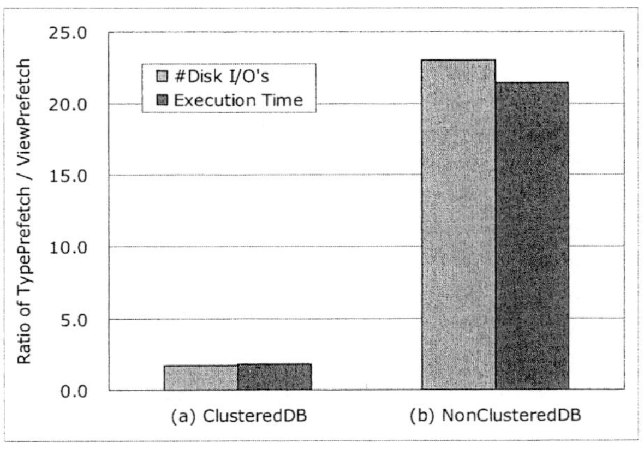

Fig. 8. Experiment Result of the XML Application

TypePrefetch. The execution time is the wall clock time measured from the start to the finish of the navigational applications, and contains the time for CPU operations, object fetches, and disk accesses. In Figure 7, ViewPrefetch is improved than TypePrefetch by up to 2.07 times for the number of disk accesses and 2.34 times for the execution time in the ClusteredDB. ViewPrefetch is improved by up to 33.0 times and 21.4 times, respectively, in the NonClusteredDB. The reason that the improvement ratios in the NonClusteredDB are much more significant than in the ClusteredDB is that the objects accessed by TypePrefetch are gathered in small number of disk pages in the ClusteredDB while those are scattered over the diverse disk pages in the NonClusteredDB.

Figure 8 shows the result of experiment (2), and the Y axis represents the ratio $\frac{TypePrefetch}{ViewPrefetch}$ as in Figure 7. In the figure, ViewPrefetch is improved than TypePrefetch by up to 1.69 times for the number of disk accesses and 1.80 times for the execution time in the ClusteredDB. ViewPrefetch is improved by up to 23.0 times and 21.4 times, respectively, in the NonClusteredDB. The reason that the improvement ratios in the NonClusteredDB are much more significant than in the ClusteredDB is the same as in the experiment (1). Since most of the databases of the real-world navigational applications are the NonClusteredDB, the applications can obtain significant performance enhancement by using the prefetch technique proposed in this paper.

5 Conclusions

In this paper, we proposed a technique to enhance the performance of the prefetch method based on the type-level access pattern proposed by Han et al. [7]. The ratio of the performance enhancement of the prefetch method by Han et al. compared with the context based prefetch method [2] was not as significant as the reduction ratio of the number of object fetches. Since the performance of prefetching is determined by the number of disk accesses in the server as well as the number of fetches, even though the number of fetches is reduced significantly, the overall performance would not be enhanced as much, if the number of disk accesses remains unchanged.

The major contributions of this paper are as follows. (1) For the iterative pattern, we proposed the methods for creating type-level access pattern views based on the type-level path access log graphs. (2) We presented the algorithm to find the type-level access pattern view that best matches the type-level access pattern detected by the navigational application. (3) We performed a series of experiments using the databases having the iterative pattern and the XML database to evaluate the overall performance enhancement obtained by the proposed prefetch technique. The experiments were performed on the clustered and non-clustered databases separately.

Through extensive experiments, we showed that the proposed technique reduced the number of disk accesses by up to 33.0 times and enhanced the overall performance of the navigational application by up to 21.4 times compared with the original prefetch method by Han et al. Since most of the databases of the real-world navigational applications are non-clustered ones, the applications can obtain significant performance enhancement by using the prefetch technique proposed in this paper.

Acknowledgement

This work was supported by the Ministry of Science and Technology (MOST) / Korea Science and Engineering Foundation (KOSEF) through the Advanced Information Technology Research Center (AITrc) and by the Brain Korea 21 Project.

References

1. Abiteboul, S., McHugh, J., Rys, M., Vassalos, V., and Wiener, J., "Incremental Maintenance for Materialized Views over Semistructured Data," In *Proc. Int'l Conf. Very Large Data Bases (VLDB)*, New York, New York, pp. 38-49, Aug. 1998.
2. Berstein, P. A., Pal, S., and Shutt, D., "Context-Based Prefetch for Implementing Objects on Relations," In *Proc. Int'l Conf. Very Large Data Bases (VLDB)*, Edinburgh, Scotland, pp. 327-338, Sept. 1999.

3. Bowman, I. T. and Salem, K., "Optimization of Query Streams Using Semantic Prefetching," In *Proc. Int'l Conf. Management of Data*, ACM SIGMOD, Paris, France, pp. 179-190, June 2004.
4. Colby, L., Kawaguchi, A., Lieuwen, D., Mumick, I., and Ross, K., "Supporting Multiple View Maintenance Policies," In *Proc. Int'l Conf. Management of Data*, ACM SIGMOD, Tucson, Arizona, pp. 405-416, June 1997.
5. Fraternali, P. and Paolini, P., "Model-Driven Development of Web Applications: the AutoWeb System," *ACM Trans. Information Systems (TOIS)*, Vol. 18, No. 4, pp. 323-382, Oct. 2000.
6. Han, W.-S., Whang, K.-Y., and Moon, Y.-S., "PrefetchGuide: Capturing Navigational Access Patterns for Prefetching in Client/Server Object-Oriented/Object-Relational DBMSs," *Information Sciences*, Vol. 152, pp. 47-61, June 2003.
7. Han, W.-S., Whang, K.-Y., and Moon, Y.-S., "A Formal Framework for Prefetching Based on the Type-Level Access Pattern in Object-Relational DBMSs," *IEEE Trans. Knowledge and Data Engineering (TKDE)*, Accepted to Appear, 2005.
8. Liskov, B. et al., "Safe and Efficient Sharing of Persistent Objects in Thor," In *Proc. Int'l Conf. Management of Data*, ACM SIGMOD, Montreal, Canada, pp. 318-329, June 1996.
9. Oracle Corp., Oracle9i SQL Reference, Release 9.2, Mar. 2002.
10. Stonebraker, M. and Moore, D., *Object-Relational DBMSs: The Next Great Wave*, Morgan Kaufmann, 1999.
11. Subramanian, M. and Krishnamurthy, V., "Performance Challenges in Object-Relational DBMSs," *IEEE Data Engineering Bulletin*, Vol. 22, No. 2, pp. 27-31, 1999.
12. Taylor, R. G., *Models of Computation and Formal Languages*, Oxford University Press, 1998.
13. Whang, K.-Y., Lee, M.-J., Lee, J.-G., Kim, M.-S., and Han, W.-S., "Odysseus: A High-Performance ORDBMS Tightly-Coupled with IR Features," In *Proc. Int'l Conf. Data Engineering (ICDE)*, IEEE, Tokyo, Japan, pp. 1104-1105, Apr. 2005.

The Dynamic Sweep Scheme Using Slack Time in the Zoned Disk

Sungchae Lim

Dongduk Women's University, Sungbuk-gu Seoul 136-714, Korea
sclim@dongduk.ac.kr
http://cs.dongduk.ac.kr

Abstract. Recently, on-demand streaming service of continuous media (CM) becomes crucial for successful Internet businesses. To ensure quality service of online CM streams, the Sweep scheme was proposed to provide high I/O throughput as well as hiccup-free playback. When this scheme is applied in the system using the zoned disk, however, it may suffer from significant bandwidth losses because of its inherent scheduling inflexibility. Since disk zones in a multi-zone disk have different data transfer rates, much slack time occurs when data requests are made to read data blocks located in inner disk zones. Such slack time cannot be efficiently reclaimed in Sweep. In this paper we propose an EDF-style variant of the Sweep scheme, called the Dynamic Sweep Scheme, in order to handle slack time that increases in the zoned disk.

1 Introduction

Recently, on-demand streaming service of continuous media (CM) such as digitized videos and audios becomes a fundamental factor for successful Internet businesses. To ensure quality service of online CM streams, a CM server is required to deliver CM data to a client's device while meeting temporal constraint of serviced CM streams. When a CM stream with playback rate p starts its playback at time s, the CM server has to read at least $p \times (t - s)$ worth of data until time t [1]. From such temporal constraint, every CM stream issues continuous data requests (for short, C-requests) which are given with deadlines depending on its playback rate. By yielding feasible schedules meeting C-requests' deadlines, the CM server prevents undesirable interruptions of playback, called *hiccups*.

To provide hiccup-free playbacks in the CM server, much literature has proposed disk scheduling algorithms suitable for the process of C-requests [2, 3, 4, 5, 6, 7]. Among them, cycle-based approaches are popularly accepted for the concurrent service of a variety of CM streams [4, 5, 6, 7]. In these approaches, the disk head is scheduled based on a fixed-size period called a *cycle* so that every CM stream reads its *per-cycle data* in each cycle and consumes them during the very next cycle. Here, the per-cycle data is the data that should be read during a cycle and its size is given by multiplying the playback rate with the cycle size. Since all the serviced CM streams have the same scheduling period, i.e., the cycle, a cyclic disk scheduler can easily provide hiccup-free schedules for C-requests with deadlines.

M.L. Lee, K.L. Tan, and V. Wuwongse (Eds.): DASFAA 2006, LNCS 3882, pp. 404–419, 2006.

The cycle-based approaches can be roughly categorized into three schemes of Sweep, Fixed-Stretch, and Grouped Sweep Scheme [4, 5]. Among them, the Sweep scheme outperforms others due to its high seek-time optimization. In this scheme, all of CM streams issue C-requests at the beginning of each cycle, and a sweep of the disk head completes the process of these issued C-requests within the same cycle. Since a large amount of data are retrieved in a disk sweep using the SCAN algorithm, Sweep can reduce disk bandwidth losses caused by frequent disk seeking, thereby providing high I/O throughout for the presentation of CM streams [3, 4, 5].

Although this scheme provides hiccup freeness as well as low seek-time overhead, it has a problem in that slack time cannot not be utilized in efficient manner. The slack time is one arising because of a time gap between the reserved disk time and the actual time used to process a C-request. As the reserved disk time is chosen against the worst-case disk time to prevent deadline misses, such slack time inevitably arises in cycles. Moreover, since the zoned disk is usually used in the modern computing system, the amount of slack time tends to increase with growing differences among the data transfer rates of different disk zones [10].

The zoned disk is a disk type in which more than one disk zone is built in a disk plate, and the outer zones from the disk spindle have larger sizes of disk tracks than inner ones [10]. Because of a longer track length and a constant revolution speed of the disk plate, the outer zones have higher transfer rates, compared to inner zones. Since the reservation of disk time is based on the worst-case data transfer rate of the innermost zone, significant slack time occurs whenever we process C-requests asking for data blocks in outer zones.

In this paper, we propose an EDF-style variant of the Sweep scheme, called the Dynamic Sweep Scheme (DSS), to handle slack time that increases in the zoned disk. To this end, we enable a CM stream to prefetch more data than its per-cycle data by using slack time, thereby expanding its scheduling period. Because the expanded period contributes to less bandwidth usage of CM streams, the proposed DSS can play back a larger number of CM streams than in the Sweep scheme. The various sizes of scheduling periods entail a complicated situation where the numbers and deadlines of C-requests being issued in the same cycle are not fixed, differently from the Sweep scheme. To cope with varying workloads and deadlines of C-requests in every cycle, the DSS adopts the earliest deadline first (EDF) algorithm for disk scheduling, and uses a new mechanism for admission control. Since our DSS also provides hiccup-freeness as well as high I/O throughput, this scheme can be used to guarantee quality streaming service in the multimedia system.

The rest of the paper is organized as follows. In Section 2, we give a brief technical background for this research, including storage model and the earlier Sweep scheme. Section 3 presents the proposed algorithm, and Section 4 shows that the DSS outperforms other scheme. Lastly, we conclude this paper in Section 5.

2 Technical Background

2.1 Track-Sized Data Clustering

A modern disk drive has a large internal cache memory and can cache a whole data passed beneath its disk head while synchronizing with rotation of the disk plates [8]. Such a disk drive can significantly reduce the rotational delay time when it reads a large size of data strip that is continuously stored within a disk track. If it reads a whole disk track of data, the time of data transfer plus rotation delay is bounded by one revolution time [8, 9]. To fully utilize such a characteristic, the scheme of track-sized data clustering is widely accepted to store CM data on the disk. In this scheme, only one kind of CM data is saved in a disk track and its disk location is continuous within the disk track. By using this track-sized data clustering, we can provide high I/O utilization and flexible disk management of CM data.

When CM data is managed in the track-sized cluster policy, each C-request is enforced to request a continuous data strip stored in a single disk track. The data strip requested by a C-request can be addressed with a location identifier of $(Offset1, Offset2, X)$. Here, X is *id* of the target disk track, and $Offset1$ and $Offset2$ are the start and end positions of requested data in track X, respectively. Therefore, if a CM stream has to read its data stored across n disk tracks of $X_1, X_2, \ldots, X_n$, the same number of C-requests should be issued for each disk track. The C-requests for X_1 and X_n may request part of a disk track, while others ask for a whole of disk track each.

2.2 Revisiting the Sweep Scheme

As before mentioned, the Sweep scheme enforces CM streams to issue C-requests at every beginning of the cycle, and processes them in that cycle. To serve the C-requests without deadline miss, this scheme admits CM streams while disk time to read all the per-cycle data of them is not greater than the cycle length. For this, the notion of the worst-case scan time is used. Let $WCST(\eta)$ be the lowest upper bound of disk time taken to read η disk tracks through a disk scan. Since a C-request always asks for data continuously located in a disk track, a scan time for processing η C-requests is never greater than $WCST(\eta)$. From this, we can have the *admission capacity* $\mathcal{K}$ of Sweep by solving $WCST(\mathcal{K}) \leq L_{cycle} < WCST(\mathcal{K}+1)$, where L_{cycle} is the cycle length. By admitting CM streams so that their workloads are managed within admission capacity $\mathcal{K}$, the Sweep scheme can serve CM streams without hiccups.

To see this in detail, consider a CM stream S that has per-cycle data size of D. Let the size of the innermost track be $T_{|1|}$. Then, S can read its per-cycle data by issuing W C-requests in each cycle, if $W = \lceil D/T_{|1|} \rceil$. Here, we call the integer W the *workload value* of S, which is disk bandwidth needed to serve S. By managing the sum of workload values of admitted CM streams below $\mathcal{K}$, hiccup-freeness is preserved. For this, a new CM stream with workload value W is admitted only when $W + \sum_{i=1}^{n} W_i \leq \mathcal{K}$, where W_i are workload values of already admitted CM streams.

Although the Sweep scheme can process W_i C-requests for S_i in every cycle, it cannot utterly eliminate the occurrence of hiccups of CM streams in some cases. To see this, consider a CM stream S that requests $0.7T_{|1|}$ size of per-cycle data and has its workload value of size one. Suppose that the data of S is stored in the disk tracks of $X_1, X_2, \ldots, X_\eta$, and those tracks are all located in the innermost zone. In this case, S is made to issue a C-request to read its first per-cycle data that is addressed with $(0, 0.7T_{|1|}, X_1)$. The second per-cycle data of S is located across two disk tracks of $(0.7T_{|1|}, T_{|1|}, X_1)$ and $(0, 0.4T_{|1|}, X_2)$, and thus S needs two C-requests to read that data although its size is not greater than $T_{|1|}$. Such a problem frequently arises when we manage CM data as the track-sized segments.

Against the problem, the Sweep scheme can adopt a simple prefetch scheme that performs read-ahead whenever fragmentation of per-cycle data across multiple tracks may cause the need for an extra issue of a C-request. The followings are steps for this prefetch, where $Track(X)$ denotes the size of track X.

(1) Let $(Offset1, Offset2, X)$ be the location identifier of the data strip asked for by a C-request.
(2) **If** $(Track(X) - Offset2) < (D \textbf{ mod } Track(X))$
(3) **Then** Modify that identifier of $(Offset1, Offset2, X)$ into $(Offset1, Track(X), X)$. /* Prefetch is applied for the read-ahead of the data in $(Offset2, Track(X), X)$ */
(4) **Else** Use the location of $(Offset1, Offset2, X)$ without modification. /* Prefetch is not used */

Figure 1 illustrates an example where the prefetch scheme is applied for the CM stream S above. In this example, read-ahead arises in cycles i, $i+1$, and $i+3$, and the read-ahead data sizes are $0.3T_{|1|}$, $0.6T_{|1|}$, and $0.2T_{|1|}$, respectively. By means of such read-ahead, S can read its per-cycle data by issuing only one C-request in a cycle.

$$\frac{(0, T_{|1|}, X_1)}{cycle\ i} \Rightarrow \frac{(0, T_{|1|}, X_2)}{cycle\ i+1} \Rightarrow \frac{(0, \frac{T_{|1|}}{10}, X_3)}{cycle\ i+2} \Rightarrow \frac{(\frac{T_{|1|}}{10}, T_{|1|}, X_3)}{cycle\ i+3} \Rightarrow \cdots$$

Fig. 1. A prefetch example for a CM stream that has $0.7 \cdot T_{|1|}$ size of per-cycle data.

According to Ruemmler [8], a seek-time to reposition the disk head across l cylinders, denoted by *seek_time(l)*, can be modeled as follows:

$$seek\_time(l) = \begin{cases} C_1 + C_2\sqrt{l} \text{ if } l \leq L, \\ C_3 + C_4 * l \text{ otherwise,} \end{cases}$$

where C_i is disk parameters and L is a boundary from which the seek-time increases linearly with l.

Since *seek_time(l)* is a convex and non-decreasing function, the overall seek time for a disk scan is maximized when requested data are evenly distributed over disk cylinders [9]. With track-sized clustering, we make each of C-requests ask a data script located in a single disk track. Therefore, the upper bound of a scan time to process η C-requests, denoted by $T^u(\eta)$, is given by:

$$T^u(\eta) = \eta * Revolution\_Time + (\eta + 1)seek\_time(\lceil \frac{N_{cyl}}{\eta + 1} \rceil) \quad (1)$$

where N_{cyl} is the total number of disk cylinders.

This means that $T^u(\eta)$ is the worst-case time for a disk sweep to process any set of η C-requests. Therefore, we can use $T^u(\eta)$ as $WCST(\eta)$ that was used for computing admission capacity $\mathcal{K}$ in Section 2.2.

3 The Proposed Dynamic Sweep Scheme

3.1 Motivations to This Research

A. Slack time in the zoned disk

Although the Sweep scheme provides hiccup-freeness as well as high seek-optimization, it still suffers from a large amount of bandwidth wastes in disk scheduling. This results from differences between disk time reserved to a CM stream against worst-case disk operations and actually used disk time. For example, consider a CM stream S_1 that requests per-cycle data of size $0.6T_{|1|}$, where $T_{|1|}$ is the track size of the innermost zone. Assume that S_1's data is stored in η disk tracks of X_1, X_2, ..., X_η, and $Track(X_1) = T_{|1|}$, $Track(X_2) = 1.2T_{|1|}$, and $Track(X_3) = 1.5T_{|1|}$, respectively.

When we schedule S_1 from cycle i, the data read by S_1 looks like that in Fig. 2. During the five cycles below, S_1 reads two disk tracks of X_1 and X_2, along with part of X_3. In this schedule, the simple prefetch scheme is applied for S_1 in cycles i and $i + 2$, and thus S_1 is able to read per-cycle data by issuing a single C-request.

$$\frac{(0, T_{|1|}, X_1)}{cycle\ i} \Rightarrow \frac{(0, 0.2T_{|1|}, X_2)}{cycle\ i+1} \Rightarrow \frac{(0.2T_{|1|}, 1.2T_{|1|}, X_2)}{cycle\ i+2} \Rightarrow \frac{(0, 0.2T_{|1|}, X_3)}{cycle\ i+3} \Rightarrow \frac{(0.2T_{|1|}, 0.8T_{|1|}, X_3)}{cycle\ i+4}$$

Fig. 2. The data read by a CM stream with per-cycle data of size $0.6 \cdot T_{|1|}$.

In Fig. 2, the total size of the data read by S_1 is $3T_{|1|}$, although bandwidth reserved to S_1 is enough to read five disk tracks of X_1 to X_5, whose total size is equal to or larger than $5.7T_{|1|}$. This means that around 50% of bandwidth is wasted by S_1 with respect to its reserved bandwidth. Such a waste of bandwidth is inevitable as long as we take the cycle-based approach that schedules C-requests in the unit of a cycle.

To solve this problem in the cycle-based approach, we propose a new method capable of expanding the scheduling period by using slack time in the zoned disk. Image a situation where S_1 reads more data using the slack time in Fig. 2, and becomes to cache around $2T_{|1|}$ size of data in memory until the end of cycle $i+3$. The amount of this data is enough to fulfill S_1's data requirement during three cycles, and thus we could expand the scheduling period of S_1 from one cycle to three cycles at that point. Simultaneously, image that S_1 is made to issue two C-requests per three cycles to read $1.8T_{|1|}$ size of data, i.e., its new per-period data. This change of the pattern of C-request issuing reduces the bandwidth requirement of S_1. By assigning the saved bandwidth that can issue a C-request per three cycles to other CM streams, our proposed method can serve a larger number of concurrent CM streams than in Sweep.

To enable period expansion, we introduce the concept of the DRP (Data Request Pattern) for each CM stream served in our system. The DRP consists of two integers k and p that indicate the number of issued C-requests and the length of the scheduling period of a CM stream, respectively. When a CM stream has a DRP $\langle k, p\rangle$, it can issue k C-requests with a scheduling period of p cycles.

We also call the fraction of k/p the *workload rate* that is proportional to the amount of bandwidth usage of the corresponding CM stream. This workload rate is used for admission control in our method. When a CM stream is newly admitted with workload value W, its DRP becomes to be $\langle W, 1\rangle$, and its workload value and the workload rate remain the same until it expands the scheduling period.

B. The mechanism of period expansion

To expand a scheduling period without hiccups, we need to read more data in advance for the CM stream trying to make period expansion. If a CM stream S with DRP $\langle W, 1\rangle$ intends to expand its DRP into $\langle k, p\rangle$, $(p > 1)$, then S has to cache data that is enough for p cycles' consumption. That is, if S wants to expand its scheduling period at time t, then S needs cached data of size $d \times p$ at least, where d is the per-cycle data of S. After such a period expansion, S will issue k C-requests at t, which must be processed by $t + p \times L_{cycle}$. Since S has cached data capable of being consumed during p cycles, it does not experience hiccups if the newly issued C-requests are processed within p cycles.

---

1. Compute $DataSize = 2 \times d \times p$. /* d is the size of per-cycle data of S. */
2. Let the size of currently cached data be denoted by $CachedSize$.
3. Solve the least integer k' satisfying that
$$CachedSize + \sum_{i=1}^{k'} Track(Y_i) \geq DataSize.$$
4. Issue k' C-requests to read data of $(0, Track(Y_1), Y_1), (0, Track(Y_2), Y_2), \ldots, (0, Track(Y_{k'}), Y_{k'})$.

Fig. 3. Algorithm for the aggressive prefetch scheme for a CM stream

To efficiently utilize slack time, we use the aggressive prefetch scheme of Fig. 3. The algorithm in Fig. 3 is for a CM stream S with DRP $\langle k, p\rangle$, and this algorithm is executed at the beginning points of the scheduling period of S. In Fig. 3, the disk tracks to be read for S are denoted by $Y_1, Y_2, Y_3, \ldots, Y_\eta$, and $Track(Y_i)$ is the size of Y_i. k' $(k' < k)$ is the number of C-requests to be issued for S and those C-requests should be processed in the time of $p \times L_{cycle}$. Each CM stream may have cached data of size $2 \times p \times d$ in Fig. 3, and thus the total memory requirement is around $M = \sum_{j=1}^{n}(2 \times d_j \times p_j)$, where $d_j \times p_j$ is per-period data size of S_i.

To show how to expand a scheduling period, we use the example of Fig. 2 again. As before, we assume that the per-cycle data of S_1 is $0.6T_{|1|}$, and its

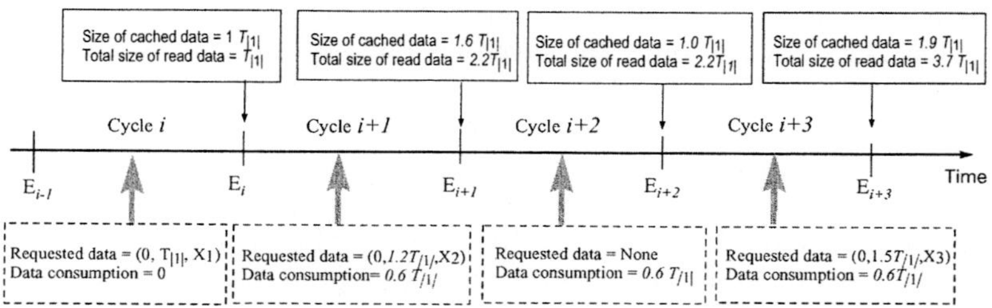

Fig. 4. Disk scheduling for S_1 with per-cycle data of size $0.6T_{|1|}$

current DRP is $\langle 1, 1\rangle$. When S_1 is scheduled according to the aggressive prefetch scheme, we have the schedule of Fig. 4. Here, we assume that S_1 issues its first C-request at point E_{i-1}.

The sizes of cached data and the total sizes of read data are depicted for the points of E_j $(i \leq j \leq i+3)$. Since the scheduling period of S_1 is a cycle in size, the aggressive prefetch algorithm is executed at every E_j. Look at the situation of E_{i+1}. At this point, S_1 has cached data of size $1.6T_{|1|}$ and thus it could expand its scheduling period to the length of two cycles since the cached data can be consumed for two cycles. Such period expansion requires that S_1 issue two C-requests with a period of two cycles. In this case, we have no saving of disk bandwidth from this period expansion. Therefore, we do not execute period expansion at this point. Instead, S_1 does not issue a new C-requests at E_{i+1} by conforming to the aggressive prefetch algorithm of Fig. 3. Due to data consumption in cycle $i+2$, the size of S_1' cached data decreases by $0.6T_{|1|}$, which is the size of its per-cycle data. Next, by issuing a C-request reading X_3 in cycle $i+3$, S_1 becomes to cache $1.9T_{|1|}$ worth of data at E_{i+3}. Then, we can expand the scheduling period of S_1 into a length of three cycles so that a new DRP $\langle 2, 3\rangle$ is given to S_1. This period expansion saves bandwidth capable of reading a disk track per three cycles, and the new DRP still meets data requirement of S_1 since $\frac{2T_{|1|}}{3} > 0.6T_{|1|}$. From the point of E_{i+3}, S_1 is scheduled with DRP $\langle 2, 3\rangle$.

3.2 System Components

Fig. 5 shows the proposed CM server that consists of a stream management component (SMC) and a disk scheduling component (DSC). The former is responsible for admission control, transferring retrieved data to clients' devices, issuing of C-requests, and expansions of scheduling periods. By creating a session context for each serviced CM stream, the SMC keeps track of the playback status of that. The latter component is to process C-requests issued by the SMC so as to load the requested data into proper memory space. For this, the DSC repetitively selects a proper number of C-requests from the C-request queue and then processes them through a disk scan.

We assume that these two components are implemented as different processes and they run in parallel. While the DSC is busy in doing a disk scan, the SMC

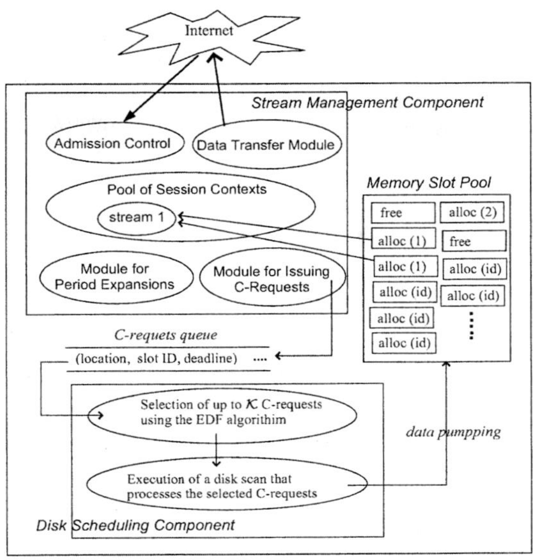

Fig. 5. The architecture of the proposed CM server

can do its tasks. For cooperation between these components, the IPC (Inter-Process Communication) mechanism are used for implementation. C-requests are put into the request queue lying between the SMC and DSC.

A data object representing a C-request includes a location identifier of the requested data strip, the given deadline, and the *id* of the used memory slot. The slot *id* indicates the memory address where the read disk track is loaded. Before issuing a C-request, the SMC allocates a free memory slot from the memory slot pool. The memory slot pool comprises of the fixed-size memory slots and the slot size is equal to that of a disk track in the outermost disk zone.

3.3 Scheduling Based on the DRP

A. EDF-style disk scheduling

A DRP specifies how many and how often C-requests are issued for a corresponding CM stream. More specifically, the use of a DRP $\langle k, p\rangle$ requires that k C-requests be issued with a period of p cycles. Assume that streams S_1, S_2, and S_3 having DRPs of $\langle 1, 1\rangle$, $\langle 3, 2\rangle$, and $\langle 5, 3\rangle$, respectively, issue their C-requests at E_{i-1}, which is the end of cycle $i-1$. The C-requests from these streams are as in Fig. 6(a), where $C_n(j)$ for S_i represents the nth C-request of S_i whose deadline is E_j. Since every C-request should be served prior to the beginning of its next scheduling period, a C-request issued at E_i with a scheduling period of p cycles is given with its deadline of E_{i+p}. As known from Fig. 6(a), the total number of issued C-requests and their deadlines are not fixed. This is different from the Sweep scheme in which the number of issued C-requests is not changed

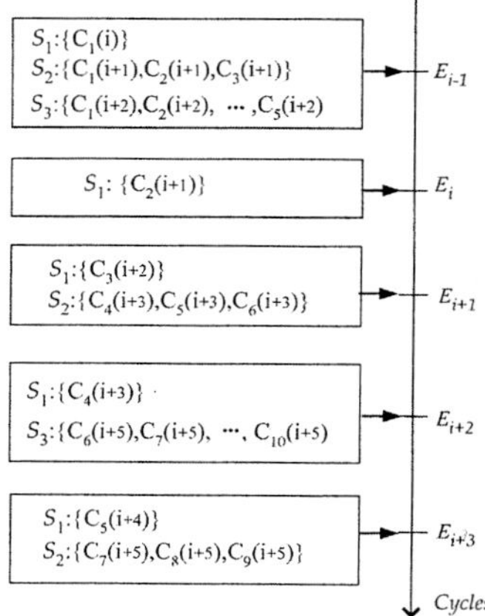

(a) Periodic issuing of C-requests

Time	Enqueued C-requests	Selected C-requests
at E_{i-1}	S_1:{C_1(i)} S_2:{C_1(i+1),C_2(i+1),C_3(i+1)} S_3:{C_1(i+2),C_2(i+2), ...,C_5(i+2)}	S_1:{C_1(i)} S_2:{C_1(i+1),C_2(i+1),C_3(i+1)} S_3:{C_1(i+2)}
at E_i	S_1:{C_2(i+1)} S_2:{} S_3:{C_2(i+2),C_3(i+2), ...,C_5(i+2)}	S_1:{C_1(i+1)} S_2:{} S_3:{C_2(i+2),C_3(i+2), ...,C_5(i+2)}
at E_{i+1}	S_1:{C_3(i+2)} S_2:{C_4(i+3),C_5(i+3),C_6(i+3)} S_3:{}	S_1:{C_1(i)} S_2:{C_4(i+3),C_5(i+3),C_6(i+3)} S_3:{}
at E_{i+2}	S_1:{C_4(i+3)} S_2:{} S_3:{C_6(i+5),C_7(i+5), ...,C_{10}(i+5)}	S_1:{C_4(i+3)} S_2:{} S_3:{C_6(i+5),C_7(i+5), ...,C_9(i+5)}
at E_{i+3}	S_1:{C_5(i+4)} S_2:{C_7(i+5),C_8(i+5),C_9(i+5)} S_3:{C_{10}(i+5)}	S_1:{C_5(i+4)} S_2:{C_7(i+5),C_8(i+5),C_9(i+5)} S_3:{C_{10}(i+5)}

(b) A feasible schedule for (a)

Fig. 6. Periodic issues of C-requests and process of them

for the same set of CM streams and the C-requests issued in a cycle have the same deadline, i.e., the end of that cycle.

In turn we describe our disk scheduling algorithm that is used to process C-requests. Suppose that we have the admission capacity of $\mathcal{K} = 5$, and thus process up to five C-requests in each cycle. By applying the EDF algorithm, we can get a feasible disk scheduling as in Fig. 6(b). In Fig. 6(b), the enqueued C-requests represent the ones waiting for process at each beginning of the cycles. For example, at E_{i-1}, there exist nine enqueued C-requests, while five ones are waiting for the service at E_i.

The selected C-requests at $E_j (i-1 \leq j \leq i+3)$ represent C-requests that are selected to be processed during E_j to E_{j+1}. This selection of C-requests is based on deadline urgency, that is, we use the EDF algorithm to give scheduling order to the enqueued C-requests. By making the number of selected C-requests equal to or less than admission capacity, i.e., five, the selected C-requests are always processed prior to the next cycle.

Let $W_j(i)$ be the number of enqueued C-requests having deadline E_i at the point of E_j. Then, situations when we miss deadlines of any C-requests are classified into two cases; (i) $E_j(j+1) > \mathcal{K}$, or (ii) $E_j(i) > 0$ for any $i \leq j$. From this observation, we can have the following criterion for the hiccup-freeness in our CM server. We call this a *hiccup-prevention condition.*

Criteria 1. For every $j > 0$, the followings should be satisfied:
$W_j(j+1) \leq \mathcal{K}$ and $W_j(j-l) = W_j(j-l+1) = \ldots = W_j(j-1) = W_j(j) = 0$, where l is the largest one of p_i.

B. Admission control

To make the hiccup-prevention condition hold all the time, a mechanism for admission control is required to manage workloads of C-requests below admission capacity. Recall that the workload rate is computed as k/p in the case of a DRP

$\langle k, p \rangle$, and the value of a workload rate determines the amount of reserved disk bandwidth. Since the workloads of CM streams depend on their workload rates, our proposed mechanism for admission control is executed to make sure that $\sum w_i \le \mathcal{K}$, where w_i is the workload rate of S_i.

We call this condition the *admission condition*, and it is a sufficient condition for preserving the hiccup-prevention condition. Based on the admission condition, we admit new CM streams. When a playback request for a CM object is issued and its workload value is W, we check if $W + \sum w_i \le \mathcal{K}$. If this is true, the CM stream is admitted; otherwise, it will be made to wait for the time any serviced CM stream ends its playback.

The admission condition is driven from the schedulability feature of the original EDF algorithm that schedules periodic tasks using CPU time. In this scheduler, a period CPU task is specified by the needed CPU time, the length of its period, and the first release time. When a periodic CPU task τ has C and P as required CPU time and period, respectively, the CPU utilization of τ is computed by C/P. While the sum of CPU utilization of scheduled tasks is not greater than 1, the original EDF scheduler can schedule all the tasks without deadline miss. If we would map a CM stream onto such a CPU periodic task, a CM stream with $\langle k, p \rangle$ can be considered a periodic CPU task with the needed CPU time of $k/\mathcal{K}$ and a period of p seconds. From this mapping, the CPU utilization of admitted CM streams is computed as $\frac{1}{\mathcal{K}} \cdot \sum k_i/p_i$, for DRPs $\langle k_i, p_i \rangle$. By maintaining $\frac{1}{\mathcal{K}} \cdot \sum k_i/p_i \le 1$, i.e., $\sum k_i/p_i \le \mathcal{K}$, we can preserve hiccup-freeness of C-requests. The formal proof can be found in [5].

The admission condition above should be held while we are doing period expansion. Let w_i^j be the workload rate of S_i after S_i has expanded its scheduling period j times. In this notation, w_i^0 represents the workload value that is calculated for S_i at admission time. To satisfy the admission condition all the time, we always perform the period expansion such that $w_i^0 > w_i^1 > w_i^2 > \ldots > w_i^j$ during j times of period expansions. In other words, we allow period expansion only when it can contribute to reduction of bandwidth usage by diminishing the value of corresponding workload rate. Because of such period expansion, we can always preserve our admission condition while DRPs are being expanded.

3.4 Analysis of Memory Usage

In this section, we estimate the size of main memory that is required to build the memory slot pool of our CM server. The memory slot pool is comprised of the same sized slots and its size is equal to the track size of the outermost zone. Since a CM steam with DRP $\langle k, p \rangle$ may cache up to $2k$ disk tracks, its maximum requirement for main memory corresponds to $2k \cdot T_{|Z|}$, where $T_{|Z|}$ is the track size in the outermost zone. From this, the maximum memory requirements of $\{S_1, S_2, \ldots, S_\eta\}$, denoted by M_{UB}, is given as follows:

$$M_{UB} = UpperBound(2 \times T_{|Z|} \times \sum_{i=1}^{\eta} k_i) = 2 \times T_{|Z|} \times UpperBound(\sum_{i=1}^{\eta} k_i), \quad (2)$$

where $\langle k_i, p_i \rangle$ is the DRP of S_i.

Because of our admission control, the sum of workload rates of the admitted CM streams is kept below $\mathcal{K}$. From this, we have the inequality below:

$$\sum_{i=1}^{\eta}(k_i/p_i) \leq \mathcal{K}. \quad (3)$$

To prevent shortage of memory slots, we give an upper bound on the size of scheduling periods of CM streams. By setting this upper bound to $MaxP$, we have the following equality:

$$p_i \leq MaxP \quad (4)$$

From (3) and (4), we can drive the inequality below.

$$\sum_{i=1}^{\eta} k_i \leq \sum_{i=1}^{\eta}(k_i \cdot \frac{MaxP}{p_i}) = MaxP \cdot \sum_{i=1}^{\eta}(k_i/p_i) \leq MaxP \times \mathcal{K}. \quad (5)$$

From (2) and (5), we can get M_{UB} of (2) as follows:

$$M_{UB} = 2 \times T_{|Z|} \times UpperBound(\sum_{i=1}^{n} k_i) \leq 2 \times T_{|Z|} \times MaxP \times \mathcal{K}. \quad (6)$$

From (6), we have a theoretical upper bound of M_{UB} that is equal to $2 \times T_{|Z|} \times MaxP \times \mathcal{K}$. In reality, the actual memory size for servicing CM streams is much less such an upper bound. This comes from two observations. First, since many CM streams share disk bandwidth and memory slots are released, the actual memory requirement for cached data is much less than M_{UB}. Here, a released memory slot means that it no longer contains cached data to be consumed, since overall data have been consumed by an involved CM stream. This release of memory slots contributes to the reduction of memory requirement in the system. Second, since the size of memory slot is for the outermost zone, the number of used memory slots is usually less than $2k$ for DRP $\langle k, p \rangle$. This is because a smaller number of memory slots can save the cached data of size $2 \times d \times p$, where $d \times p$ is the per-period data size.

3.5 Algorithms for the Proposed DSS

A. Algorithm for the Stream Management Component (SMC)

Fig. 7 shows the algorithm that is performed by the SMC during the interval of E_{i-1} to E_i. During that time, the SMC does its jobs such as admission control, period expansion, and issuing of C-requests. The new C-requests are managed in the queue of $\mathcal{Q}_{req}$, and information regarding the C-requests of $\mathcal{Q}_{req}$ is sent to the DSC so that it can produce feasible disk schedules for those C-requests.

The step for admission control is described in lines 3 to 14. A user request for playback is extracted and its workload value is computed based on its per-cycle data size. With the workload value, the SMC checks if it is admissible. If there is available bandwidth to admit this request, the SMC creates a data object that represents a corresponding scheduling context as in line 9. Such a stream context is

1. Return free memory slots back to the memory slot pool, and set $\mathcal{Q}_{req} = \emptyset$
2. Let $\mathcal{S}_{CM}$ be the stream context pool of already admitted CM streams.
3. **While** [*Time* $< E_i - \epsilon$] **Do**
4. Dequeue a user request $\mathcal{R}$ from the queue containing users' playback requests in a FIFO manner.
5. Let *PerCycle* be the quantity of per-cycle data of $\mathcal{R}$.
6. Compute the workload value of R as $W = \lceil PerCycle/T_{|1|} \rceil$. /* $T_{|1|}$ is the track size of the innermost zone */
7. Calculate the total workload $\mathcal{W}_t$ of $\mathcal{S}_{CM}$ such that
$$\mathcal{W}_t = \sum_{j=1}^{\eta} (k_j/p_j), \text{ where } S_j \in \mathcal{S}_{CM} \text{ has DRP } \langle k_j, p_j \rangle.$$
8. **If** [$\mathcal{W}_t + W \leq \mathcal{K}$] **Then**
9. Create a new stream context for R and denote it by *Obj*.
10. Allocate $2 \cdot W$ free slots from the memory slot pool and assign them to *Obj* for data read.
11. Set *Obj.deadline* $= E_i$, *Obj.k* $= W$, and *Obj.p* $= 1$, respectively. /* $\langle Obj.k, Obj.p \rangle$ is the DRP of *Obj* */
12. Admit *Obj* by putting it into $\mathcal{S}_{CM}$. /* *Obj* is kept in $\mathcal{S}_{CM}$ until it completes playback */
13. **Else** Go to a blocking state until the time point of $E_i - \epsilon$. /* Bandwidth shortage */
14. **EndWhile** /* Loop for admission control */
15. **For** [each *Obj* $\in \mathcal{S}_{CM}$] **Do**
16. **If** [*Obj.deadline* $= E_i$] **Then**
17. Perform the period expansion for *Obj*, if possible.
18. Update the deadline of *Obj* by setting *Obj.deadline* $= E_{i+Obj.p}$. /* The new deadline becomes the beginning point of the next scheduling period */
19. Issue new C-requests with deadline $E_{i+Obj.p}$ for *Obj*; put them into $\mathcal{Q}_{req}$.
20. **Else** Do nothing for this *Obj*. /* The current scheduling period does not end */
21. **EndFor** /* Loop for issuing C-requests */
22. Send the information regarding the C-requests in $\mathcal{Q}_{req}$ towards the disk scheduling component.

Fig. 7. Algorithm for the session management component which is performed during the interval of $[E_{i-1}, E_i]$

expressed by Obj, and the set of active stream contexts is denoted by $\mathcal{S}_{CM}$. To initialize Obj, its deadline and DRP is set to E_i and $\langle W, 1 \rangle$, respectively, as in line 11. If the user request is not admissible for bandwidth shortage, the SMC quits the actions of admission control and gets into a blocking state until the point of $E_i - \epsilon$. Here, ϵ is a time for executing the remaining lines of 15 to 22. Since the rest lines can be done in a quick time, the size of ϵ lies below 1 msec, by using a Pentium-III class processor. In step 16, the SMC selects every session context with $Obj.deadline = E_i$ to expand scheduling periods and issue new C-requests. In line 18 the deadline of the session context is modified by considering its scheduling period, that is, $Obj.deadline$ is set to $E_{i+Obj.p}$. Lastly, the C-requests in $\mathcal{Q}_{req}$ are sent towards the DSM in line 22. Then the DSM updates its C-request queue. The DSM selects at most $\mathcal{K}$ C-requests out of the EDF C-request queue and serves them in a disk scan that ends before E_{i+1}. While that disk scan is in process, the algorithm of Fig. 7 will be executed again at E_i.

B. Algorithm for period expansion

We here describe the detailed algorithm for the step in lines 15 to 21 of Fig. 7. For any CM stream with DRP $\langle k, p \rangle$ to expand its scheduling period, it is required to satisfy two conditions: (i) its cached data is large enough to be consumed

1. Set $\mathcal{S}_{normal} = \emptyset$ and $\mathcal{S}_{expand} = \emptyset$, respectively.
2. **For** [each $Obj \in \mathcal{S}_{CM}$ satisfying $Obj.deadline = E_i$] **Do**
3. Compute $Duration = \lfloor Obj.CachedSize / Obj.PerCycleData \rfloor$.
4. If $Duration > MaxP$, then set $Duration = MaxP$. /* $MaxP$ is the permissible maximum length of scheduling periods */
5. Select two least integers of k' and p' ($Obj.p < p' \leq Duration$) satisfying that
$$k'/p' < Obj.k/Obj.p \text{ and } k' \times T_{|1|} \geq Obj.PerCycleData \times p'.$$
6. If there exist both of k' and p' satisfying the inequality above, then put Obj into $\mathcal{S}_{expand}$; otherwise, put Obj into $\mathcal{S}_{normal}$.
7. **EndFor** /* building of $\mathcal{S}_{expand}$ and $\mathcal{S}_{normal}$ */
8. Set $MemUsed$ to $N_{free} - 2 \times \lceil \mathcal{K} - \mathcal{W} \rceil$. /* N_{free} is the number of free memory slots in the memory slot pool */
9. **For** [Each $Obj \in \mathcal{S}_{normal}$] **Do**
10. Solve the least integer N such that
$$Obj.CachedSize + N \times T_{|1|} \geq 2 \times Obj.PerCycleData \times Obj.p.$$
11. Allocate N free memory slots from the memory slot pool and decrease $MemUsed$ by N.
12. Issue N C-requests to load the data of Obj into the allocated memory slot each. These C-requests are given with the deadline of $E_{i+Obj.p}$ and they are put into Q_{req}.
13. Update the deadline of Obj by setting $Obj.deadline = E_{i+Obj.p}$.
14. **EndFor** /* Loop for issuing C-requests without period expansion */
15. **While** [$\mathcal{S}_{expand} \neq \emptyset$] **Do**
16. Extact Obj with the largest $(\frac{Obj.k \cdot p' - k' \cdot Obj.p}{Obj.p \cdot p'})/(p' - Obj.p)$ from $\mathcal{S}_{expand}$.
17. Compute the least integer N satisfying that
$$Obj.CachedSize + N \times T_{|1|} \geq 2 \times Obj.PerCycleData \times p'.$$
18. **If** [$N \leq MemUsed$] **Then**
19. Allocate N free memory slots from the slot pool and decrease $MemUsed$ by N.
20. Issue N C-requests to load the data of Obj into the allocated memory slot each. These C-requests are given with the deadline of $E_{i+Obj.p}$ and they are put into Q_{req}.
21. Update Obj's DRP and deadline by setting $Obj.k = k'$, $Obj.p = p'$, and $Obj.deadline = E_{i+p'}$, respectively.
22. **Else** Set $Obj.deadline = E_{i+1}$ without issuing new C-requests for this Obj.
23. **EndWhile** /* Loop for period expansion */

Fig. 8. The detailed algorithm for period expansion and issue of C-requests

during p' cycles ($p' > p$), and (ii) if its expanded DRP is denoted by $\langle k', p' \rangle$, then the new workload rate, i.e., k'/p', must be less than the previous one of k/p. If stream Obj has such integers of k' and p', satisfying the conditions above, it will be classified into S_{expand}; otherwise, it will be put into S_{normal} in line 6 of Fig. 8. The step for building S_{expand} and S_{normal} is given in lines 2 to 7.

Issuing of C-requests for S_{normal} is done in lines 9 to 14. The number of C-requests to be issued is determined based on the aggressive prefetch scheme in line 10. To issue C-requests, we need to allocate the same number of memory slots, on which requested disk tracks are loaded by the DSC. The number of memory slots available for S_{normal} and S_{expand} is computed as $MemUsed$ in line 8, where N_{free} denotes the number of free memory slots in the memory pool. Among N_{free}, $2 \cdot \lceil \mathcal{K} - \mathcal{W} \rceil$ memory slots are not used for S_{normal} and S_{expand}. Instead, they are reserved to admit new CM streams during the next cycles. By reserving those memory slots, we can avoid memory shortage at the admission time. Recall that we assign $2W$ memory slots to a CM stream that is admitted with workload value W.

In lines 15 to 23, we execute the step of period expansion for S_{expand}. While expanding scheduling periods, shortage of memory slots may not enable period expansions of any CM streams in S_{expand}. In the face of memory slot shortage, we expand the DRPs of Obj with the largest value of $(\frac{Obj.k \cdot p' - k' \cdot Obj.p}{Obj.p \cdot p'})/(p' - Obj.p)$, favorably over others with smaller ones. These two values, $(\frac{Obj.k \cdot p' - k' \cdot Obj.p}{Obj.p \cdot p'})$ and $(p' - Obj.p)$, represent the reduced quantity in workload rate and the additional requirement for memory slots in the presence of period expansion, respectively.

4 Performance Evaluations

The simulator runs with a realistic disk model based on IBM SCSI disk drive, whose physical characteristics are given in Table 1. The disk drive has 17 disk zones in a disk plate. Its outermost zone has 750 sectors per disk track, while the innermost has around half of them. The size of a memory slot is adjusted to that of zone 1 of the table.

Table 1. Disk parameters: IBM Ultrastar 73LZX

Parameters	Base Values
Sector size	512 bytes
No. of cylinders	20,847
No. of disk zones	17
Sectors in zone 1	750
Sectors in zone 17	390
seek_time(d)	$1.85 + 0.07\sqrt{d}$ ms, If $d < 383$ $5.47 + 2.5 \times 10^{-4}d$ ms, Otherwise

In our simulations, the users' requests for playback is assumed to arrive by following the Poisson process, and both of playback rates and playback durations arise with the uniform distributions. In the case of playback rates, we assume that they are randomly distributed in the range of [250 Kbps, 700 Kbps]. This range covers most of requirements of video clips and music that are now being serviced in the Internet, except for very high-quality video streams. To be more realistic, our simulator will handle an environment where rather lower playback rates are required. Since the Web sites usually service CM streams with lower playback rates, we also use the range of [250 Kbps, 500 Kbps]. To differentiate between these two ranges of playback rates, we denote the wider one by $\mathcal{P}_{wide}$ and the lower one by $\mathcal{P}_{low}$, respectively. The playback durations are distributed in the range of [3 minutes, 5 minutes] and the cycle length is fixed as one second.

Fig. 9 shows the supported workloads with respect to the varying sizes of used main memory. SWEEP and DSS(l) represent the Sweep scheme and the DSS with $MaxP = l$, respectively. With the increasing memory size, the maximum

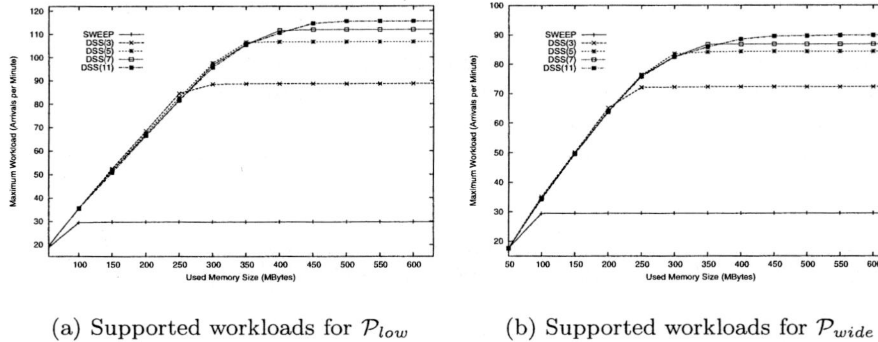

(a) Supported workloads for $\mathcal{P}_{low}$ (b) Supported workloads for $\mathcal{P}_{wide}$

Fig. 9. Maximum workloads with respect to varying memory sizes

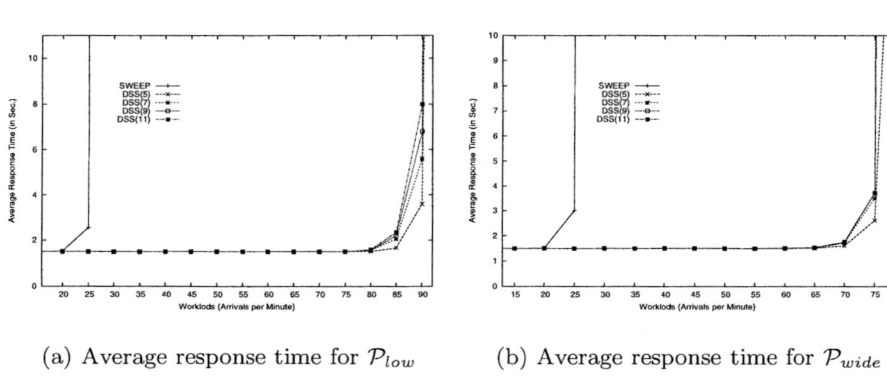

(a) Average response time for $\mathcal{P}_{low}$ (b) Average response time for $\mathcal{P}_{wide}$

Fig. 10. Average response time with memory of 300 Mbytes

workloads supported by SWEEP and DSS(x) are calculated. In Fig. 9(a), the maximum workload supported by DSS(3) is around the arrival rate of 87 per minute, which is three times as large as that of SWEEP. In the case of DSS(11), it supports up to the arrival rate of 115 per minute with memory size of 450 Mbytes. In Fig. 9(b), the supported maximum workloads are given for $\mathcal{P}_{wide}$. As known from Fig. 9(b), the DSS for $\mathcal{P}_{wide}$ requires more memory and supports a lower arrival rate than in $\mathcal{P}_{low}$.

Fig. 10 depicts the average response time to the varying arrival rates of playback requests. The response is the interval between the arrival time of a playback request and its start time for playback. In SWEEP and DSS, the start time for playback coincides with the end point of the cycle in which the first per-cycle data is read for a corresponding CM stream. The simulation in Fig. 10 was performed with memory of 300 Mbytes. In the modern computing system, this memory size is a small one for the service of CM streams. The average response time is around 1.5 seconds before the simulator is overloaded. Because the maximum workload guaranteed by SWEEP is very low, the average response time grows very fast after the arrival rate exceeds 25 per minute.

5 Conclusion

In this paper we proposed a noble disk scheduling scheme able to reclaim slack time that usually arises because of differences between reserved disk time and actually used one. Since slack times from such time gaps increase in the zoned disk, it is important to efficiently use slack time for a good I/O throughput. For this, the proposed scheme takes an approach that allows serviced CM streams to expand their scheduling periods from a cycle to a longer one. To schedule concurrent CM streams with different scheduling periods, the proposed scheme runs based on a more flexible scheduling algorithm and a new mechanism for admission control. The proposed scheme guarantees a better performance than in the Sweep scheme, while meeting the deadlines of issued C-requests.

References

1. D. James Gemmell, Harrick M. Vin, Dilip D. Kandlur, and P. Venkat Rangan. "Multimedia Storage Servers: A Tutorial and Survey". *IEEE Computer*, 28(5): 40–49, 1995.
2. A.L.N. Reddy and J.C. Wyllie. "I/O Issues in a Multimedia System". *IEEE Computer*, 27(3):69–74, 1994.
3. E. Balafoutis, M. Paterkakis, and P. Triantafillou. "Clustered Scheduling Algorithms for Mixed-Media Disk Workloads in a Multimedia Server". *Cluster Computing Journal*, 6(1):75–86, 2003.
4. Edward Y. Chang and Hector Garcia-Molina. "Effective Memory Use in a Media Server". In *Proc. of the Intl. Conference on Very Large Databases*, pages 496–505, 1997.
5. Sungchae Lim and Myoung Ho Kim. "Real-time Disk Scanning for Timely Retrieval of Continuous Media Objects". *Information and Software Technology*, 45(9): 547–558, June 2003.
6. Ibrahim Kamel, T. Niranjan, and Shahram Ghandeharizedah. "A Novel Deadline Driven Disk Scheduling Algorithms for Multi-Priority Multimedia Objects". In *Proc. of the Intl. Conference on Data Engineering*, pages 349–358, 2000.
7. V. S. Subrahmanian. *Principles of Multimedia Database Systems.* Morgan Kaufmann Pub., 1998.
8. C. Ruemmler and J. Wilkes. "An Introduction to Disk Modeling". *IEEE Computer*, 27(3):17–28, March 1994.
9. Yen-Jen Qyang. "A Tight Upper Bound of the Lumped Disk Seek Time for the SCAN Disk Scheduling Policy". *Information Processing Letters*, 54(6):323–329, 1997.
10. Rodney Van Meter. " Observing the Effects of Multi-Zone Disks ". *Proc. of the USENIX Conference* , pages 57–62, 1997.

Authentication of Outsourced Databases Using Signature Aggregation and Chaining

Maithili Narasimha and Gene Tsudik

Computer Science Department,
School of Information and Computer Science,
University of California, Irvine
{mnarasim, gts}@ics.uci.edu

Abstract. Database outsourcing is an important emerging trend which involves data owners delegating their data management needs to an external service provider. Since a service provider is almost never fully trusted, security and privacy of outsourced data are important concerns. A core security requirement is the integrity and authenticity of outsourced databases. Whenever someone queries a hosted database, the results must be demonstrably authentic (with respect to the actual data owner) to ensure that the data has not been tampered with. Furthermore, the results must carry a proof of completeness which will allow the querier to verify that the server has not omitted any valid tuples that match the query predicate. Notable prior work ([4][9][15]) focused on various types of *Authenticated Data Structures*. Another prior approach involved the use of specialized digital signature schemes. In this paper, we extend the state-of-the-art to provide both authenticity and completeness guarantees of query replies. Our work analyzes the new approach for various base query types and compares it with Authenticated Data Structures. We also point out some possible security flaws in the approach suggested in the recent work of [15].

1 Introduction

Database outsourcing [7] is a prominent example of the general commercial trend of outsourcing non-core competencies. In the Outsourced Database (ODB) Model, a third-party database service provider offers adequate software, hardware and network resources to host its clients' databases as well as mechanisms to efficiently create, update and access outsourced data.

The ODB model poses numerous research challenges which influence overall performance, usability and scalability. One of the biggest challenges is the security of hosted data. A *client* stores its data (which is usually a critical asset) at an external, and potentially untrusted, database service provider. It is thus important to secure outsourced data from potential attacks not only by malicious outsiders but also from the service provider itself. The two pillars of data security are secrecy and integrity. The central problem in the context of secrecy [5, 8] is how to allow a client to efficiently query its own data – which is hosted

M.L. Lee, K.L. Tan, and V. Wuwongse (Eds.): DASFAA 2006, LNCS 3882, pp. 420–436, 2006.

by a third-party service provider – while revealing to the provider neither the actual query nor the data over which the query is executed. In contrast, this paper focuses on the integrity of query replies for queries posed for outsourced databases. We want to ensure that query results returned by the server are: (i) correct - the tuples in the result set have not been tampered with, and (ii) complete - no valid tuples have been omitted from the result set.

Other relevant prior work [4][15][6] examined integrity issues in outsourced databases and suggested solutions using Authenticated Data Structures. Another recent paper [12] investigated the notion of signature aggregation which enables bandwidth- and computation-efficient integrity verification of query replies. However, signature aggregation mechanism ensures only *correctness* of query replies. In this paper, we extend [12] by proposing new techniques to provide *completeness* guarantees. We provide a detailed study of the applicability of our techniques for various base type queries. We also compare our approach with prior results which use Authenticated Data Structures.

Scope. We assume the relational data model, i.e., data owners and service providers manage data using a typical RDBMS and that queries are formulated using SQL. We want to provide efficient mechanisms to ensure correctness and completeness (to be defined shortly) of range selection queries, projections, joins and set operation queries. We specifically **do not** address queries that involve data aggregation (exemplified by arithmetic operations, such as SUM or AVERAGE) which usually return a single value as the answer to the posed query.

Organization. The rest of this paper is organized as follows: Section 2 motivates our work. Section 3 discusses Authenticated Data Structures approach, followed by Section 4 which describes signature aggregation. This section also proposes the extensions to achieve completeness guarantees. Section 5 describes our approach by considering various query types. Section 6 presents the analysis. We outline some directions for future work and conclude in sections 7 and 8 respectively.

2 Motivation

This paper addresses the integrity of outsourced data in the ODB model. (We note that data secrecy in ODB is orthogonal to integrity.) Specifically, we focus on integrity-critical databases which are outsourced to untrusted servers and are accessed over insecure public networks. We assume that servers can be malicious and/or incompetent and, thus, might be processing and storing hosted data incorrectly. Furthermore, since it is difficult, in general, to guarantee absolute security of large on-line systems, we assume that the server can be compromised, e.g., by a worm or virus attack. Therefore, we need efficient mechanisms to reduce the level of trust placed in the server and provide integrity guarantees to the clients. From a technical perspective, candidate solutions must include the following properties:

Correctness. Whenever a client queries outsourced data, it expects a set of tuples satisfying all query predicates. It also needs assurance that the results have been originated by the actual data owner and have not been tampered with either by an outside attacker or by the server itself. Note that the reply size (in terms of tuples) can vary between zero and n, where n is the total number of tuples in the database. Thus, a query reply can potentially be any one of the 2^n tuple subsets. Correctness enables secure and efficient authentication of tuples contained in all possible query replies.

Completeness. Whenever a client queries outsourced data, it expects to obtain **all** tuples satisfying query predicates. *Completeness* implies that the querier can verify that the server returned **all** such tuples. Note that, a server, which is either malicious or lazy, might not execute the query over the entire database and return no – or only partial – results.

3 Prior Work

We now summarize the general approach of using authenticated data structures to provide authentication of query replies and discuss two related bodies of work that use this approach, in the contexts of "Third-Party Publication" and "Edge Computing", respectively.

The basis for these two bodies of work is the seminal work by Merkle [11]. This work introduced a data structure called a "Merkle Hash Tree" (MHT) which is intended to authenticate a set of n values $x_1, x_2, ..., x_n$. MHT is constructed as a binary tree where the leaves correspond to the hashes of the n values. Thus, a leaf associated with element x_i contains $h(x_i)$, where $h()$ is a cryptographic one-way hash function, such as SHA [13]. The values of non-leaf nodes correspond to the hash of the concatenation of its two children (maintaining their order). A node with children v_1 and v_2 is assigned $h(v_1||v_2)$. The tree root is signed using a public key signature scheme (e.g., RSA or DSA). An MHT can be used to securely and efficiently prove that an element (leaf) is in the set with the help of a *verification object* (VO). A VO is a collection of $log(n)$ internal tree nodes which allow the verifier to re-compute the root of the MHT the signature of which can be verified. Although an MHT can be very large, one only needs the signed root and a short (logarithmic in the number of leaves) VO in order to verify that a particular leaf element is part of the tree. For example, the VO for leaf node 5 in Figure 1 contains $5, h_1 and h_{34}$ as well as the root signature. The verifier computes: $h'_2 = h(5)$, $h'_{12} = h(h_1||h_2)$ and $h'_{1234} = h(h'_{12}||h_{34})$ and then checks the root by verifies its signature.

3.1 Authentic Third Party Data Publication

In [4] and several related publications, Devanbu, et al. focus on Third-Party Publication. We refer to this approach as the Authenticated Data Structures (or **AuthDS**) approach. In this setting, like in ODB, data owners publish their

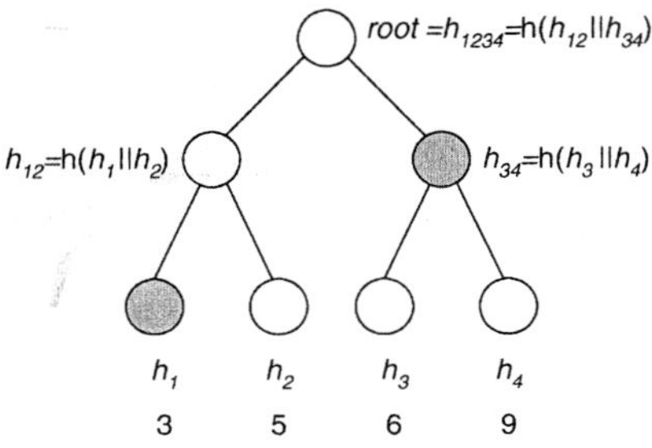

Fig. 1. MHT Example: shaded nodes represent the verification object for leaf value 5

content at untrusted third-party service providers. Notable contributions of this work are two-fold: (1) It demonstrates how to construct efficient and compact verification objects if a pre-computed authenticated data structure for that type of query exists. The terms *efficient and compact* generally mean logarithmic complexity in terms of the database size. (2) Instead of using standard binary tree MHTs as authenticated dictionaries, balanced and I/O efficient data structures, such as B-trees, are used.

Discussion. One limitation of the AuthDS approach is the need to pre-compute and store a potentially large number of authenticated data structures, in order to efficiently answer queries. Without pre-computed trees, the AuthDS approach cannot provide small verification objects. More importantly, without pre-computed trees for each sort-order, it becomes impossible to prove completeness of query replies. This results in significant setup costs for the owner and high storage overhead for the server. Also, storing multiple trees for the same relation increases the cost of updates.

3.2 Authenticating Query Results in Edge Computing

In a recent paper, Pang, et al. [15] focused on authentication in edge computing applications. In it, a trusted central server outsources parts of the database to proxy servers situated at the edge of the network. The data structure used here is a VB-tree, which is basically a modified MHT built using a B-Tree where – instead of signing only the root – all leaf nodes as well as all internal nodes are also signed. (We refer to this work as the **VB-tree approach**). As a result, verification objects are independent of the database size and hence, "potentially" much smaller. In comparison, the most efficient VO in the AuthDS approach [4] is logarithmic in the size of the entire database.

Discussion. The VB-tree approach does not address the completeness problem. Also, since a single VB-tree is used, there is no easy way to extend this scheme to provide completeness guarantees. The proposed scheme replaces a conventional cryptographic hash function used to compute the digests of individual values in a MHT with a computationally more expensive, homomorphic function which essentially computes a discrete exponentiation in a finite field. This function is insecure and can lead to forgery attacks as shown below:

> The digest is computed as $h(x) = g^x \mod q$. The modulus q is chosen as $q = 2^r$ for some random r. This choice is insecure because computing discrete logs in multiplicative, algebraic groups (thus reversing the function h) is known to be hard if q is a large prime of at least 512 bits. If q, however, is a composite integer, then the problem of computing discrete logarithms is polynomially reducible to the combination of integer factorization of q and computing discrete logarithms in $\mathbb{Z}_p^*$ for each prime factor p of q. Now in the current context, since q is chosen as 2^r, $h()$ can be reversed efficiently which can lead to forgery attacks. We refer the interested readers to [10] for details on solving discrete-logarithm problems.

Also, the experimental analysis of [15] assumes that the size of a signed digest is 16 bytes. It demonstrates that, with this overhead, the overall approach is efficient in terms of storage and VO size. However, a 16-byte signed digest is **insecure**, since there is no cryptographically strong digital signature scheme that produces signatures of only 16 bytes in size. For example, RSA, which is the most well-known signature scheme, has a signature size of at least 128 bytes (1024 bits). [1] If we repeat the calculations with a digest size of 128 bytes and recompute storage overheads, the VB-tree approach becomes quite expensive in terms of both computation and storage.

Furthermore, VB-tree approach can be very expensive in terms of VO verification time for queriers, especially, for projection queries. This is because the verification object includes signed digests for all the attributes that are filtered out as well as all the tuples that do not belong to the query result set but do fall inside the enveloping tree [2] for a given query. In order to authenticate the query results, the scheme requires the querier to verify the signatures of all these filtered attributes and tuples that are not part of the actual result set. Clearly, receiving (recall that a signature is at least 128 bytes long) and verifying (a single RSA signature verification takes 0.16 msec on P3-977 MHz machine) all these signatures can be computationally very expensive for the querier.

Finally, VB-tree approach builds a single B-tree for each table (which is computed on the sorted order of the primary key of that table). If the query predicate requires searching on a non-key attribute, then the result set is no longer a set of contiguous tuples. This translates to an increase in the height of the enveloping tree and can result in extremely high bandwidth and computation overheads.

[1] A DSA signature is at least 40 bytes (320 bits) long, but verification of a DSA signature is more expensive computationally (It takes 0.16 msec to verify a RSA signature whereas it takes 8.52 msec to verify a DSA signature on a P3-977 MHz machine).

[2] The enveloping tree is the smallest subtree within the VB-tree that envelops all the result tuples of the query

Recall that the VO verification involves verifying the signatures of all the tuples that are not part of the actual result set but do fall inside the enveloping tree.

4 Digital Signature Aggregation and Chaining (DSAC)

The main disadvantage of AuthDS is the relatively high overhead associated with building, storing and updating complex index structures. We now propose an alternative approach that is efficient for most base-level queries, without requiring any complex data structures. We refer to our approach as the Digital Signature Aggregation and Chaining - **DSAC**.

A natural and naïve alternative to AuthDS is to use digital signatures at the granularity of individual tuples. The data owner signs each tuple before storing it at the server's site. The server stores the tuple signature along with each tuple. In response to a query, the server simply sends the matching tuples and their signatures to prove integrity and authenticity of the result. Although this naïve solution provides a proof of correctness, it has some drawbacks: first and foremost, the resultant VO (which contains a set of signatures corresponding to each tuple in the result set) is neither bandwidth- nor computation-efficient for the querier. Further, there is no easy way to provide a proof of completeness. In the remainder of this section, we develop modifications and enhancements that address the drawbacks of the naïve strategy described above.

Remark. If the outsourced data is *static* or *archival* in nature, correctness and completeness can be provided easily, as described in Appendix A. However, in this paper, we focus on the more general (and challenging) case of dynamic databases.

4.1 Correctness

The ideal VO for providing correctness would involve minimal querier computation overhead and constant (in terms of integrity information) querier bandwidth overhead. The work in [12] proposed two signature schemes that enable such ideal (or near-ideal) solutions. These signature schemes allow us to aggregate multiple individual signatures into one *unified* signature, verifying which is *equivalent* to verifying ALL individual component signatures. The size of the aggregated signature equals that of a single plain digital signature (which is constant), irrespective of either the database size or the query reply size. In the ODB model, when the server receives a query, it executes the query to obtain the tuples matching the query predicate as well as their corresponding signatures. The server combines these individual signatures into a single aggregated signature and returns the result set comprised of the tuples along with the aggregated signature. Upon receipt, the querier simply verifies the latter.

The first signature scheme proposed in [12] is the Condensed-RSA signature scheme. Condensed-RSA allows aggregation of a single signer's signatures which is possible due to the fact that RSA is *multiplicatively homomorphic*. The second is the Aggregated-BGLS scheme due to Boneh, et al. [3] which allows signatures produced by multiple signers to be aggregated into a single quantity. Appendix B discusses these schemes briefly.

4.2 Completeness

Both signature schemes in [12] offer efficient proofs of correctness, however, they provide no completeness guarantees. In this section, we propose novel extensions to achieve query completeness. To achieve this goal, we propose secure linking of tuple-level signatures to form a so-called *signature chain.*[3] In order to construct the signature chains, we modify the tuple signature generation algorithm in the following way:

Definition 1. *Signature of a tuple r is computed as:*

$$Sign(r) = h(h(r)||h(IPR_1(r))|| \ldots h(IPR_l(r)))_{SK}$$

where $h()$ is a cryptographic hash function such as SHA, $||$ denotes concatenation, IPR_i denotes the immediate predecessor tuple along dimension i, l is the number of searchable dimensions of that relation and SK is the private signing key of the data owner.

The immediate predecessors of a tuple are computed as follows: (1) Sort the tuples in increasing order along each searchable dimension (i.e., according to the attribute value for each searchable attribute); (2) The immediate predecessor of a given tuple along a given dimension is a tuple with the highest value for that attribute that is less than the value of the given tuple (highest lower bound) along that attribute.[4] Thus, each tuple has as many immediate predecessors as there are searchable attributes, i.e., l.

To provide completeness, a tuple signature is computed by including the hashes of all immediate predecessor tuples, thereby explicitly chaining (linking) the signatures. We illustrate this with an example in figure 2. Suppose that there are three searchable attributes. First, the tuples are sorted along each dimension. Consider tuple R_5. According to the figure, the immediate predecessors of R_5 along dimensions A_1, A_2 and A_3 are: R_6, R_2 and R_7, respectively. Now, compute the signature of R_5 as:[5] $Sign(R_5) = h(h(R_5)||h(R_6)||h(R_2) ||h(R_7))_{SK}$.

With signatures chained in the above fashion, the server answers a range query by releasing all matching tuples, the two *boundary tuples* which are just beyond the query range (to provide a proof of completeness) as well as the aggregated signature corresponding to the result set. The signature chain proves to the querier that the server has indeed returned all tuples in the query range. For range (or exact value) queries that result in no matches, the server composes

[3] Not to be confused with *hash chains.*

[4] If the attribute values of two tuples are the same, it is necessary to use an additional mechanism (for example: use the tuple id) to break the tie.

[5] The signature scheme here can be either condensed-RSA or aggregated-BGLS. Therefore, we do not specify the details of the SIGN algorithm.

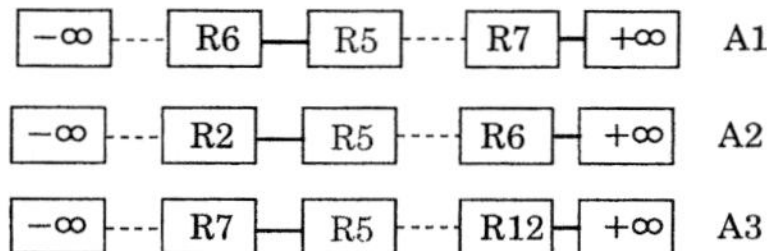

Fig. 2. Signature Chain

an *Empty Proof* by returning only the two boundary tuples that subsume the non-existent value or range.

5 Operational Details

We now describe the overall procedure for computing authentic replies.

5.1 Selection

A selection query $\sigma_C(R)$ is denoted as follows: $\sigma_C(R) = \{t|t \in R \text{ and } C(t)\}$ where R is a relation, C is a condition of the form $A_i\theta c$, A_i is an attribute of R, c is a constant value and $\theta \in \{=, \neq, <, \leq, >, \geq\}$.

Given a selection query, the server computes a result set which is a set of contiguous (along that dimension) tuples. (It could also be an empty set.) Below, we outline our technique for composing a VO for selection queries.

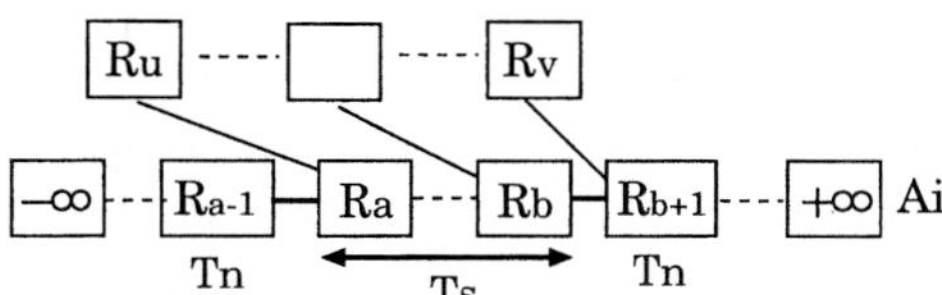

The server composes the query reply as follows:

1. computes the tuple set T_s consisting of all the tuples that match the query posed. $T_s = \{R_a, \ldots, R_b\}$
2. computes the set T_n consisting of immediate predecessor and successor nodes of the first and last nodes respectively along the search dimension (i.e., the boundary tuples). $T_n = \{R_{a-1}, R_{b+1}\}$. These values are required to prove completeness. We note that the server needs to release only the relevant attributes' value in plain text and simply send the hashes of the remaining attributes. We assume that the relation R has r attributes $\{A_1, ..., A_r\}$ and C is a condition on attribute A_i. In this case, the server only needs to reveal $R_{a-1}.A_i$ and $R_{b+1}.A_i$ in plaintext and send the hashes $h(A_j)$ for the other $(r-1)$ attributes of R_{a-1} and R_{j+1}. Thus it is possible to prevent exposure of data (i.e., pertaining to the tuples that are beyond the query result set) to potentially unauthorized queriers.

3. obtains the corresponding signatures $\{Sign(R_a), \ldots, Sign(R_{b+1})\}$[6]
4. aggregates individual signatures: $\sigma = Aggregate(Sign(R_a), \ldots, Sign(R_{b+1}))$
5. for each tuple in T_s and tuple R_{b+1}, collects the hashes of immediate predecessor tuples along all other searchable dimensions $\{A_1, \ldots, A_{i-1}, A_{i+1}, \ldots, A_l\}$, where l is the number of searchable attributes. Then for each tuple R_i, server computes 2 values: $H_1(R_i) = h(IPR_1(R_i))|| \ldots h(IPR_{i-1}(R_i)))$ and $H_2(R_i) = h(IPR_{i+1}(R_i))|| \ldots h(IPR_l(R_i)))$ Therefore, $T_m = \{H_1(R_a), H_2(R_a), \ldots, H_1(R_{b+1}), H_2(R_{b+1})\}$ Specifically, the size of T_m is $((l-1) * (b+1-a) * |hash|)$ where $|hash|$ is the hash value of each of these tuples and is usually 160 bits long. Thus the result set contains $\{T_s, T_n, T_m, \sigma\}$.

5.2 Join

A basic join operation $R \bowtie_C S$ involves two relations R and S where C is a condition of the form $A_i \theta A_j$, A_i and A_j are attributes of relation R and S respectively and $\theta \in \{=, \neq, <, \leq, >, \geq\}$. Both AuthDS and VB-tree approaches assume that all join queries are known *a priori* and require *additional* pre-computed B-trees to ensure authentication.

In the discussion that follows, we focus mainly on the equi-join operation. Given a query of the type $R \bowtie_{A_r = A_s} S$, proving correctness is relatively simple using our approach. The server executes the join query and computes the list of tuples ($t \in R$ and $s \in S$) that match the equality predicate and obtains the corresponding signatures of t and s from R and S respectively. Server combines all individual signatures of tuples in the result set to compute the aggregated signature of the entire result set. Note that the aggregated signature is sufficient to prove correctness.

However, proving completeness of a join query is not straight-forward. The querier needs to be assured that all tuples matching the equality predicate from R and S are present in the result set T_s. One way, albeit quite inefficient, to accomplish this is to pick the smaller relation (say S) and for each tuple s (or each contiguous set of tuples) in the set $S - T_s$, show an empty proof that s (more precisely $s.A_s$) does not exist in R. Note that if the server needs to show empty proofs for m tuples, server, instead of releasing m individual signatures, aggregates the m signatures into a single condensed/aggregated signature. Such a proof is clearly linear in the size of S. It remains an interesting open problem to modify the signature chaining mechanism to yield efficient completeness proofs which are linear in the size of the result set for arbitrary Join queries.

Using DSAC approach, it is possible to construct more efficient proofs of completeness if the join queries are known *a priori*. Then, while computing the signature of a tuple that is part of a join query result set, the hash of its immediate predecessor which is also in result set of the same join query is included in the tuple signature. This creates an explicit signature chain corresponding

[6] Note that it is necessary to include $Sign(R_{b+1})$ to check for completeness. However, $Sign(R_{a-1})$ is not required since hash of R_{a-1} is included in $Sign(R_a)$.

to the join query. Now, when a pre-computed $A \bowtie B$ query is executed, the server simply sends an aggregated signature that represents the signature chain of $A \bowtie B$. Note that, unlike the other two approaches, pre-computing a join query in our approach does not entail additional storage overhead.

5.3 Set Operations

Union: $T_s = U \cup V$**.** Server aggregate individual signatures for all tuples of U and all tuples of V to obtain a single signature for $U \cup V$; if U and V are intermediate results of a query evaluation or subsets of some other relations R and S, collects boundary tuples for U and V; finally constructs the VO as described above for selection queries.

Intersection: $T_s = U \cap V$**.** To prove completeness and correctness, the server needs to convince the querier that each tuple in T_s is present in both U and V. Our approach is similar to that of AuthDS: the server picks the smaller of the two sets (say U) and for each element in $U - T_s$ the server sends back empty proof that that element (tuple) does not exist in V. This proof is linear in the size of U. It shows that the result is correct and every element in $(U - (U \cap V))$ is not in V; thus, the result is complete.

5.4 Projections

$\pi_L(R)$ is the projection of relation R onto the list L where L is typically a list of (some of the) attributes of R. $\pi_L(R) = \{< t.A_j, ..., t.A_k > | t \in R\}$ where A_i's are attributes of relation R. In order to support projections, a tuple hash is computed as: $h(t) = h(h(t.A_1)||h(t.A_2)|| \dots ||t.h(A_k))$. In other words, instead of hashing the entire tuple, we hash each attribute, concatenate the resulting hashes and hash them once again. Then, we compute a tuple signature of tuple as described in section 4.2. This way, the server needs to send only the hashes (instead of actual plaintext values) for each filtered attribute. Unfortunately, this basic solution is not very efficient in terms of bandwidth since it requires us to send individual hashes for each filtered attribute (It is necessary to send individual values to allow the querier to recompute the tuple signature since the tuple hash is computed by concatenating these individual attribute hash values.).

One way to lower bandwidth overhead involves the owner generating attribute-level, instead of tuple-level, signatures. Although this increases the owner's load, projection queries become more efficient. We give a brief description of this variant below. However, the full details are beyond the scope of this paper. The owner generates the hash of attribute A_i of tuple t as $h(t.A_i) = h(t.ID||t.A_i)$ where $t.ID$ denotes the unique identifier of tuple t. Moreover, the owner generates individual signature chains along each searchable attribute as before. Since the signatures are generated at the attribute level, in response to a projection query, only the requested attribute values along with the relevant signatures chains will be returned by the server.

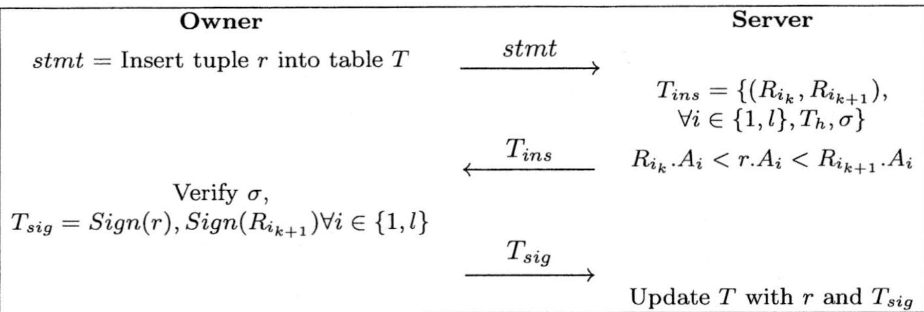

Fig. 3. Protocol to insert a new tuple into a table

5.5 Database Updates

Insertion. To insert a tuple r into table T (refer to figure 3), the owner sends the new tuple to the server. The server calculates the actual position of insertion along all l chains (where l is the number of searchable attributes) by examining the values of the individual attributes. The server computes the set of pairs of adjacent tuples $\{(R_{i_k}, R_{i_{k+1}})\}$ for inserting the new tuple, collects the signatures of all successor nodes $R_{i_{k+1}}$, aggregates these individual signatures to obtain σ and sends back these values (T_{ins}) to the data owner. Note that since the server returns pairs of adjacent tuples $\{(R_{i_k}, R_{i_{k+1}})\}$ along all l dimensions along with the signatures of all $R_{i_{k+1}}$ nodes, the owner can verify for herself that the position for inserting the new tuple is indeed the correct one. T_h contains the additional hashes required to recompute the signatures of the successor nodes[7]. Upon successful verification of σ, the owner computes the tuple signature for r by including the immediate predecessors' (i.e., all R_{i_k}) hash values and also updates the signature chains for the successor nodes (i.e., all $R_{i_{k+1}}$) by including r's hash value (along with the other appropriate hashes from T_h). The owner then sends back all $l+1$ new signatures T_{sig}.

Deletion. Performing a delete is similar to insert operation and is a multi-round protocol. Due to space restrictions, we only present a high-level description of the protocol. Owner specifies the tuple(s) to be deleted. Server isolates parts of all the l signature chains that get affected by this operation and sends back sets of tuples that surround the tuple to be deleted back to the owner. Once again, since the signatures are all linked the owner can verify that the server indeed has returned the relevant parts of all the signature chains. The owner recomputes the signatures of the successor node of the node to be deleted, along each dimension, by replacing the hash of the node to be deleted with the hash of its predecessor and returns the l new signatures back to the server.

[7] Note that each of the successor node $R_{i_{k+1}}$ has l "immediate predecessor nodes". When the predecessor along one dimension changes due to the new insertion, it becomes necessary to recompute the signatures of each of $R_{i_{k+1}}$. In order to do this, the hashes corresponding to the other $l-1$ dimensions need to be sent back to the owner.

6 Analysis

In this section, we analyze costs and overhead factors associated with DSAC and then compare its performance with AuthDS and VB-tree approaches. We begin by summarizing the notation used in this section.

n	Total number of tuples in the relation
s	Number of tuples in the result set
t	Total number of attributes in the relation
l	Total number of searchable attributes; $1 \leq l \leq t$
$\|sign\|$	Size of a digital signature: 128 bytes for RSA, 64 bytes for BGLS
$\|hash\|$	Size of a hash. Default = 20 bytes

We first illustrate the bandwidth and computation advantages of DSAC over the naïve approach of sending and verifying individual tuple signatures. In our experiments, tuples are signed with the RSA signature scheme using a 1024-bit public modulus. The experiments were conducted on a P3-977MHz Linux PC. We used the popular OpenSSL library[14] to implement all cryptographic functions. Figure 4(a) compares the time (in msec) for query verification for varying size of the result set. We can see that signature aggregation greatly reduces the computational overhead required to verify the integrity of the result set.

Figure 4(b) contrasts measured bandwidth overhead for the naïve approach with that in DSAC. Recall that the naïve approach does not provide completeness guarantees. In DSAC, since the signatures are chained, we need to send additional hashes. Specifically, when the search predicate involves a particular attribute A_i, for each tuple in the result set, we need to send additional hashes corresponding to the immediate predecessor tuples along the remaining $(l-1)$ searchable attributes. We show the overhead for varying sizes of the result set (in records), for $l = 5$. It is easy to see that although DSAC incurs additional overhead to provide completeness, it still is much more bandwidth efficient than the naïve approach.

Storage Costs. In AuthDS scheme, to obtain an efficient VO on the order of $O(log|n|)$ in size and, more importantly, to prove completeness of a range query,

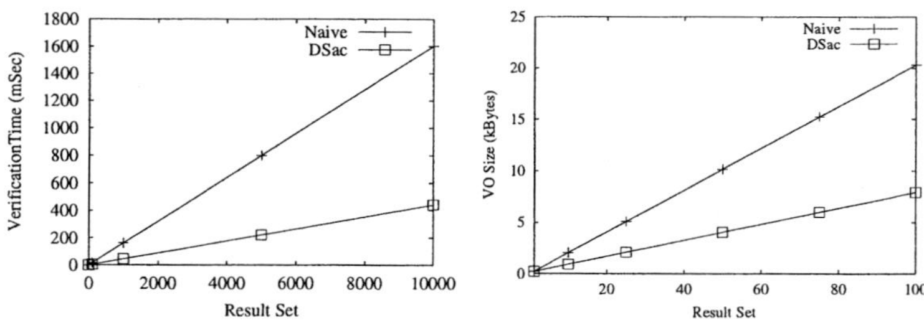

Fig. 4. (a) Query Verification Costs compared to naïve, (b) Bandwidth Costs compared to naïve

a separate B-tree for each search order is required. Therefore, for l searchable attributes, a total of l separate B-trees need to be pre-computed and stored at the server. Furthermore, to support other, more advanced queries, such as joins, the scheme requires separate data structures for each possible query. Storing these trees can result in enormous storage overhead. Also, storing multiple trees for the same relation increases the cost and complexity of the update operations since each update operation results in recomputing the tree hashes and the root signatures for all the trees and potentially some tree re-balancing operations.

In VB-tree scheme, each attribute value of a tuple is signed by the owner and each tuple is also signed in its entirety. Finally, a single VB-tree is constructed per table where individual nodes of the tree are also signed. This incurs a substantial storage overhead of $O(n * t * |sign| + t * |sign|)$ in addition to the cost of storing the VB tree itself. Thus, VB-tree is significantly more expensive than DSAC in terms of storage. Furthermore, as with AuthDS approach, VB-tree requires separate pre-computed data structures in order to support Join queries.

In comparison, DSAC incurs fixed storage overhead of one signature per tuple irrespective of the number of searchable attributes or the number of queries to be supported.

VO Size. In AuthDS, the VO size for a selection/projection query is:$VO_{size} = |s| \times \sum_i^k |hash| + (2\log|n| - 1) \times |hash| + |sign| + 2(|tuple|)$ where $\{A_i \ldots A_k\}$ are the filtered attributes of each tuple. $2(|tuple|)$ corresponds to 2 boundary tuples which are released to prove completeness and $|sign|$ corresponds to the size of the signature of the root. Note that $|s| \times \sum_i^k |hash|$ measures the hashes corresponding to filtered attributes and $(2\log|n|-1)\times|hash|$ measures additional hashes that must be sent to re-compute the root of the B-tree.

In VB-tree, the VO size for a selection/projection query is: $VO_{size} = |s| \times \sum_i^k |sign| + (2\log|s| - 1) \times |sign|$ where $\log|s|$ is the height of the enveloping tree and $\{A_i \ldots A_k\}$ are the filtered attributes of each tuple. Note that this VO cost assumes that the search is being done on the primary key. In this case, a set of contiguous tuples is returned and the additional overhead is $O(log|s|)$ signed digests. However, if the search is on a non-primary key attribute, then the enveloping tree can become quite large and signed digests corresponding to all tuples that are not part of the result set need to be returned.

For the proposed DSAC approach, the VO size is expressed as: $VO_{size} = |sign| + |s| \times (\sum_i^k |hash| + \sum_1^{l-1} |hash|) + 2(|tuple|)$. We send back a condensed/aggregated signature to verify the correctness and completeness of the result set. Figure 5 shows the VO size overheads for the AuthDS, VB-tree and DSAC approaches. As can be seen from the figure, VB-tree approach incurs very high bandwidth overheads. DSAC approach is as efficient as the AuthDS approach while requiring the storage of a single signature per record.

Our scheme incurs an overhead of $(|s| \times \sum_1^{l-1} |hash|)$ for guaranteeing completeness. This is because we need to include the hashes of the immediate predecessor tuples along every searchable attribute while computing the signature of a tuple. It is possible to reduce this overhead by trading storage efficiency to

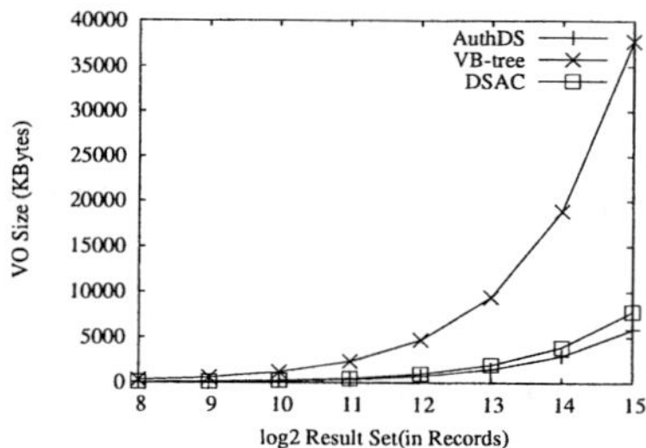

Fig. 5. VO Size Costs compared to AuthDS and VB-tree

gain bandwidth efficiency by using multiple signature chains. Another way to reduce this overhead would be to generate attribute level signatures as outlined in the prior section. We note that it is possible to reduce the VO size while maintaining a single signature chain by utilizing secure hashing techniques described in [1][2]. These incremental hashing techniques compute the hash of a message by breaking the message into smaller blocks and combining the hashes of individual blocks by using a "compression function". We would like to mention that this family of hash functions may be adapted for use in our scheme in order to send back a single "compressed" hash for each tuple. Furthermore, the same technique can also be used to reduce the bandwidth overhead associated with Projection queries. The detailed description of this technique is out of the scope of the current work.

Query Verification Costs. Query verification in both AuthDS and DSAC approaches involve computing simple hashes and combining them and verifying a single signature to verify the correctness and completeness of the result set. In comparison, VB-tree involves performing a number of signature verifications (since the scheme returns "signed" digests). Since signature verification is very expensive as compared to hashing, this scheme is computationally more expensive.

In summary, as compared to the VB-tree approach, the proposed DSAC scheme is clearly more efficient in terms of computation, storage, bandwidth and also provides a richer set of features. When compared to AuthDS, DSAC is more efficient in terms of storage and is similar in efficiency for VO size and verification costs. Both AuthDS and DSAC handle same set of queries and both require expensive signature recomputations for tuple inserts and deletes. However, as tuples are inserted and deleted over time, AuthDS involves additional intensive operations, such as re-balancing (one or more) b-trees in addition to re-calculating signatures for all roots.

7 Future Directions

Another desired property of ODB integrity is to ensure *freshness* of query replies. *Freshness* means the assurance that the query reply was generated with respect to the most recent snapshot of the database. One possible mechanism to provide freshness involves using a single Merkle Hash Tree – referred to as an FTree – for the entire relation. The root of the FTree is signed by the data owner and is assumed to be published and/or sent to all the queriers. Querier can verify freshness by verifying the owner's signature. The signature of the root is refreshed periodically (by the owner) in accordance with a system-wide freshness policy, thus ensuring that the data is fairly recent. As part of our future work, we plan to study this problem in depth. We also plan to conduct a detailed study of the applicability of our approach to other more advanced query types.

8 Conclusions

This work explored the problem of authenticity and integrity of query replies in outsourced databases. In particular, we developed a new approach (DSAC) based of signature aggregation and chaining which achieves authentication of query replies. The main contributions of this work are the proposed signature chaining mechanism which provides evidence of completeness of query result set and the analysis which sheds light on the applicability of our scheme for various query types in the relational model. We also compared our approach to the state-of-the-art in authenticated publishing.

References

1. M. Bellare, O. Goldreich, and S. Goldwasser. Incremental cryptography and application to virus protection. In *27th Annual Symposium of Theory of Computing*, 1995.
2. M. Bellare and D. Micciancio. A new paradigm for collsion-free hashing: Incrementality at reduced cost. In *EUROCRYPT '1997*.
3. D. Boneh, C. Gentry, B. Lynn, and H. Shacham. Aggregate and Verifiably Encrypted Signatures from Bilinear Maps. In *EUROCRYPT '2003*, 2003.
4. P. Devanbu, M. Gertz, C. Martel, and S. G. Stubblebine. Authentic third-party data publication. In *14th IFIP Working Conference in Database Security*, 2000.
5. H. Hacigümüş, B. Iyer, C. Li, and S. Mehrotra. Executing SQL over Encrypted Data in the Database-Service-Provider Model. In *SIGMOD*, 2002.
6. H. Hacigümüş, B. Iyer, and S. Mehrotra. Encrypted Database Integrity in Database Service Provider Model. In *CSES'02 IFIP WCC*, 2002.
7. H. Hacigümüş, B. Iyer, and S. Mehrotra. Providing Database as a Service. In *ICDE*, 2002.
8. B. Hore, S. Mehrotra, and G. Tsudik. A Privacy-Preserving Index for Range Queries. In *VLDB*, 2004.
9. C. Martel, G. Nuckolls, P. Devanbu, M. Gertz, A. Kwong, and S. G. Stubblebine. A general model for authenticated data structures. *Algorithmica*, 39(1), January 2004.
10. A. J. Menezes, P. C. van Oorschot, and S. A. Vanstone. *Handbook of applied cryptography*. CRC Press, 1997. ISBN 0-8493-8523-7.
11. R. Merkle. Protocols for public key cryptosystems. In *IEEE Symposium on Research in Security and Privacy*, 1980.

12. E. Mykletun, M. Narasimha, and G. Tsudik. Authentication and Integrity in Outsourced Databases. In *Network and Distributed Systems Security*, 2004.
13. National Institute of Standards and Technology (NIST). Secure Hash Standard. FIPS PUB 180-1, April 1995.
14. OpenSSL Project, `http://www.openssl.org`.
15. H. Pang and K-L Tan. Authenticating Query Results in Edge Computing. In *ICDE*, 2004.
16. R. L. Rivest, A. Shamir, and L. M. Adleman. A method for obtaining digital signatures and public-key cryptosystems. *Communications of the ACM*, 21(2), 1978.

A Static Data

If the outsourced data is static or archival in nature, e.g., a census database, proofs of completeness can be provided quite easily as follows:

(1)Sort all tuples in increasing order along each searchable dimension, i.e., according to the attribute value for each searchable attribute. (2) Compute a signature of each tuple by signing the "Running Hash" of all the tuples in the chain from the starting node to the current tuple as described below.

Assume that there is only one searchable dimension. (This solution is applicable for multi-dimensional queries as well.) The owner sorts tuples in ascending order along this dimension to obtain: $\{R_1, R_2, \ldots, R_n\}$. Owner then includes two boundary values: $(-\infty, +\infty)$ in the table and computes the signatures of R_1 through R_n as: $Sign(R_i) = h(R_i||h(R_{i-1}|| \ldots ||h(-\infty) \ldots))_{SK}$. At the end, it computes the signature of $+\infty$. The tuples and their signatures are stored at the server as before. Now, in order to prove both completeness and correctness of a range $\{R_i, R_j\}$, the server simply releases tuples $\{R_i, R_j\}$, running hash of R_{i-1}, and $Sign(R_j)$. Since the signatures are computed on running hashes, it can be easily seen that the reply set provides a concise proof of correctness and completeness. Note that, we do not require any signature aggregation in this scenario.

B Signature Aggregation

B.1 Condensed-RSA

The RSA [16] signature scheme is multiplicatively homomorphic which makes it suitable for combining multiple signatures generated by a single signer into one *condensed* signature. We use the term *condensed* in the context of a single signer and *aggregated* in the context of multiple signers. Clearly, former is a special case of the latter. A valid condensed signature signifies to the verifier that each individual signature contained in the condensed signature is valid, i.e., generated by the purported signer. Aggregation of single-signer RSA signatures can be performed incrementally by anyone in possession of individual RSA signatures. By incrementally, we mean that the signatures can be combined in any order and the aggregation need not be carried out in a single operation. In standard

RSA signature scheme, a party has a public key $pk = (n, e)$ and a secret key $sk = (n, d)$. A standard RSA signature on message m is computed as: $\sigma = h(m)^d \pmod{n}$ where $h()$ denotes a cryptographically strong hash function (such as, SHA-1). Verifying a signature involves checking that $\sigma^e \equiv h(m) \mod n$.

Condensed-RSA Signature Scheme. Given t different messages $\{m_1, ..., m_t\}$ and their corresponding signatures $\{\sigma_1, ..., \sigma_t\}$ generated by the same signer, a Condensed-RSA signature is computed as the product of all t individual signatures: $\sigma_{1,t} = \prod_{i=1}^{t} \sigma_i \pmod{n}$ The resulting aggregated (or condensed) signature $\sigma_{1,t}$ is of the same size as a single standard RSA signature. Verifying an aggregated signature requires the verifier to multiply the hashes of all t messages and checking that: $(\sigma_{1,t})^e \equiv \prod_{i=1}^{t} h(m_i) \pmod{n}$.

B.2 BGLS

Boneh, et al. in [3] construct an interesting aggregated signature scheme that allows aggregation of signatures generated by multiple signers on different messages into one short signature based on elliptic curves and bilinear mappings. This scheme (BGLS) operates in a Gap Diffie-Hellman group (GDH). Refer to [3] for a detailed discussion on the signature scheme and its proof of security.

A Practitioner's Approach to Normalizing XQuery Expressions

Ki-Hoon Lee, Seo-Young Kim, Euijong Whang, and Jae-Gil Lee

Department of Computer Science and
Advanced Information Technology Research Center (AITrc)*,
Korea Advanced Institute of Science and Technology (KAIST),
373-1 Guseong-dong, Yuseong-gu,
Daejeon 305-701, Korea
{khlee, sykim, euijong, jglee}@mozart.kaist.ac.kr
Fax: +82-42-867-3562

Abstract. XQuery becomes a standard of the XML query language. Just like in SQL, XQuery allows nested expressions. To optimize XQuery processing, a lot of research has been done on normalization, i.e., transforming nested expressions to equivalent unnested ones. Previous normalization rules are classified into two categories - *source-level* and *algebra-level* - depending on whether a construct is specified by using a query language or an algebraic expression. In implementation point of view, we contend that the source-level rule is preferable to the algebra-level rule because algebras used for normalization are hard to be directly exploited in a typical DBMS. However, a complete set of source-level rules is yet to be developed. In this paper, we propose source-level rules for normalizing XQuery expressions and present an implementation mechanism. We show that our rules are correct and complete according to the nesting types classified by Kim. Our mechanism is easily implementable since it adapts the well-known Query Graph Model (QGM) representation. We have successfully implemented this mechanism into our XML DBMS named *Odysseus/XML*.

1 Introduction

Recently, XML has emerged as a standard for representing, storing, and exchanging data on the Internet. Various query languages for XML data, such as XQL [9], XML-QL [1], XPath [13], and XQuery [14], have been proposed accordingly. Among them, XPath and XQuery, both proposed by World Wide Web Consortium (W3C), are the most widely used ones.

XPath supports a path expression that designates a specific element or attribute in XML data. XQuery encompasses XPath and supports a FLWR expression that is similar to a `select-from-where` expression in SQL. A FLWR expression is composed of the `for`, `let`, `where`, and `return` clauses. Each clause in a FLWR expression can include another FLWR expression, thus allowing nested expressions [14].

* This work was supported by the Ministry of Science and Technology (MOST) / Korea Science and Engineering Foundation (KOSEF) through the Advanced Information Technology Research Center (AITrc).

M.L. Lee, K.L. Tan, and V. Wuwongse (Eds.): DASFAA 2006, LNCS 3882, pp. 437–453, 2006.

Processing queries that contain nested expressions tends to be time-consuming since nested expressions can be repeatedly executed. Thus, a lot of research effort has been devoted to normalization, i.e., transforming nested expressions to equivalent unnested ones. In his seminal paper, Kim [5] opened the area of unnesting nested queries in the relational context. With the advent of the XQuery language, several normalization rules [2] [6] [7] have been reported also in the XML context.

Previous normalization rules are classified into two categories – *source-level* and *algebra-level* – depending on whether a construct is specified by using a query language or an algebraic expression. Examples of the former include the ones proposed by Kim [5] and Manolescu et al. [6], and those of the latter the ones proposed by Fegaras et al. [3] and May et al. [7]. We note that the algebras used for the latter – the monoid calculus [3] and the NAL-Algebra [7] – are very complex since nested expressions are represented in an algebraic form. The strengths and weaknesses of the two categories are as follows. The source-level rule is intuitive, but is rather error-prone (e.g., the famous count bug [4]). In contrast, the algebra-level rule is not intuitive due to those complex algebras, but is less error-prone [7].

In implementation point of view, we contend that the source-level rule is preferable to the algebra-level rule. The reason is twofold. First, those algebras used for normalization are hard to be directly exploited in a typical DBMS since they are quite different from well-known relational algebra. Second, algebra optimization is typically based on heuristics (e.g., selection as early as possible), and thus, does not guarantee optimality [12]. Nevertheless, to implement normalization of XQuery using the source-level rule, a complete set of source-level rules is yet to be developed. Source-level rules proposed earlier are not quite complete. For example, the normalization rules proposed by Manolescu et al. [6] cannot handle nested expressions in the `where` clause.

In this paper, we propose source-level rules for normalizing XQuery expressions and present an implementation mechanism. The main advantages of our approach are summarized as follows. First, our rules are complete according to the nesting types classified by Kim [5], and their correctness is proven. That is, we support all of the nesting types: Type-A, Type-N, Type-J, Type-JA, and Type-D. Especially, supporting Type-D is a unique capability of our rules. Second, our mechanism is easily implementable since it adapts the well-known Query Graph Model (QGM) [8] representation. We present detailed algorithms for normalization in Section 5. This mechanism has been successfully implemented into our XML DBMS named *Odysseus/XML* [1], showing validity of our approach.

The rest of this paper is organized as follows. Section 2 introduces the XQuery language. Section 3 summarizes prior work on normalization rules for XQuery. Section 4 proposes our normalization rules and proves their correctness. Section 5 presents our implementation mechanism. Finally, Section 6 concludes this paper.

2 Preliminaries

In this section, we briefly review the XQuery [14] language and present a few example queries. XQuery is an XML query language that is being standardized by W3C. The basic unit of XQuery is an *expression*. We introduce the FLWR expression and comparison expression [14].

[1] Odysseus/XML is part of the Odysseus DBMS family [11] that has been under development at KAIST since 1990.

– A *FLWR expression* consists of the `for`, `let`, `where`, and `return` clauses. The `for`, `where`, and `return` clauses correspond to the `from`, `where`, and `select` clauses in SQL, respectively. The `let` clause allows us to substitute an expression with a variable.
– A *comparison expression* compares the results of two expressions (i.e., E_1 *op* E_2) and returns *true* or *false*. E_1 and E_2 produce either a *single* value or a *sequence* of values. In contrast to SQL, XQuery allows us to compare two sequences. Given two sequences E_1 and E_2, E_1 *op* E_2 is true if there exists at least one pair (x, y) such that x *op* y is true where $x \in E_1$ and $y \in E_2$.

Now, we present a few example queries to facilitate understanding of XQuery. Figure 1 shows three XML documents used throughout this paper. *Departments.xml* represents the information of departments in a company; *Projects.xml* that of projects being carried out by departments; *WorksOn.xml* that of employees involved in projects.

```
<Departments>
  <Dept>
    <DNO> D2 </DNO>
    <DName> Research </DName>
    <DLoc> Bellaire </DLoc>
    <DLoc> Houston </DLoc>
    <Emp>
      <SSN> 123456789 </SSN>
      <EName> John </EName>
    </Emp>
    <Emp>
      <SSN> 333445555 </SSN>
      <EName> Franklin </EName>
    </Emp>
  </Dept>
</Departments>
```

Departments.xml

```
<Projects>
  <Proj>
    <PNO> P1 </PNO>
    <PName> Newbenefits </PName>
    <PLoc> Houston </PLoc>
    <DNO> D2 </DNO>
  </Proj>
  <Proj>
    <PNO> P2 </PNO>
    <PName> Reorganization </PName>
    <PLoc> Bellaire </PLoc>
    <DNO> D2 </DNO>
  </Proj>
</Projects>
```

Projects.xml

```
<WorksOnList>
  <WorksOn>
    <SSN> 123456789 </SSN>
    <PNO> P1 </PNO>
    <Hours> 32.5 </Hours>
  </WorksOn>
  <WorksOn>
    <SSN> 333445555 </SSN>
    <PNO> P2 </PNO>
    <Hours> 40.0 </Hours>
  </WorksOn>
</WorksOnList>
```

WorksOnList.xml

Fig. 1. Examples of XML documents

Query 1 is a path expression, which searches for employees named "John." Here, a bracket represents a predicate. Query 2 is a FLWR expression, which finds the location of the "Research" department. In Query 2, the `for` clause binds each *Dept* element to the variable x; the `where` clause checks whether *x/DName* is equal to "Research;" the `return` clause outputs *x/DLocs* that satisfy the condition in the `where` clause.

QUERY 1: Search for employees named "John."

```
document("Departments.xml")/Departments/Dept/Emp[EName="John"]
```

QUERY 2: Find the location of the "Research" department.

```
for    $x in document("Departments.xml")/Departments/Dept
where  $x/DName = "Research"
return $x/DLoc
```

We note that XQuery allows nested expressions [14]. That is, each clause in a FLWR expression can include another FLWR expression. A surrounding FLWR expression is called an *outer FLWR expression*, and a nested one an *inner FLWR expression*. Query 3 is an example query that contains a nested expression. In Query 3, the inner FLWR expression returns the *DNO's* of the departments having at least one project, and the outer FLWR expression the names of those departments.

QUERY 3: Find the names of the departments that have at least one project.

```
for    $x in document("Departments.xml")/Departments/Dept
where  $x/DNO = (for    $y in document("Projects.xml")/Projects/Proj
                 return $y/DNO)
return $x/DName
```

3 Related Work

In this section, we explain prior work on normalization rules for nested XQuery expressions. These rules transform nested XQuery expressions to equivalent unnested ones. As stated before, normalization rules are classified into the source-level rule and the algebra-level rule. The former is specified by using a query language, and the latter by using an algebraic expression.

The Source-Level Rules: Manolescu et al. [6] have proposed source-level normalization rules for XQuery. Their normalization aims at facilitating the translation of XQuery into SQL. We explain some notations used in the reference [6]. For each rule, *$x* and *$y* are variables, and E_n is an expression. E_n*($x)* means that the variable *$x* appears inside the expression E_n.

Rule 1 unnests nested expressions in the `for` clause. It first merges the `for` clauses of the outer and inner FLWR expressions, and then, the `where` clauses of those two FLWR expressions using the *and* operator. Next, it replaces the variable $\$y$, to which the inner FLWR expression is bound, with the expression $E_4(\$x, \$z)$ in the `return` clause of the inner FLWR expression.

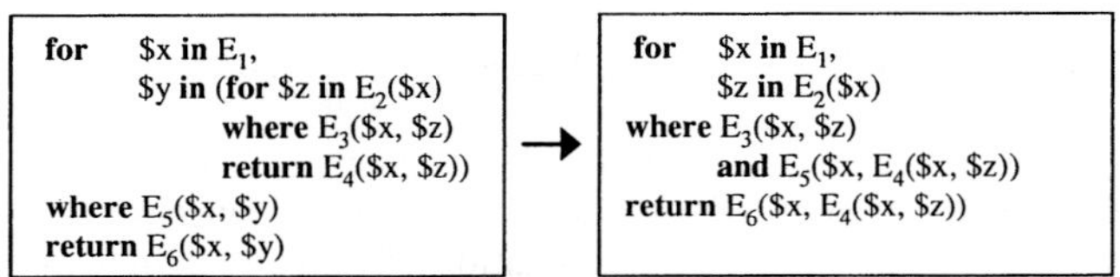

```
for    $x in E1,                          for    $x in E1,
       $y in (for $z in E2($x)                   $z in E2($x)
              where E3($x, $z)       →    where E3($x, $z)
              return E4($x, $z))                and E5($x, E4($x, $z))
where E5($x, $y)                          return E6($x, E4($x, $z))
return E6($x, $y)
```

RULE 1 [6]: Unnesting nested expressions in the `for` clause

Rule 2 unnests nested expressions in the `return` clause. It first merges the `for` clauses of the outer and inner FLWR expressions, and then, the `where` clauses of those two FLWR expressions using the *and* operator. Next, it replaces the `return` clause of the outer FLWR expression with that of the inner FLWR expression.

```
for    $x in E1                           for    $x in E1,
where E2($x)                                     $y in E3($x)
return (for $y in E3($x)             →    where E2($x)
        where E4($x, $y)                        and E4($x, $y)
        return E5($x, $y))                return E5($x, $y)
```

RULE 2 [6]: Unnesting nested expressions in the `return` clause

This work is the first attempt to normalize XQuery expressions. However, the rules are not complete because nested expressions in the `where` clause and in an aggregation function are not considered.

The Algebra-Level Rules: May et al. [7] have proposed algebra-level normalization rules for XQuery. These rules are based on the NAL-Algebra proposed by the same authors. This approach first translates an XQuery expression into an algebraic expression. Of course, this algebraic expression contains nested expressions. Then, normalization rules shown in Figure 2 are applied so as to produce an algebraic expression without nested expressions. These rules can handle Type-A, Type-N, Type-J, and Type-JA, but cannot handle Type-D.

$$\chi_{g:f(\sigma_{A_1\theta A_2}(e_2))}(e_1) = e_1 \Gamma_{g;A_1\theta A_2;f} e_2$$
$$\chi_{g:f(\sigma_{A_1=A_2}(e_2))}(e_1) = \Pi_{\overline{A_2}}(e_1 \,⟕\!\!\bowtie^{g:f(\epsilon)}_{A_1=A_2} (\Gamma_{g;=A_2;f}(e_2)))$$
$$\chi_{g:f(\sigma_{A_1\theta A_2}(e_2))}(e_1) = \Pi_{A_1:A_2}(\Gamma_{g;\theta A_2;f}(e_2)) \text{ if } e_1 = \Pi^D_{A_1:A_2}(\Pi_{A_2}(e_2))$$
$$\chi_{g:f(\sigma_{A_1\epsilon a_2}(e_2))}(e_1) = \Pi_{\overline{A_2}}(e_1 \,⟕\!\!\bowtie^{g:f(\epsilon)}_{A_1=A_2} \Gamma_{g;=A_2;f}(\mu^D_{a_2}(e_2)))$$
$$\chi_{g:f(\sigma_{A_1\epsilon a_2}(e_2))}(e_1) = \Pi_{A_1:A_2}(\Gamma_{g;=A_2;f}(\mu^D_{a_2}(e_2))) \text{ if } e_1 = \Pi^D_{A_1:A_2}(\Pi_{A_2}(\mu_{a_2}(e_2)))$$
$$\sigma_{\exists x\in(\Pi_{x'}(\sigma_{A_1=A_2}(e_2)))p}(e_1) = e_1 \ltimes_{A_1=A_2\wedge p'} e_2$$
$$\sigma_{\forall x\in(\Pi_{x'}(\sigma_{A_1=A_2}(e_2)))p}(e_1) = e_1 \triangleright_{A_1=A_2\wedge\neg p'} e_2$$

Fig. 2. Unnesting equivalences [7]

As shown by Figure 2, their algebra is quite different from the well-known relational algebra. In addition, May et al. do not propose a method of re-translating a normalized algebraic expression into a normalized XQuery expression. Thus, these rules are hard to be directly exploited in a typical DBMS.

4 Normalization Rules for XQuery Expressions

In this section, we propose our source-level normalization rules. Section 4.1 classifies nesting types of XQuery expressions. Section 4.2 shows completeness of our normalization rules. Section 4.3 proposes normalization rules for each nesting type.

4.1 Classification of Nesting Types

We classify nesting types in XQuery using the classification done by Kim [5] for SQL: Type-A, Type-N, Type-J, Type-JA, and Type-D. These nesting types are classified depending on the existence of correlation and aggregation in the same manner as in SQL. We define *correlation* and *aggregation* in Definitions 1 and 2.

DEFINITION 1: *Correlation* exists if a variable in the `for` clause of an outer FLWR expression appears in the `where` clause of an inner FLWR expression.

DEFINITION 2: *Aggregation* exists if an inner FLWR expression is used as an argument of the `count`, `avg`, `max`, `min`, or `sum` functions.

Based on the definitions above, all of the nesting types except Type-D are easily described as shown by Table 1.

Table 1. Descriptions of Type-A, Type-N, Type-J, and Type-JA

correlation \ aggregation	no	yes
no	Type-N	Type-A
yes	Type-J	Type-JA

An XQuery expression of Type-D has two inner FLWR expressions connected by an operator in the `where` clause of the outer FLWR expression. At least one of the inner FLWR expressions must have correlation. Zero or more inner FLWR expressions may have aggregation. Thus, Type-D does not belong to any category in Table 1; it falls into either (i) no aggregation and yes correlation or (ii) yes aggregation and yes correlation. This definition is also the same as that for SQL.

4.2 Completeness of Normalization Rules

XQuery allows nested expressions in the `for`, `where`, and `return` clauses. Hence, we subdivide those nesting types into three sub-categories depending on the clause where nested expressions occur.

Table 2 summarizes the nesting types considered in this paper. Type-D in the `for` and `return` clauses is not available by definition. The cells with a white circle indicate the rules proposed by Manolescu et al. [6]. The cells with a black circle indicate the rules proposed in this paper. The rule in a parenthesis deals with the corresponding nesting type.

Table 2. Classification of nesting types of XQuery FLWR expressions

Type \ Clause	for	where	return
Type-A	● (Rule 3)	● (Rule 4)	● (Rule 5)
Type-N	○ (Rule 1)	● (Rule 6)	○ (Rule 2)
Type-J	○ (Rule 1)	● (Rule 7)	○ (Rule 2)
Type-JA	● (Rule 8)	● (Rule 9)	● (Rule 10)
Type-D	N/A	● (Rule 11)	N/A

○: Normalization rule proposed in the literature [6]
●: Normalization rule proposed in this paper

Table 2 shows that our normalization rules are complete according to the classification by Kim [5]. That is, we support all of the nesting types (i.e., Type-A, Type-N, Type-J, Type-JA, and Type-D) for every clause (i.e., `for`, `where`, and `return`).

4.3 Normalization Rules for Each Nesting Type

Now, we propose source-level normalization rules for each nesting type in Table 2. We describe our normalization rules by using the notation by Manolescu et al. [6]. Every rule transforms nested queries to equivalent unnested ones. We first define *equivalence* of two queries in Definition 3.

DEFINITION 3: Two queries are *equivalent* if they produce the same results without considering order.

Normalization Rules for Type-A

We present Rules 3, 4, and 5 for nested expressions of Type-A in the `for`, `where`, and `return` clauses, respectively. In Type-A, the inner FLWR expression can be evaluated independently of the outer FLWR expression since there is no correlation. We pre-evaluate the inner FLWR expression and bind the result, which is a single value, to the variable T. Then, we substitute the inner FLWR expression with T. These rules extend the NEST-A rule [5] so as to accommodate the XQuery language.

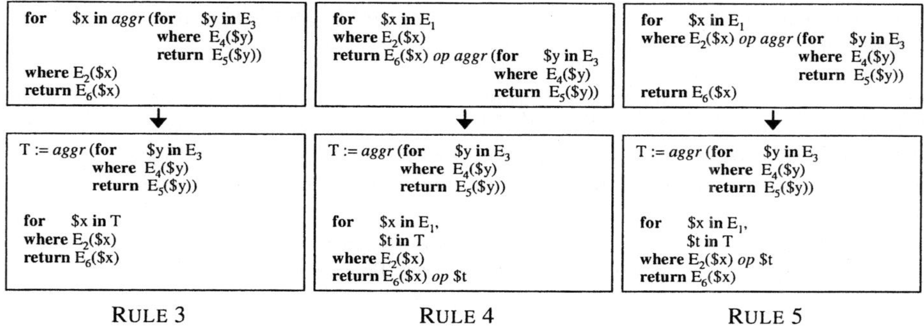

RULES 3 ∼ 5: Normalization rules for Type-A

CORRECTNESS OF RULES 3∼5: Having no correlation implies that outer and inner FLWR expressions are independent of each other. Thus, substituting the inner FLWR expression with the pre-evaluated result guarantees the same query results. □

Normalization Rule for Type-N

We present Rule 6 for nested expressions of Type-N in the `where` clause. Type-N can be handled in a manner similar to that for Type-A. The only difference is that the result of the inner FLWR expression is not a single value, but a sequence of values. We apply the `distinct` function to the inner FLWR expression before binding it to the variable T. The `distinct` function is required to avoid duplication of the query

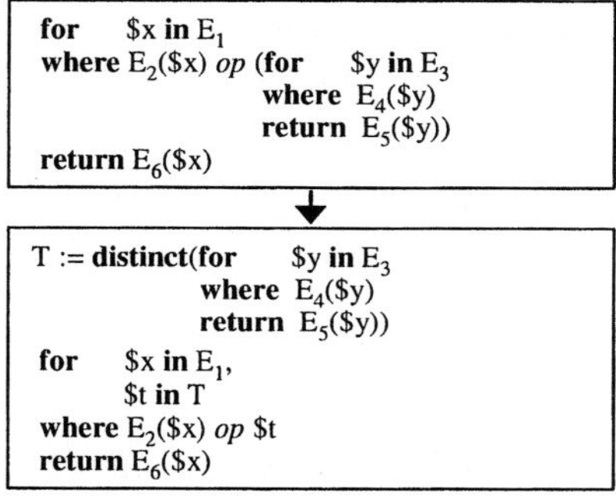

RULE 6: A normalization rule for Type-N

results. This rules extends the NEST-N-J rule by Kim [5] so as to accommodate the XQuery language.

One might argue that Rule 6 is different from NEST-N-J since Rule 6 creates a temporary relation T instead of directly joining the inner query with the outer query as in NEST-N-J. We note that, however, NEST-N-J has an important assumption that duplication in the result of the inner query should be eliminated before the join [5]. Hence, if we embody this assumption in Rule 6, it becomes identical to NEST-N-J.

CORRECTNESS OF RULE 6: As in Type-A, outer and inner FLWR expressions are independent of each other. In addition, the `distinct` function applied removes duplicates from the result of the inner FLWR expression. Thus, substituting the inner FLWR expression with the pre-evaluated result guarantees the same query results. □

EXAMPLE 1: Query 3, shown in Section 2, contains a nested expression of Type-N. Result 3 shows a possible result of Query 3. We obtain Query 3′ by applying Rule 6 to Query 3. We easily know that Queries 3 and 3′ produce the same query results. We note that, if the `distinct` function were omitted from Query 3′, Result 3 would be repeated twice since the variable T contains duplicate values (i.e., two D2's). □

RESULT 3: Result of Query 3.

<DName> Research </DName>

QUERY 3 ′: Normalize Query 3 using Rule 6.

```
T := distinct(for   $y in document("Projects.xml")/Projects/Proj
                    return $y/DNO)
for    $x in document("Departments.xml")/Departments/Dept,
       $t in T
where $x/DNO = $t
return $x/DName
```

Normalization Rule for Type-J

In Type-J, the inner FLWR expression cannot be pre-evaluated since there exists correlation. To pre-evaluate the inner FLWR expression, we define the *isolation* of the inner FLWR expression through Definitions 4 and 5.

DEFINITION 4: *Correlated expressions* are two expressions connected by comparison operators in the `where` clause of an inner FLWR expression, where at least one of them contains a variable defined in the `for` clause of an outer FLWR expression.

DEFINITION 5: *Isolation* of an inner FLWR expression is to remove all of the correlated expressions from the inner FLWR expression.

We present Rule 7 for nested expressions of Type-J in the `where` clause. We first isolate the inner FLWR expression, rendering the correlated expression $E_4(\$y)\ op_2\ E_5(\$x)$ removed. Then, we pre-evaluate the inner FLWR expression and substitute it with the pre-evaluated result, resulting in $E_2(\$x)\ op_1\ \$t/result/t1$. Finally, we add the correlated expression into the `where` clause of the outer FLWR expression, resulting in $\$t/result/t2\ op_2\ E_5(\$x)$.

```
for    $x in E1
where E2($x) op1 (for    $y in E3
                  where E4($y) op2 E5($x)
                  return E6($y))
return E7($x)
```

↓

```
T := distinct(for    $y in E3
              return <result>
                        <t1>{E6($y)}</t1>
                        <t2>{E4($y)}</t2>
                     </result>)
for    $x in E1,
       $t in T
where E2($x) op1 $t/result/t1 and $t/result/t2 op2 E5($x)
return E7($x)
```

RULE 7: A normalization rule for Type-J

CORRECTNESS OF RULE 7: There are two conditions that need to be satisfied in the original query: (i) $E_2(\$x)\ op_1\ E_6(\$y)$ and (ii) $E_4(\$y)\ op_2\ E_5(\$x)$. After isolating the inner FLWR expression, we pre-evaluate it and return the pairs of $E_6(\$y)$ and $E_4(\$y)$. Here, $E_6(\$y)$ (i.e., $\$t/result/t1$) is used for evaluating the former condition, and $E_4(\$y)$ (i.e., $\$t/result/t2$) for the latter one. Thus, the normalized query is equivalent to the original one. □

EXAMPLE 2: Query 4 contains a nested expression of Type-J. We obtain Query 4′ by applying Rule 7 to Query 4. □

We note that normalization does not always guarantee better performance. In the original query of Rule 7, suppose that the number of elements in E_3 is very large, but the inner FLWR expression itself is very cheap to compute by virtue of an index available for the predicate in the `where` clause. In this case, the cost of repeatedly evaluating the inner FLWR expression may be smaller than that of creating a temporary relation T. Here, the latter is almost the same as the cost of copying the whole elements of E_3 into T. Thus, we need a sophisticated query optimizer that can decide whether normalization is beneficial by using the estimated costs of the normalized and original queries. We leave this optimization as a topic of a future paper.

QUERY 4: Find the department where at least one project is processed in the department location.

```
for    $x in document("Departments.xml")/Departments/Dept
where  $x/DLoc = (for    $y in document("Projects.xml")/Projects/Proj
                  where  $y/DNO = $x/DNO
                  return $y/PLoc)
return $x/DName
```

QUERY 4′: Normalize Query 4 using Rule 7.

```
T := distinct(for    $y in document("Projects.xml")/Projects/Proj
              return <result><t1>{$y/PLoc}</t1><t2>{$y/DNO}</t2></result>)
for    $x in document("Departments.xml")/Departments/Dept,
       $t in T
where $x/DLoc = $t/result/t1 and $x/DNO = $t/result/t2
return $x/DName
```

Normalization Rules for Type-JA

We present Rules 8, 9, and 10 for nested expressions of Type-JA in the `for`, `where`, and `return` clauses, respectively. These rules consist of two steps. In the first step, we transform the nested expression of Type-JA to that of Type-J. In the second step, we apply our normalization rules for Type-J. Here, we elaborate on the first step.

We first isolate the inner FLWR expression, rendering the correlated expression $E_4(\$y)$ *op* $E_5(\$x)$ removed. Then, we pre-evaluate the aggregated values for each value of $E_4(\$y)$, which includes the variable $y defined in the `for` clause of the inner FLWR expression. During this pre-aggregation, the `group by` operator is required. We specify the `group by` operator using the extension proposed by Deutsch et al. [2] since the XQuery standard does not have it currently. Next, we substitute the `return` clause of the inner FLWR expression with the pre-aggregated result. Finally, we omit the aggregation operator in the outer FLWR expression. These rules extend the NEST-JA rule [5] so as to accommodate the XQuery language.

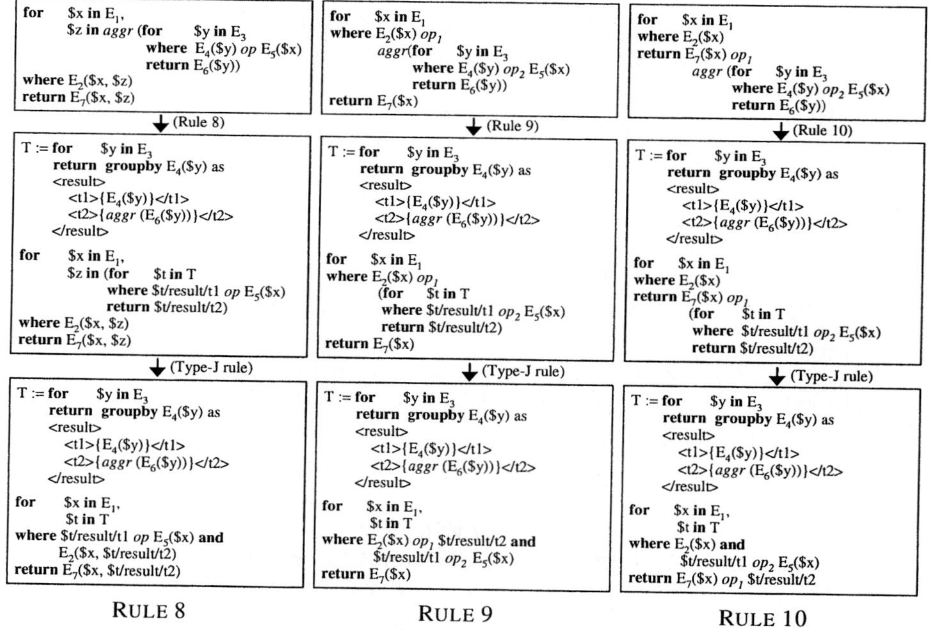

RULES 8 ~ 10: Normalization rules for Type-JA

As discussed in the literature, these rules can incur the count bug [4]. Thus, when the count bug can occur, we exploit the *Magic Decorrelation* method proposed by Seshadri et al. [10] for correcting the count bug. This method is regarded as the state-of-the-art method. It uses grouping and outer join. We omit the explanation of the Magic Decorrelation due to space limit.

CORRECTNESS OF RULES 8~10: The first step pre-evaluates the aggregated values for each value of a grouping attribute. Thus, this step preserves all of aggregated values. By pre-evaluating (i.e., removing) the aggregation, the nested expression of

Type-JA is transformed to that of Type-J. We note that the only difference between Type-JA and Type-J is existence of aggregation. Applying rules for Type-J completes the normalization. □

EXAMPLE 3: Query 5 contains a nested expression of Type-JA with nesting in the `where` clause. We obtain Query 5′ by applying Rule 9. □

QUERY 5: Find the names of the departments with at least two projects.

```
for   $x in document("Departments.xml")/Departments/Dept
where 2 <= count(for   $y in document("Projects.xml")/Projects/Proj
                 where $y/DNO = $x/DNO
                 return $y/PNO)
return $x/DName
```

QUERY 5′: Normalize Query 5 using Rule 9.

```
T := for   $y in document("Projects.xml")/Projects/Proj
     return groupby $y/DNO as
     <result><t1>{$y/DNO}</t1><t2>{count($y/PNO)}</t2></result>

for   $x in document("Departments.xml")/Departments/Dept,
      $t in T
where 2 <= $t/result/t2 and $t/result/t1 = $x/DNO
return $x/DName
```

Normalization Rule for Type-D

We present Rule 11 for nested expressions of Type-D in the `where` clause. We first define some additional notations.

- $FLWR_n$ denotes a FLWR expression.
- $FLWR_n^{Isolated}$ denotes the inner FLWR expression obtained by isolating $FLWR_n$.
- $E_n^{Correlated}(\$x)$ denotes the correlated expression of $FLWR_n$, which includes the variable \$x. If there is no correlated expression, TRUE is returned.

Since the inner FLWR expressions $FLWR_1$ and $FLWR_2$ do not have correlation between each other, we isolate them independently into the variables T_1 and T_2, respectively. Then, we perform join between T_1 and T_2. Here, we assume $\$t_1/result/t1$ and $\$t_2/result/t1$ are the return values of $FLWR_1$ and $FLWR_2$, while $\$t_1/result/t2$ and $\$t_2/result/t2$ are the values used in the correlated expressions. Next, we bind the result of this join to the variable T_3 and remove duplicates. Finally, we replace $FLWR_1$ *op* $FLWR_2$ in the `where` clause of the outer FLWR expression with the correlated expressions of $FLWR_1$ and $FLWR_2$ (i.e., $E_1^{Correlated}(\$t_3/result/t1)$ and $E_2^{Correlated}(\$t_3/result/t2)$).

CORRECTNESS OF RULE 11: We can isolate $FLWR_1$ and $FLWR_2$ separately into T_1 and T_2. Using T_1 and T_2, we compute $FLWR_1$ *op* $FLWR_2$ and store the result into T_3. Then, to compensate for lack of the correlated expressions, we add $E_1^{Correlated}(\$t_3/result/t1)$ and $E_2^{Correlated}(\$t_3/result/t2)$, which are evaluated against T_3, to the `where` clause of the outer FLWR expression. Hence, the normalized query is equivalent to the original one. □

```
for     $x in E1,
where FLWR1 op FLWR2
return E2($x)
```

↓

```
T1 := FLWR1^Isolated
T2 := FLWR2^Isolated
T3 := distinct(for   $t1 in T1,
                     $t2 in T2
               where $t1/result/t1 op $t2/result/t1
               return <result>
                        <t1>{$t1/result/t2}</t1>
                        <t2>{$t2/result/t2}</t2>
                      </result>)
for    $x in E1,
       $t3 in T3
where E1^Correlated ($t3/result/t1) and
      E2^Correlated ($t3/result/t2)
return E2($x)
```

RULE 11: A normalization rule for Type-D

EXAMPLE 4: Query 6 contains a nested expression of Type-D. We obtain Query 6′ by applying Rule 11 to Query 6. □

QUERY 6: Find the names of the employees who are working for a project located in "Houston."

```
for    $x in document("Departments.xml")/Departments/Dept/Emp
where (for   $y in document("WorksOn.xml")/WorksOnList/WorksOn
       where $y/SSN = $x/SSN
       return $y/PNO)
      =
      (for   $z in document("Projects.xml")/Projects/Proj
       where $z/PLoc = "Houston"
       return $z/PNO)
return $x/EName
```

QUERY 6′: Normalize Query 6 using Rule 11.

```
T1 := for   $y in document("WorksOn.xml")/WorksOnList/WorksOn
      return <result><t1>{$y/PNO}</t1><t2>{$y/SSN}</t2></result>

T2 := for   $z in document("Projects.xml")/Projects/Proj
      where $z/PLoc = "Houston"
      return $z/PNO

T3 := distinct(for   $t1 in T1,
                     $t2 in T2
               where $t1/result/t1 = $t2
               return $t1/result/t2)

for    $x in document("Departments.xml")/Departments/Dept/Emp,
       $t3 in T3
where $x/SSN = $t3
return $x/EName
```

5 Implementation Mechanism for Normalization Rules

In this section, we explain our implementation mechanism for the rules proposed in Section 4. We adopt the Query Graph Model (QGM) [8] to internally represent an XQuery expression. Section 5.1 introduces the QGM. Section 5.2 presents a normalization algorithm based on the QGM.

5.1 Query Graph Model

A query graph in the QGM is a data structure devised to internally represent an SQL query. It has been used for processing and optimizing an SQL query in IBM DB2. We slightly modify the original model so as to accommodate XQuery.

A query graph consists of query blocks. Each query block represents a FLWR expression and consists of a head and body. A head corresponds to the `return` clause, and thus, contains the elements that are returned as the query result. A body consists of nodes and edges. A node represents an element[2]; the clause where binding occurs is specified in a parenthesis at the side of the node. Edges are classified into the *binding edge* and *predicate edge*. The former binds a node to either an element or a query block. The latter connects nodes and represents a conjunct in the `where` clause. We denote the former as a dotted line and the latter as a solid line with a rectangle. A *loop* predicate edge attached to a node $z represents a local predicate on $z. We note that an *inter-block* predicate edge indicates that two query blocks have correlation. Each query block may additionally have a flag that indicates whether `distinct`, `group by`, or `order by` are used.

Figure 3 shows the query graphs of Queries (a), (b), and (c). We explain only Query (b) to avoid repetitive explanation. Query (b) finds the names of the departments that have at least two projects. The inner FLWR expression that counts the number of projects in a department is nested in the `where` clause of the outer FLWR expression. The outer and inner FLWR expressions correspond to the query blocks QB_1 and QB_2, respectively. In the outer FLWR expression, the `for` clause is represented as the node $\$x$ to which the *Dept* element is bound; the `where` clause as the loop predicate edge on the node $\$z$ bound to the query block QB_2; and the `return` clause as the head $\$x/DName$. In the inner FLWR expression, the `for` clause is represented as the node $\$y$ to which the *Proj* element is bound; the `where` clause as the predicate edge between the nodes $\$x$ and $\$y$; and the `return` clause as the head $count(\$y/PNO)$. We note that the predicate edge between the nodes $x and $y indicates correlation.

5.2 Normalization Algorithm

Our algorithm consists of two procedures: *Normalize_QG* and *ApplyNormalizationRules*. The former finds out the clause where a nested expression occurs, and the latter the nesting type.

In the Normalize_QG procedure, we determine the clause that contains a nested expression in the following manner. First, if a binding edge is connected from a node with "(for)" in the query block QB_1 to the query block QB_2 (e.g., between $z and QB_2 in Figure 3 (a)), the `for` clause has a nested expression. Second, if a

---

[2] Since we deal with XQuery, we use the term "element variable" corresponding to "tuple variable" in the relational context.

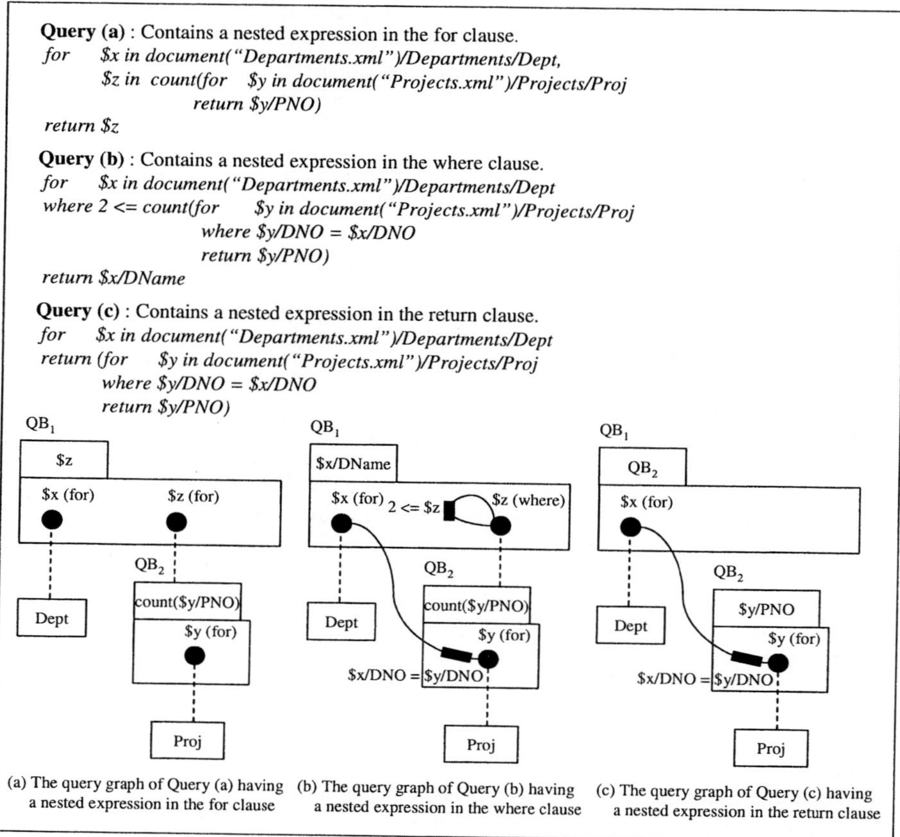

(a) The query graph of Query (a) having a nested expression in the for clause (b) The query graph of Query (b) having a nested expression in the where clause (c) The query graph of Query (c) having a nested expression in the return clause

Fig. 3. The query graphs of example queries

binding edge is connected from a node with "(where)" in the query block QB_1 to the query block QB_2 (e.g., between $z and QB_2 in Figure 3 (b)), the `where` clause has a nested expression. Third, if the head of the query block QB_1 contains another query block QB_2 (e.g., as shown in Figure 3 (c)), the `return` clause has a nested expression.

Figure 4 shows the Normalize_QG procedure. As described above, it detects nested expressions in the `for` clause (lines 3~6), in the `where` clause (lines 7~17), and in the `return` clause (lines 18~21). Then, it calls the ApplyNormalizationRules procedure with the clause information. If there exists two inner FLWR expressions in the `where` clause, it applies Rule 11 for Type-D immediately (line 15).

In the ApplyNormalizationRules procedure, we determine the nesting type in the following manner. The nesting type is dependent on existence of correlation and aggregation. Correlation exists if the inner query block QB_2 has a predicate edge connected to a node in the outer query block QB_1. On the other hand, aggregation exists if there is an aggregate function in the head of QB_2. Hence, we can easily detect correlation and aggregation using the query graph. After detecting them, the nesting type is determined as shown in Table 1.

```
1: Procedure Normalize_QG (query block QB1)
2: begin
      /* Remove nesting from the for clause */
3:    if (A binding edge is connected from a node
         with "(for)" in QB1 to QB2)
4:    then begin
5:       ApplyNormalizationRules(QB2, for)
6:    end
      /* Remove nesting from the where clause */
7:    if (A binding edge is connected from a node
         with "(where)" in QB1 to QB2)
8:    then begin
9:       if (only one operand is a query block (QB2))
10:      then begin
11:         ApplyNormalizationRules(QB2, where)
12:      end
13:      if (both operands are query blocks)
14:      then begin
15:         Apply Rule 11.
16:      end
17:   end
      /* Remove nesting from the return clause */
18:   if (The head of QB1 contains QB2)
19:   then begin
20:      ApplyNormalizationRules(QB2, return)
21:   end
22: end
```

```
1:  Procedure ApplyNormalizationRules (query block QB2, clause)
2:  begin
3:     Normalize_QG(QB2)
4:     if (QB2 has a predicate edge connected to a node in
          the outer query block)
5:     then begin
          /* Normalize a nested expression of Type-JA */
6:        if (QB2 has an aggregate function in its head)
7:        then begin
8:           Apply Rules 8,9, or 10 depending on the clause that contains
             a nested expression
9:        end
          /* Normalize a nested expression of Type-J */
10:       else
11:          Apply Rules 1,2, or 7 depending on the clause that contains
             a nested expression
12:       end
13:    end
14:    else
          /* Normalize a nested expression of Type-A */
15:       if (QB2 has an aggregate function in its head)
16:       then begin
17:          Apply Rules 3,4, or 5 depending on the clause that contains
             a nested expression
18:       end
          /* Normalize a nested expression of Type-N */
19:       else
20:          Apply Rules 1,2, or 6 depending on the clause that contains
             a nested expression
21:       end
22:    end
23: end
```

Fig. 4. The Normalize_QG and ApplyNormalizationRules procedure

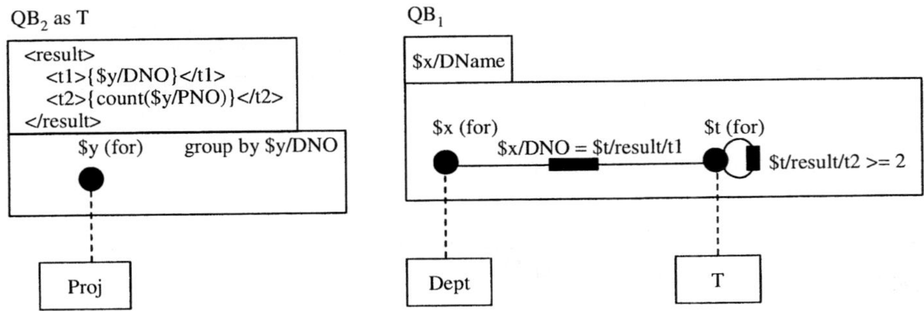

Fig. 5. The query graph obtained by normalizing Figure 3 (b)

Figure 4 also shows the ApplyNormalizationRule procedure. As described above, it finds out the nesting type and applies the normalization rule using both of the clause information and the nesting type. It applies Rules 8, 9, and 10 for Type-JA (lines 6~9); Rules 1, 2, and 7 for Type-J (lines 10~12); Rules 3, 4, and 5 for Type-A (lines 15~18); and Rules 1, 2, and 4.3 for Type-N (lines 19~21).

EXAMPLE 5: Figure 5 shows the query graph obtained by normalizing Figure 3 (b). During this normalization, the condition in line 7 of Normalize_QG is satisfied, and then, Rule 9 is applied in line 8 of ApplyNormalizationRules. We note that two query blocks are separated after normalization is completed. These two query blocks are serially executed. □

Our algorithm is also applicable when nested expressions occur in more than two levels. In that case, we apply our algorithm recursively until all of nested expressions are normalized.

6 Conclusions

In this paper, we have reported preliminary results in developing our XML DBMS named Odysseus/XML. For efficient processing of XQuery expressions, we have implemented the normalization procedure into Odysseus/XML. Our approach focuses on a practical implementation. To propose normalization rules, we have adopted the source-level rule, which is easy to implement. We have shown that our rules are correct and complete according to Kim's classification. Then, we have presented a normalization algorithm based on the QGM. The normalization rules that should be applied can be easily detected using the QGM. Overall, our work provides a practical approach to implementing normalization of XQuery expressions.

As a future work, we intend to verify the advantages of normalization by the cost formula and extensive experiments.

References

1. Deutsch, A. et al., "A Query Language for XML," In *Proc. 8th Int'l Conf. on World Wide Web*, pp. 1155–1169, May 1999.
2. Deutsch, A., Papakonstantinou, Y., and Xu, Y., "Minimization and Group-By Detection for Nested XQueries," In *Proc. 30th Int'l Conf. on Data Engineering* (ICDE), p. 839, Mar. 2004.
3. Fegaras, L. and Maier, D., "Optimizing Object Queries Using an Effective Calculus," *ACM Trans. on Database Systems*, Vol. 25, No. 4, pp. 457–516, Dec. 2000.
4. Kiessling, W., SQL-like and Quel-like Correlation Queries with Aggregates Revisited, UCB/ERL Memo 84/75, Electronics Research Laboratory, California, Berkeley, Sept. 1984.
5. Kim, W., "On Optimizing an SQL-like Nested Query," *ACM Trans. on Database Systems*, Vol. 7, No. 3, pp. 443–469, Sept. 1982.
6. Manolescu, I., Florescu, D., and Kossmann, D., "Answering XML Queries over Heterogeneous Data Sources," In *Proc. 27th Int'l Conf. on Very Large Data Bases*, pp. 241–250, Sept. 2001.
7. May, N., Helmer, S., and Moerkotte, G., "Nested Queries and Quantifiers in an Ordered Context," In *Proc. 30th Int'l Conf. on Data Engineering* (ICDE), pp. 239–250, Mar. 2004.
8. Pirahesh, H., Hellerstein, J.M., and Hasan, W., "Extensible/Rule Based Query Rewrite Optimization in Starburst," In *Proc. Int'l Conf. on Management of Data*, ACM SIGMOD, pp. 39–48, June 1992.
9. Robie, J., Lapp, J., and Schach, D., "XML Query Language (XQL)," In *Proc. the Query Languages Workshop*, Dec. 1998.
10. Seshadri, P., Pirahesh, H., and Leung, T., "Complex Query Decorrelation," In *Proc. 17th Int'l Conf. on Data Engineering* (ICDE), pp. 450–458, Feb. 1996.
11. Whang, K., Lee, M., Lee, J., Kim, M., and Han, W., "Odysseus: a High-Performance ORDBMS Tightly-Coupled with IR Features," In *Proc. 21th Int'l Conf. on Data Engineering* (ICDE), pp. 1004–1005, Apr. 2005. This paper received the Best Demonstration Award.

12. Whang, K. and Krishnamurthy, R., "Query Optimization in a Memory-Resident Domain Relational Calculus Database System," *ACM Trans. on Database Systems*, Vol. 15, No. 1, pp. 67–95, Mar. 1990.
13. World Wide Web Consortium, XML Path Language (XPath) Version 2.0, W3C Recommendation, Apr. 2005 (available from http://www.w3.org/TR/xpath20/).
14. World Wide Web Consortium, XQuery 1.0: An XML Query Language, W3C Working Draft, Apr. 2005 (available from http://www.w3.org/TR/xquery/).

Hidden Conditioned Homomorphism for XPath Fragment Containment*

Yuguo Liao, Jianhua Feng, Yong Zhang, and Lizhu Zhou

Department of Computer Science and Technology,
Tsinghua University, Beijing 100084, P.R. China
liaoyg03@mails.tsinghua.edu.cn, zhangy@tsinghua.org.cn
{fengjh, dcszlz}@mail.tsinghua.edu.cn

Abstract. As a query language for navigating XML trees and selecting a set of element nodes, XPath is ubiquitous in XML applications. One important issue of XPath queries is checking containment. In particular, we investigate a frequently used fragment of XPath that consists of node tests, the child axis (/), the descendant axis (//), branches ([]) and label wildcards (*). For special classes of pattern trees, the homomorphism algorithm returns false negatives. In order to address this problem, we propose two containment techniques, conditioned homomorphism and hidden conditioned homomorphism, and then present sound algorithms to check containment. The analytical result is given with an experiment.

1 Introduction

XPath is a simple query language for navigating XML trees and selecting a set of element nodes. It is ubiquitous in XML applications as a common sub-language of XQuery[4], XLink[10], XPointer[11] and XSLT[8]. One of the most important issues of XPath queries is checking containment. Query containment is crucial in many contexts, such as query optimization, query reformulation, information integration and integrity checking. In general, the efficiency of finding the result of a query on a given input database depends on the size of the query. Queries submitted to the query processor might contain redundant branches that can be removed independent of any integrity constraint. This fact spurred the research on query minimization in query optimization domain. Most minimization algorithms for tree pattern queries follow the general process: first pruning the query tree, then checking equivalence between the pruned query tree and the original one. Since query tree equivalence and containment are mutually reducible, the key problem is eventually reduced to checking containment between two query trees. Moreover, in the query minimization algorithms, the building block of checking containment/equivalence always contributes the most computation complexity. Hence, the efficiency of the containment algorithm is critical for the overall performance.

* Supported by the National Natural Science Foundation of China under Grant No. 60573094, Tsinghua Basic Research Foundation under Grant No. JCqn2005022 and Zhejiang Natural Science Foundation under Grant No. Y105230.

M.L. Lee, K.L. Tan, and V. Wuwongse (Eds.): DASFAA 2006, LNCS 3882, pp. 454 – 467, 2006.

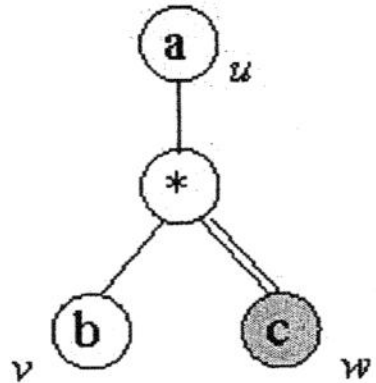

Fig. 1. A simple tree pattern corresponding to XPath expression *a*/*[*b*]//*c*

The focus of this paper is the containment checking for a fragment of XPath, with applications in all the contexts mentioned above. This fragment consists of node tests, the child axis (/), the descendant axis (//), branches ([]) and label wildcards (*). Isolating the most important features, we call this class of queries $XP^{\{[],\ *,\ //\}}$. This fragment is used frequently in practice; further restrictions seem impractical since each of the features occurs often. Every expression in $XP^{\{[],\ *,\ //\}}$ can be translated into a *tree pattern* with the same semantics [12,16]. For example, XPath expression *a*/*[*b*]//*c* is presented by the tree pattern in Fig. 1 where double-slashes represent descendant edges, * is a label wildcard, and the return node is marked with a solid circle. Starting at the root, this pattern first checks if the root node is labeled *a*. If not, it returns the empty set; otherwise, it then checks if the *a*-node has a child with both a *b*-child and a *c*-descendant. If not, it returns the empty set; otherwise, it returns all the matched *c*-descendants. The *b*-child and *c*-descendant of document tree may occur in any order.

For a given XPath expression *p* and input tree *t*, *p*(*t*) is the set of nodes in *t* returned by the evaluation of *p*. Given two expressions *p* and *q*, we say that *p* is contained in *q* (denoted by $p \subseteq q$) iff $\forall t.\ p(t) \subseteq q(t)$.

1.1 Related Work

Query containment is a well-studied area of database systems. One of the first results was that of Chandra and Merlin [7] who showed that for a class of relational database queries, called conjunctive queries, the containment problem is NP complete. Peter Buneman et al. [5] provided a PTIME algorithm for linear patterns in $XP^{\{//\}}$. Linear queries in $XP^{\{*,\ //\}}$ are a special case of regular expressions on strings, for which a linear-time containment algorithm is claimed in [13]. Queries in $XP^{\{*,\ []\}}$ can be viewed as the acyclic conjunctive queries over tree structures, from which it follows that the containment of this fragment is solvable in PTIME [19]. Containment for $XP^{\{[],\ //\}}$ was shown to be in PTIME in [1]. The class of patterns that include descendant edges ($XP^{\{[],\ //\}}$, $XP^{\{[],\ *,\ //\}}$) can be expressed in datalog with recursion, for which the containment is undecidable in general [17]. In [20] the author showed, using chase techniques, that the datalog fragment needed for $XP^{\{[],\ *,\ //\}}$ has a decidable containment problem. Using canonical model technique, [12] showed that containment in fragment $XP^{\{[],\ *,\ //\}}$ is co-NP complete, and proposed a complete algorithm for containment, which is EXPTIME complexity. The authors also proposed a sound but incomplete algorithm, which is based on homomorphism and may return false negatives. As an overview, [16] introduced some of the main algorithmic techniques that had been proposed for XPath query containment.

1.2 Motivation, Contributions and Overview

By the definition of containment, to check containment $p \subseteq q$ for two XPath expressions, we need to check that $p(t) \subseteq q(t)$ holds for all trees t. Since there are infinite many trees, it is not even clear that the problem is decidable. The method of *canonical model*, introduced in [12], prunes the check space into a finite set, and arrives at an exponential-time algorithm for checking containment. On the other hand, the *homomorphism* technique, coming from a classical characterization result for conjunctive queries against relational databases, arrives at a much more efficient but incomplete algorithm. Then, how to narrow the gap between canonical model and homomorphism? Is there any technique which is more efficient than canonical model, meanwhile more complete, that is, returns less false negatives, than homomorphism? In this paper, we address this challenge and make the following contributions:

- To address the problem that homomorphism algorithm proposed in [12] may return false negatives, we introduce a technique called *conditioned homomorphism* and present an efficient algorithm.
- For another class of tree pattern pairs, conditioned homomorphism still returns false negatives. The conditioned homomorphism is extended to *hidden conditioned homomorphism*, and an efficient algorithm is presented.
- The experiments demonstrate both the practicality and efficiency of our techniques.

The rest of this paper is organized as follows: Section 2 contains the basic notations, definitions and background materials. Section 3 and 4 contain the core of our work, that is, conditioned homomorphism and hidden conditioned homomorphism techniques. Experimental results are presented in Section 5. Finally, we conclude our work in Section 6.

2 Preliminaries

2.1 XML Tree, XPath Fragment and Tree Pattern

We model XML documents as trees over an infinite alphabet. Following the definition in [12], for a tree t, NODES (t) and EDGES (t) are the sets of nodes and edges, respectively, ROOT (t) denotes its root node, and LABLE (x) denotes the label on node x. EDGES$^+$ (t) is the transitive closure of EDGES (t): EDGES$^+$ (t) = EDGES (t)$\cup$EDGES (t)$\circ$EDGES$^+$ (t), and EDGES* (t) is the reflexive and transitive closure of EDGES (t): EDGES* (t) = NODES^2 (t)$\cup$EDGES$^+$ (t). EDGE (x) is the edge connecting node x and its parent. The size of a tree t, in notation $|t|$, is the number of edges in t.

The fragment of XPath studied in this paper, denoted by $XP^{\{[\,],\,*,\,//\}}$, consists of expressions given by the following grammar where "n" is an element and "." means the current node:

$$q \rightarrow n \mid * \mid . \mid q/q \mid q//q \mid q[q] \qquad (1)$$

Attributes and text values are handled similarly to elements and are omitted from our discussion.

The tree patterns are used to represent expressions of XPath queries [12,16]. The set of tree patterns corresponding to XPath fragment $XP^{\{[\,],\,*,\,//\}}$ is denoted by $P^{\{[\,],\,*,\,//\}}$. The definitions on XML trees can also be applied to tree patterns. Besides, for tree pattern p, C-EDGES (p) is the set of child edges and D-EDGES (p) is the set of all descendant edges. Obviously, C-EDGES (p) $\cup$ D-EDGES (p)=EDGES (p).

An *embedding* from tree pattern p to XML tree t is a function e: NODES (p) $\rightarrow$ NODES (t) satisfying:

(1) e (ROOT (p)) = ROOT(t);
(2) for each $x \in$ NODES (p), LABEL (x) = * or LABEL (x) = LABEL (e (x));
(3) for each x, $y \in$ NODES (p), if (x, y) $\in$ C-EDGES (p) then (e (x), e (y)) $\in$ EDGES (t), if (x, y) $\in$ D-EDGES (p) then (e (x), e (y)) $\in$ EDGES$^+$ (t).

The process of checking whether there exists an embedding from a tree pattern p to a tree t and getting the result sets is called *evaluation* of p on t. The set of tree nodes returned by evaluating p on t is denoted by p (t). If there exists an embedding from tree pattern p to tree t, the tree t *satisfies* the tree pattern p.

2.2 Boolean Tree Pattern

The number of return nodes in a tree pattern is called *arity*. The arity of tree patterns transformed from XPath expression is always 1. In the case of a tree pattern p with arity zero, p (t) evaluates to the empty-tuple if there exists an embedding from p to t. Otherwise, p (t) is the empty-set. Such patterns are viewed as *boolean tree patterns or boolean patterns*, and p (t) is true if an embedding exists and false otherwise. Thus, evaluation of boolean tree pattern p on tree t is to check whether p (t) is true. For boolean patterns, containment reduces to implication: $p \subseteq q$ iff $\forall t.\ p(t) \rightarrow q(t)$.

For the purpose of the containment problem, [12] claimed that it is sufficient to limit our discussion to boolean tree patterns. In fact, there is a translation of k-ary tree pattern to boolean pattern such that for any k-ary patterns p, q and their respective translations p', q', $p \subseteq q$ iff $p' \subseteq q'$.

In the rest of this paper, all tree patterns are assumed to be boolean tree patterns, unless otherwise stated.

2.3 Prior Techniques Overview

One way to reason about containment is by way of *canonical model* [12]. To check that p (t) $\rightarrow$ q (t) holds for all trees t, this technique restricts the search to "canonical" trees t', which "look like" p and are "no bigger" than q. It arrives at an exponential-time algorithm for checking containment. The second approach is homomorphism [7,19,2], which will be discussed in detail in section 2.4. The third technique, *automata* technique [14], represents the set of counter examples by a finite device, a tree automaton. It combines the tree automata corresponding to the involved expressions and checks whether the resulting automaton accepts a non-empty set. As the canonical model technique, the algorithm derived from automata technique runs in exponential time. The last technique is the *chase* technique [19,2,18]. It is mainly used as an extension of homomorphism technique to check containment in the presence of integrity constraints.

2.4 Homomorphism Technique

2.4.1 Definition of Homomorphism

Homomorphism was first proposed in [7] to check containment between conjunctive queries of relational database. It can also be applied to queries over tree structures. Given tree patterns p and q, a homomorphism *h*: $q \rightarrow p$ is a function from NODES (q) to NODES (p) that satisfies the following conditions:

Root-preserving. h (ROOT(q)) = ROOT(p),

Label-preserving. For each x $\in$ NODES (q), LABEL (x) = * or LABEL (x) = LABEL ($h(x)$),

Child-edge-preserving. For each $(x, y) \in$ C-EDGES (q), $(h(x), h(y)) \in$ C-EDGES (p), and

Descendant-edge-preserving. For each $(x, y) \in$ D-EDGES (q), $(h(x), h(y)) \in$ EDGES$^+$ (p).

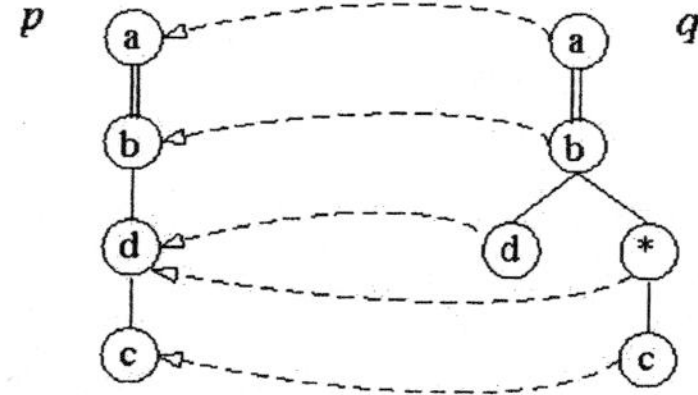

Fig. 2. A simple homomorphism from tree pattern q to tree pattern p

Homomorphism does not need to be an injective function. Fig. 2 illustrates such a homomorphism. If a homomorphism *h:* $q \rightarrow p$ exists, we say that there is a homomorphism from pattern q to pattern p. In [12], the authors showed that given two patterns p and q, one can determine in time O ($|p| \times |q|$) whether there exists a homomorphism from q to p. Moreover, if it exists, $p \subseteq q$ holds. Thus, an efficient practical algorithm for checking containment is to search for a homomorphism.

2.4.2 Adorned Tree Pattern

However, homomorphism algorithm is not always complete. It is already observed in [13] that the existence of a homomorphism fails to be a necessary criterion for patterns in $P^{\{*, //\}}$. Fig. 3(a) illustrates a scenario for that. The two tree patterns correspond to XPath expressions *p=a/*//b*, *q=a//*/b*. Although p and q are equivalent, that is $p \subseteq q$ and $q \subseteq p$, there is no homomorphism from q to p because the wildcard in q can't be mapped to any node in p. The solution is to eliminate the * node in q and *adorn* the descendant edge with "[1, ∞)" meaning that there is at least one intermediate node on this path. This is shown in Fig. 3(b), which illustrate a homomorphism from the adorned tree pattern q' to pattern p.

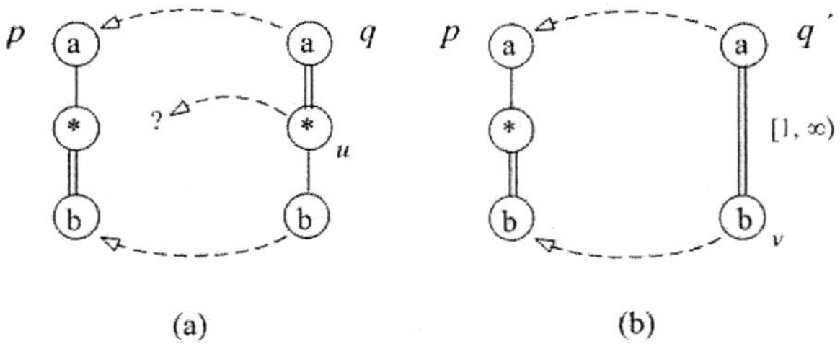

Fig. 3. (a) Two equivalent tree patterns *p* and *q* with no homomorphism from *q* to *p*; (b) After tree pattern *q* being reduced to adorned tree pattern *q*′, a homomorphism exists from *q*′ to *p*

Before formally introducing the adornments, we define *length of edge* as the number of intermediate nodes that the edge can cover. Obviously, the length of a child edge is 0, and the length of a descendant edge is an interval number. Since a node in the tree pattern can have at most one parent node, we define *edge length* of a node *x* as the length of edge connecting node *x* and its parent node, denoted by *edge-length* (*x*). For example, in Fig. 3(a), *edge-length* (*u*) = [0, ∞), and in Fig. 3(b), *edge-length* (*v*) = [1, ∞). In tree patterns, the interval is put near the corresponding edge, like the picture in Fig. 3(b).

To transform a tree pattern into an adorned one, the length of every descendant edge is initialized to be [0, ∞) and the length of every child edge is initialized to be [0, 0]. Then if there is an edge shares a * node with an adjacent edge, the * node is eliminated and the two edges are combined into a new descendant edge. The interval of the length of the new descendant edge is computed by superimposing the respective intervals of the lengths of the two edges and then increasing both the upper and lower bound of the interval by 1 (to count in the eliminated * node). And only * nodes that have a unique child may be eliminated this way, that is, if a * node has two or more child nodes then it cannot be eliminated. This process can also be described as a set of rewrite rules described as follows:

$$\begin{array}{c} \ldots//x\ldots \rightarrow \ldots//x\ldots,\ \text{edge-length}\ (x) = [0, \infty); \\ \ldots/*/x\ldots \rightarrow \ldots//x\ldots,\ \text{edge-length}\ (x) = [1, 1]; \\ \ldots//*/x\ldots,\ \text{edge-length}\ (*) = [m, n] \rightarrow \ldots//x\ldots,\ \text{edge-length}\ (x) = [m+1, n+1]; \\ \ldots/*//x\ldots,\ \text{edge-length}\ (x) = [m, n] \rightarrow \ldots//x\ldots,\ \text{edge-length}\ (x) = [m+1, n+1]; \\ \ldots//*//x\ldots,\ \text{edge-length}\ (*) = [m_0, n_0],\ \text{edge-length}\ (x) = [m_1, n_1] \rightarrow \ldots//x\ldots, \\ \text{edge-length}\ (x) = [m_0+m_1+1, n_0+n_1+1]. \end{array} \tag{2}$$

For example, the adorned tree pattern of $q = a/*/b//*/c//*/*//d$ is $q' = a//^{[1,\ 1]}b//^{[1,\ \infty]}c//^{[2,\ \infty]}d$.

2.4.3 Homomorphism with Adorned Tree Pattern

The *distance* between two nodes of tree pattern is defined as the number of edges between them on the path. If there is no ancestor-descent relationship between the two nodes, then the distance should be ∞. Take tree pattern *p* in Fig. 1 for example, *distance* (*u*, *v*) = 2, and *distance* (*w*, *v*) = ∞. A homomorphism *h* from adorned tree pattern *q* to tree pattern *p* satisfies the following conditions:

(1) h (ROOT (q)) = ROOT (p),
(2) if $x \in$ NODES (q), then LABEL (x) = * or LABEL (x) = LABEL (h (x)),
(3) if (x, y) $\in$ EDGES (q), (*distance* (h(x), h(y)) - 1) $\in$ *edge-length* (y).

Every unadorned tree pattern admits a trivial adornment by setting length of every child edge to be [0, 0], and length of every descendant edge to be [0, ∞). Hence discussions on adorned tree patterns can be also applied to unadorned tree patterns.

It is showed in [13] that the existence of homomorphism from adorned tree pattern to tree pattern is a necessary and sufficient condition for containment when both patterns are linear. To illustrate the example in Fig. 3, the tree pattern q is reduced to the adorned tree pattern q', making a homomorphism possible. [12] proposed an algorithm for finding homomorphism from adorned tree pattern q' to tree pattern p which runs in time O ($|p| \times |q'|$). Based on this algorithm, [12] proposed an algorithm for checking containment. It is sound, and runs in time O ($|p| \times |q|$) where p and q are two tree patterns. However, in general this algorithm is incomplete.

3 Conditioned Homomorphism Technique

3.1 More Complete Homomorphism?

In fact, in fragment of XP$^{\{[], *, //\}}$, existence of homomorphism from q to p is sufficient but not necessarily complete for $p \subseteq q$. This is exemplified by the tree patterns p and q in Fig. 4(a). In this example, $p \subseteq q$ but no homomorphism exists from q to p. We explain this example in next paragraph.

For convenience, every node in p and q is assigned with a unique identifier, marked at the bottom right corner of each node in Fig. 4(a). Following the steps introduced in Section 2.4.2, tree pattern q is reduced to adorned tree pattern q'. The *node6* of q is eliminated, and edge-length (*node8*) of q' becomes [1, ∞). Although there seems to be two possible targets for the *node2* of q', none of them really makes a homomorphism. But a closer inspection shows that $p \subseteq q$ holds. Given an XML tree t, p (t) = true, and e is an embedding from p to t, the number of intermediate nodes between e (*node6*) and e (*node9*) in the XML tree t must be either =0 or $\geqslant$1. According to this observation, we construct two tree patterns p_1 and p_2 in Fig. 4(b) and Fig. 4(c). The tree pattern p_1 is almost the same as the tree pattern p except that no intermediate node is allowed between *node6* and *node9*. And tree pattern p_2 specifies that there should be at least one intermediate node between *node6* and *node9*. Obviously, XML trees satisfying tree pattern p can also satisfy tree pattern p_1 or p_2. In Fig. 4(b) there is homomorphism from q' to p_1, and in Fig. 4(c) there is a homomorphism from q' to p_2. It means that $p_1 \subseteq q$ and $p_2 \subseteq q$. In another word, XML trees satisfying tree pattern p_1 or p_2 can satisfy tree pattern q. Then, $\forall t.\ p(t)$ = true$\rightarrow q(t)$ = true, that is $p \subseteq q$.

Intuitively, in the example above, tree pattern p_1 and p_2 impose certain *conditions* on the number of intermediate nodes on the path of descendant edges of tree pattern p. If tree pattern p satisfies the condition that *edge-length* (*node9*) = [0, 0], then according to Fig. 4(b), there exists homomorphism from q' to p, that is $p \subseteq q$; and if tree

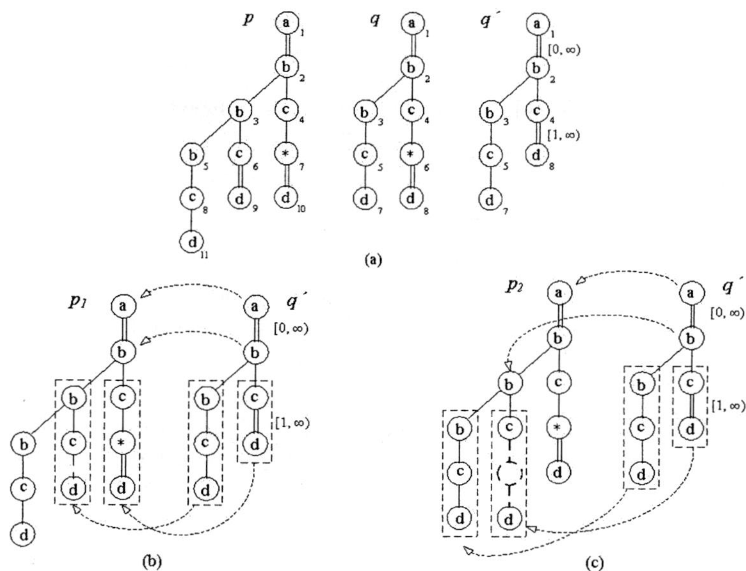

Fig. 4. (a) Tree patterns p and q with no corresponding homomorphism, q' is adorned from tree pattern q; (b) Homomorphism from q' to p_1; (c) Homomorphism from q' to p_2

pattern p satisfies the condition that *edge-length* (*node9*) = [1, ∞), similarly, according to Fig. 4(c), $p \subseteq q$. Then after union the two conditions together, it is concluded that $p \subseteq q$ under the condition *edge-length* (*node9*) = [0, ∞) in pattern p. Since the edge between *node9* and its parent *node6* in pattern p is a descendant edge, the condition *edge-length* (*node9*) = [0, ∞) can always be satisfied. That is to say, $p \subseteq q$ always holds.

3.2 Conditioned Homomorphism

The *condition term* is defined as constraint on the edge length of one or more descendant edges of a tree pattern. For tree pattern p, *edge-length* (x) = [m, n], $x \in$ NODES (p) is called a condition term; and *edge-length* (x) + *edge-length* (y) = [m, n], x, $y \in$ NODES (p) is also a condition term, "+" is superposition on intervals. For example, condition term *edge-length* (x) = [1, ∞) means that there should be more than one intermediate nodes on EDGE (x); condition term *edge-length* (y) + *edge-length* (z) = [3, ∞) means that the sum of number of intermediate nodes on EDGE (y) and EDGE (z) should be between [3, ∞). A *condition* for a tree pattern is a conjunction of condition terms. For example, a possible condition for tree pattern p is *edge-length* (x) = [1, ∞) ∧ *edge-length* (y) = [1, 1]. We define *base condition* of a tree pattern as a condition which can always be satisfied. Take tree pattern p in Fig. 4(a) for example, *base-condition* (p) = {*edge-length* (*node2*) = [0, ∞) ∧ *edge-length* (*node9*) = [0, ∞) ∧ *edge-length* (*node10*) = [0, ∞)}.

Definition 1. Let p be a tree pattern and q be an adorned tree pattern. If when p satisfies condition c, there is a homomorphism from q to p, then there is a conditioned homomorphism from q to p under condition c, denoted by $h: q \xrightarrow{c} p$.

Obviously, if there is a conditioned homomorphism from tree pattern q to p under condition *base-condition* (p), then $p \subseteq q$. Moreover, if $h_1: q \xrightarrow{c1} p$, $h_2: q \xrightarrow{c2} p \ldots h_n: q \xrightarrow{cn} p$, and $c_1 \vee c_2 \vee \cdots \vee c_n =$ *base-condition* (p), then $p \subseteq q$.

3.3 Computing Conditioned Homomorphism

For node x of tree pattern p, *sub-tree*(x) is the sub-tree of pattern p rooted at node x, and *sub-edge-tree* (x) is the *sub-tree*(x) pluses the parent node of node x and the edge between them.

Theorem 1. Let p be a tree pattern and q be an adorned tree pattern, and ROOT (q) has k child nodes $n_1, n_2..., n_k$. If there is a conditioned homomorphism from *sub-edge-tree* (n_i) to p under condition c_i, i=1...k, then there exists conditioned homomorphism from q to p under condition $c_1 \wedge c_2 \wedge \cdots \wedge c_k$.

Theorem 2. Let p be a tree pattern and q be an adorned tree pattern, and x is a non-leaf node of p, y is a non-root node of q. If ROOT (p) and the parent node of y are compatible (label preserving), and there is a homomorphism from *sub-tree* (y) to a descendant node x' of x under condition c, then a condition c' could be figured out under which a homomorphism from *sub-edge-tree* (y) to *sub-tree* (x) exists.

On the path from node x to x', let there be k child edges and l descendant edges, and the nodes on the bottom side of every descendant edges are respectively $n_1, n_2 ..., n_l$. Then, a condition term is constructed, i.e., α: *edge-length* (n_1) + *edge-length* (n_2) + ... + *edge-length* (n_l) = *edge-length* (y) - $[k, k]$. Then $c' = \alpha \wedge c$.

A condition is conjunction of condition terms. If one of the condition terms can not be satisfied, e.g. *edge-length* (x) = [-3, -2], or two condition terms conflict with each other, e.g. *edge-length* (x) = [0, 0] and *edge-length* (x) = $[1, \infty)$, this condition is called *unsatisfiable*, hence no homomorphism exists.

The above theorems allow iteratively computing conditions of homomorphism between sub-patterns bottom up. Our algorithms computing conditions of homomorphism are derived from these theorems. Algorithm 1 takes tree pattern p and adorned tree pattern q, and returns the condition under which there is a conditioned homomorphism from q to p. It proceeds bottom up in both q and p, and computes two tables *Con* (x, y) and Con^* (x, y) with $x \in$ NODES (p) and $y \in$ NODES (q). *Con* (x, y) is a condition of tree pattern p under which there is a homomorphism from *sub-tree* (y) to *sub-tree* (x). Con^* (x, y) is a condition of tree pattern p under which there is a homomorphism from *sub-edge-tree* (y) to *sub-tree* (x).

In line 7 of function COMPUTE-CONDITION*, k is the number of child edges between x and x', and n_i is the bottom side nodes of descendant edges between x and x'.While computing conditions, NULL condition means an unsatisfiable condition, and can be treated as boolean *false*. The result of conjunction of a NULL condition with other condition is also a NULL condition.

Algorithm 1. Finding conditions for conditioned homomorphism $q \rightarrow p$

```
Function: FIND-CONDITIONED-HOMOMORPHISM(p,q)
Input: tree pattern p, adorned tree pattern q
Output: boolean value indicating whether a homomorphism exists from q to
p under base-condition of p
Begin
    condition base = base-condition(p)
    for y in NODES(q) do {bottom up iteration}
       for x in NODES(p) do {bottom up iteration}
          if(LABEL(x) == * or LABEL(y) == LABEL(x))
             if(y is leaf node)
                Con(x,y) = base
             else
                condition c = ∧(y,y')∈EDGES(q) Con*(x,y')
                if c is satisfiable
                   Con(x,y)=c
                else
                   Con(x,y) = NULL
                end if
             end if
          end if
          if((y!=ROOT(q))and(LABEL(x)==* or LABEL(y.parent)==LABEL(x)))
             Con*(x,y)=COMPUTE-CONDITION*(x,y)
          end if
       end for
    end for
    if(Con(ROOT(p),ROOT(q))=base-condition(p))
       return true
    else return false
    end if
End
```

```
Function: COMPUTE-CONDITION*(x,y)
Input: node x of tree pattern p, non-root node y of tree pattern q
Output: Con*(x,y)
Begin
   if(x is a leaf node)
      return null
   else
      condition c
      for each descendant node x' of x and Con(x',y)!=NULL
         int k=number of child edges between x and x'
         c=c∨(Con(x',y)∧(Σedge-length(n_i)=edge-length(y) - [k,k]))
      end for
      return c
   end if
End
```

3.4 Checking Containment with Conditioned Homomorphism

From Definition 1 in Section 3.2, containment of two tree patterns can be checked by conditioned homomorphism. Algorithm 2 checks containment of two tree patterns p and q. Line 1 reduces tree pattern q to adorned tree pattern q' following a bottom up manner, which runs in time O (q). Then it calls function FIND-CONDITIONED-HOMOMORPHISM to check containment between p and q'. In Algorithm 1, each pair of (x, y) should be computed once for *Con* (x, y) and Con^* (x, y). When computing *Con* (x, y), each child node y' of y is retrieved for Con^* (x, y'), the number of child nodes is less than $|q|$. In computing Con^* (x, y), each descendant node x' of x is retrieved for *Con* (x', y), the number of descendant nodes is less than $|p|$. Then checking containment with conditioned homomorphism runs in time O ($|p|^2 \times |q| + |p| \times |q|^2$). Algorithm 2 is sound and efficient. It can check containment for tree patterns in frequently used cases where prior homomorphism algorithm may return false negatives.

Algorithm 2. Checking containment $p \subseteq q$

```
Function: CHECK-CONTAINMENT
Input: tree pattern p and q
Output: boolean value indicating whether p⊆q holds
Begin
    Apply the rewrite rules in (2) to q repeatedly, reducing it to q′
    return FIND-CONDITIONED-HOMOMORPHISM(p, q′)
End
```

4 Hidden Conditioned Homomorphism Technique

There are special cases in which conditioned homomorphism may return false negatives. To solve this problem, conditioned homomorphism is extended to *hidden conditioned homomorphism* which generates a more complete containment algorithm than the one proposed in previous section with the same complexity.

4.1 Special Case Study

Fig. 5(a) shows that conditioned homomorphism still fails in some cases. Since *node2* in tree pattern *q* has two child nodes, it will not be eliminated when apply the rewriting rules of (2) on *q*. Tree pattern *q* can be only embedded into tree pattern *p* under condition *edge-length* (*node2*) = [0, 0]. But, if the descendant edge of *p* is stretched, as illustrated in Fig. 5(b), *sub-tree* (*node2*) of tree pattern *q* can be embedded into any sub-tree pattern rooted at the node on the stretched path of *p*, including, of course, the sub-tree pattern rooted at the child node of *node1* in *p*. Thus, in fact, $p \subseteq q$ holds.

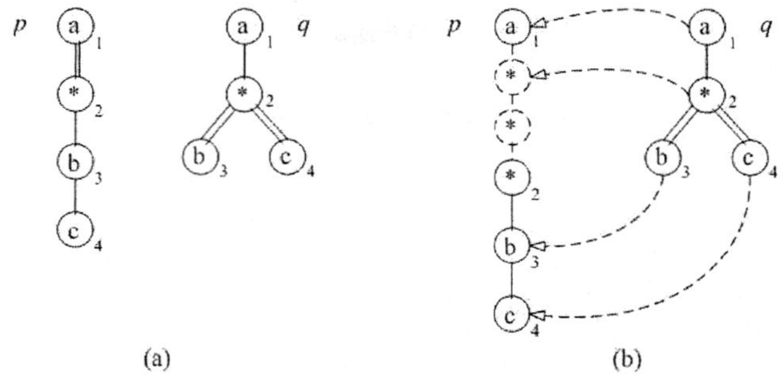

Fig. 5. (a) Two tree patterns *p* and *q*, $p \subseteq q$, but conditioned homomorphism fails to check containment; (b) Embedding from *q* to *q* after stretch the descendant nodes of *p*

4.2 Hidden Conditioned Homomorphism

For a tree pattern p, let p^k be the tree pattern constructed by adding a * node as new root node and a child edge connecting the * node and the root node of tree pattern p^{k-1}, and $p^0=p$. Let $\Gamma(p)$ be the set of tree patterns:

$$\Gamma(p) = \{p^k \mid k=0, 1, 2..., \infty\} \tag{3}$$

Hence, in the example of Fig. 5(a) where $p \subseteq q$ holds but conditioned homomorphism not exists, there is homomorphism from *sub-tree* (*node2*) of pattern q to pattern in Γ (*sub-tree* (*node2*)) of pattern p.

Theorem 3. Let p be a tree pattern and q be an adorned tree pattern, and there exists conditioned homomorphism from q to p under condition c. If LABEL (ROOT(q)) = *, and all edges connecting ROOT(q) and its child nodes are descendant edges, then there also exists conditioned homomorphism from q to each pattern in $\Gamma(p)$ under condition c.

Definition 2. Let p be a tree pattern and q be an adorned tree pattern, and there exists conditioned homomorphism from q to patterns in $\Gamma(p)$ under condition c, and let tree patterns $p' = x//p$, $q' = y/q$, LABEL (x)=* or LABEL (x) = LABEL (y), then there exists a hidden conditioned homomorphism from q' to p' under condition c.

It can be observed that, there is no explicit conditioned homomorphism from q' to p'. In Fig. 5(b), *node2* of tree pattern q is mapped to nodes hidden in the descendant edge of tree pattern p. That is why it is called hidden conditioned homomorphism.

4.3 Checking Containment with Hidden Conditioned Homomorphism

According to Theorem 3 and Definition 2, it is easy to determine the existence of a hidden conditioned homomorphism. To incorporate hidden conditioned homomorphism into the containment checking process, it is only needed to replace the line 7 of the function COMPUTE-COMDITION* proposed in previous section with lines as follows:

```
if(EDGE(y)∈C-EDGES(q) and EDGE(x)∈D-EDGES(p) and (EDGE(y′)∈D-EDGES(q) for all child nodes y′of y))
    c=c∨Con(x′,y)
else
    c=c∨(Con(x′,y)∧(Σedge-length(n_i)=edge-length(y) - [k,k]))
end if
```

Obviously, the modified algorithm for checking containment still runs in time $O(|p|^2 \times |q| + |p| \times |q|^2)$, and is more complete than the one proposed in Section 3.

5 Experimental Results

Four algorithms have been implemented: canonical model (CM for short), homomorphism (HO), conditioned homomorphism (CH) and hidden conditioned homomorphism (HCH). CM and HO are both derived from [12].

Table 1. Some of the pairs of boolean tree patterns for experiments and containment results

No.	*p*	*q*	HO	CM	CH	HCH
no.1	a//b[c]//d	a//*[.//c]//d	True	True	True	True
no.2	a/b[c]/e/c	a/*/*/c	True	True	True	True
no.3	a//b[*//c]/b[b/c]//c	a//b[*//c]b/c	True	True	True	True
no.4	a//b[c/*//d]/b[c//d]/b/c/d	a//b[c/*//d]/b/c/d	False	True	True	True
no.5	a//*/b/c	a/*[.//c]//b	False	True	False	True
no.6	a//*/b//b/c	a/*/*/*/c	False	False	False	False
no.7	a/b[.//c]//d	a//b[c]/d	False	False	False	False

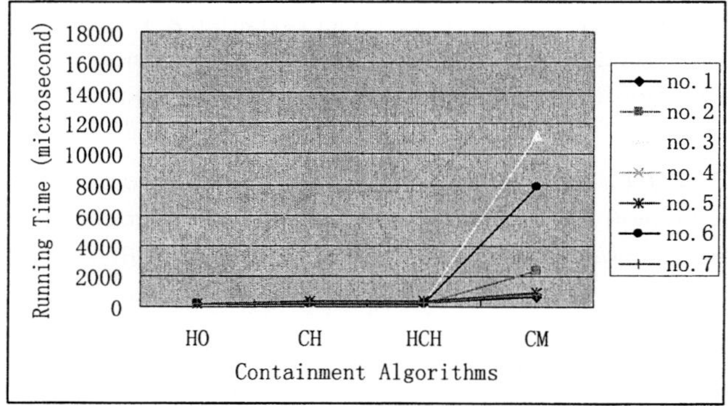

Fig. 6. Experimental results for query containment

The inputs of all algorithms are boolean tree patterns, not XPath expressions. Some of the most representative test cases are given in Table 1, where boolean tree patterns are represented using XPath syntax. Intuitively, the structure and size of tree patterns inputted for containment checking have great effect on the running time of the algorithms. The test cases in Table 1 demonstrate these variations. The size of tree pattern ranges from 4 to 11, which is reasonable for frequently used queries, and the fragment of tree patterns are in $XP^{\{[\,],*\}}$, $XP^{\{[\,],//\}}$, $XP^{\{*,//\}}$ and $XP^{\{[\,],*,//\}}$.

In the first five test cases, *p* is contained in *q*, and in the last two cases, *p* is not contained in *q*. The containment results of algorithms are shown in Table 1. Algorithm HO and CH returned false negatives in some cases, but HCH and CM didn't. Running time of the algorithms on test cases is illustrated in Fig. 6, where Y-axis represents running time in microseconds. Obviously, HCH is always more efficient than CM.

6 Conclusion

This paper investigates the checking of containment for an important core fragment of XPath. Many XML applications could benefit from a practical and efficient algorithm for checking containment of such expressions. Two techniques - conditioned homomorphism and hidden conditioned homomorphism are provided for the checking of containment. The experiment shows that these techniques are more complete than homomorphism technique, and the derived algorithms are more efficient than that of canonical model technique.

References

[1] Sihem Amer-Yahia, SungRan Cho, Laks V. S. Lakshmanan, Divesh Srivastava. *Minimization of tree pattern queries.* In Proc of the 2001 ACM SIGMOD Conf. on Management of Data, 2001.

[2] Sihem Amer-Yahia, SungRan Cho, Laks V. S. Laksshmanan, and Divesh Srivastava. *Tree pattern query minimization.* The VLDB Journal, 11(4):315-331, 2002.

[3] Michael Benedikt, Wenfei Fan, and Gabriel M. Kuper. *Structural properties of XPath fragments.* In ICDT 2003.

[4] Scott Boag, Don Chamberlin, Mary F. Fernández, Daniela Florescu, Jonathan Robie, Jérôme Siméon. *XQuery 1.0: An XML Query Language.* http://www.w3.org/TR/xquery. W3C Working draft.

[5] P. Buneman, S. Davidson, W. Fan, C. Hara, and W. Tan. *Reasoning about keys for xml.* 2000.

[6] D. Calvanese, G. DeGiacomo, and M. Vadi. *Decidable containment of recursive queries.* In Proc. Database Theory – ICDT '03, 9th International Conference, pages 330-345, 2003.

[7] A. Chandra and P. Merlin. *Optimal implementation of conjunctive queries in relational data bases.* In Proceedings of 9th ACM Symposium on Theory of Computing, pages 77-90, 1977.

[8] James Clark. *XSL Transformations (XSLT).* http://www.w3.org/TR/xslt. W3C Working draft.

[9] James Clark, Steve DeRose. *XML Path Language (XPath) Version 1.0.* http:/ www.w3.org/TR/xpath. W3C Working draft.

[10] Steven DeRose, Eve Maler, David Orchard. *XML Linking Language (XLink) Version 1.0.* http://www.w3.org/TR/xpath. W3C Working draft.

[11] Steven DeRose, Ron Daniel Jr., Paul Grosso, Eve Maler, Jonathan Marsh, Norman Walsh. *XML Pointer Language (XPointer).* http://www.w3.org/TR/xptr. W3C Working draft.

[12] G. Miklau and D. Suciu. *Containment and equivalence for a fragment of XPath.* Journal of the ACM, 51(1):2-45, 2004.

[13] T. Milo and D. Suciu. *Index structures for path expressions.* In ICDT, pages 277-295, 1999.

[14] Frank Neven. *Automata Theory for XML researchers.* SIGMOD Record, 31(3):39-46, 2002.

[15] F. Neven and T. schwentick. *XPath containment in the presence of disjunction, DTDs, and variables.* In Proc. 9th Int. Conf. on Database Theory (ICDT), Siena, pages 315-329, 2003.

[16] Thomas Schwentick. *XPath query containment.* ACM SIGMOD Database priciples Column, 2004.

[17] O. Shmueli. *Equivalence of datalog queries is undecidable.* The Journal of Logic Programming, 15(3):231-242, 1993.

[18] P. T. Wood. *Containment for XPath fragments under DTD constraints.* In Proc. Database Theory – ICDT'03, 9th International Conference, pages 300-314, 2003.

[19] P. T. Wood. *Minimizing simple xpath expressions.* Fourth International Workshop on the Web and Databases (WebDB'2001), 2001.

[20] P. T. Wood. *On the equivalence of xml patterns.* International Conference on Deductive and Object-Oriented Databases (DOOD), pages 1152-1166, 2000.

Efficient Query Processing for Streamed XML Fragments

Huan Huo, Guoren Wang, Xiaoyun Hui, Rui Zhou,
Bo Ning, and Chuan Xiao

Institute of Computer System, Northeastern University, Shenyang, China
wanggr@mail.neu.edu.cn

Abstract. Unlike in traditional databases, queries on XML streams are bounded not only by memory but also by real time processing. Recently proposed Hole-Filler model is promising for information transmission and publication, by slicing XML data into low consuming, easy synchronized fragments. However, XPath queries evaluate the elements in streamed XML data, not the XML fragments, and operation dependence caused by fragments decelerates processing efficiency. By taking advantage of schema information for XML, this paper proposes a model of tid tree to optimize queries over XML fragments by removing "redundant" operations. It then proposes XFPro for processing XPath queries on XML fragments to achieve processing and memory efficiency. Our performance study shows that XFPro performs well both on execution time and memory metrics.

1 Introduction

XML [1]is emerging as a *de facto* standard for information representation and data exchange over the web. As semi-structural data, XML can be represented as a tree-structural model with data contents and structural relationships among them. Evaluating XML queries, such as XPath [2] and XQuery [3], is thus widely studied in database management systems. Figure 1 gives an XML document and its DOM tree, which acts as an example of our work.

However, being inherently hierarchical, stored XML data poses an overwhelming overhead on runtime factors, which is not suitable for stream processing. In stream model, data arrives in continuous streams and has to be analyzed in real-time by one pass. Hence, queries on XML streams are bounded not only by memory but also by real time processing. Many applications, such as network intrusion detection, sensor network monitoring, business transactions and earth climate monitoring, involve analysis of streaming data.

Recently, many research work focus on answering queries on streamed XML data, such as XFrag [4], XStreamCast [5] and etc. In XFrag framework, large XML documents are fragmented into manageable chunks of information and XQueries are processed on steamed XML fragments in a pipelined model, without having to wait for the entire XML document to be received and materialized. In [5], a query algebra for XQuery that operates on fragmented XML stream data is presented. All these framework are built on streamed XML fragment model.

M.L. Lee, K.L. Tan, and V. Wuwongse (Eds.): DASFAA 2006, LNCS 3882, pp. 468–482, 2006.

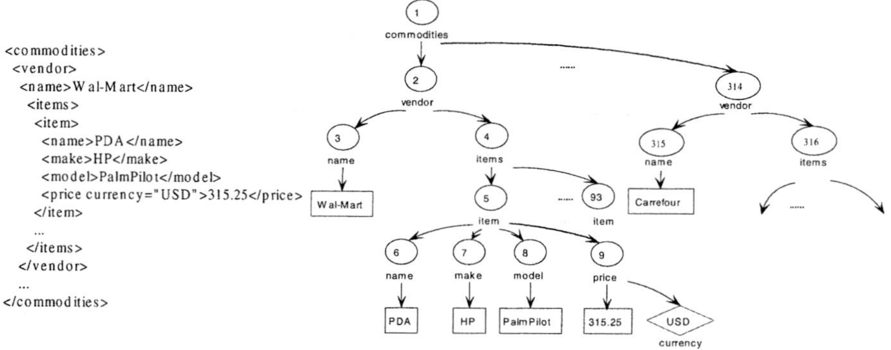

Fig. 1. An XML Document and its DOM Tree

In order to correlate each XML fragments, *Hole-Filler* model is proposed in [6]. In the model, a hole represents a placeholder into which another rooted subtree (a fragment), called a filler, could be positioned to complete the tree. In this way, infinite XML streams turn out to be a sequence of XML fragments, and queries on parts of XML data require less memory and processing time. Furthermore, changes to XML data may pose less overhead by sending only fragments corresponding to the changes, instead of sending the entire document.

Unfortunately, processing XML fragments instead of whole XML document is fraught with challenges. It has to maintain the context of the fragments for us to navigate from fragment to fragment and to cache the fragments related to the query answer when necessary. Since not all the fragments can be available at the same time and the fragments may arrive in any order, reducing the processing cost is the key for queries on XML fragments.

In XFrag, XML fragments are processed as and when they arrive and only those messages that may effect on the query results are kept in the association table. However, the XFrag pipeline is still space consuming in maintaining the links in the association tables and time consuming in scheduling the operations for each fragment. Furthermore, since fragments are forwarded through operators on the pipeline, XFrag has to check the fragments' head information on each operator, which decelerates the processing efficiency. And it can not avoid "redundant" operations when dependence occurs between adjacent operators.

This paper presents a new framework and a set of techniques for processing XPath queries over streamed XML fragment. As compared to the existing work on supporting XPath/XQuery over streamed XML fragment, we make the following contributions: (i)we present techniques for enabling the transformation from XPath expression to optimized query plan. We model the query expressions using *tid tree* and apply a series of transformations, which enable further analysis and optimizations on query operations. Furthermore, such transformations reduce the query workload by specifying query operations such as "//" and "*". (ii)based on tid tree, we present a pruning scheme to cut off redundant operations after query rewriting. In this way, we save the memory space and processing power. (iii)based on optimized tid tree, we propose query plan transformation techniques, which map a tid tree directly into an XML fragment query processor, named XFPro, and generate an efficient query execution plan. Note that, we assume the query clients cannot reconstruct the entire XML data before processing the queries.

The rest of this paper is organized as follows. Section 2 presents the related work in the area of XML stream query processing. Section 3 introduces *Hole-Filler* model as the base for our XML fragments. Section 4 gives a detailed statement of our XML fragment processing framework. Section 5 shows experimental results from our implementation and shows the processing efficiency of our framework. Our conclusions are contained in Section 6.

2 Related Work

Many recent projects relate to query processing on streamed XML, such as NiagaraCQ [7], XRQL [8] and FluXQuery [9]. The BEA/XQRL processor [8] supports pipelined processing of streams by implementing the iterator model at the expression level. However, query optimizations specially designed for XML streams are limited in this system, and large documents cannot be processed. Transducer networks [10] have also been used to handle a subset of XQuery for streaming XML data. In Flux [9], XQuery is translated into event-based intermediate representation (IR) and the buffer size is optimized by analyzing the DTD as well as the query syntax.

Instead of evaluating infinite XML stream by token, several recent efforts have focused on continuous processing of fragmented XML. The hole-filler model was first proposed in [11]. However, it is used in the context of pull-based content navigation over mediated views of XML data from disparate data sources. In Xstream [12], the advantages of a semantics-based fragmentation of XML data for efficient transmission over a wireless medium are highlighted. An alternative fragmented XML processing model, suitable for pull-based web-service applications, is presented in Active XML [13].

In XstreamCast [5], XML fragments are broadcasted to clients in a push-based streaming model and continuous query is processed in a historical timeline. In comparison, we present systematic and powerful techniques for optimizing and transforming queries that are not specifically written for fragment processing. As we stated earlier, our additional contribution is specifying query expressions and pruning "redundant" operations in them.

3 Model for Streamed Fragmented XML Data

In our approach, we adopt the hole-filler model [6] to describe XML fragments, which hold both the data contents and structural relationships. In order to simplify representation for further processing, a coding scheme is proposed to compress such information.

3.1 Preliminary Hole-Filler Model

We assume that a single document D is a node labelled acyclic tree with the set V of infinite nodes and the set E of finite edges. XML stream begins with finite XML documents and runs on as and when new elements are added into the document or updates occur upon the existing elements. The following definitions introduce some fundamental notions used in the rest of the paper.

Definition 1. *An XML document D is a tree $T_d = (V_d, E_d, \Sigma_d, root_d, oid)$, where V_d is an infinite set of nodes, including element nodes, attribute nodes and text nodes; E_d is a finite set of directed edges, indicating parent-child relationship between element nodes or containment relationship between element nodes and attribute nodes; each node has a type and is identified by oid, Σ_d is the set of node types; $root_d$ ($\in V_d$) is the root element of D.*

Definition 2. *A filler F is a subtree of XML document $T_f = (V_f, E_f, \Sigma_f, root_f, fid, head_f, H_d)$, where V_f is the subset of V_d, E_f is the subset of E_d and Σ_f is the subset of Σ_d; each filler is identified by fid, which is included in $head_f$; H_d is a finite set of holes; $root_f$ ($\in V_f$)is the root element of the subtree.*

Definition 3. *A hole H is an empty node $n(n \in H_d)$ assigned with unique hid, into which a filler with the same fid value could be positioned to complete the tree.*

Given an XML document tree, we can fragment it by recursively inserting a hole at every point where a subtree is pruned, i.e. a filler is generated, and associating it with an ID(the *fid* of the filler fragment). Note that the filler can in turn have holes in it, which will be filled by other fillers. And we can reconstruct the original XML document by substituting holes with the corresponding fillers at the destination as it was in the source. However, reconstructing the entire XML tree is not a good idea since the query has to wait for the end of the stream to begin processing, which is not accommodated for infinite streamed XML fragments. As will be discussed in the next section, our approach is to process XML fragments as and when they become available in streamed model.

Definition 4. *Tag structure is a fragment of XML document with the highest priority $TS = (V_t, E_t, root_t, ID_t, Did)$, where V_t is an infinite set of tag nodes in XML document; E_t is a finite set of edges; ID_t is a set of number identifying the tag nodes in XML document; Did is the XML document identifier.*

Tag structure is a structure summary for XML fragments. It provides structural information for XML and captures all the valid paths [6]. In the hole-filler model, tag structure not only provides the relationships between each element nodes, but also involves fragmentation information of the XML data. It can be generated according to XML Schema or DTD, and also can be obtained when fragmenting an XML document without DTD.

3.2 Encoding Scheme

The DTD and tag structure of the XML document (given in Figure 1) in Section 1 are depicted in Figure 2.

Here, we encode the *tag* attribute "ID" and "Filler" together as a tag code. For "$Filler = true$", we set the end of the tag code with "1", otherwise we set it with "0". And for attribute "ID", we separate it from the "Filler" code by a point. The tag code for tag "vendor" in the previous example is 2.1, while the tag code for tag "items" is 4.0. In this way, we can obtain the fragmentation information by checking the end of the tag code.

Figure 3 gives two fragments of the XML document in Figure 1. Here, we number the root filler (i.e. the root of the fragmented document) with fid 0. And other filler IDs can be generated by pre-order traversing XML document tree at the server site. Attribute $tsid$ [4](i.e. tag structure id) indicates the ID of the fragment's root element in XML document DTD.

We associate fillers with holes by matching filler IDs with hole IDs. Fragment 2's fid corresponds to a Fragment 1's hid, which means Fragment 2 fills the corresponding hole in Fragment 1 as a subtree when reconstructing the XML document.

It is obvious that the contents in Fragment 1 remain relative stable to Fragment 2, i.e. texts (or elements) in Fragment 2 (such as "price") may be updated more frequently. We can save transmission cost by sending Fragment 2

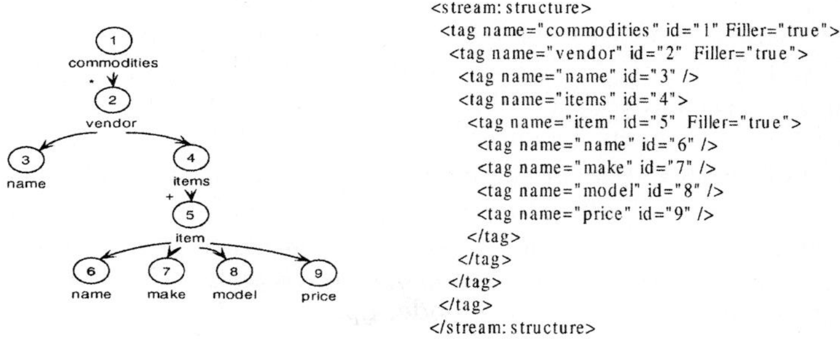

Fig. 2. Tag Structure of Hole-Filler Model

```
Fragment 1:
<commodities filler id="0" tsid="1">
  <vendor>
    <name>Wal-Mart</name>
     <items>
       <stream: hole id="10" />
       <stream: hole id="20" />
       ...
  </vendor>
  ....
</commodities>
```

```
Fragment 2:
<stream: filler id="10" tsid="5">
  <item>
    <name>PDA</name>
    <make>HP</make>
    <model>PalmPilot</model>
    <price currency="USD">315.25</price>
  </item>
</stream: filler>
```

Fig. 3. XML document Fragments

rather than the whole XML document. Furthermore, we can cut "price" as a single fragment to save update transmission cost. This will lead to higher cost in querying item/price, for the elements now are in two different fragments. There is a trade-off between transmission cost and query cost. In this paper, we assume that XML documents have been fragmented already. What we focus on is query execution on XML streaming fragments at client site. Fragmenting algorithm is stated in [14] and omitted here.

4 XFPro Query Handling

Based on hole-filler model, infinite XML streams turn out to be a sequence of XML fragments, which become the basic processing units of the query. However, input queries evaluate the elements in the XML document, not the XML fragments. Since fragments with the same tag code share the same structure, we can skip evaluating the structural relationship inside the fragments and expedite processing time by rewriting the queries for XML fragments.

This section focuses on the analysis and optimization we perform for queries on fragments. Our goal is to correctly rewrite the query so that it can be processed directly on fragments, and to prune off the redundant path evaluations. Initially, we give an overview of our framework.

4.1 Overview

In this paper, we consider the class of XPath queries that are formed using only the following axes: child, attribute, or descendant axes, denoted as forward XPath. The following query, referred to as *Query 1*, is an example on the XML document described in Section 1.

```
Query 1: /commodities/vendor/items/item[name=''PDA'']/price
```

The analysis we perform in this paper is based on the following key observations on queries over streamed XML fragments. In a path expression consisting of predecessor node and successor node, operation dependence (see definition 6)occurs if the following conditions hold true:

- The query result to predecessor node and successor node are in the same fragment, or
- Any fragment matching the predecessor node also matches the successor nodes.

The first condition is straightforward. Let us consider the second condition. When the query nodes involve predicates, the result set of the successor query must be a subset of that of the predecessor query. When the query nodes have no predicates, the first condition holds true, which means that the query result only depends on the predecessor node. Queries that satisfy this propriety are referred to as subsumption dependence [15], which in most cases can be made subsumption-free by removing the successor nodes.

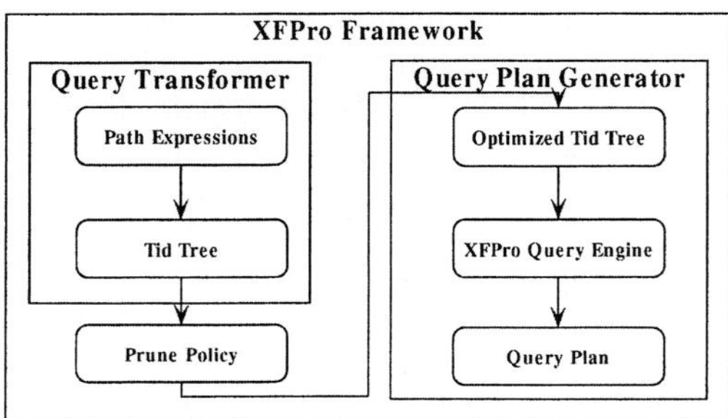

Fig. 4. Overview of the Framework

Take *Query 1* for example. According to the fragmentation information indicated in tag structure, "commodities", "vendor" and "item" are root nodes of the fillers while "items", "price" and"name" are not. Considering that a "vendor" fragment with tsid 5, filler id 7 and hole ids from 10 to 100, arrives and is evaluated against the path expression from query node "commodities", since query nodes "items" and "vendor" belong to a common fragment according to the fragmentation information in tag structure, fragments that match "vendor" obviously match "items"(without considering predicates). And such fragments need not to be evaluated for structural relationship between "vendor" and "items".

Much of our analysis bases on such query operation dependencies. Figure 4 shows the key phases in our XFPro system. First, we construct the tid tree from query expression and tag structure. Then, according to tag structure, we apply a series of policies to prune and optimize the tid tree. Such techniques not only rewrite some queries to avoid redundant operations, but most importantly, they save the memory space and processing power. After optimization, we transform the tid tree into query processor, and efficient query execution plan is generated.

4.2 Tid Tree

We introduce tid tree to represent the query expression and enable further analysis and optimizations on query operations.

Definition 5. *Let N be the set of query nodes in a query Q. Tid tree is a tree* $TT = (T_t, E_t, root_t, P_t, O_t)$, *where* T_t *is the set of corresponding tag codes of the nodes in set N;* E_t *is a set of edges describing the structural relationship between two nodes;* P_t *is a text set of the predicate values;* O_t *is an operator set including boolean connectors;* $root_t$ $(\in V_t)$ *is the root element of the tree.*

We introduce *subroot* node denoted as the root of a filler, and *subelement* node that locates in a filler but is not the root of the subtree. By taking advantage of tag codes, we can easily tell subroot nodes from subelement nodes by checking the end of the code.

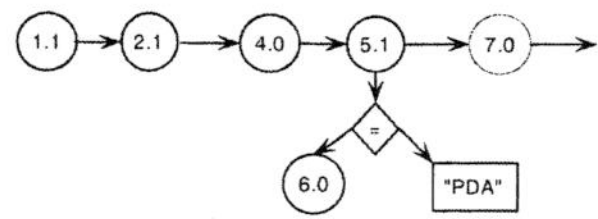

Fig. 5. Tid Tree of Query 1

And parent-child relationship between nodes is represented by a single arrow, while ancestor-descendant relationship between nodes is represented by a double arrow. In the case that the descendant node corresponds to multiple tag codes, we duplicate the descendant node and assign different tag codes to them (see Section 4.3 for details). The output of the query is depicted by an arrow.

In order to distinguish between the node that represents a tag code and the node that represents an atomic predicate, we represent tag nodes with circles and values of predicates with rectangles. The operators (such as $<$, $>$, $\geq$, $\leq$, $=$) and boolean connectors are represented with diamonds. The tid tree for the *Query 1* described in the previous section is shown in Figure 5. 1.1 is the tag code of "commodities" and similarly, 2.1, 4.0, 5.1, 6.0 and 7.0 are the tag codes of "vendor", "items", "item", "price" and "name". Here, "=" and "PDA" are treated as operator node and predicate node respectively in the tid tree.

4.3 Optimizing Tid Tree

In XFrag [4], each query primitive corresponds to an XFrag operator, which processes the fragment only if the tsid of the fragment matches that of the operator. In the case that they do not match, the fragment is simply passed on to the subsequent operator in the query tree.

However, in the case of operator dependence (as illustrated in Section 4.1), the fragments that do not match the predecessor operator need not to be evaluated against the successive one.

Definition 6. *Given any pair of nodes in tid tree n_1,n_2, if the query result of n_2 is valid only if that of n_1 is valid, n_2 is considered dependent on n_1. We use directed edge $e = (n_1, n_2)$ to imply the dependence between n_1 and n_2.*

Definition 7. *Given any pair of nodes in tid tree n_1,n_2, n_2 is subsumption dependent on n_1 if: (i) n_2 is dependent on n_1, and (ii) the query result of n_2 is a subset of the query result of n_1.*

Subsumption-free queries are intuitively queries that do not contain "redundancies". Some queries can be rewritten to be subsumption-free, by eliminating redundant portions. Much of our analysis focuses on finding such dependencies on tsid nodes, to eliminate "redundant" query evaluations on structural relationship. In pruning process, we use dashed arrows to represent subsumption dependencies, and solid arrows for subsumption-free dependencies.

Path Pattern Query. Path pattern query is the simplest type of queries. Meanwhile it is the base of tree pattern query. Firstly, we assume that the query does not contain "//" and "*". This class of query covers most of the structural relationship "redundancies". For example, *Query 2* is a simple path pattern query with only "/" involved.

```
Query 2: /commodities/vendor/items/item/name
```

The original query involves three fragments with tsid 1, tsid 2 and tsid 5 and the tid tree includes five steps with tsid 1, tsid 2, tsid 4, tsid 5 and tsid 6. However, since fragments that don't match tsid 2 obviously don't match tsid 4, i.e. tsid 4 subsumption depends on tsid 2.

We can rewrite the query to avoid such redundant operations by deleting subelement nodes which have no predicates and are not the leaf nodes in tid tree. According to tag code, subroot nodes ended with "1" are kept in the tid tree while subelement nodes ended with "0" and without predicate node in their children are removed. Since tsid 6 is a subelement node with predicate and tsid 7 is the leaf node in tid tree, they are kept in the tree. Figure 6 shows the optimized tid tree after pruning off the dependent node 4.0 (depicted by "X").

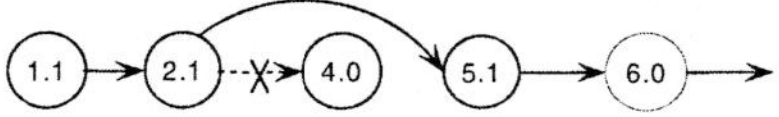

Fig. 6. The Pruned Tid Tree after removing Subsumption Dependence of Query 2

However, pruning path pattern query may lead to incorrect results, when "//" and "*" are considered. This is because the ancestor node A before "//" and the descendant node D after "//" may belong to different fragments. Hence the fragment matches A may not match D. Similarly, "*" may not match in the same filler and we cannot determine subsumption dependence directly.

In such cases, we need to rewrite the tid tree into "//" or "*" excluded form. Taking "//" for consideration, we first capture all the paths from A to D when traversing the tag structure. Then we insert the tag codes of corresponding subroot nodes of D into tid tree and link them with A according to the path. In this way, "//" is replaced by "/" and the query result is the merge set of each output node in tid tree. Now we can apply the pruning scheme for "/" to the rewritten tid tree. Figure 7 presents the tid tree of *Query 3*, which returns the descendants "name" of "vendor".

```
Query 3: /commodities/vendor//name
```

In Figure 7 (a), tsids of "name" are 3.0 and 6.0 and represented in two descendant nodes of "vendor", with tsid 2.1. In Figure 7 (b), the ancestor-descendant relationship between "vendor" and "name" is substituted by parent-child relationship and all kinds of the fragments involved in this query are indicated.

Pruning path pattern query with "*" involved takes the similar scheme. Since path pattern query is the base of tree pattern query, pruning scheme for path pattern query can be applied to all kinds of the XPath expressions.

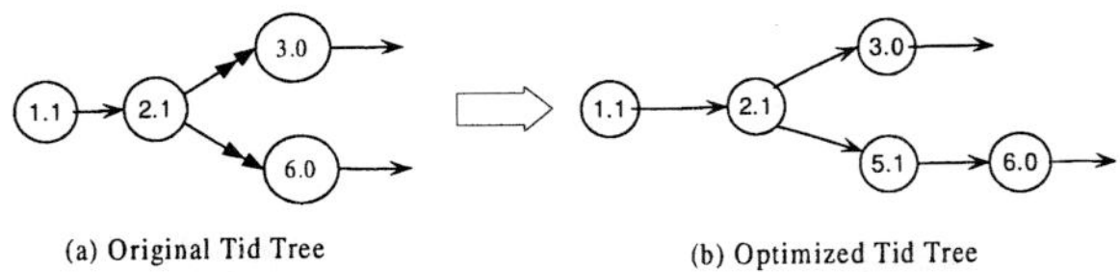

Fig. 7. Tid Tree of Query 3

Twig Pattern Query. Typically, a twig pattern query is a linear path pattern query if predicates are eliminated. This linear path expression is called main path expression, while other expressions inside predicates are called predicate path expressions. Since we have discussed the pruning scheme for main path expression, only the structural relationship between testing node and predicate node is considered here.

There are two cases in twig pattern query, as depicted in Figure 8. One is the case that the predicate expression and the testing node are in a common filler, while the other case is not.

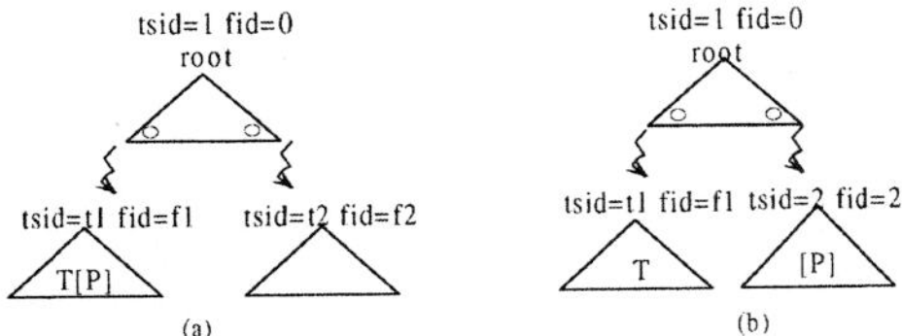

Fig. 8. Two Cases in Twig Pattern Query

In (a), the testing node T and predicate P share the same filler id. We prune P only when it is a path expression but not value testing expression. This is because the fragments with the same tsid share the same structure.

In (b), the testing node T and predicate P belong to different fragments. We cannot prune P directly. However, after rewriting the tid tree by inserting the subroot node of P, we can prune P when it is only a path expression but not value testing expression.

4.4 Query Plan Generation

As described in the previous section, we rewrite original query into tid tree. However, the tid tree only represents a view of relationships between tsid nodes and predicates, while the details of query processing are not modelled. This section focuses on the transformation from tid tree to the corresponding query plan and gives a processing example of XFPro.

The transformation from tid tree of *Query 1* into the XFPro processor is depicted in Figure 9. Each subroot node in tid tree corresponds to an entry of hash table, which is tagged by a value of true, false, undecided ($\perp$). And each subelement node is added in a bucket tagged by an odd value linked to the

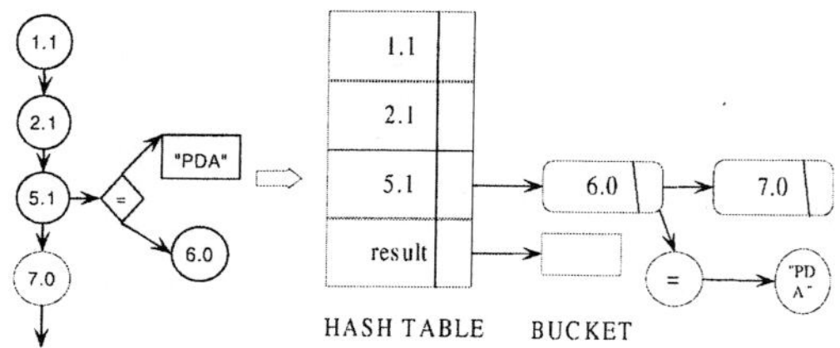

Fig. 9. Transformation from Tid Tree to XFPro

corresponding entry of the subroot node, while each predicate node is added in a bucket tagged by an even value linked to the corresponding entry. There is a result entry at the end of the hash table, which has a linked bucket to cache the candidate output. It conjuncts all the entries' value and is set true only if all the predecessor entries are set true.

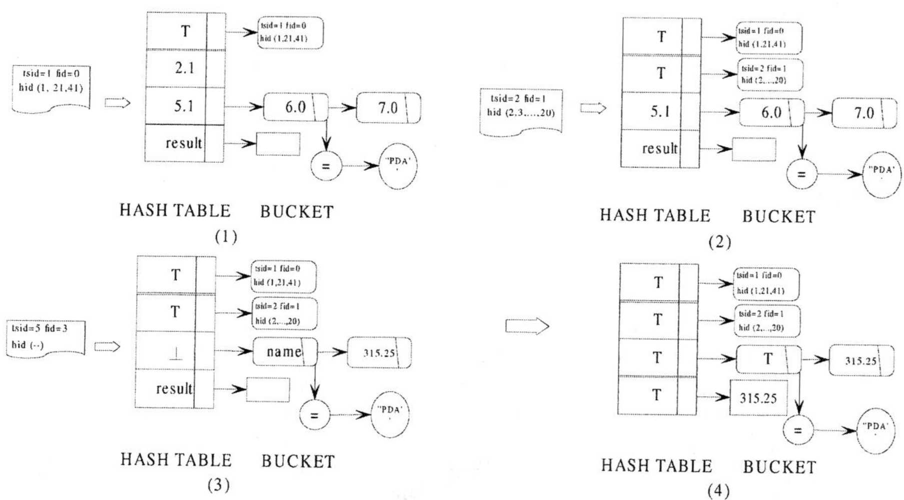

Fig. 10. XFPro Processing Example

The XFPro processing for *Query 1* is depicted in Figure 10. When the "commodities" fragment with tsid "1", filler id "0" and hole ids "1, 21, 41" arrives, the query hash table set the entry 1 with T and the information is saved in the bucket linked to the entry. More over, the fragment with tsid "1" is tagged with an undecided value when it has predicate and the condition has not been evaluated for this fragment. Note that, at the point, the "commodities" filler can be discarded as it is no more needed to produce the result and the hole filler association is already captured. This results in memory conservation on the fly. Similarly, when the "vendor" fragment with the corresponding tsid "2" arrives, the entry 2 saves the information into the bucket and is set T, as there is no condition for it. When the "item" fragment with tsid "5", filler id "3" arrives, the entry 5 is set '⊥', since it has predicate bucket. After determining that the information in filler "3" matches the predicate, it sets the entry T. The "item" fragment may also be discarded at the point conserving memory, for the result value, which is a subset of the fragment, is already captured in the linked bucket. Since all the entries in the hash table are set "true", the value of price is output as the result. The algorithms listed below describe the processing method.

```
Algorithm1 FindQueryChild()
 {Input an element node and trigger descendant operators}
  IF (isHashTerminalNode(element)) THEN output element;
   ELSE
    q <- HashBucketFirstnode(QueryNextnode(element));
    WHILE(q!=null)DO
     IF (q.fid==elemnet.fid)
      THEN  q.val=element.val; FindQueryChild(q); q=q.next;
      ELSE
       FOR(p=element.hid;p!=null&&p.hid!=q.fid;p=p.next);
         IF (p.hid==q.fid)
          THEN q.val= element.val; FindQueryChild(q);q = q.next;
         END IF END FOR
     END IF
    END WHILE
  END IF
```

Algorithm 1 and 2 change the corresponding values of the hash table to schedule triggering the descendant operator and inquiring the parent operator.

```
Algorithm2 FindQueryParent()
 {Input an element node and inquire parent operator}
  IF (HashQueryFirstnode(element)) THEN element.val=TRUE;
   ELSE
    q <- HashBucketFirstnode(QueryPrenode(element));
    WHILE(q!=null)DO
      FOR ( ; q!= null;q = q.next )
       IF (q.fid==element.fid) THEN element.val = q.val;
        ELSE
         FOR (phid=q.hid; phid!= null; phid = phid.next);
          IF(p.hid==element.fid) THEN element.val = q.value;
          END IF  END FOR
       END IF  END FOR
    END WHILE
    element.val=UNDECIDED;
  END IF
```

5 Performance Evaluation

We have implemented the XFPro translator engine in Java, which rewrites XPath expressions into tid-tree based query plans for XML fragments. Our XFPro query engine on fragmented XML streams processes the optimized queries directly on the filler fragments before reconstructing the entire XML document.

All experiments are run on a PC with 2.6GHz CPU, 512M of memory and 80G hard disk. The operating system is WindowsXP. The experiments are run on data sets generated by the xmlgen program. We have written an XML fragmenter that fragments an XML document into filler fragments to produce an XML stream, based on the tag structure defining the fragmentation layout.

We have selected three representative queries (Q_1,Q_2 and Q_3) on the generated XML documents and compared the results with the XFrag Processor [4].

```
Query1:doc("book.xml")/book/sections/section/subsection/title
Query2:doc("book.xml")/book/section[difficulty>="default"]/title
Query3:doc("book.xml")/book/title/section[difficulty>="default"]
```

To illustrate the differences in the query execution methods on the filler fragments, consider the *Query 1* that returns the subsection title of the books. Since "section", "subsection" and "title" are in common filler fragments, according to the fragmentation information in tag structure, our query operates "subsection" and "title" over fragment only when the fragment tsid matches that of the operator. Furthermore, each fragment is only evaluated once and hashed to corresponding item if tsid matches. While in XFrag, each fragment needs to be passed on through the pipeline and evaluated step by step. In this way,

Query	*File size*	*Fragmented File Size*	*Method*	*Run time*	*memory*
Q1	10Mb	11.04Mb	XFPro	518.27ms	0.36Mb
			XFrag	1875.00ms	0.62Mb
	15Mb	17.56Mb	XFPro	1377.05ms	0.81Mb
			XFrag	3926.50ms	1.35Mb
	20Mb	23.18Mb	XFPro	2121.59ms	1.18Mb
			XFrag	5245.56ms	1.83Mb
Q2	10Mb	11.98Mb	XFPro	3015.92ms	1.87Mb
			XFrag	7329.70ms	2.13Mb
	15Mb	19.20Mb	XFPro	4585.60ms	5.39Mb
			XFrag	11444.55ms	6.95Mb
	20Mb	24.12Mb	XFPro	6727.93ms	6.78Mb
			XFrag	15259.40ms	9.83Mb
Q3	10Mb	11.78Mb	XFPro	3005.86ms	2.08Mb
			XFrag	7239.07ms	2.03Mb
	15Mb	19.38Mb	XFPro	4550.15ms	5.01Mb
			XFrag	11429.71ms	6.64Mb
	20Mb	24.33Mb	XFPro	6674.87ms	6.73Mb
			XFrag	15154.78ms	8.86Mb

Fig. 11. Experimental Results

our method performs better than XFrag. The results of the experiments are summarized in Figure 11.

From the experimental results, we observe that the XFPro method outperforms the XFrag method mainly on running time, while the memory cost of these two methods makes little difference. That is because both of the methods adopt the policy of keeping the output-related information of the fragments while hash buckets use less links than association table. For the query processing time, the XFPro method saves CPU time by avoiding subsumption operations. Furthermore, the XFrag method has to schedule the operations for each fragment, while the XFPro only changes the corresponding value of the hash table.

6 Conclusions

This paper has presented a framework and a set of techniques for processing XPath queries over streamed XML fragments. We present techniques for enabling the transformation from XPath expression to optimized query plan. Our query model of tid tree helps to transform queries on element nodes to queries on XML fragments and analyze "redundant" operations in them. Furthermore, such transformations specify query operations such as "//" and "*" and reduce the query workload. Based on optimized tid tree, we present a scheme to map a tid tree directly into an XML fragment query processor, and thus efficient query execution plan is generated. Our experiments show that our framework performs well on saving processing power and memory space.

Acknowledgments. This research was partially supported by the National Natural Science Foundation of China (Grant No. 60473074 and 60573089) and Specialized Research Fund for the Doctoral Program of Higher Education (SRFDP).

References

1. W3C Recommendation: Extensible Markup Language (XML) 1.0 (Second Edition). (2000) http://www.w3.org/TR/REC-xml.
2. W3C Working Draft: XML Path Languages (XPath), ver 2.0. (2001) Tech. Report WD-xpath20-20011220, W3C, 2001, http://www.w3.org/TR/WD-xpath20-20011220.
3. W3C working draft: XQuery 1.0: An XML Query Language. (2001) Technical Report WD-xquery-20010607, World Wide Web Consortium.
4. Bose, S., Fegaras, L.: XFrag: A query processing framework for fragmented XML data. In: Eighth International Workshop on the Web and Databases (WebDB 2005), Baltimore, Maryland (June 16–17,2005)
5. Bose, S., Fegaras, L., Levine, D., Chaluvadi, V.: A query algebra for fragmented XML stream data. In: Proceedings of the 9th International Conference on Data Base Programming Languages(DBPL 2003), Potsdan, Germany (September 6–8, 2003)
6. Fegaras, L., Levine, D., Bose, S., Chaluvadi, V.: Query processing of streamed XML data. In: Eleventh International Conference on Information and Knowledge Management (CIKM 2002), McLean, Virginia, USA (November 4–9, 2002)

7. Chen, J., J.DeWitt, D., Tian, F., Wang, Y.: NiagaraCQ: A scalable continuous query system for internet databases. In Chen, W., Naughton, J.F., Bernstein, P.A., eds.: SIGMOD Conference, Dallas, Texas, USA, ACM (2000) 379–390
8. Florescu, D., Hillery, C., Kossmann, D., Lucas, P., Riccardi, F., Westmann, T., Carey, M.J., Sundararajan, A.: The BEA/XQRL streaming xquery processor. In Freytag, J.C., Lockemann, P.C., Abiteboul, S., Carey, M.J., Selinger, P.G., Heuer, A., eds.: Proceedings of the 29th International Conference on Very Large Data Bases, Berlin, Germany (2003)
9. Koch, C., Scherzinger, S., Schweikardt, N., Stegmaier, B.: FluXQuery: An optimizing xquery processor for streaming XML data. [16] 1309–1312
10. Ludäscher, B., Mukhopadhyay, P., Papakonstantinou, Y.: A transducer-based XML query processor. In Bernstein, P.A., Ioannidis, Y.E., Ramakrishnan, R., Papadias, D., eds.: Proceedings of the 28th International Conference on Very Large Data Bases, Hong Kong SAR, China (2002) 227–238
11. Ludäscher, B., Papakonstantinou, Y., Velikhov, P.: Navigation-driven evaluation of virtual mediated views. In: Proceedings of the 7th International Conference on Extending Data Base Technology(EDBT 2000), Konstanz, Germany (March 27–31, 2000) 150–165
12. Wang, E., et al.: Efficient management of XML contents over wireless environment by Xstream. In: ACM-SAC 2004. (March, 2004) 1122–1127
13. Abiteboul, S., Benjelloun, O., Cautis, B., Manolescu, I., Milo, T., Preda, N.: Lazy evaluation for active XML. In Weikum, G., König, A.C., Deßloch, S., eds.: SIGMOD Conference, Paris, France, ACM (2004) 227–238
14. Huo, H., Hui, X., Wang, G.: Document fragmentation for XML streams based on hole-filler model. In: 2005 China National Computer Conference, Wu Han, China (October 13–15,2005)
15. Bar-Yossef, Z., Fontoura, M., Josifovski, V.: On the memory requirements of xpath evaluation over XML streams. [16]
16. Nascimento, M.A., Özsu, M.T., Kossmann, D., Miller, R.J., Blakeley, J.A., Schiefer, K.B., eds.: (e)Proceedings of the Thirtieth International Conference on Very Large Data Bases. In Nascimento, M.A., Özsu, M.T., Kossmann, D., Miller, R.J., Blakeley, J.A., Schiefer, K.B., eds.: Proceedings of the 30th International Conference on Very Large Data Bases, Toronto, Canada, Morgan Kaufmann (2004)

An Efficient Algorithm for Computing Range-Groupby Queries

Young-Koo Lee[1,*], Woong-Kee Loh[1,**], Yang-Sae Moon[2], Kyu-Young Whang[1], and Il-Yeol Song[3]

[1] Department of Computer Science & Advanced Information Technology Research Center (AITrc), Korea Advanced Institute of Science and Technology (KAIST), Daejeon, Korea
{yklee, woong, kywhang}@mozart.kaist.ac.kr

[2] Department of Computer Science, Kangwon National University, Chunchon, Kangwon, Korea
ysmoon@kangwon.ac.kr

[3] College of Information Science and Technology, Drexel University, Philadelphia, Pennsylvania, USA
song@drexel.edu

Abstract. Aggregation queries for arbitrary regions in an n-dimensional space are powerful tools for data analysis in OLAP. A GROUP BY query in OLAP is very important since it allows us to summarize various trends along with any combination of dimensions. In this paper, we extend the previous aggregation queries by including the GROUP BY clause for arbitrary regions. We call the extension *range-groupby queries* and present an efficient algorithm for processing them. A typical method of achieving fast response time for aggregation queries is using the prefix-sum array, which stores precomputed partial aggregation values. A naive method for range-groupby queries maintains a prefix-sum array for each combination of the grouping dimensions in an n-dimensional cube, which incurs enormous storage overhead. Our algorithm maintains only one prefix-sum array and still effectively processes range-groupby queries for all possible combinations of multiple grouping dimensions. Compared with the naive method, our algorithm reduces the space overhead by $O(\frac{1}{2^n})$, while accessing almost the identical number of cells.

Keywords: range-groupby queries, aggregation queries, prefix-sum arrays, data cubes.

1 Introduction

On-Line Analytical Processing (OLAP) is a database application that allows users to easily analyze a large volume of data in order to extract information necessary for decision-making [3]. The summarized trends derived from the data are

* He is currently with the School of Electronics & Information, Kyunghee University, Korea.

** Corresponding author.

M.L. Lee, K.L. Tan, and V. Wuwongse (Eds.): DASFAA 2006, LNCS 3882, pp. 483–497, 2006.

more useful for decision-making than the individual ones. Thus, OLAP queries heavily compute aggregations for summarizing data. Since computing aggregations is very expensive, the efficient aggregation algorithms are crucial for achieving good performance in OLAP systems [2, 4, 8].

OLAP is based on a multidimensional data model that employs multidimensional arrays for modeling data, and the multidimensional arrays are called *data cubes* [1, 3]. In OLAP, aggregation queries processed against arbitrary regions are frequently used as powerful tools for data analysis [2, 4, 6, 7, 9, 11]. We call the queries *range-aggregation queries.* In range-aggregation queries, *query range* are imposed in the form of arbitrary contiguous ranges for each dimension. These query ranges frequently have the numerical domains such as age, income, and time, where the order between the values can be naturally defined [2, 4, 8].

Depending on the existence of grouping dimensions, range-aggregation queries in an n-dimensional cube can be classified into two categories: those without grouping dimensions and those with grouping dimensions. We call the former *range-non-groupby queries* or *range queries* [8], and the latter *range-groupby queries.* The range queries compute a single aggregation value from all the cells in the specified region, and the range-groupby queries compute an aggregation value for each combination of values of grouping dimensions. We call each combination of values of grouping dimensions as a *group key value.*

Figure 1 shows the typical forms of SQL statements for the range queries and the range-groupby queries. For a data cube C whose dimensions are $D_1, \ldots, D_n$ and whose measure is M, the range query and the range-groupby query are shown in Figures 1(a) and 1(b), respectively, where n is the number of dimensions, and $[l_i, h_i](1 \leq i \leq n)$ represents the query range for each dimension D_i. Without loss of generality, we assume that the first $m(\leq n)$ dimensions are used for grouping, i.e., $D_1, \ldots, D_m$ are the grouping dimensions and $D_{m+1}, \ldots, D_n$ are the non-grouping dimensions, throughout this paper.

Ho et al. [8] proposed a method that can effectively process the range queries. In order to process range-sum queries, their method uses a *prefix-sum array,* which stores precomputed partial sum results. The method has an advantage that it always accesses the same number of cells (2^n) regardless of the size of the query region. Following this work, extensive research has been done for update-efficient [2, 4, 5], approximate [6, 7], and progressive [9, 11] processing of range queries. Recently, a similar idea was adopted for processing temporal aggregation queries [12, 13], which retrieve summarized information from the time-evolving attributes.

To our knowledge, no previous method for processing range-groupby queries has been presented in the literature. In this paper, we propose an efficient method for computing range-groupby queries. A simple extension of the prefix-sum array method proposed by Ho et al. [8] maintains a prefix-sum array for each combination of grouping dimensions, which we call a *naive prefix-sum method.* However, such a method incurs enormous storage overhead. We explain more on the method in Section 3.

SELECT	**SUM**($C.M$)
FROM	C
WHERE	$l_1 \leq C.D_1 \leq h_1$
	...
AND	$l_n \leq C.D_n \leq h_n$;

(a) A Range Query

SELECT	$C.D_1, \ldots, C.D_m$, **SUM**($C.M$)
FROM	C
WHERE	$l_1 \leq C.D_1 \leq h_1$
	...
AND	$l_n \leq C.D_n \leq h_n$
GROUP BY	$C.D_1, \ldots, C.D_m$;

(b) A Range-Groupby Query

Fig. 1. Classification of Range-Aggregation Queries

We present a novel method that maintains only one prefix-sum array while achieving almost the identical performance compared with the naive prefix-sum method. We show that some clusters are formed from the cells accessed when computing the range-groupby queries using a prefix-sum array. The proposed algorithm takes advantage of the notion of cluster. In addition, through formal analysis, we demonstrate the effectiveness of our algorithm in terms of the number of accessed cells and the storage overhead. Our method accesses the cells by the unit of cluster instead of individual cells and avoids duplicated accesses of the same cells, which may incur performance degradation. Compared with the naive prefix-sum method, our algorithm reduces the space overhead by $O(\frac{1}{2^n})$, while requiring to access a similar number of cells. Moreover, compared with the method that directly accesses the data cube, our algorithm reduces the number of accessed cells by $O(rs^{n-m})$, where rs is the size of the query region for a dimension.

The rest of this paper is organized as follows. Section 2 reviews the concept of prefix-sum array and the method for computing range-sum queries using the prefix-sum array. Section 3 presents the naive prefix-sum method for computing range-groupby queries. Section 4 proposes our range-groupby algorithm using only one prefix-sum array. Section 5 presents the results of the analysis on our algorithm. Finally, Section 6 concludes this paper.

2 Related Work: Prefix-Sum Array and Range-Sum Queries

Our method for computing range-groupby queries is based on the prefix-sum array proposed by Ho et al. [8]. In this section, we review the prefix-sum array and the range-sum queries. A prefix-sum array is defined as follows: For an

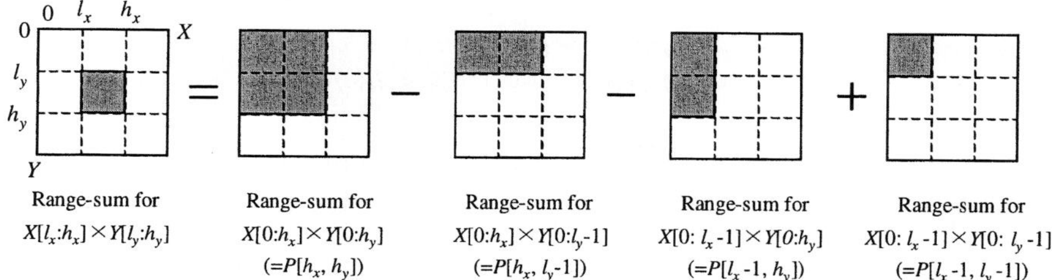

Fig. 2. Computation of a Range-Sum Query Using a Prefix-Sum Array

OLAP database consisting of dimensions $D_1, \ldots, D_n$, let array A be the data cube for the database, and P be the prefix-sum array of A. In addition, let the domain of D_i be $\{0, 1, \ldots, |D_i|-1\}$, where $|D_i|$ is the cardinality of the dimension D_i [1]. Then, a cell $P[p_1, \ldots, p_n]$ is defined as the aggregation value of the cells in the region specified by two boundary points $A[0, \ldots, 0]$ and $A[p_1, \ldots, p_n]$. The following Eq. (1) formally defines the value of a cell in P.

$$P[p_1, \ldots, p_n] = \sum_{v_1=0}^{p_1} \cdots \sum_{v_n=0}^{p_n} A[v_1, \ldots, v_n] \tag{1}$$

Figure 2 shows an example of processing a range-sum query that computes the range-sum of a region $X[l_x : h_x] \times Y[l_y : h_y]$ in a two-dimensional data cube. As shown in the figure, the range-sum for $X[l_x : h_x] \times Y[l_y : h_y]$ is equal to the range-sum of $X[0 : h_x] \times Y[0 : h_y]$, subtracted by the ones of $X[0 : h_x] \times Y[0 : l_y - 1]$ and $X[0 : l_x - 1] \times Y[0 : h_y]$, and added by the one of $X[0 : l_x - 1] \times Y[0 : l_y - 1]$. The four range-sums correspond to $P[h_x, h_y]$, $P[h_x, l_y - 1]$, $P[l_x - 1, h_y]$, and $P[l_x - 1, l_y - 1]$, respectively. Thus, the range-sum of $X[l_x : h_x] \times Y[l_y : h_y]$ can be easily computed by $P[h_x, h_y] - P[h_x, l_y - 1] - P[l_x - 1, h_y] + P[l_x - 1, l_y - 1]$.

The technique can also be applied to COUNT and AVERAGE. The following Lemma 1 [8] formally defines the equation for processing range-sum queries using a prefix-sum array in an n-dimensional space.

Lemma 1. Consider an array A representing a data cube C consisting of dimensions $D_1, \ldots, D_n$, and the prefix-sum array P for A. Then, the range-sum query that has the query range $[l_i, h_i]$ for each dimension D_i can be computed by the following Eq. (2):

$$\sum_{v_1=l_1}^{h_1} \cdots \sum_{v_n=l_n}^{h_n} A[v_1, \ldots, v_n] = \sum_{v_1 \in \{l_1-1, h_1\}} \cdots \sum_{v_n \in \{l_n-1, h_n\}} (-1)^{\alpha} P[v_1, \ldots, v_n] \, , \tag{2}$$

[1] The dimension with the continuous domain values such as income uses a transformed domain, which is called a *rank domain* [8]. A rank domain is created using a mapping function that maps the continuous domain values to the finite number of discrete domain values while preserving the order.

where α is the number of v_i's such that $v_i = l_i - 1$ among v_i's in $P[v_1, \ldots, v_n]$. We note that when $l_i = 0$, v_i becomes -1. For notational convenience, we set $P[v_1, \ldots, v_n] = 0$ if $v_i = -1$ (this value does not exist) for at least one v_i. □

Ho et al. [8] showed that, when computing a range-sum query using Eq. (2), the number of cells to be accessed from P is 2^n.

3 The Naive Prefix-Sum Method for Computing Range-Groupby

In this section, we describe the naive prefix-sum method for computing range-groupby queries using multiple prefix-sum arrays. Consider a range-groupby query over a data cube A consisting of dimensions $D_1, \ldots, D_n$, whose query ranges are $[l_i, h_i](1 \leq i \leq n)$, and $D_1, \ldots, D_m$ are grouping dimensions as assumed in Section 1. (Non-grouping dimensions are $D_{m+1}, \ldots, D_n$.) A range-groupby query computes the aggregated values for each group key value $(D_1, \ldots, D_m) = (a_1, \ldots, a_m)$ $(l_j \leq a_j \leq h_j)(1 \leq j \leq m)$ using the following Eq. (3):

$$\sum_{v_{m+1}=l_{m+1}}^{h_{m+1}} \cdots \sum_{v_n=l_n}^{h_n} A[a_1, \ldots, a_m, v_{m+1}, \ldots, v_n] \,. \tag{3}$$

The aggregation values in Eq. (3) can be efficiently computed by maintaining a data structure having a prefix-sum array *for each group key value* of the grouping dimensions. We define such a data structure in Definition 1 and formalize the computation method of the range-groupby queries using the data structure in Lemma 2.

Definition 1. Consider an array A representing a data cube C consisting of dimensions $D_1, \ldots, D_n$. We define $GP_{1..m}$ as the *group prefix-sum array* of grouping dimensions $D_1, \ldots, D_m$ for array A. The value in the cell $(D_1, \ldots, D_m, D_{m+1}, \ldots, D_n) = (q_1, \ldots, q_m, q_{m+1}, \ldots, q_n)$ of $GP_{1..m}$ is defined as follows:

$$GP_{1..m}[q_1, \ldots, q_m, q_{m+1}, \ldots, q_n] = \sum_{v_{m+1}=0}^{q_{m+1}} \cdots \sum_{v_n=0}^{q_n} A[q_1, \ldots, q_m, v_{m+1}, \ldots, v_n] \,. \tag{4}$$

□

Lemma 2. Consider an array A representing a data cube C consisting of dimensions $D_1, \ldots, D_n$. Suppose that we process a range-groupby query with grouping dimensions $D_1, \ldots, D_m$ using $GP_{1..m}$, and each dimension $D_i(1 \leq i \leq n)$ has the query range $[l_i, h_i]$. Then, the aggregated value for each group key value $(a_1, \ldots, a_m)$ can be computed by Eq. (5) below:

$$\sum_{v_{m+1}=l_{m+1}}^{h_{m+1}} \cdots \sum_{v_n=l_n}^{h_n} A[a_1,\ldots,a_m,v_{m+1},\ldots,v_n] =$$

$$\sum_{v_{m+1}\in\{l_{m+1}-1,h_{m+1}\}} \cdots \sum_{v_n\in\{l_n-1,h_n\}} (-1)^{\alpha} GP_{1..m}[a_1,\ldots,a_m,v_{m+1},\ldots,v_n] \ , \quad (5)$$

where α is the number of v_k's $(m < k \leq n)$ such that $v_k = l_k - 1$ among the v_k's in $GP_{1..m}[a_1,\ldots,a_m,v_{m+1},\ldots,v_n]$. □

The proofs for all the Theorems, Lemmas, and Corollaries in this paper are given in [10]. For the rest of the paper, we use GP instead of $GP_{1..m}$ for simplicity.

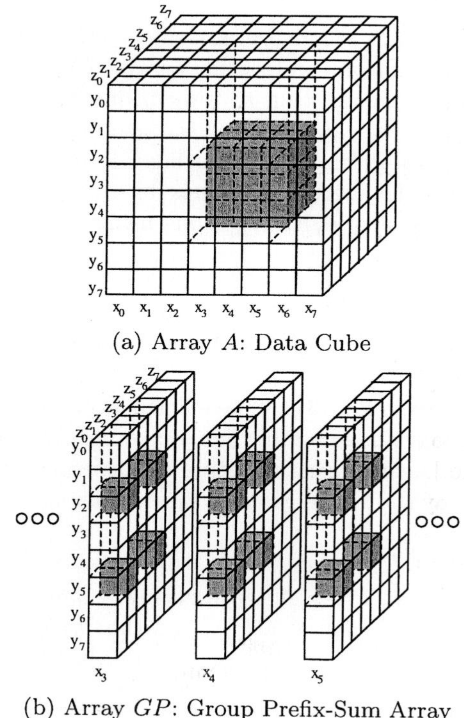

(a) Array A: Data Cube

(b) Array GP: Group Prefix-Sum Array

Fig. 3. Naive Prefix-Sum Method (Grouping Dimension = $\{X\}$)

Figure 3 shows an example of processing a range-groupby query in a data cube with dimensions X, Y, and Z. The query has a grouping dimension X and the range conditions $[x_3, x_5]$, $[y_3, y_5]$, and $[z_2, z_4]$ for X, Y, and Z, respectively. Figure 3(a) is the array A representing the data cube. Figure 3(b) is a group prefix-sum array GP of the grouping dimension is X. As shown in Figure 3(b), the array GP has a prefix-sum array consisting of dimensions Y and Z for each group key value x_i of the grouping dimension X. For each group key value, the cells accessed to compute the range-groupby query are represented as follows:

- $X = x_3$: $\sum_{v_Y=y_3}^{y_5} \sum_{v_Z=z_2}^{z_4} A[x_3, v_Y, v_Z] =$
$GP[x_3, y_5, z_4] - GP[x_3, y_5, z_1] - GP[x_3, y_2, z_4] + GP[x_3, y_2, z_1]$
- $X = x_4$: $\sum_{v_Y=y_3}^{y_5} \sum_{v_Z=z_2}^{z_4} A[x_4, v_Y, v_Z] =$
$GP[x_4, y_5, z_4] - GP[x_4, y_5, z_1] - GP[x_4, y_2, z_4] + GP[x_4, y_2, z_1]$
- $X = x_5$: $\sum_{v_Y=y_3}^{y_5} \sum_{v_Z=z_2}^{z_4} A[x_5, v_Y, v_Z] =$
$GP[x_5, y_5, z_4] - GP[x_5, y_5, z_1] - GP[x_5, y_2, z_4] + GP[x_5, y_2, z_1]$

We compute the range-groupby query by computing the range-sum queries for each group key value of X. In Figure 3(b), the shaded cells indicate the accessed cells.

Corollary 1. When computing a range-groupby query using Eq. (5) in Lemma 2, the number of cells accessed from the array GP is $2^{n-m} \times \prod_{j(1 \le j \le m)}(h_j - l_j + 1)$. □

In order to compute a range-groupby query, we have to read $\prod_{i(1 \le i \le n)}(h_i - l_i + 1)$ cells when using a data cube. On the other hand, we only need to access $2^{n-m} \times \prod_{j(1 \le j \le m)}(h_j - l_j + 1)$ cells when using the group prefix-sum array GP. However, the method is still impractical because it has to maintain a precomputed group prefix-sum array GP for each of 2^n combinations of the grouping dimensions.

4 The Proposed Prefix-Sum Method for Computing Range-Groupby

In this section, we propose an algorithm that solves the storage problem of the naive prefix-sum method. Our algorithm computes range-groupby queries using only one prefix-sum array.

4.1 Characteristics of Range-Groupby Queries and Prefix-Sum Arrays

We observe that the range-groupby queries have the following characteristics. First, a range-groupby query can be divided into range-sum queries of $\prod_{j(1 \le j \le m)}$ $(h_j - l_j + 1)$ subregions. Each subregion consists of the cells that belong to one group key value. That is, the cells whose group key value is $(a_1, \ldots, a_m)$ form a subregion delimited by range conditions $[a_j, a_j]$ of size 1 for grouping dimensions D_j's $(1 \le j \le m)$, and by range conditions $[l_k, h_k]$ for non-grouping dimensions D_k's $(m < k \le n)$. Second, these subregions are adjacent to each other.

We observe that the prefix-sum arrays have the following characteristics. First, as shown in Lemma 1, range-sum queries using a prefix-sum array access the same number (2^n) of cells regardless of the sizes and shapes of query ranges. Second, some cells accessed to process range-groupby queries for the subregions that are adjacent to each other are repeatedly accessed. We discuss on this issue in detail using examples in the next section.

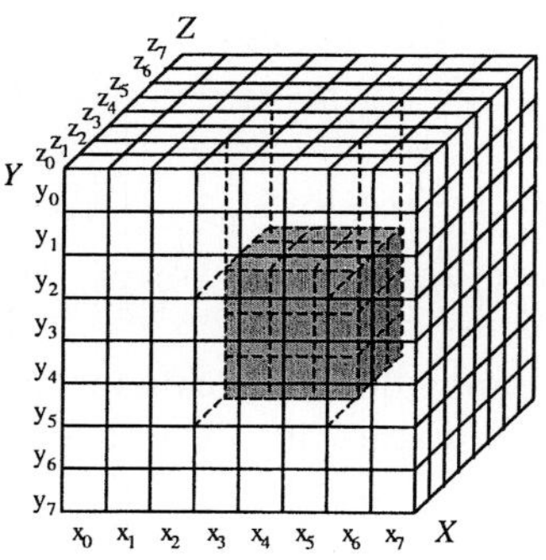

(a) Aggregation Region in the Data Cube (Array A)

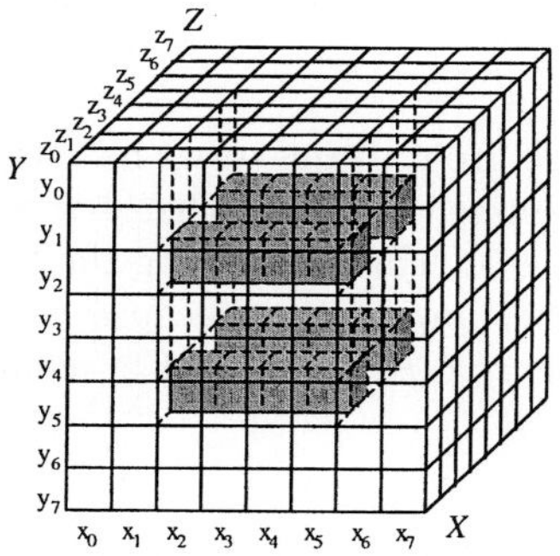

(b) Cells Accessed in the Prefix-Sum Array (Array P)

Fig. 4. Range-Groupby Query Using One Prefix-Sum Array (Grouping Dimension $= \{X\}$)

4.2 Patterns of Accessed Cells

We first discuss the case with one grouping dimension, and then generalize it to the case with multiple grouping dimensions.

Clusters with One Grouping Dimension. Figure 4 shows an example of the range-groupby query using a prefix-sum array of three dimensions X, Y, and Z. The query has a grouping dimension X and range conditions $[x_3, x_5]$, $[y_3, y_5]$, and $[z_2, z_4]$ for X, Y, and Z, respectively. Figure 4(a) represents the region specified for aggregation in the data cube (array A); Figure 4(b) the cells accessed in the prefix-sum array (array P) of A. For each group key value of the grouping dimension X, the cells accessed to compute the range-groupby query are as follows:

- $X = x_3$: $\sum_{v_Y=y_3}^{y_5} \sum_{v_Z=z_2}^{z_4} A[x_3, v_Y, v_Z] =$
  $P[x_3, y_5, z_4] - P[x_3, y_5, z_1] - P[x_3, y_2, z_4] + P[x_3, y_2, z_1]$
  $-P[x_2, y_5, z_4] + P[x_2, y_5, z_1] + P[x_2, y_2, z_4] - P[x_2, y_2, z_1]$
- $X = x_4$: $\sum_{v_Y=y_3}^{y_5} \sum_{v_Z=z_2}^{z_4} A[x_4, v_Y, v_Z] =$
  $P[x_4, y_5, z_4] - P[x_4, y_5, z_1] - P[x_4, y_2, z_4] + P[x_4, y_2, z_1]$
  $-P[x_3, y_5, z_4] + P[x_3, y_5, z_1] + P[x_3, y_2, z_4] - P[x_3, y_2, z_1]$

- $X = x_5$: $\sum_{v_Y=y_3}^{y_5} \sum_{v_Z=z_2}^{z_4} A[x_5, v_Y, v_Z] =$
$P[x_5, y_5, z_4] - P[x_5, y_5, z_1] - P[x_5, y_2, z_4] + P[x_5, y_2, z_1]$
$-P[x_4, y_5, z_4] + P[x_4, y_5, z_1] + P[x_4, y_2, z_4] - P[x_4, y_2, z_1]$

Now we analyze the pattern of the accessed cells. When processing $X = x_3$ and $X = x_4$, the prefix-sum array cells $P[x_3, y_5, z_4]$, $P[x_3, y_5, z_1]$, $P[x_3, y_2, z_1]$, and $P[x_3, y_2, z_1]$ are repeatedly accessed. Likewise, when processing $X = x_4$ and $X = x_5$, the prefix-sum array cells $P[x_4, y_5, z_4]$, $P[x_4, y_5, z_1]$, $P[x_4, y_2, z_4]$ and $P[x_4, y_2, z_1]$ are repeatedly accessed. Since eight cells are accessed for each value of X, we need to access 24 cells in total. However, if we remove the repeated accesses, we only need to access 16 different cells. We note that the accessed cells form four clusters (strips, in this case) that are parallel to the grouping dimension X.

Lemma 3. Let P be the prefix-sum array for a data cube consisting of dimensions $D_1, \ldots, D_n$. Consider a range-groupby query, where D_i has the query range $[l_i, h_i]$ and the grouping dimension is D_1. Then, when processing the range-groupby query with P, the set U' of cells accessed from P is given by Eq. (6):

$$U' = \bigcup_{v_1=l_1-1}^{h_1} \bigcup_{v_2 \in \{l_2-1, h_2\}} \cdots \bigcup_{v_n \in \{l_n-1, h_n\}} \{P[v_1, v_2, \ldots, v_n]\} . \tag{6}$$

□

Corollary 2. When computing a range-groupby query with one grouping dimension, the number of cells to be accessed from the prefix-sum array P is $2^{n-1} \times (h_1 - l_1 + 2)$ according to Lemma 3. □

By Lemma 3, the cells accessed form 2^{n-1} clusters (or strips) along the grouping dimension D_1. Each cluster has the range $[l_1 - 1, h_1]$ for the grouping dimension D_1 and a value of either $l_k - 1$ or h_k for each non-grouping dimension $D_k (1 < k \leq n)$.

Clusters with Multiple Grouping Dimensions. Figure 5 shows an example of the range-groupby query using a prefix-sum array of three dimensions X, Y, and Z. The query has two grouping dimensions X and Y, and range conditions $[x_3, x_5]$, $[y_3, y_5]$, and $[z_2, z_4]$ for X, Y, and Z, respectively. Figure 5(a) represents the region specified for aggregation in the data cube (array A); Figure 5(b) the cells accessed in the prefix-sum array (array P) of A. For each group key value, the cells accessed to compute the range-groupby query are as follows:

- $X = x_3, Y = y_3$: $\sum_{v_Z=z_2}^{z_4} A[x_3, y_3, v_Z] =$
$P[x_3, y_3, z_4] - P[x_3, y_3, z_1] - P[x_3, y_2, z_4] + P[x_3, y_2, z_1]$
$-P[x_2, y_3, z_4] + P[x_2, y_3, z_1] + P[x_2, y_2, z_4] - P[x_2, y_2, z_1]$
- $X = x_3, Y = y_4$: $\sum_{v_Z=z_2}^{z_4} A[x_3, y_4, v_Z] =$
$P[x_3, y_4, z_4] - P[x_3, y_4, z_1] - P[x_3, y_3, z_4] + P[x_3, y_3, z_1]$
$-P[x_2, y_4, z_4] + P[x_2, y_4, z_1] + P[x_2, y_3, z_4] - P[x_2, y_3, z_1]$

...

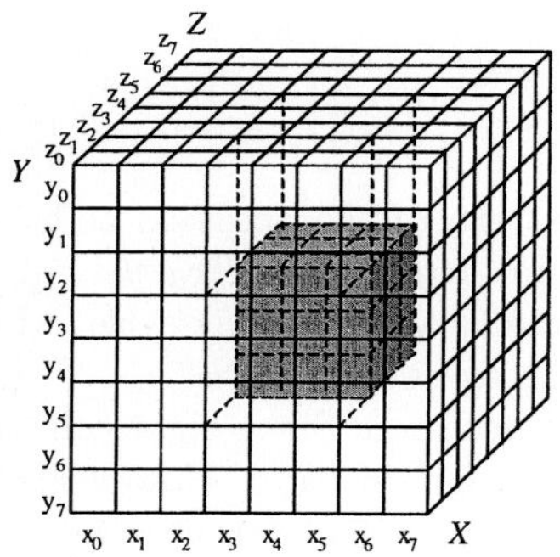

(a) Aggregation Region in the Data Cube (Array A)

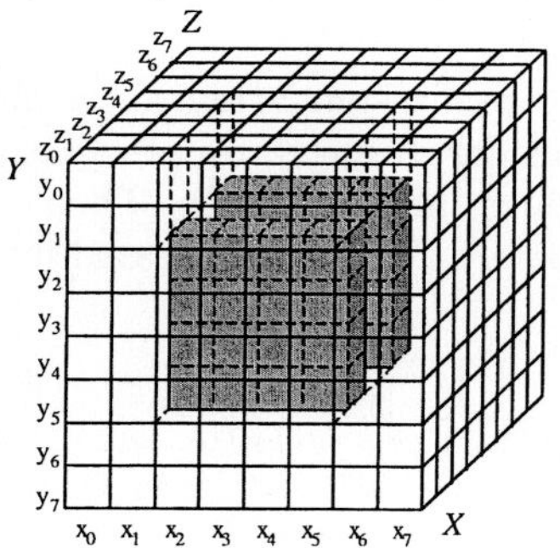

(b) Cells Accessed in the Prefix-Sum Array (Array P)

Fig. 5. Range-Groupby Query Using One Prefix-Sum Array (Grouping Dimensions = $\{X, Y\}$)

– $X = x_5, Y = y_5$: $\sum_{v_Z=z_2}^{z_4} A[x_5, y_5, v_Z] =$
$$P[x_5, y_5, z_4] - P[x_5, y_5, z_1] - P[x_5, y_4, z_4] + P[x_5, y_4, z_1]$$
$$-P[x_4, y_5, z_4] + P[x_4, y_5, z_1] + P[x_4, y_4, z_4] - P[x_4, y_4, z_1]$$

Now we analyze the pattern of the accessed cells. We can see that when either the X or Y value is increased by one, four cells are repeatedly accessed. When both X and Y values increase by one, two cells are repeatedly accessed. Since we have nine possible combinations of X and Y values, and eight cells are accessed for each combination, we need to access 72 cells in total. However, if we remove the repeated accesses, we only access 32 different cells. We note that the accessed cells form two planes parallel to the X-Y plane.

In general, these clusters are m-dimensional rectangles, where m is the number of the grouping dimensions. Theorem 1 generalizes the pattern of accessed cells for multiple grouping dimensions.

Theorem 1. Let P be the prefix-sum array for a data cube consisting of dimensions $D_1, \ldots, D_n$. Consider a range-groupby query, where D_i has the query range $[l_i, h_i]$ and the grouping dimensions are $D_1, \ldots, D_m$. Then, the set U' of cells accessed to process the query using P is represented by Eq. (7):

$$U' = \bigcup_{v_1=l_1-1}^{h_1} \cdots \bigcup_{v_m=l_m-1}^{h_m} \bigcup_{v_{m+1}\in\{l_{m+1}-1,h_{m+1}\}} \cdots \bigcup_{v_n\in\{l_n-1,h_n\}} P[v_1,\ldots,v_m,v_{m+1},\ldots,v_n] \,. \quad (7)$$

□

Corollary 3. When computing a range-groupby query, the number of cells to be accessed from the prefix-sum array P is $2^{n-m} \times \prod_{j(1\leq j\leq m)}(h_j - l_j + 2)$ according to Theorem 1. □

By Theorem 1, we can see that the accessed cells form 2^{n-m} m-dimensional rectangles parallel to the subspace consisting of the grouping dimensions. In other words, the cells form 2^{n-m} clusters, where each of the clusters consists of the values in the interval $[l_j - 1, h_j]$ for a grouping dimension D_j $(1 \leq j \leq m)$ and $l_k - 1$ or h_k for a non-grouping dimension D_k $(m < k \leq n)$.

4.3 Range_Groupby: Proposed Algorithm

Figure 6 shows the algorithm Range_Groupby that processes range-groupby queries by taking advantage of the pattern of accessed cells as presented in Theorem 1. The key idea of the algorithm is that, by accessing the cells in P only once for processing a range-groupby query, the algorithm avoids any possible disk accesses caused by the duplicated accesses of the same cells in P, which may incur performance degradation. The inputs are an n-dimensional prefix-sum array P and the query ranges $[l_i, h_i](1 \leq i \leq n)$ for each dimension. Let $G = \{D_1, \ldots, D_m\}$ be grouping dimensions.

Step 1 reads the cells of the prefix-sum array needed for computing the range-groupby query into main memory. The cells are read in the unit of cluster. Since even the total clusters are much smaller in size than the whole prefix-sum array P, they can fit in main memory. According to Theorem 1, each cluster consists of the region bounded by the interval $[l_j - 1, h_j]$ for grouping dimensions $D_j(1 \leq j \leq m)$, and $[v_k, v_k]$ of size 1 for non-grouping dimensions $D_k(m < k \leq n)$, where v_k is either $l_k - 1$ or h_k. Step 2 computes aggregation for each group key value by using the cells retrieved in Step 1.2 and Eq. (8).

5 Performance Analysis

In this section, we compare the performance and the storage overhead of the proposed algorithm Range_Groupby with two other methods for computing range-groupby queries. As the performance measure, we use the number of cells accessed from disk.

No_Precomp. This method processes a range-groupby query by directly accessing the cells within the given query region in the data cube. This method does not use precomputed results, and has no extra storage overhead. However, the method accesses the largest number of cells.

Algorithm. Range_Groupby

Input:
(1) An n-dimensional prefix-sum array P
(2) A query range $[l_i, h_i]$ for each dimension $D_i (1 \le i \le n)$
Output:
Result of aggregation

1 [Read the cells of P for each cluster into main memory to be used for processing the range-groupby query]
Let $D_{m+1}, \ldots, D_n$ be non-grouping dimensions. For each cluster, i.e., for each value $(v_{m+1}, \ldots, v_n)$ of $(D_{m+1}, \ldots, D_n)$, where $v_k \in \{l_k - 1, h_k\}$ $(m < k \le n)$, DO
1.1 Construct a cluster whose region is bounded by the interval $[l_j - 1, h_j]$ for grouping dimensions $D_j (1 \le j \le m)$ and $[v_k, v_k]$ for non-grouping dimensions $D_k (m < k \le n)$.
1.2 Retrieve the cells in the cluster into main memory.
2 [Compute the aggregation value for each group key value]
For each value $(v_1, \ldots, v_m)$ of $(D_1, \ldots, D_m)$, where $v_j \in [l_j, h_j] (1 \le j \le m)$, DO
2.1 Compute the range-sum whose region is bounded by the interval $[v_j, v_j]$ for grouping dimensions D_j and $[l_k, h_k]$ for non-grouping dimensions $D_k (m < k \le n)$. It can be computed using the cells of P retrieved in Step 1.2 and the following Eq. (8):

$$\sum_{v_{m+1}=l_{m+1}}^{h_{m+1}} \cdots \sum_{v_n=l_n}^{h_n} A[v_1, \ldots, v_m, v_{m+1}, \ldots, v_n] = \sum_{v_{m+1} \in \{l_{m+1}-1, h_{m+1}\}} \cdots \sum_{v_n \in \{l_n - 1, h_n\}} (-1)^\alpha P[v_1, \ldots, v_m, v_{m+1}, \ldots, v_n] \; . \quad (8)$$

Fig. 6. Range-Groupby Algorithm Using One Prefix-Sum Array

Full_Precomp. This is the naive prefix-sum method described in Section 3. It maintains 2^n prefix-sum arrays for every possible combination of grouping dimensions.

Range_Groupby. This method uses the algorithm Range_Groupby presented in Section 4.2, which uses only one prefix-sum array. This method reads the cells from the array only once, thereby avoiding multiple accesses to the same cells.

Table 1 summarizes the number of cells accessed from disk and the storage overhead for processing range-groupby queries. Table 1 shows that the number of cells accessed by Range_Groupby is very close to that by Full_Precomp. It shows the effectiveness of the notion of cluster, which enables avoiding repetitive accesses of the same cells. The storage overhead is measured in the total number of cells. Full_Precomp needs to store one prefix-sum array for each of 2^n combinations of grouping dimensions, and needs to store $2^n \times \prod_{i(1 \le i \le n)} |D_i|$ number of cells in total, where $|D_i|$ is the cardinality of dimension D_i.

Table 1. Comparison of Three Range-Groupby Algorithms

	Number of Accessed Cells	Storage Overhead
No_Precomp	$\prod_{i(1\leq i\leq n)}(h_i - l_i + 1)$	$\prod_{i(1\leq i\leq n)} \lvert D_i\rvert$
Full_Precomp	$2^{n-m} \times \prod_{j(1\leq j\leq m)}(h_j - l_j + 1)$	$2^n \times \prod_{i(1\leq i\leq n)} \lvert D_i\rvert$
Range_Groupby	$2^{n-m} \times \prod_{j(1\leq j\leq m)}(h_j - l_j + 2)$	$\prod_{i(1\leq i\leq n)} \lvert D_i\rvert$

We now illustrate the results in Table 1 using graphs. Figure 7 shows the number of accessed cells as the query range $(h - l + 1)$ varies. For simplicity, we assume that the sizes of the query ranges are equal for all the dimensions. In the figure, we set $n = 5$ and $m = 3$. The horizontal axis represents the normalized size of the query range, which is computed by dividing the size of the query range $(h-l+1)$ by the cardinality of the dimension $|D|$. The vertical axis represents the normalized number of accessed cells computed by dividing the number of cells accessed while processing the query by the total number of cells in the grouping dimension space $\prod_{j(1\leq j\leq m)}(h_j - l_j + 1)$.

In Figure 7, we note that Range_Groupby accesses almost the same number of cells as Full_Precomp as shown in Table 1. (The ratio of the numbers of accessed cells is $\prod_{j(1\leq j\leq m)} \frac{h_j-l_j+2}{h_j-l_j+1}$, which is very close to one.) No_Precomp accesses $\prod_{k(m<k\leq n)} \frac{h_k-l_k+1}{2}$ times as many cells as Full_Precomp. Since the size of the query range (h_i-l_i+1) is much larger than 2, No_Precomp accesses a far greater number of cells than Full_Precomp.

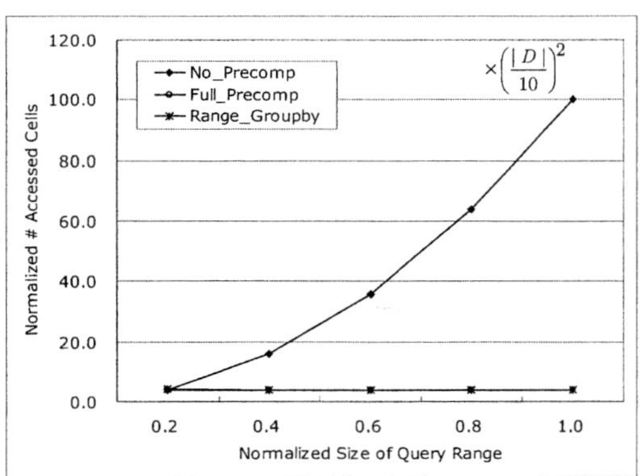

Fig. 7. Number of Cells Accessed for Processing Range-Groupby Queries

Figure 8 shows the storage overhead as the dimension cardinality varies. In the figure, we set $n = 5$. For simplicity, we assume that all the dimensions have the same cardinalities. We represent the storage overhead in gigabytes of storage space. Figure 8 shows that Full_Precomp requires $32(= 2^n)$ times as much storage as Range_Groupby.

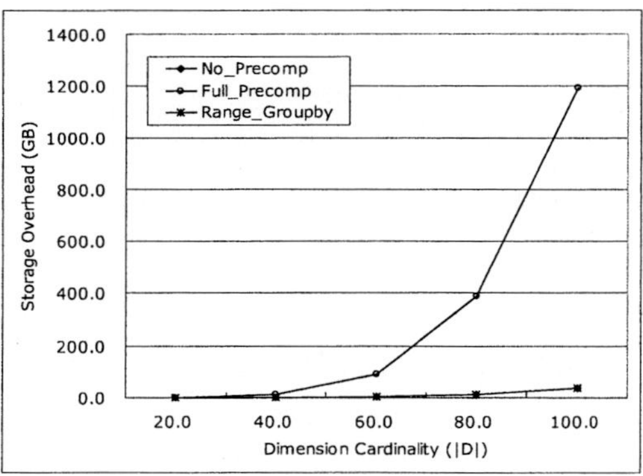

Fig. 8. Storage Overhead for the Whole Prefix-Sum Arrays

6 Conclusions

In this paper, we defined the range-groupby query and presented an efficient algorithm for processing the query. A range-groupby query is a GROUP BY query for an arbitrary region in an n-dimensional data cube. The range-groupby queries are frequent in many of OLAP applications, since the queries allow us to analyze various trends in a specified region from the diverse perspectives (dimensions). To our knowledge, there has been no effort for finding an efficient algorithm for range-groupby queries. The major contribution of this paper is that we proposed an algorithm for processing range-groupby queries in an n-dimensional data cube using only one prefix-sum array, regardless of combinations of grouping dimensions, thereby significantly reducing the storage requirements.

Through formal analysis, we showed the effectiveness of the proposed algorithm in terms of the number of cells accessed while process the query and the storage overhead. Compared with the method that directly accesses the data cube, the proposed algorithm reduces the number of accessed cells by $O(rs^{n-m})$, where rs is the size of the query region for a non-grouping dimension. Compared with the method that maintains precomputed results for all the possible combinations of the grouping dimensions, the proposed algorithm reduces the space overhead by $O(\frac{1}{2^n})$ while requiring no more number of accessed cells.

Acknowledgement

This work was supported by the Ministry of Science and Technology (MOST) / Korea Science and Engineering Foundation (KOSEF) through the Advanced Information Technology Research Center (AITrc) and by the Brain Korea 21 Project.

References

1. Agrawal, R., Gupta, A., and Sarawagi, S., "Modeling Multidimensional Databases," In *Proc. Int'l Conf. on Data Engineering*, pp. 232-243, Birmingham, U.K., Apr. 1997.
2. Chan, C.-Y. and Ioannidis, Y. E., "Hierarchical Cubes for Range-Sum Queries," In *Proc. Int'l Conf. on Very Large Data Bases*, pp. 675-686, Edinburgh, Scotland, 1999.
3. Chaudhuri, S. and Dayal, U., "An Overview of Data Warehousing and OLAP Technology," *ACM SIGMOD Record*, Vol. 26, No. 1, pp. 65-74, Mar. 1997.
4. Geffner, S., Agrawal, D., Abbadi, A. E, and Smith, T., "Relative Prefix Sums: An Efficient Approach for Querying Dynamic OLAP Data Cubes," In *Proc. Int'l Conf. on Data Engineering*, pp. 328-335, Sydney, Australia, Mar. 1999.
5. Geffner, S., Agrawal, D., and Abbadi, A. E., "The Dynamic Data Cube," In *Proc. Int'l Conf. on Extending Database Technology*, pp. 237-253, Konstanz, Germany, Mar. 2000.
6. Gilbert, A. C., Kotidis, Y., Muthukrishnan, S., and Strauss, M. J., "Optimal and Approximate Computation of Summary Statistics for Range Queries," In *Proc. ACM SIGACT-SIGMOD-SIGART Symp. on Principles of Database Systems*, pp. 228-237, Santa Babara, California, May 2001.
7. Gunopulos, D., Kollios, G., Tsotras, V. J., and Domeniconi, C., "Approximating Multi-dimensional Aggregate Range Queries over Real Attributes," In *Proc. Int'l Conf. on Management of Data*, pp. 463-474, ACM SIGMOD, Dallas, Texas, May 2000.
8. Ho, C.-T., Agrawal, R., Megiddo, N., and Srikant R., "Range Queries in OLAP Data Cubes," In *Proc. Int'l Conf. on Management of Data*, pp. 73-88, ACM SIGMOD, Tucson, Arizona, June 1997.
9. Lazaridis, I. and Mehrotra, S., "Progressive Approximate Aggregate Queries with a Multi-Resolution Tree Structure," In *Proc. Int'l Conf. on Management of Data*, pp. 401-412, ACM SIGMOD, Santa Babara, California, May 2001.
10. Lee, Y.-K., Whang, K.-Y., Moon, Y.-S., Song, I.-Y., and Loh, W.-K., An Algorithm for Computing Range-Groupby Queries, Technical Report, Advanced Information Technology Research Center (AITrc), Korea Advanced Institute of Science and Technology (KAIST), Sept. 2005.
11. Schmidt, R. R. and Shahabi, C., "ProPolyne: A Fast Wavelet-Based Techniques for Progressive Evaluation of Polynomial Range-Sum Queries," In *Proc. Int'l Conf. on Extending Database Technology*, pp. 664-681, Prague, Czech Republic, Mar. 2002.
12. Tao, Y., Papadias, D., and Faloutsos, C., "Approximate Temporal Aggregation," In *Proc. Int'l Conf. on Data Engineering*, pp. 190-201, Boston, Massachusetts, Mar. 2004.
13. Yang, J. and Widom, J., "Incremental Computation and Maintenance of Temporal Aggregates," *The VLDB Journal*, Vol. 12, No. 3, pp. 262-283, Oct. 2003.

Ag-Tree: A Novel Structure for Range Queries in Data Warehouse Environments

Yaokai Feng and Akifumi Makinouchi

Graduate School of Information Science and Electrical Engineering,
Kyushu University Hakozaki 6-10-1, Fukuoka City, Japan
{fengyk, akifumi}@is.kyushu-u.ac.jp

Abstract. In order to efficiently evaluate range-aggregate queries in data warehouse environments, several works on data cubes (such as the aggregate cubetree) are proposed. In the aggregate cubetree, each entry in every node stores the aggregate values of its corresponding subtree. Therefore, range-aggregate queries can be processed without visiting the child nodes whose parent nodes are fully included in the query range. However, the aggregate cubetree does not take range queries using partial dimensions and range queries without aggregation operations into account. That is, 1) a great deal of information that is irrelevant to the queries also has to be read from the disk for partially-dimensional range queries and 2) while it improves the performance of range queries with aggregate operations, it degrades the performance of the range queries without aggregate operations. In this paper, we proposed a novel index structure, called *Aggregate-Tree* (denoted as Ag-Tree), which gets rid of the above-mentioned weaknesses of the aggregate cubetree without any side effects. The experiments and discussions presented in this paper indicate that the new proposal is significant for range queries in data warehouse environments.

1 Introduction

Several terms that are necessary to understand this paper are explained and the background of this paper is presented.

1.1 Terms

Range-aggregate queries. An example of range-aggregate queries over a relation F (D_1, D_2,$\cdots$, D_n, M) is as follows

SELECT $AggregateFunction(M)$
FROM F
WHERE $l_1 \leq D_1 \leq h_1$
AND $l_2 \leq D_2 \leq h_2$
AND $\cdots$
AND $l_k \leq D_k \leq h_k$,

where F is a fact table that a range-aggregate query is executed on. D_1, D_2, ..., and D_n are dimension attributes, M is a measure attribute, and k dimension

M.L. Lee, K.L. Tan, and V. Wuwongse (Eds.): DASFAA 2006, LNCS 3882, pp. 498–512, 2006.

attributes (D_1, D_2, $\cdots$, D_k) ($k \leq n$) are used to determine the query range. The attributes used for the query condition in the where-clause are called *query attributes* (*dimensions*). Generally, possible range-aggregate queries include range-COUNT/SUM/AVG/MIN/MAX queries. If the queries provided from users are not with any aggregate operations, then the queries aim at the tuples in the query ranges.

Partially-dimensional range queries. The existing studies on multidimensional indexing have been directed to all-dimensional queries (referred to herein as *AD queries*), in which the queries are evaluated using all the index dimensions. However, in many applications, the query conditions (ranges) are often formed with partial (not all) dimensions, which are called *partially- dimensional range queries* (referred to herein as *PD range queries*).

Let us see PD range queries by an example. For a relational table T with eight attributes of A_1 - A_8. Assume that the actual attribute combinations possibly used in query conditions be $\{\{A_1, A_3\}$, $\{A_2, A_5\}$,$\{A_3, A_4\}$,$\{A_5, A_6\}$, $\{A_1, A_2\}$, $\{A_2, A_4\}$, $\{A_1, A_3, A_5\}$, $\{A_2, A_4, A_6\}\}$. All of these queries are PD range queries. Probably, there are many actual combinations of query attributes used in all possible PD range queries. Thus, it is not always feasible in applications with large datasets for one index to be built for each possible combination of query attributes, because (1) numerous indices have to be constructed and managed, (2) many attributes are repeatedly included in different indices (e.g., A_1 in three indices in the above example), which is too space-consuming for large datasets and results in a large maintaining cost, and (3) the combinations of index attributes that can possibly be used in the user-provided PD queries are often unpredictable. Note that, there are a total of $(2^n - 1)$ different combinations for n possible query attributes.

1.2 Background

Data warehouse [1] is a database system for analysis, which extracts, integrates, and transforms data from an OLTP database, and stores them in efficient structures for analysis. Relational databases use star schemas [2] for representing analysis data. The fact table is the center of the star schema, and it consists of dimension attributes related to the dimension tables and measure attributes that are numeric values and may be aggregated. In data warehouse environments, generally, the size of the fact table is so large that the query processing can be time consuming. Various methods have been proposed to solve this problem. The scheme maintaining materialized views [3, 9, 10] for the fact table through the data cube [4, 11, 12] is one of those. The data cube is an operator that computes aggregate functions over all possible groups in the fact table. By keeping the result of the data cube operation as a materialized view, fast query execution is possible through the summary information of the fact table. This materialized view is stored as a relation, which may be large. Therefore, overhead is heavy for creating an additional index on the materialized view in order to improve the query performance.

In order to improve the performance of cube queries, cubetree [7, 8] is proposed and used as a technique materializing a data cube through an R-tree-like structure. But the queries have to traverse all internal and leaf nodes in the query range to compute range-aggregate queries [6]. Countering this problem, the work [15] proposes an enhanced cubetree, called aggregate cubetree, in which each entry of all internal nodes stores the aggregate value(s) of the whole subtree rooted it. Therefore, by using these aggregate values, range-aggregate queries can be processed without visiting the child nodes whose parent nodes are fully included in the query range. The aggregate cubetree is better than the original cubetree because it can evaluate queries with a smaller number of node accesses.

Obviously, however, the aggregate cubetree suffers from the following two important drawbacks. 1) It does not take into account PD range queries, which is very popular in data warehouse environments. A great deal of information that is irrelevant to the queries also has to be read from the disk for PD range queries. 2) It does not take into account the queries without aggregation operations. In actual applications, not all queries given from users are with aggregate operations. That is, many queries may aim at the tuples in the given range. Certainly, the structure of the aggregate cubetree also can be used for range queries without aggregate operations. However, while it improves the performance of range queries with aggregate operations, it degrades the performance of the range queries without aggregate operations. This is because many aggregation values (especially when several aggregate functions are simultaneously necessary) in the accessed nodes also have to be read from the disk, although they are not used in the queries at all.

In this paper, countering the weaknesses of the aggregate cubetree, we proposed a novel index structure, called *Aggregate-Tree* (denoted as Ag-Tree), which has the following two outstanding properties. 1) For PD range queries with or without aggregate operations, only the information that is relevant to the queries is read from the disk. 2) For the range queries without aggregate operations, no matter they are AD range queries or PD range queries, the aggregate values are not read from the disk. By this proposal, the above-mentioned drawbacks of the aggregate cubetree are overcome without any side effects. In short, we propose a novel structure that can efficiently evaluate both PD range queries and AD range queries, no matter they are with aggregate operations or not.

The rest of this paper is organized as follows. Section 2 introduces some related works. Our proposal, the Ag-Tree, is presented in Section 3 along with some necessary algorithms and discussions. The experiment result is in Section 4. And, Section 5 concludes this paper.

2 Related Works

In order to improve the performance of the range queries with the aggregate operations, many works have been done, especially around data cube [15, 19, 20, 21, 23]. The work [19] is on a technique called quotient cube, which is a summary structure for a data cube that preserves its semantics, with applications for online exploration and visualization. The work [20] is on how to reduce the size of data cubes. The work [21] is on how to perform aggregations on multiple dimensions simultaneously. And the work [23] is on high-dimensional OLAP (e.g., 100 dimensions). In this paper, we propose a novel structure that can efficiently evaluate both PD range queries and AD range queries, no matter they are with aggregate operations or not. Although no existing works are directed to multidimensional indices for PD range queries, we found that the aggregate cubetree [15] is related to our study. Before the introduction of the aggregate cubetree, let us briefly review its predecessor, cubetree.

2.1 Cubetree

Cubetree is a tree structure for storing a data cube. If the data cube is built on the fact table having n dimension attributes, then it is composed of hyper-planes from n-dimension to zero-dimension. The basic idea of the cubetree [7, 8] is mapping these n to zero-dimensional hyper-planes into n-dimensional space, and storing them in an R-tree. The data cube organized as n-1 to zero-dimensional data except for the original n-dimensional data is called dataless cubetree, and the cubetrees made up of several n-1 dimensional R-trees from dataless cubetree is called reduced cubetree. When the data cube is composed as the reduced cubetree, the size of data cube can be reduced and the clustering effects can be improved. Other techniques such as sorting and bulk loading can also be applied to improve the clustering effects. However, the cubetree requires accessing all the leaf nodes within the query range to process a range-aggregate query, which is a primary factor that reduces the query performance as the size of query ranges get larger. In data warehouse environments, aggregate queries are frequently requested on large ranges, in which a large part of leaf nodes have to be accessed. Thus, the original cubetree possibly show worse performance for such queries than scanning the entire table [15].

2.2 Aggregate Cubetree

The basic structure of the aggregate cubetree is similar to that of the original cubetree based on R*-tree. In the aggregate cubetree, each node is composed of a number of entries. Each leaf node entry is made up of dimension attributes and aggregate value of measure attributes, and each internal node entry is composed of an MBR (Minimum Bounding Rectangle), child node pointer, and an aggregate value. The aggregate value in each internal node entry is the aggregate value of all the tuples in the corresponding subtree. Each aggregate value in internal nodes can be calculated from the aggregate values in all its child node entries.

The range queries on R-tree-like structures are performed by recursively searching nodes overlapping the query range. In the cubetree, all of the nodes overlapping the query range must be accessed for range-aggregate queries. In the aggregate cubetree, however, by using the aggregate values in the entries of the internal nodes, range-aggregate queries can be performed without visiting the child nodes whose parent nodes are fully included in the query range. Therefore, the number of node accesses can be reduced compared with the cubetree.

Although the aggregate cubetree is originally directed to data cubes, its structure certainly can be used for range queries exerted on relational datasets. In fact, it can be used to both AD and PD range queries, with or without aggregate operations. Each entry in the leaf nodes corresponds to one tuple. Besides the index attributes, the measure attributes are also contained in the leaf nodes.

3 Ag-Tree

The proposed method, Ag-Tree, is presented after a brief description of weaknesses of the aggregate cubetree.

3.1 Weaknesses of Aggregate Cubetree

As mentioned above, by storing all necessary aggregate values in intermediate nodes, the aggregate Cubetree can improve the performance of range-aggregate queries. However, it suffers from the following two weaknesses.

1. It does not take PD range queries into account. Like the other existing multidimensional indices, in the aggregate cubetree, all the objects (tuples) are clustered in the leaf nodes according to their information in all index dimensions and, every node contains the information of its entries in all the index dimensions (i.e., each node entry includes MBR edges in all index dimensions). That is, the aggregate cubetree is also directed to evaluating AD range queries. Using an n-dimensional aggregate cubetree, PD range query having k ($k < n$) query dimensions can be evaluated by simply extending the query range in each of the remaining $(n - k)$ irrelevant index dimensions to their whole data ranges. The weakness is that, each node of the aggregate cubetree contains n-dimensional information, but only k-dimensional information is necessary for an k-dimensional PD range query, which means that a great deal of unnecessary information (i.e., the information in the irrelevant dimensions) also has to be read from disk. This certainly greatly degrades the query performance.

2. It does not take the queries without aggregation operations into account. The aggregate cubetree is directed to the queries having aggregate operations. Actually, there are still many queries that need not aggregate operations (e.g., those aiming at the tuples in the query range). If the aggregate cubetree is used to evaluate such queries, then so many aggregation values in the accessed nodes also have to be read from the disk, although they are not used in the queries at all. In other words, the aggregate values in the aggregate cubetree nodes reduce the capacity of each node, especially, in the cases that several aggregate values of COUNT, SUM, AVG, MIN and MAX are necessary.

By the proposed method in this paper, both of the above problems can be solved without any side effects. That is, for PD range queries, the information

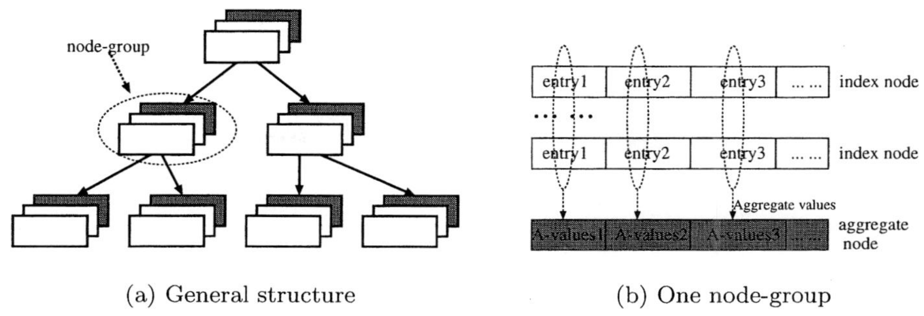

(a) General structure (b) One node-group

Fig. 1. Structure of Ag-Tree

in the irrelevant dimensions need not be read from disk, and for the queries having no aggregate operations, no aggregate values are read from disk. Thus,the proposed method can efficiently evaluate both PD range queries and AD range queries, no matter they are with aggregate operations or not.

3.2 Ag-Tree

The key idea of the Ag-Tree includes the following points. 1) Every node of the n-dimensional aggregate cubetree is divided into n one-dimensional nodes, each of which only holds information in one dimension. Thus, for PD range queries with or without aggregate operations, only the nodes corresponding to the query dimensions are possibly accessed. The nodes in the irrelevant dimensions can be skipped. 2) Unlike the aggregate cubetree, all the aggregate values are contained in some special nodes, which are independent of the index parts of the Ag-Tree. In this way, the nodes for aggregate values need not be accessed for the queries without aggregate operations. General structure of Ag-Tree is depicted in Fig. 1(a), in which the white nodes form the index part and the black nodes, called *aggregate nodes*, store aggregate values. Figure 1(b) shows one node-group, in which *A-values* means "aggregate values", i.e., all or part of {COUNT, SUM, AVG, MIN, MAX}. All the entries with the same index in different nodes of each node-group (i.e., all the entries in each ellipse) form one complete MBR whose aggregate values are contained in the aggregate node in the same location (index).

In the aggregate cubetree, each node entry corresponds to one complete MBR (one subspace in the index space). In the Ag-Tree, however, each node entry only corresponds to one edge of the corresponding MBR, i.e., a complete n-dimensional MBR is divided into n edges, which are stored in different nodes of one node-group with the same index location. In other words, the entries in the same location (index) of the node-group forms a complete MBR, which is shown in Fig. 2.

Figure 2 is an example of entries in a node-group of the Ag-Tree in a two-dimensional index space. In this example, each complete MBR is divided into two parts, which are separately contained in two nodes of one node-group. For example, $Xentry_i$ and $Yentry_i$ in Fig. 2 correspond to the two edges of MBR_i

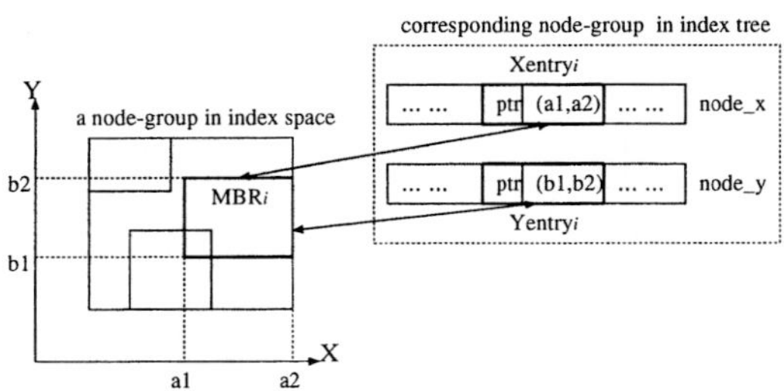

Fig. 2. Example of entries in node-groups (aggregate nodes are not shown)

paralleling the X-axis and the Y-axis, respectively. That is, $Xentry_i + Yentry_i = MBR_i$. Note that, for simplicity, Figure 2 does not include the aggregate nodes.

Here, the following two questions may occur.

How to determine the capacity of each node-group? Obviously, all of the nodes in each node-group must have the same number of entries. Based on the principle of "one node one page", we can determine the capacity of each node in the index part (say f_x) and that of the aggregate node (say f_a). Then, the final fanout/capacity of each node-group should be the smaller one of f_x and f_a, i.e., $\min\{f_x, f_a\}$. Generally, $f_a > f_x$. Thus, commonly speaking, the final fanout/capacity of each node-group is determined by the index-part. In other words, the aggregate nodes generally do not influence the fanout of the index part.

Whether or not the "node-dividing" of the Ag-Tree results in a great increase in the total number of nodes? The answer is "*No*". This is because each node of the Ag-Tree only contains the information in one dimension and no aggregate values in it, which means each node of the Ag-Tree can contain much more number of entries than each node in the aggregate cubetree.

3.3 Algorithms

Insert and delete algorithms. The insert algorithm of the Ag-Tree is naive extensions of the counterparts of R*-tree. When the new tuple reaches a leaf node-group, it is divided and stored in different nodes according to dimensions. If split is necessary for an overflowed node-group, all its nodes have to be split at the same time and the split may be up propagated. After a delete operation, if the node-group under-flowed, all its nodes should be deleted at the same time and all its entries are inserted again. That is, all the nodes in each node-group must be born simultaneously and die simultaneously. For the aggregate nodes, as the new tuples are inserted, the corresponding aggregate values in the ancestor node-groups should be updated. The insert and delete algorithms are omitted here.

Algorithm for range queries without aggregate operations. This algorithm can be used for AD range queries and PD range queries without aggregate operations, which is shown in Table 1.

Table 1. Algorithm for range queries without aggregate operations

```
Procedure RangeQuery (rect, node-group)
Input:    rect: query range
    node-group: initial node-group of the query
Output: result: all the tuples in rect
Begin
For each entry e *) in node-group Do
      If e INTERSECT rect in all the query dimensions **) Then
        If (node-group is not at leaf) Then
          RangeQuery (rect, e.child); //e.child means the child node-group of e
        Else result ← e
EndFor
End
```

*) An entry includes all parts with the same index in the different nodes of this node -group.

**) When an entry is investigated to determine whether it intersects the query range, only the nodes corresponding to the query dimensions need be accessed. EVEN, in the visited node-groups, not all nodes corresponding to the query dimensions are necessary to be checked because that the investigation of the current entry can be stopped if it is found not to intersect the query range in the current query dimension.

Table 2. Algorithm for range queries with aggregate operations

```
Procedure RangeSUM (rect, node-group)
Input:    rect: query range
    node-group: initial node-group of the query
Output: result: sum of aggregate values in the query range
Begin
    SUM_type result ← 0;
    For each entry e in node-group Do
      If e IsFullyContainedBy rect in all the query dimensions (condition1) Then
        result ← result+e.aggregateSUM
        // e.aggregateSUM is SUM value corresponding to e.
      Else If (node-group is not at leaf) AND
            (e NotSeparatedFrom rect in all the query dimensions) (condition2)
          Then
            result ← result+RangeSUM (rect, e.child);
            //e.child means the child node-group corresponding to e
    EndFor
    Return result
End
```

Algorithm for range queries with aggregate operations. An algorithm for Range-SUM queries is shown in Table 2. The algorithms for other aggregate functions are similar.

Like the algorithm in Table 1, when an entry is checked to determine its relationship (*IsFullyContainedBy*, *NotSeparatedFrom*) with the query range, only the nodes corresponding to the query dimensions need be accessed. EVEN, not all the nodes in the query dimensions are necessary to be checked (see Table 1).

Once the current entry e is found not fully to be contained in the query range in some query dimension (*condition*1 in this algorithm) and *node-group* is not at leaf level, the relationship of *NotSeparatedFrom* will be checked (*condition*2). In *condition*2, once the current entry e is found not to intersect the query range in some query dimension, the investigation of e is concluded.

When the search reaches at leaf nodes, *condition*1 is used to judge whether or not each entry is contained in the query range. The measure attribute values of the entries that are located in the query range will be add to the result.

3.4 Discussion on Query Performance

The unique features of the Ag-Tree are that, the information in different dimensions is divided and stored in different nodes, and the aggregate values are stored in independent nodes. Thus, the Ag-Tree appears to be efficient for PD range queries. No matter they are with or without aggregate operations.

Certainly, we also can build two aggregate cubetrees for range queries without aggregate operations and with aggregate operations, respectively. This way, however, (a) heavily wastes space, especially for large datasets, (b) maintaining two indices needs extra cost, and (3) the above problem of PD range queries still remains even two indices are built.

The structure of the Ag-Tree guarantees that it can be applied to PD range queries with any combinations of the query dimensions, no matter such PD range queries are with or without aggregate operations. The information in the dimensions that are irrelevant to the current query is not read from disk for PD range queries and the aggregate values are read from disk only when they are necessary. Moreover, as mentioned in the discussion of Table 1, even not all nodes (of the visited node-groups) corresponding to the query dimensions are necessary to be checked.

Next, let us see AD range queries. The Ag-Tree still appears to have advantage over the aggregate cubetree considering 1) aggregate values are read from disk only when they are necessary and 2) although all of the nodes in the visited node-groups intuitively have to been accessed for AD range queries, it is actually not true. Let us see the reason by an example in a three-dimensional index space, which is shown in Fig. 3.

In Fig. 3, because the MBR of the current node-group intersects the query range, the entries (the dotted cuboides) in this node-group should be investigated. Anyway, since all these entries do not intersect the query range in the X-Y plane, the Z-axis need not be checked. That is, the node corresponding to the Z-axis in this node-group can be skipped and the information in the Z-axis in this node-group need not be read from disk. Note that, if the X-Z plane is first checked, the node corresponding to the Y-axis can be skipped. More importantly, for the higher-dimensional spaces, because the MBRs (entries) in each

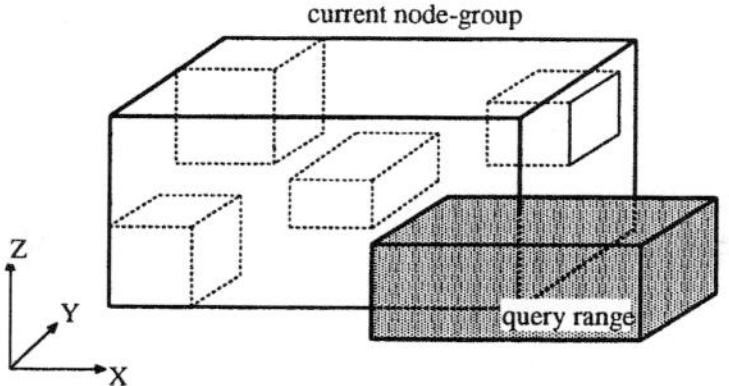

Fig. 3. Example of AD range queries

node-group become sparser, it generally becomes possible to skip more nodes in the visited node-groups. This means that, in the visited node-groups, the information in one or more dimensions possibly need not be read from secondary storage even for all-dimensional range queries. On the contrary, for all-dimensional indices (e.g., the aggregate cubetree), the information corresponding to all of the dimensions in the visited nodes have to be read from disk.

Thus, even for AD range queries, the Ag-Tree also probably has better query performance than the aggregate cubetree, especially for AD range queries without aggregate operations (so many aggregate values have to be read from disk in the case of the aggregate cubetree, although they are not used at all).

4 Experiments

Datasets having Zipf distribution with a constant of 1.5 (like the works [15, 17]) are used to examine the behavior of the Ag-Tree for range queries with or without aggregate operations. The datasets have 200000, 300000 and 500000 tuples, each of which have six attributes. Only the results for the dataset with 200000 tuples are presented in this paper because of the limitation on the number of pages. Note that the performance advantage of the Ag-Tree becomes slightly larger as the size of dataset grows.

All the experiments were performed with FreeBSD 4.5 release and the node size is 4096 bytes. Query performance is measured in term of the number of leaf node accesses because (1) I/O cost is still the performance bottleneck for many systems. Thus, the number of accessed nodes is tested and compared in many studies on multidimensional indexing, (2) the leaf nodes constitute the overwhelming majority of the total nodes and they tend to be stored in secondary storage [18], and (3) The Ag-Tree is wider than the aggregate cubetree and it is possibly lower than the Aggregate Cubetree since each node-group can holds more tuples. Thus, comparing the number of accessed leaf nodes is fairer.

The range queries having various numbers of query dimensions (from one to six) are tested with different range sizes. The ratio of the side length of query range to domain size of the corresponding query dimension varies from 10% to 100% in increments of 10%. The range query for the range of the same size is repeatedly 100 times with random locations and the average performance is presented. From the experiment results, we can see that the Ag-Tree can be used more efficiently to range queries, no matter they are with or without aggregate operations.

4.1 Range Queries Without Aggregate Operations

The experimental results are depicted in Fig. 4, where the X-axis represents range size and the Y-axis represents the number of accessed leaf nodes.

Figure 4 shows that

(1) as the number of query dimensions increases, the performance advantage of the Ag-Tree compared to the aggregate cubetree becomes weaker. Anyway, even for AD range queries, the advantage is still clear in most cases (see Section 3.4 for the reason),

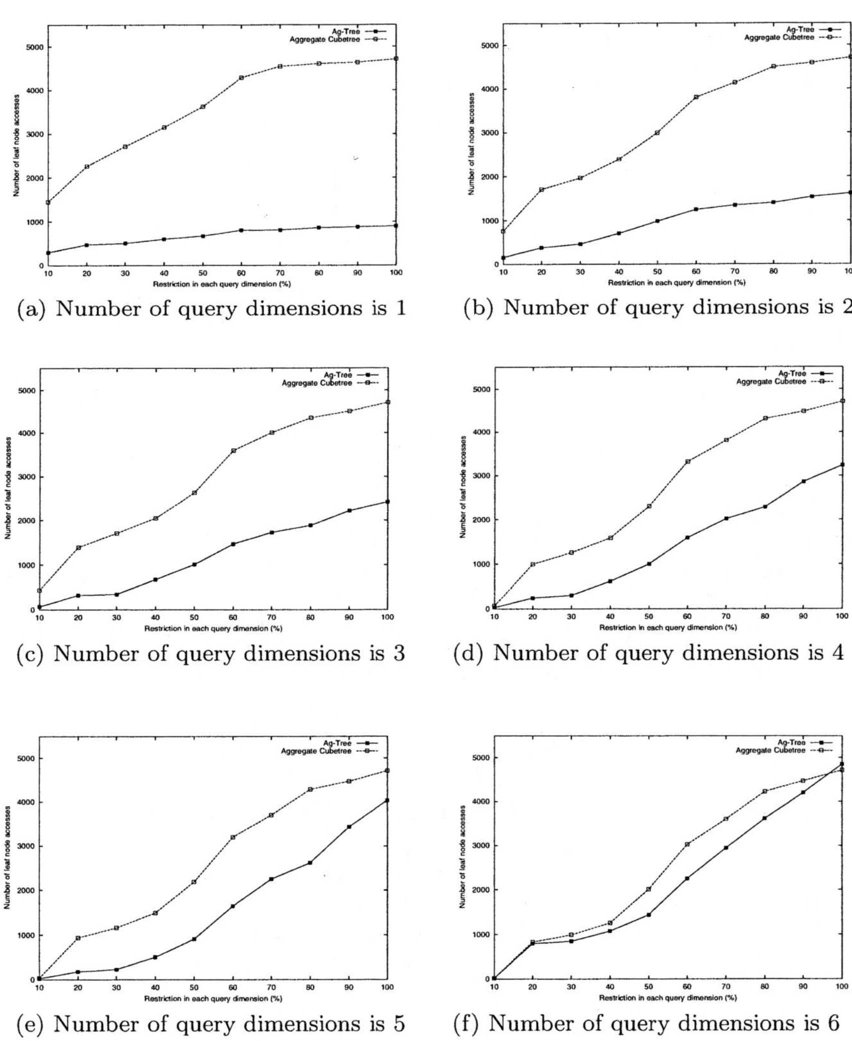

(a) Number of query dimensions is 1

(b) Number of query dimensions is 2

(c) Number of query dimensions is 3

(d) Number of query dimensions is 4

(e) Number of query dimensions is 5

(f) Number of query dimensions is 6

Fig. 4. Experimental result for range queries without aggregate operations

(2) the performance of range queries exerted on the aggregate cubetree becomes better as the number of query dimensions increases. This is because that the search region can be limited in more dimensions, and

(3) as the number of query dimensions increase, the query performance of the Ag-Tree varies in an interesting way. On the one hand, the number of accessed node-group decreases in the same reason as (2). On the other hand, the number of the accessed nodes in each accessed node-group may increases. Under these two conflicting influences, as the number of query dimensions increases, the query performance of the Ag-Tree does not change much in cases that the query size is not greater than 40%. However, if the query size exceeds 50%, the query performance of the Ag-Tree degrades clearly as the number of query dimensions grows. This seems because that more nodes generally have to be accessed in each visited node-group (see Fig. 3).

4.2 Range Queries with Aggregate Operations

The Range-SUM query is chosen as an example. The experiment result is shown in Fig. 5, in which the results for one and three query dimensions are not presented because the limitation of the number of pages and they do not lead to any new observations.

Figure 5 shows that both the query performance of the aggregate cubetree and that of the Ag-Tree degrade slowly as the query size grows. It appears

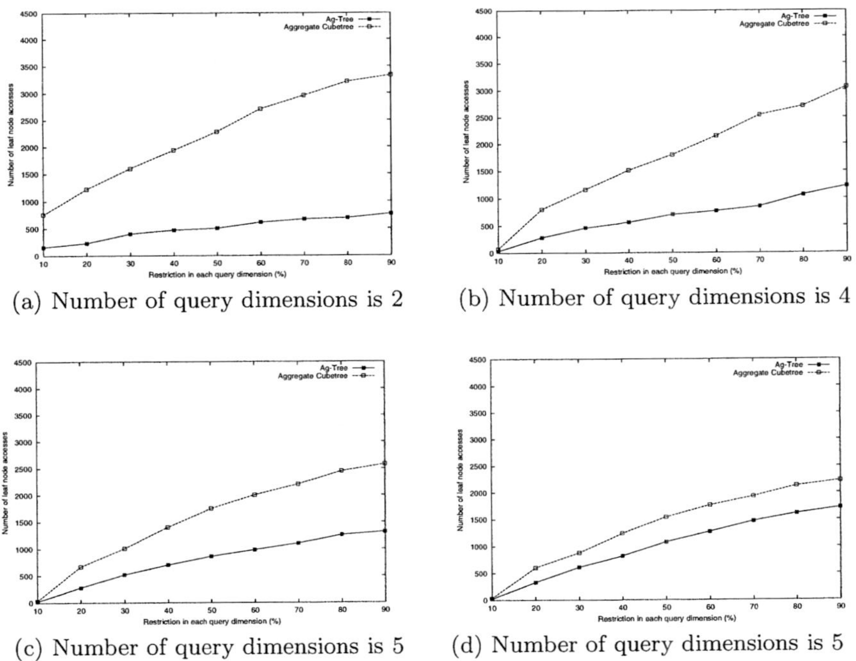

(a) Number of query dimensions is 2 (b) Number of query dimensions is 4

(c) Number of query dimensions is 5 (d) Number of query dimensions is 5

Fig. 5. Experimental result for range queries with Range-SUM

because that there are the following two conflicting tendencies as the query size increases.

1. More nodes intersect the query range.
2. More nodes are fully contained in the query range and their child/descendant nodes need not be checked.

The other observations are the same as those in Section 4.1.

5 Conclusion

In this paper, a novel structure for range queries in data warehouse environments is proposed. The proposed structure is called Aggregate-Tree and denoted as Ag-Tree, in which the information of each node entry is divided and stored in individual nodes according to the index dimensions. In addition, the necessary aggregate values are stored in separated nodes that are independent of the index nodes. In this way, for the partially-dimensional range queries (denoted as PD range queries in this paper) with or without aggregate operations, only the information in the query dimensions is possibly read from the disk. And, for the range queries without aggregate operations, no matter they are all dimensional range queries or partially-dimensional range ones, the aggregate values are not read from disk. The discussions and various experiments indicate that the proposed method can be efficiently used for range queries, no matter they are with or without aggregate operations. Although the proposed method is based on R*-tree, many other structures also can be employed. The basic requirements for applying the proposed method to an index structure are that (1) the index is MBR-based and, (2) in the index, the region that is covered by every node must be completely contained within the region of its parent node. Note that, the idea of the proposed method can not be used for the hyper-sphere-based structures (such as SS-tree), which are directed to nearest neighbor queries (e.g., similarity queries) and can not be efficiently used for range queries.

Acknowledgment

This research was supported in part by the Japan Society for the Promotion of Science through Grants-in-Aid for Scientific Research 17650031 and 16200005. In addition, the authors would like to thank Mr. Zhibin Wang, who conducted some of the experiments.

References

1. S. Chaudhuri, and U. Dayal: An overview of data warehousing and OLAP technology. ACM SIGMOD Record 26(1), pages 65-74, 1997.
2. R. Kimball: The Data Warehouse Toolkit. John Wiley & Sons, 1996.

3. N. Roussopoulos: Materialized Views and Data Warehouses. ACM SIGMOD Record, 27(1), pages 21-26, March 1998.
4. J. Gray, A. Bosworth, A. Layman, and H.Piramish: Data Cube: A Relational Aggregation Operator Generalizing Group-By, Crosstab, and Sub-Totals. Proc. International Conference on Data Engineering (ICDE), pages 152-159, 1996.
5. A. Guttman: R-Trees: A Dynamic Index Structure for Spatial Searching. Proc. ACM SIGMOD International Conference on Management of Data, pages 47-57, 1984.
6. C.Ho, R.Agrawal, N.Megiddo, and R.Srikant: Range Queries in OLAP Data Cubes. Proc. ACM SIGMOD International Conference on Management of Data, pages 73-88, 1997.
7. Nick Roussopoulos, Yannis Kotdis, and Mena Roussopoulos: Cubetree: Organization of and Bulk Incremental Update on the Data Cube. Proc. ACM SIGMOD International Conference on Management of Data, pages 89-99, 1997.
8. Yannis Kotdis, Nick Roussopoulos: An Alternative Storage Organization for ROLAP Aggregate Views Based on Cubetrees. Proc. ACM SIGMOD International Conference on Management of Data, pages 249-258, 1998.
9. H. Gupta: Selections of Views to Materialize in a Data Warehouse. Proc. International Conference on Database Theory (ICDT), pages 98-112, Delphi, January 1997.
10. I. S. Mumick, D. Quass, and B. S. Mumick: Maintenance of Data Cubes and Summary Tables in a Warehouse. Proc. ACM SIGMOD International Conference on Management of Data, pages 100-111, Tucson, Arizona, May 1997.
11. V. Harinarayan, A. Rajaraman, J. D. Ullman: Implementing data cubes efficiently. Proc. ACM SIGMOD International Conference on Management of Data, pages 205-216, 1996.
12. S.Sarawagi, R. Agrawal, and A. Gupta: On the computing the data cube. Research Report, IBM Almaden Research Center, Sanjose, Ca, 1996.
13. N. Beckmann, H. P. Kriegel, R. Schneider, and B. Seeger: The R*-tree: an Efficient and Robust Access Method for Points and Pectangles. Proc. ACM SIGMOD International Conference on Management of Data, pages 322-331, Atlantic City, NJ, May 1990.
14. S. Agrawal, R. Agrawal, P. Deshpande, and et al.: On the Computation of Multidimensional Aggregates. Proc.International Conference on Very Large Databases (VLDB), pages 506-521, August 1996.
15. S. Hong, B. Song, and S. Lee: Efficient Execution of Range Aggregate Queries in Data Warehouse Environments. Proc. International Conference on the Entity Relationship Approach (ER), page 299-310, 2001.
16. Y. Feng, A. Makinouchi: Adaptive R*-tree: An Efficient Access Method for Large Relational Datasets. IEICE Transaction on Information and Systems (submitted).
17. C. Zhang, J. Naughton, et.al.: On Supporting Containment Queries in Relational Database Management Systems. Proc. SIGMOD International Conference on Management of Data, pages 425-436, 2001.
18. G.R. Hjaltason and H.Samet: Distance Browsing in Spatial Database. ACM Trans. on Database Systems, 24(2), page 265-318, June, 1999.
19. L. V.S. Lakshmanan, J. Pei, and Y. Zhao: Qctrees: An Efficient Summary Structure for Semantic OLAP. Proc. ACM SIGMOD International Conference on Management of Data, 2003.
20. W. Wang, H.LU, J.Feng, And J.X.Yu: Condensed cube: An Effective Approach to Reducing Data Cube Size. Proc.Internatial Conference on Data Engineering (ICDE), 2002.

21. D. Xin, J. Han, X. Li, and B. W. Wah: Star-cubing: Computing Iceberg Cubes by Top-down and Bottom-up Integration. Proc.International Conference on Very Large Databases (VLDB), 2003.
22. Y. Feng, A. Makinouchi: Batch-Incremental Nearest Neighbor Search Algorithm and Its Performance Evaluation. IEICE Transaction on Information and Systems, Vol.E86-D, No.9, pp1856-1867, 2003.
23. X. Li, J. Han, H. Gonzalez: High-Dimensional OLAP: A Minimal Cubing Approach. Proc. International Conference on Very Large Databases (VLDB), page 528-539, 2004.

An XML Document Warehouse Model

Vicky Nassis[1], Tharam S. Dillon[2], Rajugan Rajagopalapillai[2], and Wenny Rahayu[1]

[1] Dept. of CS-CE, La Trobe University, Melbourne, Australia
{vnassis, wenny}@cs.latrobe.edu.au
[2] Faculty of Information Technology, University of Technology, Sydney, Australia
{tharam, rajugan}@it.uts.edu.au

Abstract. EXtensible Markup Language (XML) has rapidly gained importance as a mechanism for the exchange of information amongst heterogeneous sources over the web. In order to deal with the challenging task of managing the large volumes of data appearing, encoded in XML transactional databases, the need to explore the XML Document Warehouse (XDW) approach is initiated. The applications of the Requirement Engineering (RE) process and Object-Oriented conceptual models have proven their usefulness in building successful software models and solutions. In this paper we introduce an integration methodology for the development of XDWs. Initially we provide a formal notation of the structural design for the XDW conceptual model. Secondly we focus on deriving requirements for the XDWs by exploring the Goal-Question Metric (GQM) approach. We adapt and extend this concept to XDWs and introduce a method for developing warehouse requirements considering user viewpoints and organizational objectives. The implementation of our proposed warehouse requirement derivation model is demonstrated using a case study example extracted from a simplified real-world scenario.

1 Introduction

Data Warehouses contain data extracted from various transactional databases, which have been cleaned, aligned and combined. A great quantity of document data, web data and other semi-structured data is being increasingly encoded in XML transactional databases. EXtensible Markup Language (XML) has recently gained importance as a mechanism for the exchange of information between heterogeneous data sources over the web [1]. It is likely that a vast number of XML documents will comprise the would-be repository and include many disparate transactional XML databases. The need to efficiently manage large amounts of XML data motivated us to examine the data warehouse approach for XML data and documents, through the use of XML document marts and XML document warehouses.

1.2 Related Work

1.2.1 Data Warehouse

Since the introduction of dimensional modeling (which revolves around facts and dimensions), various design techniques have been introduced to capture multi-dimensional data (MD) at the conceptual level. These include: Ralph Kimball's Star

M.L. Lee, K.L. Tan, and V. Wuwongse (Eds.): DASFAA 2006, LNCS 3882, pp. 513 – 529, 2006.

Schema [2] from which the SnowFlake and StarFlake conceptual models were derived. In [3] [4] and [5], two different OO modelling approaches are demonstrated where data is described in n-dimensional cubes. In [6] the Object-Relational Star schema concentrates on data models and Object-Relational data warehouses with a distinct focus to provide support for the representation of two types of hierarchical relationships, which are aggregation and inheritance. These models both object and relational have a number of limitations if they were to be applied to XML Document Warehouses. The two major reasons include: (a) given XML's non-scalar, set-based and semi-structured nature, the object and relational data design model types lack the ability to accommodate XML design level constructs in an abstract and implemen tation-independent form, and (b) there is insufficient emphasis on capturing user requirements early at the design stage. Despite the success and dominance of data warehouse models, to our knowledge, no research directions exist that formally define and incorporate a requirement derivation model into a high-level conceptual model for semi-structured data (namely XML).

1.2.2 Goal Question Metric (GQM) Approach

Measurement is defined as a method that supports answering a range of questions and provides sufficient feedback in relation to the performance of a software development process in its entire duration. Given the measurement outcome it is then important to determine the degree of necessity for implementing activities to assist with the improvement of the software engineering process. At this stage a significant aspect involves examining each activity's overall impact to the software's development. The GQM approach was established for organizations that require meaningful measurement in terms of their thoroughly identified goals and projects, within the software engineering development process. Applying the GQM method mainly involves obtaining and utilizing essential data to: (a) identify organizational goals operationally and (b) interpret these (collected data) in terms of the related elements of the stated goals.

Gradually the use of the GQM approach deviated from its conventional purpose of identifying project deficiencies and evaluating goals. Nowadays it is currently encompassed in quality enhancement as a goal formation technique, targeting software development enterprises [7, 8]. Based on numerous studies [7, 8] in relation to the utilization of metrics and models in the industry, measurement proves valuable when it is instigated in a top-down approach and entails to: (a) concentrate on precisely identified goals, (b) apply to all objects (products, activities, resources) in the software development process and, (c) be interpreted based on the study of the organizational context, which includes its environment and goals as a whole.

1.3 Brief Overview of Our XML Document Warehouse (XDW) Model

The elements that comprise our proposed conceptual modeling approach for XML document warehouses, illustrated in [9], make this a distinct method as it utilizes two major components, which include: (a) the capability of *XML Document Structure*, to accommodate and explicitly describe heterogeneous, semi-structured data along with their relationship semantics (unlike flat-relational data), and (b) *XML Schema*, to describe, validate and provide semantics for its corresponding instance document (XML document). It also has the ability to capture OO concepts and relationships as well as intuitive XML specific constructs derived from class decompositions and granularity of components. (i.e. ordering and homogeneous aggregation relation-ships).

The proposed XDW model is composed of three levels: **(1) Requirement Level (RL):** Assists to the derivation of different dimensions (perspectives) of the document warehouse. This is accomplished through the development and elicitation of requirements based on the users viewpoints and organizational objectives. This level includes two main sub-components, namely: (a) *Warehouse Requirement Document*: Corresponds to the non-technically written outline of the XDW requirements, and (b) *OO Requirement Model*: Expresses all non-technical requirements into technical terms and software specific concepts using UML. **(2) XDW Conceptual Level:** Consists of two major components, which are: (a) The *XML FACT (xFACT) Repository*, which is a snapshot of the underlying transactional system for a given *context*, and (b) a collection of logically grouped *Conceptual Views*, which provide possible perspectives of the XML document hierarchy stored in the xFACT repository. These conceptual views can be grouped into logical groups, where each one is very similar to that of a given *subject area* [12] appearing in Object-Oriented conceptual modelling techniques. Each subject-area in the XDW model is referred to as a *Virtual Dimension* (VDim). VDim is called *virtual* since it is modelled using a *conceptual view* [13] (which is an *imaginary* XML document) and behaves as a dimension to a given xFACT. A requirement, which is captured in the *OO Requirement Model*, is transformed into one or more *Conceptual Views* [13], in association with the given xFACT. Therefore a valid requirement can be satisfied by one or more XML conceptual views for a given context (i.e. xFACT). **(3) Logical Level:** Involves the systematic transformation of the entire XDW conceptual model, into a major XML schema along with its corresponding XML document, through the use of generic transformation rules. This conversion process is demonstrated elaborately in our previous work [14].

1.4 Outline of Our XML Document Warehouse (XDW) Requirement Model

In [10, 15] we examined the concept of Requirement Engineering (RE), more specifically the *Goal-Oriented approach,* and proposed the XDW Requirement Model. RE, similar with the GQM approach, is concerned with the activities carried out by the system and the objectives of different stakeholders. Our XDW Requirement Model focuses on capturing and eliciting requirements early at the design stage, by taking into consideration organizational objectives as well as user viewpoints. Furthermore these are particularly related to the XDW on deriving dimensions as opposed to associating organizational objectives to the system functions, which is traditionally carried out in RE. The key issue is the principal of correspondence between the real world representation and its domain. This involves the mapping of real world entities in the system, which tends to facilitate a system's evaluation. Our XDW Requirement Modeling approach is unique as up to now there have been no attempts to capture requirements and the entirety of their semantic nature.

1.5 Contribution of the Paper

In this paper we concentrate on the first two levels of the XDW Model namely the Requirement Level and the XDW Conceptual Level. Our primary purpose is to introduce an integration methodology for the development of XDW's. In section 2 we provide a formal notation for our XDW conceptual model. This is achieved by using set theory approach to express the numerous types of components and relationships comprising the XDW conceptual model, which includes the XML FACT (xFACT) repository and the warehouse dimensions also referred to as Virtual Dimensions (VDim). Section 3 focuses on requirement formation for XDWs. It is important to recognize that until now, goal oriented approaches have been largely targeted at the development of software systems rather than focused on document warehouses involving embedded XML structures. This fact motivated us to explore the *Goal Question Metric (GQM) approach.* We adapt and extend this concept to accommodate XDW's and to propose a formal technique for deriving warehouse requirements considering the users viewpoints and organizational goals.

Based on the existing requirement-driven data warehouse models and/or research directions (mainly for relational data), requirements are identified and defined from given operational data. Our work differs from these directions as, users' views and organizational goals take priority rather than available operational data, semantics and/or formats. Therefore in our work operational data and its semantics are complementary and used to *refine* organizational goals as opposed to just *define* these.

The proposed Requirement Derivation Model using the GQM approach will be illustrated in detail with the use of a case study example. We investigate a possible XDW of a simplified version of a ***"Conference Publication"*** system used for managing and distributing conference proceedings of various international conferences held in different cities throughout the year. Conference proceedings consist of a collection of papers (past and present) stored in various geographically distributed conference databases/systems, in varying formats such as ACM, LNCS, IEEE. The system is similar to that of existing systems such as ACM Portal [16], SpringerLink [17] or IEEE Xplore® [18]. Logically, we treat all the different conferences and their proceedings as one big (logical) conference proceeding on the web (similar to the concept of a "global view" in enterprise systems).

2 Formal Model Definition for XML Document Warehouses (XDW)

The XDW conceptual model is composed of: (a) the XML FACT (xFACT) repository and (b) the Virtual Dimensions (VDims). A detailed illustration of the formal model definitions for the XDW Model is outlined in the following section.

2.1 Development of the XML FACT (xFACT) Repository

Definition A: *A context is more than a measure but instead is an item that is of interest for the organization as a whole [3, 11]. The xFACT repository is a snapshot of the underlying transactional system for a given context.*

The real world is comprised of a collection of entities and the relationships among them. A segment from the real world is referred to as a context, for instance our case study context is ***"Conference Publication"***.

At this stage, it is important to clarify the distinct meaning and representation of the xFACT repository, at the conceptual and logical levels respectively. At the conceptual level the data of a system's context is captured and represented into the xFACT conceptual model (Figure 1) using UML with the use of objects, object attributes and relationships. At the logical level, the use of generic rules accomplishes a systematic transformation of our Object-Oriented (OO) conceptual model (xFACT) into XML Schema along with its corresponding XML Document. The objects represented in UML at the conceptual level become object instances at the logical level. Therefore one major xFACT XML Document is a collection of instances of the objects in the xFACT conceptual model. That is to say that the xFACT model is a document repository but the object instances at the logical level are not considered as separate XML documents as they are in fact translated as XML elements. The complete transformation methodology for the xFACT model from conceptual level into logical level is illustrated in detail in [14] using generic rules.

The process of building the xFACT (Figure 1) for a given context involves to: (a) initially identify and name the real world objects, their attributes and relationships that may exist amongst these. The obtainment of the required information through descriptive declaration sets in the real world is a sufficient way to achieve this, and (b) map the identified components into equivalent UML objects, attributes and relationships.

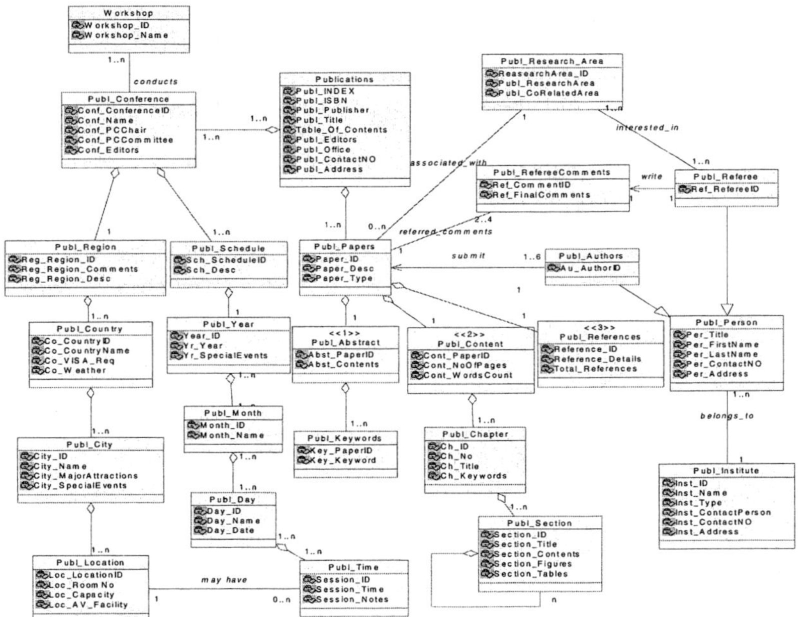

Fig. 1. The complete xFACT model of the *Conference Publication* Case Study

The list of equations below aims to uniquely discover real-world components and map these into appropriate objects and/or semantic relationships. For instance the real world object `Product` is mapped and named `Product` as a UML object in the xFACT conceptual model.

Z_o = *{The set of declarations that exclusively distinguish real world objects that map to UML objects}*

Z_α = *{The set of declarations that exclusively distinguish real world object properties that map to UML object attributes}*

Z_ρ = *{The set of declarations that exclusively distinguish real world object relationships that map to UML object relationships}*

Z = *{The set of declarations that exclusively distinguish all real world components}*

$$Z = Z_o \cup Z_a \cup Z_\rho \tag{1}$$

Equation (1) states that the union of all the declaration sets in the real world including, objects, objects attributes and objects relationships, composes **Z**.

The different types of relationships amongst objects appearing in the xFACT conceptual model may include: association, inheritance and forms of aggregation such as: ordered (a composite object consists of sub-objects which have a specific ordering), and homogeneous (one 'whole' object consists of 'part' objects that are of the same type) [9]. Based on a given context each of the identified object's relationship is expressed by cardinality which specifies how many instances of one class may be associated with a single instance of another class. Below $\boldsymbol{\beta}$ represents the cardinality set of values to be used:

$$\beta = \{0, 1, n\} \tag{2}$$

The cardinality values in (2) can form the following tuples which are presented in lower-bound upper bound format: (a) **(0..0)** *No* object instances may be connected to another. (b) **(0..1)** Indicates that *none* to maximum of *one* object instance to be connected to another. (c) **(0..n)** Signifies that *none* or *many* objects instances can be connected to another. (d) **(1..1)** Means that exactly *one* corresponding object instance is possible. (e) **(1..n)** Denotes that at least *one* object instance is connected to another and f) **(n)** means that there are no boundaries on minimum and maximum number of objects instances connected to another.

2.2 XML FACT (xFACT) Repository Domain

A *domain,* in general terms, relates with a set of possible values for a given entity, event, or subject matter. A universal real world domain is immense and having that a single context is one of its segments, signifies that all possible context domains are extracted from the one universal domain.

In equation (1) we stated that one important component is the set of declarations that identify real world object *properties*. At the conceptual level, in the xFACT model, these will correspond as object attribute values and similarly at the logical level as XML elements and/or XML attributes. Hence the value domain at each level namely, the real world, conceptual and logical levels, is composed of the collection of: real world object properties, conceptual object attributes and XML elements and/or XML attributes respectively.

Below the relationship between a real world context ψ_x where $1\leq x \leq n$ and the universal real world **w** is expressed, where each module has a domain **dom.**

$$dom(\psi_x) \subseteq dom(w) \quad (3)$$

Equation (3) indicates that a given real world context ψ_x domain is a proper subset of the entire real world **w** domain as there is at least one element/value in **w** that is not in ψ_x.

Let each of the real world object/s Δ_x, the corresponding conceptual object/s δ_x and for each object's XML schema and XML document, D_x at the logical level, to all have an individual domain **dom** where $1\leq x \leq n$. The domain mapping process starting from the real world level to conceptual level and finally to the logical level can be expressed as:

$$dom(\Delta_x) \rightarrow dom(\delta_x) \rightarrow dom(D_x) \quad (4)$$

The following equations (5) shows the mapping stages of a given real world context ψ_x, to its equivalent xFACT K_x at the conceptual level and the corresponding XML schema and XML document C_x at the logical level, where each level has a domain **dom** where $1\leq x \leq n$.

$$dom(\psi_x) \rightarrow dom(K_x) \rightarrow dom(C_x) \quad (5)$$

From the equations presented up to now, we can state that for a given context ψ_x, developing the conceptual model xFACT K_x is a matter of identifying and collecting the associated objects, attributes and relationships. Translating the conceptual model into the logical level becomes an entire XML schema together with an XML document, C_x. The concepts introduced so far are expressed as follows:

$$\begin{array}{lll} \textit{Real World Domain } \Delta_x \subseteq \psi_x & \text{and} & dom(\Delta_x) \subseteq dom(\psi_x) \\ \textit{Conceptual Level Domain } \delta_x \subseteq K_x & \text{and} & dom(\delta_x) \subseteq dom(K_x) \\ \text{Logical Level Domain } D_x \subseteq C_x & \text{and} & dom(D_x) \subseteq dom(C_x) \end{array} \quad (6)$$

2.3 Context Perspectives (Virtual Dimensions) Domains

In section 2.2 we stated that a context is a segment of the real world and can therefore be considered as one of the possible real world *perspectives*. In section 1.3 we defined that the various perspectives of the document hierarchy stored in the xFACT repository at the conceptual level are referred to as *Conceptual Views*. A logical group of conceptual views forms a *Virtual Dimension (VDim).* Requirements are formed based on the of the user's viewpoints and organizational objectives and are valid when fulfilled by one or more Conceptual View/VDim (section 1.3).

Let η_x equal to a real world perspective, also allow the corresponding generated Conceptual View/VDim equal to CV_x and at the logical level let the VDim XML schema and XML document to equal V_x, where all have value domains **dom** and $1\leq x \leq n$. These are expressed in (7).

$$\begin{array}{rl} \textit{Real World Level Domain} & \mathrm{dom}(\eta_x) \subseteq \mathrm{dom}(\psi_x) \\ \textit{Conceptual Level Domain} & \mathrm{dom}(CV_x) \subseteq \mathrm{dom}(K_x) \\ \textit{Logical Level Domain} & \mathrm{dom}(V_x) \subseteq \mathrm{dom}(C_x) \end{array} \quad (7)$$

Equation (8) shows the domain-mapping channel of all three levels.

$$\mathrm{dom}(\eta_x) \rightarrow \mathrm{dom}(CV_x) \rightarrow \mathrm{dom}(V_x) \quad (8)$$

Definition B: *A Virtual Dimension (VDim) is a subset of a given XML FACT (xFACT) model at the conceptual level. A collection of Virtual Dimensions composes the xFACT model, which denotes that the xFACT is a superset of the all the existing Virtual Dimensions.*

3 Requirement Derivation Model Using the Goal-Question Metric (GQM) Approach

In this section we will concentrate on the **Requirement Level** of the XDW model by introducing a requirement derivation technique using the principles of the Goal-Question Metric (GQM) approach.

Data warehouse requirements may arise from three main sources: (a) present and future organizational objectives based on current and past data, (b) user needs aligned with organizational objectives and (c) analytics used to fulfil organizational operations, such as frequent query paths (both internal and external) from the data warehouse.

Rather than focusing on the quality of a system's functionality, as it occurs in traditional goal-oriented approaches, we concentrate on the quality of products and/or services outlined in a given organizational context. What follows is a brief overview of our proposed Requirement Derivation Model for XDWs, shown in figure 3, which encompasses four main levels. (1) Establish primary organizational goals and define these based on the major principles of an organization, such as the products and services offered, the activities and resources used and ultimately the user viewpoints. The next step involves to decompose the derived high-level goals, where possible, to allow for new sub-goals to emerge. (2) Develop a set of questions for each stated goal to help discover various possible ways for their fulfillment. The questions formed are then used to assist in the discovery process of warehouse requirements. (3) The derived warehouse requirements are captured and modeled using our XDW Requirement Model, as illustrated in [10, 15], that will assist to generate the corresponding document warehouse dimensions. We use our requirement modeling approach because it is designed for XDWs and considering the presence of XML documents, the task of modeling the requirements and capturing their semantic nature, would otherwise be very challenging to attain. (4) Form a set of metrics in conjunction with the stated requirements that allows expressing each derived question in quantifiable terms. Metrics enable evaluation of the initial identified goals and determine the degree of their accomplishment. The implementation of our introduced Requirement Derivation methodology will be illustrated in more detail in section 3.2.

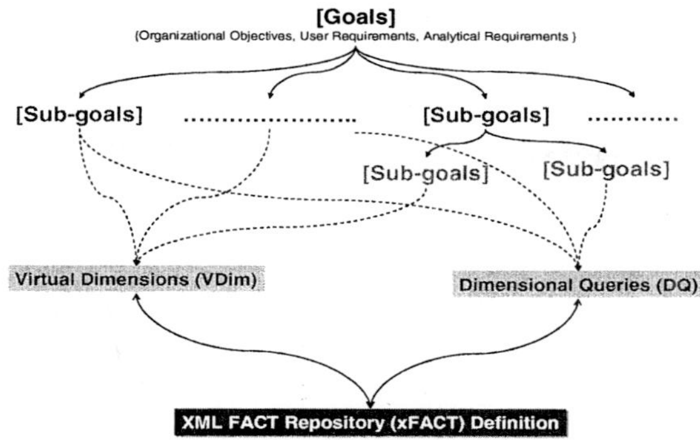

Fig. 2. Path from Goals to xFACT Repository Definition

We state that a *high-level goal* is a simplified, yet well-formulated and defined concept. The decomposition process involves breaking down one major component into several sub-segments. Goal decomposition generates one or more sub-goals, which provide an in-depth view and an enhanced understanding underlying the complexity of the concerned goal. Each well defined sub-goal corresponds to one or more *XML Warehouse Requirement*/(s), (XWR) which in turn corresponds to a collection of *definitions* for the *Virtual Dimension* (VDim) in the XDW model or warehouse (dimensional) queries. In simple terms, XWRs provide the blueprint for the VDims (and the dimensional queries) at the required level of complexity, abstraction and detail. The resulting collection of VDim (and the dimensional query) definitions, provide the formal blueprint of the xFACT. Conversely, a well-formulated xFACT should satisfy data and semantic requirements of all the VDims and dimensional queries that are formulated from the XWR. This concept is expressed in Figure 2.

3.1 Outline of the Requirement Derivation Model for XDWs

The Requirement Derivation Model is the initial stage that provides the foundation to help guide the design of the overall XDW structure. The intention is to map the derived requirements to corresponding data warehouse dimensions and subsequently configure the xFACT repository. The main themes of this methodology are to:

(1) Identify high-level goals based on the organizational objectives as well as user viewpoints.
(2) Understand the current stated goals and through hierarchical decomposition to derive one or more sub-goals. It is important to note that the level of decomposition varies for each goal as it depends on degree of their complexity. The higher the goal complexity, the more decomposition required.
(3) Explore the possibility for each sub-goal to be further elicited to promote new goals, which would have not been otherwise considered.
(4) Obtain the leaf goals, meaning the goals formed from the resulting decomposition process, and for each one to derive a set of corresponding questions that define this in *operational terms*. In other words to identify probable ways that will lead to goal fulfillment.

(5) Derive a set of warehouse requirements (XWRs) to address each formed question and represent these requirements using the XDW Requirement Model. This process will determine *'what'* data is to be collected and *'how'* it will be carried out depending initially on the data stored in the xFACT repository. In the case where a requirement cannot be fulfilled with the current available data, it is then necessary to refer to the XML transactional document databases and obtain the additional data.

(6) Develop a set of metrics by using the already established warehouse requirements (XWRs), to address each question and express it in *quantifiable terms.* A metric outcome assists in goal evaluation and determines the degree of its accomplishment.

Our proposed Requirement Derivation Model's (Figure 3) foundation lies in the GQM principles. This model is composed of four main levels: **(1) Abstraction Level:** This has two sub-levels namely the *High-Level Goal* and the *Sub-Goal Level.* **(2) Operational Level:** Form questions to express the stated goals in operational terms and lead to the derivation of warehouse requirements. **(3) Requirement Modeling Level:** Apply the XDW Requirement Modeling approach [10, 15] to capture and represent the developed warehouse requirements. The modeling of requirements reveals the kind of data required to be obtained for their fulfillment. **(4) Quantitative Level:** Develop a set of metrics using the formerly defined warehouse requirements. These metrics help to answer the formed questions stated at the *Operational Level* and evaluate the degree of accomplishment of the goals derived at the *Abstraction Level.* What follows is a detailed discussion of each level.

1. Abstraction Level

This level represents the possible goals that can be formed based on a given organizational context. In order to obtain the specifications that will be used to construct goals, the main factors to consider are, the configuration and the intentions of the organization as well as the user viewpoints. Goal development relies on three main sources of information, which includes to: (a) conduct an initial study of the organizational policy statements and strategic plans. (b) Obtain the descriptions of the organizational objects (products, services, activities and resources) and (c) assess the organizational model in order to reveal the possible user viewpoints of a given goal.

Definition C: *A goal is defined as a component which includes the following elements: (1) The object of study, (2) the products and services offered by an organization, (3) the activities involved for the successful establishment of the products and services, (4) the resources used in order to produce the products and services and (5) the likely user viewpoints.*

There are two sub-levels as shown in Figure 3: The *High-Level Goal* and the *Sub Goal Level.* A high-level or an abstract goal indicates its wide-ranging nature. In mostcases, abstract goals tend to be accompanied by high levels of complexity andtherefore might be difficult to fulfill at first. Hence it is necessary to decompose the high-level goal into several sub-goals. This leads to the creation of the *Sub-Goal Level.* Decomposition provides an enhanced understanding of the current goals and identifies new avenues for their accomplishment. In our proposed requirement derivation plan (Figure 3) where the high level goal has an arrow pointing to itself,

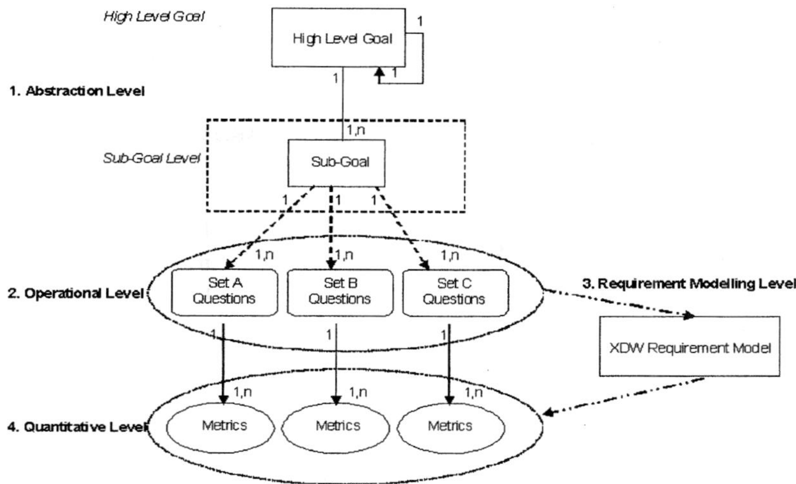

Fig. 3. Requirement Derivation Model for XDWs Using the GQM Approach

indicates that a goal does not always need to be decomposed but instead can remain in its current state, given that its level of complexity is low. This justifies that it is possible for a direct link to exist from the *Abstraction Level's, High-Level Goal* to the *Operational Level.* The dotted rectangle surrounding the sub-goal level, shown in Figure 3, indicates an optional component.

2. Operational Level

As discussed previously a direct connection may exist amongst the *Operational Level* and the two preceding sub-levels, meaning that it can be immediately related either to a high-level goal or a newly formed sub-goal. The structure of the questions formed at the *Operational Level* depends entirely on the specifications of the identified goals. A set of corresponding questions is generated for the each derived leaf goal (using the decomposition process) to express this in operational terms.

The purpose of using questions is to discover possible ways for goal fulfillment and based on the data availability to determine the capabilities encompassed or lack of, to satisfy given requirements. There are three categories for each question set, which are as follows:

- **Set A:** How can the object (product/service, activity, resource) in question, which relates to the overall goal as a whole be described?
- **Set B:** How can the object's attributes in question, which relate to the concerned issue of the stated goal, be expressed?
- **Set C:** How can the object's characteristics in question, which relate to the concerned issue of the given goal, be evaluated?

3. Requirement Modeling Level

The questions formed at the *Operational Level* bring to the surface the main elements composing a given goal. Warehouse requirements (XWRs) consist of the collection of key components identified in the questions. Our definition of a *requirement* as stated in [10, 15], denotes the expectant outcome of the data warehouse for a given context. Requirement accomplishment correlates with *'what'* kind data is required and *'how'* to obtain these from the XML transactional document database. The established requirements are then modeled using our XDW Requirement Modeling approach [10, 15]. The aims of this approach are to: (a) capture requirements early in the design process, (b) understand the current and newly formed requirements, (c) use each requirement(s) to create a corresponding XDW dimension, (d) ensure that the required data to construct a dimension is available and extracted from the XML transactional document database, and (e) certify that the collected data used for the formation of all warehouse dimensions, is assembled to build the entire xFACT repository. The full illustration of the modeling of requirements using the XDW Requirement Model can be found in our existing work [10, 15]. In this paper we will only demonstrate the derivation of requirements.

4. Quantitative Level
A set of metrics is formed through the combination of one or more of the already identified requirements, with the aim to address each question created at the *Operational Level.* Hence a single metric consists of one or a collection of warehouse requirements (XWR). Tracing each metric outcome to the concerned goal carries out the evaluation of its fulfillment. In the case where a metric cannot be fulfilled indicates that one or more of its included requirement components, cannot be satisfied with the information at hand and therefore it is necessary, only at the design stage, to refer back to the XML transactional document databases to obtain the additional required data. At this point it is important to visualize the link amongst the three major components including: XML transactional document databases, the Virtual Dimensions (warehouse dimensions) and the XML FACT (xFACT) repository. Hence it is critical to be able to move through this link from any direction to certify the correct assembly of the XDW. In this paper we will demonstrate the formation of metrics to be used for goal evaluation. The actual goal evaluation process based on the metrics outcomes will be demonstrated in future work.

3.2 Implementation of the Requirement Derivation Model for XDWs

This section provides an illustration of the outlined components of our proposed methodology for deriving requirements using the GQM approach. The sample context that will be used throughout is a ***"Conference Publication"*** case study.

The *Abstraction Level,* shown in Figure 4, is a framework of the possible goals that can be derived based on the case study context. Given the five main sources of information to define a goal, as stated in section 3, definition C, we form a sample high-level goal which is to *'Secure a Well Renowned Conference Status'*. Applying the decomposition process of the high-level goal derives smaller segments, namely the sub-goals. This process proves beneficial as it provides a clear overview and anenhanced understanding of the current complexity issue surrounding the goal in question, which assists to identify appropriate solutions in an efficient and direct manner. The decomposition process for each goal ceases depending on the developer's judgment and level of satisfaction. For instance the first sub-goal *"Improve the Paper Review Process"* is further decomposed to two more secondary

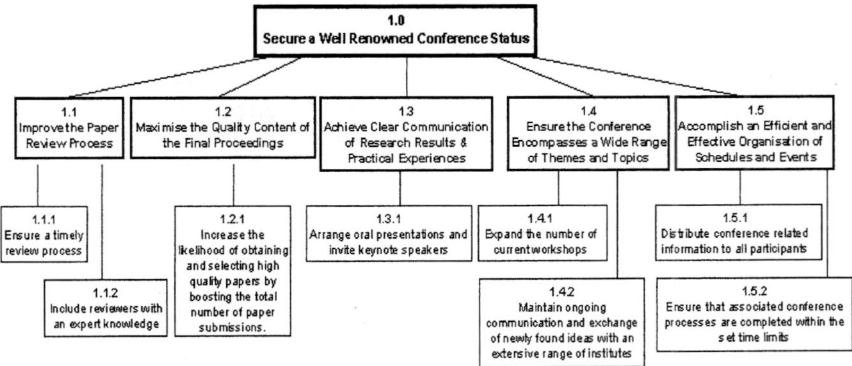

Fig. 4. "Abstraction Level" of the *Conference Publication* Context

goals, also referred to as 'leafs', which include to *"Ensure a timely review process"* and *"Include reviewers with an expert knowledge"*. This indicates that all the identified sub-goals when combined contribute to the achievement of their parent goal and subsequently the major high-level goal.

Provided the specifications of the derived leaf goals, proceeding to the *Operational Level* involves forming questions that express each of the obtained goals in operational terms. Questions bring to the surface probable ways of achieving each goal, as well as determining whether the adequate data exists to satisfy these. The major elements identified in the questions, will help form the warehouse requirements (XWRs), which will then be modeled at the *Requirement Modeling Level.* At the *Quantitative Level,* by using the identified warehouse requirements, a set of metrics is developed which relate with the process of the overall goal evaluation. As stated previously, due to space limitations the actual modeling of the requirements and the evaluations for goal accomplishment will not be carried out in this paper.

The section that follows is a demonstration of the remaining three components, namely the *Operational Level, Requirement Modeling Level and Quantitative Level,* of our proposed model to derive warehouse requirements. We choose the sample case study sub-goal to *"Maximize the Quality Content of the Final Proceedings"* which is further decomposed and one of the goals formed is to "*Increase the likelihood of obtaining and selecting high quality papers by boosting the total number of paper submissions.*

– Goal 1.2 Maximize the Quality Content of the Final Proceedings

Sub-Goal 1.2.1 Increase the likelihood of obtaining and selecting high quality papers by boosting the total number of paper submissions.

Set A Questions: *How can the object (product/service, activity, resource) in question, which relates to the overall goal as a whole, be described?*

1. What is the current number of submitted papers?
2. Is conference related information actually distributed to a wide range of audience and highly prominent institutions?
3. How many of the accepted papers have been awarded outstanding reviews?

Requirements:
1. Total number of papers submitted for the year 2005 listed by conference name.
2. List of methods for communication.
3. Total time consumed distributing conference related information.
4. Total number of accepted papers listed by conference name.
5. Total number of accepted papers where reviewers rating equals '1'.

Metrics:
1. Total number of submitted papers for the year 2005 listed by conference name.
2. Total time dedicated and in distributing conference related information displayed in ascending order with cross reference to the method used.
3. Total number of accepted papers where reviewers rating equals '1' ordered by conference name.

Comments:
The requirements *"List of methods for communication"* and *"Total time consumed distributing conference related information"* (numbered 2 and 3), are derived based on the second question *"Is conference related information actually distributed to a wide range of audience and highly prominent institutions?"* Based on the xFACT model (figure 1), its objects and the data stored, the second metric (2), which is formed based on the combination of these two requirements, cannot not be fulfilled, as the data required is inexistent. Therefore it is required to refer to the XML transactional document databases to obtain the necessary data and create two more objects in the xFACT model, such as: "Technology" which will contain information on the current technological processes and equipment used, and "Recipient" which will include all the details of contacts for correspondence. Regarding the remainder list of requirements, there is adequate information stored in the xFACT to facilitate their full accomplishment.

Set B Questions: *How can the object's attributes in question, which relate to the concerned issue of the stated goal, be expressed?*
1. What is the standard deviation of the current actual number of papers submitted from the rough estimate?
2. What is the rate of the submitted papers where the authors belong to well-known associations?
3. Does the group of reviewers allocated in each conference theme acquire the sufficient expert knowledge?
4. Has there been a significant change in the total number of paper submissions between 2004 and 2005?
5. What is the rate of acceptance from the total number of submissions?

Requirements:
1. List of papers with cross-reference to authors' details ordered by institute and region.
2. List of reviewers' details.
3. Total number of submitted papers ordered by conference and by year.
4. Estimated number of papers to be submitted ordered by conference name.
5. Total number of accepted papers.

Metrics:

1 {(Current number of submitted papers – Estimated number of paper submissions)/ number of submitted papers} * 100

2. (Number of papers with authors belonging to well-known associations / Total number of submitted papers) * 100
3. List of reviewers' details ordered by their strongest area of expertise, and displayed under each allocated conference theme.
4. Difference (subtraction) of the total numbers of papers submitted between 2005 and 2004.
5. Percentage (%) increase or decrease of papers submitted compared to the year 2004.
6. (Total number of accepted papers / Total number of submitted papers) * 100

Comments:

The requirements *"Total number of submitted papers ordered by conference and by year"* and *"Estimated number of papers to be submitted ordered by conference name"* (numbered 3, 4), are derived given the first question *"What is the standard deviation of the current actual number of papers submitted from the rough estimate?"* The metric (1) cannot not be achieved, as the data required to carry out estimation calculations is not stored in the xFACT model. It is required to obtain additional data from the XML transactional document databases and include another object, titled "Budget", which will include all future estimations and future approximations for each conference.

Set C Questions: *How can the object's characteristics in question, which relate to the concerned issue of the given goal, be evaluated?*

1. Is the overall quality content of the final proceedings satisfying from the program committee viewpoint?
2. Is there a noticeable improvement on the quality of the final selected papers in 2005 compared to the year 2004?

Requirements:

1. Average evaluation score for each conference.
2. Total score of the feedback evaluation for each conference for the year 2005.
3. Total number of evaluation forms completed.

Metrics:

1. Total score of evaluation for each conference / Total number of evaluation forms completed.
2. Total score of evaluation for each conference for the years 2004 and 2005 displayed in descending order.
3. Difference (subtraction) of the total evaluation scores for each 2004 and 2005.
4. Percentage (%) increase or decrease of evaluation scores of the proceedings for each conference in comparison with the previous year 2004.
5. Subjective evaluation from the program committee and targeted audience.

Comments:

There are two ways to fulfill the questions created regarding the quality of the conference proceedings: (1) Objective evaluation of the proceedings quality, which cannot be fulfilled given the current data contained in the objects of the xFACT model. Conducting an evaluation process by distributing feedback forms, where individual scoring and comments are permitted, can perform this. An object named "Feedback" to contain additional is required in the xFACT model, and (2) subjective evaluation, which is based mainly on the personal opinion and judgment from the viewpoint of which it is taken.

4 Conclusions and Future Work

XML supports the representation and exchange of information amongst heterogeneous data sources over the web. It is likely that the presence of XML documents in the would-be repositories will grow rapidly. The challenge to effectively manage such a vast number of XML documents, initiates the need to explore the data warehouse approach through the use of XML document marts and XML Document Warehouses (XDWs).

In this paper, at the conceptual level we provide a formal model with derived sets of rules for our XDW model, which includes the XML FACT (xFACT) repository and the Virtual Dimensions (VDims). The second major aspect concentrates on the derivation of XDW requirements. This is accomplished by exploring the Goal Question Metric (GQM) approach and in conjunction with our existing XDW Requirement Modeling approach we introduced a methodology for generating warehouse requirements (XWRs). We illustrated the implementation of this approach, using a walk through of examples extracted from our case study.

For future work many issues deserve investigation. Primarily to propose a formal step algorithm to demonstrate the association between the three major components: XML Document Warehouse requirements (XWR), Virtual Dimensions (VDims) and the XML FACT (xFACT) repository and to show each component's role and significance in contribution to the overall construction of the XDW. Next is to build an empirical study plan to validate the XDW model. Also we need to investigate feasible technologies to automate the mapping between the XDW content and the XDW repositories along with their semantics intact (conceptual and operational). Performance issues associated with this challenging task need to also be addressed.

References

1. J. Pokorn'y, "XML Data Warehouse: Modelling and Querying," Proc. of the Baltic Conf. (BalticDB-IS '02), 2002.
2. R. Kimball and J. Caserta, *The data warehouse ETL toolkit : practical techniques for extracting, cleaning, conforming, and delivering data.* Hoboken, NJ: Wiley, 2004.
3. J. Trujillo, et al., "Designing Data Warehouses with OO Conceptual Models," in *IEEE Computer Society, "Computer"*, 2001, pp. 66-75.
4. S. Lujan-Mora, et al., "Extending the UML for Multidimensional Modeling," Fifth Int. Conf. on the Unified Modeling Language and its applications (UML '02), Dresden, Germany, 2002.
5. A. Abelló, J. Samos, and F. Saltor, "Understanding facts in a multidimensional object-oriented model," 4th Int. Workshop on Data Warehousing and OLAP (DOLAP '01), 2001.
6. W. Rahayu, T. S. Dillon, et al., "Object-Relational Star Schemas," 13th IASTED Int. Conf. on Parallel & Dist. Comp. and Sys. (PDCS '01), USA, 2001.
7. Basili, V. Caldiera, G. and Rombach, D. *"The Goal Question Metric Approach"* Encyclopedia of Software Engineering. Wiley, 1994.
8. Fuggetta, A., et al.., *"Applying GQM in an Industrial Software Factory"* ACM Transactions on Software Eng. and Methodology, Vol. 7, No. 4, October, 411-488, 1998.
9. V. Nassis, R.Rajugan, T. S. Dillon, and W. Rahayu, "XML Document Warehouse Design," 6th Int. Conf. on DaWaK '04, Zaragoza, Spain, 2004.
10. V. Nassis, et al., "Goal-Oriented Requirement Engineering for XML Document Warehouses," in *Proc. and Managing Complex Data for Decision Support,*: IGP, 2006.

11. M. Golfarelli, et al., "The Dimensional Fact Model: A Conceptual Model for Data Warehouses," *Int. J. of Cooperative Information Systems*, vol. 7, pp. 215-247, 1998.
12. T. S. Dillon and P. L. Tan, *Object-Oriented Conceptual Modeling*: Prentice Hall, Australia, 1993.
13. R.Rajugan, et al., "A Three-Layered XML View Model: A Practical Approach," 24th Int. Conf. on Conceptual Modeling (ER '05), Klagenfurt, Austria, 2005.
14. V. Nassis, et al., "Conceptual and Systematic Design Approach for XML Document Warehouses," *Int. Journal of Data Warehousing and Mining*, vol. 1, No 3, 2005.
15. V. Nassis, R.Rajugan, T. S. Dillon, and J. W. Rahayu, "A Requirement Engineering Approach for Designing XML-View Driven, XML Document Warehouses," The 29th Int. Computer Software and Applications Conf. (COMPSAC '05), Edinburgh, Scotland, 2005.
16. A. Portal, "(http://portal.acm.org/)," ACM, 2005
17. Springer, "SpringerLink: http://www.springerlink.com," Springer, 2005.
18. IEEE, "IEEE Xplore®: http://ieeexplore.ieee.org," Rel 1.8 ed: IEEE, 2004.

An Evaluation of Concurrency Control Protocols for Web Services Oriented E-Commerce

Hong-Ren Chen

Graduate Institute of Technology Development and Communication,
National University of Tainan, Tainan 70005, Taiwan, R.O.C
hrchen@mail.nutn.edu.tw

Abstract. Web services oriented computing is a hot topic for many e-commerce applications recently. It dramatically speeds up the application process and becomes more agile in responding to changing business needs. In this paper, we study the concurrency control problems among interleaved transactions for web services oriented e-commerce. We propose a new method called two-phase locking with adjustable slack time (2PL-AST) based on a high priority mechanism, which resolves the concurrent data access for both real-time and non-real-time support operations. The design issue aims to meet the deadline requirements of real-time transactions and minimize the response time of non-real-time transactions in the web services family at the same time. Experiments are conducted to evaluate the performance under different concurrency control protocols.

1 Introduction

Web services oriented technologies are important for building distributed applications, which are typically constructed from a set of services that are independently designed. The widespread adoption of web services offers advantages including: interoperability, stability, and implementation reuse. The structure of a typical web services application is shown in Fig. 1 [1]. It consists of resources, application logic, and a message-processing layer that deals with message exchanges. When a services oriented message arrives at a web services the message processing changes it into something more tangible for applications to deal with. Such web services transactions include the execution of short-running transactions within an organization and long-running transactions across organizations [2].

Each activity in web services transactions may request access data executing by subtransactions in real-time or non-real-time situations. For practical purposes, the activity is considered to consist of a nested web services transaction. An Internet purchasing example as illustrated in Fig. 2 involves the following four steps: (1) selecting the product, (2) providing personal data that allows the credit card to be authorized, (3) checking the number of products in the inventory management services, and (4) confirming a customer's order and total payment [3-5]. The activities of credit authorization and customer accounting must be executed timely, and the inventory management services are commonly encapsulated with several activities to execute. In the familiar example of stock market analysis and program trading,

M.L. Lee, K.L. Tan, and V. Wuwongse (Eds.): DASFAA 2006, LNCS 3882, pp. 530 – 540, 2006.

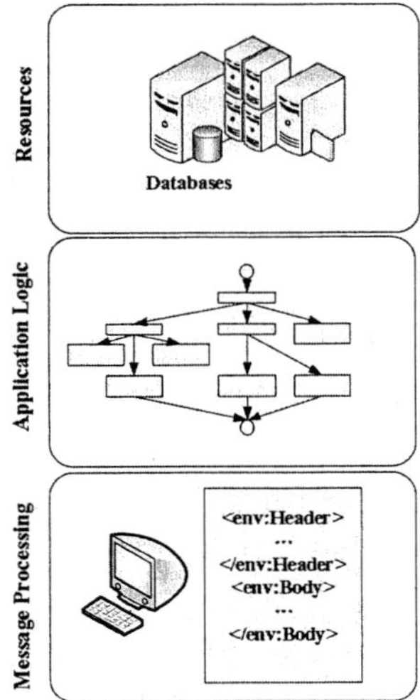

Fig. 1. The web services oriented architecture [1]

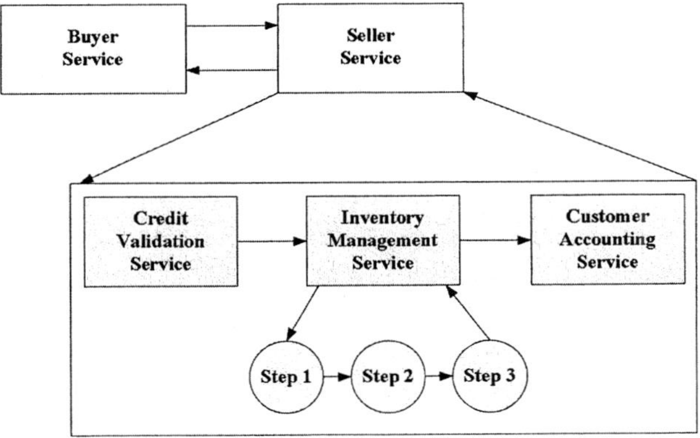

Fig. 2. The business process of an internet purchasing [5]

information on stock prices is gathered through multiple sources and piped through a series of filters for refinement. The information is then used by an expert system that spots trading opportunities. Some serious activities in web-based stock trading systems perhaps involve real-time supports. The purpose of activities for system management belongs to traditional web-based transactions [6].

In fact, the need to manage different styles of resource access conflicts and ensure the consistency of data in web services is based on concurrency control protocols. The services broker gets a lot of requests for its information and; it needs to be able to decide who wants what and whether or not they are granted access. Locking mechanisms are the standard method of concurrency control for most web-based database applications. The idea behind locking is intuitively simple and effective as stated in many previous publications [7]. Each data object has a lock associated with it. Before a web services transaction can access a data object, the concurrency control must first examine the lock associated with that data object. If the lock is free, the lock is granted to the web services transaction and the data object can be accessed by the web services transaction. The two-phase locking with high priority (2PL-HP) used in most commercially available database systems gives good performance for processing real-time transactions on the Internet [4,6,8]. This approach ensures that a higher priority transaction is never blocked by a lower priority transaction, and the conditional restart avoids the starvation problem through the high priority technique. The problem of priority inversion is resolved by using priority inheritance [4]. In spite of many research efforts concerning the concurrency control problem, the findings often assume that the system may consist of only one single type of data that is required in real-time. We know that real-time or non-real-time activities may exist simultaneously in the nested web services transactions described in Fig 2. The impacts of different non-real-time features on these concurrency control protocols have been conspicuously been ignored in previous studies in this topic. To correct this omission, a new concurrency control protocol must incorporate the access needs of real-time and non-real-time features. The design must minimize the number of missed real-time transactions and maximize the throughput of non-real-time transactions. A new concurrency control protocol called two phased locking with adjustable slack time (2PL-AST) is proposed to satisfy the concurrent data access of nested web services transactions supporting different degrees of real-time constraints. The main concepts of 2PL-AST are (1) give priority data access to real-time web services transactions, (2) utilize slack time to allow non-real-time web services transactions to access data, and (3) use conditional restart and priority inheritance to avoid the problem of starvation and priority inversion as stated in [4]. Simulations demonstrate that 2PL-AST delivers good performance when web services applications require data access in different real-time supports in the system.

The remainder of this paper is organized as follows. Section 2 describes the related work and the proposed concurrency control protocol. Section 3 provides the simulation model and performance results. Finally, a conclusion is made in Section 4.

2 The Proposed Concurrency Control Protocol

The web services oriented application is generally defined as a distributed database system where some transactions have deadlines on their completion times. Missing the deadlines can seriously affect the usefulness of completing the transactions. The goals are to satisfy transaction deadlines and to maintain database consistency. Concurrency control protocols strive to schedule data and to resolve data conflicts in such a way that transaction deadlines are taken into account [8]. The web services stack as shown in Fig. 3. Here we focus on the problem of data access conflicts among interleaved web services transactions in real-time and non-real-time support operations resolved by concurrency control protocols [2].

Concurrency control protocols are designed to maintain database consistency despite concurrent execution of transactions [8]. The two-phase locking protocol has been a popular mechanism to solve the problem of concurrent accesses to shared data

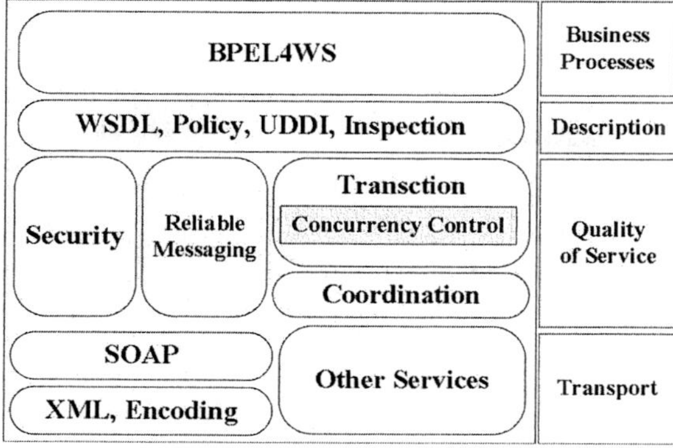

Fig. 3. The web services stack [2]

objects in most web-based database applications [7]. Some notable concurrency control protocols based on two-phase locking mechanism are introduced and notations used are listed briefly below. T_i denotes a (sub)transaction in the system. $S(T_i)$ means the slack time of transaction T_i. The remaining execution time of transaction T_i is denoted $E_{rt}(T_i)$.

2.1 Conventional Two-Phase Locking (2PL)

In 2PL, the execution of a transaction consists of two phases: the grow phase and the shrink phase. In the grow phase, locks are acquired but may not be released. In the shrink phase, locks are released but new locks may not be acquired [8]. For transactions to be executed timely, priority inversion occurs when a transaction with high priority is blocked by a transaction with lower priority.

2.2 Two-Phase Locking with High Priority (2PL-HP)

2PL-HP proposes restarting the lower priority lock holder and letting the higher priority lock requester get the lock. This resolves the problem of priority inversion for transactions with real-time constraints. Fig. 4 states the rule of 2PL-HP: if the priority of a lock-requesting transaction is higher than the lock-holding transaction, the lock-holding transaction is restarted. Otherwise, the lock-requesting transaction is blocked. Although it eliminates priority inversion, 2PL-HP causes severe access conflicts of

```
Algorithm 2PL-HP
Input: transaction Ti and Tj for accessing data object X, ∀Ti and Tj ∈ transaction set
Output: Ti or Tj accesses data object X
Begin
   If for all Tj holding a lock on data object X and P(Ti)>P(Tj) Then
      Restart each lock holder on data object X
   Else Ti blocked until release lock on data object X
   End-if
End-begin
```

Fig. 4. Pseudo code of 2PL-HP

system resources among transactions with different real-time support operations, and does not use the nested structure of web services applications.

2.3 Two-Phase Locking with Adjustable Slack Time (2PL-AST)

In 2PL-HP, the basic principle in resolving data conflicts between two web services transactions is to restart the lower-priority transaction [8]. In web services applications supporting real-time and non-real-time constraints, real-time transactions are always assigned higher priorities than non-real-time transactions. Thus, when there is an access conflict between a real-time transaction and a non-real-time transaction in web services applications, the non-real-time transaction is likely to be restarted leading to a poor performance of non-real-time transactions. To improve the total system performance, 2PL-AST (as shown in Fig. 5) is proposed using the key idea of adjustable slack time based on the high priority approach.

```
Algorithm 2PL-AST
Input: (sub)transaction Ti and Tj for accessing data object X, ∀Ti and Tj ∈ transaction set
Output: Ti or Tj accesses data object X
Begin
  Case 1: for all Tj holding a lock on data object X are same family members of Ti
          Ti blocked until release lock on data object X
          If P(Tj)<P(Ti) for transactions with real-time constraints Then
            Tj inherits P(Ti)
          End-if
  Case 2: for not all Tj holding a lock on data object X are same family members of Ti
          If P(Ti)>the highest P(Tj) with real-time constraints for non-family member Then
            If β×S(Ti) ≥ Σ_{j=1}^{m} Ert(Tj) with real-time constraints then
              If β×S(Ti)-Σ_{j=1}^{m} Ert(Tj) with real-time constraints ≥ Σ_{j=1}^{m} Ert(Tj) with non-real-time constraints Then
                Ti blocked until release lock on data object X
                Tj inherits P(Ti)
              Else
                Ti blocked until release lock on data object X
                Tj with real-time constraints inherits P(Ti)
                abort Tj with non-real-time constraints
              End-if
            Else
              abort all Tj except family members
            End-if
          Else
            Ti blocked until release lock on data object X
          End-if
          available family member Tj is processed by case 1
End-begin
```

Fig. 5. pseudo code of 2PL-AST

2PL-AST assigns the unique lowest priority value to all web services transactions with non-real-time constraints, because those transactions have no deadlines. When web services (sub)transactions have access conflicts among different interleaved web services transaction families, the high priority technique is used: it blocks or aborts the lower priority of web services (sub)transactions. The conditional restart procedure using adjustable slack time is incorporated in 2PL-AST to avoid the starvation problem of the high priority approach. This allows web services (sub)transactions with a lower priority to access data first instead of aborting, if the slack time is long

Table 1. Conflict resolution strategies in 2PL-AST

Lock-requester / Lock-holder	The same web services family		The different web services family	
	Real-time	Non-real-time	Real-time	Non-real-time
Real-time / Non-real-time	A, B	A	A, B, C	A

enough. Otherwise, lower priority web services (sub)transactions must be aborted. In a nested structure of web services oriented applications, (sub)transactions execute on behalf of their root transaction. Thus, subtransactions of the same web services family should not abort each other when access conflict occurs. When access conflict does occur within the members of a web services family, the priority inheritance method is used to avoid the problem of priority inversion [4].

The adjustable value of β is designed in response to the load of the practice system. β satisfies deadlines for real-time web services transactions and maximizes the throughput of non-real-time web services transactions. Table 1 shows the nested structure of web services transactions; the different conflict resolution strategies adopted in 2PL-AST are listed within and across a web services family. The symbol A represents blocking the lock-requester; B represents the technique of inheritance priority; and C represents using adjustable slack time to evaluate the opportunity of non-aborted (sub)transactions.

3 Simulation Model and Performance Evaluation

The architecture of simulation model as shown in Fig. 6 is defined as an open queuing model that has a network of n sites with a single external source and destination for transactions [9, 10]. Tsi indicates a transaction leaving the source for the queue in the site i and Tid presents a transaction leaving the queue in the site i for the destination. A transaction leaving the queue in the site i for the queue in site j is Tij. All accesses of local transactions existing in the central subsystem keep circulating from one queue to the next and reenter the system immediately. When a remote transaction issues the remote request, the central subsystem has external arrivals and departures. The simulation model at each site consists of four CPUs and two disks. This structure is similar to that of [3, 4, 8, 11, 12].

3.1 Workload Model and Performance Metric

Most of the workload parameters have similar values to those used in previous studies [3, 4, 11, 12]. Table 2 lists the workload model parameters and their baseline values. The parameters *page_cpu* and *page_io* determine the CPU and disk time needed to access a data page, respectively. The parameter used to model the load of the system is arrival_rate, which specifies the mean rate of transaction arrivals and has a Poisson

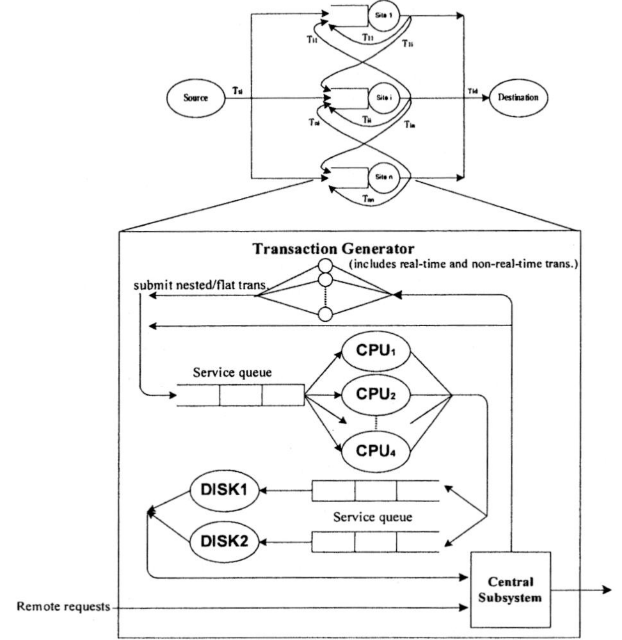

Fig. 6. The architecture of simulation model

distribution. In other words, the inter-arrival time of nested transaction is in exponential distribution with mean 1/arrival_rate. *Restart_delay* gives the delay timecaused by restarting a transaction. *Write_prob* determines the probability of updating data pages after a transaction has read the data pages. *Sub_trans* signifies the number of subtransactions varying randomly in a (sub)transaction tree. *Tran_size* represents the number of leaf subtransactions in a nested transaction, which is the mean of a uniform distribution varying range between 0.5**tran_size** and 1.5**tran_size**. The parameter *leaf_size* determines the number of operations per leaf subtransaction varying uniformly between 0.25**leaf_size** and 1.75**leaf_size**. The parameter *level_size* represents the depth of a nested transaction tree varying uniformly from 0.25**level_size** to 1.75**level_size**.

The performance metric of *MissRatio* as given in [3, 4, 8] were used:

$$MissRatio = \frac{\text{number of transactions missing the deadline}}{\text{total number of submitted transactions}} \times 100\%$$

A smaller the *MissRatio* implies the better performance. We compared the performance of the concurrency control protocols of the 2PL, 2PL-HP and 2PL-AST under various conditions, and also investigated the variety of response times for non-real-time transactions. For the transaction scheduling policy, we used the approach of earliest deadline first adopted widely for most types of real-time database research [6,11].

Table 2. Workload parameters and baseline values

Parameter	Description	Value
System		
num_sites	number of sites in the system	4
num_proc	number of processors in the site	4
page_cpu	CPU time for accessing a data page	0.03 ms
page_io	disk time for accessing a data page	4.8 ms
arrival_rate	the rate of real-time transaction arrivals the rate of non-real-time transaction arrivals	40 trans/sec 10 trans/sec
restart_delay	delay time to restart a transaction	5 ms
remote_trans	the ratio of remote transactions in the system	0.3
min_slack	minimal slack factor	2
max_slack	maximal slack factor	8
Transaction		
sub_trans	number of subtransactions in a (sub)transaction	4
tran_size	number of leaf subtransactions in a nested transaction tree	8
leaf_size	number of operations per real-time leaf subtransaction number of operations per non-real-time leaf subtransaction	4 8
level_size	the depth of a nested transaction tree	4
remote_op	the ratio of remote operations for a remote transaction	0.5
Database & Network		
db_size	number of pages in database	1600 pages
write_prob	write probability for accessing a data page	0.5
transfer_rate	transfer rate of the network	100Mbps
commit_time	commit time for completing a decision phase	40ms
comm_delay	communication delay between any two sites	dynamic

3.2 The Experiment of Basic Model

The settings for the basic parameters listed in Table 2 are based on the previous studies [3, 4, 11, 12]. In this experiment, we varied the arrival rate from 20 real-time Web services transactions/second (abbreviated as real-time trans/sec) to 120 real-time trans/sec in increasing steps of 20 in order to model different system loads. As shown in Fig. 7a, the performance order based on the *MissRatio* metrics is 2PL-AST > 2PL-HP > 2PL. From the figure, we see that the system misses more deadlines as the workload increases. This is consistent with our intuition: a heavier workload induces a longer queuing time, a higher probability of data conflicts and transaction blocking, and thus fewer transactions can meet their deadlines. 2PL performs the worst because the requesting transaction always blocks and waits for the data object to become free. This is the standard method for most database management systems which do not execute real-time transactions. 2PL causes some real-time demands to be delayed. The 2PL-AST algorithm gives real-time demands access to data without delay, and avoids useless restarts. 2PL-AST uses slack time to execute the transactions with lower priorities completely instead of restarting them. 2PL-AST uses the techniques

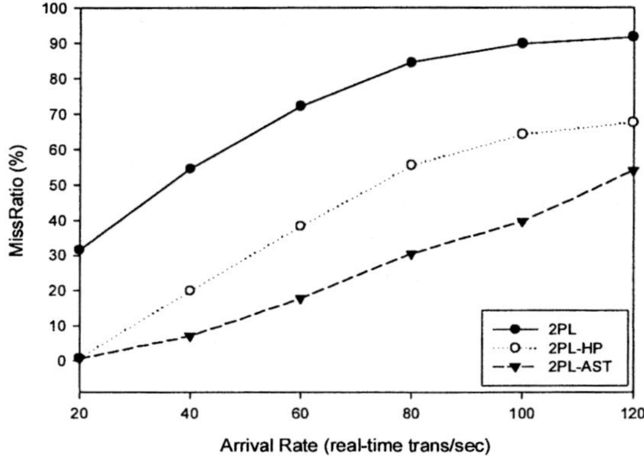

Fig. 7a. Miss ratio for basic model

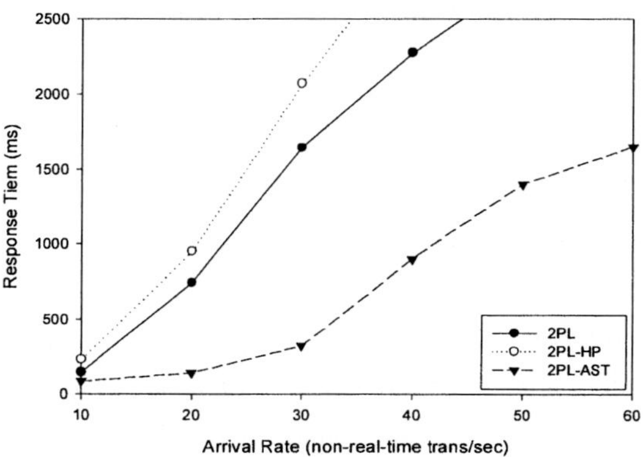

Fig. 7b. Response time for basic model

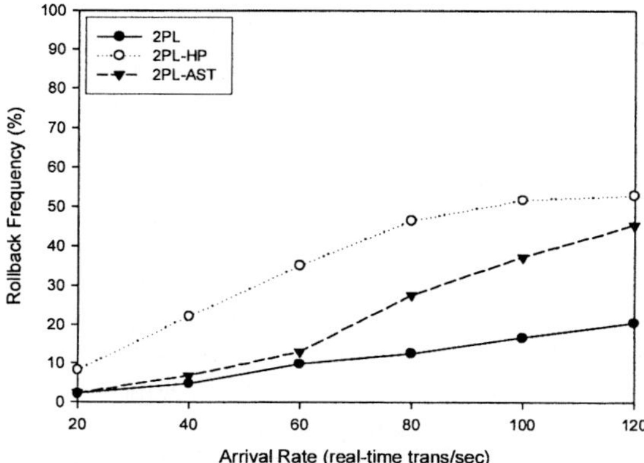

Fig. 7c. Rollback Frequency for basic model

of conditional restart and priority inheritance [4] so that access conflict will not cause the subtransactions of the same Web services family to abort each other. The 2PL-AST delivers better performance than 2PL-HP, which directly restarts lower-priority transactions when they have data access conflicts with high-priority transactions. Since the restarted transaction would have much less slack time than its first incarnation, chances are that the restarted transaction will miss its deadline too. For the performance of non-real-time transactions as illustrated in Fig. 7b, we found that 2PL-AST using the factor of adjustable slack time can maintain a faster response time than 2PL and 2PL-HP with a normal real-time transaction workload.

To study how data contention affects the performance, we plot the transaction rollback frequencies in Fig. 7c. We see that 2PL-AST causes fewer restarts than 2PL-HP does. This is because 2PL-AST keeps adjustable slack time to execute the lower-priority transactions, and fewer transactions must be restarted. However, the restart problem only occurs in 2PL when a previously aborted transaction is restarted in the deadlock processing.

4 Conclusion

It is difficult to keep up with the rapid changes in technology. The advent of web services oriented architectures intensifies competition, because these technologies are fundamentally changing the way we build our systems and how internal and external systems will interact. Various concurrency control protocols have been studied for different types of web services transactions. With the increasing pressure of response time requirements, many advanced databases now must provide real-time performance to certain services. The techniques proposed for the concurrency control of real-time transactions may not be suitable to e-commerce web services applications due to the existence of non-real-time requests because their conflict resolution mechanisms may significantly affect the performance of non-real-time web services transactions.

In this paper, a new method called 2PL-AST based on high priority algorithms is proposed to provide concurrent data access for both real-time and non-real-time requests. The concepts of 2PL-AST include (1) giving prompt data access to real-time requests, (2) utilizing slack time for non-real-time data access, and (3) using the techniques of conditional restart and priority inheritance to avoid the problems of starvation and priority inversion. Simulation results demonstrate the performance order from the best to the worst based on the metric of *MissRatio* is 2PL-AST > 2PL-HP > 2PL as workload increases. 2PL performs poorly because the requesting transaction always blocks and waits for the data object to become free. Therefore, 2PL increases the chances of real-time web services transactions missing its deadlines. 2PL-HP causes more restarts than 2PL-AST does because 2PL-HP does not consider the possibility of utilizing slack time to execute restarted transactions. For the performance of non-real-time transactions, 2PL-AST can maintain quick response times at normal real-time transaction workload.

References

1. Atkinson, M., DeRoure, D., Dunlop, A., Fox, G., Henderson, P.: Web ServiceGrids: An evolutionary Approach. UKeS Technique Report (2004) 1-13.
2. Curbera, F., Khalaf, R., Mukhi, N., Tai, S., Weerawarana, S.: The Next Step In Web Services. Comm. of the ACM 46(10) (2003) 29-34.
3. Chen, H.R., Chin, Y.H.:An Adaptive Scheduler for Distributed Real-Time Database Systems. Int. Info. Science. 153 (2003) 55-83.
4. Chen, H.R., Chin, Y.H.: Scheduling Value-Based Nested Transactions in Distributed Real-Time Database Systems. Real-Time Sys. 27 (2004) 237-269.
5. Kreger, H.:Web Services Conceptual Architecture. IBM Software Group (2001).
6. Lam, K.Y., Kuo, T.W., Kao, B., Lee, T.S.H., Cheng, R.: Evaluation of concurrency control strategies for mixed soft real-time database systems. Info. Sys. 27 (2002) 123-149.
7. Gray, J., Reuter, A.: Transaction Processing: Concepts and Techniques.Morgan Kaufmann Publishers (1993).
8. Lee, V.C.S., Lam, K.Y., Dao, B.: Priority Scheduling of Transactions in Distributed Real-Time Databases. Real-Time Sys. 16 (1999) 31-62.
9. Jain, R. The Art of Computer Systems Performance Analysis: Techniques for Experimental Design, Measurement, Simulation, and Modeling. Wiley, New York (1991).
10. Robertazzi, T.G. Computer Networks and Systems: Queuing Theory and Performance Evaluation, 3rd Edition Springer-Verlag, New York (2000).
11. Agrwal, R., Carey, M.J., Livny, M. Concurrency control performance modeling: alternative and implications. ACM Trans. On Data Sys. 12(4) (1987) 609-654.
12. El-Sayed, A.A., Hassanein, H.S., El-Sharkawi, M.E. Effect of shapingcharacteristics on the performance of nested transactions. Infomration and Software Technology 43(10) (2001) 579-590.

COWES: Clustering Web Users Based on Historical Web Sessions

Ling Chen[1,2], Sourav S. Bhowmick[1], and Jinyan Li[2]

[1] School of Computer Engineering, Nanyang Technological University, Singapore, 639798
[2] Institute for Infocomm Research, Singapore, 119613

Abstract. Clustering web users is one of the most important research topics in web usage mining. Existing approaches cluster web users based on the snapshots of web user sessions. They do not take into account the dynamic nature of web usage data. In this paper, we focus on discovering novel knowledge by clustering web users based on the evolutions of their historical web sessions. We present an algorithm called *COWES* to cluster web users in three steps. First, given a set of web users, we mine the history of their web sessions to extract interesting patterns that capture the characteristics of their usage data evolution. Then, the similarity between web users is computed based on their common interesting patterns. Then, the desired clusters are generated by a partitioning clustering technique. Web user clusters generated based on their historical web sessions are useful in intelligent web advertisement and web caching.

1 Introduction

Web Usage Mining (WUM)—the application of data mining techniques to discover usage patterns from web data—has been an active area of research and commercialization [9]. Existing web usage data mining techniques include statistical analysis [9], association rules [8], sequential patterns [13], classification [7]etc. An important topic in web usage mining is clustering web users—discovering clusters of users that exhibit similar information needs, e.g., users that access similar pages. By analyzing the characteristics of the clusters, web designers may understand the users better and thus can provide more suitable, customized services to the users [12]. There are quite a few methods for clustering web users proposed in the literature [5] [12] [11].

Generally, existing web user clustering consists of three phases: *data preparation*, *cluster discovery*, and *cluster analysis*. Since the last phase is application-dependent, let us briefly describe the first two phases. In the first phase, *web sessions* of users are extracted from the web server log by using some user identification and session identification techniques [4]. A web session, which is an episode of interaction between a web user and the web server, consists of pages visited by a user in the episode [5]. For example, Figure 1 (a) shows four requests from one session. The first line means that the user at *foo.ntu.edu* accessed the page *www.uow.edu/sce/Jeffrey/pub.html* at 10:30:05 on January 01, 2005. In the second phase, clustering techniques are applied to generate clusters of users. For

M.L. Lee, K.L. Tan, and V. Wuwongse (Eds.): DASFAA 2006, LNCS 3882, pp. 541–556, 2006.

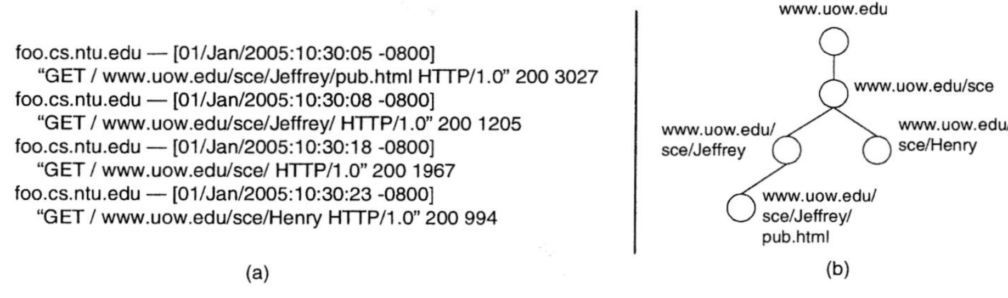

Fig. 1. Web session and page hierarchy

example, given the web sessions of three users, u_1, u_2 and u_3 as in Figure 2 (c) (left part), where only the accessed pages are presented, existing web user clustering methods [5] will group them together as their sessions share common web pages.

1.1 Motivating Example

Existing web user clustering methods cluster users based on the snapshots of their web sessions. However, the web usage data is dynamic in nature. For example, Figures 2 (a), (b) and (c) (left parts) show the historical web sessions of users u_1, u_2 and u_3 at time T_1, T_2 and T_3 respectively with a specific time granularity (e.g. *day, week, month* etc). It can be observed that pages visited by web users at different time points are different. This can be attributed to various factors, such as users' variation of their information needs and changes to the content of the web site etc.

Such dynamic nature of web usage data poses both challenges and opportunities to web user clustering. In particular, the dynamic nature of web usage data leads to the following two challenging problems:

- **Maintenance of web user clustering results**: Take the web sessions in Figure 2 as an example. Web user clusters generated by existing techniques at time T_1 does not include the usage data at time T_2 and beyond. Hence, the clustering results have to be updated constantly along with the change of web usage data. This requires development of efficient incremental web user clustering techniques.
- **Discovery of novel web user clusters**: Web user clusters generated by existing techniques at time T_3 does not include the usage data at time T_2 and before. While knowledge extracted from the snapshots of web sessions is important and useful, interesting and novel knowledge can be discovered from the historical web sessions. For example, we can discover clusters of users that exhibit similar characteristics in the evolution of their usage data, e.g. users share common *change patterns* in their historical web sessions.

In this paper, we focus on discovering novel knowledge by clustering web users based on the *change patterns* in their historical web sessions. Various types of

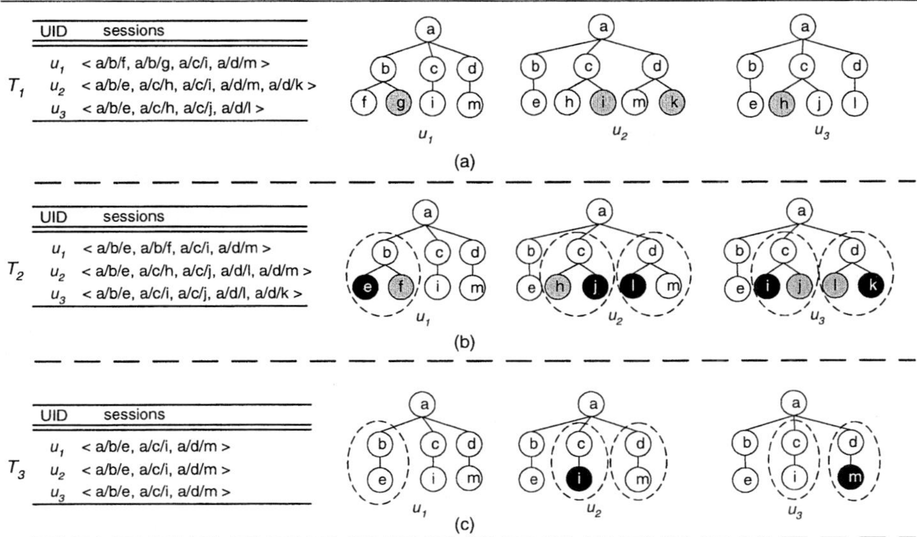

Fig. 2. Historical web sessions

change patterns can be mined from historical web usage data. In this paper, we mine a particular change pattern called *Frequently Changed Subtree Patterns* (*FCSP*), which was proposed by us in the context of XML documents in [3] before. We briefly introduce the idea of *FCSP* as follows. Pages accessed in a web session can be organized into a hierarchical structure, called a *page hierarchy*, based on the URLs of the pages [5]. For example, the page hierarchy constructed for the pages in the web session in Figure 1 (*a*) is shown in Figure 1 (*b*). Obviously, a page hierarchy represents the information needs of a user. Similarly, the sequences of historical web sessions of web users u_1, u_2 and u_3 are represented as sequences of page hierarchies in Figure 2 (right part), where a gray node represents a page that will disappear in the next web session, and a dark node is a page that newly occurs in current session. The changes to the structure of a page hierarchy, e.g. the insertions and deletions of nodes, reflect the variation of user's information needs. *A FCSP is a set of subtrees, in a page hierarchy, whose structures frequently change together in a sequence of historical web sessions.* For example, since the structures of the subtrees rooted at nodes c and d (depicted by dotted line) frequently changed together in the historical sessions of user u_2, the two subtrees will be discovered as a *2-FCSP* of u_2, according to some metrics we define later in Section 2 (A *k-FCSP* is a *FCSP* consisting of k subtrees). Similarly, the two subtrees will be discovered as a *2-FCSP* for user u_3 as well. For user u_1, the subtree rooted at node b will be discovered as a *1-FCSP*. We use the set of *FCSPs*, mined from the historical web sessions of a user, as the *change patterns* to capture the characteristics of the evolution of his usage data. Hence, users having similar *FCSPs* will be clustered. For example, the users u_2

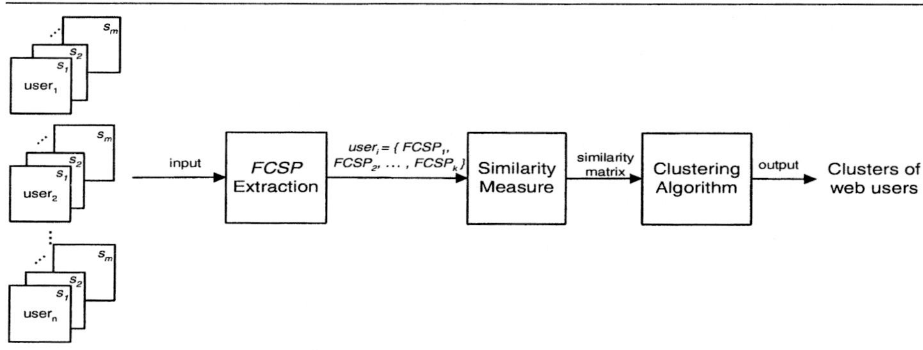

Fig. 3. Overview of *COWES*

and u_3 in Figure 2 will be grouped together as they share the common *FCSP* while u_1 will be a singular cluster.

We present an algorithm for **C**lustering **O**f **W**eb users based on their historical w**E**b **S**essions, called *COWES*. The overview of *COWES* is presented in Figure 3. Given a collection of web users $\{u_1, \cdots, u_n\}$, where each user is associated with a sequence of historical web sessions, we extract *FCSPs* from their historical web sessions first. Then, each web user is represented as a set of *FCSPs*. We define a *similarity* metric to measure the proximity between each pair of users based on their *FCSP*s. The output of the this step is a similarity matrix of web users. Finally, we perform a partitioning clustering algorithm on the similarity matrix to generate the clusters.

1.2 Applications

Web user clusters generated by *COWES* are useful at least in the following two applications:

- **Intelligent Web Advertisement:** 99% of all web sites offer standard banner advertisements [1]. This shows the importance of this form of online advertising. One of the ways to maximize revenues for the party who owns the advertising space is to design intelligent techniques for the selection of an appropriate set of advertisements to display in appropriate web pages. Web user clusters generated by *COWES* can be beneficial for designing intelligent advertisement placement strategies. For example, after clustering users in Figure 2 based on historical web sessions, we knew that the variation of information needs of u_1 is different from that of users u_2 as well as u_3. Although all users accessed the page $a/b/e$ at time T_3, u_1 frequently changes his information needs under a/b. Thus, it makes sense to put relevant advertisement banners in page a/b instead of page $a/b/e$ for u_1 in order to maximize revenues.
- **Proxy Cache Management:** Web caching is an interesting problem in web research area [2] [13] as web caches can reduce not only network traffic

but also downloading latency. Because of the limited size of cache region, it is important to design effective replacement strategies to maximize hit rates. One of the frequently used replacement strategies is LRU, which assigns priorities to the most recently accessed pages. Web user clusters generated by *COWES* can be used with LRU to manage the caching region more optimally. For example, after time T_3, LRU will cache the pages under a/c and a/d for user u_2 (u_3). When u_2 accesses pages at next time point such as T_4, once it is detected that u_2 changed his information needs under a/c, we can degrade the priority of pages under a/d and hasten the eviction of these pages. This is based on the knowledge obtained from the results of *COWES*, which indicates that u_2 frequently changes his information needs under a/c and a/d together.

The rest of the paper is organized as follows. In Section 2, we explain the notion of *FCSP* that is used as the clustering feature in our algorithm. We define the similarity metrics in Section 3. In Section 4, we present the framework of *COWES*. We evaluate the performance of *COWES* in Section 5 and review related works in Section 6. Section 7 concludes this paper.

2 Frequently Changed Subtree Pattern (FCSP)

As mentioned above, in order to cluster web users based on their historical web sessions, we extract the set of *FCSPs* first to capture the characteristics in the evolution of their usage data. We briefly introduce the notion of *FCSP* in this section. Readers can refer to our previous work [3] for details.

As in [5], pages in a web session can be organized into a *page hierarchy* based on their URLs. Hereafter, we refer to a page hierarchy of a web session as a *web session tree*. Formally, a web session tree is an unordered tree $T =< N, E >$, where N is the set of nodes where a leaf node represents a web page corresponding to a file in the web server and a non-leaf node represents a web page corresponding to a directory in the server, E is the set of edges where each edge from a parent node to a child node represents the consisting-of relationship between the corresponding pages. Particularly, a node r, $r \in N$, is the root of the tree which represents the home page of a web site. An example web session tree is shown in Figure 1. Accordingly, a tree $t_i =< N_i, E_i >$ is a web session subtree, denoted as $t_i \prec T$, iff $N_i \subseteq N$ and for all $(x,\ y) \in E_i$, x is a parent of y in T.

Given a sequence of historical web session trees of a web user, we are interested in how the structures of the trees change, which reflects the variation of the user's information needs. Hence, we first define two basic operations that change the structure of a tree as follows.

- *Insert*(x, y): This operation creates a new node x as a child node of node y in a web session tree.
- *Delete*(x): This operation is the inverse of the insertion one. It removes node x from a web session tree.

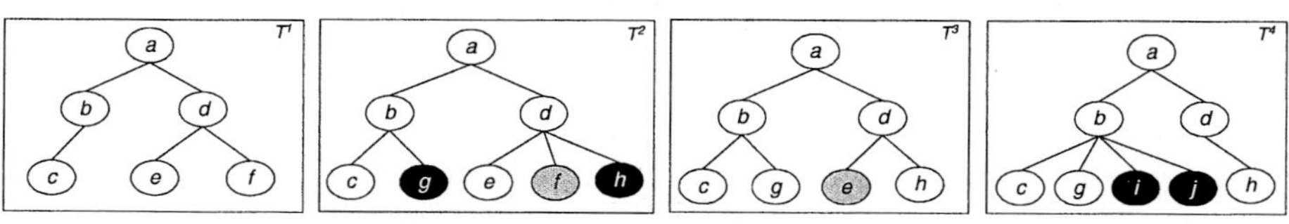

Fig. 4. Four historical sessions of a web user

A web session tree (subtree) is considered as *changed* once a change operation, i.e. insertion or deletion, occurs to it. Figure 4 shows four historical web session trees of a web user in sequence, where the black nodes depict the newly inserted nodes in the current session and the grey nodes depict the nodes that will be deleted in the next session. Compared with the session tree T^1, a new node g is inserted in the subtree a/b (Hereafter, we use the path from the root to node x to denote a web session subtree rooted at x). Thus, the subtree a/b is considered as changed in session T^2. Similarly, the subtree changed in session T^4 again.

Each changed web session subtree is associated with a value which reflects its change degree. Intuitively, the more number of nodes inserted to/removed from a subtree, the more significantly the subtree changed. Then, a metric called *Degree of Change* (*DoC*) is defined as follows.

Definition 1 (*DoC*). *Let* $t^i = < N^i, E^i >$, $t^{i+1} = < N^{i+1}, E^{i+1} >$ *be two versions of a web session subtree* t. *The Degree of Change for subtree* t *is:*

$$DoC(t, i, i+1) = \frac{|\{x|x \in \{N^i \cup N^{i+1}\} \ \&\& \ x \notin \{N^i \cap N^{i+1}\}\}|}{|\{x|x \in \{N^i \cup N^{i+1}\}\}|} \qquad \Box$$

That is, the *DoC* of a subtree in two versions is computed as the ratio of the number of inserted/deleted nodes to the total number of unique nodes of the subtree in the two versions. For example, in Figure 4, the *DoC* of the subtree a/b in the first two sessions is 1/3.

Basically, a *FCSP* is a set of web session subtrees satisfying the following two conditions: *i*) the set of subtrees frequently change together; *ii*) the set of subtrees frequently undergo significant changes together. Correspondingly, we define two metrics, *Frequency of Change* (*FoC*) and *Significance of Change* (*SoC*), to measure the change frequency and change significance of a set of subtrees.

Definition 2 (*FoC*). *Let* $< T^1, T^2, \ldots, T^n >$ *be a sequence of* n *historical web session trees of a web user. Let* P *be a set of subtrees,* $P = \{t_1, t_2, \ldots, t_m\}$, *where* $t_i^j \prec T^j$ $(1 \leq j \leq n)$. *Let* $DoC(t_i, j, j+1)$ *be the Degree of Change for subtree* t_i *from* j*th version to* $(j+1)$*th version. The Frequency of Change for the set of* P *is:*

$$FoC(P) = \frac{\sum_{j=1}^{n-1} V_j}{n-1}$$

$$where\ V_j = \prod_{i=1}^{m} V_{j_i}\ and\ V_{j_i} = \begin{cases} 1, & if\ \ DoC(t_i, j, j+1) \neq 0 \\ 0, & if\ \ DoC(t_i, j, j+1) = 0 \end{cases}$$ □

Obviously, FoC of a set of subtrees P is the fraction of sessions where all subtrees in P changed. For example, let P be two subtrees, a/b and a/d, in Figure 4. Then, $FoC(P) = 2/3$ as both subtrees changed together in sessions T^2 and T^4.

Definition 3 (*SoC*). *Let* $< T^1, T^2, \ldots, T^n >$ *be a sequence of n historical web session trees of a web user. Let P be a set of subtrees,* $P = \{t_1, t_2, \ldots, t_m\}$*. The Significance of Change of the set of subtrees is defined as follows:*

$$SoC(P) = \frac{\sum_{j=1}^{n-1} D_j}{(n-1) * FoC(P)}$$

$$where\ D_j = \prod_{i=1}^{m} D_{j_i}\ and\ D_{j_i} = \begin{cases} 1, & if\ \ DoC(t_i, j, j+1) \geq \alpha \\ 0, & otherwise \end{cases}$$ □

That is, the SoC of a set of subtrees P is computed as the ratio of the number of sessions all subtrees in P change significantly (compared with the threshold of DoC) to the number of sessions all subtrees in P changed together. Let P be the two subtrees of a/b and a/d in Figure 4. Suppose the threshold of DoC is 0.3. Then, $SoC(P) = 1/2$ as the two subtrees changed together in two sessions and both of them changed significantly only in the session T^4.

Based on the above metrics, the *Frequently Changed Subtree Pattern* can be defined as follows.

Definition 4 (*FCSP*). *Let* $< T^1, T^2, \ldots, T^n >$ *be a sequence of n historical web session trees of a web user. Let P be a set of subtrees,* $P = \{t_1, t_2, \ldots, t_m\}$*. Given the user-defined minimum DoC* α*, minimum FoC* β *and minimum SoC* γ*, P is a Frequently Changed Subtree Pattern FCSP if it satisfies the following two conditions: i)* $FoC(P) \geq \beta$*;ii)* $SoC(P) \geq \gamma$*.* □

That is, a *FCSP* is a set of web sessions subtrees that frequently change together and frequently undergo significant changes together.

3 Similarity Measure

As we use the set of *FCSPs*, mined from the historical web sessions of each user, as our clustering feature, we need to define the similarity between web users based on their *FCSPs*. In this section, we first define two types of *FCSPs* that can be shared by web users. Then, we define the *Similarity of FCSPs* and the *Similarity of Users* sequentially.

3.1 Types of Shared *FCSP*s

Recall that each *FCSP* is a set of web session subtrees. We define two types of *FCSP*s that can be shared by two web users, *Identical FCSP*s and *Approximate FCSP*s, based on their subtrees.

C - Company, P - Products, T - Training, S - Service, p_1- product$_1$, p_2 - product$_2$, c_1- course$_1$, c_2 - course$_2$

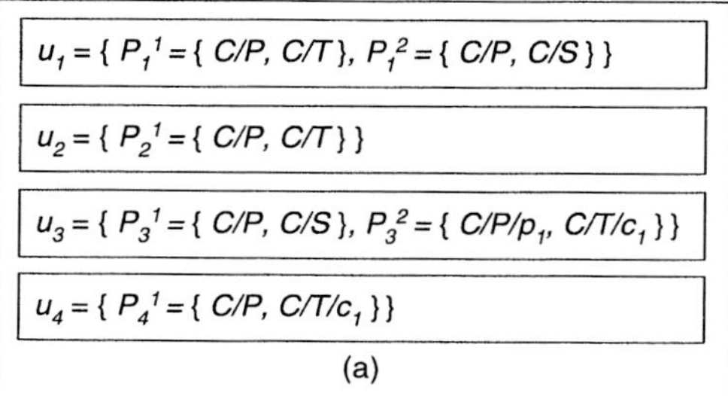

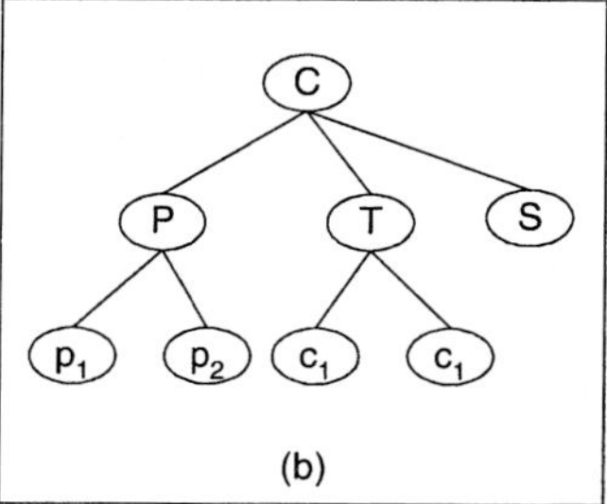

Fig. 5. *FCSP*s of web users

Before giving the definitions of the two types of *FCSPs*, we explain them with an example. Figure 5 (a) shows four web users $\{u_1, u_2, u_3, u_4\}$, where each user is associated a set of *FCSPs*, e.g. $u_1 = \{P_1^1, P_1^2\}$ (we use the subscript to denote the identity of the user and the superscript to denote the identity of the *FCSP* of the user). Each *FCSP* is a set of web session subtrees, e.g. $P_1^1 = \{Company/Products, Company/Training\}$. Figure 5 (b) shows the ancestor relationship between the web session subtrees. Consider the two *FCSP*s P_1^1 and P_2^1. Both indicate the two subtrees, *Company/Products* and *Company/Training*, frequently changed together in a sequence of historical web sessions. Hence, P_1^1 and P_2^1 contribute in the similarity of the evolution of usage data for users u_1 and u_2. We call such a pair of *FCSPs Identical FCSPs*.

Definition 5 (*Identical FCSPs*). *Let* $P_1 = \{t_1, \cdots, t_m\}$, $P_2 = \{t_1, \cdots, t_n\}$ *be two FCSPs. Let* $L(t)$ *be the path from the root of the web session tree to the root of the web session subtree* t. *If* $m = n$ *and* $\forall i(1 \leq i \leq m)$, $\exists j(1 \leq j \leq n)$ *s.t.* $L(t_i) = L(t_j)$ *and vice versa, then the two FCSPs are Identical FCSPs, denoted as* $P_1 = P_2$. □

That is, two *FCSP*s are *Identical FCSPs* if there is a one-to-one mapping between the subtrees of the two *FCSPs* and the corresponding subtrees are rooted at the same node. For example, the two users u_1 and u_3 in Figure 5 share the pair of *Identical FCSPs* P_1^2 and P_3^1.

Consider the example in Figure 5 again. Although P_1^1 and P_3^2 are not *Identical FCSP*s, they are similar to some extend in their semantics because their corresponding web session subtrees have the ancestor relationships. Hence, this pair of *FCSPs* contribute to the similarity of the evolution of usage data for u_1 and u_3 as well. We call such a pair of *FCSP*s *Approximate FCSPs*, which is defined as follows.

Definition 6 (*Approximate FCSPs*). *Let* $P_1 = \{t_1, \ldots, t_m\}$ *and* $P_2 = \{t_1, \ldots, t_n\}$ *be two FCSPs. Let* $L(t)$ *be the path from the root of the web session* *tree to the root of the web session subtree t. A subtree t_i is an ancestor of another subtree t_j, denoted as $t_j \preceq t_i$, if $L(t_i)$ is a prefix of $L(t_j)$. If $m = n$ and $\forall i(1 \le i \le m)$, $\exists j(1 \le j \le n)$ s.t. $t_i \preceq t_j$ or $t_i \succeq t_j$ and vice versa, then the two FCSPs are Approximate FCSPs, denoted as $P_1 \approx P_2$.* □

For example, the two users u_1 and u_4 in Figure 5 share the pair of *Approximate FCSPs* P_1^1 and P_4^1. Note that, the definition of *Identical FCSPs* is a special case of that of *Approximate FCSPs.*

3.2 Similarity of *FCSP*s

According to above discussion, two web users share *Identical FCSPs* and/or *Approximate FCSPs.* For each pair of shared *FCSPs*, we need to measure how similar they are. Note that each *FCSP* has a set of elements (subtrees) and is associated with two values, *FoC* and *SoC*, which reflect its strength. We then define the *Similarity of FCSPs* based on their *Element Similarity* and *Strength Similarity.* The former measures the proximity of two *FCSPs* in terms of their subtrees and the later measures the proximity of two *FCSPs* in terms of their *FoC* and *SoC.*

Element Similarity. Since a pair of *Approximate FCSPs* are different in their contained subtrees, we define the *Element Similarity* to measure the distance between a pair of *FCSPs* in terms of their subtrees. Intuitively, the closer the corresponding subtrees of the *FCSP*s in their ancestor relationship, the more similar the pair of *FCSPs.* Hence, we first define the *Ancestor Level* to measure the distance of two subtrees in their ancestor relationship.

Definition 7 (*Ancestor Level*). *Let t_i and t_j be two web session subtrees s.t. $t_j \preceq t_i$. The ancestor level between t_i and t_j, denoted as $AL(t_i, t_j)$, is the length of the path from the root of t_i to the root of t_j.* □

Consider the example in Figure 5 again. Let t_i be the subtree *Company/Products* and t_j be the subtree *Company/Products/product*$_1$. Then, $AL(t_i, t_j)$ is 1.

Definition 8 (*Element Similarity*). *Let $P_1 = \{t_1^1, \dots, t_1^m\}$ and $P_2 = \{t_2^1, \dots, t_2^m\}$ be a pair of Identical/Approximate FCSPs s.t. $t_1^i \preceq t_2^i$ or $t_1^i \succeq t_2^i$ $(1 \le i \le m)$. The Element Similarity of the pair of FCSPs, denoted as $ES(P_1, P_2)$, is defined as,*

$$ES(P_1, P_2) = 2^{-\sum_{i=1}^{m} AL(t_1^i, t_2^i)}$$ □

The *Element Similarity* of a pair of *Identical/Approximate FCSPs* has value in (0, 1]. When the pair of *FCSPs* is *Identical FCSPs*, the *Element Similarity* has the maximum value 1 since the *Ancestor Level* of each pair of corresponding subtrees is zero. The higher the value, the more similar the two *FCSPs* in terms of their subtrees. For example, consider the pair of *Approximate FCSPs* in Figure 5, $\{P_1^1 = \{C/P, C/T\}, P_3^2 = \{C/P/p_1, C/T/c_1\}\}$. $ES(P_1^1, P_3^2)$=2^{-2}=1/4.

Strength Similarity. With regard to *Strength Similarity*, we consider the similarity between a pair of *FCSPs* in terms of the values of their *FoC* and *SoC*, which reflect the change frequency and the change significance of the pattern respectively. We adopt the *Euclidean distance* to measure the distance between the values of the two metrics for a pair of shared *FCSPs* and then convert the distance to a similarity measure by using a monotonic decreasing function.

Definition 9 (*Strength Similarity*). *Let P_1 and P_2 be a pair of Identical/ Approximate FCSPs. Suppose $FoC(P_1) = f_1$, $SoC(P_1) = s_1$, $FoC(P_2) = f_2$ and $SoC(P_2) = s_2$. Then the Strength Similarity of the pair of FCSPs, denoted as $SS(P_1, P_2)$, is defined as,*

$$SS(P_1, P_2) = e^{-d(P_1,P_2)}, \quad where \ d(P_1, P_2) = \sqrt{(f_1 - f_2)^2 + (s_1 - s_2)^2} \quad \square$$

The *Strength Similarity* has value in $(0, 1]$. The closer the values of *FoC* and *SoC* of the two *FCSP*s, the higher the *Strength Similarity*. For example, suppose the *FoC* and *SoC* of the *FCSP*s in Figure 5 with respect to each user are shown in Figure 6. For the pair of *Identical FCSPs* $\{P_1^1, P_2^1\}$, its *SS* is $e^{-\sqrt{(0.6-0.55)^2+(0.75-0.8)^2}} = 0.931$.

Similarity of *FCSP*s. Now we define the *Similarity of FCSPs* by considering both *Element Similarity* and *Strength Similarity*.

Definition 10 (*Similarity of FCSPs*). *Let P_1 and P_2 be a pair of FCSPs. Let $ES(P_1, P_2)$ be their Element Similarity and $SS(P_1, P_2)$ be their Strength Similarity. Then, the similarity of the two FCSPs, denoted as $SoF(P_1, P_2)$, is defined as,*

$$SoF(P_1, P_2) = \begin{cases} ES(P_1, P_2) * SS(P_1, P_2), & \text{if } P_1 = P_2 \text{ or } P_1 \approx P_2 \\ 0, & \text{otherwise} \end{cases} \quad \square$$

That is, if a pair of *FCSPs* is *Identical/Approximate FCSPs*, then the *Similarity of FCSPs* is the product of their *Element Similarity* and their *Strength Similarity*. If the two *FCSPs* are neither *Identical* nor *Approximate*, their similarity is zero. Hence, *SoF* has value in [0,1]. The higher the value, the more similar the two *FCSPs*.

		u_1		u_2		u_3		u_4	
FCSP_ID	FCSP	FoC	SoC	FoC	SoC	FoC	SoC	FoC	SoC
$1(P_1^1, P_2^1)$	{C/P, C/T}	0.6	0.75	0.55	0.8				
$2(P_1^2, P_3^1)$	{C/P, C/S}	0.4	0.7			0.6	0.9		
$3(P_3^2)$	{C/P/p$_1$, C/T/c$_1$}					0.5	0.8		
$4(P_4^1)$	{C/P, C/T/c$_1$}							0.65	0.85

Fig. 6. *FoC* and *Weight* of *FCSPs*

3.3 Similarity of Web Users

For two web users that are represented as two sets of *FCSPs*, we should measure their proximity by taking into account not only the number of shared *FCSP*s but also the *SoF* of shared *FCSP*s. Thus, we define the *Similarity of User* as follows.

Definition 11 (*Similarity of Users*). *Let* $u_1 = \{P_1^1, P_1^2, \ldots, P_1^m\}$ *and* $u_2 = \{P_2^1, P_2^2, \ldots, P_2^n\}$ *be two web users that are represented as two sets of FCSPs. Suppose there exists* k $(0 \leq k \leq m \leq n)$ *s.t.* $P_1^1 = P_2^1$ *or* $P_1^1 \approx P_2^1$, $\cdots$, $P_1^k = P_2^k$ *or* $P_1^k \approx P_2^k$. *The Similarity of Users, denoted as* $SoU(u_1, u_2)$, *is defined as,*

$$SoU(u_1, u_2) = \frac{\sum_{i=1}^{k} SoF(P_1^i, P_2^i)}{\frac{m+n}{2}} \qquad \square$$

If two web users share all their *FCSP*s and each pair of shared *FCSP*s has the *SoF* of 1, then the *Similarity of Users* has the maximum value of 1. Otherwise, if the two web users share no *FCSP*, the *Similarity of Users* is 0.

4 Framework of *COWES*

Given a collection of web users, where each user is associated with a sequence of his historical web sessions, *COWES* generates the clusters of users in the follows phases:

- Phase I. From the historical web sessions of each user, we extract a set of *FCSP*s, which will be treated as a vector of features for clustering.
- Phase II. Compute the similarity between pairs of web users in terms of their *FCSP*s based on defined similarity metrics.
- Phase III. Perform clustering on the generated similarity matrix of web users.

In [3], we proposed an algorithm that discovers *FCSPs* from a sequence of historical tree structures. Thus, we omit the details of Phase I and interested readers can refer to [3] for the details. We discuss the Phases II and III in the following subsections.

4.1 Similarity Computation

As the output of Phase I, each web user is represented as a set of *FCSPs*. We need to compute the similarity between each pair of users in the second phase.

Given two sets of *FCSPs* of two users, we first compute an optimal alignment of their *FCSPs* so that the total *Element Similarity* between matching *FCSP*s can be maximized. For example, suppose $u_1 = \{P_1^1\}$ where $P_1^1 = \{$*Company/Products*, *Company/Training*$\}$, and $u_2 = \{P_2^1, P_2^2\}$ where $P_2^1 =$ *Company/Products*, *Company/Training /course*$_1\}$ and $P_2^2 = \{$*Company/Products /product*$_1$, *Company/Training/course*$_1\}$. Although P_1^1 is approximate with both P_2^1 and P_2^2, we align P_1^1 with P_2^1 so that the total *Element Similarity* between the matching *FCSP*s is maximized. After getting the optimal alignment, the *SOF* of the matching *FCSPs* can be computed and the *SoU* of the two users can be obtained accordingly.

4.2 Cluster Generation

After Phase II, we can get a similarity matrix of web users. Then, many appropriate algorithms can be used to generate the clusters. However, different algorithms will have different performance with respect to the characteristics of the data. Here, we employ the well-known K-medoid [6] clustering technique. Obviously, K-medoid is by no means the only available method for clustering based on the similarity matrix, but it is the more preferable one as shown by our experimental results. We need to point out that the novelty here is not the clustering algorithm, but the extraction of appropriate information from historical web sessions as a base for clustering and the similarity metrics we defined to measure the proximity of web users in terms of their characteristics in usage data evolution.

5 Experimental Results

In this section, we evaluate the performance of *COWES* via experiments on both synthetic and real data sets. All experiments are carried out on a Pentium IV 2.8GHz PC with 512MB memory. The operating system is Windows 2000 professional.

5.1 Experiments on Synthetic Data

We conduct two experiments on the synthetic data. The first experiment is carried out to illustrate our decision on employing a partitioning clustering algorithm. The second experiment is used to show the processing costs of different phases of our clustering approach.

We implemented a synthetic *FCSPs* generator which is a process of the following steps. First, we generate a general web session tree with the given number of nodes. Then, we select subtrees from the tree structure to compose *FCSP*s. We organize the *FCSPs* into groups by controlling the overlap between each pair of groups. We select *FCSP* groups for each web user and assign *FoC* and *SoC* to each *FCSP*. Parameters of the synthetic *FCSPs* generating process is shown in Table 1 (a), where the third column shows the default values of the parameters.

Table 1. Parameter and Results

D	Number of web users	5000
S	Average number of *FCSP*s per user	5
G	Number of *FCSP* groups	40
F	Average number of *FCSP*s of each group	4
P	Number of *FCSP*s	150
T	Average number of subtrees of each *FCSP*	3
N	Number of nodes of general session tree	500

(a) Parameter List

D	Step 2	Step 3
2K	10.31	5.92
3K	25.91	17.00
4K	41.39	23.20
5K	79.19	38.98
6K	96.66	95.12
7K	140.65	199.13

(b) Time

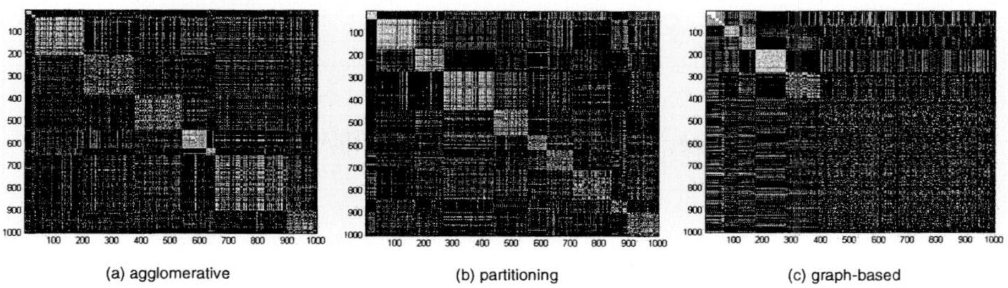

(a) agglomerative (b) partitioning (c) graph-based

Fig. 7. Similarity matrix ordered by clustering results

Result Analysis. Firstly, we conduct experiments to show why we decide to employ a partitioning clustering algorithm. Particularly, we compare the following three well-known clustering algorithms: the agglomerative algorithm, the partitioning algorithm and the graph-based algorithm [14]. Figure 7 shows the gray scale images of the same similarity matrix ordered by the clusters generated by the three algorithms. The shade of each point in the images represents the value of the corresponding entry in similarity matrix. In extreme cases, white and black correspond to the similarity values of 1 and 0 respectively. Hence, for a good clustering, the rectangles on the diagonal should be as white as possible as they represent the web users in same clusters, while the remaining areas should be as black as possible. From Figure 7, we observe that the partitioning algorithm performs the best not only in achieving the best accuracy but also in controlling the balance of the cardinality of the clusters.

We also conduct experiments on the set of synthetic data to evaluate the processing costs of the different phases of *COWES*. Since the performance of the first phase has been evaluated in our previous work [3], we do not report it again. Table 1 (*b*) shows the execution time of the second and third phases of *COWES* with respect to the variation of the number of users. It can be observed that both the costs of computing SoU and generating clusters increase quadratically with the number of users.

5.2 Experiments on Real Data

We conducted two experiments on real-life data. The first one is carried out to evaluate the accuracy of *COWES* and to demonstrate the novel clusters that can be discovered by *COWES*. The second one is conducted to compare the effectiveness of our similarity metric against an alternative one which ignores the *Approximate FCSPs*.

DataSets. The real-life datasets are collected from Internet Traffic Archive (http://ita.ee.lbl. gov), sponsored by ACM SIGCOMM. We use the trace that contains a day's worth of all HTTP requests to the EPA WWW server located at Research Triangle Park, NC. In considering the evolution of web usage data, the requests of a host are grouped with a time interval of one hour. All the

Num of Clusters	Dataset I				Num of Clusters	Dataset II			
	COWES		STRUCTURE			COWES		STRUCTURE	
	IS	ES	IS	ES		IS	ES	IS	ES
5	0.36	0.013	0.09	0.007	3	0.67	0.24	0.35	0.24
6	0.22	0.014	0.08	0.006	4	0.72	0.39	0.37	0.24
7	0.38	0.017	0.21	0.006	5	0.73	0.34	0.38	0.23
8	0.39	0.019	0.18	0.008	6	0.72	0.32	0.40	0.22

Fig. 8. Comparison of clustering algorithms

Num of Clusters	Dataset I				Num of Clusters	Dataset II			
	Approximate		Identical			Approximate		Identical	
	IS	ES	IS	ES		IS	ES	IS	ES
5	0.36	0.013	0.21	0.015	3	0.67	0.24	0.59	0.21
6	0.36	0.014	0.22	0.015	4	0.72	0.39	0.67	0.34
7	0.38	0.017	0.38	0.019	5	0.73	0.34	0.65	0.31
8	0.39	0.019	0.30	0.024	6	0.72	0.32	0.65	0.29

Fig. 9. Comparison of similarity metrics

requests of all 2333 hosts in the trace form the Dataset I. In order to study the novel knowledge that can be discovered by *COWES*, we collect the requests of 57 hosts that browse the subtree of the two paths, "/docs/WhatsNew.html" and "/docs/WhatsHot.html" to form the Dataset II. Since hosts in the Dataset II are similar in their requests, they may not be distinguished by existing cluster algorithms. We study to see whether *COWES* can generate clusters of high quality based on evolutionary features of the requests.

Result Analysis. We first conduct experiments to evaluate the accuracy of *COWES*. The results are shown in Figure 8. The quality of the clustering results is measured with two metrics, the *overall mean inner cluster similarity* and the *overall mean inter cluster similarity*, that are defined in [6] and referred to as *IS* and *ES* respectively in Figure 8. Basically, for a good clustering, the former should be large while the latter should be small. In order to evaluate the values of *IS* and *ES* of *COWES*, we employed an algorithm [10], which is referred to as *STRUCTURE* in Figure 8, that clusters the web users by the similarity in the structure of web session trees and ignores the evolutions of the sessions. We observed from Figure 8 that for Dataset I, *COWES* can achieve competitive accuracy. For Dataset II where users share similar structures in web sessions, *COWES* can distinguish them with their evolutionary features and generate clusters with much higher quality.

Then we conduct experiments to compare the effectiveness of our similarity metric, which is referred to as "Approximate" in Figure 9, with an alternative similarity metric considering the *Identical FCSPs* only, which is referred to as "Identical" in Figure 9. As shown by the results in Figure 9, although both similarity metrics have similar performance in *ES*, our similarity metric works better in *IS*.

6 Related Work

Clustering of web users is an important task of web usage mining. Existing works on web user clustering usually extract access patterns of users from web server log files and organize them into web sessions. Xiao et al. [12] clustered web user sessions based on various similarity measures, such as the number of shared web pages, the frequency of accessing the shared web pages etc. Rather than clustering the web users based on web sessions directly, Fu et al. [5] first generalized the sessions so that pages representing the similar semantics are collapsed. By this manner, the dimension of clustering feature can be reduced significantly. Wang and Zaiane [11] also cluster web users based on snapshots of web sessions. They represented web sessions as vectors of encoded page IDs and then a clustering algorithm handling categorical data was employed. The critical difference between existing works on clustering web users and our effort is that we address the dynamic nature of web usage data. We measure the proximity of web users based on the characteristics of their usage data evolution. Existing works measure the likeness between web users based on the information in snapshot web sessions. Consequently, the clusters generated by our algorithm indicate different knowledge and thus have different applications.

7 Conclusions

In this paper, we take into account the dynamic nature of web usage data to cluster web users. A novel method, *COWES*, for clustering web users by historical web sessions is presented. From a sequence of historical web sessions of each user, we first mine a set of *Frequently Changed Subtree Patterns* (*FCSPs*) to capture the characteristics in the evolution of his usage data. Then, the similarity between web users are computed based on their common *FCSPs* in terms of the *Element Similarity* as well as the *Strength Similarity*. Finally, a partitioning clustering technique is employed to generate clusters of web users. The experimental results show that our approach is effective in distinguishing web users with different characteristics in usage data evolution.

References

1. C. Buchwalter, M. Ryan, and D. Martin. The state of online advertising: data covering 4^{th}Q 2000. In *TR Adrelevance*, 2001.
2. P. Cao and S. Irani. Cost-aware www proxy caching algorithms. In *Proc. of USENIX SITSY*, 1997.
3. L. Chen, S. S. Bhowmick, and L. T. Chia. Mining association rules from structural deltas of historical xml documents. In *Proc. of PAKDD*, 2004.
4. R. Cooley, B. Mobasher, and J. Srivastava. Data preparation for mining world wide web browsing patterns. In *Knowledge and Information Systems. No. 1*, 1999.
5. Y. Fu, K. Sandhu, and M. Shih. A generalization-based approach to clustering of web usage sessions. In *Proc. of WEBKDD'99*, 1999.

6. L. Kaufman and P. Pousseeuw. Finding groups in data: An introduction to cluster analysis. In *John Wiley and Sons*, 1990.
7. T. Li, Q. Yang, and K. Wang. Classification pruning for web-request prediction. In *Proc. of WWW*, 2001.
8. B. Mobasher, H. Dai, T. Luo, and M. Nakagawa. Effective personalization based on association rule discovery from web usage data. In *Proc. of WIDM*, 2001.
9. J. Srivastava, R. Cooley, M. Deshpande, and P.-N. Tan. Web usage mining: Discovery and applications of usage patterns from web data. In *SIGKDD Explorations, 1(2):12-23*, 2000.
10. L. Wang, D. W.-L. Cheung, N. Mamoulis, and S.-M. Yiu. An efficient and scalable algorithm for clustering xml documents by structure. In *IEEE TKDE, 16(1): 82-96*, 2004.
11. W. Wang and O. R. Zaiane. Clustering web sessions by sequence alignment. In *Proc. of DEXA*, 2002.
12. J. Xiao and Y. Zhang. Clustering of web users using session-based similarity measures. In *Proc. of ICCNMC'01*, 2001.
13. Q. Yang, H. H. Zhang, and T. Li. Mining web logs for predicition models in www caching and prefetching. In *Proc. of ACM SIGKDD*, 2001.
14. Y. Zhao and G. Karypis. Evaluation of hierarchical clustering algorithms for document datasets. In *Proc. of CIKM*, 2002.

A Precise Metric for Measuring How Much Web Pages Change*

Shin Young Kwon[1], Sang Ho Lee[1], and Sung Jin Kim[2]

[1] School of Computing, Soongsil University,
1-1 Sangdo-dong Dongjak-gu, Seoul 156-743, Korea
{sykwon, shlee}@comp.ssu.ac.kr
[2] School of Computer Science and Engineering, Seoul National University,
San 56-1 Shinlim-dong Kwanak-gu, Seoul 151-744, Korea
sjkim@oopsla.snu.ac.kr

Abstract. A number of similarity metrics have been used to measure the degree of web page changes in the literature. When a web page changes, the metrics often represent the change differently. In this paper, we first define criteria for web page changes to evaluate the effectiveness of the metrics in terms of six important types of web page changes. Second, we propose a new similarity metric appropriate for measuring the degree of web page changes. Using real web pages and synthesized pages, we analyze the five existing metrics (i.e., the byte-wise comparison, the TF·IDF cosine distance, the word distance, the edit distance, and the shingling) and ours under the proposed criteria. The analysis result shows that our metric represents the changes more effectively than other metrics. We expect that our study can help users select an appropriate metric for particular web applications.

1 Introduction

In many web applications, administrators create and manage web databases (a collection of web pages). Major web search service providers such as Google or Yahoo create web databases, with which users can conduct search activities. Proxy servers and web browsers maintain web databases to cache web pages and reduce repeated downloading of the web pages. As web pages change dynamically, web databases become obsolete and need to be updated. Updating all the web pages in the databases often entails making unnecessary requests and downloading unchanged web pages. Administrators would like to update only changed (or significantly changed) web pages in the databases, hence it is important to know how much the contents of web pages changed.

A number of similarity metrics for textual data have been used to measure the degree of web page changes. The simplest way to see if a web page changes is to compare web pages in a byte-by-byte level, which is used in [1, 3, 7]. Ntoulas et al. [9] used the TF·IDF cosine distance and the word distance. Lim et al. [8] used a metric based on the edit distance. Broder et al. [2] and Fetterly et al. [6] used the shingling metric. Each of the metrics often represents the same change of web pages

* This work was supported by Korea Research Foundation Grant (KRF-2004-005-D00172).

M.L. Lee, K.L. Tan, and V. Wuwongse (Eds.): DASFAA 2006, LNCS 3882, pp. 557 – 571, 2006.

differently. Users may have a difficulty with selecting an appropriate metric for their specific applications. In our best knowledge, there have been no research activities to intensively compare (or evaluate) the existing metrics in terms of web page changes.

In this paper, we propose criteria for web page changes in order to evaluate existing similarity metrics. In the criteria, web page changes are classified into six types (namely, "add", "drop", "copy", "shrink", "replace", and "move"). We believe that the six types represent common changes on the web. For each of the six change types, each criterion is defined. Each criterion gives appropriate values of change degree for the web pages changed by each change type. A metric is defined to be effective if the metric is close to the criteria. A metric is defined to be oversensitive (undersensitive) if the metric is always higher (lower respectively) than the criteria. In this paper, we also present a new similarity metric measuring the degree of web page changes effectively. The metric is designed to reflect our criteria well in terms of the six change types.

We conducted two kinds of experiments. The first experiment shows how differently the five existing metrics (i.e., the byte-wise comparison, the TF·IDF cosine distance, the word distance, the edit distance, and the shingling metrics) and ours represent the same change of web pages with 41,469 real web pages. In the second experiment, we evaluate the effectiveness of the six metrics with synthesized pages under the criteria. From the results, we substantiate that the existing metrics have some drawbacks and our metric is more effective than the existing metrics for web page changes.

This paper is organized as follows. Section 2 explains the existing metrics briefly. In section 3, the change types of web pages are defined, and the criteria for web page changes are described. In section 4, we propose an effective similarity metric for measuring the degree of web page changes. Experimental results are reported in section 5. Finally, section 6 contains the closing remarks.

2 Existing Metrics

We introduce five metrics that have been used to measure the degree of web page changes in the literature. Throughout this paper, p denotes an original web page and p' a changed page of p. The byte-wise comparison metric [1, 3, 7], which compares two web pages p and p' sequentially character by character, is the simplest (but most rigid) method for measuring the degree of web page changes. The metric returns 0 when there is no change at all, and returns 1 otherwise. The byte-wise comparison metric returns 1 even for very trivial changes (for example, insertion of one blank space). That metric is oversensitive and does not represent the degree of changes.

The TF·IDF cosine distance metric is commonly used for determining relevance of documents to a search query in the field of information retrieval. This metric transforms p and p' to the TF·IDF weighted vectors v_p and $v_{p'}$ respectively [10], and calculates cosine distance between the two vectors as equation (1). $v_p \cdot v_{p'}$ denotes the inner product of v_p and $v_{p'}$, and $\|v_i\|_2$ denotes the second norm of vector v_i.

$$D_{COS}(p, p') = 1 - \frac{v_p \cdot v_{p'}}{\|v_p\|_2 \|v_{p'}\|_2} \qquad (1)$$

The word distance metric calculates how many of the words on a page have changed. In this metric, the distance between p and p' is calculated as equation (2), where m and n denote the numbers of words on p and p' respectively. Ntoulas et al. [9] used the TF·IDF cosine distance and the word distance to measure the degree of web page changes.

$$D_{WD}(p, p') = 1 - \frac{2 \cdot |common\ words|}{m+n} \tag{2}$$

The TF·IDF cosine distance and the word distance metrics cannot consider the change of word orders because they regard web pages as bags of words. The change of word orders frequently takes place and may be critical. For example, a change of word orders in a shopping site could represent a change of articles' priorities, which is important to customers.

The edit distance is the least expensive cost for sequences of edit operations (generally, "insertion", "deletion", and "substitution") required to transform one sequence to another sequence [5]. For example, suppose that the cost of every edit operation is 1. The edit distance from a sequence <A, G, B, A, A> to <A, B, A, T, A> is 2 because at least two edit operations (one "deletion" of G and one "insertion" of T) are needed. To measure the degree of web page changes, Lim et al. [8] defined a distance metric as equation (3), where m and n denote the numbers of words on p and p' respectively and δ denotes the edit distance between p and p'. Each page is regarded as a word sequence. Only two operations (i.e., "insertion" and "deletion") are used as edit operations, and the cost of the operations is 1. When the two pages are identical, δ becomes 0 and the metric returns 0. On the other hand, when the two pages are completely different, δ is $(m + n)$ because m old words are deleted and n new words are inserted. In this case, the metric returns 1.

$$D_{ED}(p, p') = \frac{\delta}{m+n} \tag{3}$$

The word distance and the edit distance metrics cannot distinguish insertion (deletion) of unique words from insertion (deletion, respectively) of duplicate words, even though such changes could have different implications. For example, if a web page $<w_1, w_2, w_3, w_4>$ changes to $<w_1, w_2, w_3, w_4, w_2, w_3>$, both metrics return 0.2. If the same page changes to $<w_1, w_2, w_3, w_4, w_5, w_6>$, they also return 0.2. However, it may be necessary to distinguish the two changes, because some applications like to consider them differently.

In the shingling metric, each web page is represented as a set of k-word continuous, ordered subsequences. Each subsequence is called a "shingle", and k represents the number of words on a shingle. Every word on the document starts a shingle wrapping at the end of the document. For example, the 3-shingling of a document $<w_1, w_2, w_3, w_4>$ is the set $\{<w_1, w_2, w_3>, <w_2, w_3, w_4>, <w_3, w_4, w_1>, <w_4, w_1, w_2>\}$. For a given shingle size, the distance between p and p' is shown in equation (4), where $S(p)$ is the set of shingles on p, and $|S(p)|$ is the number of elements on the set $S(p)$. Broder et al. [2] defined the shingling metric and tried to cluster web pages that have the similar contents using the metric. Fetterly et al. [6] used the metric to investigate how web pages evolve.

$$D_{k-SH}(p, p') = 1 - \frac{|S(p) \cap S(p')|}{|S(p) \cup S(p')|} \tag{4}$$

The shingling metric is oversensitive to the changes on small web pages. For example, assume that a web page <w_1, w_2, w_3, w_4, w_5> changes to <w_1, w_2, w_3, w_6, w_5>, and the shingle size k is 3. Even though only one word (w_4) changes, the metric returns 0.75. The result could cause users to misinterpret to mean that 75% of the page has changed. Moreover, if w_1 moves between w_3 and w_4 on a page <w_1, w_2, w_3, w_4, w_5>, the metric returns 1.

3 Criteria for Evaluating the Metrics

In this section, we define criteria for web page changes to evaluate how effectively the metrics measure the degree of web page changes. Prior to defining the criteria, we classify web page changes into six types (namely, "add", "copy", "drop" "shrink", "replace", and "move"). Examples of the six change types are given in Fig. 1.

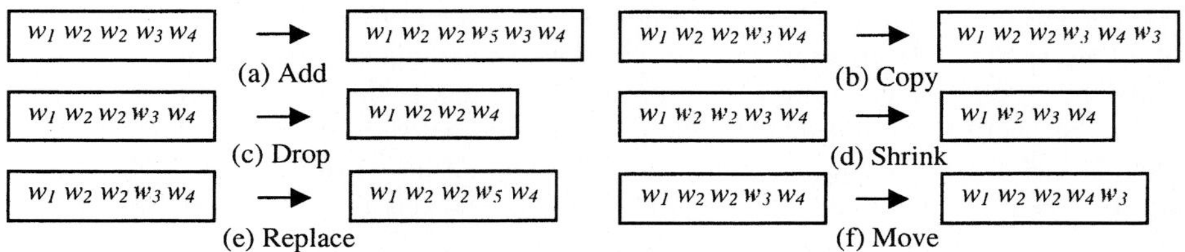

Fig. 1. Six types of web page changes

Definition 1. When new words (i.e., words not occurring on p) are inserted into p, we say that an "*add*" change takes place on the page. When old words (i.e., words occurring on p) are inserted into p, we say that a "*copy*" change takes place on the page.

Definition 2. When unique words (i.e., words occurring only once on p) are deleted from p, we say that a "*drop*" change takes place on the page. The deleted words do not exist any more on p' after the "drop" change. When duplicate words (i.e., words occurring more than once on p) are deleted from p, we say that a "*shrink*" change takes place on the page. The deleted words still occur on p' even after the "shrink" change.

Definition 3. When words on p are substituted by different words, we say that a "*replace*" change takes place on the page.

Definition 4. When the positions of words on p change, we say that a "*move*" change takes place on the page.

We give an example to illustrate how the six change types are applicable. Suppose an e-commerce site that displays a list of book information such as titles, summaries, prices, popularities (i.e., the total number of books sold), and customers' opinions, in

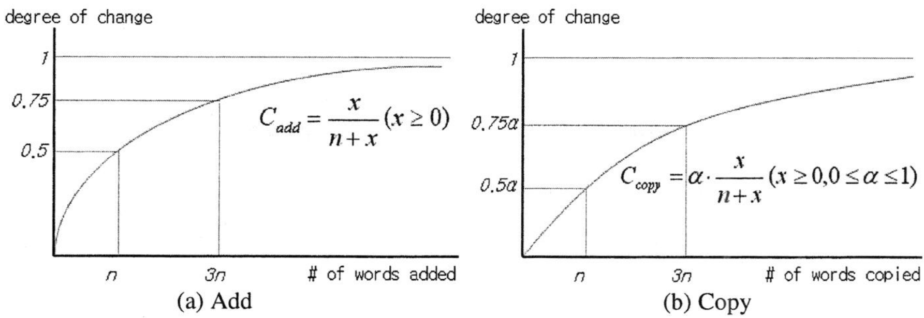

(a) Add (b) Copy

Fig. 2. Criteria for "Add" and "Copy"

an order of popularity. First, suppose that a customer writes his opinion on the page. When the opinion is different from existing opinions, the inserted words are likely to be unique (i.e., "add" change). When the opinion is similar to existing opinions, the inserted words are likely to be duplicated (i.e., "copy" change). Next, suppose that a customer deletes his opinion from the page. When the opinion is unique from existing ones, the deleted words are likely to be absent on the page (i.e., "drop" change). When the opinion is similar to other ones, the deleted words are still likely to occur on the page (i.e., "shrink" change). We distinguish the "add" change (the "drop" change) from the "copy" change (the "shrink" change, respectively), because the change of unique information is more significant than the change of duplicate information in general. On the price change, the old price of the book is updated by the new one on the page (i.e., "replace" change). When the popularities of books change, the order of book information in the list is changed (i.e., "move" change).

Figs. 2 to 4 illustrate the criterion of each change type. Let n and x denote the number of words on p and the number of changed words, respectively. The x-axis represents the number of changed words on a web page and the y-axis represents the change degree of a page.

The criterion for the "add" change is defined as $(x / (n+x))$, as illustrated in Fig. 2(a). For example, when n words are added to p with n words, the change degree is 0.5 $(= n / (n+n))$. Similarly, when $3n$ words are added to p with n words, the change degree is 0.75 $(= 3n / (3n+n))$. As the number of added words increases, the change degree becomes to be close to 1. The criterion for the "copy" change is defined as $(\alpha x / (n+x))$, which is illustrated in Fig. 2(b). The parameter α, which ranges from 0 to 1, denotes the user-defined weight of the "copy" change against the "add" change. As a user considers the "copy" change more significantly (or trivially), α becomes higher (or lower, respectively). For example, if a user considers the effect of adding one word to be equivalent to the effect of copying two words, α should be set to be 1/2. If a user considers the effect of adding one word to be equivalent to the effect of copying three words, α should be set to be 1/3.

The criterion for the "drop" change is defined as (x / n), as in Fig. 3(a). For example, when n words are dropped from p with n words, the degree of change is one $(= n / n)$. More than n words cannot be dropped from a page with n words. The criterion for the "shrink" change is defined as $(\alpha x / n)$, as in Fig. 3(b). The parameter α, which is defined before, is used to denote the user-defined weight of the "shrink"

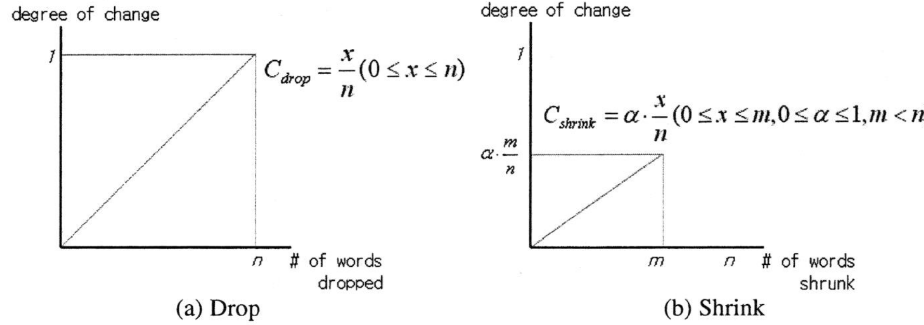

Fig. 3. Criteria for "Drop" and "Shrink"

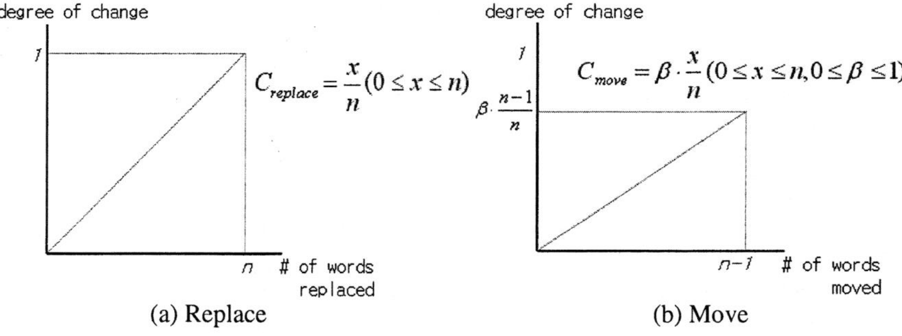

Fig. 4. Criteria for "Replace" and "Move"

change against the "drop" change. *m* denotes the maximum number of duplicate words on *p*, hence more than *m* words cannot be shrunk.

The criterion for the "replace" change is defined as (x / n), as shown in Fig. 4(a). For example, when *n* words on *p* with *n* words are replaced to other words, the degree of change is one ($= n / n$). The criterion for the "move" change is defined as $(\beta x / n)$, as in Fig. 4(b). The parameter β, which ranges from 0 to 1, denotes the user-defined weight of the "move" change against the "replace' change. As a user considers the "move" change more significantly (or trivially), β becomes higher (or lower, respectively). $(n\text{-}1)$ is the maximum number of movable words on a page with *n* words.

4 A New Metric

In this section, we propose an effective metric. Our metric is an improved version of the edit distance metric. The metric considers all the six change types described in section 3. Note that the edit distance is the least expensive cost for sequences of edit operations (generally, "insertion", "deletion", and "substitution") required to transform one sequence to another sequence. In our metric, we extend the edit operations to be the following six ones: "add", "drop", "copy", "shrink", "replace", and "move". The cost of "add", "drop", and "replace" operations is 1. The cost of "copy" and "shrink" is a, and the cost of "move" operation is b, where a and b range from 0 to 1. The extended edit distance δ_E of two web pages is defined as equation (5), where each page is regarded as a word sequence as done in [8]. k means the maximum number of sequences of the extended edit operations, and $COST_i(op)$ denotes the cost of the given edit operation in the ith sequence.

$$\delta_E = \min_{i=1..k} \left\{ \sum_{op\in\{add,\ drop,\ copy,\ shrink,\ replace,\ move\}} COST_i(op) \right\} \quad (5)$$

The extended edit distance δ_E between two word sequences A and B can be obtained through the following steps (see Example 1).

Phase 1: Finding the longest common subsequence

We first find the longest common subsequence *LCS(A, B)* of two word sequences, A and B. A subsequence of a sequence is simply a sequence with some elements (possibly none) left out. For example, a sequence $<w_2, w_3, w_4, w_2>$ is a subsequence of a sequence $<w_1, w_2, w_3, w_2, w_4, w_1, w_2>$ with corresponding index sequence $<2, 3, 5, 7>$ [5]. Using *LCS(A, B)*, we create two word sequences excluding *LCS(A, B)* from A and B (hereafter referred to as A' and B', respectively).

Phase 2: Taking care of the "move" operations

The candidate words for "move" operation (referred to as CW_{move}) are the common words on both A' and B'. If b is bigger than $2a$, we exclude some words occurring more than once on both A and B, from CW_{move}. The excluded words become the candidate words for "copy" and "shrink" operations in the next phase so as to minimize the cost of the edit operation sequence. Then, remained CW_{move} are considered as moved words. The number of "move" operations becomes the number of moved words, and the moved words are removed from A' and B'.

Phase 3: Taking care of the "copy" and "shrink" operations

The words that exist on B' and occur on B more than once are the candidates for "copy" operation (referred to as CW_{copy}). And the words that exist on A' and occur on A more than once are the candidate words for "shrink" operation (referred to as CW_{shrink}). First, each of the common words in CW_{copy} and CW_{shrink} is considered as a shrunk and copied word; the common words exist only when b is bigger than $2a$. The numbers of "copy" and "shrink" operations become the number of the common words, and the words are removed from A', B', CW_{copy}, and CW_{shrink}. Second, note that one "copy" and one "shrink" operations may also be represented by one "replace" operation. If a is smaller than 0.5, the cost (i.e., $2a$) of one "copy" operation and one "shrink" operation is cheaper than the cost (i.e., 1) of one "replace" operation. Hence, we find words such that a word in CW_{copy} and a word in CW_{shrink} occur on the same index of B and A respectively. Each of the detected words is considered as a shrunk and copied word. The numbers of "copy" and "shrink" operations increase as many as the number of the detected words, and the words are removed from A', B', CW_{copy}, and CW_{shrink}. If a is bigger than 0.5, we exclude the detected words from CW_{copy} and CW_{shrink}. The excluded words are considered as replaced words in the next phase. Finally, remained CW_{copy} and CW_{shrink} are considered as copied and shrunk words respectively. Hence, the numbers of "copy" and "shrink" operations increase as many as the numbers of copied words and the number of shrunk words respectively. The copied words are removed from *B'* and the shrunk words are removed from *A'*.

Phase 4: Taking care of the "replace", "add" and "drop" operations
The words on *A'* and *B'* with the same indexes on both *A* and *B* are considered as replaced words. The number of "replace" operations becomes the number of replaced words and the replaced words are removed from *A'* and *B'*. Next, the words on *A'* and *B'* are considered as dropped and added words respectively. Hence the numbers of "add" and "drop" operations become the numbers of the words on *B'* and *A'* respectively.

Phase 5: Calculating the extended edit distance
The extended edit distance from *A* to *B* is calculated from the numbers of edit operations and their costs.

Example 1. Suppose that a web page $A = <w_1, w_2, w_2, w_2, w_3, w_3, w_4, w_5, w_2>$ changes to $B = <w_3, w_1, w_4, w_2, w_3, w_5, w_5, w_6, w_6, w_7>$. The parameters *a* and *b* are set to be 0.4 and 0.9, respectively. We compute the extended edit distance from *A* to *B* as follows.

At the first phase, we find the longest common subsequence of *A* and *B*:

$LCS(A, B) = <w_1, w_2, w_3, w_5>$
$A' = <w_2, w_2, w_3, \mathbf{w_4}, w_2>$
$B' = <w_3, \mathbf{w_4}, w_5, w_6, w_6, w_7>$
|add| = 0, |drop| = 0, |copy| = 0, |shrink| = 0, |replace| = 0, |move| = 0

At the second phase, CW_{move} are w_3 and w_4 since the two words occur on both *A'* and *B'*. But, since *b* is bigger than *2a* and w_3 occurs twice on both *A* and *B*, w_3 is excluded from CW_{move}. Hence, only w_4 is considered as a moved word. The number of "move" operations becomes one and w_4 is removed from *A'* and *B'*:

$A' = <w_2, w_2, \mathbf{w_3}, w_2>$
$B' = <\mathbf{w_3}, w_5, w_6, w_6, w_7>$
|add| = 0, |drop| = 0, |copy| = 0, |shrink| = 0, |replace| = 0, |move| = 1

At the third phase, CW_{copy} are w_3, w_5, and w_6, and CW_{shrink} are w_2, w_2, w_2, and w_3. First, w_3 is considered as a shrunk and copied word because the word is a common word in CW_{copy} and CW_{shrink}. Hence, the number of "copy" and "shrink" operations becomes one and w_3 is removed from *A'*, *B'*, CW_{copy}, and CW_{shrink}. At this time, we have:

$A' = <w_2, w_2, \mathbf{w_2}>$, $CW_{shrink} = w_2, w_2, w_2$
$B' = <w_5, w_6, \mathbf{w_6}, w_7>$, $CW_{copy} = w_5, w_6$
|add| = 0, |drop| = 0, |copy| = 1, |shrink| = 1, |replace| = 0, |move| = 1

Next, we find the words with the same indexes on both *A* and *B* from CW_{copy} and CW_{shrink}, which are w_2 and w_6; w_2 occurs on *A* with the ninth index and w_6 occurs on *B* with the ninth index. Since *a* is smaller than 0.5, w_2 and w_6 are considered as a shrunk word and a copied word respectively. Hence, the numbers of "copy" and "shrink" operations increase by one. w_2 is removed from A' and CW_{shrink}, and w_6 is removed from B' and CW_{copy}:

$A' = <w_2, w_2>$, $CW_{shrink} = w_2, w_2$
$B' = <w_5, w_6, w_7>$, $CW_{copy} = w_5$
|add| = 0, |drop| = 0, |copy| = 2, |shrink| = 2, |replace| = 0, |move| = 1

Next, remained CW_{copy} and CW_{shrink} are considered as copied words and shrunk words respectively. Hence, the number of "copy" operations increases by one and the number of "shrink" operations increases by two. w_2 and w_2 are removed from A', and w_5 is removed from B':

$A' = <>$
$B' = <w_6, w_7>$
|add| = 0, |drop| = 0, |copy| = 3, |shrink| = 4, |replace| = 0, |move| = 1

At the fourth phase, there are no any replaced or dropped words since A' is empty. w_6 and w_7 are considered as added words, hence the number of "add" operations becomes two. Finally we have the numbers of all the extended edit operations in the least expensive sequence of the operations:

|add| = 2, |drop| = 0, |copy| = 3, |shrink| = 4, |replace| = 0, |move| = 1

At the fifth phase, we calculate the extended edit distance from A to B:

$\delta_E = (2\cdot1) + (0\cdot1) + (3\cdot0.4) + (4\cdot0.4) + (1\cdot0) + (1\cdot0.9) = 5.7$ ■

Using the extended edit distance, we calculate the distance between two web pages p and p' as equation (6), where m and n denote the numbers of words on p and p' respectively.

$$D_{IED}(p, p') = \frac{\delta_E}{\max(m, n)} \tag{6}$$

5 Experiments

We conducted two experiments. First, using real web pages, we show how differently each similarity metric measures the degree of web page changes. Second, we present the effectiveness of the metrics under the proposed criteria. We compare the following six metrics: the byte-wise comparison (in short, BW), the TF·IDF cosine distance (COS), the word distance (WD), the edit distance (ED), the 10-shingling (10SH), and our metric improving the edit distance metric (IED). Markups of web pages were excluded in the experiments, as done in the literature [2, 6, 8, 9]. The parameters a and b of our metric were set to be 0.75.

5.1 Difference of the Metrics

We randomly crawled 41,469 Korean web pages in August 2005. The web pages were downloaded twice in a two-day interval. From two versions of the web pages, we measured the degree of changes using the six metrics. Fig. 5 shows the change

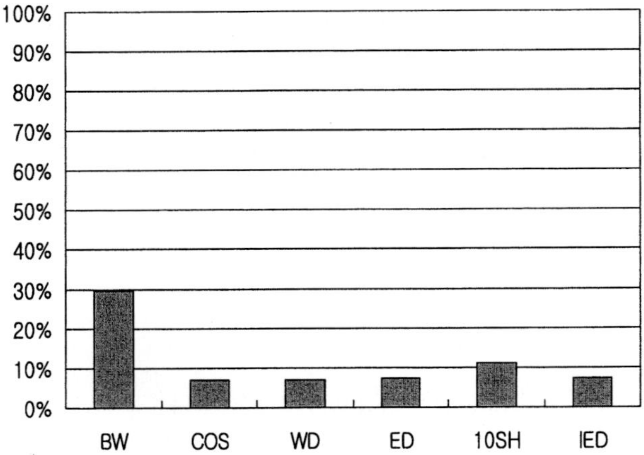

Fig. 5. Difference of sensitivity (I)

degrees of the pages under the six metrics. *y*-axis represents the sum of the change degrees of all the pages as percentage. The BW result implies that 30% of the pages changed, since it always returns 1 despite of very trivial changes (say, insertion of a blank space). For the same 30% of the pages, other metrics respond differently. 10SH determines that about 12% of all the page contents changed, while COS, WD, ED, and IED say that about 7% of them changed. As Fig. 5 shows, BW is the most sensitive metric among the six metrics. We also learn that 10SH is more sensitive to the page changes than COS, WD, ED, and IED are.

Fig. 6 shows how differently 10SH, COS, and ED respond to the same changes of web pages. The *x*-axis represents the identifier of each web page, and the *y*-axis represents the change degree of the corresponding web page. The identifiers of web pages are sorted in an ascending order of 10SH and COS in Fig. 6(a) and 6(b) respectively, in order to clearly visualize the difference of the metrics. We have observed the similar results for other combinations of metrics, which are not explicitly

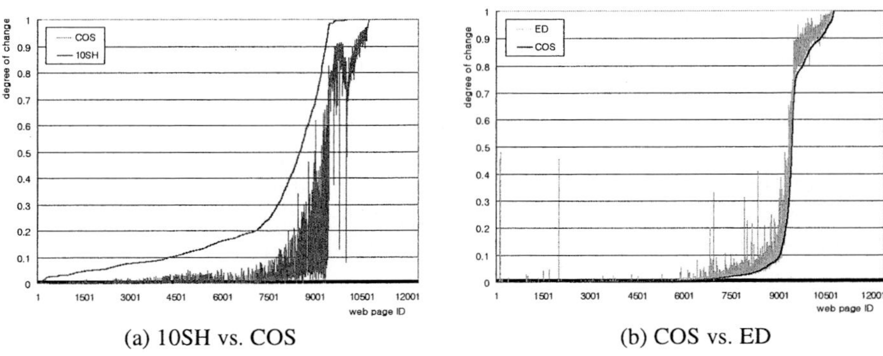

(a) 10SH vs. COS (b) COS vs. ED

Fig. 6. Difference of sensitivity (II)

presented though. As the figures show, each metric returns different values on almost all the pages. Sometimes, the difference is as large as 0.92 as shown in Fig. 6(a). This experiment implies that the degree of web page changes is heavily dependent on which metric is used to measure the page changes. Users need to select an appropriate metric when they precisely measure the degree of web page changes; otherwise they would misunderstand web page changes. These experimental results motivated our study.

5.2 Evaluation of the Metrics

We conducted experiments to evaluate the effectiveness of the metrics under the proposed criteria. These experiments were done with synthesized pages, which are constructed to reflect the characteristics on the web. A metric is defined to be effective if the results of the metric are close to the criteria. In addition, if the results of a metric are always higher (or lower) than the criteria, we say that the metric is oversensitive (or undersensitive, respectively). α and β in the criteria were set to be 0.75.

First, we evaluated the metrics when various numbers of words on a page with 1,000 words were changing. We chose a page with 1000 words, since web pages with 1,000 words occupy about 25% on the web [6]. The changed words were clustered (i.e., not distributed) on the pages, because the changes of real web pages were generally clustered [8]. In Fig. 7, the x-axis represents the number of changed words on a page, and the y-axis denotes the change degree of the corresponding page. 10SH is effective for the "add" and "drop" changes, but is oversensitive for the other changes. If α in the criteria were set to be one, the metric would be effective for the "copy" and "shrink" changes. In our experiment, COS is always undersensitive. COS returns very low values for the "copy" and "shrink" changes, which implies that COS treats the "copy" and "shrink" changes to be minor. COS and WD always return zero on the "move" change because they do not consider the changes of word order at all. WD is effective for the "replace" change but is undersensitive for the other changes. If α in the criteria were to be 0.5, the metric would be effective for the "copy" change. On the other words, WD would be the right choice for users who consider the effect of adding one word to be equivalent to the effect of copying two words. ED works similar to WD, except for the "move" change. ED treats the "move" change and "replace" change identically. IED returns the most effective results in all cases.

Next, we evaluated the metrics on various sizes of pages (i.e., 2^2, 2^3, 2^4, … , or 2^{13} words). Note that web pages with 2^2 to 2^{13} words occupy about 95% on the web [6]. We maintained the fraction of changed words on each page to be 1/4; one word on a 2^2 word page, two words on a 2^3 word page, three words on a 2^4 word page, and so on. The x-axis in Fig. 8 represents the number of words on a page before change. From this result, we found out that 10SH becomes more oversensitive as web pages become smaller on all the change types. The sensitivities of the other metrics are not dependent to the page size in most cases; COS also varies in sensitivity according to the page size, but it is not serious.

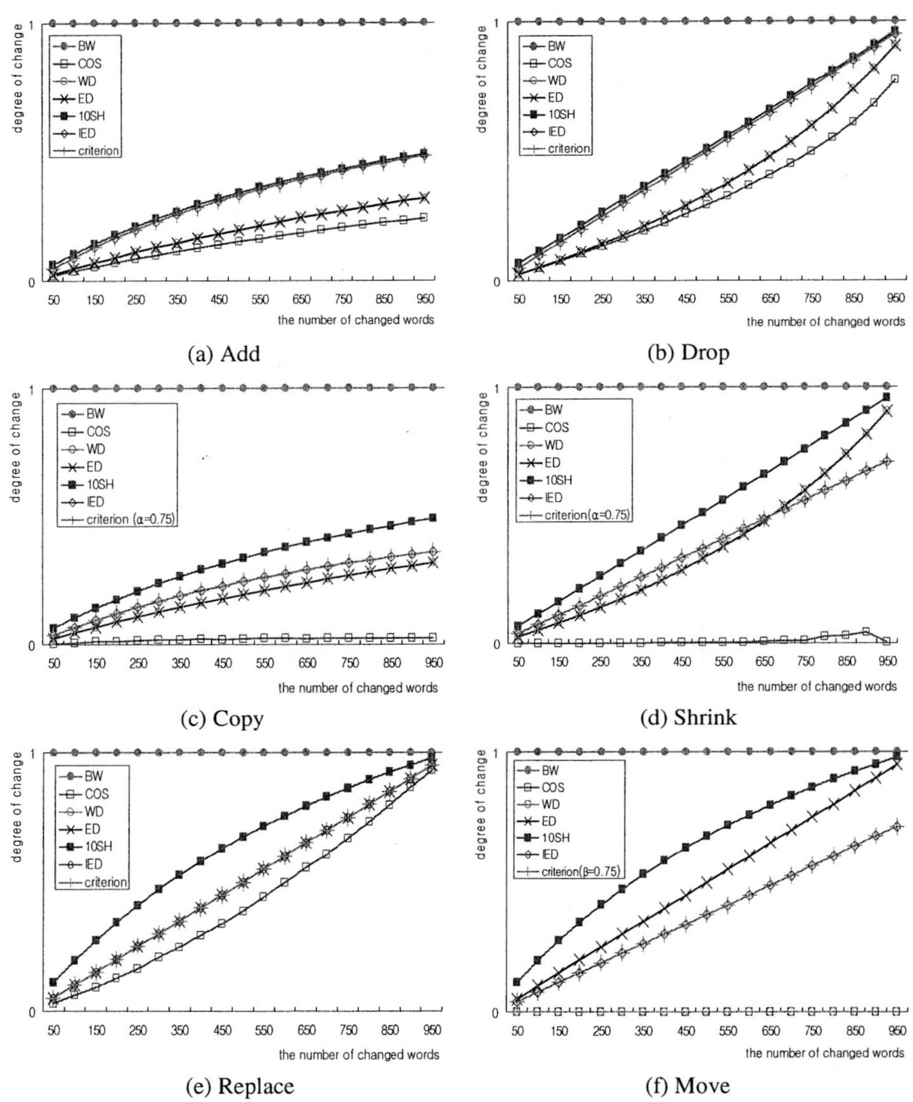

(a) Add (b) Drop

(c) Copy (d) Shrink

(e) Replace (f) Move

Fig. 7. Comparison of metrics

Note that the experiments were done with $\alpha = 0.75$ and $\beta = 0.75$. If parameters α and β were set differently, the sensitivities (or effectiveness) of the metrics would be differently evaluated under the "copy", "shrink", and "move" changes. It should be observed that the criteria graphs with other values of α and β could be easily predicted; only the slope of the criteria graph changes.

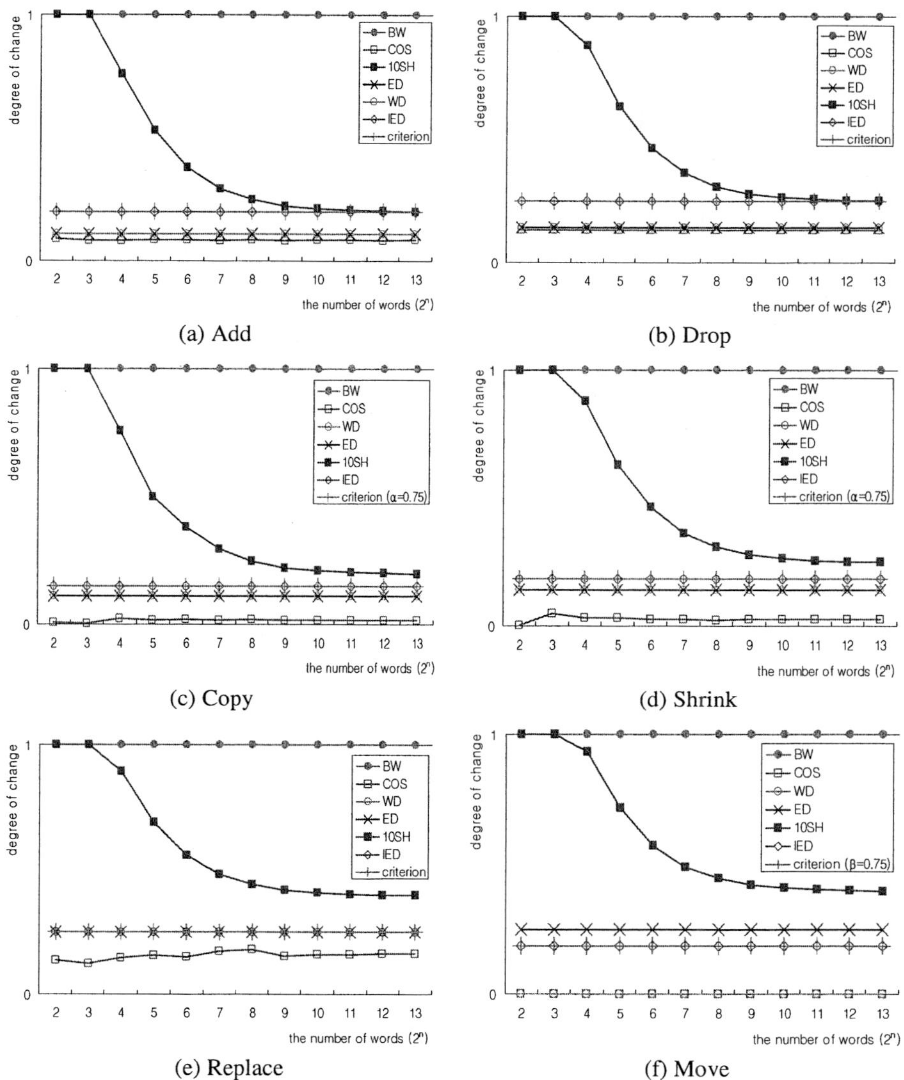

(a) Add (b) Drop

(c) Copy (d) Shrink

(e) Replace (f) Move

Fig. 8. Sensitivity versus page size

We now summarize what we have learned in our experiments.

1. 10SH is oversensitive to the changes of web pages (especially under the "move" change). The smaller the page size is, the more sensitive 10SH is. 10S H is effective for the "add" and the "drop" changes. 10SH measures the "add" change and the "copy" change similarly. The "drop" and "shrink" changes are similarly treated under 10SH.

2. COS is an undersensitive metric. COS does not consider the “move” change at all. In particular, the “copy” and the “shrink” changes are regarded as minor changes.
3. WD does not consider the “move” change at all. WD is undersensitive to the “add” and the “drop” changes. The “copy” changes (or the “shrink” changes) of two words are approximately regarded as the “add” change (or the “drop”change, respectively) of one word. WD is well effective for the “replace”change.
4. ED shows the same results as WD except the “move” change. The “move” change is considered similarly with the “drop” or “replace” change.
5. IED is the most effective metric under our proposed criteria. Mostly, IED responds to the changes of web pages identically to the criteria. IED can be used effectively in various applications because it can adjust the weights of the “copy”, “shrink”, and “move” changes.

6 Closing Remarks

In this paper, we classified the changes of web pages into six types, which are “add”, “copy”, “drop” “shrink”, “replace”, and “move”, then we defined a criterion for each type. We also proposed a new metric designed to reflect the criteria well. Under the criteria, we evaluated the effectiveness of the six metrics (namely, the byte-wise comparison, the TF·IDF cosine distance, the word distance, the edit distance, the shingling, and ours). Based on this evaluation, we found that the proposed metric is the most effective metric in terms of all the six change types. Our study presents how significantly the metrics consider each change type and which metric is effective on each change type. We believe that this study is the first attempt to evaluate the metrics and could be used as a guideline for selecting an appropriate metric measuring the degree of web page changes.

With our criteria, the metrics can be evaluated separately in terms of one of the six change types. Even though more than one change type often occurs simultaneously on real web pages, our criteria have some limitations to measure multiple changes. Further research on the criteria for evaluating which metrics represent simultaneous changes effectively is necessary.

References

1. Brewington, B. E., Cybenko, G.: How Dynamic is the Web? the 9th International World Wide Web Conference (2000) 257-276
2. Broder, A. Z., Glassman, S. C., Manasse, M. S., Zweig, G.: Syntactic Clustering of the Web. Computer Networks and ISDN Systems Vol. 29. No. 8-13. (1997) 1157-1166
3. Cho, J., Garcia-Molina, H.: The Evolution of the Web and Implications for an Incremental Crawler. the 26th International Conference on Very Large Data Bases (2000) 200-209
4. Cho, J., Garcia-Molina, H.: Synchronizing a Database to Improve Freshness. the ACM SIGMOD International Conference on Management of Data (2000) 117-128
5. Cormen, T. H., Leiserson, C. E., Rivest, R. L.: Introduction to Algorithm. the Massachusetts Institute of Technology (2001)

6. Fetterly, D., Manasse, M., Najork, M., Wiener, J. L.: A Large-Scale Study of the Evolution of Web Pages. Software: Practice & Experience, Vol. 34, No. 2 (2003) 213-237
7. Kim, S. J., Lee, S. H.: An Empirical Study on the Change of Web Pages. the 7th Asia Pacific Web Conference (2005) 632-642
8. Lim, L., Wang, M., Padmanabhan, S., Vitter, J. S., Agarwal, R.: Characterizing Web Document Change. the 2nd International Conference on Advances in Web-Age Information Management (2001) 133-144
9. Ntoulas, A., Cho, J., Olston, C.: What's New on the Web? The Evolution of the Web from a Search Engine Perspective. the 13th International World Wide Web Conference (2004) 1-12
10. Salton, G., McGill, M. J.: Introduction to Modern Information Retrieval. McGraw-Hill (1983)

Similarity Search in Transaction Databases with a Two-Level Bounding Mechanism

Jo-Chun Chuang[1], Chung-Wen Cho[1], and Arbee L.P. Chen [2]

[1] Department of Computer Science, National Tsing Hua University, Taiwan, R.O.C
[2] Department of Computer Science, National Chengchi University, Taiwan, R.O.C
alpchen@cs.nccu.edu.tw

Abstract. In this paper, we propose a novel indexing method for similarity search in transaction databases where the frequency of database updates can be high. In our method, the incoming transactions are incrementally classified into clusters. The transactions in a cluster are represented using two features, namely the union and the intersection of all the transactions. Based on these two features, the transactions in a cluster are further divided into disjoint groups. As a result, all the transactions are organized as a two-level index structure. With this index, the insertion of a transaction can be quickly done because only a particular cluster needs to be modified. Moreover, when conducting a similarity search, we can compute for each level the lower and upper bounds on the distance between the query and each transaction in the cluster. Based on these bounds, the costs on the distance computation can be greatly reduced.

1 Introduction

Mining knowledge from transaction databases is an essential step in decision-making applications. Recently, some researchers have been integrating the database techniques into the mining process to improve the quality of mining results. Similarity search in transaction databases is one of the important techniques. For example, consider the transaction database db as shown in Table 1, each transaction in the database indicates the items purchased by a customer. For a given transaction corresponding to a customer, similar transactions can be found from db and used to provide recommendations about items which the customer may be interested in. In this paper, the similarity search problem on the transaction database is considered. For a user given transaction t_q (in the rest of this paper, we call this given transaction the *query*) and a distance threshold δ, the transactions in the database whose distance to t_q is less than or equal to δ will be returned as the result for similar transactions. The *hamming distance* is a well known operator from set theory and is widely used to calculate the distance between two transactions 3, 4, 5. The hamming distance between transactions t_i and t_j $dist(t_i,t_j)$ is defined as the cardinality of the union of t_i and t_j minus the intersection of t_i and t_j. For example, assume that a customer buys the set of items (abd), the hamming distance between (abd) and t_1, t_2, … t_5 in db is 2, 2, 3, 4 and 1, respectively. If the distance threshold is set to 2, t_1, t_2, and t_5 will be returned as the

M.L. Lee, K.L. Tan, and V. Wuwongse (Eds.): DASFAA 2006, LNCS 3882, pp. 572–586, 2006.

Table 1. The transaction database db

TID	Transaction
1	(abc)
2	(acd)
3	(bdef)
4	(def)
5	(ab)

similar transactions to (abd). In this paper, we adopt the hamming distance as the distance metric for transactions.

In recent years, several works 1, 3, 4, 5 have noted the problem of similarity search on transaction data. Most of the existing approaches focus on the construction of a transaction index structure such that similar transactions can be efficiently retrieved via the index structure. The concept of *signature* is widely used in the existing approaches to index transactions. A signature is a bit vector where each bit is associated with a set of distinct items. For each transaction, a bit of the corresponding signature is set to 1 if the transaction contains a sufficient number of the items associated with the bit. The transactions represented by the same signature are considered as similar transactions. According to different purposes, the existing approaches can be classified into table-based approaches 1, 3 and R-tree based approaches 4, 5. The table-based approaches assume that the correlation among items is consistent in the transaction database. In these papers, the probability analysis is applied on the items in the transaction database such that the transactions containing high correlative items can be represented by an identical signature. Accordingly, the similar transactions can be efficiently found based on the signature. However, the correlation among items can change since the customer behavior can change from time to time. That is, after inserting a certain number of transactions, the correlation among items has to be reevaluated such that the transactions with highly correlated items can still be represented by the same signature. However, the evaluation of the correlation among items is time consuming. Therefore, these approaches are not suitable for the database with a high update rate.

On the other hand, the R-tree based approaches focus on the flexibility of index updates. Whenever a transaction is inserted into the database, the index structure is immediately updated. In general, the leaf node of the R-tree based index structure is associated with a set of transactions. Each internal node contains a set of signatures and their associated pointers each pointing to a child node of the internal node. Each signature in the internal node represents the transactions associated with the sub-tree rooted at the child node pointed by the associated pointer. In the R-tree based approaches, since the nodes in a higher level, i.e., the nodes which are closer to the root, cover more transactions in its descendants, most of the bits in the corresponding signatures will be 1. Therefore, it is hard to distinguish whether the query is similar to the transactions indexed by the descendants of the nodes. In addition, similar to the node splitting in R-tree, these approaches adopt non-trivial algorithms to evaluate the signatures in the two split nodes such that the number of the bits of a signature set to 1 in the two nodes is as small as possible. However, since the size of a node (number of signatures in a node) can be very large, these procedures can be time consuming. For example, assume the node size is m, the time complexity of *ga-split* proposed in 4 will be $O(m^4)$ (In 4, the node size is set to 4000. This is unsuitable for the dynamic environment).

When conducting a similarity search, all the existing approaches use signatures in the index structures to compute lower bounds on distance, which is between the transactions represented by the signatures and the query. Therefore, transactions which are impossible to be the answers can be pruned based on the lower bounds.

There are some other approaches which focus on the problem of similarity search. In 2, a query can be efficiently processed since the approximate set of answers can be quickly found; however, some answers will be lost. In addition to the similarity search problem on set data, a variety of approaches such as 1, 7, 8, 11 focus on the problem of similarity search on the numerical data. However, as noted in 3, these approaches are not suitable for set data since the domain of the elements in the set data does not have a natural order and the dimensionality of the items in the transactions is huge.

In this paper, we consider the problem on the database which can be updated frequently and denote such database as a *dynamic database*. Our algorithm can be applied to both insertion and deletion cases of the database. However, due to space limit, we only discuss the case of insertions in this paper. Given a query t_q and a distance threshold, our goal is to provide an index structure such that most of the dissimilar transactions to t_q can be efficiently pruned. Moreover, most of the similar transactions to t_q can be returned without having to compute their distances to t_q. The latter is important in on-line applications. For example, assume the database shown in Table 1 records the transactions for an e-store. Since what we want is to find the similar transaction to (abd) to provide on-line recommendations, the real distance/similarity between them are not important. However, in all the existing approaches, only the lower bounds on distance are used to prune the dissimilar transactions, the distance computation is necessary to verify whether the other transactions are similar to the query. In this paper, a novel index structure for the dynamic database is proposed such that the similarity search mechanism and index updates can be performed efficiently.

In the proposed approach, the incoming transactions are incrementally classified into clusters. The transactions in a cluster are represented by two sets of items, particularly the union and the intersection of all the transactions in the cluster. Based on these two features, the transactions in a cluster containing the same number of items are further grouped. For each summary of the cluster, the corresponding distance to the transactions in a group will be identical and used to represent the transactions in the group. As a result, all the transactions are organized in a two-level index structure and the corresponding features of clusters and groups are recorded. The lower bound and upper bound on distance between a query and the transactions in the cluster and a group of the cluster can be computed based on the recorded information. Based on the computed distance bounds, dissimilar transactions can be pruned and similar transactions can be found without computing their distances to the query. Therefore, the cost of distance computation can be substantially reduced.[1] While inserting a transaction, only one particular cluster needs to be modified and the time complexity of updating a

---

[1] Several approaches for clustering transactions have been proposed such as 6, 9, 10. However, these methods are not suitable for a database with a high frequency of updates, and do not provide a bound on the distance between the transactions in a cluster and a given query.

cluster is linear to the number of groups in the cluster. As a result, the proposed framework is robust for a dynamic database. For performance evaluation, we compare our approach with SG-Tree approach 4 on the similarity search time, pruning efficiency and update time. The results show that our approach outperforms the SG-Tree approach in all these aspects.

The rest of the paper is organized as follows. In Section 2, we first introduce the proposed index structure, and then present the two-level similarity search mechanism. In Section 3, we describe how to efficiently cluster the transactions and update the index structure. The performance evaluation and experiment results are shown in Section 4. Finally, we conclude this paper with some remarks on future research in Section 5.

2 The Index Structure and Similarity Search

As described in Section 1, each cluster C in the index is represented by its two features, i.e., the union and the intersection of all the transactions in the cluster. In this paper, we call the former *outer border* of C and the later *inner border* of C, denoted as C_O and C_I , respectively. Intuitively, the inner border of a cluster must be a subset of each transaction in the cluster while the outer border of the cluster must be the superset of each transaction in the cluster. Let $diff(t_i,t_j)$ denote the set operator *difference* of t_i and t_j (i.e., $|t_i - t_j|$. In addition, $dist(t_i,t_j)$ can be regarded as $diff(t_i,t_j)$ + $diff(t_j,t_i)$). Property 1 shows that the distance between any two transactions in a cluster is bounded by the difference of the corresponding outer and inner borders.

Property 1. Given a cluster C, the corresponding C_O and C_I, if t_i, $t_j \in C$, $dist(t_i,t_j) \leq diff(C_O,C_I)$.

Proof. Since t_i, $t_j \subseteq C_O$ and $C_I \subseteq t_i$, $t_j \Rightarrow |t_i \cup t_j| \leq |C_O|$ and $|C_I| \leq |t_i \cap t_j| \Rightarrow dist(t_i,t_j) = (|t_i \cup t_j| - |t_i \cap t_j|) \leq (|C_O| - |C_I|)$. Because $C_I \subseteq C_O \Rightarrow |C_O| - |C_I| = |C_O - C_I| = diff(C_O,C_I)$. □

From Property 1, we observe that the smaller the difference of the outer and inner borders of a cluster, the smaller the distance between any two transactions in the cluster; that is, transactions in the cluster are more similar to each other. Therefore, the principle of incrementally clustering the incoming transactions is to keep the $diff(C_O,C_I)$ of each cluster C as small as possible. The transactions in a cluster are further grouped into *batches*. For any two transactions t_i and t_j in a batch, the number of items in each of them is the same. Property 2 states that the difference for each transaction in a batch to the outer border and inner border of the cluster.

Property 2. Given a cluster C, the corresponding C_O and C_I, and a batch B of C, if t_i, $t_j \in$ B, $diff(C_O,t_i) = diff(C_O,t_j)$ and $diff(t_i, C_I) = diff(t_j,C_I)$.

Proof. Because t_i, $t_j \subseteq C_O$, $diff(C_O,t_i) = |C_O - t_i| = |C_O| - |t_i|$ and $diff(C_O,t_j) = |C_O - t_j| = |C_O| - |t_j|$. Because $|t_i| = |t_j| \Rightarrow diff(C_O,t_i) = diff(C_O,t_j)$. The case for $diff(t_i,C_I) = diff(t_j,C_I)$ can be proved in the similar way. □

Since the difference between C_O and each transaction in B is identical, we use $dv_O(C,B)$ to summarize $diff(C_O,t)$ for each transaction t in B. Similarly, we use

$dv_I(C,B)$ to summarize diff(t,C_I) for each transaction t in B. Moreover, we call *$dv_O(C,B)$ and $dv_I(C,B)$ the difference-value pair* of B. In the proposed index structure, the two borders and the difference-value pair of each batch in each cluster will be recorded. The two borders and the difference-value pairs of a cluster will be used to estimate the distance bounds for a query to the transactions in the cluster and in a batch of the cluster.

Example 1. Let the transactions (abc), (ab), and (bc) be contained in the cluster C, Figure 1 shows the index structure and illustrates the content of cluster C. The out border and inner border corresponding to C are (abc) and (b), respectively. The three transactions are further grouped into batches B_1 and B_2 in C based on the number of items in the transactions. The difference-value pair associated with each batch is represented in the header of the corresponding batch. □

Next, we present the similarity search on the proposed index structure. Given the query t_q and a cluster C, estimating the distance bounds for t_q to the transactions in C helps us to prune some of the transactions and recognize them as the answers to the query before their distances to t_q are computed. For a transaction t in C, dist(t_q,t) can be regarded as diff(t_q,t) + diff(t,t_q). The distance bounds of dist(t_q,t) can be derived from the difference bounds of diff(t_q,t) and diff(t,t_q). Given two transactions t_1 and t_2, if $t_1 \subseteq t \subseteq t_2$, diff($t_q$,$t_2$) $\leq$ diff(t_q,t) $\leq$ diff(t_q,t_1). Accordingly, diff(t_q,t_2) and diff(t_q,t_1) can be regarded as the lower and upper bounds of diff(t_q,t), respectively (The difference bounds of diff(t,t_q) can be computed in the similar way). This inspires us to extract the outer and inner borders from a cluster and use them along with the query to compute the corresponding distance bounds. In the following Lemmas, the distance bounds for a query to all the transactions in a cluster and to the transactions in a batch of the cluster are presented in Lemma 1 and Lemma 2, respectively. In Lemma 2, the difference-value pair of a batch is also considered when computing the corresponding distance bounds.

Lemma 1. Given a transaction t_q, the cluster C, the corresponding C_O and C_I, for the distance between t_q and each transaction t in C, the following formula always holds.

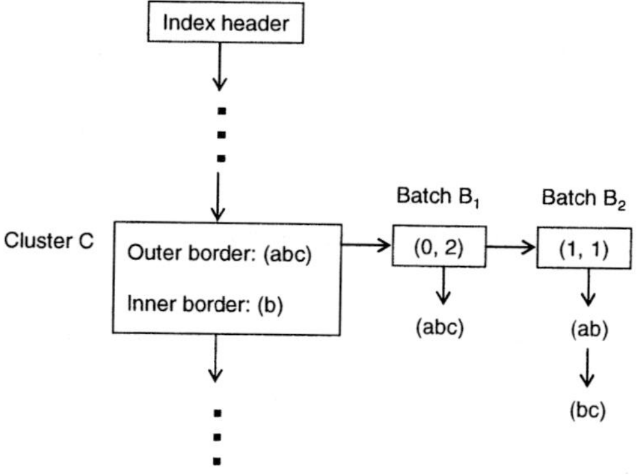

Fig. 1. The index structure

$$(diff(t_q,C_O) + diff(C_I,t_q)) \le dist(t_q,t) \le (diff(t_q,C_I) + diff(C_O,t_q)). \quad (1)$$

Proof. Because $C_I \subseteq t \subseteq C_O$, $diff(t_q,C_O) \le diff(t_q,t) \le diff(t_q,C_I)$. (1.1)
Moreover, $diff(C_I,t_q) \le diff(t,t_q) \le diff(C_O,t_q)$. (1.2)
By (1.1) and (1.2),

$$(diff(t_q,C_O) + diff(C_I,t_q)) \le (diff(t_q,t) + diff(t,t_q)) \le (diff(t_q,C_I) + diff(C_O,t_q)).$$
$$\Rightarrow (diff(t_q,C_O) + diff(C_I,t_q)) \le dist(t_q,t) \le (diff(t_q,C_I) + diff(C_O,t_q)).$$ □

For the ease of representation, we denote $diff(t_q,C_O) + diff(C_I,t_q)$ in formula (1) as *1st-LB(t_q,C)* while $diff(t_q,C_I) + diff(C_O,t_q)$ in formula (1) as *1st-UB(t_q,C)*. Moreover, we respectively call 1st-LB(t_q,C) and 1st-UB(t_q,C) the *first level distance lower bound* and the *first level distance upper bound* for t_q to each transaction in C. Given a query t_q, a distance threshold δ, and each cluster C in the index structure, the relationship between the 1st-LB(t_q,C) and 1st-UB(t_q,C) and δ is discussed as follows.

Case 1. 1st-LB(t_q,C) > δ. In this case, the distance between each transaction in the cluster and t_q must be larger than δ. Therefore, all the transactions in the cluster can be pruned straightforwardly.

Case 2. 1st-UB(t_q,C) ≤ δ. In this case, the distances of all the transactions in the cluster to t_q are smaller than or equal to δ. For this case, the transactions can be directly collected as the results without computing their distances to t_q.

Case 3. Both of the above two cases are not held. In this case, the distances between t_q and the transactions in C will be further evaluated to determine which transactions will be included in the results.

We call the first two cases described above and the corresponding treatments the *first level bounding mechanism*. For case 3, the difference-value pair of each batch in the cluster, the outer and inner borders corresponding to C, and the query will be used to calculate the distance lower and upper bounds of the query to the transactions in each batch. The two distance bounds are described in Lemma 2.

Lemma 2. Given a transaction t_q, the cluster C, the corresponding C_O and C_I, a batch B in C, and the difference-value pair $(dv_O(C,B),dv_I(C,B))$, for the distance between t_q and each transaction t in B, the following formula always holds.

$$(diff(t_q,C_O) + |diff(C_O,t_q) - dv_O(C,B)|) \le dist(t_q,t) \le (dist(t_q,C_I) + dv_I(C,B)). \quad (2)$$

Proof. Because $t \subseteq C_O$, $|t| = |C_O| - diff(C_O,t)$ (2.1)
Let $t_q = t_{q1} \cup t_{q2}$, where $t_{q1} \cap t_{q2} = \emptyset$, $t_{q1} \cap C_O = \emptyset$, and $t_{q2} \subseteq C_O$.
$|t_{q2}| = |C_O| - diff(C_O,t_q)$ and $diff(t_q,C_O) = |t_q| - |t_q \cap C_O| = |t_{q1}|$. (2.2) and (2.3)
$dist(t_q,t) = diff(t_q,t) + diff(t,t_q) = (|t_q| - |t_q \cap t|) + (|t| - |t_q \cap t|)$.
By the assumption, $(|t_q| - |t_q \cap t|) + (|t| - |t_q \cap t|) = (|t_q| - |t_{q2} \cap t|) + (|t| - |t_{q2} \cap t|)$
$= ((|t_{q1}| + |t_{q2}|) - |t_{q2} \cap t|) + (|t| - |t_{q2} \cap t|)$
$= |t_{q1}| + |t| + |t_{q2}| - 2|t_{q2} \cap t|$.
Because $(|t| + |t_{q2}| - 2|t_{q2} \cap t|) \ge ||t| - |t_{q2}||$
$\Rightarrow (|t_{q1}| + |t| + |t_{q2}| - 2|t_{q2} \cap t|) \ge (|t_{q1}| + ||t| - |t_{q2}||)$.

By (2.1), (2.2), and (2.3), $(|t_{q1}| + ||t| - |t_{q2}||) = (diff(t_q,C_O) + |diff(C_O,t_q) - diff(C_O,t)|)$.
$\Rightarrow dist(t_q,t) \geq (diff(t_q,C_O) + |diff(C_O,t_q) - diff(C_O,t)|)$. (2.4)
Redefine that $t_q = t_{q3} \cup t_{q4}$, where $t_{q3} \cap t_{q4} = \emptyset$, $t_{q3} \cap C_I = \emptyset$.
$\Rightarrow diff(t_q,C_I) = |t_{q3}|$ and $diff(C_I,t_q) = |C_I| - |C_I \cap t_q| = |C_I| - |t_{q4}|$. (2.5) and (2.6)
$dist(t_q,t) = (|t_q| - |t_q \cap t|) + (|t| - |t_q \cap t|)$.
Because $C_I \subseteq t$, $t_{q4} \subseteq C_I \subseteq t$, and $t_{q3} \cap t_{q4} = \emptyset$,
$(|t_q| - |t_q \cap t|) + (|t| - |t_q \cap t|) = (|t_q| - |(t_{q3} \cap t) \cup t_{q4}|) + (|t| - |(t_{q3} \cap t) \cup t_{q4}|)$
$= ((|t_{q3}| + |t_{q4}|) - |t_{q3} \cap t| - |t_{q4}|) + (|t| - |t_{q3} \cap t| - |t_{q4}|)$
$= (|t_{q3}| - |t_{q3} \cap t|) + (|t| - |t_{q3} \cap t|) - |t_{q4}|$
$\Rightarrow dist(t_q,t) = |t_{q3}| + |t| - 2|t_{q3} \cap t| - |t_{q4}|$.
Because $(|t_{q3}| + |t| - 2|t_{q3} \cap t|) \leq (|t_{q3}| + |t|)$
$\Rightarrow (|t_{q3}| + |t| - 2|t_{q3} \cap t| - |t_{q4}|) \leq (|t_{q3}| + |t| - |t_{q4}|)$.
By (2.5) and (2.6), $|t_{q3}|+ |t| - |t_{q4}| = diff(t_q,C_I) + (diff(t,C_I) + |C_I|) - |t_{q4}|$
$= diff(t_q,C_I) + diff(t,C_I) + (|C_I| - |t_{q4}|)$
$= diff(t_q,C_I) + diff(t,C_I) + diff(C_I,t_q)$
$\Rightarrow dist(t_q,t) \leq (diff(t_q,C_I) + diff(t,C_I) + diff(C_I,t_q))$. (2.7)
By (2.4) and (2.7),
$(diff(t_q,C_O) + |diff(C_O,t_q) - dv_O(C,B)|) \leq dist(t_q,t) \leq (dist(t_q,C_I) + dv_I(C,B))$. □

Similarly, we denote $diff(t_q,C_O) + |diff(C_O,t_q) - dv_O(C,B)|$ in formula (2) as *2nd-LB(t_q,C,B)* and $dist(t_q,C_I) + dv_I(C,B)$ as *2nd-UB(t_q,C,B)*. Moreover, we call 2nd-LB(t_q,C,B) and 2nd-UB(t_q,C,B) the *second level distance lower bound* and the *second level distance upper bound* for t_q to each transaction in B of C, respectively. Similar to the first level bounding mechanism, the relationship between 2nd-LB(t_q,C,B), 2nd-UB(t_q,C,B) and the distance threshold δ is considered when conducting a similarity search on a query t_q and each transaction t of batch B in cluster C. There are also three cases which are similar to the ones introduced previously. With respect to the first level bounding mechanism, the first two cases based on the second level distance bounds are used to prune the transactions in a batch and recognize them as the answers. We call these two cases and the corresponding treatments the *second level bounding mechanism*. When both the cases are not held, the distance between each transaction in the corresponding batch and the query will be computed. Due to space limit, we do not show the detailed description to these cases and the corresponding treatments here. These cases are similar to the ones in the first level bounding mechanism.

Given a query t_q and the user specified distance threshold δ, the algorithm *SearchBound* (Similarity *Search* on Two-level *Bound*ing Mechanism) is proposed to find the similar transactions to the query from the index structure. SearchBound works as follows. Initially, for each cluster C, the first level bounding mechanism with respect to t_q and the transactions in C is applied to prune the dissimilar transactions and find the answers without computing their distances to t_q. Once the first level bounding mechanism fails, the second level bounding mechanism will be triggered for each batch in C. Note that the information needed to calculate the second level distance bounds for t_q to the transactions in each batch, i.e., $diff(C_O,t_q)$, $diff(C_I,t_q)$, $diff(t_q,C_O)$, and $diff(t_q,C_I)$, have been computed in the previous steps. Therefore, the corresponding second level distance bounds can be efficiently computed. Finally, the distance for the query to a transaction t in C will be computed only when both bounding mechanisms have failed. After all the clusters have been processed, the similar transactions to the query will be collected and the algorithm will be terminated.

```
Algorithm SearchBound
Inputs: The index structure R, the query t_q, and the
distance threshold δ
Outputs: The set of transactions Σ whose distances to t_q
are smaller than or equal to δ
    Σ = ∅;
    For each cluster C in R
      If (1st-LB(t_q,C) > δ)  continue;
        Else if (1st-UB(t_q,C) ≤ δ)  Σ = Σ ∪ {t | t∈C};
        Else
          For each batch B in cluster C
            If (2nd-LB(t_q,C,B) > δ)  continue;
            Else if (2st-UB(t_q,C,B) ≤ δ)
                        Σ = Σ ∪ {t | t∈B};
            Else for each t ∈ B
              If dist(t_q,t) ≤ δ  Σ = Σ ∪ t;
     Return Σ;
```

Example 2. Consider the cluster C shown in Figure 1. Given the query t_q and the distance threshold $\delta = 2$, we illustrate the corresponding treatments on C according to different t_q.

Assume t_q = (abc), the corresponding 1st-LB(t_q,C) and 1st-UB(t_q,C) are 0 and 2, respectively. Since 1st-UB(t_q,C) $\leq \delta$, the distances of all the transactions in C to (abc) will be smaller than or equal to δ. Therefore, the three transactions in C will be considered similar to (abc) and included in the answer set.

Assume t_q = (bd), we observe that 1st-LB(t_q,C) $= 1 \leq \delta \leq 3 =$ 1st-UB(t_q,C) and the transactions in C can not be pruned. i.e., the first level bounding mechanism corresponding to t_q has failed in this case. Therefore, the second level bounding mechanism corresponding to t_q will be performed. For the first batch B_1, 2nd-LB(t_q,C,B_1) is 3, the transaction in this batch, i.e., (abc), can be pruned. For the second batch B_2, 2nd-UB(t_q,C,B_2) is 2. Therefore, all the transactions in B_2 will be directly included in the answer set.

Assume t_q = (de), the corresponding 1st-LB(t_q,C) and 1st-UB(t_q,C) are 3 and 5, respectively. Since 1st-LB(t_q,C) $> \delta$, all the transactions in C can not be considered similar to the transaction (de), therefore they are all pruned. □

3 Index Maintenance

In this section, we describe how to update the index when a transaction is inserted. There are two stages for the index updates. At first, we need to determine which cluster is the best choice for the new transaction. If we cannot find one, a new cluster will be created for the transaction. After that, the two borders and the difference-value pairs of the cluster corresponding to this transaction will be updated (Clearly, if a new cluster is created for the transaction, the two borders corresponding to the cluster will be the transaction. Moreover, there is only one batch is in the cluster which contains the transaction and the difference-value pair of the batch will be (0,0)). Next, we will first introduce the clustering algorithm. After that, we will describe how to update the corresponding cluster.

As mentioned in Property 1, smaller difference between the outer border and inner border of a cluster indicates that the transactions in the cluster are more similar to each other. A *maximum difference threshold maxd* is given in our approach to restrict the boundaries of a cluster such that the similarity of any two transactions in the cluster can be bound in maxd. Given a transaction t, the clustering algorithm works as follows.

Assume that after inserting t to the cluster C, the outer border and inner border of C will be updated as C_O' and C_I', respectively. Initially, for each cluster C, the value of diff(C_O',C_I') is first computed. If there exists no cluster such that the value of diff(C_O',C_I') is less than or equal to maxd, a new cluster will be created and t will be assigned to this cluster. If there exist more than one cluster such that the corresponding values of diff(C_O',C_I')'s are less than or equal to *maxd*, a further selection on these clusters, say *candidate clusters*, should be applied. Let Ω denote the set of candidate clusters. For each cluster C ∈ Ω, we define *the variance of C to t* as ($|C_O'| - |C_O|$) + ($|C_I| - |C_I'|$). Generally, if the distance between t and each transaction in C is small, the variance of C to t tends to be small. Therefore, the transactions in C can still be well represented by the updated C after inserting t. Therefore, the cluster with the smallest variance to t in Ω will be selected to insert t.

After the transaction clustering, the cluster C where the new transaction t was inserted to should be updated. The index update has two steps. First, C_O and C_I are replaced by $C_O \cup t$ and $C_I \cap t$, respectively. Second, the difference-value pairs in the cluster are updated. Since the differences of the transactions with the same number of items to C_O and C_I remain the same even when C_O and C_I are changed, these transactions will still be grouped in the same batch after updating C. Therefore, it is not necessary to regroup the transactions while the two borders of C change. Once the two borders are changed, only the difference-value pairs of the batches should be updated. Lemma 3 shows that the difference-value pair of a batch in C can be recomputed by referring to its original value and the two updated borders.

Lemma 3. Let C' be the cluster C after it is updated and C_O' and C_I' respectively be the outer and inner borders corresponding to C'. If the difference-value pair of batch B with respect to C is (x,y), the difference-value pair of B corresponding to C' will be (x',y'), where $x' = x + |C_O'| - |C_O|$ and $y' = y + |C_I| - |C_I'|$.

Proof. Let the number of items in each transaction in B be n. By definition, $x = |C_O| - n$ and $x' = |C_O'| - n \Rightarrow x' = |C_O'| - (|C_O| - x) \Rightarrow x + |C_O'| - |C_O|$. Moreover, $y = n - |C_I|$ and $y' = n - |C_I'| \Rightarrow y' = y + |C_I| - |C_I'|$. □

It will take a constant time to update the difference-value pair of a batch in a cluster. Moreover, the number of batches in a cluster is bounded by maxd (users can easily observe that the maximum number of batches in cluster C is diff(C_O,C_I) + 1). As a result, the cluster can be updated efficiently.

Example 3. Consider the index shown in Figure 1. For ease of presentation, we assume there is only one cluster, i.e., only the cluster C in the index. Let maxd be 3 and the transactions (de) and (abcde) be subsequently inserted.

At first, the outer and inner borders corresponding to C after inserting transaction (de) are (abcde) and (d), respectively. Since the value of diff((abcde), (d)) is 4, which is larger than maxd, a new cluster named D will be created for transaction (de) and the outer and inner borders corresponding to D are (de) itself. Moreover, only one batch is created for D ((de) is in this batch) and the corresponding difference-value pair is (0,0). Subsequently, the two borders corresponding to C and D after inserting (abcde) will be (abcde) and (d), and (abcde) and (de), respectively. Because only D satisfies maxd, (abcde) is therefore inserted to D. Finally, the corresponding two borders of D are updated to (abcde) and (de). According to Lemma 3, the difference-value pair of the batch in D will be updated as (3,0). Moreover, an additional batch associated with the difference-value pair (0,3) is created for the transaction (abcde). Figure 2 shows the updated index structure. □

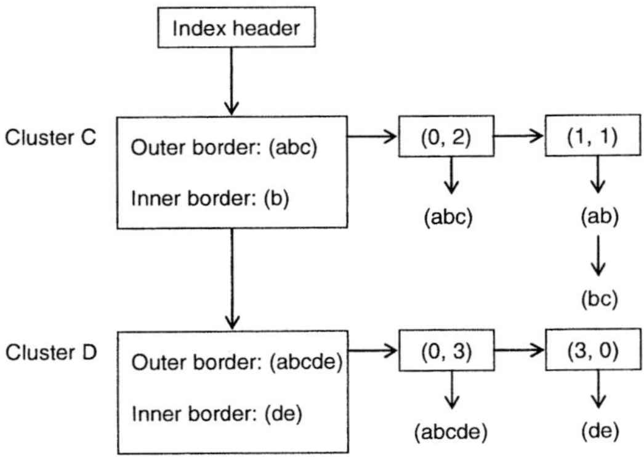

Fig. 2. The updated index

4 Experimental Results

In this section, we compare the proposed approach with the SG-Tree approach 4, which has a better performance than the other algorithm [6] on dynamic databases, on similarity search time, pruning efficiency and index update time. All the experiments are performed on a Pentium IV 2.6G PC with 1.5G RAM and under the Microsoft Windows XP environment. The two approaches are implemented by using Borland C++ 6.0. We implement the *ga_split* which is one of the three split methods proposed in the SG-Tree approach. ga-split reflects the shortest similarity search time among the three split methods. The database generating procedure introduced in 4 is used to generate the synthetic databases. Three parameters T, I and D, used to generate the synthetic databases, are the average number of items in a transaction, the average length of maximal potential frequent itemsets, and the number of transactions in the database, respectively. The number of distinct items is fixed to 1000, and the remaining not mentioned parameters are set as the same values described in 4.

For the SG-Tree approach, the node size is set to 4000, which is the same as that in 4. For our approach, we run several data sets to determine the best maxd. Most of the results show that when maxd is 100 the search time will be the shortest. Therefore, we set maxd as 100 through all the experiments.

At first, we compare the similarity search cost and pruning efficiency of SG-Tree with our approach when conducting a range search. The relative performance of the methods for various parameter settings are shown in Figure 3 through 8. For each experiment, the results were averaged over 100 queries which are randomly selected from the corresponding test datasets. Moreover, the distance threshold used in the experiments is set to either 2 or 10 which respectively corresponds to the small and large distance required by the users. Each figure shows the pruning efficiency (bars) and similarity search cost (lines) of the compared methods. The pruning efficiency is defined as the transactions accessed divided by the transactions in the datasets.

In general, when the given distance threshold is small, most of the transactions in the indices are considered dissimilar to the query. The SG-Tree and our approaches can prune the dissimilar transactions to the query efficiently by the computed distance lower bounds. On the contrary, when the distance threshold is large, a larger number of transactions in the datasets will be considered as the answers to the query. That is, many transaction groups (In our approach, the term *group* indicates the transactions in a cluster or a batch of the cluster. In the SG-Tree approach, it means the transactions represented by a signature) in both indices will be considered similar to the query. For our approach, the distance upper bound of a group can be efficiently computed such that the similar transactions in the group can be collected without computing their distances to the query. However, the SG-Tree approach cannot compute the corresponding distance upper bound of a group. A transaction in the SG-Tree will be recognized as the answer until its distance to the query is computed. Therefore, in average, our approach has a more efficient pruning mechanism than the SG-Tree approach.

Regarding the computational cost, as described in Section 1, most of the bits of the signatures in a node near to the root of the SG-Tree tend to be 1. Therefore, it is hard to distinguish whether the query is similar to the transactions indexed by the descendants of the nodes. As a result, the SG-Tree approach spends time to retrieve the nodes in the higher level of the index but fewer transactions are pruned. This is the reason, where in some cases on the below figures, the SG-Tree approach has a more efficient pruning efficiency but a worse search time than our approach.

Figures 3 through 6 show the performance of the indexes when considering the variation in the size of transactions (T) and in the size of itemsets (I), respectively. Generally, our approach has both a more efficient pruning mechanism and a lower similarity search cost than the SG-Tree approach. As the difference between the values of T and I increases, the dissimilarity of the transactions in the corresponding datasets also increases (the reason comes from the dataset generation procedure. After filling a maximal potential frequent itemset to a transaction, if the transaction has additional space for the other items, a set of items will be randomly selected by the procedure to fill up the transaction. Thus, if the difference between the values of T and I is large, the number of different items in any two transactions will tend to be

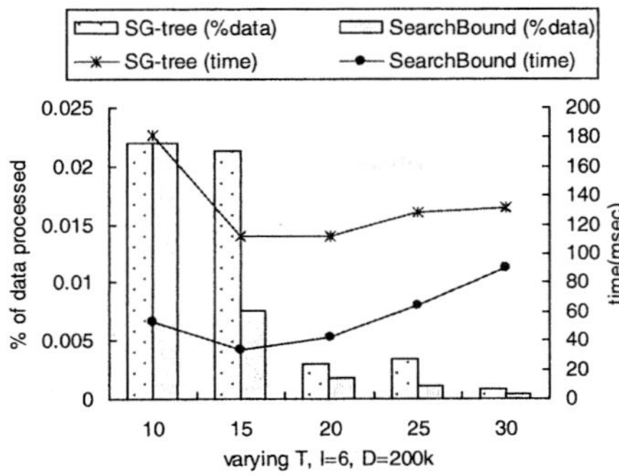

Fig. 3. Performance, varying T and distance threshold = 2

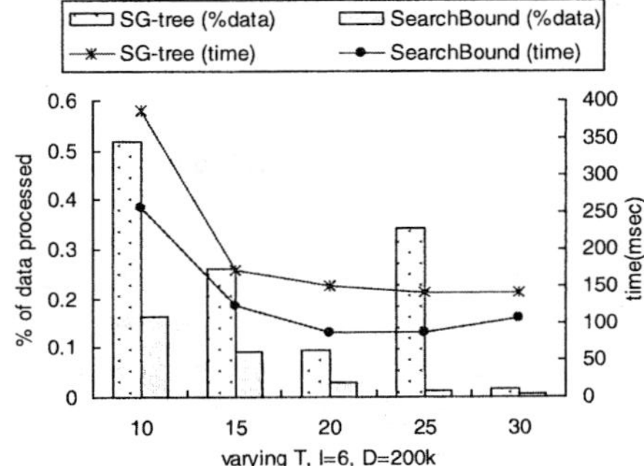

Fig. 4. Performance, varying T and distance threshold = 10

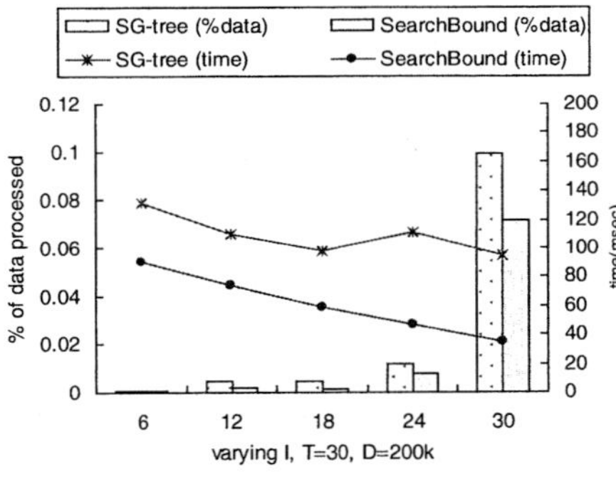

Fig. 5. Performance, varying I and distance threshold = 2

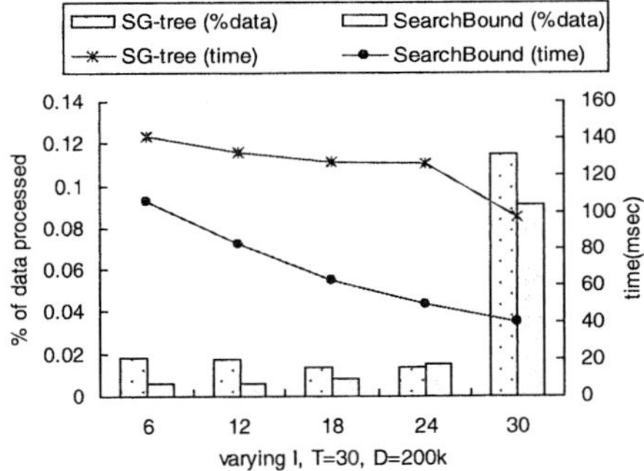

Fig. 6. Performance, varying I and distance threshold = 10

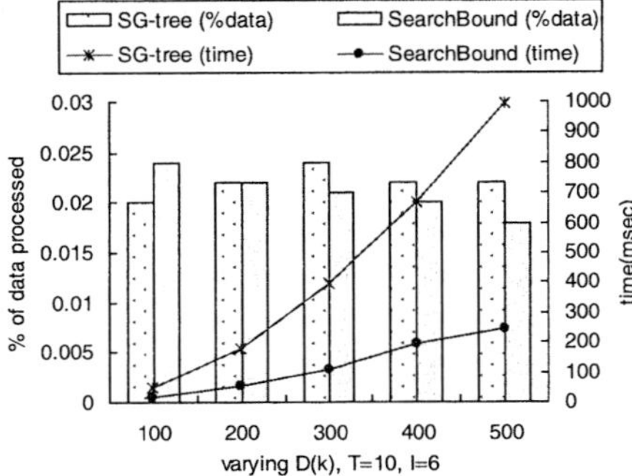

Fig. 7. Performance, varying D and distance threshold = 2

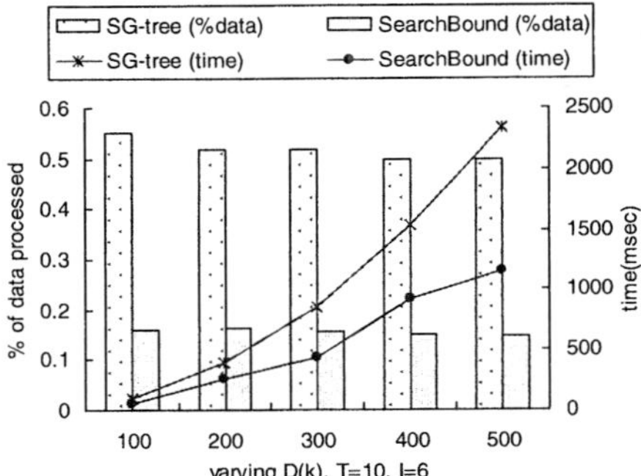

Fig. 8. Performance, varying D and distance threshold = 10

large). Therefore, a larger number of clusters will be created by our approach in order to separate dissimilar transactions. For the SG-Tree, the signature can loosely represent the corresponding transactions. As a result, both approaches will spend more time to search the corresponding indices. However, the query transactions, which are selected from the corresponding datasets, are also very different from the transactions in the datasets. Hence, more transactions can be pruned while searching the indices. In this aspect, the search time can be fast. These two conditions contradict to each other and as a result, the pruning efficiency or the similarity search cost of the two approaches are not proportional to the grow of T or I.

In Figure 7 and Figure 8, we test the robustness of the two methods to the database size. As in Figure 7 (corresponding to small distance threshold), although the pruning efficiency of SG-Tree approach is slightly worse than ours, it needs more time to search the SG-Tree. The reason is that the distance lower bounds computed corresponding to the signatures in the nodes near the root are hard to prune the transactions represented by the signatures. In Figure 8, our approach computes the distance upper bound in each index level to find the similar transactions to the query early. Therefore, our approach outperforms the SG-Tree approach in both pruning efficiency and similarity search time.

We also compare the performance of both approaches by varying the distance threshold. As shown in Figure 9, when increasing the distance threshold, the pruning efficiency of SG-Tree approach becomes worse and its processing time gets longer. In our approach, the pruning efficiency is bound in 0.27 for any distance threshold and the search cost of our approach is greatly less than that of the SG-Tree approach. Let the answers found by the distance upper bound testing in our approach be ans_l. Figure 10 shows the variance of the percentage of ans_l to the answer set corresponding to Figure 9. In Figure 10, as the distance threshold increases, the percentage of ans_l to the answer set also grows. This indicates that more answers are found by the distance upper bound testing in our approach when the given distance threshold increases. Therefore, the efficiency of the pruning mechanism of our approach can be kept as good as when given smaller distance thresholds. As a result, our approach outperforms the SG-Tree approach for any given distance threshold.

Finally, we compare the index updates of the two approaches on a synthetic dynamic environment. We separate the datasets into several blocks with 100k transactions

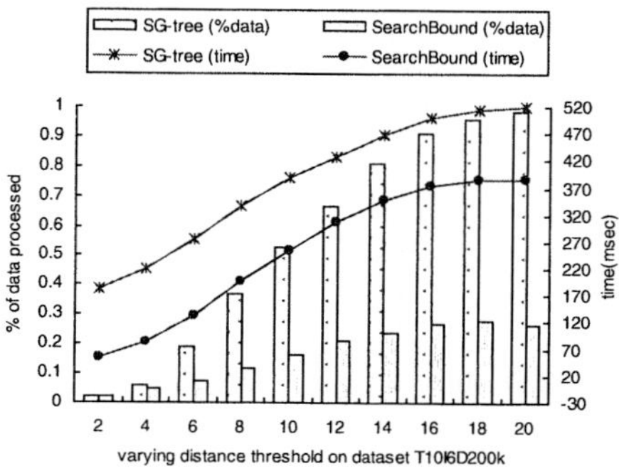

Fig. 9. Performance, varying distance threshold on T10I6D200k

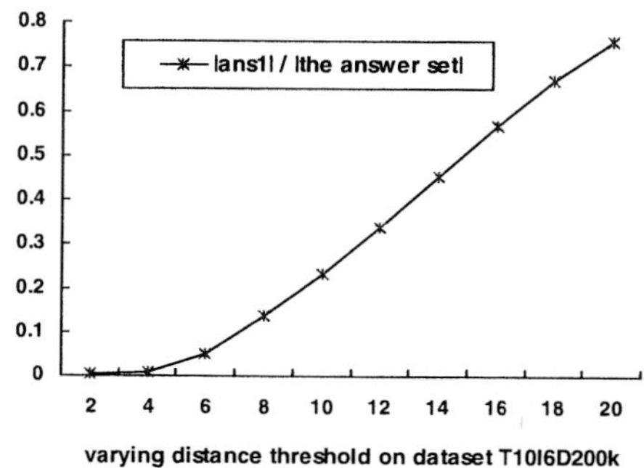

Fig. 10. The percentage of ans_l to the answer set corresponding to Fig. 9

each. Subsequently, each block is continuously inserted to the two indices. The individual block insertion time is recorded for each the index. As described in Section 1, the SG-Tree approach requires considerable time for the node splitting process. For our approach, it takes about 5 msec to update the index no matter how many blocks have been inserted. Therefore, our approach is more robust than the SG-Tree approach in an environment where the frequency of index updates is high. Due to the limit of space, we do not show the related experiments.

5 Conclusion and Future Works

In this paper, a framework for efficient similar transaction search on dynamic databases is presented. The inner border, outer border, and the difference-value pair for a cluster and the batches in the cluster are introduced to represent similar transactions in the proposed index structure. Based on the proposed index structure, the two-level bounding mechanism is developed for a query transaction to prune dissimilar transactions and find the similar transactions without computing their distances to the query. Moreover, our framework processes the index update very fast because only the cluster to which the transaction is inserted needs to be modified. Therefore, our approach is more robust than previous approaches on dynamic databases. For the performance evaluation, we compare the proposed approach with SG-Tree approach on the similarity search time, pruning efficiency and index update time. The results show that the proposed approach is superior to the SG-Tree approach in all these aspects.

Two directions are considered for future works. First, we wish to improve the proposed index structure by developing a hierarchical representation for the transactions. Consulted from the drawback of SG-Tree, the distance between the outer border and inner border of a cluster in the highest level of the hierarchical index structure should be limited. Second, we will extend the proposed framework to work on a transaction data stream.

Acknowledgements

This work was partially supported by the NSC Program for Promoting Academic Excellence of Universities (Phase II) under the grant number NSC 94-2752-E-007-004-PAE, and the NSC under the contract number 94-2213-E-004-010-.

References

1. Aggarwal, C. C., J. L. Wolf, and P. S. Yu. A New Method for Similarity Indexing of Market Basket Data. Proceedings of ACM International Conference on Management of Data (SIGMOD), 1999, 407-418.
2. Dempster, A. P., N. M. Laird, and D. B. Rubin. Maximum Likelihood from Incomplete Data via EM Algorithm. Journal of the Royal Statistical Society, B (39), 1977, 1-38.

3. Gionis, A., D. Gunopulos, and N. Koudas. Efficient and Tunable Similar Set Retrieval. Proceedings of ACM International Conference on Management of Data (SIGMOD), 2001, 247-258.
4. Jing, Q. and R. Yang. Localized Signature Table: Fast Similarity Search on Transaction Data. Proceedings of ACM International Conference on Information and Knowledge Management (CIKM), 2004, 314-323.
5. Mamoulis, N., W. D. Cheung, and W. Lian. Similarity Search in Sets and Categorical Data Using the Signature Tree. Proceedings of IEEE International Conference on Data Engineering (ICDE), 2003, 73-83.
6. Nanopoulos, A. and Y. Manolopoulos. Efficient Similarity Search for Market Basket Data. The VLDB Journal, 11, 2, 2002, 138-152.
7. Ordonez, C., E. Omiecinski, and N. Ezquerra. A Fast Algorithm to Cluster High Dimensional Basket Data. Proceedings of IEEE International Conference on Data Mining (ICDM), 2001, 633-636.
8. Roussopoulos, N., S. Kelley, and F. Vincent. Nearest Neighbor Queries. Proceedings of ACM International Conference on Management of Data (SIGMOD), 1995, 71-79.
9. Wojna, A. Center-Based Indexing for Nearest Neighbors Search. Proceedings of IEEE International Conference on Data Mining (ICDM), 2003, 681-684.
10. Yang, Y., X. Guan, and J. You. CLOPE: A Fast and Efficient Clustering Algorithm for Transactional Data. Proceedings of ACM International Conference on Knowledge Discovery and Data Mining (SIGKDD), 2002, 682-687.
11. Yang, Y. and B. Padmanabhan. Segmenting Customer Transaction Using a Pattern-Based Clustering Approach. Proceedings of IEEE International Conference on Data Mining (ICDM), 2003, 441-448.
12. Weber R., H. J. Schek, and S. Blott. A Quantitative Analysis and Performance Study for Similarity Search Methods in High-Dimensional Spaces, Proceedings of International Conference on Very Large Data Bases (VLDB), 1998, 194-20

RAF: An Activation Framework for Refining Similarity Queries Using Learning Techniques

Yiming Ma, Sharad Mehrotra, Dawit Yimam Seid, and Qi Zhong

Department of Computer Science, University of California, Irvine, USA
{maym, sharad, dseid, qzhong}@ics.uci.edu

Abstract. In numerous applications that deal with similarity search, a user may not have an exact specification of his information need and/or may not be able to formulate a query that exactly captures his notion of similarity. A promising approach to mitigate this problem is to enable the user to submit a rough approximation of the desired query and use relevance feedback on retrieved objects to refine the query. In this paper, we explore such a refinement strategy for a general class of structured similarity queries. Our approach casts the refinement problem as that of learning concepts using the tuples on which the user provides feedback as a labeled training set. Under this setup, similarity query refinement consists of two learning tasks: learning the structure of the query and learning the relative importance of query components. The paper develops machine learning approaches suitable for the two learning tasks. The primary contribution of the paper is the Refinement Activation Framework (RAF) that decides when each learner is invoked. Experimental analysis over many real life datasets shows that our strategy significantly outperforms existing approaches in terms of retrieval quality.

1 Introduction

With the proliferation of the web and emergence of applications requiring flexible search over diverse data types, effective support for personalized similarity search in database systems has emerged as an important research challenge. Similarity based retrieval systems are also increasingly used for exploratory data analysis and retrieval where a user may not initially have a clear mental model of his exact information need [1]. A promising approach to overcome the "initial query" and "subjectivity" problems is that of automatic query refinement via user feedback. In such an approach, a user starts with an approximate initial query and communicates his preferences to the system by providing feedback (judgments on the relevance or quality of answers). The system then modifies the query internally (e.g., changes the levels of importance of the different search criteria, and adds/removes search criteria) to better focus on the distinguishing features of tuples deemed relevant. The modified query is re-evaluated and the cycle of refinement continues until the user is satisfied with the results.

Query refinement via feedback has been explored extensively in the context of text document retrieval [16, 1]. More recently, its effectiveness in feature-based image and multimedia similarity retrieval [14, 18, 7] as well as similarity search

M.L. Lee, K.L. Tan, and V. Wuwongse (Eds.): DASFAA 2006, LNCS 3882, pp. 587–601, 2006.

over metric spaces [20] has also been established. Authors in [13] considered the problem of refining SQL queries from user interactions in an object relational database. This paper explored a limited set of SQL queries and illustrated that even simple extensions of refinement approaches studied in the IR literature can significantly enhance users' search experience.

This paper considers the problem of refining a general class of SQL queries. In contrast to the ad-hoc approaches in [13], we postulate the SQL refinement problem as that of concept learning from examples to which many existing machine learning solutions can be applied. A direct (naive) strategy to modify the query is to view the records on which the user provides feedback as a labeled training set and use a classifier (e.g., decision tree [15]) to learn a new query representation that will replace the original query. However, such a naive strategy does not perform well in practice. Reasons for this include the fact that classifiers do not work well when the training set is very small as is the case in our setting where a user may provide feedback on only a few records. Furthermore, being purely based on training data, the naive strategy ignores the initial query provided by the user. Consequently it may get trapped in a wrong hypothesis simply because the hypothesis fits the few examples. In addition, it is very difficult to incorporate user defined types and similarity functions into existing classifiers. Consistency is also an important issue in the refinement task. Many existing classifiers are sensitive to the inputs causing the models built at different refinement iterations to excessively differ from each other.

We view query refinement from feedback as consisting of two interrelated learning tasks – learning the query structure, and learning the query weights that capture the relative importance of different query components. These two learning tasks have different motivations and serve different purposes. For instance, structural changes to the query are very useful when the initial user query is incomplete which may happen if either a user is not familiar with the database or finds it too laborious to postulate a proper query. In contrast, weight adjustment serves the purpose of customizing/tuning the ranking of results to reflect the subjective importance of the different query components to the user. Thus, determining when to invoke the structure/weight learners becomes a key issue in refining a query. We develop a formal basis for making such a decision based on which the *Refinement Activation Framework (RAF)* is designed.

The main contributions of this paper are summarized as follows:

1. We provide a powerful framework for refining a general class of SQL similarity queries that uses a multi-modal refinement activation procedure to adjust both query predicate weights and query structure using learning techniques.
2. We provide and experimentally validate a novel query structure refinement technique that is based on a decision tree learner.

The remainder of the paper is organized as follows. Section 2 describes background concepts that form the basis of our work. Section 3 discusses our approach to query refinement. Section 4 presents our experiments. Section 5 discusses related work. We conclude with Section 6.

2 Background

2.1 Similarity Queries

A similarity query consists of three components: a set of similarity predicates structured in DNF form, a set of weights assigned to each similarity predicate and a ranking function. In this section, we describe these components.

The search condition in a similarity query is represented as a Boolean DNF (Disjunctive Normal Form) expression over similarity predicates. Formally a query $Q = C_1 \vee C_2 \vee \ldots \vee C_n$ is a DNF expression where $C_i = C_{i1} \wedge C_{i2} \ldots, C_{in}$ is a conjunction, and each C_{ij} is a similarity predicate. A **similarity predicate** is defined over a domain of a given data type. It is a function with two inputs: (1) an attribute value from a tuple, t, (2) a target value which can be a point or a range. It returns a similarity *score* in the range [0,1]. Notice that restricting ourselves to DNF queries does not limit the generality of our approach since any query condition can be mapped to its DNF representation. As will become evident later, using a DNF representation facilitates structural learning.

A **DNF ranking function** is a domain-specific function used to compute the score of a tuple by aggregating scores from individual similarity predicates according to the DNF structure of a search condition and its corresponding set (template) of **weights** that indicate the importance of each similarity predicate. The *template of weights* matches the structure of the search condition and associates a weight to each predicate in a conjunction and also to each conjunction in the overall disjunction.

A DNF Ranking Function first uses *predicate weights* to assign aggregate scores for each conjunction, and it then uses *conjunction weights* to assign an overall score for the query(disjunction). We aggregate the similarity scores of predicates in a conjunction with a weighted L_1 metric (weighted summation). Using weighted L_1 metric as a conjunction aggregation function has been widely used in text IR query models where a query is typically expressed as a single conjunction [16, 1]. To compute an overall score of a query (disjunction), we use the MAX function over the weighted conjunction scores. MAX is one of the most popular disjunction aggregation functions [4]. The weight learning algorithm used in this paper is optimized for these settings. However, our overall refinement algorithm is extensible enough to take other alternative ranking functions [19, 12] as long as a weight learning module is properly defined.

All predicate weights in a conjunction add up to 1. All conjunction weights in a disjunction may not add up to 1. A conjunction weight is in the range of [0, 1], and represents the importance of the conjunction to the user. For example, a conjunction's importance can be measured as the percentage of relevant tuples covered by it. The final aggregated scores produced by a ranking function are used for ranking the tuples. A similarity query returns a set of records with $score \geq \alpha$ (also called α *cut* or *threshold*).

Example 1. Table 1 shows an example data table to be used throughout this paper to illustrate our approach. It is a contract job listing table containing four attributes: location, salary, employment duration, and job description. Consider

Table 1. Example data table

ID	Loc	Sal	Dur(yr)	Desc
1	SN	65K	1.5	DB Developer
2	LA	70K	1	DBA
3	SD	60K	1.5	DB Designer
4	SF	70K	1.5	DB Developer
5	...	...	...	...

Table 2. Example feedback table

ID	Loc	Sal	Dur	Desc	Feedback
1	SN	65K	1.5	DB Developer	OK
2	LA	70K	1	DBA	NOK
3	SD	60K	1.5	DB Designer	OK
4	SF	70K	1.5	DB Developer	OK
...	...	...	...	...	...

the following query that asks for jobs located near SN or that pay more than 65K and have a duration close to 2 years (expressed as a DNF search condition):

(LocNear (Loc, "SN") **AND** DurClose(Dur, 2)) **OR** (SalGreater (Sal, 65000) **AND** DurClose(Dur, 2))

This search condition can be directly implemented on top of a RDBMS that supports user-defined functions (UDFs) as follows:

```
WITH Score AS (SELECT ID,
        LocNear (Loc, "SN") AS l_s,
        DurClose(Dur, 2) AS D_s1,
        SalGreater (Sal, 65000) AS S_s FROM Job)
SELECT RankVal(W_1, Score.l_s, w_11, Score.D_s1, w_12,
    W_2, Score.S_s, w_21, Score.D_s1, w_22) AS S,
    Loc, Sal, Dur, Desc
    FROM Job, Score WHERE Job.ID=Score.ID AND S ≥ α
    ORDER BY S DESC
```

A corresponding weight template may be: $(W_1(w_{11}, w_{12}), W_2(w_{21}, w_{22})) = (0.9(0.4, 0.6), 0.8(0.4, 0.6))$. The ranking function $RankVal$ uses this template to aggregate similarity scores as: $MAX[0.9 \times (0.4 \times l_s + 0.6 \times D_{s1}), 0.8 \times (0.4 \times S_s + 0.6 \times D_{s1})]$. The condition includes three similarity predicates: $LocNear$, $SalGreater$ and $DurClose$ with obvious semantics. For example, $SalGreater$ may return 1 if $salary \geq 65K$. For $30K < salary < 65K$, it returns $\left(1 - \frac{|sal-65K|}{40K}\right)^r$, where r is an integer. It returns 0 if $salary < 30K$. Such functions are application specific and designed by domain experts and implemented by database developers as UDFs. As indicated by the higher weight assigned to the $DurClose$ predicate, the user is more interested in a job that has duration close to 2 years than one that is close to SN or pays more than 65K. Although tuples with ID 1 and 4 receive the same conjunction scores from the first and second conjunction, the first tuple is ranked higher since the weight for the first conjunction is higher. Therefore, the tuple with ID 1 should be returned as the top result.

2.2 Similarity Query Refinement

Given a search condition q, a set r of top-k records returned by q, and relevance feedback f on these records (i.e., a triple $\langle q, r, f \rangle$), the similarity query refinement problem is to modify the search condition q in such a way that, when re-executed, it will rank more relevant records at the top. The interactive search process to find satisfactory answers to a particular query is called a *query session.* A query session can include one or more *refinement iterations* where the user provides feedback and the system refines the query based on the feedback and returns another set of ranked results. A query refinement in an iteration may involve adapting the predicates, the DNF condition structure as well as the weights.

Example 2. Before arriving at the condition given in example 1 that returns the best results, suppose the user started the query session with the following query that approximately captures his information need: (($LocNear(loc, \text{"}SN'')$ **AND** $DescClose(Desc, \text{"}DBA'')$), with a corresponding weight template of (1(0.5, 0.5)). At this point the user may, for example, be unfamiliar with the data stored in the database. As a result, he used "*Description* similar to 'DBA' " as one of the search conditions. Then, after seeing a few records returned by the initial query whose description matches "DBA" but whose other attributes do not match his interest, he may use relevance feedback to invoke a refinement iteration to guide the query away from this search condition eventually leading to its removal in the final query shown in example 1.

3 Learning Queries from User Feedback

3.1 Problem Formulation

For each query session we maintain two tables: an *answer table* which contains the ranked answer tuples along with the similarity scores assigned to these tuples, and a *feedback table* that stores the relevance feedback [1] given by the user on tuples in the answer table. Table 2 shows an example of such a table. The problem of query refinement can now be cast as a problem of utilizing *feedback table* to learn a classifier. In principle, any concept learning method can be employed provided that it performs well on a small number of examples. However, to be effective, query refinement requires a careful application of learning methods. In particular, simply replacing the original query with the newly learned query can have undesirable consequences. This leads to the important question of how to modify the original query based on the learned classifier.

In this section, we consider two different types of learning algorithms (classifiers). One focuses on query weight tuning, and another focuses on query structure tuning. An activation algorithm is used to control the overall learning process that consists of these two interrelated learning tasks.

3.2 Refinement Activation Framework (RAF)

Given a query and user feedback on its results, RAF determines which of the two learning task to invoke. Structural changes result in addition (deletion) of a new (old) conjunction to the DNF query or addition (deletion) of a new (old) predicate within a conjunction. In contrast to gradual weight adjustment that results in fine tuning of rank order, structural changes can dramatically change the return set even causing objects deemed irrelevant to the original query to be ranked at the top of the result set. Hence, structural changes to the query must be made conservatively since an incorrect change may lead a refinement along a wrong path. RAF invokes structural modifications only when

[1] For simplicity, we assume binary relevance judgments (i.e. "Relevant" or "Not Relevant") although our approach can also support finer grained distinctions.

ID	ConjID=1:LocNear (Loc,"SN")	ConjID=2:DescClose (Desc,"DBA")	Feedback
1	1	0.8	OK
2	0.8	1	NOK
3	0.7	0.6	OK
4	0.5	0.8	OK

Fig. 1. Example CSS table

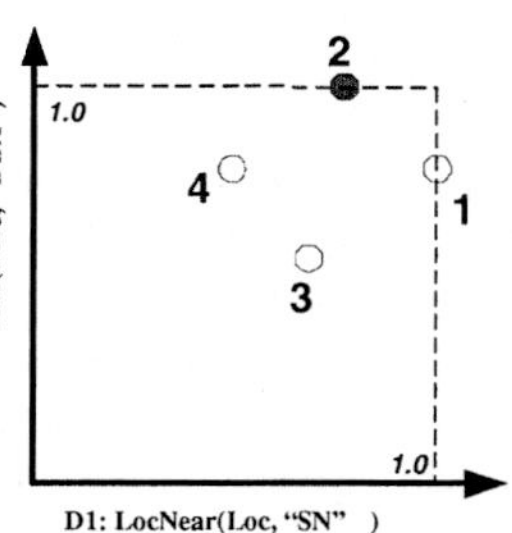

Fig. 2. CSS for Fig 1

feedback provided by the user requires that such modifications be made and the desired effect cannot be achieved by re-weighting query components. In order to identifying situations where structural modifications are needed, below we explore the limitations of weight learning in the context of refinement.

We begin by developing some notation. Consider a single conjunction $C_i = C_{i1} \wedge C_{i2} \ldots, C_{in}$ of a DNF query. Since each predicate (i.e., C_{ij}) in the conjunction returns a similarity value in the range of [0,1], together they form a *Conjunction Similarity Space* (CSS). Each dimension in the CSS represents a predicate and a tuple can be mapped to a point in the CSS. We store these mapped points in a table called *CSS table*. For example, figure 1 shows an example CSS table for the tuples in the feedback table shown in table 2. This space is also depicted in figure 2. Next, we define the notions of *CSS domination* and *CSS conflict* as follows:

Definition 1 (CSS domination). *In a given CSS, a tuple $t1$ dominates $t2$ if $t1$ is as good or better (that is, $t1$ has an equal or higher similarity value) in all dimensions and better in at least one dimension compared to $t2$.*

For example, in the Figure 2, tuple 2 dominates tuples 3 and 4, but does not dominate tuple 1. Similarly, tuple 1 dominates tuples 3 and 4, but not tuple 2.

Definition 2 (CSS conflict). *In a given CSS, a pair of feedback tuples $(t1, t2)$ conflict with each other if $t1$ receives negative feedback, $t2$ receives positive feedback, and either $t1$ dominates $t2$ or $t1$ and $t2$ have equal values in all dimensions.*

The conflicts in the CSS space in Figure 2 are between tuples 2 and 3, as well as tuples 2 and 4, but not between tuples 2 and 1. Presence of conflicts in the return set of a query means that the query is ranking an irrelevant tuple higher than a tuple deemed relevant by the user. Hence, the query does not capture the user's information need and must be modified. Unfortunately, simply modifying weights associated with the predicates can not resolve the conflict as is stated in the following lemma.

Lemma 1. *For a given CSS, if there is a conflicting tuple pair $(t1, t2)$, there is no monotonic aggregation function that can resolve this conflict by assigning a larger score to $t2$.*

Proof. From [5], an aggregation function f is *monotone* if $f(x_1, \ldots, x_m) \leq f(x'_1, \ldots, x'_m)$ whenever $x_i \leq x'_i$ for every i. Recall that we use weighted summation, which is monotonic, to aggregate scores in a CSS. Let $(t1, t2)$ be a conflicting tuple pair where $t1$ receives negative and $t2$ receives positive feedback. Since $t1$ has as good or better value in all dimensions, it is not possible to assign a bigger score to $t2$ since any weight assignment (done on predicates) applies to all tuples. Note that, even without the last condition in definition 2 (i.e., $t1$ and $t2$ have equal values in all dimensions), lemma 1 is still true. By adding this condition, we capture cases that could not be resolved by weight tuning □

We have, thus far, established the limitation of the weight learning approach in the context of refinement. Resolving conflicts requires structural modifications to the query. The activation procedure we develop utilizes the above observation to determine when to invoke such modifications.

Let $Q = C_1 \vee C_2 \vee C_n$ be a DNF query where $C_i = C_{i1} \wedge C_{i2} \ldots, C_{in}$ is a conjunction. To refine Q, first the activation procedure will decide how the feedback on each tuple is used for refinement. Specifically, it decides, for each tuple with a feedback, which conjunction should be refined by it. The activation procedure attaches feedback to different conjunctions by assigning each feedback to the highest scored conjunction[2]. For each conjunction C_i, it then determines if the assigned feedback contains any conflict. If a conflict is identified, structural modification to the query is invoked based on the conflicting set. For example, in Figure 2 where empty circles represent positive feedback, tuple 2 conflicts with tuples 3 and 4. To resolve these conflicts, the activation procedure invokes structural learning using tuples 2, 3, and 4. The structure learning algorithm will attempt to learn a predicate that, when added to the conjunction, will resolve the conflict. In the current example, it may suggest the addition of a predicate $Duration \geq 1.5$ to the conjunction. In general, depending on the mechanism used, the conjunction may be augmented by not only a single predicate but also a logical formula F consisting of multiple predicates connected by logical connectives. In the new formula (i.e., $newConj = C_i \wedge F$), most (or all) of the conflicts associated with the original conjunction can be resolved. We temporarily treat F as a pseudo-predicate so the new formula becomes a conjunction. The weights of predicates in this conjunction are rebalanced using a predicate weight learning method where, a predicate is dropped if its weight falls below a threshold. We designate the assigned weight of F by W_F.

In this paper, we assume a logic formula $F = F_1 \vee F_2 \vee \cdots \vee F_k$ is itself in DNF. The predicates in C_i of $newConj$ can be distributed over the F_p, resulting in a new candidate set of conjunctions $(C_i \wedge F_1) \vee (C_i \wedge F_2) \vee \cdots \vee (C_i \wedge F_k)$. Hence, when resolving conflict tuples in a conjunction C_i, we may potentially learn new conjunctions. During this process, the actual predicate weight of F_p in a conjunction is assigned to be W_F. We also use the original conjunction (C_i) weight to initialize the weights of candidate conjunctions (i.e., $C_i \wedge F_p$).

[2] Since the disjunction aggregation function is MAX, assigning a feedback tuple to the highest scored conjunction is appropriate. Different assignment schemes may be needed for other aggregation functions.

RAF-Algo()

```
1: Input: Query (Q), FeedbackTable (FT)
2: Output: New Query (Q')
3: compute_CSS_tables(Q, FT)
4: New Conjunctions: newConjs = ∅; newConjsCunt = 0
5: for each conjunction C_i in a query Q do
6:    CSST = get_CSS_table(C_i)
7:    Conflicts= computeConflictSet(CSST)
8:    F = ∅
9:    if |Conflicts| ≥ 1 then
10:      F= learnStructure(C_i, Conflicts)
11:   newConj=C_i ∧ F
12:   predicateWeightLearning (newConj, CSST)
13:   drop any predicate C_ij frome newConj, if C_ij.weight < τ_p
14:   if F ≠ ∅ then
15:      for each conjunction F_p in F = F_1 ∨ F_2 ∨ ··· ∨ F_k do
16:         if p == 1 then C_i = C_i ∧ F_1
17:         else newConjs[newConjsCunt + +] = C_i ∧ F_p
18: Q' = Q
19: for each new conjunction C_new_i in newConjs do
20:    Q' = Q' ∨ C_new_i
21: compute_CSS_tables(Q', FT)
22: Q' = assignConjunctionWeight (Q')
23: drop any conjunction C_i frome Q', if C_i.weight < τ_c
```

After all conjunctions are individually modified, their final conjunction weights need to be determined. Again, we use the conjunction's CSS table. Intuitively, non-conflicting positive cases in the CSS boost the importance of the conjunction in the query. Given a set of tuples in the CSS, we can measure how well the conjunction performed in the query after refinement by computing the ratio of non-conflicting positive cases captured by this conjunction and the total number of positive cases. We use this ratio as an overall conjunction weight measure. We specify our overall RAF query refinement algorithm in pseudo-code as follows:

The algorithm takes the previous query and the feedback table as input and generates a refined query. In the above algorithm, two things have been left unspecified (1) the algorithm to resolve the conflict set of a conjunction (line 10), and (2) the algorithm to learn the weight template for a given conjunction (line 12). As RAF is an open framework, different approaches can be used for the two learning tasks. Below, we provide algorithms we developed for this purpose.

3.3 Learning Predicate Weights of a Conjunction

Learning predicate weights corresponds to learning their relative importance in a conjunction. Since each dimension in the CSS corresponds to the similarity value of a predicate in a conjunction, we can map the weight learning problem to a classification problem over the CSS. Since we use the weighted summation model, we seek a hyper-plane in the CSS that separates the set of tuples marked deemed relevant, R, from the set of tuples deemed irrelevant, IR. We adapt the linear optimization process described in [8] for this purpose. The average complexity of this process is $O(n\times \mid p \mid)$, where n is the number of tuples with feedback and $|p|$ is the number of predicates in the conjunction.

Table 3. Conjunction Scores table example

ID	Loc		Sal	Dur	Desc		FB
	"SD"	"SF"			"DB Dsger"	"DB Dvper"	
2	0.8	0.4	70K	1	0.7	0.8	NOK
3	1	0.3	60K	1.5	1	0.7	OK
4	0.3	1	70K	1.5	0.7	1	OK

3.4 Learning New Structure of a Conjunction

The purpose of modifying a conjunction is to resolve conflicts present in the result set. Therefore, given a CSS table, we choose only the tuples that have conflicts, and use them in structural learning. For example, tuples 2, 3 and 4 in Figure 2 will be used in this learning. The original tuples in a `feedback table` form a learning set (*LSet*). Before we can apply our learning algorithm to this set, we need to convert it to a suitable format called a `scores table`. This conversion is needed because performing query refinement directly on the *LSet* is not always possible as database attributes can have complex and non-ordinal (numeric) attributes. The `scores table`, which consists of conflicting tuples, contains only ordinal values.

Data Preparation: Scores Table Generation.– This table is generated by retaining columns for ordinal attributes from the conflicting tuples in the *LSet* and converting complex and non-ordinal attributes into similarity measures. This similarity measure is computed by taking every value of each complex attribute in the *LSet* and calculating its similarity to all the other values of that attribute in the *LSet*. For example, tuples 2, 3 and 4 (i.e., the conflicting set) in Figure 2 form the conjunction scores table shown in Table 3. In this example, columns for ordinal attributes like Salary and Duration are identical to those in the `feedback table`. For the remaining non-ordinal attributes we created a column for each attribute–value pair. Each entry in these columns measures the similarity between the value in the heading and the attribute values from the tuples in the `feedback table`. For instance, the first entry under the column Location="SD" (i.e. 0.8) is the similarity score of the value "SD" and the location value of tuple 2 which is "LA". Since we want to learn predicates that focus on relevant tuples, only attribute values from records that are marked "Relevant" are used to from columns in the scores table. Consequently, no column is created for attribute values like "LA" because the tuple having this value is marked "Not Relevant".

Learning New Structures from a Scores Table.– Given a conjunction scores table, we can use any DNF learner (see section 5 for a review) to extract a set of hypotheses that explains/classifies the scores table. In this paper, we use a modified decision tree learner, namely C4.5 [15]. The original C4.5 employs a greedy divide-and-conquer strategy to build a decision tree. Given a labeled data such as a `scores table`, the algorithm initializes a decision tree with one leaf node that represents the whole data. It tests each attribute, and chooses the best attribute (A) and value (v) pair, which, if used to split the data into two portions – one with values in attribute $A \geq v$, another with values $< v$ – results in maximum entropy gain. It also records this split in the decision tree by splitting the original leaf nodes to two new leaf nodes; the old leaf node becomes the root of the two new leaf nodes. The algorithm recursively tests and splits the leaves until either all points in each partition belongs to one class (e.g., all marked with positive feedback or all marked with negative feedback), or it becomes statistically insignificant to split further. C4.5 then generates DNF rules/conjunctions from the decision tree.

Our main modification to C4.5 is an additional stopping condition. If we allow C4.5 to keep splitting its leaf nodes that represents a portion of data, the leaf nodes will get purer and purer towards a class. We instead stop splitting the node once a leaf node no longer has conflicts. Then, once the decision tree is constructed, a set of rules/conjunctions are derived from it. We, then, filter out the conjunctions that do not have any associated feedback tuples. The remaining conjunctions form the logical formula F used in the activation algorithm. Note that these conjunctions are also similarity based conjunctions since they are learned from the scores table. For example, from the `scores table`, table 3, the classifier generates a predicate $Dur \geq 1.5$, that removes the original conflicts.

To improve efficiency, we push similarity computations into the tree building process. This approach also avoids materialization of the `scores table`. Furthermore, we do not need to construct all `scores table` columns if we have already obtained a reasonable split point. The worst case complexity of this algorithm is $O(\mid R \mid \times d \times n \times (log(n))^2)$, in which $\mid R \mid$ is the number of relevant cases, d is the number of dimensions of the original feedback table, and n is the size of the feedback table. In practice, the number of the distinct relevant values of an attribute (e.g., Loc) is considerably smaller than $\mid R \mid$. Therefore, the complexity is close to standard decision tree complexity, which is $O(d \times n \times (log(n))^2)$.

4 Experiments

In this section, evaluate the effectiveness of RAF. We first present our experimental setup including the datasets we used and our synthetic query generator. We then evaluate RAF against four well-known algorithms.

4.1 Experimental Setup

We ran all our experiments using a P3-800MHZ PC with 256MB RAM. The similarity retrieval component is implemented using UDF features in IBM DB2. The refinement component is implemented as a stored procedure in IBM DB2. We use IBM OSL package [6] as our linear problem solver.

We used 12 datasets from the UCI machine learning repository [10], all of which have class labels. These datasets represent different domains of interests. For discrete attributes, we analyzed each pair of values of an attribute to decide the similarity value between them. For continuous attributes, we used the formula in section 2.1 to compute the similarity value of any two intervals.

To evaluate our query refinement method, we formulate two related queries, a *target* query q_t which simulates a user's real information need, and an *initial* query q_i which simulates his initial knowledge when starting the search. The query q_t can be more *general* or *specific* than q_i in terms of its DNF structure. We built a query generator that generates a set of query pairs $\langle q_1, q_2 \rangle$, where q_1 is more specific than q_2. If we set $q_t = q_1$ and $q_i = q_2$ we evaluate our algorithms on refining a general query to a specific query (i.e. G2S in our experiments). Conversely, if $q_t = q_2$ and $q_i = q_1$, we evaluate our algorithms on refining a specific query to a general query (i.e. S2G in our experiments). We generated 20 target and initial query pairs for each dataset getting a total of 240 pairs. Also, to simulate a realistic query, the size of results from q_t should be small compared to the database size. We only take top 20 records from q_t as its return set. The largest dataset we tried has nearly 32,000 records; this makes the target size less than 0.06% of the database size.

Algorithms Tested. We compare RAF with four existing methods. The first method, which we refer to as OCM (from the authors' last name initials) focuses on learning conjunctions [13]. OCM is similar to our approach in that it also refines the initial query structure using relevance feedback. The second method is FALCON [20], which does not refine the initial query explicitly, but uses the positive feedback to rank the data. The third method, Rocchio's method [16], is a standard vector based IR approach. In our experiment, we use attribute-value pairs as the vectors. Hence, Rocchio's method ignores the query structure and also similarity measures on the attributes. Since our refinement task essentially performs a classification based on the relevance feedback, one can directly apply an existing classification package if the data types can be mapped to the required types. This can be easily done for the 12 datasets we used, but not in general. Hence, the fourth method we compare our approach to is a well-known decision tree classifier C4.5 [15]. C4.5 takes the feedback data as a training set, and generates a classifier. It ignores the initial query structure, and predefined similarity measures on the data attributes. The refinement system uses this classifier to assign confidence levels as scores to the remaining data tuples.

Evaluation Process. The above algorithms are evaluated based on:

1. Efficiency: time taken to refine a query
2. Effectiveness: precision and recall measures
3. Simplicity of a refined query: number of the predicates in the query

To evaluate the effectiveness of a refinement algorithm, we simulate the desired user concept by first executing a target query and placing the top 20 tuples that satisfy the target query into a set R, the *relevant* records. Then, we execute the initial query (i.e., iteration 1). We compute the precision level at every 5% of recall interval (i.e. every relevant point retrieved) until all the relevant tuples are retrieved. To study effectiveness, we form the first learning set L by adding the top retrieved tuples containing exactly two relevant tuples from the initial query result. If a refinement algorithm performs well at a refinement iteration, it should have good precision level in all recall intervals. The refinement algorithm uses

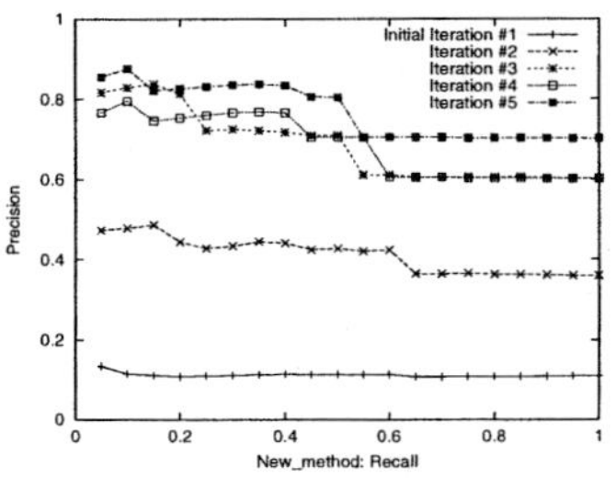

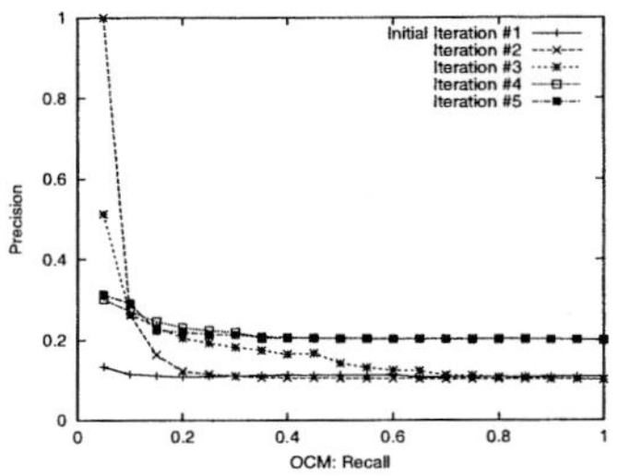

Fig. 3. Precision-Recall: RAF Vs. OCM

set L as the `feedback table` to learn a refined query. In subsequent iterations, the learning set L is updated by adding the top ranked tuples of each iteration that contain two new relevant tuples. Hence, L continues to grow accumulating all the relevance feedback gathered starting from the initial iteration. In our experiments, we execute the refinement algorithm four times (i.e., five iterations) to evaluate its performance in different iterations.

4.2 Results

As shown in table 4, average execution time for a refinement cycle in our algorithm averages around 0.5 seconds and ranges between 0.2 to 0.7 seconds. Falcon and Rocchio algorithm are not included in this table since they do not generate queries explicitly. RAF is consistently more efficient than OCM. This is because OCM always starts structure tuning which is typically more expensive than weight tuning. In RAF, the activation procedure does not choose structure tuning if there are no conflicts. RAF runs slower than C4.5. This is expected since the feature space (i.e., scores table) used in RAF is larger than the original data's feature space. Furthermore, RAF also performs weight tuning.

In Figure 3, we show the refinement effectiveness of RAF and OCM on the dataset *adult*, which is the largest dataset in our experiment. In each of the two graphs, each line represents average precision over 20 similarity queries at every 5% of recall interval. We use the average precision at each 5% recall interval as a measure of retrieval quality. If a method does well in an iteration, this average should be high. For example, average precision of RAF at iteration 1 is 11%, and after one refinement cycle it increases to 40%. OCM still remains at 11%. Hence, RAF outperforms OCM after the first refinement cycle.

Table 4. Average Refinement Time per Query (sec.)

G2S Avg. Refine Time(sec.)			S2G Avg. Refine Time(sec.)		
RAF	*OCM*	*C4.5*	*RAF*	*OCM*	*C4.5*
0.4	0.8	0.2	0.5	0.8	0.3

Table 5. Avg. Number of Predicates in Query

Dataset	G2S				S2G	
	Init	*It2*	*It5*	*Target*	*It2*	*It5*
RAF	4.8	5.1	5.6	6.7	6.9	5.1
OCM	4.8	15.1	15.9	6.7	15.3	9.7
Rocchio	4.8	69.6	76.3	6.7	76.3	97.9
C4.5	4.8	1.1	1.8	6.7	0.8	1.5

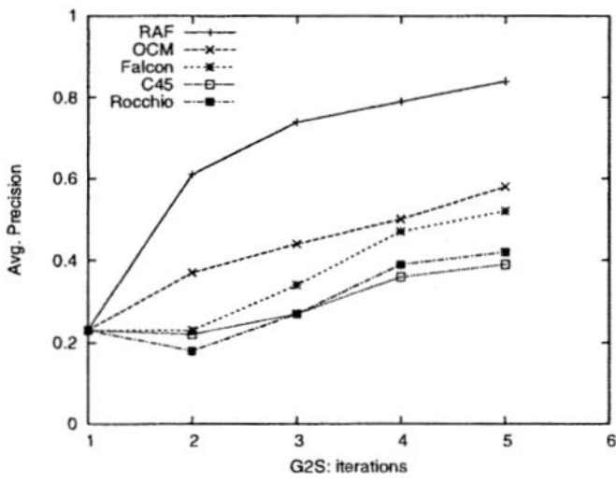

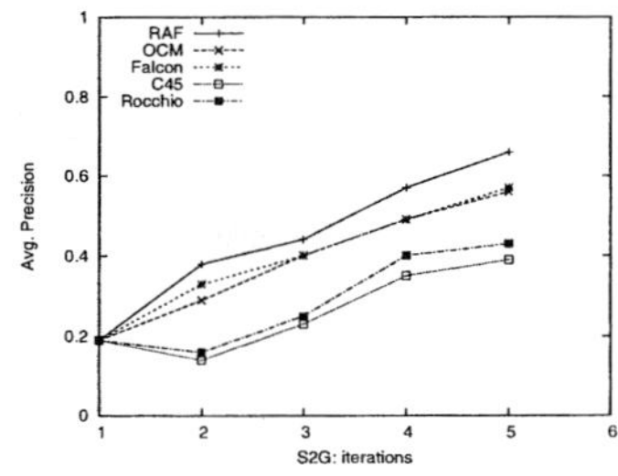

Fig. 4. Precision Average at Each Iteration

To further evaluate the learning behaviors of each algorithm in different iterations, Figure 4 plots the overall average over different iterations. We observe that RAF has very good learning behaviors in both learning scenarios (i.e., G2S and S2G), such that it has much better precision at each iteration. We also notice that without learning, the initial query performs badly in general (i.e., iteration 1). Although OCM attempts to improve the retrieval quality by modifying the initial query concept, it performs worse than RAF. The main reason is that RAF focuses directly on resolving the essential feedback conflicts, but OCM simply tries to fit concepts (i.e., predicates) that match to the feedback. Also, for some cases OCM may wrongly add a set of predicates while simple weight modification can achieve the correct ranking. RAF outperforms OCM on average by 24% in terms of average precision after first refinement cycle for G2S learning. This average is computed over the 240 query pairs. RAF and OCM outperform the other three methods in both $G2S$ and $S2G$ learning scenarios. This clearly shows the merit of considering the initial query structure during the refinement process. C4.5 and Rocchio perform the worst since they ignore the initial query structure and the predefined attribute level similarity functions during refinement cycles.

In addition to precision and recall measures, another interesting measure of a refinement algorithm is the simplicity/complexity of its refined queries. Table 5 shows the average number of predicates over the 240 queries at different iterations. The initial queries for G2S case contain 4.8 predicates on average, and target queries have 6.7. For the S2G case, the number is reversed. As we observed, the number of average predicates in RAF at different iterations lies in between the average number of predicates in initial and target queries. This increases query understandability since the refined query is not far away from the target query. OCM has about twice as many predicates on average as the target. The main reason of this is that OCM cannot represent disjunctive concepts explicitly; it uses additional predicates to simulate disjuncts. We also report the average number of vectors used by the Rocchio's method at different iterations, and the number of vectors used could be 10 times bigger than the number of target predicates. C4.5 is at another extreme, which, due to the small number of positive feedback available at each iteration, generates very small number of rules with only one or two conditions. Falcon is not included because it does not produce queries.

5 Related Work

The work most related to this paper is [13], which proposed a query refinement framework on top of ORDBMSs for learning SQL queries from user interactions. There are two major limitations in [13]. Firstly, it did not consider weight and structure learning separately, and at each iteration both weight and structure were modified while modification of only one of the two would have sufficed. This resulted in, at times, an over aggressive policy that adds/drops wrong predicates from the query. Secondly, [13] considered only learning a limited set of conjunctive queries; it did not support learning disjuncts. If the optimal query the user had in mind and the feedback was consistent with a disjunctive query (e.g., *Salary* $>$ *65K OR Duration* $>$ *2 years*), the approach would attempt to simulate a disjunction via a conjunction. That is, it would attempt to learn the query of *Salary* $>$ *65K AND Duration* $>$ *2 years*. This results in a suboptimal query with poor retrieval performance and poor interpretability.

Query refinement via feedback has been explored extensively in the context of text document retrieval in the information retrieval literature [16, 1]. Generally, a vector space model is assumed (i.e., Rocchios method [16]). Refinement tasks focus on how to weight the elements in the vector space. There is no explicit query formulation and attribute similarity measures. IR models have also been generalized to multimedia domain. Query refinement techniques have also been exploited in the multimedia domains, e.g., MARS [17, 9], Mindreader [7], FALCON [20]. FALCON generalizes the refinement model to any suitably defined metric distance function. As long as the distance between two tuples can be properly defined, FALCON can be applied. It uses the relevant examples as the query, and rank the database based on the aggregate distance measure. However, since FALCON does not consider the original query formulation, it performs poorly when the relevant set is very small.

Although not from the point of view of database queries, there is a considerable body of work on learning DNF and CNF formulas from examples. DNF learners in the literature can be grouped into two as divide-and-conquer based (e.g. decision tree learners [15]) and separate-and-conquer based or covering algorithms. Among the large number of algorithms in the latter category, the AQ family of algorithms [2], CN2 [3] and PFOIL [11] are popular. In these approaches, predicates have no similarity semantics (i.e., are crisp conditions). It is also unclear how to incorporate initial queries and similarity functions into these approaches. Furthermore, these algorithms normally require large amount of input (i.e., training and testing ratio) before deriving good hypothesis.

6 Conclusions

In many search environments, a user normally has imprecise specification of what he wants. We provide a system to enable users express imprecise queries, and refine it interactively by supplying relevance feedback. We identified two distinct tasks of similarity query refinement: refining query structure and determining the relative importance of predicates and conjunctions. We proposed a set of novel algorithms to control weight and structure learning. We implemented these algorithms and the extensive experiments we conducted showed that RAF consistently outperforms previously suggested techniques both in terms of retrieval quality and query simplicity.

References

1. Ricardo Baeza-Yates and Ribeiro-Neto. *Modern Information Retrieval.* ACM Press Series/Addison Wesley, New York, May 1999.
2. E. Bloedorn, R. S. Michalski, and J. Wnek. Multistrategy constructive induction: AQ17-MCI. In *Proc. of the 2nd Int. Workshop on Multistrategy Learning*, pages 188–203, 1993.
3. P. Clark and T. Niblett. The CN2 Induction Algorithm. *Machine Learning*, 3(4):261–283, 1989.
4. Ronald Fagin. Combining Fuzzy Information from Multiple Systems. *Proc. of the 15th ACM Symp. on PODS*, 1996.
5. Ronald Fagin, Amnon Lotem, and Moni Naor. Optimal aggregation algorithms for middleware. In *PODS*, 2001.
6. IBM. IBM linear optimization package: http://www-3.ibm.com/software/data/bi/osl/pubs/lpsol/lpuser.htm.
7. Y. Ishikawa, R. Subramanya, and C. Faloutsos. Mindreader: Querying databases through multiple examples. In *VLDB*, 1998.
8. O.L. Mangasarian, R. Setiono, and W.H. Wolberg. Pattern recognition via linear programming: Theory and application to medical diagnosis. In *SIAM*. 1990.
9. S. Mehrotra, Y. Rui, M. Ortega, and T. Huang. Supporting content-based queries over images in mars. *Proc. of IEEE-ICMCS97*, 1997.
10. C. J. Merz and P. Murphy. UCI Repository of Machine Learning Databases. http://www.cs.uci.edu/ mlearn/MLRepository.html, 1996.
11. Raymond J. Mooney. Encouraging Experimental Results on learning CNF. *Machine Learning*, 19(1):79–92, 1995.
12. M. Ortega, Y. Rui, K. Chakrabarti, K. Porkaew, S. Mehrotra, , and T. Huang. Supporting ranked boolean similarity queries in mars. *IEEE Trans. on Data Engineering*, 10(6), December 1998.
13. Michael Ortega-Binderberger, Kaushik Chakrabarti, and Sharad Mehrotra. An Approach to Integrating Query Refinement in SQL. In *Proc. EDBT*, March 2002.
14. Kriengkrai Porkaew, Sharad Mehrotra, Michael Ortega, and Kaushik Chakrabarti. Similarity search using multiple examples in mars. In *Proc. Visual'99*, June 1999.
15. R. Quinlan. *C4.5: Program for Machine Learning.* Morgan Kaufmann, 1992.
16. J. Rocchio. Relevance feedback in information retrieval. In G. Salton, editor, *The SMART Retrieval System: Experiments in Automatic Document Processing*, pages 313–323. Prentice Hall, 1971.
17. Y. Rui, T. Huang, and S. Mehrotra. Content-based image retrieval with relevance feedback in mars. *IEEE Proc. of Int. Conf. on Image Processing*, 1997.
18. Y. Rui, T. Huang, M. Ortega, and S. Mehrotra. Relevance feedback: A power tool for interactive content-based image retrieval. *IEEE Trans. Circuits and Systems for Video Technology*, 1998.
19. G. Salton. The use of extended boolean logic in information retrieval. In *SIGMOD*. 1984.
20. L. Wu, C. Faloutsos, K. Sycara, and T. Payne. FALCON: Feedback adaptive loop for content-based retrieval. *VLDB*, 2000.

Query Optimization for a Graph Database with Visual Queries

Greg Butler, Guang Wang, Yue Wang, and Liqian Zou

Department of Computer Science and Software Engineering,
Concordia University,
1455 de Maisonneuve Blvd. West,
Montréal, Québec, H3G 1M8, Canada
{gregb, gwang_1, wang_yue, l_zou}@cse.concordia.ca

Abstract. We have constructed a graph database system where a query can be expressed intuitively as a diagram. The query result is also visualized as a diagram based on the intrinsic relationship among the returned data. In this database system, CORAL plays the role of a query execution engine to evaluate queries and deduce results. In order to understand the effectiveness of CORAL optimization techniques on visual query processing.We present and analyze the performance and scalability of CORAL's query rewriting strategies, which include *Supplementary Magic Templates*, *Magic Templates*, *Context Factoring*, *Naïve Backtracking*, and *Without Rewriting* method. Our research surprisingly shows that the *Without Rewriting* method takes the minimum total time to process the benchmark queries. Furthermore, CORAL's default optimization method *Supplementary Magic Templates* is not uniformly the best choice for every query. The "optimization" of visual queries is beneficial if one could select the right optimization approach for each query.

1 Introduction

Scientific and industrial projects have been generating large volumes of data. This tremendous amount of data need storage and analysis. A key issue is that the data management software needs to be easy–to–use, yet provides fast response time. It is not trivial to make a database system simple and intuitive enough for the end-users to query in a sophisticated way. Our graph database system [1] is toward solving this important problem. We believe that the diagrammatic query and visual result display will ease the task of data management and data analysis. We have applied the benefits of deductive query language, diagrammatic queries, and data visualization so as to provide the end-users, who are not familiar with or do not want to bother with writing SQL queries, a helpful system to pose queries and represent query results in a diagram.

In brief, our graphical user interface allows the end–users to construct queries by drawing diagrams. It is implemented in JAVA. The supported graphical query language we have implemented is GraphLog [2]. The query result set is visualized as diagrams with the same icon and style as in the query. CORAL [3] is the system's database engine. The raw data are stored in a MySQL [4] relational

M.L. Lee, K.L. Tan, and V. Wuwongse (Eds.): DASFAA 2006, LNCS 3882, pp. 602–616, 2006.

database. The detailed description about our system's query formulation and result visualization mechanism can be found at [1].

In order to handle the huge size data in a real–world application, we need to study the possible optimization techniques that are effective for diagrammatical queries so as to speed up the query processing. There have been quite a number of graph database systems presented in the literature. In general, they have been lack of full studies of the query language expressiveness, semantics and optimization. To the best of our knowledge, no performance studies of optimization strategies for graph databases have been done prior to our work.

Our first step towards an optimization solution is to understand the effect of CORAL's optimization techniques on the diagrammatical queries in our context. In this paper, we will present the study of CORAL's query optimization techniques in our context. We have used a benchmark of 24 queries across a range of different data sizes. This query set on the University model are carefully chosen and typical enough to evaluate our system's ability to express queries at different complex levels. The data sets used for our experiment range from 640,000 pieces of ground facts to 5,100,000. The wide range of data sets are comprehensive enough to examine our system's capability to handle large data sets.

The capabilities of the system has been expanded to include all features of GraphLog. Our tests and demonstration were performed with a system capable of handling selection, projection, queries with negation, and transitive queries. It also supports blobs, which help to modularize queries with hierarchical relationships and layout the results in the orthogonal shape.

The rest of this paper is organized as follows: Section 1.1 introduces the evaluation framework. Section 2 illustrates the structure of the Graph Database System. Section 2.1 gives an example of query and its translations across the system. Section 3 presents and analyzes the performance experiment results for various CORAL query optimization strategies. Section 4 discusses the related work and Section 5 concludes the paper.

1.1 Test Benchmark

The benchmark used in the test was a framework for object-oriented query language evaluation [5]. It was built on a University Model. Originally, it was a guideline for designing a new query language and improving the performance of existing languages.

The University Model is a simplified version of a university administration system that manages the personal and academic information of students and staff members. The structural relationships among the classes defined in the schema are given in Figure 1.

The class `Person` has two subclasses `Staff` and `Student`. `Visiting_staff` is the subclass of the `Staff`. Both an object of class `Staff` and an object of class `Student` can be an object of class `Tutor`. A student may be supervised by one or more staff members. A staff member may be a supervisor for one or more students. However, some students do not have a supervisor and some staff members do not supervise a student. Every staff member works in a `Department`

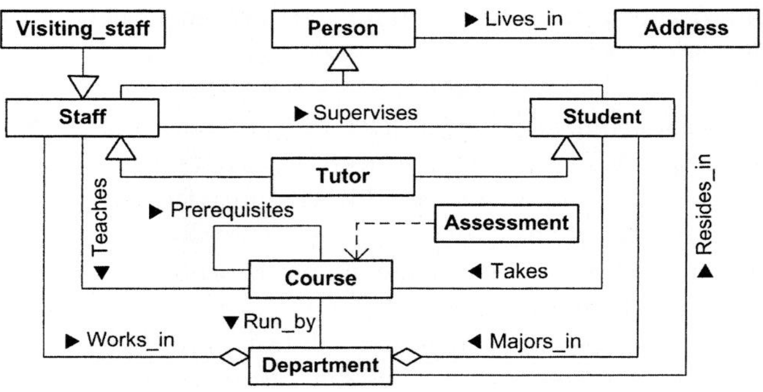

Fig. 1. The university model structure

and every student studies a specific major in a department. Each department offers `Course` for students. The staff members are lecturers for these courses. In some cases, the students need to take and pass the prerequisite courses before taking a course. Each course has an object of `Assessment` that specifies its credits and schools terms that offer it. Every person lives in a place that is defined by `Address`. Each department has a location, which is an object of class `Address`.

The benchmark contains four evaluation dimensions: *expressive power*, *support of object-orientation*, *support of collections* and *usability*. Each evaluation dimension is composed of a set of criteria and each criteria is assessed by a set of proposed queries on the University Model (Appendix A). The support of *object-orientation* mainly concerns the object identity, method calling, complex objects, class hierarchy and dynamic binding of the system. The *expressive power* approach is to test the object manipulation features of the system, such as nested queries and relational completeness. The support of *collections* tries to find a set of operations on the system that can obtain consistent performance on different collection classes. It is also used to test on the mixing of and conversion between different collection classes. The *usability* aims at examining the ease of using query notations.

2 System Architecture

Our Graph Database System takes up four subsystems. They are **Graphical User Interface**, **TGL Translator**, **Query Processing Engine** and **MySQL Data Storage**. The system architecture is shown in Figure 2.

The **Graphical User Interface (GUI)** is the system's interface to end-users. Users can draw a query diagram in the query editor. The GUI translates the user's query that is defined as a diagram into XML format and sends it to the next layer of the system: TGL Translator. The GUI is also responsible to visualize the query result set into a graph.

The **TGL Translator** consists of the *query translation component* and the *result translation component*. The query translation component accepts the query

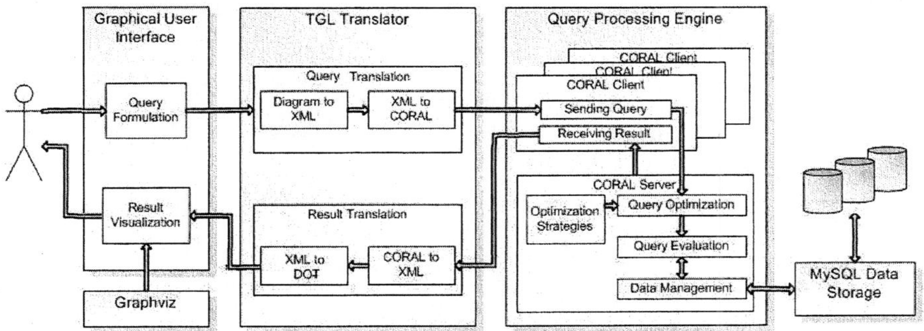

Fig. 2. Graph database system architecture

diagram from the GUI and first translates it into the XML format with pre–defined tags. Then it translates the XML–formatted query into a CORAL query program. The result translation component translates the query result returned by CORAL into XML and passes the XML–formatted query result to the upper GUI layer.

The **Query Processing Engine** is responsible for evaluating the query and deducing the result. It consists of two components: the CORAL client and the CORAL server. The CORAL client interacts with the TGL Translator and the MySQL Data Storage. It is responsible to receive the query plan from the TGL Translator and the query result from the CORAL server. The CORAL client terminates when the query finishes, whereas the CORAL server will live until the user requires to shut it down.

The CORAL Server is the deductive engine to optimize the query and execute the query. The *query optimization* part transforms the incoming queries to an internal representation based on the optimization(rewriting) methods used in the query. In the *optimization strategies*, several control annotations are added to the original query program. This optimized program is transferred to the *query evaluation* part. The *query evaluation* part takes the annotated program and in-memory facts as input and executes the program under the direction of annotations. The *data management* part is in charge of maintaining and manipulating the facts for each query. It loads data from the client interface of MySQL Data Storage and converts the data into CORAL facts on demand [11].

The **MySQL Data Storage** stores the data source physically in MySQL database. The conventional data manipulations can be performed on data in MySQL. The CORAL server initiates a connection with MySQL. All records in the target database are loaded into the CORAL server's computer main memory as a runtime database for CORAL.

2.1 A Query Example

The translation of queries adds flexibility to the system. The transformation of a query from a diagram to XML representation is a process of depicting

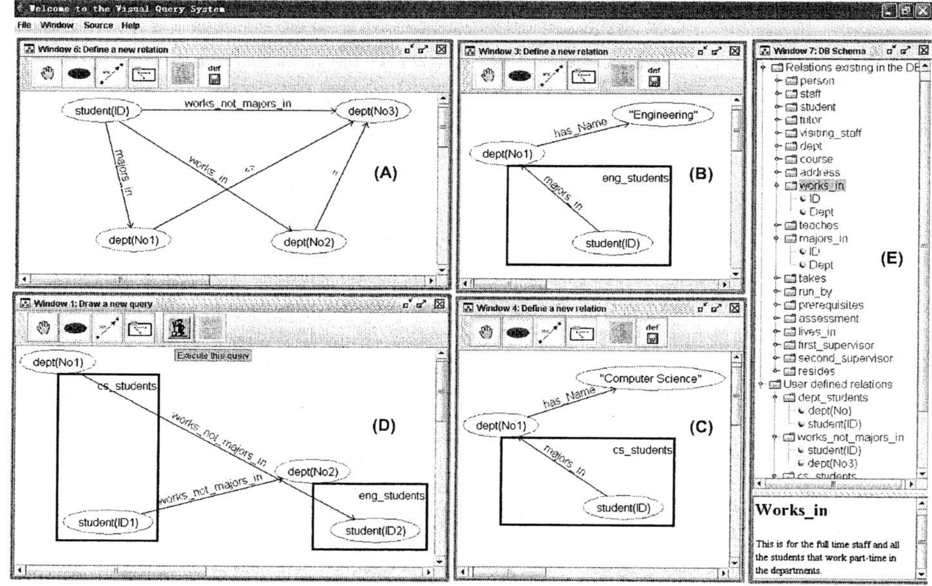

Fig. 3. The query interface. The user posed a query which returns all of the Computer Science and Engineering students who do part-time jobs across these two departments. **(A)** Defining a new relation called `works_not_majors_in`. All students who work part–time in a department that is different from their major department satisfy this concept. **(B)** Defining another new relation `eng_students`. A **blob** is used, which is a container containing all students in the Engineering department. **(C)** Similarly, defining a relation called `eng_students` for all the Computer Science students. **(D)** This is the query diagram. It makes use of the relations defined in the first three windows. **(E)** An overview of all the relations present in the database and the user–defined relations.

the query diagram in format of XML with pre–defined tags. The structure of an XML representation for a query diagram follows the Transferable Graphic Language (TGL) schema. The TGL translator builds up a mapping between an XML document that conforms to the TGL schema and a CORAL program. The detailed description about how this mapping is done can be found in [6].

In order to illustrate this procedure, we provide an example query, which returns all of the Computer Science and Engineering students who are doing part–time jobs across these two departments. Its query diagram in our graph database system is shown in Figure 3. The detailed description about our system's query formulation and result visualization mechanism can be found at [1].

The TGL translator translates both the relation definition diagrams and the query diagram into the XML–formatted documents. The following XML document is translated from the query diagram in Figure 3. There are four elements under the `<distinguished-show>` element, meaning that these four elements should be returned as the query result. It consists of two `<edge>` elements for `works_not_majors_in` as well as two `<blob>` elements named `cs_students` and

eng_students. In contrast, the nodes student(ID1), student(ID2), dept(ID1) and dept(ID2) are under the <content> element. They make up the context of the query diagram.

```
<graphlog>
<showGraphlog>
 <id>tempQueryResult</id>
 <distinguished-show>
   <edge>
     <id>EID3_0</id>
     <predicate>works_not_majors_in</predicate>
     <FromNodeID>NID0003</FromNodeID>
     <ToNodeID>NID0000</ToNodeID>
   </edge>
   <edge>
     <id>EID1_2</id>
     <predicate>works_not_majors_in</predicate>
     <FromNodeID>NID0001</FromNodeID>
     <ToNodeID>NID0002</ToNodeID>
    </edge>
   <blob>
     <id>BID0006</id>
     <predicate>cs_students</predicate>
     <outerNodeID>NID0000</outerNodeID>
     <innerNodeID>NID0001</innerNodeID>
   </blob>
   <blob>
     <id>BID0007</id>
     <predicate>eng_students</predicate>
     <outerNodeID>NID0002</outerNodeID>
     <innerNodeID>NID0003</innerNodeID>
   </blob>
 </distinguished-show>
 <content>
   <node>
     <id>NID0000</id>
     <entity>
       <name>dept</name>
       <field>No1</field>
     </entity>
   </node>
   <node>
     <id>NID0001</id>
     <entity>
       <name>student</name>
       <field>ID1</field>
     </entity>
   </node>
   <node>
     <id>NID0002</id>
     <entity>
       <name>dept</name>
       <field>No2</field>
     </entity>
   </node>
   <node>
     <id>NID0003</id>
     <entity>
       <name>student</name>
       <field>ID2</field>
     </entity>
   </node>
 </content>
</showGraphlog>
</graphlog>
```

The following two CORAL program modules are generated by the TGL Translator. They are translated as the definition of relation **works_not_majors_in** and relation **cs_students**. The TGL translator generates a similar CORAL query program for **eng_students**. The CORAL query program translated directly from the XML query in the previous page makes use of these three CORAL relation definitions in order to generate the final answer.

```
module cs_students.
export cs_students(ff).
eid1_0(ID,No1) :- majors_in(ID,No1).
cs_students (No1,ID) :-
   dept(No1,"Computing Science"),
   eid1_0(ID,No1).
end_module.
```

```
module works_not_majors_in.
export works_not_majors_in(ff).
  eid0_3(ID,No2) :- works_in(ID,No2).
  eid0_2(ID,No1) :- majors_in(ID,No1).
  works_not_majors_in(ID , No3):-
        eid0_3(ID,No2),
        eid0_2(ID,No1),
        No2 = No3, No1 <> No3.
end_module.
```

The CORAL query program translated directly from the XML query in the pervious page makes use of these three CORAL relation definitions in order to generate the final answer.

Figure 4 shows the query result for the example query. The diagram clearly shows two clusters, one for CS department students and the other for Engineering department students. In addition, all of these students are working part-time

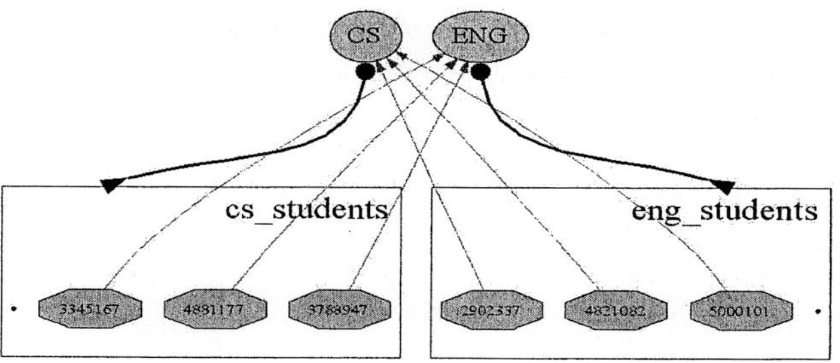

Fig. 4. Query result for the example query

across these two departments: three Engineering students identified by their student IDs are working in the CS department, and three CS students are working in the Engineering department.

3 Optimization Experiment

Deductive databases allow a view to be defined using logical rules, and allow logical queries against the view. Since the rules allow recursive definitions, the resulting expressive power of the query language is greater than the relational query languages. Graph query languages are even more expressive, and provide a visual representation.

In our graph database system, CORAL works as the deductive engine to evaluate queries and deduce results. We chose CORAL for its flexibility to connect to relational database, and its declarative nature for ease of translation from/to a GraphLog query diagram. In order to find the possible optimization solutions for our visual queries, we first test the effectiveness of CORAL's optimization strategies in our context.

3.1 Preliminaries

CORAL is a deductive database system that supports a declarative language. Every CORAL program is a collection of modules, each of which can be separately compiled into CORAL internal data structures. The modules may include facts and rules. In a declarative environment, a fact is the same thing as a tuple in a relation or a row in an SQL table. A rule is a way to derive new facts. We can say the facts are the unconditional rules. The collection of all facts are stored physically in the database, called the *existential database*. The set of all facts that we can derive from the base set of facts are not stored physically in the database, called the *intensional database*.

Modules are the units of optimization and also the units of evaluation. Evaluation techniques can be chosen on a per-module basis, and different modules with different evaluation techniques can interact in a transparent fashion. Although

CORAL developed a number of query evaluation strategies, it still uses heuristic programming rather than a cost estimation package to choose evaluation methods.

The user can specify high-level annotations at the level of each module, to guide the query optimization. User-level annotations can be added directly to the source code and they give the programmer freedom to control query's optimization as well as evaluation. CORAL's user-level annotations are divided into Rewriting Annotations, Execution Annotations, and Per-Predicate Annotations. Presently, CORAL's Rewriting Annotations, include *Supplementary Magic Templates* [7], *Magic Templates* [8], *Context Factoring* [9], *Naïve backtracking* [10], and *Without Rewriting* method. CORAL's default rewriting (optimization) method is *Supplementary Magic Templates.*

3.2 Data Loading

The test platform was a SunFire 280R with two 900MHz UltraSparc-III+ CPUs and 4GB physical memory. The operating system is Solaris 9. We tried the five annotations mentioned above individually on each query and recorded the query execution time on the CORAL server.

We have used eight data sets for our experiment to subjectively evaluate CORAL's optimization performance. Our script generates a MySQL program which inserts the data records into MySQL database. The total number of records in a data set is a function of the number of person records. The number of courses and addresses are constants, which is 500 and 2000 respectively. The size of the other tables depends on the number of person records, and(or) the number of course records, and(or) the number of address records.

Figure 5 plots the data loading time from MySQL data storage to CORAL run-time workspace for each data set. The x–axis shows the variable of number of person records, and y–axis, shows the range of the variable of data loading time in units of hours. Thus, the graph is showing us the change in loading

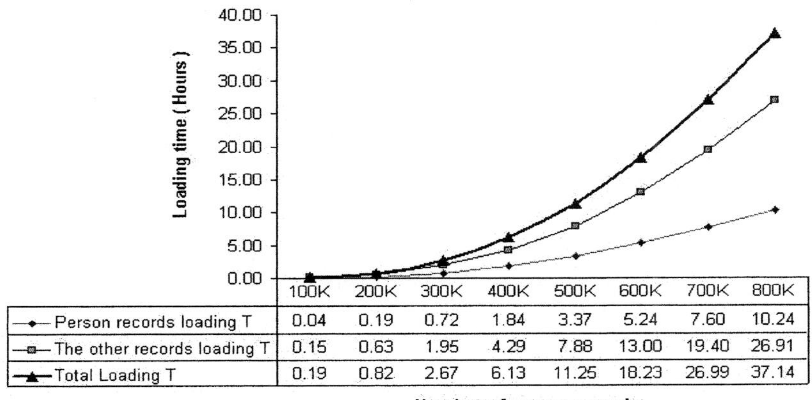

	100K	200K	300K	400K	500K	600K	700K	800K
Person records loading T	0.04	0.19	0.72	1.84	3.37	5.24	7.60	10.24
The other records loading T	0.15	0.63	1.95	4.29	7.88	13.00	19.40	26.91
Total Loading T	0.19	0.82	2.67	6.13	11.25	18.23	26.99	37.14

Fig. 5. MySQL to CORAL workspace data loading time

time from MySQL to CORAL over the increasing data set size. The curve at the bottom shows the time CORAL takes to load the person records. The curve in the middle shows represents the time CORAL takes to load all of the rest recodes. The curve at the top most of the graph demonstrates the total time CORAL takes to load all of the records in the database.

On the graph, it is easy to see that the total time CORAL takes to load MySQL data steadily rise over the data set size, from a low of about 0.2 hour in the data set based on 100,000 person records to a level of about 37 hours in the largest data set based on 800, 000 person records. It is observed that when the data set size is doubled, the loading time is about six times longer. It is tolerable for CORAL to spend hours loading in the data, as it is only the one- time cost for loading all the data to the CORAL workspace.

3.3 Query Processing

In each test run, all five optimization techniques mentioned above were tried out on each query. Figure 6 is showing CORAL total execution time for 24 queries across five optimization methods at each test run by using the cluster columns.

In detail, the x–axis shows the variable of number of person records, and the y–axis shows the range of the variable of CORAL execution time in units of seconds. On the graph, there are altogether eight cluster columns representing eight test runs. One cluster column is for one test run on a particular data set. Each cluster is made up of six vertical bars, for six kinds of CORAL optimization methods, in sequence of *No rewriting*, *Supplementary magic*, *Magic*, *Factoring*, *Naïve backtracking*, and *Hypothetical method*. The higher a vertical bar, the longer time that CORAL takes to execute all of the 24 queries using the optimization method the vertical bar represents.

CORAL has implemented the first five optimization methods. The sixth optimization method, as its name tells, is our assumption of such a method's presence. This "hypothetical method" can intelligently choose a fastest optimization method among CORAL's five optimization methods. It is not implemented as an optimization method in CORAL.

We have used 30 queries in the test benchmark for our experiment. However, in Figure 6, we omitted some queries (Q12, Q15, Q16, Q28, Q29, Q30). For the case of Q12, Q15 and Q16, CORAL does not return the query result after 15–20 minutes even for the smallest data set. We found out that the problem of Q12 is that its translated CORAL program involves cycles on negation of a sub–query, which is not supported by CORAL. Q15's problem is that, it has to include the same relation twice in the query program body. Q16 introduces a free variable which makes the CORAL program unsafe. For the case of Q28, Q29, and Q30, none of CORAL's rewriting methods has a response after 15–20 minutes except for the smallest data set.

3.4 Analysis

With the experiment results summarized in Figure 6, we have the following three main findings:

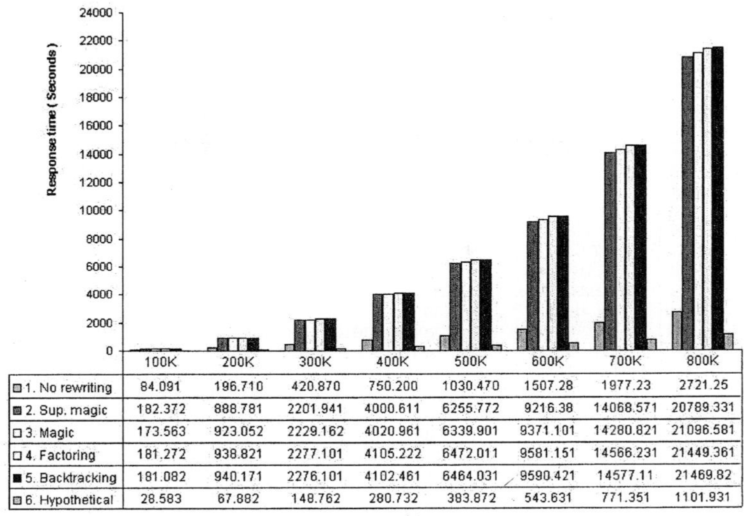

	100K	200K	300K	400K	500K	600K	700K	800K
1. No rewriting	84.091	196.710	420.870	750.200	1030.470	1507.28	1977.23	2721.25
2. Sup. magic	182.372	888.781	2201.941	4000.611	6255.772	9216.38	14068.571	20789.331
3. Magic	173.563	923.052	2229.162	4020.961	6339.901	9371.101	14280.821	21096.581
4. Factoring	181.272	938.821	2277.101	4105.222	6472.011	9581.151	14566.231	21449.361
5. Backtracking	181.082	940.171	2276.101	4102.461	6464.031	9590.421	14577.11	21469.82
6. Hypothetical	28.583	67.882	148.762	280.732	383.872	543.631	771.351	1101.931

Fig. 6. CORAL response time for 8 test runs (24 queries in each run)

(A) There is neither sudden drop nor rise in terms of each vertical bar (representing a rewriting method). Regardless of the rewriting strategies, the CORAL's response time for all of 24 queries continually rise over the data set sizes, from a low of about 29 seconds in the smallest data set to a level of 24,000 seconds ($\approx$ 6 hours). It is a reasonable growth as the larger data set consumes longer time for CORAL to execute the queries.

(B) It is common for every test run that CORAL's four rewriting methods take much longer than its no–rewriting method. This implies that CORAL's four rewriting methods slow down the query processing in certain queries: namely Q11 and Q13, and Q19 (From Table 1). For these three queries, CORAL's rewriting methods should not be used. Q11 asks for students taking a course given by "Steve Johnson". Q13 asks for all the names of the students. Q19 asks for students living in the area of Hillhead, Kelvinside and Dowanhill.

(C) The"hypothetical method" significantly outperforms the other five optimization techniques. Recall that this "hypothetical method" is one of our assumptions about CORAL's optimization strategies. It can intelligently pick the fastest optimization method among CORAL's five optimization methods.

A common behavior among CORAL's optimization methods is that the CORAL response time for each query of a certain optimization method continually rises up over the data set. Under an optimization method, the larger the data set, the longer time that CORAL takes for a query. Table 1 shows the CORAL response time particularly for the largest data set based on 800,000 person records. The numeric values in the table is in unit of seconds. Combining it with the other seven experiment results, we have discovered the following interesting facts:

Table 1. CORAL response time in unit of seconds with 5 rewriting strategies for the data set of 800,000 persons, totally 5,000,000 records

	No rewriting	Sup. magic	Magic	Factoring	Back tracking
Q1	3.000	1.570	1.600	1.570	1.560
Q2	13.550	13.850	14.700	14.180	14.480
Q3	105.550	0.040	0.030	0.030	0.040
Q4	492.950	1.270	0.810	0.830	0.830
Q5	0.010	0.020	0.010	0.020	0.030
Q6	1.320	1.320	1.340	1.320	1.320
Q7	527.690	105.980	113.650	114.740	114.880
Q8	6.160	6.380	6.410	6.430	6.450
Q9	12.330	12.290	12.720	12.620	12.620
Q10	16.480	18.760	20.060	20.180	20.240
Q11	11.540	18561.200	19013.000	19000.800	19022.400
Q13	791.740	1032.840	1216.960	1226.420	1229.840
Q14	0.150	0.190	0.180	0.200	0.190
Q17	12.490	13.090	13.610	13.050	13.380
Q18	9.650	0.001	0.001	0.001	0.010
Q19	109.110	994.400	662.670	1012.790	1007.290
Q20	2.370	2.440	2.440	2.460	2.450
Q21	0.110	0.110	0.110	0.100	0.100
Q22	233.650	1.110	0.110	0.130	0.130
Q23	134.740	17.500	11.690	17.040	17.070
Q24	0.150	0.160	0.160	0.150	0.160
Q25	0.100	0.110	0.120	0.110	0.110
Q26	0.810	0.800	0.810	0.800	0.800
Q27	235.600	3.900	3.390	3.390	3.440

(1) CORAL's rewriting techniques have pronounced effect on 8 queries (Q1, Q3, Q4, Q7, Q18, Q22, Q23, Q27), with the improvement from the low of 2 times faster in Q1 with Supplementary Magic method for the data set based on 800,000 person records, to the level of 2500 times faster in Q18 for the same data set. In contrast, the remaining 13 queries do not benefit or suffer when using CORAL's rewriting techniques in every experiment, since the improvement with an optimization technique is marginal ($\leq 20\%$).

(2) CORAL's default optimization method *Supplementary Magic* is not guaranteed to defeat CORAL's the other three optimization methods under all circumstances. The evidence is from Q3, Q4, Q22, Q23, and Q27 across all the test runs. Due to the space limitation, we only discuss the case of 800,000 person records data set as an evidence, as it is shown in Table 1. In Q3, both *Magic* and *Factoring* takes only 75% of the time consumed by applying *Supplementary Magic* method. In Q4 and Q22, *Magic* takes as low as 63% and 66% respectively of the time consumed by using *Supplementary Magic* method. For Q22's case, the *Supplementary Magic* method is even more worse: the other three methods takes only around 10% of the time consumed by *Supplementary Magic*.

(3) There is no universal best nor worst optimization technique. If one optimization technique fails, so do the other three techniques.

We categorized the benchmark queries into three classes: queries that benefit from optimization, queries that suffer from optimization, and queries that keep neutral about optimization. We have summarized their CORAL query program(s) characteristics in the Table 2.

Table 2. Characterizing queries based upon their optimization effect

	Optimization is beneficial								Optimization is harmful					
	Q1	Q3	Q4	Q7	Q18	Q22	Q23	Q27	Q11	Q13	Q19	Q28	Q29	Q30
atomic values	+			+		+	+	+	o		o	o	o	
don't care symbols	+	+									o		o	
$\geq$ 3 joins		+	+	+			+		o			o	o	o
recursion					+									
relations union						+		+			o	o		
naïve										o				

4 Related Work

There have been numerous graph database systems presented in the literature [15, 16, 17, 18, 19, 20, 21, 22]. In general, they have been research prototypes that lack full studies of the query language expressiveness, semantics and optimization. The implementations have been limited. To the best of our knowledge no performance studies of optimization strategies for graph databases have been done prior to our work.

Our work builds upon the Hy+ system [2] developed by Alberto Mendelzon in Toronto. They designed the GraphLog language, studied its expressive power, and implemented a prototype system in Smalltalk. Their implementation translated GraphLog into several logic-based systems including CORAL. However, the only performance study [23] that they did was a comparison of the naïve translation to Datalog/CORAL with a translation to factored Datalog using automata.

In the field of deductive databases there has been extensive research on the optimization of queries for Datalog (and its variants). The major interest has been the optimization of recursive queries. Ceri et al. [14] provide an excellent summary of the field. The evaluation or comparison of optimization strategies is typified by Bancilhon and Ramakrishnan [12, 13] who develop analytical cost models for the optimization strategies when applied to four queries (related to the parent and ancestor relations) and then generate numerical data from the analytical models using synthetic data driven by three shapes — tree, inverted tree, and cylinder — for the "family tree". The state-of-the-art is perhaps best summarized in a quote [24]: *"Related work on the performance of recursive queries and their evaluation algorithms has considered either worst case performance, or performance over structured synthetic databases, or empirically measured performance over randomly generated relations."* The community has not developed extensive benchmarks nor carried out extensive performance comparisons.

5 Conclusion

In this paper, we have studied the optimization of visual queries for our graph database using a benchmark of 24 queries across a range of different data sizes. Our aim is to understand the effectiveness of CORAL's optimization techniques on the diagrammatic queries. Recall that our database supports defining queries in a diagrammatic form and visualization of the query results. With the extensive experiment results, we are able to conclude that it is beneficial to optimize a visual query. Nevertheless, within the scope of the 24 benchmark queries, applying one optimization technique uniformly in general was worse than applying no optimization to the queries. It is important to utilize the optimization strategies in CORAL when appropriate as there is very slow execution for some queries if no optimization is used. Our research indicates that, a "smart" selection that is able to determine which kind of rewriting method to apply on a given query may profoundly improve the performance of the query execution engine.

References

1. Butler, G., Wang, G., Wang, Y., Zou, L.: A Graph Database with Visual Queries for Genomics. Procs. of the 3rd Asia-Pacific Bioinformatics Conf. (2005) 31–40
2. Consens, M.P.,Eigler, F.Ch., Hasan, M.Z., Mendelzon, A.O., Noik, E.G., Ryman, A.G., Vista, D.: Architecture & Applications of the Hy+ Visualization System. IBM Systems Journal, Vol. 33, No. 3 (1994) 458–476
3. Ramakrishnan, R., Srivastava, D., Sudarshan, S., Seshadri, P.: The CORAL Deductive System. VLDB Journal, Vol. 3, No. 2 (1994) 161–210
4. Widenjus, M., Axmark, D.: MySQL Reference Manual. O'Reilly (2002)
5. Chan, K.C., Trinder, P.W., Welland, R.: Evaluating Object-Oriented Query Languages. The Computer Journal, Vol 37, No. 10 (1994) 858–872
6. Zou, L.: GraphLog: Its Representation in XML & Translation to CORAL. Masters Thesis. Dept. of Computer Science, Concordia University (2003)
7. Beeri, C., Ramakrishnan, R.: On the Power of Magic. Procs. of the ACM Symp. on Principles of Database Systems (1987) 269–283
8. Ramakrishnam, R.: Magic Templates: A Spellbinding Approach to Logic Programs. Procs. of the Intl. Conf. on Logic Programming (1988) 140–159
9. Naughton, J.F., Seshadri, S.: Argument Reduction Through Factoring. Procs. of the 15th Intl. Conf. on Very Large Databases (1989) 173–182
10. Ramakrishnan, R., Srivastava, D., Sudarshan, S.: Rule ordering in bottom-up fixpoint evaluation of logic programs. Procs of the 16th Intl. Conf. on Very Large Databases (1990) 359–371
11. Wang, G.: Linking CORAL to MySQL & PostgreSQL. Master Thesis. Dept. of Computer Science, Concordia University (2004)
12. Bancilhon, F., Ramakrishnan, R.: An amateur's introduction to recursive query processing strategies. Procs. of ACM SIGMOD (1986) 16–52
13. Bancilhon, F., Ramakrishnan, R.: Performance evaluation of data intensive logic programs. Foundations of Deductive Databases & Logic Programming. J. Minker ed., Morgan Kaufmann (1988) 439–517
14. Ceri, S., Gottlob, G., Tanca, L.: What You Always Wanted to Know About Datalog. IEEE Trans. on Knowledge & Data Eng., Vol. 1, No. 1. (1989) 146–166
15. Giugno, R., Shasha, D.: A Fast & Universal Method for Querying Graphs. Proc. of the Intl. Conf. in Pattern Recognition. (2002) 112–115
16. Cruz, I.F., Leveille, P.S.: Implementation of a Constraint-Based Visualization System. Procs. of IEEE Intl. Symp. on Visual Languages (2000) 13–21
17. Gyssens, M., Paredaens, J., Gutch, D.V.: A graph-oriented object model for database end-user interfaces. Procs. of ACM SIGMOD (1990) 24–33

18. Paredaens, J., Peelman, P., Tanca, L.: G-Log: A Declarative Graphical Query Language. Procs. of 2nd Intl. Conf. on Deductive & Object–oriented Databases (1991) 108–128
19. Poulovassilis, A., Hild, S.G.: Hyperlog: a graph-based system for database browsing, querying & update. Trans. on Knowledge & Data Eng., Vol. 13, No. 2 (2001)
20. Olston, C.: VIQING: Visual Interactive QueryING. Procs. of 4th IEEE Symp. on Visual Languages. (1998) 162–169
21. Erwig, M.: XING: a visual XML query language. Journal of Visual Languages & Computing, Vol 14 (2003) 5–45
22. Ni, W., Ling, T.W.: GLASS: A Graphical Query Language for Semi-Structured Data. Procs. of 8th Intl. Conf. on Database Systems for Advanced Applications (2003) 362–369
23. Vista, D., Wood, P.T.: Efficient Evaluation of Visual Queries Using Deductive Databases. Workshop on Programming with Logic Databases. (1993) 143–161
24. Seshadri S., Naughton, J.F.: On the expected size of recursive Datalog queries. Procs. of ACM Symp. on Principles of Database Systems. (1991) 268–279

Appendix A: Benchmark Evaluation Dimensions and Queries

1. Support of object-orientation
   (a) Method calling
   Q1. Return staff members named Steve Johnson.
   (b) Dynamic binding
   Q2. Return staff members earning more than 2000 per month.
   (c) Complex objects
   Q3. Return tutors living in Glasgow.
   (d) Object identity
   Q4 Return tutors working and studying in the same department.
   (e) Class hierarchy
   Q5 Return all visiting staff in the university.
   Q6 Return all visiting staff members in the university who earn more than 2000 per month.
2. Expressive power
   (a) Multiple generators
   Q7 Return students studying in the same department as Steve Johnson.
   (b) Dependent generators
   Q8 Return courses taken by the students.
   (c) Returning new objects
   Q9 Return students and the courses taken by them.
   (d) Nested queries
   Q10 Return students and the courses taken by them that have more than one credit.
   (e) Quantifiers
   Q11 Return students taking a course given by Steve Johnson.
   Q12 Return students taking only courses given by Steve Johnson.
   (f) Relational completeness
   Q13 Return the names of students.
   Q14 Return all the possible combinations between departments and courses.
   Q15 Return staff members and students in the Computing Science Department.
   Q16 Return areas where students, but no staff live.

   (g) Nested relational extension
      Q17 Return income tax of staff as 40
   (h) Recursion
      Q18 Return all direct and indirect prerequisite courses of the "DB4" course.
3. Support of collections
   (a) Collection literals
      Q19 Return students living in the following areas: Hillhead, Kelvinside and Dowanhill.
   (b) Collection equality
      Q20 Return courses with no prerequisite courses.
   (c) Aggregate functions
      Q21 Return courses with less than two assessments.
   (d) Positioning and ordering
      Q22 Return the first and second supervisors of Steve Johnson.
      Q23 Return students having Steve Johnson before Bob Campbell in their supervisor lists.
   (e) Occurrences and counting
      Q24 Return courses with 4 assessments of the same percentage weight.
      Q25 Return the number of assessments worth 25
   (f) Converting collections
      Q26 Return the salary of tutors and keep the possible duplicate values.
   (g) Combining collections
      Q27 Return the students supervised by Steve Johnson.
   (h) Mixing collections
      Q28 Return courses taught by the supervisors of Steve Johnson
4. Usability
   (a) Local definitions
      Q29 Return students whose major departments are in either Hillhead Street or University Avenue.
   (b) Query functions
      Q30 Return students taking some course run by their departments.

A Four Dimensional Petri Net Approach for Workflow Management

Ping-Yu Hsu[1], Yen-Liang Chen[2], and Yuan-Bin Chang[2]

[1] Department of Business Administration, National Central University, No.300, Jungda Rd., Jhongli City, Taoyuan, Taiwan 320
[2] Department of Information Management, National Central University, No.300, Jungda Rd., Jhongli City, Taoyuan, Taiwan 320

Abstract. Workflow management is a fast evolving technology which can support business process reengineering and realize the full or partial automatic process of a business. A formal model of workflow should contain at least four major dimensions: the process, resource, case and time dimensions. Although much research has been devoted to this subject, to the best of our knowledge, no existing research is able to model workflow with the four dimensions at the same time. In this paper, a formal model, named as WF-RAPN (A Resource Assignment Petri Net for Workflow Management) is shown. The model extends traditional Petri Nets with resource assignments and case handling. To guarantee that resources are correctly consumed and execution time of each case is soundly calculated in the modeled processes, a formal set of WF-RAPN composition rules are designed and the proof of the correctness is also shown in the paper.

Keywords: Petri nets, WF-RAPN, workflow, resource assignment.

1 Introduction

Workflow management is a fast evolving technology which can support business process reengineering and realize the full or partial automatic process of a business. The term workflow defined by the Workflow Management Coalition (WfMC) refers to the automation of a business process which passes the information or tasks from one participant to another according to a set of procedural rules [9].

A formal model should contain at least four major dimensions: the process, resource, case, and time dimensions [8]. The process dimension describes the routing of the activities in a workflow. The basic types of routing include sequential, parallel, conditional, and iteration routing [4]. Sequential routing means tasks are executed sequentially, parallel routing specifies tasks are executed in parallel, conditional routing indicates a decision of routing among tasks, and iterative routing organizes tasks into loops. In the resource dimension, the resource allocation and assignment strategies are concerned. Especially, when resources are limited and shared by multiple tasks. The availability of resources in turn depends on the resource assignment strategies when conflicts occur. The case

M.L. Lee, K.L. Tan, and V. Wuwongse (Eds.): DASFAA 2006, LNCS 3882, pp. 617–627, 2006.

dimension displays the fact that workflows are case-based. Each case is an instance of a workflow process, and does not directly influence another case. They influence each other indirectly by sharing the same resources. In the time dimension, we have to keep the total elapsed time of each case, and this temporal information can help workflow managers to improve the workflow design.

Petri Nets is a class of graphical and mathematical models suitable to model concurrent, parallel, asynchronous and dynamic systems [5],[6]. Being a powerful modeling tool for dynamic systems, much research has used Petri nets to model and analyze real-world and workflow management system [1],[2],[3],[4],[7],[8]. WF-net [8] gives only process control specification for workflow modeling. TCPN [7] and TCWF-net [4] extend Petri net by adding *minimun*, *maximun* and *durational timing* constraints to places or transitions. However, they do not take account of the issues of case and resource assignment of workflow management. Jongwook [3] proposes an interactive Petri net model which incorporates resource sharing constraints for planning and scheduling, but the model lacks resource assignment mechanism and does not specify composition rules to correctly construct a work flow related net.

Although each of these four dimensions has been separately addressed by some previous researches, to the best of our knowledge, no existing research has been devoted to model workflow with the four dimensions at the same time. In this paper, we present a model based on Petri Net, named WF-RAPN (A Resource Assignment Petri Net for Workflow Management), to model the four dimensions of workflow at the same time. The contribution of the model is that four patterns of sub-Petri Net along with algorithms are proposed to model resource allocation and assignment decision, a set of composition rules are proposed to guarantee that the patterns and the rest of the Petri-Net integrated well and no residual tokens are left behind when a case is closed, a notation of case is proposed to record each job processed on the workflow and a mechanism to compute the elapse time for each case is also included.

The rest of the paper is organized as follows. In Section 2, the components of WF-RAPN are introduced. The firing rules and firing conditions of new components are also formally stated in the section. Based on the components, the patterns that are used in workflow to describe resource sharing and assignments are introduced in Section 3. To correctly construct a workflow, a well formed expressions of WF-RAPN is defined in Section 4. The correctness of the well formed expressions is proved in Section 5. Conclusion and future work are drawn in Section 6.

2 The Construct of WF-RAPN

2.1 Places

Two types of places are designed in WF-RAPN. A *CP* (Conventional Place) corresponds to the process condition and is the same as the place of classical Petri nets. Every token in a condition place has a case identity used to distinguish the case or batch that it belongs to. Each *RP* (Resource Place) is a repository of one type of resources. A RP with tokens means a particular type of resources are available. RPs may hold more than one token to denote the availability of multiple resources. The two types of places are shown in Fig. 1.

In WF-RAPN, every case has two attributes: case identity (CID) and the accumulated elapse time (AET). The case identity attribute is the identifier that uniquely distinguishes a case from the others. The AET of a case records the accumulated time of this particular case taken so far.

2.2 Transitions

WF-RAPN has two types of transitions, namely, Conventional Transition (CT) and Resource Dispatching Transition (RDT). CTs correspond to tasks and have the same meanings and behavior as the transitions of classical Petri nets. For each shared resource, a RDT is created to assign the resource to activities. RDTs can only dispatch one type of resources to tasks and thus can have only one input RP. Fig. 2 shows the graphical representation of the two types of transitions.

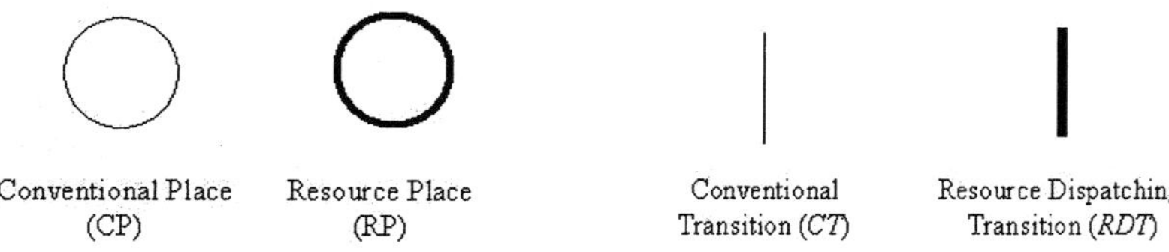

Fig. 1. WF-RAPN places

Fig. 2. WF-RAPN transitions

To simplify WF-RAPN diagrams, the convention for marks on edges connecting into and out of CTs is one. The detailed firing conditions and firing rules of each type of transitions are explained in Sections 2.4 and 2.5.

2.3 The WF-RAPN Model

The construct of a WF-RAPN machine is defined as $< P, T, E, SYMP, SYMT, W, C, D, WT, PRI, ResourcePair, DF, S_0 >$, where

$P = \{P_1, \ldots, P_i\}$, where i is the number of places
$T = \{T_1, \ldots, T_j\}$, where j is the number of transitions
$E \subset P \times T \cup T \times P \to \{True, False\}$
$SYMP : P \to \{CP, RP\}$
$SYMT : T \to \{CT, RDT\}$
$W : P \times T \cup T \times P \to \{0, 1, \ldots\}$
$C : \{C_1, \ldots, C_k\}$, where k is the number of cases
$D : T \to$ Real Number
$WT : P \times C \to$ Real Number
$PRI : CP \to$ Real Number
$DF : T \times 2^P \to P$
S_0 : initial state

P is a non-empty finite set of places, T is a non-empty finite set of transitions, and E is a non-empty finite set of arcs connecting places and transitions. $P \cap T = \phi$ *and* $P \cup T \neq \phi$. C is a non-empty set of cases. $SYMP$ and $SYMT$ express the types of places and transitions. W is the weights on E. D denotes durations of transitions. WT is a set of functions defined on the tokens of CPs to keep track of the waiting time when the tokens are kept in the CPs. PRI is a set of priority functions defined on CPs. DF is a set of decision functions defined on the transitions of type RDT to simulate the resource assignment decision in the event of resource contention. S_0 is an initial state and has the form of $< M_0, AET_0 >$, where the attributes denote the initial markings and the accumulative executing times, respectively.

M: {p—p in P and $SYMP(p) = CP$} $\times C \rightarrow$ {0, 1},
M: {p—p in P and $SYMP(p) = RP$} $\rightarrow$ {0, 1,. . . },
To simplify the notation of firing rules, M: {p—p in P and $SYMP(p) = RP$} $= M$: {p—p in P and $SYMP(p) = CP$} $\times C$ in the paper,
$AET : C \rightarrow$ Real Number

For a CP place, M records the number of tokens in the place designated for each case. For a RP place, M records the number of tokens (resources) ready to be distributed. The detailed behaviors of state functions are further explained in their firing rules.

2.4 Enabling and Firing Conditions

A CT transition is enabled if all of their input places have at least $W(P, T_i)$ tokens designated to the same case. A RDT transition, T_i, is enabled if its input RP, say RP_k, has at least $W(RP_k, T_i)$ tokens and at least one of its input CP_s has a token. In WF-RAPN, a transition T_i for case *cid* is enabled at j-state if one of the following conditions holds:

1. when $SYMT(T_i) = RDT$,
   (a) $\exists! P\ SYMP(P) = RP \wedge E(P, T_i) \wedge M_j(P) \geq W_j(P, T_i)$, and
   (b) $\exists P\ SYMP(P) = CP \wedge E(P, T_i) \wedge M_j(P, cid) = 1$
2. when $SYMT(T_i) = CT$,
   $\forall P\ E(P, T_i) \wedge M_j(P, cid) \geq W_j(P, T_i)$

2.5 Firing Rules

An enabled conventional transition (CT) may fire. However, an enabled RDT must fire at once. The state of a WF-RAPN machine is advanced when a transition starts to fire or when a transaction completes a firing. The duration is the time needed to complete the transition. The j-th state of the machine is represented by $< M_j, AET_j >$. When transition T_i fires or completes in the (j-1)-th state with relative time θ, the state is advanced to the j-th state with functions defined below.

- If the enabled transition T_i fires for case *cid*, only markings of those places which tokens leave are updated accordingly and the others remain the same. If $SYMP(P) = CP$, then

$$M_j(P,x) = \begin{cases} M_{j-1}(P,cid) - W(P,T_i) & \text{if } E(P,T_i) \wedge x = cid \\ M_{j-1}(P,cid) & \text{otherwise} \end{cases}$$

for all conventional places in P. Variable x denotes a variable of a case identification.
If $SYMP(P) = RP$, then

$$M_j(P) = \begin{cases} M_{j-1}(P) - W(P,T_i) & \text{if } E(P,T_i) \\ M_{j-1}(P) & \text{otherwise} \end{cases}$$

for all resource places in P.
- When a firing transition T_i for case *cid* completes, if T_i is not a RDT, then only markings of those places where tokens arrive are updated accordingly and the others remain the same. If T_i is a RDT transition, one of its output RPs will be selected to receive the resource token according to the resource assignment decision function DF of T_i.
If $SYMP(P) = CP$, then

$$M_j(P,x) = \begin{cases} M_{j-1}(P,x) + W(T_i,P) & \text{if } SYMT(T_i) \neq RDT \wedge E(T_i,P) \wedge x = cid \\ M_{j-1}(P,x) & otherwise \end{cases}$$

for all conventional places in P.
If $SYMP(P) = RP$, then

$$M_j(P) = \begin{cases} M_{j-1}(P) + W(T_i,P) & \text{if } SYMT(T_i) \neq RDT \wedge E(T_i,P) \\ M_{j-1}(P) + W(T_i,P) & \text{if } SYMT(T_i) = RDT \wedge E(T_i,P) \wedge \\ & \quad DF(T_i, \{P_h \mid \exists y E(P_h,T_i) \wedge M_{j-1}(P_h,y) = 1\}) = P \\ M_{j-1}(P) & otherwise \end{cases}$$

for all resource places in P.
When two or more activities compete for the same resources, the DF function of a RDT will assign the resource to the activity which input CP has a higher priority. If the priorities among competitive activities are the same, the activity with a longer waiting time recorded in its input CP gets the resource.
- The accumulative executing time (AET) will be accumulated and kept for each case. The initial AET of a case is zero and never changes when the token of the case stays in the source place P_b. When the state advances, we will add extra θ to AETs of all cases which are still running. Once a token of a case arrives at sink place, P_e, the AET of the case stops accumulating.

$$AET_j(cid) = \begin{cases} AET_{j-1}(cid) & \text{if } M_j(P_b,cid) > 0 \text{ or } M_j(P_e,cid) > 0 \\ \\ AET_{j-1}(cid) + \theta & otherwise \end{cases} \qquad (1)$$

for all cases in P.

3 Modeling Resource Assignment with WF-RAPN

In WF-RAPN, resources are divided into two categories, consumable (e.g. parts and materials), and reusable (e.g., human and devices) resources. After being utilized, a consumable resource is consumed and exhausted but the reusable resource can be reused.

A resource can be shared by multiple activities with random or deterministic assignment strategies. Random assignments assign shared resources among competing activities in a random manner; on the other hand, deterministic assignments allow users to explicitly assign resources to specific activities according to decision functions. Fig. 3 represents the pattern of sharing common consumable resource rp_1 randomly between two traditional transitions t_1 and t_2. If p_1 and p_3 both have a token arrived, t_1 and t_2 will be enabled simultaneously. In this case, a token of rp_1 will be assigned to t_1 or t_2 randomly.

Fig. 4 shows the pattern in which reusable resource rp_1 is randomly shared by tasks t_1 and t_2. The pattern is similar to that presented in Fig. 3 except that

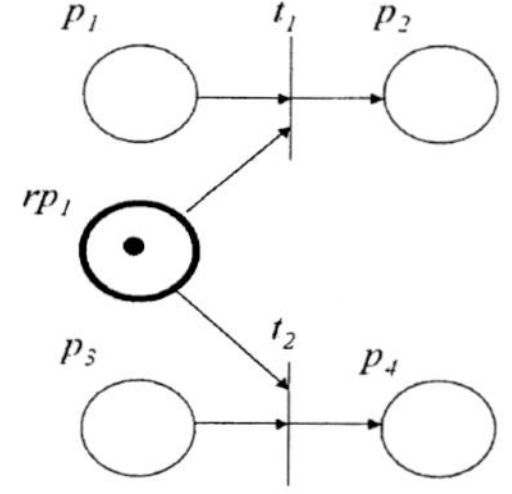

Fig. 3. Consumable resource rp_1 is randomly assigned to t_1 or t_2

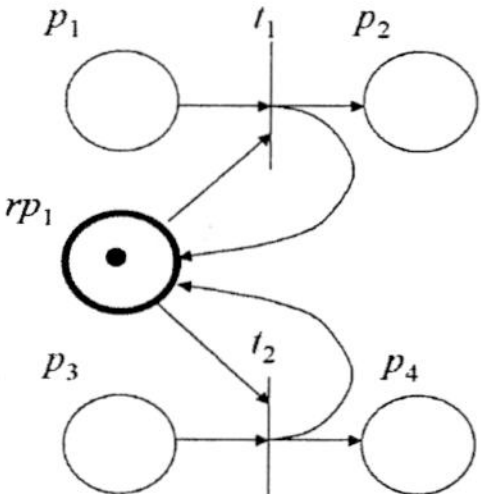

Fig. 4. Reusable resource rp_1 is randomly assigned to t_1 or t_2

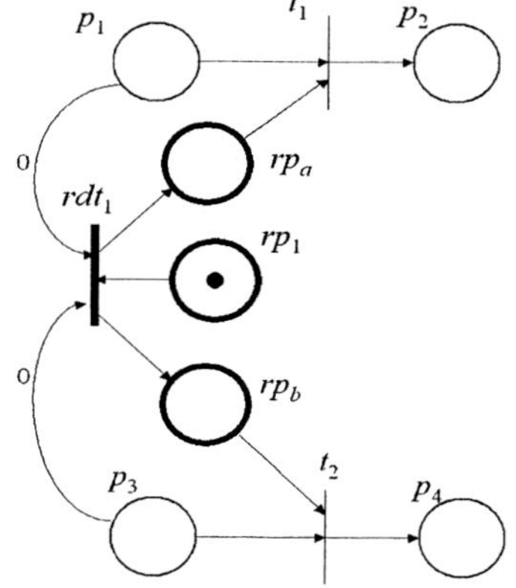

Fig. 5. Consumable resource rp_1 is assigned to t_1 or t_2 by rdt_1

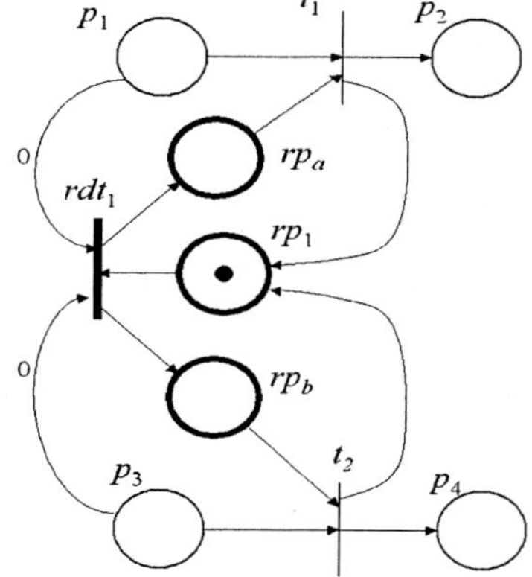

Fig. 6. Reusable resource rp_1 is assigned to t_1 or t_2 by rdt_1

the token would flow back to rp_1. When the firing of t_1 or t_2 completes, a token will flow back to rp_1.

Fig. 5 presents the pattern of assigning resource to a specific activity by a decision function. When rdt_1 fires, its decision function can decide which output place, namely, rp_a or rp_b, can have the resource token. If the token is assigned to rp_b, the CT t_2 will be enabled, and may fire. If the transition type of t_2 is EFT, t_2 will fire at once when it is enabled.

Fig. 6 presents the pattern that reusable resource rp_1 is assigned to t_1 or t_2 according to the result of decision function rdt_1. The pattern is similar to that presented in Fig. 5 with the addition of two arcs from t_1 and t_2 to rp_1, which send resource tokens back to rp_1 when the firing of $t_1$or t_2 completes.

4 Formal Expressions of WF-RAPN

This section is devoted to develop a formal construction rules of WF-RAPN so that the workflows constructed according to the rules are always correct We leave the proof of its correctness in the next section.

To make the rules succinct, following vocabulary is defined. Let T be a set of non-RDT transitions, P be a set of conventional places, RT be a set of RDT transitions and RP be a set of resource places. A place or transition is called a singleton if it is not connected with any edges.

Definition 1. *$\{< p,t >\}$ and $\{< t,p >\}$ are atomic terms based on T and P if t in T, p in P and both t and p are singleton.*

Fig. 7 shows two types of atomic terms. On the left side, the start element is a place and the end element a transition. On the right side, the start element is a transition and the end element a place.

Definition 2. *A simple term based on T and P is defined as follows:*

1. *Atomic terms are simple terms.*
2. *IfTM is a simple term based on T and P and starts and ends with transition t_s and t_e (or place p_s and p_e), respectively, and p_x in P (or t_x in T) is a singleton then TM union $\{< p_x, t_s >\}$and TM union $\{< t_e, p_x >\}$ (or $\{< t_x,p_s >, < p_e,t_x >\}$) are extension terms, which are also simple terms.*
3. *If TM_1 and TM_2 are mutually exclusive simple terms based on T and P and TM_1 ends with transition t_e (or place p_e), and TM_2 starts with place p_s in P (or transition t_s) then TM_1 union TM_2 union $\{< t_e, p_s >\}$ (or $\{< p_e,t_s >\}$) are concatenation terms, which are also simple terms.*
4. *Specifically, a simple term is called a PP simple term, if both the start and end elements are places, and similarly called a TT simple term, if both the start and end elements are transitions. Fig. 8 shows the two types of simple terms.*
5. *A parallel term and an iterative term, to be defined in Definitions 3 and 5, are TT simple terms, and a conditional term, given in Definition 4, is a PP simple term.*

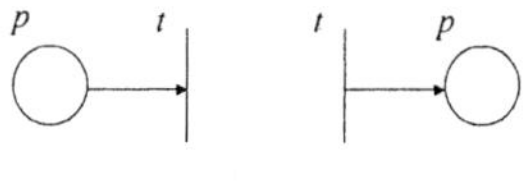

Fig. 7. Two types of atomic terms

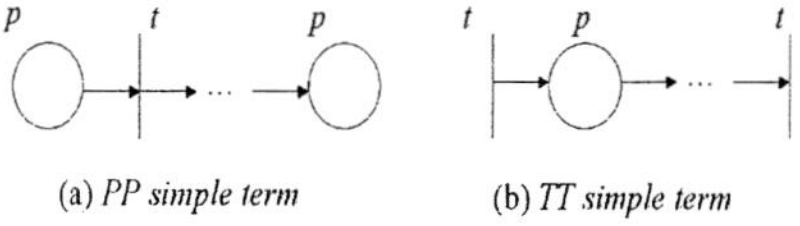

Fig. 8. Two types of simple terms

Definition 3. *Given a set of mutually exclusive PP simple terms* $TM_1,\ldots,$ TM_n *based on* T *and* P*, where the start and end elements of* TM_j *are* ps_j *and* pe_j *respectively for* $1 \leq j \leq n$, t_j, t_k *in* T *and are singleton, then* $\{< t_i,$ $ps_1 >,\ldots,< t_i,\ ps_n >\}$ *union* TM_1 *union* TM_2 $\ldots$ *union* TM_n *union* $\{< pe_1,$ $t_k >,\ldots,< pe_n,\ t_k >\}$ *is a parallel term based on* T *and* P*. Fig. 9 shows the pattern of a parallel term.*

Definition 4. *Given a set of mutually exclusive TT simple terms* $TM_1,\ldots,$ TM_n *based on* T*, and* P*, where the start and end elements of* TM_j *are* ts_j *and* te_j *respectively for* $1 \leq j \leq n$*, and* p_j, p_k *in* T *and are singleton, then* $\{< p_i,$ $ts_1 >,\ldots,< p_i,\ ts_n >\}$ *union* TM_1 *union* TM_2 $\ldots$ *union* TM_n *union* $\{< te_1,$ $p_k >,\ldots,< te_n,\ p_k >\}$ *is a conditional term based on* T *and* P*. Fig. 10 shows an example of a conditional term.*

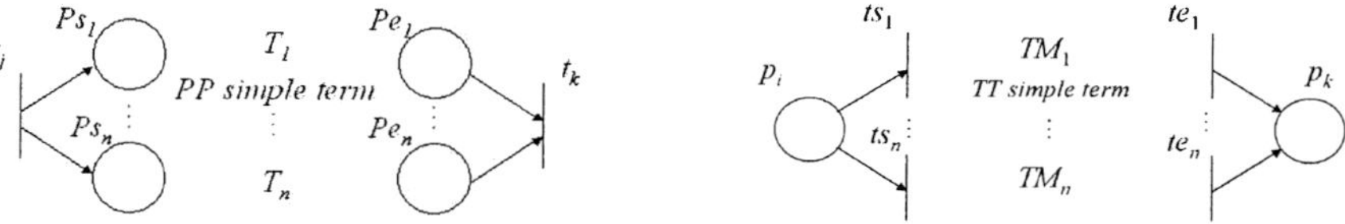

Fig. 9. An example of parallel terms

Fig. 10. An example of conditional terms

Definition 5. *Given two mutually exclusive TT terms, namely,* TM_1 *and* TM_2*, based on* T *and* P*. If* TM_1 *starts and ends with atomic terms,* $< t_1,\ p_1 >$ *and* $< p_2,\ t_2 >$*, respectively and* TM_2 *starts and ends with transitions* t_3 *and* t_4*, respectively, then* TM_1 *union* TM_2 *union* $\{< p_2, t_3, < t_4, p_1 >\}$ *is an iterative term based on* T *and* P*. Fig. 11 shows an example of an iterative term.*

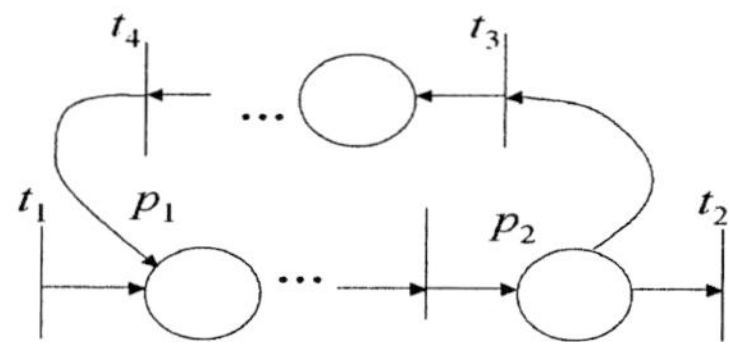

Fig. 11. An example of iterative terms

Definition 6. *A simple TT term based on* T *and* P *is a workflow based on* T *union* RT*, and* P *union* RP*.*

Definition 7. *Given a workflow, w, based on T union RT and P union RP, a singleton resource place, r in RP,* t_1*,* t_2*,...,*t_r *in w, w′ is a workflow based on the same sets if*

1. $w' = w \cup \{< r, t_i > | i = 1, \ldots, r\}$*, or*
2. $w' = w \cup \{< r, t_i >, < t_i, r > | i = 1, \ldots, r\}$

Fig. 3 and Fig. 4 illustrate two samples defined in Definition 7.

Definition 8. *Given a workflow, w, based on T union RT and P union RP, singleton resource places,* $r, r_1 \ldots r_k$ *in R, and* $t_1, t_2, \ldots, t_k, ps_1..ps_k$ *in w, w' is a workflow based on the same sets if:*

1. $w' = \{< r, trdt >\} \cup \{< ps_i, trdt >, < trdt, rp_i >, < rp_i, ts_i > | i = 1, \ldots, k\} \cup w$*, or*
2. $w' = \{< r, trdt >\} \cup \{< ps_i, trdt >, < trdt, rp_i >, < rp_i, ts_i >, < ts_i, r > | i = 1, \ldots, k\} \cup w$

Fig. 5 and 6 show samples defined in Definition 8.

When using WF-RAPN to model a workflow, the system designer must follow the following composition rules. A WF-RAPN must have a source place and a sink place. The source place has no input transitions and connect to a workflow with its begin transition. A token in the source place denotes the beginning of a case. A sink place is used to denote the ending of a case and has no output transitions and is connected to a workflow with its ending transition. Once a token comes to a sink place, the corresponding case finishes.

Definition 9. *Given a workflow, w, based on T union RT and P union RP, two singleton places* p_e *and* p_s *in P, if* t_s *and* t_e *are the start and end transitions of w, respectively, then any WF-RAPN starts with* $< P$ *union* RP, T *union* RT*, w union* $\{< ps, ts >, < te, pe >\}, SYMP, SYMT, W >$ *is a well form formula, where SYMP and SYMT are defined according to P, RP, T, and RT, and W follows the convention stated in section 2.3.*

5 Correctness Proofs

To show the correctness of the model, two issues should be proved, including: (1) The routing process of multiple cases can be run correctly; (2) The time AET of each case is computed correctly. As for the first issue, we show that in a well formed WF-RAPN, when the token of a case goes from the source into the sink place, no tokens of this case remain in the workflow. The second issue is resolved by showing that the elapse time of state changes are correctly accumulated, and therefore the total accumulated elapse time of a case in a workflow is exactly the total execution time of the case.

Theorem 1. *In a simple term where edges are marked with conventions, when a token in the end place or the end transition, no token with the same cid is left in other places or transitions in the simple term.*

Proof.
The proof is proceeded with induction.

The statement is true when the simple term is an atomic term.

Given a set of simple terms, S, based on T and P and that make the statement true, we will prove that extending the simple terms in the set with rules defined in definition 2 to 6 yield simple terms that also make the statement true.

Case 1. Let s in S, if s is extended with the extension rule then an element can be affixed to the term with either start and end elements. In both scenarios, the new terms do not have extra branches and will still make the statement true.

Case 2. Let s_1, s_2 in S, if a new term is formed by concatenating s_1 and s_2 then when a token is in either the part of s_1 or s_2, no token with the same *cid* should be left in the other term. Thus the new term still support the statement.

Case 3. Let $s_1, \ldots, s_n$ are TT terms in S then combining the set of terms with the parallel rule forms a new term. In the new term, n tokens with the same *cid* are sent to the n sub terms at the same time and when the last transition is fired, a token with the same *cid* is taken away from each of the n sub terms. Therefore, no token with the same *cid* is left in the sub terms.

Case 4. Let $s_1, \ldots, s_n$ be PP terms in S then combing the set of terms with the conditional rule forms new term, in which when the first transition completes its fire for a token, only one sub term gets a token with the same *cid*. Hence, when the last transitions fired with the same *cid*, no sub terms have any token with the same *cid* left.

Case 5. Let s_1 and s_2 be TT terms and the start and end elements of s_1 are connected to s_2 with the iterative rule to form a new term. Before the end transition of the original s_1 fires, a token must exist in the last place of s_1 which means no token with the same *cid* has left in s_2 or other parts of s_1.

Thus, the new terms derived from S also make the statement true and the theorem is proved.

Theorem 2. *For a well-formed WF-RAPN with a state sequence of* $< S_0, \ldots, S_n >$, *if* S_k *is the first state where the sink place* P_s *has a token with case identity cid, then* $AET_j(cid)$ = *the elapse time of the case for* $j \geq k$.

Proof.
Let S_i be the first state where the token of the case leaves the source place. Then, according to the firing rule shown in formula (1) stated in Section 2.5, we have $AET(cid)$=0 before state i. After state i but before state k, the firing rule in formula (1) indicates that the elapse time of case cid will be accumulated at each state change. Finally, once we have reached state k or after state k, the time accumulation stops according to formula (1). As a result, $AET_j(cid)$, where $j \geq k$, holds the elapse time of the case.

6 Conclusion

A formal model of workflow should be able to describe the semantic of process routing, resource assignment, case identification and execution time computation.

WF-RAPN is designed to fulfill these requirements. WF-RAPN extends classical Petri nets with resource places and resource dispatching transition. With WF-RAPN, we can formally describe all these details and compute the execution time of each case. Although WF-RAPN can describe basic resource assignment and sequencing relationships, more research is needed in modeling resource consumptions. For example, the model cannot describe scenarios where activities consume partial resource, instead of the entire units, or activities utilize and release the same resource intermittently. Hence, future research is needed to model resource utilization and assignments in more complicated scenarios of workflow.

References

1. J. Wang D. Liu, S.C.F. Chan, and L. Zhang J. Sun. Modeling workflow processes with colored petri nets. *Computers in Industry*, 49:267–281, 2002.
2. K. Hasegawa, P. E. Miyagi, D. J. Santos, K. Takahashi, L. Ma, and M. Sugisawa. On resource arc for petri net modeling of complex resource sharing system. *Journal of International Robotic Systems Theory and Applications*, 26:423–437, 1999.
3. Jongwook Kim, Desrochers A.A., and Sanderson A.C. Task planning and project management using petri nets. *IEEE International Symposium on Assembly and Task Planning*, 10:265–271, 1995.
4. J. Li, Y. S. Fan, and M. C. Zhou. Timing constraint workflow nets for workflow analysis. *IEEE Transactions on Systems*, 33:179–193, 2003.
5. T. Murata. Petri nets: properties, analysis and applications. In *Proc. IEEE*, volume 77, pages 541–580, 1989.
6. J. L. Peterson. *Petri Net Theory and the Modeling of Systems*. Prentice-Hall, 1981.
7. J. P. Tsai and S.J. Yang. Timing constraint petri nets and their application to schedulability analysis of real-time system specifications. *IEEE Trans on Software Eng.*, 21:32–49, 1995.
8. W. M. P. van der Aalst. The application of petri nets to workflow management. *Journal of Circuits, Systems and Computers*, 8:21–66, 1998.
9. WfMC. *Workflow Management Coalition Terminology and Glossary (WFMC-TC-1011 Issue 3.0)*. Workflow Management Coalition, 1999.

Containment of Conjunctive Queries over Conceptual Schemata

Andrea Calì

Faculty of Computer Science, Free University of Bozen-Bolzano,
piazza Domenicani 3, I-39100 Bolzano, Italy
ac@andreacali.com

Abstract. Conceptual Modelling plays a fundamental role in database design since Chen's Entity-Relationship (ER) model. In this paper we consider a conceptual model capable of capturing classes of objects with their attributes, relationships among classes, cardinality constraints in the participation of entities to relationships, and is-a relations among both classes and relationships. We provide a formal semantics for such model in terms of predicates and constraints over their extensions. We address the problem of containment of conjunctive queries over a conceptual schema, and we show an algorithm for solving the problem, that achieves better computational complexity than the techniques found in the literature. The results presented here are directly applicable in query answering on incomplete databases, and in data integration under constraints.

1 Introduction

Conceptual models, and in particular the Entity-Relationship (ER) model [9], play a fundamental role in database design. Conceptual schemata used in database design have the necessary expressiveness and flexibility for effectively representing the domain of interest, and are precise enough to allow the implementation on DBMSs.

In this paper we address the problem of query containment, where queries are conjunctive queries expressed over a conceptual schema. As a conceptual model, we adopt a formalism that we call *Extended Entity-Relationship (EER) Model*, able to represent classes of objects with their attributes, relationships among classes, cardinality constraints in the participation of entities to relationships, and is-a relations among both classes and relationships. Since our conceptual model deals with classes (entities) and relations (relationships) on classes, we provide a formal semantics to our conceptual model in terms of the relational database model. In our setting, conjunctive queries are expressed by using predicates (relations) appearing in the relational representation of the conceptual schema.

The problem of determining containment of queries is highly relevant for query optimisation [8]; in general a query Q_1 is contained in another query Q_2 if for every database D the answers to Q_1 evaluated over D are a subset of the

M.L. Lee, K.L. Tan, and V. Wuwongse (Eds.): DASFAA 2006, LNCS 3882, pp. 628–643, 2006.

answers to Q_2 evaluated over D. The query containment problem is complicated, in our setting, by the high expressiveness of the EER model. In fact, we represent a conceptual schema by means of a relational schema, on whose predicates the queries are formulated, and therefore we need to make use of *integrity constraints* to capture the expressiveness of the EER model.

The problem of determining whether a query Q_1 is contained in a query Q_2 under a set Σ of constraints, written $Q_1 \subseteq_\Sigma Q_2$, consists in determining whether *for every database* D *satisfying* Σ the answers to Q_1 evaluated over D are a subset of the answers to Q_2 evaluated over D. Consider the following example, adapted from [11] and entirely based on the relational database model. We have two relations

$$\begin{array}{ll} \mathsf{employee} & [emp\_no, emp\_name, salary, dept] \\ \mathsf{dept} & [dept\_no, dept\_name, location] \end{array}$$

with a single integrity constraint $\mathsf{employee}[4] \subseteq \mathsf{dept}[1]$, stating that every department number appearing in the fourth column of employee must be the number of some department, therefore it must appear in the first column of dept. Now, consider the two conjunctive queries

$$\begin{array}{l} Q_1(U) \leftarrow \mathsf{employee}(U, agenor, X, Y) \\ Q_2(U) \leftarrow \mathsf{employee}(U, agenor, X, Y), \mathsf{dept}(Y, Z, W) \end{array}$$

Without constraints we have that Q_1 is not contained in Q_2, while in the presence of the constraint the queries are equivalent, i.e. they are contained in each other.

In the rest of the paper we will present an algorithm that checks containment of queries expressed over an EER schema, represented by means of a relational schema with constraints. The class of constraints we deal with does not fall in the class of IDs and FDs for which containment is known to be decidable (see [4]); indeed, the decidability of the problem is already known from a work that addresses containment in the context of a Description Logics that is able to capture the EER model [6]. However, our technique, besides providing an in-depth look at the issue of containment of queries over EER schemata, yelds an upper bound for the complexity of the problem that is better than the one of [6].

2 Preliminaries

In this section we give a formal definition of the relational data model, of database constraints, of conjunctive queries, and of containment of conjunctive queries under constraints.

The relational data model. In the relational data model [10], predicate symbols are used to denote the relations in the database, whereas constant symbols denote the objects and the values stored in relations. We assume to have two distinct, fixed and infinite alphabets Γ and Γ_f of constants and *fresh constants* respectively, and we consider only databases over $\Gamma \cup \Gamma_f$. We adopt the so-called *unique name assumption*, i.e. we assume that different constants denote different objects.

A *relational schema* $\mathcal{R}$ consists of an alphabet of *predicate* (or *relation*) symbols, each one with an associated arity denoting the number of arguments of the predicate (or attributes of the relation). When a relation symbol R has arity n, it can be denoted by R/n.

A *relational database* (or simply database) D over a schema $\mathcal{R}$ is a set of relations with constants as atomic values. We have one relation of arity n for each predicate symbol of arity n in the alphabet $\mathcal{R}$. The relation R^D in D corresponding to the predicate symbol R consists of a set of tuples of constants, that are the tuples satisfying the predicate R in D.

When, given a database D for a schema $\mathcal{R}$, a tuple $t = (c_1, \ldots, c_n)$ is in R^D, where $R \in \mathcal{R}$, we say that the fact $R(c_1, \ldots, c_n)$ holds in D. Henceforth, we will use interchangeably the notion of fact and tuple.

Integrity constraints. *Integrity constraints* are assertions on the symbols of the alphabet $\mathcal{R}$ that are intended to be satisfied in every database for the schema. The notion of satisfaction depends on the type of constraints defined over the schema. A database D over a schema $\mathcal{R}$ is said to *satisfy* a set of integrity constraints Σ expressed over $\mathcal{R}$, written $D \models \Sigma$, if every constraint in Σ is satisfied by D.

The database constraints of our interest are *functional dependencies (FDs)*, *inclusion dependencies (IDs)* and *key dependencies (KDs)* (see e.g. [2]). We denote with boldface uppercase letters (e.g. $\mathbf{X}$) both sequences and sets of attributes of relations. Given a tuple t in relation R^D, i.e. a fact $R(t)$ in a database D for a schema $\mathcal{R}$, and a set of attributes $\mathbf{X}$ of R, we denote with $t[\mathbf{X}]$ the *projection* (see e.g. [2]) of t on the attributes in $\mathbf{X}$.

(i) Functional dependencies (FDs). A functional dependency on a relation R is denoted by $R : \mathbf{X} \rightarrow \mathbf{Y}$. Such a constraint is satisfied in a database D iff for each $t_1, t_2 \in R^D$ we have that if $t_1[\mathbf{X}] = t_2[\mathbf{X}]$ then $t_1[\mathbf{Y}] = t_2[\mathbf{Y}]$.

(ii) Inclusion dependencies (IDs). An inclusion dependency between relations R_1 and R_2 is denoted by $R_1[\mathbf{X}] \subseteq R_2[\mathbf{Y}]$. Such a constraint is satisfied in a database D iff for each tuple t_1 in R_1^D there exists a tuple t_2 in R_2^D such that $t_1[\mathbf{X}] = t_2[\mathbf{Y}]$.

(iii) Key dependencies (KDs). A key constraint over relation R is denoted by $key(R) = \mathbf{K}$, where $\mathbf{K}$ is a subset of the attributes of R. Such a constraint is satisfied in a database D iff for each $t_1, t_2 \in R^D$ we have $t_1[\mathbf{K}] \neq t_2[\mathbf{K}]$. Observe that this constraints is equivalent to the functional dependency $R : \mathbf{K} \rightarrow \mathbf{A}_R$, where $\mathbf{A}_R$ is the set of all attributes of R, therefore KDs are a special case of FDs.

Queries. A *relational query* is a formula that specifies a set of data to be retrieved from a database. In the following we will refer to the class of *conjunctive queries*. A *conjunctive query* (CQ) Q of arity n over a schema $\mathcal{R}$ is written in the form $Q(\boldsymbol{X}) \leftarrow body(\boldsymbol{X}, \boldsymbol{Y})$ where:

(1) Q belongs to a new alphabet $\mathcal{Q}$ (the alphabet of queries, that is disjoint from both Γ, Γ_f and $\mathcal{R}$);
(2) $Q(\boldsymbol{X})$ is the *head* of the conjunctive query, denoted $head(Q)$;
(3) $body(\boldsymbol{X}, \boldsymbol{Y})$ is the *body* of the conjunctive query, denoted $body(Q)$, and is a conjunction of atoms involving the variables $\boldsymbol{X} = X_1, \ldots, X_n$ and $\boldsymbol{Y} = Y_1, \ldots, Y_m$, and constants from Γ;
(4) the predicate symbols of the atoms are in $\mathcal{R}$,
(5) the number of variables of $\boldsymbol{X}$ is called the *arity* of Q.

Every variable appearing more than once in Q (more than once in the body, or both in the body and in the head) is called *distinguished variable (DV)*; every othervariable is called *non-distinguished variable (NDV)*. We denote with $Var(Q)$ the set of all variables of Q.

Given a database D, the answer to Q over D, denoted $Q(D)$, is the set of n-tuples of constants $(c_1, \ldots, c_n)$, such that, when substituting each x_i with c_i, for $1 \leq i \leq n$, the formula $\exists \boldsymbol{Y}.body(\boldsymbol{X}, \boldsymbol{Y})$ evaluates to *true* in D, where $\exists \boldsymbol{Y}$ is a shorhand for $\exists Y_1 \cdots \exists Y_m$.

Query containment. Given two CQs Q_1, Q_2 over a relational schema $\mathcal{R}$, we say that Q_1 is *contained in* Q_2, denoted $Q_1 \subseteq Q_2$, if for every database D for $\mathcal{R}$ we have $Q_1(D) \subseteq Q_2(D)$. Given two CQs Q_1, Q_2 over a relational schema $\mathcal{R}$, and a set Σ of constraints on $\mathcal{R}$, we say that Q_1 is *contained in* Q_2 *under* Σ, denoted $Q_1 \subseteq_\Sigma Q_2$, if for every database D for $\mathcal{R}$ we have that $D \models \Sigma$ implies $Q_1(D) \subseteq Q_2(D)$.

3 The Conceptual Model

In this section we present the conceptual model we shall deal with in the rest of the paper, and we give its semantics in terms of relational database schemata with constraints.

Our model incorporates the basic features of the ER model [9] and OO models, including subset (or is-a) constraints on both entities and relationships. It is an extension of the one presented in [3], and here we use a notation analogous to that of [3]. Henceforth, we will call our model *Extended Entity-Relationship (EER) model*, and we will call schemata expressed in the EER model *Extended Entity-Relationship (EER) schemata.*

An *EER schema* consists of a collection of entity, relationship, and attribute definitions over an *alphabet Sym of symbols.* The alphabet *Sym* is partitioned into a set of entity symbols (denoted by *Ent*), a set of relationship symbols (denoted by *Rel*), and a set of attribute symbols (denoted by *Att*).

An *entity definition* has the form

entity E
  isa: $E_1, \ldots, E_h$
  participates(≥ 1): $R_1 : c_1, \ldots, R_\ell : c_\ell$
  participates(≤ 1): $R'_1 : c'_1, \ldots, R'_{\ell'} : c'_{\ell'}$

where: *(i)* $E \in Ent$ is the entity to be defined; *(ii)* the isa clause specifies a set of entities to which E is related via is-a (i.e., the set of entities that are supersets of E); *(iii)* the participates(≥ 1) clause specifies those relationships to which an instance of E must necessarily participate; and for each relationship R_i, the clause specifies that E participates as c_i-th component to R_i; *(iv)* the participates(≤ 1) clause specifies those relationships to which an instance of E cannot participate more than once (components are specified as in the previous case). The isa, participates(≥ 1) and participates(≤ 1) clauses are optional. A *relationship definition* has the form

relationship R among $E_1, \ldots, E_n$
  isa: $R_1[j_{1\,1}, \ldots, j_{1\,n}], \ldots, R_h[j_{h\,1}, \ldots, j_{h\,n}]$

where: *(i)* $R \in Rel$ is the relationship to be defined; *(ii)* the entities of Ent listed in the among clause are those among which the relationship is defined (i.e., component i of R is an instance of entity E_i); *(iii)* the isa clause specifies a set of relationships to which R is related via is-a; for each relation R_i, we specify in square brackets how the components $[1, \ldots, n]$ are related to those of E_i, by specifying a permutation $[j_{i\,1}, \ldots, j_{i\,n}]$ of the components of E_i; *(iv)* the number n of entities in the among clause is the *arity* of R. The isa, clause is optional. An *attribute definition* has the form

attribute A of X
  qualification

where: *(i)* $A \in Att$ is the attribute to be defined; *(ii)* X is the entity or relationship to which the attribute is associated; *(iii) qualification* consists of none, one, or both of the keywords functional and mandatory, specifying respectively that each instance of X has a unique value for attribute A, and that each instance of X needs to have at least a value for attribute A. If the functional or mandatory keywords are missing, the attribute is assumed by default to be multivalued and optional, respectively.

For the sake of simplicity, and without any loss of generality, we assume that in our EER model different entities and relationships have disjoint sets of attributes; also, we do not consider the domains of the attributes, i.e. the specification of the domains to which values of attributes must belong.

The semantics of an EER schema is defined by specifying when a database for that schema satisfies all constraints imposed by the constructs of the schema. First of all, we formally define a database schema from an EER diagram. Such a database schema is defined in terms of *predicates*, that represent the so-called concepts (entities, relationships and attributes) of the conceptual schema. Therefore, we define a relational database schema that encodes the properties of the EER schema $\mathcal{C}$.

(a) Each entity E in $\mathcal{C}$ has an associated predicate E of arity 1. Informally, a fact of the form $E(c)$ asserts that c is an instance of entity E.
(b) Each attribute A for an entity E in $\mathcal{C}$ has an associated predicate A of arity 2. Informally, a fact of the form $A(c, d)$ asserts that d is the value of attribute A associated to c, where c is an instance of entity E.

(c) Each relationship R among the entities $E_1, \ldots, E_n$ in $\mathcal{C}$ has an associated predicate R of arity n. Informally, a fact of the form $R(c_1, \ldots, c_n)$ asserts that $(c_1, \ldots, c_n)$ is an instance of relationship R, where $c_1, \ldots, c_n$ are instances of $E_1, \ldots, E_n$ respectively.
(d) Each attribute A for a relationship R among the entities $E_1, \ldots, E_n$ in $\mathcal{C}$ has an associated predicate A of arity $n + 1$. Informally, a fact of the form $A(c_1, \ldots, c_n, d)$ asserts that $(c_1, \ldots, c_n)$ is an instance of relationship R and d is the value of attribute A associated to $(c_1, \ldots, c_n)$.

Once we have defined the database schema $\mathcal{R}$ for an EER schema $\mathcal{C}$, we give the semantics of each construct of the EER model; this is done by specifying what databases (i.e. extension of the predicates of $\mathcal{R}$) *satisfy* the constraints imposed by the constructs of the EER diagram. We do that by making use of the relational database constraints introduced in Section 2.

(1) For each attribute $A/2$ for an entity E in an attribute definition in $\mathcal{C}$, we have the ID $A[1] \subseteq E[1]$.
(2) For each attribute $A/(n+1)$ for a relationship R/n in an attribute definition in $\mathcal{C}$, we have the ID $A[1, \ldots, n] \subseteq R[a, \ldots, n]$.
(3) For each relationship R involving an entity E_i as i-th component according to the corresponding relationship definition in $\mathcal{C}$, we have the ID $R[i] \subseteq E_i[1]$.
(4) For each mandatory attribute $A/2$ of an entity E in an attribute definition in $\mathcal{C}$, we have the ID $E[1] \subseteq A[1]$.
(5) For each mandatory attribute $A/(n+1)$ of a relationship R/n in an attribute definition in $\mathcal{C}$, we have the ID $R[1, \ldots, n] \subseteq A[1, \ldots, n]$.
(6) For each functional attribute $A/2$ of an entity E in an attribute definition in $\mathcal{C}$, we have the KD $key(A) = \{1\}$. In fact, there cannot be more than one value for attribute A that is assigned to a single instance of E.
(7) For each functional attribute $A/(n+1)$ of a relationship R/n in an attribute definition of $\mathcal{C}$, we have the KD $key(A) = \{1, \ldots, n\}$. In fact, there cannot be more than one value for attribute A that is assigned to a single instance of R.
(8) For each is-a relation between entities E_1 and E_2, in an entity definition in $\mathcal{C}$, we have the ID $E_1[1] \subseteq E_2[1]$. In fact, the is-a relation specifies a set containment between entities E_1 and E_2.
(9) For each is-a relation between relationships R_1 and R_2, where components $1, \ldots, n$ of R_1 correspond to components $j_1, \ldots, j_n$, in a relationship definition in $\mathcal{C}$, we have the ID: $R_1[1, \ldots, n] \subseteq R_2[j_1, \ldots, j_n]$. In fact, the is-a relation specifies a set containment between relationships R_1 and R_2.
(10) For each mandatory participation (participation with minimum cardinality 1) as c-th component of an entity E in a relationship R, specified by a clause participates$\geq$ 1: $R : c$ in an entity definition in $\mathcal{C}$, we have the ID $E[1] \subseteq R[c]$.
(11) For each participation with maximum cardinality 1 as c-th component of an entity E in a relationship R, specified by a clause participates$\leq$ 1: $R : c$ in an entity definition in $\mathcal{C}$, we have the ID $key(R) = \{c\}$

The class of constraints we obtain, which is a subclass of key and inclusion dependencies, is a novel class of relational database dependencies, that we shall

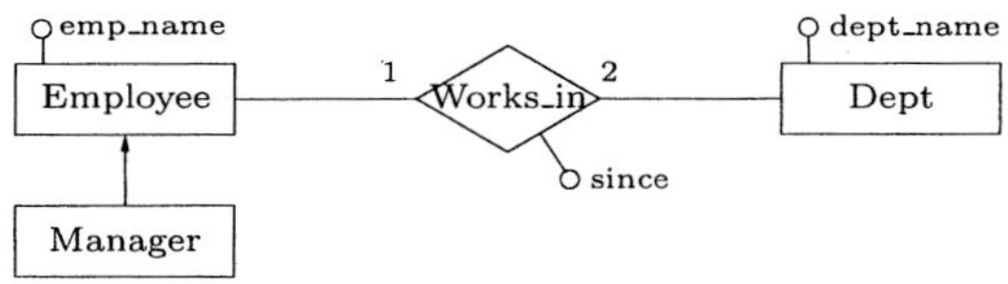

Fig. 1. EER schema for Example 1

call *conceptual dependencies (CDs)* for obvious reasons. The conjunctive queries we consider are formulated using the predicates in the relational schema we obtain from the EER schema as described above.

Example 1. Consider the EER schema shown in Figure 1, depicted in the usual graphical notation for the ER model (components are indicated for the relationship Works_in). The elements of such a schema are manager/1, employee/1, dept/1, works_in/2, emp_name/2, dept_name/2, since/3. The schema describes employees working in departments of a firm, and managers that are also employees. We omit the formal specification of the schema and the constraints on its relational representation. Suppose we want to know the names of the managers who work in the toy department (named *toy_dept*) since 1999. The corresponding conjunctive query is

$$Q(Z) \leftarrow \mathsf{manager}(X), \mathsf{emp\_name}(X,Z), \mathsf{works\_in}(X,Y), \mathsf{since}(X,Y,1999)$$
$$\mathsf{dept}(Y), \mathsf{dept\_name}(Y, \mathit{toy\_dept})$$

4 Chase and Containment

In this section we first present the notion of *chase*, which is a fundamental tool for dealing with database constraints; then we prove some relevant properties of the chase under conceptual dependencies (CDs), by means of which we prove the decidability of the problem of containment of conjunctive queries under such dependencies.

The *chase* of a conjunctive query [13, 11] is a key concept in particular in the context of functional and inclusion dependencies. Intuitively, given a conjunctive query, its conjuncts are "frozen" and seen as facts in a database, where each variable is associated to a distinct value. Since this collection of facts in general does not satisfy the inclusion and functional dependencies, the idea is to convert the initial facts into a new set of facts constituting a database that satisfies the dependencies, possibly by collapsing facts (according to FDs) or adding new facts (according to IDs). Since a frozen query is a database, as we will see in the next section, we will define the notion of chase of a database having, in general, fresh and non-fresh constants.

Construction of the chase. Consider a database instance D for a relational schema $\mathcal{R}$, and a set Σ of dependencies on $\mathcal{R}$; in particular, $\Sigma = \Sigma_I \cup \Sigma_F$, where Σ_I is a set of inclusion dependencies and Σ_F is a set of functional dependencies.

In general, D does not satisfy Σ, written $D \not\models \Sigma$. In this case, we construct the chase of D w.r.t. Σ, denoted $chase_\Sigma(D)$, by repeatedly applying the rules defined below. We denote with $chase^*_\Sigma(D)$ the part of the chase that is already constructed before the rule is applied.

INCLUSION DEPENDENCY CHASE RULE. Let R, S be relational symbols in $\mathcal{R}$. Suppose there is a tuple t in $R^{chase^*_\Sigma(D)}$, and there is an ID $\sigma \in \Sigma_I$ of the form $R[\mathbf{Y}_R] \subseteq S[\mathbf{Y}_S]$. If there is no tuple t' in S^D such that $t'[\mathbf{X}_S] = t[\mathbf{X}_R]$ (in this case we say the rule is *applicable*), then we add a new tuple t_{chase} in S^D such that $t_{chase}[\mathbf{X}_S] = t[\mathbf{X}_R]$, and for every attribute A_i of S, with $1 \leq i \leq m$ and $A_i \notin \mathbf{X}_S$, $t_{chase}[A_i]$ is a fresh value in Γ_f that *follows*, according to lexicographic order, all the values already present in the chase.

FUNCTIONAL DEPENDENCY CHASE RULE. Let R be a relational symbol in $\mathcal{R}$. Suppose there is a FD φ of the form $R : \mathbf{X} \to \mathbf{Y}$. If there are two tuples $t, t' \in \mathcal{R}^{chase^*_\Sigma(D)}$ such that $t[\mathbf{X}] = t'[\mathbf{X}]$ and $t[\mathbf{Y}] \neq t'[\mathbf{Y}]$ (in this case we say the rule is *applicable*), make the symbols in $t[\mathbf{Y}]$ and $t'[\mathbf{Y}]$ equal in the following way. Let $\mathbf{Y} = Y_1, \ldots, Y_\ell$; for all $i \in \{1, \ldots, \ell\}$, make $t[Y_i]$ and $t'[Y_i]$ merge into a combined symbol according to the following criterion: *(i)* if both are constants in Γ, halt the process, since the initial database cannot be chased; *(ii)* if one is in Γ and the other is a fresh constant in Γ_f, let the combined symbol be the non-fresh constant; *(iii)* if both are fresh constants in Γ_f, let the combined symbol be the one preceding the other in lexicographic order. Finally, replace all occurrences in $chase^*_\Sigma(D)$ of $t[Y_i]$ and $t'[Y_i]$ with their combined symbol.

In the following, we will need the notion of *level* of a tuple in the chase; intuitively, the lower the level of a tuple, the earlier the tuple has been constructed in the chase.

Definition 1. *Given a database instance D for a relational schema $\mathcal{R}$, and a set Σ of FDs and IDs, the* level *of a tuple t in $chase_\Sigma(D)$, denoted by $level(t)$, is defined as follows:*

(1) if t is in D then $level(t) = 0$;
(2) if t_2 is generated from t_1 by application of the ID chase rule, and $level(t_1) = k$, then $level(t_2) = k + 1$;
(3) if a FD is applied on a pair of tuples t_1, t_2, they keep their level, except when they are turned into the same tuple; in such a case, the new tuple gets the minimum of the levels of t_1 and t_2.

Now we come to the formal definition of the chase.

Definition 2. *We call* chase *of a relational database D for a schema $\mathcal{R}$, according to a set Σ of FDs and IDs, denoted $chase_\Sigma(D)$, the database constructed from the initial database D, by repeatedly executing the following steps, while the FD and ID chase rules are applicable.*

(1) while there are pairs of tuples on which the FD chase rule is applicable, apply the FD chase rule on a pair, arbitrarily chosen;

(2) *if there are tuples on which the ID chase rule is applicable, choose* the one *at the lowest level and apply the ID chase rule on it.*

As we pointed out before, the aim of the construction of the chase is to make the initial database satisfy the FDs and the IDs. This is formally stated by the following result.

Theorem 1. *Given a database schema $\mathcal{R}$ with a set Σ of FDs and IDs, and given a database D for $\mathcal{R}$, the database $chase_\Sigma(D)$ satisfies Σ.*

Proof. We prove the result by contradiction. We start from IDs; suppose a fact $R(c_1, \ldots, c_m)$ in $chase_{\Sigma_I}(D)$ violates an ID of the form $R[\mathbf{X}_R] \subseteq S[\mathbf{X}_S]$. This means that there is a tuple $t_R = (c_1, \ldots, c_m)$ in $R^{chase_\Sigma(D)}$ and there is no tuple t_S in $S^{chase_{\Sigma_I}(D)}$ such that $t_R[\mathbf{X}_R] = t_S[\mathbf{X}_S]$. But this is a contradiction, since these are exactly the conditions for the application of the chase rule for IDs, that has already been applied during the construction of $chase_{\Sigma_I}(D)$. As for FDs, suppose that two tuples t, t' in $chase_\Sigma(D)$ violate a FD of the form $R : \mathbf{X} \to \mathbf{Y}$, i.e. $t[\mathbf{X}] = t'[\mathbf{X}]$ and $t[\mathbf{Y}] \neq t'[\mathbf{Y}]$; this is the condition of application of the FD chase rule, therefore we have a contradiction, since the FD chase rule must have already been applied during the construction of the chase. This proves the claim. □

We remind the reader of the following definition (see e.g. [2]): a set Σ_I of IDs is *cyclic* if in Σ_I there is a sequence of dependencies $R_i[\mathbf{X}_i] \subseteq S_i[\mathbf{Y}_i]$, with $1 \leq i \leq n$, where $R_{i+1} = S_i$ for $1 \leq i \leq n$, and $R_1 = S_n$. Otherwise, Σ_I is said to be *acyclic*. It is easy to see that $chase_\Sigma(D)$ can be infinite only if the set if IDs in Σ is cyclic.

Associated to the chase, we have a *chase graph* that encodes the process of construction of the chase itself.

Definition 3. *Given a database D, and a set of inclusion dependencies Σ_I, let $chase_{\Sigma_I}(D)$ be the (possibly infinite) chase of D according to Σ_I. The* chase graph *associated to $chase_{\Sigma_I}(D)$ is a graph defined as follows.*

(i) The set of the nodes is the set of facts in $chase_{\Sigma_I}(D)$.
(ii) The edges are labelled with IDs in Σ_I.
(iii) Given two facts f_1, f_2 of $chase_{\Sigma_I}(D)$, the arc (f_1, f_2) is in the graph if f_2 is added to the chase in an application of the chase rule for a dependency $\sigma \in \Sigma_I$; in this case, the arc (f_1, f_2) is labelled by σ.
(iv) If there is a fact $f_1 = R(c_1, \ldots, c_n)$ and an ID of the form $R[\mathbf{Y}_R] \subseteq S[\mathbf{Y}_S]$, but the required fact f_2 is already in the chase, then there is a special arc from f_1 to f_2, that we will call cross-arc *according to the notation of [11].*

Notice that every chase graph, if we exclude the cross-arcs, is a forest of trees whose roots are the facts in the original database D.

Example 2. Consider the relations R and S, both of arity 2, and a set of IDs $\Sigma = \{\sigma_1, \sigma_2, \sigma_3\}$, with:

$$\sigma_1 : R[1] \subseteq S[1]$$
$$\sigma_2 : S[2] \subseteq R[1]$$
$$\sigma_3 : S[2] \subseteq S[1]$$

Let D be a database containing the facts $R(a, b)$ and $R(a, c)$. The chase graph associated to $chase_\Sigma(D)$ is shown in Figure 2, where the newly introduced values are α_i $(i = 1, 2, \ldots)$ and the dashed arcs are cross-arcs.

The chase is a powerful tool for reasoning about dependencies [13, 14, 16, 11]. In the next following we will show how the chase can be used in testing the containment of queries under database dependencies.

Testing query containment with the chase. In their milestone paper about query containment under functional and inclusion dependencies [11], Johnson and Klug proved that, under FDs and IDs, a containment $Q_1 \subseteq_\Sigma Q_2$ between two conjunctive queries can be tested by verifying whether there is a query homomorphism from Q_2 to the chase of the database obtained by "freezing" Q_2, i.e. turning its conjuncts into facts. A homomorphism from a conjunctive query Q to a database D is a function f from the variables and constants appearing in a query Q to $\Gamma \cup \Gamma_f$ such that every conjunct $R(X_1, \ldots, X_n)$ (where every X_i is a variable or constant) is mapped to a fact of the form $R(c_1, \ldots, c_n)$ in D, where $c_i = f(X_i)$ for all $i \in \{1, \ldots, n\}$.

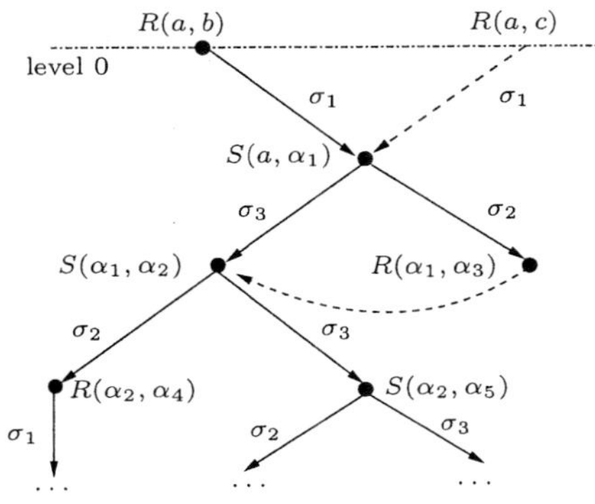

Fig. 2. Chase graph for Example 2

Definition 4. *Consider a a conjunctive query Q; the* frozen query Q, *denoted $fr(Q)$, is a pair $\langle fr(head(Q)), fr(bodyQ)\rangle$, where $\langle fr(head(Q))$ is a fact and $fr(bodyQ)\rangle$ is a database, that is obtained by choosing a homomorphism $\mu : \Gamma \cup Var(Q) \rightarrow \Gamma \cup \Gamma_f$ such that μ sends each constant of Γ into itself, and each variable in $Var(Q)$ to a fresh constant in Γ_f. Each conjunct in $body(Q)$ is sent by μ to a fact in $fr(body(Q))$, and $head(Q)$ to $fr(head(Q))$. For technical reasons, the fresh constants to which μ maps the DVs must precede in lexicographic order* all *the (fresh) constants to which μ maps the NDVs.*

Theorem 2 (see [11]). *Let Q_1, Q_2 be conjunctive queries, and Σ a set of FDs and IDs. Then $Q_1 \subseteq_\Sigma Q_2$ if and only if there is a homomorphism that sends each constant of Γ to itself, and maps $body(Q_2)$ to $chase_\Sigma(fr(body(Q_1)))$ and $head(Q_2)$ to $fr(head(Q_1))$.*

To test containment of conjunctive queries under IDs alone or *key-based* dependencies (a special class of FDs and IDs that is more general than the combination of key and foreign key dependencies), Johnson and Klug proved that it is sufficient to consider a *finite* portion of the chase; this leads to the decidability of the problem of containment, and it is also shown that the complexity of the problem of testing containment is PSPACE-complete. This result was extended in [4] to a broader class of dependencies, namely key dependencies and *non-key-conflicting*

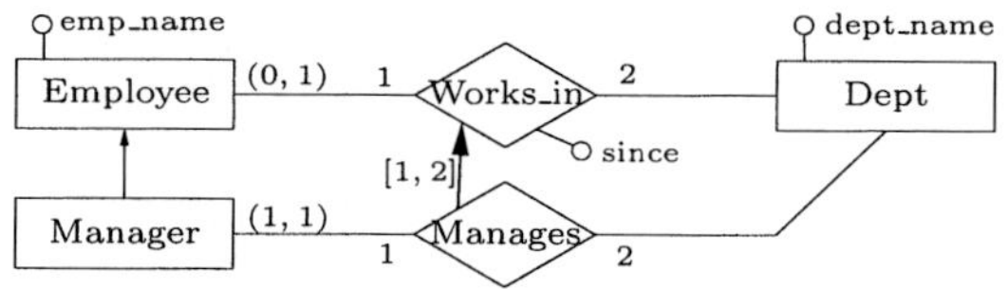

Fig. 3. EER schema for Example 3

inclusion dependencies (NKCIDs), in the context of query answering on incomplete and inconsistent databases; the NKCIDs, in fact, behave like IDs alone because they do not interfere with KDs in the construction of the chase. In our case we are in the presence of CDs, i.e. a special class of key dependencies and inclusion dependencies; IDs are not non-key-conflicting (or better *key-conflicting*); therefore the decidability of query containment is yet to be proved. In the presence of CDs, the construction of the chase presents some problems, as shown in the following example.

Example 3. Consider the EER schema shown in Figure 3, derived from that of Example 1, and depicted in the usual graphical notation for the ER model, where the label $[1,2]$ in the is-a relation between the two relationships denotes that the components of Manages correspond, in their order, to components $1,2$ (in this order) of Works_in, and the cardinality constraint $(0,1)$ for Employee denotes that each instance of Employee must participate a minimum of 0 times and a mazimum of 1 times to Works_in; the cardinality constraint for the participation of Manager to Manages is analogous. We have an additional predicate manages/2 with respect to Example 1. Suppose we have a database, obtained by freezing a query, with the facts manager(m) and works_in(m, d). If we construct the chase, we obtain the facts employee(m), manages(m, α_1), works_in(m, α_1), dept(α_1), where α_1 is a fresh constant. Observe that m cannot participate more than once to works_in, so we deduce $\alpha_1 = d$. We must therefore replace α_1 with d in the rest of the chase, including the part that has been constructed so far.

Fortunately, also in the case of CDs, a finite portion of the chase is sufficient to test conjunctive query containment. This result can be proved analogously to the corresponding result in [11], but now things are complicated by the fact that an application of the FD chase rule can lead to a sequence of cascading applications of the same rule. This affects lower levels of the chase, so that we cannot be sure, once we stop at a certain level, whether the collapse of a pair of facts (due to the application of the FD chase rule) in a level that is far larger than the limit level can affect the portion of the chase we have constructed. In other words, in principle we do not know what the first portion of the chase actually is, before we construct the rest of the possibly infinite chase, since the application of the FD chase rule in a far level could propagate, like a crack in a high wall, down to the first portion.

First, we show that, after a certain number of levels, it is impossible that the construction of the chase of a frozen query Q_1 w.r.t. a set of CDs fails (see the

FD chase rule), leading to the conclusion that Q_1 is contained in all queries. We state our result for the chase of a database.

Lemma 1. *Let D be a database and Σ a set of CDs. We have that if the construction of $chase_\Sigma(D)$ does not fail after level $W!$, where W is the maximum width of an ID in Σ (i.e. the maximum number of attributes involved in an ID), then it does not fail in any level greater than $W!$.*

Proof (sketch). It is easy to see that the construction of the chase may fail only if the FD chase rule is applied between two tuples, containing *only* non-fresh constants in Γ, and belonging to a relation that represent a relationship of an EER schema; in fact, all other tuples of the same kind contain at most one non-fresh constant. Since tuples containing only constants in Γ propagate only through IDs that represent is-a relations between two relationships, such tuples do not "survive" after $W!$ levels. □

Lemma 2. *Let Q_1, Q_2 be two conjunctive queries, $\Sigma = \Sigma_K \cup \Sigma_I$ a set of CDs, where Σ_K and Σ_I are sets of KDs and IDs respectively. If there exists a homomorphism μ sending each constant of Γ to itself, and mapping $body(Q_2)$ to facts of $chase_\Sigma(fr(body(Q_1)))$ and $head(Q_2)$ to $fr(head(Q_1))$, then there exists another homomorphism μ' having the same properties, that sends all the facts of $body(Q_2)$ to facts in $chase_\Sigma(fr(body(Q_1)))$ appearing at levels that are lower than $|Q_2| \cdot |\Sigma| \cdot W!$, where $|Q_2|$ is the number of conjuncts in Q_2, $|\Sigma|$ is the number of dependencies in Σ, and W is the maximum width of an ID in Σ.*

Proof (sketch). The proof of this theorem goes very much like the proof of the analogous result for the case of IDs alone or *key-based* dependencies [11]: all the results hold also in the presence of CDs. We do not provide the details here, due to the fact that the proof is long and rather complicated. The only difference between our result and the result of [11] is the term $W!$, that is replaced by $(W+1)^W$ in the result of that paper. This is because $W!$ is the maximum length of a path in the chase graph made up of ordinary arcs only, starting from a fact θ, and such that there are no two *equivalent* facts in the path, where two facts θ_1, θ_2 are said to be equivalent if: *(i)* they have the incoming arc labelled with the same ID; *(ii)* for every attribute A_i, if either $\theta_1[A_i]$ or $\theta_2[A_i]$ appears in θ, it holds $\theta_1[A_i] = \theta_2[A_i]$. In our case, differently from [11], the maximum length of such a path is $W!$. □

We now come to the decidability of query containment. Our plan of attack consists in showing a *principle of locality* of KDs in the chase: in practice, we show that collapses due to the application of the FD chase rule propagate their effects at most δ levels back in the chase, where δ is a value depending on the dependencies. Therefore, in order to test whether $Q_1 \subseteq_\Sigma Q_2$, we need to construct the chase until level $\ell_{JK} = |Q_2| \cdot |\Sigma| \cdot W!$, and continue for extra δ levels; after that point, no changes will occur in the first ℓ_{JK} levels of the chase. We first need an auxiliary lemma.

Lemma 3. *Let D be a database instance (over Γ and Γ_f) for a relational schema $\mathcal{R}$, and $\Sigma = \Sigma_K \cup \Sigma_I$ a set of CDs, where Σ_K and Σ_I are sets of KDs and IDs respectively. Consider a fact θ containing a symbol $c \in (\Gamma \cup \Gamma_f)$, at level ℓ in $chase_\Sigma(D)$; then, c does not appear in any fact at levels greater than $\ell + |\Sigma| \cdot W! = \ell + \delta$.*

Proof. First, observe that only the IDs encoding is-a arcs between relationships are non-unary in Σ. Clearly, c can appear for $|\Sigma|$ more levels, but also for more, if there are cyclic non-unary IDs. If we consider a path of ordinary arcs (non-cross-arcs) corresponding to the application of the ID chase rule w.r.t. IDs $\sigma_1, \ldots, \sigma_k$ that form a cycle, if σ_i is unary for some $i \in \{1, \ldots, k\}$, c cannot survive for more than $|\Sigma|$ levels after ℓ; instead, if $\sigma_1, \ldots, \sigma_k$ are all non-unary, and therefore forced to have the same width U, the cycle of IDs formed by $\sigma_1, \ldots, \sigma_k$ can be traversed (in the application of the ID chase rule) $U!$ times, where all the generated facts are obtained by permutating the values in the U positions of θ. After that, no further propagation of c is possible. Since k is limited by $|\Sigma|$ and U by W, the thesis follows. □

Lemma 4. *Let D be a database instance (over Γ and Γ_f) for a relational schema $\mathcal{R}$, and $\Sigma = \Sigma_K \cup \Sigma_I$ a set of CDs, where Σ_K and Σ_I are sets of KDs and IDs respectively. Suppose that, during the construction of $chase_\Sigma(D)$, we apply the FD chase rule to two facts θ_1, θ_2 in $chase_\Sigma(D)$; then all the applications of the FD chase rule that are done in consequence of the first one involve facts that are at level greater or equal than* $\max(level(\theta_1), level(\theta_2)) - \delta$*, where $\delta = |\Sigma| \cdot W!$.*

Proof. Let $key(R) = \{k\}$ be a KD in Σ_K, $\theta_1 = R(\alpha_1, \ldots, \alpha_{k-1}, c, \alpha_{k+1}, \ldots, \alpha_n)$, and $\theta_2 = R(\beta_1, \ldots, \beta_{k-1}, c, \beta_{k+1}, \ldots, \beta_n)$. We refer the reader to Figure 4, that shows the chase graph for $chase_\Sigma(D)$ (higher levels are below in the figure). We assume that $\alpha_1, \ldots, \alpha_n, \beta_1, \ldots, \beta_n$ are fresh constants in Γ_f (at the end of the proof we shall consider the case where one of the two facts θ_1, θ_2 is in D). In the following we shall not consider IDs and FDs regarding attributes, since they are acyclic and have a marginal role in the construction of the chase. Also, we assume $\ell_1 = level(\theta_1) \geq level(\theta_2) = \ell_2$; this is done without loss of generality, since the other case is symmetric to this one. Since θ_1 and θ_2 agree on the key, we need to turn α_i into β_i for all i such that $1 \leq i \leq n$ and $i \neq k$; in fact, since

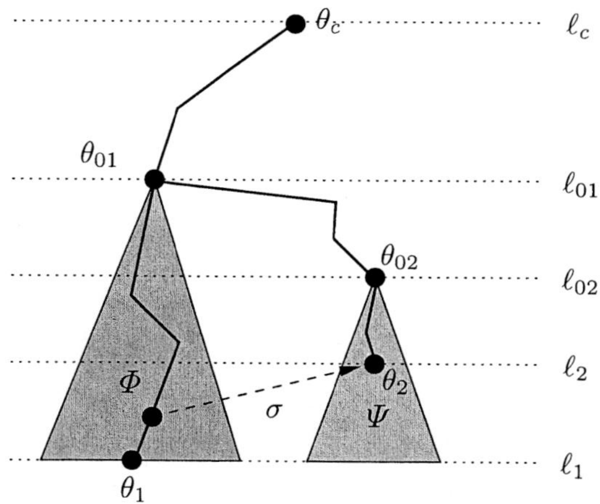

Fig. 4. Figure for the proof of Lemma 4

θ_2 was generated earlier that θ_1, its fresh constants have higher lexicographic rank; as a consequence, θ_1 is turned into θ_2, so that the arc incoming into θ_1 becomes a cross-arc incoming into θ_2, labelled with the ID σ in Figure 4. Since c appears both in θ_1 and θ_2, it must have appeared for the first time al level ℓ_c, in the fact θ_c; then it propagated in the chase to θ_1 and θ_2.

Let θ_{01} and θ_{02} be the facts where the α_i and β_i appear for the first time, respectively; notice that in general, when fresh constants appear for the first time at levels greater than 0, they occupy all positions in a fact, except one, that contains a constant appearing at the previous level. In the figure, the level ℓ_{01} of θ_{01} is lower than the level ℓ_{02} of θ_{02}: the other case is treated analogously, since it is symmetrical. The shaded subgraphs Φ, Ψ in Figure 4 are the subtrees (considering ordinary arcs only) rooted in θ_{01} and θ_{02} repectively. Therefore: in Φ we find constants $\alpha_1, \ldots, \alpha_{k-1}, c, \alpha_{k+1}, \ldots, \alpha_n$, plus fresh constants introduced in Φ for the first time; in Ψ we find constants $\beta_1, \ldots, \beta_{k-1}, c, \beta_{k+1}, \ldots, \beta_n$, plus fresh constants introduced in Ψ for the first time; moreover, α_1 and β_i appear *only* in Φ, Ψ respectively. By Lemma 3, $\ell_1 - \ell_{01} \leq \delta$, where $\ell_1 = level(\theta_1)$; therefore, changing α_i into β_1 ($1 \leq i \leq n$ and $i \neq k$) affects portions of the chase that are less than δ levels far from θ_1; moreover, applications of the FD chase rule on facts in $\Phi \cup \Psi$ will clearly affect only facts in $\Phi \cup \Psi$ itself. Finally, in the case where θ_{01} (or θ_{02}) is in D, Lemma 3 show immediately that the thesis holds. This proves the claim. □

Lemma 5. *Let Q_1, Q_2 be two conjunctive queries, $\Sigma = \Sigma_K \cup \Sigma_I$ a set of CDs, where Σ_K and Σ_I are sets of KDs and IDs respectively. If there exists a homomorphism μ sending each constant of Γ to itself, and mapping $body(Q_2)$ to facts of $chase_\Sigma(fr(body(Q_1)))$ and $head(Q_2)$ to $fr(head(Q_1))$, then there exists another homomorphism μ' having the same properties, that sends all the facts of $body(Q_2)$ to facts of the database obtained by constructing the first $(|Q_2| + 1) \cdot \delta$ levels of $chase_\Sigma(fr(body(Q_1)))$, where $\delta = |\Sigma| \cdot W!$, according to the given procedure of applications of the chase rules (Definition 2).*

Proof. The proof descends straightforwardly from Lemmata 2 and 4, as discussed above. □

The following theorem is a direct consequence of the previous lemma.

Theorem 3. *Let Q_1, Q_2 be two conjunctive queries, $\Sigma = \Sigma_K \cup \Sigma_I$ a set of CDs, Where Σ_K and Σ_I are sets of KDs and IDs respectively. Checking whether $Q_1 \subseteq_\Sigma Q_2$ is decidable, and can be done by constructing the first $(|Q_2|+1) \cdot |\Sigma| \cdot W!$ levels of $chase_\Sigma(fr(body(Q_1)))$, and checking for the existence of a homomorphism μ' as in Theorem 5.*

As for the complexity of the algorithm for checking a containment $Q_1 \subseteq_\Sigma Q_2$ in case Σ is a set of CDs, we first focus on the complexity w.r.t. $|Q_1|$ and $|Q_2|$ (number of atoms of Q_1 and Q_2 respectively); it is easy to see that our algorithm can be run in time polynomial in $|Q_1|$, and exponential in $|Q_2|$. This because the depth of our finite segment of chase does not depend on $|Q_1|$, and it is linear in $|Q_2|$. The algorithm is also double exponential in W.

The complexity w.r.t. $|Q_1|$ is especially important because, when considering the correspondence between query containment and query answering over a knowledge base or incomplete data [1, 4], Q_1 plays the role of the data, and the complexity w.r.t. $|Q_1|$, called *data complexity*, is highly relevant, since the size of the data is usually much larger that that of the schema. Though decidability of query containment in our case could be proved from the results in [6], our techniques provides a better insight on the complexity of the problem, as discussed in the following section.

5 Discussion

In this paper we have presented a conceptual model based on the ER model, and we have given its semantics in terms of the relational database model with integrity constraints. We have considered conjunctive queries expressed over conceptual schemata, and we have shown that containment of such queries is decidable by means of an algorithm that performs better than all the known ones.

Containment of queries is a fundamental topic in database theory [7, 6, 11, 12]. [3] deals with conceptual schemata in the context of data integration, but the cardinality constraints are more restricted than in our approach. Another work that deals with dependencies similar to those presented here is [5], however the is-a relation among relationships is not considered in it. Also [15] addresses the problem of query containment using a formalism for the schema that is more expressive than the one presented here; however, the problem here is proved to be coNP-hard. In [6], the authors address the problem of query containment for queries on schemata expressed in a formalism that is able to capture our EER model; in this work it is shown that checking containment is decidable and its complexity is exponential in the number of variables and constants of Q_1 and Q_2, and double exponential in the number ov existentially quantified variables that appear in a cycle of the *tuple-graph* of Q_2 (we refer the reader to the paper for further details). Since the complexity is studied by encoding the problem in a different logic, it is not possible to analyse in detail the complexity w.r.t. $|Q_1|$ and $|Q_2|$, which by the technique of [6] is in general exponential. Our work provides a more detailed analysis of the computational cost, showing a lower complexity w.r.t. $|Q_1|$.

The complexity results about query containment are directly applicable in certain cases of answering queries on incomplete databases or knowledge bases, and also in data integration under constraints; still, effective and efficient algorithms are yet to be developed. As for future work, we plan to tackle the problem of answering queries over data integration sytems where the schema is expressed in the EER model, in a way that is similar to the one followed in [3].

Acknowledgments. This work was partly supported by the EU project TONES (IST-007603), and by the Italian national project MAIS. I wish to warmly thank Maurizio Lenzerini, who suggested me to investigate the topic of this paper; I am also grateful to Leopoldo Bertossi, Diego Calvanese and Michael Kifer for valuable comments about this material.

References

1. Serge Abiteboul and Oliver Duschka. Complexity of answering queries using materialized views. In *Proc. of PODS'98*, pages 254–265, 1998.
2. Serge Abiteboul, Richard Hull, and Victor Vianu. *Foundations of Databases.* Addison Wesley Publ. Co., 1995.
3. Andrea Calì, Diego Calvanese, Giuseppe De Giacomo, and Maurizio Lenzerini. Accessing data integration systems through conceptual schemas. In *Proc. of ER 2001*, pages 270–284, 2001.
4. Andrea Calì, Domenico Lembo, and Riccardo Rosati. On the decidability and complexity of query answering over inconsistent and incomplete databases. In *Proc. of PODS 2003*, pages 260–271, 2003.
5. Diego Calvanese, Giuseppe De Giacomo, Domenico Lembo, Maurizio Lenzerini, and Riccardo Rosati. DL-Lite: Tractable description logics for ontologies. In *Proc. of AAAI 2005*, pages 602–607, 2005.
6. Diego Calvanese, Giuseppe De Giacomo, and Maurizio Lenzerini. On the decidability of query containment under constraints. In *Proc. of PODS'98*, pages 149–158, 1998.
7. Edward P. F. Chan. Containment and minimization of positive conjunctive queries in OODB's. In *Proc. of PODS'92*, pages 202–211, 1992.
8. Ashok K. Chandra and Philip M. Merlin. Optimal implementation of conjunctive queries in relational data bases. In *Proc. of STOC'77*, pages 77–90, 1977.
9. P. P. Chen. The Entity-Relationship model: Toward a unified view of data. *ACM Trans. on Database Systems*, 1(1):9–36, March 1976.
10. E. F. Codd. A relational model of data for large shared data banks. *Comm. of the ACM*, 13(6):377–387, 1970.
11. David S. Johnson and Anthony C. Klug. Testing containment of conjunctive queries under functional and inclusion dependencies. *J. of Computer and System Sciences*, 28(1):167–189, 1984.
12. Phokion G. Kolaitis and Moshe Y. Vardi. Conjunctive-query containment and constraint satisfaction. In *Proc. of PODS'98*, pages 205–213, 1998.
13. David Maier, Alberto O. Mendelzon, and Yehoshua Sagiv. Testing implications of data dependencies. *ACM Trans. on Database Systems*, 4:455–469, 1979.
14. David Maier, Yehoshua Sagiv, and M. Yannakakis. On the complexity of testing implications of functional and join dependencies. *J. of the ACM*, 28(4):680–695, 1981.
15. Maria Magdalena Ortiz de la Fuente, Diego Calvanese, Thomas Eiter, and Enrico Franconi. Data complexity of answering conjunctive queries over SHIQ knowledge bases. Technical report, Free University of Bozen-Bolzano, 2005. http://arxiv.org/abs/cs.LO/0507059/.
16. Moshe Vardi. Inferring multivalued dependencies from functional and join dependencies. *Acta Informatica*, 19:305–324, 1983.

Data Tables with Similarity Relations: Functional Dependencies, Complete Rules and Non-redundant Bases*

Radim Bělohlávek and Vilém Vychodil

Department of Computer Science, Palacky University, Olomouc
Tomkova 40, CZ-779 00 Olomouc, Czech Republic
{radim.belohlavek, vilem.vychodil}@upol.cz

Abstract. We study rules $A \Rightarrow B$ describing attribute dependencies in tables over domains with similarity relations. $A \Rightarrow B$ reads "for any two table rows: similar values of attributes from A imply similar values of attributes from B". The rules generalize ordinary functional dependencies in that they allow for processing of similarity of attribute values. Similarity is modeled by reflexive and symmetric fuzzy relations. We show a system of Armstrong-like derivation rules and prove its completeness (two versions). Furthermore, we describe a non-redundant basis of all rules which are true in a data table and present an algorithm to compute bases.

1 Introduction and Related Work

Introduction. Rules of the form $A \Rightarrow B$ where A and B are collections of attributes have been studied in several areas of computer science. We are interested in their role as describing dependencies known as functional dependencies [2, 12]. The interpretation of an ordinary functional dependence $A \Rightarrow B$ in a given data table $\mathcal{D}$ is the following: any two table rows in $\mathcal{D}$ which have the same values of attributes from A have also the same values of attributes from B.

In a paper by 29 leading experts in database systems [1], it has been pointed out that one of the important future topics in database research is management of uncertainty. In particular, one should extend existing tools to allow for imprecision. For instance, not only exact matches but also approximate matches of data items, i.e. matches w.r.t. some underlying similarity, need to be taken into account in the very foundations of data processing. From this point of view, it seems necessary to extend the notion and interpretation of classical functional dependencies so as to take into account similarity in attribute values. A natural idea is to interpret a functional dependence $A \Rightarrow B$ as follows: any two objects which have similar values of attributes from A have also similar values of attributes from B.

* Supported by grant No. 1ET101370417 of GA AV ČR, by grant No. 201/05/0079 of the Czech Science Foundation, and by institutional support, research plan MSM 6198959214.

M.L. Lee, K.L. Tan, and V. Wuwongse (Eds.): DASFAA 2006, LNCS 3882, pp. 644–658, 2006.

Table 1. Data table: there are no non-trivial ordinary functional dependencies but there are approximate dependencies

	dist.	diam.	weight	moons
Mercury	57.9	4878	0.056	0
Venus	108.2	12103	0.815	0
Earth	149.6	12714	1.000	1
Mars	227.9	6787	0.107	2
Jupiter	778.3	134700	317.700	39
Saturn	1427.0	120000	95.200	30
Uranus	2870.0	50800	14.660	21
Neptune	4496.7	48600	17.230	8
Pluto	5900.0	2300	0.002	1

As an illustrative example, consider a table from Tab. 1 describing planets of our solar system. The table contains the following attributes: *distance from sun* (in thousands of kilometers), *equatorial diameter* (in kilometers), *weight* (in weights of Earth), *number of known moons*; and objects *Mercury*, *Venus*,... As one can see, there are no non-trivial ordinary functional dependencies in the data table. However, one can see that with an intuitive notion of similarity, there are dependencies saying that similar values of some attributes imply similar values in other attributes. For instance, similar distance from sun implies similar number of moons. On the other hand, Uranus and Neptune serve as a counterexample to a dependency saying that similar diameter implies similar number of moons. Needless to say, a precise meaning the above described dependencies depends on the definition of the similarity relations and the definition of validity of a functional dependency involving similarity relations. We come back to this example in Section 6.

One can think of many other examples of functional dependencies over domains with similarity relations and there is a question of an appropriate framework to put this idea into work. A feasible option is offered by fuzzy logic [11]. Suppose a domain D_y (i.e., the set of all values) of each attribute y is equipped with a fuzzy similarity $\approx_y$ (a particular fuzzy relation assigning to any values $a, b \in D_y$ a degree $a \approx_y b \in [0,1]$ to which a is similar to b). Then one may consider formulas $A \Rightarrow B$ with A and B being fuzzy sets of attributes, and the following meaning of $A \Rightarrow B$: for any two objects x_1, x_2, if the degree $x_1[y] \approx_y x_2[y]$ of similarity of their y-values $x_1[y], x_2[y] \in D_y$ is at least $A(y)$ for each attribute y, then for each attribute y' the degree $x_1[y'] \approx_{y'} x_2[y']$ is at least $B(y')$. Therefore, degrees $A(y) \in [0,1]$ and $B(y) \in [0,1]$ act as thresholds for similarities in attribute values. It is easily seen that this approach extends the classical one. Namely, if A and B are crisp sets, i.e. $A(y) \in \{0,1\}$ and $B(y) \in \{0,1\}$ for each $y \in Y$, and each $\approx_y$ is an ordinary equality then the above meaning coincides with the meaning of attribute dependencies.

In the present paper, we introduce a concept of a functional dependence and its interpretation in data tables over domains with similarities. We present a system of axioms (deduction rules) and show its completeness as well as its graded completeness. We describe non-reduntant bases of all functional dependencies which are true in a data table and present an algorithm for their computation.

Related Work. For an overview of modeling uncertainty and imprecision in data engineering and databases we refer to [6]. Various aspects of functional dependencies over domains equipped with similarity relations have already been studied, see e.g. [13, 14, 15], a good overview is [15]. Compared to our notion of a functional dependence and its validity, neither of these approaches does allow for using thresholds (see above). Therefore, our dependencies have more expressive capability. For instance, we can have dependencies like "age similarity in degree at least 0.7 and income similarity in degree at least 0.9 implies similarity in life insurance costs in degree 0.5" which is quite reasonable rule since it captures the possibly different influences of age and income on the conclusion concerning similarity in life insurance costs. Furthermore, we describe bases and an algorithm for their computation which the above-cited works did not.

2 Preliminaries

Fuzzy logic and fuzzy set theory are formal frameworks for a manipulation of a particular form of imperfection called fuzziness (vagueness). For an introduction to fuzzy logic we refer to [3, 9, 11]. In this section, we recall some concepts we need.

Contrary to classical logic, fuzzy logic uses a scale L of truth degrees, a most common choice being $L = [0,1]$ (real unit interval) or some subchain of $[0,1]$. This enables us to consider intermediate truth degrees of propositions, e.g. "x_1 is similar to x_2" has a truth degree 0.8, indicating that the proposition is almost true. In addition to L, one has to pick an appropriate collection of logical connectives (implication, conjunction, ...). A general choice covering almost all particular structures used in applications is a complete residuated lattice with a truth-stressing hedge (shortly, a hedge) [9], i.e. a structure $\mathbf{L} = \langle L, \wedge, \vee, \otimes, \rightarrow, {}^*, 0, 1\rangle$ such that $\langle L, \wedge, \vee, 0, 1\rangle$ is a complete lattice with 0 and 1 being the least and greatest element of L, respectively; $\otimes$ is commutative, associative, and $a \otimes 1 = 1 \otimes a = a$ for each $a \in L$; $\otimes$ and $\rightarrow$ satisfy so-called adjointness: $a \otimes b \leq c$ iff $a \leq b \rightarrow c$ for each $a, b, c \in L$; hedge * satisfies $1^* = 1$, $a^* \leq a$, $(a \rightarrow b)^* \leq a^* \rightarrow b^*$, $a^{**} = a^*$. Elements a of L are called truth degrees. $\otimes$ and $\rightarrow$ are (truth functions of) "fuzzy conjunction" and "fuzzy implication". Hedge * is a (truth function of) logical connective "very true". The above properties have natural logical interpretations [9].

A common choice of $\mathbf{L}$ is a structure with $L = [0,1]$ (unit interval), $\wedge$ and $\vee$ being minimum and maximum. Three most important pairs of $\otimes$ and $\rightarrow$ are Łukasiewicz: $a \otimes b = \max(a+b-1, 0)$, $a \rightarrow b = \min(1-a+b, 1)$; Gödel (minimum): $a \otimes b = \min(a, b)$, $a \rightarrow b = 1$ for $a \leq b$ and $a \rightarrow b = b$ for $a > b$; Goguen (product): $a \otimes b = a \cdot b$, $a \rightarrow b = 1$ for $a \leq b$ and $a \rightarrow b = \frac{b}{a}$ for $a > b$. Another common choice is $L = \{a_0 = 0, a_1, \ldots, a_n = 1\} \subseteq [0,1]$ $(a_0 < \cdots < a_n)$ with $\otimes$ given by $a_k \otimes a_l = a_{\max(k+l-n,0)}$ and the corresponding $\rightarrow$ given by $a_k \rightarrow a_l = a_{\min(n-k+l,n)}$. Such an $\mathbf{L}$ is called a finite Łukasiewicz chain. Another possibility is a finite Gödel chain which consists of L and restrictions of Gödel operations on $[0, 1]$ to L. Two boundary cases of (truth-stressing) hedges are (i) identity, i.e. $a^* = a$ $(a \in L)$; (ii) globalization: $a^* = 1$ for $a = 1$, and $a^* = 0$ for $a \neq 1$.

Having $\mathbf{L}$, we define usual notions: an $\mathbf{L}$-set (fuzzy set) A in universe U is a mapping $A\colon U \to L$, $A(u)$ being interpreted as "the degree to which u belongs to A". If $U = \{u_1, \dots, u_n\}$ then A can be denoted by $A = \{^{a_1}/u_1, \dots, {}^{a_n}/u_n\}$ meaning that $A(u_i)$ equals a_i for each $i = 1, \dots, n$. For brevity, we write $\{\dots, u, \dots\}$ instead of $\{\dots, {}^1/u, \dots\}$. Let $\mathbf{L}^U$ denote the collection of all $\mathbf{L}$-sets in U. Operations with $\mathbf{L}$-sets are defined in the usual way, i.e. componentwise [11]. An $\mathbf{L}$-set $A \in \mathbf{L}^X$ is called crisp if $A(x) \in \{0, 1\}$ for each $x \in X$. Crisp $\mathbf{L}$-sets can be identified with ordinary sets. For $a \in L$ and $A \in \mathbf{L}^X$, $a \otimes A \in \mathbf{L}^X$ is defined by $(a \otimes A)(x) = a \otimes A(x)$.

Given $A, B \in \mathbf{L}^U$, we define a subsethood degree

$$S(A, B) = \textstyle\bigwedge_{u \in U} \big(A(u) \to B(u)\big), \tag{1}$$

which generalizes the classical subsethood relation "$\subseteq$". $S(A, B)$ represents a degree to which A is a subset of B. In particular, we write $A \subseteq B$ iff $S(A, B) = 1$. As a consequence, $A \subseteq B$ iff $A(u) \leq B(u)$ for each $u \in U$.

A binary $\mathbf{L}$-relation $\approx$ in U, i.e. a mapping $\approx\colon U \times U \to L$, is called reflexive if for each $u \in U$ we have $u \approx u = 1$; symmetric if for each $u, v \in U$ we have $u \approx v = v \approx u$; transitive if for each $u, v, w \in U$ we have $(u \approx v) \otimes (v \approx w) \leq (u \approx w)$; $\mathbf{L}$-equivalence if it is reflexive, symmetric, and transitive. We will use reflexive and symmetric $\mathbf{L}$-relations to represent similarity on domains of attribute values.

Throughout the rest of the paper, $\mathbf{L}$ denotes an arbitrary complete residuated lattice with a hedge.

3 Functional Dependencies over Domains with Similarity Relations

3.1 Functional Dependencies and Their Validity

Suppose Y is a finite set of attributes. A *(fuzzy) functional dependence (over attributes Y)* is an expression $A \Rightarrow B$, where $A, B \in \mathbf{L}^Y$ are fuzzy sets of attributes. We use also "FD" for "functional dependence".

Functional dependencies will be evaluated in the following data tables: A *data table over domains with similarity relations* is a tuple

$$\mathcal{D} = \langle X, Y, \{\langle D_y, \approx_y \rangle \mid y \in Y\}, T \rangle, \text{ where}$$

- X is a non-empty set (of objects, table rows),
- Y is a non-empty finite set (of attributes, table columns),
- for each $y \in Y$, D_y is a non-empty set (of values of attribute y) and $\approx_y$ is a binary fuzzy relation in D_y which is reflexive and symmetric (similarity),
- T is a mapping assigning to each $x \in X$ and $y \in Y$ a value $T(x, y) \in D_y$ (value of attribute y on object x).

$\mathcal{D}$ always denotes some data table over domains with similarity relations with its components denoted as above, $A \Rightarrow B$ always denotes a FD.

Remark 1. (1) $\mathcal{D}$ can be seen as a table with rows and columns corresponding to $x \in X$ and $y \in Y$, respectively, and with table entries containing values $T(x, y) \in D_y$. Moreover, each domain D_y is equipped with an additional information about similarity of elements from D_y.

(2) Consider $L = \{0, 1\}$ (case of classical logic). If each $\approx_y$ is an equality (i.e. $a \approx_y b = 1$ iff $a = b$), then $\mathcal{D}$ can be identified with what is called a relation on relation scheme Y with domains D_y ($y \in Y$) [12].

(3) We may assume that attributes from Y are numbered, i.e. $Y = \{y_1, \ldots, y_n\}$. Then, for $x \in X$ and $Z \subseteq Y$, $x[Z]$ denotes a tuple of values $T(x, y)$ for $y \in Z$. For instance, if $Y = \{y_1, \ldots, y_{10}\}$ and $Z = \{y_2, y_3, y_{10}\}$, then $x[Z] = \langle T(x, y_2), T(x, y_3), T(x, y_{10})\rangle$. Moreover, we denote $x[\{y\}]$ by $x[y]$ and identify it with $T(x, y)$.

We want to consider $A \Rightarrow B$ true in $\mathcal{D}$ if "for any two objects $x_1, x_2 \in X$: if x_1 and x_2 have similar values on attributes from A then x_1 and x_2 have similar values on attributes from B". In general, we will consider a degree $a \in L$ to which $A \Rightarrow B$ is true in $\mathcal{D}$, with $a = 1$ meaning that $A \Rightarrow B$ is (fully) true. Define first for a given $\mathcal{D}$, objects $x_1, x_2 \in X$, and a fuzzy set $C \in \mathbf{L}^Y$ of attributes a *degree $x_1(C) \approx x_2(C)$ to which x_1 and x_2 have similar values on attributes from C* (agree on attributes from C) by

$$x_1(C) \approx x_2(C) = \textstyle\bigwedge_{y \in Y} \bigl(C(y) \rightarrow (x_1[y] \approx_y x_2[y])\bigr). \qquad (2)$$

That is, $x_1(C) \approx x_2(C)$ is truth degree of "for each attribute $y \in Y$: if y belongs to C then the value $x_1[y]$ of x_1 on y is similar to the value $x_2[y]$ of x_2 on y". Then, validity of a FD is captured by the following definition. A *degree $||A \Rightarrow B||_{\mathcal{D}}$ to which $A \Rightarrow B$ is true in $\mathcal{D}$* is defined by

$$||A \Rightarrow B||_{\mathcal{D}} = \textstyle\bigwedge_{x_1, x_2 \in X} \bigl((x_1(A) \approx x_2(A))^* \rightarrow (x_1(B) \approx x_2(B))\bigr). \qquad (3)$$

Remark 2. (1) $||A \Rightarrow B||_{\mathcal{D}}$ is a truth degree of "for any objects $x_1, x_2 \in X$: if it is true that x_1 and x_2 have similar values on attributes from A then x_1 and x_2 have similar values on attributes from B".

(2) If A and B are crisp sets (i.e. $A(y) \in \{0, 1\}$ and $B(y) \in \{0, 1\}$ for each $y \in Y$) then A and B may be considered as ordinary sets and $A \Rightarrow B$ may be seen as an ordinary FD. Then, if $\approx_y$ is a crisp equality (i.e., $a \approx_y b = 1$ iff $a = b$ and $a \approx_y b = 0$ iff $a \neq b$), $x_1(A) \approx x_2(A) = 1$ iff $x_1[A] = x_2[A]$ and similarly for B. Therefore, $||A \Rightarrow B||_{\mathcal{D}} = 1$ iff $A \Rightarrow B$ is true in $\mathcal{D}$ in the usual sense of validity of ordinary FDs.

(3) We now show that for a FD $A \Rightarrow B$, degrees $A(y) \in L$ and $B(y) \in L$ act as thresholds. This is best seen when * is globalization, i.e. $1^* = 1$ and $a^* = 0$ for $a < 1$. Since for $a, b \in L$ we have $a \leq b$ iff $a \rightarrow b = 1$ (see [9]), we have

$$(a \rightarrow b)^* = \begin{cases} 1 & \text{iff } a \leq b, \\ 0 & \text{iff } a \not\leq b. \end{cases}$$

Therefore, $||A \Rightarrow B||_{\mathcal{D}} = 1$ means that proposition "for any objects $x_1, x_2 \in X$: if for each attribute $y \in Y$, $A(y) \leq (x_1[y] \approx_y x_2[y])$, then for each attribute $y' \in Y$, $B(y') \leq (x_1[y'] \approx_y x_2[y'])$" is (fully) true. As a particular example, if $A(y) = a$ for $y \in Y_A \subseteq Y$ (and $A(y) = 0$ for $y \notin Y_A$) $B(y) = b$ for $y \in Y_B \subseteq Y$ (and $B(y) = 0$ for $y \notin Y_B$), the proposition becomes "for any objects $x_1, x_2 \in X$: if for each attribute $y \in Y_A$, $x_1[y]$ is similar to $x_2[y]$ in degree at least a, then for each attribute $y' \in Y_B$, $x_1[y']$ is similar to $x_2[y']$ in degree at least b". That is, having A and B fuzzy sets allows for a rich expressibility of relationships between attributes which is why we want A and B to be fuzzy sets in general.

3.2 Semantic Entailment

We are going to define the meaning of "$A \Rightarrow B$ follows from a collection T of FDs". Since FDs may be valid to various degrees, we assume that, in general, T encompasses FDs with their degrees of validity. That is, we assume that T is a fuzzy set of FDs and that $T(C \Rightarrow D)$, i.e. degree to which $C \Rightarrow D$ belongs to T, is a degree of validity of $C \Rightarrow D$, cf. also [8]. This covers the case when T is crisp (i.e. $T(C \Rightarrow D) = 1$ or $T(C \Rightarrow D) = 0$), i.e. a given FD either is assumed valid or not; then we write $A \Rightarrow B \in T$ if $T(A \Rightarrow B) = 1$ and $A \Rightarrow B \notin T$ if $T(A \Rightarrow B) = 0$.

For a fuzzy set T of fuzzy FDs, the set $\mathrm{Mod}(T)$ of all *models* of T is defined by

$$\mathrm{Mod}(T) = \{\mathcal{D} \,|\, \text{for each } A, B \in \mathbf{L}^Y : T(A \Rightarrow B) \leq ||A \Rightarrow B||_{\mathcal{D}}\},$$

where $\mathcal{D}$ stands for an arbitrary data table over domains with similarities. That is, $\mathcal{D} \in \mathrm{Mod}(T)$ means that for each FD $A \Rightarrow B$, a degree to which $A \Rightarrow B$ holds in $\mathcal{D}$ is higher than or at least equal to a degree $T(A \Rightarrow B)$ prescribed by T. Particularly, for a crisp T, $\mathrm{Mod}(T) = \{\mathcal{D} \,|\, \text{for each } A \Rightarrow B \in T\text{: } ||A \Rightarrow B||_{\mathcal{D}} = 1\}$.

A degree $||A \Rightarrow B||_T \in L$ to which $A \Rightarrow B$ *semantically follows* from a fuzzy set T of functional dependencies is defined by

$$||A \Rightarrow B||_T = \textstyle\bigwedge_{\mathcal{D} \in \mathrm{Mod}(T)} ||A \Rightarrow B||_{\mathcal{D}}.$$

That is, $||A \Rightarrow B||_T$ is a truth degree of "$A \Rightarrow B$ is true in all models of T".

Lemma 1. *For $A, B \in \mathbf{L}^Y$, a data table $\mathcal{D}$ over domains with similarities, and $c \in L$ we have*

$$c \leq ||A \Rightarrow B||_{\mathcal{D}} \quad \textit{iff} \quad ||A \Rightarrow c \otimes B||_{\mathcal{D}} = 1. \tag{4}$$

Proof. Sketch: it can be shown that $c \leq ||A \Rightarrow B||_{\mathcal{D}}$ iff $c \rightarrow ||A \Rightarrow B||_{\mathcal{D}} = 1$ iff $||A \Rightarrow c \otimes B||_{\mathcal{D}} = 1$.

Lemma 1 enables us to reduce the concept of a model of a fuzzy set of FDs to the concept of a model of an ordinary set of FDs, and to reduce the concept of semantic entailment from a fuzzy set of FDs to the concept of semantic entailment from an ordinary set of FDs:

Lemma 2. *Let T be a fuzzy set of FDs and $A, B \in \mathbf{L}^Y$. Define an ordinary set* $\mathrm{c}(T)$ *of FDs by*

$$\mathrm{c}(T) = \{A \Rightarrow T(A \Rightarrow B) \otimes B \mid A, B \in \mathbf{L}^Y \text{ and } T(A \Rightarrow B) \otimes B \neq \emptyset\}. \quad (5)$$

Then we have

$$\mathrm{Mod}(T) = \mathrm{Mod}(\mathrm{c}(T)), \quad (6)$$

$$||A \Rightarrow B||_T = ||A \Rightarrow B||_{\mathrm{c}(T)}, \quad (7)$$

and thus

$$||A \Rightarrow B||_T = \bigvee\{c \in L \mid ||A \Rightarrow c \otimes B||_T = 1\}, \quad (8)$$

$$||A \Rightarrow B||_T = \bigvee\{c \in L \mid ||A \Rightarrow c \otimes B||_{\mathrm{c}(T)} = 1\}. \quad (9)$$

Proof. Using definitions and Lemma 1.

Note that due to (9), the concept of a degree of entailment from a fuzzy set of FDs can be reduced to entailment in degree 1 from a set of FDs.

4 Complete System of Rules for Functional Dependencies

We now introduce an axiomatic system for reasoning with FDs and prove its completeness in two versions. First, we prove that a FD $A \Rightarrow B$ is provable from an ordinary set T of FDs iff $A \Rightarrow B$ semantically follows from T in degree 1 (completeness). Second, we introduce a concept of a degree $|A \Rightarrow B|_T$ of provability of a FD $A \Rightarrow B$ from a fuzzy set T of FDs and show that $|A \Rightarrow B|_T = ||A \Rightarrow B||_T$ (graded completeness, see [8]).

4.1 Axioms and Some Derived Rules

Our axiomatic system consists of the following *deduction rules.*

(Ax) infer $A \cup B \Rightarrow A$,
(Cut) from $A \Rightarrow B$ and $B \cup C \Rightarrow D$ infer $A \cup C \Rightarrow D$,
(Mul) from $A \Rightarrow B$ infer $c^* \otimes A \Rightarrow c^* \otimes B$

for each $A, B, C, D \in \mathbf{L}^Y$, and $c \in L$. Rules (Ax)–(Mul) are to be understood as usual deduction rules: having FDs which are of the form of FDs in the input part (the part preceding "infer") of a rule, a rule allows us to infer the corresponding FD in the output part (the part following "infer") of a rule.

Remark 3. (1) Rules (Ax) and (Cut) are taken from [10]. A difference from [10] is that A, B, C, D are fuzzy sets in (Ax) and (Cut) while in [10], A, B, C, D are ordinary sets.

(2) Rule (Mul) is a new rule in our fuzzy setting.

A FD $A \Rightarrow B$ is called *provable* from a set T of FDs, written $T \vdash A \Rightarrow B$, if there is a sequence $\varphi_1, \ldots, \varphi_n$ of FDs such that φ_n is $A \Rightarrow B$ and for each φ_i we either have $\varphi_i \in T$ or φ_i is inferred (in one step) from some of the preceding FDs (i.e., $\varphi_1, \ldots, \varphi_{i-1}$) using some deduction rule (Ax)–(Mul). A deduction rule "from $\varphi_1, \ldots, \varphi_n$ infer φ" (φ_i, φ are FDs) is said to be *derivable* from (Ax)–(Mul) if $\{\varphi_1, \ldots, \varphi_n\} \vdash \varphi$.

Lemma 3. *If "from $\varphi_1, \ldots, \varphi_n$ infer φ" is a rule derivable from the ordinary Armstrong axioms (see [12]) then replacing symbols of sets by symbols of fuzzy sets, the resulting rule is derivable from* (Ax) *and* (Cut).

Proof. It follows from [10] that each deduction rule derivable from the ordinary Armstrong axioms is derivable from (Ax_c) and (Cut_c) where (Ax_c) and (Cut_c) result from (Ax) and (Cut) by replacing fuzzy sets by ordinary sets. Now, observe that replacing ordinary sets with fuzzy sets in any proof from (Ax_c) and (Cut_c), we get a proof from (Ax) and (Cut).

Remark 4. Lemma 3 shows that, for instance, the following deduction rules are derivable from (Ax) and (Cut):

(Ref) infer $A \Rightarrow A$,
(Wea) from $A \Rightarrow B$ infer $A \cup C \Rightarrow B$,
(Add) from $A \Rightarrow B$ and $A \Rightarrow C$ infer $A \Rightarrow B \cup C$,
(Pro) from $A \Rightarrow B \cup C$ infer $A \Rightarrow B$,
(Tra) from $A \Rightarrow B$ and $B \Rightarrow C$ infer $A \Rightarrow C$,

for each $A, B, C, D \in \mathbf{L}^Y$.

4.2 Completeness

A deduction rule "from $\varphi_1, \ldots, \varphi_n$ infer φ" is said to be *sound* if

$$\mathrm{Mod}(\{\varphi_1, \ldots, \varphi_n\}) \subseteq \mathrm{Mod}(\{\varphi\}),$$

i.e. if each model of all $\varphi_1, \ldots, \varphi_n$ is also a model of φ.

Lemma 4. *Each of the rules* (Ax)–(Mul) *is sound.*

Proof. Omitted due to lack of space (proof is straightforward from definitions).

Let T be a set of FDs. T is called *syntactically closed* if $T \vdash A \Rightarrow B$ iff $A \Rightarrow B \in T$, i.e. if $T = \{A \Rightarrow B \,|\, T \vdash A \Rightarrow B\}$. T is called *semantically closed* if $||A \Rightarrow B||_T = 1$ iff $A \Rightarrow B \in T$, i.e. if $T = \{A \Rightarrow B \,|\, ||A \Rightarrow B||_T = 1\}$.

Lemma 5. *Let T be a set of FDs. If T is semantically closed then T is syntactically closed.*

Proof. Sketch: First it can be shown that a set T of FDs is syntactically closed iff we have: $A \cup B \Rightarrow A \in T$; if $A \Rightarrow B \in T$ and $B \cup C \Rightarrow D \in T$ then $A \cup C \Rightarrow D \in T$; if $A \Rightarrow B \in T$ then $c^* \otimes A \Rightarrow c^* \otimes B \in T$, for each $A, B, C, D \in \mathbf{L}^Y$, and $c \in L$. These conditions are satisfied for if "from $\varphi_1, \ldots, \varphi_n$ infer φ" is one of (Ax)–(Mul), then if $\varphi_1, \ldots \varphi_n \in T$, we have $\mathrm{Mod}(T) \subseteq \mathrm{Mod}(\{\varphi_1, \ldots \varphi_n\}) \subseteq \mathrm{Mod}(\{\varphi\})$

by soundness of (Ax)–(Mul). This says each model of T is a model of φ, i.e. $||\varphi||_T = 1$. Since T is semantically closed, i.e. $T = \{A \Rightarrow B \mid ||A \Rightarrow B||_T = 1\}$, we get $\varphi \in T$.

Lemma 6. *Let T be a set of FDs, let both Y and L be finite. If T is syntactically closed then T is semantically closed.*

Proof. Sketch: Let T be syntactically closed. In order to show that T is semantically closed, it suffices to show $\{A \Rightarrow B \mid ||A \Rightarrow B||_T = 1\} \subseteq T$. We prove this by showing that if $A \Rightarrow B \notin T$ then $A \Rightarrow B \notin \{A \Rightarrow B \mid ||A \Rightarrow B||_T = 1\}$. By Lemma 4, since T is syntactically closed, it is closed under all of the rules which result from Armstrong axioms (and thus also their consequences) by replacing sets with fuzzy sets. Let thus $A \Rightarrow B \notin T$. To see $A \Rightarrow B \notin \{A \Rightarrow B \mid ||A \Rightarrow B||_T = 1\}$, we show that there is $\mathcal{D} \in \mathrm{Mod}(T)$ which is not a model of $A \Rightarrow B$. For this purpose, let first A^+ be the largest fuzzy set C such that $A \Rightarrow C \in T$. A^+ exists. Namely, $V = \{C \mid A \Rightarrow C \in T\}$ is non-empty since $A \Rightarrow A \in T$ by (Ref), V is finite by finiteness of Y and L, and for $A \Rightarrow C_1, \ldots, A \Rightarrow C_n \in T$, we have $A \Rightarrow \bigcup_{i=1}^n C_i \in T$ by a repeated use of (Add). Now, take a data table $\mathcal{D}$ with $X = \{x_1, x_2\}$ such that for $y \in Y$ we have: if $A^+(y) = 1$ then $D_y = \{a\}$, $T(x_1, y) = T(x_2, y) = a$, $a \approx_y a = 1$; if $A^+(y) \neq 1$ then $D_y = \{a, b\}$, $T(x_1, y) = a$, $T(x_2, y) = b$, $a \approx_y a = b \approx_y b = 1$, $a \approx_y b = b \approx_y a = A^+(y)$. Then for each $y \in Y$, $\approx_y$ is reflexive and symmetric (and even transitive).

Now, it can be shown that $\mathcal{D}$ is a model of T but not of $A \Rightarrow B$ (details omitted due to lack of space).

We thus have completeness of (Ax)–(Mul).

Theorem 1 (completeness). *Let $\mathbf{L}$ and Y be finite. Let T be a set of FDs. Then*

$$T \vdash A \Rightarrow B \quad \textit{iff} \quad ||A \Rightarrow B||_T = 1.$$

Proof. Sketch: Denote by $syn(T)$ the least syntactically closed set of FDs which contains T. It can be shown that $syn(T) = \{A \Rightarrow B \mid T \vdash A \Rightarrow B\}$. Furthermore, denote by $sem(T)$ the least semantically closed set of FDs which contains T. It can be shown that $sem(T) = \{A \Rightarrow B \mid ||A \Rightarrow B||_T = 1\}$. To prove the claim, we need to show $syn(T) = sem(T)$. As $syn(T)$ is syntactically closed, it is also semantically closed by Lemma 6 which means $sem(syn(T)) \subseteq syn(T)$. Therefore, by $T \subseteq syn(T)$ we get

$$sem(T) \subseteq sem(syn(T)) \subseteq syn(T).$$

In a similar manner we get $syn(T) \subseteq sem(T)$, showing $syn(T) = sem(T)$. The proof is complete.

4.3 Graded Completeness

Theorem 1 says that for an *ordinary set* T and a FD $A \Rightarrow B$, $A \Rightarrow B$ follows from T *in degree 1* iff $A \Rightarrow B$ is provable from T. A question is whether for a *fuzzy set* T, *a degree to which* $A \Rightarrow B$ *follows from* T can be somehow approximated using a suitable notion of a proof [8, 9]. In this section, we will see that this is possible, i.e. that (Ax)–(Mul) obey even *completeness in degrees.*

For a fuzzy set T of FDs and for $A \Rightarrow B$ define a *degree* $|A \Rightarrow B|_T \in L$ *to which* $A \Rightarrow B$ *is provable from* T by

$$|A \Rightarrow B|_T = \bigvee\{c \in L \mid \mathrm{c}(T) \vdash A \Rightarrow c \otimes B\}, \tag{10}$$

where $\mathrm{c}(T)$ is defined by (5). The following theorem shows that the concept of a degree of provability coincides with that of a degree of semantic entailment.

Theorem 2 (graded completeness). *Let* $\mathbf{L}$ *and* Y *be finite. Then for every fuzzy set* T *of fuzzy attribute implications and* $A \Rightarrow B$ *we have* $|A \Rightarrow B|_T = ||A \Rightarrow B||_T$.

Proof. Consequence of Lemma 2 and Theorem 1.

5 Computing Non-redundant Bases of All True Functional Dependencies

In the previous sections, we showed that semantic entailment from sets of functional dependencies can be characterized syntactically (by a suitably defined notion of provability / provability degree), i.e. we showed a *completeness* of (Ax)–(Mul). In knowledge engineering, completeness is used still in another sense: "complete" means "fully describing all dependencies which are true in a given data table / model". Therefore, call a set T of functional dependencies *complete in* $\mathcal{D}$ if

$$||A \Rightarrow B||_T = ||A \Rightarrow B||_{\mathcal{D}} \tag{11}$$

for each $A \Rightarrow B$ (degree to which $A \Rightarrow B$ semantically follows from T equals degree to which $A \Rightarrow B$ is true in $\mathcal{D}$). Thus, a set T which is complete in $\mathcal{D}$ conveys all information about dependencies in $\mathcal{D}$ via the concept of semantic entailment. Moreover, if T is complete in $\mathcal{D}$ and no proper subset of T is complete in $\mathcal{D}$, we call T a *non-redundant basis of* $\mathcal{D}$. In other words, a non-redundant basis T is a complete set from which one cannot remove any $A \Rightarrow B \in T$ without losing completeness. From this point of view, we are interested in finding non-redundant bases because they are basically "the minimal sets of FDs conveying the maximal information about $\mathcal{D}$".

Note if T is complete w.r.t. $\mathcal{D}$, it follows immediately from Theorem 1 and the definition of completeness w.r.t. $\mathcal{D}$ that an arbitrary FD $A \Rightarrow B$ can be proved from T using (Ax)–(Mul) iff $A \Rightarrow B$ is true in $\mathcal{D}$ in degree 1.

In the sequel we show a way to compute a non-redundant basis of any $\mathcal{D}$. Since the proofs are technically involved, we omit them due to lack of space.

Given an $\mathbf{L}$-set B of attributes, we define a binary $\mathbf{L}$-relation $\mathrm{Eq}(B)$ on X (rows of $\mathcal{D}$) as follows

$$(\mathrm{Eq}(B))(x, x') = x(B) \approx x'(B). \tag{12}$$

Eq(B) is a binary **L**-relation indicating *similarity of table rows* on attributes from B, cf. (2). For any binary **L**-relation *Sim* on X we define an **L**-set At(*Sim*) of attributes by

$$(\mathrm{At}(Sim))(y) = \bigwedge_{x,x'}(Sim(x,x') \rightarrow (x[y] \approx_y x'[y])). \tag{13}$$

If *Sim* is interpreted as a similarity relation, $(\mathrm{At}(Sim))(y)$ is a truth degree of "any table rows which are *Sim*-similar are also *Sim*-similar on the value of attribute y". Finally, we define an operator $\mathrm{C}\colon \mathbf{L}^Y \rightarrow \mathbf{L}^Y$ (i.e., C is an operator on **L**-sets of attributes) as follows

$$\mathrm{C}(B) = \mathrm{At}((\mathrm{Eq}(B))^*). \tag{14}$$

In words, $(\mathrm{C}(B))(y)$ is a truth degree of proposition: "any table rows which are (very) similar on attributes from B are also similar on the value of attribute y". It can be shown that Eq, At, and C given by (12), (13), and (14), respectively, have the following properties (for the notions involved, see e.g. [7]):

Theorem 3. Eq *and* At *form a Galois connection.* C *is a closure operator.* □

It can be shown that the set $T = \{B \Rightarrow \mathrm{C}(B) \mid B \in \mathbf{L}^Y\}$ of functional dependencies is complete in $\mathcal{D}$. However, T is not interesting since it is too large and redundant. Nevertheless, T contains non-redundant bases which are based on the following concept.

For any $M \in \mathbf{L}^Y$ (i.e., M is an fuzzy set of attributes) define a data table $\mathcal{D}_M = \langle X, Y, \{\langle D_y, \approx_y\rangle \mid y \in Y\}, T\rangle$ where

- $X = \{x, x'\}$,
- for $y \in Y$, if $M(y) = 1$ then $D_y = \{a\}$, $a \approx_y a = 1$, $T(x,y) = a$, and $T(x',y) = a$,
- for $y \in Y$, if $M(y) \neq 1$ then $D_y = \{a,b\}$, $a \approx_y a = b \approx_y b = 1$, $a \approx_y b = b \approx_y a = M(y)$, $T(x,y) = a$, and $T(x',y) = b$.

Given a data table $\mathcal{D}$ over domains with similarities, $\mathcal{P} \subseteq \mathbf{L}^Y$ (a system of fuzzy sets of attributes) is called a *system of pseudo-intents of* $\mathcal{D}$ if for each $P \in \mathbf{L}^Y$ we have:

$$\begin{aligned} P \in \mathcal{P} \quad \text{iff} \quad & P \neq \mathrm{C}(P) \text{ and } ||Q \Rightarrow \mathrm{C}(Q)||_{\mathcal{D}_P} = 1 \\ & \text{for each } Q \in \mathcal{P} \text{ with } Q \neq P. \end{aligned}$$

The following assertion says that in order to get a non-redundant basis it suffices to pick from $\{B \Rightarrow \mathrm{C}(B) \mid B \in \mathbf{L}^Y\}$ only those FDs where B's belong to a system of pseudo-intents:

Theorem 4. *Let* $\mathcal{D} = \langle X, Y, \{\langle D_y, \approx_y\rangle \mid y \in Y\}, T\rangle$ *be a data table over domains with similarities,* $\mathcal{P}$ *be a system of pseudo-intents of* $\mathcal{D}$*. Then* $T = \{P \Rightarrow \mathrm{C}(P) \mid P \in \mathcal{P}\}$ *is a non-redundant basis of* $\mathcal{D}$*.* □

We now show a way to compute a system of pseudo-intents in an efficient way. For brevity, we discuss only particular case for a hedge * being globalization, i.e.

$a^* = 1$ for $a = 1$ and $a^* = 0$ for $a \neq 1$. First, if * is globalization then C can be described as follows

$$(\mathrm{C}(B))(y) = \bigwedge\{x[y] \approx_y x'[y] \mid x < x', \text{ and } \text{for any } y' \in Y\colon B(y') \leq x[y'] \approx_y x'[y']\}.$$

Furthermore, define an operator $cl_{T^*} : \mathbf{L}^Y \to \mathbf{L}^Y$ (operator on fuzzy sets of attributes) by putting for each $Z \in \mathbf{L}^Y$:

$$Z^{T^*} = Z \cup \bigcup\{B \otimes S(A, Z)^* \mid A \Rightarrow B \in T \text{ and } A \neq Z\},$$

$$Z^{T^*_n} = \begin{cases} Z & \text{if } n = 0, \\ (Z^{T^*_{n-1}})^{T^*} & \text{if } n \geq 1, \end{cases}$$

$$cl_{T^*}(Z) = \bigcup_{n=0}^{\infty} Z^{T^*_n}.$$

The existence and uniqueness of $\mathcal{P}$ is characterized by the following assertion.

Theorem 5. *Let* $\mathbf{L}$ *be a finite linearly ordered residuated lattice with globalization,* $\mathcal{D} = \langle X, Y, \{\langle D_y, \approx_y\rangle \mid y \in Y\}, T\rangle$ *be a data table over domains with similarities. Then*

(i) *there is a unique system* $\mathcal{P}$ *of pseudo-intents of* $\mathcal{D}$;
(ii) *for* $T = \{P \Rightarrow \mathrm{C}(P) \mid P \in \mathcal{P}\}$, cl_{T^*} *is a closure operator and* $\mathcal{P} \cup \{\mathrm{C}(M) \mid M \in \mathbf{L}^Y\}$ *is the set of all its fixpoints.* □

Hence, in case of globalization and finite linearly ordered structure of truth degrees, one can find $\mathcal{P}$ as a subset of fixpoints of a closure operator. This can be done with polynomial time delay by the following algorithm (inspired by Ganter's NextClosure algorithm [7]):

Algorithm 1.
Input: $\mathcal{D}$ (data table over dom. with similarity relations).
Output: $\mathcal{P}$ (system of pseudo-intents).

$B := \emptyset$
if $B \neq \mathrm{C}(B)$: *add* B *to* $\mathcal{P}$
while $B \neq Y$:
  $T := \{P \Rightarrow \mathrm{C}(P) \mid P \in \mathcal{P}\}$
  $B := B^+$ (B^+ is lectically smallest fixed point of cl_{T^*} which is a successor of B)
  if $B \neq \mathrm{C}(B)$: *add* B *to* $\mathcal{P}$

The efficiency of the previous algorithm depends on computation of $cl_{T^*}(Z)$. A straightforward method to compute $cl_{T^*}(Z)$ leads to an algorithm similar to the CLOSURE algorithm known from database systems [12]. An improved version of CLOSURE, also known as LINCLOSURE [12], can also be adopted in our setting. This and related topics will be discussed in a forthcoming paper.

6 Illustrative Examples

Consider again Tab. 1. To get a data table $\mathcal{D} = \langle X, Y, \{\langle D_y, \approx_y\rangle \mid y \in Y\}, T\rangle$ over domains with similarity relations, denote by X and Y the sets of planets and their attributes, respectively, put $D_y = [0, \infty)$ for each $y \in Y$, and consider Fig. 1. Fig. 1 depicts similarities on the domains D_y. The similarities $\approx_y$ on domains D_y can be described as follows: As a structure of truth degrees, take a real unit interval $[0, 1]$ equipped with Łukasiewicz operations and globalization, and denote by E_a^b a fuzzy set in $[0, \infty)$ defined by

$$E_a^b(x) = \begin{cases} 1 & \text{if } x < a, \\ \frac{b-x}{b-a} & \text{if } x \geq a \text{ and } x \leq b, \\ 0 & \text{otherwise.} \end{cases}$$

E_a^b expresses that if the distance between two reals drops below a, then the reals are indistinguishable (with respect to E_a^b); if the distance exceeds b, the reals are fully distinct (with respect to E_a^b); reals with distances between a and b are given proportional truth degrees between 1 and 0. Thus, for any real numbers x_1 and x_2 we can define their E_a^b-similarity degree to be $E_a^b(|x_1 - x_2|)$, i.e. the degree to which $|x_1 - x_2|$ belongs to E_a^b. This says that two objects are similar to a degree to which is it true that the objects are "close". Now, the curves depicted in Fig. 1 correspond to similarities defined as follows:

$$x_1 \approx_s x_2 = E_{50}^{500}(|x_1 - x_2|), \quad x_1 \approx_d x_2 = E_{5000}^{20000}(|x_1 - x_2|),$$
$$x_1 \approx_w x_2 = E_1^{10}(|x_1 - x_2|), \quad x_1 \approx_m x_2 = E_1^5(|x_1 - x_2|),$$

where $s \in Y$ denotes distance from sun, $d \in Y$ denotes diameter, $w \in Y$ denotes weight, and $m \in Y$ denotes number of moons. For instance, if x_1 denotes *Earth* and x_2 denotes *Mars* then "$x_1[m] \approx_m x_2[m] = 1$" (i.e., proposition "Earth and Mars have similar number of moons" is fully true), "$x_1[s] \approx_m x_2[s] \doteq 0.93$" (i.e., proposition "Earth and Mars have similar distance from sun" is true in degree 0.93), etc. Note that "being similar" is subjective and that we can replace the above similarities by other ones.

For technical reasons, we round the exact values of $L = [0, 1]$ from $\approx_y$ $(y \in Y)$ down to values of $L = \{0, 0.1, 0.2, \ldots, 0.9, 1\}$. This way we obtain a finite linearly ordered structure of truth degrees with globalization suitable to generate the non-redundant basis of $\mathcal{D}$. In our case, the basis obtained by Algorithm 1 contains the following formulas (for brevity, we do not repeat attributes from premises,

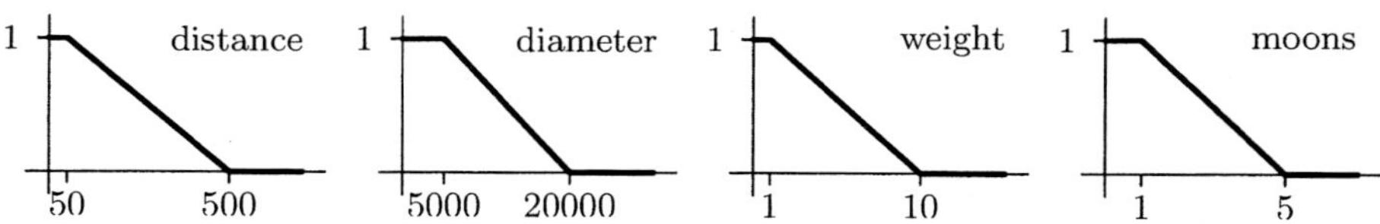

Fig. 1. Similarity relations

i.e. instead of FD $A \Rightarrow B$, we list a FD $A \Rightarrow B'$ where B' results from B by deleting all y with $A(y) = B(y)$):

$$\{s, {}^{0.8}\!/d, w, m\} \Rightarrow \{d\}, \qquad \{{}^{0.9}\!/s, {}^{0.8}\!/d, w, {}^{0.7}\!/m\} \Rightarrow \{m\},$$
$$\{{}^{0.8}\!/s, d, w, {}^{0.7}\!/m\} \Rightarrow \{s, m\}, \qquad \{{}^{0.7}\!/s, {}^{0.8}\!/d, w, m\} \Rightarrow \{{}^{0.9}\!/s\},$$
$$\{{}^{0.1}\!/s\} \Rightarrow \{{}^{0.7}\!/s, {}^{0.8}\!/d, w, {}^{0.7}\!/m\}, \qquad \{{}^{0.7}\!/d, {}^{0.8}\!/w\} \Rightarrow \{{}^{0.8}\!/d\},$$
$$\{{}^{0.6}\!/d, w, {}^{0.8}\!/m\} \Rightarrow \{m\}, \qquad \{{}^{0.6}\!/d, {}^{0.9}\!/w\} \Rightarrow \{w, {}^{0.7}\!/m\},$$
$$\{{}^{0.4}\!/d\} \Rightarrow \{{}^{0.6}\!/d, {}^{0.8}\!/w\}, \qquad \{{}^{0.1}\!/d\} \Rightarrow \{{}^{0.3}\!/d\},$$
$$\{{}^{0.1}\!/w\} \Rightarrow \{{}^{0.6}\!/d, {}^{0.8}\!/w\}, \qquad \{{}^{0.1}\!/m\} \Rightarrow \{{}^{0.6}\!/d, w, {}^{0.7}\!/m\}.$$

A FD $A \Rightarrow B$ holds in $\mathcal{D}$ in degree to which follows (syntactically/semantically) from the above-mentioned FDs. One can see that all of the FDs of the basis have a natural meaning in the data table $\mathcal{D}$.

For instance, $\{{}^{0.1}\!/m\} \Rightarrow \{{}^{0.6}\!/d, w, {}^{0.7}\!/m\}$, says "if the numbers of moons are similar in degree (at least) 0.1, then the diameters are similar in degree 0.6, the weights are fully similar, and the numbers of moons are similar in degree 0.7". Taking into account the underlying similarities, the formula can be read:

$$\text{“if } |x[m] - x[m]| \leq 4 \text{ then } |x[d] - x'[d]| \leq 11000,$$
$$|x[w] - x'[w]| \leq 1, \text{ and } |x[m] - x'[m] \leq 2|\text{”},$$

i.e., the implication says: "if the difference between numbers of moons of x and x' is at most 4 then the difference between their diameters is at most 11000, the difference between their weights is at most one weight of Earth, and the difference between numbers of moons is at most 2.

7 Concluding Remarks

We introduced functional dependencies for data tables over domains with similarity relations. We presented basic semantic notions (validity, entailment), a complete axiom system, description of non-redundant bases of all functional dependencies which are true in a given table, and presented an algorithm for its computation. In addition to that, in a full version of this paper, we will show

- other complete systems of derivation rules;
- algorithm and related results for other hedges than globalization;
- complete proofs of our theorems.

Note that in a related paper [5] we show a close connection to so-called attribute implications which makes it possible to reduce some problems considered here to analogous problems of fuzzy attribute implications. Our future research will focus on:

- algorithms for various problems of FDs ([12] is a good survey of problems and algorithms in classical FDs);
- further types of data dependencies in a fuzzy setting, like multivalued dependencies (cf. [6]).

References

1. Abiteboul S. *et al.*: The Lowell database research self-assessment. *Communications of ACM* **48**(5)(2005), 111–118.
2. Armstrong W. W.: Dependency structures in data base relationships. *IFIP Congress*, Geneva, Switzerland, 1974, pp. 580–583.
3. Bělohlávek R.: *Fuzzy Relational Systems: Foundations and Principles.* Kluwer, Academic/Plenum Publishers, New York, 2002.
4. Bělohlávek R., Chlupová M., Vychodil V.: Implications from data with fuzzy attributes. AISTA 2004 in Cooperation with the IEEE Computer Society Proceedings, 2004, 5 pages, ISBN 2–9599776–8–8.
5. Bělohlávek R., Vychodil V.: Functional dependencies of data tables over domains with similarity relations (to appear).
6. Buckles B. P., Petry F. E.: Fuzzy databases in the new era. Proceedings of the 1995 ACM symposium on Applied computing, pp. 497–502, Nashville, Tennessee, ISBN 0-89791-658-1, 1995.
7. Ganter B., Wille R.: *Formal Concept Analysis. Mathematical Foundations.* Springer, Berlin, 1999.
8. Gerla G.: *Fuzzy Logic. Mathematical Tools for Approximate Reasoning.* Kluwer, Dordrecht, 2001.
9. Hájek P.: *Metamathematics of Fuzzy Logic.* Kluwer, Dordrecht, 1998.
10. Holzer R.: Knowledge Acquisition under Incomplete Knowledge using Methods from Formal Concept Analysis: Part I. *Fundamenta Informaticae,* **63**(1)(2004), 17–39.
11. Klir G. J., Yuan B.: *Fuzzy Sets and Fuzzy Logic. Theory and Applications.* Prentice Hall, 1995.
12. Maier D.: *The Theory of Relational Databases.* Computer Science Press, Rockville, 1983.
13. Prade H., Testemale C.: Generalizing database relational algebra for the treatment of incomplete or uncertain information and vague queries. *Information Sciences* **34**(1984), 115–143.
14. Raju K. V. S. V. N., Majumdar A. K.: Fuzzy functional dependencies and lossless join decomposition of fuzzy relational database systems. *ACM Trans. Database Systems* Vol. 13, No. 2, 1988, pp. 129–166.
15. Tyagi B. K., Sharfuddin A., Dutta R. N., Tayal D. K.: A complete axiomatization of fuzzy functional dependencies using fuzzy function. *Fuzzy Sets and Systems* **151**(2)(2005), 363–379.

Reuse or Never Reuse the Deleted Labels in XML Query Processing Based on Labeling Schemes

Changqing Li[1], Tok Wang Ling[1], and Min Hu[2]

[1] Dept. of CS, National University of Singapore, Singapore, 117543
{lichangq, lingtw}@comp.nus.edu.sg
[2] Dept. of COFM, National University of Singapore, Singapore, 119260
g0406391@nus.edu.sg

Abstract. To facilitate the XML query processing, several kinds of labeling schemes have been proposed. Based on the labeling schemes, the ancestor-descendant and parent-child relationships in XML queries can be quickly determined without accessing the original XML file. Recently, more researches are focused on how to update the labels when nodes are inserted into the XML. However how to process the deleted labels are not discussed previously. We think that the deleted labels can be processed in two different directions: (1) reuse all the deleted labels to control the label size increasing speed and improve the query performance; (2) never reuse the deleted labels to query different versions of the XML data based on labeling schemes. In this paper, we firstly introduce our previous work, called QED, which can completely avoid the re-labeling in XML updates. Secondly based on QED we propose a new algorithm, called Reuse, which can reuse all the deleted labels to control the label size increasing speed; meanwhile the Reuse algorithm can completely avoid the re-labeling also. Thirdly to query different versions of the XML data, we propose another new algorithm, called NeverReuse, which is the only approach that never reuses any deleted labels. Extensive experimental results show that the algorithms proposed in this paper can control the label size increasing speed when reusing all the deleted labels, and is the only approach to query different versions of the XML data based on labeling schemes.

1 Introduction

XML query processing has been thoroughly studied in the past few years. Many techniques, e.g. structural index [11, 12] and labeling scheme [1, 6, 18], have been proposed to facilitate XML queries. The structural index is a structure summary from the original data which can help to traverse the hierarchy of XML, but this traversal is costly and the overhead of the traversal can be substantial if the path lengths are very long or unknown. On the other hand, The labeling scheme requires smaller storage space, yet it can efficiently determine the ancestor-descendant (A-D) and parent-child (P-C) relationships between any two elements of the XML. In this paper, we focus on the labeling scheme.

Recently how to efficiently update the XML has gained a lot of attention [2, 6, 8, 13, 14, 15, 18]. Different algorithms have been proposed to decrease the update cost,

M.L. Lee, K.L. Tan, and V. Wuwongse (Eds.): DASFAA 2006, LNCS 3882, pp. 659 – 673, 2006.

however the updates are focused on how to process the labels when a node is *inserted* into the XML. How to process the deleted labels is not considered in the previous researches.

We think that the deleted labels can be processed in two different directions: (1) reuse all the deleted labels to control the label size increasing speed; (2) never reuse the deleted labels to query different versions of the XML. Thus the objective of this paper is to propose algorithms to process the deleted labels in these two different directions, and meanwhile to keep the low update cost.

The main contributions of this paper are summarized as follows:

- We propose a new algorithm which can reuse all the deleted labels. In this way, we control the label size increasing speed when nodes are deleted and inserted in the XML data. This Reuse algorithm need not re-label the existing nodes in updates.
- We propose another new algorithm that is the first one which never reuses the deleted labels; it is the only approach that truly maintains different XML label versions and supports the query of different XML versions based on labeling schemes.
- We conduct several experiments which show that the Reuse algorithm can efficiently control the label size increasing speed, and the NeverReuse algorithm can truly maintain the different label versions (the labels in different versions are unique).

The rest of the paper is organized as follows. Section 2 reviews the related work. We introduce our previous work on how to update the XML without re-labeling the existing nodes and give the motivation of this paper in Section 3. In Section 4, We propose the algorithm to reuse all the deleted labels which can control the label size increasing speed in the update environment with both insertions and deletions. We propose another algorithm which never reuses the deleted labels and accordingly supports the query of different XML versions based on labeling schemes in Section 5. The experimental results are illustrated in Section 6, and we conclude in Section 7.

2 Related Work

2.1 XML Labeling Schemes

We present three families of XML labeling schemes, namely containment [1, 9, 19, 20], prefix [6, 13, 15] and prime [18].

Containment Scheme. Zhang et al [20] use a labeling scheme in which every node is assigned three values: "start", "end" and "level". For any two nodes u and v, u is an ancestor of v iff u.start < v.start and v.end < u.end. In other words, the interval of v is contained in the interval of u. Node u is a parent of node v iff u is an ancestor of v and v.level – u.level = 1.

In Figure 1, "5,6,3" is a child of "2,7,2" since interval [5, 6] is contained in interval [2, 7] and levels 3 – 2 = 1.

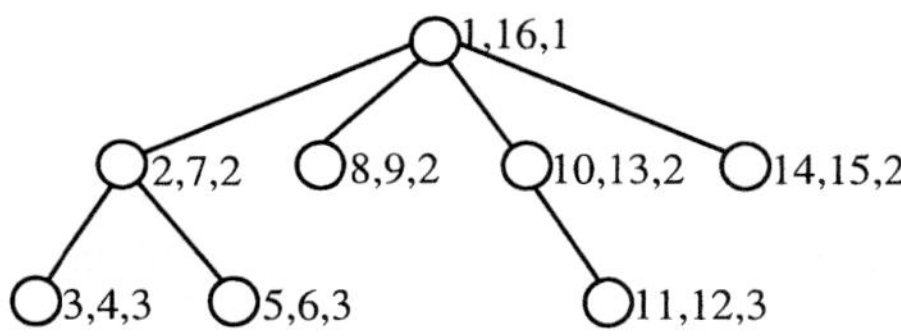

Fig. 1. Containment scheme

Although the containment scheme is efficient to determine the ancestor-descendant relationship, the insertion of a node will lead to a re-labeling of all the ancestor nodes of this inserted node and all the nodes after this inserted node in document order. This problem may be alleviated if the interval size is increased with some values unused. However, large interval sizes waste a lot of numbers which causes the increase of storage, while small interval sizes are easy to lead to re-labeling.

To solve the re-labeling problem, [2] uses Float-point values for the "start" and "end" of the interval. It seems that Float-point solves the re-labeling problem [15]. But in practice, the Float-point is represented in a computer with a fixed number of bits [2, 15]. As a result, only 18 values [2] can be inserted between any two real values since [2] uses the consecutive integer values at the initial labeling. Even if [2] uses values with large gaps, it still can not avoid the re-labeling due to the float-point precision. Therefore, using real values instead of integers does not provide any benefit for the node updating [15, 18].

When a node is inserted at a place where a node has ever been deleted, it is natural for the containment scheme to reuse the deleted labels to reduce the storage space. On the other hand, if we need to maintain different XML versions, we should not use the deleted labels in the previous XML versions. All the current containment labeling schemes can not achieve this objective since there are a finite number of values between any two values in a computer; when the finite number of values are used up, the current containment schemes have to reuse the deleted labels or re-label the nodes.

Prefix Scheme. In the prefix labeling scheme, the label of a node is that its parent's label (prefix) concatenates its own (self) label. For any two nodes u and v, u is an ancestor of v iff label(u) is a prefix of label(v). Node u is a parent of node v iff label(v) has no prefix when removing label(u) from the left side of label(v).

DeweyID [15] labels the nth child of a node with an integer n, and this n should be concatenated to the prefix (its parent's label) to form the complete label of this child node.

OrdPath [13] is similar to DeweyID, but it only uses the odd numbers at the initial labeling. When the XML tree is updated, it uses the even number between two odd numbers to concatenate another odd number for the inserted node. OrdPath wastes many numbers which makes its label size larger. The query performance of OrdPath is worse as it needs more time to decide the prefix levels based on the odd and even numbers (see [7] for the experimental results).

Cohen et al [6] uses Binary String to label the nodes (called BinaryString in this paper). The root of the tree is labeled with an empty string. The first child of the root is labeled with "0", the second child with "10", the third with "110", and the fourth with "1110" etc. Similarly for any node u, the first child of u is labeled with label(u)."0", the second child of u is labeled with label(u)."10", and the ith child with label(u)."$1^{i-1}0$".

When a node is inserted into the XML, DeweyID and BinaryString need to re-label the sibling nodes after this inserted node and the descendants of these siblings. Though OrdPath need not re-label the existing nodes, it increases the label size and decreases the query performance.

It is natural for DeweyID and BinaryString to reuse the deleted labels, but when all the labels between two labels are used up, they have to re-label the existing nodes. Therefore they can not truly maintain the different label versions of the XML since they need re-labeling. OrdPath can reuse the deleted labels, but it does not consider how to avoid reusing the deleted labels.

Prime Scheme. Wu et al [18] use Prime numbers to label XML trees. The root node is labeled with "1" (integer). Based on a top-down approach, each node is given a unique prime number (self_label) and the label of each node is the product of its parent node's label (parent_label) and its own self_label. For any two nodes u and v, u is an ancestor of v iff label(v) mod label(u) = 0. Node u is a parent of node v iff label(v)/self_label(v) = label(u).

We have compared Prime with other labeling schemes in [7]. Prime has very bad query performance because it has very large label size and it employs the modular and division operations to determine the ancestor-descendant and parent-child relationships. Its update performance is also much worse (see [7]). Therefore we do not discuss Prime further in this paper.

QED. In [7], we propose a compact dynamic binary string approach to efficiently process XML updates, furthermore we propose a dynamic quaternary encoding (called QED) in [8] which can *completely* (no overflow problem) avoid the re-labeling when a node is inserted into the XML. We will in detail introduce QED in Section 3, and the *reuse* and *never reuse* algorithms in Sections 4 and 5 respectively are all based on QED.

2.2 XML Version Control

It is important to maintain and query different versions of the XML [3, 4, 5, 10, 16, 17]. The Reference-Based Version Model [4] discusses the storage performance of multiversion documents. [10] stores the latest version of a document and the sequence of changes of different versions of the XML. [3] queries the historical XML data in which parts of the XML data are always updated. All of these papers are about the version control of the documents. To the best of our knowledge, no one has ever studied how to maintain the different versions of the labels of labeling schemes and how to use the labeling scheme to query different versions of the XML data.

If we want to query different versions of the XML data based on labeling schemes, we should not reuse the deleted labels especially when the deleted labels have order relationships with the new inserted labels.

3 Preliminary and Motivation

Here we introduce our QED [8] based on examples.

3.1 Label the XML Based on QED

Definition 3.1 (Quaternary code). *Four numbers "0", "1", "2" and "3" are used in the code and each number is stored with two bits, i.e. "00", "01", "10" and "11".*

Definition 3.2 (QED code). *QED code is a quaternary code. The number "0" is used as the separator and only "1", "2" and "3" are used in the QED code itself.*

The separator "0" can be used to separate different codes, and it will never encounter the overflow problem, thus QED can completely avoid re-labeling (see [8] for more details). The most important feature of our QED encoding is that it is based on the lexicographical order for efficient updates.

Definition 3.3 (Lexicographical order $\prec$). *Given two Quaternary codes C_A and C_B, C_A is lexicographically equal to C_B iff they are exactly the same. C_A is said to be lexicographically smaller than C_B ($C_A \prec C_B$) iff*

a) "0" $\prec$ "1" $\prec$ "2" $\prec$ "3" (this is always true and is used by condition b)), or
b) compare C_A and C_B symbol by symbol from left to right. If the current symbol of C_A and the current symbol of C_B satisfy (a), then $C_A \prec C_B$ and stop the comparison, or
c) C_A is a prefix of C_B.

From Figure 1, it can be seen that the "start" and "end" values are from 1 to 16. Table 1 shows the QED codes for these 16 numbers, and the following steps are the details of how to get the QED codes. Note that 16 is only an example; any other number is well also. See [8] for the formal QED algorithms.

Step 1. In the encoding of the 16 numbers, we suppose there is one more number before number 1, say number 0, and one more number after number 16, say number 17.

Step 2. The $(1/3)^{th}$ number is encoded with "**2**", and the $(2/3)^{th}$ number is encoded with "**3**". The $(1/3)^{th}$ number is number **6**, which is calculated in this way, 6 = round(0+(17–0)/3). The $(2/3)^{th}$ number is number **11** (11 = round(0+(17–0)$\times$2/3)).

Step 3. The $(1/3)^{th}$ and $(2/3)^{th}$ numbers between number 0 and number 6 are number 2 (2 = round(0+(6–0)/3)) and number 4 (4 = round(0+(6–0)$\times$2/3)). The QED code of number 0 (left code) is now empty with size 0 and the QED code of number 6 (right code) is now "2" with size 1 (here 1 refers to 2 bits). This is **Case (a) where the left code size is smaller than the right code size**. In this case, the $(1/3)^{th}$ code is that we change the last symbol of the *right* code to "1" and concatenate one more "2", i.e. the code of number **2** is "***12***" ("2"$\rightarrow$"1" and "1"$\oplus$"2"$\rightarrow$"12"), and the $(2/3)^{th}$ code is that we change the last symbol of the *right* code to "1" and concatenate one more "3", i.e. the code of number **4** is "***13***" ("2"$\rightarrow$"1" and "1"$\oplus$"3"$\rightarrow$"13").

Table 1. QED encoding

Decimal number	QED codes
1	112
2	12
3	122
4	13
5	132
6	2
7	212
8	22
9	23
10	232
11	3
12	312
13	32
14	322
15	33
16	332

Step 4. The $(1/3)^{th}$ and $(2/3)^{th}$ numbers between numbers 6 and 11 are numbers 8 (8 = round(6+(11–6)/3)) and 9 (9 = round(6+(11–6)×2/3)). The QED code of number 6 (left code) is "2" with size 1 (here 1 refers to 2 bits) and the code of number 11 (right code) is "3" with size 1 (here 1 refers to 2 bits). This is **Case (b) where the left code size is larger than or equal to the right code size**. In this case, the $(1/3)^{th}$ code is that we directly contatenate one more "2" after the *left* code, i.e. the code of number **8** is "***22***" ("2" ⊕ "2" → "22"), and the $(2/3)^{th}$ code is that we directly concatenate one more "3" after the *left* code, i.e. the code of number **9** is "***23***" ("2" ⊕ "3" → "23").

Step 5. The $(1/3)^{th}$ and $(2/3)^{th}$ numbers between numbers 11 and 17 are numbers 13 (13 = round(11+(17–11)/3)) and 15 (15 = round(11+(17–11)×2/3)). The code of number 11 (left code) is "3" with size 1 and the code of number 17 (right code) is empty now with size 0. This is still **Case (b)**. Therefore the QED code of number **13** is "***32***" ("3" ⊕ "2" → "32"), and the code of number **15** is "***33***" ("3" ⊕ "3" → "33").

In this way, all the numbers will be encoded.

Lemma 3.1. *All the QED codes are ended with either "2" or "3".*

Theorem 3.1. *Our QED codes are lexicographically ordered.*

Example 3.1. The QED codes in Table 1 are lexicographically ordered from top to down. "132" ≺ "2" lexicographically because the comparison is from left to right, and the 1st symbol of "132" is "1", while the 1st symbol of "2" is "2". "23" ≺ "232" because "23" is a prefix of "232".

When we replace the "start"s and "end"s (1-16) in Figure 1 with our QED codes, and based on the lexicographical comparison, a QED containment scheme is formed.

3.2 Order-Sensitive Updates

The following algorithm shows how we can insert nodes without re-labeling the existing nodes.

Algorithm 1. AssignInsertedCode

Input: Left_Code, Right_Code

Output: Inserted_Code, such that Left_Code $\prec$ Inserted_Code $\prec$ Right_Code lexicographically.

Description:

```
 1: get the sizes, i.e. number of bits, of Left_Code and Right_Code
 2: if size(Left_Code) < size(Right_Code)  //size is the number of bits of the code
 3:    then Inserted_Code = the Right_Code with the last
                              symbol changed to "1" ⊕ "2"
 4: else if size(Left_Code) > size(Right_Code)
 5:    if the last symbol of Left_Code is "2"
 6:       then Inserted_Code = the Left_Code with the
                          last symbol changed from "2" to "3"
 7:    else if the last symbol of Left_Code is "3"
 8:       then Inserted_Code = Left_Code ⊕ "2"
 9: else if size(Left_Code) = size(Right_Code)
10:    then Inserted_Code = Left_Code ⊕ "2"
```

Fig. 2. AssignInsertedCode algorithm

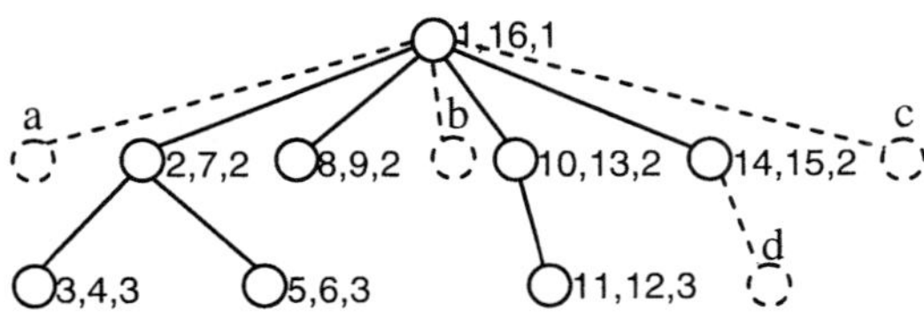

Fig. 3. Update

Example 3.2. When inserting node "**a**" (see Figure 3), we should insert a number between the "start" of the parent "1" (Left_Code) and the "start" of the first sibling "2" (Right_Code). If we use the existing approach, we can not insert a number between "1" and "2", and we must re-label the nodes. However, when referring to Table 1, our QED codes for "1" and "2" are "112" and "12". Based on the AssignInsertedCode algorithm, we insert a QED code between "112" and "12", then the "start" of the inserted node "a" is "**113**" (see lines 4-6 of the AssignInsertedCode algorithm in Figure 2). The "end" of node "a" is an insertion between the new "start" "113" and the "start" of the first sibling "12", thus the "end" of "a" is "**1132**" (see lines 4, 7 and 8 in Figure 2). Obviously, "112" $\prec$ "113" $\prec$ "1132" $\prec$ "12". We need not re-label any existing nodes, but we can keep the containment scheme working correctly. It is similar for the insertions of nodes "b", "c" and "d".

3.3 Motivation

It can be seen that QED avoids the node re-labeling when a node is inserted into the XML. But it has the following deficiencies. QED does not consider how to process the deleted labels. The deleted label with larger size than its neighbor labels will be reused, but the deleted label with smaller size will not be reused.

Example 3.3. When we delete the QED code "12" between "112" and "122" (see Table 1) and want to insert another code at this place, the inserted code will be "1122" (see lines 9 and 10 in Figure 2). The deleted code "12" is not reused because it has smaller size than its neighbors ("112" and "122"), and the re-inserted code "1122" has larger size than the deleted code "12", therefore the size increases fast. On the other hand, if we delete the QED code "122" between "12" and "13" (see Table 1) and insert another code at this place, the inserted code is still "122" (see lines 9 and 10 in Figure 2). The deleted code "122" is reused because it has larger size than its neighbors ("12" and "13").

It is not good to process the deleted labels in this way. If we want to improve the query performance, all the deleted labels should be reused which will hinder the label size from increasing fast. On the other hand, if we want to query different versions of the XML, we should never reuse the deleted labels. That is to say, our current approach is not for the reuse objective and also not for the version control objective. Therefore in Sections 4 and 5, we propose algorithms to reuse the deleted labels and never reuse the deleted labels respectively.

4 Reuse the Deleted Labels (Reuse)

If there are no deletions, the original QED algorithm [8] (Algorithm 1 in this paper) can guarantee that the inserted label has the smallest size between two labels, also the cost of Algorithm 1 is very cheap which only needs to modify the last 2 bits of the neighbor label. However, if there are deletions, Algorithm 1 can not guarantee that the inserted label is with the smallest size. Figure 4 shows the Reuse algorithm. The idea of this algorithm is to find the *smallest* possible code *lexicographically between* two given codes by comparing left_code and right_code symbol by symbol from left to right. From Lemma 3.1, we know that all the QED codes can only be ended with either "2" or "3", therefore the cases and conditions in Figure 4 are complete.

Example 4.1. Suppose the QED code "12" between "112" and "122" (see Table 1) is deleted and we need to insert a new code between "112" and "122". The new inserted code is "1122" based on Algorithm 1 in Figure 2. The deleted code "12" is not reused. On the other hand, based on Algorithm 2 in Figure 4, we compare "112" and "122" symbol by symbol from left to right. The second symbol of left_code ("112") is "1" and the second symbol of right_code ("122") is "2" (see Case (d) in Figure 4). The difference position is at the 2nd symbol (see line 33 in Figure 4), therefore S_L = getPartCode(left_code, *P*, *P*) = getPartCode("112", 2, 2) = "1", i.e. the second symbol of "112", and S_R = getPartCode(right_code, *P*, *P*) = getPartCode("122", 2, 2) = "2". S_L == "1" and S_R == "2", hence the condition at line 36 in Figure 4 is satisfied. Based on line 37, temp_code = getPartCode(left_code, 1, *P*-1) $\oplus$ "2" = getPartCode("112", 1,

2-1) ⊕ "2" = "1" ⊕ "2" = "12". "12" $\prec$ "122" lexicographically, i.e. temp_code $\prec$ right_code lexicographically, therefore the condition at line 38 is satisfied. As a result, inserted_code = temp_code = "12". It can be seen the deleted code "12" is reused.

Algorithm 2. AssignInsertedCodeWithReuse

Input: left_code, right_code
Output: inserted_code (reuse the deleted code)

Description:

1: Case (a) left_code and right_code are both empty
2: inserted_code = "2"

3: Case (b) left_code is NOT empty but right_code is empty
4: **if** "2" does not appear in left_code //left_code contains "1" and "3", or contains only "3"
5: **if** all the symbols of left_code are "3"
6: **then** inserted_code = left_code ⊕ "2"
7: **else**
8: **then** denote the position of the firstly encountered "1" as P
9: inserted_code = getPartCode(left_code, 1, P-1) ⊕ "2"
10: **else if** "1" does not appear in left_code //left_code contains "2" and "3", or contains only "2", or contains only "3"; //the case that all the symbols of left_code are "3" has been discussed at line 5
11: **then** denote the position of the firstly encountered "2" as P
12: inserted_code = getPartCode(left_code, 1, P-1) ⊕ "3"
13: **else if** both "1" and "2" appear in left_code //left_code contains "1", "2" and "3", or contains only "1" and "2"
14: **then** denote the position of the firstly encountered "1" as P_A, and denote the position of the firstly encountered "2" as P_B
15: **if** $P_A < P_B$
16: **then** inserted_code = getPartCode(left_code, 1, P_A -1) ⊕ "2"
17: **else if** $P_A > P_B$ //note that P_A can not be equal to P_B
18: **then** inserted_code = getPartCode(left_code, 1, P_B -1) ⊕ "3"

19: Case (c) left_code is empty but right_code is NOT empty
20: **if** "2" does not appear in right_code //right_code contains "1" and "3", or contains only "3"
21: **then** denote the position of the firstly encountered "3" as P
22: inserted_code = getPartCode(right_code, 1, P-1) ⊕ "2"
23: **else if** "3" does not appear in right_code //right_code contains "1" and "2", or contains only "2"
24: **then** denote the position of the firstly encountered "2" as P
25: inserted_code = getPartCode(right_code, 1, P-1) ⊕ "12"
26: **else if** "2" and "3" both appear in right_code //right_code contains "1", "2" and "3", or contains only "2" and "3"
27: **then** denote the position of the firstly encountered "2" as P_A, and denote the position of the firstly encountered "3" as P_B
28: **if** $P_A < P_B$
29: **then** inserted_code = getPartCode(right_code, 1, P_A -1) ⊕ "12"
30: **else if** $P_A > P_B$ //note that P_A can not be equal to P_B
31: **then** inserted_code = getPartCode(right_code, 1, P_B -1) ⊕ "2"

32: Case (d) conditions (a) and (b) in Definition 3.3
33: denote the first difference position of left_code and right_code as P; in other words, getPartCode(left_code, 1, P-1) is equal to getPartCode(right_code, 1, P-1) and getPartCode(left_code, P, P) is different from getPartCode(right_code, P, P); denote getPartCode(left_code, P, P) as S_L ($Symbol_{Left}$) and getPartCode(right_code, P, P) as S_R ($Symbol_{Right}$)
34: **if** (S_L == "1") and (S_R == "3")
35: **then** inserted_code = getPartCode(left_code, 1, P-1) ⊕ "2"
36: **else if** (S_L == "1") and (S_R == "2")

Fig. 4. AssignInsertedCodeWithReuse algorithm

```
37: then temp_code = getPartCode(left_code, 1, P-1) ⊕ "2"
38:        if temp_code ≺ right_code lexicographically
39:           then inserted_code = temp_code
40:        else
41:           then suppose there is a temp_left_code which is equal to getPartCode(left_code, P,
                  left_code.size()) and suppose there is a temp_right_code which is empty
                  //left_code.size() return the total symbol number of left_code
42:               process temp_left_code and temp_right_code based on Case (b); denote the returned
                  result by Case (b) as temp_code
43:               inserted_code = getPartCode(left_code, 1, P) ⊕ temp_code
44: else if (S_L == "2") and (S_R == "3")
45: then temp_code = getPartCode(left_code, 1, P-1) ⊕ "3"
46:        if temp_code ≺ right_code lexicographically
47:           then inserted_code = temp_code
48:        else
49:           then suppose there is a temp_left_code which is equal to getPartCode(left_code, P,
                  left_code.size()) and suppose there is a temp_right_code which is empty
                  //left_code.size() return the total symbol number of left_code
50:               process temp_left_code and temp_right_code based on Case (b); denote the returned
                  result by Case (b) as temp_code
51:               inserted_code = getPartCode(left_code, 1, P) ⊕ temp_code

52: Case (e) condition (c) in Definition 3.3
53: left_code is a prefix of right_code; suppose there is a temp_left_code which is empty and suppose
there is a
    temp_right_code which is equal to getPartCode(right_code, left_code.size()+1, right_code.size())
54: process temp_left_code and temp_right_code based on Case (c); denote the returned result by Case
(c) as temp_code
55: inserted_code = getPartCode(right_code, 1, left_code.size()) ⊕ temp_code

Function getPartCode(code, P1, P2)
  1: return the symbols of code between position P1 and P2.
```

Fig. 4. (*continued*)

Theorem 4.1. *Algorithms 1 and 2 guarantee that the order can be kept no matter how many codes are inserted at any place of the QED codes.*

Example 4.2. After insertion, the new inserted code based on Algorithm 1 is "1122" and the new inserted code based on Algorithm 2 is "12". Based on Algorithm 1 or 2, we can insert infinite number of QED codes between "112" and "1122" and between "1122" and "122", or between "112" and "12" and between "12" and "122". That means that the Reuse algorithm in this paper can completely avoid the re-labeling also, yet it makes the label size increase slowly.

Theorem 4.2. *Suppose some codes are deleted between left_code and right_code, and suppose the minimum size of these deleted codes is MS. Algorithm 2 guarantees that the inserted code between left_code and right_code is with size MS.*

Example 4.3. Suppose the QED codes "212", "22" and "23" between "2" and "232" (see Table 1) are deleted and we need to insert a new code between "2" and "232". Based on Algorithm 2 in Figure 4, left_code "2" is a prefix of right_code "232", thus it is Case (e). Based on line 53, temp_left_code is empty and temp_right_code = getPartCode(right_code, *left_code.size()*+1, *right_code.size()*) = getPartCode("232", 1+1, 3) = "32". Based on line 54, we need to go to Case (c). The condition at line 26 is satisfied. When we go to line 27, the firstly encountered "2" in "32" is at the 2nd symbol, and the firstly encountered "3" in "32" is at the 1st symbol, i.e. $P_A = 2$ and $P_B = 1$. Thus the condition at line 30 is satisfied, i.e. $P_A > P_B$. Therefore based on line 31, inserted_code = getPartCode(right_code, 1, P_B -1) $\oplus$ "2" = getPartCode("32", 1, 1-1) $\oplus$ "2" = "" $\oplus$ "2" = "2". Next we go back to line 54, and temp_code = "2". When going to line 55, the final inserted_code = getPartCode(right_code, 1, *left_code.size()*) $\oplus$ temp_code = getPartCode("232", 1, 1) $\oplus$ "2" = "2" $\oplus$ "2" = "22". The deleted code "22" is reused, and it can be seen that the size of "22" is less than or equal to the size of the deleted codes "212" and "23". That means the deleted code with smaller size is reused firstly. Similarly when we insert a code between "2" and "22", lines 52, 53, 54, 19, 23, 24, 25 and 55 in Figure 4 will be used and the returned result is "212" which is equal to the deleted code "212". When we insert a code between "22" and "232", lines 32, 33, 44, 45, 46 and 47 in Figure 4 will be used and the returned result is "23" which is equal to the deleted code "23".

Based on Theorem 4.2, the label size will not increase fast.

5 Never Reuse the Deleted Labels (NeverReuse)

If a deleted code has larger size than its neighbors, Algorithm 1 will reuse this deleted code (see the last two sentences of Example 3.3). If we want to query different versions of the XML based on the labeling schemes, Algorithm 1 is not appropriate. We propose another algorithm which never reuses the deleted codes; it truly maintains the different label versions of the XML.

Case (a) in Algorithm 3 (see Figure 5) is easy to understand. Intuitively Case (b) (lines 4-11 in Figure 5) can be summarized as: inserting a code between left_code and the first deleted_code, inserting between any two consecutive deleted codes, and inserting between the last deleted code and right_code using Algorithm 1 (see Figure 2); the final inserted code is the code of all these inserted codes with the smallest size.

Algorithm 3. AssignInsertedCodeWithoutReuse

Input: left_code, right_code, middle_codes (between left_code and right_code)
Output: inserted_code, and inserted_code ≠ any one of the deleted_codes

Description:

```
1: Case (a) process the deleted codes
2: if middle_codes are deleted
3:     then do not delete middle_codes physically, but mark them as "deleted"

4: Case (b) process the inserted code
5: suppose there are n-2 deleted codes between left_code and right_code
6: put left_code, deleted_codes, and right_code in an array with size n called LDRcodes
7: suppose there is another array called temp_inserted_code with size n-1
8: for (int i=0; i<(n-1); i++) {
9:     temp_inserted_code[i] = AssignInsertedCode(LDRcodes[i], LDRcodes[i+1])
10: } //AssignInsertedCode is Algorithm 1 in Figure 2
11: inserted_code = min{temp_inserted_code[i] | i∈ [0, n-2]} (min means the minimal size)
```

Fig. 5. AssignInsertedCodeWithoutReuse algorithm

When a node is deleted, it is not physically deleted but instead is marked as "deleted" and is stored ordered with other undeleted nodes. At line 9 of Algorithm 3, we use AssignInsertedCode (Algorithm 1) rather than Algorithm 2 because in fact there are no physical deletions and the cost of Algorithm 1 is smaller than Algorithm 2. We use an example to illustrate Algorithm 3.

Example 5.1. Suppose the QED codes "122", "13" and "132" between "12" and "2" (see Table 1) need to be deleted. We do not delete them physically, but mark them as "deleted". When a new code needs to be inserted between "12" and "2", the new code will be "13" based on Algorithm 1 (Figure 2). The deleted code "13" is reused that is not what we expect. Based on Algorithm 3, we insert codes between left_code "12" and the first deleted_code "122", between deleted_codes "122" and "13", between deleted_codes "13" and "132", and between the last deleted_code "132" and right_code "2"; the inserted codes will be "1212", "123", "1312" and "133" based on Algorithm 1. We select the inserted code with the smallest size, e.g. "123", as the final inserted code. "123" and "133" are the codes between "12" and "2" with the smallest sizes which do not reuse the deleted codes.

Theorem 5.1. *All the deleted codes will NOT be reused based on Algorithm 3.*

Based on Algorithm 3, we will never reuse the deleted codes, as well Algorithm 3 guarantees that a code with smaller size is used before a code with larger size is used.

Algorithm 3 intends to make the label size increase slowly (called NeverReuse-I) However, Algorithm 3 needs more time to calculate the inserted code especially when there are a lot of deleted codes between left_code and right_code. If we want to reduce the insertion time, we can directly use any inserted code (see line 9 in Figure 5) as the final inserted code (called NeverReuse-II), but this can not guarantee that the inserted code is with the smallest size. Furthermore, if a code is required to be inserted between two specific deleted codes (the inserted code should have order relationships with the two specific deleted codes), then insert a code between these two specific deleted codes (called NeverReuse-III) instead of using Algorithm 3. We will further test NeverReuse-I, NeverReuse-II, NeverReuse-III in Section 6.2.

6 Performance Study

The query and update performance of different labeling schemes have been studied in [8]. In this paper, we mainly compare the Reuse and NeverReuse algorithms proposed in this paper with the original QED encoding in [8]. All the experiments are implemented in Java and all the experiments are carried out on a 3.0 GHz Pentium 4 processor with 1 GB RAM running Windows XP Professional.

6.1 Performance Study on Reusing the Deleted Codes

Based on the original QED [8], we generate 1,000,000 QED codes. We test the case that codes are deleted then inserted at the *odd* positions of the 1,000,000 codes; after the deletions and insertions, we call these new codes *CodeSet2*; this is case 1. Secondly we test that the codes are deleted then inserted at the *even* positions of

CodeSet2, thirdly *odd* positions of *CodeSet3*, fourthly *even* positions of *CodeSet4*, and so on.

We compare the performance of QED (based on Algorithm 1 in Figure 2) and Reuse (based on Algorithm 2 in Figure 4). Figure 6 shows that the code size of Reuse does not increase in all the ten cases (since we reuse all the deleted codes). On the other hand, the code size of QED increases linearly (for these ten cases) which is fast. Note if there are only insertions (no deletions) at different places of the QED codes, the code size of QED increases logarithmically but not linearly.

The experimental results confirm that our Reuse algorithm (Figure 4) can reuse all the deleted codes, thus it efficiently controls the increasing speed of the code size.

6.2 Performance Study on Never Reusing the Deleted Codes

We delete and insert at any place of the 1,000,000 QED codes generated in Section 6.1. The experimental results confirm that our NeverReuse algorithm(s) (NeverReuse-I, NeverReuse-II, and NeverReuse-III; see the discussions after Theorem 5.1) never reuse any deleted codes, hence the NeverReuse algorithm(s) can truly maintain different label versions of the XML data. There are no other researches about how to never reuse the deleted labels in labeling schemes. Therefore we do not compare different schemes on label version control in the experiments. The other containment and prefix labeling schemes can not truly maintain different XML label versions because they must reuse the deleted labels no matter how large gaps are leaved between two values.

We compare the size and the update time increasing speeds of NeverReuse-I, NeverReuse-II and NeverReuse-III. Figure 7(a) shows that the size (only the size of the inserted codes) differences among the three approaches are not very large though NeverReuse-I is better. On the other hand, Figure 7(b) shows that the update time (only the processing time) of NeverReuse-I increases very fast, but the update time of NeverReuse-II and NeverReuse-III is almost 0 millisecond (ms). Therefore in practice, we suggest using NeverReuse-III because its update time is small, its code size is not large, and the most important reason is that NeverReuse-III can maintain the order relationships among the deleted codes. Maintaining the orders of the deleted codes can only be achieved by our approach.

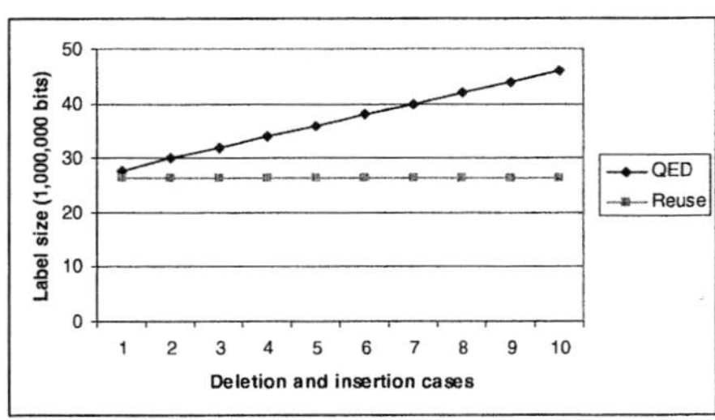

Fig. 6. Sizes of QED and Reuse

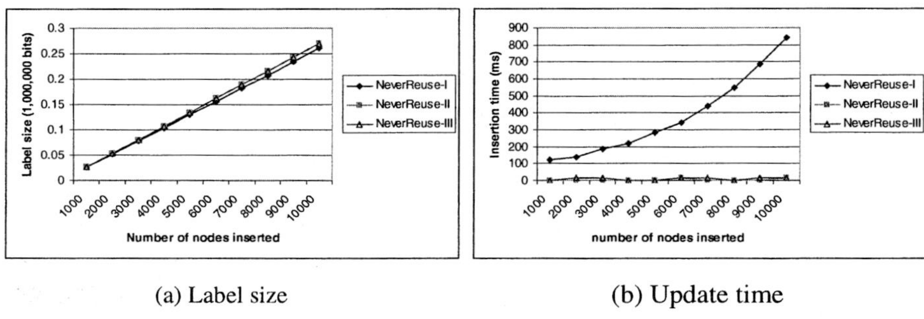

(a) Label size (b) Update time

Fig. 7. NeverReuse

7 Conclusion

In this paper, we propose a new algorithm which can reuse all the deleted labels. In this way, we efficiently control the label size increasing speed. The experimental results also show that with this algorithm we can greatly decrease the label size when a lot of nodes are deleted and inserted. Meanwhile, the Reuse algorithm can completely avoid the re-labeling in XML updates also. In summary, Reuse is more appropriate to efficiently process the updates with both insertions and deletions (QED is more appropriate for the updates with insertions only).

No one has ever studied how to query different versions of the XML based on labeling schemes, therefore in this paper we propose algorithm(s) that never reuse the deleted labels; this truly maintains the different label versions (the labels in different versions are unique). The existing labeling schemes can not truly maintain the label versions since they must re-label the exiting nodes when many nodes are inserted.

References

1. R. Agrawal, A. Borgida, H. V. Jagadish. Efficient Management of Transitive Relationships in Large Data and Knowledge Bases. In Proc. of ACM SIGMOD, pages 253-262, 1989.
2. T. Amagasa, M. Yoshikawa, S. Uemura. QRS: A Robust Numbering Scheme for XML Documents. In *Proc. of ICDE*, pages 705-707, 2003.
3. S. Bose, L. Fegaras. Data Stream Management for Historical XML Data. In *Proc. of ACM SIGMOD*, pages 239-250, 2004.
4. S. Chien, V. J. Tsotras, C. Zaniolo. Efficient Management of Multiversion Documents by Object Referencing. In *Proc. of VLDB*, pages 291-300, 2001.
5. S.Y. Chien, V. Tsotras, C. Zaniolo, D. Zhang. Supporting Complex Queries on Multiversion XML Documents. In *ACM Trans. on Office Information Systems*, pages 1-42, 2005.
6. E. Cohen, H. Kaplan, T. Milo. Labeling Dynamic XML Trees. In *Proc. of PODS*, pages 271-281, 2002.
7. Changqing Li, Tok Wang Ling, Min Hu. Efficient Processing of Updates in Dynamic XML Data. To appear in *Proc. of ICDE*, 2006.

8. Changqing Li, Tok Wang Ling. QED: A Novel Quaternary Encoding to Completely Avoid Re-labeling in XML Updates. In *Proc. of CIKM*, pages 501-508, 2005.
9. Q. Li, B. Moon. Indexing and Querying XML Data for Regular Path Expressions. In *Proc. of VLDB*, pages 361-370, 2001.
10. A. Marian, S. Abiteboul, G. Cobena, L. Mignet. Change-Centric Management of Versions in an XML Warehouse. In *Prof. of VLDB*, pages 581-590, 2001.
11. J. McHugh, S. Abiteboul, R. Goldman, D. Quass, J. Widom. Lore: A Database Management System for Semistructured Data. In *SIGMOD Record 26(3)*, pages 54-66, 1997.
12. S. Nestorov, J. D. Ullman, J. L. Wiener, S. S. Chawathe. Representative Objects: Concise Representations of Semistructured, Hierarchial Data. In *Prof. of ICDE*, pages 79-90, 1997.
13. P. E. O'Neil, E. J. O'Neil, S. Pal, I. Cseri, G. Schaller, N. Westbury. ORDPATHs: Insert-Friendly XML Node Labels. In *Prof of ACM SIGMOD*, pages 903-908, 2004.
14. A. Silberstein, H. He, K. Yi, J. Yang. BOXes: Efficient Maintenance of Order-Based Labeling for Dynamic XML Data. In *Proc. of ICDE*, pages 285-296, 2005.
15. I. Tatarinov, S. Viglas, K. S. Beyer, J. Shanmugasundaram, E. J. Shekita, C. Zhang. Storing and querying ordered XML using a relational database system. In *Proc. of ACM SIGMOD*, pages 204-215, 2002.
16. F. Wang, C. Zaniolo, X. Zhou, H.J. Moon. Managing Multiversion Documents & Historical Databases: a Unified Solution Based on XML. In *Proc. of WebDB*, pages 151-153, 2005.
17. F. Wang, X. Zhou, C. Zaniolo. An XML-Based Approach to Publishing and Querying the History of Databases. In *World Wide Web Journal*, pages 1-30, 2005.
18. X. Wu, M. L. Lee, W. Hsu. A Prime Number Labeling Scheme for Dynamic Ordered XML Trees. In *Proc. of ICDE*, pages 66-78, 2004.
19. M. Yoshikawa, T. Amagasa, T. Shimura, S. Uemura. XRel: a path-based approach to storage and retrieval of XML documents using relational databases. In *ACM Trans. Internet Techn. 1(1)*, pages 110-141, 2001.
20. C. Zhang, J. F. Naughton, D. J. DeWitt, Q. Luo, G. M. Lohman. On Supporting Containment Queries in Relational Database Management Systems. In *Proc. of ACM SIGMOD*, pages 425-436, 2001.

Fast Reachability Query Processing

Jiefeng Cheng, Jeffrey Xu Yu, and Nan Tang

The Chinese University of Hong Kong, China
{jfcheng, yu, ntang}@se.cuhk.edu.hk

Abstract. Graph has great expressive power to describe the complex relationships among data objects, and there are large graph datasets available. In this paper, we focus ourselves on processing a primitive graph query. We call it *reachability query*. The reachability query, denoted $A \leadsto D$, is to find all elements of a type D that are reachable from some elements in another type A. The problem is challenging because the existing structural join algorithms, studied in XML query processing, cannot be directly applied to it, because those techniques make use of the tree-structure heavily. We propose a novel approach which can process reachability queries on the fly while keeping the space consumption small that is needed to keep the required information for processing reachability queries. In brief, our approach is based on 2-hop labeling for a directed graph G which consumes $O(|V| \cdot \log |E|)$ space. We construct a novel join-index which is built on a small table and B+-tree. With the join-index, the high efficiency is achieved. We conducted extensive experimental studies, and we confirm that our approach can efficiently process reachability queries over a graph or a tree.

1 Introduction

Due to the advanced Web technology and the new techniques for data archiving and analyzing, there is a huge volume of data available in public, which are graph structured in nature including hypertext data, semi-structured data and XML [1]. For instance, in Web mining, the navigation patterns of Web surfers is modeled as directed acyclic graphs to improve the analysis of the navigation behavior of user groups [4]. In Genome biology, graph and network models have been used, for example, gene-regulatory networks or metabolic networks. HumanCyc [13] and Cyc [11] are two such databases where graph is used to represent their inter-reactions.

Graph has great expressive power to describe the complex relationships among data objects. Real applications use different facilities/systems to handle their data as either directed graphs, or directed acyclic graphs, or trees. As a major standard for representing data on the World-Wide-Web, XML provides facilities for users to model data as trees or to view data as graphs with two different links, the parent-child links (document-internal links) and reference links (cross-document links) where the cross-document links are supported by value matching using ID/IDREF in XML. In addition, the XLink (XML Linking Language) [8] and XPointer (XML Pointer Language) [9] provide more opportunities for users to manage their complex data as graphs and integrate data effectively.

In this paper, we study a primitive graph query, called *reachability query*, that is needed in any types of graphs (directed graphs, directed acyclic graphs, or trees). In

M.L. Lee, K.L. Tan, and V. Wuwongse (Eds.): DASFAA 2006, LNCS 3882, pp. 674–688, 2006.

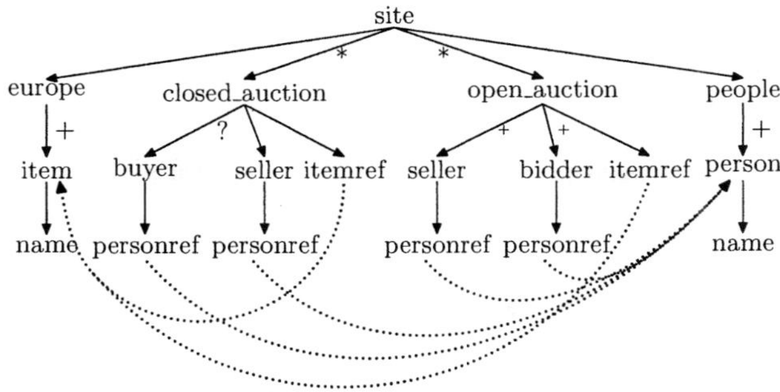

Fig. 1. A part of DTD used in XMark Benchmark [16]

brief, given two types of elements in a graph, A and D, the reachability query, denoted $A \rightsquigarrow D$, is to find all elements of the type D that are reachable from some elements in the type A.

The needs of such a reachability query can be even found in XML. Consider the DTD graph in Fig. 1, which is a part of DTD used in XMark Benchmark [16]. The DTD specifies `person`, `seller`, and `bidder`, where a `person` has a `name`, and a `seller`/`bidder` may have ID/IDREF to reference a `person`, because `seller` and `bidder` are `person`. In Fig. 1, solid links represent document-internal links whereas dashed links represent cross-document links (ID/IDREF). Suppose that we want to know seller's names. It becomes difficult to find `names` of `sellers` using the XPath operator // (descendants-or-self-axis) alone, because // does not traverse the cross-document links supported by ID/IDREF. It needs more joins to process this reachability query using XPath even the underneath DTD is known. It requests even great effort to process a reachability query if there is no DTD available, and may need to traverse the whole graph. It is unreasonable for users not to be able to find such information in a graph effectively and efficiently, where users are recommended to model data by sharing the commonly-used parts (e.g., seller as person) as much as possible.

It is important to note that the reachability query we are studying is a more general facility to find relevant information in arbitrary graphs (including trees). $A//D$ is a special case of $A \rightsquigarrow D$ when data is a tree. There exist many advanced techniques to process structural join or containment join, $A//D$, for XML including [3, 6, 10]. Those techniques cannot be directly applied to reachability queries, $A \rightsquigarrow D$, because they all at maximum make use of the XML tree-structure without ID/IDREF. As an exemption, in [17], Wang et al studied reachability queries, $A \rightsquigarrow D$, and proposed two algorithms based on a graph coding scheme [2] and structural join techniques used in XML.

In this paper, we propose a novel index-based approach that can efficiently process reachability queries, $A \rightsquigarrow D$, over a graph (including tree). Our approach achieves high efficiency while keeping space consumption small. First, we adapt a graph coding scheme which consumes $O(|V| \cdot \log |E|)$ space for a directed graph $G(V, E)$. The coding scheme is based on the 2-hop labeling for a graph [7]. We report a simple yet effective technique that can further reduce the space consumption of 2-hop cover. Note: There are several recent works on computing 2-hop cover using a divide-and-conquer approach [14, 15] or a geometry-based approach [5]. The incremental maintenance of such 2-hop cover was also reported in [15]. Second, we propose an algorithm for reachability queries based on 2-hop labeling. In order to be more efficiently processing reachability queries, we construct a novel join index consisting of a table and a B+-tree. Our join index allows us to process any $A \rightsquigarrow D$ queries in a graph on the fly. As shown in our extensive experimental studies, our index-based approach consumes the similar amount of space like the interval-based graph coding scheme as reported in [17], and significantly outperforms the algorithms given in [17]. Third, we confirm that our approach can also process structural joins for XML tree data efficiently.

The rest of the paper is organized as follows. Section 2 discusses graph data and defines reachability queries. Section 3 introduces the only existing algorithm for reachability queries over graphs, which serves the baseline for us to compare. Section 4 discusses our approach in detail. We will give the graph coding we used, the query processing techniques and its join index. Experimental results are presented in Section 5. Finally, Section 6 concludes the paper.

2 Graph Data and Reachability Query

We consider a large directed node-labeled graph $G = (V, E, \lambda, L)$, to represent a complex data set which can be semi-structured data or XML data. Here, V is a set of elements, E is a set of edges, L is a set of labels, and λ is a function which assigns a node a label. Given a label $l \in L$, the extent of l is defined as a set of nodes whose label is l, denoted $ext(l)$. An example is given below.

Example 1. *A simple XML document is shown in Fig. 2. The example shows two relationships between elements in XML. One represents the parent-child relationship between two elements in XML. For example, the element* `<site>` *has* `<europe>` *as its subelement (parent-child). The parent-child relationships for an XML document form a tree representation. Fig. 3 (a) shows the tree representation of Fig. 2. The other is a general reference from one element to another using* `id` *and* `idref` *based on value-matching, where* `id` *specifies a unique user-assigned identifier for an element, and* `idref` *specifies a link to the element with the same identifier. For example, in Fig. 2, line-4, an item is associated with an identifier (*`id="item1"`*). In the middle of Fig. 2, there is an element* `itemref` *which points to (*`id="item1"`*) using* `idref="item1"`. *Both parent-child and id-idref relationships together form a graph representation for an XML document. Fig. 3 (b) shows the graph representation of Fig. 2. Note: in both Fig. 3 (a) and (b), every node is associated with a system-assigned object identifier, for example 16.*

Given a directed node-labeled graph $G = (V, E, \lambda, L)$, we define a *reachability query*, denoted $A \rightsquigarrow D$, as to find whether elements with label A can reach elements with label D. In other words, let A and D be two labels in L. $A \rightsquigarrow D$ finds all pairs of (u, v) such as v is reachable from u where $u \in ext(A)$ and $v \in ext(D)$ in the graph G.

We consider two cases for a query $seller \rightsquigarrow name$ against the simple XML document (Fig. 2). First, we issue the query against its tree representation (Fig. 3 (a)), the query result is empty, because there does not exist a data path from an element of `seller` to an element of `name`. It is important to note that, when XML is modeled as

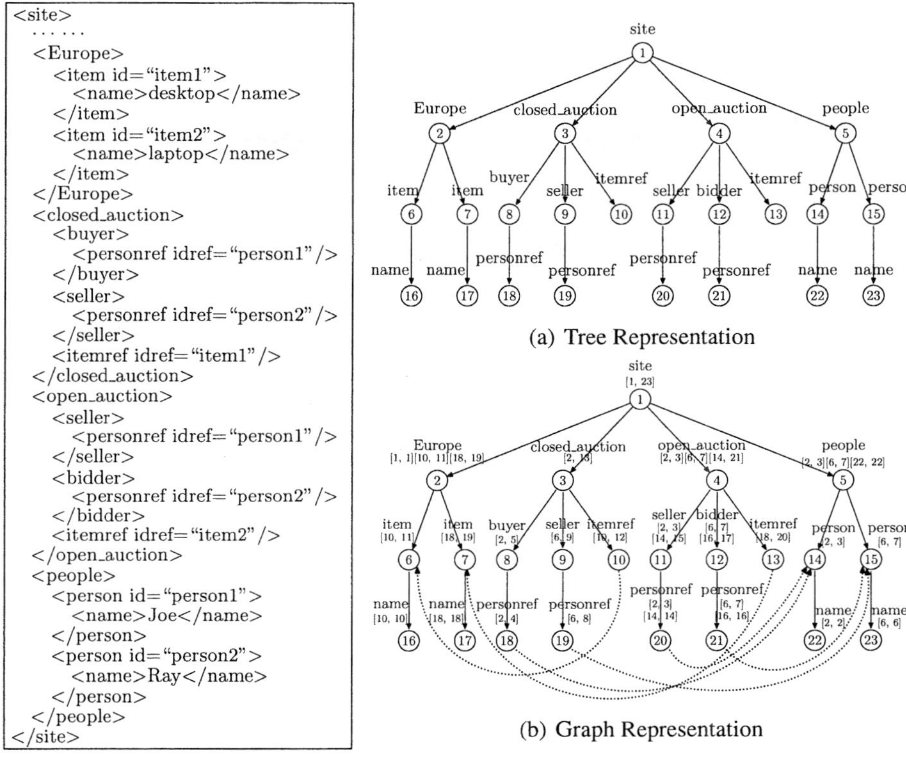

```
<site>
  ......
  <Europe>
    <item id="item1">
      <name>desktop</name>
    </item>
    <item id="item2">
      <name>laptop</name>
    </item>
  </Europe>
  <closed_auction>
    <buyer>
      <personref idref="person1"/>
    </buyer>
    <seller>
      <personref idref="person2"/>
    </seller>
    <itemref idref="item1"/>
  </closed_auction>
  <open_auction>
    <seller>
      <personref idref="person1"/>
    </seller>
    <bidder>
      <personref idref="person2"/>
    </bidder>
    <itemref idref="item2"/>
  </open_auction>
  <people>
    <person id="person1">
      <name>Joe</name>
    </person>
    <person id="person2">
      <name>Ray</name>
    </person>
  </people>
</site>
```


(a) Tree Representation

(b) Graph Representation

Fig. 2. A Sample XML Document Fragment

Fig. 3. Document Representation

a tree, $A \rightsquigarrow D$ is the same as $A//D$ used in XPath queries. Second, we issue the query against its graph representation (Fig. 3 (b)), there are two pairs, namely, (9, 23) and (11, 22), because sellers are persons and therefore persons names are sellers names. An acute reader may ask whether the second case can be processed using // in XPath with value index efficiently. The answer is rather negative. For getting the sellers names, 22 and 23, the XQuery is as follows.

```
for $p in //seller
let $n := for $s in //person
          where $p/personref/@idref = $s/@id
return $n/name
```

The above XQuery finds all `sellers` and all `persons` followed by id/idref matching, and is time-consuming. It is worth of noting that it requests users to know the underneath schema of XML data. In fact, even when a user knows the underneath schema, sometime, it is rather complicated to process $A \rightsquigarrow D$ using // and id/idref. For example, the reachability query, $closed\_auction \rightsquigarrow name$, requires more joins on id/idref if it is processed using XQuery.

3 An Existing Approach

For processing reachability queries, $A \leadsto D$, two algorithms were processed in [17] using a structural join method based on an interval-based coding scheme for arbitrary directed graphs. In brief, given a directed graph, G. First, it constructs a directed acyclic graph G' by condensing a maximal strongly connected component in G as a node in G'. Second, it generates interval-based codes for G' the directed acyclic graph based on [2]. Third, all nodes in a strongly connected component in G share the same code assigned to the corresponding representative node condensed in G'.

Agrawal et al [2] proposed a method for labeling directed acyclic graphs using intervals. The labeling is done in three steps for a directed acyclic graph, G_D. 1) Construct an optimum tree-cover $\mathcal{T}$. An optimum tree-cover is defined as to minimize the number of intervals. 2) Every node, v, in the $\mathcal{T}$ is labeled using an interval $[s, e]$. A node v has a *postorder number*, denoted *po*, which is the number assigned following a postorder traversal of the tree starting from 1. The e value in $[s, e]$ for a node v is the postorder number of the node v, and the s value in the interval is the smallest postorder number of its descendants, where $s = e$ if v is a leaf node. 3) After $\mathcal{T}$ is labeled, it examines all nodes of $G_D$in the reverse topological order. During the traversal, for each node u, add all the intervals associated with v, if there exists an edge (u, v), into the interval associated with u. Note: an interval can be eliminated if it is contained in another. Let I_u be a list of intervals assigned to a node u. Suppose there are two nodes u and v where $I_u = \{[s_1, e_1], [s_2, e_2], \cdots, [s_n, e_n]\}$, and $I_v = \{[s'_1, e'_1], [s'_2, e'_2], \cdots, [s'_m, e'_m]\}$. There exists a path from u to v if the postorder of v is in an interval, $[s_j, e_j]$, of u. The interval-based graph code for the sample XML documents as a directed graph is given in Fig. 3 (b).

Two algorithms, *GMJ* and *IGMJ*, were studied in [17]. We introduce the algorithm *IGMJ* (Improved Graph-Merge Join) below, because it outperforms *GMJ*.

As shown in Algorithm 1, for $A \leadsto D$, *IGMJ* takes two lists $Alist$ and $Dlist$ as its input. Here, $Alist$ and $Dlist$ are two lists of nodes belonging to label A and D respectively. $Alist$ is sorted on the intervals $[x, y]$ by the ascending order of x and then

Algorithm 1. *IGMJ* $(Alist, Dlist)$

```
a := Alist.head();   d := Dlist.head();
R := ∅;
while a ≠ ∅ ∨ d ≠ ∅ do
   if a.x ≤ d.postid then
      rstree.trim(a.x);   rstree.insert(a);   a := a.next();
   else
      rstree.trim(d.postid);
      for all elements a ∈ rstree do
         R.insert(a.id, d.id);
      end for
      d := d.next();
   end if
end while
return R;
```

the descending order of y. If a node of A has n intervals, then it will have n entries in the $Alist$. $Dlist$ is sorted by the ascending order of postorder. The motivation is to leverage the order in the intervals and postorder to accelerate join processing. The $rstree$ is a range search tree. In the range search tree, the intervals are indexed and organized according to their y values. Two operations, $trim(v)$ and $insert(n)$, are used such as $trim(v)$ is to batch delete the intervals whose y values smaller than v and $insert(n)$ is to insert a node to the range search tree.

4 A Novel Join Index

In this paper, we propose a novel join index for a set of reachability queries $A \rightsquigarrow D$ in a graph $G = (V, E, \lambda, L)$. Note, there are in total ${}_nC_2$ combinations of such $A \rightsquigarrow D$ if n is the size of the set of labels, L. The goal is to minimize the query processing cost for any reachability query $A \rightsquigarrow D$ in a graph G on the condition that the size of the join index is small.

Intuitively, it is seen as difficult to minimize both query processing cost and the space required for such a join-index. Let's consider the simplest approach. That is to materialize all ${}_nC_2$ combinations of such $A \rightsquigarrow D$ on disk, $\langle L_1, L_1\rangle$, $\langle L_1, L_2\rangle$, $\cdots$, $\langle L_{n-1}, L_n\rangle$, $\langle L_n, L_n\rangle$ if there are n labels. In doing so, we can answer any reachability query, $A \rightsquigarrow D$, by simply loading the corresponding materialized join-index from disk. However, the simplest approach here processes reachability queries efficiently at the expense of huge disk space. Suppose that there are n labels, The worst case is that the extent of a label, $ext(L_i)$, may occur n times because there are n reachability queries from L_i to any other L_j for $j = 1, \cdots, n$. It also implies that the join-index can be possibly n times of $|V|$ where V is the set of nodes in graph G. Such simplest approach is infeasible.

In the following, we propose a novel join index which takes space less than that of the data in general. We will show that we can process any reachability query efficiently with the proposed join index. Below, we will first introduce a graph coding, our query processing techniques based on the graph coding, and the join index structure.

4.1 2-Hop Reachability Labeling

The 2-hop reachability labeling is defined in [7]. We introduce it below in brief. Let $G = (V, E)$ be a directed graph. A 2-hop reachability labeling on graph G assigns every node $v \in V$ a label $L(v) = (L_{in}(v), L_{out}(v))$, where $L_{in}(v), L_{out}(v) \subseteq V$, such that every node x in $L_{in}(v)$ connects to every node y in $L_{out}(v)$. A node v is reachable from a node u, denoted $u \rightsquigarrow v$, if and only if $L_{out}(u) \cap L_{in}(v) \neq \emptyset$. The size of the 2-hop reachability labeling over a graph $G(V, E)$, is given as L, below.

$$L = \sum_{v \in V(G)} |L_{in}(v)| + |L_{out}(v)| \quad (1)$$

Consider $L(v)$ for a node v, the name of 2-hop comes from the idea that the reachability from a node $x \in L_{in}(v)$ to node $y \in L_{out}(v)$ is via the node v in the middle way, so that the first hop is from x to v and the second hop is from v to y. In order to solve the 2-hop reachability labeling, Cohen et al introduce 2-hop cover which is a set of paths in the graph G. The definition is given below [7].

Definition 1 (2-hop cover). *Given a directed graph $G = (V, E)$. Let $P_{u \rightsquigarrow v}$ be a set of paths from node u to node v in G, and P be a set of all such $P_{u \rightsquigarrow v}$ in G. A hop, h_u, is defined as $h_u = (p_u, u)$, where p_u is a path in G and u is one of the endpoints of p_u. A 2-hop cover, denoted H, is a set of hops that covers P, such as, if node v is reachable from node u then there exists a path p in the non-empty $P_{u \rightsquigarrow v}$ where the path p is concatenation of p_u and p_v, denoted $p = p_u p_v$, and $h_u = (p_u, u)$ and $h_v = (p_v, v)$.*

The 2-hop reachability labeling can be derived from a 2-hop cover [7]. Formally, given a 2-hop cover H, the label for node v, $L(v) = (L_{in}(v), L_{out}(v))$ becomes $L_{in}(v) = \{x \mid ((x, v), v) \in H\}$ and $L_{out}(v) = \{x \mid ((v, x), v) \in H\}$. Given a 2-hop reachability labeling, $H = \cup_{v \in V} H_v$ where $H_v = \{((x, v), v) | x \in L_{in}(v)\} \cup \{((v, x), v) | x \in L_{out}(v)\}$. In addition, the size of the 2-hop cover, $|H|$, for a graph G, is the same as that of 2-hop reachability labeling ($|H| = L$).

The 2-hop cover problem is to find the minimum size of 2-hop cover for a given graph $G(V, E)$, which is proved to be NP-hard [7]. Cohen et al show that a greedy algorithm exists to compute a near optimal solution for the 2-hop cover problem. The resulting size of the greedy algorithm is larger than the optimal at most $O(\log n)$ where $n = |V|$. In [14, 15], Schenkel et al studied a partition-based approach to efficiently generate 2-hop cover for a large graph. The incremental maintenance of such 2-hop code for a graph was also discussed in [15]. In [5], we also propose a novel geometry-based algorithm to improve the efficiency of computing 2-hop cover for even large dense graphs.

The computed 2-hop labeling for the graph representation of the XML document (Fig. 3 (b)) is listed in Table 1. Here, The table has four attributes L (label), v (node), L_{in} of v and L_{out} of v. For example, $8 \rightsquigarrow 14$, because $L_{out}(8) \cap L_{in}(14) = \{8\} \neq \emptyset$.

We observe that the 2-hop labeling can be further compressed by removing hops in the form of $(v \rightsquigarrow v, v)$. Table 2 shows the compact 2-hop labeling for the sample example. We use the compact 2-hop labeling in our work. When compact 2-hop labeling is used, the condition of checking reachability needs to be modified as below: if $u \rightsquigarrow v$ is true, then one of the three conditions must be true, (a) $L_{out}(u) \cap L_{in}(v) \neq \emptyset$, (b) $u \in L_{in}(v)$ and (c) $v \in L_{out}(u)$. As can be seen in Table 2, $8 \rightsquigarrow 14$ is true, because $8 \in L_{in}(14)$.

Table 1. 2-hop labeling for the graph in Fig. 3 (b)

$\mathcal{T}$	v	L_{in}	L_{out}	$\mathcal{T}$	v	L_{in}	L_{out}	$\mathcal{T}$	v	L_{in}	L_{out}
site	1	$\emptyset$	2, 3, 4, 5	item	7	2, 4	$\emptyset$	person	15	3, 4, 15	15
europe	2	2	2	buyer	8	3, 8	8	name	16	2, 3, 6	$\emptyset$
closed_auction	3	3	3	seller	9	3	15	name	17	2, 4, 7	$\emptyset$
open_auction	4	4	4	seller	11	4	14	name	22	3, 4, 8, 14	$\emptyset$
people	5	5	5, 14, 15	bidder	12	4	15	name	23	3, 4, 15	$\emptyset$
item	6	2, 3, 6	6	person	14	3, 4, 8, 14	15				

Table 2. Compact 2-hop labeling for the graph in Fig. 3 (b)

L	v	L_{in}	L_{out}	L	v	L_{in}	L_{out}	L	v	L_{in}	L_{out}
site	1	$\emptyset$	$2, 3, 4, 5$	item	7	$2, 4$	$\emptyset$	person	15	$3, 4$	$\emptyset$
europe	2	$\emptyset$	$\emptyset$	buyer	8	3	$\emptyset$	name	16	$2, 3, 6$	$\emptyset$
closed_auction	3	$\emptyset$	$\emptyset$	seller	9	3	15	name	17	$2, 4, 7$	$\emptyset$
open_auction	4	$\emptyset$	$\emptyset$	seller	11	4	14	name	22	$3, 4, 8, 14$	$\emptyset$
people	5	$\emptyset$	$14, 15$	bidder	12	4	15	name	23	$3, 4, 15$	$\emptyset$
item	6	$2, 3$	$\emptyset$	person	14	$3, 4, 8$	$\emptyset$				

In the following, for simplicity, we use the non-compact 2-hop labeling to explain our ideas and we use the compact 2-hop labeling in our testing.

4.2 Reachability Query Processing Based on 2-Hop Labeling

We discuss reachability query processing below based on hops (Definition 1). Recall: given a hop, $h_u = (p_u, u)$, p_u is a path and u is one of the endpoints of p_u. Suppose w is the other endpoint. There are only two possible cases for p_u. One is $p_u = w \rightsquigarrow u$, and the other is $p_u = u \rightsquigarrow w$. Here, w is the center of the hop. In Table 1, all centers appear in either L_{in} or L_{out}. Given a set of hops, $\mathcal{H}$, constructed for a graph G. We can obtain such a set of centers, denoted W. For each $w \in W$, we can also construct two sets, $H^+(w)$ and $H^-(w)$ as below.

$$H^+(w) = \{u \mid w \rightsquigarrow u, (w \rightsquigarrow u, u) \in H\} \quad (2)$$

$$H^-(w) = \{u \mid u \rightsquigarrow w, (u \rightsquigarrow w, u) \in H\} \quad (3)$$

Here, $H^+(w)$ consists of all nodes that can be reached from the center w, and $H^-(w)$ consists of all nodes that can reach the center w. Both $H^-(w)$ and $H^+(w)$ together serve as an inverted index showing that every node in $H^+(w)$ can be reached from all nodes in $H^-(w)$. Furthermore, we can efficiently find the nodes in either $H^+(w)$ or $H^-(w)$ that are associated with a label L_i.

$$H^+(L_i, w) = \{u \mid u \in H^+(w) \wedge \lambda(u) = L_i\} \quad (4)$$

$$H^-(L_i, w) = \{u \mid u \in H^-(w) \wedge \lambda(u) = L_i\} \quad (5)$$

As an example, consider Table 1. $H^+(14) = \{22\}$ and $H^-(14) = \{5, 11\}$. It suggests that 22 can be reached from 5 and 11. Furthermore, we have $H^+(name, 14) = \{22\}$, $H^-(people, 14) = \{5\}$, and $H^-(seller, 14) = \{11\}$. It suggests that the `seller` identified by node identifier 11 has a `name` identified by 22.

Reachability query processing. Given the above equations, a reachability query, $A \rightsquigarrow D$, can be processed in two steps. First, it finds all centers $w \in W$ in which $H^+(A, w)$ and $H^-(D, w)$ are non-empty. Note: both A and D are labels. Second, it produces the query result by simply pairing every element in $H^-(A, w)$ with every element in $H^+(D, w)$, because they must be reachable. The correctness of our reachability query processing is ensured based on the correctness of 2-hop labeling. Recall: 2-hop labeling

Table 3. Code Sizes for different XMark Datasets

Name	Factor	Data Set (M)	Graph		Tree	
			2-Hop (M)	Interval (M)	2-Hop (M)	Interval (M)
10M	0.1	11.88	3.97	3.43	4.15	3.11
20M	0.2	23.93	7.97	6.89	8.35	6.26
30M	0.3	39.24	11.89	12.43	12.43	9.32
40M	0.4	47.51	15.83	13.66	16.53	12.40
50M	0.5	59.03	19.81	17.07	20.61	15.45

ensures that, if node v can be reachable from node u in a graph G, there must exist a center w such as w is reachable from u and v is reachable from w. We maintain the 2-hop labeling. For a reachability query $A \rightsquigarrow D$, we check all possible centers w, and we only report those elements of A that can reach elements D. In other words, we do not include any results which shall not be include and we do not miss any results.

The size of graph code. The code size of 2-hop labeling in general is similar with the interval-based code. We will discuss it in our experimental studies. As shown in Table 3, for example, when the XMark dataset [16] is 59.03MB, the size of 2-hop labeling is less than a half of the raw dataset, 19.81MB, whereas the interval-based code is 17.07MB. It implicitly suggests that the space needed for 2-hop labeling is reasonable small. In the next subsection, we discuss the efficiency of reachability query processing using an join index.

4.3 Join Index

As discussed in the previous section, our reachability query processing is done in two steps for $A \rightsquigarrow D$: i) finding all centers $w \in W$ in which $H^+(A, w)$ and $H^-(D, w)$ are non-empty, and ii) pairing every element in $H^+(A, w)$ with every element in $H^-(D, w)$. In order to process these two steps efficiently, we propose an join index which consists of two parts, namely, a center-table and a balanced B+-tree. The center-table is an implementation of a function, $W(A, D)$, which returns all centers $w \in W$ such as both $H^-(A, w)$ and $H^+(D, w)$ are non-empty. The B+-tree is illustrated in Fig. 4. The search key on the B+-tree is a pair $\langle L_i, w\rangle$, where L_i is a

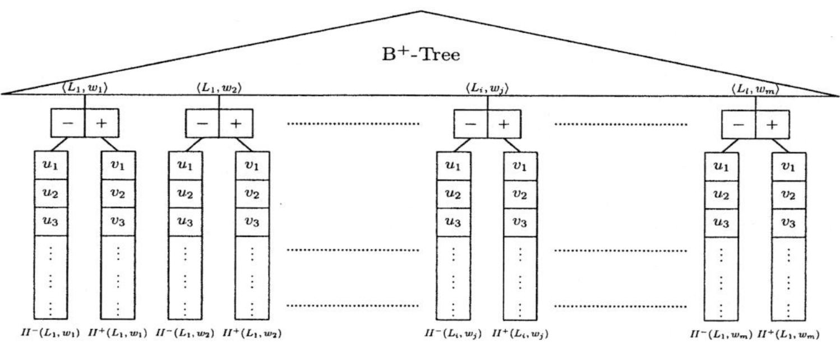

Fig. 4. B+-tree

Algorithm 2. *HPSJ*(A,D)

1: $\mathcal{W} \leftarrow W(A, D)$;
2: **for each** $w \in \mathcal{W}$ **do**
3: Search for $H^-(A, w)$ and $H^+(D, w)$ on the B$^+$-Tree;
4: pair every element in $H^-(A, w)$ with all elements in $H^+(D, w)$ and output the result;
5: **end for**

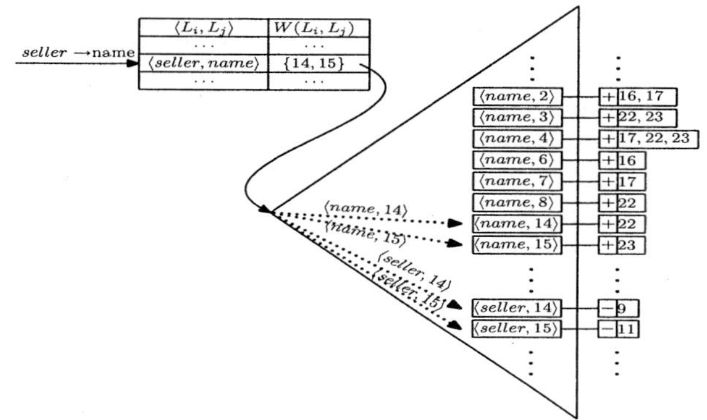

Fig. 5. An Example

label and w is a center. In the leaf nodes of B+-tree, there are two pointers for a search key $\langle L_i, w\rangle$, namely, $H^-_{L_i}(w)$ and $H^+_{L_i}(w)$. The B+-tree can be fast constructed using 2-hops, and is easy to maintain. Due to limit of space, we do not discuss the maintenance issues in this paper.

Our *HPSJ* algorithm is outlined in Algorithm 2, which takes two labels, A and D, as input, for a reachability query, $A \rightsquigarrow D$, and process $A \rightsquigarrow D$ over a graph which is stored in our join-index. In the algorithm, we first find the list of centers, $\mathcal{W}$, from the center-table (line-1). Note: $W(A, D)$ returns centers, w, where both $H^-(A, w)$ and $H^+(D, w)$ are non-empty. For each of the centers, $w \in \mathcal{W}$, we search the B+-tree part of the join-index; and report the join results by pairing every elements in $H^-(A, w)$ and $H^+(D, w)$.

As an example, we show how to process a reachability query, $seller \rightsquigarrow name$, against the graph representation of XML (Fig. 3 (b)), in Figure 5. First, we identify all the centers by calling $W(seller, name)$ using the center-table. We obtain two centers, 14 and 15 (Note: $\mathcal{W} = \{14, 15\}$). We then obtain all `seller` that can reach `name` in both centers, 14 and 15, by searching B+-tree. For example, with the search key $\langle saller, 14\rangle$, we find 9 in $H^-(seller, 14)$; with the search key $\langle name, 14\rangle$, we find 22 in $H^+(name, 14)$; and therefore, the seller (9) has a name (22).

5 Performance Study

Our approach can process reachability queries, $A \rightsquigarrow D$, over graphs and trees. We conducted extensive performance studies, in comparison with those algorithms that are designed for reachability queries over graphs and reachability queries over trees, respectively. For the former, we compare our proposed *HPSJ* algorithm against the *IGMJ* algorithm [17] over large graphs. For the latter, we compare our *HPSJ* algorithm with two index-based structural join algorithms, *XR-tree* [10] and *B+-tree* [6] over trees. We report our results in this section.

The datasets we used for testing are generated using the XMark benchmark [16]. Five factors are used, namely, from 0.1 to 0.5. Given an XMark dataset generated with a factor. We generate graph data by treating both document-internal links (parent-child) and cross-document links (ID/IDREF) as edges in the same manner, and we generate tree data with the document-internal only. The details are given in Table 3. In Table 3, the first column is the dataset name for easy reference, the second column is the factor used to generate a XMark dataset. The third column shows the size of the dataset used. The fourth and fifth columns show the size of the compact 2-hop labeling and the interval [2], for the graph, respectively. The last two columns show the size of the compact 2-hop labeling and the interval [2], for the tree, respectively. All sizes are of the unit of Megabyte. It is worth noting that, for both graph and tree, the size of the 2-hop labeling and the size of the interval coding are marginally different. Given a graph and a tree generated from the same XMark dataset with a certain factor. The size of the 2-hop labeling code for the graph is smaller than that for the tree, because 2-hop labeling can cover a rather large number of nodes in graph, in comparison with the case of tree. On the other hand, the size of the interval code for the graph is larger than that for the tree, as expected.

We implemented our *HPSJ* algorithm and the *IGMJ* algorithm using MS VC++. We used the code implemented by Jiang and Wang [10] for testing *XR-tree* [10] and *B+-tree* [6] over trees. We conducted our testing on a PC with Pentium 2GHz CPU, 1G main memory and an 80G SCSI disk. The OS is Windows 2000 Professional.

5.1 Reachability Query Processing over Graphs

For the XMark benchmark, there are many labels in its DTD. A part of the XMark DTD is given in Fig. 1. We conducted testing over a large number of combinations of two labels, and report 10 queries in this testing. The 10 queries are selected as they give different results with different distributions. Table 4 lists the 10 selected queries, in which the first column is the query id, the second column shows the reachability query, $A \leadsto D$, the following 5 pairs show the sizes of $|A|$ and $|D|$ for each XMark dataset, namely, 10M, 20M, etc, for graphs. Here, for $A \leadsto D$, $|A|$ indicates the total number of A elements that can match D elements, and $|D|$ indicates the total number of D elements that can match A elements.

We process the 10 selected reachability queries, using *HPSJ* and *IGMJ*. The performance results are shown in Fig. 6. There are 5 subfigures, for 5 different datasets, 10M, 20M, 30M, 40M and 50M, respectively, in Fig. 6. In each subfigure, x-axis is the 10 queries, and y-axis is the elapse time in msec. Our algorithm, *HPSJ*, significantly outperforms *IGMJ* in all cases, even though our algorithm uses a slightly larger size of graph labeling. We explain the reason below. Give a reachability query, $A \leadsto D$. There are $|W(A, D)|$ centers found in the first step in our algorithm. In the second step, we only need to search over the B+-Tree of our join-index for $|W(A, D)|$ times. We don't

Table 4. Queries for XMark Data Sets as Graphs

	$A \rightsquigarrow D$	10M		20M		30M		40M		50M	
		$\lvert A\rvert$	$\lvert D\rvert$	$\lvert A\rvert$	$\lvert D\rvert$	$\lvert A\rvert$	$\lvert D\rvert$	$\lvert A\rvert$	$\lvert D\rvert$	$\lvert A\rvert$	$\lvert D\rvert$
Q1	$africa \rightsquigarrow item$	1	55	1	110	1	181	1	220	1	269
Q2	$closed\_auctions \rightsquigarrow reserve$	1	592	1	1175	1	1891	1	2319	1	2854
Q3	$closed\_auctions \rightsquigarrow item$	1	2152	1	4317	1	7111	1	8626	1	10565
Q4	$europe \rightsquigarrow incategory$	1	2307	1	4490	1	7375	1	8974	1	10945
Q5	$namerica \rightsquigarrow incategory$	1	3756	1	7427	1	12531	1	15261	1	18630
Q6	$people \rightsquigarrow incategory$	1	4456	1	8888	1	14686	1	17997	1	21762
Q7	$closed\_auctions \rightsquigarrow bidder$	1	6059	1	11937	1	18889	1	23077	1	28755
Q8	$item \rightsquigarrow keyword$	2055	4331	4199	8627	6855	14233	8317	17128	10148	20844
Q9	$item \rightsquigarrow text$	2175	6462	4350	12830	7177	21257	8700	25664	10657	31371
Q10	$item \rightsquigarrow incategory$	2175	8219	4350	16290	7177	27037	8700	32787	10657	40232

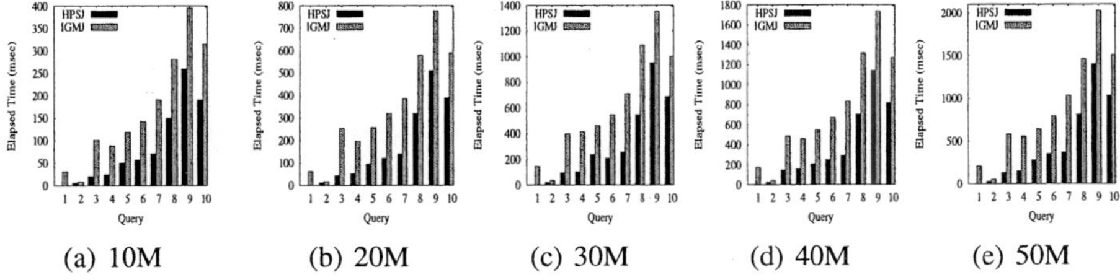

(a) 10M (b) 20M (c) 30M (d) 40M (e) 50M

Fig. 6. Reachability Query Processing over Different Graphs

need to check any join conditions but simply pair the results retrieved from B+-tree. Note: the size of $|W(A, D)|$ has the impacts on the number of searching over B+-tree used in our join-index. *IGMJ* behaves like a structural join algorithm, which has to scan the two interval lists, A and D, once. *IGMJ* needs to check join condition with some run-time data structures to support it as shown in Algorithm 1. The cost depends on the sizes of the two lists, A and D, rather than the size of query result.

We also show the scalability results in Fig. 7 for query Q1, Q3, Q4, Q9 and Q10, respectively. In each subfigure in Fig. 7, the x-axis is the dataset size, and y-axis is the elapse time in msec. There are two cases. First, Fig. 7 (a), (b) and (c) show that, for query Q1, Q2 and Q3, the processing time of *HPSJ* takes the similar amount of time, despite the size of dataset increases. On the other hand, the processing time used in *IGMJ* increases linearly. It is mainly because that the result size is small. There is no time needed for *HPSJ* to check join condition whereas *IGMJ* needs more time to

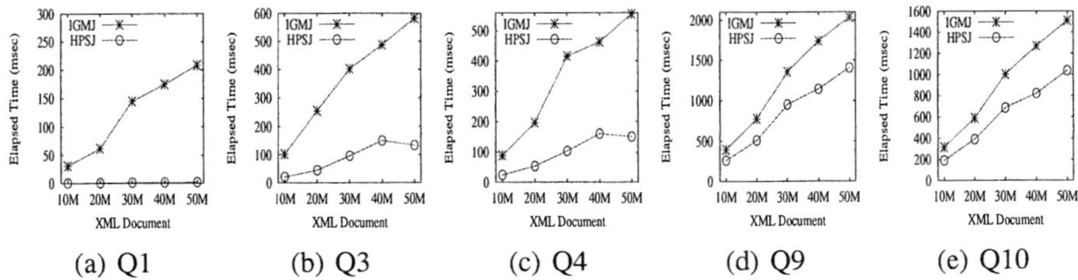

(a) Q1 (b) Q3 (c) Q4 (d) Q9 (e) Q10

Fig. 7. Scalability of Reachability Query Processing over Graphs

check the join condition when the dataset becomes larger. For Q1, *HPSJ* beats *IGMJ* by nearly 100 times. Second, Fig. 7 (d) and (e) show that, for query Q9 and Q10, both the processing time of *HPSJ* and *IGMJ* increase while the size of dataset increases. It is because the result size for query Q9 and Q10 are large. *HPSJ* takes more time to retrieve data from disk with more B+-tree searches, because the number of centers can be large accordingly. Nevertheless, *HPSJ* is faster than *IGMJ* in all cases. In particular, for query Q9, almost all $item$ elements have $text$ sub-elements. It implies that *HPSJ* needs more time to retrieve data like *IGMJ* does to process the two lists. Nevertheless, *HPSJ* is about 1.4 times faster than *IGMJ*.

5.2 Reachability Query Processing over Trees

We show our testing results over XML trees in comparing our *HPSJ* algorithm with the two index-based structural join algorithms, namely, *XR-Tree* [10] and *B+-tree* [6]. Because the XML trees are used, in this testing, $A \rightsquigarrow D$ is the same as $A//D$. In this testing, we use 5 tree datasets given in Table 3. We only show our result using 6 queries, Q1, Q4, Q5, Q8, Q9 and Q10. Like Table 4, the result sizes for these queries with are listed in Table 5.

Table 5. Queries for XMark Data Sets as Trees

	$A//D$	10M		20M		30M		40M		50M	
		$\|A\|$	$\|D\|$	$\|A\|$	$\|D\|$	$\|A\|$	$\|D\|$	$\|A\|$	$\|D\|$	$\|A\|$	$\|D\|$
Q1	$africa//item$	1	55	1	110	1	165	1	220	1	275
Q4	$europe//incategory$	1	2307	1	4490	1	6696	1	8974	1	11187
Q5	$namerica//incategory$	1	3756	1	7427	1	11414	1	15261	1	19003
Q8	$item//keyword$	1510	4189	3026	8330	4512	12456	6023	16582	7483	20544
Q9	$item//text$	2175	6246	4350	12454	6525	18669	8700	24848	10875	30972
Q10	$item//incategory$	2175	8219	4350	16290	6525	24509	8700	32787	10875	40925

Fig. 8 shows the testing result. As can be seen in Fig. 8, *HPSJ*, *XR-tree* and *B+-tree* all perform in a similar way due to the similar I/O complexity [10]. *HPSJ* is faster than *XR-Tree* in all the cases, but is slower than the *B+-tree* algorithm in the cases where the number of results is large. The testing results for *XR-tree* and *B+-tree* show the similar trends as reported in [12]. In brief, *XR-tree* cannot perform well if they need to access the stab lists multiple times, which requires more I/O costs. *B+-tree* based algorithm needs to access most of the leaf pages of the index structure. It can be faster than *HPSJ* when the result size is large. Another reason that *B+-tree* outperforms *HPSJ* is that there are possible random I/Os when using *HPSJ*. In other words, $H^+(L_i, w)$ and $H^-(L_j, w)$ are stored in different disk pages.

Fig. 9 shows the elapsed time of processing reachability queries while increasing the size of the trees. As seen in Fig. 9 (a) and (b), when there is a small number of query results, *HPSJ* outperforms the indexed structural join algorithms at most 44.79 times and 23.99 times on average. When the query results become big, as shown in Fig. 9 (c), (d) and (e), *HPSJ* outperforms *XR-tree*, and *B+-tree* outperforms *HPSJ*, for the reasons discussed above.

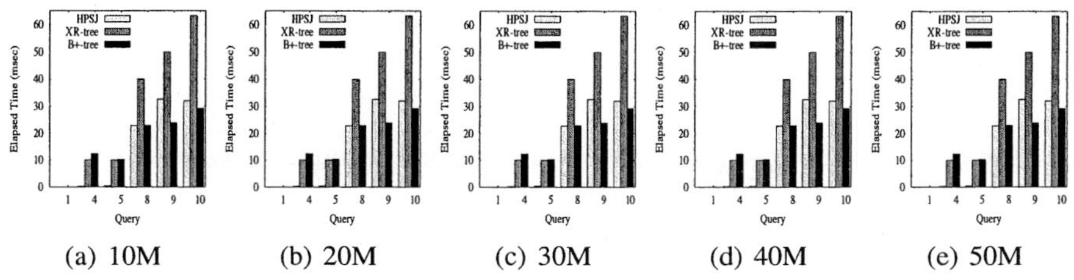

(a) 10M (b) 20M (c) 30M (d) 40M (e) 50M

Fig. 8. Performance on Different Data Sets as Trees

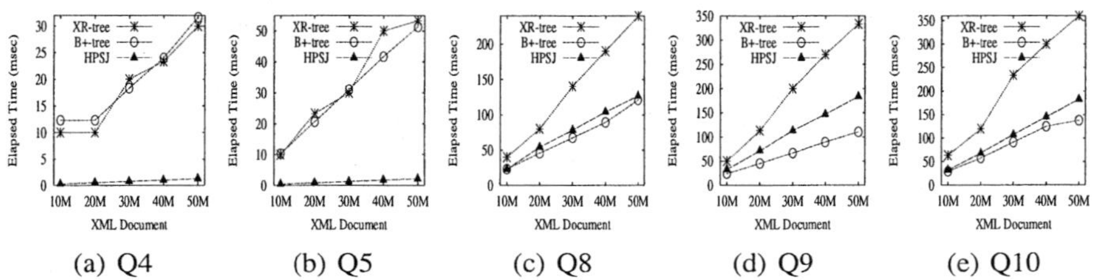

(a) Q4 (b) Q5 (c) Q8 (d) Q9 (e) Q10

Fig. 9. Scalability on Trees

6 Conclusion

We studied reachability query processing, which is to find all elements of a type D that are reachable from some elements in another type A, denoted $A \leadsto D$. We proposed a novel approach which processes reachability queries on the fly. In other words, we do not need to check any join conditions while processing reachability queries. Our approach is based on 2-hop labeling for a directed graph G which consumes $O(|V| \cdot \log |E|)$ space. A novel join-index was proposed in this paper which is built on a small table and B+-tree. With the join-index, the high efficiency is achieved. We conducted extensive experimental studies. We showed that our approach can significantly outperform the up-to-date algorithm for reachability queries over graphs, and achieve high efficiency for processing reachability queries over trees.

Acknowledgement

The work described in this paper was supported by grant from the Research Grants Council of the Hong Kong Special Administrative Region, China (CUHK418205).

References

1. S. Abiteboul, P. Buneman, and D. Suciu. *Data on the Web: from relations to semistructured data and XML*. Morgan Kaufmann Publishers Inc., San Francisco, CA, USA, 2000.
2. R. Agrawal, A. Borgida, and H. V. Jagadish. Efficient management of transitive relationships in large data and knowledge bases. In *Proc. of SIGMOD'89*, 1989.

3. S. Al-Khalifa, H. V. Jagadish, J. M. Patel, Y. Wu, N. Koudas, and D. Srivastava. Structural joins: A primitive for efficient xml query pattern matching. In *Proceedings of the 18th International Conference on Data Engineering (ICDE'02)*, page 141. IEEE Computer Society, 2002.
4. B. Berendt and M. Spiliopoulou. Analysis of navigation behaviour in web sites integrating multiple information systems. *The VLDB Journal*, 9(1):56–75, 2000.
5. J. Cheng, J. X. Yu, X. Lin, H. Wang, and P. S. Yu. Fast computation of reachability labeling for large graphs. Submitted for publication, 2005.
6. S.-Y. Chien, Z. Vagena, D. Zhang, V. J. Tsotras, and C. Zaniolo. Efficient structural joins on indexed xml documents. In *Proc. of 28th International Conference on Very Large Data Bases (VLDB)*, pages 263–274, Hong Kong, China, August 2002.
7. E. Cohen, E. Halperin, H. Kaplan, and U. Zwick. Reachability and distance queries via 2-hop labels. In *Proc. of SODA'02*, 2002.
8. S. DeRose, E. Maler, and D. Orchard. XML linking language (XLink) version 1.0. `http://www.w3.org/TR/xlink`, 2001.
9. S. DeRose, E. Maler, and D. Orchard. XML pointer language (XPointer) version 1.0. `http://www.w3.org/TR/xptr`, 2001.
10. H. Jiang, H. Lu, W. Wang, and B. Ooi. Xr-tree: Indexing xml data for efficient structural join. In *Proceedings of the 19th International Conference on Data Engineering (ICDE'03)*. IEEE Computer Society, 2003.
11. I. Keseler, J. Collado-Vides, S. Gama-Castro, J. Ingraham, S. Paley, I. Paulsen, M. Peralta-Gil, and P. Karp. Ecocyc: A omprehensive database resource for escherichia coli. *Nucleic Acids Research*, 33(D334-D337), 2005.
12. H. Li, M. L. Lee, W. Hsu, and C. Chen. An evaluation of xml indexes for structural join. *SIGMOD Rec.*, 33(3):28–33, 2004.
13. P. Romero, J. Wagg, M. L. Green, D. Kaiser, M. Krummenacker, and P. D. Karp. Computational prediction of human metabolic pathways from the complete human genome. *Genome Biology*, 6(1):1–17, 2004.
14. R. Schenkel, A. Theobald, and G. Weikum. Hopi: An efficient connection index for complex xml document collections. In *Proc. of EDBT'04*, 2004.
15. R. Schenkel, A. Theobald, and G. Weikum. Efficient creation and incremental maintenance of the HOPI index for complex XML document collections. In *Proc. of ICDE'05*, 2005.
16. A. Schmidt, F. Waas, M. Kersten, M. J. Carey, I. Manolescu, and R. Busse. Xmark: A benchmark for xml data management. In *Proc. of VLDB'02*, 2002.
17. H. Wang, W. Wang, X. Lin, and J. Li. Labeling scheme and structural joins for graph-structured xml data. In *Proc. of The 7th Asia Pacific Web Conference*, 2005.

Relation-Based Document Retrieval for Biomedical Literature Databases*

Xiaohua Zhou, Xiaohua Hu, Xia Lin, Hyoil Han, and Xiaodan Zhang

College of Information Science & Technology, Drexel University,
3141 Chestnut Street, Philadelphia, PA 19104
xiaohua.zhou@drexel.edu,
{thu, xlin, hhan, xzhang}@cis.drexel.edu

Abstract. In this paper, we explore the direct use of relations in information retrieval for precision-focused biomedical literature search. A relation is defined as a pair of two concepts which are semantically and syntactically related to each other. Unlike the traditional term-based IR models, our model represents a document by a set of controlled concepts and their binary relations. Since document level co-occurrence of two concepts, in many cases, does not mean this document really addresses their relationships, the direct use of relation may improve the precision of very specific search, e.g. *searching documents that mention genes regulated by Smad4*. For this purpose, we develop a generic ontology-based approach to extract concepts and their relations; a prototyped IR system supporting relation-based search is then built for Medline abstract search. We then use this novel IR system to improve the retrieval result of all official runs in TREC-2004 Genomics Track. The experiment shows promising performance of relation-based IR. The mean of P@100 (the precision of top 100 documents) for all 50 topics is raised from 26.37 %(the P@100 of the best run is 42.10%) to 53.69% while the recall is kept at an acceptable level of 44.31%. The experiment also demonstrates the expressiveness of relations for the representation of genomic information needs.

1 Introduction

Precision and recall are two basic metrics measuring the performance of an Information Retrieval (IR) system. Often, high precision is at the cost of low recall, and vice versa. Nowadays, precision-focused searching is getting more and more attention most likely due to the following two reasons. First, in a lot of domain-specific search, such as searching the Medline, which collects 14 millions of biomedical abstracts published in more than 4600 journals, the professionals normally know what they need and their search queries are often very specific and only like to receive those documents which meet their specific query; thus, they do not expect a large number of documents. Second, the absolute number of returned relevant document is still large enough for most retrieval tasks even if the recall is low because of the exponentially increasing size of the document collection.

* This research work is supported in part from the NSF Career grant (NSF IIS 0448023). NSF CCF 0514679 and the research grant from PA Dept of Health.

M.L. Lee, K.L. Tan, and V. Wuwongse (Eds.): DASFAA 2006, LNCS 3882, pp. 689 – 701, 2006.

Traditional IR models often use a set of terms to index and search documents. A term might be a concept from a controlled vocabulary, or a word or a phrase in a natural language statement, or a thesaurus entry representing a set of synonymous terms [14]. Term-based indexing and searching is convenient for text processing. However, this mechanism might lose some useful information such as the correspondence between terms strongly addressed in the original documents. There are full of various explicitly asserted biological relationships in genomic and biomedical literature, e.g. protein interactions and disease complications; these biological relationships are exactly what scientists are interested in. Therefore, we hypothesize that the direct use of relationships would improve the precision of genomic information retrieval (GIR).

Term-based IR models have to use term co-occurrence to approximate relations because there are no direct relations available in their indices. However, the co-occurrence of two terms in a document, in many cases, does not mean this document really addresses their relationships, especially when the co-occurrence count is low (e.g. in abstract-based search such as PubMed). Thus, the precision would be compromised. We conducted a simple experiment that tried to retrieve documents addressing the interaction of *obesity* and *hypertension* from PubMed[1] by specifying the co-occurrence of term *hypertension* and *obesity* in abstract or title. We then took the top 100 abstracts for human relevance judgment. Unfortunately, as expected, only 33 of them were relevant.

obesity [TIAB] AND hypertension [TIAB] AND hasabstract [text]
AND ("1900"[PDAT] : "2005/03/08"[PDAT])

Fig. 1. The query used to retrieve documents addressing the interaction of obesity and hypertension from PubMed. A ranked hit list of 6687 documents is returned.

In literature, there are volumes of work using term relationships to improve IR. However, their definition of the relationship and the motivation to use relationships are different from ours. Their relationships could be roughly classified into two classes. One is the co-occurrence relationship; the range for co-occurrence might be a document, a paragraph, a sentence, or a fix-sized sliding window [1, 2, 20]. The other is the general semantic relationship such as is-a, part-of and synonym [2]. Their applications of relationships in IR also fall into two categories. One line of work applies the correspondence between query terms and document terms into query expansion [1]. The other line of work uses the syntactic relationship between document terms to estimate a more accurate dependency document model such as bigram and trigram [5, 11]. The effect of the dependency model on IR is similar to that of using phrases instead of words as the indexing unit.

Our relation is defined as a pair of two concepts which are semantically and syntactically related to each other. The semantic constraint could be but not limited to general is-a, part-of and synonym. In most cases, they refer to domain-specific relationships. For GIR, the semantic relationships could be interaction, binding, affecting, producing, etc. The syntactic constraint is the explicit assertion of the binary relation between two concepts in a natural language statement. Many general (e.g. WordNet)

[1] http://www.ncbi.nlm.nih.gov/entrez/query.fcgi

or domain thesaurus (e.g. UMLS) already define lots of semantic relationships. But if the concepts of a relation are not syntactically related in the document they appear, we would not treat them as a relationship during both indexing phase and searching phase. Thus, our definition of relationship is stricter than that in the previous literature. Our motivation for relationship is also different from previous work. We directly use relationships in conjunction with concepts to index and search documents whereas previous work indirectly uses relationships for query expansion or dependency document model estimation.

The extraction of binary relations from text is a challenging task. We think this is one of the major reasons that no relation-based search engine is reported so far. The concept (term) extraction is the first step of the relation extraction. The methods for term extraction fall into two categories, with dictionary [13, 21] or without dictionary [9, 12, 17, 18]. The later is characterized by its high extracting speed and no reliance on dictionary and the capability of predicting new terms. However, it does not extract the meaning of a term. Thus, it does not fit for our application. Instead, we apply a dictionary-based approach [21] to the concept extraction. The majority of the literature use patterns learned by supervised approaches [12] or unsupervised approaches [7, 13], or coded by hand to identify binary relations in a natural language statement. We apply hand-coded patterns to the extraction of binary relations.

We finally develop a generic ontology-based approach to extract concepts and their binary relations. Based on that, we build a prototyped IR system supporting relation-based search for Medline abstracts. We use this novel IR system to improve the retrieval result of all official runs in TREC-04 Genomics Track. The experiment shows promising performance of relation-based IR. The mean of P@100 (the precision of top 100 documents) for all 50 topics is raised from 26.37 %(the P@100 of the best run is 42.10%) to 53.69% while the recall is kept at an acceptable level of 44.31%. The experiment also shows the expressiveness of relations for the representation of information needs, especially in the area of biomedical literature which are full of various biological relations.

The rest of the paper is organized as follows: Section 2 describes the representation of documents and queries. Section 3 presents a generic approach to the extraction of concepts and relations. Section 4 shows the experiment design and result. A short conclusion finishes the paper.

2 Representation of Document and Query

Traditional IR models a document and a query as a set of terms. A term might be a concept from a controlled vocabulary, or a word or a phrase in a natural language statement, or a thesaurus entry representing a set of synonymous terms. The different indexing units may produce slightly different performance for IR. But neither of them explicitly addresses the relation between terms, i.e. terms in a document are unstructured. Obviously, a document is full of various relations. For example, biomedical literatures contain a large number of biological relationships among gene, protein, mutation, disease, drug, etc. Intuitively, the incorporation of such knowledge (represented by relations) will help improve the precision of an IR system. For this purpose, we propose a relation-based document representation mechanism below.

2.1 Document Representation

In the relation-based IR model, we represent a document by a set of concepts from UMLS and their binary relations as shown in Figure 2. We use controlled concepts rather than words in natural language to index the documents because of the characteristics of the GIR. In genomic-related literature, a term is often comprised of multiple words; the word-based unigram IR model might lose the semantics of the term. Meanwhile, severe synonym and polysemy problem in GIR might cause trouble while an IR system tries to match query terms with indexing terms according to their names instead of meanings [15, 19]. A UMLS concept is a meaning with a unique ID representing a set of synonymous terms. Thus, the introduction of UMLS concept for indexing may relieve the two above-mentioned problems.

Terms (CUI, Name, Semantic Type, Frequency)
T1 (C0003818, arsenic, Hazardous or Poisonous Substance, 9)
T2 (C0870082, hyperkeratosis, Disease or Syndrome, 4)
T3 (C1333356, XPD, Gene, 6)
T4 (C0007114, skin cancer, Neoplastic Process, 1)
T5 (C0012899, DNA repair, Genetic Function, 3)
T6 (C0241105, hyperkeratotic skin lesion, Finding, 2)
T7 (C0936225, inorganic arsenic, Inorganic Chemical, 1)
......

Relations (First Concept, Second Concept, Frequency)

R1 (T1, T3, 3)	R2 (T2, T4, 1)
R3 (T2, T5, 2)	R4 (T2, T3, 2)
R5 (T4, T5, 1)	R6 (T3, T4, 1)

......

Fig. 2. A real example of document representation. The document (PMID: 12749816) can be found through PubMed. CUI is the unique ID of a concept in UMLS[2].

However, we keep term names in the index because term names do provide additional information for IR. For example, in the experiment of TREC 2004 Genomics Track (see Section 2.2 and Section 4), we use term names to decide if a term (protein) belongs to certain protein family. Also, we record the semantic type of a term, the category a term belongs to. The semantic type is also useful to express information needs (see Section 2.2).

A relation is defined as a pair of two concepts which are semantically and syntactically related to each other. We extract all such concept pairs in a document and record their frequency. For the simplicity, the relation in our model is undirected.

2.2 Query Representation

The query representation is often subject to the mechanism of document representation. Under traditional term-based IR model, we often use term vector or term-based Boolean expression to represent information needs. In this section, we will first

[2] http://www.nlm.nih.gov/research/umls/

briefly introduce the syntax of relation-based Boolean expression and then demonstrate the effectiveness of this query representation mechanism by the examples from TREC 2004 Genomics Track.

Two types of predicates denoted by concept (T) and relation (R) are available to build Boolean expression. A concept can be specified by any combination of its name (STR), unique ID (CUI), and semantic type (TUI). All predicates can be combined by AND or OR operator. Here, we use the ad hoc retrieval topics in TREC 2004 Genomics Track[3] to illustrate how to use relation-based Boolean expression to represent user information needs.

Topic #1: Ferroportin-1 in humans
Query: T (CUI=C0915115)
Notes: C0915115 is the concept ID of *Ferroportin-1* in the dictionary of UMLS (Unified Medical Language System). All concepts IDs in this paper are based on UMLS.

Topic #12: Genes regulated by Smad4
Query: R (CUI_1=C0694891 and TUI_2=T028)
Notes: C0694891 is the concept ID of *Smad4* and T028 stands for the semantic type if *Gene*. Because a relation is undirected, the query should contain the symmetric predicate R (CUI_2=C0694891 and TUI_1=T028). However, for the simplicity, we let the IR system automatically generate the symmetric predicate R.

Topic #14: Expression or Regulation of TGFB in HNSCC cancers
Query: R (CUI_1=C1515406 and CUI_2=C1168401)
Notes: C1515406 is the concept ID of *TGFB* and C1168401 is the concept ID of *HNSCC*

Topic #30: Regulatory targets of the Nkx gene family members
Query: R (STR_1 like nkx% and TUI_1=T028 and TUI_2=T028)
Notes: we assume a term with its name beginning with nkx and with semantic type of gene is the member of *Nkx gene family*.

We can see that relation-based Boolean expression is neat and powerful to express user information needs from above examples. In topic #1, we simply use one T predicate though Ferroportion-1 has lots of synonyms. In topic #12 and #30, we use one R predicate in conjunction with semantic types to express a question-answering type information need that is very difficult to be represented by term vector or term-based Boolean expression.

3 Extraction of Concepts and Relations

In this section, we propose a generic ontology-based approach to the extraction of concepts and relations. As shown in Figure 3, we first extract term names using do main ontology in conjunction with part of speech patterns [21]; then use surrounding words to narrow down the meaning of the extracted term, i.e. identifying the concept the term refers to in the context. Finally we employ several heuristic approaches to the extraction of binary relations.

---

[3] http://trec.nist.gov/data/genomics/04.adhoc.topics.txt

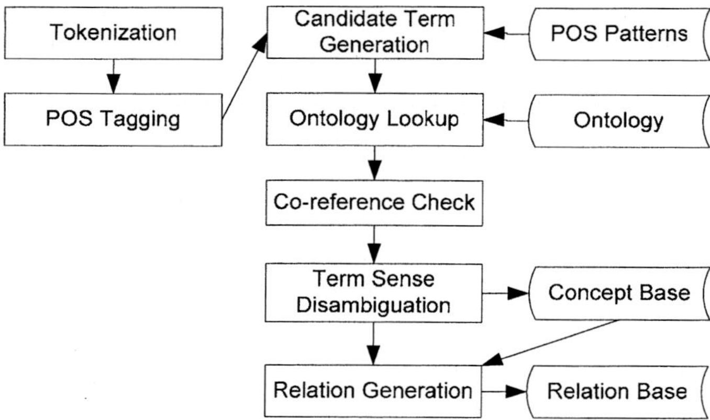

Fig. 3. The architecture of the concept and relation extraction system

3.1 Extraction of Terms

There are volumes of work on the topic of term extraction from biomedical literatures. Most of them use either hand-created rules or machine-learned rules to extract terms from text. However, neither of them extracts the meaning of a term that is important to our document representation model. For instance, the information extraction (IE) system may tell you that *Ferroportin-1* is a protein but not tell you what protein it is. For this reason, we implement a generic ontology-based approach [21] that identifies not only the semantic type of the term, but also its possible meanings. This approach begins with part of speech (POS) tagging, then generates candidate terms using POS patterns, and finally determines if it is a term by looking up the ontology.

In this particular project, we take UMLS as the domain ontology. UMLS is built from the electronic versions of many different thesauri, classifications, code sets, and lists of controlled terms in the area of biomedicine and health. The Metathesaurus of UMLS is organized by concept or meaning of terms and provides their various names (synonyms), and the relationships among them. By checking with the synonym table, we can easily determine if the candidate (generated by POS patterns listed in Table 1) is a term and retrieve possible meanings if yes.

Table 1. Part of Speech Patterns and Examples. NN, NUM, and JJ denote noun, number, and adjective, respectively. All article, preposition, and conjunction words will be removed from the original text before pattern matching.

Part of Speech Pattern	Examples
NN NN NN	Cancer of Head and Neck
NN NUM NN	DO 1 Antibody
JJ NN NN	High Blood Pressure
NN NN	DNA Repair
NN NUM	Ferroportin 1
JJ NN	Sleeping Beauty
NN	FancD2

A term sometimes appears in the form of a pronoun such as *it* or its abbreviation. It is then necessary to figure out what the pronoun or the abbreviation refers to in the local context. We then develop a simple heuristic approach to handle abbreviations and implement a light method [3] to solve pronominal references.

3.2 Term Sense Disambiguation

Using the approach proposed by [21], we may extract more than one meaning for a term. For example, *Ferroportin-1* has two meanings in UMLS (*C0915115: metal transporting protein 1*; *C1452618: Slc40a1 protein, mouse*). Thus, we need a sense disambiguation component to further clarify the meaning the term refers to in the context.

Inspired by the finding that the ambiguity of many UMLS terms in text is caused by the use of short name, abbreviation, or partial name, we develop an unsupervised term sense disambiguation approach adapted from Lesk's word sense disambiguation (WSD) approach. The Lesk's WSD approach basically tags sense by maximizing the number of common words between the definition of candidate senses and the surrounding words of the target [10]. Different from Lesk's approach, our approach first use surrounding words (3 words in the left side of the target and 3 word in the right side of the target) to narrow down sense candidates. If there is still more than one sense left, we then score each candidate. In Lesk's approach, any word in any sense has same weight. Obviously it is not a good assumption for term sense disambiguation. Instead, we borrow the idea from term weighting research and use TF*IDF to score the importance of a word for a sense [8]. Then the final formula for sense tagging is:

$$S = \arg\max_j \sum_i IDF_i \times TF_{ij} = \arg\max_j \sum_i \log\frac{N}{n_i} \times \frac{F_{ij}}{F_j}$$

Where:
N is the number of senses in dictionary
n_i is the number of senses containing $Word_i$
F_{ij} is the occurrence of $Word_i$ in various names of $Sense_j$
F_j is the total occurrence of words in various names of $Sense_j$

3.3 Extraction of Relations

A relation is defined as a pair of two concepts which are semantically and syntactically related to each other. If there is a pre-defined relation between the semantic types of two concepts in the domain ontology, these two concepts are simply viewed as semantically related. However, the judgment of syntactic relation between two concepts is difficult. We propose a heuristic approach for syntactic relation judgment.

The extraction of biological relationships is a hot topic in the area of information extraction. The essence of this line of work is to generalize the syntactic rules for certain types of relations in a supervised or unsupervised manner. However, there are two major problems when applying these methods to extract biological relations for our IR indexing. First, the indexing component of our IR system is interested in various biological relationships. But most of these reported extracting methods are merely tested on protein-protein interactions. Second, the recall of these extracting methods seems to low for IR use. For example, the IE system reported by [13] only extracts 53 relationships with 43 correct from 1,000 Medline abstracts containing the keyword "protein interaction". Instead, we develop a simple but effective heuristic approach that first uses clause level co-occurrence to generate concept-pair candidates and then apply a set of rules to filter out some candidates. This approach is able to identify various biological relationships with high recall and good precision for IR use.

Term co-occurrence is frequently used to determine if two terms are connected in graph-based data mining. Some work takes any pair of two words in a sentence as a relation [16]. However, as reported by [4], sentences in Medline abstracts are often very long and complex. Thus, if we follow the strategy of [16], many noisy relations may be introduced. Instead, we use a clause as the boundary of a relation because concepts within a clause are more cohesive than within a sentence in general. We implement a light approach that basically uses comma and a set of conjunction words (including *although, because, but, if, that, though, when, whether, while* and so on) to split a complex sentence into one main clause and several subordinating clauses. In example 1, there are three terms underlined and one relation (*obesity* and *periodontal disease*). The term *epidemiological study* has no relation with any of the other two terms because it is in a separate clause.

Rule for relation: *If two concepts are co-occurred within a clause, but are not coordinating components, and their semantic types are related to each other in domain ontology, this concept pair is identified as a binary relation.*

Example 1: *A recent epidemiological study revealed that obesity is an independent risk factor for periodontal disease.*

Example 2: *Diabetes is associated with many metabolic disorders including insulin resistance, dyslipidemia, hypertension and atherosclerosis.*

Also, Ding et al. [4] pointed out that coordinating was a frequently occurred phenomenon in biomedical documents and interactions (relations) between coordinating components was rare in Medline abstract. Thus, in example 2, *diabetes* has relations with remaining four concepts respectively. But *insulin resistance, dyslipidemia, hypertension,* and *atherosclerosis* don't have relations with each other because they are coordinating components.

In short, we consider a concept pair a binary relation if these two concepts are co-occurred within a clause, but are not coordinating components, and their semantic types are related to each other in the domain ontology.

4 Experiment

In this section, we discuss the experiment design and the search engine and document collection used for experiment. Then we analyze the experiment result and compare the performance of proposed relation-based IR model with other work.

4.1 Search Engine and Collection for Experiment

To our best knowledge, no search engines support relation-based search so far. For this reason, we developed a prototyped IR system supporting relation-based Boolean search. We implemented conceptual document representation in Figure 2 with a DB2 database. When a query represented by relation-based Boolean expression (see Section 2.2) is submitted, the system automatically converts the Boolean expression to ANSI SQL statement and submits the SQL statement to the DB2 system. The prototyped IR system is function-limited. It does not support document ranking, but simply returns documents that satisfy all predicates specified in the query.

We use the collection of TREC 2004 Genomics Track in our experiment. The document collection is a 10-year subset (1994-2003, 4.6 million documents) of the MEDLINE bibliographic database of the biomedical literature that can be searched by PubMed. Relevance judgments were done using the conventional "pooling method" whereby a fixed number of top-ranking documents from each official run were pooled and provided to an individual for relevance judgment. The pools were built from the top-precedence run from each of the 27 groups. They took the top 75 documents for each topic and eliminated the duplicates to create a single pool for each topic. The average pool size (average number of documents judged per topic) was 976, with a range of 476-1450. Based on the human relevance judgment, the performance of each official run could be evaluated (All facts and evaluation result of TREC-04 Genomics Track in Section 5 are from [6]).

Since our goal is to see whether our relation-based IR methods can further improve TREC 2004 participants' retrieval results, we build our search engine on top of search engines participated in TREC 2004. For this, we take the documents in pools for each topic and eliminate repeated documents across topics to create a single pool for our experiment use. The indexing and searching of our prototyped IR system is based on this mini-pool containing 42, 255 documents.

4.2 Experiment Design

Our goal is to build a precision-focused IR system. The major research question of this paper is *if relation-based IR outperforms term-based IR in terms of precision.* Because the current prototyped system does not support ranking, we compare overall precision (the precision of all retrieved documents) of our run with P@100 of all runs participated in TREC 2004 Genomics Track. Our run retrieved 125 documents on average. Thus, the comparison is fair to runs in TREC-04.

The hypothesis that relation-based IR outperforms term-based IR in terms of precision is actually based on the assumption that explicit assertion of term relation is more useful than document level term co-occurrence when judging if a document addresses certain relationship. To test the truth of this assumption, we study if the query $R(t_1, t_2)$ provides higher precision than the query $T(t_1)$ *and* $T(t_2)$ in our experiment.

We are also interested in the recall of relation-based IR though it is not our focus. On one hand, the use of relation will lower the recall because the number of documents returned by $R(t_1, t_2)$ is always equal or less than by $T(t_1)$ *and* $T(t_2)$. On the other hand, the use of concept instead of term name well solves the synonym problem; thus it may increase the recall. So we will study the effect of use of concept and relation on the recall of IR.

4.3 Analysis of Experiment Result

Our run retrieves 124.80 documents on average and achieves 53.69% overall precision and 44.31% overall recall (see Table 5). Because our prototyped system does not support ranking, we compare our overall precision with P@100 of TREC 2004 Genomics Track. This comparison is fair to runs of TREC since our system retrieves more than 100 documents on average.

We first compare the precision on 50 individual topics. Except for topic 16, the precision of ours outperforms P@100 of TREC on all other 49 topics as shown in Fig. 4. Then we compare the precision of our run with P@100 of all official runs in TREC. As shown in Table 2, the precision of our run (53.69%) is significantly higher than P@100 of the top 3 runs and the mean of all official runs (26.37%). It is worth noting that we can not say that the precision of our IR system is better than that of other IR systems because our search is based on the returns of all other IR systems. But the experiment result really tells us that the relation based model is very promising for precision-focused IR because it significantly improves the precision of other IR systems.

For seven topics that use a single R predicate like $R\ (CUI_1{=}A \text{ and } CUI_2{=}B)$, we further change the Boolean expression to *T (CUI=A) and T (CUI=B)* and search again. As expected, the precision is lowered while the recall is improved (see Table 3). That is, the binary relation provides higher precision than document level term co-occurrence when retrieving documents addressing certain relationships. This is the foundation of the claim of the whole paper that relation-based IR model contributes higher precision to domain-specific research than term-based IR models.

The concept-based search can raise the recall of IR especially when a term has lots of synonyms because all synonyms share one concept ID. To test this hypothesis, we change seven single T predicate searches listed in Table 4 to term-based searches. As expected, the recall of topic 1 and 35 is significantly lowered because both of them have many synonyms.

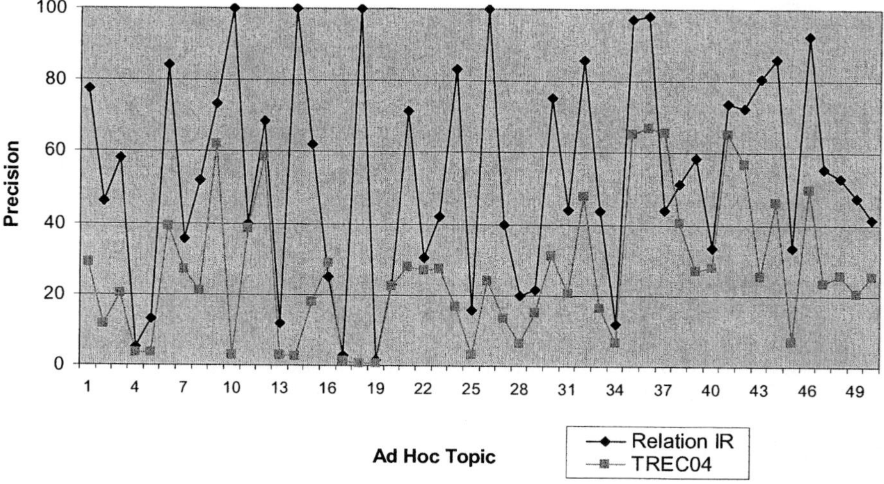

Fig. 4. The comparison of the overall precision of our relation-based IR system with the mean P@100 of all official runs in TREC 2004 Genomic Track on 50 ad hoc retrieval topics

Table 2. The comparison of the precision of our run with official runs participated in TREC 2004 Genomics Track. Runs in TREC are sorted by Mean Average Precision (MAP) [6]. Because our retrieval is not ranked, MAP and P@10 are not available; the P@100 of our run is actually the overall precision.

Run	MAP	P@10	P@100
Relation IR (Our Run)	N/A	N/A	53.69
pllsgen4a2 (the best)	40.75	60.04	41.96
uwntDg04tn (the second)	38.67	62.40	42.10
pllsgen4a1 (the third)	36.89	57.00	39.36
edinauto5 (the worst)	0.12	0.36	1.3
Mean@TREC04	21.72	42.69	26.37

Table 3. The comparison of the use of relation and concept co-occurrence in IR

Topic	$R\ (t_1, t_2)$		$T\ (t_1)$ and $T\ (t_2)$		P@100 TREC04 (%)
	P (%)	R (%)	P (%)	R (%)	
7	35.71	8.70	24.62	27.83	27.04
8	52.00	8.07	41.05	24.22	20.94
13	12.00	12.50	8.77	20.83	2.74
14	100.00	23.81	80.00	23.81	2.70
15	61.90	14.44	48.08	27.78	18.00
21	71.43	18.75	52.83	35.00	27.96
22	30.52	44.76	25.14	65.71	27.09

Table 4. The comparison of concept-based search and term-based search

Topic	Name B	T(CUI=A)		T (STR like %B%)		T(STR=B)	
		P (%)	R (%)	P (%)	R (%)	P (%)	R
1	Ferroportin	77.59	56.96	84.62	41.77	88.46	29.11
6	FancD2	84.09	39.36	84.09	39.36	85.29	30.85
9	mutY	73.38	98.26	81.75	97.39	81.48	95.65
35	WD40	97.16	63.10	99.28	50.55	98.28	21.03
36	RAB3A	98.10	81.50	98.10	81.50	98.53	79.13
43	Sleeping Beauty	80.56	14.87	77.42	12.31	77.42	12.31
46	RSK2	92.59	12.69	82.76	12.18	89.47	8.63

5 Conclusions and Future Work

In this paper, we proposed a novel relation-based information retrieval approach for biomedical literature search. Unlike traditional term-based IR models that use terms to index and search documents, our relation model uses controlled concepts and their binary relations to index and search documents. Because explicitly asserted biological relationships are exactly what scientists are interested in, the direct use of relation for document indexing and searching may improve the precision of genomic information retrieval. The experiment on the collection of TREC 2004 Genomics Track successfully tested this hypothesis. Besides, we could draw another three conclusions from the experiment:

- An explicitly asserted relation in text is a stronger indicator of a document that addresses a binary relation than the document level concepts co-occurrence.
- Concept-based search will bring higher recall than term-based search especially when a searching term has many synonyms.
- Relation-based Boolean expression is powerful and effective to express genomic information needs.

For future work, we will develop a ranking algorithm for relation-based IR and implement a full-functioned search engine supporting relation-based searching. We will also take effort on the extraction of concepts and relations that would further improve the performance of the relation-based search.

References

1. Bai, J., Song, D., Bruza, P., Nie, J.Y., and Cao, G., "Query Expansion Using Term Relationships in Language Models for Information Retrieval", *In Proceedings of the ACM 14th Conference on Information and Knowledge Management (CIKM)*, November 2005, Bremen, Germany.
2. Cao, G., Nie, J.Y., and Bai, J., "Integrating Word Relationships into Language Models", *Proceedings of the 28th annual international ACM SIGIR conference on Research and Development in Information Retrieval*, 2005, pp. 298 - 305
3. Dimitrov, M., Bontcheva, K., Cunningham, H., and Maynard, D., "A Light-weight Approach to Coreference Resolution for Named Entities in Text", *Proceedings of the Fourth Discourse Anaphora and Anaphor Resolution Colloquium (DAARC)*, Lisbon, 2002.
4. Ding, J., Berleant, D., Xu, J., and Fulmer, A.W., "Extracting Biochemical Interactions from MEDLINE Using a Link Grammar Parser", *In the 15th IEEE International Conference on Tools with Artificial Intelligence (ICTAI'03)*, 2003.
5. Gao, J., Nie, J.Y., Wu, G. and Cao G., "Dependency Language Model for Information Retrieval", *Proceedings of the 27th annual international ACM SIGIR conference on Research and Development in Information Retrieval*, 2004, pp. 170 - 177
6. Hersh W, et al. "TREC 2004 Genomics Track Overview", The thirteenth Text Retrieval Conference, 2004.
7. Hu, X., Yoo, I., Song, I.Y., Song, M., Han, J., and Lechner, M., "Extracting and Mining Protein-Protein Interaction Network from Biomedical Literature", *Proceedings of the 2004 IEEE Symposium on Computational Intelligence in Bioinformatics and Computational Biology*, 2004.
8. Jones, K.S., "Exhaustivity and specificity", *Journal of Documentation*, 1972, Vol. 28, pp.11-21.
9. Kim, J.T. and Moldovan, D.I., "Acquisition of Linguistic Patterns for Knowledge-Based Information Extraction", *IEEE Transactions on Knowledge and Data Engineering*, 1995, 7(5), pp. 713-724.
10. Lesk, M., "Automatic Sense Disambiguation: How to Tell a Pine Cone from and Ice Cream Cone", *Proceedings of the SIGDOC'86 Conference, ACM*, 1986.

11. Miller, D., Leek, T., and Schwartz M.R., "A Hidden Markov Model Information Retrieval System", Proceedings of SIGIR-99, 22nd ACM International Conference on Research and Development in Information Retrieval, 1999, pp 214-221.
12. Mooney, R. J. and Bunescu, R. "Mining Knowledge from Text Using Information Extraction", *SIGKDD Explorations* (special issue on Text Mining and Natural Language Processing), 7, 1 (2005), pp. 3-10.
13. Palakal, M., Stephens, M.; Mukhopadhyay, S., Raje, R., Rhodes, S., "A multi-level text mining method to extract biological relationships" , *Proceedings of the IEEE Computer Society Bioinformatics Conference (CBS2002)*, 14-16 Aug. 2002 Page(s):97 – 108
14. Salton, G. and Buckley, C., "Improving retrieval performance by relevance feedback", *Journal of the American Society for Information Science*, 1990, vol. 41, pp. 288-97
15. Sanderson, M. 1994, "Word sense disambiguation and information retrieval", *Proceedings of the 17th annual international ACM SIGIR conference on Research and development in information retrieval*, p.142-151, July 03-06, 1994, Dublin, Ireland.
16. Schenker, A., Last, M., Bunke, H., and Kandel, A., "Clustering of Web Documents Using a Graph Model", *In A. Antonacopoulos & J. Hu (Eds.), Web Document Analysis: Challenges and Opportunities*, 2003.
17. Soderland, S., Fisher, D., Aseltine, J., and Lehnert, W., "CRYSTAL: Inducing a Conceptual Dictionary", *Proceedings of the Fourteenth International Joint Conference on Artificial Intelligence*, 1995, pp. 1314-1319.
18. Soderland, S., "Learning Information Extraction rules for Semi-structured and free text", *Machine Learning*, Vol. 34, 1998, pp. 233-272.
19. Stokoe, C. and Tait, J. I. 2004. Towards a Sense Based Document Representation for Information Retrieval, in *Proceedings of the Twelfth Text REtrieval Conference (TREC)*, Gaithersburg M.D.
20. van Rijsbergen, C.J., "A theoretical basis for the use of cooccurrence data in information retrieval", *Journal of Documentation*, 1977, 33(2), pp 106-119.
21. Zhou, X., Han, H., Chankai, I., Prestrud, A., and Brooks, A., "Converting Semi-structured Clinical Medical Records into Information and Knowledge", *Proceeding of The International Workshop on Biomedical Data Engineering (BMDE) in conjunction with the 21st International Conference on Data Engineering (ICDE)*, Tokyo, Japan, April 5-8, 2005.

Effective Keyword Search in XML Documents Based on MIU

Jianjun Xu[1], Jiaheng Lu[2], Wei Wang[1], and Baile Shi[1]

[1] Department of Computing and Information Technology,
Fudan University, China
{xjj, weiwang1, blshi}@fudan.edu.cn
[2] Department of Computer Science,
National University of Singapore
lujiahen@comp.nus.edu.sg

Abstract. Keyword search is an effective approach for most users to search for information because they do not need to learn complex query languages or the underlying structures of the data. This paper focuses on effective keyword search in XML documents which are modeled as labeled trees. We first analyze the problems caused by the refinement of result granularity during XML keyword search and then propose to partition an XML document into XML fragments with the granularity of Minimal Information Unit (MIU). Furthermore, we present efficient index structures and the corresponding search algorithms. Finally, our comprehensive experiments demonstrate the benefits of our method over previously proposed methods in terms of result quality, index size and execution time.

1 Introduction

Keyword search is now the most popular information discovery method because the user does not need to learn any query language, or know the underlying structure of the data. Google, as the most famous search engine, provides keyword search on the HTML documents of World Wide Web. When the user just inputs several keywords on its simple-style homepage, Google can return all the HTML documents that are associated with these keywords. Therefore, the search engines of this kind can greatly facilitate naïve users to search for information on WWW.

With XML gradually becoming the *de facto* standard for data representation and exchange, keyword search on XML documents has become an important research direction. Although an XML document can be regarded as an HTML document, and thus the existing search engine techniques can be used for XML keyword search, the XML document has its own characteristics to be exploited. The biggest difference between HTML keyword search and XML keyword search lies in the granularities of their results. HTML keyword search returns the whole HTML document. The tags in the HTML document are just display instructions with no semantic information, so it is difficult to partition an HTML document into fragments. On the contrary, the tags in the XML document contain certain semantic information, indicating the meaning of the data nested. Therefore, we can return just the fragments of the XML document

M.L. Lee, K.L. Tan, and V. Wuwongse (Eds.): DASFAA 2006, LNCS 3882, pp. 702–716, 2006.

associated with the keywords, rather than the whole XML document. In XML keyword search, the granularity of the search result is refined from document into element, which is called Refinement of Result Granularity. Refinement of result granularity is very useful and effective in searching on large XML documents, because it can help the user filter out a great deal of irrelevant information. Besides, because XML documents in most practical applications are often far larger than HTML documents in size, if we just return to the user the whole XML document, the high cost of network transfer will greatly degrade the search performance.

However, refinement of result granularity also gives rise to several problems. First, if some result element is partitioned from the XML document and returned to the user, it will be semantically incomplete with its context lost. Consider a sample XML document shown in Figure 1. Suppose that the user inputs a single keyword "Ullman", for he wants to search for the information about Ullman's publications. In this situation, all the known researches will return to the user the elements directly containing "Ullman", such as the second *author* element in Figure 1, i.e. <author>Jeffrey D. Ullman</author>. Nevertheless, for the user, the context information is insufficient in such a simple result. He cannot understand whether Ullman is the author of a book or that of a paper, needless to say what on earth this publication is. Obviously, such search results will never satisfy the user. Therefore, how to make the search results semantically complete with necessary context information becomes a pressing problem to be solved.

```
<publication>
  <books>
    <publisher>Prentice Hall</publisher>
    <book>
      <title>Database Concepts</title>
      <author>David M Kroenke</author>
    </book>
    <book>
      <title>A First Course in Database Systems</title>
      <author>Jeffrey D. Ullman</author>
    </book>
    ...
  </books>
  ...
</publication>
```

Fig. 1. A Sample XML Document

Second, the search results gained through using the existing techniques still contain much irrelevant information. Still consider the XML document in Figure 1. Suppose that the user wants to search for the information about Ullman's books published by Prentice Hall, and thus he may input the keywords "Ullman Prentice Hall". All the known researches return the smallest elements containing "Ullman", "Prentice" and "Hall" in the XML document, such as the first *books* element. Obviously, such a result will not satisfy the user as well, because it contains all the information of the books published by Prentice Hall. Thus, what the user really wants is still submerged in the sea of irrelevant information. Of course, in comparison with returning the whole XML document, it is a big step forward to simply return the first *books* element, because all the information of the books published by other presses has been filtered out. Yet, all in all, it is still a problem how to achieve a finer result granularity to filter out irrelevant information.

Third, refinement of result granularity may lead to invalid search results. The commonest situation is that different keywords are matched with different parts of the XML document. Because there is no or weak relationship among these parts, such search results mean little to the user. The root cause of the problem lies in that the keywords belong to different entities, among which there exists weak relationship. Thus, how to identify entities in the XML document and their relationships to reduce invalid search results as much as possible becomes another challenge.

This paper makes the following contributions: (1) Based on the analysis of the problems caused by refinement of result granularity, we give the definition of Minimal Information Unit (MIU) and present the algorithm of partitioning the XML document into MIUs. (2) Regarding MIU as the granularity of indexing and searching, we design efficient index structures and the corresponding search algorithms. (3) We conduct an extensive experimental study with real-life as well as synthetic XML data sets to validate the effectiveness and efficiency of our method. Our results demonstrate significantly improved result quality and search performance.

The rest of this paper is organized as follows. In Section 2, we review related work about XML keyword search. In Section 3, we present the data model that we use and the query semantics. Then, Section 4 states the definition of MIU in the XML document and the algorithm of partitioning the XML document into MIUs. Section 5 presents efficient index structures and the corresponding search algorithms. Section 6 contains experiments that show the effectiveness and efficiency of our method. Finally, Section 7 concludes this paper.

2 Related Work

At the present time, there are mainly two directions in the researches on XML keyword search. One is to add full-text search features and ranking to accurate XML query languages such as XML-QL[5, 6, 7]. The advantage of these languages after extension is the accuracy of the search results. However, all these languages are not suitable for naïve users, because they need to learn the syntax of complex query languages, and know the structures of XML documents.

The researches in the other direction make good use of the characteristics of the XML document to carry out keyword search. These researches mainly include: XRANK[1], XKeyword[2], XSEarch[3] and XKSearch[4]. XRANK is the first to realize that the granularity of the search result can be element. And it puts forward DIL algorithm, which merges the lists of inverted index items to find out all the elements containing all the keywords. XKeyword is the extension of keyword search in the relational databases—DISCOVER[8]. Regarding an XML document as a graph, XKeyword transforms XML keyword search into proximity search among the keywords in the graph. From the angle of semantics, XSEarch solves, to some degree, the problem of invalid search results. XKSearch brings forward ILE algorithm, which is used to search for all the SLCAs (Smallest Lowest Common Ancestor) in the XML tree. ILE algorithm outperforms DIL algorithm when the search contains the keywords with significantly different frequencies. The SE variant is tuned for the case where the keywords have similar frequencies.

The above-mentioned researches all make contributions to the development of XML keyword search in the second direction, but most of them do not realize the problems caused by refinement of result granularity. Therefore, the problems stated in Section 1 will appear in their search systems. In addition, there also exist in them some other defects, which are pointed out in the following sections.

3 Data Model and Query Semantics

3.1 XML Data Model

An XML document can be regarded as a labeled tree. The leaf node is the data value, and the inner node the element. An XML document contains nested elements, and each element has its own attributes, values or subelements. To facilitate the expression, attributes can be regarded as subelements, too. In the XML tree, a value node is represented with a pane, and an element node with a circle.

Definition 1. XML Data Graph DG = (N, E, ROOT, $Label_{NE}$, $Value_{NV}$, Order). N=NE $\cup$NV. N is the set of nodes, in which NE is the set of element nodes, and NV is the set of value nodes. A node n has its unique global number id(n). E$\subseteq$N×N. E is the set of containment edges. ROOT$\in$NE. ROOT is the unique root node. Function $Label_{NE}(n)$ returns the tag of element node n, and function $Value_{NV}(n)$ returns the value of value node n. The child nodes of an element node are in order. Function Order(n) returns a number that represents the relative position of node n among its siblings.

Definition 2. XML Schema Graph SG = (NE, E, ROOT, $Label_{NE}$, $Cardinality_E$). NE is the set of element nodes. E$\in$NE×NE. E is the set of containment edges. ROOT$\in$ NE. ROOT is the unique root node. Function $Label_{NE}(n)$ returns the tag of element node n, and function $Cardinality_E(e)$ returns the cardinality of containment edge e. Suppose that, in the XML schema graph, e connects node n_1 with node n_2, and n_1 is the parent node of n_2. Function $Cardinality_E(e)$ calculates the scope of times n_2 may appear as the child nodes of some specific node n_1 in the corresponding XML data graph. $Cardinality_E(e)$ is represented as c_1:c_2, in which c_1 is the minimum times of appearance, while c_2 the maximum times. If $c_1 = c_2 = m$, c_1:c_2 can be simplified as m. Please note that the difference between the XML schema graph and the ordinary DTD graph lies in that the former exactly records the cardinalities of containment edges in a specific XML document, whereas the cardinalities in the latter may just represent approximate scopes, sometimes even far different from the real situation of the document.

In the XML schema graph, if the cardinality of containment edge e is 1 or 0:1, e is called the edge of low frequency, otherwise the edge of high frequency. Figure 2 is the text of an XML document, and Figure 3 is the XML data graph of the document. We can see that only the leaf nodes, which are the value nodes, contain the really useful information. Figure 4 is the XML schema graph of the document, in which the edges of high frequency are represented with the thick lines. Moreover, the cardinality

```
<dblp>
   <conference>
      <name>SIGMOD</name>
      <year>
         <confyear>2003</confyear>
         <paper pages=4-15>
            <title>Querying Structured Text in an XML Database</title>
            <author>Shurug Al-Khalifa</author>
         </paper>
         <paper pages=16-27>
            <title>XRANK: Ranked Keyword Search over XML Documents</title>
            <author>Lin Guo</author>
         </paper>
         … …
      </year>
      <year>
         <confyear>2004</confyear>
         … …
      </year>
      … …
   </conference>
   … …
</dblp>
```

Fig. 2. XML Document (DBLP)

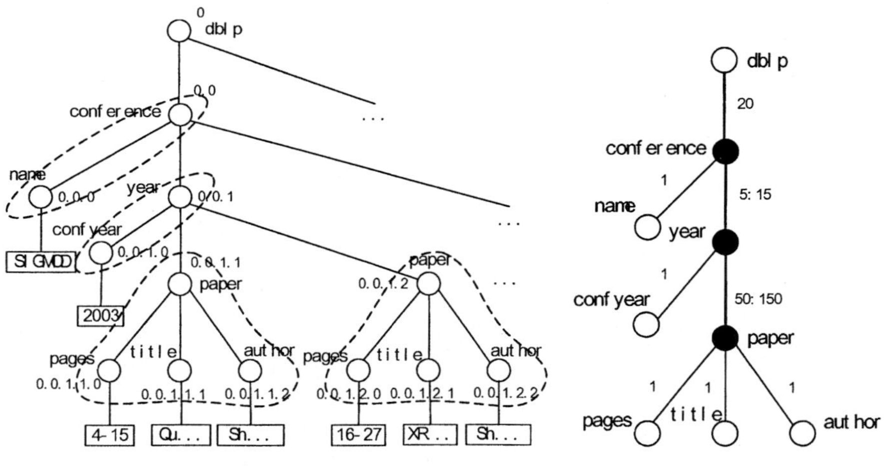

Fig. 3. Data Graph (DBLP)

Fig. 4. Schema Graph (DBLP)

of each containment edge is marked beside the edge. For instance, the cardinality of the edge between node *conference* and node *year* is 5:15, which means that for any conference, it has been held at least for five years and at most for fifteen years.

3.2 Result Definition of Keyword Search

Keyword search Q is the keywords submitted by the user. Suppose that Q = {w_1, w_2, ..., w_k}. XKSearch defines the result set of keyword search as all the SLCAs. The so-called SLCA node is the element node in the XML tree and satisfies the following two conditions: (1) the subtree rooted at the node contains w_1, w_2, ..., w_k; (2) there does not exist any subtree of the subtree mentioned in (1), which also contains w_1, w_2, ..., w_k.

XKSearch defines the result set as all the SLCAs, so it may lose some results. For example, in the XML tree of Figure 5, suppose that k_1 and k_2 are the keywords submitted by the user. Through observation, it is not difficult to find out that the search results should be the two XML fragments shown in Figure 5, whose root nodes are node 1 and node 4 respectively. However, in XKSearch, because node 1 is the ancestor node of node 4, node 1 will, according to ILE algorithm, be removed by the procedure *removeAncestor()*. Obviously, such removal is not appropriate. The root cause of this problem just lies in that the definition of the result set made in XKSearch has its deficiency.

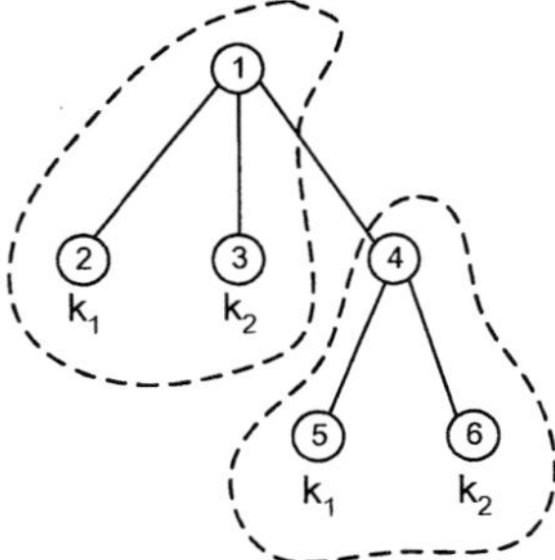

Fig. 5. SLCA & XLCA

To solve the above-mentioned problem, XLCA (eXclusive Lowest Common Ancestor) is proposed on the basis of SLCA and defined as follows: first of all, for an XML data graph T, find out all the SLCAs of T; these SLCAs are just XLCAs; second, remove from T the fragments rooted at these SLCA nodes, and then find out again all the SLCAs of T, which are left out by ILE algorithm but revealed after the removal; these SLCAs are also XLCAs; the second step repeats until there is no SLCA in T. It can be seen that all the XLCAs are exclusive, i.e. non-overlapped. From the definition, SLCA must be XLCA, while XLCA is not necessarily SLCA.

Suppose that xlca(T) is the set of all the XLCAs in an XML data graph T, and that slca(T) is the set of all the SLCAs. We define the result set of XML keyword search as all the XLCAs, that is, xlca(T). For T, slca(T)$\subseteq$xlca(T). We can see that the definition of the result set made in XKSearch is not complete, because it cannot find out xlca(T)$-$slca(T). For example, in Figure 5, XKSearch cannot find out the fragment rooted at node 1, but we can because the XLCA node set just includes node 1 and node 4. Note that from Section 4 MIU is regarded as the granularity of indexing and searching. Therefore, since then, XLCA is composed of MIUs, rather than elements.

4 Minimal Information Unit

4.1 Definition of MIU

Keyword search aims at searching for the information of the entities associated with the keywords. Entity should be the finest granularity of the search result, otherwise the information returned to the user may be semantically incomplete. The search result should also contain the necessary context information, which requires returning to the user the entities closely related to those directly containing the keywords. Meanwhile, the entities that have no or weak relationship to those directly containing the keywords should also be filtered out as much as possible. Therefore, the first step in keyword search is to identify all the entities in the search target.

An XML document is a set of entities. The element in the document represents the entity in the real world or its attribute. For example, in Figure 3, the *paper* element refers to the paper entity, and its *title* subelement serves as the title attribute of the paper entity. Each entity can have one or more attributes. Attributes can be simple or composite. A specific entity is just an instance of certain entity type. In the XML document, it means that there exist elements of the same type but with different contents. Besides, there exists certain relationship of containment between entities. Similarly, in the XML document, it means that there exists nesting between elements. For example, dblp is the set of several conferences. Since a conference is held in different years, it can be further divided by year. Then, in a specified year, the conference contains many papers.

Definition 3. Minimal Information Unit (MIU) of DG is an XML fragment in DG. Its root node refers to the entity it represents, and all the descendant nodes refer to the attributes of the entity. This fragment as a whole makes up an information unit with relatively complete semantics. Similarly, we can also define the Minimal Information Unit of SG. To distinguish between them, we name MIU of DG dMIU, and MIU of SG sMIU. The former represents the specific entity, while the latter refers to the entity type. Usually, there are several dMIUs corresponding to one sMIU.

The introduction of MIU is conducive to solving the problems caused by refinement of result granularity. First, after the recognition of dMIUs, the search result can be composed of dMIUs representing entities, rather than arbitrary elements. This makes its components semantically complete. Second, only after the recognition can the entities in the context be identified and returned to the user. In this way the search result can contain the necessary context information. Third, it is not until the recognition of dMIUs that we can filter out the entities unrelated to those directly containing the keywords in order to further reduce the irrelevant information.

XSEarch solves the problem of invalid results by means of judging the relationship between two elements. XSearch holds that different elements with the same tag represent different entities of the same type, and so concludes that they are semantically unrelated. This kind of judging method is so severe that it probably judges some valid results to be invalid. Take the XML tree in Figure 6 for example. Suppose the user submits the keywords "Prentice Hall Database", for he wants to search for the

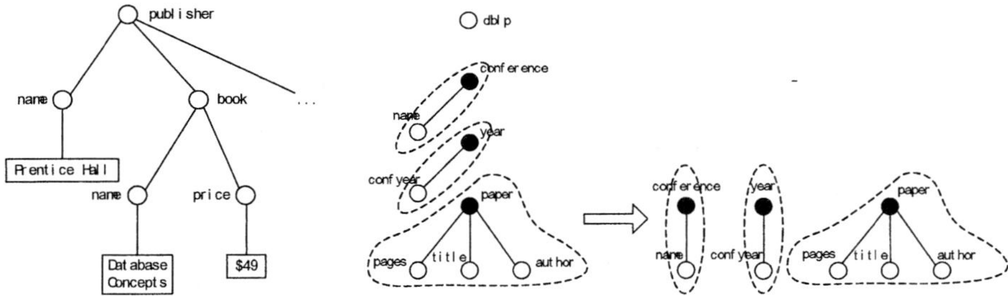

Fig. 6. A Sample XML Tree

Fig. 7. Partitioning of Schema Graph

Information about books on Database published by Prentice Hall. However, because"Prentice Hall" and "Database" are both in the elements with the same tag "*name*", XSEarch will hold that "Prentice Hall" and "Database" belong to different entities of the same type, and so they are semantically unrelated. Therefore, it will not return the result to the user. Yet, it is not the fact. After partitioning an XML document into MIUs, the different elements with the same tag must belong to different dMIUs. So what can be solved by XSEarch can also be achieved by our method. What's more, our method has its own advantage. We do not think that there is no relationship between different dMIUs. Instead, in Section 5, we give a mechanism to judge the quality of the result according to its classification.

4.2 Partitioning of MIU

Some nodes in the XML tree have no real meanings, and usually have no attributes. The nodes of this kind only serve for connection, like node *dblp* in Figure 3, so we call them connection nodes, or dumb nodes.

The algorithm of partitioning SG into sMIUs is described as follows: In SG, through removing all the edges of high frequency and then removing all the isolated nodes (i.e. connection nodes), all the subgraphs acquired are sMIUs of this SG. Take the SG in Figure 4 for example, the partitioning is demonstrated in Figure 7.

To partition the XML document into dMIUs, we first carry out the preprocessing, i.e. scanning over its XML DG. After the acquisition of its corresponding XML SG, we partition SG into sMIUs according to the above-mentioned algorithm. Then, we can partition DG into dMIUs according to the acquired sMIUs.

4.3 Tuning of MIU

The edges of high frequency can be further divided into the weak edges of high frequency and the strong edges of high frequency. The former are the edges of $c_2 \leq \alpha$, in which α is a tunable parameter, while the latter are the edges of $c_2 > \alpha$.

In some situations, because of practical needs, we can tune the partition of SG to gain sMIUs with the coarser granularity. After fixing the value of α, we can regard all the weak edges of high frequency as the edges of low frequency, and repartition SG.

4.4 Indexing of MIU

Dewey encoding is a numbering technique widely used in the context of general knowledge classification. The common used numbering method in XML keyword search is as follows: (1) the dewey number of the root node is 0; (2) suppose that the dewey number of some node is x, then the dewey number of its first child node is x.0, the second is x.1, and so on. In Figure 3, each node of the XML tree is numbered according to dewey encoding. The length of a dewey number is defined as the number of components it contains, like $|0.0.1| = 3$. The length is just the depth of the corresponding node in the XML tree. We can also know whose value is bigger between two dewey numbers by comparing the first component at first; if the same, then the second, and so on, like 0.0.1.1.0<0.1.1.1. Furthermore, the number of the root node can be specified as the document number as well, thus supporting the global numbering of the document set. Note that what we index is the root nodes of dMIUs, so we can greatly reduce the lengths of the dewey numbers as well as the quantity of them.

5 Search Algorithms Based on MIU

5.1 Classification of Search Results and System Indexes

According to the result quality in terms of semantics, the results of keyword search Q $= \{w_1, w_2, ..., w_k\}$ can fall into two categories: the optimal results and the common results. The optimal result means that $w_1, w_2, ..., w_k$ appear in the same entity, i.e. in the same MIU. The common result means that $w_1, w_2, ..., w_k$ appear in several entities, i.e. in several MIUs. The common results can be further divided into the linear common results and the non-linear common results. The linear common result means that $w_1, w_2, ..., w_k$ appear in several entities which have close context relationship with each other. In other words, $w_1, w_2, ..., w_k$ appear in several MIUs which have ancestor-descendant relationship. They appear on the same path originating from the root. And the non-linear common result means that $w_1, w_2, ..., w_k$ appear in several entities which have loose relationship. In other words, $w_1, w_2, ..., w_k$ appear in several MIUs and no path originating from the root can contain all of these MIUs.

The known researches all regard element as the finest granularity. Consequently, it is difficult, from the angle of semantics, to classify the search results. The existing researches usually acquire at first all the results and then sort them using information retrieval techniques. By contrast, this paper takes MIU as the finest granularity. The search results are divided into three categories: the optimal, linear common and non-linear common results. Obviously, from the angle of semantics, the optimal results are superior to the common ones, and, in most situation, the linear common results are superior to the non-linear common ones. Therefore, we can calculate successively the results of the three categories. If the result output of the search system is based on *top-k*, the search may finish earlier when the optimal result set (or the linear common result set) is searched out. Furthermore, from section 5.2, we can see that the time and space cost is quite low in searching for the optimal results and the linear common ones.

To support keyword search, we design efficient index structures. First of all, with regard to the XML document to be searched, we establish an inverted index of MIU numbers in the external storage. For each keyword w in the document, there is a list of inverted index items, miuIL[w], which contains all the dewey numbers of the MIUs where w appears directly. Besides, the MIU numbers in the list are arranged at first in the descending order according to length, and then, for those with the same length, they are arranged in the ascending order according to value. For the XML document in Figure 2, miuIL(SIGMOD)={0.0, ...}, miuIL(2003)={0.0.1, ...}, miuIL (Querying) ={0.0.1.1, ...}, miuIL(XRANK)={0.0.1.2, ...}, ... Second, we establish an inverted index of PATH numbers. For each keyword w, there is a list of inverted index items, pathIL[w], which contains all the numbers of the paths where w appears. The PATH numbers in the list are arranged in the ascending order according to value. For the XML document in Figure 2, pathIL(SIGMOD)={P1, P2, ...}, pathIL(2003)={P1, P2, ...}, pathIL(Querying)={P1, ...}, pathIL(XRANK)={P2, ...}, ...

5.2 Searching for Optimal Results and Linear Common Results

The optimal result is an MIU which contains w_1, w_2, ..., w_k. Suppose that the miuIL lists corresponding to w_1, w_2, ..., w_k are respectively miuIL[w_1], miuIL[w_2], ..., miuIL[w_k]. Algorithm 5.1 can calculate the optimal results through merging miuIL[w_1], miuIL[w_2], ..., miuIL[w_k]. It optimizes the process of merging as well. The search for the results is carried out successively from the low level to high level. Thus, if different are the lengths of the MIU numbers that the current k pointers point, the MIU numbers on lower levels can be directly skipped. In this way, we only need to compare their lengths, rather than the specific redundant MIU numbers.

Algorithm 5.1 computeOptimalResults

```
while (miuIL[w1]<>Ø & ... & miuIL[wk]<>Ø) {
  minlength=min{|top(miuIL[w1])|, ..., |top(miuIL[wk])|}
  for(i=1;i<=k;i++)
    while (|top(miuIL[wi])|>minlength) {
      remove(top(miuIL[wi]));
      if (miuIL[wi]==Ø) exit;}
  rearrange the order of miuIL[w1], ..., miuIL[wk]
    to make the value of top(miuIL[w1]) the smallest
  temp=remove(top(miuIL[w1]));
  for(i=2;i<=k;i++)
    if (top(miuIL[wi])==top(miuIL[w1])) remove(miuIL[wi])
    else break;
  if (i==k+1) output(temp);
}
```

Fig. 8. Searching for the Optimal Results

The linear common result is composed of several MIUs, and each MIU contains at least one keyword. Moreover, there exists ancestor-descendant relationship among these MIUs, that is to say, they appear on the same path originating from the root. Suppose that the pathIL lists corresponding to w_1, w_2, ..., w_k are respectively pathIL[w_1], pathIL[w_2], ..., pathIL[w_k]. We can calculate the linear common results through merging pathIL[w_1], pathIL[w_2], ..., pathIL[w_k]. The algorithm is similar to that of searching for the optimal results. With limited space, the detailed description of the algorithm is omitted here.

5.3 Searching for Non-linear Common Results

Algorithm 5.2 presents the algorithm of evaluating the non-linear common result set, which is called BUP (Bottom-up Pass) algorithm. The basic idea of BUP algorithm is as follows: the search process starts from the lowest level of the XML tree, bottoming up one level after another; during the process, the information on the keywords is passed upwards along the path level by level; once some MIU node contains all the keywords (some of them may be passed here from the lower levels), the corresponding XML fragment will be regarded as a search result.

This algorithm uses a list, miuList, to store the relevant information on the MIU nodes in the current level which contain the keywords or whose subtrees contain the keywords. The steps of the algorithm are described below. For the current level *l*, (1) check the miuList to see if there exist the MIU nodes containing all the keywords. If there do exist, remove the nodes from the miuList. Then check the removed nodes. If they do not belong to the optimal or linear common results, output the XML fragments corresponding to them; 2) after checking level *l*, pass the information on the keywords of the remaining nodes in the miuList to their parent nodes(level *l*-1), and replace all the child nodes with their parent nodes. If there exist several child nodes with the same parent node, merge the subtrees together and meanwhile record in the parent node the position of each child node containing keywords; 3) read the numbers of the MIU nodes in level *l*-1 from the miuIL list of each keyword, and merge them with the miuList. Note that, in step 2, we record the accurate information on the positions of the keywords, so the XML fragment returned is not necessarily the whole subtree which probably contains much irrelevant information. In step 3, if there does not exist the keyword w_i in level *l*-1 or in its upper levels, further check if w_i exists in the miuList. If there is none, either, then the algorithm can finish earlier.

In algorithm 5.2 *l* is the level currently under review. miuList.KS represents the set of keywords appearing in miuList. miuList[i].KS represents the set of keywords appearing in the subtree which takes miuList[i] as its root. Function *prefix()* returns the prefix of the dewey number with the designated length. *merge(miuStart, miuEnd-1)* is to replace the nodes in the miuList from *miuStart* to *miuEnd-1* with their parent node. Simultaneously, the information on the positions of these child nodes is recorded to filter out irrelevant information later. Function *miuILLevel(w_i, level)* returns the set of the MIU numbers in miuIL[w_i], each of which has the same level *level*.

BUP algorithm will be further demonstrated with the example in Figure 5. First, review the lowest level, i.e. the third level to examine every node where k_1 or k_2 appears. Because there is no node which contains all the keywords, every node where k_1 or k_2 appears on the third level passes upwards to its own parent node the information on the keywords. Thus, node 5 passes the keyword k_1 to node 4, and node 6 passes the keyword k_2 to node 4. And when it comes to the nodes on the second level, it is found that node 4 contains all the keywords, and thus the corresponding XML fragment is output. Likewise, node 2 and node 3 pass k_1 and k_2 respectively to node 1, and when it comes to the nodes on the first level, it is found that node 1 contains all the keywords, and thus the corresponding XML fragment is output.

Algorithm 5.2 BUP Algorithm

```
miuList=∅;
level=docdepth+1;
while (level>0) {
   //check for results
   if (miuList<>∅) {
      for (i=0;i<size(miuList);i++) {
         if (miuList[i].KS contains all keyword) {
            if ((miuList[i] not in OptimalResultSet)
              & (miuList[i] not in LinearCommonResultSet))
            output(miuList[i])
         delete(miuList[i])}}
   }
   //pass keyword information to their parents
   if ((miuList<>∅) & (level>1)){
      miuStart=0;
      while (miuStart<size(miuList)) {
         miuEnd=miuStart+1;
         while ((miuEnd<size(miuList))
              & (prefix(miuList[miuStart],level-1)==prefix(miuList[miuEnd],level-1)))
            miuEnd++;
         merge(miuStart, miuEnd-1)}
   }
   //read keyword information of the upper level
   level--;
   if (level>0) insert miuILLevel(w1,level), ..., miuILLevel(wk,level) into miuList
   for (i=0; i<k; i++) {
      if ((miuILLevel(wi,level)=∅) & ... & (miuILLevel(wi,1)=∅) & !(miuList.KS contains wi))
         exit;
}
```

Fig. 9. Searching for the Non-linear Common Results

Now we compare our work with XRANK. First, DIL algorithm proposed in XRANK searches for the results from left to right with the sequence of the results having no regularity in terms of semantics. By contrast, BUP algorithm presented in this paper adopts the bottom-up search strategy. Intuitively speaking, the deeper results contain the richer context information, so they are usually the better results from the angle of semantics. The bottom-up search strategy can guarantee that the deeper results will be produced first, that is to say, the results with richer context information will be produced first. Therefore, in terms of semantics, the sequence of the results produced by BUP algorithm is obviously better than that of DIL algorithm. Thus, in the situation where the response time is strictly demanded, the results produced by BUP algorithm can be directly output. Second, for DIL algorithm, even if, at some moment in the process of search, it is predictable that the index items left will not produce results any more, it is not until all the index items are scanned that the results can be output. Whereas, BUP algorithm carries out a predictable check whenever it finishes its search on one level; if it is predicted that no new result will be produced, the search can finish earlier. In addition, the stack-based DIL algorithm searches from left to right, and so will involve large quantities of push and pop operations on the stack when the keywords appear randomly in the XML tree. However, the above-mentioned operations do not exist in BUP algorithm with its adopting the bottom-up search strategy, and it only needs to neglect the several components in the rear part of the dewey numbers when passing upwards the information on the keywords.

6 Experimental Evaluation

We experimentally evaluate the techniques presented in this paper. First, we investigate the space savings due to the MIU partition. Second, we present some evidence that our search results are of high quality from the angle of semantics. Finally, we evaluate the performance of our search algorithms.

6.1 Experimental Setup

For our experiments, we use both the DBLP and XMark data sets. DBLP, the popular computer science bibliography database, is widely used in XML benchmarking. In the version we use, there are almost 100,000 records, totaling about 80MB of data. We filter out the references and other information only related to the DBLP website and group first by journal/conference name, then by year. We also generate an 100MB XMark data set. We choose to experiment with the DBLP and XMark data sets for they represent real-life and synthetic data sets, respectively. The experiments have been carried out on a PC with a 3.0GHz Pentium IV processor and 1GB of RAM.

6.2 Space Savings

To the best of our knowledge, the existing works all take element as the finest granularity. However, we take MIU. Table 1 gives the space requirements of the two approaches. As shown, the element approach incurs a significant space overhead for both DBLP and XMark. It is because the indexing scope of the element approach covers all the elements. By contrast, the MIU approach requires less space because its indexing scope covers all the MIUs, and one MIU just contains several elements. In our experiments, the average number of elements in one MIU is 7.8. Furthermore, the index item in the MIU approach has a shorter length because the dewey number of the MIU is just that of the root node of the MIU.

Table 1. Space Requirements of the Different Approaches

	DBLP		XMark	
	Inv. List	PATH List	Inv. List	PATH List
For element (XRANK)	136MB	N/A	205MB	N/A
For element (XKSearch)	177MB	N/A	258MB	N/A
For MIU	78MB	21MB	132MB	26MB

6.3 Result Quality

Each search result produced by our system is composed of MIUs rather than elements. Thus, the components of the search result have semantically complete information. Moreover, the existing works do not take the context information into consideration and their search mechanism cannot obtain the necessary context information automatically. By contrast, in our search system, it is easy to obtain such information.

We choose four typical keyword searches for the experiments in this and the next sections. Q1={Ullman}, Q2={keyword, search}, Q3={SIGMOD, XML}, Q4={XML,

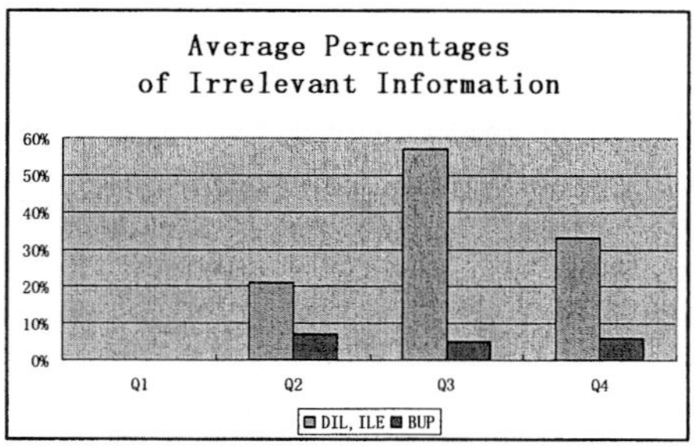

Fig. 10. Percentages of Irrelevant Information

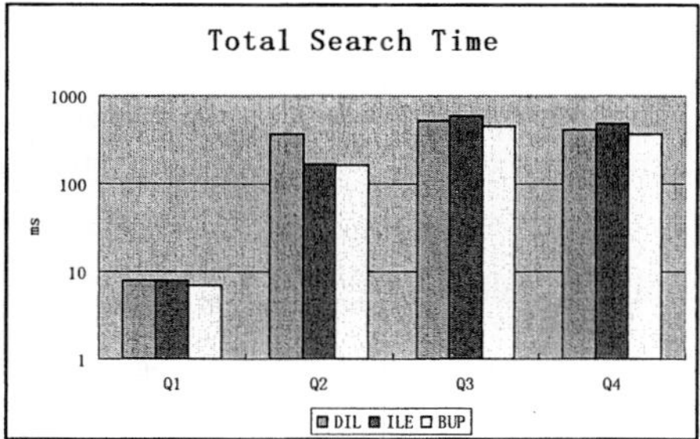

Fig. 11. Total Search Time

relational}. First, we compare the percentages that irrelevant information occupies in the search results acquired through DIL algorithm, ILE algorithm and our search algorithms respectively, which is shown in Figure 10. In terms of refinement of result granularity, the existing researches can only reach the level of element without further filtering out the irrelevant information in the elements. Our search algorithms outweigh DIL algorithm and ILE algorithm in this aspect, especially in the situation the keywords appear across levels, which means that the keywords submitted by the user do not appear in the same level, when a great deal of irrelevant information may appear in the lower levels. From the figure, we can find out that the percentages that irrelevant information occupies in our search results remains steady and in a comparatively lower level, while those in the results of DIL algorithm and ILE algorithm are in a higher level and vary a lot.

6.4 Search Performance

We now evaluate the search performance of the different algorithms. Figure 11 shows the total search time of DIL algorithm, ILE algorithm and BUP algorithms respectively. From the figure, we can find out that the total search time taken in BUP algorithm is the least, while DIL a little more, and ILE the most. In the experiments, we also validate that when keywords have significantly different frequencies, the search speed of ILE algorithm is faster than DIL algorithm and BUP algorithms, which is determined by its algorithm scheme. However, for ILE algorithm, it is just the performance in the special situations of this kind. Usually, ILE algorithm has no such predominance, and just as stated in Section 3, it cannot guarantee that all the possible results will be found out.

7 Conclusion

In this paper, with the focus on effective keyword search in XML documents, we first analyze the problems caused by the refinement of result granularity during XML keyword search, and then give the description of how to partition an XML document into XML fragments with the granularity of Minimal Information Unit (MIU). By regarding MIU as the granularity of indexing and searching, we design efficient index structures and the corresponding search algorithms. Through the sufficient experimental evaluation, we demonstrate that our index structures and query evaluation techniques do provide significant space saving and performance gains. And our search results are semantically complete with necessary context information remaining and irrelevant information filtered out.

References

1. Lin Guo, Feng Shao, Chavdar Botev, and Jayavel Shanmugasundaram. XRANK: Ranked Keyword Search over XML Documents. In *Proc. of SIGMOD*, 2003.
2. Vagelis Hristidis, Yannis Papakonstantinou, and Andrey Balmin. Keyword Proximity Search on XML Graphs. In *Proc. of ICDE*, 2003.
3. Sara Cohen, Jonathan Mamou, Yaron Kanza, and Yehoshua Sagiv. XSEarch: A Semantic Search Engine for XML. In *Proc. of VLDB*, 2003.
4. Yu Xu and Yannis Papakonstantinou. Efficient Keyword Search for Smallest LCAs in XML Databases. In *Proc. of SIGMOD*, 2005.
5. Daniela Florescu, Donald Kossmann, and Ioana Manolescu. Integrating Keyword Search into XML Query Processing. In *Proc. of IJCTN*, 2000.
6. Norbert Fuhr and Kai Großjohann. XIRQL: A Query Language for Information Retrieval in XML Documents. In *Proc. of SIGIR*, 2001.
7. Anja Theobald and Gerhard Weikum. The Index-based XXL Search Engine for Querying XML Data with Relevance Ranking. In *Proc. of ICEDT*, 2002.
8. Vagelis Hristidis and Yannis Papakonstantinou. DISCOVER: Keyword Search in Relational Databases. In *Proc. of VLDB*, 2002.
9. Sanjay Agrawal, Surajit Chaudhuri, and Gautam Das. DBXplorer: A System for Keyword-Based Search over Relational Databases. In *Proc. of ICDE*, 2002.
10. Gaurav Bhalotia, Arvind Hulgeri, Charuta Nakhe, Soumen Chakrabarti, and S. Sudarshan. Keyword Searching and Browsing in Databases using BANKS. In *Proc. of ICDE*, 2002.
11. Shurug Al-Khalifa, Cong Yu, and H. V. Jagadish. Querying Structured Text in an XML Database. In *Proc. of SIGMOD*, 2003.
12. Jiaheng Lu, Tok Wang Ling, Chee-Yong Chan, and Ting Chen. From Region Encoding To Extended Dewey: On Efficient Processing of XML Twig Pattern Matching. In *Proc. of VLDB*, 2005.
13. World Wide Web Consortium. http://www.w3.org
14. DBLP XML Records. http://dblp.uni-trier.de/xml/dblp.xml.gz

Assessing the Completeness of Sensor Data

Jit Biswas[1], Felix Naumann[2], and Qiang Qiu[1]

[1] Institute for Infocomm Research (I^2R), Singapore
{biswas, qiu}@i2r.a-star.edu.sg
[2] Humboldt-Universität zu Berlin, Germany
naumann@informatik.hu-berlin.de

Abstract. In this paper we present a quality model highlighting the completeness of sensor data with respect to its application. The model allows consistent handling of information loss as data propagates through a sensor network. The tradeoffs between various factors that influence completeness are quantified thereby allowing an integrated view of completeness at various levels in a system. The paper is presented in the context of the fast emerging field of *smart spaces*. All concepts in the paper have a foundation in real-life problems arising in this context. Preliminary implementation results are presented to illustrate the value of the completeness based approach versus one that does not use completeness.

1 Introduction and Motivation

Applications in the fast emerging field of smart spaces [1, 2] use data collected and aggregated from sensors of many modalities to monitor entities and environments and assist in decision making. Information rich sensor data, such as image and audio, is used in conjunction with basic context information such as location, identity, and time to carry out classification, inferencing, and other categories of recognition tasks.

A major problem in such systems is information- or data-loss. Data may be lost at many stations from the sensor to the application. Besides the sensors themselves, losses may arise from the transmission medium, e.g., radio attenuation or network congestion. In this paper we present a quantitative model for such loss. The model is based on an intuitive notion of sensor data completeness that measures the amount of data reaching a point of consumption compared to the maximum amount of data possible at that point. In related work [3] we have investigated data loss that arises from delay or congestion within the networking layer, and present an admission control scheme for regulation of such loss.

1.1 A Smart Home Application

We consider as an example, an application that analyzes the pacing behavior of elderly dementia patients in their homes [4]. This application relies on sensor readings that need to be updated and reasoned about rapidly, while at the same time analyzing the knowledge thus generated to answer complex high level queries about the patient. For example, in connection with the home of a dementia patient (Fig. 1), a doctor might ask “Does the person become highly agitated while he is exhibiting abnormal pacing behavior in the living room?” [5]. An answer to this query involves accessing a set of

M.L. Lee, K.L. Tan, and V. Wuwongse (Eds.): DASFAA 2006, LNCS 3882, pp. 717–732, 2006.

location sensors that determine position and can accurately classify pacing behavior from other forms of movement, and a number of body worn accelerometers, which generate 2D or 3D instantaneous acceleration data. From this data it is possible to infer through some high-level pattern classification algorithms, what was the type of behavior that the person was exhibiting.

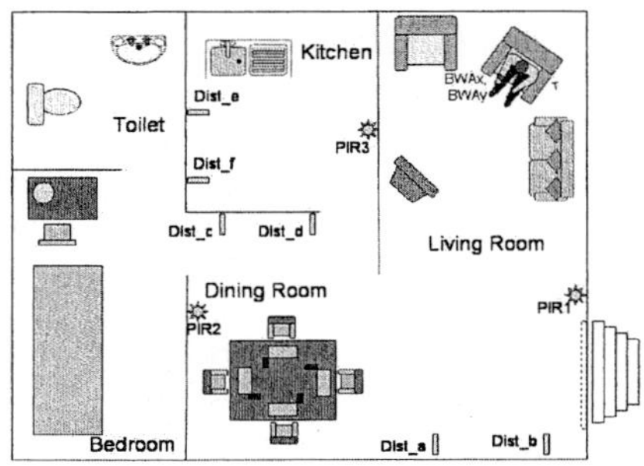

Fig. 1. Home Layout

Each of three rooms of Fig. 1 is equipped with a passive infra-red sensor PIR1, PIR2 and PIR3, passing information to a proxy (Fig. 2), whether a person is in that room.

Because we assume only a single person in the house, the proxy translates this data into a single attribute stating the room in which the person is. In addition, each room is equipped with two ultrasound distance sensors (D_a, D_b, ..., D_f), which measure the distance of some object to the sensor. Usually, the distance of the opposite wall is reported, but when the person is in the room, the sensors report the distance to that person. The data from the two sensors of each room are passed to the proxy, which derives the position of the person in the room. Finally, the person is equipped with an on-body sensor, namely a 2D body worn accelerometer, which generates two readings BWAx and BWAy.

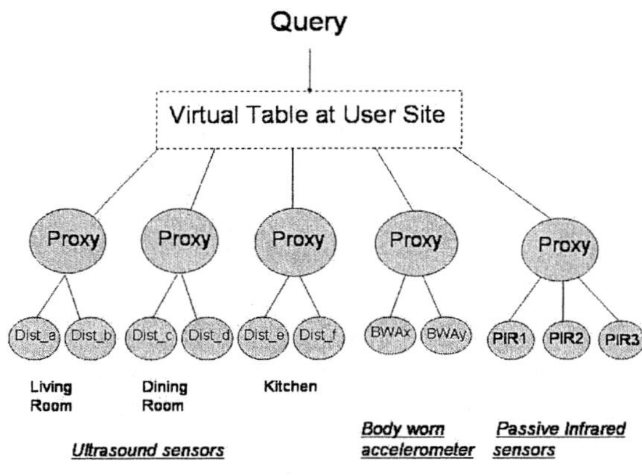

Fig. 2. An Example Sensor Query System Scenario showing the Virtual Table

Tab. 1 (left) shows the raw data as produced by the sensors. We assume that the smallest granularity time period (system data rate) for this application is 1 second. We will measure completeness as the ability of the overall system to produce data values for each relevant measure in each time period. The following completeness-relevant observations can be made from Tab. 1:

Table 1. Raw data from sensors (left) and data produced by the set of proxies (right)

	Living Room		Dining Room		Kitchen						
Time (s)	Dist_a	Dist_b	Dist_c	Dist_d	Dist_e	Dist_f	BWAx	BWAy	PIR1	PIR2	PIR3
1	0,8889	1,5335	2,9245	1,9658	2,1119	1,9637	394	372	1	0	0
2	1,2945	1,5846					395	372	1	0	0
3	1,7001	1,6580	2,9245	1,9658	2,1119	1,9637	396	374	1	1	0
4	2,1057	1,7537					396	374	1	0	0
5	2,5114	1,8717	2,9245	1,9658	2,1119	1,9637	398	375	1	0	0
6	2,9170	2,0120					398	375	1	0	0
7	1,1571	1,6198	2,9245	1,9658	2,1119	1,9637	399	376	1	0	0
8	1,2830	1,6500					399	376	1	0	0
9	1,4089		2,9245	1,9658	2,1119	1,9637	400	377	1	0	0
10	1,5348						400	377	1	0	0
11	1,6607		2,9245		2,1119	1,9637	401	378	1	0	0
12	1,7866			1,9658			401	378	1	0	0
13	2,9170		2,9245		0,8526	1,5616	402	378	0	0	1
14	2,9170	2,0120		1,9658			402	378	0	0	1
15	2,9170	2,0120	2,9245		0,7945	1,5480	403	379	0	0	1
16	2,9170	2,0120		1,9658			403	379	1	0	1
17	2,9170	2,0120	2,9245		0,7363	1,5357	404	379	0	0	1
18	2,9170	2,0120					404	382	0	0	1
19	2,9170	2,0120	2,9245	1,9658	0,6782	1,5248	402	379	0	0	1
20	2,9170	2,0120					403	382	0	0	1
21	2,9170	2,0120	2,9245	1,9658	0,6201	1,5151	404	380	0	0	1
22	2,9170	2,0120					402	379	0	0	0
23	2,9170	2,0120	0,5818	1,4957	2,1119	1,9637	403	383	0	1	0
24	2,9170	2,0120					404	379	0	1	0
25	2,9170	2,0120	1,1193	1,1078	2,1119	1,9637	403	383	0	1	0
26	2,9170	2,0120					404	384	0	1	0
27	2,9170	2,0120	1,1553	1,5829	2,1119	1,9637	405	379	0	1	0
28	2,9170	2,0120					403	380	0	1	0
29	2,9170	2,0120	1,1787	1,5959	2,1119	1,9637	405	380	0	1	0

	Living Room		Dining Room		Kitchen				
Time (s)	PosX_ab	PosY_ab	PosX_cd	PosY_cd	PosX_ef	PosY_ef	BWAx	BWAy	Room
1	1,52	1,68	2	2,71	1,71	3			Living Room
2	1,41	2,1							Living Room
3	1,73	2,46	2	2,71	1,71	3			Living Room
4	1,81	2,81						374	Living Room
5	1,64	3,31	2	2,71	1,71	3			Living Room
6	1,8	2,3							Living Room
7	1,67	1,95	2	2,71	1,71	3			Living Room
8	1,56	2,13							Living Room
9			2	2,71	1,71	3	400	377	Living Room
10									Living Room
11					1,71	3			Living Room
12									Living Room
13					1,61	1,67			Kitchen
14	1,8	2,3						378	Kitchen
15	1,8	2,3			1,52	1,67			Kitchen
16	1,8	2,3							-
17	1,8	2,3			1,59	1,57			Kitchen
18	1,8	2,3							Kitchen
19	1,8	2,3	2	2,71	1,58	1,52			Kitchen
20	1,8	2,3					403	382	Kitchen
21	1,8	2,3	2	2,71	1,57	1,46			Kitchen
22	1,8	2,3							-
23	1,8	2,3	1,86	1,29	1,71	3			Dining Room
24	1,8	2,3							Dining Room
25	1,8	2,3	1,43	2	1,71	3		383	Dining Room
26	1,8	2,3							Dining Room
27	1,8	2,3	1,14	1,71	1,71	3			Dining Room
28	1,8	2,3							Dining Room
29	1,8	2,3	1,71	1,86	1,71	3			Dining Room

- The ultrasound sensors have long stretches of almost constant data. During those periods they are measuring their distance to the opposite wall.
- Sensor D_b stopped working for seconds 9 - 13.
- At second 22 no passive infrared sensor detects a person. This can happen during transition of the person from one room to the other.
- Sensor D_d has a too fast internal clock. Originally it was synchronized with sensor D_c to deliver distance data simultaneously. This is important to derive exact position data at the proxy. After a while, D_d reports data for second 12, even though the measurement actually occurred in second 11. After corrective actions of the proxy in second 19, the two sensors are in synch again.

Tab. 1 (right) shows the data produced by the set of proxies. The following completeness relevant observations can be made:

- The system data rate remains (by definition) at 1 second. This rate is globally set and true at all levels, except for the query data rate as specified in the user requirements.
- The distance data was used to derive positional information for each room. Accordingly, as soon as one of the two distance values was missing, no positional value can be derives (lines 9-13).
- Some rounding has taken place.
- Both the accelerometer readings have undergone PCA (Piecewise Constant Approximation) compression. Thus, only a few values remain.
- The passive infra-red (PIR) data was aggregated to form the "Room" attribute values. In cases where the PIR values conflict (line 16) or give no information (line 22) no value is provided.

1.2 Sample Queries with Completeness Awareness

In this section we present three sample queries that illustrate how completeness may be used in the system. The high level queries are as follows: a) "Is there a person in one of the three rooms?", b) "Is the person in the room pacing abnormally?" and c) "Is the person highly agitated?"

Passive infrared sensors are used to determine the presence of a person in one of the three rooms. Upon detection, ultrasound sensors are used to get accurate pacing trajectories to classify them as normal or abnormal. Once abnormal pacing is identified, body worn accelerometer readings are taken to detect the onset of agitation.

Query 1: "Every 10 seconds generate a PIR sensor reading for each room."

The above sample query indicates whether a person is present in one of the rooms. The completeness level of the information provided could be increased by upgrading to a greater requirement of completeness to get precise position information once a person is detected to have entered a given room.

Query 2: "Every second generate the position of the person in the Living Room."

The previous sample query gathers position information through external observation, with a high degree of completeness. Once the pacing is detected to be abnormal, an additional query at a still higher level of completeness is issued to the body worn accelerometer to gather data and collect it for fine grained motion analysis at the analyst's workstation.

Query 3: "Every 0.1 second generate a set of accelerometer readings."

In a typical sensor query system, sensors can switch between *sleep*, *idle*, and *active* states to prolong battery life. Due to lack of any well defined conventions, sensors are generally operating at a predefined constant sampling rate while switching into a active state. In addition, to meet the requirements of a certain range of applications, sensors are easily to be operated at a sampling rate that is higher than necessary for some applications. Such over-fed data unnecessarily reduces the query processing performance and wastes system resources in terms of transmission bandwidth and battery power.

1.3 Contributions and Paper Structure

The main contribution of this paper is a model highlighting the *completeness* of sensor data: (i) The model allows consistent handling of information content losses as data propagates through a sensor network. (ii) The model considers factors that influence completeness and allows trade-offs between the sensor data completeness and system resource consumption to be configured based on application requirements. (iii) An implementation of the model in a "smart home" application context demonstrates all the concepts introduced in the paper. Our implementation results illustrate the value of the completeness based approach versus one that does not use completeness. Query running times are greatly reduced and system resources are conserved as over-fed data are cleared from the data operation and transmission paths.

We have presented thus far, a simple example of a "smart home" that is able to monitor the health and well-being of its resident. We have emphasized the importance of information completeness in such an application. We have also put together the concepts discussed in this paper into an example system that illustrates various types of processing taking place, and some sample queries in this environment. In order to keep the presentation and analysis simple, we have only introduced only three modalities of sensors. In our current deployment of sensors in a hospital ward ([5]) we have a much richer diversity of sensing modalities including pressure sensors, microphones and video cameras. Feature extraction allows us to filter massive amounts of source data into streams of relevant information which are then stored in a relational database. The remainder of the paper is structured as follows. In Sec. 2 we present a completeness model for sensor data. The model permits us to express query completeness as well as data completeness in a unified framework. Sec. 3 introduces the notion of *predicting quality* highlighting the fact that such predictions allow fine-tuning and optimization of sensor configuration. Sec. 4 discusses a proof of concept implementation set up in our laboratory, and introduces preliminary results. Sec. 5 discusses related work; conclusions and future work are discussed in Sec. 6.

2 A Completeness Model for Sensor Data

Completeness is but one of several information quality criteria, albeit an important one. It is a measure for *how much* data reaches a point of consumption compared to the *maximum amount* of data possible at that point. The more complete some data is, the higher the quality of conclusions on that data are. Examples for conclusions are aggregations on the data, which again have a completeness value, and medical diagnosis, which are not measured by their completeness but by their clinical success.

In this section we lay the foundation of our completeness model for sensor data by first defining what the maximum amount of data is, i.e., our reference point. Then we formally define completeness and show in the following sections how it is affected by different operations along the sensor query system components and operations performed by them.

2.1 Data Rates in Sensor Systems

Given a component, the rate at which data is produced by the component is called its data rate. Rates are defined as the average number of data items produced within some fixed duration, usually millisecond. There are five types of data rates that are important for us:

System data rate (SysDR). The system data rate is the maximum data rate that prevails for all sources and end users in a system. The system rate should be at least the maximum of all other data rates. It is fixed once at setup and merely serves as a point of reference. SysDR is chosen so that all other rates can be defined as multiples of SysDR.

A system producing data at system data rate is the maximum a system can produce. Typical rates at the user-end of a sensor system are much lower. The typical system data rate of a monitoring system, such as the one described in Sec. 1.1, is 1/msec (or 1000/sec), i.e., no component produces data at a higher rate than that.

Sampling data rate (SampDR). The sampling data rate is the rate at which a sensor obtains samples from its environment, as determined by physical limitations or by configuration settings. The sampling rate may be set during setup or changed dynamically by an application or by the sensor itself.

Typical sampling data rates are 0.1/sec for the IR sensors, 0.1/sec for idle distance sensors, and 1/sec for active distance sensors.

Sensor data rate (SensDR). The sensor data rate is the rate at which a sensor communicates data to the outside world—usually to a base station, or to the next hop in a multi-hop sensor network. Sensor data rate can be lower than the sample data rate to save energy. For instance, a sensor might measure temperature once per second, but is configured to only communicate if there is a change in temperature.

Operator data rate (OpDR). The operator data rate is the rate at which a logical operator in the sensor network produces data. Usually the operation is an aggregation, but could also be a selection, projection, transformation, or even a dispatch-type operation. Operator data rate can be lower or higher than the data rates of its input. For instance, an aggregation operator might aggregate groups of ten data items received from a sensor, and thus have an operator data rate of on tenth of the sensor data rate. On the other hand, an operator might produce data at a higher rate than its input if it fills input gaps with data. In the temperature example above, an operator might receive data only if the temperature changes but produces a constant stream of data, using the last available input data. Also note that input is not necessarily sensor data, but can in turn be data from another operator.

Query data rate (QDR). The query data rate is the rate at which the end user or application would like to see data delivered in a query response. It is dictated by the application requirements. For instance, an clinician might be satisfied with a averaged temperature data for a patient that is based on a temperature reading every minute: The query data rate is $1/60000$ per millisecond. On the other hand, an application tracking fast objects, such as automobiles, can only produce reliable results with a data rate of $1/100$, i.e., 10 readings per second.

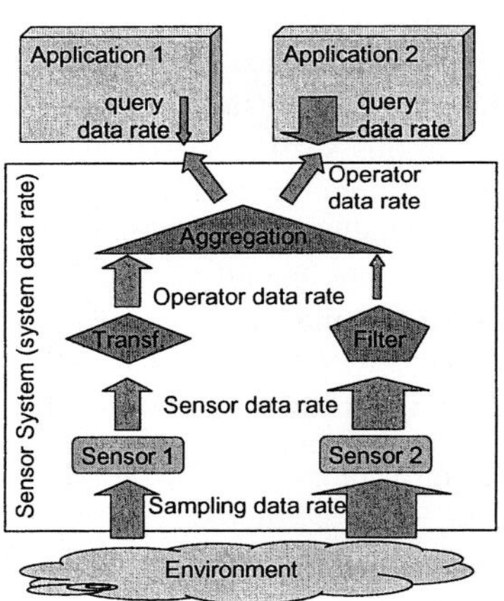

Fig. 3. Different data rates in a sensor system (wide arrows indicate high data rate)

We use the query data rate to measure the quality of the system. If the operator data rate of the final operator is at least as high as the query data rate, the setup and configuration of the sensor system is acceptable. If it is lower, the overall quality is diminished.

For brevity from here on, we omit the term "data" from the different data rates. Fig. 3 shows the points in a sensor system where the individual data rates are defined. The system itself has an overall system rate. Two sensors measure the environment at different sampling rates and produce data at different sensor rates. A transformation operator leaves the data rate unchanged; a filter operator reduces the data rate and thus has a lower operator rate. An aggregation again produces data at some operator rate, which is consumed by two applications, each with different requirements, expressed as query rate. Application 1 has a lower query rate and is thus adequately supplied by the sensor system. Application 2 has higher query rate than the incoming operator rate. Thus, its overall quality is diminished.

The mentioned data rates are determined by different means: Data rates of sensors (SampDR and SensDR) are usually determined by the manufacturer and can be configured using embedded software. The operator data rate is dynamically set during runtime. It depends on the algorithms involved and their internal parameters. Finally, and most important is a means to determine the query data rate QDR. This involves two subproblems: First determining the "right" QDR for the application at hand, and second specifying the QDR in a query. We leave the first problem to the expert and provide a model for the second.

2.2 Completeness

In this section we describe how we translate actual data rates of a running system into a single completeness value measured over a certain period, which can be compared with the requirements of the query. To this end we construct one virtual relation VR for each data transfer level of the system. The first column of VR always represents the time-dimension. Time increments are determined by the system data rate, i.e., if SysDR is 1 /sec, there is a row for each second. The other columns represent different sensors or operators producing data at that level of the system.

We distinguish two kinds of completeness for columns (see definitions later):

- System completeness: Completeness with respect to the system data rate.
- Query completeness: Completeness with respect to the query data rate.

Tab. 1 show the virtual tables of the smart home scenario as described in Sec. 1.1. If we regard each data item in a relation as a cell, some of the cells could be unoccupied or occupied by null value, i.e., SensDR and OpDR are less that SyDR. The proportion of data bearing cells to null valued cells in a set of cells indicates the completeness of the group of cells. Regard the $Dist_b$ column of Tab. 1. The sensor stopped producing output values for five second, thus, the system completeness of this column for the overall period of 29 seconds is $24/29$ or 0.83. Regarding the entire table, we calculate its completeness as $\frac{29+24+15+14+15+15+29+29+29+29+29}{29*11} = \frac{257}{319} \approx 0.81$. Due to aggregation, some columns of Tab. 1 naturally contains less values. To account for this effect, completeness for aggregated columns is calculated differently as we explain in the following paragraphs.

Definition 1 (System completeness). *Let n be the number of sensors represented in the virtual relation VR, let d be the duration of measurement for a given application or query, and let v be the number of non-null values in VR. Then* system completeness *of VR is $SysComp(VR) := \frac{v}{n \cdot d}$.*

In the previous and the next definition we assume all sensors represented in VR to be relevant for a query. Next, query completeness reflects the fact that the usually very high system rate is higher than the requirement of the query. Thus for query completeness, we take as a basis the query rate QDR and not the system rate SysDR.

Definition 2 (Query Completeness). *Corresponding to Definition 1,* query completeness *is defined $QComp(VR) := \frac{SysComp(VR) \cdot SysDR}{QDR}$.*

Consider for instance a system data rate of 1 per millisecond and a query data rate of 1 per min or 1/60000 per millisecond. Consider further a series of sensors and operators producing a final system completeness of 1/1000 (1 per second) at the querying site. Then query completeness is $\frac{1}{1000}/\frac{1}{60000} = 60$, i.e., the query requirements are well met. In fact, completeness is 60 times higher than necessary, indicating potential to decrease sensor data rates. A QDR of 2 per second on the other hand evaluates to a query completeness of $\frac{1}{1000}/\frac{1}{500} = 1/2$, i.e., the query requirements are not met indicating a need to increase sensor data rates or operator data rates.

In Sec. 3 we show how to calculate system completeness without knowing the precise value of v, thus utilizing the completeness measure to gauge the effectiveness of the sensor networks for different applications.

3 Predicting Quality

The main idea of calculating completeness and propagating its scores from the sensors over proxies to the final application is to model the information using a virtual table between each level of nodes. The schema of this table represents the data that is passed between the nodes. This schema includes columns for the "split" values for different sensors. The completeness of this virtual table can easily and formally be defined by counting NULL-values. In real-world scenarios, this virtual table is never materialized, so one cannot count values. Instead, it is necessary to predict the number of null-values based on setup of sensor data rates, properties of the sensors themselves, and operations at the proxy levels. This calculation should be performed bottom up: Given the completeness of the sensor data, completeness values at various higher levels (proxies, application, and query) can be mathematically predicted.

The following paragraphs list formulas to calculate completeness through various operations. Together, these formulas build a completeness model, similar to the known cost-models of conventional DBMS optimizers.

3.1 Completeness of Sensor Output

Sensors output data at their individual sensors data rate, thus "filling" the virtual relation. If $SensDR(s_i)$ is the sensor data rate of sensor s_i, the output data completeness of s_i is, $SysComp(s_i) = \frac{SensDR(s_i)}{SysDR}$. By ignoring for now various factors that influence completeness, the system completeness of VR that is filled with only raw sensor data from n sensors is $SysComp(VR) = \frac{\sum_i SensDR(s_i)}{SysDR \cdot n}$.

As SensDR of a sensor closely depends on its SampDR, which can generally be set to a wide range of different values on the fly, one possible dimension to manipulate data completeness is through dynamically configuring SampDR of a sensor.

3.2 Completeness Through Several Typical Sensor System Operations

Virtual relations are not only filled with raw sensor data, but, at higher levels, by various operations. A comprehensive algebra to manipulate data completeness through every possible sensor system operation is left for further work. In this section we consider a few logical data operators that are most commonly encountered in typical smart home systems of the type described in Sec. 1.1, and their effects on completeness are characterized. It is noted that the formulas listed below for completeness calculation are not necessarily unique, nor the most precise ones, but based on our experience they are simple and effective to provide a good estimation on completeness in real systems. A more general discussion on the completeness influence of data operations is left to future work.

Logic-OR Data Operator: This type of data operation can be abstracted as an operation that integrates N time series inputs, $\{s_1, s_2, \ldots, s_n\}$, into one time series output, s_{or}, and the integration logic is OR, that is, for each time, a non-null value reading from any among the N inputs lead to a non-null value in the output. This type of operation is mainly to describe in-network data aggregation ([6]), which is essential for wireless sensor networks where resources such as bandwidth and energy are limited. In such in-network data aggregation, intermediate nodes may aggregate several events reported from different sources into one event as sensor readings can be correlated, e.g., detection of the same phenomenon. Based on our experience, a good estimation of OpDR for this type of operation is $OpDR_{or}(s_1, s_2, \ldots, s_n) = max(SensDR(s_1), SensDR(s_2), \ldots, SensDR(s_n))$.

Therefore, the system completeness of the aggregated output can be estimated as $SysComp(s_{or}) = max(SysComp(s_1), SysComp(s_2), \ldots, SysComp(s_n))$.

Logic-AND Data Operator: This type of data operation can be abstracted as an operation that integrates N time series inputs, $\{s_1, s_2, \ldots, s_n\}$, into one time series output, s_{and}, and the integration logic is AND, that is, for each time, a null value reading from any among the N inputs lead to a null value in the output. The operation is mainly to describe that columns in VR can possibly be the results by fusing raw sensor data from multiple sources. For example, in an object tracking system, the position data can be the integrated results of fusing the distance readings from two nearby ultrasonic sensors. A typical join operation on sensor data based on only the timestamp can also be described as this type of operation. Based on our experience, a good estimation of OpDR for this type of operation is

$$OpDR_{and}(s_1, s_2, \ldots, s_n) = min(SensDR(s_1), SensDR(s_2), \ldots, SensDR(s_n))$$

Therefore, the system completeness of the fused output can be estimated as,

$$SysComp(s_{and}) = min(SysComp(s_1), SysComp(s_2), \ldots, SysComp(s_n))$$

Compression Operator: In sensor networks, wireless communication is the key factor to consume resources in terms of bandwidth and energy. It is common for sensors to compress time series readings instead of sending them in raw form. One of simplest yet effective sensor data compression method is Piecewise Constant Approximation (PCA) ([7]), which is adopted in the system we built. In PCA, the time data series D to be processed is represented as a sequence of n segments, $PCA(D) = (v_1, e_1), (v_2, e_2), \ldots, (v_n, e_n)$, where e_n is the end point of a segment and v_n is a constant value for time in $[e_{n-1}+1, e_n]$. Here we assume the value at $e_{n-1}+1$ is used for v_n. With such approximation, d(i) is estimated as

$$d(i) = \begin{cases} v_1 & \text{if } i \leq e_1 \\ v_m & \text{if } e_{m-1}+1 \leq i \leq e_m \end{cases}$$

Let $k = e_m - e_{m-1}$, that is, every k samples share a constant, and s_{compr} be the compressed output, OpDR for this type of data compression is, $OpDR_{compr} = \frac{SampDR}{k}$. Therefore, the system completeness of the compressed output can be estimated as, $SysComp(s_{compr}) = \frac{SysComp(D)}{k}$.

Aggregation Query Operator: Aggregation queries, such as COUNT, MIN, MAX and SUM, occur frequently in such systems and their completeness handling requires a slight twist. By definition, an aggregation operator has multiple values, $\{s_1, s_2, \ldots, s_n\}$, as input and a single value, s_{aggr}, as output. Completeness associated with such operators should reflect the completeness of the input, i.e., relatively how much data went into the calculation of the aggregate, and not the single output value. Therefore, the system completeness of the single aggregated output value is defined as,

$$SysComp(s_{aggr}) = avg(SysComp(s_1), SysComp(s_2), \ldots, SysComp(s_n))$$

4 Prototype and Experimental Results

In this section, a preliminary prototype implementation of the concepts discussed in this paper is presented. The prototype demonstrates the value of the proposed completeness model through an experimental implementation of the patient behavior monitoring system described in Sec. 1.1.

4.1 A Sensor Query Engine with Completeness Awareness

A sensor query engine with completeness awareness is built to perform a preliminary evaluation of the proposed data completeness model. This sensor query engine is implemented by introducing a middleware layer on top of the relational SQL engine, MySQL. The main functions of this layer include,

- Self-discovery of the available sensors in the system,
- Maintenance of a relational table in MySQL for each sensor with real-time update,
- Generation of appropriate views of the full Virtual Relation, by full-outer-join operation on all the relevant tables within a particular time window,
- Adjustment of the sampling rate of each sensor on the fly, based on data completeness.

In the prototype, original SQL queries are supported with two new clauses, COMP and TIME, as shown in Fig. 4. The COMP clause enables the possibility to explicitly indicate the completeness requirement of any available attribute in the VR. The completeness requirement indicated may be used for both configuring the system and accessing the quality of query results. In this initial version of our prototype, completeness is closely coupled with sampling rate adjustment of related sensors for future queries and PCA [7] compression ratio selection for past queries. The TIME clause is used to support simple continuous queries by specifying the beginning and end of the monitoring duration as well as the frequency at which the query is to be executed.

4.2 Experimental Setup and Measurements

A replica of the home layout shown in Fig. 1 is set up in the lab. Each of the three rooms—kitchen, dining room and living room—is equipped with two ultrasonic sensors and one passive infra (PIR) sensor. A person with body worn accelerometer is assumed to be wandering inside the house. All sensors are installed on the CrossBow MicaZ mote platform. The data gathering process is shown in Fig. 2. Due to the small number of sensors used, and also the small spatial separation among sensors, a very simple network topology is employed, in which each sensor directly communicates through a wireless link with a common proxy attached to a PC. Thus, all proxies and the user node of Fig. 2 are actually co-located at the same node. To emphasize the effect of the completeness model, no additional sensor management scheme is employed; in other words, all sensors are kept active during the monitoring period.

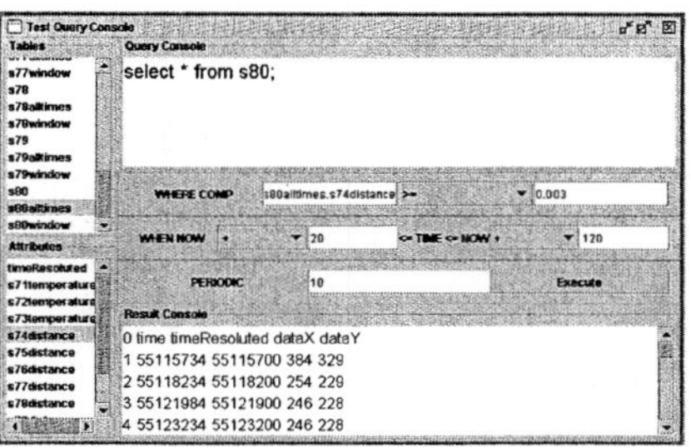

Fig. 4. Sensor Query Engine with Completeness Awareness

As discussed above, in such patient behavior monitoring systems, a wide range of factors are available for us, e.g., sensor sampling rate, data operation or sensor scheduling, to explore the flexibility of meeting query completeness requirements but simultaneously reducing system resource consumption and increasing query performance. In our experiments, we wished to see how the completeness model could help in improving query performance and system resource planning for future queries through the selection of appropriate sensor sampling rate. Without completeness awareness, to satisfy the requirements of all three queries described in Sec. 1.2, the predefined constant sampling rates for PIRs, ultrasonic sensors and BWA needed to be set to at least 0.1, 1, and 10 samples per second continuously. The system with such a set of minimal constant sampling rate settings is used as a comparison against a system with completeness awareness, where the sampling rate of each sensor is dynamically selected based on query completeness requirement, while answering Query 2.

The VR for Query 2, shown in Tab. 1, is generated as a view of combining the output of all five proxies:

```
CREATE VIEW HOUSEHOLD
      SELECT *  FROM P1, P2, P3, P4, P5
      FULL OUTERJOIN ON Time
```

The SysDR is defined here as 1 per millisecond. As indicated, the required QDR in Query 2 for position data, which are represented as X and Y coordinates $(PosX_{ab}, PosY_{ab})$, is 1 per second. To achieve full query completeness, the following condition should be satisfied:

$$QComp(PosX_{ab}) \geq 1.$$

Based on the definition of query completeness,

$$QComp(PosX_{ab}) = \frac{SysComp(PosX_{ab}) \cdot SysDR}{QDR},$$

The SysComp requirement to be specified in the query is,

$$SysComp(PosX_{ab}) \geq \frac{QDR}{SysDR}$$

With the new completeness clause COMP, Query 2 can be posed as:

```
SELECT PosX_ab, PosY_ab  FROM HOUSEHOLD
WHERE  Room = "Living Room"
AND    COMP(PosX_ab) >= 0.001
```

As shown here, the required QDR for the application, which may be provided by experts, is implicitly specified in the query through the indication of system completeness requirement. For attributes without any completeness requirements a default system completeness value, 0.0001 in this experiment, is assumed.

As a logic-AND type operator is used to derive the position information by fusing distance data from two ultrasonic sensors $Dist_b$ and $Dist_b$, based on the algebra discussed in Sec. 3, we have,

$$SysComp(PosX_{ab}) = min(SysComp(Dist_a), SysComp(Dist_b)),$$

Based on the discussion in Sec. 3 we have

$$SysComp(Dist_a) = \frac{SensDR(Dist_a)}{SysDR}, \quad SysComp(Dist_b) = \frac{SensDR(Dist_b)}{SysDR}$$

and

$$SensDR(Dist_a) = SampDR(Dist_a), \; SensDR(Dist_b) = SampDR(Dist_b)$$

As specified in the query, to satisfy the query completeness we should have

$$SysComp(PosX_{ab}) \geq 0.001$$

With the set of equations above, we found such completeness requirement can be satisfied with

$$SampDR(Dist_a) \geq 1 \text{ per second}, \quad SampDR(Dist_b) \geq 1 \text{ per second}$$

Results were collected by posing Query 2 over our sensor query system with and without completeness awareness respectively. The query period, which is the duration of measurement for a query each time, is varied in experiments.

From the experimental results, we observe that by satisfying just the necessary query completeness, through our completeness planning, we can achieve much better query response performance as shown on the left of Fig. 5. This is the case, even though the overall system completeness is low as shown on the right. In addition, there is greater system resource saving, in terms of bandwidth and energy, as shown on the left of Fig. 6 and better query completeness satisfaction as shown on the right.

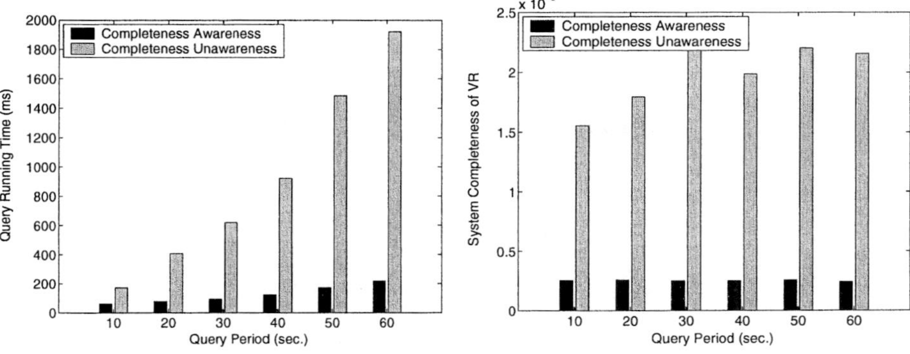

Fig. 5. Running Time (left) and System Compl. of VR (right) of Query 2

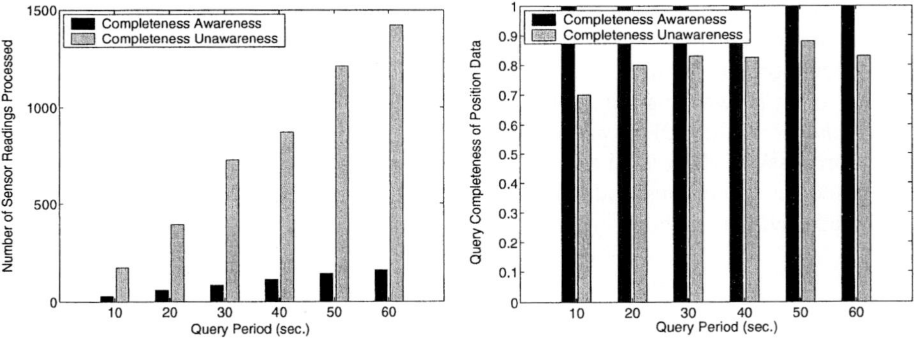

Fig. 6. Amount of Data Processed (left) and Query Completeness of Position Data (right) for Query 2

5 Related Work

There are two major areas of related work, namely information quality and Data Stream Management Systems (DSMS). A systematic and formal approach to the measurement of information quality, and the combination of such measurements for information integration are presented in [8]. These approaches are based on notions of coverage, density of information, ranking of information sources, query-specific attribute weightings, and a number of ways of selecting between multiple sources of data. IQ bounds are discussed in [9] and related to the notion of query completeness in this paper. Determining the "size" of a data source, i.e., its *coverage*, its not a new problem. Most notably, Motro and Rakov define a "completeness" criterion, which matches our coverage criterion [10]. Motro suggests to add "completeness assertions" to the query result, adding more meaning to the result [11]. Completeness assertions are statements, such as "the data contains *all* recordings on the CBS label". These assertions are aggregated along query plans in a similar fashion to our coverage along mapping paths. Thus, the author can give qualitative statements about the completeness of results, but not quantitative statements as we do. Finally, Florescu et al. quantitatively describe the content of distributed autonomous document sources using probabilistic measures [12]. Their model calculates two values: "Coverage" of data sources, determining the probability that a matching document is found in the source, and "overlap" between two data sources, determining the probability that an arbitrary document is found in both sources. These probabilities are calculated with the help of word-count statistics.

The early work in the area of continuous queries led to the identification of stream processing as as new problem [13, 14, 15, 16]. It is found in [15, 16] that a key challenge for the design of a DSMS is to provide approximation and adaptivity in executing continuous queries, because data rates and query load may exceed available resource. Our proposed completeness model can provide a quantitative approach to handle the interaction between resource management and query approximation in such DSMS by simply treating those approximation techniques [16, 17], such as synopsis compression, sampling and load shedding, as various knobs in our model.

The most well known and distributed sensor based system is the Berkeley MOTE. In [18] the authors describe the query language for the MOTE, the database TinyDB and its support for continuous queries. In [19] is presented ideas on tree-based processing of in-network aggregation and the subtleties of its cost-benefit analysis, and *wave scheduling*. In [20] the authors discuss the main issues that apply to sensor based query processing. High level approaches have been outlined in [21] and [22]. Finally, [23] discusses continuously adaptive queries over streams in the face of changing query workloads and data rates.

6 Conclusions

As a first step we have introduced a simple model for information completeness, which is a criterion for information quality. The model is evaluated in a unique application setting that is based primarily on sensor data sources. Factors affecting completeness are characterized and a simple analytical model illustrates how a trade-off can be made between avoidable and unavoidable factors that affect completeness, thereby giving some means for achieving desired completeness levels without paying too high a price. Although a system should contain components such as reasoning systems, knowledge-bases, databases, and stream management, only the lower portion of such a system has actually been modeled and analyzed in this paper. Higher level components of such systems must be integrated to gauge the effectiveness of the entire scheme of dealing with information completeness.

On the positive side, query completeness is a notion that can be used in many ways and to many ends. This paper illustrates how query completeness can be used to alleviate sensors from unnecessarily high sampling rates. Other uses are conceivable, such as sensor selection and sensor management as well as resource management. In future work we shall be continuing to develop a sound understanding of important criteria for information quality such as completeness. Our aim is to apply these ideas in a manner that permits easy development of context aware applications for smart spaces.

We also intend to develop a formal model for completeness based on the informal model presented herein.

Acknowledgment. This research was supported in part by the German Research Society (DFG grant no. NA 432).

References

1. Wang, X., Dong, J.S., Zhang, D., Chin, C.Y., Hettiarachchi, S.R.: Semantic space: An infrastructure for smart spaces. IEEE Pervasive Computing Magazine (2004) 32–39
2. Bardram, J.E.: Applications of context-aware computing in hospital work - examples and design principles. In: Proceedings of the 2004 ACM Symposium on Applied Computing. (2004)
3. Tolstikov, A., Biswas, J., Chen-Khong, T.: Data loss regulation to ensure information quality in sensor networks. In: Proceedings of the 2005 Intelligent Sensors, Sensor Networks and Information Processing Conference. (2005)
4. Biswas, J., Das, S., Qiu, Q., Chava, V.S., Thang, P.: Quality aware elderly people monitoring using ultrasonic sensors. In: Proceedings of the International Conference On Smart Homes and Health Telematics (ICOST). (2005) 107–115
5. Biswas, J., Yap, P., Foo, V., Qiu, Q., Aung, A.P.W., Thang, P.V., Guopei, Q.: Use of pervasive monitoring technology as compared to direct observational methods using the soapd scale in the measurement of agitation in patients with dementia. In: Research Collaboration between Institute for Infocomm Research (I2R) and Alexandra Hospital, Singapore. (2005)
6. Intanagonwiwat, C., Govindan, R., Estrin, D.: Directed diffusion: A scalable and robust communication paradigm for sensor networks. In: Proceedings of the International Conference on Mobile Computing and Networking (MobiCom). (2000)
7. Lazaridis, I., Mehrotra, S.: Capturing sensor-generated time series with quality guarantees. In: Proceedings of the International Conference on Data Engineering (ICDE). (2003)
8. Naumann, F., Freytag, J.C., Leser, U.: Completeness of integrated information sources. Information Systems **29**(7) (2004) 583–615
9. Leser, U., Naumann, F.: Query planning with information quality bounds. In: Proceedings of the International Conference on Flexible Query Answering Systems (FQAS). Advances in Soft Computing, Warsaw, Poland, Springer Verlag (2000)
10. Motro, A., Rakov, I.: Estimating the quality of databases. In: Proceedings of the International Conference on Flexible Query Answering Systems (FQAS), Roskilde, Denmark, Springer Verlag (1998) 298–307
11. Motro, A.: Completeness information and its application to query processing. In: Proceedings of the International Conference on Very Large Databases (VLDB), Kyoto (1986) 170–178
12. Florescu, D., Koller, D., Levy, A.: Using probabilistic information in data integration. In: Proceedings of the International Conference on Very Large Databases (VLDB), Athens, Greece (1997) 216–225
13. Terry, D., Goldberg, D., Nichols, D., Oki, B.: Continuous queries over append-only databases. In: Proceedings of the ACM International Conference on Management of Data (SIGMOD). (1992)
14. Babu, S., Widom, J.: Continuous queries over data streams. In: SIGMOD Record. (2001) 109–120
15. Babcock, B., Babu, S., Datar, M., Motwani, R., Widom, J.: Models and issues in data stream systems. In: Proceedings of the Symposium on Principles of Database Systems (PODS). (2002)

16. Motwani, R., Widom, J., Arasu, A., Babcock, B., Babu, S., Datar, M., Manku, G., Olston, C., Rosenstein, J., Varma, R.: Query processing, resource management, and approximation in a data stream management system. In: Proceedings of the Conference on Innovative Data Systems Research (CIDR). (2003) 245–256
17. Abadi, D.J., Carney, D., Cetintemel, U., Cherniack, M., Convey, C., Lee, S., Stonebraker, M., Tatbul, N., Zdonik, S.: Aurora: A new model and architecture for data stream management. VLDB Journal **12**(2) (2003) 120–139
18. Madden, S.R., Franklin, M.J., Hellerstein, J.M., Hong, W.: Tinydb: An acquisitional query processing system for sensor networks. ACM Transactions on Database Systems (TODS) **30**(1) (2005) 122–173
19. Demers, A., Gehrke, J., Rajaraman, R., Trigoni, N., Yao, Y.: The Cougar project: A work-in-progress report. In: SIGMOD Record. Volume 32. (2003)
20. Yao, Y., Gehrke, J.: Query processing for sensor networks. In: Proceedings of the Conference on Innovative Data Systems Research (CIDR). (2003)
21. Bonnet, P., Gehrke, J., Seshadri, P.: Towards sensor database systems. Technical Report TR2000-1819, Cornell University (2000)
22. Gedik, B., Liu, L.: Mobieyes: Distributed processing of continuously moving queries on moving objects in a mobile system. In: Proceedings of the International Conference on Extending Database Technology (EDBT). (2004)
23. Madden, S., Shah, M.A., Hellerstein, J.M., Raman, V.: Continuously adaptive continuous queries over streams. In: Proceedings of the ACM International Conference on Management of Data (SIGMOD). (2002)

Intelligent Statistics Management in Sybase ASE 15.0

Satya Sreenivasan, Xiao Ming Zhou, and Tat Keong Loh

Sybase Asia Development Center,
438B Alexandra Road #04-01, Singapore 119668
{ssreeniv, xzhou, tloh}@sybase.com

Abstract. Sybase ASE (Adaptive Server Enterprise) is a cost based database system. Statistics information plays a key role in the costing model of ASE optimizer. Typically, up-to-date statistics is critical in selecting an optimal query plan with good performance. However, updating statistics is a resource intensive maintenance operation. A common user concern is the lack of input on when statistics needs to be updated and also the time taken to maintain the statistics. In this paper, we introduce a new solution for automating statistics maintenance in Sybase ASE 15.0. Our solution includes a new metric for evaluating data changes due to DMLs (Data Management Language), the use of a scheduler to generate rules to gather statistics based on feedback from the metric and random sampling of data when gathering statistics. This approach will make statistics maintenance more intelligent and efficient, and reduce the TCO (Total Cost of Ownership) significantly.

1 Introduction

Commercial databases have increased in size and complexity due to the proliferation of enterprise data. Recent survey results indicate an unprecedented growth in data volume, with OLTP systems as large as 23 TB [1]. Based on the logical and physical state of the system and the kind of query being optimized, there is an expectation on the query processor to evaluate many different access plans and provide the most efficient plan. To achieve this, modern query processors rely on accurate statistics that represent the underlying distribution of data in the system. Such statistical data typically includes the number of rows in a table, number of leaf pages in an index, histograms representing distribution of data in a column, and the number of distinct values in a column. The query optimizer uses this information to estimate the number of rows processed at each step of a plan, thereby assessing the cost of all competing plans and picking the plan that has the least cost. In the absence of accurate statistics, cost estimates can be different from the actual values, which can result in poor choice of a query execution plan and affect performance dramatically.

In applications that have sudden bursts of data coming in, or columns that encounter frequent data changes, statistics can become stale very rapidly causing unreliable throughput and response times. Some statistics such as the number of rows in a table or the leaf count of an index are dynamically updated whenever there are DMLs (Data Management Language). It is expensive to dynamically maintain column level statistics. Hence, such statistics have to be refreshed by manually configuring

M.L. Lee, K.L. Tan, and V. Wuwongse (Eds.): DASFAA 2006, LNCS 3882, pp. 733 – 740, 2006.

statistics maintenance. However, updating statistics is a resource intensive operation that must be scheduled at appropriate maintenance windows when the load on the system is light.

A key pain point in statistics maintenance is the difficulty in determining which columns would benefit from having statistics and which existing statistics require a refresh. The second issue is that while not having accurate statistics could lead to a less-than-optimal plan, running statistics maintenance operations too frequently could greatly impede critical operations. The time taken to refresh statistics is a matter of concern as well, since this operation requires table scans and leaf-level scans of indexes and the use of CPU cycles to perform data sorts together with a significant use of data cache. Hence, statistics maintenance is an onerous task for database administrators.

All of the above issues can be addressed to make statistics gathering more intelligent in order to free up valuable administration time and move towards a self-administering system.

The rest of the paper is organized as follows: In Section 2, we introduce some related works and background of this topic. In Section 3, we introduce the Sybase solution in ASE15.0. An outline of the sampling algorithm and some experimental results showing its effectiveness is presented in Section 4. We conclude and address our future enhancement in Section 5.

2 Background

Efficient processing of statistics is a requirement of all major commercial databases. Identifying which objects in the database need statistics, how often to refresh these statistics and when to schedule this maintenance operation are issues that need to be addressed by every intelligent statistics system. To this end, several major players have developed automatic statistics update mechanisms such as Microsoft SQL Server [8], Oracle 10g[2], ASA as well as DB2 UDB [4].

The Sybase solution to intelligent statistics maintenance is a three-pronged approach. The user problems described earlier can be divided into three areas:

- When to update statistics
- How to automate this task
- How to make statistics maintenance more efficient.

We introduce a new "datachange" metric that functions as a measure of the change of data distribution in an object since the last statistics refresh. This provides administrators with some guidance to determine if the existing statistics have become stale. We propose the infrastructure for power users to be able to update statistics through pre-canned templates in order to conserve resources. Finally, statistics maintenance is made more efficient by reducing the size of the dataset.

This is achieved in two ways. The first is by the use of random data sampling when statistics is being gathered. The second way is by the use of semantic data partitions, wherein the data is partitioned and stored in smaller chunks and statistics maintained at the level of the partition (see Fig.1). Semantic data partitioning is not the focus of this paper and will not be discussed at length.

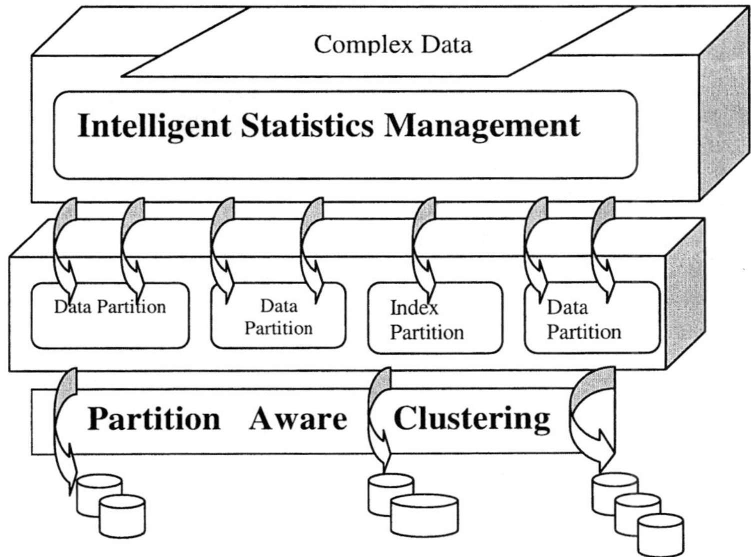

Fig. 1. Framework for intelligent statistics management

3 Intelligent Statistics Management in Sybase ASE 15.0

3.1 Overview of Statistics in ASE

Statistics in Sybase ASE is stored in system catalogs. This includes table level statistics such as the number of rows in a table, number of pages etc and column level information. The "update statistics" command is used to collect and maintain these statistics. This command allows for statistics to be gathered at various levels of granularity, such as for all indexes of the table, for all columns in a partition of the table, or for non-indexed columns. It also allows the configuration of the number of steps to be used in creating the histogram that represent data distribution in a column and the number of parallel threads to be used in gathering statistics.

3.2 Datachange

The datachange function monitors DML activities and measures the number of INSERTS, DELETES and UPDATES on an object, column or partition since update statistics was last run. The function measures the changes to data distribution as a percent of number of rows in the table or partition.

To keep track of the changes to the data distribution, three internal counters are maintained, one each for INSERTS, DELETES and UPDATES. These counters are maintained per partition. They are stored in the partition descriptor and cached in-memory. The in-memory values are flushed to disk periodically through an idle-soaker thread. As the counters are available in-memory, no additional I/O is required to maintain them.

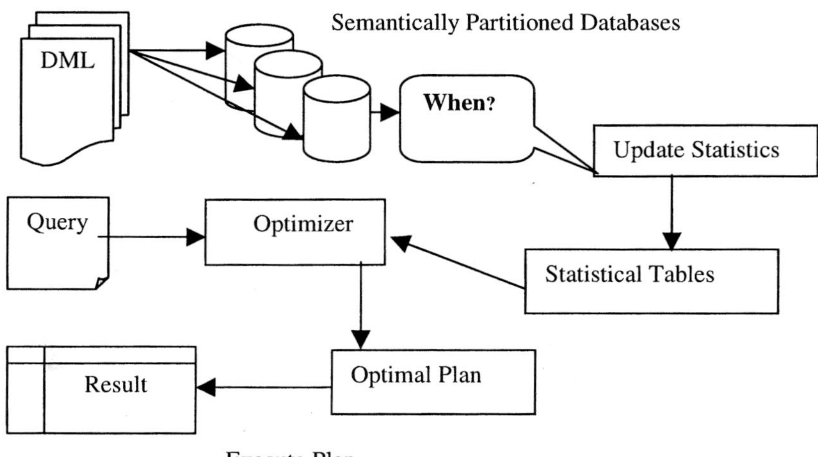

Fig. 2. A typical system with a data distribution that is changing rapidly due to a high rate of DMLs. The query optimizer chooses the best plan for incoming queries by using statistics for the data distribution, stored in the system catalogs. The database administrator routinely issues an "update statistics command" to refresh the statistics.

For a column "i" in a table "O" that has "n" rows, let "I" be the number of inserts, "D" the number of deletes and "U" the number of updates. Then the datachange for column "i", "DC(i)" is calculated as:

$$DC(i) = (I + D + 2*U)/2$$

For object "O", the datachange at object level is calculated as:

$$DC(O) = (\ \mathrm{Max}((I + D + 2*U) \text{ for each column "i" having statistics}))\ /\ n$$

Whenever there is a DML on the table, the corresponding counter is incremented. The counters are reset when statistics are updated for the object/partition or during a clean shutdown of the server.

Database administrators can use the output of this function to set thresholds for various objects with a job-scheduling task. When the datachange metric indicates that the threshold has been exceeded, the scheduler task will execute the "update statistics" command.

There are many flavors of the update statistics command. This is to allow granularity in gathering statistics. Correspondingly, the datachange function can be used to determine the changes at these same levels of granularity.

3.3 Automating Statistics Collection

The Job Scheduler feature in Sybase ASE 15.0 enables database administrators to define and schedule database tasks. The Job Scheduler provides a single interface for managing multiple system-wide servers. It helps to automate routine management tasks, with jobs written in Sybase Transact-SQL. The Job Scheduler comprises of an internal scheduler task, an external scheduling agent and a system catalog to store the history, status and other data related to scheduled and completed jobs.

The internal scheduler task determines when scheduled jobs are run. It feeds the external scheduling agent with the necessary job information. The scheduling agent retrieves the job definition from the system catalog and issues the job commands to the target databases. It then logs the results back to the system catalog.

Sybase ASE 15.0 provides templates, which are shortcuts to common jobs, leaving database administrators to fill in only the parameters required to create the job definition. In addition, an intelligent wizard can be invoked to guide database administrators in filling the templates, generate jobs and to schedule these jobs at appropriate times.

For automating statistics gathering, an object level template or a database level template can be used. The object level template allows the administrator to define the datachange threshold for each object, partition or column that needs to be tracked, the window when the maintenance task should be run as well as the options available for the update statistics command, such as the desired number of steps in the histogram or the number of consumer threads to be used. The database level template will sweep through all the indexes in the database and update the statistics on all the indexes based on a pre-configured threshold. After statistics is gathered successfully, the datachange function values are reset to 0.

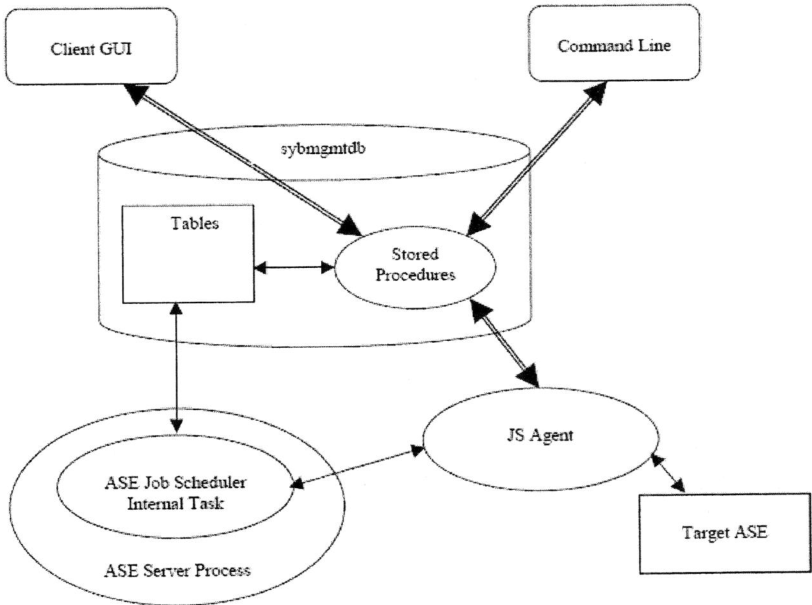

Fig. 3. Job scheduler architecture depicting interactions between the internal scheduler task and external scheduling agent and the system catalog containing information on the completed jobs

3.4 Sampling for Update Statistics

Updating column level statistics requires table scans of non-indexed columns and leaf-level scans of index pages. This operation uses a large number of system resources besides requiring very large maintenance windows when the datasets are large or are rapidly changing. The use of sampling in databases has been proposed for a number of problems such as estimating result size for a query, as well as estimating and constructing histograms [3,5,6,7]. Sampling for update statistics, is an option designed to reduce the resources required to gather statistics.

Depending on the user specified sampling rate, a random subset of pages of the table/partition are read into a temporary table, which is then sorted and statistics is gathered from this sorted subset. With a smaller subset of data, the I/O contention while reading data, the number sort buffers required for the sorts and the overall time taken to gather statistics are all reduced. Sampling is not carried out at the row level, since scanning one row from a page can be quite inefficient. So all rows from a sampled page are used in statistics gathering. The disadvantage of this approach is that if the values in a page are correlated, then the sampled statistics might be skewed. When there is a high degree of correlation, a larger sampling percent should be configured. This will allow a larger number of pages to be read which will uncover more distinct values in the table. However, as the distribution of data may not be known beforehand, some level of experimentation has to be done to arrive at an appropriate sampling percent that presents the best approximation for the dataset in hand.

The update statistics command that is generated by the Job Scheduler uses a default sampling rate of 20% of the table size. This use of sampling helps in decreasing the time taken to automatically update statistics. This sample percentage can be configured with the help of the scheduler template to the value that provides the most accurate approximation for the dataset.

4 System Evaluation

The following experimental results were obtained by updating statistics on a single column of a table that has 10,556,400 records and 105,564 pages.

From the results in Table 1 and Table 2, it is seen that for this dataset, a 50% sampling of the dataset reduces the execution time by 58% and the number of

Table 1. Elapsed time during update statistics on a single column using different sampling percentages

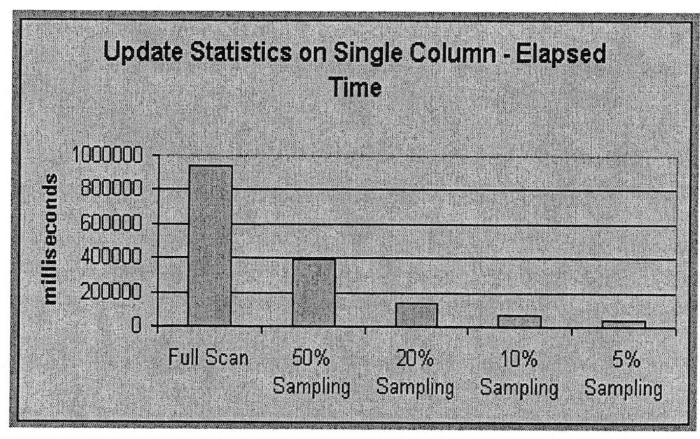

Table 2. Physical I/Os during update statistics on a single column using different sampling percentages

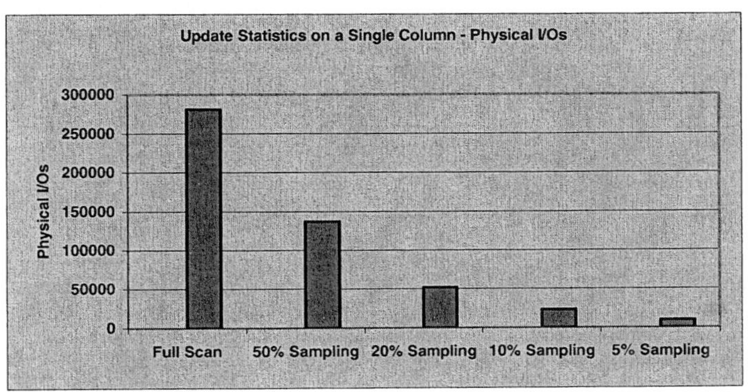

Table 3. Comparison of cost estimate with sampled index statistics in TPC-D queries

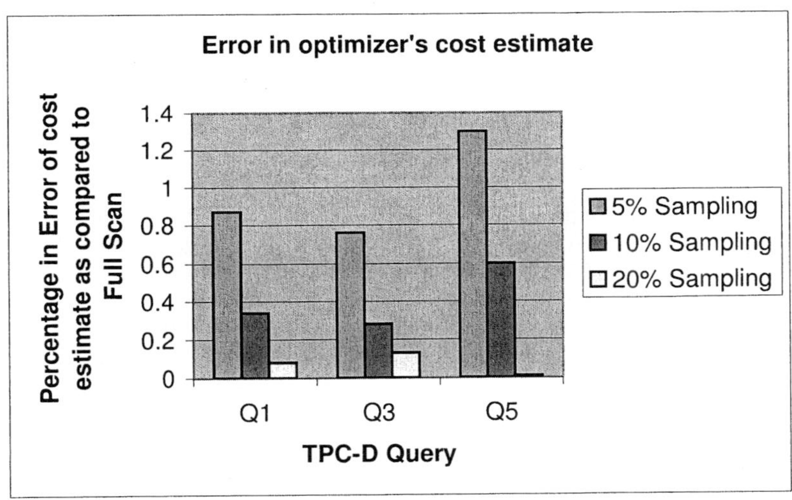

physical I/Os by 51% and a 10% sampling of the same dataset reduces execution time by 92% and the number of physical I/Os by 91%. The percentage of sampling used and the accuracy of statistics gathered will be dependent on the characteristics of the underlying dataset.

When the same dataset was partitioned 10 ways, and the update statistics query executed with 20% sampling rate, which is the default sampling rate used by the job scheduler, the elapsed time was observed to be 14 seconds. This is a substantial drop from the 940 seconds needed for a full scan of the un-partitioned dataset. With the scheduling routine kicking in to refresh statistics on smaller partitioned datasets only when the datachange metric indicates significant DMLs, the window for maintaining statistics is significantly reduced without impeding critical system activities.

A separate experiment was conducted on a 1 GB TPC-D database to verify that the optimizer's cost estimates were not significantly affected by the use of sampling. The indexes of the largest tables in the dataset, lineitem and orders, were sampled at 5%, 10% and 20% and a selection of queries run to record the cost estimates for these queries. A comparison of these values with the cost estimates for these queries after a full scan is depicted in the Table 3 and shows that the error in estimation is within an acceptable range.

5 Conclusion

Statistics aids the optimizer in choosing the least cost query access plan. To this end, maintaining accurate statistics is essential in the performance of the database. The "Automatic Update Statistics" solution in ASE 15.0 can help database administrators in statistics maintenance. For near-zero manual deployments, ASE 15.0 Job Scheduler templates can be configured and tuned to activate statistics update with minimum impact to critical operations.

Some future enhancements could include automatic generation and delete of statistics where applicable, auto refresh of statistics if a column's minimum or maximum value changes due to DMLs, use of feedback mechanism to determine optimal sampling.

Acknowledgements

We acknowledge the contributions of the "Job Scheduler", "Auto update statistics" and "optimizer" development groups and all other Sybase development teams involved in ASE15.0.

References

1. 2005 Winter TopTen Award Winners, Winter Corporation, 2005.
2. M. Ault, M. Tumma, D. Liu, D.Burleson. Oracle Database 10g New Features: Oracle 10g Reference for Advanced Tuning and Administration. Rampant TechPress, 2003.
3. S. Chaudhuri, R. Motwani, V. Narasayya, Random Sampling for Histogram Construction: How much is enough? In Proc. ACM SIGMOD Conference, 1998.
4. DB2 Universal Database for iSeries – Database Performance and Query Optimization, IBM Corp., 2002.
5. Y. Ling and W. Sun. An Evaluation of Sampling-Based Size Estimation Methods for Selections in Database Systems. In Proc. IEEE Conference on Data Engineering, 1995.
6. R.J. Lipton and J.F. Naughton. Query Size Estimation by Adaptive Sampling. In Proc. ACM PODS, 1990.
7. G.Piatesky-Shapiro and C. Connell. Accurate estimation of the number of tuples satisfying a condition. In Proc. ACM SIGMOD Conference, 1984.
8. SQL Server 2000 Books Online v8.00.02. Microsoft Corp., 2004

Holistic Schema Mappings for XML-on-RDBMS

Priti Patil* and Jayant R. Haritsa

Database Systems Lab, SERC,
Indian Institute of Science, Bangalore 560012, INDIA

Abstract. When hosting XML information on relational backends, a mapping has to be established between the schemas of the information source and the target storage repositories. A rich body of recent literature exists for mapping *isolated* components of XML Schema to their relational counterparts, especially with regard to table configurations. In this paper, we present the Elixir system for designing "industrial-strength" mappings for real-world applications. Specifically, it produces an *information-preserving holistic* mapping that transforms the complete XML world-view (XML schema with constraints, XML documents XQuery queries including triggers and views) into a full-scale relational mapping (table definitions, integrity constraints, indices, triggers and views) that is tuned to the application workload. A key design feature of Elixir is that it performs *all* its mapping-related optimizations in the XML source space, rather than in the relational target space. Further, unlike the XML mapping tools of commercial database systems, which rely heavily on user inputs, Elixir takes a principled cost-based approach to automatically find an efficient relational mapping. A prototype of Elixir is operational and we quantitatively demonstrate its functionality and efficacy on a variety of real-life XML schemas.

1 Introduction

For persistently storing information from XML sources, there are primarily two technological choices available: A specialized native XML store (e.g. Tamino [25], Natix [11], Timber [10]), or a standard relational engine (e.g. IBM DB2 [20], Oracle [24], MS-SQL Server [22]). From a pragmatic viewpoint, the latter approach brings with it the benefits of highly-functional, efficient and mature technology. Therefore, a rich body of literature has emerged in the last five years on the mechanics of hosting XML documents on relational backends. Specifically, there have been several proposals for generating efficient mappings between XML schema (e.g. DTDs [17] or XML Schema [29]) and relational schema. A common feature of much of this work is that it has focused on *isolated* components of the relational schema, typically the table configurations. However, viable XML-to-relational systems that intend to support real-world applications will need to provide an *information-preserving holistic* mapping that transforms the complete XML world-view (XML schema with constraints, XML documents, XQuery

* Currently with IBM India Software Lab.

M.L. Lee, K.L. Tan, and V. Wuwongse (Eds.): DASFAA 2006, LNCS 3882, pp. 741–756, 2006.

queries including triggers and views) into a full-scale relational schema (table definitions, integrity constraints, indices, triggers and views). In this paper, we address this issue by presenting a system called ELIXIR (Establishing hoLIstic schemas for XML In Rdbms) which produces such "industrial-strength" XML-to-RDBMS mappings.

By taking a principled cost-based approach to mapping design, Elixir *automatically* delivers efficient mappings that are *tuned* to the XML application. This is in marked contrast to the XML mapping tools currently provided by commercial database systems, wherein the user is expected to play a significant role in the design and the tuning is largely manual. For example, in DB2's XML Extender, the user needs to have intimate knowledge of the application to specify mapping of each XML node to either a table or a column using the Document Access Definition (DAD) medium [20].

A novel feature of Elixir is that it performs *all* its mapping-related optimizations in the XML source space, rather than in the relational target space. The evaluation of the quality of these optimizations is done at the target database engine, and the feedback is used to guide the optimization process in the XML space, in an iterative manner, resulting in a *dynamically-derived* mapping that is *tuned to the application*. This approach is based on our observation that an organic understanding of the XML source can result in more informed choices from a performance perspective – as a case in point, making index choices at the XML source and then mapping them to relational equivalents proves to be substantially better than directly using the relational engine's index advisor, which is the current industrial practice [6]. An additional benefit of source-based index choices is that the knowledge can be used to guide the XQuery-to-SQL translation during query processing, consistent with the observation in [12] that schema decomposition and query translation are interdependent and should therefore be handled in an integrated manner.

A related feature of Elixir is its *integrated* approach to producing efficient holistic schemas – for example, the choice of indices is affected by the XML constraints. This integration ensures that all the interactions between the XML inputs and the effects of these inputs on the relational outputs are automatically taken into account during the optimization process.

Currently, a prototype of Elixir is operational on the DB2 relational engine [20], and can be easily ported to any standard RDBMS. The prototype is implemented in Ocamlc (Objective Caml) [23], a strongly-typed functional programming language, and has been successfully evaluated on a variety of real-world and synthetic XML schemas [29] for representative XQuery [2] queries. To make our objectives concrete, a sample fragment of inputs from an XML banking application and a relational mapping derived from Elixir for these inputs is shown in Figure 1.

To the best of our knowledge, Elixir is the first system to aim towards delivering industrial-strength mappings for XML-to-RDBMS. In the remainder of this paper, we describe its highlights – the complete technical details are available in [14].

– – XML Schema

```
<xs:element name="country" type="CountryType"
          minOccurs="0" maxOccurs="unbounded">
 <xs:key name="acc-num-key">
   <xs:selector xpath=".//account"/>
   <xs:field xpath="./sav-acc-num |
                   ./check-acc-num"/>
 </xs:key>
 <xs:keyref name="cust-acc" refer="acc-num-key">
   <xs:selector xpath=".//customer"/>
   <xs:field xpath="./acc-num"/>
 <xs:keyref>
</xs:element>
...
```

– – XML Documents

```
<bank>
   <country>
      <name>India</name>
      <customer>
         <cust-id>1</cust-id>
         <acc-num>101</acc-num> ...
      </customer> ...
      <city>
         ...
         <account>
            <sav-acc-num>101</sav-acc-num>
            <balance>1232423</balance>
         </account>
      </city> ...
  </country> ...
</bank>
```

– – XML Query workload

```
FOR $cust IN //customer
FOR $acc IN //account
WHERE ($cust/acc-num = $acc/sav-acc-num
OR $cust/acc-num = $acc/check-acc-num)
AND $cust/cust-id = '1000'
return <balance>$acc/balance</balance>
# Frequency 20000
```

– – XQuery Triggers

```
CREATE TRIGGER Increment-Counter
AFTER INSERT OF //Customer
...
CREATE TRIGGER NewCityTrigger
AFTER INSERT OF /bank/country/city
...
```

– – XML Views

```
CREATE VIEW imp_cust AS
 FOR $cust IN //customer
 FOR $acc IN //account
 WHERE ($cust/acc-num = $acc/sav-acc-num
 OR $cust/acc-num = $acc/check-acc-num)
 AND $acc/balance > 100000
 return <acc-num>$cust/acc-num</acc-num>
       <balance>$acc/balance</balance>
...
```

(a) Input

– – Tables

```
CREATE TABLE Customer (Cust-id-key
INTEGER PRIMARY KEY, id INTEGER NOT NULL,
name VARCHAR(25),...);
CREATE TABLE Account (Acc-id-key
INTEGER PRIMARY KEY, ...);
...
```

– – Relational keys equivalent to XML keys

```
ALTER TABLE Account ADD CONSTRAINT Acc-key
UNIQUE (sav-or-check-acc-num, parent-Country);
ALTER TABLE Customer ADD CONSTRAINT Acc-fkey
FOREIGN KEY (acc-num, parent-Country)
REFERENCES Account(sav-or-check-acc-num,
parent-Country);
...
```

– – Recommended Indices

```
CREATE INDEX name-index ON Customer(name);
CREATE INDEX acc-num-index ON Account
(sav-or-check-acc-num, parent-Country);
...
```

– – SQL Triggers

```
CREATE TRIGGER Increment-Counter
AFTER INSERT ON Customer
REFERENCING NEW AS new_row
FOR EACH ROW
BEGIN ATOMIC
  UPDATE Branch-office
  SET Acc-counter = Acc-counter + 1
  WHERE Branch-office.Id = new_row.Branch
END

...
```

– – Stored Procedure

```
CREATE PROCEDURE NewCityTrigger(...)
BEGIN
  Send-mail(cust-name, city-name, ...)
END

...
```

– – Relational views

```
CREATE VIEW imp_cust AS
(SELECT C.acc-num, A.balance
 FROM   Customer C, Account A
 WHERE  C.acc-num = A.sav-or-check-acc-num
 AND    A.balance > 10000)


...
```

(b) Output

Fig. 1. Example Elixir Mapping

2 Architecture of Elixir System

The overall architecture of the Elixir system is depicted in Figure 2. Given an XML schema, a set of documents valid under this schema, and the user query workload, the system first creates an equivalent canonical "fully-normalized" initial XML schema [9], corresponding to an extremely fine-grained relational mapping, and in the rest of the procedure attempts to design more efficient schemas by merging relations of this initial schema.

Summary statistical information of the documents for the canonical schema is collected using the StatsCollector module. The estimated runtime cost of the XML workload, after translation to SQL, on this schema is determined by accessing the relational engine's query optimizer. Subsequently, the original XML schema is transformed in a variety of ways using various schema transformations, the relational runtime costs for each of these new schemas is evaluated, and the transformed schema with the lowest cost is identified. This whole process is repeated with the new XML schema, and the iteration continues until the cost cannot be improved with any of the transformed schemas. The choice of transformations is conditional on their adhering to the constraints specified in the XML schema, and this is ensured by the Translation Module.

In each iteration, the Index Processor component selects the set of XML path-indices that fit within the disk space budget (measured with respect to the equivalent *relational* indices), and deliver the greatest reduction in the query runtime cost. These path indices are then converted to an equivalent set of

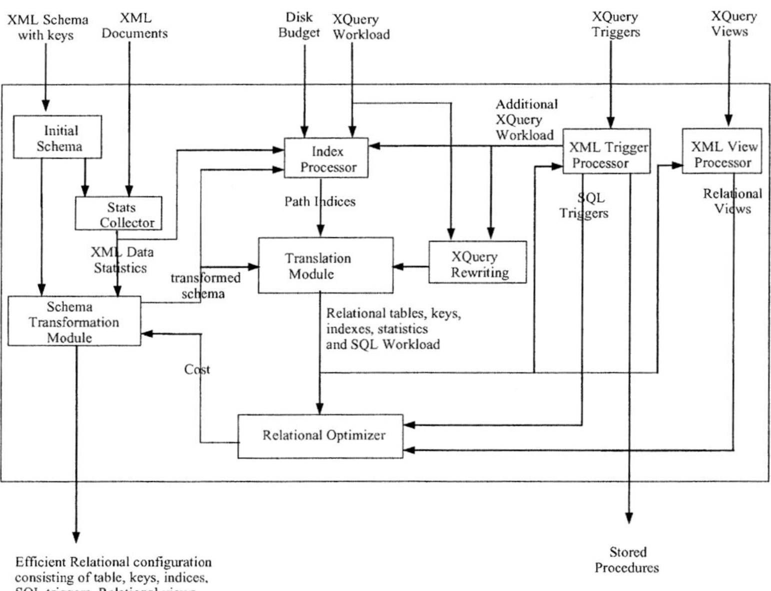

Fig. 2. Architecture of the Elixir system

relational indices. The XQuery queries are also rewritten to benefit from the path indices, with the query rewriting based on the concept of *path equivalence classes* [16] of XML Schema.

The XML Trigger Processor is responsible for handling all XML triggers – it maps each trigger to either an equivalent SQL trigger, or if it is not mappable (as discussed in Section 5), represents it with a stored procedure that can be called by the middleware at runtime. To account for the cost of the non-mappable triggers, queries equivalent to these triggers are added to the input query workload. Finally, the XML View Processor maps XML views and materialized XML views specified by the user to relational views and materialized query tables, respectively.

To implement the above architecture, we have consciously attempted, wherever possible, to incorporate the ideas and systems previously presented in the literature. Specifically, for schema transformations, we leverage the LegoDB framework [3], with its associated FleXMap search tool [15] and StatiX [9] statistics tool; the Index Processor component is based on the XIST path-index selection technique [16]; and, the DB2 relational engine [20] is used as the backend.

In the following sections, we discuss in detail the generation of the various components of the holistic relational schema, including Table Configurations, Key Constraints, Indices, Triggers and Views.

3 Generating Constraint-Preserving Relations

XML Schema supports a rich set of integrity and cardinality constraints. The *Translation Module* takes an XML schema with such constraints as input and produces a constraint-preserving equivalent relational schema. For example, XML Schema supports three integrity constraints: *unique*, *key* and *keyref*, with similar semantics to their relational counterparts – *unique* ensures no duplication among non-null values; *key* ensures all values are unique and non-null; and *keyref* ensures reference to XML nodes. Due to hierarchical data model of XML, *context* is also specified for integrity constraints to define the different sets of nodes to be distinguished.

Using the syntax of [5], example constraints for the sample *bank.xml* document shown in Figure 3 are given below:

- *acc-num-key*: (//country,(.//account, {sav-acc-num | check-acc-num}))
  Within a country (here country is a *context*), each account is uniquely identified by a savings or checking account number.
- *cust-acc*: (//country,(./customer,{acc-num})) KEYREF *acc-num-key*
  Within a country, each customer refers to a savings or checking account number by acc-num.

An obvious way of supporting XML constraints in an RDBMS is to use triggered procedures, but this is highly inefficient [8], and should therefore only be used for those constraints (such as cardinality constraints) that do not have a relational equivalent. Specifically, the XML *key* and *keyref* constraints should

```
<bank>
    <country>
        <name>India</name>
        <customer>
            <cust-id>1</cust-id>
            <acc-num>101</acc-num> ...
         </customer> ...
         <city>
            <name>Bangalore</name>
            <state>Karnataka</state>
            <head-office> ... </head-office>
            <branch-office> ... </branch-office> ...
            <atm> ... </atm> ...
            <account>
                <sav-acc-num>101</sav-acc-num>
                <balance>1232423</balance>
            </account>
            <account>
                <check-acc-num>102</check-acc-num>
                <balance>645634</balance>
            </account>...
        </city> ...
    </country> ...
</bank>
```

Fig. 3. Sample XML Document (bank.xml)

```
TABLE Account(
    Acc-id-key INT,
    sav-acc-num INT,
    check-acc-num INT,
    balance INT,
    parent-City INT)
```

(a) Using LegoDB mapping

```
TABLE Account(
    Acc-id-key INT,
    sav-or-check-acc-num INT,
    parent-Country INT,
    acc-num-flag INT,
    balance INT,
    parent-City INT)
```

(b) Inclusion of relational key

Fig. 4. Generating relational keys for XML key – *acc-num-key*

be mapped to relational key and foreign-key constructs. We have developed a three-step algorithm for implementing this mapping – this technique is superficially similar to the X2R storage mapping algorithm [7], but a crucial difference is that they tailor the schema to fit the key constraints, thereby risking efficiency, whereas we take the opposite approach of integrating the key constraints with an efficient schema.

Specifically, Elixir starts by converting the XML schema into the *schema tree* representation proposed in FleXMap [15]. Then, in the first step, subtrees corresponding to different paths that need to be mapped to a single column are "associated", with the need for association determined from the XML keys. For example, for *acc-num-key*, the subtrees corresponding to sav-acc-num and check-acc-num have to be associated. In the next step, the XML-to-relational mapping procedure proposed in [3] is extended to create table configurations in the presence of the associated trees. After mapping the XML schema to tables, the final step is to incorporate the relational keys that are equivalent to the original XML keys.

An example output for the initial generic mapping of Figure 4(a)) is shown in Figure 4(b). Here, the elements sav-acc-num and check-acc-num are mapped to a single column `sav-or-check-acc-num`, and an additional column, `acc-num-flag`, is created for identifying the account number type. Further, since the context element for *acc-num-key* is country, which is not an immediate parent of **Account**, a `parent-Country` column, which refers to `country-id-key`, is added to distinguish between different contexts.

Similarly we can define an equivalent relational foreign key for the *cust-acc* XML keyref. Specifically, create the following relation:

```
TABLE Customer (Cust-id-key INT, Cust-id INT, Name STRING, Address
STRING, Acc-num STRING, parent-Country INT)
```

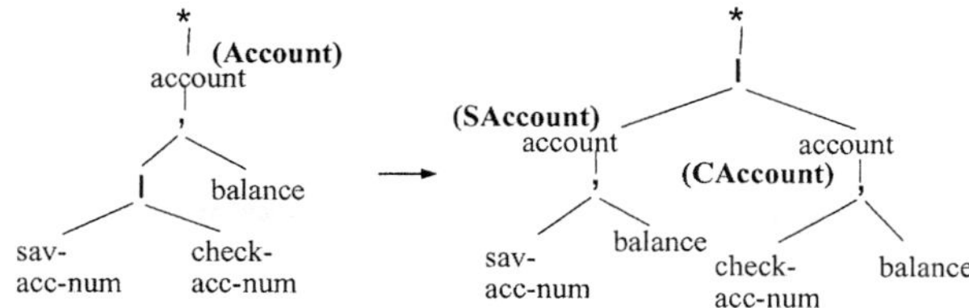

Fig. 5. Invalid union distribution due to *acc-num-key* constraint

where the foreign key is {`Acc-num`, `parent-Country`}, referring to the key attribute pair of the `Account` relation.

Cost-based strategies, such as those proposed in [3], explore the optimization space by applying various transformations to the XML schema (which exploit the standard rules of regular expressions in XML Schema for *unions* and *repetitions*), and evaluating the costs of the corresponding relational configurations. Elixir restricts the mapping search space to only *constraint-valid schema trees* by filtering out the invalid schema transformations. For example, consider the union account = sav-acc-num | check-acc-num shown before and after distribution in Figure 5. The corresponding relational configuration will have account numbers stored in two relations as follows:

```
TABLE SAccount(SAcc-id-key INT, sav-acc-num INT, balance INT, parent-City
INT)
TABLE CAccount(CAcc-id-key INT, check-acc-num INT, balance INT,
parent-City INT)
```

Here our goal is to map the XML key and keyref in the form of primary key and foreign key, respectively. However, according to the *acc-num-key* constraint, sav-acc-num and check-acc-num should be mapped to a single column, in order to define the relational key, thereby rendering the union distribution invalid.

This example shows that not all relational configurations obtained by schema transformations are valid. Thus, while exploring the search space of relational configurations, we should explore only the space of valid configurations. The simple solution for this is to carry out the transformation on the schema tree and then check if relational keys equivalent to the given XML constraints can be defined on the resulting relational configuration. If it is not possible then that relational configuration can be ignored, otherwise it should be evaluated for the given query workload. However, this solution results in considerable unnecessary work, which can be avoided if we can detect the invalidity schema transformations *before* carrying out the schema transformation.

For example, assume that union $t_1|t_2$ is being distributed, where t_1 and t_2 are subtrees of the schema tree. Now we will try to analyze the cause for invalidation. Note that both the subtrees, corresponding to sav-acc-num (t_1) and check-acc-num (t_2), are on the same field path of the *acc-num-key* constraint. Thus, if the union distribution of this tree i.e. $t_1|t_2$ is distributed, then in the resulting configuration, t_1 and t_2 will be mapped to different relations. In general, **if subtrees t_1 and t_2 are both on the same field path, then union distribution of $t_1|t_2$**

is invalid. The complete set of rules to detect when schema transformations are invalid w.r.t. XML schema constraints is given in [14]. A useful side-effect of incorporating the constraints during the schema design process is that the mapping process completes faster due to the reduction of the optimization search space.

4 Index Selection in Elixir

We move on in this section to a different component of the holistic mapping, namely deciding on the best choice of relational *indices*, given a disk space budget. As mentioned earlier, Elixir takes the approach of finding a good set of indices in the XML space and then mapping them to equivalent indices in the relational space. This is in marked contrast to current industrial practice [6], where the index advisor of the relational engine is used to propose a good set of indices after the schema mapping has been carried out.

For finding good XML indices, we leverage the recently proposed XIST tool [16], which makes *path-index* recommendations given an input consisting of an XML schema, query workload, data statistics, and disk budget. We have extended XIST to make use of semantic information such as keys, which are closely linked to index selection, by giving priority to the paths corresponding to keys during the index selection process. This is in keeping with Elixir's general philosophy of exploring the *combined* search space of logical design (i.e. schema transformations) and physical design (i.e. indices) since solving them independently leads to suboptimal performance [6].

After making the choice of XML path-indices, a strategy to convert path indices to the equivalent relational indices has to be designed. Secondly, the disk usage of the *relational indices* should be within the user-specified budget – therefore, an equivalence mapping between the disk occupancies in the XML and relational spaces has to be formulated. Finally, the XQuery-to-SQL translation process should take advantage of the presence of the relational indices. In the remainder of this section, we describe our approach to handle the first and third issues – the second issue is discussed in [14].

4.1 Path Index to Relational Index Conversion

Consider an XML-to-relational mapping, as shown in Figure 6 for a fragment of the XMark benchmark schema [28]. Here, a non-leaf node is annotated with a relation name, while a leaf node is annotated with the name of a relational column. Relations `Site`, `Africa`, ..., `Samerica`, `Item`, and `Mailbox` are created for elements site, africa, ..., samerica, item, mailbox, respectively. For this environment, assume that the following path index, PI, has been recommended: /site/regions/africa/item/mailbox/mail/from. To evaluate PI, the four relations {`Site`, `Africa`, `Item`, and `Mailbox`} have to be joined.

An obvious translation process is to simply build the indices on the key and foreign-key pair for each parent-child involved in PI. However, the drawback of

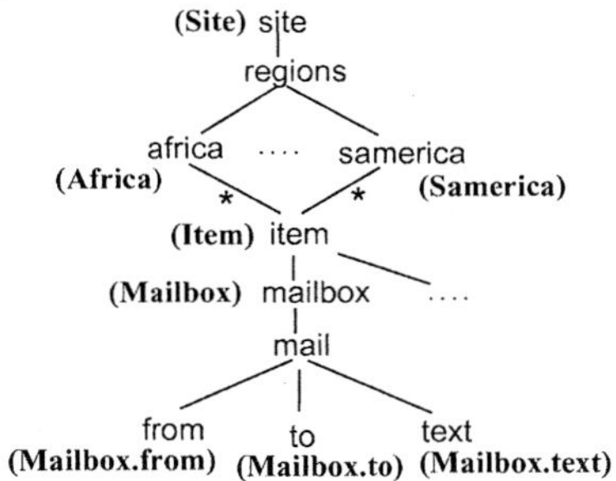

Fig. 6. Example relational configuration

1. `Mailbox.parent-africa`
2. `Mailbox.from`

(a) Equivalence Class-based Approach

1. `Africa.parent-Site`
2. `Item.parent-Africa`
3. `Mailbox.parent-Item`
4. `Mailbox.from`

(b) Direct Approach

Fig. 7. Relational indices for path index /site/regions/africa/item/mailbox/mail/from

this direct approach is that the number of relational indices created for a path-index is a function of the *path-length*, and can therefore become very expensive to create and maintain. An alternative and less expensive approach is to use the concept of *equivalence classes* [16] to reduce the number of relational indices. Two paths P_1 and P_2 are in the same equivalence class if the evaluation of both paths against XML data results in selection of the same nodes. These equivalence classes can be determined directly from the XML schema and are valid for all XML documents conforming to the XML schema.

We have developed a procedure (details in [14]) that uses these path equivalence classes (EQs) to convert the path-index only to the relational indices corresponding to each EQ on the path. For example, if we assume that for each relation, the column which stores IDs is the primary key, and that an index exists on the primary key by default, then the equivalent relational indices for PI are as shown in Figure 7(a) (for comparative purposes, the indices recommended by the Direct approach are shown in Figure 7(b)).

4.2 Query Rewriting for Path Indices

The use of integrity constraints to guide XQuery-to-SQL query translation has been recently discussed in [13]. Here, we focus on the use of available path indices to guide XQuery-to-SQL query translation, and thereby derive a more efficient rewriting of the query. For example, consider the query:

```
for    $mail = /site/regions/africa/item/mailbox/mail
where $mail/from/text() = "priti@dsl.serc.iisc.ernet.in"
return count($mail)
```

The relevant path P here is /site/regions/africa/item/ mailbox/mail/from. If there is no path index on P, then the SQL translation of the above query will be:

```
select  count(*)
from   Site S, Africa A,  Item I, Mailbox M
```

```
where S.site-key = A.parent-site
      and A.africa-key = I.parent-africa
      and I.item-key = M.parent-item
      and M.from = 'priti@dsl.serc.iisc.ernet.in'
```

On the other hand, if a path index on P is available, the translation module uses this information to translate the query as follows:

```
select  count(*)
from   Africa A, Mailbox M
where A.africa-key = M.parent-africa
      and M.from = 'priti@dsl.serc.iisc.ernet.in'
```

While the above was an illustrative example, the complete algorithm for incorporating indices in the XQuery-to-SQL translation process is given in [14].

5 Mapping XML Triggers and Views

We now move on to the advanced components of XML triggers [4] and XML views [1]. Triggers are primarily used to execute a specific logic upon updates to the database. To leverage the power of relational databases, our aim is to map the XML triggers to relational triggers, an example of which is shown in Figure 8.

```
CREATE TRIGGER Increment-Counter
AFTER INSERT OF //CUSTOMER
FOR EACH NODE
 LET $branch_id = NEW_NODE/branch
 LET $branch_node =
         //branch-office[id=$branch_id]
 LET $counter = $branch_node/acc-counter
DO (
FOR $branch_node
UPDATE $branch_node
REPLACE $counter WITH $counter + 1 )
```

(a) XML trigger

```
CREATE TRIGGER Increment-Counter
AFTER INSERT ON Customer
REFERENCING NEW AS new_row
FOR EACH ROW
BEGIN ATOMIC
  UPDATE Branch-office
  SET Acc-counter=Acc-counter+1
  WHERE Branch-office.Id =
                  new_row.Branch
END
```

(b) Equivalent SQL trigger

Fig. 8. Mapping XML triggers to SQL triggers

A problem specific to the XML domain, however, is that compared to relational updates, XQuery updates may be seen as *bulk* statements since they may involve arbitrarily large fragments of documents that are inserted or dropped through a single statement. For example, when a bank sets up operations in a new city, the corresponding XQuery update could result in several SQL insert statements on the tables corresponding to the update path.

In this situation, consider the following XML trigger, sending e-mail to advertise the new office to all customers from the same country as the inserted city:

```
CREATE TRIGGER NewCityTrigger AFTER INSERT OF /bank/country/city
FOR EACH NODE DO (
   LET $city-name = NEW_NODE/name
   LET $city-state = NEW_NODE/state
   LET $city-head-office-id = NEW_NODE/head-office-id
   LET $city-branch-offices = NEW_NODE/branch-office
   ...
   FOR $customer IN NEW_NODE/../country/customer
     send-email ($customer, $city-name, $city-state,
                $city-head-office-id, $city-branch-offices, ...) )
```

The above trigger needs to be executed after all the insert statements to the `City`, `Branch-office`, `Office-Id`, `Atm`, `Account` relations have been executed. However, in the current SQL standard, triggers cannot be specified relative to a set of operations on different tables. We refer to such triggers as *non-mappable XML triggers* and model them instead as stored procedures that can be called by the middleware at runtime.

While the costs of mappable triggers are natively modeled by the relational optimizer, an additional query workload equivalent to the non-mappable triggers is included in the XML query workload. Our experiments have shown that in practice XML triggers play an important role in determining the choice of the final relational configuration.

Turning our attention to XML views, Elixir maps these views to relational views by first converting the XML view definition to the equivalent SQL view definition, and then translating XQuery queries on the XML views to SQL queries on relational views. Additionally, if the user specifies a *materialized* XML view, then this view is mapped to materialized relational views. The complete mapping algorithm is given in [14], and an illustrative example is shown below.

Consider a user specifying the following materialized XML view to make the balance inquiry query execute faster:

```
CREATE MATERIALIZED VIEW customer_balance AS
    FOR $customer IN //customer
    FOR $account IN //account
    WHERE $customer/acc-num = $account/sav-acc-num or
          $customer/acc-num = $account/check-acc-num
    return
        <customer-balance>
            <id>$customer/cust-id</id>
            <acc-num>$customer/acc-num</acc-num>
            <balance>$customer/balance</balance>
        </customer-balance>
DATA INITIALLY IMMEDIATE REFRESH IMMEDIATE
```

Elixir maps this XML materialized view to the following equivalent relational materialized view:

```
CREATE TABLE customer_balance AS
    (SELECT C.id, C.acc-num, A.balance
     FROM   Customer C, Account A
     WHERE  C.acc-num = A.sav-or-check-acc-num)
DATA INITIALLY IMMEDIATE REFRESH IMMEDIATE
```

6 Experimental Evaluation

In this section, we present our experimental evaluation of the Elixir system. Our experiments were run on a Pentium-IV PC running Linux, with DB2 UDB v8.1 [20] as the backend database engine. Four representative real-world XML schemas: *Genex* [19], *EPML* [18], *ICRFS* [21] and *TourML* [26], which deal with gene expressions, business processes, enterprise analysis and tourism, respectively, are used in our study. In addition, we also evaluate the performance for the synthetic XMark benchmark schema [28].[1]

6.1 Effect of Keys

To serve as a baseline for assessing the effect of key inclusion, we compare the performance of Elixir (in the absence of indices, triggers, and views) with that of FleXMap (FM) [15], a framework for expressing XML schema transformations and for searching the equivalent relational configuration space. Using the ToXgene tool [27], three types of documents were generated for each XML schema by varying the distribution of elements as *all-uniform*, *uniform-exponential*, and *all-exponential*, resulting in documents with uniform data, moderately skewed data, and highly skewed data, respectively. The query workload involves 10 representative queries for each XML schema.

We compare the runtime efficiency of Elixir and FleXMap with regard to the following metrics: (a) The percentage reduction in search space, and (b) The response time speedup due to this reduction. The average number of transformations evaluated by Elixir and FM are shown in Figure 9(a) for the five XML schemas. We see there that the reduction ranges from 30% to 60%, arising from the filtering out of invalid transformations, discussed in Section 3. For example, on the ICRFS schema, the average number of transformations performed by FleXMap are about 1860, whereas Elixir only requires about 860.

The time speedup due to the search space reduction is shown in Figure 9(b), which captures the average time required to obtain the final relational configuration for the same set of schemas. Here, we observe that the runtime reductions range from 50% to 85%. It is interesting to note that the speedup is *super-linear* in the percentage space reduction. For example, the 50% search space reduction for ICRFS may be expected to result in a speedup of 2, but the speedup actually obtained is greater than 4. The reason for this is as follows: A given XQuery workload satisfies more paths in the fully decomposed schema of FleXMap resulting in *more subqueries* in the equivalent SQL workload, as compared to the

[1] Since XMark is available only as a DTD, we created the equivalent XML Schema and incorporated keys by mapping the IDs and IDREFs.

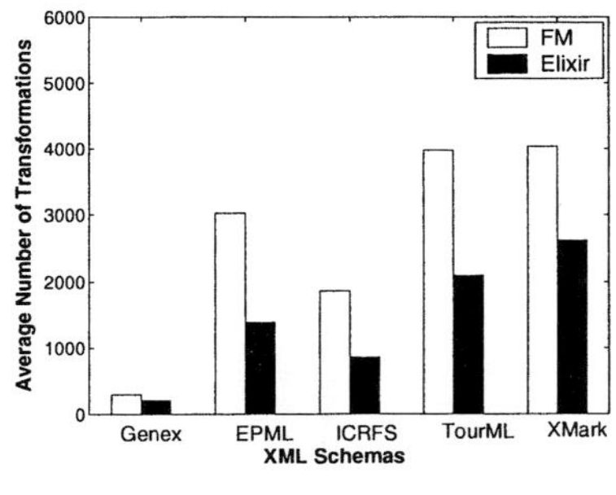

(a) Search space

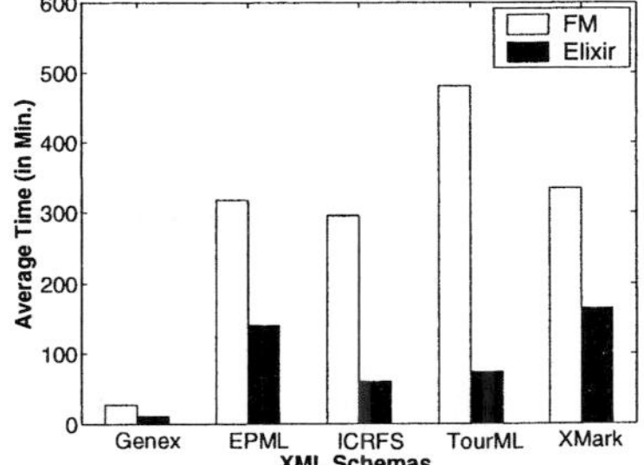

(b) Time efficiency

Fig. 9. Impact of Keys

number derived from the restrictive decomposed schema of Elixir. Thus, the time required for evaluating the cost of an individual transformation using the relational optimizer is more for FleXMap than for Elixir. In a nutshell, Elixir has "fewer and cheaper" transformations.

6.2 Effect of Index Selection

We now move on to evaluating the impact of index selection. Specifically, we compare Elixir, with its path-index-based selection, against two alternatives: *BasicDB2*, where the system has only its default primary key indices, and *DB2Advisor*, where DB2's Index Advisor tool is used to suggest a good set of indices, similar to [6].

We report here the results of experiments on the EPML schema [18] with various sizes of XML documents ranging from 1 MB to 500 MB. The query workload involves 20 representative queries. The index disk budget was set to be 10 percent of the space occupied by the XML document repository, a common rule-of-thumb in practice. The results for this set of experiments are shown in Figure 10, where we see that the cost of the final relational configuration is significantly lower for Elixir as compared to *BasicDB2* as well as *DB2Advisor*. The results obtained on other schemas were similar and are available in [14].

Analysis of the set of indices chosen by Elixir and *DB2Advisor* indicates the following: The SQL workload equivalent to the given XQuery workload involves several joins. DB2 attempts to improve the query performance by creating multicolumn indexes or single column indexes (with `include` clause). Elixir, on the other hand, uses the path indices suggested by XIST and converts path indices to equivalent single column relational indices. Further, the sets of indexes chosen by DB2Advisor and Elixir are quite different in that the overlap is only between 20% to 50%.

6.3 Overall Performance of Elixir System

While the previous experiments evaluated the performance in isolation for various components (the trigger and view performance is available in [14]), the

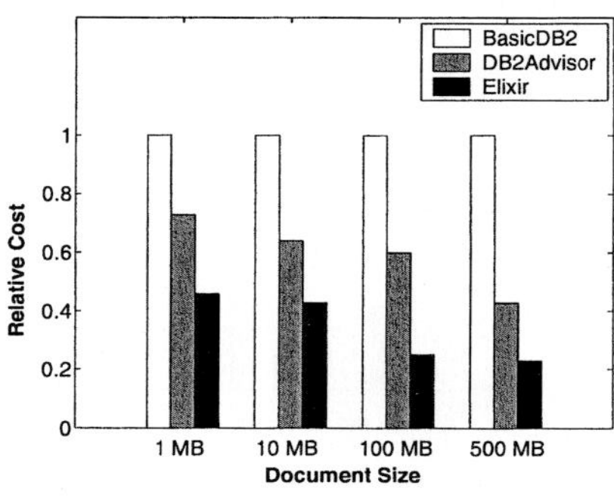

Fig. 10. Index selection

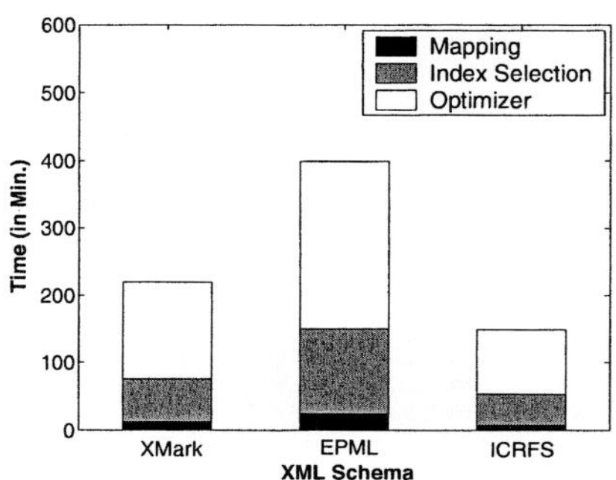

Fig. 11. Elixir Performance

overall performance when all components are integrated is shown in Figure 11. This figure shows both the total time for producing the final relational schema as well as the breakup of this time in different steps of the tuning process – Mapping, Index selection, and Optimizer. With regard to overall time, we find that it is in the range of a few hours for each schema. While this may seem excessive at first glance, note that (a) the schema generation process is typically a one-shot process, and therefore time may not be a major issue; and, further, (b) the breakup of the runtime indicates significant potential for improvement – the heavy overhead (60% to 70%) is largely attributable to our using the optimizer *from the outside*, which involves fresh creation of tables, loading of statistics, costing the mapping and table deletion, in *each* iteration of the mapping process. We expect that this overhead would be substantially reduced if the Elixir system were implemented inside the relational engine since the optimizer could be instrumented to directly provide the cost for the new mappings. Finally, note that due to the absence of comparable systems for producing holistic schemas, we only provide absolute performance results here.

7 Conclusions and Future Work

In this paper, we studied the problem of producing *information-preserving holistic schema* mappings from XML repositories to relational backends. Specifically, we proposed the Elixir system, which captures most significant aspects of the XML world and delivers relational schemas that include table configurations, keys, indices, triggers, and views, featuring an integrated, cost-based and source-centric optimization of the mapping process. A detailed experimental study on real-world and synthetic schemas demonstrated the effectiveness of our techniques with regard to both the final quality of the relational configuration as well as the mapping time. In a nutshell, the Elixir system achieves "industrial-strength" mappings for XML-on-RDBMS providing lossless translation (structure and semantics including constraints and triggers) and performance tuning (indices and materialized views). Our future plans include implementation of the

Elixir system inside public-domain relational engines and extending the schema mapping to include security components.

Acknowledgements. This work was supported in part by a Swarnajayanti Fellowship from the Dept. of Science & Technology, Govt. of India.

References

1. S. Abiteboul. On Views and XML. In *Proc. of 18th ACM Symp. on Principles of Database Systems (PODS)*, May 1999.
2. S. Boag et al. XQuery 1.0: An XML Query Language, May 2001. `http://www.w3.org/TR/xquery/`.
3. P. Bohannon, J. Freire, P. Roy and J. Siméon. From XML schema to relations: A cost based approach to XML storage. In *Proc. of 18th IEEE Intl. Conf. on Data Engineering (ICDE)*, March 2002.
4. A. Bonifati, D. Braga, A. Campi and S. Ceri. Active XQuery. In *Proc. of 18th IEEE Intl. Conf. on Data Engineering (ICDE)*, February 2002.
5. P. Buneman, S. Davidson, W. Fan, C. Hara and W. Tan. Keys for XML. *Computer Networks*, 39(5), 2002.
6. S. Chaudhuri, Z. Chen, K. Shim and Y. Wu. Storing XML (with XSD) in SQL Databases: Interplay of Logical and Physical Designs. In *Proc. of 20th IEEE Intl. Conf. on Data Engineering (ICDE)*, March 2004.
7. Y. Chen, S. Davidson and Y. Zheng. Constraints preserving schema mapping from XML to relations. In *Proc. of 5th Intl. Workshop on Web and Databases (WebDB)*, June 2002.
8. Y. Chen, S. Davidson and Y. Zheng. Validating constraints in XML. Tech. Report MS-CIS-02-03, Dept. of Computer and Information Science, Univ. of Pennsylvania, 2002.
9. J. Freire, J. Haritsa, M. Ramanath, P. Roy and J. Siméon. Statix: Making XML count. In *Proc. of ACM SIGMOD Intl. Conf. on Management of Data*, June 2002.
10. H. Jagadish et al. TIMBER: A Native XML Database. *VLDB Journal*, 11(4), 2002.
11. C. Kanne and G. Moerkotte. Efficient Storage of XML data. In *Proc. of 16th IEEE Intl. Conf. on Data Engineering (ICDE)*, February 2000.
12. R. Krishnamurthy, V. Chakaravarthy and J. Naughton. On the Difficulty of Finding Optimal Relational Decompositions for XML Workloads: a Complexity Theoretic Perspective. In *Proc. of 9th Intl. Conf. on Database Theory (ICDT)*, January 2003.
13. R. Krishnamurthy, R. Kaushik and J. Naughton. Efficient XML-to-SQL Query Translation: Where to Add the Intelligence? In *Proc. of 30th Intl. Conf. on Very Large Data Bases (VLDB)*, August 2004.
14. P. Patil and J. Haritsa. Holistic Schema Mappings for XML-on-RDBMS. Tech. Report `http://dsl.serc.iisc.ernet.in/publications/report/TR/TR-2005-02.pdf`.
15. M. Ramanath, J. Freire, J. Haritsa and P. Roy. Searching for efficient XML-to-relational mappings. In *Proc. of 1st Intl. XML Database Symp. (XSym)*, September 2003.
16. K. Runapongsa, J. Patel, R. Bordawekar and S. Padmanabhan. XIST: An XML Index Selection Tool. In *Proc. of 2nd Intl. XML Database Symp. (XSym)*, August 2004.

17. DTD. http://www.w3.org/XML/1998/06/xmlspec-report.
18. EPML (EPC Markup Language). http://wi.wu-wien.ac.at/~mendling/EPML/.
19. GENEX (Gene Expression Markup Language). http://www.ncgr.org/genex.
20. IBM DB2 XML Extender. http://www-3.ibm.com/software/data/db2/extenders/xmlext/library.html.
21. ICRFS (ICRFS XML schema). http://www.insureware.com/abouti/mlines.shtml.
22. A survey of MS-SQL Server 2000 XML features. http://msdn.microsoft.com/library/en-us/dnexxml/html/xml07162001.asp?frame=true.
23. Objective Caml. http://caml.inria.fr/ocaml.
24. Oracle XML DB: An oracle technical white paper. http://technet.oracle.com/tech/xml/content.html.
25. Tamino. http://www1.softwareag.com/Corporate/products/tamino/prod_info/default.asp.
26. Tourism Markup Language. http://www.opentourism.org.
27. ToXgene (ToX XML Data Generator). http://www.cs.toronto.edu/tox/toxgene/.
28. XMark. http://monetdb.cwi.nl/xml/.
29. XML schema. http://www.w3.org/TR/xmlschema-1/.

Semi-supervised Classification Based on Smooth Graphs

Xueyuan Zhou and Chunping Li

School of software, Tsinghua University, 100084 Beijing, P.R. China
zhou-xy03@mails.tsinghua.edu.cn, cli@tsinghua.edu.cn

Abstract. In semi-supervised classification, labels smoothness and cluster assumption are the key point of many successful methods. In graph-based semi-supervised classification, graph representations of the data are quite important. Different graph representations can affect the classification results greatly. Considering the two assumptions and graph representations, we propose a novel method to build a better graph for semi-supervised classification. The graph in our method is called m-step Markov random walk graph (mMRW graph). The smoothness of this graph can be controlled by a parameter m. We believe that a relatively much smoother graph will benefit transductive learning. We also discuss some benefits brought by our smooth graphs. A cluster cohesion based parameter learning method can be efficiently applied to find a proper m. Experiments on artificial and real world dataset indicate that our method has a superior classification accuracy over several state-of-the-art methods.

1 Introduction

One basic assumption employed directly or indirectly by semi-supervised classification is the labels smoothness [10] or cluster assumption [1]. In labels smoothness assumption, neighboring data points tend to have the same label. This is true in many real world problems and human intuition. In cluster assumption, two points are likely to have the same label if there is a path connecting them passing through regions of high density only, or to say that the decision boundary should lie in regions of low density. These two assumptions have been successfully applied in semi-supervised classification. Seeger [5] and Zhu [10] have given extensive reviews about semi-supervised classification methods.

Based on these two assumption, some methods are successfully applied in semi-supervised classification. In harmonic function method [9], value of f at each unlabeled data point is the average of f at neighboring points. The regularization method is used to smooth the values of unlabeled data points in [8]. In these methods, a common feature lies in that the aim is to make sure that neighboring points have approximately the same indicating function value. In cluster kernel [1], kernels are designed such that induced distance is smaller for points in the same cluster and larger for points in different clusters. In [2], low density regions are identified to separate clusters.

M.L. Lee, K.L. Tan, and V. Wuwongse (Eds.): DASFAA 2006, LNCS 3882, pp. 757–766, 2006.

Although these two assumptions seem different on the surface, they reflect the same nature in classification, that is the data of one class is usually distributed continuously in a relatively high density region, different classes generally do not overlap with each other, and low density regions usually separate clusters. From this point of view, labels smoothness and cluster assumption share the same meaning. However, real world data might not be distributed so smoothly, especially in high dimension cases. For example, text data in bag-of-words representation. In this case, cluster assumption might be damaged to some extent. Low density regions may lie inside some cluster. Labels smoothness assumption is also difficult to be held. Because the density of data varies greatly, so it is difficult to distinguish if the concept of "neighboring" in one region is proper for "neighboring" in another region. Therefore, it is important to build a much smoother graph representation of the data for graph-based semi-supervised classification.

To overcome the difficulties of bad data distribution, we build a smooth graph using Markov random walk model, then label the huge amount of unlabeled data using any other graph-based semi-supervised classification methods. This method fits the graphical representation better, and can reveal the distribution of labeled and unlabeled data. With different steps, it gradually combines local and global distributions of all the data points at different levels.

In this paper, we introduce basic concepts about Markov random walk in Sect. 2. In Sect. 3, a novel graph representation of data is presented, which employs Markov random walk model. And a cluster based parameter learning method is given in Sect. 4. With the experiment analysis of the artificial and real world data sets, the results and evaluations are shown in Sect. 5. In Sect. 6, we give the discussion and concluding remark.

2 Markov Random Walk Model

The theory and application of random walk are ubiquitous in the modern probability literature, and random walks perhaps form the simplest and most important examples of stochastic processes, i.e. random phenomena unfolding with time. In this paper, we only consider random walk on graph, which is not exactly the same as original random walk.

Let the graph $G = (V, E)$ be a pair consisting of a set V of vertices, and a set E of edges joining some pairs of vertices. For each $x \in V$, we may consider the set N_x of neighbors of x, formed by vertices y with an edge joining x to y. The random walk is based on this graph, where the step from x to y $(y \in N_x)$ has probability p_{xy}. Under the assumption of Markovian property, such a random walk on graph can be viewed as a Markov chain. Details for random walks on graph are given in [6]. Rudnick and Gaspari [4] give an advanced discussion about original form of random walk.

In the Markov random walk for classification, data points are mapped to the vertices in a graph or states in a Markov chain. The transition probability can be seen as the similarity between data pairs. Given that a dataset consists of data pairs $\{(x_1, y_1), \cdots, (x_n, y_n)\}$, we can construct a graph on the input data x_i, and the weight of edge is defined as

$$w_{ij} = exp(-\frac{d(x_i, x_j)}{\sigma^2}) \quad (1)$$

where $d(\cdot)$ can be Euclidean distance or other distance measure, and σ is a parameter for exponential weights. Let the one-step transition probability be

$$p_{ij} = \frac{w_{ij}}{\sum_k w_{ik}} \quad (2)$$

We can get the transition matrix $P = [p_{ij}]$. Some semi-supervised classification methods [1, 7, 8, 9] are based on such a basic representation. In this paper, we assume $w_{ii} = 0$, which forms a non-lazy random walk.

3 m-Step Markov Random Walk Graph Model

Under labels smoothness and cluster assumption [10, 1], some methods have been proposed to smooth functions on graphs in order to get a better classification result [8, 9]. However, most of these methods focus on the model itself to smooth the graph. We attempt to construct a smooth graph first, and then label the unlabeled data.

3.1 m-Step Markov Random Walk Graph

Based on Sect. 2, we can get a full connected graph G and its transition matrix P. We can also further construct a kNN graph G_k from graph G. The transition matrix P reflects the local structure of the graph. Data points usually have higher probabilities to walk to the ones nearby, and tend to walk to denser regions more likely than sparser ones.

The smoothness here can be explained as the distribution of data changes slowly in one cluster, which can also be explained as the transition probabilities from one point to its neighbors change slowly in a small region. Therefore, we propose the following graph as the basic representation for semi-supervised classification: connection matrix of graph $G^{(m)}$ is

$$P^* = P^m \quad (3)$$

where P is the original transition matrix defined in Sect. 2.

Therefore, if we treat P as the connection matrix of graph G, then $P \times P$ is the connection matrix of another graph $G^{(2)}$, and $P \times P \times P$ is the connection matrix of graph $G^{(3)}$, and so on.

3.2 Analysis of the Smoothness

Now we give an analysis about graph $G^{(m)}$. To facilitate analysis we first map the graph representation of data into a Markov chain. The vertices of graph are mapped into states in the chain. And the vertex set V is mapped into state set I. The weight of graph defined in Sect. 2 is mapped into transition probability between states in Markov chain. Then from the view of Markov chain, if P^m exists when $m \to \infty$, there is an uniform distribution π_j $(1 \leq j \leq n)$ over all the data, where $n =\mid I \mid$, is the total number of states in I or points in graph G. That means the probability from any data point to one fixed point is the same. In this case, the graph is "flat". We can define the smoothness of a graph according to its "flat" state if it exists. We define the smoothness function as:

$$Q^{(m)} = \sum_{i,j=1}^{n} (p_{ij}^{(m)} - \pi_j)^2 \tag{4}$$

$Q^{(m)}$ reflects the smoothness of one graph. The smaller value of $Q^{(m)}$ means a much smoother graph. Then we can predict that graph $G^{(2)}$ is much smoother than $G^{(1)}$. This can be explained from the view of Markov chain. We give a brief proof here.

By treating graph G as a Markov chain, it is easy to satisfy the following conditions: it is a finite-state Markov chain with no two disjoint closed sets, and it is aperiodic. After mapping the graph into a Markov chain, we have the following result [3]: there exists a probability distribution $\{\pi_j, j \in I\}$ and numbers $\alpha > 0$ and $0 < \beta < 1$ such that, for all $i, j \in I$,

$$\mid p_{ij}^{(n)} - \pi_j \mid \leq \alpha\beta^n, \quad n = 1, 2, \cdots \tag{5}$$

In particular,

$$\lim_{n \to \infty} p_{ij}^{(n)} = \pi_j \quad for\ all \quad i, j \in I \tag{6}$$

In equation (5), $p_{ij}^{(n)}$ is an element in matrix P^n. From equation (5), we know that as n gets larger, $p_{ij}^{(n)}$ gets closer to the fixed value π_j.

From equation (4) and (5), we have

$$Q^{(m)} = \sum_{i,j=1}^{n} (p_{ij}^{(m)} - \pi_j)^2 \leq \sum_{i,j=1}^{n} \alpha^2\beta^{2m} = n^2\alpha^2\beta^{2m}$$

For some fixed graph, n is a constant. Therefore, $Q^{(m)}$ gets smaller and smaller as m grows, then we can say that the graph gets smoother and smoother.

We call this graph as m-step Markov random walk graph (mMRW graph). Different m values will result in different graphs. In special case when $m = 1$, it is the original graph G. However, m should not get too large. When $m \to \infty$, P^m will become an uniform distribution for each point, which provides little information about the classification.

The following example can aptly illustrate this point. Assume that a is the transition matrix of some graph G.

$$\mathbf{a} = \begin{pmatrix} 0.40 & 0.60 & 0.00 & 0.00 \\ 0.20 & 0.70 & 0.10 & 0.00 \\ 0.00 & 0.10 & 0.60 & 0.30 \\ 0.00 & 0.00 & 0.80 & 0.20 \end{pmatrix} \quad \mathbf{a}^4 = \begin{pmatrix} 0.22 & 0.60 & 0.14 & 0.04 \\ 0.20 & 0.55 & 0.19 & 0.06 \\ 0.05 & 0.19 & 0.54 & 0.22 \\ 0.03 & 0.16 & 0.58 & 0.23 \end{pmatrix}$$

$$\mathbf{a}^{16} = \begin{pmatrix} 0.14 & 0.41 & 0.33 & 0.12 \\ 0.14 & 0.40 & 0.34 & 0.12 \\ 0.11 & 0.34 & 0.40 & 0.15 \\ 0.11 & 0.33 & 0.41 & 0.15 \end{pmatrix} \quad \mathbf{a}^{64} = \begin{pmatrix} 0.12 & 0.37 & 0.37 & 0.14 \\ 0.12 & 0.37 & 0.37 & 0.14 \\ 0.12 & 0.37 & 0.37 & 0.14 \\ 0.12 & 0.37 & 0.37 & 0.14 \end{pmatrix}$$

We can see that $Q^{(1)} = 1.00$, $Q^{(4)} = 0.39$, $Q^{(16)} = 0.01$, $Q^{(64)} = 0.00$. As the number of steps increases, the graph gets flatter and flatter, and at last becomes an uniform distribution for each column.

3.3 Why the Smoothness May Help

One way to explain why the smooth graph can be better than the original one is from the distances between points. From equation (1) and (2), we know that the transition probabilities are related to the weights of a graph. Larger probabilities mean larger weights. As the number of steps m gets larger, p_{ij} between far points in the same cluster becomes larger, which means its corresponding weight gets larger. And in turn, it means the distance of the two points far away now is smaller. Furthermore, this kind of distance shortening is based on the density of data. Distances between points in one cluster are shortened more and in different clusters are shortened less.

Another way is from the spectral decomposition theory. The transition matrix P^* can be decomposed as: $P^* = \Phi\Lambda\Psi$, where Λ is a diagonal matrix. Then we have

$$p_{ij}^{(m)} = \sum_k \lambda_k^{(m)} \phi_{ik} \psi_{kj} \tag{7}$$

Because P is a transition probability matrix, we have $\lambda_0 = 1 > \lambda_1 > \lambda_2 \cdots > \lambda_n$. From spectral and harmonic analysis we know that small eigenvalues correspond to high frequency eigenfunctions. Then from equation (7) we can see that the power of transition matrix P in fact reduces the magnitudes of high frequency components much more than low frequency ones which correspond to larger eigenvalues. Therefore, the power of matrix P behaves like a low-pass filter and smoothes the distribution of the graph. In real world data, high frequency components usually correspond to the noise, and low frequency ones reflect the distribution of data more confidently. So a smooth graph reduces the noise greatly and represents the distribution of data better than the original one.

4 Parameter Learning

The parameters in our model are m, k in kNN graph and σ (if we use $exp((x_i - x_j)^2/\sigma)$ to construct P). If we use the cosine of two vectors to get P, which is:

$$r(x_i, x_j) = \frac{< x_i, x_j >}{\sqrt{< x_i, x_i >< x_j, x_j >}} \tag{8}$$

then we have only paramters m and k. In reality, it is easy to ensure $\sum_k r_{ik} \neq 0$. Zhu [9] has proposed a method for learning σ. The parameter k is difficult to learn for different data distribution. We enumerate several values of k to give some clues about affection of k in Sect. 5. In the following part, we focus on how to learn m in our model.

In semi-supervised classification, labeled data usually has a relatively small size, e.g. in case of only two labeled data points, one for each class. In this case, we can not fully trust these two points. Because they may be noises or biased by noises greatly. Therefore, many parameter learning methods only relying on labeled data can not be used here. Based on the cluster assumption, we know that when two clusters are separated well, no lower density region exists in any cluster. From this intuition, we propose the following function to select a proper m:

$$g_m(C_i) = \frac{\sum_{i,j=1}^{n} p(x_i, x_j)}{\mid C_i \mid^2} \tag{9}$$

$p(x_i, x_j)$ is the probability from x_i to x_j. We call $g_m(C_i)$ as the cohesion function of one class, and it can be viewed as the density of one cluster. For some m, when $g_m(C_i)$ becomes relatively stable, that is $\Delta g(C_i) < \epsilon$, then we can stop the walk and pick up the value of m at this time.

5 Experimental Results

Many graph based methods for semi-supervised classification can be viewed as Markov random walks [7, 8, 9]. These methods have clear explanations and have done well in semi-supervised classification. In order to take advantage of our smooth graph representations, we employ a random walk related method, i.e. harmonic function in [9] to label those unlabeled data points.

5.1 Artificial Data

We use the switch or two-moon data [7] in many semi-supervised learning papers. The weight is formed using equation (1), and $d(\cdot)$ is Euclidean distance. From Fig. 1 we can see that, as the value of m gets larger and larger, the graph becomes much smoother. Furthermore, when $m = 1$ and $\sigma = 0.04 \sim 0.06$, classification can be totally correct using method in [9]. However, keeping the accuracy at 100%, the mMRW graph enlarges the range of parameter σ to $\sigma = 0.04 \sim 0.45$ with different m.

The smoothness of mMRW is different from smoothness in [8, 9]. In this paper, we use smoothness to describe the transition probabilities between points. Rough transition probabilities between points might easily spread the effect of errors. If the bridge noise has a high transition probability, it will bias the label. However, a smooth transition probability can reduce this error.

5.2 Text Classification

We apply our method to text classification task, with few labeled documents but many unlabeled ones. Text documents are represented by high dimension

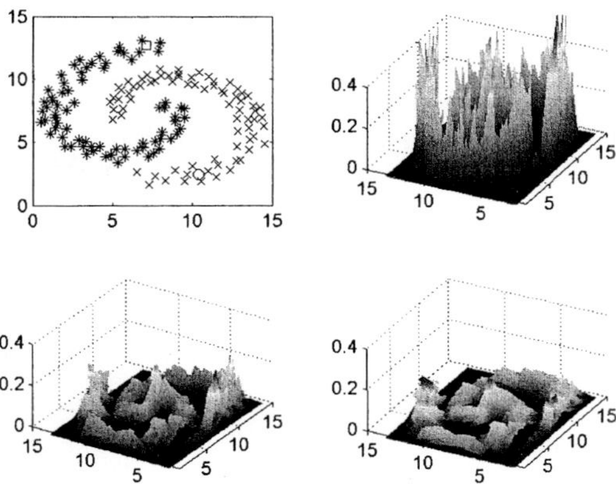

Fig. 1. mMRW graph on artificial data. $\sigma = 0.45$. Right up: $m = 1$; Left bottom: $m = 5$; Right bottom: $m = 9$.

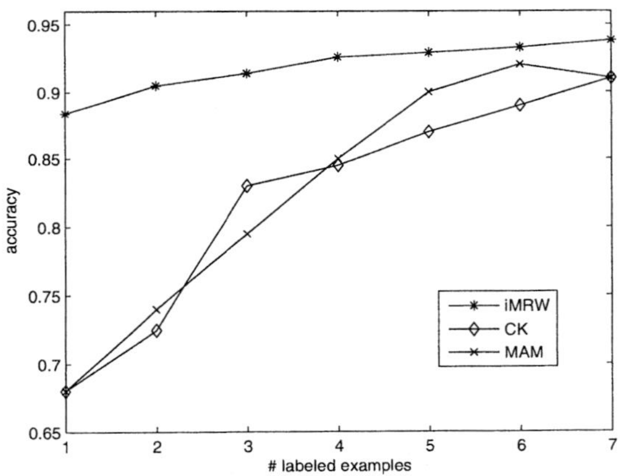

Fig. 2. Classification results of mMRW graph on text data set Windows vs Mac using cohesion factor method

vectors, which are usually very sparse. We expect that our method can construct a smooth graph which benefits the classification.

We train our model with real-world dataset: windows vs mac in 20 Newsgroups, also used by [1, 7], electronic vs space, and baseball vs hocky. The first dataset has two categories, windows and mac with respectively 961 and 958 examples with dimension 7511. Out of all the examples, 987 examples are taken away to form the test set. From 2 to 128 labeled data points are randomly selected to form X_L. We use cosine values of vectors to form the transition matrix P. We train on 100 randomly splits balanced for class labels, test on a fixed separate set of 987 points. The value of m ranges from 1 to 16. Then we compare kNN and mMRW graph with different k and m values. The settings for electronic vs space and baseball vs hocky are nearly the same.

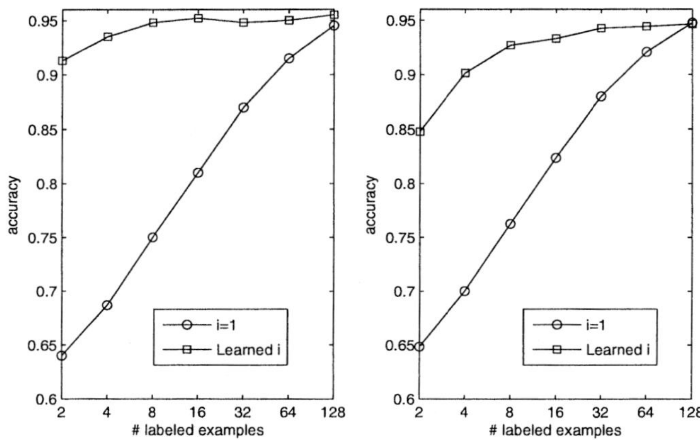

Fig. 3. Classification results. Left: Electronics vs Space; Right: Baseball vs Hocky.

In Fig. 2, mMRW is the accuracy of our method with parameter m learned in Sect.4. MAM is the result of [7] and CK is the result of [1]. We can see a clear advantage of mMRW graph method, especially when the number of labeled examples is relatively small. Fig. 3 is the classification results of our method and the original harmonic function [9], where $m = 1$ is the result of harmonic function and learned m is the result of our method.

5.3 Benefits from Smooth Graphs

The smooth graphs can bring many benefits for graph-based semi-supervised classification. We will discuss these benefits in the following part.

1. Large ranges for the parameter σ
If we select equation (1) as the weight of graph G, then we have to learn the parameter σ. This parameter in fact brings a decay to the distance metric $d(x_i, x_j)$. We can view each data point as a sample of the true data distribution. Then this form of weight can be viewed as to reconstruct the true distribution using a exponential function with parameter σ. When σ is too small, then the surface of the data in one cluster may vary greatly at different point and low density regions are likely to exist inside each cluster. When σ is too large, exponential function may connect different true clusters. Therefore, proper value of σ is critical.

However, if we use smooth graphs, the range of this parameter can be enlarged. This contributes to the low-pass filter effect of the power of P, which smoothes the distribution of data. In artificial dataset, the range of σ is enlarged from $0.04 \sim 0.06$ to $0.04 \sim 0.45$. This is because Markov random walk reshapes the cluster first.

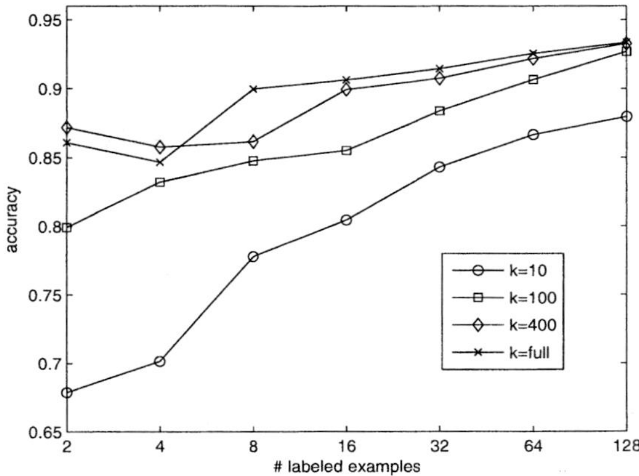

Fig. 4. Classification accuracy with different kNN graphs. Windows vs Mac data set.

2. No need for kNN graphs
Many semi-supervised classification methods employ kNN graphs to represent data. However, using smooth graphs, kNN graphs may not be so important. Experiments have shown that sometimes full connected graphs are better than kNN graphes when k is small. See Fig. 4.

3. Reduce the effect of few labeled examples
Classification accuracies of many semi-supervised classification methods decrease as the labeled examples get fewer and fewer [1, 7, 9]. However, in clustering, classification accuracy has no relation to labeled example. This shows that when labeled examples are few, we can still get a classification accuracy as high as that with more labeled examples, or at least accuracy should not change greatly.

With the help of smooth graphs, we can first "reshape" each cluster clearly. And labeled examples only tell you each cluster's label. In the case, with few labeled examples, smooth graphs method can still result in high classification accuracy. This can be seen from Fig. 2 and Fig. 3.

6 Discussion

In this paper, a new form of graph is proposed, which is called m-step Markov random walk graph. We combine the smooth graph representations with the graph-based semi-supervised classification method. The graph is constructed using Markov random walk model, and is different from kNN and εNN graph. Experimental results show that the combination of better graphs and the graph-based semi-supervised classification method has many advantages in classification task. However, more efficient methods to find a proper m might be interesting to investigate.

Acknowledgment

This work was supported by Chinese 973 Research Project under grant No. 2004CB719401.

References

1. Chapelle, O., Weston, J., Schölkopf, B.: Cluster Kernels for Semi-Supervised Learning. Advances in Neural Information Processing Systems 15, MIT Press (2003) 585-592
2. Chapelle, O. and A. Zien: Semi-Supervised Classification by Low Density Separation. Proceedings of the Tenth International Workshop on Artificial Intelligence and Statistics (2005) 57-64
3. Henk C. T.:Stochastic Models: An Algorithmic Approach, John Wiley & Sons (1994)
4. Rudnick, J., Gaspari, G.: Elements of the Random Walk: An Introduction for Advanced Students and Researchers. Cambridge University Press (2004)
5. Seeger, M.: Learning with labeled and unlabeled data. Technical report , Edinburgh University (2000)
6. Shanbhag, D. N. Rao, C. R., eds.: Handbook of Stochastic, Vol 19, Elsevier Science (2001)
7. Szummer, M., Jaakkola, T.: Partially labeled classification with Markov random walks. Neural Information Processing Systems (NIPS), Vol 14 (2001)
8. Zhou, D. et al.: Learning with local and global consistency. In Advances in Neural Information Processing System 16 (2004)
9. Zhu, X., Lafferty, J., Ghahramani, Z.: Semi-Supervised Learning Using Gaussian Fields and Harmonic Function. In Proceedings of The Twentieth International Conference on Machine Learning (2003)
10. Zhu, X.: Semi-Supervised Learning with Graphs. Doctoral Thesis. CMU-LTI-05-192, Carnegie Mellon University (2005)

Compacting XML Data

Shuohao Zhang, Curtis Dyreson, and Zhe Dang

P. O. Box 642752,
Washington State University,
Pullman, WA 99164-2752, USA
{szhang2, cdyreson, zdang}@eecs.wsu.edu

Abstract. *Compression* aims to reduce the size of data without loss of information. *Compaction* is a special kind of compression in which the output is in the same language as the input. Compaction of an XML data forest produces a smaller XML forest, without losing any data. This paper develops a formal framework for the compaction of XML data and presents two compaction techniques.

1 Introduction

Compression aims to reduce the size of data without loss of information. It is useful because smaller data can save storage space and also network bandwidth when data is transmitted. A *compressor* generates a file smaller in size than the original; feeding this file to a *de-compressor* can recover the original.

XML is rapidly becoming a dominant media for data exchange over the Internet. Because XML data is usually quite verbose, compression is an important issue for XML. Several tools are already available for XML compression. One can use either a general purpose compressor such as gzip, or an XML-specific compressor (such as XMill [2]) to compress XML data.

This paper addresses a special kind of compression, called compaction, where the compressed output remains as XML. Existing compression techniques do not compact the data because they all produce a compressed file in a non-XML format, which only a special-purpose de-compressor can understand. The main benefit of compaction is that it is orthogonal to other compression techniques, so an XML file can be compacted and then compressed.

The general idea behind compaction is that the same data can be represented in XML in (several) different structures. Consider two XML data documents, author.xml and pub.xml, shown respectively in Fig. 1 and Fig. 2. The data is simple enough that we can rely on readers of the data to agree on its intended semantics. In author.xml author n1 writes a book t1, published by p1; author n2 is a co-author on book t1 and also independently writes a book t2, published by p2. pub.xml contains exactly the same information except that the structure is different. Both documents have data about the same two authors, the same two publishers, and the same two books. Each document similarly relates each book, author, and publisher, e.g., in both documents book t2 is authored by author n2 and published by publisher p2. Section 3 develops a formal framework that allows the implicit meaning or semantics of an XML data

M.L. Lee, K.L. Tan, and V. Wuwongse (Eds.): DASFAA 2006, LNCS 3882, pp. 767 – 776, 2006.

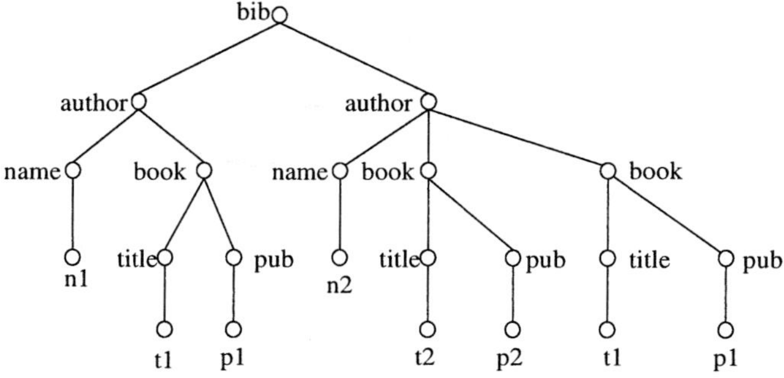

Fig. 1. author.xml

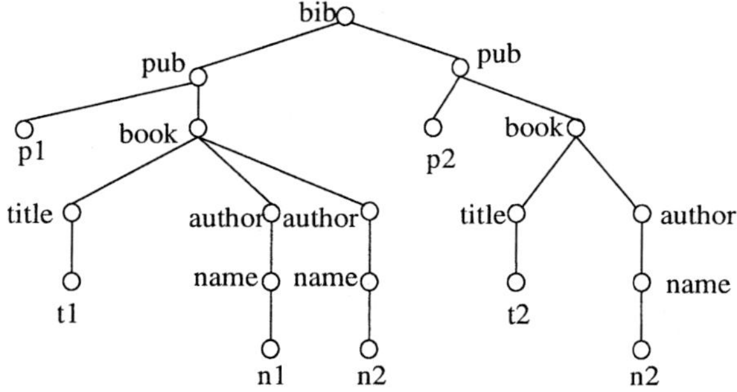

Fig. 2. pub.xml

collection to be determined and compared. For compaction, what interests us is the fact that author.xml and pub.xml have the same data but are of different sizes. Excluding text data, there are 14 elements in author.xml but only 13 elements in pub.xml. This suggests that author.xml could be compacted to at least the size of pub.xml. Of course, other compression techniques could potentially reduce the physical size of author.xml much further; however, only compacting produces output in XML.

Compaction is concerned with *logical* redundancy as much as *physical* redundancy. Note that in compaction we can measure the size of XML data by the number of elements. This differs from common compression tasks in which the size of a compressed file can only be measured by the disk space it occupies. While file size reflects the physical redundancy in a file, the number of *duplicate* nodes gives a better measure for redundancy on the logical level. By preserving the XML syntax in the output, compaction rearranges the original data to a new form with fewer places that are subject to update anomaly. Certainly, compacting an XML file may potentially (and usually does) compress the data at the same time. Though fewer elements does not guarantee a physically smaller file in general, it is usually so in practice.

This paper is organized as follows. Section 2 introduces preliminary concepts and Section 3 presents a semantics for XML that translates an XML data collection to a graph. Section 4 presents a compaction technique called *restructuring*, which transform a forest to another without affecting the semantics. Section 5 presents related work, and Section 6 concludes the paper.

2 Preliminaries

This section defines preliminary concepts. We start with tree and forest.

Definition [tree]. A tree is a five tuple (V, E, Σ, L, C), where V is the *node* set, E:$V\times V$ is the *edge* set, Σ is an *alphabet* of labels and text values, L:$V\rightarrow\Sigma$ is a *label function* that maps a node to its label, and C:$V\rightarrow\Sigma$ is a *value function* that maps a node to its *value*. ∎

This tree data model is different from the DOM data model [5]. It ignores sibling order and it does not model other kinds of DOM nodes such as attributes and comments. But the simpler model is sufficient for our purposes.

We often need to deal with an XML *data collection*, which is a group of XML documents or parts of XML documents. This can be modeled as a *forest* in general.

Labels can be used to partially identify nodes in a forest, but not to distinguish nodes of the same label. To further identify nodes of the same label, we need another characterization. One such characterization is a *type identifier*. Here we define nodes to be of the same *type* if they have the same label; *type identifier* is defined to be an identifier that identifies nodes of the same type. (Note that the term "type" is commonly used in the XML database literature but with varying meanings in different researches. In this paper, the type of a node is simply its label.) Such type identifiers observe the dependency among nodes of different types in a forest. For example, we may have the following dependencies in author.xml and pub.xml:

- an author depends on its corresponding name,
- a book depends on its corresponding title, and
- a name, title or publisher each depends on its value.

In each of these dependencies, one type is dependent on some other types or its own value. In a specific dependency, we call a node of the depending type a *depending* node; a depending node is identified by nodes or value corresponding to the deciding types, which we call the *identifying information* of the depending node. In general, we shall allow identifying information to be a combination of both nodes and values.

Usually, a node's identifying information is its immediate children (nodes or values). We further observe that, regardless of the relative position of the depending types and the deciding types, the identifying information is always "closest" to a dependent node. For example, if a book is identified by its title, then in the forest that title is closer to the book it identifies than it is to other books.

More precisely, suppose v is a dependent node and u is a type t identifying node of v, then u is closest in distance to v among all type t nodes. This observation suggests that we can employ this notion of *closeness* to locate the identifying information.

Definition [related nodes]. Let v be a node of type x. Then *related*(v, t) = $\{x \mid x$ is a node of type t and from among all the nodes of type t, x is *closest* in distance to $v\}$. The distance between a pair of nodes is measured by the length of the path that connects the nodes. ∎

Using the notion of closest, related nodes, we formalize a type identifier as follows.

Definition [type identifier]. A type identifier I of a type t is a two-tuple (I_{Type}, I_{Text}), where $I_{Type} = \{x_1,\ldots, x_m\}$ and $I_{Text} = \{y_1,\ldots, y_n\}$ are each a set of types, m and n are non-negative integers and they are not both zero, and $t \notin I_{Type}$. Two type t nodes u and v are *identical*, denoted $u \doteq v$, if and only if the following holds.

- When $m > 0$, for each q in *related*(v, x_i), $1 \le i \le m$, there exists a node p in *related*(u, x_i) such that $p \doteq q$; for each p in *related*(u, x_i), there exists a node q in *related*(v, x_i) such that $p \doteq q$.
- When $n > 0$, for each q in *related*(v, y_i), $1 \le i \le n$, there exists a node p in *related*(u, y_i) such that $C(p)=C(q)$; for each q in *related*(u, y_i), there exists a node p in *related*(v, y_i) such that $C(p)=C(q)$.

The following notation represents the dependency of type t on the other types:

$$t \leftarrow x_1,\ldots, x_m; y_1,\ldots, y_n$$

where the delimiter symbol ";" is required, even if m or n is zero. ∎

The above definition recursively describes how a depending node is identified by a combination of nodes of other types and some values. The base case in the recursive definition is when the set I_{Type} of type t is empty. In this case, whether two type t nodes u and v are identical is decided by comparing some values. If I_{Type} is non-empty, then whether u and v are identical is recursively determined by whether nodes of some other types are identical. As a special case, u and v are identical if they are the same node. Using the type identifier notation, the dependencies in the motivating example are: 1) "author ← name;", 2) "book ← title;", 3) "name ← ; name", 4) "title ← ; title", and 5) "publisher ← ; publisher".

3 A Semantics for XML

We now illustrate a semantics for XML using the example in Section 1. We show a series of semantics-preserving operations that derives the semantics of a tree, which is a graph. As both author.xml and pub.xml are mapped to the same graph, they are regarded semantically equivalent.

First, we identify duplicate information, i.e., data that represents the same real-world entity. Duplicates are identified by the type identifiers. In author.xml, since the first and third book have the same title, and we have identifiers "book ← title;" and "title ← ; title", the fist and third book elements are duplicates.

Similarly, in pub.xml, the second and third author elements represent the same author, because of the identifiers "author ← name; " and "name ← ; name". The duplicate information is removed through a process called *node gluing*. Gluing removes a duplicate, leaving only a single copy of the data. Fig. 3 shows the gluing for the two documents. In author.xml, for example, a book element is duplicated. We remove one copy by gluing the two subtrees together (shown by dotted lines), and also move the edge from the book element to the remaining copy of the author element (shown by dashed lines).

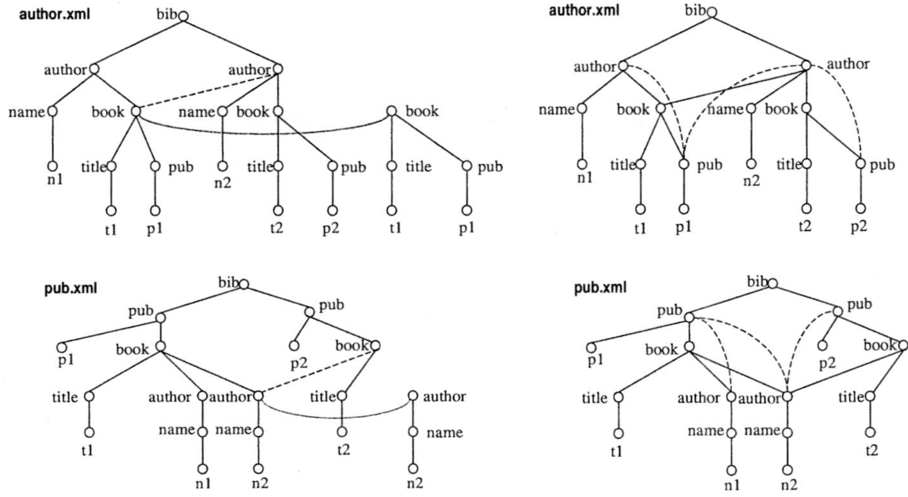

Fig. 3. Node gluing

Fig. 4. Node connecting

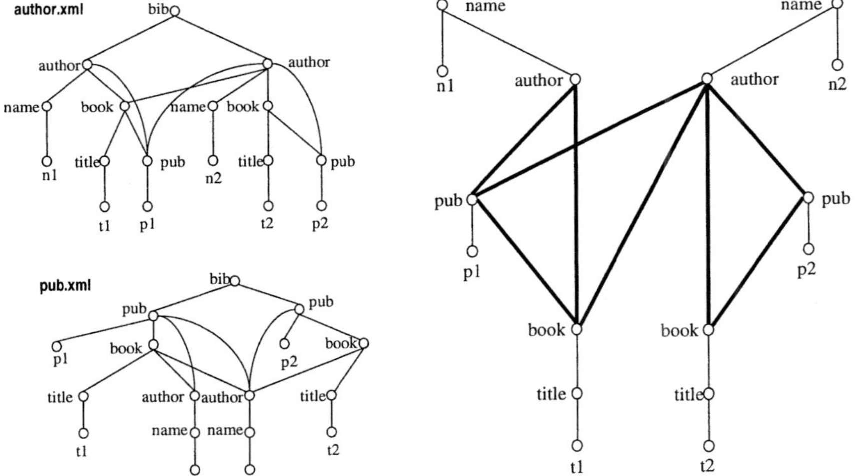

Fig. 5. The final graphs

Fig. 6. A graph isomorphic to the two final graphs

The next step is to add edges between "related" nodes. In author.xml, authors are related to the books they wrote, and also to the publishers that publish those books. A tree can only (directly) capture relationships between parent and child nodes. The proposed semantics represents every such relationship with an edge, hence creating a graph that will usually contain cycles. We call the process of relating nodes as *node connecting*. Fig. 4 illustrates node connecting (shown by dashed lines). In the figure, only author, name and publisher nodes are connected. To reduce clutter in the depicted graphs we have chosen not to represent some of the relationships. A connection between the n2 name node and the t2 title node, for example, is not shown. This connection can be inferred because there is a one-to-one correspondence between book and title (as well as author and name). Hence, any node connected to a name node is also connected to the corresponding (its parent) author node. How do we decide which types of nodes to connect and which not to? It depends on the possible parent-child relationships in forests to be semantically compared. For example, since author is always a parent of a name in any possible forest that we compare, we only connect author, but not name, with other types of nodes. On the other hand, since an author node can be either a parent or a child of a book node, we need to make connection between them in the graph. Not adding these edges keeps Fig. 4 less cluttered. More importantly, it saves a certain amount of cost (depending on the property of the data) not to physically materialize these edges. Logically, however, these edges are present in the graph.

Note that the root node bib is, as we would infer, equally related to all nodes in each document. For ease and clarity of presentation, we choose to remove this bib node in both graphs. The final graphs resulting from node connecting are shown in Fig. 5. The two graphs in Fig. 5 are isomorphic. To illustrate this more clearly, a graph that is isomorphic to both is depicted in Fig. 6. It is semantically equivalent to the two initial trees because neither subtree gluing nor node connecting changes the "meaning" of the data. It is also a "minimal" form of the original trees in the sense that duplicate data has been eliminated. The graph in Fig. 6 (as well as the graphs in Fig. 5) is a *canonical* representation of the two initial trees, because it is semantically equivalent to the original data, yet syntactically minimal.

Formally, deriving this semantics consists of the following two steps.

1. **Node Gluing:** Two nodes are glued together if and only if they are identical. i.e., they are of the same type and their identifiers evaluate to the same value. The idea is that, if u and v are identical, then it is only necessary to keep one copy. We can replace every edge (v,y) with (u,y) and then remove v. Adding new edges to the forest may result in cycles. Thus gluing produces a graph in general. When nodes are glued in this process, the size of V decreases, and the size of E does not increase (and may decrease). As we can see, semantically comparing two forests is only possible when given the set of identifiers for all types of nodes. Identifiers carry the information about how nodes are related, and are crucial to reason about data semantics.
2. **Node Connecting:** In the next step, related nodes are connected. The idea is that every pair of related nodes is now explicitly identified by an edge that connects them. Before node connecting, a pair of related nodes may or may not be adjacent, while semantically whether they are connected or not should not make any difference. Connecting effectively changes a tree to a graph by adding edges. The number of edges in E may either increase or decrease depending on the specific situation. There is no change to V, Σ, L, or C.

4 Compaction

With a semantics for XML data defined, a formal discussion on compaction is now possible. Compaction aims to transform a forest to a smaller forest. The two forests will have the same semantics, i.e., the forest-to-graph translation maps them to the same graph. Compaction can be achieved by changing the structure of a forest. A *restructuring* is a transformation that changes the structure of the forest but keeps its semantics intact. A forest can be restructured by mapping it to its canonical graph, and then creating a semantically equivalent forest with a different structure. Ideally, the restructuring will yield a forest that is *smaller* in size than the original. Here we employ a structural specification called a *signature* that designates the target's structural characteristics. For example, the signature for pub.xml is

bib#pub#book#(author#name,title)

in which the symbol # denotes parent-child relationship and siblings are separated by commas and enclosed within a pair of parentheses.

We have devised a restructuring algorithm that takes a canonical graph and a target signature as input, and outputs a new forest that conforms to the specification. (Due to space limit, the detail is omitted in this paper; it can be found at [8]). Essentially, this restructuring algorithm is an inverse of the combination of node gluing and node connecting. In changing the canonical graph to a forest, the restructuring algorithm *disconnects* and *unglues* nodes. It disconnects since the output has to contain no cycle, and it unglues (makes duplicates) since the semantics encoded in every edge in the canonical graph must be faithfully preserved.

In restructuring, different target signatures will yield forests of different sizes. To find the most compact forest among them, we could simply enumerate all the possible target forests. However, this is computational intractable. The number of different target signatures is more than exponential.[1]

While in general the problem is hard, there is a simple technique to generate a compact forest for some forests. The idea is to take advantage of the *cardinality ratio*. The ratio characterizes the relationship between pairs of element types as one of the following: one-to-one, one-to-many, or many-to-many. For example, the relationship between publisher and book is one-to-many: a book is published by exactly one publisher but a publisher publishes many books. On the other hand, the relationship between book and author is many-to-many.

Cardinality ratio may come with the data as a predefined constraint; if not, it can be quickly determined by traversing the canonical graph. (In contrast, we do not infer type identifiers and assume they must be given.) Table 1 shows the cardinality ratios for the example graph. The relationship between author and name is one-to-one (recall that authors are glued by name, hence each author is associated with a single name, and vice-versa). Author to book is many-to-many since an author can write many books, and a book can have many authors. (Note that exact, average ratios could be computed, e.g., 4.2 to 2.7.)

---

[1] Given a label set of size n, suppose the number of distinct unordered trees is $t(n)$ and the number of distinct unordered forests is $f(n)$, we have,

$t(1) = 1$, $t(n) = (2n\text{-}2) \bullet t(n\text{-}1) = (2n\text{-}2) \bullet (2n\text{-}4) \dots 2 \bullet t(1) = (2n\text{-}2) \bullet (2n\text{-}4) \dots \bullet 2$, and

$f(1) = 1$, $f(n) = (2n\text{-}1) \bullet f(n\text{-}1) = (2n\text{-}1) \bullet (2n\text{-}3) \dots 3 \bullet f(1) = (2n\text{-}1) \bullet (2n\text{-}3) \dots \bullet 3$.

Table 1. Cardinality ratios for the example graph

	pub	title	book	name
author	n-m	n-m	n-m	1-1
name	n-m	n-m	n-m	
book	n-1	1-1		
title	n-1			

The key to achieving compactness is to focus on types that are related in one-to-many relationships. Specifically, assume types X and Y are in a one-to-many relationship. Then a target signature that has X above Y leads to a forest that is more compact than a forest with Y above X. Consider the example of publisher and book, which have a one-to-many relationship. If publishers are above books in the target signature, then in the target forest there are no duplicate publishers (or duplicate books). Every book is placed under the publisher to which it belongs. If books are above publishers in the target signature, then the same publisher may be duplicated several times. Such a forest is less compact and hence need not to be considered.

The technique for generating a target signature for a compact forest begins by considering one-to-one relationships. One side of the relationship is made a child of the other side. If one side is involved in gluing the other, then it should be made the child, otherwise either side can be made the child. Consider book and title in the example graph. Their relationship is one-to-one. Furthermore, book is glued using title. Hence book should be a parent of title in the potentially compact output. The target signature after this step is book#title and author#name. Next, one-to-many relationships are processed by making the one side the parent. In the example, after considering the one-to-many relationships, the target is pub#book#title and author#name. Finally, only many-to-many relationships remain. The remaining types are placed as high as possible in the forest. In the example graph, this means that author is made a child of book resulting in the signature pub#book#(title,author#name).

Once the target signature has been generated, the original forest is restructured using the target signature. The restructured forest may or may not be smaller, i.e., the technique does not generate the *most compact* forest. Finding the signature that leads to the most compact restructuring is theoretically intractable. However, we expect the technique outlined above to lead to a "reasonable" target signature in practice. The technique can be further refined by utilizing the average cardinality ratio of many-to-many relationships, e.g., if the ratio is thirty-to-two, then the two side of the relationship should be made the parent. But such refinements are beyond the scope of this paper.

To gauge how well compaction performs on real-world data, we did an experiment to compact DBLP data. The test data has a size of 309KB and contains 7312 elements. Restructuring the data using a compact signature yields a 252KB data collection that contains 5441 elements. The compacted data has an 18% reduction in file size and a 25% reduction in number of elements. The detail of the experiment can be found at [8].

5 Related Work

Compaction for XML is similar to XML compression in the sense that they both aim to describe the same information with shorter representation. However, compaction differs from usual compression since the output has to retain XML syntax. To the best of our knowledge, the problem of compaction has not been previously researched. In this section, we briefly review general and XML-specific compression techniques, and relate them to compaction when pertinent.

Most modern data compression techniques have their genesis in the Huffman algorithm [767] or the LZ77 algorithm [7]. Huffman coding is *statistical*; it assigns shorter codes to more frequent characters and longer codes to less frequent ones. Popular data compression tools such as gzip and pkzip are based on LZ77. A later version of LZ77, the LZW algorithm [6], is more suitable for practical implementation. The essence of the LZ77 family of compression techniques is to store repetitive sequences just once. Any repetition of a sequence that previously occurred is replaced by a pointer to that sequence. Such techniques are called *pattern-based.*

Specialized compressors take advantage of the specific properties of the data to be compressed. For XML data in particular, several compression techniques have been proposed. The earliest such work is XMill [2]. Incorporating existing compressors, XMill compresses XML structures and values separately, uses type specific compressors for different types of data, and allows user-defined compressors for domain specific data-types. Data compressed by XMill cannot be directly queried; doing so would entail a complete decompression. XGrind [4] and XPRESS [3] are both compressors that support direct query evaluations on compressed XML data. XGrind uses a compression scheme based on Huffman coding, while XPRESS adopts an encoding method called reverse arithmetic encoding. It is worthwhile to note that both compression techniques are *homomorphic* because the structure of the original XML data is preserved in the compressed XML data. In contrast, an important compaction technique proposed in this paper, restructuring, changes the structure of the original data. Homomorphism is important for the compressed data to be efficiently queried. Compaction, on the other hand, is useful to ascertain the semantic redundancy in the data. Compacted XML data is not supposed to be queried directly by the query intended for the original data. Among the three compressors, XGrind is the only one that tries to utilize schema information such as a DTD to enhance the compression ratio. In comparison, finding an appropriate schema (target signature in our situation) is the goal of compaction. To enhance compaction ratio, knowledge of identifiers in the original data is required, and knowledge of cardinality ratio is helpful.

6 Conclusion

XML compaction aims to produce a smaller, compact XML forest, without losing information. This paper develops a formal framework for the compaction of XML data. It first formalizes XML data by introducing a forest data model and defining types and identifiers. A translative semantics for XML is then presented. This semantics translates an XML data collection to a canonical graph, depending on a given set of identifiers. Data collections that translate to the same canonical graph are deemed to have the same semantics. Based on this formalization, two compaction techniques, restructuring and grouping, are discussed. Though finding the *most* compact forest is computationally prohibitive in general, we developed simple techniques to find a *more* compact forest at low cost using restructuring or grouping.

In future we plan to explore the relationship between compaction and compression. General compression techniques are not confined to produce the same file format as the input. Hence, it is reasonable to expect that they can achieve a better compression than compaction. However, a file can be first compacted and then compressed. Does combining the compaction with compression produce better performance than compression alone? An interesting work is to examine this problem on both the theoretical and experimental grounds.

References

1. D. Huffman. A Method for Construction of Minimum-Redundancy Codes, Proc. of IRE, September 1952.
2. H. Liefke and D. Suciu. Xmill: An Efficient Compressor for XML Data, SIGMOD Conference, 2000.
3. J. Min, M. Park, and C. Chung. XPRESS: A Queriable Compression for XML Data, SIGMOD Conference, 2003.
4. P. M. Tolani and J. R. Haritsa. XGRIND: A Query-friendly XML Compressor, ICDE 2002.
5. W3C. Document Object Model (DOM), www.w3.org/DOM.
6. T. Welch. A Technique for High-Performance Data Compression, Computer, pp. 8-18, 1984.
7. J. Ziv and A. Lempel. A Universal Algorithm for Sequential Data Compression, IEEE Transactions on Information Theory, 23:3, pp. 337-343, 1977.
8. http://www.eecs.wsu.edu/~cdyreson/pub/compaction.

Fast Structural Join with a Location Function*

Nan Tang[1], Jeffrey Xu Yu[1], Kam-Fai Wong[1], and Haifeng Jiang[2]

[1] The Chinese University of Hong Kong, Hong Kong, China
[2] IBM Almaden Research Center, 650 Harry Road, San Jose, USA
{ntang, yu, kfwong}@se.cuhk.edu.hk, jianghf@us.ibm.com

Abstract. A structural join evaluates structural relationship (parent-child or ancestor-descendant) between XML elements. It serves as an important computation unit in XML pattern matching, such as twig joins. There exists many work on efficient structural joins. In particular, indexes can expedite structural joins by skipping unmatchable elements. A typical use of indexes is to retrieve, for a given element, all its ancestor (or descendant) elements from an indexed set. However we observed two possible limitations with such index probes, namely *false hit* and *false locate*. A false hit means that an index probe touches unnecessary data besides real results; a false locate stands for a (wasted) probe that has zero answers. Obviously false hit and false locate can affect negatively the efficiency of structural joins. In this paper, we challenge ourselves to develop new structural join algorithm with *no false hit* and *no false locate*. We illustrate that *R-Tree* has the no false hit property (in contrast to B^+*-Tree*) and hence is a good candidate for our algorithm. For no false locate, we propose a new function called *Location* which tells the probing points that will result in matches. We design and implement the Location function using a space-efficient structure, and present our algorithm using *R-Tree* together with the Location function. Extensive experiments show the efficiency of our algorithm.

1 Introduction

Structural join is known as an important computation primitive in XML query processing. The Stack-Tree join algorithm proposed in [1] improved the traditional merge based algorithms with stack mechanism. Only one sequential scan is needed for two input ordered lists *A-List* and *D-List*. Index-based algorithms [2,3] improve the join performance. The essential idea is to use indexes on the participating element sets to directly (or near directly) find the matching elements and skip those without matches.

Despite of their success in performance improvement over merge-based algorithms, the current indexed-based algorithms are bound to two limitations, namely *false hit* and *false locate*. Given an element, find its ancestor (or descendant) elements from an indexed set, through an index probe. A *false hit* means

* This work is partially supported by the CUHK strategic grant (numbered 4410001) and the grant from the Research Grants Council of the Hong Kong Special Administrative Region, China (CUHK418205).

M.L. Lee, K.L. Tan, and V. Wuwongse (Eds.): DASFAA 2006, LNCS 3882, pp. 777–786, 2006.

that an index probe touches unnecessary data besides real results; a *false locate* stands for a (wasted) probe that has zero answers. *False hit* and *false locate* can affect negatively the efficiency of structural joins.

We summarize the contributions of this paper as follows:

1. We make a comparison between *R-Tree* and *B*$^+$*-Tree* on their support to structural searches. We conclude that structural search on *R-Tree* indexed data does not incur *false hit* while that on *B*$^+$*-Tree* has *false hit.*
2. We propose a `Location` function to accurately locate the matchable elements. It is built on top of a succinct and space-efficient bit-vector structure, namely *Locator*, which stores the distribution information of element nodes in a set and can be used to retrieve index probing points for no *false locate.*
3. We present a new index-based structural join algorithm, *R-Locator*, which combines *R-Tree* and *Locator* to achieve no *false hit* and no *false locate.*

Section 2 presents the motivation. Then Section 3 compares *R-Tree* over *B*$^+$*-Tree* on indexing region encode. We propose in Section 4 the space-efficient bit-vector index *Locator* and show how to use *Locator* for no *false locate.* Section 5 proposes a new structural join algorithm based on *R-Tree* and *Locator.* Section 6 analyzes the experiments. Finally Section 7 concludes this paper.

2 Motivation

Stack-Tree-Desc/Anc [1], is a milestone in structural join algorithm by maintaining an in-memory stack, with which we need only once scan of two input ordered lists. Many optimization comes from the observation that many unmatchable elements may attend the join operation depending on the characters of documents and queries. To efficiently skip these unmatchable elements, two approaches, *B*$^+$*-Tree* and *XR-Tree* based structural join algorithms, are proposed in [2, 3] respectively. Consider the ancestor-descendant query $a//d$, Figure 1 shows the cases for different skip apporaches. Without indexes, the *Stack-tree* join algorithm will retrieve all the a elements and d elements, including $a_1 \ldots a_{11}$, $d_1 \ldots d_5$. The results are just (a_7, d_1) and (a_{11}, d_5), many nodes are *false hit.*

Chien [2] utilized the property that if a tree element x is not the ancestor of z, then any descendant y of x cannot be the ancestor of z either. We use $S(e)$ and $E(e)$ to represent node e's *startpos* and *endpos* under region encode, respectively. With *B*$^+$*-Tree* index, when a_1 is not the ancestor of d_1, we could find the first

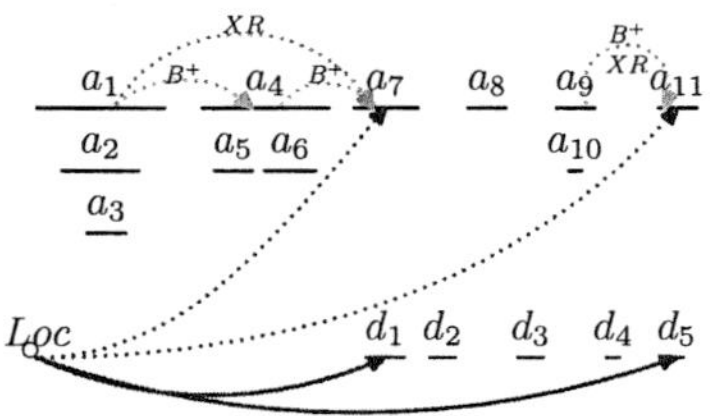

Fig. 1. Skip Elements Cases

element e satisfying $S(e) > E(a_1)$ and $S(e) < S(d_1)$, so to get a_4 as shown in Figure 1, similarly we could get a_7, etc. With this skip technique, however, many useless elements are still *false located*, including $a_1, a_4, a_8, a_9, d_2, d_3, d_4$.

XR-Tree proposed in [3] could keep extra structural relationship so that, given an element e and an indexed set R, all e's ancestors (or descendants) in R can be identified efficiently. With *XR-Tree*, we could jump from a_1 to a_7 when we judge that a_1 is an unmatchable ancestor element and d_1 is stabbed by a_7. However, still many unmatchable elements are *false located* as $a_1, a_8, a_9, d_2, d_3, d_4$. *XR-Tree* outperforms B^+-*Tree* in the point that the less hit of a_4.

The reason of *false locate* of both B^+-*Tree* and *XR-Tree* is that they only grasp the local structural information instead of the global structural information, which drives the design of `Location` function. The goal of `Location` function is that, when we get a_1 which has no matches, we could retrieve d_1 and a_7; when we get d_2 which has no matches, we could retrieve d_5 and a_{11}.

3 *R-Tree* vs. B^+-*Tree*: No False Hit vs. False Hit

Encoding Selection: Consider the two most commonly used encodings: Region encoding and Dietz encoding. We use $S(e)$ and $E(e)$ to represent node e's *startpos* and *endpos* under region encoding, respectively. One special character of region encoding is that, for an element x, $(S(x), E(x))$ is a region, any descendant y of x, its region $(S(y), E(y))$ is covered by $(S(x), E(x))$. We adopts region encoding in this paper to show the advantage of this unique character.

3.1 R-tree for No False Hit

Figure 2 shows an XML data tree with region encoding. In general, one index structure is built for each tagname of element. For example, if we use B^+-*Tree*, we have one B^+-*Tree* for a and one for d. It is similar when using *R-Tree*.

Figure 3 shows a B^+-*Tree* index for a. If we want to retrieve the ancestors of d_3, we can search on it with *key* value less than $S(d_3) = 11$, and get a_1, a_2, a_3, a_4 while not the results a_1, a_4. This is called *false hit* and validation is needed. Region encode is a 2-dimensional data, using 1-dimensional index structure (B^+-*Tree*), we lost some information when dropping dimension.

As is well known, *R-Tree* is an excellent high-dimensional index structure, especially for 2-dimensional data. Figure 4 shows the areas to be retrieved under

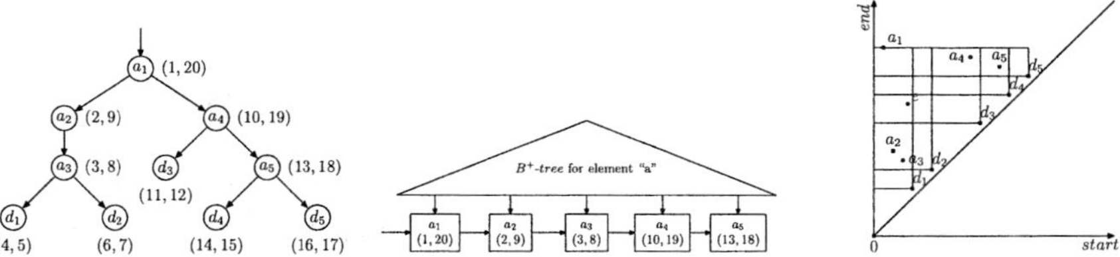

Fig. 2. An XML Document **Fig. 3.** An B$^+$-tree Index **Fig. 4.** R-tree Retrieve Area

R-Tree. Review above example, when querying the ancestors of d_3, only the rectangle area including a_1 and a_4 is returned without redundant data. This is also the truth for any other element and other XPath axes. Therefore, *R-Tree* produces no *false hit* for XPath axes.

With above analysis, we may conclude that *R-Tree* outperforms B^+*-Tree* in scanning. The *false hit* of B^+*-Tree* retrieves all possible data including not only all the results but also redundant data; while the *R-Tree* with no *false hit* merely retrieve the results. To further optimize the *R-Tree* performance in structural join, we utilize the bulk-loading process and *R-Tree* packing [4] techniques to keep the *start* order in leaf page when we insert node in increasing *startpos*. This leads to a full storage utilization in the *R-Tree* leaves and consequently improves the query performance.

3.2 Stack Mechanism for R-tree

Assume the stack is represented as $\mathcal{T}$, the stack operations for B^+*-Tree* proceed as follows: first get a_1 and d_1, push a_1 into $\mathcal{T}$, and then get a_2, compare a_2 with $\mathcal{T}.top()$ to see whether $S(a_2) > E(\mathcal{T}.top())$ for popping stack. We get $false$ for this operation so next we compare $S(a_2)$ and $S(d_1)$, we *push* a_2 into $\mathcal{T}$ because $S(a_2) < S(d_1)$. The operations of *d*s are similar,for a new d, we compare it with $\mathcal{T}.top()$ iteratively to pop elements in $\mathcal{T}$ that are not the ancestors of d. The deficiency of B^+*-Tree* is the redundant comparison operation together with potential redundant *push* and *pop* stack operations coming from the *false hit.*

R-Tree also outperforms B^+*-Tree* in this aspect as follows. We get the first element of descendant d_1, then retrieve on *R-Tree* to get a_1, a_2 and a_3 with ascending order on *start* value. Then we could directly do the operation $\mathcal{T}.push(a_1)$, $\mathcal{T}.push(a_2)$, $\mathcal{T}.push(a_3)$. We insure the *start* order through bulk-loading process and *R-Tree* packing. a_1, a_2 and a_3 are insured to be the ancestors of d_1 because of the *no false hit* of *R-Tree.* Next we explain why a_1 must be a_2's ancestor and a_2 must be a_3's ancestor without comparison. See Figure 4, assume there is another node e which is d_1's ancestor, a_1's descendant and a_2's sibling node. Now d_1 have two ancestors a_2 and e that are sibling relationship, this contradict the character of tree structure. Thus this kind of node does e not exist, which insures the correctness of our put operation. We also save time on *pop* operation because we have no *false* elements in $\mathcal{T}$.

4 Locator for No False Locate

4.1 Locator: The Structure

Table 1 shows a group of assumptive encodings which is better than Figure 2 for explaining *Locator*, here N represents node name and C represents encoding. We build a *Locator* for each distinct tagname e, denoted as $\mathcal{L}_e$.

We maintain two *Locator*s for ancestor and descendant, separately. Figure 5 shows the *Locator* for element d, $\mathcal{L}_d$ and element a, $\mathcal{L}_a$. Each bit just represents the region length 1. Initially all bits are set to 0, if some element d_i intersects with

Table 1. Encoded Elements

N	C	N	C	N	C	N	C	N	C	N	C
a_1	(1,6)	a_2	(2,5)	a_3	(3,4)	a_4	(7, 12)	a_5	(8,9)	a_6	(10,11)
a_7	(13,16)	a_8	(19, 20)	a_9	(23,26)	a_{10}	(24,25)	a_{11}	(29,32)	d_1	(14, 15)
d_2	(17,18)	d_3	(21,22)	d_4	(27,28)	d_5	(30, 31)				

some bits of $\mathcal{L}_d$, the corresponding bits are set to 1. Even if each bit represents only length 1, the *Locator* is still a very space-efficient structure, for a large XML document, 100M for example, the number of elements is about 10^6 and the region range is about 2×10^6, about $200K$, which is not a problem for current memory capacity. Furthermore, we could use many mature techniques for compressing bit-vector structure.

L_a	1	1	1	1	1	1	1	1	1	1	1	1	1	1	1	1	0	0	1	1	0	0	1	1	1	1	0	0	1	1	1	1
L_d	0	0	0	0	0	0	0	0	0	0	0	0	0	1	1	0	1	1	0	0	1	1	0	0	0	0	1	1	0	1	1	0

Fig. 5. Locator for a and d

For instance, d_1's encoding is $(14, 15)$, so the 14th and 15th bits of $\mathcal{L}_d$ are set to 1. The construction of $\mathcal{L}_a$ is similar. Note that a bit may be set to 1 many times but only the first operation takes effect.

With $\mathcal{L}_d$, we could shrink the search space of *R-Tree*. Assume the query is $a//d$ for ancestor-descendant relationship, instead of using the tree height measure to shrink the query window, we could shrink the query window to $\{(29, 29), (32, 32)\}$ for d_5, here $(29, 29)$ is the coordinate of the lower left corner of rectangle query window and $(32, 32)$ is upper right corner. The query windows for other elements are similar. Sometimes when there are some region continuous ancestors such as a_1, a_4 and a_7, the shrink using tree height h may be better. We denote the region of the continuous 1 by r, so if $\frac{r}{2} \leq h$, we use the region code to shrink the query window, otherwise we use h.

4.2 Optimized Locator for No False Locate

Can we perform *no false locate*? The answer is positive. There seems to be two ways as shown in Figure 1, one way is to *locate* a_7 and a_{11}, the other way is to *locate* d_1 and d_5. We trace the second way. The basic *Locator* $\mathcal{L}_d$ cannot do this because it could only locate d_1, d_2, d_3, d_4, d_5 for *false locate*. Therefore we propose an optimization technique represented as: $\mathcal{L}'_d = \mathcal{L}_a \& \mathcal{L}_d$

The optimized $\mathcal{L}'_d$ is shown in Figure 6. With $\mathcal{L}'_d$, we could easily locate d_1 and d_5, which has *no false locate*. Then we could directly retrieve only a_7 and a_{11} with the *no false hit* property discussed above. This is a perfect structural join process.

The '&' operation is safe, which means no results are lost. Note that this optimization technique could only be used on $\mathcal{L}_d$ while not on $\mathcal{L}_a$, which reflects the

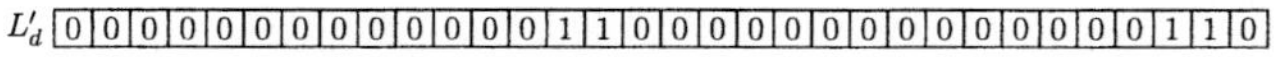

L'_d | 0 | 0 | 0 | 0 | 0 | 0 | 0 | 0 | 0 | 0 | 0 | 0 | 0 | 1 | 1 | 0 | 0 | 0 | 0 | 0 | 0 | 0 | 0 | 0 | 0 | 0 | 0 | 0 | 0 | 1 | 1 | 0 |

Fig. 6. Optimized Locator for d

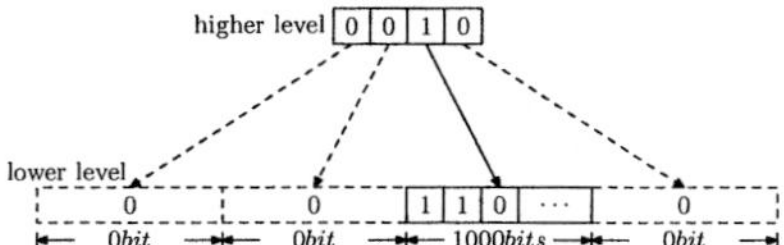

Fig. 7. Hierarchical Locator

dissymmetrical relationship between a and d in ancestor-descendant structural query. We explain this phenomenon as follows. When some continuous 1 of $\mathcal{L}_d$ are set to 0 affected by $\mathcal{L}_a$, the descendants whose *start* values in these revalued bits must have no ancestors. Otherwise, it violates the containment relationship of the ancestor and descendant's region encoding: the region of ancestor's encoding always covers that of its descendants. For $\mathcal{L}_a$, in contrast, if some continuous 1 in $\mathcal{L}_a$ correspond to 0 in $\mathcal{L}_d$, it is very possible that some elements a whose *start* values fall in this area will have descendants in others regions. It also validates that the region of continuous 1 of the ancestor's *Locator* always covers that of its descendants. Therefore the opposite optimization $\mathcal{L}'_a = \mathcal{L}_d \& \mathcal{L}_a$ is not *safe*, which will lost some information to trace ancestors. This disproportional relationship between ancestor and descendant should be seriously considered in many cases about structural join using region encoding.

An Analysis of Locator: Assume the page size is 4K (32768 bits), for a large XML document, say, 10^6 elements, we need only $\frac{2\times10^6}{32768} \approx 61$ pages, about $244K$, which could be easily loaded into main memory. If the XML document is huge, however, 10^9 elements for example, the size of *Locator* is $244M$. We could easily build a hierarchical *Locator* structure, we use 1 bit in the higher level to represent 1000 bits of its lower level; we set the higher bit 0 if all the lower 1000 bits are 0 but we store the lower 1000 bits as a virtual structure for saving storage space, otherwise we set it 1, which is shown in Figure 7. We preprocess the higher level to guide which part of the lower level should be read, and the higher level is just $244K$ that will be stayed in the main memory.

The cost of *Locator* is easy to analyze. Assume the number of element is $|X|$, the space and time complexities of using *Locator* are $O(|X|)$ for both $\mathcal{L}_a$ and $\mathcal{L}_d$ because at most one scan each is enough for performing all *location*. The I/O complexity analysis is straightforward as well. Each page of *Locator* is read once, hence we get the I/O complexity $O(\frac{|X|}{B})$, where B is the blocking factor.

5 Structural Joins Using *R-Tree* and *Locator*

In this section, we propose a structural join algorithms *R-Locator*. When some elements which have no matches are met, we use *Locator* to perform the *Location* function and adopt *R-Tree* instead of B^+-*Tree* for retrieving elements.

Basic *Locator* Operation: The operation FINDFIRST($L, pos, val, orien$) is just a bit-vector operation. FINDFIRST() is used to find the first val in L from a given position pos in the direction $orien$. We need scan the *Locator* only once, thus the upper limit of operating the *Locator* is the size of *Locator*.

R-Locator Structural Join Algorithm: *Locator* is a self-governed structure for `Location` function, which could be seamlessly combined with other index structures such as B^+-*Tree* and *R-Tree*. We use *Locator* to efficiently find the position where the descendant elements must have matchable ancestors and use B^+-*Tree* or *R-Tree* to retrieve the physical encodings. Here we select *R-Tree* for indexing because *R-Tree* could perform no *false hit*. *Locator* could also help to improve the performance of B^+-*Tree* in locating but it is not optimal. For instance, assuming we have three encoded ancestors $a_1(40,45), a_2(50,60), a_3(61,70)$ and two encoded descendants $d_1(30,35), d_2(63,67)$; with $\mathcal{L}_d$, we know that d_2 must have matchable ancestors, and then we find corresponding continuous 1 in $\mathcal{L}_a$, which is $(50,70)$. This is what *Locator* could do, with B^+-*Tree*, we will get a_2, a_3; while with *R-Tree*, we could get the result a_3. *R-Locator* algorithm is listed as:

Algorithm 1. *R-Locator* (A, D)

input: A: the ancestor set and D: the descendant set
output: Query results of $A//D$

```
 1: a := First(A);   d := First(D)   stack := ∅;   L_d := L_d & L_a
 2: while (a ≠ End(A) ∧ d ≠ End(D)) ∨ ¬stack.empty() do
 3:   if (a.start > stack → top.end) ∧ (d.start > stack → top.end) then
 4:     stack → pop()
 5:   else if (a.start < d.start) then
 6:     stack → push(a);   a := a → next
 7:   else if (¬stack.empty()) then
 8:     output pairs(a ∈ stack, d)
 9:   else
10:     pos := FINDFIRST(L_d, d.end + 1, 1, True)
11:     d := Rtree_d → find(pos, pos)
12:     pos := FINDFIRST(L_a, d.start − 1, 0, False)
13:     pos := max(a.start + 1, pos + 1)
14:     a := Rtree_a → find(pos, pos)
15:   end if
16: end while
```

The algorithm keeps two cursors, a and d for current elements checked. The stack is adopted to hold the elements in A; and we also maintain the ancestor-descendant relationship in *stack*. The idea of this algorithm is also based on stack mechanism, but when elements having no matches are met, better than previous approaches to skip unmatchable elements and test the elements that may have matches, we adopt *Locator* to perform the `Location` function (line 10) and use *R-Tree* to find ancestors (line 14).

6 Performance Evaluation

6.1 Experiment Setup

Our test-bed is an experimental database system which includes a storage manager, a buffer pool manger, *B^+-Tree*, *R-Tree*, *XR-Tree* and *Locator*. All the algorithms were coded with Visual Studio .NET. All the experiments were conducted on a Pentium IV 2.80GHz PC with 1024M RAM and a 80G hard disk, running Windows XP. The page size used is 4K and we use the file system as the storage. All the experimental results presented below were obtained with a fixed buffer pool size: 100 pages, just large enough to cache the hot elements.

We use synthetic data for all our experiments in order to control the structural and consequently join characteristics of the XML documents. We adopt two DTDs based on *DBLP* DTD and *Department* DTD which is similar to that in [3]. We generated two 20M raw data for each DTD using the IBM XML data generator with default parameters.

6.2 No False Hit vs. False Hit

This group of experiments was conducted to study the performance of *R-Tree* vs. *B^+-Tree* for *false hit*. We first use optimized $\mathcal{L}'_d$ to exactly locate descendants, then we search the possible bit range on $\mathcal{L}_a$ for possible ancestors, and then we use *R-Tree* or *B^+-Tree* for retrieving the ancestors. We use the stack here to store the nested ancestors, so the number of ancestors retrieved by *R-Tree* is the exact number of results. The queries selected are listed in Table 8, we choose these queries to thoroughly test all the nested and distributive cases.

Figure 9 shows the number of ancestors retrieved by *R-Tree* and *B^+-Tree*. If the ancestor elements whose ranges are covered by $\mathcal{L}_a$ are all matches of corresponding d got from $\mathcal{L}_d$, both *R-Tree* and *B^+-Tree* could get *no false hit*. Therefore the number of ancestors retrieved by *R-Tree* and *B^+-Tree* is the same, as shown in Figure 9 of the cases Q_2 and Q_3. In most cases, otherwise, some ancestor elements have continuous encodings but some are not matches of corresponding d got from $\mathcal{L}_d$, in which case *R-Tree* will still perform *no false hit* while *B^+-Tree* will get many useless ancestor elements because of *false hit*. Therefore *B^+-Tree* will retrieve much more ancestor elements than that of *R-Tree*. In Figure 9, the queries Q_1, Q_4, Q_5, Q_6 show this case.

	Query	Document
Q_1	*employee//email*	*Department*
Q_2	*employee//name*	*Department*
Q_3	*inproceedings//title*	*DBLP*
Q_4	*book//homepage*	*DBLP*
Q_5	*article//homepage*	*DBLP*
Q_6	*article//editor*	*DBLP*

Fig. 8. Sample Queries

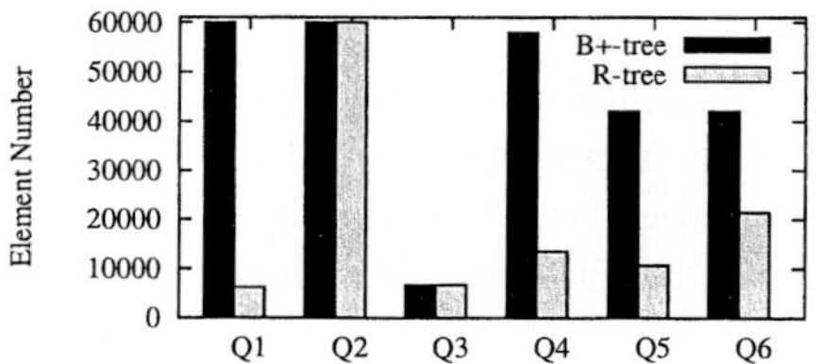

Fig. 9. *R-Tree* vs. *B^+-Tree*

6.3 Varying Selectivity on Elements

The objective of this set of experiments is to study the capabilities of various algorithms to skip elements. Among all experiments, we show the results for the case where the join selectivity on the ancestor set and the descendant set varied together, starting from 90% down to 1%.

Varying Selectivity on Ancestors: The first group of experiments is to vary join selectivity on ancestors. During this experiments, we kept the percentage of descendants that match at least one ancestor high (99%) and varied the selectivity on ancestors, i.e., the percentage of ancestors that have descendants. Figure 6.3(a) and 6.3(b) display the elapsed time for various algorithms. As can be observed from the figures, elapsed time with all algorithms decrease with the decrease of selectivity on ancestors. All approaches improve the performance by skipping unmatchable elements. Furthermore, *R-Locator* has the best overall performance. We also notice that *XR-Tree* is better than B^+*-Tree* in the case, this is because that *XR-Tree* is structured by maintaining stab lists in the ancestor, thus *XR-Tree* performs less *false locate* than that of B^+*-Tree*. One interesting to note that even only few elements can be skipped, despite of the possible overhead of index probing, all approaches perform no worse than the basic *Stack-tree* join algorithm.

Varying Selectivity on Descendants: The second group of experiments is to test the performance when varying join selectivity on descendants. We keep the

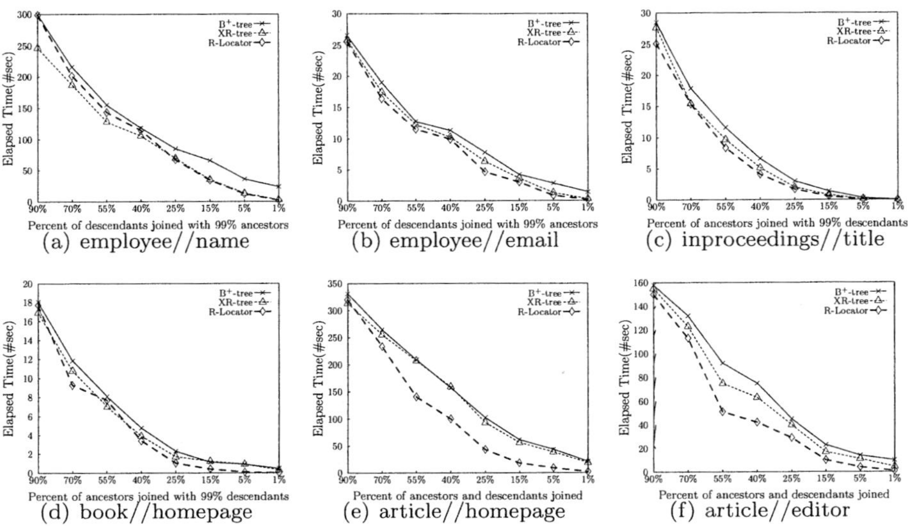

Fig. 10. Elapsed time (in second) for different join selectivity. (a) (b): 99% of descendants join with varying proportion of ancestors; (c) (d): 99% of ancestors join with varying proportion of descendants; (e) (f): varying proportion of ancestors and descendants are joined.

join selectivity on ancestors high (99%) and vary the join selectivity on descendants. Figure 6.3(c) and 6.3(d) show the overall performance of the algorithms tested. As observed from the figures, *R-Locator* perform the best performance. The *XR-Tree* is better than B^+*-Tree* in that it keeps more information than B^+*-Tree*, therefore has the less chance for *false locate.* While one potential higher overhead of *XR-Tree* is caused by two additional fields (ps, pe) in key entries, hence more index pages.

Varying Selectivity on Both Ancestors and Descendants: In the last set of experiments, we vary the join selectivity on both ancestors and descendants. The results for these experiments are shown in Figure 6.3(e) and 6.3(f). As shown in the figures, *R-Locator* still performs the best overall performance. This can be explained as follows: as we vary the selectivity on both ancestors and descendants, the case of interleaving elements of unmatchable elements on ancestors and descendants increases, which increases the number of inevitable *false locate* on both B^+*-Tree* and *XR-Tree.* However, the distribution of elements has no effect on *Locator* for *no false locate.*

The diversity of the algorithms is best illustrated by this group of experiments, where there is potential to perform *Location* function. *Locator* could perform the *Location* function with low overhead, therefore it provides the best performance among all. *XR-Tree*, on the other hand, keeps more information than B^+*-Tree*, so it has more chance to achieve the *Location* function, thus it performs the second and B^+*-Tree* performs the worst overall performance.

7 Conclusion

In this paper, we propose a new `Location` function for fast structural join. Previous approaches are all failed in performing this function, the reason is that they use index to test whether the elements retrieved have matches by skipping unmatchable elements. The design of our space-efficient structure *Locator* is to efficiently perform `Location` function. The extensive performance evaluation show the significance of our proposed algorithm over previous approaches.

References

1. S. Al-Khalifa, H. V. Jagadish, N. Koudas, J. M. Patel, D. Srivastava, and Y. Wu. Structural Joins: A Primitive for Efficient XML Query Pattern Matching. In *Proceedings of ICDE '02*, 2002.
2. S.-Y. Chien, Z. Vagena, D. Zhang, V. J. Tsotras, and C. Zaniolo. Efficient structural joins on indexed XML documents. In *Proceedings of VLDB '02*, 2002.
3. H. Jiang, H. Lu, W. Wang, and B. C. Ooi. XR-Tree: Indexing XML data for efficient stuctural join. In *Proceedings of ICDE '03*, 2003.
4. I. Kamel and C. Faloutsos. Updates for structure indexes. In *Proceedings of the 2nd Int'l Conference on Information and Knowledge Management(CIKM)*, 1993.

Adapting Prime Number Labeling Scheme for Directed Acyclic Graphs

Gang Wu, Kuo Zhang, Can Liu, and Juanzi Li

Knowledge Engineering Lab, Department of Computer Science,
Tsinghua University, Beijing 100084, P.R. China

Abstract. Directed Acyclic Graph(DAG) could be used for modeling subsumption hierarchies. Several labeling schemes have been proposed or tailored for indexing DAG in order to efficiently explore relationships in such hierarchy. However few of them can satisfy all the requirements in response time, space, and effect of updates simultaneously. In this paper, the prime number labeling scheme is extended for DAG. The scheme invests intrinsic mapping between integer divisibility and subsumption hierarchy, which simplifies the transitive closure computations and diminishes storage redundancy, as well as inherits the dynamic labeling ability from original scheme. Performance is further improved by introducing some optimization techniques. Our extensive experimental results show that prime number labeling scheme for DAG outperforms interval-based and prefix-based labeling schemes in most cases.

1 Introduction

Directed Acyclic Graph(DAG) is an effective data structure for representing subsumption hierarchies in applications, e.g. OO programming, software engineering, and knowledge representation. The growing number and volume of DAGs in such systems inspire the demands for appropriate index structures for DAG.

Labeling schemes[8] are widely used in indexing tree or graph structured data considering their avoiding expensive join operations for transitive closure computations. Determinacy, compaction, dynamicity, and flexibility are factors for labeling scheme design besides speedup [10]. However, the state of art labeling schemes for DAG could not satisfy most above requirements simultaneously.

One major category of labeling schemes for DAG is spanning tree based. Ordinarily, they first find a spanning tree and assign labels for vertices following the tree's edges, and then propagate additional labels to record relationships of the non-tree edges. Christophides compared two such schemes [4], i.e. interval-based [7] and prefix-based [3]. Evaluations to the non-tree edges relationships cannot take advantage of the deterministic tree label characters. Non-tree labels need not only additional storage but also special efforts in query processing. Also interval-based scheme studied in [4] has a poor re-labeling ability for updates.

There are also labeling schemes having no concern with spanning tree, such as bit vector [9] and 2-hops [5]. Though bit vector can process operations on DAG more efficiently, it is static and requires global rebuilding of labels when

M.L. Lee, K.L. Tan, and V. Wuwongse (Eds.): DASFAA 2006, LNCS 3882, pp. 787–796, 2006.

updates happen. Moreover, studies show that recent 2-hops approach introduces false positives in basic reachability testing.

A novel labeling scheme for XML tree depending on the properties of prime number is proposed in [10]. Prime number labeling scheme associates each vertex with a unique prime number, and labels each vertex by multiplying parents' labels and the prime number owned by the vertex. Compared with prefix-based scheme, the effect of updating is almost the same, and the query response time and the size requirements are even smaller. However, no further work has been performed on extending the idea to the case of DAG.

We extend the scheme by labeling each vertex with an integer which equals to the arithmetic product of the prime numbers associating with the vertex and all its ancestors. Independent of spanning tree, the scheme can efficiently explore the subsumption hierarchies in a DAG by checking the divisibility among the labels. It also inherits dynamic update ability and compact size feature from its predecessor. Experimental results indicate that prime number labeling scheme is an efficient and scalable scheme for indexing DAG with appropriate extensions and optimizations. The major contributions are summarized as follows.

- Extend original prime number scheme[10] for labeling DAG and supporting the processing of typical operations on DAG.
- Optimize the scheme on space and time requirements in terms of the characteristics of DAG and prime numbers.
- A generator is implemented to generate arbitrary complex synthetic DAG for the extensive experiments. Space requirement, construction time, scalability, and the impact of selectivity and update are all studied in the experiments.

2 Prime Number Labeling Scheme for DAG

Given vertices v and w in DAG G, we will use $parents(v)$, $children(v)$, $ancestors(v)$, $descendants(v)$, $leaves(v)$, $siblings(v)$ and $nca(v, w)$ indicating queries on those known typical operations related to *reachability*[1]. (See [4] for formal expressions). Vertex update is another kind of operation worthy of note because it may bring reorganizations to the index structure.

2.1 Prime Number Labeling Scheme for DAG - Lite

Definition 1. *Let $G = (V, E)$ be a DAG. A **Prime Number Labeling Scheme for DAG - Lite** (PLSD-Lite) associates each vertex $v \in V$ with an exclusive prime number $p[v]$, and assigns to v a label $L_{lite}(v) = (c[v])$, where*

$$c[v] = p[v] \cdot \begin{cases} \prod_{v' \in parents(v)} c[v'], & in\text{-}degree(v)>0 \\ 1, & in\text{-}degree(v)=0 \end{cases} \quad (1)$$

In Figure 1, PLSD-Lite assigns each vertex an exclusive prime number increasingly from "2" with a depth-first traversal of the DAG. The first multiplier factor in the brackets of each vertex is the prime number assigned.

[1] DAG(*directed acyclic graph*), and *reachability* are general definitions in graph theory. Given two vertices v and w, $v \rightsquigarrow w$ is used to indicate that w is reachable from v.

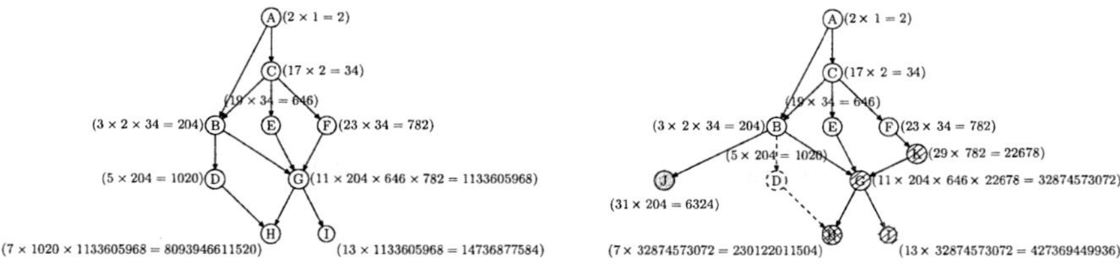

Fig. 1. PLSD-Lite

Fig. 2. Updates in PLSD-Lite

Lemma 1. *Let $G = (V, E)$ be a DAG. Composite number $c[v]$ in the $L_{lite}(v) = (c[v])$ of a vertex $v \in V$ can be written in exactly one way as a product*

$$c[v] = p[v] \cdot \prod_{v' \in ancestors(v)} p[v']^{m_{v'}} \tag{2}$$

where $m_{v'} \in \mathbb{N}$.

Lemma 1 [2] implies that for any vertex with PLSD-Lite, there is a bijection between an ancestor of the vertex and a prime factor of the label value.

Theorem 1. *Let $G = (V, E)$ be a DAG. For any two vertices $v, w \in V$ where $L_{lite}(v) = (c[v])$ and $L_{lite}(w) = (c[w])$, $v \rightsquigarrow w \iff c[v] | c[w]$.*

Consequently, whether two vertices have the relation of ancestor/descendant can be simply determined with PLSD-Lite. For example, in Figure 1, we have $A \rightsquigarrow D$ because $2|1020$. Finding out all the ancestors or descendants of a given vertex is realizable by testing the divisibility of the vertex's label with the other vertices' labels in the DAG or conversely. Moreover, a vertex is a leaf if any other vertex's label value could not be divided by its label value. There is also a simple solution to nca evaluating. First put all the common ancestors of both vertices into a set. Then filter out vertices whose descendants are also within the set.

As stated in [10], re-labeling happens with the insertion or deletion of a vertex, and only affects the descendants. After deleting vertex D, inserting leaf vertex J and non-leaf vertex K, we have Figure 2. As a new leaf, J does not affect other vertices in the DAG. Insertion of K only affects descendants G, H, I and K itself. Vertex H is affected by the deletion of ancestor D too.

However, PLSD-Lite lacks enough information to identify parents/child relation. In order to support this operation, we need to separately record the prime number that identifies the vertex and the additional information about parents.

2.2 Prime Number Labeling Scheme for DAG - Full

Definition 2. *Let $G = (V, E)$ be a DAG. A* ***Prime Number Labeling Scheme for DAG - Full*** *(PLSD-Full) associates each vertex $v \in V$ with an exclusive prime number $p[v]$, and assigns to v a label $L_{full}(v) = (p[v], c_a[v], c_p[v])$, where*

[2] All the proofs in this paper are omitted for the length limited.

$$c_a[v] = p[v] \cdot \begin{cases} \prod_{v' \in parents(v)} c_a[v'], & in\!-\!degree(v)\!>\!0 \\ 1, & in\!-\!degree(v)\!=\!0 \end{cases} \tag{3}$$

and

$$c_p[v] = \begin{cases} \prod_{v' \in parents(v)} p[v'], & in\!-\!degree(v)\!>\!0 \\ 1, & in\!-\!degree(v)\!=\!0 \end{cases} \tag{4}$$

We term $p[v]$ as "self-label", $c_a[v]$ ($c[v]$ in Definition 1) as "ancestors-label", and $c_p[v]$ as "parents-label". In Figure 3, three parts in one bracket is self-label, ancestors-label, and parents-label. Theorem 1 is still applicable.

Theorem 2. *Let $G = (V, E)$ be a DAG, and vertex $v \in V$ has $L_{full}(v) = (p[v], c_a[v], c_p[v])$. If the unique factorization of composite integer $c_a[v]$ results r different prime numbers, $p_1 < ... < p_r$, then there is exactly one vertex $w \in V$ that takes p_i as the self-label for $1 \leq i \leq r$, and w is one of the ancestors of v. If the unique factorization of composite integer $c_p[v]$ results s different prime numbers, $p'_1 < ... < p'_s$, then there is exactly one vertex $u \in V$ that takes p'_i as the self-label for $1 \leq i \leq s$, and u is one of the parents of v.*

Therefore, we can find out all the parents of any vertex by factorizing the parents-label. For instance, since vertex G in Figure 3 has a parents-label $1311 = 3 \times 19 \times 23$, vertices B, E and F are considered to be all the parents of G. We still have the rights to determine the parent/child relation of two vertices by checking divisibility between one's parents-label and the other's self-label in terms of Definition 2. Unique factorization also can be used to obtain ancestors. Three ancestors A, B and C of vertex D could be identified by factoring "1020". Though trial division itself could be used to do integer factorization, we can choose faster integer factorization algorithm alternately especially for small integers. Corollary 1 further expresses PLSD-Full's sibling evaluation ability.

Corollary 1. *Let $G = (V, E)$ be a DAG. For any two vertices $v, w \in V$ where $L_{full}(v) = (p[v], c_a[v], c_p[v])$ and $L_{full}(w) = (p[w], c_a[w], c_p[w])$, w and v are siblings if and only if the greatest common divisor* $\gcd(c_p[v], c_p[w]) \neq 1$.

Corollary 1 enables us to discover the siblings of a vertex by testing whether the greatest common divisor of the parents-labels equals 1. In Figure 3, vertex B has two siblings E and F because $\gcd(34, 17) = 17 \neq 1$.

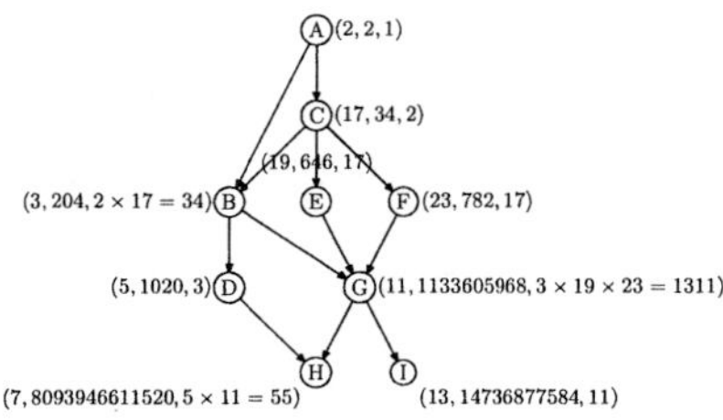

Fig. 3. PLSD-Full

3 Optimization Techniques

Elementary arithmetic operations employed by PLSD become time-consuming when their inputs are large numbers. Some optimizations are introduced here.

Least Common Multiple. There is apparent redundancy in previous construction of ancestors-label that power $m_{v'}$ in Equation 2 magnifies the size of ancestors-label exponentially, but it is helpless for evaluating the operations of DAG. It is straightforward to remove the redundancy by simply setting $m_{v'}$ to 1 in Equation 2. We have Equation 5.

$$c[v] = p[v] \cdot \prod_{v' \in ancestors(v)} p[v'] \tag{5}$$

Theorems 1 and 2 still hold. Define $lcm(a_1, a_2, ..., a_n)$ to be the *least common multiple* of n integers $a_1, a_2, ..., a_n$. In particular, we define $lcm(a) = a$ here.

$$c[v] = p[v] \cdot \begin{cases} lcm(c[v'_1], ..., c[v'_n]), & in-degree(v)>0 \ and \ v'_1, ..., v'_n \in parents(v) \\ 1, & in-degree(v)=0 \end{cases} \tag{6}$$

Equation 6 implies that an ancestors-label can be simply constructed by multiplying self-label by the least common multiple of all the parents' ancestors-labels. Thereafter, Equation 5 holds. With this optimization technique, the max-length of ancestors-label in DAG is only on terms with the total count of vertices and the count of ancestors. Figure 4 has a smaller max-length of ancestors-label.

Topological Sort. Previous selection of prime number for the self-label is arbitrary as long as any two vertices have different self-label. A naive approach is assigning each vertex met in depth-first search of DAG a prime number ascendingly. Unfortunately, Equation 5 and 2 imply that the size of a vertex's self-label has influence on all the ancestors-labels of its descendants. So vertices on the top of the hierarchy should be assigned small prime numbers as early as possible. Topological sort[6] of a DAG provides the character we need. One of the topological sort of the DAG in Figure 1 is "$A, C, E, F, B, D, G, H, I$". Let the self-labels to be the first 9 prime numbers "$2, 3, 5, 7, 11, 13, 17, 19, 23$" respectively, then we get Figure 5.

Leaves Marking. As an optimization for reducing label size, even numbers e.g. $2^1, 2^2, ..., 2^n$ are used as self-labels for leaf vertices in [10], which gives us another

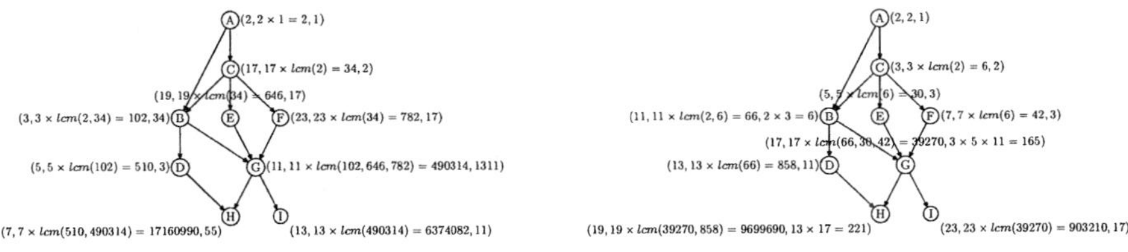

Fig. 4. Least Common Multiple

Fig. 5. Topological Sort

method to identify leaves. However, the prime number theorem indicates that the growth of prime number is slower than that of power of 2, so self-labels of even number leaves increase dramatically. An alternative is to follow the rule of PLSD-FULL and simply set leaf's ancestors-label to be negative. Whether a vertex is a leaf could be determined by the sign of its ancestors-label. It is a meaningful technique in the case of existing large number of leaves in a DAG.

Descendants-Label. In the same idea of ancestors-label, we can extend LDUP-Full by adding the following so-called "descendants-label".

$$c_a[v] = p[v] \cdot \begin{cases} \prod_{v' \in children(v)} c_a[v'], & out-degree(v)>0 \\ 1, & out-degree(v)=0 \end{cases} \tag{7}$$

Clearly, Equation 7 is a reverse version of Equation 3. Now, $descendants(v)$, can be evaluated by factoring descendants-label. In section 4 we will give empirical results on querying descendants and leaves using this technique.

4 Performance Study

This section presents some results of our extensive experiments conducted to study the effectiveness of prime number labeling scheme for DAG (PLSD).

4.1 Experiment Settings

Taking the queries on RDF class hierarchies as an application background for DAG, we setup test bed on RSSDB v2.0 [2]. In this case, each vertex stands for a class in the RDF metadata, and each edge stands for the hierarchy relationship between a pair of classes in the RDF metadata. RDF metadata is parsed and stored in PostgreSQL (win32 platform v8.0.2 with Unicode configuration).

Though least common multiple, topological sort, and leaves marking are optional optimizations, they are integrated in our default PLSD-Full implementation. PLSD-Lite and PLSD-Full without these optimizations are ignored for their apparent defects. Furthermore, descendants-label is employed to examine its effects on descendants query. We also provide the Unicode Dewey prefix-based scheme and the extended postorder interval-based scheme by Agrawal et al. Hence, there are totally four competitors in our comparisons, namely, default PLSD-Full (PLSDF), PLSD-Full with descendants-label (PLSDF-D), extended postorder interval-based scheme (PInterval) and Unicode Dewey prefix-based scheme (UPrefix). All the implementations are developed with JDK1.5.0. Database is connected through PostgreSQL 7.3.3 JDBC2 driver. All the experiments are conducted on a PC with single 2.66GHz Intel Pentium 4 CPU, 1GB DDR-SDRAM, 80GB IDE hard disk, and Microsoft Windows 2003 Server.

The relational representations of UPrefix and PInterval, including tables, indexes, and buffer settings, are the same to [4]. As for PLSDF, we create a table with four attributes: PLSDF(self-label: text, label: text, parent-label: text, uri: text). It is not surprising that we use PostgreSQL data type *text* instead of the longest integer data type *bigint* to represent the first three attributes considering that a vertex with 15 ancestors has an ancestors-label value at least 32589158477190044730 which exceeds the bound of *bigint* (8 bytes, between ±9223372036854775808). The conversion from text to number is available on host language Java. Thus the number-theoretic algorithms used for PLSDF could be performed outside PostgreSQL in main memory. Similarly, we use PLSDF-D(self-label: text, label: text, parent-label: text, descendants-label: text, uri: text) to represent PLSDF-D. For PLSDF and PLSDF-D, we only build B-tree indexes on self-labels. Buffer settings are the same to those of UPrefix and PInterval.

4.2 Data Sets

To simulate diverse cases of DAG, we implement a RDF metadata generator to generate RDF file with arbitrary complexity and scale of RDF class hierarchies. Generator's input includes the count of vertices, the max depth of spanning tree, the max fan-out of vertices, and the portion of fan-in (*ancestors/precedings*). The output is a valid RDF file. We concatenate the values of above four parameters and the count of edges with hyphens to identify a DAG. Listed in Table 1, two groups of DAGs are generated for evaluating the performance.

Table 1. Data Sets

RDF Metadata DAG	Size (MB)	Classes/ Vertices	SubClassOf/ Edges	Depth Max	Fan-out Max	Fan-in Portion	Fan-in Max
1300-8-4-0.2-50504	2.55	1300	50504	8	4	0.2	219
1300-8-4-0.4-100132	4.62	1300	100132	8	4	0.4	458
1300-8-4-0.6-149451	6.34	1300	149451	8	4	0.6	373
1300-8-4-0.8-199774	8.05	1300	199774	8	4	0.8	897
1300-8-4-1.0-250222	9.32	1300	250222	8	4	1.0	562
90000-16-2-0.000053-44946	16.3	90000	44946	16	2	0.000053	3

4.3 Space Requirement and Construction Time

As shown in Figure 6(a), PLSDF and PLSDF-D have much smaller average space requirement and mild trend of increase. The underlying cause is twofold. First, both are simply composed of only one table whose row size equals to the count of vertices, and one B-tree index. In contrast, Interval and UPrefix consist of three tables (and more indexes) to record additional information besides spanning tree. Another cause is that all the data type in the table of PLSDF or PLSDF-D are *text* which will be "compressed by the system automatically, so the physical requirement on disk may be less"[1]. Figure 6(b) illustrates that PLSDF and PLSFD-D have the same gentle tendency but less construction time to UPrefix, whereas the construction time of Interval is the worst. It is obvious that the count of non-spanning tree edges impacts the space requirement and label construction time for UPrefix and Interval. Another observation is that PLSDF needs few space and construction time relative to PLSDF-D. This is reasonable considering that PLSDF-D equals to PLSDF plus descendants-label.

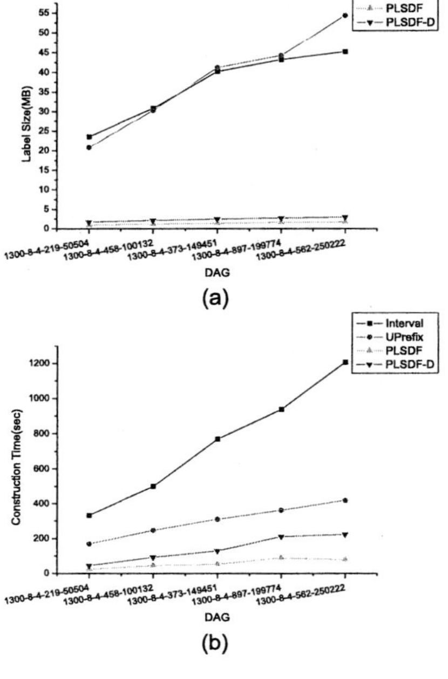

Fig. 6. Label Size(a) & Construction Time(b)

	Operation Type	Selectivity
Q1	ancestors	2.53%
Q2	descendants	20.08%
Q3	siblings	2.98%
Q4	leaves	38.67%
Q5	nca	0.011%

Fig. 7. Test Typical Operations for Overall Performance

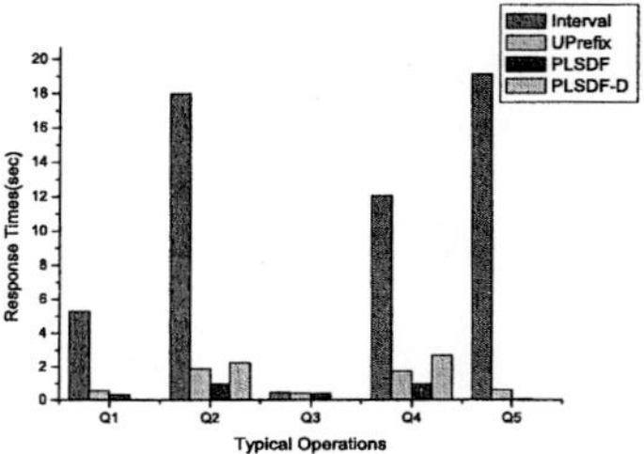

Fig. 8. Overall Performance

4.4 Response Time of Typical Operations

Overall Performance. DAG "9000-8-4-0.004-45182" is used here. The operations are listed in Figure 7. The total elapsed time is shown in Figure 8. PLSDF-D is applied only to Q2 and Q4 to examine the effectiveness of descendants-label, because it is the same to PLSDF for the other three queries. For the given selectivity, PLSDF processes all the operations faster than the others. PLSDF-D exhibits accepted performance in Q2 and Q4 as well. The concise table structure of PLSDF/PLSDF-D and computative elementary arithmetic operations avoid massive database access. For instance, the evaluation of a vertex's ancestors includes only two steps. Firstly retrieve the self-label and ancestors-label of the vertex from the table. Then do factorization using the labels. The only database access happens in the first step.

Impact of Varying Selectivity. Selectivity experiment result is shown in Figure 9. Diagrams in the figure correspond to operations from Q1 to Q5 respectively. The metric of X-axis is the results selectivity of the operation except that the fifth diagram for nca uses X-axis to indicate the average length from the spanning-tree root. The metric of Y-axis is the response time. PLSDF displays almost constant time performance for all operations. Though the change of response time is indistinguishable in some extensions, PLSDF stays at a disadvantage at a very low selectivity especially for Q2 and Q4. Fortunately, PLSDF-D

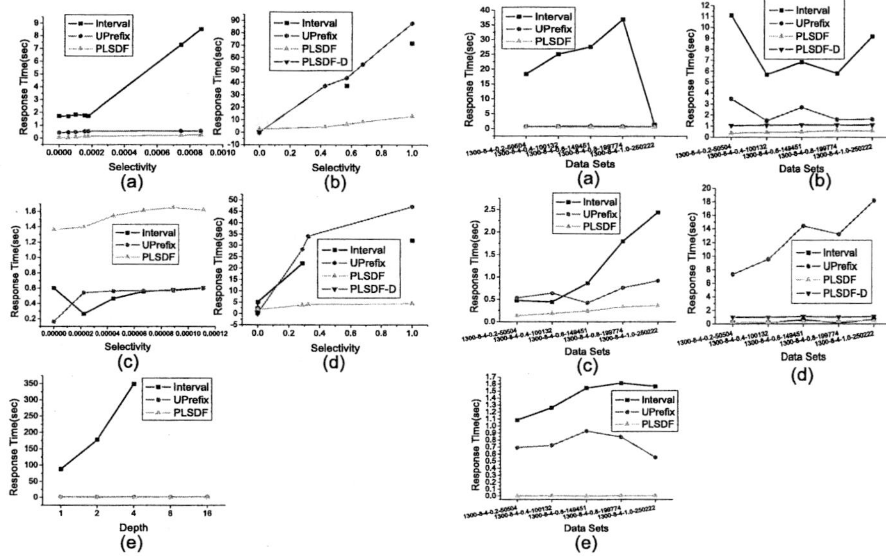

Fig. 9. Impact of varying selectivity

Fig. 10. Scale-up Performance

counterbalances this with descendants-label. It is a better plan to choose PLSDF-D at a low selectivity and switch to PLSDF when the selectivity exceeds some threshold. However, no good solution is found for PLSDF in Q3 where it costs more response time at a low selectivity. PLSDF has to traverse among the vertices and compute greatest common divisor one at a time.

Scale-Up Performance. We carry out scalability tests with the first group of DAGs in Table 1. Operations are made to have the equal selectivity (equal length on path for nca) for each scale of DAG size. Five diagrams in Figure 10 corresponds to operations from Q1 to Q5 respectively. Interval and UPrefix are affected by both the size of the DAG. Unlike the other two labeling schemes, PLSDF and PLSDF-D perform good scalability in all cases.

4.5 Effect of Updates

The "Un-ordered Updates" experiments exhibited in [10] are repeated. Here we only give the results of updates on non-leaf vertices (updates on leaf have the same results to that of XML tree, see Section 2.1). Ten DAGs whose vertices increase from 1000 to 10000 are generated. We insert a new vertex into each DAG between bottom left leaf and the leaf's parent in the spanning tree. Figure 11 shows our experimental results which coincides with that of XML tree. PLSDF has exactly the same effect of update as Uprefix. While additional label of PLSDF-D questionless causes more vertices to be re-labeled.

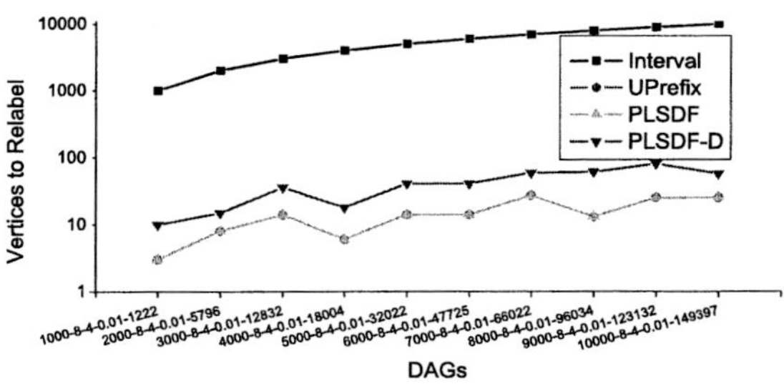

Fig. 11. Effect of Updates

5 Conclusion

Prime number labeling scheme for DAG takes advantage of the mapping between integers divisibility and vertices reachability. No extra information is required to be stored for non-spanning tree edges, and the utilizations of elementary arithmetic operations avoid time-consuming database operations. Performance is further improved with the optimization techniques. Analysis also indicates that re-labeling only happens when a non-leaf vertex is inserted or removed.

References

[1] Postgresql 8.0.3 documentation. available at http://www.postgresql.org/docs/8.0/interactive/index.html.

[2] D. Beckett. Scalability and storage: Survey of free software / open source rdf storage systems. Technical Report 1016, ILRT, June 2003. http://www.w3.org/2001/sw/Europe/reports/rdf_scalable_storage_report/.

[3] O. C. L. Center. Dewey decimal classification. available at http://www.oclc.org/dewey.

[4] V. Christophides, G. Karvounarakis, D. Plexousakis, M. Scholl, and S. Tourtounis. Optimizing taxonomic semantic web queries using labeling schemes. *Journal of Web Semantics*, 11(001):207–228, November 2003.

[5] E. Cohen, E. Halperin, H. Kaplan, and U. Zwick. Reachability and distance queries via 2-hop labels. *SIAM J. Comput.*, 32(5):1338–1355, 2003.

[6] T. H. Cormen, C. E. Leiserson, R. L. Rivest, and C. Stein. *Introduction to Algorithms, Second Edition.* The MIT Press, September 2001.

[7] Q. Li and B. Moon. Indexing and querying xml data for regular path expressions. In P. M. G. Apers, P. Atzeni, S. Ceri, S. Paraboschi, K. Ramamohanarao, and R. T. Snodgrass, editors, *Proceedings of the 27th International Conference on Very Large Data Bases*, pages 361–370, Roma, Italy, 2001.

[8] N. Santoro and R. Khatib. Labelling and implicit routing in networks. *Comput. J.*, 28(1):5–8, 1985.

[9] N. Wirth. Type extensions. *ACM Trans. Program. Lang. Syst.*, 10(2):204–214, 1988.

[10] X. Wu, M.-L. Lee, and W. Hsu. A prime number labeling scheme for dynamic ordered xml trees. In *ICDE*, pages 66–78. IEEE Computer Society, 2004.

KEYNOTE: Keyword Search by Node Selection for Text Retrieval on DHT-Based P2P Networks*

Zheng Zhang, Shuigeng Zhou, Weining Qian, and Aoying Zhou

Department of Computer Science and Engineering,
Fudan University, Shanghai 200433, China
{zhzhang1981, sgzhou, wnqian, ayzhou}@fudan.edu.cn

Abstract. Efficient full-text keyword search remains a challenging problem in P2P systems. Most of the traditional keyword search systems on DHT overlay networks perform the join operation of keywords at document level, which consumes a huge amount of storage and bandwidth. In this paper, we present KEYNOTE, a novel keyword search system that performs the join operation at node level. Compared to the traditional keyword search systems on DHTs, KEYNOTE can greatly reduce the storage and communication cost. To forward a query to the relevant nodes for searching documents, two effective node selection methods are presented. To address the hot spot problem in Chord overlay networks, an efficient load balancing scheme is introduced. Simulated experimental evaluation with up to 8,000 nodes and over 600,000 real-world documents validates the practicality of the proposed system.

1 Introduction

Recently Peer-to-Peer (P2P) systems have emerged as a scalable infrastructure that can provide large-scale and decentralized lookup services. Filename-based P2P search systems are already popular, while content-based search remains a challenge in P2P network context. Compared to the other complex P2P information retrieval systems, keyword search systems on DHTs [1, 2, 3, 4] are particularly attractive due to their simple yet efficient searching mechanism and high search accuracy. Meanwhile, along with the development of centralized search engines, such as Google, it is interesting and worth of studying whether P2P-based Web and text search can achieve equivalent precision, and similar or even better performance, for the low cost, ease of deployment, and scalability characteristics of P2P systems.

As with the centralized Web search engines, the users may be interested only in top-k documents that are most relevant to the query in the P2P networks. Since the top-k documents usually exist in a small number of nodes(or peers), how to select the relevant peers without maintaining the information of all peers is the first challenge for making P2P-based content search a reality.

Existing DHT-based keyword search technologies perform the join operation at the document level, consuming a large amount of storage and bandwidth. In the rest part of

* This work was supported by the National Natural Science Foundation of China (NSFC) under grant numbers 60373019, 60573183 ,60496325 and 60503034, Shuguang Program of Shanghai Education Development Foundation, and Shanghai Rising-Star Program (04QMX1404).

M.L. Lee, K.L. Tan, and V. Wuwongse (Eds.): DASFAA 2006, LNCS 3882, pp. 797–806, 2006.

this paper, it is called the document join approach. Fig. 1 illustrates its basic scheme. In this approach, the keywords and the computers in this system are hashed into the same range. A computer hosts those keywords whose hashed values are between its address and the address of the next computer in the network. When a node joins the network, it publishes the inverted index including the term, the global document ID and other meta data (e.g., the weight of the term in the document). To perform the multi-term query, the system has to transfer the posting information of one term from one node to other nodes holding other terms. This approach is problematic in the situations where a huge number of documents exist in the P2P network, and the node hosting the index of the terms must spend considerable storage space for the index and metadata, while answering a multi-term query, much bandwidth is consumed to transfer the large amount of indices. As indicated by [1], even with promising optimization techniques, current keyword search systems are not feasible for Internet-scale search.

Furthermore, for the existing systems, queries are not distributed evenly. Even with the randomized DHT, the query processing workload is not balanced in the P2P systems. keeping load balance on top of DHT overlay is a critical requirement for P2P-based keyword search systems.

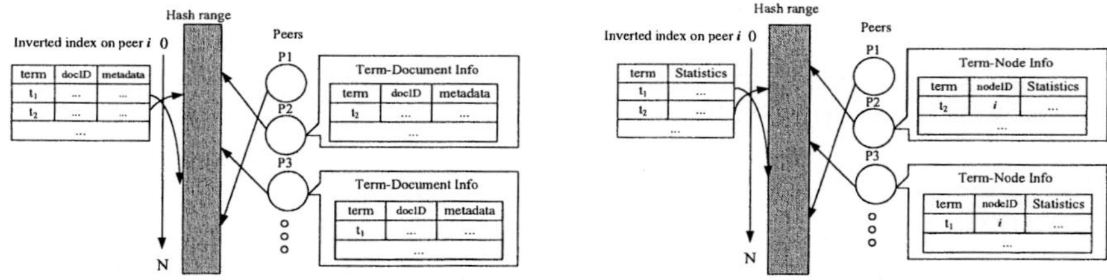

Fig. 1. Document-join System

Fig. 2. Node-join System

To deal with the above three challenges, we present a novel search system. The basic idea is to select those peers having most of relevant documents to the query. To reduce storage and bandwidth cost, our system performs the join operation at the node level. Fig. 2 illustrates its scheme. Instead of publishing the term-document information, our system publishes term-node data. The distributed indices include the terms, the source node identifiers and the statistics regarding the terms in the source nodes. To perform queries consisting of two terms, we need only to transmit the term-node statistics from one node to another node. We call our system KEYNOTE, KEYword-search using NOde-selection for TExt-retrieval. We also provide an efficient load balancing algorithm on top of the DHT overlay, Chord [5] in our system.

In this paper, our contributions include:

- We propose KEYNOTE, a novel keyword search system over Chord overlay networks using node-level join, which can greatly reduce both communication and storage cost.
- Two simple yet effective methods for node selection are proposed, which can be implemented in distributed way.

- A load balancing algorithm is presented for the Chord overlay, which can guarantee that the load balancing of each hot term on one given node could be achieved in $O(\log N)$ steps(N is the number of nodes in the network).

1.1 Related Work

PlanetP[6] uses Bloom Filter to summarize the content of each node and distributes this summarization to the whole network. In [7], Lu et. al studies content-based resource selection and document retrieval in hybrid P2P networks. pSearch[8] is a peer-to-peer information retrieval system based on CAN[9], which employs statistically derived conceptual indices for retrieval. P2P keyword search on top of DHTs are most relevant to our work. To reduce the communication cost for the keyword join, some optimization techniques have been proposed. In [2], Reynolds et. al adopt Bloom filters, caches and incremental results to reduce the join cost. [1] reported that by combing all the existing optimization techniques , it is still impossible to make P2P web search feasible on top of DHTs. In [4], Tang et. al propose eSearch, a hybrid global-local indexing mechanism to make the communication cost independent of the number of documents in the network. However, this method consumes 6.8 times storage cost of traditional keyword join systems. In [10], Zhong et. al report that the communication cost of keyword join system could be reduced to 0.0175 times by combining the techniques of Bloom Filter, caching , pre-computation, query log mining and incremental set intersection.

The remainder of this paper is organized as follows. Section 2 presents KEYNOTE in details. Section 3 describes a load balancing algorithm in Chord overlay. Section 4 gives the experimental evaluation of our system. Section 5 concludes our paper.

2 Techniques of the KEYNOTE System

In KEYNOTE, a large number of computers are organized by DHT into a Chord[5] ring. Fig. 3 illustrates the system architecture of KEYNOTE. When a new peer wants to join the network, it first joins the Chord network using the join protocol of Chord. Afterward, the new peer publishes the term-node statistics to other peers which are

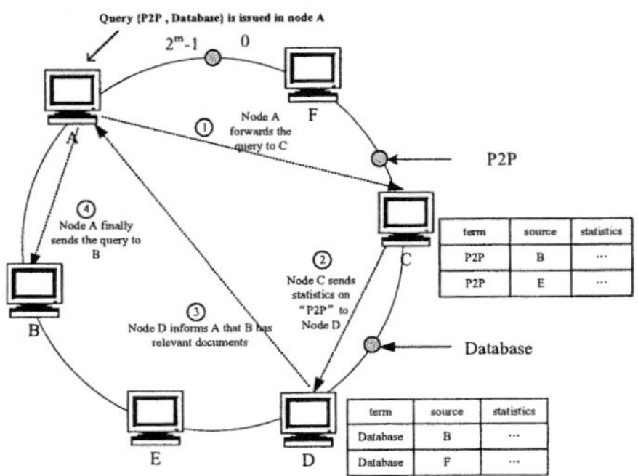

Fig. 3. Query processing in KEYNOTE

responsible for the terms in the Chord ring. When a multi-term query is issued, the term-node information regarding these terms are transmitted from one node to other nodes for performing the node-level join. From those nodes which contain all the terms, the peer selection methods are used to select top-L (where L is the system parameter in our system) relevant peers to which the query is finally forwarded for processing. After all local top-k results from these selected peers are returned to the query peer, these partial results are merged into the final top-k documents. The node leaving and failure are handled similarly in Chord.

In the following, we would present peer selection methods, term-node information publication , query processing and analysis of system resources in details.

2.1 Peer Selection Methods

Peer Selection Using Sum Statistics: *PS-sum*. Our first peer selection method(simply *PS-sum*) is inspired by the gGlOSS system[11], which proposes an approach to estimate the goodness of each text database for a given query and then ranks these text databases according to the estimated goodness. In KEYNOTE, an estimation of the *goodness* of peer P_j with regard to the query vector $q = \{q_1, q_2, \ldots, q_m\}$ is given as follows.

$$G_{sum}(q, P_j) = \sum_{i=1,\ldots,m} q_i \times w_{sum}(i, j) = \sum_{i=1,\ldots,m} q_i \times sum\_tf_i(P_j) \times idf_i \quad (1)$$

where $w_{sum}(i, j)$is the sum weight of term t_i appearing in different documents in P_j. And $sum\_tf_i(P_j)$ is the sum of TF weight of t_i appearing in different documents in P_j, *i.e.*, $sum\_tf_i(P_j) = \sum_{d_k \in P_j \wedge t_i \in d_k} tf_{ik}$, where tf_{ik} is the TF weight of t_i in document d_k.

In KEYNOTE we compute the weight of each term based on the global information. Therefore, in equation 1, idf_i is defined as the global value of $log\frac{N}{n_i}$, where n_i is the number of documents that contains t_i in the whole network and N is the total number of documents in the network.

Peer Selection Using Sum and Max Statistics: *PS-sum_max*. The *PS-sum* method could fail in the following occasion. Peer A contains only one relevant document *d* to the query *q*. Peer B contains many relevant documents whose summed relevance is much greater than the relevance of *d*, but the maximum relevance of these documents is less than the relevance of *d*. Now the users issue a top-1 search for the query q and use *PS-sum* to select one peer for searching, peer B would be selected for processing the query. In this case, the users would miss the most relevant document *d* in peer A . To address this problem, here we propose a new method, *PS-sum_max*, which considers both the summed relevance and the maximum relevance. Formally, we define the goodness of P_j to *q* as follows:

$$G_{sum\_max}(q, P_j) = \frac{G_{sum}(q, P_j)}{2 * Max\_G_{sum}(q)} + \frac{G_{max}(q, P_j)}{2 * Max\_G_{max}(q)} \quad (2)$$

where $Max\_G_{sum}(q) = Max\{G_{sum}(q, P_j)\}$, $Max\_G_{max}(q) = Max\{G_{max}(q, P_j)\}$ and

$$G_{max}(q, P_j) = \sum_{i=1,\ldots,m} q_i \times w_{max}(i, j) = \sum_{i=1,\ldots,m} q_i \times max\_tf_i(P_j) \times idf_i \quad (3)$$

where $w_{max}(i, j)$ is the maximum weight of term t_i among all the documents in P_j, $max\_tf_i(P_j) = max\{tf_{ik}|d_k \in P_j\}$ and idf_i has the same meaning in equation 1.

2.2 Term-Node Information Publishing and Query Processing

To implement *PS-sum* and *PS-sum_max*, we need to know the global value of $w_{sum}(i, j)$ and $w_{max}(i, j)$ for each term t_i in peer P_j, which further requires global values of N and n_i. For the value of n_i, we could look up the node holding t_i . But there is no dedicated node storing the value of N. In KEYNOTE, we let those nodes responsible for stop-words store the value of N. Our process of publishing statistics for each term t_i in P_j consists of three steps.

1. We publish the number of documents containing t_i to the node holding t_i .
2. We get the global value of N and n_i from the nodes containing stop-words and the node holding t_i respectively and then compute the global weight of t_i in each document in P_j. Afterward, $w_{sum}(i, j)$ and $w_{max}(i, j)$ are computed .
3. Finally, the information which constitute a tuple (t_i, P_j, $w_{sum}(i, j)$, $w_{max}(i, j)$) is published to the node responsible for t_i .

To answer a multi-term query, the term-node information of each term is first located using the routing protocol in Chord. Then inverted lists of these terms are transmitted from one node to other nodes for performing the join operation. From those nodes which contain all these terms, we choose the top-L relevant nodes and forward the query to these L nodes in parallel to get the local top-k documents from each of these L nodes. Finally, the global top-k documents are obtained by merging the local top-k documents from each of these L nodes.

2.3 Analysis of System Resource Usage and Search Latency

For the convenience of analysis, we make the following assumptions: (1)The query involves two terms t_1 and t_2. The user is interested in seeing the top-10 results for the query and the system parameter L is 15. (2)The link between each peer and its successors on the chord ring is pre-established TCP-IP link. When two non-neighbors want to transmit data, they have to establish the temporal UDP link.(3) The available network bandwidth per query is 1.5Mbps, the bandwidth of a T1 link. (4) The link latency to establish the temporal link is 40ms and the time involved in the local searching and computing in each site is omitted in our analysis since in P2P systems we focus on the network latency.

Storage Cost. The storage cost is the total storage consumption for holding the distributed index over the whole network. In traditional document-join systems, we assume that these systems need 8 bytes to represent the document ID and another 4 bytes to store the meta-data (e.g., the weight of the term). Thus, the total storage consumption in these systems is $12 \times n \times t \times d$ Bytes, where n is the number of nodes in the network, t is the averaged number of distinct terms per node and d is the averaged number of term-relevant documents per term on each node. In KEYNOTE , we use 4 bytes to represent the node ID(or node IP) and another 8 bytes to store the sum weight and max weight of each term. Thus, the storage cost in KEYNOTE is $12 \times n \times t$ Bytes. Compared to the document-join systems, KEYNOTE reduces the storage cost by a factor of d. Obviously, the value of d is data collection dependent. In our Reuter news collection, this value is around 17.

Communication Cost. The communication cost is the bandwidth cost for transmitting the data after the link is established.

We first analyze the communication cost of document-join systems. To locate the two nodes holding t_1 and t_2, the communication cost is $2 * \frac{1}{2} * \log(n) * (40+1+40) = 81 * \log n$, where $\frac{1}{2} * \log(n)$ is the averaged routing hops in the Chord overlay consisting of n nodes, (40+1+40) is the size of the query message(including 40-byte TCP-IP header, 1-byte message ID and 40-byte query text). To perform the join operation of t_1 and t_2, the communication cost is $12 * N_{term\_doc}$ bytes, where N_{term_doc} is the averaged number of documents in which a term appears. We assume that the optimization techniques for the join operation (including Bloom Filter, caching , pre-computation, query log mining and incremental set intersection) are used in the traditional document-join system and these techniques could lead to 0.0175 times reduction[1]. To return the search results, the communication cost is $28 + 1 + 10 * (8 + 4) = 149$(including 28-byte UDP-IP header, 1-byte message ID, 8-byte document ID and 4-byte similarity score for the top-10 results). Therefore, the total communication cost of document join systems with optimization techniques is $81 * \log n + 0.0175 * 12 * N_{term\_doc} + 149$ Bytes.

Now we begin to analyze the communication cost in KEYNOTE. The cost to locate the two nodes holding t_1 and t_2 is the same as that in document-join systems. The communication cost of node-level join operation is $12 * N_{term\_node}$, where N_{term_node} is the averaged number of nodes in which a term appears . The cost of returning the list of selected peers to the query peer is $28 + 1 + 15 * (4 + 4) = 149$(including 28-byte UDP-IP header, 1-byte message ID, 4-byte node ID and 4-byte similarity score for the top-15 nodes). The communication cost of returning the final document list to the query peer is $28 + 1 + 15 * 10 * (8 + 4) = 1829$(including 8-byte document ID and 4-byte similarity score of the top-10 documents from each of the selected 15 peers). Therefore, the total communication cost of KEYNOTE with optimization techniques is $81 * \log n + 0.0175 * 12 * N_{term\_node} + 149 + 1829$ Bytes.

We can observe that compared to document-join systems KEYNOTE could reduce the communication cost for Web searching roughly by a factor of $N_{term\_doc}/N_{term\_node}$. In our data set, $N_{term\_doc}/N_{term\_node}$ is roughly around 13.

Search Latency. The search latency in the document join system is $2 * T_{link\_latency} + \frac{C_{doc-join}*8}{1.5*10^6}$ seconds, where two latencies to establish the UDP links are consumed. One link latency is used to establish the UDP link for transmitting the data in the join operation, and the other link latency is consumed to build the link for transmitting the top-k results to the query peer. The search latency in KEYNOTE is $3 * T_{link\_latency} + \frac{C_{KEYNOTE}*8}{1.5*10^6}$ seconds where totally 3 link latencies are involved. One link latency is used for performing the join operation. The second latency is used for returning the

[1] [10] reports that by combining these techniques together could lead to 0.0175 times reduction in communication cost for the join operation.

list of selected peers to the query peer. The last latency is consumed for locating the selected peers.

3 Load Balancing

The load balancing issue includes balancing both the storage load and query execution load. In KEYNOTE, the storage cost on each node is greatly reduced by our term-node information publication mechanism. Thus, in this paper we focus on balancing the query execution cost. In [12], Dabek et al. propose the idea of replicating the popular files on all the nodes in the search path. We call this strategy "all-cache" method. In KEYNOTE, we only cache the hot keys on the carefully selected nodes and we call our method "selective cache".

Algorithm1 gives a formal description of our load balancing algorithm when a node N_i becomes overloaded for the hot key *k*.

Algorithm 1. ShedLoad (Node N_i, Key *k*)

$i = 0$
if N_i is not the original host for key k **then**
    Let $d=(k + 2^m - N_i) \bmod 2^m$
    while $i < m$ AND $d > 2^i$ **do**
        $i = i + 1$
    end while
end if
repeat
    Let N_j be the predecessor who hosts the key $(k + 2^m - 2^i) \bmod 2^m$
    $i = i + 1$
until $i \geq m$ OR N_j has no copy of the key k
Copy key k to N_j
if N_i is still overloaded due to the frequent access of key k **then**
    ShedLoad (N_i, k)
end if

Theorem 1. *In KEYNOTE, for one given node N_i and key k, our load balancing algorithm could make N_i's load for key k become light in O($\log N$) steps.*

For the detailed description of our algorithm and the proof of theorem 1, please refer to our technical report[13].

4 Experimental Evaluation

We use the Reuters news as our evaluation dataset, which contains over 600,000 news from the date 08.20.1996 to 08.19.1997. Each document in this data set is stored in the XML format and has the tag "location.name" that denotes the source location of this news. We divide the Retuers news into different collections based on the tag "location.name" . The total number of collections is 8,722 , which represents 8,722 nodes in

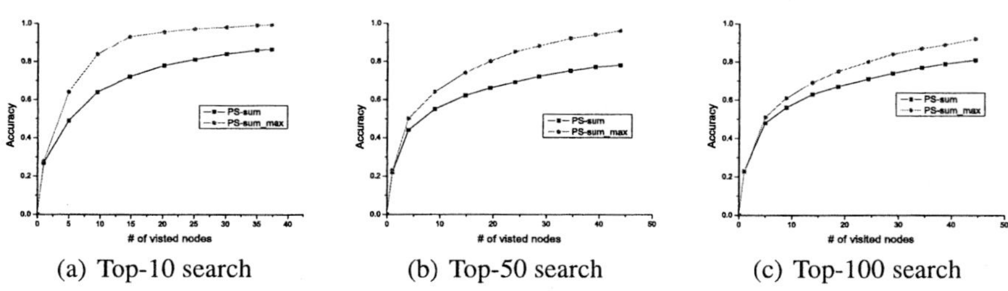

(a) Top-10 search (b) Top-50 search (c) Top-100 search

Fig. 4. Top-k search performance of KEYNOTE on a 2000-node network

the Chord overlay networks. To test the performance of our system on networks with different sizes, we scale the network size from 500 to 8,000. Four types of queries are used to evaluate the search performance of KEYNOTE: one-term , two-term , three-term and four-term. We give each of the four types the same probability to appear and generate 1, 000 queries . All the experimental results presented are obtained by averaging the results of the 1000 queries.

We measure the accuracy of our system by comparing the results returned by our system with the results from centralized searching. For each top-k query, let A be the searching result in centralized context, and B be the returned result of our system. The accuracy is defined as $\frac{|A \cap B|}{|A|}$. To test the effectiveness of our load-balancing method, we conduct the experiment both on the full Chord ring and half-full Chord ring when $m = 16$. We assume that there is one hot key in the network and a node that receives more than 100 request per time unit would become overloaded. The number of requests for the hot key ranges from 1,000 to 11,000 per time unit, and all requests are evenly distributed in the Chord ring.

Fig. 4 illustrates the top-k search performance of KEYNOTE using our two peer selection methods on a 2000-node network. Fig. 4(a) shows the performance comparison between *PS-sum* and *PS-sum_max* for the top-10 search. From Fig. 4(a) we can observe that *PS-sum_max* outperforms *PS-sum* since by visiting the same number of nodes *PS-sum_max* could return more accurate documents than *PS-sum* could. We could have the similar observation in Fig. 4(b) and Fig. 4(c). From Fig. 4, we could see that our peer selection methods are very effective in determining the relevances of each peer to the query. For the top-10 search, we could get an accuracy of 93% by visiting only 15 nodes on a 2000-node network. Even for the top-100 search, we could get an accuracy of 87% by visiting 35 nodes on a 2000-node network.

Fig. 5 shows the system performance on different network sizes. In Fig. 5 we let the accuracy be 90% and test the number of visited nodes required to achieve this accuracy on different network sizes. In Fig. 5(a), we could see that the number of visited nodes in KEYNOTE doesn't grow linearly with the network size. For the top-100 search, the system needs to visit 19 nodes when network size is 500. But when the network size is 8000 (16 $\times$ increment), the system visits only 50 nodes(2.5 $\times$ increment). For the top-10 and top-50 search, the number of visited nodes almost remains constant when the network size grows from 4,000 to 8,000. Fig. 5(b) shows that the percentage of the visited nodes to the network size decreases as the network size grows larger.

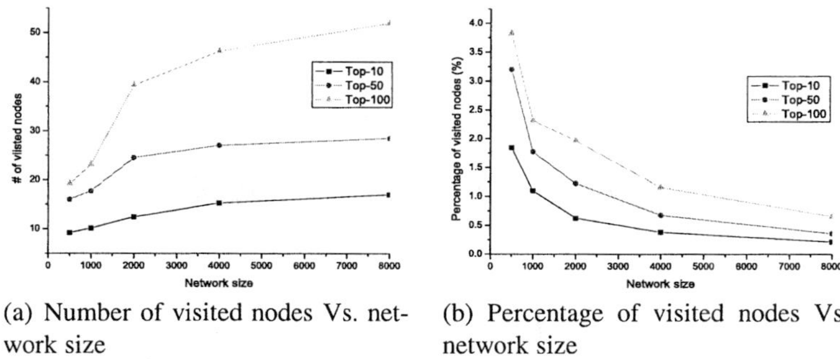

(a) Number of visited nodes Vs. network size

(b) Percentage of visited nodes Vs. network size

Fig. 5. The impact of varying network size on system performance

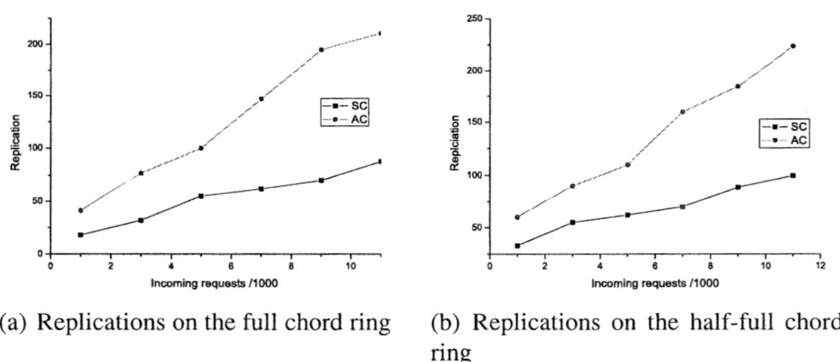

(a) Replications on the full chord ring

(b) Replications on the half-full chord ring

Fig. 6. The performance of the load balancing algorithm

Table 1. The scaled performance of top-10 search on a $6 * 10^7$-node network with $8 * 10^9$ pages

Techniques	Document-join	KEYNOTE
Total storage cost	7814GB	439GB
Averaged Comm. cost	7.03 M	541KB
Latency per query	37.5 seconds	3.0 seconds
Accuracy	100%	91%

Fig. 6 gives the performance comparison of two load balancing techniques, our "selective cache" (simply SC) method and the "all cache" (simply AC) method. We could see that our "selective cache" method uses significantly few replications to achieve load balancing than the "all cache" method both on the full Chord ring and the half-full ring.

To project the performance of our system and the document-join system for the Internet-level search, we *scale* our evaluation results to $8 * 10^9$ Web pages and $6 * 10^7$ nodes. Table 1 shows that by compromising 10% accuracy we get over $10\times$ reduction in communication and bandwidth cost as well as the search latency, which makes KEYNOTE feasible for the Internet-level search.

5 Conclusion

In this paper, we present KEYNOTE, a novel full-text search system on DHTs. By performing the join operation at node level, KEYNOTE can greatly reduce storage and bandwidth cost. For tackling the hot-spot problem on the Chord overlay, an efficient load-balance algorithm is introduced. The experimental results validate the performance of KEYNOTE and indicate the feasibility of KEYNOTE for Internet-scale search.

References

1. Li, J., Loo, B.T., Hellerstein, J., Kaashoek, F., Karger, D.R., Morris, R.: On the feasibility of peer-to-peer web indexing and search. In: Proceedings of IPTPS'03. (2003)
2. Reynolds, P., Vahdat, A.: Efficient peer-to-peer keyword searching. In: Middleware03. (2003)
3. Shi, S., Yang, G., Wang, D., Yu, J., Qu, S., Chen, M.: Making peer-to-peer keyword searching feasible using multi-level partitioning. In: Proceedings of IPTPS'04. (2004)
4. Tang, C., Dwarkadas, S.: Hybrid global-local indexing for effcient peer-to-peer information retrieval. In: Proceedings of NSDI04. (2004)
5. Stoica, I., Morris, R., Karger, D., Kaashoek, F., Balakrishnan, H.: Chord: A scalabel peer-to-peer lookup service for internet applicaitons. In: Proceedings of SIGCOMM01. (2001)
6. Cuenca-Acuna, F., Peery, C., Martin, R., Nguyen, T.: Planetp: Using gossiping to build content addressbale peer-to-peer information sharing communities. In: Proceedings of HPDC03. (2003)
7. Lu, J., Callan, J.: Content-based retrieval in hybrid peer-to-peer networks. In: Proceedings of CIKM03. (2003)
8. Tang, C., Xu, Z., Dwarkadas, S.: Peer-to-peer information retrieval using selforganizing semantic overlay networks. In: Proceedings of SIGCOMM03. (2003)
9. Ratnasamy, S., Francis, P., Handley, M., Karp, R., Shenker, S.: A scalable content addressable network. In: Proceedings of SIGCOMM01. (2001)
10. Zhong, M., Moore, J., Shen, K., Murphy, A.: An evaluation and comparison of current peer-to-peer full-text keyword search techniques. In: Proceedings of Webdb05. (2005)
11. Gravano, L., Garcia-Molina, H.: Generalizing gloss to vector-space databases and broker hierarchies. In: Proceedings of the 21st VLDB conference. (1995)
12. Dabek, F., Brunskill, E., Kaashoek, M.F., Karger, D., Morris, R., Stoica, I., Balakrishnan, H.: Building peer-to-peer systems with chord, a distributed lookup service. In: Proceedings of HotOS-VIII. (2001)
13. Zhang, Z., Zhou, S., Qian, W., Zhou, A.: KEYNOTE: Keyword search using node selection for text retrieval on DHT-based P2P networks. Technical report, Fudan University (2005)

How to BLAST Your Database — A Study of Stored Procedures for BLAST Searches

Uwe Röhm and Thanh-Mai Diep

University of Sydney, School of Information Technologies,
Sydney NSW 2006, Australia

Abstract. Stored procedures are an important feature of all major database systems that allows to execute application logic within database servers. This paper reports on experiences to implement a popular scientific algorithm, the Basic Local Alignment Search Tool (BLAST), as stored procedures within a relational database. We implemented the un-gapped, nucleotide version of the BLAST algorithm with four different relational database engines, both commercial and open source. In an experimental evaluation, we compared our *dbBLAST* implementations with a standard file-based BLAST implementation from NCBI with regard to the implementation effort, runtime performance, and scalability. It shows that although our dbBLAST runs faster than the file-based BLAST program for short query sequences, all implementations lack scalability. However, the results also indicate that stored procedures require significant less development effort—both in time and space—than traditional programming approaches.

1 Introduction

The objective of this paper is to investigate the suitability of today's database systems for scientific computing, and to identify possible shortcomings of database engines for those applications. We concentrate on relational database systems. As an example application, we take the basic local alignment search tool (BLAST) for gene sequence databases [1, 2]. The idea is to store the sequence data in a database and to implement the standard BLAST algorithm *within* the database systems using stored procedures.

All major commercial database engines support stored procedures and even some open source database systems recently extended into this direction (e.g. PostgreSQL 8 or MySQL 5). The 'traditional' stored procedure capability in the spirit of the SQL/PSM standard is basically an extension of SQL with statement grouping, local variables, control flow and condition statements [3, 4]. Besides, there is also the possibility of externally defined stored procedures written in a 3GL programming language — for example in C, Java, or recently also any language supported by the common language runtime (CLR) of .NET.

The main benefits of stored procedures are reduced communication between client and server, and better code maintainability. In the context of scientific computing, stored procedures are interesting because they allow the implementation of data analysis algorithms beyond the capabilities of SQL queries, and to run those tasks near the data analysed. In addition, it would introduce set-oriented processing and declarative querying, both of which would be very benefitial in scientific programs. The main contributions of this paper are as follows:

M.L. Lee, K.L. Tan, and V. Wuwongse (Eds.): DASFAA 2006, LNCS 3882, pp. 807–816, 2006.

- We developed a database-centric version of the BLAST algorithm, called *dbBLAST*, using stored procedures and an optimised physical design for relational databases.
- We implemented *dbBLAST* with different relational database systems — three commercial DBMS, and one open source DBMS (PostgreSQL 8) — and report on our experiences doing so.
- In a quantitative evaluation, we compared our four *dbBLAST* implementations with a state-of-the-art, file-based BLAST program from NCBI.
- Based on our experiences and evaluation results, we make suggestions for further improvements of database engines to better support scientific database applications.

Please note that we do not strive to improve or replace the BLAST algorithm itself. Rather we take this well established algorithm as given and implement it using a different technology, namely with 4GL programming languages inside a database.

Our main results are that we could implement the BLAST algorithm much faster and shorter using stored procedures than using a 'traditional' programming language such as C. At least for shorter query sequences, dbBLAST is also faster than NCBI-BLAST, but it is significantly less scalable. This can be mainly attributed to the limited support of extensive string processing and the weak integration of stored procedures within the query processor of current database engines. There were also significant performance differences between the database systems used. But although dbBLAST in its current form lacks scalability, it successfully demonstrates the power of declarative querying for scientific computing, and how to enrich pure BLAST searches with access to all meta-data of the stored sequence database.

2 The Basic Local Alignment Search Tool

The Basic Local Alignment Search Tool (BLAST) is an algorithm which searches a nucleotide or protein sequence database for matches to a given nucleotide or protein sequence [1]. The search is based on local similarity, that is, it aligns two sequences based on short segments of relatively conserved subsequences. This algorithm is widely used in bioinformatics to identify sequence homology. It consists of two phases:

Phase 1 – Finding Hot Spots. In the first phase of BLAST, the query sequence is broken down into smaller subsequences known as *words* of length w. A protein sequence database is searched for *hot spots*, local subsequences which exactly match a query word or are 'related' to a query word. A related word is equal in length to a query word and has a similarity score above or equal to a threshold value t. On the other hand, hot spots in a nucleotide database are exact matches to the query words. Alignment scores are calculated using a substitution matrix in the case of proteins. In the case of nucleotides, a reward value (positive) is given for a pair of matching bases and a penalty value (negative) is given for a pair of mismatched bases. Scores for each individual pair of aligned residues are summated to give the total score.

Phase 2 – Hot Spot Extension. For each *hot spot* found, the alignment comparison is extended in both directions for both query and database sequences, attempting to find a maximal segment pair (MSP): that is a segment pair with a maximum score over all segment pairs of sequences in comparison. The extension of hot spots in one direction is terminated when either one of the sequences reached its ends, or when the score of the segment pair falls below x number of arbitrary units below the best score yet found. On completion, the algorithm reports all MSPs found during this process with substitution matrix score above a cut-off score s, called the *high-scoring pairs* (HSP). The extension step usually accounts for over 90% of NCBI-BLAST's execution time [2].

2.1 NCBI-BLAST

There are several highly optimised, file-based implementations of the BLAST algorithms available [9, 5]; one of the most popular is from the National Center for Biotechnology Information (NCBI) [9]. NCBI-BLAST runs as a standalone program that scans the entire nucleotide or protein sequence databases in order to search for matches to an input sequence. Note that in the context of NCBI-BLAST, 'database' actually means a compressed binary file containing the sequence data. NCBI-BLAST differs in a few notable aspects from the original BLAST algorithm as published in [1]:

- NCBI-BLAST searches for both the query nucleotide sequence and its complementary strand due to the double stranded nature of DNA. The query sequence may match a nucleotide sequence in the database as is, or be the complement of a nucleotide sequence.
- NCBI-BLAST finds *hot spots* by searching for exact matches between query words and a corresponding subsequence from a nucleotide database. This means that it does not do an initial similarity match using a substitution matrix and that the t threshold is actually ignored.
- The implementation contains an optimisation that avoids extensions leading to an already identified MSP. Before NCBI-BLAST extends a hot spot, it checks whether it lies within an already found MSP. Such hot spots would extend to the very same MSP and hence are discarded.

NCBI-BLAST is implemented in C and compiles on every major operating system. The distribution also includes a *formatdb* tool which must be run first to prepare the sequence 'database' for processing. Formatdb takes sequences in FASTA format and does a straight-forward bit-compression on the nucleotide sequences: every base is encoded with two bits. Some nucleotide sequences have degenerate symbols which represent a set of nucleotides (such as 'N', which denotes 'A, 'T', 'C' OR 'G'). As two bits can encode only four different symbols, NCBI-BLAST actually ignores those degenerated symbols and replaces them with a randomly selected one.

3 dbBLAST: BLAST Using Stored Procedures

We have developed a database-centric version of the well established BLAST algorithm using a relational database management system, containing both code and the sequence data (including all other data such as sequence origin and modification date, source organism, article references, etc.). This way, our solution can easily enrich the sequences with any sequence details, e.g., where the matches have been published. In order to be able to compare the performance of this *dbBLAST* approach with NCBI-BLAST, we followed the implementation specifics of it as much as possible. However, only the nucleotide search was implemented, for the sake of simplicity.

3.1 Database Design

The central idea of the database design for dbBLAST is to avoid scanning the whole database for a query. This is achieved in two ways: First, we introduce an inverted index over all sequences in the database. Secondly, the sequence data is segmented so that not the whole sequence data has to be loaded into the database buffer to check a possible hit, but only the segment matching with a query word.

Inverted Index. The inverted index utilises ideas from text-based information retrieval for sequence indexing [6]. Every w-residue word found in the database is indexed in a `Words` table. A second `WordIndex` table holds the inverted index with the exact occurrences (sequence IDs and residue index) of each indexed word. This indexing approach is feasible because the database is updated only very infrequently (and then, mostly insertions). A drawback is that for each queried word length w an own inverted index is needed.

Sequence Segmenting. Sequences can become very long — e.g. in the human genome database, sequences consisting of several ten thousands of base pairs are not uncommon. This means that BLAST has to handle sequence attributes of several kilobytes size and one needs string manipulation functions to access individual characters and substrings within them. The solution of dbBLAST is to partition each database sequence into smaller segments which fit one string attribute[1]. The extension phase of the BLAST algorithm normally does not need access to the whole sequence; rather, it extends hot spots just a few dozen residues to the left and to the right to find a MSP. Hence, the chances are high that we can find the complete MSP within one segment. Additionally, our dbBLAST implementations do also include a 'paging' algorithm which allows us to extend MSPs which span more than one segment.

3.2 dbBLAST Implementation

The BLAST algorithm is implemented as a set of stored procedures inside the database server. The front-end is the `blastn()` function that can be called with a query sequence and the central BLAST parameters[2] as arguments. The two central problems for implementing BLAST as stored procedure are that the query sequences can potentially become very long, and that the algorithm's result is set-valued. Ideally, database systems should support arbitrarily sized strings as parameters and either set-valued output parameters or return values. However, both features are not very common in today's systems. Hence, our approach returns the matches, depending on the host database capabilities, either as a multi-valued return value, or they are stored in a table in the database from which they have to be retrieved by the caller. The dbBLAST algorithm is organised in five steps:

[1] Depending on the DBMS engine, we had to use either 4KB or 8KB segments.

[2] *reward* and *penalty* values and s, t, and x thresholds.

Step 1: Query Preparation. First, it computes the complement of the query sequence (cf. NCBI-BLAST description). Then, both the original query sequence and its complement are split into m words of length w. This word list is stored in a temporary table(or, where possible, in a local table variable) for further processing.

Step 2: Hot-Spot Search. In the next step, the set of hot spots candidates in the sequence database is identified. Here, dbBLAST makes use of the inverted index — basically, it is a join between the query words table and the inverted index table. Please note that similar to NCBI-BLAST, our algorithm searches for exact matches.

Step 3: Duplicate Check. Similar to the approach taken by NCBI-BLAST, dbBLAST tries to minimise the number of extensions by checking for each hot spot candidate whether it lies within the boundaries of an extension that has already been made. If that is the case, the hot spot candidate is discarded and no extension will be done.

Step 4: MSP Extension. This step corresponds to phase two of the BLAST algorithm and is the computationally most expensive step. For every hot spot found, the matching sequence segment is retrieved from the database and a MSP is attempted to be found by extending the match into both directions. If the match extends beyond the segment's border, the adjacent segment is paged in. If the resulting MSP has a score exceeding the cut-off threshold s, it is inserted into the results table. Whenever possible, either a local table or table variable is used for this.

Step 5: Result Output. The entries in the result table are returned as return value of the call to `blastn()`. In the case that a system does not support table-valued stored procedures, clients have to explicitly request the results.

3.3 Stored Procedure Capabilities of Different Database Engines

We implemented dbBLAST on three commercial database management systems, in the following anonymously referred to as DBMS A, DBMS B, and DBMS C, and on PostgreSQL 8. Due to limited space, we only can give a short overview of the implementation details here; the interested reader finds a more detailed discussion in [7].

DBMS A. dbBLAST has been implemented on the first commerical DBMS with separate stored procedures for each step. Due to a size limitations of character strings in that system, the database sequences are segmented into 4 KB segments. The implementation makes use of join-hints in both step 2 (hot-spot search) and 3 (duplicate check). As DBMS A does not directly support table-valued functions, the results are inserted into a persistent table to be retrieved later by clients.

DBMS B. We implemented dbBLAST on commercial DBMS B in its proprietary 4GL language. As an interesting feature, DBMS B allows for set-valued local variables. The words of the query sequence are stored and processed in such a local table variable. The database sequences were segmented into 8KB segments, and all sequence processing could be programmed using VARCHARs. The high-scoring pairs are collected in a local table variable and returned to the client as a table-valued result.

DBMS C. We implemented dbBLAST on a third commercial DBMS, referred to as DBMS C, that supports stored procedures hosted in a CLR runtime environment. We used a combination of the internal 4GL language and CLR managed functions written in

C# for the most time-consuming part of BLAST: The MSP extension step. Syntactically and from the development side, this integration was quite straight forward. However, DBMS C only provides pass-by-value for arguments of .NET stored procedures, which requires additional copying of the query sequence and the database segments.

PostgreSQL 8. We were also interested in the comparison with an open source database supporting stored procedures. Hence, dbBLAST has also been implemented in PostgreSQL 8 using PL/pgSQL stored procedures, respectively stored functions. The query words are stored in a temporary table, and the database sequences are segmented into 8KB segments. The `blastn()` function is actually table-valued: the results are returned as table where the matching query and database sequence sections are shown.

4 Evaluation

4.1 Experimental Setup

The following performance and scalability tests were performed on a standard PC server with a 3 GHz Pentium 4 CPU (with hyper-threading enabled) and 2GB RAM under Microsoft Windows Server 2003 Standard Edition. For each test, the only database system running was the system under test. The test database was populated with 5217 nucleotide sequences from the Lycopersicon esculentum genome (tomato) as found in the `nc1130` data file obtained from the GenBank database. As a base line, we compare our dbBLAST implementations with NCBI-BLAST version 2.2.10 that is configured to run under version 1.4 settings (ungapped, single hit).

4.2 Implementation Efforts

The BLAST algorithm was implemented by the same programmer in four different relational database engines using the available stored procedure facilities. We kept track of the development time and the code size for all five implementations and compared them with the approximate values for NCBI-BLAST. The implementation efforts with all database systems (DBMS A, B, C, and PostgeSQL) are very comparable: all have a program complexity of about 500 lines of code with only one to three days development time for an experienced developer (cf. [7]).

The results indicate that database stored procedures require significant less development effort – both in time and space – than traditional programming based on low-level file access and 3GL programming languages such as C. We attribute this to the higher abstraction levels and set-oriented interfaces available in stored procedure languages. We should also note that for a more meaningful conclusions one would need to conduct a more formalised investigation with different programmers and also a more comparable BLAST implementation in C.

4.3 Response Times and Scalability

We are interested in the response times and the scalability of the different implementations. We have measured the response times of each implementation for different query lengths from 20 up to 8000 base pairs. For each query length, five different randomly

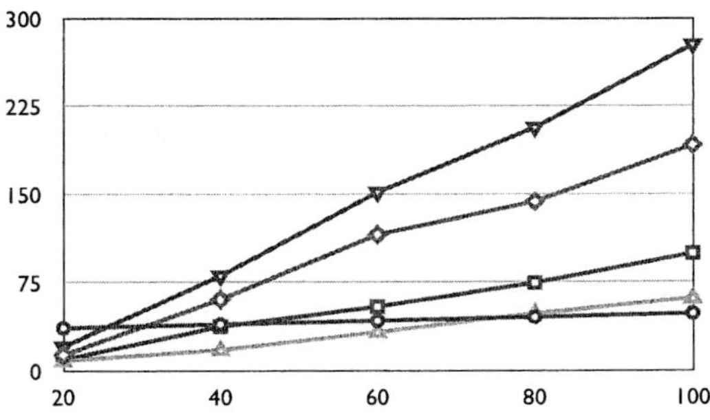

Fig. 1. Response times for small query sequences

generated queries have been executed. The numbers in Figures 1 and 2 are the averages over five executions of those five random queries. The same set of queries has been executed by all databases for consistency.

Figure 1 shows the response times for small query sequences between 20 and 100 base pairs. Because BLAST has a runtime complexity of $O(nm)$, all implementations show a linear increase of their response time with the query length (including NCBI-BLAST although the increase is almost invisible). The gradient of the curves however varies depending on the runtime efficiency of the different implementations. We will give a more detailed analysis of that in the next section.

Of the dbBLAST implementations, PostgeSQL shows the slowest performance, followed by DBMS A, B and C. DBMS C is just a bit slower than DBMS B but scales much worse as can be seen in the results of the scalability test in Figure 2. A promising result is that in particular DBMS B shows a very comparable, up to query length 60 even better performance than NCBI BLAST. So far the approach of reducing the search space by filtering of hot spots through an inverted index works. Please note again that NCBI BLAST is a highly-optimised C-program running on a 3 GHz machine with lots of main memory — certainly a tough competitor for a database solution.

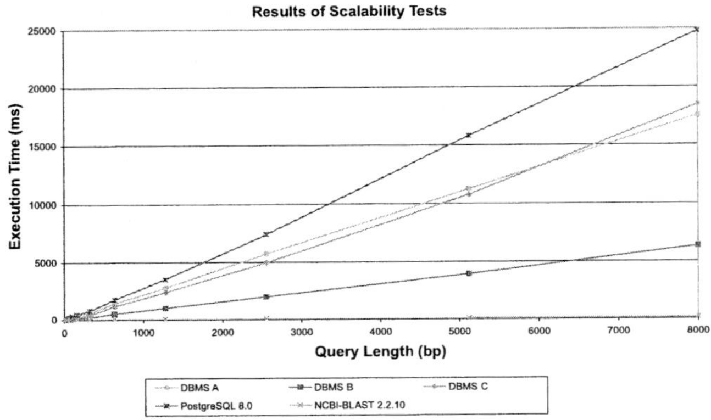

Fig. 2. Scalability of response times

Figure 2 shows the results of our scalability test, i.e. the response times for query lengths up to 8000 base pairs. The trends seen in the previous chart become now much clearer. The slowest implementation of dbBLAST is on PostgeSQL. Then follows DBMS A and DBMS C, both of which show very similar performances for larger queries. Interestingly, the DBMS C is significantly slower DBMS B, despite the fact that it implemented the computational intensive expansion-phase in .NET. However, one should note that we could not evaluate a release version.

Finally, NCBI-BLAST shows the best scalability with the lowest runtime increase, clearly outperforming all stored procedure implementations for larger queries longer than 60 base pairs. This is not too much of a surprise because the test database fits completely into main memory.

4.4 Execution Time Analysis

In Figure 3 we analyse how much of the total execution time had been spent in the different parts of the dbBLAST algorithm (query length was 1280 base pairs). Finding possible hot-spots through the inverted index is actually a very fast step for most database system: the *hot-spot search* phase is basically a join between the inverted index and the query words table. The only exemption is PostgreSQL. It originally suffered even worse from the sub-optimal decisions of its query optimizer that always chose an join plan involving a complete scan through the (quite large) inverted index table[3]. In the end, we manually programmed an index-nested loop join in the stored procedure using a cursor. As the result in Figure 3 shows, still a far from optimal work-around.

The largest part with 50-80% of the total execution time attributes to the *MSP extension* phase of the BLAST algorithm. This is the computationally expensive part that mainly consists of string operations and accesses to single character positions — a usage pattern only very rudimentary supported by current stored procedure implementations. It also depends linearly on the query length — the longer the query, the more words, i.e., possible hits to check and to expand. Hence, it is here where the performance of the implementations could be improved most.

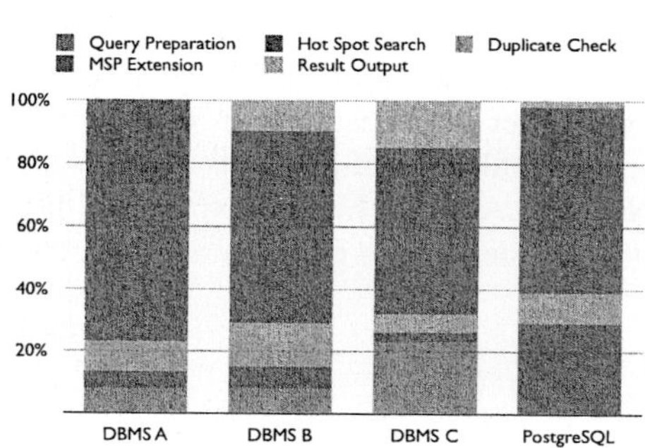

Fig. 3. Execution times of dbBLAST steps

The second crucial part for the performance and scalability of dbBLAST is the *duplicate check*. This is actually an optimisation borrowed from the NCBI-BLAST implementation which checks, for each hot spot candidate, whether it lies in a previously computed match. An extension is performed only if the hot spot candidate has not already been reported. As the *MSP extension*, this phase depends linearly on the length of the query sequence. It could be much improved if one could combine this check with the

[3] One reason might be that PostgreSQL does not maintain statistics on indexes [8].

previous finding hits query. Unfortunately, this is not supported by current database engines because the results table is modified within the expansion step and today's query engines don't allow side-effects on queried tables. So in the current implementations, the duplicate check is done by separate queries on the results table for each word in the query sequence.

The remaining phases of the algorithm, query preparation and result output, are of minor impact on the overall runtime. The query preparation time in DBMS C is larger than that of DBMS B because it was using a persistent table for the query words, while the DBMS B implementation, although functionally very similar, was using a table variable in the stored procedure. DBMS A does not show an explicit time for the result output because it does not support table-valued stored procedures — rather dbBLAST did leave the matches in a result table which has to be scanned by the caller in an additional step.

5 Related Work

Oracle included both nucleotide and protein BLAST searches in their latest ODM data mining component for Oracle 10g [10, 11, 12]. The algorithm is implemented by means of table-valued stored procedures and using the Oracle Data Cartridge Interface. In contrast to this work, there are no optimisations to the physical database design such as an inverted index on the possible hotspots or a paging for the sequences. Instead, sequences are always stored as CLOBs. Unfortunately, it was not possible to compare it with the presented three implementations on DBMS A, B, and C.

Recently, the Laboratory of Neuro Imaging at UCLA did publish *BLASTgres*, an extension of PostgreSQL with biological datatypes such as particularly sequence ranges and locations, and BLAST functions [13]. In contrast to our work, BLASTgres concentrates on leveraging user-defined datatypes and tree-structured indexes (i.e. PostgreSQL's GiST index) to support biological algorithms, while dbBLAST is using standard SQL datatypes and an optimized database schema incorporating an inverted index.

A number of different research groups have developed BLAST with the use of grid technologies, e.g, [14, 15, 16]. The focus is here typically on the parallelisation of the BLAST computation over several grid nodes. Some systems even use one of the standard BLAST implementations on each of the participating sites [17]. However, in none of these approaches does database technology play any major role. Only in a different context (astronomy) one recent work did successfully combine grid and database technologies: [18] discusses an SQL-implementation of the data-intensive MaxBCG algorithm that finds galaxy clusters in a large astronomical database.

Stored procedures themselves have been covered only very rarely in the database community, at least lately. [19] discussed some techniques for developing Enterprise JavaBeans (EJBs) to leverage existing database stored procedures for use in web applications. This is exactly the opposite approach to this paper which strives to implement an algorithm already existing outside the DBMS into the database. Recently, Microsoft did give an overview of the integration of the .NET CLR within its upcoming version of SQL Server [20]. A good overview of the SQL/PSM standard is given by Melton in [4], of which a kind of executive summary can be found in [3].

6 Conclusions

We presented dbBLAST, a database-centric version of the popular BLAST algorithm for sequence alignment search. Our approach leverages the stored procedures capabilities of today's relational database engines and used an optimised physical design with an inverted index over the (segmented) sequence database.

In a prototype study, we compared different implementations of dbBLAST with regard to implementation complexity and runtime performance. For smaller query sizes of up to 60 base pairs, dbBLAST was faster than the file-based NCBI-BLAST, but it was lacking the scalability of a file-based BLAST search. We showed that this is mainly due to the computationally expensive step in the BLAST computation. Current stored procedure implementations obviously have problems with efficient processing of large character strings. But it also showed that we could implement the BLAST algorithm much faster and more compact using stored procedures than using a 3GL language.

References

1. Altschul, S.F., Gish, W., Miller, W., Myers, E.W., Lipman, D.J.: Basic local alignment search tool. Journal of Molecular Biology **215** (1990) 403–410
2. Altschul, S.F., et al.: Gapped Blast and PSI-Blast: a new generation of protein database search programs. Nucleic Acids Research **25** (1997) 3389–3402
3. Eisenberg, A.: New standard for stored procedures in sql. ACM SIGMOD Record **25** (1996)
4. Melton, J.: Understanding sql stored procedures: a complete guide to sql/psm. M.K. (1998)
5. NCBI: NCBI-BLAST. (URL: http://www.ncbi.nlm.nih.gov/BLAST)
6. Grossmann, D.A., Friedler, O.: Information Retrieval: Algorithms and Heuristics. Kuwler Academic Publishers (1998)
7. Diep, T.M., Röhm, U.: dbBLAST: A comparison study of BLAST implementations with stored procedures in different RDBMS. Technical report, University of Sydney. (2006)
8. The PostgreSQL Global Development Group: PostgreSQL 8.0.1 documentation.
9. Washington University: WU-BLAST 2.0. (URL: http://blast.wustl.edu/blast/)
10. Stephens, S., Chen, J.Y., Thomas, S.: ODM BLAST: Sequence homology search in the RDBMS. IEEE Data Engineering Bulletin **27** (2004) 20–23
11. Stephens, S., et al.: Oracle Database 10g: A platform for BLAST search and regular expression pattern matching in life sciences. Nucleic Acids Research **33** (2005) D675–D679
12. Oracle Coorp.: Oracle Data Mining Application Developer's Guide 10g Release 1. (2004)
13. Laboratory of Neuro Imaging (LONI): BLASTgres User Guide. UCLA. 1.0 edn. (2005)
14. Liu, Y.: Grid-BLAST: Building a cyberinfrastructure for large-scale comparative genomics research. In: 2003 Virtual Conference on Genomics and Bioinformatics. (2003)
15. Konishi, F., Shiroto, Y., Umetsu, R., Konagaya: A scalable BLAST service in OBIGrid environment. Genome Informatics **14** (2003) 535–536
16. Chen, C.W., Röhm, U.: A service-oriented approach for parallelising data-intensive algorithms in grid-enabled cluster. In: 1st Int. Workshop on Biomedical Data Engineering. (2005)
17. Krishnan, A.: GridBLAST: A globus based high-throughput implementation of BLAST in a grid framework. In: Concurrency and Computation: Practice and Experience. (2000) 1–7
18. Nieto-Santisteban, M.A., Gray, J., et al.: When database systems meet the grid. In: 2nd Biennial Conference on Innovative Data Systems Research (CIDR). (2005) 154–161
19. Saracco, C.M.: Leveraging stored procedures through enterprise javabeans. IBM (2000)
20. Acheson, A., et al.: Hosting the .NET runtime in Microsoft SQL server. In: Proceedings of the 23th ACM SIGMOD Int. Conf. on Management of Data, Paris, France. (2004) 860–865

DTD-Diff: A Change Detection Algorithm for DTDs

Erwin Leonardi[1], Tran T. Hoai[1], Sourav S. Bhowmick[1], and Sanjay Madria[2]

[1] School of Computer Engineering,
Nanyang Technological University, Singapore
[2] Department of Computer Science,
University of Missouri-Rolla, MO 65409, USA
{pk909134, assourav}@ntu.edu.sg, madrias@umr.edu

Abstract. The DTD of a set of XML documents may change due to many reasons such as changes to the real world events, changes to the user's requirements, and mistakes in the initial design. In this paper, we present a novel algorithm called DTD-Diff to detect the changes to DTDs that defines the structure of a set of XML documents. Such change detection tool can be useful in several ways such as maintenance of XML documents, incremental maintenance of relational schema for storing XML data, and XML schema integration. We compare DTD-Diff with existing XML change detection approaches and show that converting DTD to XML Schema (XSD) (which is in XML document format) and detecting the changes using existing XML change detection algorithms is not a feasible option. Our experimental results show that DTD-Diff is 5–325 times faster than X-Diff when it detects the changes to the XSD files. We also study the result quality of detected deltas.

1 Introduction

XML has emerged as the leading textual language for representing and exchanging data over the Web. In many applications a schema (i.e., *Document Type Definition* (DTD) or *XML schema* (XSD) [3] is associated with a set of XML documents to define their legal structures. Schema of such XML documents may also need to be updated to reflect a change in the real world, a change in the user's requirements, mistakes in the initial design, etc. For example, consider the DTD D_1 in Figure 1(a) at time t_1. It may evolve to D_2 (Figure 1(b)) at time t_2 because the university may wish to restructure the information due to change in the university administrators' requirements. Such DTD change detection tools can be useful in maintenance of XML documents when their DTD evolves, incremental maintenance of relational schema of the schema-conscious approach [9] for storing XML data, XML schema integration, etc. Let us elaborate further on the usage of DTD change detection tool in maintenance of XML documents. Let X be a set of XML documents where each document $x_i \in X$ conforms to DTD D. Assume that due to mistakes in the initial design, D is modified to D'. Consequently, $x_i \in X$ may not conform to D' anymore. Therefore, it is necessary

M.L. Lee, K.L. Tan, and V. Wuwongse (Eds.): DASFAA 2006, LNCS 3882, pp. 817–827, 2006.

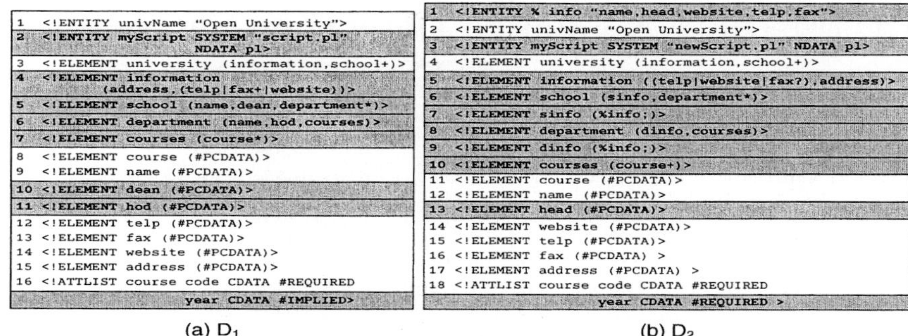

Fig. 1. Two versions of a DTD

to detect the differences between D and D' (denoted by $\triangle(D,D')$) *automatically* so that it can be used to transform $x_i \in X$ to x'_i such that x'_i conforms to D'.

In this paper, we propose a novel algorithm, called DTD-DIFF, for detecting the changes to DTDs. *To the best of our knowledge, this is the first approach that addresses the DTD change detection problem.* At first glance, it may seem that the DTD change detection problem can easily be addressed by existing change detection tools for XML documents [6, 7, 10]. Specifically, we can first transform DTDs to XSD files that are in XML format. Then, the changes to the DTDs can be detected using existing XML change detection tools (such as X-Diff [10] and XyDiff [6]). Although this approach will clearly detect changes, we argue that they suffer from these following limitations: *granularity of types of changes*, *inability to detect changes to both unordered and ordered nodes*, *detection of semantically incorrect changes*, *generation of non-optimal edit scripts*, and *performance bottleneck*. The details can be found in [8].

In summary, the main contributions of this paper are as follows. (1) In Section 2, we present data model to represent the changes to DTDs. By using this data model we are able to detect the changes to DTDs, that are discussed Section 3, correctly. (2) In Section 4, we propose a novel algorithm called DTD-DIFF for detecting the changes to DTDs. The algorithm takes as input two versions of a DTD that are represented using our DTD data model and detects the changes *directly* without converting them to XSD format. (3) Through an extensive experimental study in Section 5, we show that our approach is 5–325 times faster than X-Diff [10]. Note that in our study, we convert DTDs to XSD files prior to employing X-Diff to detect the changes.

2 DTD Data Model

A DTD consists of *entity declaration* (`<!ENTITY ...>`), *element type declaration* (`<!ELEMENT ...>`), and *attribute declaration* (`<!ATTLIST ...>`) that describe entities, elements, and attributes, respectively. Formally,

Definition 1 [DTD]. *A DTD is a 3-tuple $D = (\mathcal{E}, \mathcal{A}, \mathcal{G})$ where $\mathcal{E}$ is a set of Element Type Declarations (ETD) in D, $\mathcal{A}$ is a set of Attribute Declarations*

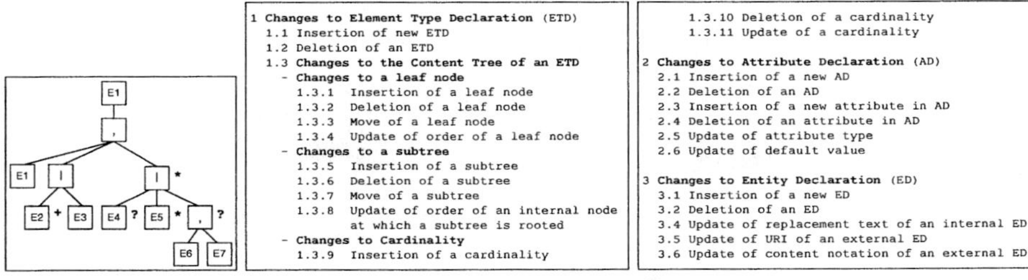

(a) Content Tree (b) Types of changes

Fig. 2. Content Tree and Type of Changes

(AD) in D, $\mathcal{G}$ is a set of internal and external Entity Declarations (ED). Also, if the numbers of ETDs, ADs, and EDs in a DTD are α, β, and γ then $|\mathcal{E}| = \alpha$, $|\mathcal{A}| = \beta$, and $|\mathcal{G}| = \gamma$. □

For example, consider the DTD D_2 in Figure 1(b). Lines 1-3, 4-17, and 18 are examples of EDs, ETDs, and AD, respectively.

Element Type Declaration (ETD): In a DTD, XML elements are declared using element type declaration. Each element type declaration E has a *name* N_E and *element content* C_E. For example, consider the DTD D_1 in Figure 1(a). The name and the content of element type `school` (line 5) are `school` and `(name,dean,department*)`, respectively. Observe that *element content* can be very complex with multiple levels of nesting. For example, `<!ELEMENT E1 (E1,(E2+|E3),(E4?|E5*|(E6,E7)?)*)>`. We represent the element content C_E as a *content tree* T_E. For example, consider the element type declaration `<!ELEMENT E1 (E1,(E2+|E3), (E4?|E5*| (E6,E7)?)*)>`. The content tree T_{E1} is depicted in Figure 2(a). Note that in an element content C_E we may have *sequence* (denoted by ",") and *choice* (denoted by "|") groups of elements. Observe that the elements in a *sequence* group must be ordered, and the order of elements in *choice* group is not significant. That is, a *content tree* T_E may have *ordered* and *unordered* parts.

Attribute Declaration (AD): The attribute declaration in a DTD is used to define the attributes of an element. Each AD A has a *name* N_A of element type to which a set of attributes S_A belongs. Each attribute a in the attribute set S_A has a *name* N_a, *type* Y_a, and an optional *default value* D_a. For example, reconsider D_1 in Figure 1(a). The attribute declaration of element type `course` is in line 16. The type of data and default value of the attribute `code` are `CDATA` and `#REQUIRED`, respectively.

Entity Declaration (ED): Entities are variables used to define shortcuts to common text. Entity references are references to entities. We have two kinds of entities: *general entity* and *parameter entity*. Consider DTD D_2 as depicted in Figure 1(b). Line 1 is an example of *parameter entity*. An example of *general entity* is in line 2. Note that we only consider the general entities. This is because the parameter entities automatically replace the entity references. Entities can be declared as *internal* or *external*. An *internal* ED I has a *name* N_I and a *replacement text* R_I. On the other hand, an *external* ED J has a *name* N_J, *universal resource indicator (URI)* U_J, and a *content notation* P_J. For example, in D_2 line 2 is an example of an internal ED. The name and replacement text of this entity are `univName` and `"Open University"`, respectively. Line 3 (Figure 1(b)) is an example of an external ED. The name, URI, and content notation are `MyScript`, `"Script1.pl"`, and `"pl"`, respectively. The details on the DTD data model can be found in [8].

3 Types of Changes

A set of DTD changes that can be detected by DTD-DIFF is depicted in Figure 2(b). We notice that a DTD indeed has richer of types of changes compared to XML documents. In DTD, we have types of changes for cardinalities of elements, more meaningful types of changes for AD and ED, etc. The details of each type of changes depicted in Figure 2(b) can be found in [8]. In this section, we only briefly discuss two issues regarding the types of changes to DTDs.

Update of Node/Attribute Name: We do not consider update of node/ attribute name for the following reason. Consider the ETDs `school` in D_1 and D_2. We cannot consider that the name of element "`name`" is updated to "`sinfo`" and element "`dean`" is deleted as it will lead us to have a delta that is semantically incorrect. On the other hand, suppose we have a "`lastname`" element whose name is updated to "`surname`". DTD-DIFF detects as a deletion of element "`lastname`" and an insertion of element "`surname`" as we do not have information of semantic relationships between "`lastname`" and "`surname`". Note that the delta is still correct even though the result quality is reduced. Therefore, we consider the update of node/attribute name as a pair of deletion and insertion of a node in order to avoid semantically incorrect deltas in some cases.

Changes to Entity Type: If an entity g is changed from being an *internal entity* to being an *external entity*, or vice versa, then we consider as a pair of a deletion of an entity and an insertion of an entity.

4 DTD-Diff Algorithm

In this section, we present the DTD-DIFF algorithm. The outline of the algorithm is depicted in Figure 3(a). It takes as input two DTDs $D_1 = (\mathcal{E}_1, \mathcal{A}_1, \mathcal{G}_1)$ and $D_2 = (\mathcal{E}_2, \mathcal{A}_2, \mathcal{G}_2)$ representing old and new versions of a DTD and returns an edit script Z containing the differences between D_1 and D_2. The algorithm consists of six phases (Figure 3(a)). We shall discuss each phase in turns.

The Parsing and Hashing Phase: Given two DTDs, D_1 and D_2, DTD-DIFF parses D_1 and D_2 into $(\mathcal{T}_1, \mathcal{A}_1, \mathcal{G}_1)$ and $(\mathcal{T}_2, \mathcal{A}_2, \mathcal{G}_2)$ respectively and computes their hash values. Note that $\mathcal{T}_1$ and $\mathcal{T}_2$ are two sets of content trees of $\mathcal{E}_1$ and $\mathcal{E}_2$, respectively. Since content tree of an element type declaration has both *ordered*

```
Input:  DTD D1=(E1,A1,G1)
        DTD D2=(E2,A2,G2)
Output: Edit Script Z

  /* Phase 1:
     Parsing and Hashing */
  (TE1,A1,G1) <-- ParseHash(D1)
  (TE2,A2,G2) <-- ParseHash(D2)
  /* Phase 2: Finding the changes
     to element type declaration */
  FOR EACH t1 IN TE1 DO
    FOR EACH t2 IN TE2 DO
      IF t1 and t2 has the same name
       THEN
        Mmin <-- Matching(t1,t2)
        BREAK
      END IF
    END FOR
  END FOR
  /* Phase 3: Detect Move Operation */
  Mmin <-- DetectMove(TE1, TE2, Mmin)
  /* Phase 4: Finding the changes to
     attribute declaration */
  Mmin <-- DetectAttributeChanges(A1 , A2 )
  /* Phase 5: Finding the changes to
     entity declaration */
  Mmin <-- DetectEntityChanges( G1 , G2 )
  /* Phase 6: Generating Edit scripts */
  Z <-- GenerateEditScripts(Mmin)
  RETURN Z
```

(a) Outline of DTDDiff Algorithm

```
Input: Node N
Output: The hash value of node N

IF N is leaf node THEN
  RETURN MD5Value(label(N) • cardinality(N))
ELSE IF N is non-leaf node THEN
  conentenated_text = empty text
  FOR EACH child IN children OF N
    CalculateHashValue ( child )
  END FOR
  IF N is choice group THEN
    sort children of N by their hash values
  END IF
  FOR EACH child IN children OF N
    conentenated_text •= HashValue(child)
  END FOR
  conentenated_text •= label(N) • cardinality(N)
  RETURN MD5Value(conentenated_text)
END IF
```

(b) The *CalculateHashValue* Algorithm

Fig. 3. Outline of DTD-DIFF Algorithm and The *CalculateHashValue* Algorithm

```
Input: Two root node r1 and r2
Output: a set of matching pairs M

M = empty set
push pair {r1,r2} into queue Q
WHILE (Q is not empty)
  pop a pair {r1,r2} from queue Q
  M = M ∪ {r1,r2}
  IF HashValue(r1)<>HashValue(r2) AND
       N1, N2 are non-leaf nodes THEN
     /* compute the cost of matching every
        pair of child nodes of r1 and r2 */
    FOR EACH child1 IN children of r1
      FOR EACH child2 IN children of r2
        IF label(child1)=label(child2) THEN
          ComputeCost(child1, child2)
        ELSE
          Cost(child1,child2) = ∞
        END IF
      END FOR
    END FOR
    matched_pairs = set of pairs resulting from
        minimum-cost bipartite-matching among
        child nodes of r1 and r2
    FOR EACH pair{x,y} IN matched_pairs
      push pair{x,y} into queue Q
    END FOR
  END IF
END WHILE
RETURN M
```

Fig. 4. The *Matching* Algorithm

and *unordered* parts (the child nodes of the sequence and choice groups respectively), the algorithm for computing the hash values must be able to address this issue. We use the *CalculateHashValue* algorithm as shown in Figure 3(b). Note that "•" in Figure 3(b) denotes concatenation of strings. Function **MD5Value** is a hash function based on the MD5 Message-Digest algorithm [1].

We also calculate the hash values of AD in $\mathcal{A}$ and ED in $\mathcal{G}$. The hash value of AD $A \in \mathcal{A}$ is calculated as follows. $Hash(A)$ = **MD5-Value**($Hash(N_A)$ • $Hash(s_1)$ • ... • $Hash(s_x)$), where $Hash(s_x)$ = **MD5-Value**($Hash(N_s)$ • $Hash(Y_s)$ • $Hash(D_s)$), $s_x \in S_A$, and $Hash(s_1) < Hash(s_2) < \ldots < Hash(s_x)$. The hash value of ED $E \in \mathcal{G}$ is calculated as follows. $Hash(E)$ = **MD5-Value**($Hash(N_E)$ • $\mathcal{H}$), where if E is an internal entity declaration, then $\mathcal{H} = Hash(R_E)$. Otherwise, E is an external entity declaration, and $\mathcal{H} = Hash(U_E) \bullet Hash(P_E)$. The overall complexity of calculating the hash values is $O(\sum_{i=1}^{|\mathcal{T}_1|}(|T_{Ei}| \times d_i) + \sum_{j=1}^{|\mathcal{T}_2|}(|T_{Ej}| \times d_j) + |\mathcal{A}_1| + |\mathcal{A}_2| + |\mathcal{G}_1| + |\mathcal{G}_2|)$ where $|\mathcal{T}_1|$ and $|\mathcal{T}_2|$ are the numbers of content trees in $\mathcal{T}_1$ and $\mathcal{T}_2$, respectively, $|T_{Ei}|$ is the number of nodes in T_{Ei}, and d_i is the average out-degree of T_{Ei}.

The Matching Phase: Given two content trees of ETDs E_1 and E_2, denoted as T_{E1} and T_{E2} respectively, DTD-DIFF invokes the *Matching* algorithm as depicted in Figure 4. The *Matching* algorithm returns a set of matching pairs M_{min}. The principle behind the *Matching* algorithm in DTD-DIFF is based on

```
Input: Two node r1 and r2
Output: C, Cost of matching r1 and r2

1   C = 0
2   IF HashValue(r1) = HashValue(r2) THEN RETURN 0
    /*Cost of update operation*/
3   IF cardinality(r1) <> cardinality(r2) THEN C=1
4   IF r1 and r2 are leaf node THEN RETURN C
     /* recursively compute the cost of matching every
        pair of child nodes of r1 and r2 */
5   FOR EACH child1 IN children of r1
6     FOR EACH child2 IN children of r2
7       IF label(child1)=label(child2) THEN
8         ComputeCost(child1, child2)
9       ELSE
10        Cost(child1,child2) = ∞
11      END IF
12    END FOR
13  END FOR
14  matched_pairs = set of pairs resulting from minimum-cost
       bipartite-matching among child nodes of r1 and r2
15  C = C + cost of minimum-cost bipartite-matching
       among child nodes of r1 and r2
16  FOR EACH child1 IN children of r1
17    IF child1  matched_pairs THEN
18      C = C + 1 /* cost of delete operation*/
19    END IF
20  END FOR
21  FOR EACH child2 IN children of r2
22    IF child2  matched_pairs THEN
23      C = C + size of child2 /* cost of insert operation*/
24    END IF
25  END FOR
26  IF r1 and r2 are sequence group THEN
27    C = C + number of local move operations required
28  END IF
29  RETURN C
```

Fig. 5. The *ComputeCost* Algorithm

the one in X-Diff [10]. That is, our matching technique finds the minimum-cost bipartite matchings of two content trees. However, there are critical differences between the *Matching* algorithm in DTD-DIFF and the one in X-Diff as we exploit the unique structural and semantic features of a DTD. First, the *Matching* algorithm in X-Diff is invoked once. DTD-DIFF invokes the *Matching* algorithm as many as the number of ETDs. Observe that each ETD in a DTD has a unique name and hierarchy. Each root node in the content tree appears only once and mapping occurs only between nodes with the same signature. So each smaller content tree will be compared with another smaller tree from the second version having the root node with same name. Note that this computation is independent from the remaining content trees. Second, the *ComputeCost* algorithm in Figure 5 that is invoked by the *Matching* algorithm in DTD-DIFF to compute the cost matching between r_1 and r_2 considers the cardinality changes (line 3, Figure 5). Note that the *Matching* algorithm in X-Diff does not consider the cardinality changes as it deals with XML documents, not DTDs. Third, unlike X-Diff which is based on unordered trees, a content tree can have ordered and unordered subtrees. Hence, in order to ensure our matching technique works on ordered subtrees as well, we adopt the technique used in XyDiff [6] to find the largest order preserving sequences among those matching pairs in sequence groups (line 26-28, Figure 5). The overall complexity of this phase is $O(min\{\alpha_1, \alpha_2\} \times \overline{|T_{\mathcal{E}1}|} \times \overline{|T_{\mathcal{E}2}|} \times max\{\overline{d_1}, \overline{d_2}\} \times log(max\{\overline{d_1}, \overline{d_2}\})$, where $\overline{|T_{\mathcal{E}1}|}$ and $\overline{|T_{\mathcal{E}2}|}$ are the average numbers of nodes of the content trees in $T_{\mathcal{E}1}$ and $T_{\mathcal{E}2}$, respectively, $\overline{d_1}$ and $\overline{d_2}$ are the average out-degree of the content trees in $T_{\mathcal{E}1}$ and $T_{\mathcal{E}2}$, respectively, and α_1 and α_2 are the numbers of ETDs in D_1 and D_2, respectively.

The Move Detection Phase: After we have a set of matching pairs M_{min}, DTD-DIFF detects move operations. Formally, the move operation is defined as follows. Let n_1 and n_2 be two nodes in T_{E1} and T_{E2} respectively. Let $parent(n)$ be the parent node of node n. Then, node n_1 is moved to be node n_2 iff $(parent(n_1), parent(n_2)) \notin M_{min}$ and $Hash(n_1) = Hash(n_2)$. Note that we only consider a move operation if the hash values of n_1 and

n_2 are the same. This is because if the hash values of n_1 and n_2 are different, then we need to check the differences in the subtrees rooted at n_1 and n_2. If the hash values of n_1 and n_2 are different, then the algorithm detects it as a deletion of n_1 and an insertion of n_2. Now, we discuss how the move operations are detected. Let P and Q be two lists of the subtrees from the first and second versions respectively that have no matching subtrees in M_{min}. Subtrees in P and Q are sorted by their size in decreasing order. For each subtree in P, the algorithm checks whether there is a subtree in Q that have the same hash value. If $p_i \in P$ and $q_j \in Q$ have the same hash value, then the algorithm marks that subtree p_i in the first version is moved to be subtree q_j in the second version. The complexity of this phase is $O(n \times log(n))$, where n is the number of nodes in the content tree.

The Attribute Declaration Change Detection Phase: Recall that attribute list can be seen as a collection of attributes. The algorithm for detecting the changes to attribute declarations works as follows. Given two ADs, $A_1 \in \mathcal{A}_1$ and $A_2 \in \mathcal{A}_1$, we compare the hash values of these ADs. If $Hash(A_1) = Hash(A_2)$, then A_1 is the same as A_2 and we mark them to indicate that they have been matched and are not changed. Otherwise, we start to compare the attributes in the attribute list of A_1 to the ones in the attribute list of A_2. We use the hash values and the attribute name of these attributes. If the hash values of two attributes are the same, then they are not changed. Otherwise, we compare their attribute names. If their names are the same, then we check their attribute types and default values. Observe that if their attribute names are different, then we do not need to compare their attribute types and default values as we do not consider the update of the attribute name for the reasons discussed in Section 3. The cost of detecting the changes to attribute declarations is $O(n \times log(n))$, where n is the number of attributes defined in the DTD.

The Entity Declaration Change Detection Phase: The change detection mechanism of EDs is quite straightforward and similar to the approach for detecting changes to attribute declarations. Hence, we do not elaborate on this step further. The complexity of the algorithm for finding the changes on the entity declarations is $O(n \times log(n))$, where n is the number of entity declarations defined in the DTD.

Edit Scripts Generation Phase: The edit script Z is generated as follows. (1) An edit script Z is initialized as a set of *move operations* detected in the preceding step. (2) Then, for all unmatching nodes in the first tree, *delete operations* are added into edit script Z. (3) Next, for all unmatching nodes in the second tree, *insert operations* are added into edit script Z. (4) For all pairs of matching nodes that have different cardinality, *cardinality update operations* are added into edit script Z. (5) For all pairs of matching nodes that belong to sequence groups and have incorrect local order, *local order move operations* are added into edit script Z. (6) The *changes to the attributes lists* are added into edit script Z. (7) Finally, the *changes to the entity declarations* are added into edit script Z. The overall complexity of this step is $O(\sum_{i=1}^{|\mathcal{T}_1|}(|T_{Ei}|)+\sum_{j=1}^{|\mathcal{T}_2|}(|T_{Ej}|)+|\mathcal{A}_1|+|\mathcal{A}_2|+|\mathcal{G}_1|+|\mathcal{G}_2|)$.

5 Experimental Results

We have implemented DTD-DIFF entirely in Java. The experiments were conducted on a Microsoft Windows XP Professional machine having Pentium 4 1.7 GHz processor with 512 MB of memory. We use both real world DTDs and a set of synthetic DTDs generated by using our DTD generator. The second versions of DTDs are generated by using our DTD changes generator. We vary the *numbers of element types*, the *percentage of changes*, the *out-degree* of each element types, and the *depth* of each element types. We compare the performance of DTD-DIFF with the state-of-the-art approaches. Unfortunately, despite our best efforts (including contacting the authors), we could not get the Java version of XyDiff. Hence, we compared our approach to the Java version of X-Diff [10] (downloaded from http://www.cs.wisc.edu/~yuanwang/xdiff.html) only. As X-Diff is not designed for detecting the changes on DTDs, we convert the DTDs into XSD [3] using *Syntex dtd2xs* (downloaded from http://www.syntext.com/downloads/) before detecting the changes. Note that the results of X-Diff suffer from the limitations discussed in Section 1. We also study the result quality of DTD-DIFF.

Execution Time vs Number of Element Types: We set the *out-degree* and *depth* of each element type to "5" and "3" respectively. Note that the average of the maximum depth of real DTDs is "3" [5]. The number of attributes of each element is set to "3". We set the percentage of changes to "9%". The characteristic of the data sets used in this set of experiments is depicted in Figure 6(a).

Code	# Element Types	DTD (DTD-Diff)		XSD (X-Diff)	
		File size (Kb)	# Nodes	File size (Kb)	# Nodes
E005-B05-D02	5	2	105	7	390
E010-B05-D02	10	3	175	12	691
E015-B05-D02	15	4	275	17	1,031
E025-B05-D02	25	6	490	30	1,847
E050-B05-D02	50	12	900	56	3,460

Code	# Element Types	DTD (DTD-Diff)		XSD (X-Diff)	
		File size (Kb)	# Nodes	File size (Kb)	# Nodes
E075-B05-D02	75	18	1,430	87	5,360
E100-B05-D02	100	23	1,880	113	7,044
E150-B05-D02	150	36	2,785	170	10,564
E250-B05-D02	250	59	4,410	273	16,903
E500-B05-D02	500	122	9,280	570	35,076

(a) Different Number of Element Types

DTD	# Element Type	# Attribute List
SigmodRecord	11	1
PSD	66	10
Policy7	56	26
DBLP	36	12
NewsML_1.1	117	114

(d) Real DTD Characteristics

Code	Out-degree	DTD (DTD-Diff)		XSD (X-Diff)	
		Filesize (Kb)	# Nodes	Filesize (Kb)	# Nodes
E025-B05-D02	5	6	485	30	1,837
E025-B10-D02	10	12	1,585	82	5,022
E025-B15-D02	15	21	3,265	162	10,047
E025-B25-D02	25	45	7,975	385	24,021
E025-B40-D02	40	114	21,625	1,032	64,611
E025-B50-D02	50	167	31,325	1,500	94,014

(b) Different Number of Out-degree

Code	Depth	DTD (DTD-Diff)		XSD (X-Diff)	
		Filesize (Kb)	# Nodes	Filesize (Kb)	# Nodes
E025-B05-D01	1	5	150	13	868
E025-B05-D02	2	6	465	28	1,731
E025-B05-D03	3	10	1,215	68	3,896
E025-B05-D04	4	21	3,585	194	10,444
E025-B05-D05	5	46	9,045	500	25,720
E025-B05-D06	6	86	17,305	994	49,068
E025-B05-D07	7	209	43,465	2,853	122,182
E025-B05-D08	8	557	117,180	7,231	328,862

(c) Different Number of Depth

Fig. 6. Data Sets

Figure 7(a) depicts the performance of DTD-DIFF and X-Diff. We observed that DTD-DIFF significantly outperforms X-Diff. DTD-DIFF is 5–272 times faster than X-Diff. X-Diff failed to detect the changes when the numbers of elements are more than or equal to 250 due to lack of main memory. The inability of X-Diff to process large number of nodes in XML data is also highlighted in [7]. We now briefly discuss why our approach significantly outperforms X-Diff. First,

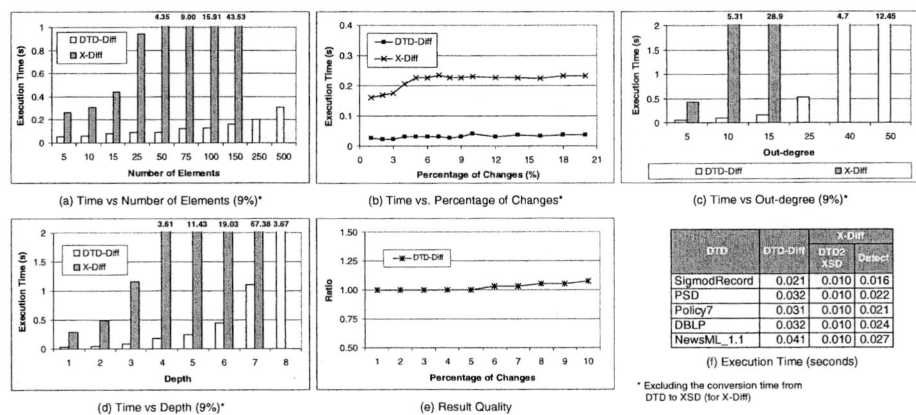

(a) Time vs Number of Elements (9%)*

(b) Time vs. Percentage of Changes*

(c) Time vs Out-degree (9%)*

(d) Time vs Depth (9%)*

(e) Result Quality

DTD	DTD-Diff	X-Diff	
		DTD2 XSD	Detect
SigmodRecord	0.021	0.010	0.016
PSD	0.032	0.010	0.022
Policy7	0.031	0.010	0.021
DBLP	0.032	0.010	0.024
NewsML_1.1	0.041	0.010	0.027

(f) Execution Time (seconds)

* Excluding the conversion time from DTD to XSD (for X-Diff)

Fig. 7. Experimental Results

the tree representations of XSD files (XSD tree) contain elements with same names. On the other hand, in DTD-DIFF, each root node of the content trees in a DTD has a unique name. As a result, there exists a one-to-one mapping between a content tree in the old version to another content tree in the new version. Hence, X-Diff does more number of bipartite matching compared to DTD-DIFF. Second, the number of nodes in the content trees is lesser in most cases compared to an XSD tree. This further reduces the number and cost of bipartite matching in DTD-DIFF. The details can be found in [8]. Furthermore, numbers of nodes in the XSD files are larger than the number of nodes in the content trees (from 2.8 up to 5.8 times larger, Figure 6).

We also study the performance of DTD-DIFF and X-Diff by using real world DTDs [2, 4]. Figure 6(d) depicts the characteristics of the real world DTDs. We set the percentage of changes to 3%. Figure 7(f) depicts the performances of DTD-DIFF and X-Diff. We notice that X-Diff has slightly better performance than DTD-DIFF. This is primarily due to the characteristics of the data. For instance, although *NewsML_1.1* has 117 elements, the performance of DTD-DIFF is comparable to X-Diff! Observe that for synthetic data set with similar size, DTD-DIFF outperforms X-Diff significantly. This is because in *NewsML_1.1*, only 6 out of 117 ETDs have nested content and the maximum depth of *NewsML_1.1* DTD is only 2. Hence, cost of bipartite matching is almost the same. In summary, X-Diff performs relatively better than DTD-DIFF when the DTDs have simple and "flat" structure. When the DTD structure is complex, DTD-DIFF outperforms X-Diff as shown using synthetic dataset. Also, note that DTD-DIFF is still better than X-Diff because of the inaccuracies and incompleteness in the results generated by X-Diff [8].

Execution Time vs Percentage of Changes: We use the E025-B05-D02 data set, whose number of element types, out-degree, and depth are 25, 5, and 2 respectively, as the first version of the DTD. We vary the percentages of changes from "1%" to "20%". Figure 7(b) depicts the execution time of DTD-DIFF and

X-Diff for different percentages of changes. We observe that the percentage of changes slightly affect the performance of DTD-Diff and X-Diff.

Execution Time vs Out Degree: We set the number of element types and the depth to "25" and "2" respectively. We set the percentage of changes to "9%". We vary the out-degree of each element type from "5" to "50". The characteristic of the data sets used in this set of experiments is depicted in Figure 6(b). Figure 7(c) depicts the performance of DTD-Diff and X-Diff for different numbers of out-degree of each element type. We observe that DTD-Diff is up to 325 times faster than X-Diff. This is because of the reasons discussed above. We also notice that X-Diff cannot detect the changes to XSD files when the out-degree is more than or equal to 25 due to the lack of main memory.

Execution Time vs Depth: We set the number of element types and the out-degree to "25" and "5" respectively. We set the percentage of changes to "9%". We vary the out-degree of each element type from "1" to "8". The characteristic of the data sets used in this set of experiments is depicted in Figure 6(c). Figure 7(d) depicts the performance of DTD-Diff and X-Diff for different depth of each content tree. We observe that DTD-Diff is up to 89 times faster than X-Diff. X-Diff failed to detect the changes when the depth is more than or equal to 8 due to the lack of main memory.

Result Quality: We also examine the quality of deltas detected by DTD-Diff. We use `E010-B05-D02` data set and the percentages of changes are varied between "1%" to "10%". Then, we calculate the result quality, that is, the ratio between the number of edit operations detected by DTD-Diff and the optimal one. Figure 7(e) depicts the ratios. We observe that DTD-Diff is able to detect the optimal deltas until percentage of changes is set to "5%". Afterwards, DTD-Diff detects almost optimal deltas. This is because, in some cases, a move operation is detected as a pair of deletion and insertion. Note that we do not compare the result quality of DTD-Diff to other approaches as, to the best of our knowledge, DTD-Diff is the first approach for detecting the changes to DTDs. We do not compare the result quality of DTD-Diff to the one of X-Diff (when we use XSD files) as the types of changes of DTD and XML are different.

6 Conclusions

A DTD change detection tool can be useful in several ways such as maintenance of XML documents and incremental maintenance of relational schema for storing XML data. In this paper, we present a novel technique for detecting the changes to DTDs. Our work is motivated by the problem that converting DTD to XML Schema (XSD) (which is in XML document format) and detecting the changes using existing XML change detection algorithms (X-Diff and XyDiff) is not a feasible option. Such effort is expensive and may generate semantically incorrect and non-optimal edit scripts. We propose an algorithm DTD-Diff that directly computes the changes between two versions of DTDs by taking into account the structural and semantic features of DTDs. We experimentally demonstrate that X-Diff performs relatively better than DTD-DIFF when the DTDs have simple and "flat" structure. When the DTD structure is complex, DTD-DIFF runs significantly faster (5–325 times) than X-Diff for given data set. DTD-DIFF is also able to produce optimal or at least near-optimal deltas.

References

1. RONALD L. RIVEST. The MD5 Message Digest Algorithm. *Internet RFC 1321*, April 1992. http://www.faqs.org/rfcs/rfc1321.html.
2. UW XML Repository. *Database Research Group, University of Washington.* http://www.cs.washington.edu/research/xmldatasets/.
3. XML Schema. *World Wide Web Consortium.* http://www.w3.org/XML/Schema.
4. XML.ORG Registry and Repository for XML Schemas. http://www.xml.org/xml/registry.jsp.
5. B. CHOI. What are real DTDs like?. *In WebDB*, 2002.
6. G. COBENA, S. ABITEBOUL, A. MARIAN. Detecting Changes in XML Documents. *In ICDE*, 2002.
7. E. LEONARDI, S. S. BHOWMICK. Detecting Changes on XML Documents Using Relational Databases: A Schema-Conscious Approach. *In ACM CIKM*, 2005.
8. E. LEONARDI, T. T. HOAI, S. S. BHOWMICK, S. MADRIA. DTD-DIFF: A Change Detection Algorithm for DTDs. *Technical Report, Center for Advanced Information System, Nanyang Technological University*, Singapore, 2005.
9. J. SHANMUGASUNDARAM, K. TUFTE, C. ZHANG, G. HE, D. J. DEWITT, AND J. F. NAUGHTON. Relational Databases for Querying XML Documents: Limitations and Opportunities. *In VLDB*, 1999.
10. Y. WANG, D. J. DEWITT, J. CAI. X-Diff: An Effective Change Detection Algorithm for XML Documents. *In ICDE*, 2003.

Mining Models of Composite Web Services for Performance Analysis

Aiqiang Gao[1], Dongqing Yang[1], Shiwei Tang[2], and Ming Zhang[1]

[1] School of Electronics Engineering and Computer Science,
Peking University, Beijing 100871, China
{aqgao, ydq, mzhang}@db.pku.edu.cn
[2] National Laboratory on Machine Perception,
Peking University, Beijing 100871, China
tsw@pku.edu.cn

Abstract. Web service composition provides a way to build value-added services and web applications by integrating and composing existing web services. In this paper, a composite web service is modeled using queueing network for the purpose of performance analysis. Each component web service participating the composite web service corresponds to one service center. The control flow between component web services is represented by the Markov chain that describes the transition of customers between service centers. To perform performance analysis, the Markov chain should be known first. However, a web service is usually a black box and only its interfaces can be seen externally, so the internal control flow can be only estimated from history execution logs. This paper gives a method that mines the Markov chain of a composite web service from its execution logs. Then, bottlenecks identification and performance analysis are conducted for the queueing network model. Experimental results show that this model mining method is effective and efficient.

1 Introduction

The emerging paradigm of web services promises to bring to distributed computation and services the flexibility that the web has brought to the sharing of documents (see [1]).

Web service composition ([1, 2]) is to build value-added services and web applications by integrating and composing existing elementary web services(also called component web services). Though the existence of considerable works on automatic composition and verification([1, 3]), performance aspects of a composite web service has received relatively limited attention. The task of performance analysis for composite web services becomes a non-trivial task due to the existence of control logic between component web services.

In this paper, queueing network modeling is used to model a composite web service for the purpose of performance analysis. To conduct performance analysis, the transition probability between service centers should be known first. That is to say, the Markov chain describing the transition of customers must be determined.

M.L. Lee, K.L. Tan, and V. Wuwongse (Eds.): DASFAA 2006, LNCS 3882, pp. 828–837, 2006.

Because web services provide only external interfaces definition (for example, WSDL [4]), the transition relationships between component services are usually unknown. Whereas, the transitions can be derived from externally visible behaviors. This paper gives a method that derives Markov chain of a composite web service from execution logs.

The mined Markov chain describes the transition probability of service centers in the queueing network model. Based on this observation, bottleneck identification and performance analysis can be done for the corresponding queueing network model. Given the arrival rate, service demands for all service centers are computed, which are then used to identify bottlenecks of the queueing network. Other performance parameters such as utilization and average queue length can also be obtained.

Though it is not new to model a composite web service using Markov chain, the method described in this paper for mining the embedded Markov chain of a queueing network model from logs and utilizing the model for performance analysis is interesting. The main contributions of this paper are:

1. Queueing Network modeling is used to model a composite web service for the purpose of bottlenecks identification and performance analysis, where the service centers correspond to the component web services that participate the composite service. And a process mining method is used to mine a model for the composite web service. The discovered model is just the embedded markov chain of the queueing network.
2. With the mined markov chain of the queueing network, bottleneck identification and performance analysis are conducted. The experiments and performance analysis shows that it is an effective way to evaluate the efficiency and performance behavior of a composite service.

The rest of this paper is organized as follows. Section 2 gives a description of web services and presents queueing network based model for a composite web service; Section 3 discusses a method for mining Markov chain from service execution logs; Section 4 illustrates the usage of the derived model for bottlenecks identification and performance analysis; Section 5 shows some experimental results to illustrate that this method is effective and efficient; Section 6 reviews related works and Section 7 concludes this paper and discusses future work.

2 Modeling Composite Web Services Using Queueing Network

2.1 Web Services and Composite Web Services

For an application to use a web service, the programmatic interface of the web service must be precisely described. WSDL [4] is an XML grammar for specifying properties of a web service such as *what* it does, *where* it is located and *how* it is invoked([2]).

Web service composition is the process of building value-added services and web applications by integrating and composing existing elementary web services.

The constructs and composition patterns for web service composition in the industrial standards or languages(such as BPEL4WS [5] and OWL-S(DAML-S)[6]) can be summarized using workflow patterns discussed in [7]. The usually used patterns are sequential, conditional choice (exclusive), parallel and iterative.

In this paper, the elementary web services that are used to synthesize a composite one are called *component web services.* Both the component and composite web services used in this paper are WSDL-described and SOAP-based.

2.2 Preliminary Concepts

Definition 1 *(Markov Property). Consider a system that is observed at times 0,1,2,$\cdots$. Let X_n be the state of the system at time n for $n = 0, 1, 2, \cdots$. Suppose the system is at time n, say. That is, the system states have been observed as $X_0, X_1, \cdots, X_n$. The question is: can the state of the system at time $n+1$ be predicted, in a probabilistic way? If the next state X_{n+1} depends only on X_n, given the complete history of $X_0, X_1, \cdots, X_n$, the question is considerably simplified. If the system has this property at all times n, it is said to have a Markov property (see [8]).*

Definition 2 *(Markov Chain). For observation time $n = 0, 1, 2, \cdots$, the stochastic process $\{X_n, n \geq 0\}$ on state space S is said to be a Discrete-Time Markov Chain (DTMC) if it has a Markov property.*

If a system is observed continuously, with $X(t)$ being the state at time $t, t \geq 0$, the stochastic process is called a Continuous-Time Markov Chain (CTMC) if it has a Markov property.

For a composite web service, each participating component web service T(called task, also) is an activity. At each time point, it is either active or not active. Thus, each task can be captured by a binary random variable T, where T=1 represents task T is active while T=0 for not active. Let a *system state* X_t at time t defined as a set of activities which are active at that time. Then, X_t is a random variable because the result of web service invocation is uncertain. If the system is observed at times $t_1, t_2, \ldots$, this sequence of random variables $X_{t_1}, X_{t_2}, \ldots$ form a stochastic process. By assuming the conditional probability of each task node given its parents in the composite web service, i.e. by assuming the Markov property, the stochastic process for a composite web service can be seen as a Markov chain([9, 10, 11]).

2.3 Queueing Network for Composite Web Services

Queueing network modeling is a particular approach to computer system modeling in which the computer system is represented as a network of queues which is evaluated analytically. A *network of queues* is a collection of *service centers* representing the system resources that provide service to a collection of *customers* that represent the users or transactions([8, 12, 13]).

Queueing Network Model for Composite Web Services. Each component service participating in a composite web service corresponds to one *service center* in the queueing network model. The control flow between component services is described by the *transitions* of customers between service centers in the queueing network model. The *customers* are the service requestors that invoke web service operations.

The transition of customers between service centers is inherently a Markov chain. The fact that customers are served at a service center i implies that service center i is active during that time period. So, the transition of customers between service centers corresponds to the state transition of the Markov chain for the composite web service. Based on this fact, to quantify a queueing network model that corresponds to a composite service, it is necessary to quantify the Markov chain first.

3 Deriving Markov Chain of Queueing Network

According to Section 2, a composite web service is represented by the embedded Markov chain. Its execution logs can be regarded as realizations of the underlying stochastic process. Motivated by [9], this section discusses a method to identify all states and their transitions according to the Markov assumption.

3.1 Execution Log

Suppose the execution log $L = \{L_1, L_2, \cdots, L_m\}$ consists of m records each describing a single execution trace of the composite service.

Each record is a sequence of log elements: *service*(*starttime*, *endtime*), separated by comma. Each log element represents an execution of *service* starting at time *starttime* and ending at time *endtime*.

Each service execution starts with state S_0, i.e., the empty set of active services. When S_0 is entered again, one execution ends.

When system is in state S_i, the set of active services is denoted as $Active(S_i)$. The transition from state S_i to S_j is the result of the execution of some service s_k that makes $Active(S_j) = Active(S_i) \bigcup \{s_k\}$. When a service s_k ends, a transition from the current state S_i to state S_j occurs with $Active(S_j) = Active(S_i) - \{s_k\}$.

3.2 Method for Deriving Markov Chain

According to Markov property, system state S_j will only depend on state S_{j-1}. This implies a method for building the Markov chain by scanning the log, identifying system states and linking consecutive states.

The procedure for building Markov chain is shown in Algorithm 1 and Algorithm 2. Algorithm 1 is used to compute the event occurrence frequencies and Algorithm 2 is used to compute the state transition probability.

In Algorithm 1, the events are sorted in ascending order of timestamp and then scanned to find the overlapping services and their transitions. This algorithm remembers previous state by an auxiliary variable, so it can identify a loop from the logs under the assumption that there are no duplicate activities.

Algorithm 1. Computing the Event Occurrence Frequency

```
1: read a line from log file;
2: while (!in.eof()) do
3:     set prevSet and tmpSet to be empty;
4:     get an ordered set allLogElement of event with "start" or "end" labeled;
5:     add prevSet to states if prevSet ∉ states
6:     for pos ← 0, allLogElement.size() do
7:         tmp:=log element at position pos;
8:         if (tmp.label == "start") then
9:             currSet := prevSet;
10:            currSet.add(tmp.getServiceName()); prevSet := currSet;
11:        end if
12:        if (tmp.label == "end") then
13:            currSet.remove(tmp.getServiceName());
14:            if (prevSet.size() ≥ 1 and currSet.isEmpty()) then
15:                continue;              ▷ to find a joint state for parallel activities
16:            end if
17:            if (currSet.isEmpty()) then
18:                If (states.contains(prevSet)), add a new state to states;
19:                ElseIf (tmpSet == prevSet) handle loop; continue;
20:                compute sojourn time for state prevSet;
21:            end if
22:            if (transition.contains("tmpSet− > prevSet")) then
23:                numOfTransition := numOfTransition + 1;
24:            else
25:                transition.add("tmpSet− > prevSet"); numOfTransition := 1;
26:            end if
27:        end if                         ▷ end of if on condition "label==end"
28:    end for                            ▷ end of "for" loop
29:    line := in.readLine();
30: end while
```

Now, the time complexity is analyzed for Algorithm 1. Suppose there are m logs and n services. For each execution log, lines 3 to 28 are executed. There may be $O(n)$ activities in each log, so lines 6 to 28 needs to be executed $O(n)$ times. Because there may be $O(n^2)$ transitions at most, so lines 22 to 26 take $O(n^2)$ time to determine whether a corresponding transition exists. According to the above analysis, a total of $O(n^3)$ time is needed for each log record. Thus,Algorithm 1 computes the model in $O(mn^3)$ time. Algorithm 2 can be executed in $O(n^3)$. Hence, the whole process for mining a Markov chain takes $O(mn^3)$.

In the following, a simple example is used to illustrate the process to construct a Markov chain from services logs. Suppose, the set $L = \{L_1\}$ consists of the following service log:

$$L_1 = \{D(1,2), A(3,9), B(4,11), C(6,12), E(13,14)\}.$$

Table 1 shows the intermediate variables during the computation. The set of states is: $\{S_0, S_{\{D\}}, S_{\{A,B,C\}}, S_{\{E\}}\}$. In Tab. 1, S_0, S_1, S_2, S_3 are used to represent

Algorithm 2. Computing State Transition Probability

```
for all state ∈ states do
    t_num ← the number of transitions from state;
    v_num ← the number of transition to state;
    for all transition t do
        if (t.getSource() == state) then
            tnum ← the count of t;
            target ← target of t;
            matrix[state][target] := tnum/t_num;
            averageSojourn := sojourn.get(state)/v_num;
        end if
    end for
end for
```

Table 1. Result of processing log L

step	currSet	prevSet	tmpSet	states	transition
initial	∅	∅	∅	∅	∅
step1	{D}	{D}	∅	$\{S_0\}$	∅
step2	∅	∅	{D}	$\{S_0, S_1\}$	$\{S_0 \rightarrow S_1\}$
step3	{A}	{A}	{D}	$\{S_0, S_1\}$	$\{S_0 \rightarrow S_1\}$
step4	{A,B}	{A,B}	{D}	$\{S_0, S_1\}$	$\{S_0 \rightarrow S_1\}$
step5	{A,B,C}	{A,B,C}	{D}	$\{S_0, S_1\}$	$\{S_0 \rightarrow S_1\}$
step6	{B,C}	{A,B,C}	{D}	$\{S_0, S_1\}$	$\{S_0 \rightarrow S_1\}$
step7	{C}	{A,B,C}	{D}	$\{S_0, S_1\}$	$\{S_0 \rightarrow S_1\}$
step8	∅	∅	{A,B,C}	$\{S_0, S_2, S_1\}$	$\{S_0 \rightarrow S_1, S_1 \rightarrow S_2\}$
step9	{E}	{E}	{A,B,C}	$\{S_0, S_2, S_1\}$	$\{S_0 \rightarrow S_1, S_1 \rightarrow S_2\}$
step10	∅	∅	{E}	$\{S_0, S_2, S_1, S_3\}$	$\{S_0 \rightarrow S_1, S_1 \rightarrow S_2, S_2 \rightarrow S_3\}$

Fig. 1. Markov chain for the example

states $S_0, S_{\{D\}}, S_{\{A,B,C\}}, S_{\{E\}}$,respectively. The corresponding Markov chain is shown in Fig. 1. This example is a tandem queueing network according to [8].

4 Performance Analysis for Queueing Network Model

With the Markov chain derived from Section 3, the queueing network model for a composite web service can be analyzed quantitatively. Parameters such as service demand, utilization and residence time can be computed given the arrival rate. Then, the bottleneck(s) can be identified.

4.1 Bottleneck Identification for Single-Class Queueing Network

According to [14], the bottleneck for single class model is the service center i with the largest service demand $D_i = S_i \times V_i$, with service time S_i and visit ratio V_i. So the problem of finding bottleneck of single class network reduces to finding the service center with largest service demand. Because service time has been known according to Algorithm 1 in Section 3, the focus is to compute visit ratio vector $[V_i]$ for all service centers.

The queueing network model for composite web service is itself an open network. When a customer arrives, the probability that he will enter service center i is b_i. While he completes the service at service center i, he can switch to service center j or leave the network.

Suppose the arrival rate for the whole composite service is λ. Because the network model for composite web service is a steady one, so the departure rate is also λ. At the same time, for each service center, the rate of arrival and departure is also equivalent. So, for all component service centers $j = 1, 2, \cdots, M$, formula 1 holds (see [13]).

$$v_j = \sum_{i=1}^{M} p_{ij} v_i + b_j \lambda \tag{1}$$

For entry center, the visit ratio is λ. So, given a arrival rate λ, with the transition probability matrix $\{p_{ij}\}$ derived in Section 3, the set of linear equations 1 are solved to get the visit ratio for each service center. The algorithm for solving linear equations is Gauss Principal Element Elimination [15].

Then, the service demand of each service center is computed using visit ratio V_i and service time S_i. As a result of this, the service center with largest service demand is identified. Bottleneck identification for multi-class queueing network is also performed using a method according to [16], in which a method is discussed to give a set of potential bottlenecks for multi-class queueing network. The implementation details are not included here due to space limitation.

4.2 Delay in Transmission

In the above discussion, the transmission channels are an abstraction for sending and receiving messages. So far their effect on system performance has been neglected. In reality, transmission delays can increase the system response time. Particularly, in the web service settings, messages are contained in a SOAP-based envelope and transmitted over HTTP or SMTP, which is regarded to cost much transmission delay.

Service centers could be used to model transmission channels: this model assumes that only one message can be in transit at a time and may produce inflated response times. In this case, it can be considered that a resource is dedicated to a request, so the channel is modeled as a *delay center* ([12, 17]). The arrival rate for such a service center is equal to the arrival rate at the component fed by the channel. Each channel has a delay time property, representing the average time it takes a message to traverse the channel([18]).

A channel's transmission delay affects the system response time: the delay of each channel traversed by a job is added to the job's response time. However, it does not affect component performance or bottlenecks.

5 Experiments

Experiments are performed to evaluate the methods discussed in this paper. Composite web services are defined using BPEL4WS [5]. The execution engine for BPEL process is ActiveBPEL (http://www.activebpel.org/) engine, which uses Axis (http://ws.apache.org/axis) to hold external web services.

The loan approval example in BPEL4WS specification is employed as the base of the composite service. It is extended to include a three-branch conditional construct and a two-branch parallel construct. For more information about loan approval example, the readers are referred to [5]. It is deployed and executed in an engine, with logs collected. Then Algorithm 1 is executed to mine the underlying model from the logs.

With the mined Markov chain and the visit ratio formulas, we can get visit ratio V_i and service time S_i of service center i. Then the performance measure such as service demands, resource utilization, average residence time and average queue length can be computed. The formulas used are the following ones(see [12]): the service demand for i is $D_i = S_i \times V_i$; the utilization for i is $U_i = \lambda \times D_i$; the average residence time is $R_i = D_i/(1-U_i)$; average queue length is computed by Little's law with $Q_i = \lambda \times R_i = \lambda \times D_i/(1-U_i) = U_i/(1-U_i)$. The details of computation results won't be shown here for lack of space.

Experiments are also conducted to evaluate the performance of Algorithm 1. The computer used for experiments is with the following configurations: Pentium 4 1.5GHZ with 512M RAM, Windows 2000, jdk1.4.2.

Nodes are randomly added to the process definition for varied model sizes. Table 2 shows the execution time. It can be seen that this method is efficient and scales linearly with the size of the input for a given model size. It also scales well with the size of model in the experiments.

Table 2. Execution time of Algorithm 1 (in Seconds)

Number of Logs	Number of Nodes			
	10	30	50	100
100	0.04	0.16	0.39	1.25
1000	0.27	1.61	3.75	12.51
10000	2.56	17.02	39.82	124.41

6 Related Works

The field of modeling web services and their interaction has received considerable attention in recent years. A variety of formalisms have been proposed in the following directions: web service composition specifications [5, 6], formal model of services composition, automatic composition, analysis and verification(see [1, 3] for a survey of these topics).

Though the existence of considerable works on automatic composition, QoS-driven service composition([19]) and semantic web service composition, performance analysis of composite web service has received relatively limited attention.

Author in [20] performs response time analysis of composite web services. While in our method, composite web service is modeled using queueing network techniques, so performance parameters such as response time, throughput and utilization can also be achieved. Moreover, this paper can deal with more composition constructs than just parallel in [20].

Agrawal et al. [21] introduced the first algorithm for mining workflow logs. A broad survey on the current work in workflow mining, or process mining,is given by van der Aalst and Wejters [22]. In [9, 11], the problem of automatic process discovery and mining is based on a probability model,i.e. by assuming Markov condition. The method discussed here is mostly motivated by CrossFlow[9] with the differences: our method is based on queueing network and its embedding Markov chain; our method can deal with concurrent states with any number of involved activities while CrossFlow[9] doesn't mention it; the method in this paper can also be used to identify loop construct.

7 Conclusion

This paper models composite web service using queueing network for the purpose of performance analysis. The transition probabilities between service centers, being a Markov chain, are mined from history execution logs. By remembering previous state, the model mining algorithm can handle sequential, exclusive choice, concurrent and iterative cases. After the Markov chain is derived, bottlenecks identification and performance analysis is conducted . Experimental results show this process mining method is efficient and effective. In future, the various challenges on process mining proposed in [22] will be further discussed.

Acknowledgement

This work is supported by the National Natural Science Foundation of China under Grant No. 90412010 and ChinaGrid project of the Ministry of Education, China.

References

1. R. Hull, M. Benedikt, V. Christophides, and J. Su.E-services: A look behind the curtain. In Proc. ACM Symp.on Principles of Database Systems, 2003.
2. Aphrodite Tsalgatidou,Thomi Pilioura,An Overview of Standards and Related Technology in Web Services,Distributed and Parallel Databases,12,125-162,2002

3. Giuseppe De Giacomo,Daniela Berardi and Massimo Mecella,Basis for Automatic Web Service Composition, tutorial at WWW2005, available at http://www.dis.uniroma1.it/~degiacom/
4. W3C, "Web Services Description Language (WSDL) Version 2.0", W3C Working Draft, March 2003. (See http://www.w3.org/TR/wsdl20/.)
5. Business Process Execution Language for Web Services, version 1.1, http://www.ibm.com/developerworks/library/ws-bpel/
6. OWL Services Coalition. OWL-S: Semantic markup for web services, November 2003.
7. W.M.P. van der Aalst,A.H.M. ter Hofstede,B.Kiepuszewski, and A.P.Barros. Workflow Patterns. Distributed and Parallel Databases,14(1):5-51,2003
8. V.G. Kulkarni, Operations Research Applied Stochastic Models (photocopy), Beijing:Tsinghua Press,China,2004
9. J.klingemann,J.Wsach,and K.Aberer. Deriving Service Models in Cross-Organizational Workflows. In Ninth International Workshop on Research Issuses in Data Engineering:Virtual Enterprise,RIDE-VE'99,Sydney,Australia,March 1999
10. J.E.Cook and A.L.Wolf,Automating process discovery through event-data analysis. In Proc.of the 17the Int.Conference on Software Engineering,April,1995
11. Ricardo Silva,Jiji Zhang,James G.Shanahan,Probabilistic Workflow Mining,KDD'05,August 21-24,2005,Chicago,Illinois,USA
12. Lazowska, E., Zahorjan, J., Graham, S., Sevcik, K., Quantitative System Performance: Computer System Analysis Using Queueing Network Models, Prentice Hall, Englewood Cliffs, N. J., 1984.
13. Hua Xing,Queueing Theory and Stochastic Service System,Shanghai Translation Press:1987(in Chinese)
14. Denning, P. J., Buzen, J. P. The Operational Analysis of Queueing Network Models. ACM Computing Surveys,1978,10(3), 225-261.
15. Changjin Jiang, Scientific Computing and C-language Programs, Hefei:Press of University of Science and Technology,China (in Chinese)
16. Giuliano C., Giuseppe S.,Politecnico di M.,Bottlenecks Identification in Multiclass Queueing Networks using Convex Polytopes, Proc.of 12th Intl. Symp. on Modeling,Analysis, and Simulation of Computer and Telecommunications Systems,2004
17. Daniel A. Menasc and Virgilio A. F. Almeida,Capacity Planning for Web Services: metrics, models, and methods, Prentice Hall, 2001,ISBN 0-13-065903-7
18. Bridget Spitznagel and David Garlan, Architecture-Based Performance Analysis, In Proc.1998 Conf. on Software Engineering and Knowledge Engineering
19. Liangzhao Z., Boualem Benatallah, Anne H.H. Ngu, Marlon Dumas, Jayant K., Henry Ch., QoS-Aware Middleware for Web Services Composition, IEEE transactions on Software Engineering , 2004,30(5):311-327
20. D.A. Menasc, "Response-Time Analysis of Composite Web Services," IEEE Internet Computing, 2004,8(1): 90-92
21. R. Agrawal, D. Gunopulos, and F. Leymann. Mining process models from workflow logs. Proc. of 6th Intl. Conf. on Extending Database Technology, 469-483, 1998.
22. Aalst and A.J.M.M. Weijters. Process Mining: A Research Agenda. Computers in Industry, 53(3):231-244, 2004.

Modeling Multimedia Data Semantics with MADS

Oleksandr Drutskyy and Stefano Spaccapietra

EPFL - Ecole Polytechnique Fédérale de Lausanne,
School of Computer and Communication Sciences,
Database Laboratory, 1015 Lausanne, Switzerland
{oleksandr.drutskyy, stefano.spaccapietra}@epfl.ch

Abstract. To bridge the gap between the over increasing ubiquity of multimedia and the lack of approaches to deal with semantics of multimedia information, an important number of research efforts has been brought out lately. Nevertheless, a vast majority of proposed techniques deal with movies or other montage-edited media sources like TV-news, football matches, etc., which are characterized by efficient temporal granularity (frames, shots, scenes, etc.). Unfortunately, this latter property does not hold in environments like, e.g, multimedia meetings, making traditional approaches not quite suitable for such settings. In this paper we present our approach to conceptual modeling of multimedia data based on MADS, a spatio-temporal data model with multi-representation support. We also provide an example for the case of multimedia meetings.

1 Introduction

Due to persistent popularization of digital cameras, PDAs, 3G cell phones, etc., multimedia gradually takes stands once dominated by classical alphanumeric data. However, despite the simplicity of taking pictures with one's digital camera, it is not that obvious, e.g. to find among those shots the photo of Liz standing the left of Bill at the last week briefing. This is partially due to the fact that the major emphasis in the field of multimedia research has been for a long time placed on such (low-level) issues as storage, coding, networking, hardware, etc., while paying a very limited attention to semantic aspects of multimedia information.

In this paper we present our approach[1] to conceptual modeling of multimedia data based on MADS [1], a spatio-temporal data model supporting multi-representation, which we extend with multimedia modeling capabilities. This permits to reuse the existing features of MADS in the multimedia context, as well as to keep the model backward-compatible for non-multimedia applications.

It is especially due to the recent raising of Semantic Web and ontologies-related research that semantics in general and multimedia semantics in particular are being paid an overgrowing attention nowadays.

[1] This work is funded by National Center of Competence in Research (NCCR) on Interactive Multimodal Information Management (IM2), supported by the Swiss National Science Foundation. http://www.im2.ch

M.L. Lee, K.L. Tan, and V. Wuwongse (Eds.): DASFAA 2006, LNCS 3882, pp. 838–848, 2006.

An important number of recent activities in the field of multimedia content description has been focused on MPEG-7, an XML Schema based standard, providing over 450 simple and complex types [2]. MPEG-7 is extensible and allows describing temporal, spatial, and spatio-temporal components of audiovisual content. Despite its benefits, the complexity and immaturity of the standard hamper its wide spreading. Moreover, its marked affixment to physical media sources does not permit to fully exploit the multimedia semantics.

A semantic multimedia meta-modeling approach based on Enhanced Multimedia Meta Objects (EMMO) is proposed in [3]. An EMMO establishes a tradable knowledge-enriched unit of multimedia content, combining media, semantic, and functional aspects. In general, EMMOs represent an interesting approach to conceptual multimedia modeling, taking advantage of ontologies, versioning support, and providing association and constructor mechanisms. Nevertheless, the model seems to be somewhat physical-media oriented, and tries to mix physical and semantic aspects of multimedia data altogether, which, in our opinion, hampers the expressiveness of semantics-oriented modeling.

Perhaps one of the most recent directions of multimedia research is focused in the domain of emergent semantics. Due to variety and multitude of user groups, whose expectancies are not known beforehand, it becomes almost impossible to foresee the all different semantic interpretations of multimedia information by various application users. In [4], several approaches to tackle this problem are presented. In particular, the media blending approach [5] has proved useful for discovering emergent semantics in multimedia settings.

The rest of the paper is structured as follows: sect. 2 provides a general description of a multimedia meeting environment, and points out its peculiar properties as compared to traditional multimedia settings. Sect. 3 introduces MADS, a spatio-temporal data model supporting multi-representation. Sect. 4 describes MADS multimedia extensions, and illustrates a sample conceptual multimedia-extended schema. Finally, sect. 5 concludes and discusses the work in progress.

2 Multimedia Meeting Framework

One of the primary directions of the IM2 project is a Smart Meeting Room application dealing with interfaces and supporting facilities to store and retrieve both the raw media data produced at the meetings (e.g. video and audio recordings of the meetings), and the corresponding metadata produced after the meetings (namely, various annotations to describe, in particular, relevant segmentations of the audio and video files and, as far as possible, their semantic content) [6].

In the context described above we are developing a conceptual multimedia modeling technique suitable in particular for the case of multimedia meetings. The interaction between multimedia meeting participants can take place either in the form of monologues or discussions. Participants are also free to use a projection board or other visualization tools for demonstrating slides, diagrams, etc. The totality of multimedia meetings is recorded by a set of audiovisual recording equipment, which could be fixed-position, fixed-trajectory, or

(a) (b)

Fig. 1. Multimedia Meeting Scenarios

free-trajectory (cameraman-driven). Two typical examples of multimedia meetings in IM2 are shown in fig. 1. In fig. 1a three wall-fixed cameras are filming 2 of the 4 meeting participants on one side of the desk, the other 2 participants on the other side of the desk, and a projection screen on the wall, respectively. In fig. 1b each meeting participant is filmed by a personal dedicated fixed camera.

Compared to traditional audio-visual multimedia applications, multimedia meetings are characterized by a number of features that make existing modeling approaches not quite suitable for meeting scenarios. Thus, for example, a great number of existing video annotation and conceptual modeling techniques are based on dividing video sequences into temporal components, namely: frames, shots, and scenes. It has been argued that shots represent the finest level of descriptive granularity for motion pictures [7]. This reasoning, however, does not necessarily hold for the case of multimedia meetings. Indeed, in a setting like the one presented in fig. 1b, shot-level division is seriously hampered by a highly static pattern of video recordings. As for frame level division, this type of segmentation is way too fine and removes temporal aspects of video content [8].

Another important peculiarity of multimedia meetings is a multitude of physical media sources. For example, each meeting participant can be represented by: a set of personal video files, parts of the video file for the projection screen, as well as parts of the common sound file. This markedly differs from the majority of classical single-media systems, often meant for motion pictures, where each media file is considered as single and is in general treated (i.e. annotated, queried, etc.) independently of the other files in the collection. It should be noted that unlike the motion pictures context, where montage is used to produce a single media file out of a series of independent footages, this solution is not appropriate to multimedia meeting scenarios. Unlike motion pictures, multimedia meetings applications do not seek to provide a unified multimedia view of the domain as seen by a single person or group of persons (e.g. movie director). Quite the contrary, in multi-user environments like that of the IM2, users/annotators are many, each having their own points of interest. It is thus important to preserve all the multimedia recordings, and make them available for multiple accesses and reuse by different users, thus prohibiting any possible semantic losses.

Further investigating the problem of multitude of physical media sources, we go on to yet another important characteristic of multimedia meetings, namely that of clearly separating semantic and physical aspects of multimedia. This, in our opinion, is one of the major requirements that a powerful conceptual multimedia modeling technique should meet. It becomes especially important when multimedia serves as a representation of real world entities (physical objects, relationships, events, etc.), while in this case the multimedia semantics actually reflects the semantics of the real world entities behind the multimedia recordings. For example, having John filmed during the meeting with a camera A, or a camera B, or not having him filmed at all, does not change the fact of John's taking part in the meeting. This means that we would like to be able to represent as much semantic information about this recorded meeting, as if we were doing so for the real meeting itself, and not just for its multimedia representation.

Summarizing the aforesaid, a powerful conceptual multimedia modeling technique should meet the following principal requirement:

- consider separately semantic and physical aspects of multimedia;
- be scalable with respect to multitude of physical media sources;
- support spatio-temporal semantics;
- be user-adaptable and support multi-representation;
- be at least as expressive as the modeling technique used to describe real world entities independently of their multimedia depiction.

3 MADS Data Model

Taking into consideration the requirements defined in sect. 2, we have hereby chosen MADS [1], [9] as the underlying base model for our conceptual multimedia modeling approach. MADS (Modeling Application Data with Spatio-temporal features) is a conceptual data model that primarily addresses the domain of spatio-temporal applications. One of the key features in MADS is the orthogonality of its 4 modeling dimensions (data structure, space, time, and representation), which makes the model easy to extend yet backward compatible.

MADS structural dimension supports such well-known features as objects, relationships, attributes, methods, and so forth, as well as a number of more complex components, such as derived attributes, is-a links, aggregation, generalization, multi-inheritance, transition relationships, etc.

MADS spatial dimension provides abstract datatypes (ADT) for representing shape and location information (points, lines, simple and complex surfaces, etc.). Each datatype has an associated set of methods for manipulating its values. The spatiality of a type is described by a predefined attribute `Geometry`, whose value domain is one of the spatial datatypes.

MADS temporal dimension provides ADTs for representing instants, intervals, and temporal elements. Temporal ADTs support time-stamping, i.e. associating a timeframe to a fact. The temporality of a type in MADS is described by a predefined attribute `Lifecycle`, and due to the model orthogonality, any object or relationship type can be specified as spatial, or temporal, or both. MADS also allows to represent time-varying and space-varying information as a function from time/space to value domains.

Another manifestation of spatio-temporal semantics in MADS is the constrained relationships. Spatial (resp. temporal) object types can participate into topological (resp. synchronization) relationship types. Such kind of relationships impose additional constraints of spatio-temporal nature on the `Geometry` (or `Lifecycle`, or both) attributes of the linked instances. MADS supports six predefined topological relationships (incl. disjoint, adjacent, inside, etc.), and seven predefined synchronization relationships (incl. before, overlaps, during, etc.).

Finally, MADS representation dimension permits to deal with issues like user-adaptability and multi-representation by introducing a mechanism of perception stamps. In MADS, object and relationship types, attributes, and methods can have different representations and therefore be stamped. Two traditional stamping criteria are viewpoints, and resolutions.

Besides a rich data description part, MADS also provides a powerful algebraic query language as well as a number of GUI tools: Query Editor for visual querying functionality, and Schema Editor for designing MADS conceptual schemata.

Let's illustrate some of MADS modeling features with an example. Fig. 5 presents a sample conceptual schema of a multimedia meeting environment. The object type `Meeting` has a lifecycle of type `IntervalSet`, which allows accounting for interruptions, or dealing with meetings that span several days. Moreover, spatiality of object type `Meeting` is described by its predefined attribute `Geometry` (not shown), whose value domain is a spatial datatype `Point` (representing the place where a meeting is held). Similarly, spatiality of meeting participants (object type `Participant`) is also of datatype `Point`, yet their current spatial position is time-varying. We further assume that participants can attend meetings either physically, or virtually using a webcam. In order to save communication bandwidth, virtual attendees can disconnect/reconnect multiple times, thus missing certain parts of the meeting. This fact is reflected on the schema by the lifecycle of a relationship type `Virtually` being an `IntervalSet`. Furthermore, relationship types `Physically` and `Virtually` show topological semantics of types `Inside` and `Disjoint`, respectively, meaning that unlike participants who attend physically, virtual attendees cannot be physically situated in the meeting room. Besides, since the exact number and identity of Internet participants is not known in advance, we decide to resort to multirepresentation features of MADS, and thus introduce two perception stamps T1 and T2, with the former reflecting the information available before the meeting has taken place, and the latter reflecting the information available after the meeting has finished. As you can notice, the relationship type `Virtually` is only available in the perception stamp T2. Finally[2], the relationship type `Presents` marks the span of the document presentation via its lifecycle of type `Interval`.

4 MADS Multimedia Extensions

Modeling multimedia representation of real world objects and events conditions some peculiarities as compared to modeling these same real world entities

[2] The rest of the elements presented in fig. 5 are described in sect. 4.4.

directly. In order to depict these special characteristics that inhere in multimedia information, we use the orthogonality principle of MADS, and propose to introduce a new modeling dimension (*Multimedia Dimension*) that serves to semantically represent various facts related to multimedia aspects of the modeled information. This approach permits to efficiently reuse all the existing features of MADS in multimedia-related applications, as well as to keep it totally backward-compatible for traditional non-multimedia use.

4.1 Multimedia Abstract Datatypes

Semantically an object in MADS is said to be of multimedia type if it has some associated multimedia representation. That is either: 1) our knowledge of the object existence comes e.g. from watching a video or listening to an audio stream, where the object is visually/aurally represented, or 2) the object has some associated multimedia representation thereof, which however does not condition our knowledge of the object existence. In other words, having a multimedia object means having an object that possesses some multimedia representation via, for example, a video file, an audio stream, etc. To precise which kind of multimedia representation is in issue, abstract multimedia datatypes are used.

Fig. 2 shows the hierarchy of multimedia datatypes in MADS. Each of the multimedia datatypes is characterized by a number of its proper methods, which provide some datatype-specific functionality. For example, the complex datatypes in fig. 2 provide the following specific operations:

1. Audio-Video (`AV`), e.g. a motion picture.
   Specific operation: lip motion assisted speech recognition.
2. Audio-Video-Text (`AVT`), e.g. movies with subtitles.
   Specific operation: subtitle production via speech recognition.
3. Picture-Audio (`PA`), e.g. TV news from a reporter calling on the phone.
   Specific operation: automatic voice-recognition-based photo selection.
4. Picture-Text (`PT`), e.g. a digital picture and its title or textual description.
   Specific operation: picture description via low-level image content analysis.

It should be noted nonetheless that fig. 2 only represents a hierarchy of abstract conceptual multimedia datatypes, which should not be confronted with a

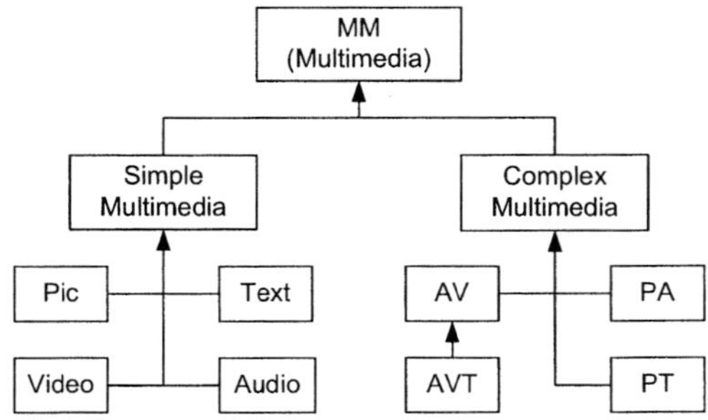

Fig. 2. Multimedia Datatype Hierarchy

list of particular multimedia formats, like JPEG, MP3, etc., supported by the multimedia-oriented application. At this stage, for example, AV only specifies that the multimedia information in question is of audio-visual type, whatever its storage, encoding, and format are. These latter characteristics, in their turn, should be considered at other modeling levels and are in general implementation-dependant. It should also be noted that the hierarchy in fig. 2 is not exhaustive and only represents the most used, in authors' point view, types of multimedia data. In order to better adapt to particular requirements of a multimodal multimedia application, any new abstract multimedia datatype whatsoever, ranging from tactile information to smell, could be introduced into the hierarchy. In this case, newly introduced datatypes could be associated with specific concepts from a domain ontology, which would make understating their semantics easier for the users of the system. On the other hand, for the sake of application simplicity, a pruned hierarchy could also be used instead, with some of the datatypes not taken into consideration and thus represented by their super-types.

Strictly adhering to the orthogonality principle of MADS, any object or relationship can be specified as multimedia, no matter if this object or relationship already has some characteristics of other MADS modeling dimensions. Thus, for example, it is possible to have an object that is at the same time spatial and multimedia, or spatial and temporal and multimedia, etc. In much the same manner as for spatial or temporal objects in MADS, a multimedia object type implies having a special attribute (`Multimedia`), whose value domain is one of the abstract multimedia datatypes (see fig. 3). Besides objects and relationships, also the attributes can be of multimedia type. A multimedia attribute is a simple (possibly multi-valuated) attribute, whose domain is a multimedia datatype.

Fig. 3 demonstrates the use of abstract multimedia datatypes in MADS. The object type `Meeting`, as well as one of its attributes (`Organizer`) are specified as multimedia (`AV` and `Pic`, respectively), which on the object type definition level means having an attribute `Multimedia` of type `AudioVisual`, as well as attribute `Organizer` of type `Picture`. Note as well, that the object type `Meeting` combines at once spatial, temporal, and multimedia characteristics.

4.2 Representational Relationships

As previously mentioned, a relationship type in MADS can be specified as multimedia by being associated with one of the abstract multimedia datatypes. In

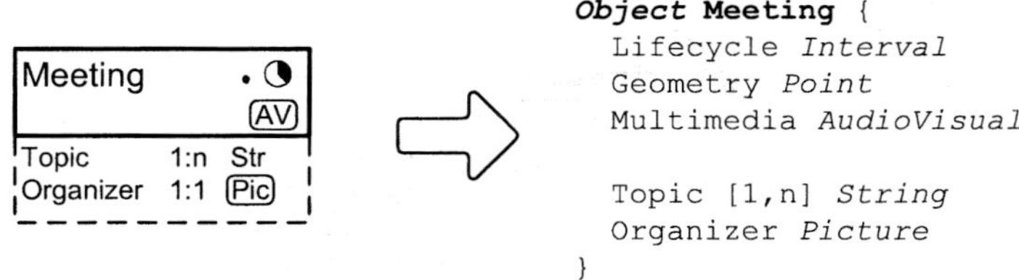

Fig. 3. Multimedia Semantics in MADS Schema and Object Type Definition

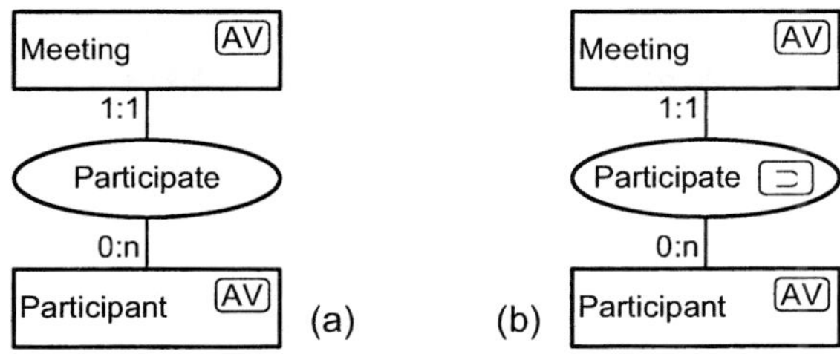

Fig. 4. Representational Relationships in MADS

addition to that, multimedia object types can participate into a special kind of relationships called *representational relationships*. Enriching a binary relationship with representational semantics implies imposing additional constraints on `Multimedia` attributes of instances linked by the relationship. For example, in fig. 4a object types `Meeting` and `Participant` are linked by a relationship type `Participate`, which we would like to constrain by imposing that only then does it hold when the assumed participant can be seen and/or heard throughout the corresponding meeting. To enforce this condition, the relationship `Participate` is further constrained by being assigned as `MultimediaInclusion` type (fig. 4b), meaning that according to the schema in fig. 4b any participant, who is said to participate in a meeting, must additionally have his multimedia representation included in the multimedia representation of the corresponding meeting. Given the example in fig. 4b, this would in particular signify (taking into account that both `Meeting` and `Participant` are of `AV` multimedia type) that the audio-visual representation of the `Participant`, which is contained in his `Multimedia` attribute, must be included in the audio-visual representation of the corresponding `Meeting`, contained in the `Meeting.Multimedia` attribute.

The following 4 generic types of representational relationships are proposed:

1. *multimedia inclusion*: multimedia representation of one linked instance is semantically included into multimedia representation of the other linked instance (see e.g. fig. 4b);
2. *multimedia intersection*: multimedia representations of two linked instances share some common semantics, however neither of the two completely includes the other one;
3. *multimedia equality*: multimedia representations of two linked instances are semantically equal, meaning that multimedia representations of neither linked instances provides more semantic content than the other one;
4. *multimedia inequality*: multimedia representations of two linked instances are semantically disjoint.

It is important to emphasize that associating relationship types in MADS with any of the representational relationship types described above only imposes additional constraints of merely conceptual nature, and does not (not necessarily) imply similar constraints on physical multimedia files, streams, etc. behind the multimedia instances linked by the concerned relationship. For example, turning back to fig. 4b, the fact of the relationship type `Participate` being of the representational type `MultimediaInclusion` does not necessarily imply that e.g. MPEG files containing multimedia representations of meetings should be physically composed of MPEG files representing meeting participants.

4.3 Multirepresentation in Multimedia

As presented in sect. 3, representation dimension of MADS allows to deal with the notion of multi-representation, in particular, by means of perception stamp mechanism. Thanks to the orthogonality principle, the representation dimension can also be used in multimedia settings, especially when dealing with such important aspects of conceptual multimedia data modeling as user-adaptability and multi-representation (see sect. 2). In particular, multirepresentation in MADS can be used to solve the following problems in the context of multimedia semantics (demonstrated here by the example of multimedia meetings):

1. Multiple values of multimedia attributes (incl. reserved `Multimedia` attribute).
   Suppose that in some multimedia-enabled meeting management system participants are represented by their photos (possibly more than one). We would like to be able to use regular passport-format photos in official settings, while keeping informal ones for coffee-breaks and banquet environments.
2. Multiple datatypes of multimedia attributes.
   Further generalizing the problem of multivalued multimedia attributes, also their datatypes may differ from one representation to another, even possibly belonging to different modeling dimensions. For example, the `Organizer` attribute in fig. 3 could be of multimedia datatype `Picture` in one representation, and of non-multimedia datatype `String` in another representation.
3. Limiting access to multimedia content.
   In the context of the IM2 project, which is characterized by a big number of users from various domains, multirepresentation coupled with an access rights mechanism can help control user access to multimedia content depending on user's access privileges on the representation that this content belongs to. This facilitates, in particular, multiple and simultaneous user access.

4.4 Multimedia-Extended MADS Schema

In fig. 5, a sample multimedia-extended conceptual schema of a multimedia meeting environment is presented. We keep on the description given in sect. 3, and characterize hereby the multimedia-related details of the presented schema. The object type `Person` displays its multimedia properties by means of a predefined attribute `Multimedia` (not shown), whose value domain is a multimedia datatype `Picture`. This allows, for example, associating a passport-size photo with each person registered in the system. Moreover, also the object type `Participant` is now additionally characterized by a `Picture`, which, in our example, is simply inherited from its super-type `Person`. In order to allow meeting participants present documents of various formats, and not restrict them to some specific

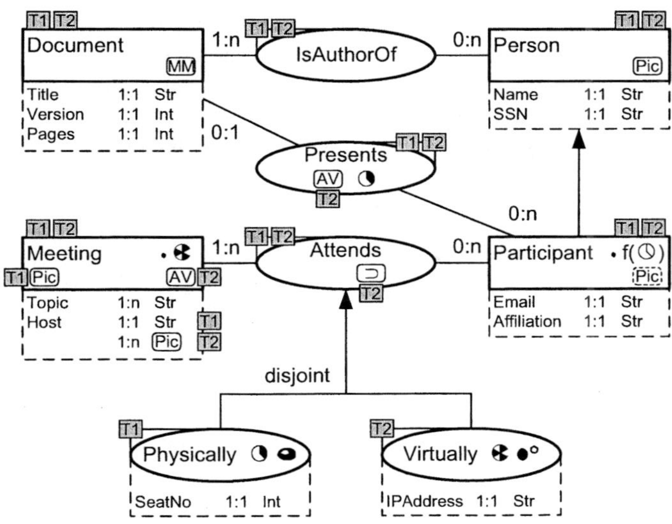

Fig. 5. Multimedia-Extended MADS Schema

one, we define the multimedia nature of the object type `Document` as being of an abstract multimedia super-type `MM` (see fig. 2). Furthermore, interested not only in storing presentation documents themselves, but also in capturing the manner in which they are presented by meeting participants, we decide to add multimedia property of complex datatype `AV` to the relationship type `Presents`. Since this latter multimedia information can only become available after the end of the meeting and not beforehand, we mark the newly-introduced audio-visual multimedia property of the relationship type `Presents` as belonging solely to the perception stamp T2. Making further use of the multirepresentation support in our multimedia-enabled environment, we decide to visually describe each `Meeting` by a `Picture` of its meeting room (already achievable in T1), and to provide instead a full-length audio-visual report of the meeting as soon as it becomes available (obviously, only accessible in T2). In order to exercise some control on the audio-visual representation of the object type `Meeting` in the perception T2, we order that all the meeting participants must be seen in the audio-visual footage in question. This is achieved by constraining the relationship type `Attends` with a representational relationship of type `MultimediaInclusion`. Finally, instead of storing the information about `Meeting.Host` as a simple character string value, we rather opt for a set of up-to-date photos taken right on the spot. Clearly, these latter are only available in T2.

5 Conclusions and Future Work

This paper presents a novel technique for multimedia data conceptual modeling.

We base ourselves on MADS, a spatio-temporal data model supporting multi-representation. Using MADS orthogonality principle, we extend the model with a new completely orthogonal multimedia modeling dimension. This permits to reuse the existing features of MADS in the multimedia context, as well as to keep the model totally backward-compatible for non-multimedia use. Although our approach is not limited to some specific multimedia setting, a sample case of multimedia meetings has been extensively used throughout the paper. We illustrate the modeling capabilities of our approach with a sample schema.

Currently, we are working on developing a complex 3-layer model, which will permit to represent multimedia data from 3 different points of view, namely: physical, logical, and conceptual. The multimedia-extended MADS, as described in this paper, is to be used at the conceptual layer of the 3-layer model in question. Our future plans also include incorporating the described multimedia extensions into MADS visual schema editing tool Schema Editor.

References

1. C. Parent, S. Spaccapietra, E. Zimanyi. The MurMur Project: Modeling and Querying Multi-Representation Spatio-Temporal Databases. In Information Systems. Elsevier, 2005
2. J. Smith. MPEG-7 Multimedia Content Description Standard. In D. Feng, W.C. Siu, H.J. Zhang (Eds.) Multimedia Information Retrieval and Management, pages 121-147. Springer-Verlag, 2003
3. S. Zillner, U. Westermann, W. Winiwarter. EMMA - A Query Algebra for Enhanced Multimedia Meta Objects. In proceedings of ODBASE 2004, Agia Napa, Cyprus, October 25-29 2004, Springer
4. K. Aberer et al. Emergent Semantics Principles and Issues. In Proceedings of the DASFAA 2004, LNCS 2973, pp. 25-38, Jeju Island, Korea, March 2004
5. E. Altman, L. Wyse. Emergent Semantics from Media Blending. In U. Srinivasan, S. Nepal (Eds.) Managing Multimdeia Semantics, pp. 351-362. IRM Press, 2005
6. H. Bounif, O. Drutskyy, F. Jouanot, S. Spaccapietra: A Multimodal Database Framework for Multimedia Meeting Annotations. In proceedings of the 10th International Multi-Media Modeling Conference, MMM 2004, Brisbane, Australia, IEEE Press (2004)
7. J. Vendrig, M. Worring. Interactive Adaptive Movie Annotation. IEEE MultiMedia, vol. 10, no. 3, pages 30-37, July 2003
8. M. Davis. Media Streams: An Iconic Visual Language for Video Representation. In Ronald M. Baecker, J. Grudin, William A.S. Buxton, S. Greenberg (Eds.) Readings in Human-Computer Interaction: Toward the Year 2000, 2nd ed., pages 854-866. Morgan Kaufmann, 1995
9. C. Parent, S. Spaccapietra, E. Zimanyi. Spatio-Temporal Conceptual Models: Data Structures + Space + Time. In Proceedings of the 7th ACM Symposium on Advances in GIS, Kansas City, Kansas, November 5-6 1999

STIL: An Extended Resource Description Framework and an Advanced Query Language for Metadatabases

Benjamin Buffereau and Philippe Picouet

École Nationale Supérieure des Télécommunications de Bretagne,
CS83818 - 29238 Brest cedex 3 - France
benjamin.buffereau@enst-bretagne.fr,
philippe.picouet@enst-bretagne.fr

Abstract. RDF, the current standard for the representation of Web metadata, is based on a simple graph model that ensures logical interoperability between metadata formats. This model is however too limited to represent natively complex metadata structures such as sets, lists, structured property values and reified triples, which are simulated using blank nodes and built-in vocabularies. This situation tend to blur the semantics of RDF graphs and complicate the expression of queries. In this article, we extend RDF with n-ary statements and statement nesting, so that complex metadata structures are expressed natively. A query language over this extended RDF is also proposed.

1 Introduction

Now widely adopted as the Web metadata representation standard, RDF [5] has found applications in many areas. Surprisingly enough, a standard query language is still missing. At the time of writing, SPARQL, the future standard RDF query language, is still under construction [7].

The concept of database of metadata, or metadatabase, is nonetheless promising. A growing number of Web resource descriptions are available on the network, notably in the form of RDF files. For the moment, those metadata can only be accessed through Web servers. The idea of metadatabases is to propose another access to metadata through query servers. Such servers could transform the Web into a huge decentralized database, allowing users to express complex queries to retrieve resources matching their needs.

As will be shown in this article, RDF is actually not fully appropriate as the data model of metadatabases. Its weakpoint is the ill-defined concept of blank node, that blurs the initial vision of RDF metadata as a graph of well-identified objects. Though inevitable to represent complex metadata structures, blank nodes introduce heterogeneity in metadata representation. As a result, querying RDF graphs is difficult as soon as blank nodes must be compared. Worst, as blank nodes may appear anywhere in RDF graphs, expressing generic queries is almost impossible.

M.L. Lee, K.L. Tan, and V. Wuwongse (Eds.): DASFAA 2006, LNCS 3882, pp. 849–858, 2006.

In this article, we propose an extended RDF called STIL, for Statements as Trees of Identifiers and Literals, and its query language STILQL. Keeping the good sides of RDF, STIL introduces n-ary statements, statements nesting, and standalone literals and identifiers. As a result, STIL natively represents all the structures that must be simulated in RDF. Moreover, in STIL, data resources (*e.g.* Web pages) are considered as a special case of metadata resources, which allows to query uniformly Web resources.

The article is organized as follows. Section 2 exposes the problematics of metadatabases, describes the potential applications of a metadata query language on a few use cases, and explains the drawbacks of RDF as a data model for such a query language. Section 3 presents the STIL data model and its benefits. Section 4 presents STILQL and its application to the use cases.

2 Problem Statement

2.1 An Example

Today's Web is composed of both data resources dedicated to human readers, and metadata resources that describe other resources. As an example, consider two (fictive) Web sites. The DASFAA2006 conference site, http://wwww.dasfaa06.org, publishes the conference papers as well as a metadata ressource (desc) that describes the papers. The database community Web site, http://www.databases.org, is a directory of Web pages and scientific papers about databases, in the Open Directory style. It also contains a metadata resource (desc) that describes the directory structure.

In the following, we use the following namespaces [2]: dasfaa06: is the alias for http://www.dasfaa06.org/, db: the alias for http://www.databases.org/, rdf: the RDF namespace, and ex: a fictive namespace used to name our predicates.

Fig. 1 presents (a possible subset of) the metadata resources dasfaa06:desc and db:desc expressed in RDF. As papers may have more than one author, and the order of authors is meaningful, blank nodes typed as RDF sequences are used to

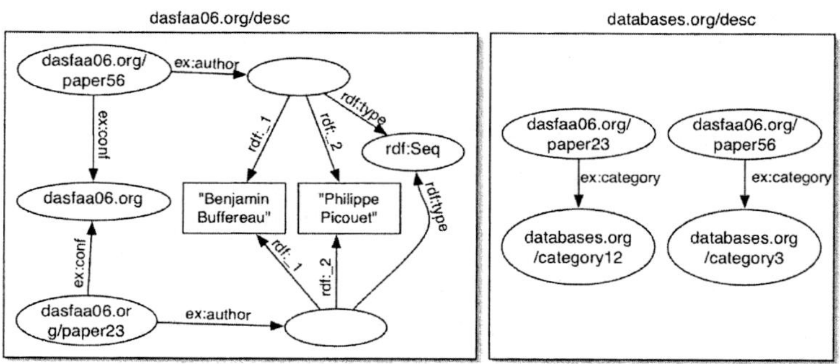

Fig. 1. Metadata resources in RDF

represent papers with more than one author. For the sake of the demonstration, we assume that two papers have the same sequence of authors represented by two different blank nodes.

2.2 Metadatabases Use Cases

For the moment, data and metadata resources are accessible only through Web servers using HTTP. The vision of metadatabases is to propose another access to those data and metadata resources through query servers. This would transform the whole Web into a world-wide database of data and metadata. In the following, we illustrate the potential of this vision on a few use cases.

Metadatabases would be a useful complement to current full-text search engines. Precise queries could be expressed, for example:

Q1: *Get the papers described in* dasfaa06:desc *as written by the same author(s).*

Q2: *Get the identifier, conference and author(s) of papers described in* dasfaa06:desc , *and classified by* db:desc *under the category* db:category12.

Metadatabases could also be useful in Web site management. As an example, the Web site of Benjamin Buffereau could be created simply by aggregating information already published on conferences Web sites. If dasfaa06:paper56 is the identifier of a paper written by Benjamin Buffereau, the following query extracts its metadata:

Q3: *Get the description from* dasfaa06:desc *of the resource* dasfaa06: paper56.

The situation above results in data and metadata duplication: the same paper is available from two sources, as well as its description. This is a problem for the people maintaining the database community Web site, as the same resource may be classified twice. In order to find duplicates, the following query could be expressed:

Q4: *Get the data resources described in* db:desc *that have different identifiers but the same content.*

2.3 Drawbacks of RDF

Though simple to express in natural langage, the queries Q1, Q3, and Q4 are difficult to write in query languages that use RDF as their data model, as briefly explained below.

First, in order to express Q4, a query language must be able to compare the contents of two data resources. This can be done easily with query languages that recognize data resources as instances of their data model. Unfortunately, though some Web resources such as HTML pages have a graph structure that can be converted in RDF, this is not the case of other resources such as images or PDF files. The contents of such resources can be seen as RDF literals, but an RDF graph is a set of triples, so a literal is not a valid instance of the RDF data model. As a conclusion, in order to express Q4, a query language using RDF as its data model must use an external function to compare the data resources.

Second, the expression of Q1 and Q3 must be independent of the structure of the queried RDF graphs. Q1 compares the author(s) of different papers, no matter if the value of this property is a single author or a list of authors. Similarly, Q3 asks for the description of a data resource without any knowledge of the structure of this description. We call such queries *generic queries*. Because of blank nodes, generic queries are difficult to express in query languages based on RDF. As an example, consider the expression of Q1 on the graph in Fig. 1. As the same sequence of authors is represented by two different blank nodes, the expression of Q1 cannot rely on blank node identifiers: blank nodes must be compared based on their descriptions. Then, the query must compute blank node descriptions and compare them. The situation would be different if the list of authors was represented as a literal node. Without any prior knowledge of the graph structure, it is difficult to express a query that would take into account every possible situation.

3 The STIL Model

As RDF is limited to binary statements, statements of a higher arity must be splitted into binary statements, and blank nodes must be introduced. In order to eliminate blank nodes, we propose to allow n-ary statements, as well as statement nesting in the style of relational complex values [1]. Moreover, in order to be able to query any type of resources including opaque data formats and file directories, standalone literals and identifiers are allowed.

After a presentation of STIL syntax and semantics (Sect. 3.1), we expose the benefits of the approach (Sect. 3.2) and investigate the conversion of RDF graphs into STIL collections (Sect. 3.3).

3.1 STIL Syntax and Semantics

STIL is a value-oriented model, i.e. constructs of the language are not objects but values. It distinguishes three types of values, namely literals, resource identifiers and statements. Literals are base type values such as strings or integers. Identifiers represent Web resources identified by a URI, or local resources identified by a symbol. Statements represent arbitrarily complex relations between values. A statement is composed of a prefix and a set of attributes. Each attribute is composed of a name and a value. The prefix and the attribute names are identifiers, while an attribute value may be an identifier, a literal or a statement. In a given statement, *attribute names must be distinct*, and give the role of each value in the statement. Finally, a collection is defined as a (possibly heterogeneous) set of values.

Graphically, a statement takes the shape of a rooted tree with labels on nodes and arcs. The root represents the statement prefix, its outgoing arcs represent the statement attributes, and the arc destinations represent the attribute values. Literals and identifiers are represented as nodes. A collection is represented as a set of trees, where a tree may be a single node.

```
<collection> = "{" "}" | "{" <values> "}"
<values> = <value> | <value> "," <values>
<value> = <literal> | <identifer> | <statement>
<statement> = <identifier> "[" "]" | <identifier> "[" <attributes> "]"
<attributes> = <attribute> | <attribute> "," <attributes>
<attribute> = <identifier> "=" <value>
```

Fig. 2. BNF grammar for STIL values

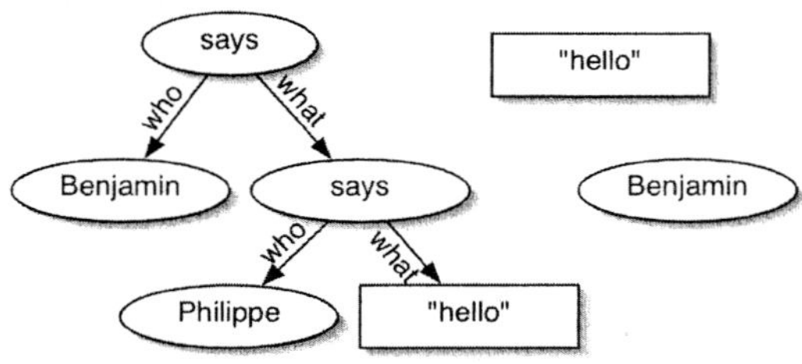

Fig. 3. An example of STIL collection

For example, the collection in Fig. 3 states that there exists a resource called `Benjamin`, a literal `"hello"`, and a statement whose expression in natural language is "Benjamin says that Philippe says hello".

A BNF grammar for STIL values is given in Fig. 2. In this syntax, the collection of Fig. 3 is expressed as follows:

```
{Benjamin, "hello", says[who=Benjamin, what=says[who=Philippe, what="hello"]]}
```

3.2 Benefits of the STIL Approach to Metadata Representation

A first benefit of STIL is its flexibility: any type of resource can be interpreted as a STIL collection. For example, a file directory is a set of identifiers, a relational database is a set of statements, and an image is a collection containing a single literal which is the resource contents. As a consequence, STIL queries can be written to get, compare, or aggregate resources of any type.

A second benefit of STIL is that it represents natively complex metadata structures, such as structured property values [5], n-ary relations [6], and reified statements. Fig. 3 gives an example of statement reification. Complex metadata structures are more easy to compare in STIL than in RDF. Moreover, extracting a resource description is straightforward: the description of a resource is the set of statements where the resource appears as an attribute value.

3.3 Converting RDF Graphs into STIL Collections

The compatibility of STIL with RDF is an important issue as a lot of metadata resources are modeled in RDF. In order to use STILQL as an RDF query language, RDF resources must be converted "on-the-fly" into STIL collections. STIL

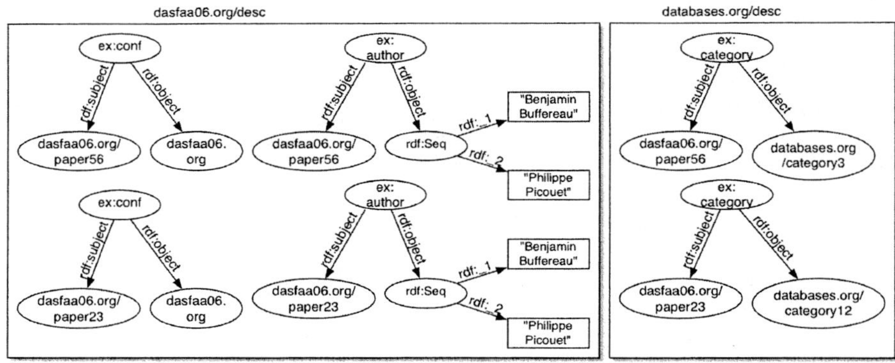

Fig. 4. STIL representation of the RDF collections in Fig. 1

is an extension of RDF ground graphs: the STIL representation of a ground RDF triple is a statement where the prefix is the triple predicate and the attributes are the triple subject and object. Thus, the only difficulty is the conversion of blank nodes. However, most RDF blank nodes actually represent complex values, that can be represented in STIL as statements. We then propose the following (lossless) conversion from an RDF graph into a STIL collection:

- a blank node typed as `rdf:Statement` is converted into a STIL statement whose prefix is the predicate of the reified statement and whose attributes are the reified statement subject and object.
- a blank node typed as `rdf:Bag`, `rdf:Alt`, `rdf:Seq` or `rdf:Collection` is converted into a STIL statement whose prefix is the blank node type and whose attributes are the elements of the list or set.
- an untyped blank node is converted into a statement whose prefix is `blank` and whose attributes are the outgoing arcs.
- the other triples of the RDF graph are converted into STIL statements whose prefix is the triple predicate and whose attributes are the triple subject and object.

Following those conversion rules, the RDF graph in Fig. 1 is converted into the STIL collection in Fig. 4. Note that the conversion fails on untyped blank nodes in two cases: first, when the RDF graph contains a cycle of untyped blank nodes; second, when there are two triples in the RDF graph that have the same predicate and the same untyped blank node as subject. Intuitively, this correspond to the few situations in which blank nodes cannot be interpreted as complex values.

4 STILQL, the STIL Query Language

In this section, we propose a quick overview of the STIL query language. STILQL is inspired from semistructured query languages such as Lorel [8] and StruQL

[4]. Its semantics is inspired from the complex value algebra [1]. More details can be found in [3].

4.1 Simple Queries

A STIL value, as well as a STIL collection defined in extension, are valid queries. The set operators can be used on STIL collections. Some unary operators are provided: `content` returns the (union of the) collection(s) referred to by the identifiers found in argument; `prefix` returns the prefixe(s) of the statements found in argument; `arity` returns the arity (i.e. the number of attributes) of the statements found in argument; `attributes` returns the attribute name(s) of the statements found in argument; `type` returns the type(s) of the values found in argument. Possible types are `Identifier`, `Literal` and `Statement`.

Path expressions can be used to navigate in statements. A path expression is a dot-separated sequence of attribute names. The wildcards ? and * can also appear in path expressions. The wildcard ? replaces any attribute name, while the wildcard * replaces any sequence of attribute names.

The syntax of STILQL also allows the declaration of namespace aliases. Aliases can be used to abbreviate URIs both in queries and query results.

4.2 "Where ... Match ... Return" Queries

In order to compose more complex queries, variables must be defined and bound to values (see Q5, Q6, Q7, Q8 in Fig. 5). Variables are prefixed with `$`. A STIL query that uses variables is at least composed of a "where" clause to define and bind variables, and a "return" clause to format the query result.

```
#### Q5 # returns the collection in Fig. 4 ########################################

where $x in content(<http://www.dasfaa06.org/desc>) return $x;

#### Q6 # returns {says[who=Benjamin,what="hello"],says[who=Philippe,what="hello"],
########## says[who=Benjamin,what="goodbye"], says[who=Philippe,what="goodbye"]} ##

where $x in {Benjamin,Philippe}, $y in {"hello","goodbye"}
return says[who=$x,what=$y];

#### Q7 # returns {res[p=ex:category, o=dasfaa06:paper56, s=db:category3], ########
######### res[p=ex:category, o=dasfaa06:paper23, s=db:category12]} ################

where $x in content(<http://www.databases.org/desc>), $p = prefix($x),
      $o = $x.rdf:object, $s = $x.rdf:subject
match attributes($x) == {rdf:object, rdf:subject}
return res[p=$p o=$o, s=$s];

#### Q8 # alternative syntax for Q7 ##############################################

where $p[rdf:subject=$s, rdf:object=$o] in content(<http://www.databases.org/desc>)
return res[p=$p o=$o, s=$s];
```

Fig. 5. Some STIL queries

The "where" clause is a comma-separated list of variable definitions. The left operand of a variable definition gives the variable name, and its right operand gives the variable value(s). The "return" clause may be a single variable (Q5), or a statement constructor where variables may appear as prefix or attribute values (Q6, Q7, Q8).

```
##########################################################################
# Some aliases
##########################################################################

alias dasfaa06: <http://www.dasfaa06.org/>
alias rdf: <http://www.w3.org/1999/02/22-rdf-syntax-ns#>
alias ex: <http://www.example.org/>
alias db: <http:www.databases.org/>

################################## Q1 ##################################
# Get papers described in dasfaa06:desc
# as written by the same author(s).
##########################################################################

where ex:author[rdf:subject=$p1, rdf:object=$a] in content(dasfaa06:desc),
      ex:author[rdf:subject=$p2, rdf:object=$a] in content(dasfaa06:desc)
match $p1 != $p2
return res[paper1=$p1, paper2=$p2];

################################## Q2 ##################################
# Get the identifier, conference and author(s) of papers described in
# dasfaa06:desc and classified by db:desc
# under the category db:category12.
##########################################################################

where ex:conf[rdf:subject=$p, rdf:object=$c] in content(dasfaa06:desc),
      ex:author[rdf:subject=$p, rdf:object=$a] in content(dasfaa06:desc),
      ex:category[rdf:subject=$p, rdf:object=db:category12]
         in content(db:desc)
return res[id=$p, conf=$c, author=$a]

################################## Q3 ##################################
# Get the description proposed by dasfaa06:desc
# of the resource dasfaa06:paper56.
##########################################################################

where $statement in content(dasfaa06:desc)
match dasfaa06:paper56 in $statement.*
return $statement;

################################## Q4 ##################################
# Get the data resources described in db:desc
# that have different identifiers but the same content.
##########################################################################

where ex:category[rdf:subject=$r1, rdf:object=$c1],
      ex:category[rdf:subject=$r2, rdf:object=$c2]
match $r1 != $r2 and content($r1) == content($r2)
return res[r1=$r1, r2=$r2];
```

Fig. 6. Expression in STILQL of queries Q1 to Q4

Variable definitions use operators and path expressions. In particular, the operator `content` is used to iterate over the values found in a STIL collection (Q5, Q7, Q8). Moreover, operators and path expressions can be applied to variables, in order to define a variable from another variable (Q7).

Results can be restricted to the values matching a predicate, which must be defined in a "match" clause between the "where" and the "return" (Q7). A syntactic shortcut can be used to abbreviate some variable definitions. It consists in using a statement pattern as the left operand of a variable definition (Q8). A statement pattern is a statement where the prefix or some attribute names are replaced with variables.

4.3 STILQL in Action

The expression of the queries defined in Sect. 2.2 is given in Fig. 6. The queries work on the STIL representation of dasfaa06:desc and db:desc proposed in Fig. 4. They illustrate many useful features of STILQL:

- it allows to express distributed queries: Q2 works both on the content of the metadata resources db:desc and dasfaa06:desc.
- it allows the expression of generic queries: Q1 returns the papers that have the same authors, no matter if the list of authors is represented as a literal, an identifier or a statement. Thanks to the uniform notion of identity in STIL, users can write queries without any particular knowledge of the description structure.
- it allows to get quite simply, and using a generic query, the description of a given resource (Q3).
- it allows to query uniformly data and metadata resources (Q4).

Note that Q1 was written assuming that the query writer wants the papers that have exactly the same authors (the same people in the same order). If the query writer actually wants the papers that have at least one author in common, the query must be expressed differently.

5 Conclusion

In this paper, we addressed the issue of defining a metadata representation model and a query language that support the distribution of metadata and the expression of generic queries. We have proposed a new value-oriented metadata model (STIL) and its query language (STILQL). STIL is flexible enough to model the contents of most resources, including RDF resources. Thus, STILQL is both a general-purpose Web query language and a powerful RDF query language.

The extension of STILQL is an ongoing work: the closure of the language opens the road to the definition of a view mechanism. An update language and a schema definition language will also be studied.

Concerning implementation, optimization issues and access methods have to be investigated. At a more fundamental level, the expressive power of STILQL should be studied to determine a taxonomy of queries related to complexity classes.

References

1. Serge Abiteboul, Richard Hull, and Vitor Vianu. *Foundations of Databases.* Addison-Wesley, 1995.
2. Tim Bray, Dave Hollander, and Andrew Layman (editors). Namespaces in xml [online]. Available from: `http://www.w3.org/TR/REC-xml-names/`.
3. Benjamin Buffereau and Philippe Picouet. STIL: an alternative, queryable resource description framework. In *Bases de données avancées 2005 (BDA2005)*, 2005.
4. M. Fernandez, D. Florescu, A. Levy, and D. Suciu. A query language for a web-site management system. In *SIGMOD Record*, pages 4–11, September 1997.
5. Frank Manola and Eric Miller (editors). Rdf primer [online]. February 2004. Available from: `http://www.w3.org/TR/2004/REC-rdf-primer-20040210/`.
6. Natasha Noy and Alan Rector (editors). Defining n-ary relations on the semantic web: Use with individuals (working draft) [online]. 21 July 2004. Available from: `http://www.w3.org/TR/swbp-n-aryRelations`.
7. Eric Prud'hommeaux and Andy Seaborne (editors). SPARQL query language for RDF (working draft) [online]. July 2005. Available from: `http://www.w3.org/TR/2005/WD-rdf-sparql-query-20050721/`.
8. Dallan Quass, Anand Rajaraman, Yehoshua Sagiv, Jeffrey Ullman, and Jennifer Widom. Querying semistructured heterogeneous information. In *Proceedings of fourth international conference on Deductive and Object-Oriented Databases (DOOD)*, pages 436–445, Singapore, 1995.

Communication-Efficient Implementation of Range-Joins in Sensor Networks

Aditi Pandit and Himanshu Gupta

SUNY, Stony Brook, NY 11754
{apandit, hgupta}@cs.sunysb.edu

Abstract. In this article, we consider energy-efficient implementation of the SQL join operation in sensor databases, when the join selection condition is a range predicate. Apart from two simple approaches, we propose distributed hash-join and index-join algorithms for implementation of range-join operations in sensor networks. Through extensive simulations, we show that hash-join as well as index-join approaches significantly outperform the simple approaches, even for moderately sized networks. Our experiments also reveal that although both approach scale well, the index-join algorithm performs better than the hash-join algorithm especially in large sensor networks.

1 Introduction

A sensor network is a multi-hop ad hoc wireless network of resource constrained sensor nodes. Each sensor node has limited computing capability and memory, and is equipped with a short-range low-power radio, a small limited battery, and various sensing devices. Sensor networks combine sensing, computing, and networking capabilities to realize high-level sensing tasks in a collaborative manner. Each sensor node in a sensor network generates a stream of data items that are readings (typically, scalar values) from its sensing devices. This motivates visualizing sensor networks as distributed database systems [4, 10, 2]. Since, message communication is the main consumer of battery energy and sensor nodes have limited battery power, it is important to implement the queries in sensor networks with minimum communication cost. Moreover, due to the limited computing and memory resources at each node, the query processing in sensor networks is necessarily distributed.

In this article, we focus on communication-efficient implementation of certain special cases of SQL join operation in sensor networks. In particular, we address in-network processing of the SQL *range-join* operation, which is a special case of the join operation when the selection condition involved is a range predicate. We propose various distributed algorithms. One of our proposed hash-join algorithm can be shown to incur optimal communication cost under certain assumptions.

2 Range Join in Sensor Networks

In this section, we start with presenting an overview of sensor network databases.

M.L. Lee, K.L. Tan, and V. Wuwongse (Eds.): DASFAA 2006, LNCS 3882, pp. 859–869, 2006.

Sensor Network Databases. A sensor network consists of a large number of sensors distributed randomly in a geographical region. Each sensor has limited processing capability, is equipped with sensing devices, and has a low-range radio. Two sensor nodes can communicate with each other if the distance between them is less than the *transmission radius*. We assume that each sensor node in the sensor network has a limited storage capacity. Also, sensors have limited battery energy, which must be conserved for prolonged unattended operation. Each sensor node in a sensor network generates a streams of data tuples, and groups of sensor nodes producing tuples with the same format contribute to a single *data stream table*. In a sensor network, such data stream tables can be looked upon as partitioned horizontally across (or generated by) a set of sensors in the network. In a sensor database system, a query is typically initiated at a node called the *query source* and the results are routed to the query source for storage and/or consumption.

Problem Formulation. The SQL join ($\bowtie$) operation is a binary operation used to correlate data from multiple tables. *Range-joins* are joins wherein the join-predicate is whether two columns (*join-attributes*, usually with the same semantics), one from each operand table, have values that are within a given range of each other. *Equi-joins* are a further specialization of range-joins wherein the join-predicate is an equality of two columns, one from each operant table. In this article, we consider the problem of efficient in-network implementation of range-joins in sensor networks. In particular, we consider a join operation, initiated by a query source node Q, involving two data streams R and S distributed across some geographic regions $\mathcal{R}$ and $\mathcal{S}$ in the network. The main performance criteria for our distributed implementation is minimum communication cost, which is defined as the total data transfer between neighboring sensor nodes.

Related Work. The vision of sensor network as a database has been proposed by many works [4, 10, 2, 14]. However, prior research has only addressed limited SQL functionality – single queries involving simple aggregations [8, 6, 15] and/or selections [9] over single tables [7], or local joins [15]. So far, it has been considered that correlations such as median computation or joins should be computed on a single node [15, 9, 1]. The problem of distributed and communication-efficient implementation for general join operation has not been addressed in the context of sensor networks, except for our recent work [3] described in the next paragraph.

Chowdhary and Gupta [3] address the problem of communication-efficient distributed implementation of the join operation in the context of sensor networks. The paper presents a provably optimal algorithm for join operation that incurs provably minimum communication cost under reasonable assumptions, and a suboptimal heuristic that performs empirically close to optimal. However, they consider the general join operation that requires matching each tuple of one operand with each tuple of the other operand. In contrast, we consider implementation of range-join operations in sensor networks, for which we develop more efficient algorithms by using hashing and indexing techniques.

3 Implementation of Range-Join in Sensor Networks

In this section, we develop various algorithms for communication-efficient implementation of range-joins in sensor networks. As described in the previous section, we consider a join operation, initiated by a query source node Q, involving two data streams R and S being generated by two geographic regions $\mathcal{R}$ and $\mathcal{S}$ in the network. We first start with describing our general approach of implementing a range-join operation in sensor networks.

General Approach. Traditional database join algorithms such as nested-loop join or merge-join are unsuitable for direct implementation in sensor networks because they are "blocking" and sensor nodes have limited memory resources. To perform the join operation in a non-blocking manner, we determine the sliding windows W_r and W_s of the data streams R and S respectively and store them at some appropriately chosen regions in the network. We use the generation time of tuples to determine their membership in sliding windows. The size, shape, and location of the regions storing the windows depends on the memory capacity of each node, maximum size of each window, and the location of the regions $\mathcal{R}$ and $\mathcal{S}$ that are generating the respective data streams.

After the sliding windows W_r and W_s have been stored in the network, we perform the following high-level operations whenever a tuple r of table R (and vice-versa for a tuple of S)[1] arrives.

1. Find tuples of the window W_s that match with the new tuple r.
2. Join the matching pairs of tuples, and route the resulting tuples to the query source Q.
3. Insert the tuple r in the region storing W_r.

It is easy to see that performing the above operations for every arriving tuple of data streams R and S will correctly compute the join of R and S. The various approaches proposed in this paper differ in the manner in how and where the sliding windows are stored and how the above three operations are performed.

Naive Algorithm. The Naive algorithm uses the simplest way of storing the sliding windows. In particular, the Naive approach stores the windows W_r and W_s around the center of the regions $\mathcal{R}$ and $\mathcal{S}$ that are generating the respective data streams. Let the regions storing the windows W_r and W_s be $\mathcal{W}_r$ and $\mathcal{W}_s$ respectively. Now, when a new tuple r of the data stream R arrives, we need to broadcast r in the $\mathcal{W}_s$ region to find matching tuples of W_s.

Centroid Algorithm. In the Centroid Algorithm, both the windows W_r and W_s are stored within a region around some point C in the network region. When a new tuple r of the data stream table R arrives, it is routed to the point C, and then, broadcast within the appropriate region around C to find matching tuples

[1] Throughout this article, we discuss the tasks performed on arrival of an R tuple. The same discussion applies to arrival of S tuples.

from the window W_s. The resulting joined tuples are routed to the query source Q. Finally, the tuple r is stored at a nearby node around C with available space.

The total communication cost incurred in the above described approach consists of the cost of routing r to C, broadcasting r in the region around C, and routing the resulting joined tuples to the query source Q. It is easy to show that the total communication cost is minimized when C is the weighted centroid of $\triangle\mathcal{RS}Q$ formed by the centers of the regions $\mathcal{R}$ and $\mathcal{S}$, and the query source Q, where the centroid is weighted by the sizes of R, S, and $R \bowtie S$ (at Q) respectively.

3.1 Hash-Join Algorithm

The Naive and Centroid algorithms involve a broadcast of every newly arriving tuple in an appropriate region. In this subsection, we present a distributed Hash-Join Algorithm that exploits the fact that the join-predicate is a range predicate.

Basic Idea. The main idea of our distributed Hash-join algorithm is to "bucketize" (partition and store) each arriving tuple into certain buckets based on its join-attribute value. In particular, for each arriving tuple r or R, we hash its join-attribute value onto geographic coordinates and insert the tuple r at a node closest to the hashed geographic coordinates (as in GHT [11, 12]). To minimize communication cost, we wish to execute the "find W_s tuples" and "insert r in W_r" operations in the same region. Thus, use the same hash function for both operand data streams, and hence, the sliding windows W_r and W_s get stored in the same common region. For each new tuple r, the node closest to the hashed geographic coordinates is delegated with the responsibility of storing r, and performing the join with the stored sliding window W_s.

Hash-Join Algorithm Steps. We now outline the sequence of steps undertaken for each arriving tuple. For simplicity of presentation, we right now restrict ourselves to equi-join operations (and assume that there is sufficient available memory at each node I to store all hashed tuples (i.e., there is no overflow). We relax both the assumptions in later paragraphs. Now, for each arriving tuple r of a data stream R, the following operations are performed.

1. Hash the join-attribute value of the tuple r to geographic coordinates.
2. Route r to the node I that is closest to the hashed geographic coordinates. We use the standard location-aided routing mechanism such as GPSR [5] to route to I.
3. Insert r at the node I.
4. Join of r with matching tuples of W_s can be computed at I, since the matching tuples (having the same join-attribute value as that of r) of W_s must be available at I.
5. Route the resulting join tuples to the query source Q.

We note here that the above described distributed Hash-join approach is similar to the symmetric hash-join [13] algorithm proposed for evaluation of equi-joins in streaming database systems. We omit the proof of the following theorem for lack of space.

Theorem 1. *Let C be the weighted centroid of the centers of the regions $\mathcal{R}$ and $\mathcal{S}$, and Q, where the weights correspond to the sizes of the tables R, S, and $R \bowtie S$ respectively. Consider the hash-function that hashes the join-attribute values uniformly around C.*

The Hash-join algorithm using the above hash-function incurs optimal communication cost for implementation of an equi-join operation if each sensor node has sufficient memory to store all the hashed tuples. □

Hash-Join for Range-Joins. In order to extend the Hash-join algorithm to perform range-join operations, we need to only modify the fourth step of finding the matching tuples of W_s. More specifically, in case of a range-join operation, the tuples of W_s that may match with r need not have the same attribute value as that of r, but would be within a range of r's join-attribute value. If we use a *locality preserving* hash function, i.e., a hash function that maps close attribute values to close geographic coordinates, then the fourth step of our distributed hash-join algorithm can be modified to the following.

- The tuples of W_s that match with r must be available at nearby nodes *around* I. Thus, the tuple r should be broadcast in a region around I to find the matching tuples. The size of the broadcast region depends on the range of the join-predicate and the locality of the hash function, assuming there are no overflows.

Hash function for Range-Joins. To enable communication-efficient processing of range-joins, we use a hash function that maps a join-attribute value to radii coordinates (d, θ) with respect to the centroid C. In particular, we use the lower-order bits of the join-attribute value to obtain d, and the higher-order bits to obtain θ. Thus, a small range of join-attribute values would get mapped from (d_1, θ) to (d_2, θ) with respect to the centroid C for some values of d_1, d_2, and θ. Then, the set of tuples of W_s for a given range of of join-attribute values will lie on a radial straight line away from the centroid (see Figure 1 (a)), which can be efficiently targeted using location-aided routing such as GPSR [5].

Managing Overflows. Due to memory limitations, a sensor node I may not be able to store all the W_r and W_s tuples hashed to it. There are many ways to solve such an overflow problem. Our technique to handle overflows at individual nodes is to store the overflow tuples in nodes close (as close as possible) to the originally hashed node I. The node I keeps track of the maximum distance of the node that stores the overflow tuples, using overflow radii variables O_r^I and O_s^I for R and S data streams respectively. The overflow radius variables are kept updated.

The third step of inserting the tuple r in W_r and the fourth step of finding the matching tuples in W_s of the Hash-join algorithm need to be modified to incorporate our overflow technique. For the third step, if the node I doesn't

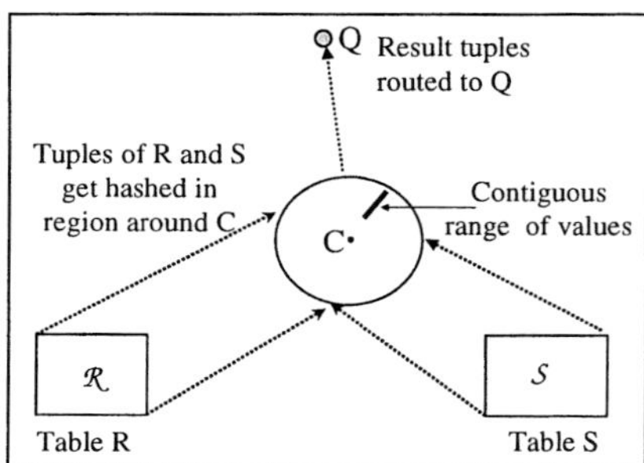

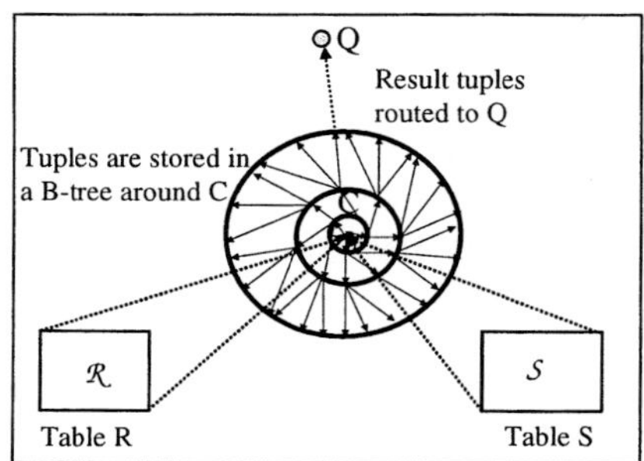

Fig. 1. (a) Hash-join algorithm, and (b) Index-join algorithm

have available memory to store the tuple r, it needs to find the closest node with available memory around it and possibly, update the O_r^I value. For the fourth step, to find matching tuples in W_s, the newly arrived tuple is broadcast in a region of radius O_s^I around I. In practice, the extent of overflow reduces the efficiency of the Hash-join algorithm.

To handle node failures and mobility, we can replicate tuples of a node I at nearby nodes.

3.2 Index-Join Algorithm

In this subsection, we propose an algorithm based on a distributed index data structure to achieve efficient searching of matching tuples for every newly arrived tuple. Essentially, the proposed Index-join algorithm uses a distributed index structure embedded within the sensor network to efficiently route the newly arrived tuple to the sensor nodes storing the matching tuples. In particular, we choose to build the classical B-tree index structure in a distributed manner in the sensor network. To avoid the cost of routing to two different regions, we use a single index structure to store both W_r and W_s windows.

B-Tree in Sensor Networks. To build a distributed B-Tree index structure in a sensor network, we need to first determine the location of the B-tree root and number of children/keys at each node (which in turn determines the height of the tree). Using similar arguments as in Theorem 1, we can show that to optimize the overall communication cost, the root of the B-tree index structure should be located at the weighted centroid C of $\triangle \mathcal{RSQ}$. The number of children (degree) at each node is determined by the memory available at each node for join processing and the number of communication-neighbors of a node in the network. Once the degree of the B-tree has been determined, we can determine the join-attribute key values to be used at each node in the B-tree starting from the root. At each node in the B-tree, the children nodes are distributed at uniform angles around the parent node. Due to limitations in the number of direct communication neighbors available, a child may not necessarily be a direct communication neighbor of its parent. In fact, the communication distance of a child from its parent may increase with the increase in the node's depth from the root.

To start building the index, the chosen root node determines its children, sets its child-pointers to its children, and sends a message to the chosen children with information about the range of join-attribute values each child is responsible for. Note that in traditional database systems, B-tree nodes use memory addresses as pointers to point to their children. However, in sensor networks, we can use geographic coordinates as pointers and use location-aided routing mechanism to reach children that are multiple hops away. The above process of creating more B-tree levels terminates when the remaining data range at each sensor node is small enough that the corresponding set of tuples of W_r and W_s can be stored at a single node. Finally, we need to set sibling pointers at the leaves, which can be done easily. To alleviate the problem of maintenance of the B-tree structure in response of insertions and deletions, we keep additional empty space in each sensor node to accommodate future insertions and do not reclaim space of expired/deleted tuples (since the overall rate of insertions is same as the overall rate of deletions).

Index-Join Algorithm. For every arriving tuple r of the data stream R, we essentially search for matching tuples in W_s using the constructed B-tree index structure, and then insert the tuple r in the index structure.

More specifically, we search for tuples in W_s with join-attribute value a, which is the lowest join-attribute value that could possible match with the join-attribute value of the tuple r. The root node finds the range in which the value a lies, and transmits the tuple to the geographic coordinates corresponding to the appropriate child. Eventually, a leaf node is reached and the sibling pointers are followed to access all the nodes storing tuples of W_s having join-attribute values from a to the maximum join-attribute value that could possibly match with the join-attribute value of r. The resulting joined tuples are finally routed to the query source.

Insertion of the tuple r happens similarly. In particular, we search for the leaf node that stores tuples of W_r with join-attribute value equal to that of r, and try to insert the tuple r at that node. Typically, the node should have enough space to store the new tuple because of the expiry of older tuples and the additional space available to accommodate insertions. In case of inavailability of empty space, we use the standard technique of insertions into B-trees. To make the distributed B-tree structure more load balanced, we replicate the higher-level nodes (ones closer to the root) into multiple nodes in a region around them.

4 Performance Evaluation

In this section, we present our simulation results which compare the performance of various range-join algorithms viz., Naive, Centroid, Hash-join, and Index-join algorithms, proposed in our article. Since incurred communication cost is the dominant consumer of limited battery power in the sensor nodes and the computation performed by all algorithms is minimal, we present only the total communication cost (in number of hops) incurred by various algorithms. Below, we present a discussion on our simulation results.

Experiment Setup. In our simulations, we generate a sensor network by randomly placing 10,000 nodes in an area of 10×10 units. Each sensor has a uniform transmission radius and two sensors can communicate with each other if they are located within each other's transmission radius. Varying the number of sensors is equivalent to varying the transmission radius, and hence, we fix the number of sensors and measure performance of our algorithms for different transmission radii. Each sensor node stores tuples in a local table of fixed size (5 tuples/node) occupying 300 bytes of memory. For the distributed Index-join algorithm, we use the same memory to also store the index structure entries, so as to be fair across various algorithms in terms of memory usage at individual nodes. Data tuples are generated at a uniform rate of 600 tuples/second by sensor nodes in the regions $\mathcal{R}$ and $\mathcal{S}$, and the (default) sliding window size consists of tuples that are at most 0.5 seconds old resulting in a sliding window size of about 300 tuples for each data stream. We perform simulations demonstrating the effect of varying various parameters such as transmission range, range of the join-predicate, size and shape of $\triangle \mathcal{RS}Q$, and the size of the sliding window.

Varying Transmission Radius for Different Predicate Ranges. In this set of experiments, we fix the locations of the regions $\mathcal{R}$ and $\mathcal{S}$ and the query source Q, and analyze the effect of increasing transmission radius on the total communication cost incurred for different values of the predicate range. The regions $\mathcal{R}$ and $\mathcal{S}$ are centered around the coordinates (1,1) and (9,1) which are the far-left and far-right corners at the bottom of the network, while the query source Q is located at (5,9) towards the top of the network. We vary the transmission radius from 0.15 to 0.24. Lower transmission radii left the sensor network disconnected, while higher transmission radius resulting in very low communication cost. We chose three different ranges of the join-predicate, viz., 10, 30, and 50. Note that range of the join-predicate signifies join-selectivity factor, and hence, determines the size of the join result.

The simulation results are shown in Figure 2. In all the figures of this section, we have not shown the plot for Naive approach, since it performed much worse (incurred twice the communication cost incurred by Centroid) than all other approaches. In Figure 2, we can see that the Hash-join and Index-join algorithms significantly outperform the Centroid approach in all three graphs. Also, the Index-join consistently outperforms the Hash-join algorithm. Note that the better performance of Index-join with respect to Hash-join does not contradict Theorem 1 due to the underlying assumptions made therein. With the increase in the transmission radius, the reduction in the number of hops leads to decrease in the overall communication cost incurred. All the three predicate ranges depict the above behavior, with the higher predicate ranges resulting in higher communication cost.

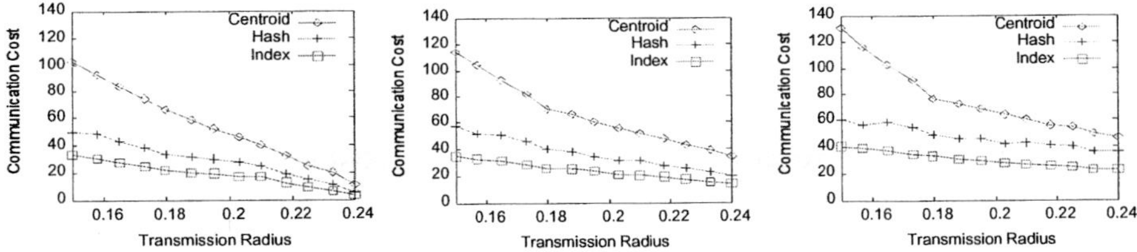

Fig. 2. Varying transmission radius for three different predicate ranges (10, 30, and 50)

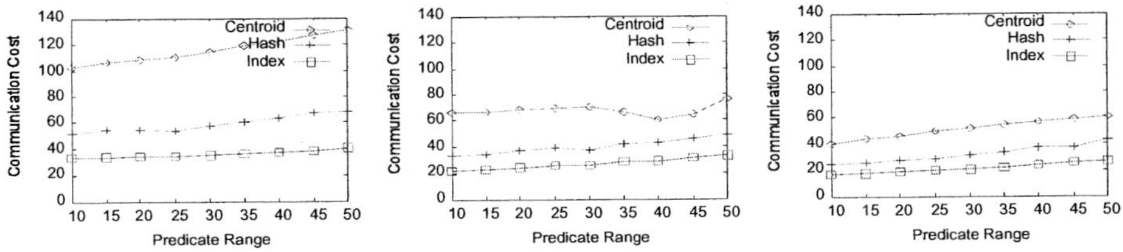

Fig. 3. Varying predicate range for three different transmission ranges viz., 0.15, 0.18, and 0.21

Varying Predicate Range for Different Transmission Radii. In this set of experiments, we fix the locations of the regions $\mathcal{R}$, $\mathcal{S}$, and $\mathcal{Q}$ as before, and analyze the effect of increasing the join-predicate range for different values of transmission radius. We vary the join-predicate range from 10 to 50, for three different transmission radii viz., 0.15, 0.18, and 0.21. The simulation results are shown in Figure 3. Here also, we observe the similar trend as in the first set of experiments, i.e., Index-join and Hash-join algorithms significantly outperform the Centroid approach, Index-join slightly outperforms the Hash-join, and increase in the transmission radius or predicate ranges causes the communication cost to decrease or increase respectively.

Varying $\triangle\mathcal{RSQ}$ for Different Predicate Ranges. In this set of experiments, we study the effect of different shapes and sizes of $\triangle\mathcal{RSQ}$ on the total communication cost, for three different predicate ranges (10, 30, and 50). Here, we fix the transmission radius to be 0.18. To vary the size and shape of the $\triangle\mathcal{RSQ}$,

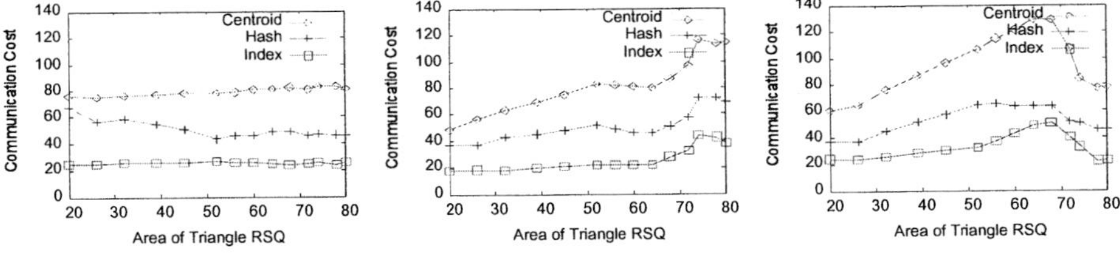

Fig. 4. Various $\triangle\mathcal{RSQ}$ for three different predicate ranges viz., 10, 30, and 50. Here, the transmission radius is 0.18.

we fix the centers of the regions $\mathcal{R}$ and $\mathcal{S}$, and change the position of the query source Q. We plot the graphs in Figure 4, where on the x-axis we represent the various instances of $\triangle\mathcal{RS}Q$ in the order of the area of the triangle. Again, we see that the Hash-join and Index-join algorithms perform significantly better than the Centroid, with Index-join consistently performing much better than the Hash-join algorithm. We note that increase in the area of the triangle for a fixed predicate range causes increase in the total communication cost incurred, since increase in the area of the triangle results in increase in the distance to the centroid.

5 Conclusion

In this article, we have proposed techniques for communication-efficient implementation of range-joins in sensor networks. We designed various approaches viz., Naive, Centroid, Hash-join, and Index-join, and evaluate their relative performance in random sensor networks. Our simulations indicate that the Hash-join and Index-join approaches perform much better than the other two simple approaches. Our designed algorithms could be incorporated in the sensor network query engines such as TinyDB. Some of the promising future directions include generalizing our technique for join for more than two tables, determining efficient join ordering, approximate evaluation of joins, and multiple query optimization involving join queries.

References

1. B. Bonfils and P. Bonnet. Adaptive and decentralized operator placement for in-network query processing. In *Proceedings of the International Workshop on Information Processing in Sensor Networks (IPSN)*, 2003.
2. P. Bonnet, J. Gehrke, and P. Seshadri. Towards sensor database systems. In *Proceeding of the International Conference on Mobile Data Management*, 2001.
3. V. Chowdhary and H. Gupta. Communication-efficient implementation of join in sensor networks. In *International Conference on Database Systems for Advanced Applications (DASFAA)*, 2005.
4. R. Govindan, J. Hellerstein, W. Hong, S. Madden, M. Franklin, and S. Shenker. The sensor network as a database. Technical report, University of Southern California, Computer Science Department, 2002.
5. B. Karp and H. Kung. Gpsr: greedy perimeter stateless routing for wireless networks. In *Proceedings of the International Conference on Mobile Computing and Networking (MobiCom)*, 2000.
6. S. Madden, M. Franklin, J. Hellerstein, and W. Hong. TAG: A tiny aggregation service for ad-hoc sensor networks. In *Proceedings of the Symposium on Operating Systems Design and Implementation (OSDI)*, 2002.
7. S. Madden and J. M. Hellerstein. Distributing queries over low-power wireless sensor networks. In *Proceedings of the ACM SIGMOD Conference on Management of Data*, pages 622–622, 2002.

8. S. Madden, R. Szewczyk, M. Franklin, and D. Culler. Supporting aggregate queries over ad-hoc wireless sensor networks. In *Workshop on Mobile Computing and Systems Applications*, 2002.
9. S. R. Madden, M. J. Franklin, J. M. Hellerstein, and W. Hong. The design of an acquisitional query processor for sensor networks. In *Proceedings of the ACM SIGMOD Conference on Management of Data*, pages 491–502, 2003.
10. S. R. Madden, J. M. Hellerstein, and W. Hong. TinyDB: In-network query processing in tinyos. http://telegraph.cs.berkeley.edu/tinydb, Sept. 2003.
11. S. Ratnasamy, B. Karp, S. Shenker, D. Estrin, R. Govindan, L. Yin, and F. Yu. Data-centric storage in sensornets with GHT, a geographic hash table. *Mobile Networks and Applications*, 8(4):427–442, 2003.
12. S. Ratnasamy, B. Karp, L. Yin, F. Yu, D. Estrin, R. Govindan, and S. Shenker. GHT: A geographic hash table for data-centric storage. In *Proceedings of ACM Intl. Workshop on Wireless Sensor Networks and Applications (WSNA)*, 2002.
13. A. N. Wilschut and P. M. G. Apers. Dataflow query execution in a parallel main memory environment. *Distributed and Parallel Databases*, 1(1):103–128, 1993.
14. Y. Yao and J. Gehrke. The cougar approach to in-network query processing in sensor networks. In *SIGMOD Record*, 2002.
15. Y. Yao and J. Gehrke. Query processing for sensor networks. In *Proceedings of the International Conference on Innovative Data Systems Research (CIDR)*, 2003.

Efficient k-Nearest Neighbor Searches for Parallel Multidimensional Index Structures

Kyoung Soo Bok[1], Seok Il Song[2], and Jae Soo Yoo[3]

[1] Department of Computer Science,
Korea Advanced Institute of Science and Technology, Korea
ksbok@dbserver.kaist.ac.kr
[2] Department of Computer Engineering, Chungju National University, Korea
sisong@chungju.ac.kr
[3] Department of Computer and Communication Engineering,
Chungbuk National University, Korea
yjs@chungbuk.ac.kr

Abstract. In this paper, we propose a parallel multidimensional index structure and range search and k-NN search methods for the index structures. The proposed index structure is nP(processor)-n×mD(disk) architecture which is the hybrid type of nP-nD and 1P-nD. Its node structure increases fan-out and reduces the height of an index tree. Also, the proposed range search methods are designed to maximize I/O parallelism of the index structure. Finally, we present a new method to transform k-NN queries to range search queries. Through various experiments, it is shown that the proposed method outperforms other parallel index structures.

1 Introduction

In the past couple of decades, multidimensional index structures play a key role in modern database applications such as GIS (Geographic Information System), LBS (Location Based Service), content based image retrieval system and so on. The applications commonly are required to manipulate multi-dimensional data. To satisfy the requirements of the modern database applications, various multi-dimensional index structures have been proposed[5, 8, 9].

There is much research on multidimensional index structures to improve retrieval performance in various ways. However, performance enhancement through a single index structure has the limitation that a single index structure may show insufficient retrieval performance for large amount of data. To solve this problems, several index methods using parallelism of processors or disk I/Os have been proposed[7, 10]. These parallel multidimensional index structures can be classified into 1P-nD and nP-mD, where nP and nD denote the number of processors and disks, respectively. In 1P-nD architecture, multiple disks are connected to one processor so as to improve performance through parallel disk I/Os, and in nP-mD architectures, multiple disks are connected to multiple processors.

M.L. Lee, K.L. Tan, and V. Wuwongse (Eds.): DASFAA 2006, LNCS 3882, pp. 870 – 879, 2006.

MXR-tree[1] and PML-tree[2] are 1P-nD parallel index structures. The MXR-tree have one master server that contains all internal nodes of the parallel R-tree. The PML-tree uses native space indexing with a disjoint space decomposition method. The PML-tree eliminates extra search paths of the R-tree and leaf node redundancy of the R^+-tree by distributing data objects into multiple data spaces. However, there is only one channel between a processor and disks so loading data to memory is processed in serial. In the nP-mD architecture, multiple disks are connected to multiple processors. nP-mD parallel index structures are constructed on special environments such as NOW (Network of Workstation). Therefore, nP-mD index structures exploit parallelism of processors and disk I/Os. MR-tree[3], MCR-tree[6] and PN-tree[4] are nP-mD parallel index structure. The MCR-tree reduces communication messages of the MR-tree. One master and multiple clients are connected through a computer network. Each client builds a complete R-tree for the portion of the data assigned to it. The PN-tree is an index structure for multidimensional spaces using multiple B^+-trees. The PN-tree can take advantage of as many processors as the dimensionality of the space.

In this paper, we propose a multidimensional index structure that supports the parallelism of processors and disk I/Os. The proposed index structure is nP-n×mD architecture which is a hybrid type of nP-nD and 1P-nD. That is, there are multiple processors and each processor have multiple disks. Our node structures increase fan-out and reduce the height of an index tree. Also, range search algorithm that maximizes I/O parallelism is presented. To the best of our knowledge, existing parallel multidimensional index structures hardly consider k-NN(k-Nearest Neighbor) queries. We propose new k-NN search methods suitable to our index structures. Through various experiments, it is shown that the proposed method outperforms other parallel index structures.

The rest of this paper is organized as follows. In section 2, we present the detailed description of our parallel multi-dimensional index structure. In section 3, we present the search algorithm for it. In section 4, the results of performance evaluation are presented. Finally, we conclude in section 5.

2 Architecture and Insertion Method of Our Index Structure

Our proposed multidimensional index structure is an nP-n×mD architecture which is a hybrid type of nP-nD and 1P-nD. That is, there are multiple processors and each processor have multiple disks. Disks are grouped evenly according to the number of servers. The groups are assigned to the servers. One primary server coordinates search processes and others are normal servers that process index operations. Each server manages a disk group and the disk group contains an independent index structure. A node in the index structure is distributed to disks in the group, i.e., a node consists of the pages of disks.

Each server manages a disk group and the disk group contains an independent index structure. Figure 1 shows the index structure of a disk group. As shown in the figure, a node in the index structure is distributed to disks in the group, i.e., a node consists of the pages of disks. An entry in the node contains child node's MBR and the pointers of those pages that consist of the node. In the figure, the first entry of the root node points the node 1. The node 1 consists of the first pages of disk A, B and C, so the entry must have the pointers of these pages and the MBR of the node 1.

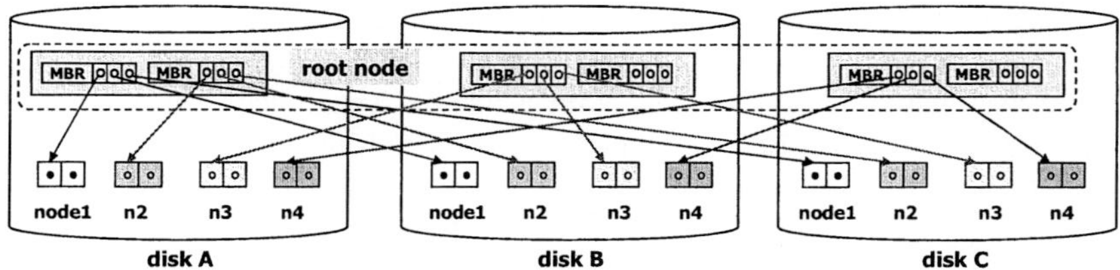

Fig. 1. Index structure of a disk group

The benefits of our architecture are as follows. First, similar data are declustered across multiple disks in the group. Since the entries in a node are distributed to multiple disks, declustering effects are maximized. Second, the height of index tree is reduced. The size of a node is determined by the page size and the number of disks in the group. As the node size increases, it takes more time to load a node into memory. However, because the index structure can load the node in parallel, the loading time is not a problem. In the R-tree family, overlaps between nodes reduce the retrieval performance. The height of a tree is one of the factors to increase overlaps. As the height of a tree becomes higher, more overlaps may be caused. Finally, in multidimensional index structures, as the dimension increases, the number of nodes to be accessed increases. That is, the number of node accesses is large when processing range search or k-NN search. Subsequently, in parallel multidimensional index structure, *uniSpread* is much more important than *minLoad*. The proposed index structure read all pages that consist of a node, so it maximizes the *uniSpread.*

2.1 Insertion

Assume that we insert entries a, b, c, d, e, f, g and h sequentially and have three disk groups. The entries are declustered across disk-groups in round robin fashion, i.e., a is inserted into the first disk-group, b is inserted into the second disk-group and so on. Various declustering techniques have been proposed, but in multidimensional data sets, the performance gap among them is not so large. Also, round-robin technique is easy and cheap to implement. In that reason, we choose round-robin technique as the declustering method. Entries assigned to each group are inserted into the index structure of the group. In the first phase, we find a proper node to insert a new entry. When a node is located, we check whether the node has enough space to accommodate the entry. Then, if overflow occurs, we start split process.

When processing node split, we need to carefully allocate pages for newly created node. In general, nodes in multidimensional index structures are not always full. Consequently, we cannot fully obtain disk I/O parallelism when accessing index nodes. To relieve this problem, we place the pages of two nodes (old node and new node) in different disks as much as possible so as to increase disk I/O parallelism when processing range search. We will describe our range search algorithm in the next section. Figure 2 shows node split process. In node 2(n2), overflow occurs. To split node 2, we assign a new node (node 3) and move partial entries of node 2 to node 3. When allocating pages to node 2 and node 3, we preferentially choose disks that have the smallest number of allocated pages. In the lower figure, disk D and E have the

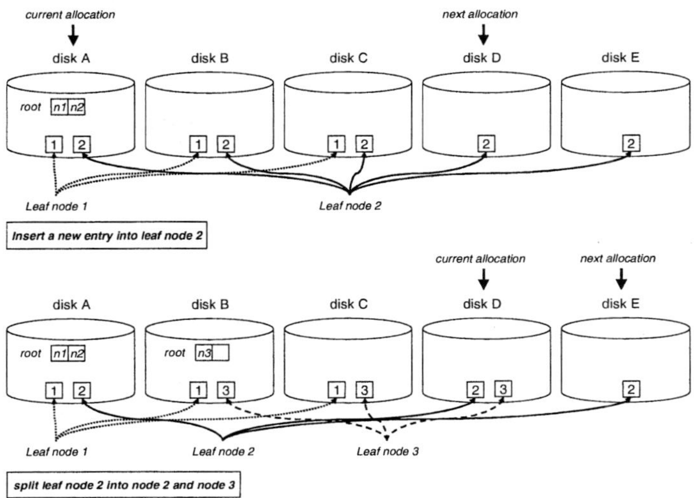

Fig. 2. Node split

smallest number of allocated pages, so pages for node 2 and node 3 are allocated from these two disks. First, we allocate three pages from D, E and A sequentially, and then allocate three pages from B, C, and D sequentially.

3 Search Algorithms

3.1 Range Search

In multidimensional index, structures have searchers take multiple paths when processing range search. That is, multiple nodes may be selected as next nodes to visit. Existing range search algorithms visit the selected child nodes sequentially. Figure 3 shows the process of existing range search algorithms. A searcher chooses entries 2, 4 and 7 from root node that are overlapped with its. The searcher visit child nodes that are pointed by 2, 4 and 7 sequentially. To read node 2, the searcher must access disk A, D and E since the pages of node 2 are distributed those disks. In a similar fashion the searcher visits node 4 and 7. The total number of disk accesses is the sum of the number of disk accesses to read root node and leaf nodes. The number of disk accesses to read root node is 1 and that of leaf nodes is 3. Therefore, the total number of disk accesses to process the range query is 4.

Our range search algorithms use different approaches to load child nodes. Once child nodes to visit are determined, we make a page loading plan according to which disks are involved to load child nodes. In figure 3, A3 means the third page of disk A. There are 8 pages to be read. We cluster these pages into groups consists of pages from different disks. For example, pages A3, B3, C3, D1 and E1 in GRP1 are from different disks. It means that those pages can be read at one I/O time. Also, A5, D4 and E2 in GRP2 are from different disks, so we can read them in parallel. If we load pages in this way, only two disk I/Os are needed to load leaf nodes. One disk I/O is saved com pared to the previously mentioned method. Figure 4 show our range search algorithm.

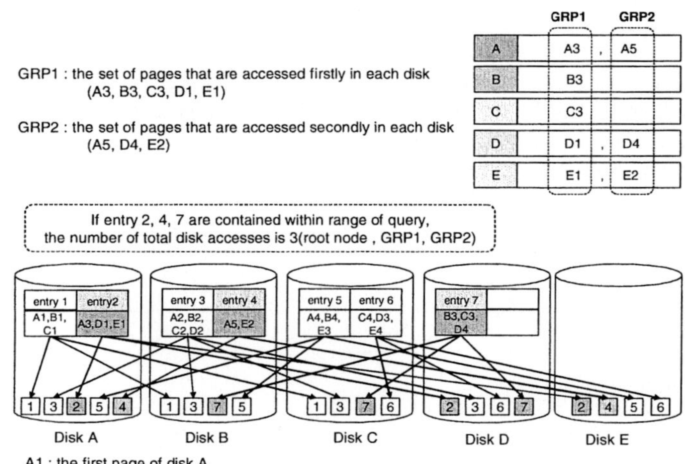

Fig. 3. Example of range search

```
Algorithm range search
<All Servers>
    transmit information of the root node to I/O scheduler;
    while(infinite loop)
        if(management information of I/O scheduler do not exist)
            break;
        end if
        cur_node := access nodes using I/O scheduler simultaneously;
        if (cur_node == leaf_node)
            calculate similarity and store it to result set;
        else
            select entries that is included in  the range;
            transmit the entry information to I/O scheduler;
        end if
    end while
    transmit the results to master server;
<Master Server>
    gather results and sort them according to similarity order;
    return the results to client;
```

Fig. 4. Range search algorithm

3.2 k-NN Search

Existing parallel multidimensional index structures hardly consider k-NN search. However, k-NN queries are important in modern database applications. We propose three k-NN algorithms and through experiments we show which one is the best. In the first method, the primary server distributes a k-NN query to servers and each server processes the k-NN query independently. Then, the servers return the k results to the primary server. The primary server filters the results from servers and makes final k results. The response time is the sum of the longest time among servers' response time and the time to filter servers' results. This method is simple and easy to implement. However, we may not use disk I/O parallelism like our range search algorithm because of the properties of the k-NN algorithm. When processing range search, a searcher chooses all child nodes to visit next that overlap with query predicates before going down to next level. Therefore, we can make a parallel page loading plan and save disk I/Os. However, in the existing k-NN search algorithm, all child nodes to visit next are not determined definitely but just one child node is determined. Consequently, we cannot make a page loading plan as in our range search algorithm. Figure 5 shows the first algorithm of k-NN search.

```
Algorithm KNN search 1
<All Servers>
    while(infinite loop)
        if(root_node == internal node)
            calculate similarities between query and entries in the node;
            sort them according to  similarity order;
        else
            calculate similarity between query and object;
            store values that are less than or equal to K to result set;
        end if
        if(a value of result set is greater than or equal to k)
            if(kth result is less than or equal to similarity of the first entry)
                break;
            end if
        end if
        root_node := access child nodes of the first entry simultaneously;
    end while
    transmit the k results to the master server;
<Master Server>
    gather results and sort them according to  similarity order;
    return the k results to the client;
```

Fig. 5. The first algorithm of k-NN search

In the second method, the primary server transforms k-NN queries to a range queries. Once a k-NN query has arrived from a client, the primary server processes the k-NN query partially. When the primary server gets first k results, it calculates the distance between k-th element and query point of the given k-NN query. It makes a range query with the distance. The range query is distributed to servers and the servers process the range query and return results. The primary server gathers the results from servers and makes k results. The time to process a k-NN query partially is quite short. Since servers can process the transformed range query, this method can get the parallelism of the range search algorithm. However, the transformed range query may become larger and reduce the overall performance. Figure 6 shows the second algorithm of k-NN search.

In the third method, once the primary server receives a k-NN query from clients, it sends the query to all servers. The servers execute partial k-NN queries with the received query, transform the k-NN query to range query similar to the primary server of type 2 and return the transformed range query to the primary server. Then, the

```
Algorithm KNN search 2
<Master Server>
    while(infinite loop)
        if(root_node == internal node)
            calculate similarities between query and entries in the node;
            sort them according to the  similarity order;
        else
            calculate similarity between query and object;
            store values that are less than or equal to k to result set;
        end if
        if(a value of result set is greater than or equal to k)
            break;
        end if
        root_node := access child nodes of the first entry simultaneously;
    end while
    calculate similarity between query and k-th object and convert to range query;
    transmit the result of the range query to the master server;
<All Servers>
    execute the proposed range search algorithm and transmit the result to the master server;
<Master Server>
    gather results and  sort them;
```

Fig. 6. The second algorithm of k-NN search

```
Algorithm KNN search 3
<All Servers>
    while(infinite loop)
        if(root_node == internal node)
            calculate similarities between query and entries in the node;
            sort them according to the  similarity order;
        else
            calculate similarity between query and object;
            store values that are less than or equal to k to result set;
        end if
        if(a value of result set is greater than or equal to k)
            break;
        end if
        root_node := access child nodes of the first entry simultaneously;
    end while
    calculate similarity between query and k-th object and convert it  to range query;
    transmit the result of the range query to the master server;
<Master Server>
    select the minimum range;
    transmit the selected range query to all servers;
<All Servers>
    execute the proposed range search algorithm and transmit the result to the master server;
<Master Server>
    gather results and sort them according to similarity order;
    return the k results to the client;
```

Fig. 7. The third algorithm of k-NN search

primary server redistributed the transformed query to servers. The servers process the range query and return their results to the primary server. Finally, the primary server makes k results from server's results. Figure 7 shows the third algorithm of k-NN search.

4 Performance Evaluation

The simulation platform is Sun Enterprise 250 with 1GB main memory and Solaris 2.7. Simulation programs are developed with gcc 2.8 compiler. We use uniformly distributed 100,000 data with 10 ~ 80 dimensionality. We measure response time and total number of disk accesses of a query to compare the retrieval performance of our index structure with the existing parallel multidimensional index structures. We perform several experiments in various environments. We present the results of experiments with varying dimension, the number of disks and page size. We compare our proposed index structure with MCR-tree. To our knowledge, the MCR-tree is the most recently proposed nP-mD parallel index structure and shows best performance among existing parallel multidimensional index structures.

We perform experiments to measure the response time and the disk accesses of k-NN queries and range queries with varying dimensions from 10 to 80, page sizes from 4k ~ 48k and disks from 3 ~ 15. Figure 8 to 10 show the response time and disk accesses of range searches and three types of k-NN searches. The graph of k-NN type 1 is omitted from the following charts since the performance difference of k-NN type 1 and others is too large to present in the charts with others. We carefully observe the performance of three k-NN queries. From the performance evaluation, we could conclude that our proposed k-NN search algorithms outperform the existing k-NN search algorithm (k-NN type 1). Also, as shown in the figures, the k-NN type 2 outperforms slightly the k-NN type 1. The reason is that even though the selectivity of transformed range query in k-NN type 3 may be smaller than that in k-NN type 2, k-NN type 3 requires more communication messages and more CPU time to gather and filter results from the servers.

We perform various experiments to measure disk accesses and response time of the range search operations of the MCR-tree and the PR-tree with varying the number of disks from 3 to 15. As shown in Figure 11, the PR-tree outperforms MCR-tree in all cases. In the MCR-tree, each server and client construct R-trees on one disk. However,

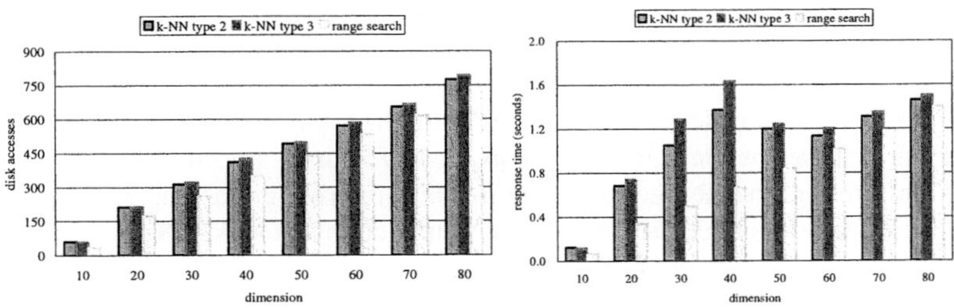

Fig. 8. Search operation with varying dimensions (data set : 100K, page size : 4k, disks : 15, servers : 3)

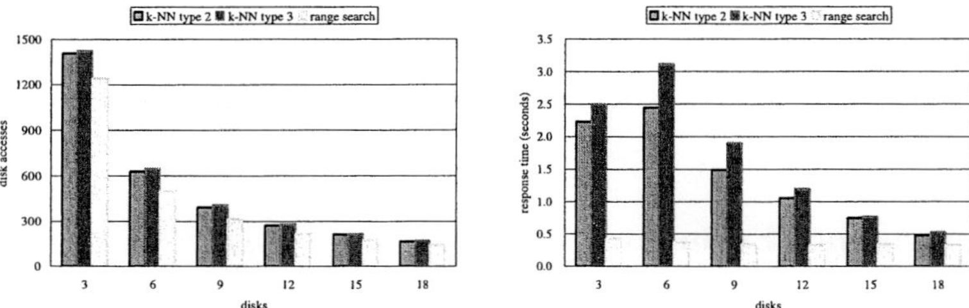

Fig. 9. Search operation with varying the number of disks (data set : 100K, page size : 4k, dimension : 20, servers : 3)

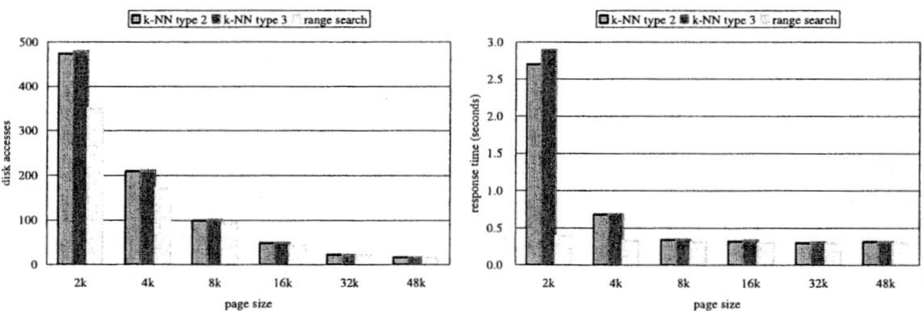

Fig. 10. Search operation with varying page size (data set : 100K, disks : 15, dimension : 20, servers : 3)

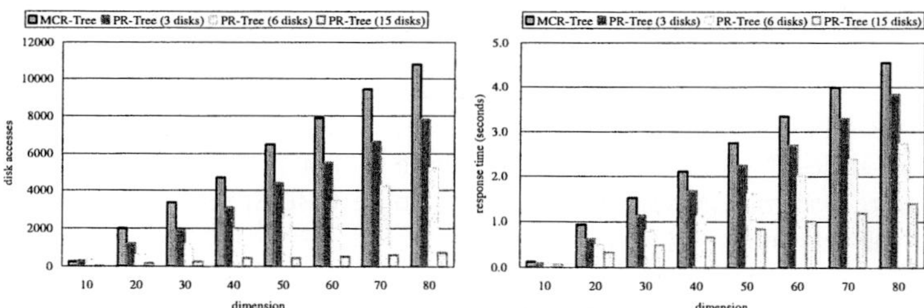

Fig. 11. Search operation with varying dimension (data set : 100K, servers : 3, page size : 4k, disks : 15)

we present an architecture where servers build R-trees on multiple disks. Also, our new range search algorithms improve the disk I/O parallelism.

Table 1 shows the results of performance comparisons between k-NN search algorithms of PR-trees and MCR-trees. As shown in the table, PR-trees outperform MCR-trees about 3 times when comparing only k-NN search algorithms. In MCR-trees, there is only one global R-tree that contains only internal nodes and leaf nodes of the global R-tree are organized as R-trees in multiple clients. The k-NN search algorithms require searchers to take paths downward and upward repeatedly. Therefore, communication messages between master and clients increase. Also, since our k-NN algorithms is to transform k-NN queries to range-queries, searchers get improved disk I/O parallelism as described in the previous section.

Table 1. Disk Accesses (DA) and Response Time (RT) of search operations (dimension : 9, data set : real 100K, disks : 3, servers : 3)

Index	Range		k-NN (type 1)		k-NN (type 2)		k-NN (type 3)	
	DA	RT	DA	RT	DA	RT	DA	RT
MCR-tree	60	0.047	76	0.12	-	-	-	-
PR-tree	33	0.21	54	0.036	47	0.031	38	0.034

5 Conclusion

We proposed a parallel multidimensional index structure based on nP-n×mD structure. We present new range search algorithms that more efficiently use disk I/O parallelism. Even though the k-NN search is one of the important query types in multidimensional index structures, research on improving k-NN search performance in parallel multidimensional index structures are hardly noticed. We present a new k-NN search algorithm that improves the disk I/O parallelism. Through various experiments, we prove that our proposed index structure outperforms exiting parallel multidimensional index structures.

References

1. Kamel and C. Faloutsos, "Parallel R-trees", Proc. ACM SIGMOD, pp.195-204, 1992.
2. K. S. Bang and H. Lu, "The PML-tree: An Efficient Parallel Spatial Index Structure for Spatial Databases", Proc. ACM Annual Computer Science Conference, pp.79-88, 1996.
3. N. Koudas, C. Faloutsos and I. Kamel, "Declustering Spatial Databases on a Multi-Computer Architecture", Proc. EDBT, pp.592-614, 1996.
4. M. H. Ali, A. A. Saad, and M. A. Ismail, "The PN-Tree: A parallel and distributed multi-dimensional index, Distributed and Parallel Databases, Vol.17, No.2, pp.111-133, 2005.
5. V. Gaede, O. Gunther, "Multidimensional access methods", ACM Computing Surveys, Vol.30, Issue. 2, pp.170-231, 1998.
6. B. Scnnitzer and S. T. Leutenegger, "Master-Client R-trees: A New Parallel R-tree Architecture", Proc. SSDBM, pp.68-77, 1999.
7. B. Wang, H. Horinokuchi, K. Kaneko and A. Makinouchi, "Parallel R-tree Search Algorithm on DSVM", Proc. DASFAA, pp.237-245, 1999.
8. J. An, Y. P. Chen, Q. Xu and X. Zhou, "A New Indexing Method for High Dimensional Dataset", Proc. DASFAA, pp.385-397, 2005.
9. X. Zhou, G. Wang, J. X. Yu and G. Yu, "M+-tree : A New Dynamical Multidimensional Index for Metric Spaces", Proc. ADC 2003, pp.161-168, 2003.
10. D. Taniar, J. W. Rahayu, "Global parallel index for multi-processors database systems", Information Science, Vol.165, No.1-2, pp.103-127, 2004.

Efficient Non-Blocking Top-k Query Processing in Distributed Networks*

Bo Deng, Yan Jia, and Shuqiang Yang

School of Computer Science,
National University of Defense Technology,
Changsha 410073, China
dengbomail@gmail.com, jiayanjy@vip.sina.com,
sqyang9999@126.com

Abstract. Incremental access can be essential for top-k queries, as users often want to sift through top answers until satisfied. In this paper, we propose the progressive rank (PR, for short) algorithm, a new non-blocking top-k query algorithm that deals with data items from remote sources via unpredictable, slow, or bursty network traffic. By accessing remote sources asynchronously and scheduling background processing reactively, PR hides intermittent delays in data arrival and produces the first few results quickly. Experiments results show that PR is an effective solution for producing fast query responses in the presence of slow and bursty remote sources, and can be scaled well.

1 Introduction

The objective of the top-k query is to find the "top *k*" results, according to a user-specified ranking function. In many database applications, top-k query processing is natural behavior, and the database research communities have studied the issue of efficient processing of top-k queries [1, 4, 5, 8, 9, 10, 16, 19] for a long time.

Incremental access can be essential for top-k queries, as users often want to sift through top answers until satisfied. Unfortunately, most state-of-the-art top-k query techniques in distributed environment [1, 2, 3, 7, 11, 14, 15] are performed in blocking mode: A query is submitted, then the system will waiting for a long time until the final answer is returned. As the number of results *k* increases, this blocking behavior becomes a serous problem in the pipelined operators and the scenarios that the results require user interaction.

In many emerging distributed applications, e.g. searching Web databases, retrieving in wide-area peer-to-peer (P2P) networks, wide-area distribution raises significant performance problems for top-k query processing techniques as data access becomes less predictable due to link congestion, load imbalances, etc. The main challenge of non-blocking top-k query processing techniques in distributed networks is how to deal with the unpredictable data accessing. However, the state-of-the-art non-blocking top-k

* This research is partly supported by the National High Technology Research and Development Plan (863 plan) of China under Grants No.2004AA112020 and No.2003AA111020.

M.L. Lee, K.L. Tan, and V. Wuwongse (Eds.): DASFAA 2006, LNCS 3882, pp. 880 – 889, 2006.

query techniques [1, 4, 11, 14] were addressed how to avoid random accesses to reduce the query cost and don't take into account network delays.

In this paper, we propose the progressive rank (PR, for short) algorithm, a new non-blocking top-k query algorithm that deals with data items from remote sources via unpredictable, slow, or bursty network traffic. The basic idea behind PR is to access remote sources asynchronously and produce an object on the fly when it is confirmed belonging to the final top-k results set. In this method, PR hides intermittent delays in data arrival and produces the first few results quickly.

The rest of the paper is organized as follows. Section 2 defines the problem of querying for top k matches in distributed networks. Section 3 discusses the related work. Section 4 introduces our new algorithm PR. Section 5 studies of the performance of PR. Finally, Section 6 concludes this paper.

2 Problem Statement

We consider a distributed environment with m + 1 nodes: a central manager node and m remote data source nodes. The central manager is connected to each remote data source node. Each remote data source node i has a data list D_i . D_i is a list of $\langle O, S_i(O)\rangle$ pairs, where O is an object and $S_i(O)$ ($S_i(O) > 0$) is the score of the object. We assume that objects in each list are sorted in descending order by their scores. If an object does not appear in a list, we say that its score in that list is 0.

For each object O, the central manager uses a monotone combining ranking function f to calculate its aggregate score across the m nodes. The top-k query q is to retrieve k objects from the m data lists $D = \{D_1, D_2, ..., D_m\}$ with the highest $f(O)$, $f(O) = f(S_1(O), S_2(O)..., S_m(O))$. For simplicity, we assume the sum function as the ranking function in this paper, i.e. $f(O) = S_1(O) + S_2(O) + ... + S_m(O)$.

A partial sum f_{psum} of an object O can be calculated as $f_{psum}(O) = S_1^{'}(O) + S_2^{'}(O) + ... + S_m^{'}(O)$, where $S_i^{'}(O) = S_i(O)$ if O has been seen by node i, and $S_i^{'}(O) = 0$ otherwise. Similarly, an upper bound f_{upper} of an object O can be calculated as $f_{upper}(O) = U_1(O) + U_2(O) + ... + U_m(O)$, where $U_i(O) = S_i(O)$ if O has been seen by node i, and $U_i(O)$ is equal to $\underline{S}_i$ otherwise, where $\underline{S}_i$ is the score of the last object seen under sorted access of node i. We assume the initial value of $\underline{S}_i$ is infinite. Obviously, $f_{upper}(O) \geq f(O) \geq f_{psum}(O)$ for any object O.

We assume that the first e results are most important to users. We assume $e/k \leq 0.1$. The goals of non-blocking top-k query algorithms in distributed networks are: (1) Minimizing the time of producing the first e results, (2) Producing results even if the remote sources occasionally get blocked, and (3) Reducing the bandwidth consumption of producing the total top-k results. We assume that the computation cost in each node is negligible since the communication cost among nodes dominates the query response time.

3 Related Work

Among the ample work on top-k query processing, the TA family of algorithms for monotonic score aggregation [9, 10, 16] stands out as an extremely efficient and highly versatile method. Two main differences between our study and these studies are (1) TA is performed in blocking mode while our algorithm is performed in non-blocking mode, and (2) in distributed systems, TA cannot hide intermittent delays in data arrival while our algorithm does.

The first TA-style non-blocking algorithm, called Stream-combine, has been presented in [11]. [1, 14] developed a non-blocking algorithm called Upper and a blocking algorithm called Pick. [4] presented a blocking algorithm called MPro and its non-blocking variation iMPro. All these algorithms were designed for special data sources that unsuitable to be accessed randomly and addressed how to avoid random accesses to reduce the query cost. In contrast, we are interested in general distributed systems that all data sources can be accessed by sorted and random access.

Our work benefited greatly from [7], which presented a fix round trips algorithm called TPUT. TPUT used three phases to get the top k results: (1) fetching the k best objects and their scores from each node and calculating the k'th highest f_{psum} as τ_1, (2) asking each of the m nodes for objects with score $\geq \tau_1/m$, then calculating the k'th highest f_{psum} as τ_2, and (3) fetching the still missing scores of the objects whose aggregate score will greater than τ_2 using random accesses. The recent work [15] addressed to reduce the communication costs of TPUT using histogram-based statistical metadata. However, these algorithms are performed in blocking mode. In our work, PR accesses data source asynchronously, and divides each node access into two phases. Every phase uses non-fix access round trips and produces results on the fly.

One of our main inspirations is from XJion [17], which extends Symmetric Hash-Jion [18] to a multi-threaded and online aggregation style [13] join operator. XJion fetches all data from remote data sources asynchronously to retrieve totally join results, while our work is interested in retrieving top k results according to a user-specified ranking function.

4 Progressive Rank

In this Section, we first introduce our new algorithm for non-blocking top-k queries in distributed networks termed Progressive Rank (PR, for short) and prove the correctness in Section 4.1, then discuss the efficiency of our approach in Section 4.2.

4.1 Algorithm

The basic idea behind PR is to access remote sources asynchronously and produce an object on the fly when it has been confirmed belong to the final top-k results set. As shown in Figure 1, PR fetches data asynchronously form each node by two phases: the sorted phase (line 3 to line 8) and the random phase (line 10 to line 18). The sorted phase finds the top-k candidate objects and the random phase looks up the candidate objects in all nodes to identify the top-k objects.

```
Algorithm. PR (Input: top-k query q, the indicator p)
Let U = Ø, the counters res= 0, n = 0, and τp = 0
For each data lists Di (1 ≤ i ≤ m) asynchronously:
   Repeat
      Do sorted access to get p ⟨O, Si(O)⟩ pairs
      Add the p objects into U and update the fpsum and fupper of objects of U
      res = ProduceOntheFly(U, res, m, n)
      Let the k'th highest fpsum of U be the partial aggregation threshold τp
   Until no data available or the score of the last object seen S_i < τp/m
   n = n + 1
   Repeat
      If there are objects of U have not been seen by node i:
         Get the first p unseen objects by node i of U, order by fpsum descending
         Do random access to get the scores of the p objects
         Add the p pairs into U and update the fpsum and fupper of objects of U
         res = ProduceOntheFly(U, res, m, n)
      Else:
         If n = m: Break
   Until res = k
Function ProduceOntheFly (U, res, m, n)
Let the sorted access threshold τsorted = Σ_{i=1}^{m} S_i
For each object O of U, order by fpsum descending
   Let the highest fupper of U - {O} be the upper threshold τupper
   If n < m: τupper = Max(τupper, τsorted)
   If fpsum(O) ≥ τupper:
      Output O
      Remove ⟨O, Si(O)⟩(1 ≤ i ≤ m) from U
      res = res + 1
      If res = k: Halt
   Else: Break
Return res
```

Fig. 1. Algorithm PR

In the sorted phase, the center manager node calculates the k'th highest f_{psum} of U as the partial aggregation threshold τ_p and asks each of the m nodes for objects with score $\geq \tau_p / m$ using sorted access, every $p \langle O, S_i(O) \rangle$ pairs of each trip, where p is an indicator to get smooth runtime behavior and $p = \gamma \cdot e$, where γ ($\gamma \geq 1$) is a factor for getting the first e results quickly and producing the rest results smoothly. We call γ the smooth parameter. We choose $\gamma = 2$ in our design.

When all sorted phases finished, PR finds at least k objects with f_{psum} greater than τ_p, and the aggregate score of objects unseen cannot greater than τ_p. Thereby, the objects belonging to the final top k results have been seen at least at one node. The random phase of a node ends if no more object needs to probe at the node (line 11 and line 17). When all random phases are finished, all top-k candidate objects have been seen at all nodes and PR can identify the top-k results.

The function ProduceOntheFly checks objects of *U*. If an object *O* has $f_{psum}(O) \geq$ the output threshold τ_{upper}, it belongs to the final top-k results set, and ProduceOntheFly outputs it. By this approach, PR produces the first few results quickly. There are two cases for choosing the output threshold τ_{upper}:

Case 1: If there are some nodes performing in the sorted phase, ProduceOntheFly chooses the bigger of τ_{sorted} and the highest f_{psum} of $U - \{O\}$ as the τ_{upper} (line 22 and line 23). Note that when $f_{psum}(O) \geq \tau_{sorted}$, the aggregate score of unseen objects cannot be greater than $f(O)$, when $f_{psum}(O) \geq$ the highest f_{upper} of $U - \{O\}$, the aggregate score of objects of $U - \{O\}$ cannot be greater than $f(O)$. Thereby, the condition of line 24 guarantees outputting top-k results in descending order by their aggregate scores.

Case 2: When all sorted phases are finished ($n = m$), ProduceOntheFly chooses the highest f_{upper} of $U - \{O\}$ as the τ_{upper}. As discussed above, the objects belonging to the final top *k* results have been seen at least at one node. Thereby, if $f_{psum}(O) \geq \tau_{upper}$, the object *O* can be outputted as the next result safely.

Note that not all sorted phases and random phases can be finished before the top-k results have been produced. PR can safely terminate in this situation because the function ProduceOntheFly guarantees outputting the exact top-k results by descending. This property makes PR hide intermittent delays in data arrival and produce results even some of nodes getting blocked.

Theorem 1. For any data input, the PR algorithm correctly produces the exact top-k objects in descending order by their aggregate scores.

Proof. As discussed above. □

The algorithm is not limited to sum, and can apply to any strict monotonic aggregation function *f* as long as there is a way to determine when to stop Sorted Phase. For example, if *f* is multiplication, the stop condition will be $\underline{S}_i < \tau_p^{1/m}$.

4.2 Efficiency

As discussed above, PR produces the first few results quickly. We discuses the bandwidth needed by PR to produce the total results in the following.

As defined in [9], instance optimality is a measure of how close an algorithm is to the optimal algorithm in the worst case. Let *A* denote the class of all deterministic algorithms, and let *D* denote the class of data series that we are interested in. For any algorithm $a \in A$, and any data series $d \in D$, we use $\text{cost}(a,d)$ to denote the cost of running *a* over *d*. An algorithm *R* is instance optimal over *A* and *D* if $R \in A$ and there exist two constants *C1* and *C2* such that for every $a \in A$ and $d \in D$:

$$\text{cost}(R,d) \leq C1 \times \text{cost}(a,d) + C2 . \tag{1}$$

The constant *C1* is called the optimality ratio of *R*.

As defined in [7], $w(j)$ is denoted as "the value of the j'th position", a data series has a log-log slope function $C(n)$, if for all j where $j \le k$, $w(C(n)\times j) < w(j)/n$, and $C(n)$ is the smallest value satisfying this criteria (n is an integer here).

Let the cost metric is the number of $\langle Object, Score\rangle$ pairs fetched, i.e. the bandwidth consumption. As proved in [7]: Let D be the class of all data series that have log-log slope function of $C(n)$. Let A be the class of all deterministic algorithms that correctly find the top k answers for each data series in D. The TPUT algorithm is instance-optimal over A and D, with optimality ratio $(m-1)\times min(C(2m), C(m)\times k) + min(C(m^2), C(m)\times k)$.

Theorem 2. Let D be the class of all data series that have log-log slope function of $C(n)$. Let A be the class of all deterministic algorithms that correctly finds the top k answers for every data series in D. If there are max and min performance times for each round trip, the PR algorithm is instance-optimal over A and D, and the optimality ratio is at most $(m-1)\times min(C(2m), C(m)\times k) + min(C(m^2), C(m)\times k)$.

Proof. Note that in the sorted phase, PR fetches at most $m\times p$ $\langle Object, Score\rangle$ pairs more than TPUT after the m nodes have sent their first $k\,\langle Object, Score\rangle$ pairs to the center manager. We investigate the stage before that the m nodes have sent their first $k\,\langle Object, Score\rangle$ pairs to the center manager in the following.

If there are a max performance time t_{max} and a min performance time t_{min} for each round trip (in general, a timeout parameter can be used as the t_{max}), let $\mu = [t_{max}/t_{min}]$, where $[t_{max}/t_{min}]$ is the big round number t_{max}/t_{min}. PR fetches at most $[k/p]\times p\times ((m-1)\times\mu+1)$ $\langle Object, Score\rangle$ pairs by sorted access when the m nodes have sent their first $k\,\langle Object, Score\rangle$ pairs to the center manager, where $[k/p]$ is the big round number of k/p. Thereby, PR fetches at most more $[k/p]\times p\times((m-1)\times\mu+1) - m\times k$ excrescent $\langle Object, Score\rangle$ pairs than TPUT by sorted access before the m nodes have sent their first k objects to the center manager. Even in extreme case, each excrescent $\langle Object, Score\rangle$ pair consists of a distinct object and has been looked up in the other $m-1$ nodes in the random phase, PR fetches at most more a constant of $m\times([k/p]\times p\times((m-1)\times\mu+1) - m\times(k-p))$ $\langle Object, Score\rangle$ pairs than TPUT.

As discussed above, according to formula (1), when all data series that have log-log slope function of $C(n)$ and there are max and min performance times for each round trip, PR is an instance-optimal algorithm, and the optimality ratio is at most $(m-1)\times min(C(2m), C(m)\times k) + min(C(m^2), C(m)\times k)$. □

Although PR consumes more bandwidth than TPUT in some extreme cases, PR needs less bandwidth in most situations because the sorted phase threshold τ_p increases when PR is running. When τ_p is greater than the first threshold of TPUT, PR could stop the sorted phase earlier than TPUT.

5 Experimentation

5.1 Experimental Setting

We experimentally evaluated the performance of our proposed algorithm PR and related algorithms in slow and bursty networks, i.e. the sources are subject to blocking. We assume that data arrive from the nodes with Pareto distribution, a distribution is widely used in case of slow and bursty networks [6]. By varying the shape factor α ($0 < \alpha < 2$) and the scale factor λ ($\lambda > 0$) of Pareto distribution, we can simulate different networks scenarios. For simplicity, we set $\lambda = 5$, which means a round trip spends 5 seconds at least. A round trip is considered to be timeout if no tuple arrives within a certain time threshold t (60s as default) and the request will be resent.

We compared the performance of our new PR algorithm with the following two techniques.

- TPUT: This is an efficient 3-phase algorithm for distributed networks as described in [7]. We choose TPUT as the blocking counterpart.
- proTA: We adapted Fagin et al.'s TA algorithm [9] for our scenario. The resulting non-blocking algorithm, proTA, probes data lists synchronously, and p objects each trip for sorted access. After every random access trip, proTA produces the objects that have been confirmed belong to the top-k results set.

We used both real-world data collections and synthetic to evaluate our new algorithm. We used the data from Protein Data Bank (PDB) as the real-world data collection. The PDB is the single worldwide repository for the processing and distribution of 3-D structure data of large molecules of proteins and nucleic acids, and consists of about 32,000 proteins structure descriptions. We chose 12 structures related to flu as templates (querying the PDB with keyword "flu"), and calculated the similarity factor as the score of the other structures with each template to be 12 data lists.

For the synthetic data collections, we kept the PDB entry IDs as object IDs in each node. We assumed that nodes exhibit different degrees of correlation of each other. First, the scores of objects of node 1 were initialized by the Zipf's distribution [20] with a Zipf factor θ . Then, a random walk mode was used to initialize the other nodes. For node $i(2 \le i \le m)$, $S_i(O) = S_{i-1}(O) + V_i(O)$, where $V_i(O)$ is a random number in the range of $\pm c \times S_1(O)$, c is the correlation factor. For simplicity, we set $c = 0.1$ in our experiments.

Our implementation of the test-bed and the related algorithms was written in GNU C++. All the experiments are conducted on Intel Pentium IV CPU 2.4GHz with 512MB RAM running Red Hat Linux 9. All experiments queries were for the top-100 results. We set $e = 10$, which means the first 10 results are most important to user. Thereby, the indicator p was set to 20 for PR and proTA. We measured the time and bandwidth needed to producing the results.

5.2 Experimental Results

5.2.1 Results for Synthetic Data Sets

Figure 2 (a) shows the time of producing the top-k results with the nodes number m = 20. We show results for $\alpha = 1.2$ and $\theta = 0.7$, (similar results occur with all other tested values of α and θ , and are omitted for the space reasons). We see that the PR shows excellent performance. For the first 10 results response time, PR outperforms proTA and TPUT by a factor approximately 1.8 and 8. For the total results response time, PR outperforms proTA by a factor approximately 2.2 and slightly better than TPUT. This is because PR accesses nodes asynchronously, while proTA and TUPT need to wait the longest delay of all nodes to continue next round trip.

Figure 2 (b) shows the bandwidth results with the setting in Figure 2 (a). The overall performance of PR outperforms proTA and TPUT by a factor approximately 1.5 and approximately 1.2. The main reason of PR outperforming proTA is that PR finds candidate top-k objects by sorted access while proTA consumes more bandwidth on random access. The main reason of PR outperforming TPUT is that PR accesses nodes with *p* objects each round trip while TPUT uses simply 3-phases to identify top-k results, which brings more bandwidth consumption for redundant data.

Figure 3 shows the first 10 results response time (Figure 3 (a)), the total results response time (Figure 3 (b)), and the bandwidth (Figure 3 (c)) in different scales with *m* = 10, 20, 50, and 100. In the case of *m* = 10, TPUT performs slightly better than PR to the term of the total results response time (Figure 3 (b)). The reason is that when the node number is small, nodes seldom get blocked, and TPUT only needs 3 round trips. As the number of nodes increases, the advantage of PR over proTA and TPUT will be magnified. The main reason is that proTA and TPUT encounter timeout almost every round trip when *m* is greater than 50.

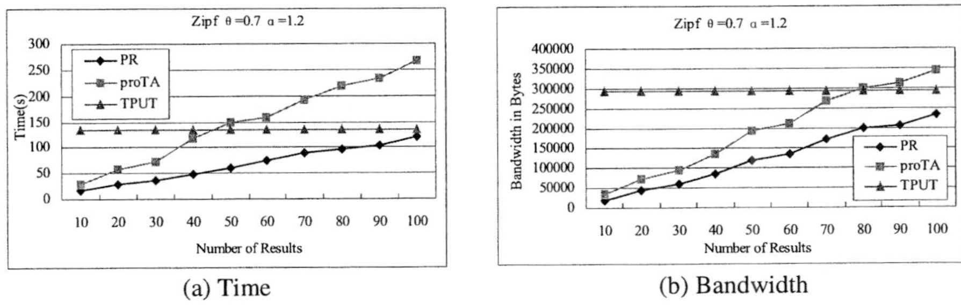

(a) Time (b) Bandwidth

Fig. 2. Performance of synthetic data sets

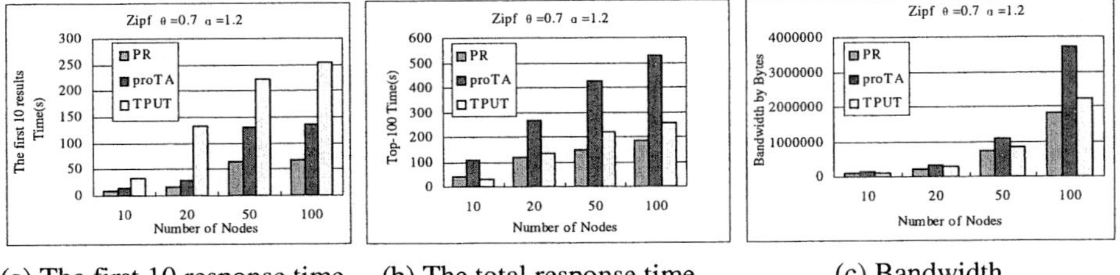

(a) The first 10 response time (b) The total response time (c) Bandwidth

Fig. 3. Performance in different scales

5.2.2 Results for Real Data Sets

Figure 4 (a) gives the time for producing the top-k result with $\alpha = 1.2$, (similar results occur with all other tested values of α, and are omitted for the space reasons). The real data set consists of 12 data lists. Similar to the case m = 10 discussed above, TPUT performs slightly better than PR in terms of the total results response time. For the first 10 results response time, PR outperforms proTA and TPUT with a factor approximately 2 and 4. For the total results response time, PR outperforms proTA with a factor approximately 2.5. Figure 4 (b) shows that in terms of bandwidth consumption, PR outperforms proTA and TPUT with a factor approximately 1.7 and 1.2.

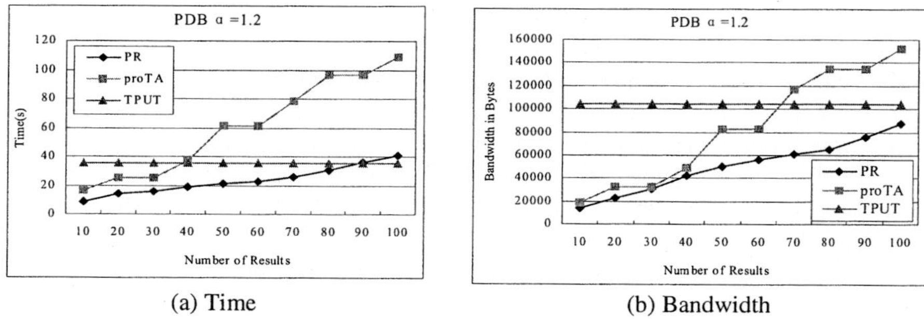

(a) Time (b) Bandwidth

Fig. 4. Performance of real data sets

6 Conclusions

In this paper, we have presented the PR algorithm, an efficient non-blocking top-k query algorithm in distributed networks. PR hides intermittent delays in data arrival and produces the first few results quickly. PR produces results even if the remote sources occasionally get blocked, and consumes low data traffic to produce the total top-k results. The experiments results have shown that PR is an effective solution for producing fast query responses in the presence of slow and bursty remote sources, and can be scaled well. Several interesting and important problems still remain open, such as how to choose appropriate p to get better runtime behavior.

Acknowledgements. We are grateful to Dr. Pei Cao and Zhe Wang for giving us the original source code of TPUT and to Di Zheng for comments that improved readability. We are also grateful to the reviewers for their helpful comments and suggestions.

References

1. N. Bruno, L. Gravano, and A. Marian. Evaluating top-k queries over web-accessible databases. In ICDE, 2002.
2. W.-T. Balke, W. Nejdl, W. Siberski, et al. Progressive Distributed Top-k Retrieval in Peer-to-Peer Networks. In ICDE 2005.
3. B. Babcock, C. Olston: Distributed Top-K Monitoring. In SIGMOD, 2003

4. K.C.-C. Chang, S.-W. Hwang: Minimal probing: supporting expensive predicates for top-k queries. In SIGMOD 2002.
5. M. J. Carey and D. Kossmann. On saying "Enough already!" in SQL. In SIGMOD, 1997.
6. M. E. Crovella, M. S. Taqqu, and A. Bestavros. Heavy-tailed probability distributions in the world wide web, chapter A practical guide to heavy tails: statistical techniques and applications, pages 3–26. Chapman Hall, 1998.
7. P. Cao, Z. Wang. Efficient top-k query calculation in distributed networks. In PODS 2004.
8. R. Fagin. Combining fuzzy information from multiple systems. In J. Comput. System Sci., pages 58:83–99, 1999.
9. R. Fagin, Amnon Lotem, and Moni Naor. Optimal aggregation algorithms for middleware. In PODS, 2001.
10. U. Güntzer, W.-T. Balke, and W. Kieβling. Optimizing multi-feature queries for image databases. In VLDB, 2000.
11. U. Güntzer, W.-T. Balke, and W. Kieβling. Towards efficient multi-feature queries in heterogeneous environments. In ITCC, 2001.
12. S. Hwang and K.C.-C. Chang. Optimizing Access Cost for Top-k Queries over Web Sources: A Unified Costbased Approach. In ICDE, 2005.
13. J. M. Hellerstein, P. J. Haas, and H. J. Wang. Online Aggregation. In Proceedings of the ACM International Conference on Management of Data, In SIGMOD, 1997.
14. A. Marian, L. Gravano, N. Bruno: Evaluating Top-k Queries over Web-Accessible Databases. TODS 29(2), 2004.
15. S. Michel, P. Triantafillou, and G. Weikum. KLEE: A Framework for Distributed Top-k Query Algorithms. In VLDB, 2005.
16. S. Nepal and M. V. Ramakrishna. Query processing issues in image (multimedia) databases. In ICDE, 1999.
17. T. Urhan and M. J. Franklin. XJoin: Getting Fast Answers From Slow and Burst Networks. Technical Report CS-TR-3994, UMIACS-TR-99-13, Computer Science Department, University of Maryland, Feb. 1999.
18. A. N. Wilschut and P. M. G. Apers. Pipelining in Query Execution. In Databases, Parallel, Architectures, and their applications, Miami, FL, 1990.
19. C. Yu, G. Philip W. Meng. Distributed Top-N Query Processing with Possibly Uncooperative Local Systems. In VLDB 2003.
20. G. K. Zipf: Human Behavior and the Principle of Least Effort. Addison-Wesley Press, 1949.

Continuous Expansion: Efficient Processing of Continuous Range Monitoring in Mobile Environments

Xiaoyuan Wang and Wei Wang

Department of Computing and Information Technology,
Fudan University, Shanghai, China
{xy_wang, weiwang1}@fudan.edu.cn

Abstract. Continuous range monitoring on moving objects has been increasingly important in mobile environments. With the computational power and memory capacity on the mobile side, the distributed processing could relieve the server from high workload and provide real-time results. The existing distributed approaches typically partition the space into subspaces and associate the monitoring regions with those subspaces. However, the spatial irrelevance of the subspaces and the monitoring regions incurs the redundant processing as well as the extra communication cost. In this paper, we propose *continuous expansion* (CEM), a novel approach for efficient processing of continuous range monitoring in mobile environments. Considering the concurrent execution of multiple continuous range queries, CEM abstracts the dynamic relations between the movement of objects and the change of query answers, and introduces the concept of query view. The query answers are affected if and only if there are objects changing their current query views, which lead to the minimum transmission cost on the moving object side. CEM eliminates the redundant processing by handling the updates only from the objects that potentially change the answers. The experimental results show that CEM achieves the good performance in terms of server load and communication cost.

1 Introduction

Given a set of spatial regions of interest, a continuous range query retrieves the moving objects inside the regions, and continuously provides real-time updates as moving objects move in and out of these regions. Efficient processing of continuous range monitoring could enable many of the location-aware applications, such as traffic monitoring and intelligent transportation systems. With various applications, a large number of continuous range queries are repeatedly evaluated in a concurrent execution environment. One challenge is the real-time response to query answers, which is critical for actual applications. Any delay of the query response results in an obsolete answer. Examples are digital battle fields and enhanced 911 services. Another challenge is the concurrent execution. With a large quantity of queries, many query regions interact and lead to

M.L. Lee, K.L. Tan, and V. Wuwongse (Eds.): DASFAA 2006, LNCS 3882, pp. 890–899, 2006.

overlapping. Movement of a single object can affect the answers of multiple queries, which increase the complexity of evaluation.

Much work has focused on the efficient evaluation of continuous range queries in a *centralized* location monitoring system [3, 4, 5, 6]. With the equipment of battery-powered mobile devices, which have constrained computational capability and memory capacity, the *distributed* processing of continuous range monitoring could reduce the expensive location updates and relieve the server from high workload. The existing typical approaches are MobiEyes [2] and MQM [1]. Both of the approaches partition the space into subspaces, such as the grid cells in MobiEyes and the subdomains in MQM, and associate the monitoring regions with those subspaces. However, since the partition of subspaces does not depend on the distribution of continuous monitoring regions, two kinds of changes, that an object enters/exits a certain monitoring region or changes its resident subspace, have to be updated separately, which incur the redundant processing and extra communication cost on both the server side and the moving object side. Furthermore, energy efficiency on the mobile side becomes a primary concern in distributed environments. Therefore the distributed processing should aim at saving the energy consumption and prolonging the lifetime of moving objects.

In this paper, we propose the *continuous expansion monitoring* (CEM) method for efficient processing of continuous range monitoring in mobile environments. Different from the existing approaches, CEM views the object's resident spaces and the monitoring regions in a unified way, and abstracts the dynamic relations between the movement of objects and the change of query answers. We introduce the concept of query view. The query answers are affected if and only if there are objects changing their current query views, which lead to the minimum transmission cost on the moving object side. Thus CEM could efficiently reduce the message communication and save the energy consumption on the mobile side. CEM handles the updates only from the objects that potentially change the answers, and eliminates the redundant processing. By storing all the queries that a query view contains beforehand, there is no need to perform the dynamic computation on the server side to determine the new queries an object falls in. We conduct a comprehensive set of simulation based experiments and show that CEM outperforms the existing approaches in terms of server load and communication cost.

The rest of the paper is organized as follows. Section 2 reviews the related work. Section 3 presents the CEM method in detail. Section 4 conducts the experimental evaluation and we conclude the paper in Section 5.

2 Related Work

Much effort has been put into the efficient evaluation of continuous range queries over moving objects in a *centralized* location monitoring system [3, 4, 5, 6]. One way is to directly evaluate queries on an object index [4] at each time, where frequent updates of the object index is a major problem. Another way is to build an index structure on queries instead of objects [3, 5, 6].

With the advances in mobile hardware, the *distributed* processing of continuous range monitoring has many advantages. The existing typical techniques are MobiEyes [2] and MQM [1].

MobiEyes [2] partitions the space into grid cells of equal sizes. For each grid cell, MobiEyes maintains the corresponding queries whose monitoring regions intersect with it. Each moving object stores a local query table LQT, which contains the queries intersecting with the grid cell the object currently lies in. When an object falls in a grid cell, it checks LQT to determine whether itself is covered by the nearby query regions. It notifies the server to update the query answers if the result is different. When an object changes its current grid cell, it notifies the server of this change. At the same time, the server determines the new queries that intersect with the new grid cell and send them to the objects.

MQM [1] dynamically partitions the space into disjoint rectangular subdomains. Each mobile object is associated with a resident domain consisting of adjacent subdomains, and maintains the list of monitoring regions inside its current resident region. When an object enters or exits a monitoring region, it sends a message to the server and updates the query results. When an object exits its current resident region, it requests a new one from the server. To decide the new redisent region, the server maintains a binary partition tree (BP-tree), which stores the subdomains and the corresponding monitoring regions. The maximum number of monitoring regions a mobile object can load and process at one time depends on its computational capability.

As in most existing mobile environments, we have three underlying assumptions on moving objects: (1) Moving objects are equipped with positioning technologies like GPS devices or embedded sensors and are able to locate their positions. (2) Moving objects have limited battery power, computational capability and memory capacity. (3) Moving objects are able to communicate with the server. As is in [5], we employ the incremental evaluation to compute only the updates of the previous answers. Positive/Negative updates indicate that a certain object needs to be added to/removed from the result set of a certain query. In our discussion, each continuous range query is represented by a rectangular region.

3 Continuous Expansion Monitoring

3.1 Motivation

The existing distributed approaches, such as MQM and MobiEyes, typically partition the space into subspaces, such as the subdomains in MQM and the grid cells in MobiEyes, and associate the monitoring regions with those subspaces. However, since the partition of subspaces does not depend on the distribution of continuous queries, there arise the following limited aspects in these approaches:

1. The spatial irrelevance of the subspaces and the continuous monitoring regions leads to the redundant processing. Whenever an object moves cross the boundary of the subspace, the client update to the server is required. The region continuity is broken up since a monitoring region can reside in multiple

subspaces. For example, the location *p1* and *p2* in the same monitoring regions might be in two different subspaces. When an object moves from *p1* and *p2*, it has to communicate with the server and makes a new request although it remains within the same monitoring regions and does not change any query answer.

2. The system performance is sensitive to the size of the subspace. If the size is too small, the frequent spanning of two resident subspaces leads to the unnecessary communication between mobile objects and the server. If the size is too large, a large number of queries maintained locally are heavy burdens on moving objects.

3. Since different monitoring regions may be applied for different applications, the concurrent execution of continuous range queries results in the continuous overlapping of monitoring regions, which increases the length of the query list maintained locally on the moving object side as well as the evaluation complexity.

Furthermore, different from the centralized approaches, the communication cost on moving objects is a primary concern in distributed processing because message communication in wireless environments is the main consumer of battery power. It has been shown that the energy consumption on communication is up to three orders of magnitude more than that required by computation [7], and transmitting data requires much more power than receiving data [7]. Therefore the distributed processing should minimize the communication cost incurred, especially the transmission cost on the moving object side.

Taking into consideration the aspects above, the basic idea behind CEM is to abstract the dynamic relations between the movement of objects and the change of query answers. We introduce the concept of query view. When an object moves within a query view, the range of its movement can be *continuously expanded* until it crosses the boundary of the query view, which indicates the change of query answers. Only at this time needs the object communicate with the server. For example, as long as the location *p1* and *p2* are in the same monitoring regions, they will be within the same query view, and no extra communication with the server is needed when an object moves from *p1* to *p2* since its movement does not change any query answer.

3.2 Query View

In this subsection we introduce the formal definition of the query view and provide the theoretical basis of CEM.

Definition 1 (Query View). *A query view is a combined query consisting of one or more continuous queries* $q_1, \ldots, q_i$. *The monitoring region of the query view, called the view region, is defined as the intersection of the monitoring regions of* $q_1, \ldots, q_i$.

Definition 2 (Relation *contains*). *A query view contains a query q if the view region is fully covered by the monitoring region of q.*

From the definition, we see that the locations are in the same query view region if and only if they are within the monitoring regions of the same queries.

Different from the subspace which is independently partitioned from the space, the query view considers both the combined effect of multiple continuous monitoring regions and the possible continuous movement of objects. From the view of queries, it is a high-level abstract of all the monitoring regions. From the view of objects, it is the continuous expanded region in which the object's movement does not affect any query answer. The change of any query answer corresponds to the event that objects enter/leave a certain view region. For the representation of query views, we introduce the concept of Minimum Bounding Rectangle and Maximum Extended Rectangle.

Definition 3 (Minimum Bounding Rectangle; Maximum Extended Rectangle). *The Minimum Bounding Rectangle (MBR) of a query view is a rectangle with the minimum size that closely bounds the view region. The extended region within the MBR is included by a minimum number of rectangles, each of which is called the Maximum Extended Rectangle (MER).*

A non-rectangular query view is represented by its MBR with one or more MERs. An example with three queries is illustrated in Figure 1. Five query views $V1$ to $V5$ are generated. They *contains* $\{q1\}$, $\{q1, q2\}$, $\{q2\}$, $\{q2, q3\}$ and $\{q3\}$ respectively. Rectangle $R1$ is the MBR closely bounding the view region $V3$. The extended regions are included by two MERs $R2$ and $R3$. Thus the query view $V3$ is represented by the form $< R1, \{R2, R3\} >$. The partition of a minimum number of rectangles (MER) guarantees the minimum information needed to represent the extended region. Moreover, the dead space can be regarded as a specific view region. Since it is not close, an approximate region is used to represent it, for example, the region $R4$ bounded by dashed lines in Figure 1.

For the construction of query views, we employ the "splitting-merging" strategy. We first divide the space into the small grid cells of the same size and map all the monitoring ranges on the grid space. For each grid cell, we check whether it is fully or partially covered by one or more query regions, and maintain a temporary structure to record the corresponding queries. Finally we collect all the grid cells, merge those that are covered by the same query regions, and generate the whole query views. Since the view regions are not overlapped, a query view is said to be an object's query view if the current location of the object is within the view region.

We introduce a theorem below, which reveals the dynamic relation between the object's movements and the query answers. Based on the theorem, Corollary 1

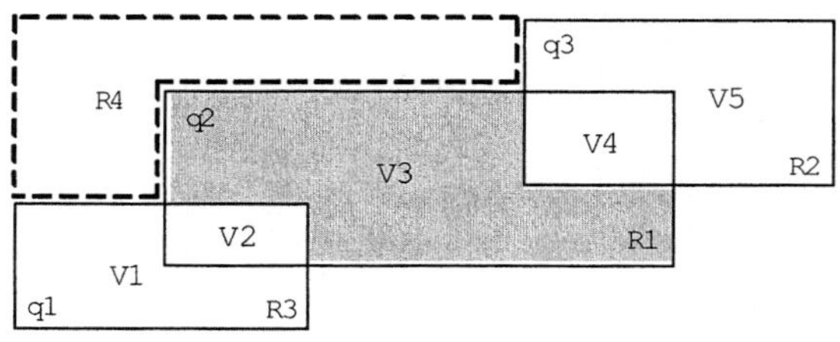

Fig. 1. An example of query views

shows that CEM minimizes the transmission cost on the mobile side, which further save the energy consumption on the moving objects.

Theorem 1 (Correlation Rule). *The query answers are changed if and only if there are objects changing their query views.*

Proof. (1) Suppose there is an object o changing its current query view from $v1$ to $v2$. $QSet1$ and $QSet2$ are the sets of the corresponding queries that $v1$ and $v2$ *contains* respectively. From the definition of query view, there at least exists one query q satisfying 1) $q \in QSet1$ and $q \notin QSet2$, or 2) $q \in QSet2$ and $q \notin QSet1$. Otherwise, $v1$ and $v2$ can be merged into one query view. Therefore the answer of q is changed by the movement of o. If in case 1, o falls into the negative answer of q, since the new query view $v2$ does not contain q and o exits the monitoring region of q. If in case 2, o falls into the positive answer of q. (2) Suppose there is a query q changing its answer. This indicates that at least one object o enters/exits the monitoring region of q, which correspond to the positive/negative answer. Thus the current query view of o is different from its previous view, because q can not be included in both of two views at the same time. So the change of q's answer corresponds to the change of o's query view.

Corollary 1 (Minimum Transmission Cost). *CEM incurs the minimum transmission cost on the moving object side.*

Proof. When its movement affects the query answers, an object is required to transmit the message to notify the server of this change, which leads to the lower bound of the transmission cost. According to Theorem 1, the change of the query answers on the server side and the change of the query views on the moving object side form a one-to-one relationship in CEM. Besides the notification of the change of query views, there is no other transmission incurred from the moving objects to the server. So CEM incurs the minimum transmission cost on the moving object side.

3.3 Data Structure

In this subsection, we describe the design of the data structures on the server side and on the moving object side. A query, query view and object are respectively identified by *QID*, *VID*, and *OID*.

During the course of its execution, CEM maintains the following data structures on the server side:

- **Query View Table (QVT).** Query views are organized within the disk-based sequential table QVT. Each entry has the form (*VID*, *VR*, *QList*). *VID* is the query view identifier, on which QVT is indexed. *VR* is the monitoring region of the query view. If it is a rectangular region, a single rectangle is used to represent it. Otherwise, its MBR with the MERs is used to represent it. *QList* is a list including all the queries that the query view *VID contains.*
- **Grid-Based View Index (GVI).** GVI is an in-memory $k*k$ grid structure to index the query views. The space is uniformly divided into $k*k$ grid cells.

For each grid cell, GVI maintains a list *VList* of *VIDs* of query views whose monitoring regions overlap with this cell.

- **Query Table (QT).** QT is a disk-based table indexed on *QID*. Each entry in QT has the form (*QID*, *QR*), where *QID* is the query identifier, and *QR* is the monitoring region of the query. QT is used only when there are new queries to be inserted or deleted.
- **Query Result Buffer (QRB).** QRB is an in-memory sequential buffer that stores the incoming query results.

  Each moving object maintains the following data structures on the mobile side:
- **Query View Region (QVR).** QVR is the monitoring region of the query view that the moving object currently lies in. The representation of QVR corresponds to that of *VR* in QVT. If the view region is non-rectangular, QVR is represented by its MBR with the MERs. Otherwise, it is represented by a rectangle.
- **Grid-Based Location Index (GLI).** GLI is an auxiliary structure used to fast determine whether the current location of the moving object is within the view region. Note that GLI is employed only when the view region is not rectangular, because with a rectangular view region we can easily know whether the position lies within it in constant time. According to the grid partition of the MBR of the non-rectangular view region, GLI is implemented as a bit vector and the details can be further found in [9].

3.4 The Processing Algorithm

In this subsection, we present the details of the CEM processing algorithm on the moving object side and the server side. The algorithm is based on the Correlation Rule in Subsection 3.2, which guarantees the correctness of the evaluation.

Processing on the moving object side. A moving object communicates with the server only when it enters or leaves the monitoring region of a query view, which means the change of query answers. While it has been within the view region *VR*, two steps are processed when the object moves at each time step:

1. Determine whether the current location is in the view region *VR* using GLI.
2. If it is not within *VR*, which indicates that it has left the old view region and might enter a new one, the object notifies the server of this change by sending its object identifier *OID*, its previous query view identifier *VID*, and its new position to the server. It also clears up its local structure QVR and GLI. After receiving the response from the server, which contains its new query view identifier and the corresponding view region, the object builds up the new location index GLI according to the grid partition of the view region. If it is still within *VR*, the object does nothing since its movement does not change any query answer.

Processing on the server side. The server communicates with the moving objects in two situations: (1) The server has received the notification from an object and then sends to it a message about the new query view. (2) When there are new queries to be inserted or deleted, the server broadcasts the related information to the objects.

When an object moves within its current view region, it falls into the answers of the queries that the current query view *contains* and does not need to communicate with the server. When an object changes its view region, the server updates the query answers in QRB upon receipt of the notification.

The processing logic is described as follows. Three parameters *OID*, *VID*, and *pos*, that is, the object identifier, the previous query view identifier, and the new position, are sent to the server by the moving object. The server first gets the old queries that the previous query view *VID contains* by QVT. Then it maps the new position *pos* to the corresponding grid cell in the view index GVI and gets the new query view where *pos* is located in. Then the server again use QVT to obtain the new queries that the new query view *contains* and the corresponding view region. Two difference operations are performed on the old query set and new query set to get the incremental positive and negative answers. The server updates the answers in QRB, and finally sends the message to the object, which contains its new query view identifier and the corresponding view region.

Note that only the query views rather than the queries are visible from the view of moving objects. All the query information and the incremental answers are kept on the server side, and no local query list is maintained on the mobile side. In fact, the main operation that an object carries out each time it moves is just to determine whether it is still within the current view region. On the server side, there is no need to perform the dynamic computation to determine the new queries an object falls in, because the object's location is tied up with the corresponding query view, and all the queries that a query view *contains* have been stored in QVT in advance.

Index maintenance. We take the similar strategy like the "splitting-merging" to deal with the change of queries. When a new query q is inserted or deleted on the server side, three steps proceed: (1) Determine the affected query views. (2) Update the index structures. (3) Broadcast the messages. Details of the update of query views can be found in [9].

4 Experimental Evaluation

We conduct a set of simulation based experiments and compare CEM with MobiEyes and MQM. All the experiments are performed on Pentium IV 2.0GHz with 512 MB RAM running Windows Server 2003. The size of disk page is set to 4KB. We use synthetic datasets generated by GSTD [8]. All the objects are uniformly distributed in a unit-square space and can move arbitrarily with a maximum moving distance of 0.1. The monitoring regions in the space follow a uniform distribution and their average sizes are 0.05. The performance measures are the I/O overhead incurred on the server side and the communication cost.

The default number of objects and queries is 10K and 1K respectively. Exactly 100 snapshots are recorded for each moving objects. We set k in GLI to 100. The grid cell side length in MobiEyes is set to 0.016 to accord with the setting in [2].

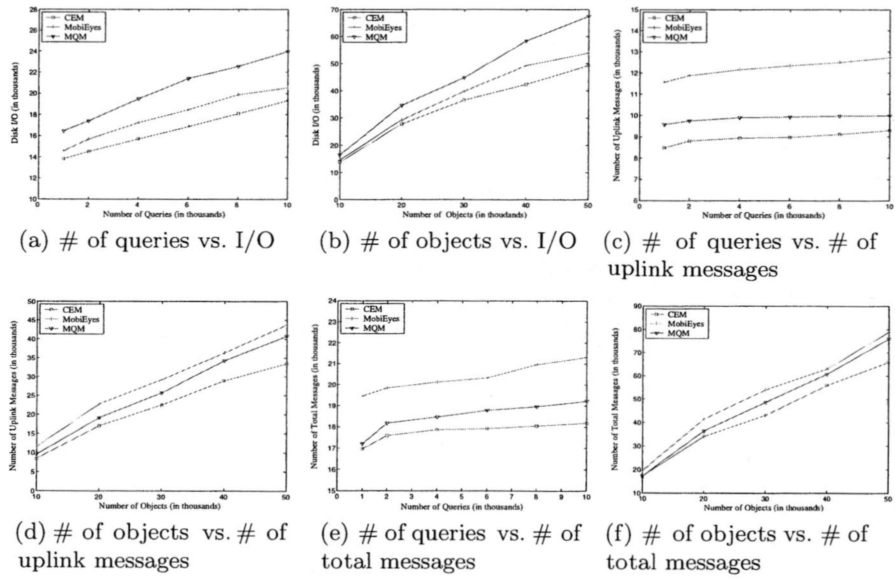

(a) # of queries vs. I/O (b) # of objects vs. I/O (c) # of queries vs. # of uplink messages

(d) # of objects vs. # of uplink messages (e) # of queries vs. # of total messages (f) # of objects vs. # of total messages

Fig. 2. Performance Results

The minimum number of monitoring regions in MQM follows the distribution from 10 to 100. For the I/O, we consider that both the SQT in MobiEyes and the BP-tree in MQM are resident on disk. At each time step the incremental answers are computed on the server side.

We first investigate the performance of server load in term of the average number of disk I/O at each time step (snapshot). Figure 2(a) and 2(b) show the effect of increasing the number of queries and objects on I/O cost respectively. In Figure 5(a), we vary the number of queries from 1K to 10K. All the approaches increase the number of disk I/O accordingly, because with more queries to be evaluated, the structures maintained for queries, that is, the SQT in MobiEyes, the BP-tree in MQM and the QVT in CEM, need more disk space, which lower the performance of one disk access. CEM improves the performance slightly due to the fact that in CEM there is no need of additional searching for the queries overlapped with the subspaces, and all the monitoring regions corresponding to a certain query view have been stored beforehand. In Figure 5(b), the number of objects varies from 10K to 50K. We see that the server processing cost becomes higher with more objects. CEM performs better than the other approaches, and the curve shows that its gain on the server performance becomes larger with the increasing number of objects.

We then investigate the communication cost in the distributed solutions. As is in [1, 2], we use the number of messages at each time step to measure the communication cost since the messages in the transmission are usually very short. Two kinds of metrics are reported, the uplink messages and the total messages (including uplink messages and downlink messages).

Figure 2(c) and 2(d) show the number of uplink messages with the different number of queries and objects. In Figure 2(c), the mobile transmission cost in MQM and CEM keep stable, and are not much affected by the increase of queries. CEM significantly saves the message cost compared with the other approaches, since by query views CEM combines the update effect of the monitoring regions and the resident spaces. For MobiEyes, it incurs the higher transmission cost, since frequent grid cell spanning increases the number of messages transmitted on the mobile side. In Figure 2(d), we see that with the increasing objects, more and more messages are transmitted on the mobile client. CEM preserves the relative gain against the other two approaches, and the gain increases with the number of objects. Figure 2(e) and 2(f) give the effect of the number of queries and objects on the total communication cost. Since the total communication cost includes the mobile transmission cost, the curves are somewhat similar to those in Figure 2(c) and 2(d). An interesting result is that in CEM the total communication cost almost has a one-to-one relationship with the mobile transmission cost, because CEM handle the updates, both on the server side and on the mobile side, in a unified way, and the number of downlink messages corresponds to that of uplink messages.

5 Conclusion

In this paper, we propose an efficient method, the *continuous expansion monitoring* (CEM), for the distributed processing of continuous range monitoring in mobile environments. In the future work, we would like to extend the basic idea to other types of continuous queries over moving objects.

References

1. Y. Cai, and K.A. Hua. Processing Range-Monitoring Queries on Heterogeneous Mobile Objects. In *Proc of MDM*, 2004.
2. B. Gedik, and L. Liu. MobiEyes: Distributed Processing of Continuously Moving Queries on Moving Objects in a Mobile System. In *Proc of EDBT*, 2004.
3. D. V. Kalashnikov, S. Prabhakar, S. E. Hambrusch, W. G. Aref. Efficient Evaluation of Continuous Range Queries on Moving Objects In *Proc of DEXA*, 2002.
4. M.L. Lee,W. Hsu, C.S. Jensen, B. Cui, K. L. Teo. Supporting Frequent Updates in R-trees: A Bottom-Up Approach. In *Proc of VLDB*, 2003.
5. M. F. Mokbel, X. Xiong, and W. G. Aref. SINA: Scalable Incremental Processing of Continuous Queries in Spatio-temporal Databases. In *Proc of SIGMOD*, 2004.
6. S. Prabhakar, Y. Xia, D. V. Kalashnikov, W. G. Aref, and S. E. Hambrusch. Query Indexing and Velocity Constrained Indexing: Scalable Techniques for Continuous Queries on Moving Objects. *IEEE Trans. on Computers*, 51: 1124-1140, Oct. 2002.
7. V. Raghunathan, C. Schurgers, S. Park and M. Srivastava. Energy Aware Wireless Microsensor Networks. *Signal Processing Magazine*, 45(2):40-50, 2002.
8. Y. Theodoridis, J.R.O. Silva, and M.A. Nascimento. On the Generation of Spatiotemporal Datasets. In *Proc of SSD*, 1999.
9. X. Wang, and W. Wang. Continuous Expansion: Efficient Processing of Continuous Range Monitoring in Mobile Environments. Technical Report, Fudan University.

Effective Low-Latency K-Nearest Neighbor Search Via Wireless Data Broadcast

KwangJin Park[1], MoonBae Song[1], Ki-Sik Kong[1], Sang-Won Kang[1], Chong-Sun Hwang[1], Kwang-Sik Chung[2], and SoonYoung Jung[3]

[1] Dept. of Computer Science and Engineering, Korea University, 5-1, Anam-dong, Seongbuk-Ku, Seoul 136-701, Korea
{kjpark, mbsong, kskong, swkang, hwang}@disys.korea.ac.kr

[2] Dept. of Computer Science and Engineering, Korea National Open University
kchung0825@knou.ac.kr

[3] Dept. of Computer Science Education, Korea University
jsy@comedu.korea.ac.kr

Abstract. To facilitate power saving via wireless data broadcast, index information is typically broadcast along with the data. By first accessing the broadcast index, the mobile client is able to predict the arrival time of the desired data. However, it suffers from the drawback that the client has to wait and tune for an index segment, in order to conserve battery power consumption. Moreover, the average time elapsed between the request for the data and its receipt may increase as a result of these additional messages. In this paper, we present a broadcast-based spatial query processing method designed to support K-NN(K-Nearest Neighbor) queries via wireless data broadcast. With the proposed schemes, the client can perform NN query processing without having to tune into an index segment. Experiments are conducted to evaluate the performance of the proposed methods. The resulting latency and energy consumption are close to the optimum values, as the analysis and simulation results indicate.

1 Introduction

The recent convergence of internet, wireless communications, mobile location-aware clients, and geo-processing has given rise to a new generation of Location-Based Service(LBS). LBS provide the ability to retrieve the geographical location of a mobile device, providing services based on location. Examples of such applications include emergency services, car navigation systems and tourist tour planning. The field of LBS, which only emerged a few years ago, presents many research and industrial challenges. An important class of queries of LBS is K-NN(K-Nearest Neighbor) queries, which finds the k-point objects closest to a query point.

Definition 1.1. For a query point q and a query parameter k, the k-nearest neighbor query returns the smallest set $NNq,(k) \subseteq S$ that contains(at least) k objects from S, and for which the following condition holds:

$$\forall Oi \subseteq NNq(k), \forall Oi' \in S - NNq(k) : dist(Oi, q) < dist(Oi', q) \qquad (1)$$

M.L. Lee, K.L. Tan, and V. Wuwongse (Eds.): DASFAA 2006, LNCS 3882, pp. 900–909, 2006.

With a large candidate data set, answering LBS via scanning through the whole data set becomes extremely expensive. Thus, index structures and related search algorithms have been proposed to provide efficient processing of LBS queries [1]. Air indexing is one technique used to address this issue, and operates by interleaving indexing information among broadcast data items. The mobile client is able to predict the arrival time of the desired data and only needs to tune into the broadcast channel when the requested data arrives, by first accessing the broadcast index. Thus, mobile client can stay in power save mode most of time, and tune into the broadcast channel only when the requested data arrives [2, 3]. Air indexing techniques can be evaluated in terms of the following factors; First, **Access latency:** The average time elapsed from the moment a user issues a query to the client to the moment when the required data item is received by the client. Second **Tuning Time:** The amount of time spent by a client listening to the channel. Then, the **Access Latency** consists of two separate components, namely: **Probe Wait:** The average duration for getting to the next index segment. If we assume that the distance between two consecutive index segment is L, then the probe wait is $L/2$. **Bcast Wait:** The average duration from the moment the index segment is encountered to the moment when the required data item is downloaded. The **Access Latency** is the sum of the **Probe Wait** and **Bcast Wait**, and these two factors work against each other.

Among the most popular indexes for LBS is R-tree [4] and its variations, notably the R*-tree. The R-tree serves as the basis of many later spatial indexing structures. All of these R-tree-based indexes share the basic assumption that spatial objects are approximated by their bounding rectangles before being inserted into the indexes.

2 Related Work

A lot of research has been carried out with regard to solving the K-NN search problem for spatial databases. In [5], authors propose a branch-and-bound R-tree traversal algorithm to find the nearest neighbor object to a point, and then generalize it to find the K-nearest neighbors. In [6], authors propose a Shared Execution Algorithm for evaluating a large set of Continuous K-NN(CKNN) queries. The authors investigate the problem of evaluating a large set of continuous K-NN queries. Within incremental evaluation, only queries affected by the motion of objects are reevaluated. In [7], the authors address the issues of supporting spatial queries of LBS via wireless data broadcast. They present a new index structure based on the Hilbert curve, which enables the linear broadcasting of data objects in a multi-dimensional space. In [8], authors present a mechanism performing an exact K-NN search over conventional sequential-access R-trees, optimizing established K-NN search algorithms. They propose an optimization technique, which improves the tune-time of K-NN search, and also discusses the tradeoffs involved in organizing the index on the broadcast medium. Furthermore, the use of histograms was investigated as a technique for improving tune-in time and memory requirements of a K-NN search.

2.1 Broadcast Sequence

In a recent paper [9], the concept of data sorting for broadcasting called Broad cast-Based location dependent data delivery Scheme (BBS) has been proposed. In this method, the server periodically broadcasts the IDs and coordinates of data objects, without an index segment and these broadcast data objects are sorted sequentially, according to the location of the data objects, before being sent to the clients. In this method, since the data objects broadcast by the server are sequentially ordered, based on their location, it is not necessary for the client to wait for the index segment, if the desired data object is able to be identified before the associated index segment has arrived. In this method, the structure of the broadcast affects the distribution of the data object. The BBS provides the fastest access time, since no index is broadcast along with the data and thus, the size of the entire broadcast cycle is minimized. Preliminary simulation-based results have shown that BBS significantly reduces the AT(access time).

Proposed algorithms are simple but efficient technique to support linear transmission of spatial data and processing of K-NN queries. A simple sequential broadcast can be generated by linearizing the two dimensional coordinates in two different ways: i.e., Horizontal Broadcasting(HB) or Vertical Broadcasting(VB). In HB, the server broadcasts the location dependent data (LDD) in horizontal order, that is, from the leftmost coordinate to the rightmost coordinate. Conversely, in VB, the server broadcasts the LDD in vertical order, that is, from the bottom coordinate to the top coordinate. In this paper, the server is assumed to broadcast data objects using HB.

2.2 Energy Efficient Selective Tuning

Previous index schemes utilize indexes to conserve battery power. The waiting time required to reach the forthcoming index segment can be reduced, by replicating the index m times in a broadcast cycle. However, the drawback of this solution is that broadcast cycles are lengthened due to the additional indexing information, and has the worst possible latency, because the clients are required to wait until the beginning of the next broadcast, even if the desired data is just in front of them. Thus, the existing indexing methods are unsuitable for LBS. With the BBS scheme [9], the clients can significantly reduce their access time, since this scheme eliminates the probe wait time(See Section 1) for the clients. However, the average TT(tuning time) may increase, since the client is required to tune into the broadcast channel until the desired data item has arrived. In the previous index schemes [3], each data item contains a pointer to the next occurrence of the index segment, additionally, every data item contains a pointer to the next data item that has the same attribute value. In our scheme, every data item contains pointers containing the IDs, locations and arrival times of the data items that will subsequently be broadcast. In this section, energy efficient K-NN schemes for the BBS environment are presented, namely the Efficient K-NN Schemes(EKS). This scheme provides clients with the ability to perform selective tuning, assisting reduction in the client's tuning time.

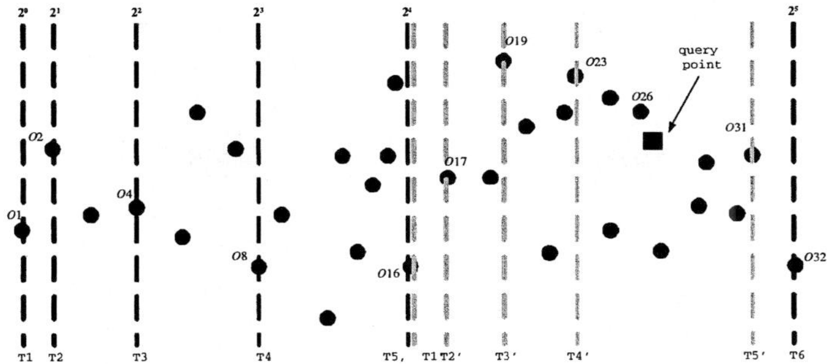

Fig. 1. Sequence of the Exponential Pointer

In this method, the client utilizes exponential pointers from each data item for the purpose of reducing energy consumption. Each data item contains the following information;

- It's ID and location information.
- Initial Pointer(IP): arrival time of the first data item to be broadcasted in the next broadcast cycle
- Exponential Pointer(EP): IDs locations and arrival times of the data items that will be broadcasted at T_i. The maximal number of EP from the each data item is $\log_e N$, where e is the exponent value and N is the number of data items that will be broadcasted(e.g., if $e = 2$ and N=32, the first broadcasted data item $O1$ has the following EPs: the data items located in $T2$, $T3$, $T4$, $T5$ and $T6$(See Fig. 1))
- Boundary Pointer(BP): EP contains y-coordinate of uppermost and lowermost lines between Ti and Ti+n as shown in Fig. 2(b).

The client obtains the ID, location information and EP from the first tuned data item. Then, the client switches to power save mode until the desired data item appears on the broadcast channel. The client repeatedly switches between the power-save and wake up modes until the desired data item is retrieved. Let us consider the example of the nearest neighbor search in Fig. 1. First, the client tunes to the broadcast channel at T1 and obtains the following pointers ID=$\{O2, O4, O8, O16, O32\}$ from data item $O1$. Then, the client switches to power-save mode until $O16$(at T5) has appeared on the broadcast channel, since T5 is the nearest boundary line on the left-hand side of the query point q up to the present time. Then, the client wakes up at T5, and obtains EP ID=$\{O17, O19, O23, O31\}$ from data item $O16$. The client again switches to power-save mode until $O23$ appears on the broadcast channel. Finally, the client wakes up at T4' and tunes the broadcast channel until $O26$ as the final result.

2.3 Exact K-NN Search

Assume the data objects are sequentially broadcast in horizontal order. If the client starts to tune into the broadcast at TN, in order to find K-NN, wrong

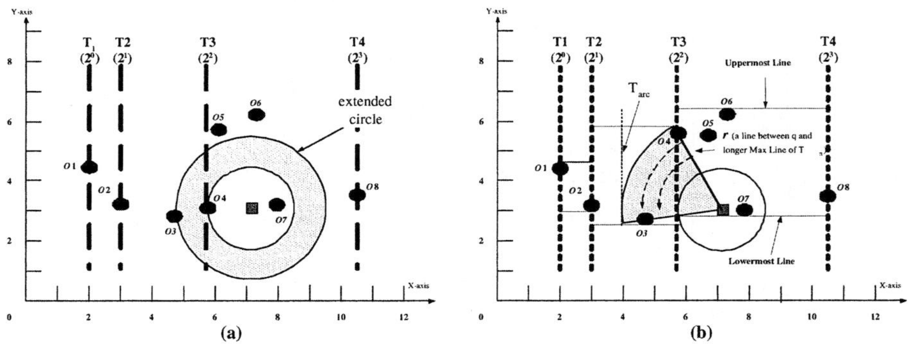

Fig. 2. Client's Processing for the Exact K-NN Search

answers may be returned. Let us consider the example in Fig. 2(a). Assume value of k=3. As shown in the figure, the client starts to tune the broadcast channel at T3(e.g., $O4$), where T3 is the nearest boundary line on the left-hand side of the q. Then, the client returns the final results as $O4$, $O5$ and $O7$, even though the exact K-NN results are $O3$, $O4$ and $O7$. This can be explained by the fact that EP only contains information regarding data items corresponding to a value of e(i.e., exponential value). That is, the client is unable to obtain information regarding data objects between Tn and Tn+1(i.e., $O3$ between T2 and T3), if the client starts to tune into the broadcast channel at T1 in Fig. 2(a)). Therefore, the client must satisfy the following conditions, in order to return exact K-NN:

Notations

- O: data object
- r: A line between q and farthest point from q and Tn, e.g., Max line or Min Line of Tn(See Fig. 2(b))
- *B-sector*(q, r): the sector centered at query point q and having r as the radius(shaded area in Fig. 2(b)).
- T_{arc}: perpendicular boundary line located on the left-side of the *B-sector*, where T_{arc} to q contains K-NN query points.
- TS: safety bound line, nearest Tn from the left-side of T_{arc}, where the x-coordinate of $TS \leq$ x-coordinate of T_{arc}
- O_f : the client's first tuned data item in the broadcast channel
- T_i: boundary lines of the current broadcast data object
- T: set of T_i,
- TN: nearest boundary line on the left-hand side of the q, e.g., T5 in Fig. 1
- ON: data object of TN, e.g., $O16$ in Fig. 1

Lemma 4.3.1. While the client processes the K-NN query, if the client start to tune the broadcast channel at Tn, where x-coordinate of Tn< x-coordinate of T_{arc}, then the client misses any K-NN.

Proof. Let T_{m-n} denote the data objects between T_m and T_n, where the x-coordinate of T_m< x-coordinate of T_n and $m,n \geq 1$. Given a query point q, let $k=3$. If a *B-sector* is drawn, centered at query point q and having r, T_{arc} is obtained. Then, the nearest T_n from the left-side of T_{arc} is selected as TS(e.g., T2 in Fig. 2(b)). Now the client can guarantee that it does not miss the K-NN, if it starts to tune the broadcast channel at T2, since the data objects of $T_{2-4} \supset$ K-NN. □

Lemma 4.3.2. Let T_{arc-k} denote the data objects between T_{arc} and T_k. If the number of T_{m-n} is larger than or equal to K-NN, then $T_{arc-k} \supseteq$ K-NN, where (x-coordinate of T_n)< (x-coordinate of T_{arc}) and (x-coordinate of T_k)> (x-coordinate of q).

Proof. It is clear that there are five objects of T_{2-3}, since $T_2=2^2$ and $T_3=2^3$. Given a query point q, let $k=5$. If a *B-sector* is drawn, centered at query point q and having r, where r be a line between q and uppermost line of $T_3(2^2)$ as shown in Fig. 2(b), and if the client begins to tune the broadcast at T2, then the client misses any K-NN(See Lemma 4.3.1). □

Theorem 4.3.1. Let us assume that the number of data objects of T_{m-n}>K-NN, where x-coordinate of T_m<x-coordinate of T_n<x-coordinate of T_{arc}. Then, the client can guarantee that it does not miss the K-NN, if it starts to tune the broadcast channel at T_m.

Definition 4.3.1. Let k^{th}-NN denote one of data objects among K-NN. Then, K-NN $\notin T_{m-n}$ or k^{th}-NN $\not\subset T_{m-n}$, if x-coordinate of T_n<x-coordinate of TS.

Algorithm 1. The client algorithm used to process the K-NN

Sn: the first tunes data object after it turns into active mode
Qi: data object from queue
FarQi: k-th NN from K-NN in the queue
queue <- initially set to ∅ **Input:** locations of the clients and the data objects;
Output: *K-NN*;
Procedure:

```
do
  wake-up and read(EP from Sn)
  find(TN)
    if(Sn=TN (i.e., (x-coordinate of Sn + 1)≥(x-coordinate of q))) // Satisfy Definition 4.3.2
      then TN=>Tn and find TS from Tn, where Tm-n satisfy Lemma 3.2 and turn into
      power-save mode until TS arrives from the broadcast channel
      wake-up at TS
        do
          read(Oc)
            if queue=∅
              then add queue(Oc)
            else sort queue by the distance from query point q
              find FarQi and delete Qi from queue, if Qi is out of K-NN
              do compare distance of (q and Oc) and (q and FarQi)
                if distance of(q and Oc)< (q and FarQi)
                  then delete FarQi from queue and add queue(Oc)
                else FarQi=>FarQi
        while (satisfy Lemma 4.3.3)
        return K-NN as a result
    else turn into power-save mode until TN
while ((x-coordinate of Sn+1)≤(x-coordinate of q))
```

Theorem 4.3.2. Let O_{candi} denote the candidate for the K-NN and farthest data object among the O_{candi} be denoted as $O_{candi'}$. While the client obtains k-th O_{candi}, if the dist($O_{candi'}$ and q)<dist(x-coordinate of q and O_i), then O_i and the rest of the broadcast data objects are located outside of the K-NN range.

Definition 4.3.2. If x-coordinate of Oi that is broadcast right after the client's first tunes data object is larger than the x-coordinate of q, then the client stops selective tuning.

Definition 4.3.3. If the x-coordinate of O_f>x-coordinate of q, the client can not identify the K-NN in the current broadcast cycle.

2.4 Analytic Evaluation

In this section, we compare the performance of the proposed BBS scheme with that of the (1, m) index scheme. Let m be the number of times broadcast indices, N be the number of data items and C be the average number of buckets containing records with the same attribute value. Let k' be the index search cost for single data item and AAT be the average access time:

Probe Wait: In the BBS method, since the data objects broadcasted by the server are sequentially ordered based on their location and thus, it is not necessary for the client to wait for an index segment. Therefore, *Probe Wait* of BBS=0.

- Previous index method: $\frac{1}{2} \times (index + \frac{N}{m})$
- BBS method: $None$

Bcast Wait:

- Previous index method: $\frac{1}{2} \times (N - k + (index \times m)) + k + (k' \times k)$
- BBS method: $\frac{N-k}{2} + k$

Since the AT is the sum of the *Probe Wait* and the *Bcast Wait*, average AT for:

Previous index method is:

$$AAT_{PRE} = \frac{1}{2} \times (index \times (m+1) + N(\frac{1}{m} + 1) - k) + k + (k' \times k) \quad (2)$$

BBS is:

$$AAT_{BBS} = \frac{N-k}{2} + k \quad (3)$$

Tuning Time. Let ATT be the average tuning time and k be the number of levels in the multileveled index tree. The ATT for previous index is:

$$ATT_{PRE} = 1 + (k' \times k) + k \times C \quad (4)$$

Let e be $Se(i)$ be the digit sum [10] and ATT_{EKS} be the average tuning time for EKS. Then, The ATT for:

$$ATT_{EKS} = \frac{\sum_{i=0}^{N-k} Se(i)}{N-k+1} + \frac{k}{2} \times C \quad (5)$$

3 Performance Evaluation

This section presents the numerical results obtained through the analysis and simulation. The broadcast channel has a bandwidth of 144 kbps. The clients are equipped with a Hobbit Chip(AT&T). The power consumption of the chip in sleep mode is 10uW and the consumption in active mode is 486.1uW [3, 11]. The server generates the broadcast data stream with appropriate index information. In the experiment, the initial probe position and the target data objects are uniformly distributed in the broadcast. The broadcast data objects are assumed to be static, such information as restaurants, hospitals and hotels.

Access Latency. In this experiment, the AT is evaluated for various parameter settings. First, the effect of the number of the broadcast data items on the access time is studied. The number is varied from 100 to 1000. The query arrival time increases proportional to the amount of data. As shown in Fig. 3(a), EKS outperforms the other schemes, since it is not necessary for the client to wait for an index segment, in order to locate the desired data items and to determine when to tune into the broadcast channel to receive them. Thus, the search cost required to identify the desired data items is significantly reduced. The proposed scheme provides superior access time, since no index is broadcast along with data items. Thus, the size of the entire broadcast is minimal in this way. Fig. 3(b) and 3(c) present the access latency as the value of k and the size of the data increases, respectively. This is due to the previous index technique of broadcasting data without considering the properties of the locality of the data, resulting in increased client search cost and access time.

Energy Consumption. Fig. 4(a) presents the energy consumption, as the size of the data items increases from 128 bytes to 4096 bytes. The average tuning time of EKS is longer than (1,m) method but provides minimum latency(See Section 2.4, Tuning Time). As shown in this figure, in this case, the proposed scheme outperforms the 1,m R-tree and 1,m Hilbert, since (1,m) method minimizes the tuning time but not the access time, while the proposed schemes reduce the TT and AT at the same time. In other words, when the energy consumption is estimated, it is necessary to consider not only the active time, but

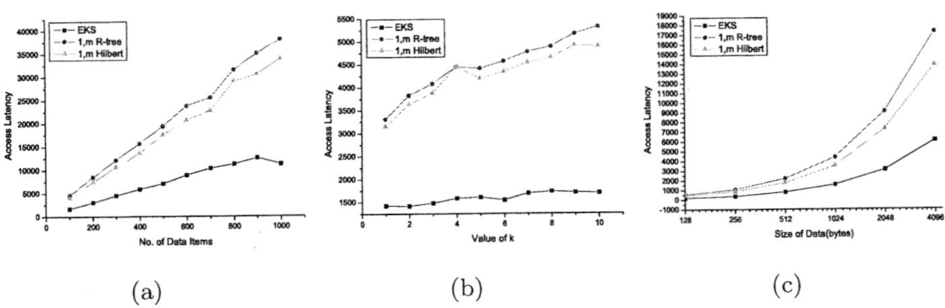

(a) (b) (c)

Fig. 3. Access Latency

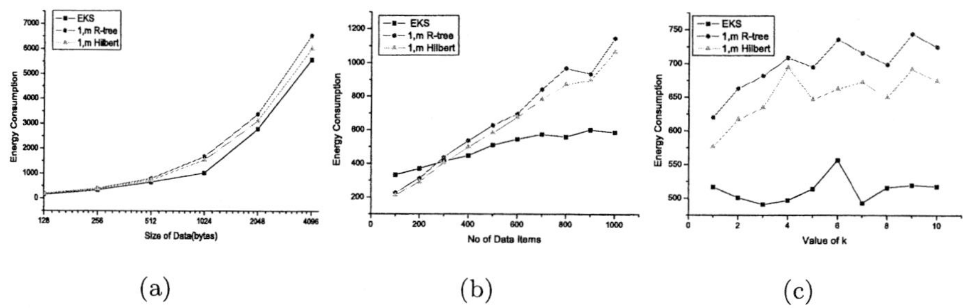

(a) (b) (c)

Fig. 4. Energy Consumption

also the doze time, even if the doze time is considerably smaller than the active time, the client also consumes battery power when it stays in power save mode. Fig. 4(b) and 4(c) present the energy consumption as the number of the data items and value of k increase, respectively. As shown in this figure, EKS demonstrates best performance as the amount of data increases, since the (1,m) with r-tree and Hilbert significantly increases access latency as the amount of the data increases.

4 Conclusion

In this paper, two issues involved with data organizing and selective tuning for K-NN queries on air were investigated. For the purpose of data broadcasting in LBSs, the BBS method is presented, and for the purpose of selective tuning with the BBS method, EKS is presented. With the proposed schemes, the client can perform K-NN query processing without having to tune into an index segment. The experimental results demonstrate that the proposed schemes significantly reduce not only the AT, but also the energy consumption, since the client does not always have to wait for the index segment. As future work, the extension of the proposed schemes for Continuous KNN(CKNN) queries on the air is being investigated. Examples of CKNN queries are everywhere in our daily life, e.g., "Continuously report the 5 nearest gas stations until I reach my destination".

References

1. B. Zheng, W.-C. Lee, D. Lee, "Search K Nearest Neighbors on Air," In *Proc. of MDM*, 2003. pp. 181-195.
2. T. Imielinski, S. Viswanathan, and B.R.Badrinath, "Energy efficient indexing on air," In *Proc. of SIGMOD*, 1994. pp. 25-36.
3. T. Imielinski, S. Viswanathan, and B.R.Badrinath, "Data on Air: Organization and Access," *IEEE Trans. Knowledge and Data Eng*, 1997, 9(3), 353-372.
4. A. Guttman, "R-trees: A dynamic index structure for spatial searching," In *Proc. of SIGMOD*, 1984. pp. 47-57.

5. N. Roussopoulos S. Kelley, and F. Vincent, "Nearest Neighbor Queries," In *Proc. of SIGMOD*, 1995. pp. 71-79.
6. X. Xiong, M. F. Mokbel, and W. G. Aref, "SEA-CNN: Scalable Processing of Continuous K-Nearest Neighbor Queries in Spatio-temporal Databases," In *Proc. of ICDE*, 2005. pp. 643-654.
7. B. Zheng, W.-chien Lee and D. L. Lee, "Spatial Queries in Wireless Broadcast Systems," *Wireless Network*, 2004, 10(6), 723-736.
8. B. Gedik, A. Singh, and L. Liu, "Energy Efficient Exact kNN Search in Wireless Broadcast Environments," In *Proc. of GIS*, 2004. pp. 137-146.
9. K. Park, M. Song, and C. Hwang, "An Efficient Data Dissemination Schemes for Location Dependent Information Services," In *Proc. of LNCS 3347 Springer-Verlag*, 2004, pp. 96-105.
10. Shallit, J.O., "On infinite products associated with sums of digits," *Journal of Number Theory 21*, 1985, pp. 128-134.
11. O. Kasten, "Energy consumption," ETH-Zurich, Swiss Federal Institute of Technology. Available at `http://www.inf.ethz.ch/~kasten/research/bathtub/energy_consumption.html`.

Nearest Neighbor Queries for R-Trees: Why Not Bottom-Up?

MoonBae Song, KwangJin Park, SeokJin Im, and Ki-Sik Kong

Dept. of Computer Science and Engineering, Korea University,
5-1, Anam-dong, Seongbuk-Ku, Seoul 136-701, Korea
{mbsong, kjpark, seokjin, kskong}@disys.korea.ac.kr

Abstract. Given a query point q, finding the nearest neighbor (NN) object is one of the most important problem in computer science. In this paper, a bottom-up search algorithm for processing NN query in R-trees is presented. An additional data structure, hash, is introduced to increase the pruning capability of the proposed algorithm. Based on hash, whole data space is disjointly partitioned into $n \times n$ cells. Each cell contains the pointers of leaf nodes which intersect with the cell. The experiment shows that the proposed approach outperforms the existing NN search algorithms including the BFS algorithm which is known as I/O optimal algorithm.

1 Introduction

Given a query point q, finding the nearest neighbor object, so-called nearest neighbor (NN) search, is one of the most important problem in computer science. As a general form of the problem, the NN search is formally defined in the following. A point set P is a set of points in a d-dimensional data space DS, point set $P = \{p_0, p_1, \ldots, p_{|P|-1}\}, p_i \in DS \subseteq \mathbb{R}^d$. Given query point q, the result of the NN search is

$$NN(q) = \{p \in P \mid \forall p' \in P : dist(p,q) \leq dist(p',q)\}. \quad (1)$$

For this purpose, we need a multidimensional data structure and a search algorithm that efficiently traverses the structure for processing the NN query. Since 1984 when Guttman proposed his work [2], R-trees have become the most popular data structure for indexing multidimensional data for various purpose. There are two different approaches to process NN queries on R-trees. One was developed by Roussopoulos et al. [4]. Owing to its searching behavior, it is referred to as depth-first search (DFS) algorithm in the following. The other, called best-first search (BFS), is proposed by Hjaltason and Samet [7]. To the best of our knowledge, the BFS algorithm is known as optimal NN search algorithm for R-trees. This means that it visits node only if necessary. Since the top-down approaches should visit from the root node to leaf node, the minimum I/O cost per query cannot be smaller than the height of R-tree.

M.L. Lee, K.L. Tan, and V. Wuwongse (Eds.): DASFAA 2006, LNCS 3882, pp. 910–919, 2006.

In this paper, we propose a new NN search algorithm in a bottom-up manner for R-trees, which outperforms existing optimal NN search algorithm. In contrast the two existing algorithms that work in a top-down manner, the proposed approach starts at the leaf level and traverses to the *Root* node. In order to select more appropriate leaf node, it exploits hash structure in which whole data space is disjointly partitioned into $n \times n$ cells. Each cell contains the pointers of leaf nodes which intersect with the cell. Experimental results show that our proposed NN search algorithm ourperforms the existing NN search algorithms including the BFS algorithm which is known as I/O optimal algorithm.

2 Nearest Neighbor Search Using R-Trees

As one of the most promising indexes for searching spatial data, R-tree was proposed by Guttman [2]. It is *d*-dimensional extension of B$^+$-tree for multidimensional objects. In the data structure, any geometric object is represented by its minimum bounding rectangle (MBR). An MBR is minimal approximation of a geometric object and a multidimensional rectangle $R = [l_1, u_1] \times \cdots \times [l_d, u_d]$, also called (hyper-)rectangle, in the data space. Every nodes have between m and M entries ($m \leq M/2$) unless it is the root node. Figure 1 shows an R-tree for point set $P = \{a, b, ..., p\}$ in which the maximum node capacity M is 3. Points that are spatially close in space (e.g., k, l, and m) are clustered in the same leaf node (E_7). Nodes are then recursively grouped together with the same principle until the top level, which consists of a single root, so-called the *Root* node.

Roussopoulos et al. [4] proposed a branch-and-bound algorithm for NN search in a depth-first manner. We refer to this algorithm as the depth-first search (DFS) algorithm. They suggested three pruning heuristics based on two distance metrics (*mindist* and *minmaxdist*) to discard candidates nodes, so that the number of disk access can be minimized. *mindist* is minimum possible distance between the query point and a node (or MBR R), while *minmaxdist* is the minimum of maximum possible distances from the query point to a face of the MBR. Conceptually speaking, *mindist* and *minmaxdist* provide a lower- and an

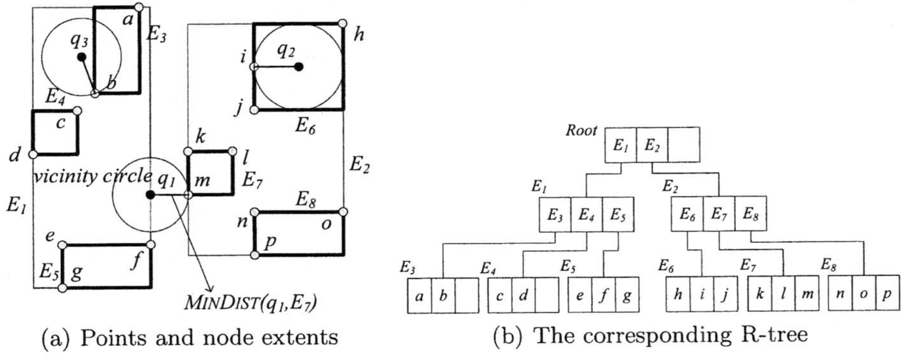

(a) Points and node extents (b) The corresponding R-tree

Fig. 1. Example R-tree and NN query processing q_1, q_2, and q_3

upperbound on the actual distance of object O from query point q respectively. Based on these metrics, Roussopoulos et al. [4] proposed the following three pruning heuristics:

- PH1: An MBR R with $mindist(q, R)$ greater than the $minmaxdist(q, R')$ of another MBR R', is discarded because it cannot contain the NN.
- PH2: An actual distance from q to a given object O, which is greater than the $minmaxdist(q, R)$ for an MBR R, can be discarded because R contains an object O' that is nearer to q.
- PH3: Every MBR R with $mindist(q, R)$ greater than the actual distance from q to a given object O is discarded because it cannot enclose an object nearer than O.

DFS algorithm visits the nodes with minimum *mindist* order from the Root. In the example of query point q_1 in Figure 1, after visiting the root node, then it visits the minimum *mindist* node (e.g., E_1) from q_1. The process is repeated recursively until the leaf node E_5 which contains the potential NN f. When backtracking to the previous level (node E_1), remaining entries (E_3 and E_4) are easily pruned by PH3. Backtracking again to the root level and following the search path E_2E_7, the actual NN m can be found. In summary, the order of nodes visited in DFS algorithm for query point q_1 is $Root, E_1, E_5, E_2, E_7$. The DFS algorithm has proven to be sub-optimal [6]. This means that it visits more nodes than actually necessary.

Given a query point q, let $VC(q)$ be the vicinity circle of query point q that centers at the query point q and has radius equal to $mindist(q, NN(q))$. As proven in [6], an optimal NN search algorithm should visit only the nodes intersecting with the vicinity circle VC. In [7], the best-first search (BFS) algorithm which achieves the optimal I/O performance has been proposed by Hjaltason and Samet. It maintains a heap $\mathcal{H}$ of the entries visited so far in ascending order by *mindist*. Similar to DFS, BFS starts from the *Root* and insert all entries in the node into heap $\mathcal{H}$. In the example of Figure 1, for instance, it insert all entries (e.g., E_1 and E_2) in the *Root* node into heap. Then the heap $\mathcal{H} = \{\langle E_2, mindist(q_1, E_2)\rangle, \langle E_1, mindist(q_1, E_1)\rangle\}$. At each step, the first item in the heap is selected to visit, and its all entries is inserted into the heap $\mathcal{H}$. The algorithm follows the same procedure until a data object is visited. Therefore, the order of nodes visited in the BFS algorithm for query point q_1 is $Root, E_1, E_2, E_7$ (without visiting E_5). To the best of our knowledge, the BFS algorithm proposed by Hjaltason and Samet is known as optimal NN search algorithm for R-trees especially in I/O cost.

3 Bottom-Up Search (BUS) Algorithm

The performance limits of conventional top-down algorithms is the height of tree owing to their algorithmic characteristic. This limit should be broken in order to support database application for high performance computing recently. This increasing demand lead us to propose a new search algorithm – bottom-up search algorithm.

3.1 Hash Structure

In order to access from the bottom (i.e., leaf level), the conventional R-trees have to be modified slightly. In this paper, we propose a hash data structure to support our bottom-up search algorithm. Definition 1 and 2, which follow, describe the basic concept of Hash and cell. For the simplicity of presentation, we assume $d = 2$ in the rest of paper. But the extension for the representation of higher-dimensional data ($d > 2$) is straightforward.

Definition 1 (Hash). *The data space DS is two-dimensional unit space* $[0, 1]^2$. *In hash structure* H, *DS is disjointly divided into* $n \times n$ *cell structure, each of size* $\frac{1}{n} \times \frac{1}{n}$. *Each cell is denoted by* $H(i, j), 0 \leq i, j \leq n - 1$ *and* n *is called the granularity of Hash.*

Definition 2 (Cell). *Each cell* $H(i, j)$ *represents a region of space* $[i\delta, (i + 1)\delta) \times [j\delta, (j + 1)\delta)$ *generated by uniform partitioning, where* δ *is the length of cell size of* $\frac{1}{n}$. *Each cell contains an intersection list, called* IL, *of all leaf nodes that intersect with the cell. For any two-dimensional query point* $q = (q_1, q_2)$, *the corresponding cell of query* q *can simply be computed as* $H(\lfloor \frac{q_1}{\delta} \rfloor, \lfloor \frac{q_2}{\delta} \rfloor)$.

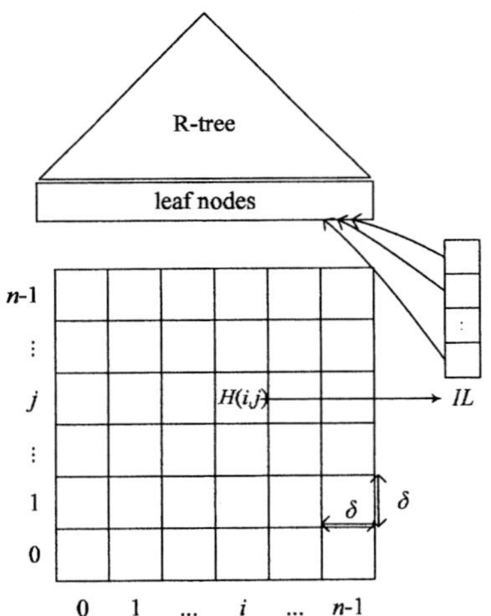

Fig. 2. R-tree and its Hash Structure

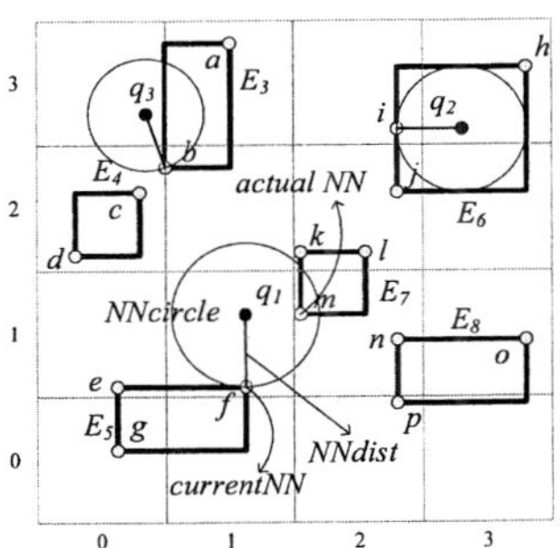

Fig. 3. An Example of Hash for a R-tree in Figure 1

In a sense, the hash data structure H is nothing but pointer information about leaf nodes that intersect with each cell $H(i, j)$. In Figure 2, the relation between R-tree and its hash structure is depicted. For the sake of brevity, the IL of each cell only contains the pointer to all leaf nodes that intersect with the cell itself. We consider, for instance, 4×4 hash structure in Figure 3. In this example, the intersection list of $H(0, 2)$ denoted as $H(0, 2).IL$ is $\{E_3, E_4\}$.

3.2 Basic Algorithm

As shown in Figure 3, the intuitive meaning of such a data structure is that it has a low-cost in finding the objects which are spatially close to the corresponding cell. We denote the potential NN obtained by hash $currentNN$ and $NNdist$ means $mindist(q, currentNN)$. Given query point q, let $NNcircle(q)$ be the circle of query q that centers at q and has radius equal to $NNdist$. This circle provides an upperbound which guarantees that the actual NN must be included within the circle. Our proposed bottom-up search algorithm is based on the hash as a starting point.

Algorithm 1. Basic BUS algorithm

Procedure BottomUpNNSearch(Query q)
1: Determine the corresponding cell of q denoted as $C = H(\lfloor \frac{q_1}{\delta} \rfloor, \lfloor \frac{q_2}{\delta} \rfloor)$.
2: Read the all leaf nodes in $C.IL$ and $currentNN \leftarrow$ nearest object.
3: Searching point $\check{N} \leftarrow$ the leaf node that contains $currentNN \in C.IL$
4: **repeat**
5:   $\check{N} \leftarrow \check{N}$'s parent
6:   **foreach** entry $E_i \in \check{N}$ **do**
7:     **if** $mindist(E_i, q) < NNdist$ **do** /* PH3 */
8:       $currentNN \leftarrow$ TopDownNNSearch(E_i, $NNdist$, q)
9:     **end-if**
10:   **end-for**
11: **until** ($\check{N}$ is the *Root* node)

This algorithm is called bottom-up search (for short BUS) depicted in Algorithm 1 The corresponding cell C of query q is obtained in line 1. In line 2, the potential NN (denoted as $currentNN$) is obtained by calculating the distances of all objects in the all leaf nodes in $C.IL$. As the *searching point* for the proposed algorithm, node $\check{N}$ is initialized to the leaf node containing $currentNN$. The **repeat-until**-loop of lines 4–11 is the main loop for the algorithm. $\check{N}$ is updated as its parent node (line 5), then TopDownNNSearch() is applied to the children of node $\check{N}$ which lying closer to q than $NNdist$ (using PH3). Starting at the node E_i, TopDownNNSearch(E_i, $dist$, q) traverses only nodes which has smaller distance from q than $dist$. As a top-down search algorithm, it is either DFS or BFS. The procedure continues until the searching point $\check{N}$ is the *Root* node. The ideal case would be that (from the leaf level to root node) the search algorithm traverses only one node for each level of the tree, which is called *one-path search.* As shown in q_1 of Figure 1(a), the more subtrees VC intersects the more nodes visited in the search algorithm. On the other hand, in the case of q_2 and q_3, the one-path search is possible, if there is no intersection between the VC and other nodes which don't belong to "search path".

4 Pruning Heuristics

In addition to PH1–3 [4], we introduce two more pruning heuristics, PH4 and PH5, on the basis of the Hash structure H.

4.1 PH4: Remnant

The $currentNN$ determined in lines 1–4 of Algorithm 1 is essentially the nearest object from q among every leaf nodes which intersects with $C(q)$. Hence the intuitive meaning of $NNdist$ is the semantically upperbound of possible distance to $NN(q)$.That is to say, $NN(q)$ must be enclosed by $NNcircle$ (simply denoted as $VC(q) \subseteq NNcircle$). From the characteristics of hash H, it is guarantee that there is no object in the region of $C \cap NNcircle$. Therefore, if there is an object which closer to q than the already found $currentNN$, then it will be exist in the region of $NNcircle - C$.

The relationship between C and $NNcircle$ in the middle of the BUS NN search is depicted in Figure 4. We will call the spherical cut of $NNcircle - C$ the "remnant" of $NNcircle$ on C (or simply called remnant). There are at most four possible remnants in case of $d = 2$.

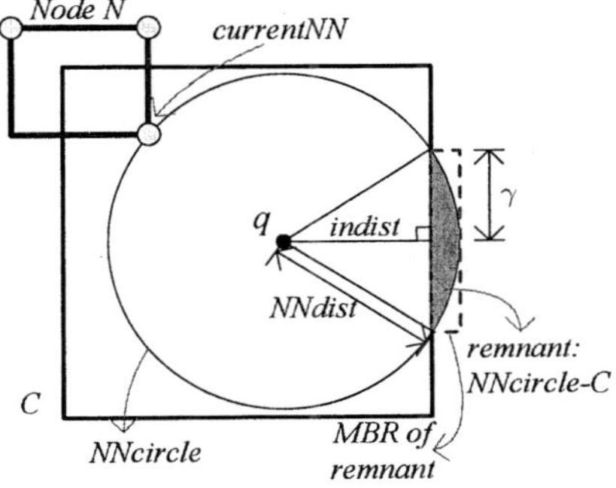

Fig. 4. Remnant and its MBR

Lemma 1 ($NNcircle$ and Remnant). *There is no object in the area of $C \cap NNcircle$. However, we cannot guarantee that such condition is also true for the region of remnant ($NNcircle - C$). Therefore, if there exists a closer object to the query point than $currentNN$, the object must reside in the remnant area.*

Proof. *Let suppose that there exists an object NN' in the area of $C \cap NNcircle$. As a result, obviously $NNdist(= mindist(q, currentNN))$ becomes greater than $mindist(q, NN')$, and this leads to a contradiction on the meaning of $NNdist$. Hence, we can guarantee that there is no object in the area of $C \cap NNcircle$. But, for the remnant area, we couldn't ensure the above guarantee because of the possible existence of other nodes that does not intersect with $C(q)$ but include any object closer than $currentNN$.* □

Based on the remnant concept, we introduce new heuristic for pruning unnecessary nodes. As stated in Lemma 1, there is no object in the region of $C \cap NNcircle$. By utilizing this characteristic, we can prune some additional nodes which are not pruned by PH3.

Lemma 2 (PH4: Remnant Property). *The nodes which only intersect with the region of $C \cap NNcircle$ can never include NN, therefore they should be pruned. Consequently, the search procedure traverses the only nodes that intersect with the remnant of $NNcircle(q)$. We call this heuristic the remnant property.*

Proof. *As we stated in Lemma 1, there is no object in the area of* $C \cap NNcircle$*. Thus, every node that intersects with* $C \cap NNcircle$ *could not contains NN also, and these nodes should be pruned.* □

Corollary 1. *From Lemma 2, if* $NNcircle \subset C$*, then* $currentNN$ *is simply evaluated as the actual NN and the search procedure will terminate.*

Proof. *Owing to the characteristic of remnant,* $NNcircle \subset C$ *leads* $remnant = \emptyset$ *properly. When* $remnant = \emptyset$*, from Lemma 2, we can guarantee that there exists no further node that intersects with the remnant. Therefore, the search procedure will terminate.* □

4.2 PH5: The Concept of Safe MBR

What is important in PH4 is that the search procedure only traverses nodes that intersect with the remnant. Therefore, it is needed to traverse the tree until there is no such node that intersects with the remnant. Similar to Corollary 1, the NN search procedure may be terminated, if it does guarantee such condition before the whole tree is traversed.

In order to guarantee such condition, each node in the tree will require some additional information. The extra information on each node is called *safe MBR*, which is defined as follows.

Definition 3 (Safe MBR). *Given node N and the set S of its siblings* $\{N_0, N_1, \ldots, N_{|S|-1}\}$*, the safe MBR of node N,* $safeMBR(N) = MIR(\bigcap(safeMBR(N'sparent), MBR(N), \bigcap_{0 \leq i \leq s-1} N_i{}^c))$ *except for root node.* $MIR(\cdot)$ *is the function of Maximum Inscribed Rectangle. The safe MBR of the root node is its MBR.*

Figure 5 illustrates two different examples of safe MBR. In general, increasing the intersection between sibling nodes leads decreasing the size of safe MBR. This is closely related to the splitting policy of R-tree [2]. The safe MBRs have no intersection between sibling nodes in character. Thus, we can introduce the following heuristic to prune unnecessary nodes.

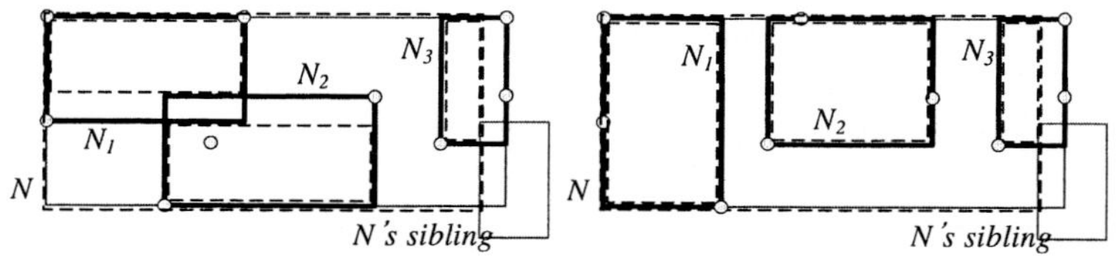

Fig. 5. Safe MBR

Lemma 3 (PH5: Safe MBR Property). *If* $NNcircle$ *is completely enclosed by the safe MBR of the searching point* $\check{N}$*, then the search procedure will terminate.*

Proof. *If* $NNcircle$ *is completely enclosed by the safe MBR of node* $\check{N}$*, the rest nodes should be pruned by PH4. The underlying reason is that those nodes will never intersect with the remnant area in the characteristic of the safe MBR.* □

By utilizing PH5, the optimal cost of the proposed algorithm is the average number of nodes in a cell while that of conventional top-down algorithms is the height of tree.

4.3 Algorithm Description and Example

The entire procedure of proposed algorithm is depicted in Algorithm 2. Lines 1–4 are the same as in Algorithm 1 except that calls TopDownNNSearch() at *Root* and returns its result in the case of $C.IL$ = **null** (line 2). At line 5, if $NNcircle$ is covered by C or the safe MBR of $\check{N}$, then return $currentNN$ and terminates the search procedure (using Corollary 1 and Lemma 3). The **repeat-until**-loop of lines 7–16 is the main loop for the algorithm. $\check{N}$ is updated as its parent node (line 8), then TopDownNNSearch() is applied to the children of node $\check{N}$ which lying closer to q than $NNdist$ (using PH3) and intersecting with at least one remnant in the remnant set $RemMBRSet$ (using PH4). The procedure continues until the searching point $\check{N}$ is the *Root* node or $NNcircle$ is totally covered by the safe MBR of $\check{N}$ (using PH5).

Algorithm 2. The entire BUS algorithm

Procedure BottomUpNNSearch(Query q)
1: Determine the corresponding cell of q denoted as $C = H(\lfloor \frac{q_1}{\delta} \rfloor, \lfloor \frac{q_2}{\delta} \rfloor)$.
2: **if** $C.IL$ is **null then return** TopDownNNSearch(*Root*, ∞, q)
3: Read the all leaf nodes in $C.IL$ and $currentNN \leftarrow$ nearest object.
4: Searching point $\check{N} \leftarrow$ the leaf node that contains $currentNN \in C.IL$
5: **if** $NNcircle$ is totally covered by C or $N.SafeMBR$ **then return** $currentNN$
6: $RemMBRSet \leftarrow$ computeRemnantMBR(q, $NNdist$, C)
7: **repeat**
8:   $\check{N}_{old} \leftarrow \check{N}$; $\check{N} \leftarrow \check{N}$'s parent
9:   **foreach** child entry E_i in $\check{N}$ and $E_i \neq \check{N}_{old}$ **do**
10:     **if** $mindist(q, E_i) < NNdist$ and $\exists\gamma$, such that
11:       E_i has intersection with $\gamma \in RemMBRSet$ **then** /* PH3,PH4 */
12:       $currentNN \leftarrow$ TopDownNNSearch(E_i, $NNdist$, q)
13:       $RemMBRSet \leftarrow$ computeRemnantMBR(q, $NNdist$, C)
14:     **end-if**
15:   **end-for**
16: **until** ($\check{N}$ is *Root* or $NNcircle$ is totally covered by $\check{N}.SafeMBR$) /* PH5 */
17: **return** $currentNN$

As an example, we reconsider the above example that we want to find the nearest neighbor to the query points q_1, q_2, and q_3 in Figure 3. For q_1, the algorithm starts by probing $currentNN$ from the hash, after which it executes the following steps: (1) $currentNN = f$, $\check{N} = E_5$, and $NNdist = mindist(q_1, f)$. (2) $currentNN = f$, $\check{N} = E_1$, and $NNdist = mindist(q_1, f)$. (3) $currentNN = f$, $\check{N} = Root$, and $NNdist = mindist(q_1, f)$. (4) $currentNN = m$ =TopDownNNSearch(E_2, $NNdist$, q_1), and $NNdist = mindist(q_1, m)$. (5) The algorithm terminates and reports m as the NN. For q_2, the algorithm executes the following steps: (1) $currentNN = i$, $\check{N} = E_6$, and $NNdist = mindist(q_2, i)$. (2) The algorithm terminates and reports i as the NN. For q_3, the algorithm executes the following steps: (1) $currentNN = b$, $\check{N} = E_3$, and $NNdist = mindist(q_3, b)$. (2) $currentNN = b$, $\check{N} = E_1$, and $NNdist = mindist(q_3, b)$ (3) The algorithm terminates and reports b as the NN.

The algorithm presented above can be easily generalized to answer kNN query, although the above algorithm and example only focused NN query. A heap is needed instead of single $currentNN$. It maintains at most k current NN results in ascending order by *mindist*. And $NNdist$ should be interpreted as *mindist* of kth entry in the heap. Obviously, the rest of generalization will be straightforward.

5 Performance Evaluation

We performed various experiments to demonstrate the significant impact of the proposed bottom-up NN search algorithm on R-trees and compared it to the conventional algorithms. First, we implements R*-tree and the conventional NN search algorithms such as DFS [4] and BFS [7] using Java language. And the proposed algorithm is implemented as three variations: basic BUS algorithm (BUS), BUS algorithm with PH4 (BUS4), and BUS algorithm with PH4 and PH5 (BUS45). All experiments were conducted on a Pentium M 900Mhz machine with 512M main memory and 60GB secondary storage. As the experimental datasets, 10k random points are generated by pseudo-random number generator within $[0, 1]^2$. The 10k query points are also generated randomly, then each query carefully evaluated by five different algorithms in the average node accesses.

Figure 6 show the result of experiment using the synthetic dataset described above in different setting in which R-tree was constructed from different M (node capacity) with a fixed m of $M/3$ (minimum entries), and Hash has a different granularity n. There is a tendency that BFS always outperforms DFS and the average I/O cost of these two top-down approaches remains greater than the height h of the tree. This observation implies that at least h node access are needed to accomplish the conventional algorithms. On the other hand, the proposed

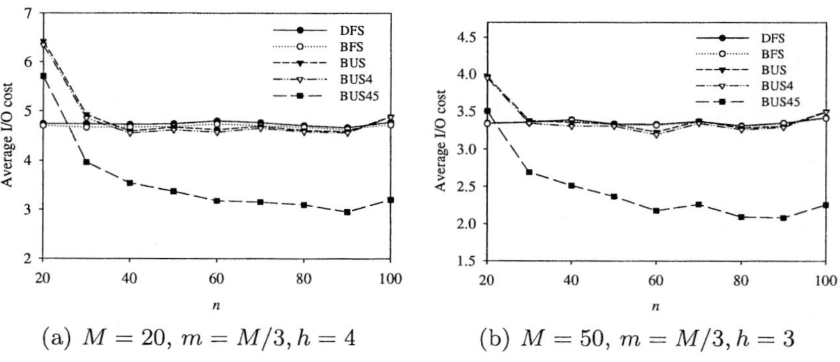

(a) $M = 20$, $m = M/3, h = 4$ (b) $M = 50$, $m = M/3, h = 3$

Fig. 6. Experimental results with different parameters

algorithm only accesses far smaller number of nodes than the tree height h especially in a reasonable granularity n of hash. The relative order of the performance of proposed algorithms is BUS $<$ BUS4 $\ll$ BUS45 properly. BUS4 shows slightly better performance than BUS in all case, and these two algorithms (BUS and BUS4) maintains a competitive performance with conventional algorithms such as DFS and BFS. BUS45 which is combined with PH5 can provide great performance benefit of 15%~61% over the conventional approaches. This improvement has a meaning that the proposed algorithm outperforms BFS algorithm which known as I/O optimal.

6 Conclusions

In this paper, we have proposed an efficient nearest neighbor algorithm for R-trees, which far outperforms the best known I/O optimal algorithm called BFS. To this end, we have proposed two new pruning heuristics based on hash structure we designed. One is the remnant property, the other is the safe MBR property. The former is that the algorithm only traverses those nodes that are intersected with a special region so-called remnant, so that more pruning capability than conventional pruning heuristic for R-trees can be achieved. The latter means that smaller number of nodes than the height of tree are only needed to answer the NN query by appending a special MBR called safe MBR to each node. In our future work, we plan to extend this work to the continuous NN query processing, high-dimensional indexing, and multiple NN query processing.

References

1. J. Bentley, "Multidimensional binary search trees used for associative searching", *Communication of ACM* 18 (9), 1975.
2. A. Guttman, "R-trees: A Dynamic Index Structure for Spatial Searching", *Proc. of SIGMOD*, 1984.
3. Norbert Beckmann, Hans-Peter Kriegel, Ralf Schneider, and Bernhard Seeger, "The R*-Tree: An Efficient and Robust Access Method for Points and Rectangles", *Proc. of SIGMOD*, 1990.
4. N. Roussopoulos, S. Kelley, F. Vincent, "Nearest neighbor queries", *Proc. of SIGMOD*, 1995.
5. Y. Theodoridis and T. Sellis, "A Model for the Prediction of R-tree Performance", *Proc. of PODS*, 1996.
6. Apostolos Papadopoulos and Yannis Manolopoulos, "Performance of Nearest Neighbor Queries in R-Trees", *Proc. of ICDT*, 1997.
7. G.R. Hjaltason and H. Samet, "Distance browsing in spatial databases", *ACM Trans. Database Systems* 24 (2), 1999.
8. C. Böhm, S. Berchtold, and D. A. Keim. "Searching in High-Dimensional Spaces: Index Structures for Improving the Performance of Multimedia Databases", *ACM Computing Surveys* 33(3), 2001.
9. Yufei Tao's A Dataset collection. `http://www.cs.cityu.edu.hk/~taoyf/ds.html`

Author Index

Lecture Notes in Computer Science

For information about Vols. 1–3827

please contact your bookseller or Springer

Vol. 3933: F. Bonchi, J.-F. Boulicaut (Eds.), Knowledge Discovery in Inductive Databases. VIII, 251 pages. 2006.

Vol. 3931: B. Apolloni, M. Marinaro, G. Nicosia, R. Tagliaferri (Eds.), Neural Nets. XIII, 370 pages. 2006.

Vol. 3928: J. Domingo-Ferrer, J. Posegga, D. Schreckling (Eds.), Smart Card Research and Advanced Applications. XI, 359 pages. 2006.

Vol. 3927: J. Hespanha, A. Tiwari (Eds.), Hybrid Systems: Computation and Control. XII, 584 pages. 2006.

Vol. 3925: A. Valmari (Ed.), Model Checking Software. X, 307 pages. 2006.

Vol. 3924: P. Sestoft (Ed.), Programming Languages and Systems. XII, 343 pages. 2006.

Vol. 3923: A. Mycroft, A. Zeller (Eds.), Compiler Construction. XIII, 277 pages. 2006.

Vol. 3922: L. Baresi, R. Heckel (Eds.), Fundamental Approaches to Software Engineering. XIII, 427 pages. 2006.

Vol. 3921: L. Aceto, A. Ingólfsdóttir (Eds.), Foundations of Software Science and Computation Structures. XV, 447 pages. 2006.

Vol. 3920: H. Hermanns, J. Palsberg (Eds.), Tools and Algorithms for the Construction and Analysis of Systems. XIV, 506 pages. 2006.

Vol. 3916: J. Li, Q. Yang, A.-H. Tan (Eds.), Data Mining for Biomedical Applications. VIII, 155 pages. 2006. (Sublibrary LNBI).

Vol. 3915: R. Nayak, M.J. Zaki (Eds.), Knowledge Discovery from XML Documents. VIII, 105 pages. 2006.

Vol. 3909: A. Apostolico, C. Guerra, S. Istrail, P.A. Pevzner, M. Waterman (Eds.), Research in Computational Molecular Biology. XVII, 612 pages. 2006. (Sublibrary LNBI).

Vol. 3907: F. Rothlauf, J. Branke, S. Cagnoni, E. Costa, C. Cotta, R. Drechsler, E. Lutton, P. Machado, J.H. Moore, J. Romero, G.D. Smith, G. Squillero, H. Takagi (Eds.), Applications of Evolutionary Computing. XXIV, 813 pages. 2006.

Vol. 3906: J. Gottlieb, G.R. Raidl (Eds.), Evolutionary Computation in Combinatorial Optimization. XI, 293 pages. 2006.

Vol. 3905: P. Collet, M. Tomassini, M. Ebner, S. Gustafson, A. Ekárt (Eds.), Genetic Programming. XI, 361 pages. 2006.

Vol. 3904: M. Baldoni, U. Endriss, A. Omicini, P. Torroni (Eds.), Declarative Agent Languages and Technologies III. XII, 245 pages. 2006. (Sublibrary LNAI).

Vol. 3903: K. Chen, R. Deng, X. Lai, J. Zhou (Eds.), Information Security Practice and Experience. XIV, 392 pages. 2006.

Vol. 3901: P.M. Hill (Ed.), Logic Based Program Synthesis and Transformation. X, 179 pages. 2006.

Vol. 3899: S. Frintrop, VOCUS: A Visual Attention System for Object Detection and Goal-Directed Search. XIV, 216 pages. 2006. (Sublibrary LNAI).

Vol. 3897: B. Preneel, S. Tavares (Eds.), Selected Areas in Cryptography. XI, 371 pages. 2006.

Vol. 3896: Y. Ioannidis, M.H. Scholl, J.W. Schmidt, F. Matthes, M. Hatzopoulos, K. Boehm, A. Kemper, T. Grust, C. Boehm (Eds.), Advances in Database Technology - EDBT 2006. XIV, 1208 pages. 2006.

Vol. 3895: O. Goldreich, A.L. Rosenberg, A.L. Selman (Eds.), Theoretical Computer Science. XII, 399 pages. 2006.

Vol. 3894: W. Grass, B. Sick, K. Waldschmidt (Eds.), Architecture of Computing Systems - ARCS 2006. XII, 496 pages. 2006.

Vol. 3890: S.G. Thompson, R. Ghanea-Hercock (Eds.), Defence Applications of Multi-Agent Systems. XII, 141 pages. 2006. (Sublibrary LNAI).

Vol. 3889: J. Rosca, D. Erdogmus, J.C. Príncipe, S. Haykin (Eds.), Independent Component Analysis and Blind Signal Separation. XXI, 980 pages. 2006.

Vol. 3888: D. Draheim, G. Weber (Eds.), Trends in Enterprise Application Architecture. IX, 145 pages. 2006.

Vol. 3887: J.R. Correa, A. Hevia, M. Kiwi (Eds.), LATIN 2006: Theoretical Informatics. XVI, 814 pages. 2006.

Vol. 3886: E.G. Bremer, J. Hakenberg, E.-H.(S.) Han, D. Berrar, W. Dubitzky (Eds.), Knowledge Discovery in Life Science Literature. XIV, 147 pages. 2006. (Sublibrary LNBI).

Vol. 3885: V. Torra, Y. Narukawa, A. Valls, J. Domingo-Ferrer (Eds.), Modeling Decisions for Artificial Intelligence. XII, 374 pages. 2006. (Sublibrary LNAI).

Vol. 3884: B. Durand, W. Thomas (Eds.), STACS 2006. XIV, 714 pages. 2006.

Vol. 3882: M.L. Lee, K.L. Tan, V. Wuwongse (Eds.), Database Systems for Advanced Applications. XIX, 923 pages. 2006.

Vol. 3881: S. Gibet, N. Courty, J.-F. Kamp (Eds.), Gesture in Human-Computer Interaction and Simulation. XIII, 344 pages. 2006. (Sublibrary LNAI).

Vol. 3880: A. Rashid, M. Aksit (Eds.), Transactions on Aspect-Oriented Software Development I. IX, 335 pages. 2006.

Vol. 3879: T. Erlebach, G. Persinao (Eds.), Approximation and Online Algorithms. X, 349 pages. 2006.

Vol. 3878: A. Gelbukh (Ed.), Computational Linguistics and Intelligent Text Processing. XVII, 589 pages. 2006.

Vol. 3877: M. Detyniecki, J.M. Jose, A. Nürnberger, C. J. '. van Rijsbergen (Eds.), Adaptive Multimedia Retrieval: User, Context, and Feedback. XI, 279 pages. 2006.

Vol. 3876: S. Halevi, T. Rabin (Eds.), Theory of Cryptography. XI, 617 pages. 2006.

Vol. 3875: S. Ur, E. Bin, Y. Wolfsthal (Eds.), Hardware and Software, Verification and Testing. X, 265 pages. 2006.

Vol. 3874: R. Missaoui, J. Schmidt (Eds.), Formal Concept Analysis. X, 309 pages. 2006. (Sublibrary LNAI).

Vol. 3873: L. Maicher, J. Park (Eds.), Charting the Topic Maps Research and Applications Landscape. VIII, 281 pages. 2006. (Sublibrary LNAI).

Vol. 3872: H. Bunke, A. L. Spitz (Eds.), Document Analysis Systems VII. XIII, 630 pages. 2006.

Vol. 3870: S. Spaccapietra, P. Atzeni, W.W. Chu, T. Catarci, K.P. Sycara (Eds.), Journal on Data Semantics V. XIII, 237 pages. 2006.

Vol. 3869: S. Renals, S. Bengio (Eds.), Machine Learning for Multimodal Interaction. XIII, 490 pages. 2006.

Vol. 3868: K. Römer, H. Karl, F. Mattern (Eds.), Wireless Sensor Networks. XI, 342 pages. 2006.

Vol. 3866: T. Dimitrakos, F. Martinelli, P.Y.A. Ryan, S. Schneider (Eds.), Formal Aspects in Security and Trust. X, 259 pages. 2006.

Vol. 3865: W. Shen, K.-M. Chao, Z. Lin, J.-P.A. Barthès, A. James (Eds.), Computer Supported Cooperative Work in Design II. XII, 659 pages. 2006.

Vol. 3863: M. Kohlhase (Ed.), Mathematical Knowledge Management. XI, 405 pages. 2006. (Sublibrary LNAI).

Vol. 3862: R.H. Bordini, M. Dastani, J. Dix, A.E.F. Seghrouchni (Eds.), Programming Multi-Agent Systems. XIV, 267 pages. 2006. (Sublibrary LNAI).

Vol. 3861: J. Dix, S.J. Hegner (Eds.), Foundations of Information and Knowledge Systems. X, 331 pages. 2006.

Vol. 3860: D. Pointcheval (Ed.), Topics in Cryptology – CT-RSA 2006. XI, 365 pages. 2006.

Vol. 3858: A. Valdes, D. Zamboni (Eds.), Recent Advances in Intrusion Detection. X, 351 pages. 2006.

Vol. 3857: M.P.C. Fossorier, H. Imai, S. Lin, A. Poli (Eds.), Applied Algebra, Algebraic Algorithms and Error-Correcting Codes. XI, 350 pages. 2006.

Vol. 3855: E. A. Emerson, K.S. Namjoshi (Eds.), Verification, Model Checking, and Abstract Interpretation. XI, 443 pages. 2005.

Vol. 3854: I. Stavrakakis, M. Smirnov (Eds.), Autonomic Communication. XIII, 303 pages. 2006.

Vol. 3853: A.J. Ijspeert, T. Masuzawa, S. Kusumoto (Eds.), Biologically Inspired Approaches to Advanced Information Technology. XIV, 388 pages. 2006.

Vol. 3852: P.J. Narayanan, S.K. Nayar, H.-Y. Shum (Eds.), Computer Vision – ACCV 2006, Part II. XXXI, 977 pages. 2006.

Vol. 3851: P.J. Narayanan, S.K. Nayar, H.-Y. Shum (Eds.), Computer Vision – ACCV 2006, Part I. XXXI, 973 pages. 2006.

Vol. 3850: R. Freund, G. Păun, G. Rozenberg, A. Salomaa (Eds.), Membrane Computing. IX, 371 pages. 2006.

Vol. 3849: I. Bloch, A. Petrosino, A.G.B. Tettamanzi (Eds.), Fuzzy Logic and Applications. XIV, 438 pages. 2006. (Sublibrary LNAI).

Vol. 3848: J.-F. Boulicaut, L. De Raedt, H. Mannila (Eds.), Constraint-Based Mining and Inductive Databases. X, 401 pages. 2006. (Sublibrary LNAI).

Vol. 3847: K.P. Jantke, A. Lunzer, N. Spyratos, Y. Tanaka (Eds.), Federation over the Web. X, 215 pages. 2006. (Sublibrary LNAI).

Vol. 3846: H. J. van den Herik, Y. Björnsson, N.S. Netanyahu (Eds.), Computers and Games. XIV, 333 pages. 2006.

Vol. 3845: J. Farré, I. Litovsky, S. Schmitz (Eds.), Implementation and Application of Automata. XIII, 360 pages. 2006.

Vol. 3844: J.-M. Bruel (Ed.), Satellite Events at the MoDELS 2005 Conference. XIII, 360 pages. 2006.

Vol. 3843: P. Healy, N.S. Nikolov (Eds.), Graph Drawing. XVII, 536 pages. 2006.

Vol. 3842: H.T. Shen, J. Li, M. Li, J. Ni, W. Wang (Eds.), Advanced Web and Network Technologies, and Applications. XXVII, 1057 pages. 2006.

Vol. 3841: X. Zhou, J. Li, H.T. Shen, M. Kitsuregawa, Y. Zhang (Eds.), Frontiers of WWW Research and Development - APWeb 2006. XXIV, 1223 pages. 2006.

Vol. 3840: M. Li, B. Boehm, L.J. Osterweil (Eds.), Unifying the Software Process Spectrum. XVI, 522 pages. 2006.

Vol. 3839: J.-C. Filliâtre, C. Paulin-Mohring, B. Werner (Eds.), Types for Proofs and Programs. VIII, 275 pages. 2006.

Vol. 3838: A. Middeldorp, V. van Oostrom, F. van Raamsdonk, R. de Vrijer (Eds.), Processes, Terms and Cycles: Steps on the Road to Infinity. XVIII, 639 pages. 2005.

Vol. 3837: K. Cho, P. Jacquet (Eds.), Technologies for Advanced Heterogeneous Networks. IX, 307 pages. 2005.

Vol. 3836: J.-M. Pierson (Ed.), Data Management in Grids. X, 143 pages. 2006.

Vol. 3835: G. Sutcliffe, A. Voronkov (Eds.), Logic for Programming, Artificial Intelligence, and Reasoning. XIV, 744 pages. 2005. (Sublibrary LNAI).

Vol. 3834: D.G. Feitelson, E. Frachtenberg, L. Rudolph, U. Schwiegelshohn (Eds.), Job Scheduling Strategies for Parallel Processing. VIII, 283 pages. 2005.

Vol. 3833: K.-J. Li, C. Vangenot (Eds.), Web and Wireless Geographical Information Systems. XI, 309 pages. 2005.

Vol. 3832: D. Zhang, A.K. Jain (Eds.), Advances in Biometrics. XX, 796 pages. 2005.

Vol. 3831: J. Wiedermann, G. Tel, J. Pokorný, M. Bieliková, J. Štuller (Eds.), SOFSEM 2006: Theory and Practice of Computer Science. XV, 576 pages. 2006.

Vol. 3830: D. Weyns, H. V.D. Parunak, F. Michel (Eds.), Environments for Multi-Agent Systems II. VIII, 291 pages. 2006. (Sublibrary LNAI).

Vol. 3829: P. Pettersson, W. Yi (Eds.), Formal Modeling and Analysis of Timed Systems. IX, 305 pages. 2005.

Vol. 3828: X. Deng, Y. Ye (Eds.), Internet and Network Economics. XVII, 1106 pages. 2005.